R. Gupta's®

POPULAR MASTER GUIDE

Jamia Millia Islamia

MBA

Master of Business Administration

Entrance Examination

Useful for

MBA (FULL TIME/EXECUTIVE)

Ample Study & Practice Material Prepared by Experts
Numerous Solved Multiple Choice Questions

by

RPH Editorial Board

RAMESH PUBLISHING HOUSE, NEW DELHI

Published by
O.P. Gupta *for* Ramesh Publishing House

Admin. Office
12-H, New Daryaganj Road, Opp. Officer' Mess,
New Delhi-110002 ✆ 23275224, 23245124

E-mail: info@rameshpublishinghouse.com
For Online Shopping: www.rameshpublishinghouse.com

Showroom
• Balaji Market, Nai Sarak, Delhi-6 ✆ 23253720, 23282525
• 4457, Nai Sarak, Delhi-6, ✆ 23918938

Book Code: R-1872

ISBN: 978-93-86298-20-1

Price: ₹ 595

Printed at: Deepak Offset, Delhi

CONTENTS

❑❑❑

Jamia Millia Islamia (JMI)

MBA Entrance Examination-2025

(Exam held on 24-05-2025)

Directions (Qs. No. 1-5): *Read the following passage and answer the question that follow it.*

To summarize the Classic Maya collapse, we can tentatively identify five strands. I acknowledge, however, that Maya archaeologists still disagree vigorously among themselves in part, because the different strands evidently varied in importance among different parts of the Maya realm; because detailed archaeological studies are available for only some Maya sites; and because it remains puzzling why most of the Maya heartland remained nearly empty of population and failed to recover after the collapse and after re-growth of forests. With those caveats, it appears to me that one strand consisted of population growth outstripping available resources: a dilemma similar to the one foreseen by Thomas Malthus in 1798 and being played out today in Rwanda, Haiti and elsewhere. As the archaeologist David Webster succinctly puts it, "Too many farmers grew too many crops on too much of landscape." Compounding that mismatch between population and resources was the second strand: the effects of deforestation and hillside erosion, which caused a decrease in the amount of useable farmland at a time when more rather than less farmland was needed, and possibly exacerbated by an anthropogenic drought resulting from deforestation, by soil nutrient depletion and other soil problems, and by the struggle to prevent bracken ferns from overrunning the fields.

The third strand consisted of increased fighting, as more and more people fought over fewer resources. Maya warfare, already endemic, peaked just before the collapse. That is not surprising when one reflects that at least five million people, perhaps many more, were crammed into an area smaller than the US state of Colorado (104,000 square miles). That warfare would have decreased further the amount of land available for agriculture, by creating no-man's lands between principalities where it was now unsafe to farm. Bringing matters to a head was the strand of climate change. The drought at the time of the Classic collapse was not the first drought that the Maya had lived through, but it was the most severe. At the time of previous droughts, there were still uninhabited parts of the Maya landscape, and people at a site affected by drought could save themselves by moving to another site. However, by the time of the Classic collapse the landscape was now full, there was no useful unoccupied land in the vicinity on which to begin anew, and the whole population could not be accommodated in the few areas that continued to have reliable water supplies.

As our fifth strand, we have to wonder why the kings and nobles failed to recognize and solve these seemingly obvious problems undermining their society. Their attention was evidently focused on their short-term concerns of enriching themselves, waging wars, erecting monuments, competing with each other, and extracting enough food from the peasants to support all those activities. Like most leaders throughout human history, the Maya kings and nobles did not heed long-term problems, insofar as they perceived them. Finally, while we still have some other past societies to consider before we switch our attention to the modern world, we must already be struck by some parallels between the Maya and the past societies. As on Mangareva, the Maya environmental and population problems led to increasing warfare and civil strife. Similarly, on Easter Island and at Chaco Canyon, the Maya peak population numbers were followed swiftly by political and social collapse. Paralleling the eventual extension of agriculture from Easter Island's coastal lowlands to its uplands, and from the Mimbres floodplain to the hills, Copan's inhabitants also expanded from the floodplain to the more fragile hill slopes, leaving them with a larger population to feed when the agricultural boom in the hills went bust. Like Easter Island chiefs erecting ever larger statues, eventually crowned by pukao, and like Anasazi elite treating themselves to necklaces of 2,000 turquoise beads, Maya kings sought to outdo each other with more and more impressive temples, covered with thicker and thicker plaster — reminiscent in turn of the extravagant conspicuous consumption by modern American CEOs. The passivity of Easter chiefs and Maya kings in the face of the real big threats to their societies completes our list of disquieting parallels.

1. According to the passage, which of the following best represents the factor that has been cited by the author in the context of Rwanda and Haiti?
   A. Various ethnic groups competing for land and other resources
   B. Various ethnic groups competing for limited land resources
   C. Various ethnic groups fighting with each other
   D. Various ethnic groups competing for political power

2. By an anthropogenic drought, the author means:
   A. a drought caused by lack of rains.
   B. a drought caused due to deforestation.
   C. a drought caused by failure to prevent bracken ferns from overrunning the fields.
   D. a drought caused by actions of human beings.

3. According to the passage, the drought at the time of Maya collapse had a different impact compared to the droughts earlier because:
   A. the Maya kings continued to be extravagant when common people were suffering.
   B. it happened at the time of collapse of leadership among Mayas.
   C. it happened when the Maya population had occupied all available land suited for agriculture.
   D. it was followed by internecine warfare among Mayans.

4. According to the author, why is it difficult to explain the reasons for Maya collapse?
   A. Copan inhabitants destroyed all records of that period.
   B. The constant deforestation and hillside erosion have wiped out all traces of the Maya kingdom.
   C. Archaeological sites of Mayas do not provide any consistent evidence.
   D. It has not been possible to ascertain which of the factors best explains why the Maya civilization collapsed.

5. Which factor has not been cited as one of the factors causing the collapse of Maya society?
   A. Environmental degradation due to excess population
   B. Social collapse due to excess population
   C. Increased warfare among Maya people
   D. Obsession of Maya population with their own short-term concerns.

Directions (Qs. No. 6-8): *Read the following passage and answer the question that follow it.*

Some artists go out in a blaze of glory. Pierre-Auguste Renoir went out in a blaze of kitsch. At least, that's the received opinion about the work of his final decades: all those pillowy nudes, sunning their abundant selves in dappled glades; all those peachy girls, strumming guitars and idling in bourgeois parlors; all that pink. In the long twilight of his career, the old man found his way to a kissable classicism that modern eyes can find awfully hard to take.

All the same, the Renoir of this period - the three very productive decades before his death in 1919 at the age of 78 - fascinated some of the chief figures of modernism. Picasso was on board; his thick -limbed 'neoclassical' women from the 1920 are indebted to Renoir. So was Matisse, who had one eye on Renoir's Orientalist dress-up fantasies like the Concert, with its flattened space and overall patterning, when he produced his odalisques. Given that so much of late Renoir seems saccharine and semi comical to us, is it still possible to see what made it modern to them?

Yes and no. To understand the Renoir in the 20th Century you have to remember that before he became a semi classicist, he was a consummate Impressionist. You need to picture him in 1874, 33 years old, painting side by side with Monet in Argenteuil, teasing out the new possibilities of sketchy brushwork to capture fleeting light as it fell across people and things in an indisputably modern world. But in the decade that followed, Renoir became one of the movement's first apostates. Impressionism affected many people in the 19th century in much the way the internet does now. It both charmed and unnerved them. It brought to painting a novel immediacy, but it also gave back a world that felt weightless and unstable. What we now call post - Impressionism was the inevitable by-product of that anxiety. Artists like Seurat and Gauguin searched for an art that owed nothing to the stale models of academicism but possessed the substance and authority that Impressionism had let fall away.

For Renoir, a turning point came during his honeymoon to Rome and Naples in 1881. Face to face with the firm outlines of Raphael and the musculature of Michelangelo, he lost faith in his flickering sunbeams. He returned to France determined to find his way to lucid, distinct forms in an art that reached for the eternal, not the momentary. By the later years of that decade, Renoir had lost his taste for the modern world anyway. As for modern women, in 1888 he could write, "I consider that women who are authors, lawyers and politicians are monsters". ("The woman who is an artist," he added graciously, "is merely ridiculous.") Ah, but the woman who is a goddess - or at least harks back to one - that is different matter. It would be Renoir's aim to reconfigure the female nude in a way that would convey the spirit of the classical world without classical trappings. Set in "timeless" outdoor settings, these women by their weight and scale and serenity alone - along with their often recognizably classical poses - would point back to antiquity.

For a time, Renoir worked with figures so strongly outlined that they could have been put down by Ingres with a jackhammer. By 1892, he had drifted back toward a fluctuating impressionist brushstroke. Firmly contoured or flickering, his softly scalped women are as full-bodied as Doric columns. This was one of the qualities that caught Picasso's eye, especially after his first trip to Italy, in 1917. He would assimilate Renoir along-side his own sources in Iberian sculpture and elsewhere to come up with a frankly more powerful, even haunting, amalgam of the antique and the modern in paintings like Woman in a White Hat.

Renoir was most valuable as a stepping - stone for artists making more potent use of the ideas he was developing. The heart of the problem is the challenge. Renoir set for himself: to reconcile classical and Renaissance models with the 18th century French painters he loved. To synthesize the force and clarity of classicism with the intimacy and charm of the Rococo is a nearly impossible trick. How do you cross the power of Phidias with the delicacy of Fragonard? The answer: at your own risk - especially the risk of admitting into your work the weaknesses of the Rococo. It's fine line between charming and insipid, and 18th century French painters crossed it all the time. So did Renoir.

6. All of the following are true in light of the passage EXCEPT.

A. Fragonard is an 18th century artist

B. Picasso combined classicism and modernism in "Woman in a white Hat".

C. Renoir was a semi - Classicist, who became an Impressionist

D. Gauguin suffered from post - Impressionism anxiety

7. We can infer from the passage that the word 'odalisques' means:

A. Pillars B. Landscapes

C. Figures D. Women

8. The passage suggests that:

A. Renoir was greatly misunderstood in his lifetime

B. Classicism and modernism don't go together

C. Renoir's later work appealed to modern tastes

D. Renoir's artistic appeal waned in the twilight of his career

Directions (Qs. No. 9-12): *Read the following passage and answer the question that follow it.*

Organic food is a two-billion pound industry grown fat on the back of celebrity endorsement and a well-heeled middle class seduced by claims that it is good for health. Prince Charles is one of its most enthusiastic and pro-active promoters. Not content with simply consuming it, he has his own lucrative line in overpriced organic products including biscuits which taste more like chalk.

But now questions are being raised about some of the basic assumption that have contributed to the popularity of organic food and the phenomenal growth of this sector in the past decade. People are asking: is organic food really worth the price which is often three times more than that of normal food?

This follows new research by a group of British scientists who found that organic food offered no extra benefit over the ordinary cheaper foodstuff. In a controversial report, exports from the London School of Hygiene and Tropical Medicine say there is no evidence that organic food is more nutritional or healthier than food produced using fertilizers. For example, the expensive free-range chicken (sold as a "premium" product) has the same nutritional value as the factory-farmed chicken; and similarly, there is no difference between organic and non-organic vegetables or dairy produce.

The research, based on data published over the past 50 years and said to be the most comprehensive review ever of the relative benefits of organic food, strikes at the very heart of what has been portrayed by campaigners as its USP - that is healthier than conventional food and therefore worth paying a "bit extra".

Dr. Alan Dangour, who led the study, was unambiguous in rejecting claims made for organic food. "Looking at all of the studies published in the last 50 years, we have concluded that there's no good evidence that consumption of organic food is beneficial to health based on the nutrient content," he said. The report, commissioned by the government's Food Standards Agency and published in the American Journal of Clinical Nutrition, concluded that "organically and conventionally produced crops and livestock products are broadly comparable in their nutrient content". A "small number of differences" were noted but these were "unlikely to be of any public health relevance."

In a pointed reference to the hype over the supposed benefits of organic food, the FSA said the research was aimed at helping people make "informed choices" about what they ate. In other words, it was concerned that the high-profile campaign for organic food, dressed up as ethical issue, was preventing people form making "informed choices" and they were being sold things on false premises.

"Ensuring people have accurate information is absolutely essential in allowing us all to more informed choices about the food we eat. This study does not mean that people should not eat organic food. What it shows is that there is little, if any, nutritional difference between organic and conventionally produced food and that there is no evidence of additional health benefits from eating organic food", said Gill Fine, FSA's Director of Consumer Choice and Dietary Health.

In the organic food circles, the report has caused fury with campaigners alleging that it is all part of a "cancerous conspiracy" to defame the organic food movement. Newspapers have been full of angry letters denouncing the report as "selective", "misleading" and "limited".

The Soil Association, which campaigns for "planet-friendly organic food and farming", is furious that the research crucially ignored the presence of higher pesticide residues in conventional food. Some have defended organic food arguing that it is not about health alone but also involves wider environmental and social issues.

However, even those who agree that the report may be "flawed" in some respects believe that it is an important contribution to the debate on organic food.

"Yet the report - for all its alleged flaws - is an important one. For a start, it is certainly not the work of dogmatic and intractably hostile opponents of the caused. In fact, it raises key global issued After all, it organic food is no more beneficial in terms of nutrition than other, standard foodstuffs, why should we pay excessive price to eat the stuff? Why devote more land to its production", asked Robin McKie, Science Editor of The Observe. There is also a view that the fad for organic food is a bit of a class thing - something to do with the idea that if something is expensive it is also good. So, a Marks & Spencer cheese sandwich is supposed to taste better than a similar sandwich at Subway next door; everything at Harrods is out of this world: and similarly you don't know what you are missing if organic food is not your preferred choice. There is said to be a whiff of snobbery about buying into an expensive lifestyle choice. Will science bring them down to earth?

9. All of the following are the author's views on organic food EXCEPT:

A. It is insipid

B. It is very costly

C. It is not more nutritious than conventional food

D. It is patronized by the rich

10. Which of the following factors/aspects, related to organic food, has the result of the FSA study primarily called into question?

A. The nutritional value

B. The health benefits

C. The celebrity endorsement

D. The presence of pesticides

11. According to the passage, defenders of organic food are of the opinion that the FSA study:

A. Is not representative and scientific

B. Has been promoted by those who have vested interest in conventional food

C. Is flawed and has been projected as ethical issue

D. Is not balanced and has not taken a comprehensive view of the issue

12. In this passage, the author essentially:

A. Analyses the pros and cons of promoting organic food

B. Debunks the findings of a study on organic food

C. Reports the findings of a research on organic food and checks the veracity of its claim

D. Discusses the debate, which has followed the findings of a study on organic food

Directions (Qs. No. 13-17): *Read the following passage and answer the question that follow it.*

A remarkable aspect of art of the present century is the range of concepts and ideologies which it embodies. It is almost tempting to see a pattern emerging within the art field - or alternatively imposed upon it a *posteriori* - similar to that which exists under the umbrella of science where the general term covers a whole range of separate, though interconnecting, activities. Any parallelism is however - in this instance at least - misleading. A scientific discipline develops systematically once its bare tenets have been established, named and categorized as conventions. Many of the concepts of modern art, by contrast, have resulted from the almost accidental meetings of groups of talented individual at certain times and certain places. The idea generated by these chance meetings had two fold consequences. Firstly, a corpus of work would be produced which, in great part, remains as a concrete record of the events. Secondly, the ideas would themselves be disseminated through many different channels of communication - seeds that often bore fruit in contexts far removed from their generation. Not all movements were exclusively concerned with innovation. Surrealism, for instance, claimed to embody a kind of insight which can be present in the art of any period. This claim has been generally accepted so that a sixteenth century painting by Spranger or a mysterious photograph by Atget can legitimately be discussed in surrealist terms. Briefly, then, the concepts of modern art are of many different (often fundamentally different) kinds and resulted from the exposures of painters, sculptors and thinkers to the more complex phenomena of the twentieth century, including our ever increasing knowledge of the thought and products of earlier centuries. Different groups of artists would collaborate in trying to make sense of a rapidly changing world of visual and spiritual experience. We should hardly be surprised if no one group succeeded completely, but achievements, though relative, have been considerable. Landmarks have been established - concrete statements of position which given a pattern to a situation which could easily have degenerated into total chaos. Beyond this, new language tools have been created for those who follow - semantic systems which can provide a springboard for further explorations.

The codifying of art is often criticized. Certainly one can understand that artists are wary of being pigeonholed since they are apt to think of themselves as individuals - sometimes with good reason. The notion of self-expression, however, no longer carries quite the weight it once did; objectivity has its defenders. There is good reason to accept the ideas codified by artists and critics, over the past sixty years or so, as having attained the status of independent existence - an independence which is not without its own value. The time factor is important here. As an art movement slips into temporal perspective, it ceases to be a living organism - becoming, rather, a fossil. This is not to say that it becomes useless or uninteresting. Just as a scientist can reconstruct the life of a prehistoric environment from the messages codified into the structure of a fossil, so can an artist decipher whole webs of intellectual and creative possibility from the recorded structure of a 'dead' art movement. The artist can match the creative patterns crystallized into this structure against the potentials and possibilities of his own time. As T.S. Eliot observed, no one starts anything from scratch; however consciously you may try to live in the present, you are still involved with a nexus of behaviour patterns bequeathed from the past. The original and creative person is not someone who ignores these patterns, but someone who is able to translate and develop them so that they conform more exactly to his - and our - present needs.

13. Many of the concepts of modern art have been the product of:

A. ideas generated from planned deliberations between artists, painters and thinkers.

B. the dissemination of idea through the state and its organizations.

C. accidental interactions among people blessed with creative muse.

D. patronage by the rich and powerful that supported art.

14. In the passage, the word 'fossil' can be interpreted as:

A. an art movement that has creased to remain interesting or useful.

B. an analogy from the physical world to indicate a historic art movement.

C. an analogy from the physical world to indicate the barrenness of artistic creations in the past.

D. an analogy from the physical world to indicate the passing of an era associated with an art movement.

15. In the passage, which of the following similarities between science and art may lead to erroneous conclusions?

A. Both, in general, include a gamut of distinct but interconnecting activities.

B. Both have movements not necessarily concerned with innovation.

C. Both depend on collaborations between talented individuals.

D. Both involve abstract through and dissemination of ideas.

16. The range of concepts and ideologies embodied in the art of the twentieth century is explained by:

A. the existence of movement such as surrealism.

B. landmark which give a pattern to the art history of the twentieth century.

C. new language tools which can be used for further explorations into new areas.

D. the fast changing world of perceptual and transcendental understanding.

17. The passage uses an observation by T.S. Eliot to imply that:

A. creative processes are not 'original' because they always borrow from the past.

B. we always carry forward the legacy of the past.

C. past behaviour and thought processes recre themselves in the present and get labeleu as 'original' or 'creative'.

D. 'innovations' and 'original thinking' interpret and develop on past thoughts to suit contemporary needs.

18. Read the following paragraph and answer the question that follows:

Arti is planning for higher studies and her future goals include working as a manager of a non-profit organization designed to provide assistance to under-represented populations. Arti researched the missior statements of various colleges and discovered that college X, a small private college with a fee of ₹ 8 lakhs per year, was dedicated to producing compassionate and curious leaders. College Y, a large institute with a fee of ₹ 9 lakh per year, promoted itself as a leading research facility. Based on her research, she decided to apply to college X rather than College Y.

Which of the following options is the most likel explanation of Arti's decision?

A. A direct relationship exists between a college's cost and the quality of the education it provides.
B. Students apply to smaller colleges that offer more personalized attention from professors.
C. A large research university cannot prepare students for a career as a non-profit executive.
D. Students apply to colleges with mission statements that align with their goals.

19. Read the following paragraph and answer the question that follows:

The size of oceanic waves is a function of the velocity of the wind and of fetch, the length of the surface of the water subject to those winds. The average impact of waves against a coastline is a function of the size of the waves and the shape of the sea bottom. The degree of erosion on coastline is a function of the average impact of waves and the geologic composition of the coastline.

According to the above paragraph, which of the following options will be true?

A. The fetch of wind is related to the shape of the sea bottom.
B. The size of oceanic waves will not fluctuate far from average.
C. The size of oceanic wave is correlated with the shape of the sea bottom.
D. Degree of erosion on coastline is related to shape of the sea-bottom.

20. In the following question, there are five sentences/paragraphs. The sentence/paragraph labelled A is in its correct place. The four that follow are labelled B, C, D and E and need to be arranged in the logical order to form a coherent paragraph/passage. From the given options, chose the most appropriate option.

A. The driving force of the 'nuclear renaissance' is a claim that nuclear power, once up and running, is a carbon-free energy source. The assertion is that a functioning nuclear reactor creates no greenhouse gases and thus contributes nothing to global warming or chaotic weather.
B. The frequently repeated notion that nuclear power is a carbon-free energy source is simply untrue.
C. At every stage of the cycle greenhouse gases are released into the atmosphere from burning diesel, manufacturing steel and cement and, in the circumpolar regions of the planet, by disturbance of the tundra, which releases large amounts of methane, a particularly potent greenhouse gas.
D. That part is almost true, but the claim ignores the total environmental impact of nuclear energy, which includes a long and complicated chain of events known in the industry as the 'nuclear cycle' which beings with finding, mining, milling and enriching uranium, then spans through plant construction and power generation to the reprocessing and eventual storage of nuclear waste, all of which creates tons of.
E. Even the claim that a functioning nuclear power facility is CO_2 - free challenged by the face that operating plant requires an external power source to run, and that electricity is almost certain to come from a fossil-fuelled plant.

A. DCEB
B. EBCD
C. DEBC
D. EDCB

Directions (Qs. 21 and 22): *In each question there are five sentences. Each sentence has pairs of words/phrases that are italicized and highlighted. From the italicized and highlighted word(s)/phrase(s), select the most appropriate word(s)/phrase(s) to from correct sentence. Then, from the options given, choose the best one.*

21. (*i*) The municipal ***councilor (A)/ counselor (B)*** promised to improve civic amenities in the suburbs.
(*ii*) Jean's ***adopted (A)/ adoptive (B)*** patents dote on her and cater to her every whim.
(*iii*) The ***venal (A)/ venial (B)*** official was caught red - handed accepting bribe.
(*iv*) We have now shifted our residence ***farther (A)/ further (B)*** away from the main city.
(*v*) She claims to be of aristocratic ***dissent (A)/ descent (B)***.

A. AAABB
B. BBABB
C. ABBAB
D. ABAAB

22. (*i*) While evacuating people from the flood ravaged areas ***precedence (A)/ precedent (B)*** was given to women and children.
(*ii*) The best was to reach the summit is by trekking up the hill, ***alternately (A)/ alternatively (B)*** you can go on horse back.
(*iii*) His impeccable manners perfectly ***complimented (A)/ complemented (B)*** his polished looks and fashionable attire.
(*iv*) There has been a ***noticeable (A)/notable (B)*** improvement in Tarun's academic performance lately.
(*v*) You must be ***discreet (A)/ discrete (B)*** about your plans.

A. AABAB
B. ABBBB
C. BABAA
D. ABBAA

Directions (Qs. No. 23-28): *In each of the following questions, the word at the top is used in four different ways. Choose the option in which the usage of the word is INCORRECT or INAPPROPRIATE.*

23. Pull

A. Pull aside the curtains and let in some fresh air.
B. I decided to pull away from the venture due to differences of opinion with my partners.
C. Being a charismatic leader that he is, he can certainly pull the crowds.
D. The municipal corporation has decided to pull down all illegal.

24. Shade

A. Nina's bedroom was painted in a soft shade of pink.
B. Abdul is a dubious character who is suspected of being involved in several shady deals.
C. The weary traveler rested for a while in the shade of a tree.
D. The people in the strife torn region have been living in the shade of fear for several years.

25. Run

A. I must run fast to catch up with him.
B. Our team scored a goal against the run of play.
C. You can't run over him like that.
D. The newly released book is enjoying a popular run.

26. Round

A. The police fired a round of tear gas shells.
B. The shop is located round the corner.
C. We took a ride on the merry-go-round.
D. I shall proceed further only after you come around to admitting it.

27. Buckle

A. After the long hike our knees were beginning to buckle.
B. The horse suddenly broke into a buckle.
C. Sometimes, an earthquake can make a bridge buckle.
D. People should learn to buckle up as soon as they get into the car.

28. File

A. You will find the paper in the file under C.
B. I need to file an insurance claim.
C. The cadets were marching in a single file.
D. When the parade was on, a soldier broke the file.

Directions (Qs. No. 29-32): *In each of the following questions there are sentences that form a paragraph. Identify the sentence(s) or part(s) of sentence(s) that is/are correct in terms of grammar and usage (including spelling, punctuation and logical consistency). Then, choose the most appropriate option.*

29. A. In 1849, a poor Bavarian imigrant named Levi Strauss
B. landed in San Francisco, California,
C. at the invitation of his brother-in-law David Stern
D. owner of dry goods business.

A. B only B. B and C
C. A and B D. A, B and D

30. A. In response to the allegations and condemnation pouring in,
B. Nike implemented comprehensive changes in their labour policy.
C. from the public would become a prominent media issue,
D. Nike sought to be a industry leader in employee relations.

A. D and A B. D only
C. A and D D. B, C and D

31. A. Charges and counter charges mean nothing.
B. to the few million who have lost their home.
C. The nightmare is far from over, for the government
D. is still unable to reach hundreds who are marooned.

A. A only B. C only
C. A and C D. A, C and D

32. A. I did not know what to make of you.
B. Because you'd lived in India, I associate you more with my parents than with me.
C. And yet you were unlike my cousins in Calcutta, who seem so innocent and obedient when I visited them.
D. You were not curious about me in the least.

A. A only B. A and B
C. B only D. A and D

Directions (Qs. No. 33-36): *In each question, there are five sentences. Each sentence has a pair of words that are italicized and highlighted. From the italicized and highlighted words, select the most appropriate words (A or B) to form correct sentences. The sentences are followed by options that indicate the words, which may be selected to correctly complete the set of sentence. From the options given, choose the most appropriate one.*

33. Anita wore a beautiful ***broach (A)/brooch (B)*** on the lapel of her jacket. If you want to complain about the amenities in your neighbourhood, please meet you ***councillor (A)/Counselor (B)***. I would like you ***advice (A)/advise (B)*** on which job I should choose. The last scene provided a ***climactic (A)/ climatic (B)*** ending to the film. Jean that ***flair (A)/ flare (B)*** at the bottom are in fashion these days.

A. BABAA B. BABAB
C. BAAAB D. ABABA

34. The cake had lots of ***currents (A)/currants(B)*** and nuts in it. If you engage in such ***exceptional (A)/ exceptionable (B)*** behaviour, I will be forced to punish you. He has the same capacity as an adult to ***consent (A)/assent (B)*** to surgical treatment. The minister is ***obliged (A)/compelled (B)*** to report regularly to a parliamentary board. His analysis of the situation is far too ***sanguine (A)/genuine (B)***.

A. BBABA B. BBAAA
C. BBBBA D. ABBAB

35. She managed to bite back the ***ironic (A)/caustic (B)*** retort on the tip of her tongue. He gave an impassioned and ***valid (A)/cogent (B)*** plea for judicial reform. I am not ***adverse (A)/averse (B)*** to helping out. The ***coupe (A)/coup (B)*** broke away as the train climbed the hill. They heard the bells ***peeling (A)/pealing (B)*** far and wide.

A. BBABA B. BBBAB
C. BAABB D. ABBAA

36. We were not successful in ***defusing (A)/diffusing (B)*** the Guru's ideas. The students ***baited (A)/ bated (B)*** the instructor with irrelevant questions. The ***hoard (A)/horde (B)*** rushed into the campus. The prisoner's ***interment (A)/internment (B)*** came to an end with his early release. The hockey team could not deal with his ***unsociable (A)/unsocial (B)*** tendencies.

A. BABBA B. BBABB
C. BABAA D. ABBAB

Directions (Qs. No. 37-40): *Each of the following questions has a sentence with two blanks. Given below each question are four pairs of words. Choose the pair that best completes the sentence.*

37. The genocides in Bosnia and Rwanda, apart from being mis-described in the most sinister and _____ manner as 'ethnic cleansing', were also blamed, in further hand-washing rhetoric, on something dark and interior to _____ and perpetrators alike.

A. innovative; communicator
B. exigent; exploiters
C. enchanting; leaders
D. disingenuous; victims

38. As navigators, calendar makers, and other _____ of the night sky accumulated evidence to the contrary, ancient astronomers were formed to _____ that certain bodies might move in circles about points, which in turn moved in circles about the earth.

A. scrutinizers; believe B. observers; concede
C. observers; agree D. students; conclude

39. Every human being, after the first few days of his life, is a product of two factors; on the one hand, there is his _____ endowment; and on the other hand, there is the effect of environment, including _____.

A. constitutional; weather
B. congenital; education
C. genetic; pedagogy
D. personal; climate

40. Exhaustion of natural resources, destruction of individual initiative by governments, control over men's minds by central _____ of education and propaganda are some of the major evils which appear to be on the increase as a result of the impact of science upon minds suited by _____ to an earlier kind of world.

A. tenets; fixation B. organs; tradition
C. aspects; inhibitions D. institutions; inhibitions

41. Sheela purchases two varieties of apples - A and B - for a total of ₹ 2800. The weight in kg of A and B purchased by Sheela are in the ratio 5 : 8 but the cost per kg of A is 20% more than that of B. Sheela sells and B with profit of 15% and 10% respectively. What is the overall profit in Rupees?

A. 340 B. 600
C. 240 D. 480

Directions (Qs. No. 42 and 43): *Each of the following questions has a paragraph from which the last sentence has been deleted. From the given options, choose the one that completes the paragraph in the most appropriate way.*

42. Jawaharlal Nehru seemed an unlikely candidate to lead India towards its vision. Under the cotton Khadi he wore in deference to the dictates of Congress, he remained the quintessential English gentleman. In a land of mysteries, he was a cool rationalist. The mind that had exulted in the discovery of science at Cambridge never ceased to be appalled by his fellow Indians who refused to stir from their homes on days proclaimed inauspicious by their favourite astrologers. He was a publicly declared agnostic in the most intensely spiritual area in the world, and he never ceased to proclaim the horror the word 'region' inspired in him. Nehru despised India's priests, her sadhus, her chanting monks and pious 'skerkhs'.

A. And yet, the India of those sadhus and the superstition-haunted masses had accepted Nehru.
B. They had only served, he felt, to impede her progress.
C. The Mahatma had made it clear that it was on his shoulders that he wished his mantle to fall.
D. Nehru's heart told him to follow the Mahatma and his heart, he would later admit, had beed right.

43. Birth rates have fallen dramatically- and voluntarily. Coercive birth control, including paying people not to have babies, was discredited and abandoned decades ago. Nearly two — thirds of the couples in poor countries now use birth control, and not because some patriarchal westerner told them to. In the 1970S, the government of Bangladesh offered people in the Matlals region low-cost contraceptive supplies and advice. Birth rates promptly fell well below those of neighbouring regions. So Bangladesh extended the service nationally and its birth rate plummeted from six children per woman to three.

A. The 'population bomb' has already gone off.

B. Given the choice, people want fewer children

C. Governments want fewer children since their own life expectancy falls with rising numbers.

D. Even when birth rates fall, there is a lag which means population keeps growing far decades until birth and death rates even out.

44. Most people at their first consultation take a furtive look at the surgeon's hands in the hope of reassurance. Prospective patients look for delicacy, sensitivity, steadiness, perhaps unblemished pallor. On this basis, Henry Perowne loses a number of cases each year. Generally, he knows it's about to happen before the patient does: the downward glance repeated, the prepared questions beginning to falter, the overemphatic thanks during the retreat to the door.

A. Other people do not communicate due to their poor observation.

B. Other patients don't like what they see but are ignorant of their right to go elsewhere.

C. But Perowne himself is not concerned.'

D. But others will take their place, he thought.

45. Trade protectionism, disguised as concern for the climate, is raising its head. Citing competitiveness concerns, powerful industrialized countries are holding out threats of a levy on imports of energy-intensive products from developing countries that refuse to accept their demands. The actual source of protectionist sentiment in the OECD countries is, of course, their current lack lustre economic performance, combined with the challenges posed by the rapid economic rise of China and India - in that order.

A. Climate change is evoked to bring trade protectionism through the back door.

B. OECD countries are taking refuge in climate change issues to erect trade barriers against these two countries.

C. Climate change concerns have come as a convenient stick to beat the rising trade power of China and India.

D. Defenders of the global economic status quo are posing as climate change champions.

46. Mattancherry is Indian Jewry's most famous settlement. Its pretty streets of pastel coloured houses, connected by first-floor passages and home to the last twelve saree-and-sarong-wearing, whiteskinned Indian Jews are visited by thousands of tourists each year. Its synagogue, built in 1568, with a floor of blue-and-white Chinese tiles, a carpet given by Haile Selassie and the frosty Yaheh selling tickets at the door, stands as an image of religious tolerance.

A. Mattancherry represents, therefore, the perfect picture of peaceful co-existence.

B. India's Jews have almost never suffered discrimination, except for European colonizers and each other.

C. Jews in India were always tolerant.

D. Religious tolerance has always been only a facade and nothing more.

47. Given the cultural and intellectual interconnections, the question of what is 'Western' and what is 'Eastern' (or 'Indian') is often heard to decide, and the issue can be discussed only in more dialectical terms. The diagnosis of a thought as 'purely Western' or 'purely Indian' can be very illusory.

A. Thoughts are not the kind of things that can be easily categorized.

B. Though 'occidentalism' and 'orientalism' as dichotomous concepts have found many adherents.

C. 'East is East and West is West' has been a discredited notion for a long time now.

D. The origin of a thought is not the kind of thing to which 'purity' happens easily.

48. Aruns present age in years is 40% of Barun's. In another few years, Arun's age will be half of Barun's. By what percentage will Barun's age increase during this period?

A. 10 B. 15

C. 30 D. 20

49. A person can complete a job in 120 days. He works alone on Day 1. On Day 2, he is joined by another person who also can complete the job in exactly 120 days. On Day 3, they are joined by another person of equal efficiency. Like this, everyday a new person with the same efficiency joins the work. How many days are required to complete the job?

A. 21 B. 17

C. 19 D. 15

50. The passage given below is followed by four alternate summaries. Choose the option that best captures the essence of the passage.

Foreign peacekeepers often exist in a bubble in the poor countries in which they are deployed, they live in posh compounds, drive fancy vehicles, and distance themselves from locals. This may be partially justified as they are outsiders, living in constant fear, performing a job that is emotionally draining. But they are often despised by the locals, and many would like them to leave. A better solution would be bottom-up peace building, which would involve their spending more time working with communities, understanding their grievances and earning their trust, rather than only meeting government officials.

A. Peacekeeping duties would be more effectively performed by local residents given their better understanding, knowledge and rapport with their own communities.
B. The environment in poor countries has tended to make foreign peacekeeping forces live in enclaves, but it is time to change this scenario.
C. Extravagant lifestyles and an aloof attitude among the foreigners working as peacekeepers in poor countries have justifiably make them the target of local anger.
D. Peacekeeping forces in foreign countries have tended to be aloof for valid reasons but would be more effective if they worked more closely with local communities.

51. Four jumbled up sentences, related to a topic, are given below. Three of them can be put together to form a coherent paragraph. Identify the odd one out and key in the number of the sentence as your answer:

A. The legal status of resources mined in space remains ambiguous; and while the market for asteroid minerals is currently nonexistent, this is likely to change as technical hurdles diminish.
B. Outer space is a commons, and all of it is open for exploration, however, space law developed in the 1950s and 60s is state-centric and arguably ill-suited to a commercial future.
C. Laws adopted by the US and Luxembourg are first steps, but they only protect firms from competing claims by their compatriots; a Chinese company will not be bound by US law.
D. Critics say the US is conferring rights that it has no authority to confer; Russia in particular has condemned this, citing the US' disrespect for international law.

Directions (Qs. No. 52-56): *Arrange the sentences A, B, C and D in a proper sequence so as to make a coherent paragraph.*

52. A. Good advertising can make people buy your products even if it sucks.
B. A dollar spent on brainwashing is more cost-effective than a dollar spent on product improvement.
C. That's important because it takes pressure off you to make good products.
D. Obviously, there's a minimum quality that every product has to achieve: it should be able to withstand the shipping process without becoming unrecognizable.

A. ACBD B. BDCA
C. ADBC D. DABC

53. A. And that the pursuit of money by whatever design within the law is always benign.
B. And it holds broadly that the greater the amount of money, the greater the intelligence.
C. This is the institutional truth of Wall Street, this you will be required to believe.
D. The institutional truth of the financial world holds that association with money implies intelligence.

A. ABCD B. BACD
C. DBAC D. BCDA

54. A. That Hollywood is a man's world is certainly true, but it is not the whole truth.
B. Even Renaissance film actress, Jodie Foster, who hosts this compendium of movie history, confesses surprise at this.
C. She says that she had no idea that women were so active in the industry even in those days.
D. During the silent era, for example, female scriptwriters outnumbered males 10 to 1.

A. ADCB B. BDAC
C. DACB D. ADBC

55. A. But Buddhism is more severely analytical.
B. In the Christian tradition there is also a concern for the fate of human society conceived as a whole, rather than merely as a sum or network of individuals.
C. Salvation is a property, or achievement of individuals.
D. Not only does it dissolve society into individuals, the individual in turn is dissolved into component parts and instants, a stream of events.

A. DCAB B. CBAD
C. ABCD D. DCBA

56. A. However, the real challenge today is in unlearning, which is much harder.
B. But the new world of business behaves differently from the world in which we grew up.
C. Learning is important for both people and organizations.
D. Each of us has a 'mental model' that we've used over the years to make sense.

A. CADB B. BDCA
C. ACDB D. CDAB

Directions (Qs. No. 57-66): *In the following questions four alternatives for the given idiom/phrase. Choose the alternative which best expresses the meaning of the given idiom/phrase.*

57. He has all his ducks in a row, he is complacent.
(*a*) has everything ready
(*b*) is well organized
(*c*) always scores a zero
(*d*) never gets confused
A. (*a*) B. (*c*)
C. (*b*) D. (*d*)

58. a damp squib
(*a*) rainy weather (*b*) a disappointing result
(*c*) a skirt in a laundry (*d*) None of the above
A. (*b*) B. (*a*)
C. (*d*) D. (*c*)

59. My sincere advice to my maid-servant fell on stony ground.
(*a*) was counter productive
(*b*) had a strong impact
(*c*) made one stubborn
(*d*) had little success
A. (*c*) B. (*a*)
C. (*d*) D. (*b*)

60. in cold blood
(*a*) angrily (*b*) deliberately
(*c*) excitedly (*d*) slowly
A. (*b*) B. (*c*)
C. (*d*) D. (*a*)

61. Adolescence is a period of halo cyan days.
(*a*) hard days (*b*) of mental pressure
(*c*) happy days (*d*) days of preparation
A. (*a*) B. (*c*)
C. (*d*) D. (*b*)

62. To smell a rat
(*a*) to smell foul (*b*) to see a rat
(*c*) to chase a rat (*d*) to be suspicious
A. (*b*) B. (*d*)
C. (*a*) D. (*c*)

63. Once the case reached the court, the police washed their hands off it.
(*a*) waited for a response to
(*b*) claimed credit for
(*c*) disassociated themselves from
(*d*) seemed eager to continue
A. (*c*) B. (*d*)
C. (*a*) D. (*b*)

64. To take someone for a ride
(*a*) to give a ride to someone
(*b*) to deceive someone
(*c*) to be indifferent
(*d*) to disclose a secret
A. (*c*) B. (*d*)
C. (*a*) D. (*b*)

65. She wanted to go hitch-hiking but her mother put her foot down and now she's 'going by bus.
(*a*) took a firm stand
(*b*) expressed her displeasure
(*c*) scolded her badly
(*d*) got irritated
A. (*b*) B. (*d*)
C. (*a*) D. (*c*)

66. To move heaven and earth
(*a*) to cause an earthquake
(*b*) to try everything possible
(*c*) to pray to all Gods
(*d*) to travel in a rocket
A. (*b*) B. (*a*)
C. (*d*) D. (*c*)

Instructions: It is sometimes mooted that there can be democracy in a two-party system. That would be correct if politics were a game like cricket or football; but politics is not sports.

67. Which of the following would strengthen the argument?
(*a*) Two party system functions well
(*b*) Politics is a dirty game.
(*c*) Two political parties limit the choice of the voters.
(*d*) None of these.
A. (*c*) B. (*a*)
C. (*d*) D. (*d*)

68. Which of the following would weaken the argument?
(*a*) The game of politics is played like any other game, for example, football.
(*b*) Politics is not a sport.
(*c*) Political parties struggle for power.
(*d*) None of these.
A. (*b*) B. (*d*)
C. (*a*) D. (*c*)

69. The assumption/assumptions of the argument is/are which of the following?

I. Politics is not a game.
II. Two party system is ideal for democracy
III. Cricket is played by two teams.

(*a*) Only I (*b*) Only II
(*c*) Only III (*d*) I, II, III

A. (*d*) B. (*c*)
C. (*a*) D. (*b*)

Instructions: We will have to take more interest in hydro-electric projects. As the prices of oil have increased, it has become vital that such renewable sources of energy are tapped.

70. The assumption/assumptions of the argument is/are which of the following?

I. Hydro electric power is a renewable source of energy.
II. Hydro electric power is comparatively cheaper.

(*a*) Only I
(*b*) Only II
(*c*) Both I and II
(*d*) Neither I nor II

A. (*b*) B. (*a*)
C. (*d*) D. (*c*)

71. Which of the following will weaken the argument?

(*a*) Generation of hydroelectric power is more costly than oil.
(*b*) OPEC increased oil prices.
(*c*) Without energy we cannot manage.
(*d*) None of these.

A. (*c*) B. (*a*)
C. (*d*) D. (*b*)

Directions (Qs. No. 72-74): *In each question there are five sentences or parts of sentences that form a paragraph. Identify the sentence(s) or part(s) of sentence(s) that is/ are correct in terms of grammar and usage. Then, choose the most appropriate option.*

72. (*a*) When I returned to home, I began to read
(*b*) everything I could get my hand on about Israel.
(*c*) That same year Israel's Jewish Agency sent
(*d*) a Shaliach a sort of recruiter to Minneapolis.
(*e*) I became one of his most active devotees.

A. (*c*) and (*e*) B. (*c*) only
C. (*e*) only D. (*b*), (*c*) & (*e*)

73. (*a*) It is sometimes told that democratic
(*b*) government originated in the city-states
(*c*) of ancient Greece. Democratic ideals have been handed to us from that time.
(*d*) In truth, however, this is an unhelpful assertion.
(*e*) The Greeks gave us the word, hence did not provide us with a model.

A. (*a*), (*b*) & (*d*) B. (*b*), (*c*) & (*d*)
C. (*b*) & (*d*) D. (*b*) only

74. (*a*) So once an economy is actually in recession,
(*b*) The authorities can, in principle, move the economy
(*c*) Out of slump - assuming hypothetically
(*d*) That they know how to - by a temporary stimulus.
(*e*) In the longer term, however, such policies have no affect on the overall behaviour of the economy.

A. (*a*), (*b*) & (*e*) B. (*b*), (*c*) & (*e*)
C. (*c*) & (*d*) D. (*d*) only

Instructions: From the given options, choose the sentence that completes the paragraph in the most appropriate way.

75. I am sometimes attacked for imposing 'rules'. Nothing could be further from the truth: I hate rules. All I do is report on how consumers react to different stimuli. I may say to a copywriter, "Research shows that commercials with celebrities are below average in persuading people to buy products. Are you sure you want to use a celebrity?" Call that a rule? Or I may say to an art director, "Research suggests that if you set the copy in black type on a white background, more people will read it than if you set it in white type on a black background."

(*a*) Guidance based on applied research can hardly qualify as 'rules'.
(*b*) Thus, all my so called 'rules' are rooted in applied research.
(*c*) A suggestion perhaps, but scarcely a rule.
(*d*) Such principles are unavoidable if one wants to be systematic about consumer behaviour.
(*e*) Fundamentally it is about consumer behaviour - not about celebrities or type settings.

A. (*c*) B. (*a*)
C. (*d*) D. (*b*)

76. We can usefully think of theoretical models as maps, which help us navigate unfamiliar territory. The most accurate map that it is possible to construct would be of no practical use whatsoever, for it would be an exact replica, on exactly the same scale, of the place where we were. Good maps pull out the most important features and throw away a huge amount of much less valuable information. Of course, maps can be bad as well as good — witness the attempts by medieval Europe to produce a map of the world. In the same way, a bad theory, no matter how impressive it may seem in principle, does little or nothing to help us understand a problem.

(*a*) But good theories, just like good maps, are invaluable, even if they are simplified.

(*b*) But good theories, just like good maps, will never represent unfamiliar concepts in detail.

(*c*) But good theories, just like good maps, need to balance detail and feasibility of representation.

(*d*) But good theories, just like good maps, are accurate only at a certain level of abstraction.

(*e*) But good theories, just like good maps, are useful in the hands of a user who knows their limitations.

A. (*d*) B. (*a*)
C. (*c*) D. (*b*)

77. Age has a curvilinear relationship with the exploitation of opportunity. Initially, age will increase the likelihood that a person will exploit an entrepreneurial opportunity because people gather much of the knowledge necessary to exploit opportunities over the course of their lives, and because age provides credibility in transmitting that information to others. However, as people become older, their willingness to bear risks declines, their opportunity costs rise, and they become less receptive to new information.

(*a*) As a result, people transmit more information rather than experiment with new ideas as they reach an advanced age.

(*b*) As a result, people are reluctant to experiment with new ideas as they reach an advanced age.

(*c*) As a result, only people with lower opportunity costs exploit opportunity when they reach an advanced age.

(*d*) As a result, people become reluctant to exploit entrepreneurial opportunities when they reach an advanced age.

(*e*) As a result, people depend on credibility rather than on novelty as they reach an advanced age.

A. (*d*) B. (*b*)
C. (*c*) D. (*a*)

78. Relations between the factory and the dealer are distant and usually strained as the factory tries to force cars on the dealers to smooth out production. Relations between the dealer and the customer are equally strained because dealers continuously adjust prices - make deals - to adjust demand with supply while maximizing profits. This becomes a system marked by 'a lack of long-term commitment' on either side, which maximizes feelings of mistrust. In order to maximize their bargaining positions, everyone holds back information - the dealer about the product and the consumer about his true desires.

(*a*) As a result, 'deal making' becomes rampant, without concern for customer satisfaction.

(*b*) As a result, inefficiencies creep into the supply chain.

(*c*) As a result, everyone treats the other as an adversary, rather than as an ally.

(*d*) As a result, fundamental innovations are becoming scarce in the automobile industry.

(*e*) As a result, everyone loses in the long run.

A. (*d*) and (*a*)
B. (*b*)
C. (*c*)
D. (*e*)

79. In the evolving world order, the comparative advantage of the United States lies in its military force: Diplomacy and international law have always been regarded as annoying encumbrances, unless they can be used to advantage against an enemy. Every active player in world affairs professes to seek only peace and to prefer negotiation to violence and coercion.

(*a*) However, diplomacy has often been used as a mask by nations which intended to use force.

(*b*) However, when the veil is lifted, we commonly see that diplomacy is understood as a disguise for the rule of force.

(*c*) However, history has shown that many of these nations do not practice what they profess.

(*d*) However, history tells us that peace is professed by those who intend to use violence.

A. (*d*) B. (*a*)
C. (*b*) D. (*c*)

80. In a certain language 'to be polite' is coded as 'fa so la', 'she is polite' is coded as 'so me pa' and 'to have manners' is coded as 'na la ma'. Which of the following is the code for 'be' in that language?

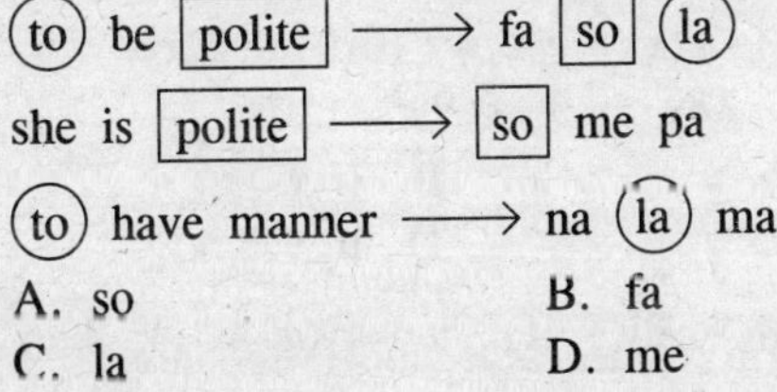

A. so B. fa
C. la D. me

81. Study the following series:

TJENUQAKIOGRMSPBHFDLVC

If in a certain code 'GRIM' is coded as 'RMOS' and 'DUSK' is coded as 'LQPI' how will 'STOP' be coded in the same code language?

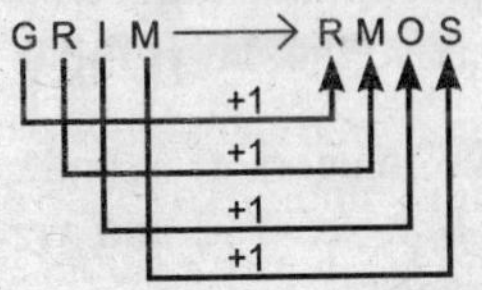

A. MJIS B. PJGB
C. JPJIS D. MJGB

82. A television channel has scheduled five half-hour shows between 9.30 pm and midnight. Out of the three family drama shows 'Main Sati Hoon' has social message for audience. The family dramas bring in maximum revenues for the channel and they are scheduled one after another. The show 'Detective Doom' is a suspense thriller, a family drama and also has social message. Two of the family dramas have social message and one not having social message has adult content. There are two shows which have adult content and they have been scheduled at 10.30 pm and 11.30 pm. The show 'HIV and India' is a news based program and also has social message. 'Midnight Murders' neither has social message nor is a family drama and is scheduled to 11.30 pm. The two news based programs but are not family dramas have been given two adjacent slots. The show 'Main Sati Hoon' has been scheduled for 10.00 to 10.30 pm slot and has a family drama preceding it. 'Laugh a while' is the fifth program.

When is 'Laugh a While' scheduled?

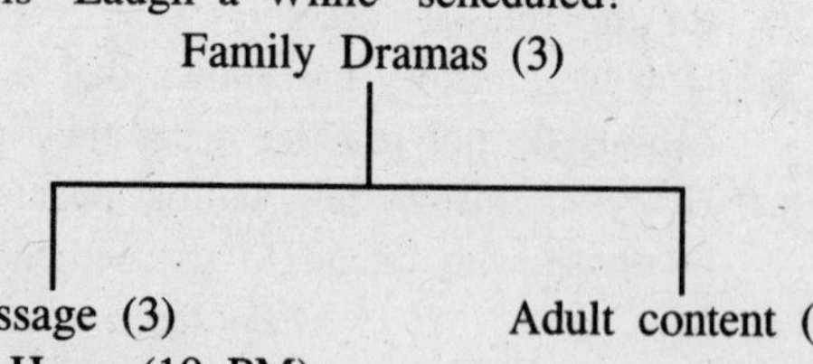

A. 9:00 pm to 9:30 pm
B. 9:30 pm to 10:00 pm
C. 10:00 pm to 10:30 pm
D. 10:30 pm to 11:00 pm

83. I. $12x^2 + 11x + 12 = 10x^2 + 22x$
II. $13y^2 - 18y + 3 = 9y^2 - 10y$

A. if $x > y$ B. if $x \geq y$
C. if $x < y$ D. if $x \leq y$

84. If $u^2 + (u - 2v - 1)^2 = -4v(u + v)$, then what is the value of $u + 3v$?

A. ¼ B. 0
C. ½ D. –1/4

85. I. $\sqrt{1225x} + \sqrt{4900} = 0$
II. $(81)^{1/4}y + (343)^{1/3} = 0$

A. if $x > y$ B. if $x \geq y$
C. if $x < y$ D. if $x \leq y$

86. Three positive integers x, y and z are in arithmetic progression. If $y - x > 2$ and $xyz = 5(x + y + z)$, then $z - x$ equals:

A. 8 B. 12
C. 14 D. 10

87. If $\log_4 m + \log_4 n = \log_2 (m + n)$ where m and n are postive real numbers, then which of the following must be true?

A. $\frac{1}{m} + \frac{1}{n} = 1$
B. $m = n$
C. $\frac{1}{m} + \frac{1}{n} = 2$
D. No values of m and n can satisfy the given equation

88. The evolution of Bring Your Own Device (BYOD) trend has been as proxfound as it has been rapid. It represents the more visible sign that the boundaries between personal life and work life are blurring. The 9 am - 5 pm model of working solely from office has become archaic and increasingly people are working extended hours from a range of locations. At the very heart of this evolution is he ability to access enterprise networks from anywhere and anytime. The concept of cloud computing serves effectively to extend the office out of office. The much-heralded benefit of BYOD is greater productivity. However, recent research has suggested that this is the greatest myth of BYOD and the reality is that BYOD in practice poses new challenges that may outweigh the benefits. A worldwide survey commissioned by Fortinet chose to look at attitude towards BYOD and security from the user's point of view instead of the IT managers. Specifically the survey was conducted in 15 territories on a group of graduate employees in their early twenties because they represent the first generation to enter the workplace with an expectation of own divide use. Moreover they also represent tomorrow's influences and decision makers. The survey findings reveal that of financial organization, the decision to embrace BYOD is extremely dangerous. Large organizations will have mature IT strategies and policies in place. But what about smaller financial businesses? They might not have such well-developed strategies to protect confidential data.

Crucially, within younger employee group, 55% of the people share an expectation that they should be allowed to use their own devices in the workplace or for work purposes. With this expectation comes the very real risk that employees may consider contravening company policy banning the use of own devices. The threats posed by this level of subversion cannot be overstated. The survey casts doubt on the idea of BYOD leading to greater productivity by revealing the real reason people wnat to use their own devices. Only 26% of people in this age group cite efficiency as the reason they want to use their own devices, while 63% admit that the main reason is so they have access to their favourite applications. But with personal applications so close to hand, the risks to the business must surely include distraction and time wasting. To support this assumption 46% of people polled acknowledged time wasting as the greatest threat to the organization, while 42% citing greater exposure to theft or loss of confidential data. Clearly, from a user perspective there is great deal of contradiction surrounding BYOD and there exists an undercurrent of selfishness where users except to use their own devices, but mostly for personal interest. They recognize the risks to the organization but are adamant that those risks are work taking.

Which of the following is not true about BYOD?

A. BYOD enables employees to access enterprise network from anywhere and anytime
B. Due to evolution of BYOD trend the 9 am - 5 pm model of working solely from office has become outdated
C. Recent research has confimed that BYOD boosts organizational productivity
D. The concept of cloud computing facilities the BYOD trend

89. Six bells commence tolling together and toll at intervals of 2, 4, 6, 8, 10 and 12 seconds respectively. In 30 minutes, how many times do they toll together?

A. 10 times B. 16 times
C. 20 times D. 25 times

90. Mr. Jose buys some eggs. After bringing the eggs home, he finds two to be rotten and throws them away. Of the remaining eggs, he puts five-ninth in his fridge, and brings the rest to his mother's house. She cooks two eggs and puts the rest in her fridge. If her fridge cannot hold more than five eggs, what is the maximum possible number of eggs bought by Mr. Jose?

A. 9 B. 17
C. 11 D. 29

Directions (Qs. No. 91-92): *Read the following passage and answer the question that follow it.*

Six friends Abhishek, Deepak, Mridul, Pritam, Ranjan and Salil married within a year in the months of February, April, July, September, November and December and in the cities of Ahmedabad, Bengaluru, Chennai, Delhi, Mumbai and Kolkata, but not necessarily following the above order. The brides' names were Geetika, Jasmine, Hema, Brinda, Ipsita and Veena once again not following any order.

The following are some facts about their weddings.

- Mridul's wedding took place in Chennai, however he was not married to Geetika or Veena
- Abhishek's wedding took place in Ahmedabad and Ranjan's in Delhi; however, neither of them was married to Jasmin or Brinda
- The wedding in Kolkata took place in February
- Hema's wedding took place in April, but not in Ahmedabad
- Geetika and Ipsita got married in February and November and in Chennai and Kolkata but not following the above order
- Pritam visited Bengaluru and Kolkata only after his marriage in December
- Salil was married to Jasmine in September

91. Hema's husband is:

A. Abhishke B. Deepak
C. Ranjan D. Pritam

92. In Mumbai, the wedding of one of the friends took place in the month of:

A. April B. September
C. November D. December

93. Identify the odd one out:

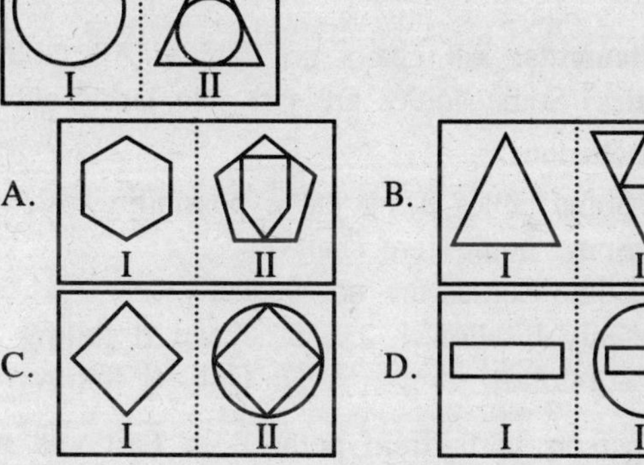

94. 29, 37, 21, 43, 13, 53, 5

A. 37 B. 53
C. 13 D. 43

95. 150, 290, 560, 1120, 2140, 4230, 8400

A. 2140 B. 560
C. 1120 D. 4230

96. An analyst is comparing the financial performance of three companies: P, Q, and R, over two consecutive years. The profits of companies P and Q increased by 20% and 15% respectively from Year 1 to Year 2, while company R saw a profit decrease of 10% in the same period. In Year 1, the ratio of the profits of companies P, Q, and R was 2 : 3 : 5 respectively. If the total combined profit of the three companies in Year 2 was ₹ 1,44,000 and the profit increase of company Q from Year 1 to Year 2 was ₹ 6,000, calculate the profit of company R in Year 1.

A. ₹ 50,000 B. ₹ 60,000
C. ₹ 75,000 D. ₹ 40,000

97. Statements: Some pearls are gems. All gems are diamonds. No diamond is stone. Some stones are coarls.

Conclusions:

I. Some stones are pearls
II. Some corals being diamond is a possibility.
III. No stone is pearl.

A. Only I follows
B. Only II follows
C. Either I or III follows
D. None of these

98. Statements: Some apartments are flats. Some flats are buildings. All buildings are bungalows. All bungalows are gardens.

Conclusions:

I. All apartments being building is a possibility
II. All bungalows are not buildings
III. No flat is garden.

A. None follows
B. Only I follows
C. Either I or III follows
D. II and III follows

99. Statements: All chairs are tables. All tables are bottles. Some bottles are jars. No jar is bucket.

Conclusions:

I. Some tables being jar is possibility.
II. Some bottles are chairs.
III. Some bottles are not bucket.

A. Only I follows B. I and II follow
C. All follow D. Only II follows

100. A person starts from point P in East and moves 12 m to point Q. Then, he moves right 8 m to point R. Again he moves right for 6 m to point S. Then, he moves 6 m in the North to point T. Finally from there he goes to left for 6 m to point U. Which of three point he would form a triangle whose all the angles are less than 90°?

A. PTQ B. QTR
C. UTS D. TSR

101. If A + B means A is the father of B. If A × B means A is the sister of B. If A \$ B means A is the wife of B. If A% B means A is the mother of B. If A ÷ B means A is the son of B. What should come in place of the question mark, to establish that J is the brother of T in the expression?

J ÷ P % H ? T % L

A. × B. ÷
C. \$ D. Either ÷ or ×

Directions (Qs. No. 102-106): *Read the following data carefully and answer the question that follow it.*

Two friends Raghu and Manav invested amount on simple and compound interest. The difference between the amount invested on by Raghu and Manav is ₹ 6000 and the total simple interest earned by Raghu and Manav is ₹ 20640. Total amount invested in compound interest by Raghu and Manav is ₹ 25000 and the ratio between the amount invested on compound interest by the two friends is 3 : 2. Raghu and Manav invested on simple interest at the rate of 20% and 24% for 5 and 2 years respectively. For compund interest, Raghu and Manav invested at the rate of interest of 10% and 20% for two years and a year respectively.

102. What per cent is the total sum invested by Raghu and Manav on the compound interest of the total sum invested on simple interest? (Manav's investment is more than that of Raghu's investment).

A. 89% B. 85%
C. 83% D. 88%

103. What is the ratio between the amounts got after 2 years and a year on the sum invested by Raghu and Manav on compound interest calculated annually.

A. 81 : 77 B. 83 : 121
C. 180 : 120 D. 121 : 180

104. What per cent more is the simple interest earned by Raghu than the simple interest earned by Manav?

A. 39% B. 41%
C. 40% D. 36%

105. What will be the average amount invested by Raghu and Manav on simple interest?

A. 18600 B. 18100
C. 15000 D. 19500

106. What will be the difference between the compound interest earned by Raghu and Manav when compounded annually?

A. ₹ 900 B. ₹ 960
C. ₹ 800 D. ₹ 600

Directions (Qs. No. 107-110): *Read the information given below and solve the questions based on it.*

	Match played	**Won**	**Drawn**	**Lost**	**Goals for**	**Goals against**
Bihar	2		1		2	4
Punjab	2				3	7
Haryana						1

107. What is the total number of matches played in the competition?

A. 6 B. 3
C. 9 D. None of these

108. What did the score card read in favour of Punjab in Punjab-Haryana match?

A. 2-5 B. 1-5
C. 1-4 D. 1-6

109. How many matches did Punjab lose?

A. 0 B. 1
C. 2 D. 0 or 1

110. How many goals did Haryana score?

A. 5 B. 1
C. 3 D. 7

111. How much you earn is less important. What is more important is how you earn, i.e., your methods of earning?

A. How you earn is an important
B. How much you earn is as important
C. How you earn is not as important

A. Only A B. Only B
C. Only C D. None of these

112.

Letters	P	M	A	E	J	K	D	R	W	H	I	U	T	F
Digits/ Symbols Conditions	4	$	1	2	3	#	5	@	©	6	%	δ	7	9

(*i*) If the first letter is a consonant and the last letter is a vowel, the codes of both these are to be interchanged.

(*ii*) If both the first and the last letters are consonants both these are to be coded as per the code of the last letter.

(*iii*) If the first letter is vowel and the last letter is a consonant both these are coded as

Note: All the remaining letters are to be coded as per their original codes.

ERWHKA

A 2@©6#1 B. 1@©6#2
C. 1@©6#1 D. 2@©6#2

113. What will be the cost of the second necklace?

I. The cost of the first necklace is more than 1/5 of the second and the cost of the third necklace is more than 2/5 of the second. The total cost of all the three necklaces is ₹ 120000.

II. The cost of the first necklace is 2/5 more than the second. The total cost of all the three necklaces is ₹ 120000.

A. If the data in statement I alone are sufficient to answer the question, while the data in statement II alone are not sufficient to answer the question.
B. If the data in statement II alone are sufficient to answer the question, while the data in statement I alone are not sufficient to answer the question.
C. If the data either in statement I alone or in statement II alone are sufficient to answer the question.
D. If the data in both the statement I and II together are not sufficient to answer the question.

114. How many children are there in the class?

I. Numbers of boys and girls are in the respective ratio of 3 : 4.

II. Number of girls is more than the number of boys by 18.

A. if the data in statement I alone are sufficient to answer question, while the data in statement II alone are not sufficient to answer the question.
B. if the data in statement II alone are sufficient to answer the question, while the data in statement I alone are not sufficient to answer the question.
C. if the data either in statement I alone or in statement II alone are sufficient to answer the question.
D. if the data in both the statements I and II together are necessary to answer the question.

Directions (Qs. No. 15 and 16): *Read the following passage and answer the question that follow it.*

There are two trains A and B. Both trains have four different types of coaches viz. General coaches, sleeper coaches, first class coaches and AC coaches. In train A, there are total 700 passengers. Train B has 30% more passengers than train A. 20% of the passengers of train A are in general coaches. One-fourth of the total number of passengers of train A are in AC coaches. 23% of the passengers of train A are in sleeper class coaches. Remaining passengers of train A are in first class coaches. Total number of passengers in AC coaches in both the trains together is 480. 30% of the number of passengers of train B is in sleeper class coaches, 10% of the total passengers of train B are in first class coaches. Remaining passengers of train B are in general class coaches.

115. If cost of per ticket of first class coach ticket is ₹ 450, what total amount will be generated from first class coaches of train A?

A. ₹ 100080 B. ₹ 108000
C. ₹ 100800 D. ₹ 10800

116. Total number of passengers in general class coaches in both the trains together is approximately. What percentage of total number of passengers in train B?

A. 35 B. 42
C. 45 D. 38

117. An increase, in the cost price of an article, by 22% leads to the value of ₹ 61. What was the original cost price of the article?

A. ₹ 40 B. ₹ 45
C. ₹ 50 D. ₹ 55

118. PBA and PDC are two secants. AD is the diameter of the circle with centre at 0. ∠A = 40°, ∠P = 20°. Find the measure of ∠DBC.

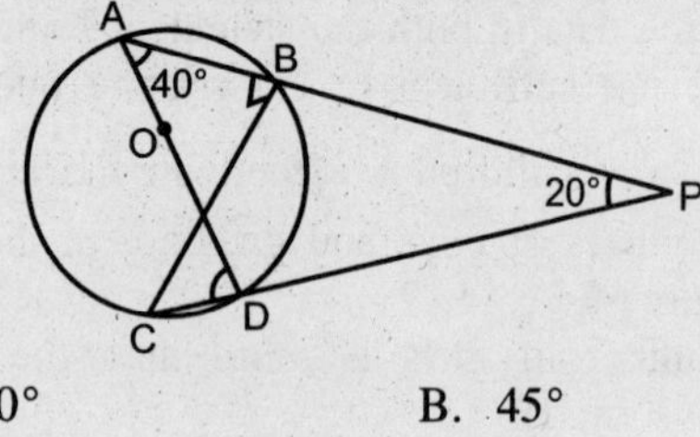

A. 30° B. 45°
C. 50° D. 40°

Directions (Qs. No. 119 and 120): *Read the following passage and answer the question that follow it.*

In a building there are thirteen flats on three floors— II, III and IV. Five flats are unoccupied. Three managers, two teachers, two lawyers and one doctor occupy the remaining flats. There are at least three flats on any floor and not more than six flats on any floor. No two persons of the same profession stay on any floor. On the second floor, out of four flats, one occupant is the lawyer and has only one neighbour. One teacher lives one floor below the other teacher. The doctor is not the neighbour of any the lawyers. No flat is unoccupied on the third floor.

119. How many flats are occupied on the fourth floor?

A. Two B. Three
C. Four D. Data inadequate

120. How many flats are there on the third floor?

A. Three or Four B. Four
C. Five D. Three

Directions (Qs. No. 121-124): *Read the following Instructions and answer the question that follow it.*

Mathematicians are assigned a number called Erdos number (named after the famous mathematician, Paul Erdos). Only Paul Erdos himself has an Erdos number of zero. Any mathematician who has written a research paper with Erdos has an Erdos number of 1.For other mathematicians, the calculation of his/her Erdos number is illustrated below:

Suppose that a mathematician X has co-authored papers with several other mathematicians. 'From among them, mathematician Y has the smallest Erdos number. Let the Erdos number of Y be y. Then X has an Erdos number of $y + 1$. Hence any mathematician with no co-authorship chain connected to Erdos has an Erdos number of infinity.: .

In a seven day long mini-conference organized in memory of Paul Erdos, a close group of eight mathematicians, call them A, B, C, D, E, F, G and H, discussed some research problems. At the beginning of the conference, A was the only participant who had an infinite Erdos number. Nobody had an Erdos number less than that of F.

On the third'day of the conference F co-authored a paper jointly with A and C. This reduced the average Erdos number of the' group of eight mathematicians to 3. The Erdos numbers of B, D, E, G and H remained unchanged with the writing of this paper. Further, no other co-authorship among any three members would have reduced the average Erdos number of the group of eight to as low as 3.

- At the end of the third day, five members of this group had identical Erdos numbers while the other three had Erdos numbers distinct from each other.
- On the fifth day, E co-authored a paper with F which reduced the group's average Erdos number by 0.5. The Erdos numbers of the remaining six were unchanged with the writing of this paper.
- No other paper was written during the conference.

121. The person having the largest Erdos number at the end of the conference must have Erdos number (at that time):

A. 5 B. 7
C. 9 D. 14

122. How many participants in the conference did not change their Erdos number during the conference?

A. 2 B. 3
C. 4 D. 5

123. The Erdos number of C at the end of the conference was:

A. 1 B. 2
C. 3 D. 4

124. The Erdos number of E at the beginning of the conference was:

A. 2 B. 5
C. 6 D. 7

125. Seven offices in an office building are to be painted. The offices, which are on one side of a hallway, are numbered consecutively. One to seven, from the front of the building to the back. Each office is to be painted one colour only according to the following conditions:

- Two offices must be painted white;
- Two offices must be painted blue
- Two offices must be painted green; and one office must be painted yellow
- Two offices painted green must be next to each other
- Two offices painted blue cannot be next to each other
- The offices painted yellow cannot be next to an office painted white
- Office 3 must be painted white

If office 5 is painted white, which of the following

must be true?

A. Office 4 is painted blue
B. Office 2 is painted yellow
C. Office 4 is painted yellow
D. Office 1 is painted blue

126. A scientist is trying to find a cure for the common cold using four ingredients. He can choose from the stable chemicals A, B and C the unstable chemicals W, X, Y and Z. In order for the formula not to explode, there must be two stable chemical in it Also, certain chemical cannot be mixed because of their reaction together. Chemical B cannot be mixed with Chemical W. Chemical Y cannot be mixed with Chemical Z.

Which of the following combinations of chemical is impossible?

I. Using chemical Y and W together
II. Using chemical B and C together
III. Using chemical W, X and Z together

A. III only
B. I and III only
C. I only
D. II only

127. Fare in rupees for three different types of vehicles:

Vehicle	Fare for distance upto					
	2 km	4 km	7 km	10 km	15 km	20 km
Type A	₹ 5.00	₹ 9.00	₹ 13.50	₹ 17.25	₹ 22.25	₹ 26.00
Type B	₹ 7.50	₹ 14.50	₹ 24.25	₹ 33.25	₹ 45.75	₹ 55.75
Type C	₹ 10.00	₹ 19.00	₹ 31.00	₹ 41.50	₹ 56.50	₹ 69.00

Note: Fare per km for intermittent distance is the same.

Ajit Singh wants to travel a distance of 15 kms. He starts his journey by Type A vehicle. After travelling 6 kms, he changes the vehicle to Type B for the remaining distance. How much money will he be spending in all?

A. ₹ 42.25
B. ₹ 36.75
C. ₹ 40.25
D. ₹ 42.75

128. Tap A can fill a tank in 20 hours, B in 25 hours but tap C can empty a full tank in 30 hours. Starting with A, followed by B and C each tap opens alternatively for one hour period till the tank gets filled up completely. In how many hour the tank will be filled up completely?

A. $51\frac{11}{15}$
B. $52\frac{2}{3}$
C. $24\frac{4}{11}$
D. $55\frac{2}{3}$

129. In a code language 'PROVIDE' is written as 'MULYFGB', then what will be code for 'BECAUSE' in same languages:

A. YZHDRVB
B. ZHYDRVB
C. YHZDRVB
D. ZYDHVBR

130. Goodricke Group Ltd. is planning to give top priority to core competence of production and marketing of tea in 2007. The company intends to increase the production of orthodox varieties of tea. Goodricke is planning to invest ₹ 10 crore to modernize the factories. The company has announced a net profit of ₹ 5.49 crore for 2006 as against ₹ 3.76 crore in 2005.

Which of the following can be deduced from the caselet?

A. Core competence can be used for furthering company's interests.
B. Production and marketing is core competence of Goodricke Group.
C. Increase in production of existing products enhances core competence.
D. Core competence leads to modernization.

131. Find the area of the shaded region if ABC is an equilateral triangle of side 6 cm.

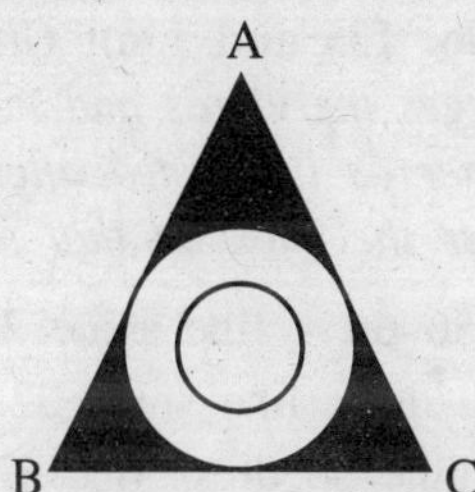

A. 6.15 cm
B. 5.15 cm
C. 4 cm
D. 3.12 cm

132. If the length of diagonals DF, AG and CE of the cube shown in the adjoining figure are equal to the three side of a triangle, then the radius of the circle circumscribing that triangle will be:

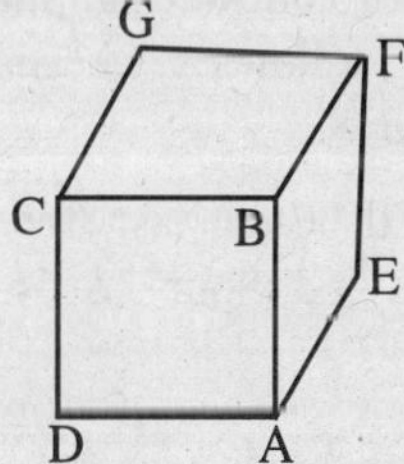

A. equal to the side of the cube
B. $\sqrt{3}$ times the side of the cube
C. $\frac{1}{\sqrt{3}}$ time the side of the cube
D. impossible to find from the given information

133. Six products — Ariel, Vivel, Rin, Nirma, Gillette Gel and Pepsodent - are to be placed in six display windows' of a shop numbered 1-6 from left to right of a shopper standing outside the shop. AS per the company requirements, Rin and Ariel should be displayed next to each other, but Ariel shoud be least three windows away from Nirma. Pepsodent is preferred to be kept between Gillette Gel and Rin but away from Vivel at least by two windows. Vivel cannot be displayed next o Rin for the reason of mixed-product identity. Also Vivel cannot be displayed in window 1.

If the positions of Rin and Ariel are interchanged, which item will be displayed in window 5?

A. Ariel B. Nirma
C. Rin D. Vivel

134. There were 42 students in a hostel. Due to the admission of 13 new students, the expenses of the mess increase by ₹ 31 per day while the average expenditure per head diminished by ₹ 3. What was the original expenditure of the mess?

A. ₹ 633.23 B. ₹ 583.3
C. ₹ 623.3 D. ₹ 632

Directions (Qs. No. 135 and 136): *Given an Input line; the machine arranges the words and numbers in steps in a systematic manner as illustrated afterwards: Study the pattern and answer the question that follows.*

Input line : 56 dress fine shine 32 66 72 offer
Step I: 72 56 dress fine shine 32 66 offer
Step II: 72 shine 56 dress fine 32 66 offer
Step III: 72 shine 66 56 dress fine 32 offer
Step IV: 72 shine 66 offer 56 dress fine 32
Step V: 72 shine 66 offer 56 fine dress 32
Step VI: 72 shine 66 offer 56 fine 32 dress

STEP VI: is the last step and the output in Step VI is the final output.

As per the rules followed in the above steps, find out in each of the following questions the appropriate step for the given input.

135. Which step will be the last step for an input whose second step is '63 Sour 18 56 grapes healthy 32 rise?

A. IV B. V
C. VIII D. None of these

136. Which of the following will be the third step for input jockey firm 36 43 growth chart 22 45?

A. 45 jockey 43 growth firm 36 chart 22
B. 45 jockey 43 firm growth 36 chart 22
C. 45 jockey 43 growth 36 firm chart 22
D. 45 jockey 43 firm 36 growth chart 22

137. Nalini has received a total of 600 WhatsApp messages from four friends Anita, Bina, Chaitra and Divya. Bina and Divya has respectively sent 30% and 20% of these messages, while Anita has sent an equal number of messages as Chaitra. Moreover, Nalini finds that of Anita's, Bina's, Chaitra's and Divya's messages, 60%, 40%, 80% and 50% respectively are jokes. What percentage of the jokes, received by Nalini, has been sent neither by Divya nor by Bina?

A. 65.12% B. 38.6%
C. 61.4% D. 57%

Directions (Qs. No. 138-142): *Read the following Instruction and answer the question that follow it.*

A farmer had a rectangular land containing 205 trees. He distributed that land among his four daughters - Abha, Bina, Chitra and Dipti by dividing the land into twelve plots along three rows (X,Y,Z) and four Columns (1,2,3,4) as shown in the figure below:

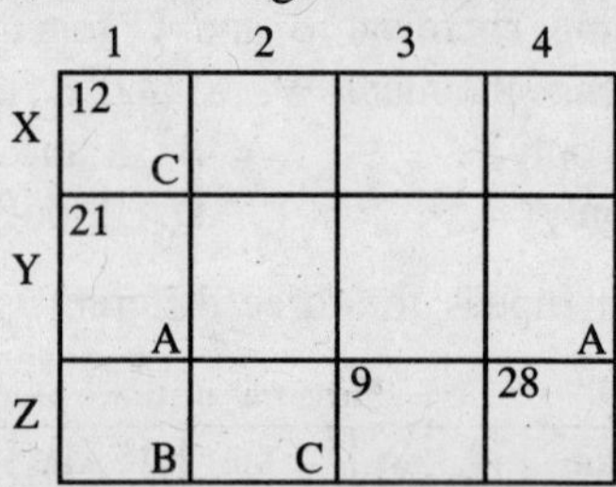

The plots in rows X, Y, Z contained mango, teak and pine trees respectively. Each plot had trees in non-zero multiples of 3 or 4 and none of the plots had the same number of trees. Each daughter got an even number of plots. In the figure, the number mentioned in top left corner of a plot is the number of trees in that plot, while the letter in the bottom right corner is the first letter of the name of the daughter who got that plot (For example, Abha got the plot in row Y and column 1 containing 21 trees). Some information in the figure got erased, but the following is known:

1. Abha got 20 trees more than Chitra but 6 trees less than Dipti.
2. The largest number of trees in a plot was 32, but it was not with Abha.
3. The number of teak trees in Column 3 was double of that in Column 2 but was half of that in Column 4
4. Both Abha and Bina got a higher number of plots than Dipti.
5. Only Bina, Chitra and Dipti got corner plots.
6. Dipti got two adjoining plots in the same row.
7. Bina was the only one who got a plot in each row and each column.
8. Chitra and Dipti did not get plots which were adjacent to each other (either in row/column/ diagonal).
9. The number of mango trees was double the number of teak trees.

138. How many mango trees were there in total?

A. 49 B. 84
C. 98 D. 126

139. Which of the following is the correct sequence of trees received by Abha, Bina, Chitra and Dipti in that order?

A. 50, 69, 30, 56 B. 54, 57, 34, 60
C. 44, 87, 24, 50 D. 60, 39, 40, 66

140. How many pine trees did Chitra receive?

A. 18 B. 30
C. 21 D. 15

141. Who got the plot with the smallest number of trees and how many trees did that plot have?

A. Dipti, 6 trees B. Bina 3 trees
C. Bina 4 trees D. Abha, 4 trees

142. Which of the following statements is NOT true?

A. Chitra got 12 mango trees
B. Bina got 32 pine trees.
C. Abha got 41 teak trees.
D. Dipti got 56 mango trees.

143. Which column had the highest number of trees?

A. 4
B. 3
C. Cannot be determined
D. 2

144.

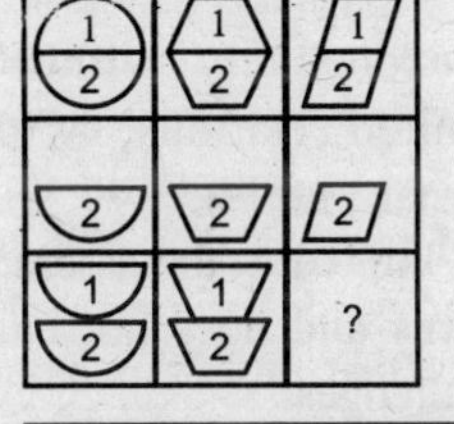

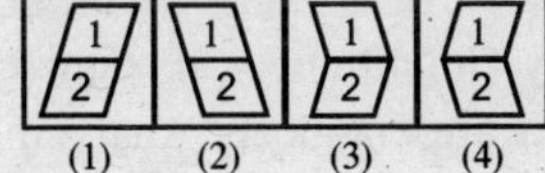

A. 1 B. 2
C. 3 D. 4

145. Given the introduction of India's 2024 National Digital Currency Policy aimed at enhancing the digital economy framework, what is the most likely immediate impact on the country's financial sector and business operations, considering current global economic trends?

A. Increased operational costs for businesses due to the high initial investment required for integrating digital currency systems.
B. Decreased reliance on traditional banking systems, leading to a shift towards more decentralized financial services.
C. Enhanced efficiency in business transactions and reduced transaction costs, driving growth in the e-commerce sector.
D. Marginal impact on the financial sector due to the existing dominance of traditional banking and low digital literacy rates.

146. As per the NITI Aayog's recent report on enhancing MSME exports, which of the following strategies is NOT recommended to address the challenges faced by Indian MSMEs in the global market?

A. Creating a unified portal for all export-related information accessible by MSMEs.
B. Differentiating between Exporter on Record (EOR) and Seller on Record (SOR) to streamline export procedures.
C. Increasing the minimum threshold for compulsory registration under the MSME category to encourage more small businesses to export.
D. Promoting the use of the Export Credit Guarantee to mitigate financial risks associated with exporting activities.

147. As of the fiscal year 2023-24, the Government of India, following the Reserve Bank of India Act, 1934, Section 47, meticulously completed its Government Securities (G-Sec) borrowing program. This action underscores the government's commitment to prudent fiscal management. Given this context, which of the following statements best reflects the implications of this completion of G-Sec borrowing for the Indian economy?

A. It reflects a cautions approach to fiscal management, aiming to ensure borrowing aligns with actual fiscal needs and expectations of receiving dividend income from the RBI.
B. It indicates a shift towards exclusive reliance on external commercial borrowings to meet future fiscal deficits.
C. It signifies a potential increase in the government's dependency on high-cost, short-term debt instruments for future financing needs.
D. It suggests an immediate reduction in the Reserve Bank of India'a Open Market Operations, leading to decreased liquidity in the financial markerts.

148. In the context of the Reserve Bank of India's omnibus framework for recognizing Self-Regulatory Organizations (SROs) within the financial sector, which of the following best encapsulates the envisioned role of SROs in augmenting the regulatory landscape?

A. To serve solely as an intermediary for grievances between financial entities and the RBI, without a mandate for compliance enforcement.
B. To assist the RBI by fostering a compliance culture among regulated entities through self-governance, code of conduct enforcement, and promoting sectoral research and innovation.

C. To replace the regulatory authority of the RBI by taking over complete regulatory and supervisory responsibilities for their respective sectors.

D. To focus primarily on lobbying activities with the government and regulatory bodies on behalf of their members, without engaging in any form of compliance or governance activities.

149. Following the strategic enhancement of the RoDTEP scheme as announced by Union Minister Piyush Goyal, which incorporates SEZs, EOUs, and AA holders into its fold, assess the nuanced impact of this extension. Specifically, what is the anticipated outcome on India's export dynamics, considering the scheme's budgetary allocation and targeted sectoral support?

A. Amplification of export volume in sectors unaffected by global market fluctuations, due to enhanced duty remissions.

B. Marginal increase in exports, confined to sectors with existing high duty levies, without broader economic implications.

C. Singular focus on reducing the trade deficit by increasing exports in sectors that primarily compete with China and the US, without addressing underlying sectoral challenges.

D. Broad-based enhancement of competitive advantage across pivotal export sectors, including engineering, pharmaceuticals, and food processing, aimed at substantial economic growth and employment generation.

150. What is the name of the operation recently launched by India to evacuate Indian Nationals from Haiti?

A. Operation Meghdoot B. Operation Shakti

C. Operation Raahat D. Operation Indravati

151. Morgan Stanley Research forecasts India's GDP growth rate for the fiscal year 2024-25 (FY25) to be:

A. 5.8%, indicating a cautious outlook due to external economic uncertainties.

B. 6.5%, reflecting a slight moderation but a constructive outlook on the economy.

C. 7.2%, suggesting a robust acceleration driven by significant reforms and investments.

D. 6.9%, mirroring the growth forecasted for FY24 and emphasizing consistent economic momentum.

152. Consider the following statements about the legal and constitutional provisions related to Rajya Sabha elections in India:

1. The open ballot system in Rajya Sabha elections was introduced by an amendment to the Representation of the People Act, 1951 to curb the practice of cross-voting.
2. The Tenth Schedule of the Indian Constitution, also known as the Anti-Defection Law, applies to Rajya Sabha elections and members can be disqualified for not adhering to party directives.
3. The Supreme Court ruling in the case of Kuldip Nayar versus Union of India validated the open ballot system but state that MLAs cannot be disqualified under the Tenth Schedule for voting against their part in Rajya Sabha elections.

Which of the above statements is/are correct?

A. Only statements 1 and 2 are correct.

B. Only statement 1 and 3 are correct.

C. All statements are correct.

D. Only statement 3 is correct.

153. In the context of international organizations and their impact on regional development, evaluate the role of the United Nations Economic and Social Commission for Asia and the Pacific (UNESCAP). Which of the following statements accurately encapsulates its objectives and initiatives?

A. UNESCAP aims to foster cooperation among its 53 member States and 9 associate members to achieve inclusive and sustainable economic and social development in the Asia-Pacific region.

B. UNESCAP focuses solely on the economic development of Asian Pacific nations through direct financial aid.

C. UNESCAP operates exclusively within the boundaries of the United Nations, without collaboration with external entities.

D. UNESCAP's mandate is limited to the assessment of environmental concerns and does not engage with socioeconomic challenges.

154. Devin AI, introduced by Cognition, is recognized as the world's first AI software engineer. Analyzing its capabilities and performance, which of the following statements is NOT true about Devin AI?

A. Devin AI can autonomously execute software development processes including coding, debugging, and problem-solving.

B. It is programmed to learn and improve over time through machine learning algorithms, adapting to new software development challenges.

C. The introduction of Devin AI into the software development landscape eliminates the need for human engineers in all aspects of software design and deployment.

D. Devin AI demonstrated a significant increase in efficiency by correctly resolving a higher percentage of issues unassisted compared to the previous model on the SWE-Bench benchmark

155. What is a key characteristic of the WTO's recently introduced regulations for international trade in services, as discussed at the 13th Ministerial Conference?

A. They promote digitization and cross-border data flows while respecting members' regulatory autonomy.
B. They restrict the provision of subsidies by member nations to domestic service providers.
C. They introduce additional tariffs on international services to encourage local consumption.
D. They offer preferential treatment exclusively to Least Developed Countries (LDCs) in the services sector.

156. Match the Articles of the Indian Constitution (Column A) with their subjects (Column B):

Column A	Column B
1. Article 14	(*a*) Right to Constitutional Remedies
2. Article 21	(*b*) Equality before the law
3. Article 32	(*c*) Procedure for amendment of the Constitution
4. Article 368	(*d*) Protection of life and personal liberty

Options:

A. 1-(*b*), 2-(*d*), 3-(*a*), 4-(*c*)
B. 1-(*d*), 2-(*b*), 3-(*c*), 4-(*a*)
C. 1-(*a*), 2-(*c*), 3-(*b*), 4-(*d*)
D. 1-(*c*), 2-(*a*), 3-(*d*), 4-(*b*)

157. The Price Stabilization Fund (PSF) in India is primarily designed to:

A. Subsidize the export of agricultural commodities.
B. Provide interest-free loans for market intervention to stabilize the prices of essential commodities.
C. Directly subsidize consumers for essential commodity purchases.
D. Offer subsidies to farmers for specific crop production only.

158. Within the ambit of Patent Rules 2024, an innovative provision has been introduced to streamline and enhance the efficiency of the patent application process. This specific amendment pertains to the facilitation of quicker responses from applicants post the issuance of the First Examination Report (FER). Identify this amendment from the options below:

A. Mandatory electronic filing for all patent applications
B. Introduction of expedited examination for startups
C. Introduction of virtual hearings for opposition proceedings
D. Reduction in the time frame for submitting responses to FERs

159. The Price Stabilization Fund (PSF) serves a critical role in India's agricultural sector. Considering its operational mechanics and strategic objectives, which of the following options correctly matches the PSF features with their implications or purposes?

A. Employs open market operations for price control: Correctly identifies a mechanism for intervention
B. Operated under the Department of Agriculture: Incorrectly suggests departmental oversight
C. Provides subsidies directly to consumers: Misinterprets fund disbursement mechanics
D. Exclusively focuses on short-term crop loans: Misconstrues the fund's scope and application

160. As of the latest developments, how many Vande Bharat trains are currently operational across India, marking a significant milestone in the country's railway infrastructure enhancement?

A. 50 B. 75
C. 120 D. 102

161. Which individual was recently honored with an honorary knighthood by King Charles III of Britain, highlighting significant contributions and strengthening ties between the two nations?

A. Ravindra Kumar B. Sunil Bharti Mittal
C. Nicholas Pooran D. Renu Sood Karnad

162. Who has been acknowledged with the prestigious 58th Jnanpith Award, honoring their exceptional contributions to literature?

A. Gulzar
B. Jagadguru Rambhadracharya
C. Both A and B
D. None of the above

163. At the World Government Summit 2024, which city served as a host, reflecting its growing significance on the global stage for international dialogue and governance?

A. Dubai B. New York
C. Tokyo D. London

164. How much has the Central Government increased the target of 'Lakhpati Didi Yojana'?

A. 3 crores B. 3.5 crores
C. 4 crores D. 4.5 crores

165. Name the 1st of its kind Standardized Health Insurance Products (SHIP) introduced by Insurance Regulatory and Development Authority of India (IRDAI) that must be offered by all general and standalone health insurers with effect from April 1, 2020?

A. Arogya Swasthiya B. Arogya Scheme
C. Arogya Sanjeevani D. None of these

166. What is a grey market?

A. The trade of a commodity for which the country of origin is not mentioned

B. The trade of a commodity through distribution channels not authorized by the manufacturer

C. The trade of a commodity which is recognized as a counterfeit product

D. The trade of a commodity for which the taxes are evaded

167. From which location, India test-fired the new generation Agni Prime missile in 2021?

A. Vikram Sarabhai Space Centre, Thiruvananthapuram (Thumba), Kerala

B. Satish Dhawan Space Centre (Sriharikota), Andhra Pradesh

C. LAPAN Rocket Launcher Station, Pameungpeuk, Garut, Indonesia

D. APJ Abdul Kalam island, Odisha

168. How much of monthly pension has been approved by cabinet to small traders, businessmen, and shopkeepers under Pradhan Mantri Kisan Pension Yojana (PM-KPY) on 31st May 2019?

A. 3000 B. 3500

C. 4000 D. None of these

169. Who heads the task force, that prepared the ₹ 102 lakh crore "National Infrastructure Pipeline for the year 2019-20 to 2024-25"?

A. Girish Murmu B. Atanu Chakraborty

C. Nirmala Sitharaman D. None of these

170. What is the full form of NFT in the context of blockchain?

A. Non-fundable tax

B. Non-fakable token

C. Non-functional tax

D. Non-fungible token

ANSWERS

1	2	3	4	5	6	7	8	9	10
A	D	C	D	D	C	D	B	C	B
11	**12**	**13**	**14**	**15**	**16**	**17**	**18**	**19**	**20**
D	D	C	D	A	D	D	D	D	A
21	**22**	**23**	**24**	**25**	**26**	**27**	**28**	**29**	**30**
D	D	B	D	C	D	B	D	C	B
31	**32**	**33**	**34**	**35**	**36**	**37**	**38**	**39**	**40**
B	D	C	B	B	A	D	C	B	A
41	**42**	**43**	**44**	**45**	**46**	**47**	**48**	**49**	**50**
A	B	B	B	D	B	D	D	D	D
51	**52**	**53**	**54**	**55**	**56**	**57**	**58**	**59**	**60**
D	A	C	D	B	A	C	A	C	D
61	**62**	**63**	**64**	**65**	**66**	**67**	**68**	**69**	**70**
A	B	A	D	C	A	A	C	B, D	A
71	**72**	**73**	**74**	**75**	**76**	**77**	**78**	**79**	**80**
B	A	C	D	A	B	A	D	C	B
81	**82**	**83**	**84**	**85**	**86**	**87**	**88**	**89**	**90**
B	D	B	D	A	C	D	C	B	C
91	**92**	**93**	**94**	**95**	**96**	**97**	**98**	**99**	**100**
C	D	A	D	C	A	D	B	C	B
101	**102**	**103**	**104**	**105**	**106**	**107**	**108**	**109**	**110**
A	C	D	A	C	A	B	B	C	D
111	**112**	**113**	**114**	**115**	**116**	**117**	**118**	**119**	**120**
D	A	A	D	C	B	C	A	B	D
121	**122**	**123**	**124**	**125**	**126**	**127**	**128**	**129**	**130**
B	D	B	C	A	A	D	A	C	C
131	**132**	**133**	**134**	**135**	**136**	**137**	**138**	**139**	**140**
A	A	C	A	D	A	C	C	A	A

141	142	143	144	145	146	147	148	149	150
B	B	A	C	C	C	A	B	D	D
151	**152**	**153**	**154**	**155**	**156**	**157**	**158**	**159**	**160**
B	B	A	C	A	A	B	D	A	D
161	**162**	**163**	**164**	**165**	**166**	**167**	**168**	**169**	**170**
B	C	A	A	C	B	D	A	B	D

EXPLANATORY ANSWERS

1. The passage refers to the Malthusian dilemma where population growth exceeds available resources, illustrated through examples like Rwanda and Haiti. In real-world contexts, especially in these regions, this pressure often manifests as competition among different ethnic groups over scarce land and other essential resources. Thus, Option A best represents the broader implication of resource competition highlighted by the author, even though the passage does not explicitly mention "ethnic groups," it aligns with the real-world situation being referenced.

2. The word "anthropogenic" means human caused. In the passage, the author suggests that deforestation may have worsened drought conditions, so the broader meaning is a drought produced by human activity. Option B is too narrow because deforestation is only one example of such human action, while Option D correctly captures the full meaning of the term.

3. The passage clearly explains that earlier droughts were survivable because there were still unoccupied areas where affected people could move and begin again. At the time of the Classic collapse, however, the landscape was already full, and there was no useful vacant land left nearby. That is what made this drought much more destructive than earlier ones.

4. At the beginning, the author says Maya archaeologists still disagree vigorously because different factors had different importance in different regions, evidence is incomplete, and some questions remain puzzling. This means no single factor can be identified with certainty as the one complete explanation. Therefore, this option best reflects why the collapse is difficult to explain.

5. The passage does mention short-term concerns, but these are specifically attributed to the "kings and nobles," not to the Maya population as a whole. The other options are clearly discussed: environmental degradation, warfare, and broader social-political collapse linked with population pressure. Hence this option is the one not cited in the form stated in the question.

6. This is the incorrect statement, so it is the right choice for "EXCEPT." The passage shows the reverse sequence. Renoir was first a major Impressionist, painting with Monet in 1874, and only later moved toward a semi-classical style after his 1881 visit to Rome and Naples. Hence this option does not fit the passage.

7. The word "odalisques" is used in the context of Matisse and Renoir's Orientalist paintings. In art history, "odalisques" refers to female figures, usually reclining or decorative women in an exoticized setting. So the meaning intended here is clearly women.

8. The opening of the passage presents the "received opinion" that Renoir's late work became kitschy, overly sweet, and difficult for modern viewers to appreciate. Although major modernists like Picasso and Matisse still admired aspects of it, the general suggestion is that his late work lost wider appeal. Therefore this option fits the passage best.

9. The author criticizes organic food as expensive, associated with elite consumers, and not nutritionally superior. However, calling it "insipid" (tasteless) is not a general view expressed by the author; only a specific sarcastic remark about biscuits is made, not a broader claim about all organic food.

10. The FSA-backed study mainly challenges the central claim that organic food provides additional health benefits. It clearly states there is no evidence that organic food is more beneficial to health, which directly questions this aspect rather than celebrity endorsement or pesticide concerns.

11. Defenders argue that the study ignored important aspects such as pesticide residues and broader environmental and social issues. This implies they consider the study incomplete and lacking a comprehensive perspective rather than entirely unscientific or biased.

12. The passage presents the study's conclusions, the reactions from supporters and critics, and the wider social context. It does not simply support or reject the study but highlights the debate arising from it, making this the most accurate description.

13. The passage clearly states that many concepts of modern art arose from "almost accidental meetings of groups of talented individuals at certain times and places." This directly supports the idea that chance interactions, rather than planned efforts, led to the development of these concepts.

14. The word "fossil" is used to describe how an art movement, once it passes into history, is no longer a "living organism" but something preserved from the past. Like a fossil, it represents a past era whose structure can still be studied and interpreted, indicating the passage of time rather than uselessness.

15. The passage notes that it is tempting to compare art with science because both seem to include a range of interrelated activities. However, this similarity is misleading, since science develops systematically while art evolves through more accidental and less structured processes.

16. The diversity of modern art concepts is attributed to artists being exposed to the "complex phenomena of the twentieth century" and attempting to interpret a rapidly changing world of visual and spiritual experience, which explains the wide range of ideologies.

17. The reference to T.S. Eliot emphasizes that creativity is not created from nothing. Instead, originality lies in adapting and transforming inherited ideas so that they fit present needs and contexts.

18. Arti's goal is to work as a manager in a non-profit helping under-represented populations. College X emphasizes producing "compassionate and curious leaders," which aligns closely with her aspirations, whereas College Y focuses on research. Her decision is best explained by alignment of mission with her goals.

19. The passage states: wave impact depends on wave size and sea-bottom shape, and erosion depends on wave impact and geological composition. Since sea-bottom shape influences wave impact, which in turn affects erosion, erosion is indirectly related to sea-bottom shape.

20. Sentence A introduces the claim that nuclear power is carbon-free. D logically follows by partially accepting this but pointing out that the claim ignores the broader nuclear cycle. C then elaborates on this cycle by explaining how greenhouse gases are released at each stage. E further strengthens the argument by stating that even operating plants depend on fossil-fuel-based electricity. Finally, B serves as the concluding statement, firmly rejecting the claim as untrue.

21. (*i*) councilor refers to a member of a municipal council → A
(*ii*) adoptive parents is the correct expression → B
(*iii*) venal means corrupt and open to bribery → A
(*iv*) farther is used for physical distance → A
(*v*) descent refers to lineage → B

22. (*i*) precedence means priority → A
(*ii*) alternatively gives a choice → B
(*iii*) complemented means enhanced → B
(*iv*) notable improvement is the standard and more appropriate collocation → A
(*v*) discreet means careful in speech/action → A

23. "Pull away" is not the correct phrasal usage here; the proper expression is "pull out of a venture."

24. The correct idiomatic expression is "shadow of fear," not "shade of fear."

25. "Run over" literally means to hit with a vehicle; the intended figurative meaning is incorrect usage here.

26. Though "come around to" is correct, the phrasing is awkward and less appropriate compared to standard idiomatic constructions.

27. Incorrect usage; the correct expression is "broke into a gallop."

28. Incorrect; the correct idiom is "break rank," not "break the file."

29. A and B combine to form a grammatically correct and meaningful core sentence. D is incorrect due to missing article ("a dry goods business"), and C cannot stand alone with correctness in available combinations.

30. Among the given options, D is the closest acceptable sentence. A is only a fragment, B has pronoun inconsistency, and C is structurally incorrect.

31. Sentence C ("The nightmare is far from over, for the government") is the most appropriate correct part in the given context. Other combinations introduce fragments (B) or depend on additional clauses for completion, whereas C maintains grammatical acceptability as a meaningful clause in the paragraph.

32. A and D are grammatically correct and complete sentences. B is awkward, and C has tense inconsistency.

33. brooch is the ornament worn on clothing; councillor is the elected local representative; advice is the noun needed after "your"; climactic ending is the correct expression for a dramatic high point; and flare refers to the widening style at the bottom of jeans.

34. currants are dried fruits; exceptionable behaviour means objectionable behaviour; consent to treatment is the correct expression; obliged to report fits the sense of duty; and sanguine means overly optimistic.

35. caustic retort means a sharp and biting reply; cogent plea means a convincing and well-reasoned appeal; averse to helping is the correct idiom; coupe can refer to a railway compartment/carriage; and bells pealing is the correct phrase for bells ringing loudly.

36. diffusing the Guru's ideas means spreading those ideas, which fits the sentence better than defusing; baited the instructor means provoked or teased; horde means a large crowd; internment means confinement or detention; and unsociable tendencies correctly refers to a person who avoids social interaction.

37. "Disingenuous" correctly conveys the misleading and insincere labeling of genocide as "ethnic cleansing." The phrase "victims and perpetrators alike" is a standard and logical pairing in this context.

38. "Observers of the night sky" is the appropriate term, and "concede" fits the idea of accepting a conclusion based on accumulating evidence.

39. "Congenital endowment" refers to innate traits, while "education" appropriately represents environmental influence, making the sentence logically complete.

40. "Central institutions of education and propaganda" is the correct and standard collocation. "Inhibitions" properly conveys the idea that minds are constrained or shaped by earlier conditions. The pair "tenets; fixation" is not suitable here because "tenets of education" is not idiomatic, and "suited by fixation" is grammatically and semantically weak.

41. Let weights be $5x$ and $8x$,

$$\text{CP of B} = y,\ \text{CP of A} = 1.2y$$
$$5x(1.2y) + 8xy = 2800$$
$$6xy + 8xy - 2800 \Rightarrow 14xy = 2800$$
$$\Rightarrow \quad xy = 200$$
$$\text{CP of A} = 6xy = 1200, \text{CP of B} = 8xy = 1600$$
$$\text{Profit} = 15\% \text{ of } 1200 + 10\% \text{ of } 1600 = 180 + 160 = 340.$$

42. The paragraph highlights Nehru's dislike for priests, sadhus, monks, and religious practices. This sentence logically concludes that he believed these elements hindered India's progress.

43. The paragraph emphasizes voluntary decline in birth rates when people are given access and awareness, making this the most appropriate conclusion.

44. The paragraph contrasts patient reactions; while some leave after observing Perowne's hands, this option logically introduces another group who stay despite dissatisfaction.

45. The paragraph argues that climate concerns are being used as a disguise for protectionism, and this option best captures that idea.

46. The passage highlights Mattancherry and its synagogue as symbols of religious tolerance. The best concluding sentence should extend this idea with historical nuance. Option B does this by acknowledging that Indian Jews largely lived without discrimination while allowing for rare exceptions. This supports and deepens the idea of tolerance rather than merely repeating it.

47. The paragraph emphasizes that strict classification of ideas as purely Western or Eastern is misleading due to cultural interconnections. This option captures that philosophical argument most precisely.

48. Let Barun's age = B, Arun's = 0.4 B

After x years:

$$0.4\text{B} + x = \frac{1}{2}(\text{B} + x)$$
$$0.4\text{B} + x = 0.5\text{B} + 0.5x$$
$$0.5x = 0.1\text{B} \Rightarrow x = 0.2\text{B}$$

Percentage increase in Barun's age

$$\frac{0.2\text{B}}{\text{B}} \times 100 = 20\%.$$

49. Daily work forms AP:

$$\frac{1+2+3+\ldots+n}{120} = 1$$
$$\frac{n(n+1)}{240} = 1$$
$$n(n+1) = 240 \Rightarrow n = 15.$$

50. The passage acknowledges both justification for distance and the need for community engagement, making this the most balanced summary.

51. B introduces the issue of outdated, state-centric space laws; A builds on this by highlighting ambiguity in legal status and future commercial prospects; C then gives concrete examples of national laws and their limitations. Sentence D, however, shifts to a specific geopolitical criticism (Russia vs. US), breaking the general analytical flow, and is therefore the odd one out.

52. A states that good advertising can make people buy a bad product. C must follow because "That's important" refers directly to the idea in A. B then strengthens that point by saying brainwashing is more cost-effective than improving the product. D works best at the end as a necessary qualification that some minimum quality is still required.

53. D introduces the institutional truth of the financial world. B extends it by saying that more money is taken to mean more intelligence. A adds the related belief that pursuit of money within the law is benign. C then closes the sequence by stating that this is the creed one is required to believe on Wall Street.

54. A opens with the contrast that Hollywood is a man's world, but that is not the whole truth. D supplies the example from the silent era. B then refers to this surprising fact through "this." C naturally explains what exactly surprised Jodie Foster.

55. C begins with the statement that salvation is an achievement of individuals. B adds that Christianity also has a concern for society as a whole. A then shifts the discussion to Buddhism by saying it is more severely analytical. D explains this by showing how Buddhism dissolves society into individuals and the individual further into component parts and instants.

56. C introduces the general idea that learning is important. A must follow because "However" creates a contrast by introducing the harder concept of unlearning. D then explains why unlearning is difficult by referring to long-formed "mental models." B concludes the paragraph by providing the reason for this need— the modern business world behaves differently, making unlearning necessary.

57. "Have all one's ducks in a row" means everything is properly arranged and organized, not complacency.

58. "A damp squib" refers to something that fails to meet expectations or ends in disappointment.

59. "Fell on stony ground" means advice or effort that was ignored or ineffective.

60. "In cold blood" means doing something intentionally without emotion.

61. "Halcyon days" refers to peaceful, happy, and carefree times (note: correct spelling is halcyon, not halo cyan).

62. "To smell a rat" means to sense something wrong or suspect deceit.

63. "Washed their hands off" means to withdraw responsibility or detach oneself from a matter.

64. "To take someone for a ride" means to cheat or trick someone.

65. "Put her foot down" means to assert authority or take a firm decision.

66. "To move heaven and earth" means to make every possible effort.

67. This strengthens the argument because it shows why a two-party system may not fully support true democracy.

68. This weakens the argument by directly contradicting the claim that politics is not like a game.

69. The argument compares politics with games like cricket and football. For this analogy to work, it must assume that such games involve two opposing sides (like two parties). Statement I is already given in the argument, so it is not an assumption. Statement II is not required. Hence, only III is the correct assumption.

70. The argument states that due to rising oil prices, we must turn to hydro-electric projects. The phrase "such renewable sources of energy" already establishes that hydro-electric power is renewable, so Statement I is not an assumption but a stated premise. The reasoning of the argument depends on the idea that hydro-electric power is economically preferable compared to expensive oil. This is not explicitly stated and must be assumed. Therefore, only Statement II is the underlying assumption.

71. The argument supports hydro-electric projects because oil has become expensive. If it is shown that hydro-electric power is actually more costly than oil, then the entire basis of the argument collapses. This directly weakens the argument by attacking its core economic reasoning.

72. (*a*) is incorrect because "returned to home" is wrong; correct usage is "returned home."

(*b*) is incorrect because "get my hand on" should be "get my hands on."

(*c*) is grammatically correct and properly structured.

(*d*) is incorrect because it lacks proper punctuation and structure; it should read "a Shaliach, a sort of recruiter."

(*e*) is grammatically correct and complete.

Therefore, only (*c*) and (*e*) are correct.

73. (*a*) is incorrect because "It is sometimes told" is not proper usage; "It is sometimes said" is correct.

(*b*) is grammatically correct.

(*c*) is incorrect because "handed to us from that time" is awkward; correct form is "handed down to us."

(*d*) is correct and clearly structured.

(*e*) is incorrect because the construction is faulty and illogical.

Thus, the correct parts are (b) and (d).

74. (*a*) is acceptable.

(*b*) is acceptable.

(*c*) is incorrect because "out of slump" should be "out of a slump."

(*d*) is grammatically correct and meaningful.

(*e*) is incorrect because "affect" should be "effect."

Since the options do not provide the combination of only correct parts without including errors, the most appropriate available answer is (*d*) only.

75. The paragraph is defensive and rhetorical, repeatedly questioning whether his advice can be called "rules." The tone is conversational and ironic. Option (*c*) matches this tone perfectly and directly answers the rhetorical question raised.

76. The passage emphasizes that useful maps (and theories) must simplify reality by ignoring less important details. The conclusion should highlight that such simplification does not reduce usefulness. Option (*a*) captures this idea most effectively.

77. The paragraph explains the curvilinear relationship: age first helps but later reduces risk-taking and openness. The final logical outcome is reduced exploitation of opportunities, which is precisely stated in option (*d*).

78. The paragraph highlights mistrust, lack of commitment, and withholding of information across all relationships. This naturally leads to adversarial behavior, making option (*c*) the best conclusion.

79. The paragraph contrasts the professed desire for peace with the actual reliance on military force. Option (*b*) most strongly exposes this contradiction by describing diplomacy as a façade for power.

80. Given:

to be polite → fa so la

she is polite → so me pa

to have manners → na la ma

Step 1: Identify common word for polite

Appears in first and second → common code = so → polite = so

Step 2: Identify common word for to

Appears in first and third → common code = la → to = la

Step 3: Now in "to be polite" → fa so la

We already know:

so = polite

la = to

Remaining word = fa = be

Hence, code for be is fa.

81. T, J, E, N, U, Q, A, K, I, O, G, R, M, S, P, B, H, F, D, L, V, C.

From the examples:

GRIM → RMOS

G → R (next letter in the series)

R → M (next)

I → O (next)

M → S (next)

DUSK → LQPI

D → L (next)

U → Q (next)

S → P (next)

K → I (next)

Thus, the rule is: each letter is replaced by the immediate next letter in the given series.

Applying to STOP:

S → P

T → J

O → G

P → B

Therefore,

STOP → PJGB.

82. Let us place the shows step by step very carefully. There are five half-hour slots between 9:30 pm and midnight:

9:30–10:00

10:00–10:30

10:30–11:00

11:00–11:30

11:30–12:00

Now use the clues:

- There are 3 family dramas, and they are scheduled one after another.
- Main Sati Hoon is a family drama with social message and is fixed at 10:00–10:30.
- Detective Doom is also a family drama and also has social message.
- Out of the 3 family dramas, 2 have social message and 1 does not.
- Therefore the third family drama must be Laugh a While, and it is the one without social message.
- It is also given that one family drama without social message has adult content. So Laugh a While has adult content.
- There are 2 adult-content shows, scheduled at 10:30 pm and 11:30 pm.

- Midnight Murders is not a family drama, has no social message, and is scheduled at 11:30 pm.
- So the other adult-content slot, namely 10:30 pm, must belong to Laugh a While.

Now check the family-drama block:

Since family dramas are consecutive, and Main Sati Hoon is at 10:00–10:30, and it also has a family drama preceding it, the three family dramas must be:

9:30–10:00
10:00–10:30
10:30–11:00

These three are:

- Detective Doom
- Main Sati Hoon
- Laugh a While

Since Laugh a While is the family drama with adult content, it must be at the adult-content slot: 10:30 pm to 11:00 pm.

83. If $x \geq y$:

Solve I: $12x^2 + 11x + 12 = 10x^2 + 22x$

$$2x^2 - 11x + 12 = 0$$
$$(2x - 3)(x - 4) = 0$$
$$x = \frac{3}{2}, 4$$

Solve II: $13y^2 - 18y + 3 = 9y^2 - 10y$

$$4y^2 - 8y + 3 = 0$$
$$(2y - 1)(2y - 3) = 0$$
$$y = \frac{1}{2}, \frac{3}{2}$$

Compare possible values:

Minimum $x = \frac{3}{2}$, maximum $y = \frac{3}{2}$ → equality possible

For all cases, x is never less than y

Thus, $x \geq y$.

84. Given:

$u^2 + (u - 2v - 1)^2 = -4v(u + v)$

Expand:

$u^2 + u^2 + 4v^2 + 1 - 4uv - 2u + 4v = -4uv - 4v^2$

$2u^2 + 4v^2 + 1 - 4uv - 2u + 4v = -4uv - 4v^2$

Bring all terms to LHS:

$2u^2 + 8v^2 - 2u + 4v + 1 = 0$

Divide by 2:

$$u^2 + 4v^2 - u + 2v + \frac{1}{2} = 0$$

Complete squares:

$$\left(u - \frac{1}{2}\right)^2 + 4\left(v + \frac{1}{4}\right)^2 = 0$$

Thus:

$$u = \frac{1}{2}, v = -\frac{1}{4}$$

Now:

$$u + 3v = \frac{1}{2} + 3\left(-\frac{1}{4}\right) = \frac{1}{2} - \frac{3}{4} = \frac{1}{4}.$$

85. If $x > y$

First interpret expressions correctly.

Equation I: $\sqrt{1125x + \sqrt{4900}} = 0$

$$35x + 70 = 0$$
$$35x = -70$$
$$x = -2$$

Equation II: $(81)^{1/4}\ y + (343)^{1/3} = 0$

$$3y + 7 = 0$$
$$3y = -7$$
$$y = -\frac{7}{3}$$

Now compare:

$$x = -2,\ y = -\frac{7}{3} \approx -2.33$$

So, $-2 > -2.33$

Thus, $x > y$.

86. Let the three positive integers in arithmetic progression be

$$x, y, z = y - d, y, y + d$$

where d is a positive integer.

Given: $y - x > 2$

Since $y - x = d$,

we get, $d > 2$.

Now use

$$xyz = 5(x + y + z).$$

Substitute $x = y - d$ and $z = y + d$:

$(y - d) \cdot y \cdot (y + d) = 5((y - d) + y + (y + d))$

$$y(y^2 - d^2) = 5(3y)$$
$$y(y^2 - d^2) = 15y$$

Since y is a positive integer, divide by y:

$$y^2 - d^2 = 15$$

Now factor:

$(y - d)(y + d) = 15$

Possible positive factor pairs of 15 are:

$$1 \times 15,\ 3 \times 5$$

Case 1: $y - d = 1,\ y + d = 15$

Adding: $2y = 16 \Rightarrow y = 8$

Then, $d = 7$

Case 2: $y - d = 3,\ y + d = 5$

Adding: $2y = 8 \Rightarrow y = 4$

Then, $d = 1$

But this does not satisfy $d > 2$.

So only valid value is:

$$d = 7$$

Now

$$z - x = (y + d) - (y - d) = 2d = 14.$$

87. Given, $\log_4 m + \log_4 n = \log_2 (m + n)$ where m and n are positive real numbers.

Using the product rule on the left side,

$$\log_4 (mn) = \log_2 (m + n)$$

Now convert the left side to base 2:

$$\log_4 (mn) = \frac{\log_2(mn)}{\log_2 4} = \frac{1}{2}\log_2(mn)$$

So,

$$\frac{1}{2}\log_2(mn) = \log_2 (m + n)$$

Multiply by 2:

$$\log_2 (mn) = 2\log_2 (m + n)$$

$$\log_2 (mn) = \log_2 (m + n)^2$$

Hence,

$$mn = (m + n)^2$$

Expand: $mn = m^2 + 2mn + n^2$

$m^2 + mn + n^2 = 0$

But m and n are positive real numbers,

so $m^2 > 0,\ mn > 0,\ n^2 > 0$

and therefore

$$m^2 + mn + n^2 > 0$$

So it can never be equal to 0. Therefore, no positive real values of m and n satisfy the equation.

88. The passage says exactly the opposite. It states that the widely advertised claim that BYOD increases productivity is actually the "greatest myth" of BYOD. The research discussed in the passage suggests that BYOD creates challenges such as distraction, time-wasting, and security risks, which may outweigh any benefits. The other three statements are supported by the passage.

89. The bells toll together again after a time equal to the LCM of 2, 4, 6, 8, 10 and 12 seconds.

$$2 = 2,\ 4 = 2^2,\ 6 = 2 \times 3,$$

$$8 = 2^3,\ 10 = 2 \times 5,\ 12 = 2^2 \times 3$$

$$\text{LCM} = 2^3 \times 3 \times 5 = 120 \text{ seconds}$$

$$= 2 \text{ minutes}$$

So they toll together once every 2 minutes. In 30 minutes, the common tolling times are:

$$0, 2, 4, 6, \ldots, 30$$

This is an arithmetic sequence with

$$\frac{30}{2}+1 = 15 + 1 = 16 \text{ terms}$$

The initial tolling at the start is also counted because they "commence tolling together."

90. Let the total number of eggs bought be x.

After throwing away 2 rotten eggs, remaining eggs:

$$x - 2$$

He puts

$$\frac{5}{9}(x-2)$$

in his fridge, so the number taken to his mother's house is

$$(x-2)-\frac{5}{9}(x-2) = \frac{4}{9}(x-2)$$

His mother cooks 2 eggs, so eggs left to keep in her fridge:

$$\frac{4}{9}(x-2)-2$$

Her fridge cannot hold more than 5 eggs,

so $$\frac{4}{9}(x-2)-2 \le 5$$

$$\frac{4}{9}(x-2) \le 7$$

$$x-2 \le \frac{63}{4} = 15.75$$

Also, $(x - 2)$ must be divisible by 9 so that five-ninths of it is an integer. The possible values are:

$$x - 2 = 9 \Rightarrow x = 11$$

$x - 2 = 18 \Rightarrow x = 20$ not possible since $18 > 15.75$

Hence the maximum possible number of eggs is 11.

91. From the clues, Salil married Jasmine in September and Pritam married in December. Mridul's wedding was in Chennai. Abhishek's wedding was in Ahmedabad and Ranjan's in Delhi. Kolkata wedding took place in February, so the person married in February must be in Kolkata. Geetika and Ipsita were married in February and November, and in Kolkata and Chennai respectively in some order. This fits only when Deepak married Geetika in February at Kolkata, and Mridul married Ipsita in November at Chennai. Then the only month left for Hema is April. Since Hema's wedding was in April and not in Ahmedabad, and April is left with Ranjan in Delhi, Hema's husband is Ranjan.

92. After fixing the arrangement, the full schedule becomes: Deepak–February–Kolkata, Ranjan–April–Delhi, Abhishek–July–Ahmedabad, Salil–September–Bengaluru, Mridul–November–Chennai, and Pritam–December–Mumbai. Hence, the wedding held in Mumbai took place in December.

93. In the question figure, pattern is that figure II contains figure I inside another enclosing shape. Also, the inner figure in II is exactly the same as I.

Checking options:

- A: Figure I is a hexagon, but in II the inner figure is not the same hexagon → pattern breaks.
- B: Triangle in I, and II contains smaller triangles → follows pattern.
- C: Diamond in I, and II has same diamond inside a circle → follows pattern.
- D: Rectangle in I, and II has same rectangle inside a circle → follows pattern.

Hence, option A does not follow the rule.

94. The series follows an alternating pattern of addition and subtraction where the numbers increase by multiples of 8:

$+8, -16, +24, -32, +40, -48$

Checking stepwise:

$29 + 8 = 37$

$37 - 16 = 21$

$21 + 24 = 45$ (but given 43 → mismatch)

$45 - 32 = 13$

$13 + 40 = 53$

$53 - 48 = 5$

All terms fit the pattern except 43, which should have been 45, hence it is the wrong term.

95. $150 \times 2 - 10 = 290$

$290 \times 2 - 20 = 560$

$560 \times 2 - 30 = 1090$ (but given 1120 → wrong)

$1090 \times 2 - 40 = 2140$

$2140 \times 2 - 50 = 4230$

$4230 \times 2 - 60 = 8400$

Thus 1120 breaks the pattern.

96. Let the Year 1 profits of P, Q and R be in the ratio 2 : 3 : 5.

So, $P_1 = 2x,\ Q_1 = 3x,\ R_1 = 5x$

Company Q's profit increased by 20%, and that increase is ₹ 6,000.

$$20\% \text{ of } Q_1 = 6000$$

$$\frac{20}{100} \times Q_1 = 6000$$

$$Q_1 = \frac{6000 \times 100}{20} = 3000$$

Since $Q_1 = 3x,$

$$3x = 30000$$

$$x = 10000$$

Therefore,

$$R_1 = 5x = 5 \times 10000 = 50000$$

Now check with the remaining data:

$$P_1 = 20000,\ Q_1 = 30000,\ R_1 = 50000$$

Year 2 profits:

$$P_2 = 20000 + 215\% \text{ of } 20000$$

$$= 20000 + 43000 = 63000$$

$Q_2 = 30000 + 20\% \text{ of } 30000 = 30000 + 6000 = 36000$

$R_2 = 50000 - 10\% \text{ of } 50000 = 50000 - 5000 = 45000$

Total Year 2 profit:

$$63000 + 36000 + 45000 = 144000$$

This matches the given total exactly. Hence the data are now fully consistent.

97. From the statements:

- Some pearls are gems → some pearls are diamonds (since all gems are diamonds).
- No diamond is stone → those pearls (which are diamonds) are not stones.
- Some stones are corals → stones and corals have partial overlap.

Now evaluate conclusions:

I. Some stones are pearls → Not definite, because pearls (linked to diamonds) are outside stones. But no complete restriction that all pearls are outside stones, so possibility cannot be confirmed.

II. Some corals being diamond is a possibility → Not possible. Corals $\subseteq$ stones, and no diamond is stone, so corals cannot be diamonds.

III. No stone is pearl → Also not definite, because only "some pearls" are diamonds, not all. So some pearls could still be stones.

Now I and III are complementary (contradictory):

I: Some stones are pearls

III: No stone is pearl

Since exactly one of these must be true, we conclude:

98. Some apartments are flats, some flats are buildings → possibility that apartments are buildings exists

All buildings are bungalows → II is false

Some flats → buildings → gardens ⇒ some flats are gardens → III false

Only I follows.

99. All chairs → tables → bottles

Some bottles are jars → overlap possible → I follows

Chairs ⊂ bottles ⇒ some bottles are chairs → II follows

Some bottles (jars) are not buckets ⇒ III follows

Hence all follow.

100. Let the positions be marked on coordinates.

$$P = (0, 0)$$

He moves 12 m east:

$$Q = (12, 0)$$

Then right from east means south 8 m:

$$R = (12, -8)$$

Again right from south means west 6 m:

$$S = (6, -8)$$

Then 6 m north:

$$T = (6, -2)$$

Now check the options.

For ΔPTQ,

$$PT^2 = 40, TQ^2 = 40, PQ^2 = 144$$

Since

$$40 + 40 < 144$$

it is an obtuse triangle.

For ΔQTR,

$$QT^2 = 40, TR^2 = 72, QR^2 = 64$$

Largest value is 72, and

$$40 + 64 > 72$$

So all angles are less than 90°. It is an acute triangle.

ΔUTS and ΔTSR are right triangles.

101. The experession is: J ÷ P % H ? T % L

Meanings:

- A ÷ B: A is the son of B
- A % B: A is the mother of B
- A × B: A is the sister of B

So, J ÷ P

means J is the son of P.

P % H

means P is the mother of H.

To make J the brother of T, T must also be the child of P. This is possible if

H × T

that is, H is the sister of T. Then H and T are siblings, and since P is mother of H, P is also mother of T. Thus J and T are children of P, and J is male, so J is the brother of T.

102. Let Raghu's and Manav's investments on simple interest be R_s and M_s.

Given: $M_s - R_s = 6000$

Simple interest earned:

$$R_s \times \frac{20 \times 5}{100} = R_s$$

$$M_s \times \frac{24 \times 2}{100} = 0.48\ M_s$$

Total simple interest:

$$R_s + 0.48M_s = 20640$$

Using

$$M_s = R_s + 6000$$

$$R_s + 0.48(R_s + 6000) = 20640$$

$$1.48R_s = 17760$$

$$R_s = 12000,\ M_s = 18000$$

Total invested on simple interest:

$$12000 + 18000 = 30000$$

Total invested on compound interest: 25000

Required percentage:

$$\frac{25000}{30000} \times 100 = 83.33\%$$

So the nearest option is 83%.

103. Total compound interest investment is ₹ 25,000 and the ratio is 3 : 2. Since Manav's investment is more than Raghu's, divide as:

$$R_c : M_c = 2 : 3$$

$$R_c = 10000,\ M_c = 15000$$

Raghu invested at 10% for 2 years:

$$A_R = 10000\left(1+\frac{10}{100}\right)^2$$

$$A_R = 10000\left(\frac{11}{10}\right)^2 = 12100$$

Manav invested at 20% for 1 year:

$$A_M = 15000\left(1+\frac{20}{100}\right) = 18000$$

Required ratio:

$$12100 : 18000 = 121 : 180.$$

104. From Question 102,

$$R_s = 12000,\ M_s = 18000$$

Simple interest earned by Raghu:

$$SI_R = 12000$$

Simple interest earned by Manav:

$$SI_M = 18000 \times \frac{24 \times 2}{100} = 8640$$

Difference:

$$12000 - 8640 = 3360$$

Percentage more:

$$\frac{3360}{8640} \times 100 = 38.88\%$$

Nearest option: 39%.

105. The amounts invested on simple interest are:

12000 and 18000

Average investment:

$$\frac{12000 + 18000}{2} = \frac{30000}{2} = 15000.$$

106. Compound interest investments are:

$$R_c = 10000, \; M_c = 15000$$

Raghu's compound interest at 10% for 2 years:

$$CI_R = 10000(1.1^2 - 1) = 10000(1.21 - 1) = 2100$$

Manav's compound interest at 20% for 1 year:

$$CI_M = 15000 \times \frac{20}{100} = 3000$$

Difference:

$$3000 - 2100 = 900.$$

107. There are three teams — Bihar, Punjab and Haryana. In such a competition, each team plays one match against each of the other two teams. So total matches are

$$\frac{3 \times 2}{2} = 3.$$

108. Let the three matches be Bihar–Punjab, Bihar–Haryana and Punjab–Haryana.

From the table:

- Bihar scored 2 and conceded 4
- Punjab scored 3 and conceded 7
- Haryana conceded 1

Total goals scored = total goals conceded, so Haryana's goals scored are

$$(4 + 7 + 1) - (2 + 3) = 12 - 5 = 7$$

Now Bihar had one drawn match. The only consistent breakup is:

- Bihar vs Punjab = 2 – 2
- Bihar vs Haryana = 0 – 2
- Punjab vs Haryana = 1 – 5

So the Punjab–Haryana score card, written in favour of Punjab, is 1 – 5.

109. From the above reconstruction, Punjab's two matches are:

- vs Bihar: 2 – 2 → draw
- vs Haryana: 1 – 5 → loss

So Punjab lost exactly one match.

110. Total goals conceded by all teams are

$$4 + 7 + 1 = 12$$

Hence total goals scored by all teams are also 12. Bihar and Punjab together scored

$$2 + 3 = 5$$

Therefore Haryana scored

$$12 - 5 = 7.$$

111. The statement clearly says that the method of earning is more important than the amount earned. Now check the three given statements carefully.

A. "How you earn is an important" — this is not a proper or complete statement in English. Even if we try to read it loosely, it does not correctly capture the comparison made in the original sentence.

B. "How much you earn is as important" — this changes the meaning. The original statement says it is less important, not equally important.

C. "How you earn is not as important" — this is the direct opposite of the given statement.

So none of A, B, or C correctly expresses the idea of the original sentence. Therefore the right choice is None of these.

112. Given coding is

E → 2, R → 5, W → @, H → ©,
I → 6, K → #, A → 1

Word: ERWHIKA

First letter = E (vowel), last letter = A (vowel). None of the special conditions apply, so normal coding is used.

Thus,

E = 2
R = 5
W = @
H = ©
I = 6
K = #
A = 1

Required code sequence matches 2@©6#1 from the options.

113. In statement I, the first necklace is only said to be more than 1/5 of the second and the third is more than 2/5 of the second, with total cost ₹ 120000. These are only inequalities, so the exact cost of the second necklace cannot be found. In statement II, the first necklace is 2/5 more than the second, but there is no information about the third necklace, so again the exact value cannot be found. Even after combining both, the third necklace remains undetermined, so the answer still cannot be uniquely obtained.

114. From statement I, boys and girls are in the ratio 3 : 4. This gives only relative values, not the total number. From statement II, girls exceed boys by 18, but this alone also does not give the total because the basic relation is missing. Combining both, let boys = $3x$ and girls = $4x$. Then

$$4x - 3x = 18$$
$$x = 18$$

So total children

$$3x + 4x = 7x = 126$$

Hence both statements together are necessary.

115. Total passengers in train A = 700. General class passengers are 20% of 700:

$$700 \times \frac{20}{100} = 140$$

AC passengers are one-fourth of 700:

$$\frac{700}{4} = 175$$

Sleeper class passengers are 23% of 700:

$$700 \times \frac{23}{100} = 161$$

So first class passengers in train A are

700 - (140 + 175 + 161) = 224

If one first class ticket costs ₹ 450, then total amount generated is

224 × 450 = 100800.

116. Total passengers in train B are 30% more than train A.

So, 700 + 30% of 700 = 700 + 210 = 910

General passengers in train A =140. Total AC passengers in both trains together = 480, while AC passengers in train A = 175. Therefore AC passengers in train B are

480 - 175 = 305

In train B, sleeper passengers are 30% of 910:

$$910 \times \frac{30}{100} = 273$$

First class passengers are 10% of 910:

$$910 \times \frac{10}{100} = 91$$

So general passengers in train B are

910 - (305 + 273 + 91) = 241

Total general passengers in both trains together are

140 + 241 = 381

Required percentage of train B passengers is

$$\frac{381}{910} \times 100 \approx 41.87\%$$

which is approximately 42%.

117. Let the original cost price be x.

Increase = 22%

So new price:

$$x + \frac{22}{100}x = 61$$

$$x\left(1 + \frac{22}{100}\right) = 61$$

$$x \times \frac{122}{100} = 61$$

$$x = \frac{61 \times 100}{122}$$

$$x = 50$$

So the original cost price is ₹ 50.

118. Given two secants PBA and PDC, and ∠P = 20°. Using the external secant angle property:

$$\angle P = \frac{1}{2}(\text{arc AC} - \text{arc BD})$$

$$20 = \frac{1}{2}(\text{arc AC} - \text{arc BD})$$

arc AC - arc BD = 40(1)

At point A, ∠A = 40° is an inscribed angle subtending arc BD:

arc BD = 2 × 40 = 80

Substitute in (1):

arc AC - 80 = 40

arc AC = 120° (this is the larger arc)

Hence minor arc AC = 360 - 120 = 240°

Now, since AD is a diameter:

arc AB + arc BD = 180°

arc AB + 80 = 180 ⇒ arc AB = 100°

Now minor arc AC consists of:

arc AB + arc BD + arc DC

= 100 + 80 + arc DC = 240

arc DC = 60°

Finally, ∠DBC is an inscribed angle subtending arc DC:

$$\angle DBC = \frac{1}{2} \times 60 = 30°.$$

119. There are 8 occupied flats in total and 5 unoccupied flats.

Second floor has exactly 4 flats. The clue says that on the second floor, one occupant is a lawyer and has only one neighbour. In a row of 4 flats, a person having only one neighbour must be in an end flat, and this works only when exactly 2 flats are occupied on that floor. So second floor has 2 occupied flats and 2 unoccupied flats.

That leaves

8 - 2 = 6

occupied flats for the third and fourth floors together. Now, no flat is unoccupied on the third floor, and every floor has at least 3 flats. If the third floor had 4 occupied flats, then only 2 occupied flats would remain for the fourth floor, which is not possible because the fourth floor must have at least 3 flats and must accommodate the floorwise profession restrictions properly.

So the third floor must have exactly 3 occupied flats.

Hence the fourth floor also has 6 – 3 = 3 occupied flats.

120. Since no flat is unoccupied on the third floor, the number of flats on the third floor equals the number of occupied flats there.

From the above distribution:

- Second floor occupied = 2
- Remaining occupied on third and fourth floors = 6
- Fourth floor must have at least 3 occupied flats

Therefore the third floor cannot have 4 occupied flats, because then the fourth floor would be left with only 2 occupied flats. So the third floor must have exactly 3 occupied flats, and hence exactly 3 flats.

121. Let F have the smallest initial Erdõs number, say x. On the third day, A, F and C co-author a paper. Since A initially has infinity and nobody has a smaller Erdõs number than F, after this paper:

$$A = x + 1$$
$$F = x$$

C = x + 1 or remains x, but from the final conditions it works out as x+1

Average Erdõs number after day 3 is 3 for 8 people, so total becomes

$$8 \times 3 = 24$$

On day 5, E co-authors with F and the group average reduces by 0.5, so total reduces by

$$8 \times 0.5 = 4$$

Thus E's number drops by 4. Since after co-authoring with F, E becomes x + 1, E must have been x + 5 before that. The consistent arrangement gives x = 1. Hence the largest Erdõs number at the end is

$$x + 6 = 7$$

So, the maximum final Erdõs number is 7.

122. Only three participants can change during the conference:

- A changes on day 3 from infinity to finite.
- C changes on day 3 because of co-authoring with F.
- E changes on day 5 because of co-authoring with F.

All the remaining five participants keep their Erdõs numbers unchanged throughout the conference. So, the number of participants whose Erdõs number did not change is 5.

123. F has the smallest Erdõs number and the consistent value is 1. C co-authors with F on the third day, so C's Erdõs number becomes

$$1 + 1 = 2$$

No further paper involving C is written. So C's Erdõs number at the end remains 2.

124. From the fifth-day condition, E co-authors with F and the average falls by 0.5. For 8 people this means the total Erdõs number falls by

$$8 \times 0.5 = 4$$

So, E alone decreases by 4. Since after co-authoring with F, E becomes F + 1, and F = 1, E becomes 2. Therefore E must have been

$$2 + 4 = 6$$

at the beginning of the conference.

125. Office 3 and office 5 are white. Since yellow cannot be next to a white office, yellow cannot be in office 2, 4 or 6. Therefore yellow must be in office 1 or 7. The two green offices must be together, and with offices 3 and 5 already white, the only possible adjacent pairs left are 1_2 or 6_7. In either case, after placing yellow at one end and the two green offices at the other end, the two remaining offices to be painted blue are forced to include office 4. So office 4 must be blue.

126. The formula uses four ingredients and must contain two stable chemicals. So it must have exactly two stable and two unstable chemicals.

I. Y and W together is possible, for example with stable chemicals A and C.

II. B and C together is also possible, with two suitable unstable chemicals such as X and Y.

III. W, X and Z together already gives three unstable chemicals. Then only one place remains for a stable chemical, but the formula requires two stable chemicals. So this combination is impossible.

127. Type A fare:

Up to 4 km = ₹ 9.00

Up to 7 km = ₹ 13.50

Fare per km from 4 to 7 km:

$$\frac{13.50 - 9.00}{3} = 1.50$$

For 6 km:

$9 + (2 \times 1.50) = 9 + 3 = 12$

Type B fare:

Up to 7 km = ₹ 24.25

Up to 10 km = ₹ 33.25

Fare per km from 7 to 10 km:

$$\frac{33.25 - 24.25}{3} = 3$$

Remaining distance = 15 – 6 = 9 km

For 9 km:

$24.25 + (2 \times 3) = 24.25 + 6 = 30.25$

Total cost:

$12 + 30.25 = 42.25.$

128. Take total capacity of the tank as the LCM of 20, 25, 30, i.e. 300 units. Then the hourly rates are:

$$A = \frac{300}{20} = 15 \text{ units/hour},$$

$$B = \frac{300}{25} = 12 \text{ units/hour},$$

$$C = \frac{300}{30} = 10 \text{ units/hour}$$

Since C empties the tank, its rate is –10 units/hour.

In one 3-hour cycle, work done is:

$15 + 12 - 10 = 17$ units

In 17 such cycles, that is in 51 hours, filled part is:

$17 \times 17 = 289$ units

Remaining part:

$300 - 289 = 11$ units

After the 51st hour, tap A opens next. Its rate is 15 units/hour, so time to fill the remaining 11 units is:

$$\frac{11}{15} \text{ hour}$$

Hence total time:

$$51 + \frac{11}{15} = 51\frac{11}{15} \text{ hours.}$$

129. In the code PROVIDE → MULYFGB, the letters are changed alternately by −3, +3, −3, +3 ... in alphabetical order.

Check:

P → M (–3)
R → U (+3)
O → L (–3)
V → Y (+3)

Apply the same rule to BECAUSE:

B → Y (–3)
E → H (+3)
C → Z (–3)
A → D (+3)
U → R (–3)
S → V (+3)
E → B (–3)

So the code becomes YHZDRVB.

130. The passage clearly states that the company "is planning to give top priority to core competence of production and marketing of tea." This is a direct statement, not an inference. Hence this conclusion follows exactly and most accurately from the caselet.

131. Triangle ABC is equilateral with side $a = 6$ cm.

Area of equilateral triangle

$$\text{Area} = \frac{\sqrt{3}}{4}a^2 = \frac{\sqrt{3}}{4} \times 36 = 9\sqrt{3}$$

$$9\sqrt{3} \approx 9 \times 1.732 = 15.588 \text{ cm}^2$$

The large circle shown is the incircle of the triangle.

Radius of incircle:

$$r = \frac{a\sqrt{3}}{6} = \frac{6\sqrt{3}}{6} = \sqrt{3}$$

Area of the circle:

$$\pi r^2 = \pi\left(\sqrt{3}\right)^2 = 3\pi \approx 3 \times 3.142$$
$$= 9.426 \text{ cm}^2$$

The shaded region is the triangle minus the circular region (inner small circle is not part of shaded subtraction here).

$$\text{Shaded area} = 15.588 - 9.426$$
$$= 6.162 \approx 6.15 \text{ cm}^2$$

Hence, the closest correct option is 6.15 cm².

132. In a cube of side a, the diagonals DF, AG, and CE are space diagonals.

Length of any space diagonal of a cube:

$$= \sqrt{a^2 + a^2 + a^2} = a\sqrt{3}$$

Thus, the triangle formed by these three diagonals has all sides:

$$a\sqrt{3}, a\sqrt{3}, a\sqrt{3}$$

So, the triangle is equilateral with side $s = a\sqrt{3}$.

Circumradius of an equilateral triangle:

$$R = \frac{s}{\sqrt{3}}$$

Substituting:

$$R = \frac{a\sqrt{3}}{\sqrt{3}} = a$$

Hence, the radius of the circumcircle is equal to the side of the cube.

133. Arrange the products as:

1 – N, 2 – V, 3 – G, 4 – P, 5 – R, 6 – A

This satisfies all given conditions. After interchanging Rin and Ariel:

1 – N, 2 – V, 3 – G, 4 – P, 5 – A, 6 – R

Thus, window 5 contains Ariel.

134. Let the original daily expenditure of the mess be x. Then the original average expenditure per head was

$$\frac{x}{42}$$

After admission of 13 students, totål students become

$$42 + 13 = 55$$

and new expenditure becomes

$$x + 31$$

The average expenditure per head diminished by ₹ 3,

So, $$\frac{x+31}{55} = \frac{x}{42} - 3$$

$$\frac{x+31}{55} = \frac{x-126}{42}$$

$$42(x + 31) = 55(x - 126)$$

$$42x + 1302 = 55x - 6930$$

$$8232 = 13x$$

$$x = \frac{8232}{13} = 633.23$$

Hence the original expenditure was ₹ 633.23.

135. The machine places the greatest remaining number first, then the alphabetically largest remaining word, then the next greatest number, and so on. Since there are 8 elements, the final arrangement is completed in Step VI, just as in the model pattern. Therefore the last step is neither IV, nor V, nor VIII. So the answer is None of these.

136. The machine places the elements alternately in this order:

- largest number
- alphabetically last word
- next largest number
- next alphabetically last word

Input:

jockeyfirm3643growthchart2245

Numbers in descending order:

45, 43, 36, 22

Words in reverse alphabetical order:

jockey, growth, firm, chart

Now form the steps:

Step I: put 45in the first place

45jockeyfirm3643growthchart22

Step II: put jockey in the second place

It is already there, so no visible change:

45jockeyfirm3643growthchart22

Step III: put 43in the third place

45jockey43firm36growthchart22

So, the third step is: D : 45 jockey 43 firm 36 growth chart 22.

137. Total messages = 600

Bina sent 30% of 600 = $\frac{30}{100} \times 600 = 180$

Divya sent 20% of 600 = $\frac{20}{100} \times 600 = 120$

So Anita and Chaitra together sent

$$600 - (180 + 120) = 300$$

Since Anita and Chaitra sent equal numbers,

Anita = 150, Chaitra = 150

Now jokes :

Anita: 60% of 150 = 90

Bina: 40% of 180 = 72

Chaitra: 80% of 150 = 120

Divya: 50% of 120 = 60

Total jokes:

$$90 + 72 + 120 + 60 = 342$$

Jokes sent neither by Divya nor by Bina means jokes sent by Anita and Chaitra:

$$90 + 120 = 210$$

Required percentage:

$$\frac{210}{342} \times 100 = 61.4035\% \approx 61.4\%.$$

So, the answer is C. 61.4%.

138. Total trees = 205.

Let teak trees = T.

Given mango trees = 2T.

Pine trees = 205 − (T + 2T) = 205 − 3T.

From column condition (3), teak values must follow ratio 1 : 2 : 4 across columns (with Y1 = 21 fixed).

The only valid multiples of 3 or 4 (all distinct) satisfying this are 21, 4, 8, 16 → total teak = 49.

Hence mango = 2 × 49 = 98.

139. Using condition (1):

Abha = Chitra + 20

and Dipti = Abha + 6.

Let Chitra = 30 ⇒ Abha = 50

⇒ Dipti = 56.

Total = 205

⇒ Bina = 205 − (50 + 30 + 56) = 69.

This set satisfies all plot and ownership constraints.

140. Chitra has total 30 trees. From placement rules (corner + non-adjacency + distribution), she gets one mango plot (12) and one pine plot.

Remaining = 30 − 12 = 18,

Hence pine trees received = 18.

141. All plots are distinct non-zero multiples of 3 or 4. Smallest possible = 3. From constraints (Bina occupies one plot in each row and column and corner allocation), the smallest plot (3) must go to Bina.

142. From full grid consistency, Bina does not receive the 32-tree plot (largest value condition and placement contradict this). Other statements match the final distribution, so this statement is not true.

143. From the completed grid (based on all constraints of Qs. 138 - 142), the distribution of trees across columns can be summed. Column 4 contains the largest values including 28 and other comparatively higher multiples (since the largest plot = 32 is also placed in a non-Abha column and fits structurally in column 4 during final arrangement).

Also, condition (3) on teak trees enforces a proportional increase from Column 2 → Column 3 → Column 4, which further pushes Column 4 total highest among all columns.

Thus, Column 4 has the maximum number of trees.

144. In the 3 × 3 grid, two clear patterns are observed—one for shapes (column-wise) and one for numbers (row-wise).

Shape pattern (by columns):

Column 1 → Circle

Column 2 → Pentagon

Column 3 → Parallelogram

So, the missing figure must also be a parallelogram.

Number pattern (by rows):

Row 1 → all figures have 1/2

Row 2 → all figures have 2

Row 3 → pattern repeats like Row 1 → 1/2

Thus, the missing figure must contain 1/2.

Orientation pattern (Row 3):

In Row 3, shapes are inverted/tilted compared to Row 1

So the parallelogram in the missing cell must follow this same orientation style.

Among the options, only option (3) matches:

Parallelogram shape

Contains 1/2

Correct orientation consistent with Row 3

Hence, the answer is C. 3.

145. India's actual 2024 digital-currency context was the RBI's digital rupee/CBDC rollout rather than a formally titled "National Digital Currency Policy." The RBI describes the e₹ as sovereign digital money with convenience and finality of settlement, which supports faster, more efficient payments rather than decentralised finance replacing banks. That makes option C the best fit.

146. NITI Aayog's MSME export report recommends a one-stop information channel, clarifying roles such as EOR and SOR in e-commerce exports, and stronger export credit/guarantee support. It does not recommend raising the MSME registration threshold as an export strategy.

147. Contemporary analysis of the FY 2023–24 completion of the G-Sec borrowing programme linked it to prudent fiscal management and the expectation of RBI surplus transfer under Section 47, not to external borrowing dependence or short-term costly debt.

148. B: To assist the RBI by fostering a compliance culture among regulated entities through self-governance, code of conduct enforcement, and promoting sectoral research and innovation: The RBI's omnibus SRO framework explicitly envisages SROs promoting best practices, code of conduct adherence, compliance culture, information sharing, and research/innovation. They are not meant to replace RBI regulation.

149. The March 2024 extension of RoDTEP to AA holders, EOUs and SEZs was presented as a competitiveness measure for key sectors such as engineering, textiles, chemicals, pharmaceuticals and food processing, within budgetary limits. That aligns best with a broad-based export boost, not a narrow or marginal effect.

150. India launched Operation Indravati in March 2024 to evacuate Indian nationals from Haiti via the Dominican Republic.

151. Morgan Stanley Research's FY25 India growth view was 6.5%, describing the outlook as constructive even with some moderation from the previous year rather than a sharp slowdown or acceleration to above 7%.

152. Statement 1 is correct because the open ballot for Rajya Sabha elections was introduced through an amendment to the Representation of the People Act, 1951 to address cross-voting concerns. Statement 2 is not correct because the Tenth Schedule does not disqualify MLAs for voting against the party line in Rajya Sabha elections. Statement 3 is correct because in Kuldip Nayar v. Union of India, the Supreme Court upheld the open ballot system and recognized that such voting does not attract disqualification under the Tenth Schedule.

153. This is the official description of ESCAP's role. It is a regional intergovernmental platform promoting cooperation and solutions for sustainable development, not a body confined only to direct financial aid or only to environmental assessment.

154. This is the statement that is not true. Devin was presented as an autonomous AI software engineer capable of coding, debugging, and solving certain tasks, and Cognition reported benchmark gains on SWE-bench. But that does not mean human engineers are eliminated from all software design and deployment work.

155. At MC13, the WTO's new disciplines on services domestic regulation were framed around good regulatory practice, simplification, transparency, and easier services trade. They are not about tariffs on services or exclusive preferences only for LDCs. Option A best captures the intended direction, especially the balance between facilitating modern services trade and preserving each member's right to regulate.

156. Article 14 deals with equality before law, Article 21 ensures protection of life and personal liberty, Article 32 provides the right to constitutional remedies, and Article 368 lays down the procedure for amendment of the Constitution. Hence the correct matching is 1-(*b*), 2-(*d*), 3-(*a*), 4-(*c*).

157. The Price Stabilization Fund is used to support price stabilization operations like buffer stock creation and market intervention for essential commodities (e.g., pulses, onions). It does not directly subsidize consumers or exports but helps manage volatility through financial support mechanisms.

158. The Patent Rules 2024 introduced a change to reduce the response time after issuance of the First Examination Report (FER), aimed at speeding up patent processing and improving efficiency in granting patents.

159. The Price Stabilization Fund is meant for market intervention to control abnormal price volatility in essential commodities, mainly through procurement, buffer stocking, and release into the market through designated agencies. That makes option A the only correctly matched feature. Options B, C, and D describe functions or structures that the PSF does not have.

160. During 2024, official government releases stated that 102 Vande Bharat train services were operational across Indian Railways. This matches the option given here.

161. Sunil Bharti Mittal was awarded an honorary knighthood by King Charles III for services to UK–India business relations.

162. The 58th Jnanpith Award was announced jointly for Gulzar and Jagadguru Rambhadracharya. A later official ceremony specifically conferred it on Rambhadracharya and also congratulated Gulzar, who could not attend, confirming both as awardees.

163. The World Governments Summit 2024 was held in Dubai, United Arab Emirates, including events at Madinat Jumeirah.

164. In the Interim Budget 2024–25, the government announced that the target under Lakhpati Didi would be enhanced from 2 crore to 3 crore women.

165. IRDAI mandated all general and standalone health insurers to offer the standard health insurance product Arogya Sanjeevani Policy with effect from April 1, 2020.

166. A grey market refers to genuine goods sold through unauthorized or unofficial distribution channels. It is different from counterfeit trade and different from simple tax evasion.

167. The new generation Agni Prime (Agni-P) missile was test-fired in 2021 from Dr APJ Abdul Kalam Island off the coast of Odisha.

168. The Cabinet decision of 31 May 2019 for shopkeepers, retail traders, and self-employed persons provided a minimum assured monthly pension of ₹ 3,000 after the age of 60.

169. The task force that prepared the National Infrastructure Pipeline was headed by Atanu Chakraborty, then Economic Affairs Secretary.

170. In blockchain terminology, NFT stands for Non-fungible token.

Previous Years' Paper

Jamia Millia Islamia (JMI)

MBA Entrance Examination-2024

(Exam held on 09-06-2024)

Directions (Qs. No. 1-4): *Read the passage and answer the question based on it.*

An ATM dispenses exactly ₹ 5000 per withdrawal using 100, 200 and 500 notes. The ATM requires every customer to give her preference for one of the three denominations of notes. It then dispenses notes such that the number of notes of the customer's preferred denomination exceeds the total number of notes of other denominations dispensed to her.

1. In how many different ways can the ATM serve a customer who gives 500-rupee notes as her preference?

A. 5 ways B. 6 ways
C. 4 ways D. 7 ways

2. If the ATM could serve only 10 customers with a stock of fifty 500-rupee notes and a sufficient number of notes of other denominations, what is the maximum number of customers among these 10 who could have given 500 rupee notes as their preference?

A. 3 B. 5
C. 4 D. 6

3. What is the maximum number of customers that the ATM can serve with a stock of fifty 500-rupee notes and a sufficient number of notes of other denominations, if all the customers are to be served with at most 20 notes per withdrawal?

A. 12 B. 13
C. 10 D. 11

4. What is the number of 500-rupee notes required to serve 50 customers with 500-rupee notes as their preferences and another 50 customers with 100-rupee notes as their preferences, if the total number of notes to be dispensed is the smallest possible?

A. 800 B. 1400
C. 900 D. 750

Directions (Qs. No. 5-8): *Read the passage and answer the question based on it.*

Adriana, Bandita, Chitra and Daisy are four female students, and Amit, Barun, Chetan and Deb are four male students. Each of them studies in one of three institutes – X, Y and Z. Each student majors in one subject among Marketing, Operations and Finance, and minors in a different one among these three subjects.

The following facts are known about the eight students:

1. The three students are from X, three from Y and the remaining two students both female, are from Z.
2. Both the male students from Y minor in Finance, while the female student from Y majors in Operations.
3. Only one male student majors in Operations, while three female students minor in Marketing.
4. One female and two male students major in Finance.
5. Adriana and Deb are from the same institute. Daisy and Amit are from the same institute.
6. Barun is from Y and majors in Operations. Chetan is from X and majors in Finance.
7. Daisy minors in Operations.

5. Who are the students from the institute Z?

A. Adriana and Daisy B. Bandita and Chitra
C. Chitra and Daisy D. Chitra and Bandita

6. Which subject does Deb minor in?

A. Finance
B. Cannot be determined uniquely from the given information
C. Marketing
D. Operations

7. Which subject does Amit major in?

A. Operations
B. Finance
C. Cannot be determined uniquely from the given information
D. Marketing

1. D	2. D	3. A	4. C	5. D	6. A	7. B

8. If Chitra majors in Finance, which subject does Bandita major in?

A. Cannot be determined uniquely from the given information
B. Marketing
C. Operations
D. Finance

Directions (Qs. No. 9-12): *Read the passage and answer the question based on it.*

You are given an $n \times n$ square matrix to be filled with numerals so that no two adjacent cells have the same numeral. Two cells are called adjacent if they touch each other horizontally, vertically or diagonally. So, a cell in one of the four corners has three cells adjacent to it, and a cell in the first or last row or column which is not in the corner has five cells adjacent to it. Any other cell has eight cells adjacent to it.

9. What is the minimum number of different numerals needed to fill a 3×3 square matrix?

A. 4 B. 3
C. 2 D. 1

10. What is the minimum number of different numerals needed to fill a 5×5 square matrix?

A. 3 B. 2
C. 4 D. 1

11. Suppose you are allowed to make one mistake, that is, one pair of adjacent cells can have the same numeral. What is the minimum number of different numerals required to fill a 5×5 matrix?

A. 16 B. 4
C. 25 D. 9

12. Suppose that all the cells adjacent to any particular cell must have different numerals. What is the maximum number of different numerals. What is the minimum number of different numerals needed to fill a 5×5 square matrix.

A. 9 B. 16
C. 4 D. 25

Directions (Qs. No. 13-16): *Answer the questions based on the conditions given:*

A company administers a written test comprising of three sections of 20 marks each — Data Interpretation (DI), Written English (WE) and General Awareness (GA), for recruitment. A composite score for a candidate (out of 80), is calculated by doubling her marks in DI and adding it to the sum of her marks in the other two sections. Candidates who score less than 70% marks in two or more sections are disqualified. From among the rest, the four with the highest composite scores are recruied. If four or less candidates qualify, all who qualify are recruited.

Ten candidates appeared for the written test. Their marks in the test are given in the table below. Some marks in the table are missing, but the following facts are known:

1. No two candidates had the same composite score.
2. Ajay was the unique highest scorer in WE.
3. Among the four recruited, Geeta had the lowest composite score.
4. Indu was recruited.
5. Danish, Harini and Indu had scored the same marks in the GA.
6. Indu and Jatin both scored 100% in exactly one section and Jatin's composite score was 10 more than Indu's.

Candidate	Marks out of 20		
	DI	WE	GA
Ajay	8		16
Bata		9	11
Chetna	19	4	12
Danish	8	15	
Ester	12	18	16
Falak	15	7	10
Geeta	14		6
Harini	5		
Indu		8	
Jatin		16	14

13. Which of the following statements MUST be true?

1. Jatin's composite score was more than that of Danish.
2. Indu scored less than Chetna in DI.
3. Jatin scored less than Indu in GA.

A. Only 2 B. Only 1
C. Both 2 and 3 D. Both 1 and 2

14. Which of the following statements MUST be FALSE?

A. Chetna scored more than Bala in DI
B. Harini's composite score was less than that of Falak
C. Bala's composite score was less than that of Ester
D. Bala scored same as Jatin in DI

8. C	9. A	10. C	11. B	12. A	13. D	14. D

15. If all the candidates except Ajay and Danish had different marks in DI, and Bala's composite score was less than Chetna's composite score, then what is the maximum marks that Bala could have scored in DI?

A. 12 B. 11
C. 13 D. 14

16. If all the candidates scored different marks in, WE then what is the maximum marks that Harini could have scored in WE?

A. 14 B. 12
C. 13 D. 11

Directions (Qs. No. 17-20): *Read the information given below and answer the question that follows.*

A new airlines company is planning to start operations in a country. The company has identified ten different cities which they plan to connect through their network to start with. The flight duration between any pair of cities will be less than one hour. To start operations, the company has to decide on a daily schedule.

The underlying principle that they are working on is the following:

Any person staying in any of these 10 cities should be able to make a trip to any other city in the morning and should be able to return by the evening of the same day.

17. If the underlying principle is to be satisfied in such a way that the journey between any two cities can be performed using only direct (non-stop) flights, then the minimum number of direct flights to be scheduled is:

A. 45 B. 90
C. 135 D. 180

18. Suppose three of the ten cities are to be developed as hubs. A hub is a city which is connected with every other city by direct flights each way, both in the morning as well as in the evening. The only direct flights which will be scheduled are originating and/or terminating in one of the hubs. Then the minimum number of direct flights that need to be scheduled so that the underlying principle of the airline to serve all the ten cities is met without visiting more than one hub during one trip is:

A. 96 B. 54
C. 120 D. 60

19. Suppose the 10 cities are divided into 4 distinct groups 01, 02, 03, 04 having 3, 3, 2 and 2 cities respectively and that G1 consists of cities named A, B and C. Further, suppose that direct flights are allowed only between two cities satisfying one of the following:

1. Both cities are in G1
2. Between A and any city in G2
3. Between B and any city in G3
4. Between C and any city in G4

A. 40 B. 20
C. 28 D. 36

20. Suppose the 10 cities are divided into 4 distinct groups G1, G2, G3, G4 having 3, 3, 2 and 2 cities respectively and that G1 consists of cities named A, B and C. Further, suppose that direct flights are allowed only between two cities satisfying one of the following:

1. Both cities are in G1
2. Between A and any city in G2
3. Between B and any city in G3
4. Between C and any city in G4

However, due to operational difficulties at A, it was later decided that the only flights that would operate at A would be those to and from B. Cities in G2 would have to be assigned to G3 or to G4.

What would be the maximum reduction in the number of direct flights as compared to the situation before the operational difficulties arose?

A. 6 B. 5
C. 3 D. 4

Directions (Qs. No. 21 & 22): *Read the information given below and answer the question that follows.*

Four cars need to travel from Akala (A) to Bakala (B). Two routes are available, one via Mamur (M) and the other via Nanur (N). The roads from A to M, and from N to B, are both short and narrow. In each case, one car takes 6 minutes to cover the distance, and each additional car increases the travel time per car by 3 minutes because of congestion. (For example, if only two cars drive from A to M, each car takes 9 minutes). On the road from A to N, one car takes 20 minutes, and each additional car increases the travel time per car by 1 minute. On the road from M to B, one car takes 20 minutes and each additional car increases the travel time per car by 0.9 minute.

The police department orders each car to take a particular route in such a manner that it is not possible for any car to reduce its travel time by not following the order, while the other cars are following the order:

15. C	16. A	17. D	18. A	19. A	20. D

21. How many cars would be asked to take the route A-N-B, that is Alaka-Nanur-Bakala route, by the police department?

A. 4 B. 2
C. 3 D. 1

22. If all the cars follow the police order, what is the difference in travel time (in minutes) between a car which takes the route A-N-B and a car that takes the route A-M-B?

A. 1 B. 0.2
C. 0.9 D. 0.1

Directions (Qs. No. 23 & 24): *Read the information given below and answer the question that follows.*

Four cars need to travel from Akala (A) to Bakala (B). Two routes are available, one via Mamur (M) and the other via Nanur (N). The roads from A to M, and from N to B, are both short and narrow. In each case, one car takes 6 minutes to cover the distance, and each additional car increases the travel time per car by 3 minutes because of congestion. (For example, if only two cars drive from A to M, each car takes 9 minutes). On the road from A to N, one car takes 20 minutes, and each additional car increases the travel time per car by 1 minute. On the road from M to B, one car takes 20 minutes, and each additional car increases the travel time per car by 0.9 minute.

The police department orders each car to take a particular route in such a manner that it is not possible for any car to reduce its travel time by not following the order, while the other cars are following the order:

A new one-way road is built from M to N. Each car now has three possible routes to travel from A to B: A-M-B, A-N-B and A-M-N-B. On the road from M to N, one car takes 7 minutes and each additional car increases the travel time per car by 1 minute. Assume that any car taking the A-M-N-B route travels the A-M portion at the same time as other cars taking the A-M-B route, and the N-B portion at the same time as other cars taking the A-N-B route.

23. How many cars would the police department order to take the A-M-N-B route so that it is not possible for any car to reduce its travel time by not following the order while the other cars follow the order? (Assume that the police department would never order all the cars to take the same route).

A. 1 B. 3
C. 4 D. 2

24. If all the cars follow the police order, what is the minimum travel time (in minutes) from A to B? (Assume that the police department would never order all the cars to take the same route.)

A. 26 B. 32
C. 29.9 D. 30

25. Arun's present age in years is 40% of Barun's. In another few years, Arun's age will be half of Barun's. By what percentage will Barun's age increase during this period?

A. 20 B. 10
C. 30 D. 25

26. A person can complete a job in 120 days. He works alone on Day 1. On Day 2, he is joined by another person who also can complete the job in exactly 120 days. On Day 3, they are joined by another person of equal efficiency. Like this, everyday a new person with the same efficiency joins the work. How many days are required to complete the job?

A. 20 B. 10
C. 25 D. 15

27. An elevator has a weight limit of 630 kg. It is carrying a group of people of whom the heaviest weighs 57 kg and the lightest weighs 53 kg. What is the maximum possible number of people in the group?

A. 11 B. 15
C. 12 D. 13

28. A man leaves his home and walks at a speed of 12 km per hour, reaching the railway station 10 minutes after the train had departed. If instead he had walked at a speed of 15 km per hour, he would have reached the station 10 minutes before the train's departure. The distance (in km) from his home to the railway station is:

A. 20 B. 25
C. 10 D. 15

29. Ravi invests 50% of his monthly savings in fixed deposits. Thirty percent of the rest of his savings is invested in stocks and the rest goes into Ravi's savings bank account. If the total amount deposited by him in the bank (for savings account and fixed deposits) is ₹ 59,500, then Ravi's total monthly savings (in ₹) is:

A. 60000 B. 50000
C. 70000 D. 40000

30. If a seller gives a discount of 15% on retail price, she still makes a profit of 2%. Which of the following ensures that she makes a profit of 20%?

A. Sell at retail price
B. Give a discount of 5% on retail price
C. Give a discount of 2% on retail price
D. Increase the retail price by 2%

21. B	22. *	23. D	24. B	25. A	26. D	27. A	28. A	29. C	30. A

31. A man travels by a motor boat down a river to his office and back. With the speed of the river unchanged, if he doubles the speed of his motor boat, then his total travel time gets reduced by 75%. The ratio of the original speed of the motor boat to the speed of the river is:

A. $\sqrt{7} : 2$ B. $\sqrt{6} : \sqrt{2}$

C. $2\sqrt{5} : 3$ D. 3 : 2

32. Suppose, C1, C2, C3, C4 and C5 are five companies. The profits made by C1, C2 and C3 are in the ratio 9 : 10 : 8 while the profits made by C2, C4 and C5 are in the ratio 18 : 19 : 20. If C5 has made a profit of ₹ 19 crore more than C1, then the total profit (in ₹) made by all five companies is:

A. 435 crore B. 348 crore

C. 345 crore D. 438 crore

33. The number of girls appearing for an admission test is twice the number of boys. If 30% of the girls and 45% of the boys get admission, the percentage of candidates who do not get admission is:

A. 65 B. 35

C. 50 D. 60

34. A stall sells popcorn and chips in packets of three sizes: large, super and jumbo. The numbers of large, super and jumbo packets in its stock are in the ratio 7 : 17 : 16 for popcorn and 6 : 15 : 14 for chips. If the total number of popcorn packets in its stock is the same as that of chips packets, then the numbers of jumbo popcorn packets and jumbo chips packets are in the ratio.

A. 1 : 1 B. 8 : 7

C. 4 : 3 D. 6 : 5

35. In a market, the price of medium quality mangoes is half that of good mangoes. A shopkeeper buys 80 kg good mangoes and 40 kg medium quality mangoes from the market and then sells all these at a common price which is 10% less than the price at which he bought the good ones. His overall profit is:

A. 6% B. 10%

C. 12% D. 8%

36. If Fatima sells 60 identical toys at a 40% discount on the printed price, then she makes 20% profit. Ten of these toys are destroyed in fire. While selling the rest, how much discount should be given on the printed price so that she can make the same amount of profit?

A. 28% B. 30%

C. 25% D. 24%

37. If a and b are integers of opposite signs such that $(a + 3) 2 : b2 = 9 : 1$ and $(a - 1) 2 : (b - 1) 2 = 4 : 1$, then the ratio $a : b$ is:

A. 9 : 4 B. 81 : 4

C. 25 : 4 D. 1 : 4

38. A class consists of 20 boys and 30 girls. In the mid-semester examination, the average score of the girls was 5 higher than that of the boys. In the final exam, however, the average score of the girls dropped by 3 while the average score of the entire class increased by 2. The increase in the average score of the boys is:

A. 10 B. 9.5

C. 4.5 D. 6

39. The area of the closed region bounded by the equation $|x| + |y| = 2$ in the two-dimensional plane is:

A. 4π B. 4

C. 8 D. 2π

40. From a triangle ABC with sides of lengths 40 ft., 25 ft. and 30 ft., a triangular portion GBC is cut off where G is the centroid of ABC. The area, in sq. ft. of the remaining portion of triangle ABC is:

A. $225 / \sqrt{3}$ B. $275 / \sqrt{3}$

C. $500 / \sqrt{3}$ D. $250 / \sqrt{3}$

41. Let ABC be a right-angled isosceles triangle with hypotenuse BC. Let BQC be a semicircle, away from A, with diameter BC. Let BPC be an arc of a circle centered at A and lying between BC and BQC. If AB has length 6 cm then the area, in sq. cm, of the region enclosed by BPC and BQC is:

A. 18 B. $9\pi - 18$

C. 9π D. 9

42. A solid metallic cube is melted to form five solid cubes whose volumes are in the ratio 1 : 1 : 8 : 27 : 27. The percentage by which the sum of the surface areas of these five cubes exceeds the surface area of the original cube is nearest to:

A. 10 B. 60

C. 20 D. 50

31. A **32.** D **33.** A **34.** A **35.** D **36.** A **37.** C **38.** B **39.** C **40.** C **41.** A **42.** D

Directions (Qs. No. 43-48): *Read the passage and answer the question based on it.*

This year alone, more than 8,600 stores could close, according to industry estimates, many of them the brand-name anchor outlets that real estate developers once stumbled over themselves to court. Already these have been 5,300 retail closing this year. Sears Holdings—which owns Kmart—said in March that there's "substantial doubt" it can stay in business altogether, and will close 300 stores this year. So far this year, nine national retail chains have filed for bankruptcy.

Local jobs are a major casualty of what analysts are calling, with only a hint of hyperbole, the retail apocalypse. Since 2002, department stores have lost 448,000 jobs, a 25% decline, while the number of store closures this year is on pace to surpass the worst depths of the Great Recession. The growth of online retailers, meanwhile, has failed to offset those losses, with the ecommerce sector adding just 178,000 jobs over the past 15 years. Some of those jobs can be found in the massive distribution centers Amazon has opened across the country, often not too far from malls the company helped shutter.

But those are work places, not gathering places. The mall is both. And in the 61 years since the first enclosed one opened in suburban Minneapolis, the shopping mall has been where a huge swath of middle-class America went for far more than shopping. It was the home of first jobs and blind dates, the place for family photos and ear piercings, where goths and grandmothers could somehow walk through the same doors and find something they all liked. Sure, the food was lousy for you and the oceans of parking lots encouraged car-heavy development, something now scorned by contemporary planners. But for better or worse, the mall has been America's public square for the last 60 years.

So, what happens when it disappears?

Think of your mall or think of the one you went to as a kid. Think of the perfume clouds in the department stores. The fountains splashing below the skylights. The cinnamon wafting from the food court. As far back as ancient Greece, societies have congregated around a central marketplace.

In medieval Europe, they were outside cathedrals. For half of the 20th century and almost 20 years into the new one, much of America has found their agora on the terrazzo between Orange Julius and Sbarro, Waldenbooks and the Gap, Sunglass Hut and Hot Topic.

That mall was an ecosystem unto itself, a combination of community and commercialism peddling everything you needed and everything you didn't: Magic Eye posters, Wind catchers, Air Jordans.

A growing number of Americans, however, don't see the need to go to any Macy's at all. Our digital lives are frictionless and ruthlessly efficient, with retail and romance available at a click. Malls were designed for leisure, abundance, ambling. You parked and planned to spend some time. Today, much of that time has been given over to busier lives and second jobs and apps that let you swipe right instead of haunt the food court. 'Malls, says Harvard business professor Leonard Schlesinger, "were built for patterns of social interaction that increasingly don't exist."

43. The central idea of this passage is that:

A. malls used to perform a social function that has been lost.

B. the closure of malls has affected the economic and social life of middle-class America.

C. the advantages of malls outweigh their disadvantages.

D. malls are closing down because people have found alternate ways to shop.

44. Why does the author say in paragraph 2, 'the massive distribution centers Amazon has opened across the country, often not too far from malls the company helped shutter'?

A. To indicate that malls and distribution centers are located in the same area

B. To show that Amazon is helping certain brands go online

C. To indicate that the shopping habits of the American middle class have changed

D. To highlight the irony of the situation

45. In paragraph I, the phrase "real estate developers once stumbled over themselves to court" suggests that they:

A. took brand-name anchor outlets to court

B. were eager to get brand-name anchor outlets to set up shop in their mall

C. collaborated with one another to get brand-name anchor outlets

D. malls are closing down because people have found alternate ways to shop

43. A	**44.** D	**45.** C

46. The author calls the mall an ecosystem unto itself because:

A. People of all ages and from all walks of life went there.
B. it was a commercial space as well as a gathering place.
C. people could shop as well as eat in one place.
D. it sold things that were needed as well as those that were not.

47. Why does the author say that the mall has been America's public square?

A. Malls did not bar anybody from entering the space.
B. Malls were a great place to shop for a huge section of the middle class.
C. Malls were a hangout place where families grew close to each other.
D. Malls were a great place for everyone to gather and interact.

48. The author describes 'Perfume clouds in the department stores' in order to:

A. describe the smells and sights of malls
B. evoke memories by painting a picture of malls
C. emphasize that all brands were available under one roof
D. show that malls smelt good because of the various stores and food court

Directions (Qs. No. 49-51): *Read the passage and answer the question based on it.*

Do sports mega events like the summer Olympic Games benefit the host city economically? It depends, but the prospects are less than rosy. The trick is converting ... several billion dollars in operating costs during the 17-day fiesta of the Games into a basis for long-term economic returns. These days, the summer Olympic Games themselves generate total revenue of $4 billion to $5 billion, but the lion's share of this goes to the International Olympics Committee, the National Olympics Committees and the International Sports Federations. Any economic benefit would have to flow from the value of the Games as an advertisement for the city, the new transportation and communications infrastructure that was created for the Games, or the ongoing use of the new facilities.

Evidence suggests that the advertising effect is far from certain. The infrastructure benefit depends on the initial condition of the city and the effectiveness of the planning. The facilities benefit is dubious at best for buildings such as velodromes or natatoriums and problematic for 100,000-seat Olympic stadiums. The latter require a conversion plan for future use, the former are usually doomed to near vacancy. Hosting the summer Games generally requires 30-plus sports venues and dozens of training centers. Today, the Bird's Nest in Beijing sits virtually empty, while the Olympic Stadium in Sydney costs some $30 million a year to operate.

Part of the problem is that Olympics planning takes place in a frenzied and time-pressured atmosphere of intense competition with the other prospective host cities – not optimal conditions for contemplating the future shape of an urban landscape.

Another part of the problem is that urban land is generally scarce and growing scarcer. The new facilities often stand for decades or longer. Even if they have future use, are they the best use of precious urban real estate?

Further, cities must consider the human cost. Residential areas often are razed and citizens relocated (without adequate preparation or compensation). Life is made more hectic and congested. There are, after all, other productive uses that can be made of vanishing fiscal resources.

49. The central point in the first paragraph is that the economic benefits of the Olympic Games:

A. are shared equally among the three organizing committees.
B. accrue to host cities, if at all, only in the long-term.
C. accrue mostly through revenue from advertisements and ticket sales.
D. are usually eroded by expenditure incurred by the host city.

50. Sports facilities built for the Olympics are not fully utilized after the Games are over because:

A. their location away from the city center usually limits easy access.
B. their scale and the costs of operating them are large.
C. the authorities do not adapt them to local conditions.
D. they become outdated having being built with little planning and under time pressure.

51. The author feels that the Games place a burden on the host city for all of the following reasons EXCEPT that:

A. they divert scarce urban land from more productive uses
B. they involve the demolition of residential structures to accommodate sports facilities and infrastructure
C. the finances used to fund the Games could be better used for other purposes
D. the influx of visitors during the Games place a huge strain on the urban infrastructure

46. B	**47.** D	**48.** B	**49.** B	**50.** B	**51.** D

Direction (Qs. No. 52): *Identify the most-appropriate summary for the paragraph.*

52. For each of the past three years, temperature have hit peaks not seen since the birth of meteorology and probably not for more than 1,10,000 years. The amount of carbon dioxide in the air is at its highest level in 4 million years. This does not cause storms like Harvey — there have always been storms and hurricanes along the Gulf of Mexico - but it makes them wetter and more powerful. As the seas warm, they evaporate more easily and provide energy to storm fronts. As the air above them warms, it holds more water vapour. For every half a degree Celsius in warming, there is about a 3% increase in atmospheric moisture content. Scientists call this the Clausius-Clapeyron equation. This means the skies fill more quickly and have more to dump. The storm surge was greater because sea levels have risen 20 cm as a result of more than 100 years of human-related global warming which has melted glaciers and thermally expanded the volume of sea water.

A. The storm Harvey is one of the regular, annual ones from the Gulf of Mexico; global warming and Harvey are unrelated phenomena.
B. Global warming does not breed storms but makes them more destructive; the Clausius-Clapeyron equation, though it predicts potential increase in atmospheric moisture content, cannot predict the scale of damage storms might wreck.
C. Global warming melts glaciers, resulting in sea water volume expansion; this enables more water vapour to fill the air above faster. Thus, modern storms contains more destructive energy.
D. It is naive to think that rising sea levels and the force of tropical storms are unrelated; Harvey was destructive as global warming has armed it with more moisture content, but this may not be true of all storms.

Directions (Qs. No. 53-59): *The five sentences (labelled 1, 2, 3, 4 and 5) gives in this question, when properly sequenced, form a coherent paragraph. Decide on the proper order for the sentence and key in this sequence of five numbers as your answer.*

53. 1. The process of handing down implies not a passive transfer, but some contestation in defining what exactly is to be handed down.
2. Wherever Western scholars have worked on the Indian past, the selection is even more apparent and the inventing of a tradition much more recognizable.
3. Every generation selects what it requires from the past and makes its innovations, some more than others.
4. It is now a truism to say that traditions are not handed down unchanged, but are invented.
5. Just as life has death as its opposite, so is tradition, by default the opposite of innovation.

A. 54132 B. 45321
C. 23145 D. 31452

54. 1. Scientists have for the first time managed to edit genes in a human embryo to repair a genetic mutation, fueling hopes that such procedures may one day be available outside laboratory conditions.
2. The cardiac disease causes sudden death in otherwise healthy young athletes and affects about one in 500 people overall.
3. Correcting the mutation in the gene would not only ensure that the child is healthy but also prevents transmission of the mutation to future generations.
4. It is caused by a mutation in a particular gene and a child will suffer from the condition even if it inherits only one copy of the mutated gene.
5. In results announced in Nature this week, scientists fixed a mutation that thickens the heart muscle, a condition called hypertrophic cardiomyopathy.

A. 54321 B. 15243
C. 43215 D. 32154

55. 1. The study suggests that the disease did not spread with such intensity, but that it may have driven human migrations across Europe and Asia.
2. The oldest sample came from an individual who lived in southeast Russia about 5,000 years ago.
3. The ages of the skeletons correspond to a time of mass exodus from today's Russia and Ukraine into western Europe and central Asia, suggesting that a pandemic could have driven these migrations.
4. In the analysis of fragments of DNA from 101 Bronze Age skeletons for sequences from Yersinia pestis, the bacterium that causes the disease, seven tested positive.
5. DNA from Bronze Age human skeletons indicate that the black plague could have emerged as early as 3,000 BCE, long before the epidemic that swept through Europe in the mid-1300s.

A. 32145 B. 12453
C. 45321 D. 54123

52. C	53. A	54. B	55. D

56. 1. This visual turn in social media has merely accentuated this announcing instinct of ours, enabling us with easy-to-create, easy-to-share, easy-to-store, easy-to-consume platforms, gadgets and apps.
2. There is absolutely nothing new about us framing the vision of who we are or what we want, visually or otherwise, in our Facebook page, for example.
3. Turning the pages of most family albums, which belong to a period well before the digital dissemination of self-created and self-curated moments and images, would reconfirm the basic instinct of documenting our presence in a particular space, on a significant occasion, with others who matter.
4. We are empowered to book our faces and act as celebrities within the confinement of our respective friend lists, and communicate our activities, companionship and locations with minimal clicks and touches.
5. What is unprecedented is not the desire to put out news feeds related to the self, but the ease with which this broadcast operation can now be executed, often provoking (un) anticipated responses from beyond one's immediate location.

A. 54123 B. 32145
C. 41235 D. 23451

57. 1. People who study children's language spend a lot of time watching how babies react to the speech they hear around them.
2. They make films of adults and babies interacting and examine them very carefully to see whether the babies show any signs of understanding what the adults say.
3. They believe that babies begin to react to language from the very moment they are born.
4. Sometimes the signs are very subtle-slight movement of the baby's eyes or the head or the hands.
5. You'd never notice them if you were just sitting with the child, but by watching a recording over and over, you can spot them.

A. 3 B. 4
C. 2 D. 5

58. 1. Neuroscientists have just begun studying exercise's impact within brain cells – on the genes themselves.
2. Even there, in the roots of our biology, they've found signs of the body's influence on the mind.
3. It turns out that moving our muscles produces proteins that travel through the bloodstream and into the brain, where they play pivotal roles in the mechanism of our highest thought processes.
4. In today's technology-driven, plasma-screened-in world, it's easy to forget that we are born movers—animals, in fact—because we've engineered movement right out of our lives.
5. It's only in the past few years that neuroscientists have begun to describe these factors and how they work, and each new discovery adds awe-inspiring depth to the picture.

A. 4 B. 3
C. 2 D. 1

59. 1. The water that made up ancient lakes and perhaps an ocean was lost.
2. Particles from the Sun collided with molecules in the atmosphere, knocking them into space or giving them an electric charge that caused them to be swept away by the solar wind.
3. Most of the planet's remaining water is now frozen or buried, but clues over the past decade suggested that some liquid water, a presumed necessity for life, might survive in underground aquifers.
4. Data from NASA's MAVEN orbiter show that solar storms stripped away most of Mars's once-thick atmosphere.
5. A recent study reveals how Mars lost much of its early water, while another indicates that some liquid water remain.

A. 3 B. 2
C. 4 D. 1

60. Although _____ in the class seemed to follow _____ the teacher said, she never intended to simplify her language.

A. no one/anything
B. anybody/anything
C. nobody/nothing
D. someone/something

61. Trademarks enable a brand to distinguish ______ products from ______ of another brand.

A. its/those B. our/this
C. their/it D. it/that

62. When the woman asked how I got ______ address, I told her that it was given by a relative of ______.

A. my/me B. mine/his
C. she/she D. her/hers

56. B **57.** A **58.** A **59.** D **60.** A **61.** A **62.** D

Directions (Qs. No. 63-65): *Find any modifiers in the following sentences that are misplaced or unclear and select the most suitable sentence among the given options which eliminates any problems.*

63. A. Browsing among the gifts for sale, I remembered my grandmother's word.
B. Browsing among the gifts for sale, my grandmother's words came to me.
C. Browsing the gifts for sale, my grandmother's words came to me.
D. Browsing gifts for sale, my grandmother's words came to me.

64. A. I got instructions on how to make a centerpiece from a fourth-grader.
B. I got instruction to make a centerpiece from a fourth-grader.
C. I got instructions from a fourth-grader to make a centerpiece.
D. I got instructions from a fourth-grader on how to make a centerpiece.

65. A. I have a list of the people who danced on the table.
B. I have a list of people who danced on the table.
C. I have a list on the table of the people who danced.
D. I have list of people who danced on the table.

Directions (Qs. No. 66-68): *Complete the given sentences with the appropriate word given below:*

66. The political party, which is in majority in the parliament, ______ support from the opposition on important bills.
A. Expect B. Expected
C. Will expect D. Expects

67. Rahul and Richa plan to get married in summer but Richa's family _______ it to happen in winter.
A. Wants B. Want
C. Wanted D. Will want

68. Among all the children in my family, only my son ______ like milk.
A. Doesn't B. Don't
C. Will not D. May not

Directions (Qs. No. 69-71): *Complete the given sentences with the appropriate Prepositions given below:*

69. I am committed _______ my word.
A. to B. for
C. by D. with

70. It is tough to go _______ troubles, but has to stay strong.
A. from B. through
C. in D. into

71. Andrew swam ________ the raging river and crossed it successfully.
A. from B. in
C. into D. through

Directions (Qs. No. 72 & 73): *Complete the given sentences with the appropriate synonyms given below:*

72. He was truly **pleased** with his life. Replace the highlighted word with an appropriate synonym from the following:
A. Regards B. Irritated
C. Contents D. Content

73. He was very **optimistic** about his future. Replace the highlighted word with an appropriate synonym from the following:
A. Desperate B. Promising
C. Pessimistic D. Hopeless

Directions (Qs. No. 74-76): *Complete the given sentences with the appropriate antonyms given below:*

74. Copious
A. Plentiful B. Revenge
C. Scarce D. None of the above

75. Boisterous
A. Lively B. Exuberant
C. None of the above D. Restrained

76. Elaborate
A. Detailed B. Simple
C. Inticrate D. None of the above

Directions (Qs. No. 77-80): *Answer the questions given below:*

1600 satellites were sent up by a country for several purposes. The purposes are classified as broadcasting (B), communication (C), surveillance (S), and others (O). A satellite can serve multiple purposes; however, a satellite serving either B, or C, or S does not serve O.

The following facts are known about the satellites:

1. The numbers of satellites serving B, C and S (though may be not exclusively) are in the ratio 2 : 1 : 1.
2. The number of satellites serving all three of B, C, and S is 100.

63. A	**64.** C	**65.** C	**66.** D	**67.** A	**68.** B	**69.** A
70. B	**71.** D	**72.** D	**73.** B	**74.** C	**75.** D	**76.** B

3. The number of satellites exclusively serving C, is the same as the number of satellites exclusively serving S. This number is 30% of the number of satellites exclusively serving B.
4. The number of satellites serving O is the same as the number of satellites serving both C and S but not B.

77. What best can be said about the number of satellites serving C?

A. Cannot be more than 800
B. Must be between 450 and 725
C. Must be between 400 and 800
D. Must be at least 100

78. What is the minimum possible number of satellites serving B exclusively?

A. 100 B. 200
C. 250 D. 500

79. If at least 100 of the 1600 satellites were serving O, what can be said about the number of satellites serving S?

A. At most 475
B. Exactly 475
C. At least 475
D. No conclusion is possible based on the given information

80. If the number of satellites serving at least two among B, C and S is 1200, which of the following MUST be FALSE?

A. The number of satellites serving B is more than 1000.
B. All 1600 satellites serve B or C or S
C. The number of satellites serving B exclusively is exactly 250
D. The number of satellites serving C cannot be uniquely determined.

81. Let S be the set of all points (x, y) in the x-y plane such that $|x| + |y| \leq 2$ and $|x| \geq 1$. Then, the area in square units, of the region represented by S equals:

A. 2 B. 1
C. 4 D. 3

82. Ramesh and Gautam are among 22 students who write an examination. Ramesh scores 82.5. The average score of the 21 students other than Gautam is 62. The average score of all the 22 students is one more than the average score of the 21 students other than Ramesh. The score of Gautam is:

A. 51 B. 49
C. 48 D. 53

83. At their usual efficiency levels, A and B together finish a task in 12 days. If A had worked half as efficiently as she usually does, and B had worked thrice as efficiently as he usually does, the task would have been completed in 9 days. How many days would A take to finish the task if she works alone after usual efficiency?

A. 24 B. 18
C. 12 D. 36

84. In a circle of radius 11 cm, CD is a diameter and AB is a chord of length 20.5 cm. If AB and CD intersect at a point E inside the circle and CE has length 7 cm, then the difference of the lengths of BE and AE, in cm, is:

A. 2.5 B. 0.5
C. 3.5 D. 1.5

85. With rectangular axes of coordinates, the number of paths from (1, 1) to (8, 10) via (4, 6), where each step from any point (x, y) is either to $(x, y + 1)$ or to $(x + 1, y)$, is:

A. 3920 B. 3820
C. 3840 D. 3940

86. Amala, Bina and Gouri invest money in the ratio 3 : 4 : 5 in fixed deposits having respective annual interest rates in the ratio 6 : 5 : 4. What is their total interest income (in ₹) after a year, if Bina's interest income exceeds Amala's by ₹ 250?

A. 6350 B. 7000
C. 6000 D. 7250

87. A club has 256 members of whom 144 can play football, 123 can play tennis, and 132 can play cricket. Moreover, 58 members can play both football and tennis, 25 can play both cricket and tennis, while 63 can play both football and cricket. If every member can play at least one game, then the number of members who can play only tennis is:

A. 45 B. 38
C. 32 D. 43

88. Let T be the triangle formed by the straight line $3x + 5y - 45 = 0$ and the coordinate axes. Let the circumcircle of T have radius of length L, measured in the same unit as the coordinate axes. Then, the integer closest to L is:

A. 9 B. 6
C. 7 D. 8

77. B **78.** C **79.** A **80.** D **81.** A **82.** A **83.** B **84.** B **85.** A **86.** D **87.** D **88.** A

89. Three men and eight machines can finish a job in half the time taken by three machines and eight men to finish the same job. If two machines can finish the job in 13 days, then how many men can finish the job in 13 days?

A. 12 men B. 13 men
C. 11 men D. 14 men

90. The wheels of bicycle A and B have radii 30 cm and 40 cm, respectively. While travelling a certain distance, each wheel of A required 5000 more revolutions than each wheel of B. If bicycle B travelled this distance in 45 minutes, then its speed, in km per hour, was:

A. 18 π B. 12 π
C. 14 π D. 16 π

91. AB is a diameter of a circle of radius 5 cm. Let P and Q be two points on the circle so that the length of PB is 6 cm, and the length of AP is twice that of AQ. Then the length, in cm, of QB is nearest to:

A. 7.8 B. 8.5
C. 9.1 D. 9.3

92. A chemist mixes two liquids 1 and 2. One litre of liquid 1 weights 1 kg and one litre of liquid 2 weighs 800 gm. If half litre of the mixture weighs 480 gm, then the percentage of liquid 1 in the mixture, in terms of volume, is:

A. 85 B. 70
C. 80 D. 75

93. One can use three different transports which move at 10, 20 and 30 kmph, respectively. To reach from A to B, Amal took each mode of transport 1/3 of his total journey time, while Bimal took each mode of transport 1/3 of the total distance. The percentage by which Bimal's travel time exceeds Amal's travel time is nearest to:

A. 21 B. 20
C. 19 D. 22

94. A person invested a total amount of ₹ 15 lakh. A part of it was invested in a fixed deposit earning 6% annual interest, and the remaining among was invested in two other deposits in the ratio 2 : 1, earning annual interest at the rates of 4% and 3%, respectively. If the total annual interest income is ₹ 76000 then the amount (in ₹ lakh) invested in the fixed deposit was:

A. 9 lakhs B. 10 lakhs
C. 8 lakhs D. 7 lakhs

95. Meena scores 40% in an examination and after review, even though her score is increased by 50%, she fails by 35 marks. If her post-review score is increased by 20%, she will have 7 marks more than the passing score. The percentage score needed for passing the examination is:

A. 60 B. 70
C. 75 D. 80

96. In a race of three horses, the first beat the second by 11 metres and the third by 90 metres. If the second beat the third by 80 metres, what was the length, in metres, of the racecourse?

A. 860 B. 890
C. 900 D. 880

97. The product of two positive numbers is 616. If the ratio of the difference of their cubes to the cube of their difference is 157:3, then the sum of the two numbers is:

A. 58 B. 95
C. 50 D. 85

98. Foot and Mouth Disease (FMD), recently seen in the news, is related to which one of the following?

A. Viral disease of livestock
B. Bacterial disease of livestock
C. Fungus disease of Birds
D. Plant disease

99. Exercise "LAMITIYE, recently seen in the news, is conducted between which two countries?

A. India and Seychelles
B. India and Australia
C. India and Japan
D. India and Egypt

100. Recently, which state government has agreed to implement the PM SHRI Schools scheme by signing an MoU with the Ministry of Education?

A. Maharashtra B. Tamil Nadu
C. Gujarat D. Uttar Pradesh

101. Bugun Liocichla, recently seen in the news, belongs to which one of the following species?

A. Bird B. Spider
C. Fish D. Butterfly

102. Noctis Volcano, a recently discovered massive volcano, was found on which planet?

A. Jupiter B. Mars
C. Neptune D. Saturn

89. B	**90.** D	**91.** C	**92.** C	**93.** D	**94.** A	**95.** B
96. D	**97.** C	**98.** A	**99.** A	**100.** C	**101.** A	**102.** B

103. What was the medals tally of India in the last Tokyo, Olympics held in 2021?
A. Six (One gold, two silver, and three bronze)
B. Six (One gold, one silver, and four bronze)
C. Seven (One gold, one silver and five bronze)
D. Seven (One gold, two silver and four bronze)

104. According to a report by TRAFFIC and WWF-India, which state has topped in the illegal trade of shark body parts?
A. Tamil Nadu B. Andhra Pradesh
C. Odisha D. Maharashtra

105. Recently, the Indian Navy has set up its first independent headquarters named 'Nausena Bhawan' at which place?
A. Chennai B. Mumbai
C. Delhi D. Jaipur

106. Atapaka Bird Sanctuary, recently seen in the news, is located in which state?
A. Andhra Pradesh B. Maharashtra
C. Kerala D. Karnataka

107. What is the theme of 'Jal Shakti Abhiyan: Catch the Rain 2024' campaign?
A. Jal Shakti se Vikas
B. Valuing Water
C. Nari Shakti se Jal Shakti
D. Source Sustainability for Drinking Water

108. Mahtari Vandana Yojana, recently seen in the news, is launched by which state?
A. Chhattisgarh B. Jharkhand
C. Odisha D. Karnataka

109. 'Gulf of Tonkin Incident', recently seen in the news, is related to which one of the following?
A. Russia-Ukraine War B. Iran Iraq War
C. World War II D. Vietnam War

110. What is 'Inflection 2.5', recently seen in the news?
A. Large Language Model
B. Black hole
C. Asteroid
D. Exoplanet

111. Yaounde Declaration, recently mentioned in the news, is associated with which one of the following issues?
A. Poverty B. Climate Change
C. Nuclear disarmament D. Malaria eradication

112. According to recent released Council on Energy, Environment and Water CEEW's report, which of the following states have been placed on the top in water management?
A. Haryana, Karnataka and Punjab
B. Maharashtra, Tamil Nadu and Kerala
C. Madhya Pradesh, Bihar and Jharkhand
D. Uttar Pradesh, Gujarat and Rajasthan

113. Recently, which university conferred President Murmu with the Honorary Degree of Doctor of Civil Law?
A. University of Chicago
B. University of Pennsylvania
C. University of Melbourne
D. University of Mauritius

114. Recently, researchers discovered a new scorpion species with 8 eyes and 8 legs in which country?
A. Maldives B. Vietnam
C. Thailand D. Indonesia

115. Recently, where was the India's first Future LABS center inaugurated?
A. C-DAC Thiruvananthapuram
B. C-DAC Bengaluru
C. C-DAC Kolkata
D. C-DAC Bengaluru

116. Blue Line term, recently seen in the news, serves as the boundary between which of the following two countries?
A. Lebanon and Israel
B. India and China
C. North Korea and South Korea
D. Sudan and Libya

117. Recently, Prime Minister of India inaugurated the first Oil Palm Processing Mill under Mission Palm in which state?
A. Karnataka B. Assam
C. Arunachal Pradesh D. Maharashtra

118. Recently, where was the India's first indoor athletics and aquatic centre inaugurated?
A. Bhubaneswar B. Chennai
C. New Delhi D. Jaipur

119. What is the rank of India in the Global Human Development Index, according to UNDP's latest report?
A. 111 B. 133
C. 134 D. 132

103. D	**104.** A	**105.** C	**106.** A	**107.** C	**108.** A	**109.** D	**110.** A	**111.** D
112. A	**113.** D	**114.** C	**115.** A	**116.** A	**117.** C	**118.** A	**119.** C	

120. Electric Mobility Promotion Scheme 2024, recently seen in the news, is introduced by which ministry?

A. Ministry of Petroleum and Natural Gas
B. Ministry of Heavy Industries
C. Ministry of Power
D. Ministry of Earth Sciences

121. Recently, where was the 12th edition of India-Italy Military Cooperation Group meeting held?

A. New Delhi B. Chandigarh
C. Chennai D. Bengaluru

122. Recently, the naval forces of which three countries launched a joint exercise near the Gulf of Oman?

A. China, Iran, and Russia
B. India, USA and China
C. Bangladesh, Myanmar and Bhutan
D. Australia, Maldives and Russia

123. Prasar Bharti - Shared Audio Visuals for Broadcast and Dissemination (PB-SHABD) is recently launched by which ministry?

A. Ministry of Electronics and Information Technology
B. Ministry of Communications
C. Ministry of Commerce and Industry
D. Ministry of Information & Broadcasting

124. What is Alzheimer's disease, recently seen in the news?

A. A progressive brain condition affecting memory and cognitive skills
B. A disorder primarily affecting the lungs
C. A contagious viral infection
D. A type of cancer

125. Which Indian, state was the theme state of World's Largest International Crafts Fair, Surajkund Mela 2024?

A. Rajasthan B. Maharashtra
C. Madhya Pradesh D. Gujarat

126. What is 'eROSITA', recently mentioned in the news?

A. Drone
B. Artificial Intelligence tool
C. Submarine
D. X-ray telescope

127. Bluetongue disease, recently seen in the news, is transmitted by which one of the following?

A. Fungi B. Insects
C. Contaminated water D. Plants

128. What is the theme of 'World Wetland Day' 2024?

A. Wetlands and Human Wellbeing
B. Wetlands for a Sustainable Urban Future
C. Wetlands and Climate Change
D. Wetlands and Water

129. Which state government recently launched 'Operation Smile X' to rescue child labourers?

A. Rajasthan B. Uttar Pradesh
C. Karnataka D. Telangana

130. Who won the Men's Singles Wimbledon Championship in 2023?

A. Alcaraz Garfia B. Nick Kyrgios
C. Novak Djokovic D. Roger Federer

Directions (Qs. No. 131-142): *Solve the following question and mark the best possible option:*

131. A ball of diameter 4 cm is kept on top of a hollow cylinder standing vertically. The height of the cylinder is 3 cm, while its volume is 9π cm^3. Then the vertical distance, in cm, of the topmost point of the ball from the base of the cylinder is:

A. 6 B. 4
C. 5 D. 3

132. Let ABC be a right-angled triangle with BC as the hypotenuse. Lengths of AB and AC are 15 km and 20 km, respectively. The minimum possible time, in minutes, required to reach the hypotenuse from A at a speed of 30 km per hour is:

A. 34 B. 24
C. 14 D. 22

133. Suppose, $\log 3x = \log 12y = a$, where x, y are positive numbers. If G is the geometric mean of x and y and log6 G is equal to:

A. $a/4$ B. $2a$
C. $a/2$ D. a

134. If $x + 1 = x^2$ and $x > 0$, then $2x^4$ is:

A. $7+3\sqrt{5}$ B. $6+4\sqrt{5}$
C. $3+5\sqrt{5}$ D. $5+3\sqrt{5}$

135. The value of $\log_{0.008}\sqrt{5}+\log_{\sqrt{3}}81-7$ is equal to:

A. 1/3 B. 2/3
C. 5/6 D. 7/6

136. If $92x - 1 - 81x - 1 = 1944$, then x is:

A. 9/4 B. 3
C. 4/9 D. 1/3

120. B	**121.** A	**122.** A	**123.** D	**124.** A	**125.** D	**126.** D	**127.** B	**128.** A
129. D	**130.** A	**131.** A	**132.** B	**133.** D	**134.** A	**135.** C	**136.** A	

137. The number of solutions (x, y, z) to the equation $x - y - z = 25$, where x, y and z are positive integers such that $x \leq 40$, $y \leq 12$ and $z \leq 12$ is:

A. 101 B. 87
C. 105 D. 99

138. For how many integers n will the inequality $(n - 5)(n - 10) - 3(n - 2) \leq 0$ be satisfied?

A. 21 B. 12
C. 11 D. 13

139. If $f_1(x) = x^2 + 11x + n$ and $f_2(x) = x$, then the largest positive integer n for which the equation $f_1(x) = f_2(x)$ has two distinct real roots, is:

A. 24 B. 34
C. 14 D. 22

140. Let AB, CD, EF, GH and JK be five diameters of a circle with center at O. In how many ways can three points be chosen out of A, B, C, D, E, F, G, H, J, K and O so as to form a triangle?

A. 140 B. 160
C. 120 D. 110

141. If the square of the 7th term of an arithmetic progression with positive common difference equals the product of the 3rd and 17th terms, then the ratio of the first term to the common difference is:

A. 2 : 3 B. 3 : 2
C. 3 : 4 D. 4 : 3

142. In how many ways can 7 identical erasers be distributed among 4 kids in such a way that each kid gets at least one eraser but nobody gets more than 3 erasers?

A. 20 B. 14
C. 15 D. 16

Directions (Qs. No. 143-146): *Solve the following question and mark the best possible option:*

The following table represents addition of two six-digit numbers given in the first and the second rows, while the sum is given in the third row. In the representation, each of the digits 0, 1, 2, 3, 4, 5, 6, 7, 8, 9 has been coded with one letter among A, B, C, D, E, F, G, H, J, K with distinct letters representing distinct digits.

		B	H	A	A	G	F
+		A	H	J	F	K	F
	A	A	F	G	C	A	F

143. Which digit does the letter A represent?

A. 1 B. 2
C. 3 D. 4

144. Which digit does the letter B represent?

A. 7 B. 9
C. 8 D. 6

145. Which among the digits 3, 4, 6 and 7 cannot be represented by the letter D?

A. 4 B. 5
C. 7 D. 6

146. Which among the digits 4, 6, 7 and 8 cannot be represented by the letter G?

A. 5 B. 4
C. 3 D. 6

Directions (Qs. No. 147-150): *Solve the following question and mark the best possible option:*

Princess, Queen, Rani and Samragni were the four finalists in a dance competition. Ashman, Badal, Gagan, and Dyu were the four music composers who individually assigned items to the dancers. Each dancer had to individually perform in two dance items assigned by the different composers. The first items performed by the four dances were all assigned by different music composers. No dancer performed her second item before the performance of the first item by any other dancers. The dancers, performed their second items in the same sequence of their performance of their first items.

The following additional facts are known.

(*i*) No composer who assigned item to Princess, assigned any item to Queen.
(*ii*) No composer who assigned item to Rani, assigned any item to Samragni.
(*iii*) The first performance was by Princess, this item was assigned by Badal.
(*iv*) The last performance was by Rani; this item was assigned by Gagan.
(*v*) The items assigned by Ashman were performed consecutively. The number of performances between items assigned by each of the remaining composers was the same.

147. Which of the following is true?

A. The third performance was composed by Ashman.
B. The second performance was composed by Gagan.
C. The third performance was composed by Dyu.
D. The second performance was composed by Dyu.

137. D **138.** C **139.** A **140.** B **141.** A **142.** D **143.** A **144.** B **145.** C **146.** D **147.** D

148. Which of the following is FALSE?

A. Rani did not perform in any item composed by Badal.
B. Samragni did not perform in any item composed by Ashman.
C. Queen did not perform in any item composed by Gagan.
D. Princess did not perform in any item composed by Dyu.

149. The sixth performance was composed by:

A. Gagan B. Ashman
C. Dyu D. Badal

150. Which pair of performances were composed by the same composed?

A. The first and the sixth
B. The second and the sixth
C. The first and the seventh
D. The third and the seventh

Directions (Qs. No. 151-154): *Solve the following question and mark the best possible option:*

Six players — Tanzi, Umeza, Wangdu, Xyla, Yonita and Zeneca competed in an archery tournament. The tournament had three compulsory rounds, Rounds 1 to 3. In each round every player shot an arrow at a target. Hitting the centre of the target (called bull's eye) fetched the highest score of 5. The only other possible scores that a player could achieve were 4, 3, 2, and 1. Every bull's eye score in the first three rounds gave a player one additional chance to shoot in the bonus rounds, Rounds 4 to 6. The possible scores in Rounds 4 to 6 were identical to the first three.

A player's total score in the tournament was the sum of his/her scores in all rounds played by him/her. The table below presents partial information on points scored by the players after completion of the tournament. In the table, NP means that the player did not participate in that round, while a hyphen means that the player participated in that round and the score information is missing.

	Round-1	Round-2	Round-3	Round-4	Round-5	Round-6
Tanzi	—	4	—	5	NP	NP
Umeza	—	—	—	1	2	NP
Wangdu	—	4	—	NP	NP	NP
Xyla	—	—	—	1	5	—
Yonita	—	—	3	5	NP	NP
Zeneca	—	—	—	5	5	NP

The following facts are also known:

1. Tanzi, Umeza and Yonita had the same total score.
2. Total scores for all players, except one, were in multiples of three.
3. The highest total score was one more than double of the lowest total score.
4. The number of players hitting bull's eye in Round 2 was double of that in Round.
5. Tanzi and Zeneca had the same score in Round 1 but different scores in Round 3.

151. What was the highest total score?

A. 25 B. 21
C. 24 D. 23

152. What was Zeneca's total score?

A. 24 B. 23
C. 21 D. 22

153. Which of the following statement is true?

A. Zeneca's score was 23.
B. Zeneca was the highest scorer.
C. Xyla's score was 23.
D. Xyla was the highest scorer.

154. What was Tanzi's score in Round 3?

A. 1 B. 3
C. 4 D. 5

Directions (Qs. No. 155-158): *Solve the following question and mark the best possible option:*

The figure below shows the street map for a certain region with the street intersections marked from a through I. A person standing at an intersection can see along straight lines to other intersections that are in her line of sight and all other people standing at these intersections.

For example, a person standing at intersection *g* can see all people standing at intersections *b*, *c*, *e*, *f*, *h* and *k*. In particular, the person standing at intersection *g* can see the person standing at intersection *e* irrespective of whether there is a person standing at intersection *f*.

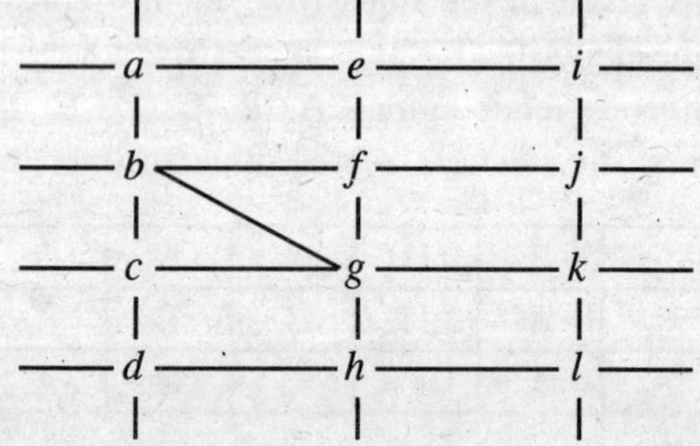

148. C **149.** D **150.** A **151.** A **152.** A **153.** D **154.** A

Six people U, V, W, X, Y and Z are standing at different intersections. No two people are standing at the same intersection.

The following additional facts are known.

1. X, U and Z are standing at the three corners of a triangle formed by three street segments.
2. X can see only U and Z.
3. Y can see only U and W.
4. U sees V standing in the next intersection behind Z.
5. W cannot see V or Z
6. No one among the six is standing at intersection *d*.

155. Who is standing at intersection *a*?

A. V B. W
C. Y D. No one

156. Who can V see?

A. U and Z only B. U only
C. U, W and Z only D. Z only

157. What is the minimum number of street segments that X must cross to reach Y?

A. 1 B. 3
C. 2 D. 4

158. Should a new person stand at intersection *d*, who among the six would she see?

A. U and Z only B. V and X only
C. U and W only D. W and X only

Directions (Qs. No. 159-162): *Solve the following question and mark the best possible option:*

A new game show on TV has 100 boxes numbered 1, 2, ..., 100 in a row, each containing a mystery prize. The prizes are items of different types, *a*, *b*, *c*, ..., in decreasing order of value. The most expensive item is of type *a*, a diamond ring, and there is exactly one of these. You are told that the number of items at least doubles as you move to the next type. For example, there would be at least twice as many items of type *b* as of type *a*, at least twice as many items of type *c* as of type *b* and so on. There is no particular order in which the prizes are placed in the boxes.

159. What is the minimum possible number of different types of prizes?

A. 2 B. 1
C. 3 D. 4

160. What is the maximum possible number of different types of prizes?

A. 3 B. 5
C. 4 D. 5

161. Which of the following is not possible?

A. There are exactly 45 items of type *c*.
B. There are exactly 30 items of type *b*.
C. There are exactly 75 items of type *e*.
D. There are exactly 60 items of type *d*.

162. You ask for the type of item in box 45. Instead of being given a direct answer, you are told that there are 31 items of the same type as box 45 in boxes 1 to 44 and 43 items of the same type as box 45 in boxes 46 to 100. What is the maximum possible number of different types of items?

A. 6 B. 3
C. 4 D. 5

Directions (Qs. No. 163-166): *Solve the following question and mark the best possible option:*

A supermarket has to place 12 items (coded A to L) in shelves numbered 1 to 16. Five of these items are type of biscuits, three are types of candies and the rest are types of savouries. Only one item can be kept in a shelf. Items are to be placed such that all items of same type are clustered together with no empty shelf between items of the same type and a least one empty shelf between two different types of items. At most two empty shelves can have consecutive numbers.

The following additional facts are known:

1. A and B are to be placed in consecutively numbered shelves in increasing order.
2. I and J are to be placed in consecutively numbered shelves both higher numbered than the shelves in which A and B are kept.
3. D, E and F are savouries and are to be placed in consecutively numbered shelves in increasing order after all the biscuits and candies.
4. K is to be placed in shelf number 16.
5. L and J are items of the same type, while H is an item of a different type.
6. C is a candy and is to be placed in a shelf preceded by two empty shelves.
7. L is to be placed in a shelf preceded by exactly one empty shelf.

163. In how many different ways can the items be arranged on the shelves?

A. 2 B. 1
C. 4 D. 8

164. Which of the following items is not a type of biscuit?

A. G B. B
C. L D. A

155. D	156. A	157. C	158. A	159. A	160. *	161. A	162. D	163. D	164. A

165. Which of the following can represent the numbers of the empty shelves in a possible arrangement?

A. 1, 7, 11, 12 B. 1, 5, 6, 12
C. 1, 2, 8, 12 D. 1, 2, 6, 12

166. Which of the following statements is necessarily true?

A. There are at least four shelves between items.
B. There are two empty shelves between the biscuits and the candies.
C. All biscuits are kept before candies.
D. All candies are kept before biscuits.

167. The income of Amala is 20% more than that of Bimala and 20% less than that of Kamala. If Kamala's income goes down by 4% and Bimala's goes up by 10%, then the percentage by which Kamala's income would exceed Bimala's is nearest to:

A. 29 B. 28
C. 32 D. 31

168. In a class, 60% of the students are girls and the rest are boys. There are 30 more girls than boys. If 68% of the students, including 30 boys, pass an examination, the percentage of the girls who do not pass is:

A. 10% B. 30%
C. 49% D. 20%

169. On selling a pen at 5% loss and a book at 15% gain, Karim gains ₹ 7. If he sells the pen at 5% gain and the book at 10% gain, he gains ₹ 13. What is the cost price of the book in Rupees?

A. 80 B. 85
C. 95 D. 100

170. Corners are cut off from an equilateral triangle T to produce a regular hexagon H. Then, the ratio of the area of H to the area of T is:

A. 2 : 3 B. 4 : 5
C. 3 : 4 D. 5 : 6

EXPLANATORY ANSWERS

1. (D): To determine the number of ways the ATM can serve a customer preferring 500-rupee notes:

Variables:

Let x = number of 500-rupee notes
y = number of 200-rupee notes
z = number of 100-rupee notes

Constraints:

Total amount: $500x + 200y + 100z = 5000$
Simplifies to $5x + 2y + z = 50$
Preference condition: $x > y + z$

Possible Solutions:

For: $x = 8$

$$5(8) + 2y + z = 50$$
$$40 + 2y + z = 50$$
$$2y + z = 10$$

With $y + z < 8$, possible combinations:
$(y = 3, z = 4)$ $(y = 4, z = 2)$ $(y = 5, z = 0)$
$\rightarrow$ 3 ways

For: $x = 9$

$$5(9) + 2y + z = 50$$
$$45 + 2y + z = 50$$
$$2y + z = 5$$

With $y + z < 9$, possible combinations:
$(y = 0, z = 5)$ $(y = 1, z = 3)$ $(y = 2, z = 1)$
$\rightarrow$ 3 ways

For: $x = 10$

$$5(10) + 2y + z = 50$$
$$50 + 2y + z = 50$$
$$2y + z = 0$$
$$y = 0, z = 0 \rightarrow 1 \text{ way}$$

Total Ways: $3 + 3 + 1 = 7$.

2. (D): To maximize the number of customers preferring 500-rupee notes with a stock of 50 notes:

Per Customer Analysis:

Each customer prefers 500-rupee notes,
So $x > y + z$.
To minimize the number of 500 notes per customer, set $y + z = x - 1$.
From $5x + 2y + z = 50$,
substituting $y + z = x - 1$ gives $y = 51 - 6x$.
Minimum x Value: y must be non-negative:

$$51 - 6x \geq 0 \rightarrow x \leq 8.5 \rightarrow x \leq 8$$

Optimal x:

$x = 8$ gives $y = 3$ and $z = 4$ per customer.

Total 500 Notes Used:

8 notes per customer $\times$ 6 customers
$= 48$ notes ≤ 50 available.
Maximum Customers: 6.

3. (A): To determine the maximum number of customers the ATM can serve with 50 fifty-rupee (500-rupee) notes and a limit of 20 notes per withdrawal:

Objective: Maximize the number of customers by minimizing the use of 500-rupee notes per customer.

165. D	**166.** A	**167.** D	**168.** D	**169.** A	**170.** A

Withdrawal Constraints:

Each customer withdraws ₹ 5000.

Let x = number of 500-rupee notes per customer. The condition is $x > y + z$, where y and z are the number of 200- and 100-rupee notes, respectively.

Total notes per withdrawal: $x + y + z \leq 20$.

Minimizing 500-Rupee Notes:

Minimum x: 4

$4 \times 500 =$ ₹ 2000

Remaining amount: ₹ 3000 to be fulfilled by 200- and 100-rupee notes.

Example combination:

$4 \times 500 + 10 \times 200 + 0 \times 100$

= ₹ 5000 using 14 notes.

This satisfies $x > y + z$ since $4 > 10 + 0$ is false. Adjusting to satisfy $x > y + z$:

$4 \times 500 + 3 \times 200 + 7 \times 100$

= ₹ 5000 using 14 notes ($4 > 3 + 7$ is false).

Optimal valid combination:

$4 \times 500 + 1 \times 200 + 3 \times 100$

= ₹ 5000 using 8 notes ($4 > 1 + 3$ is false).

To satisfy $x > y + z$,

$4 \times 500 + 0 \times 200 + 0 \times 100$

= ₹ 2000 which is insufficient.

Therefore, the minimum feasible x that satisfies all constraints is 4.

Calculating Maximum Customers:

Each customer uses at least 4 fifty-rupee notes.

Total available 500-rupee notes: 50.

Maximum number of customers: $50/4 = 12.5$, which means 12 customers can be served.

4. (C): To serve 50 customers preferring 500-rupee notes and another 50 preferring 100-rupee notes with the smallest number of 500 notes:

500-Preferring Customers:

Each uses $10 \times$ 500-rupee notes

$\rightarrow$ 50 customers $\times$ 10 = 500 notes.

100-Preferring Customers:

Optimal configuration requires each to use $8 \times$ 500-rupee notes to minimize total notes while satisfying 100-note preference constraints.

50 customers $\times$ 8 = 400 notes.

Total 500 Notes Needed: $500 + 400 = 900$.

5. (D): To identify the students from institute Z:

Institute Distribution:

Total students: 8 (4 female, 4 male)

Distribution: 3 from X, 3 from Y, 2 (both female) from Z.

Known Assignments:

From Fact 6:

Barun is from Y.

Chetan is from X.

From Fact 5:

Adriana and Deb are from the same institute (likely Y).

Daisy and Amit are from the same institute (likely X).

Female Students from Z:

Remaining females: Chitra and Bandita must be the two from Z.

6. (A): To determine Deb's minor subject:

From Fact 2: Both male students from Y minor in Finance.

From Fact 5: Adriana and Deb are from the same institute (Y).

Conclusion: Deb, being male and from Y, must minor in Finance.

7. (B): To determine Amit's major:

Given Information:

Fact 6: Chetan is from X and majors in Finance.

Fact 4: One female and two male students major in Finance.

Fact 5: Adriana and Deb are from the same institute; Daisy and Amit are from the same institute.

Fact 2: Both male students from Y minor in Finance, and the female student from Y majors in Operations.

Fact 3: Only one male student majors in Operations (Barun).

Deductions: From Fact 6 and Fact 4, the two male Finance majors are Chetan and Deb.

Barun majors in Operations (from Fact 3).

Adriana, being the female from Y, majors in Operations (from Fact 2).

Daisy and Amit are from the same institute, likely Z (since X has Chetan and two others, Y has Barun, Deb, Adriana).

Chitra is the other female from Z.

Conclusion: Since the two male Finance majors are Chetan and Deb, Amit cannot major in Finance.

The remaining subjects for Amit are Marketing and Operations.

However, Operations is already taken by Barun and Adriana. Therefore, Amit must major in Marketing.

9. (A): To fill a 3×3 matrix where no two adjacent cells (including diagonally adjacent) have the same numeral, a minimum of 4 different numerals is required. This ensures that each cell can be uniquely identified without violating the adjacency rule.

10. (C): For a 5×5 matrix with the same adjacency constraints, the minimum number of different numerals needed remains 4. This is because the chromatic number for such a grid, where each cell is adjacent to up to eight others, necessitates at least four distinct numerals to avoid any two adjacent cells sharing the same numeral.

11. (B): Allowing one mistake (one pair of adjacent cells having the same numeral) in a 5 × 5 matrix does not reduce the minimum number of different numerals required. Therefore, the minimum number remains 4 to ensure that the vast majority of adjacency constraints are satisfied while permitting just one exception.

For Qs. No. 13-16:

Candidate	Marks out of 20			
	DI	WE	GA	Composite
Ajay	8	19	16	16 + 35 = 51
Bala	16	9	11	32 + 20 = 52
Chetna	19	4	12	38 + 16 = 54
Danish	8	15	12	16 + 27 = 43
Ester	12	18	16	24 + 34 = 58
Falak	15	7	10	30 + 17 = 47
Geeta	14	14	6	28 + 20 = 48
Harini	5	10	12	10 + 22 = 32
Indu	18	8	12	36 + 20 = 56
Jatin	18	16	14	36 + 30 = 66

13. (D):

(*a*) Jatin's composite score was more than that of Danish. This statement must be true.

(*b*) Indu scored less than Chetna in DI. This statement is also true.

(*c*) Jatin scored less than Indu in GA. This statement is not true.

Hence, Option (D) Both (*a*) and (*b*) must be true.

14. (D):

(*a*) Chetna scored more than Bala in DI. This statement is true.

(*b*) Harini's composite score was less than that of Falak. This statement is true.

(*c*) Bala's composite score was less than that of Ester. This statement is also true.

(*d*) Bala scored same as Jatin in DI. This statement must be false.

15. (C): Required maximum marks that Bala could have scored in DI = 13

13 × 2 + 20 = 46 not any other composite marks.

If we put 14 then 14 × 2 + 20 = 48.

Bala's composite marks will be 48

Geeta's composite marks same = 48

Given no two candidates had the same composite score.

16. (A): Maximum marks that Harini could have scored in WE = 14

Harini composite marks will be

= 5 × 2 + 10 + 14

= 10 + 10 + 14 = 34

34 has not any other composite marks.

Hence, required maximum marks = 14.

17. (D): To satisfy the principle that any person can travel between any two of the ten cities using only direct (non-stop) flights in both the morning and evening:

Calculating Unordered Pairs: Number of unordered city pairs: $\binom{10}{2} = 45$.

Considering Directions and Times:

For each unordered pair, there are two directional flights (e.g., A to B and B to A).

Each directional flight requires both a morning and an evening flight.

Total Direct Flights:

Flights per unordered pair: 2 directions × 2 times = flights.

Total flights: 45 pairs × 4 flights = 180.

Thus, the minimum number of direct flights that need to be scheduled is 180.

18. (A): With three cities designated as hubs among the ten cities, and all direct flights originating and/or terminating at these hubs:

Connections per Hub:

Each hub connects to the remaining 7 non-hub cities.

Additionally, each hub connects to the other 2 hubs.

Flights per Hub:

Flights to non-hubs: 7 cities × 2 directions = 14 flights.

Flights to other hubs: 2 hubs × 2 directions = 4 flights.

Total per hub: 14 + 4 = 18 flights.

Total Flights for All Hubs:

3 hubs × 18 flights = 54 flights.

Considering both morning and evening schedules: 54 flights × 2 = 96 flights.

Therefore, the minimum number of direct flights that need to be scheduled is 96.

19. (A): Given the division of ten cities into four groups (G1: A, B, C; G2: 3 cities; G3: 2 cities; G4: 2 cities) with specific flight restrictions:

Allowed Direct Flights:

Within G1: Between A, B, and C.

Number of unordered pairs: $\binom{3}{2} = 3$.

Considering both directions: 3 pairs × 2 = 6 flights.

Between A and G2: A connects to each of the 3 cities in G2.

3 cities × 2 directions = 6 flights.

Between B and G3: B connects to each of the 2 cities in G3.

2 cities × 2 directions = 4 flights.

Between C and G4: C connects to each of the 2 cities in G4.
2 cities × 2 directions = 4 flights.
Total Direct Flights:
Within G1: 6 flights.
A to G2: 6 flights.
B to G3: 4 flights.
C to G4: 4 flights.
Subtotal: 6 + 6 + 4 + 4 = 20 flights.
Considering Morning and Evening:
Each direct flight operates twice (morning and evening).
Total flights: 20 × 2 = 40 flights.
Thus, the maximum reduction in the number of direct flights is 40.

20. **(D):** Due to operational difficulties at city A, the following changes occur:
Flights within G1:
Originally, all pairs in G1 had direct flights (6 flights).
Now, only flights between A and B are allowed: 2 flights.
Reduction: 6 – 2 = 4 flights.
Flights between A and G2:
These flights are eliminated because G2 is reassigned to G3 or G4.
Originally: 6 flights.
Reduction: 6 flights.
Impact on G3 and G4:
Assigning G2 to G3 or G4 increases flights in those groups but does not contribute to reduction.
Maximum reduction in the number of direct flights: 4 flights. Thus, the answer is D: 4.

21. **(B):** To determine the number of cars the police department should assign to the A-N-B route to ensure no car can reduce its travel time by deviating:
Route Assignments:
A-N-B Route: Assign 2 cars.
A-M-B Route: Assign the remaining 2 cars.
Calculating Travel Times:
A-N-B Route:
A to N: 20 + 1 × (2 – 1) = 21 minutes.
N to B: 6 + 3 × (2 – 1) = 9 minutes.
Total: 21 + 9 = 30 minutes.
A-M-B Route:
A to M: 6 + 3 × (2 – 1) = 9 minutes.
M to B: 20 + 0.9 × (2 – 1) = 20.9 minutes.
Total: 9 + 20.9 = 29.9 minutes.
Assessing Incentives to Switch:
Cars on A-M-B:
Current time: 29.9 minutes.
Switching to A-N-B would result in: 20 + 1 × (3 – 1) = 22 minutes for A to N and 6 + 3 × (3 – 1) = 12 minutes for N to B, totaling 34 minutes.
This is worse, so no incentive to switch.
Cars on A-N-B:
Current time: 30 minutes.
Switching to A-M-B would result in: 6 + 3 × (3 – 1) = 12 minutes for A to M and 20 + 0.9 × (3 – 1) = 21.8 minutes for M to B, totaling 33.8 minutes. This is worse, so no incentive to switch.
Since no car can reduce its travel time by changing routes, assigning 2 cars to the A-N-B route satisfies the required condition.

23. **(D):** To determine the number of cars the police department should assign to the A-M-N-B route to ensure no car can reduce its travel time by deviating:
Route Assignments:
A-M-N-B Route: Assign 2 cars.
A-M-B Route: Assign 1 car.
A-N-B Route: Assign 1 car.
Calculating Travel Times:
A-M-N-B Route:
A to M: 6 + 3 × (3 – 1) = 12 minutes.
M to N: 7 + 1 × (2 – 1) = 8 minutes.
N to B: 6 + 3 × (3 – 1) = 12 minutes.
Total: 12 + 8 + 12 = 32 minutes.
A-M-B Route:
A to M: 6 + 3 × (3 – 1) = 12 minutes.
M to B: 20 + 0.9 × (3 – 1) = 21.8 minutes.
Total: 12 + 21.8 = 33.8 minutes.
A-N-B Route:
A to N: 20 + 1 × (3 – 1) = 22 minutes.
N to B: 6 + 3 × (3 – 1) = 12 minutes.
Total: 22 + 12 = 34 minutes.
Assessing Incentives to Switch:
Cars on A-M-N-B:
Current time: 32 minutes.
Switching to A-M-B would take 33.8 minutes (longer).
Switching to A-N-B would take 34 minutes (longer).
Cars on A-M-B and A-N-B:
Switching to A-M-N-B would not reduce their travel time.
Since no car can reduce its travel time by switching routes, assigning 2 cars to the A-M-N-B route satisfies the required condition.
Therefore, the number of cars to assign to the A-M-N-B route is 2, corresponding to option D: 2.

24. **(B):** To determine the minimum travel time from A to B when all cars follow the police order:
Route Assignments:
A-M-N-B Route: 2 cars.
A-M-B Route: 1 car.
A-N-B Route: 1 car.

Calculating Travel Times:

A-M-N-B Route:

A to M: 6 + 3 × (3 − 1) = 12 minutes.

M to N: 7 + 1 × (2 − 1) = 8 minutes.

N to B: 6 + 3 × (3 − 1) = 12 minutes.

Total: 12 + 8 + 12 = 32 minutes.

A-M-B Route:

A to M: 6 + 3 × (3 − 1) = 12 minutes.

M to B: 20 + 0.9 × (3 − 1) = 21.8 minutes.

Total: 12 + 21.8 = 33.8 minutes.

A-N-B Route:

A to N: 20 + 1 × (3 − 1) = 22 minutes.

N to B: 6 + 3 × (3 − 1) = 12 minutes.

Total: 22 + 12 = 34 minutes.

Determining Minimum Travel Time:

The A-M-N-B route offers the shortest travel time of 32 minutes.

The other routes take longer: 33.8 minutes and 34 minutes.

Therefore, the minimum travel time from A to B, based on the assigned routes, is 32 minutes, corresponding to option B: 32.

25. **(A):** Let present age of Barun = x years.

and present age of Arun age

$$= \frac{40}{100} \times x = \frac{2x}{5} \text{ years}$$

After, y years,

$$\text{Barun's age} = (x + y) \text{ years}$$

$$\text{Arun's age} = \frac{2x}{5} + y$$

According to the question,

$$\frac{1}{2}(x + y) = \frac{2x}{5} + y$$

$$\Rightarrow \quad x + y = \frac{4x}{5} + 2y$$

$$\Rightarrow \quad x - \frac{4x}{5} = 2y - y$$

$$\Rightarrow \quad \frac{x}{5} = y \Rightarrow x = 5y$$

$$x + y = 5y + y = 6y$$

Required % increase Barun's age

$$= \left(\frac{6y - 5y}{5y}\right) \times 100 = 20\%.$$

26. **(D):** A can do a work in 120 days

1 day work is completed $\frac{1}{120}$ part

2nd day work is completed $\frac{1}{120} + \frac{1}{20} = \frac{2}{120}$ part

3rd day work is completed

$$\frac{1}{120} + \frac{1}{120} + \frac{1}{120} = \frac{3}{120} \text{ part}$$

....

....

....

15th day work is completed

$$= \frac{1}{120} + \frac{2}{120} + \frac{3}{120} + \ldots\ldots\ldots + \frac{15}{120}$$

$$= \frac{1 + 2 + 3 + \ldots\ldots\ldots + 15}{120}$$

$$= \frac{15 \times 16}{2} \times \frac{1}{120} = 120 \times \frac{1}{120} = 1$$

Hence, required no. of days to complete the work = 15 days

27. **(A):** An elevator has a weight limit of 630 kg.

Heaviest weight = 57 kg and

Lightest weight = 53 kg carrying a group

$$\text{Average weight of a group} = \frac{57 + 53}{2} = 55 \text{ kg}$$

Hence, maximum possible number of people in the

$$\text{group} = \frac{630}{55} = 11$$

28. **(A):** Let the distance from his home to the railway station = x km

According to the question,

$$\frac{x}{12} - \frac{10}{60} = \frac{x}{15} + \frac{10}{60}$$

$$\Rightarrow \quad \frac{x}{12} - \frac{x}{15} = \frac{10}{60} + \frac{10}{60}$$

$$\Rightarrow \quad \frac{5x - 4x}{60} = \frac{20}{60} \Rightarrow x = 20$$

Hence, required distance = 20 km.

29. **(C):** Let Ravi's total monthly saving = ₹ x

$$\text{Ravi invests in fixed deposit} = \frac{50}{100} \times x = \frac{x}{2}$$

$$\text{Remaining} = x - \frac{x}{2} = \frac{2x - x}{2} = \frac{x}{2}$$

$$\text{In Stock: } 30\% \text{ of } \frac{x}{2} = \frac{30}{100} \times \frac{x}{2} = \frac{3x}{20}$$

Ravi's saving account:

$$\frac{x}{2} - \frac{3x}{20} = \frac{10x - 3x}{20} = \frac{7x}{20}$$

According to the question,

$$\frac{x}{2} + \frac{7x}{20} = ₹\ 59{,}500$$

$\Rightarrow \quad \frac{10x + 7x}{20} = ₹\ 59,500$

$\Rightarrow \quad 17x = ₹\ 59,500 \times 20$

$\Rightarrow \quad x = ₹\ \frac{59,500 \times 20}{17}$

$= ₹\ 3500 \times 20 = ₹\ 70000$

Hence, Ravi's total monthly saving = ₹ 70,000

30. (A): Let the retail price is x and the cost price is C.

$\Rightarrow \quad x \times \frac{85}{100} = C \times \frac{102}{100}$

$\Rightarrow \quad \frac{x}{C} = \frac{6}{5}$ ...(*i*)

Let he gives a discount of P% on retail price to make profit 20%

$\Rightarrow \quad C \times \frac{120}{100} = \left\{\frac{(100 - P)}{100}\right\} \times x$ ...(*ii*)

By solving (*i*) and (*ii*)

$\Rightarrow$ P = 0%, So he will sell at retail price to get a 20% discount.

Hence, the required result will be 0% *i.e.*, sell at retail price.

31. (A): $\frac{d}{x+y} + \frac{d}{x-y} = t$ hrs.

$\Rightarrow \quad \frac{d[x - y + x + y]}{x^2 - y^2} = t$

$\Rightarrow \quad 2dx = t(x^2 - y^2)$

Again, $\frac{d}{2x+y} + \frac{d}{2x-y} = \frac{t}{4}$

$\frac{d\,(2x - y + 2x + y)}{4x^2 - y^2} = \frac{t}{4}$

$4dx \times 4 = t(4x^2 - y^2)$

$\frac{16dx}{2dx} = \frac{t\,(4x^2 - y^2)}{t\,(x^2 - y^2)}$

$8x^2 - 8y^2 = 4x^2 - y^2$

$4x^2 = 7y^2$

$\frac{x^2}{y^2} = \frac{7}{4}$

$x : y = \sqrt{7} : 2$

Hence, required ratio = $\sqrt{7} : 2$.

33. (A): Let no. of boys = x

and no. of girls = $2x$

$\frac{45x}{100} + \frac{30}{100} \times 2x = \frac{105x}{100}$

Total no. of students = $3x$

No. of Students who do not get admission

$= 3x - \frac{105x}{100} = \frac{300x - 105x}{100} = \frac{195x}{100}$

Required % $= \frac{\frac{195x}{100}}{3x} \times 100 = \frac{195\,x}{100 \times 3x} \times 100 = 65\%$.

34. (A):

	Large		Super		Jumbo		
Popcorn	$7x$	+	$17x$	+	$16x$	=	$40x$
Chips	$6x$	+	$15x$	+	$14x$	=	$35x$

$\frac{16x}{40x} = \frac{2}{5} \Rightarrow \frac{14x}{35x} = \frac{2}{5}$

Required ratio $= \frac{\frac{2}{5}}{\frac{2}{5}} = \frac{2}{5} \times \frac{5}{2} = \frac{1}{1}$

$= 1 : 1.$

35. (D): Medium and good

$CP = \frac{x}{2} \times 40 + x \times 80$

$= ₹\ 20x + 80x = ₹\ 100x$

$SP = \left(80 - \frac{10}{100} \times 80\right) \times \frac{3x}{2}$

$= 72 \times \frac{3x}{2} = ₹\ 108x$

Profit $= 108x - 100x = 8x$

Profit % $= \frac{8x}{100x} \times 100 = 8\%$.

36. (A): Let printed price of the toy = ₹ 100

Discount $= \frac{40}{100} \times 100 = ₹\ 40$

S.P. of each toy = ₹ 100 – 40 = ₹ 60

S.P. of 60 toys = 60 × 60 = ₹ 3600

$\because$ C.P. $= \frac{100}{120} \times 3600 = ₹\ 3000$

Now, M.P. = 50 × 100 = ₹ 5000

Discount = 5000 – 3600 = ₹ 1400

Discount % $= \frac{1400}{5000} \times 100 = 28\%$.

38. (B): No. of boys = 20

No. of girls = 30

Let average marks of boys = x

$\therefore$ Total marks of boys = $20x$

Average marks of girls = $x + 5$

$\therefore$ Total marks of girls = $30\,(x + 5)$

Total marks of the class $= 20x + 30x + 150$
$= 50x + 150$ ...(*i*)
$= 50 (x + 3)$

Again, Average score of girls $= (x + 2)$
Total marks of girls $= 30 (x + 2)$
$= 30x + 60$

Total marks of the class $= 50 (x + 5)$
$= 50x + 250$

Required average $= 50x + 250 - 30x + 60$
$= 20x + 190$

Average marks of boys increase $= \frac{190}{20} = 9.5.$

40. (C):

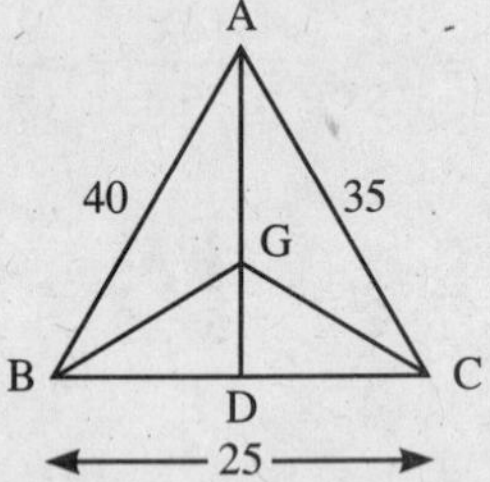

ABC be a triangle in which G is the centroid. A triangular portion GBC is cut off.

$\therefore$ Area of remaining $= \left(\frac{2}{3}\right) \times$ area of ΔABC

$\therefore \quad S = \frac{40 + 35 + 25}{2} = \frac{100}{2} = 50$ ft.

Area of $\Delta ABC = \sqrt{S (S - 40) (S - 35) (S - 25)}$
$= \sqrt{50 \times 10 \times 15 \times 25}$
$= \sqrt{5 \times 10 \times 5 \times 3 \times 5 \times 5 \times 10}$
$= 250\sqrt{3}$ ft².

$\therefore$Area of remaining $= \frac{2}{3} \times 250\sqrt{3} = \frac{500}{\sqrt{3}}$ ft².

41. (A):

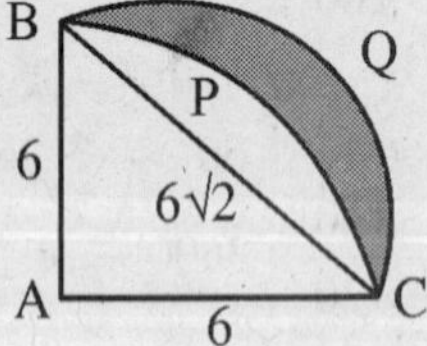

ΔABC is a right-angled isosceles triangle.
Let BCQ is a semi circle with BC diameter and BPC be an arc of a circle centred at A.

Area of semicircle BQC $= \frac{1}{2} \pi \times \left(3\sqrt{2}\right)^2 = 9\pi$

Area of BPC $= \frac{\pi}{4} \times 6^2$ area of ΔABC

$= 9\pi - \frac{1}{2} \times 6 \times 6 = 9\pi - 18$

$\therefore$ Area of shaded portion $= 9\pi - 9\pi + 18 = 18.$

42. (D): Let volumes of the cube
$= x^3 \times (1 + 1 + 8 + 27 + 27) = 64x^3$

Side of the original cube $= 3\sqrt{(64x)^3} = 4x$

Surface area of original cube $= 6 \times (4x)^2 = 96x^2$

Side of the smaller cubes are x, x, $2x$, $3x$ and $3x$ respectively.

The surface area of smaller cubes
$= 6 (x^2 + x^2 + 4x^2 + 9x^2 + 9x^2)$
$= 6 \times 24x^2 = 144x^2$

Difference of surface area
$= 144x^2 - 96x^2 = 48x^2$

Required % change $= \frac{48}{96} \times 100 = 50\%.$

43. (A): The central idea of the passage focuses on how malls once served significant social roles in middle-class America, acting as communal gathering places beyond just shopping destinations. The author elaborates on the various social interactions and community activities that took place in malls, such as first jobs, blind dates, family photos, and social gatherings. With the decline and closure of malls, these social functions are being lost, highlighting the transformation of malls from vibrant public squares to obsolete retail spaces.

44. (D): In paragraph 2, the author mentions that Amazon has opened massive distribution centers near malls it has helped close. This juxtaposition underscores the irony that while Amazon's growth in online retailing contributes to the decline of physical malls, the company simultaneously establishes a physical presence close to these very malls. The proximity of Amazon's distribution centers to shuttered malls emphasizes the contradictory nature of the situation: the same entity driving the decline of traditional retail is investing in infrastructure nearby. This ironic twist highlights the complex relationship between online and physical retail spaces.

45. (C): The phrase "real estate developers once stumbled over themselves to court" implies that real estate developers were extremely eager and proactive in their efforts. In this context, "to court" means to seek favor or attract something. Specifically, the developers were keen on attracting brand-name anchor outlets to set up in their malls. These anchor outlets are crucial for drawing in customers and ensuring the mall's success.

46. (B): The author describes the mall as an "ecosystem unto itself," emphasizing that it was a self-sustaining environment where various commercial activities and social interactions coexisted harmoniously. This description highlights that malls were not just places for shopping but also served as communal hubs where people gathered for various social purposes, such as family outings, socializing, and community events.

47. (D): The author likens malls to America's public square to illustrate their role as central hubs for social interaction and community engagement. Historically, malls provided a space where people from various backgrounds, ages, and walks of life could come together, interact, and engage in diverse activities beyond shopping.

48. (B): The author uses descriptive phrases like "Perfume clouds in the department stores" to create vivid sensory imagery that transports readers back to their experiences in malls. These sensory details—such as the scents, sounds, and sights—are intended to evoke nostalgic memories and paint a vivid picture of the mall environment.

49. (B): The first paragraph discusses the economic impact of hosting the Olympic Games on the host city. It highlights that while the Games generate substantial revenue of $4 billion to $5 billion, the majority of this revenue is allocated to the International Olympics Committee, National Olympics Committees, and International Sports Federations, rather than the host city itself. The paragraph emphasizes the challenge of converting the significant operating costs incurred during the Games into long-term economic benefits for the host city. It suggests that any economic advantages would need to stem from factors like advertising value, new infrastructure, or the continued use of facilities built for the Games.

50. (B): The passage explains that sports facilities constructed for the Olympics, such as velodromes or natatoriums, frequently remain underutilized after the Games conclude. Specifically, it mentions that the Bird's Nest in Beijing sits virtually empty, and the Olympic Stadium in Sydney incurs operational costs of approximately $30 million annually. The primary reasons for this underutilization are the large scale of these facilities and the substantial costs associated with operating and maintaining them.

51. (D): However, the passage does not mention that the influx of visitors during the Games places a significant strain on the urban infrastructure. Therefore, option (D) is the exception and is not cited by the author as a reason why the Games burden the host city.

52. (C): The passage explains the relationship between global warming and the increasing destructiveness of storms like Harvey. It states that while global warming does not create more storms, it enhances their intensity by making them wetter and more powerful. Specifically, as global temperatures rise, sea levels increase due to the melting of glaciers and the thermal expansion of seawater. Warmer seas evaporate more easily, providing additional energy to storm fronts. Additionally, warmer air holds more water vapor, leading to higher atmospheric moisture content as predicted by the Clausius-Clapeyron equation. This increased moisture results in storms that can carry more water and possess greater destructive energy. Therefore, the correct interpretation is that global warming leads to the melting of glaciers and the expansion of seawater volume, which in turn allows more water vapor to accumulate in the atmosphere, making modern storms more destructive. This explanation corresponds to option (C).

53. (A): To arrange the sentences into a coherent paragraph, follow the logical flow from general statements to specific examples and conclusions:

1. **Sentence 5:** Introduces a comparison to highlight the relationship between tradition and innovation.
   "Just as life has death as its opposite, so is tradition, so is tradition by default the opposite of innovation."
2. **Sentence 4:** States a general truth about traditions being invented rather than passed down unchanged.
   "It is now a truism to say that traditions are not handed down unchanged, but are invented."
3. **Sentence 1:** Elaborates on the process of handing down traditions, emphasizing contestation.
   "The process of handing down implies not a passive transfer, but some contestation in defining what exactly is to be handed down."
4. **Sentence 3:** Discusses how each generation selects and innovates based on their needs from the past.
   "Every generation selects what it requires from the past and makes its innovations, some more than others."
5. **Sentence 2:** Provides a specific example related to Western scholars and the Indian past.
   "Wherever Western scholars have worked on the Indian past, the selection is even more apparent and the inventing of a tradition much more recognizable."

Thus, the proper sequence is 5, 4, 1, 3, 2, corresponding to option (A).

54. (B): To form a coherent paragraph, arrange the sentences from introducing the scientific achievement, explaining the specific study, detailing the disease, and concluding with the implications:

1. **Sentence 1:** Introduces the groundbreaking achievement in gene editing.
   "Scientists have for the first time managed to edit genes in a human embryo to repair a genetic mutation, fueling hopes that such procedures may one day be available outside laboratory conditions."
2. **Sentence 5:** Provides details about the specific study and the condition addressed.
   "In results announced in Nature this week, scientists fixed a mutation that thickens the heart muscle, a condition called hypertrophic cardiomyopathy."
3. **Sentence 2:** Describes the impact of the cardiac disease.
   "The cardiac disease causes sudden death in otherwise healthy young athletes and affects about one in 500 people overall."
4. **Sentence 4:** Explains the genetic basis of the disease.
   "It is caused by a mutation in a particular gene and a child will suffer from the condition even if it inherits only one copy of the mutated gene."
5. **Sentence 3:** Highlights the broader implications of correcting the mutation.
   "Correcting the mutation in the gene would not only ensure that the child is healthy but also prevents transmission of the mutation to future generations."

Thus, the proper sequence is 1, 5, 2, 4, 3, corresponding to option B.

55. (D): To arrange the sentences into a coherent paragraph, follow the logical flow from the general findings to specific details and implications:

1. **Sentence 5:** Introduces the main finding about the early emergence of the black plague.
   "DNA from Bronze Age human skeletons indicate that the black plague could have emerged as early as 3,000 BCE, long before the epidemic that swept through Europe in the mid-1300s."
2. **Sentence 4:** Describes the methodology of the study.
   "In the analysis of fragments of DNA from 101 Bronze Age skeletons for sequences from Yersinia pestis, the bacterium that causes the disease, seven tested positive."
3. **Sentence 1:** Suggests the broader implication of the study regarding human migrations.
   "The study suggests that the disease did not spread with such intensity, but that it may have driven human migrations across Europe and Asia."
4. **Sentence 2:** Provides specific information about the oldest sample analyzed.
   "The oldest sample came from an individual who lived in southeast Russia about 5,000 years ago."
5. **Sentence 3:** Connects the ages of the skeletons to historical human movements.
   "The ages of the skeletons correspond to a time of mass exodus from today's Russia and Ukraine into western Europe and central Asia, suggesting that a pandemic could have driven these migrations."

Thus, the proper sequence is 5, 4, 1, 2, 3, corresponding to option (D).

57. (A): The task is to identify which sentence should begin the paragraph. Sentence 3 introduces the foundational belief that babies react to language from birth, setting the stage for the subsequent details about how this is studied.

1. **Sentence 3:** Introduces the foundational belief about babies' reactions to language.
   "They believed that babies begin to react to language from the very moment they are born."

This is followed logically by observations and methods used to study this phenomenon.
Therefore, the correct answer is (A): 3.

58. (A): To form a coherent paragraph, arrange the sentences to transition from the general role of movement in human biology to the specific impact of exercise on brain cells:

1. **Sentence 4:** Introduces the fundamental nature of humans as movers.
   "In today's technology-driven, plasma-screened-in world, it's easy to forget that we are born movers—animals, in fact—because we've engineered movement right out of our lives."
2. **Sentence 1:** States the current state of research into exercise's impact on brain cells.
   "Neuroscientists have just begun studying exercise's impact within brain cells – on the genes themselves."
3. **Sentence 2:** Mentions the biological connection between the body and mind.
   "Even there, in the roots of our biology, they've found signs of the body's influence on the mind."
4. **Sentence 3:** Explains the biochemical processes involved.
   "It turns out that moving our muscles produces proteins that travel through the bloodstream and into the brain, where they play pivotal roles in the mechanism of our highest thought processes."
5. **Sentence 5:** Concludes with recent advancements in understanding these factors.
   "It's only in the past few years that neuroscientists have begun to describe these factors and how they work, and each new discovery add awe-inspiring depth to the picture."

Thus, the proper sequence is 4, 1, 2, 3, 5, corresponding to option (A).

59. (D): To construct a logical paragraph, arrange the sentences to first present the data about Mars's atmosphere loss, followed by the mechanisms and implications:

1. **Sentence 4:** Presents the data from NASA's MAVEN orbiter.
   "Data from NASA's MAVEN orbiter show that solar storms stripped away most of Mars's once-thick atmosphere."
2. **Sentence 1:** States the result of atmospheric loss.
   "The water that made up ancient lakes and perhaps an ocean was lost."
3. **Sentence 2:** Explains the mechanism behind the loss of water.
   "Particles from the Sun collided with molecules in the atmosphere, knocking them into space or giving them an electric charge that caused them to be swept away by the solar wind."
4. **Sentence 5:** Discusses the current state of Mars's water.
   "A recent study reveals how Mars lost much of its early water, while another indicates that some liquid water remain."
5. **Sentence 3:** Provides additional information about the remaining water.
   "Most of the planet's remaining water is now frozen or buried, but clues over the past decade suggested that some liquid water, a necessity for life, might survive in underground aquifers."

Thus, the proper sequence is 4, 1, 2, 5, 3, corresponding to option (C).

60. (A): The sentence requires negative pronouns to indicate that nobody followed anything the teacher said. "No one" and "anything" correctly express this negative meaning without grammatical errors.

61. (A): "its" correctly refers to the brand's own products, and "those" distinguishes them from another brand's products, maintaining proper possessive forms.

62. (D): "her" serves as the objective pronoun for "address," and "hers" correctly indicates possession for "relative of hers," ensuring grammatical accuracy

63. (A): The modifier "Browsing among the gifts for sale" correctly refers to "I," ensuring that the action of browsing is clearly linked to the speaker, avoiding ambiguity.

64. (C): This sentence clearly indicates that the instructions are provided by a fourth-grader and are intended for making a centerpiece, eliminating any ambiguity about the source and purpose.

65. (C): The modifier "on the table" correctly describes the location of the list, and "of the people who danced" clearly defines the list's content, avoiding confusion.

66. (D): "The political party" is a singular subject, so the singular verb "expects" correctly agrees with it.

67. (A): "Richa's family" is treated as a singular collective noun, requiring the singular verb "wants" to maintain subject-verb agreement.

68. (B): "my son" is a singular subject, so the singular form "doesn't" is appropriate to agree with it.

69. (A): "Committed to" is the correct prepositional phrase indicating dedication or obligation.

70. (B): "Go through troubles" correctly conveys the meaning of enduring or overcoming difficulties.

71. (D): "Swam through the raging river" accurately describes swimming across it, indicating movement within and across the river.

72. (D): "Content" is an appropriate synonym for "pleased," meaning satisfied or happy with something.

73. (B): "Promising" is a suitable synonym for "optimistic," indicating a positive outlook toward the future.

74. (C): "Copious" means abundant. Its antonym is "scarce," which means limited or insufficient.

75. (D): "Boisterous" refers to noisy and energetic behavior. The antonym "restrained" means quiet or controlled.

76. (B): "Elaborate" means detailed or complicated. Its antonym is "simple," meaning easy or uncomplicated.

77. (B): Based on the given ratios and constraints, the number of satellites serving C must fall between 450 and 725.

78. (C): Calculations based on the ratios and exclusive servings determine that the minimum number of satellites serving B exclusively is 250.

79. (A): Given that at least 100 satellites serve O, the number serving S cannot exceed 475 based on the provided constraints.

80. (D): Based on the information provided, the number of satellites serving C can be uniquely determined, making option D false.

81. (A): The set S is defined by two conditions: $|x| + |y| \leq 2$ and $|x| \geq 1$.

Graphical Interpretation:

$|x| + |y| \leq 2$ represents a diamond-shaped region centered at the origin with vertices at (2, 0) (0, 2) (−2, 0) and (0, −2).

$|x| \geq 1$ restricts the region to areas where x is either greater than or equal to 1 or less than or equal to −1.

Intersection of Conditions:

The combination of these inequalities results in two separate diamond-shaped regions on either side of the y-axis:

One where $x \geq 1$

Another where $x \leq -1$

Conclusion: Thus, the set S consists of 2 distinct regions.

Therefore, the correct answer is (A): 2.

82. **(A):** Total score of student other than Gautam

$= 62 \times 21 = 1302$

$\Rightarrow$ Ramesh's score $= 82.5$

$\Rightarrow$ Average score of 21 other than Ramesh $= a$

$\Rightarrow$ Sum of 22 student score other than Ramesh

$= 21a$

$\Rightarrow$ Average of 22 students $= a + 1$

$\Rightarrow$ Sum of 22 students $= a + 1$

$\Rightarrow$ Sum of 22 students score $= 22\ (a + 1)$

$\Rightarrow$ $22\ (a + 1) - 21a = 82.5$

$\Rightarrow$ $22a + 22 - 21a = 82.5$

$\Rightarrow$ $a = 82.5 - 22$

$\Rightarrow$ $a = 60.5$

$\Rightarrow$ Sum of 22 student $= (60.5 + 1) \times 22$

$= 1353$

$\Rightarrow$ Gautam's marks $= 1353 - 1302$

$\Rightarrow$ Gautam's marks $= 51$.

83. **(B):** A and B together finish a task in 12 days

A had worked half as efficiency as she usually does, and B had worked thrice as efficiently as he usually does, the task would have been completed in 9 days.

According to the question,

$$(A + B) \times 12 = \left(\frac{A}{2} + 3B\right) \times 9$$

$$\Rightarrow 12A + 12B = \frac{9A}{2} + 27B$$

$$\Rightarrow \left(12A - \frac{9A}{2}\right) = 27B - 12B$$

$$\Rightarrow \frac{24A - 9A}{2} = 15B$$

$$\Rightarrow 15A = 30B$$

$$\Rightarrow \frac{A}{B} = \frac{2}{1}$$

A efficiency is 2 unit work in a day,

B efficiency is 1 unit work in day,

$\Rightarrow$ Total work $= (A + B) \times 12$

$\Rightarrow$ $(2 + 1) \times 12 = 36$ unit

Hence, A take to finish the task if she works alone at her usual efficiency $= \frac{36}{2} = 18$ days.

84. **(B):**

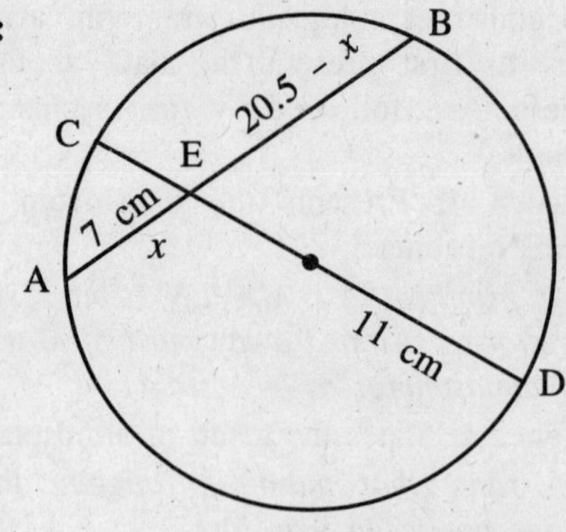

$$AE \times EB = CE \times ED$$

$$x \times (20.5 - x) = 105$$

$$20.5x - x^2 = 105$$

$$x^2 - 20.5x + 105 = 0$$

$$\Rightarrow x^2 - \frac{41}{2}x + 105 = 0$$

$$\Rightarrow 2x^2 - 41x + 210 = 0$$

$$\Rightarrow 2x^2 - 20x - 21x + 210 = 0$$

$$\Rightarrow 2x\ (x - 10) - 21\ (x - 10) = 0$$

$$\Rightarrow (x - 10)\ (2x - 21) = 0$$

$$x = 10$$

or $x = \frac{21}{2} = 10.5$

For $x = 10$

AE $= 10$ cm, BE $= 20.5 - 10 = 10.5$

Required difference $= 10.5 - 10 = 0.5$ cm.

86. **(D):**

Amala	:	Bina	:	Gouri
$3x$	:	$4x$	:	$5x$
6	:	5	:	4
$18x$	:	$20x$	:	$20x$

According to the question,

$20x - 18x = ₹\ 250$

$\Rightarrow$ $2x = 250$

$x = 125$

Total interest income

$= 18 \times 125 + 20 \times 125 + 20 \times 125$

$= 2250 + 2500 + 2500 = ₹\ 7250$.

87. **(D):** $n(A \cup B \cup C) = n(A) + n(B) + n(C) - n(A \cap B) - n(B \cap C) - n(C \cap A) + n(A \cap B \cap C)$

$\Rightarrow 256 = 144 + 123 + 132 - (58) - (25) - 63) + n(A \cap B \cap C)$

$\Rightarrow 256 = 399 - (146) + n(A \cap B \cap C)$

$\Rightarrow 256 = 253 + n(A \cap B \cap C)$

$\therefore n(A \cap B \cap C) = 256 - 253 = 3$

Hence, the number of players who can only play tennis

$= 123 - (58 - x) - (x) - (25 - x)$

$= 40 + x = 40 + 3 = 43$.

88. (A): Let T be the triangle formed by the straight line $3x + 5y - 45 = 0$ and..

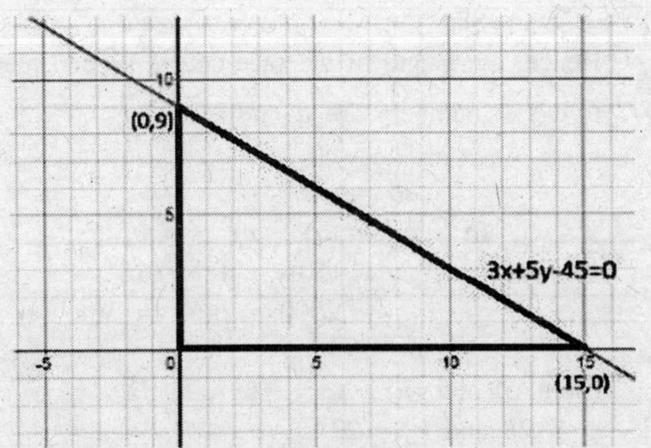

In any right triangle, the circum-radius is half of the hypotenuse.

Here, L = 1/2 × the length of the hypotenuse

$= \frac{1}{2}\left(\sqrt{15^2+9^2}\right) = \frac{1}{2}\times\sqrt{306} = \frac{1}{2}\times 17.49 = 8.74$

Hence, the integer close to L = 9.

89. (B): Let a man can finish the job in x days

Man's 1 day work $= \frac{1}{x}$

∵ 2 machines take time in 13 days

∴ 1 machine takes time in 13 × 2 = 26 days

1 machine's 1 day work = 1/26

According to the question,

$$\frac{3}{m}+\frac{8}{26} = 2\left(\frac{8}{m}+\frac{3}{26}\right)$$

$$\Rightarrow \frac{3}{m}+\frac{4}{13} = \frac{16}{m}+\frac{3}{13}$$

$$\Rightarrow \frac{16}{m}-\frac{3}{m} = \frac{4}{13}-\frac{3}{13}$$

$$\Rightarrow \frac{13}{m} = \frac{1}{13} \Rightarrow m = 169$$

A man complete the work in 169 days.

Hence, no. of men required to complete the work in 13 days $= \frac{169}{13} = 13$ men.

90. (D): Let n be the number of revolution

Circumference of a circle → 1 revolution = $2\pi r$

⇒ 1 revolution of wheel A = 2 × π × 30

= 60π cm

⇒ 1 revolution of wheel B = 2 × π × 40

= 80π cm

According to question

60π × (n + 5000) = 80π × n

⇒ $3n + 15000 = 4n$

⇒ $n = 15000$

Distance = 20000 × 60π cm

⇒ Distance = (20000 × 60π)/(100000) km

⇒ Distance = 12π

Speed = (12π)/(3/4)

⇒ Speed = 16π

∴ The speed, in km per hour, was 16π.

91. (C):

$x^2 = (10)^2 - (6)^2$

$= 100 - 36 = 64$

∴ $x = 8$

∴ AP = 8 cm

∴ AQ = 4 cm

$(QB)^2 = (10)^2 - (4)^2$

$= 100 - 16 = 84$

⇒ $QB = \sqrt{84} = 9.1$ cm.

92. (C): Liquid 1 $= \frac{1}{2}l = 500$ g

Liquid 2 $= \frac{1}{2}l = 400$ g

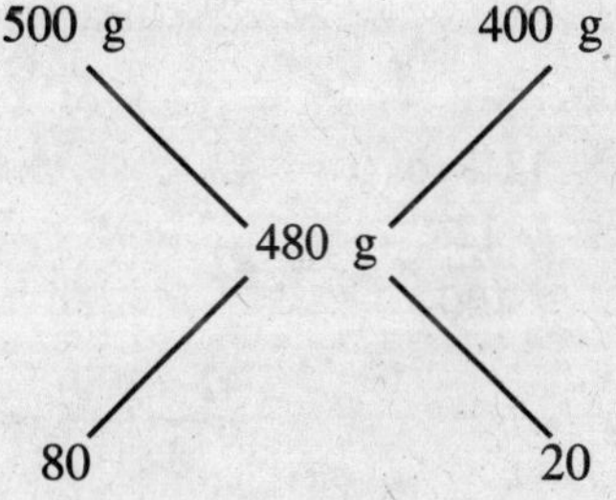

Required ratio $= \frac{80}{20} = 4 : 1$

Weight of liquid 1 $= \frac{4}{5}\times 480 = 384$ g

Weight of liquid 2 $= \frac{1}{5}\times 480 = 96$ g

% of liquid 1 in the mixture

$= \frac{384}{480}\times 100 = 80\%$.

93. (D): A|——|——|——|B

$\frac{t}{3}$ $\frac{t}{3}$ $\frac{t}{3}$

A|——|——|——|B

$\frac{D}{3}$ $\frac{D}{3}$ $\frac{D}{3}$

One can use three different transports which move at 10, 20 and 30 km/hr

Let the total distance covered LCM of 10, 20, 30 is 60 km.

Amal took each mode of transport $\frac{1}{3}$ of his total journey time.

$$\text{Distance} = \text{Speed} \times \text{time}$$

$$\Rightarrow \quad 60 = 10 \times \frac{t}{3} + 20 \times \frac{t}{3} + 30 \times \frac{t}{3}$$

$$\Rightarrow \quad 60 = 60 \times \frac{t}{3} \Rightarrow t = 3 \text{ hrs}$$

Bimal took each mode of transport $\frac{1}{3}$ of the total distance

$$\text{Time} = \frac{\text{distance}}{\text{speed}}$$

$$\Rightarrow \quad t = \frac{20}{10} + \frac{20}{20} + \frac{20}{30} = 2 + 1 + \frac{2}{3}$$

$$\Rightarrow \quad t = 3 + \frac{2}{3} \text{ hrs}$$

Bimal's travel time exceeds Amal's travel time

$$\Rightarrow 3 + \frac{2}{3} - 3 = \frac{2}{3} \text{ hrs}$$

$$\text{Required } \% = \frac{2}{3 \times 3} \times 100 = \frac{200}{9}$$

$$= 22.22\% \text{ nearest to } 22\%.$$

95. (B): 60% of $x + 35 = 72\%$ of $x - 7$

$$\Rightarrow \quad 12\% \text{ of } x = 42$$

$$\Rightarrow \quad \frac{12}{100} \times x = 42$$

$$\Rightarrow \quad x = \frac{42 \times 100}{12} = 350$$

$$\text{Pass marks} = \frac{60}{100} \times 350 + 35$$

$$= 210 + 35 = 245$$

$$\text{Pass } \% = \frac{245}{350} \times 100 = 70\%.$$

96. (D): Let the three horses be A, B and C

Let the length of the race course be S meters

According to the question,

A finished the race = S meter

B finished the race = (S – 11) meters

C finished the race = (S – 90) meters

Again, B finished the race = S meters

C finished the race = (S – 80) meters

$$\text{Now,} \quad \frac{(S-11)}{(S-90)} = \frac{S}{S-80}$$

$$\Rightarrow S(S - 90) = (S - 11)(S - 80)$$

$$\Rightarrow S^2 - 90S = S^2 - 80S - 11S + 880$$

$$\Rightarrow 91S - 90S = 880$$

$$\Rightarrow S = 880$$

Hence, the length of the race course = 880 meters.

97. (C): Let numbers are a and b

$$a + b = 50 \quad \ldots(i)$$

$$ab = 616$$

$$(a - b)^2 = (a + b)^2 - 4ab$$

$$= (50)^2 - 4 \times 616$$

$$= 2500 - 2464 = 36$$

$$\therefore \quad a - b = 6 \quad \ldots(ii)$$

From (*i*) and (*ii*)

$a = 28$ and $b = 22$

$$\text{Now,} \quad \frac{(28)^3 - (22)^3}{(28-22)^3} = \frac{21952 - 10648}{(6)^3}$$

$$= \frac{11304}{216} = \frac{157}{3}$$

$\therefore$ the sum of the two numbers

$$= a + b = 28 + 22 = 50.$$

98. (A): Foot and Mouth Disease (FMD) is a highly contagious viral disease that primarily affects livestock such as cattle, sheep, and pigs. It causes severe economic losses in the agricultural sector due to decreased productivity and trade restrictions.

99. (A): Exercise "LAMITIYE" is a bilateral naval exercise conducted between India and Seychelles. It focuses on enhancing maritime security and cooperation between the two nations.

100. (C): The PM SHRI Schools scheme is an initiative aimed at enhancing digital infrastructure and smart classrooms in schools across India. Recently, the Gujarat state government agreed to implement this scheme by signing a Memorandum of Understanding (MoU) with the Ministry of Education. This collaboration marks Gujarat's commitment to modernizing its educational facilities and integrating advanced technological tools to improve the quality of education.

101. (A): Bugun Liocichla is a species of bird. It gained attention when it was discovered in the Bugun National Park in India, highlighting its unique and endangered status.

102. (B): Noctis Volcano is located on Mars. It is part of the Tharsis volcanic region, which is home to some of the largest volcanoes in the solar system.

103. (D): In the Tokyo 2021 Olympics, India secured a total of seven medals: one gold, two silver, and four bronze. This tally reflects India's performance across various sporting events during the Games.

105. (C): The Indian Navy has established its first independent headquarters named 'Nausena Bhawan' in Delhi. This marks a significant step in enhancing the administrative infrastructure of the Navy.

106. (A): Atapaka Bird Sanctuary is located in Andhra Pradesh. It is renowned for its rich biodiversity and serves as a habitat for various bird species.

107. (C): The theme of the 'Jal Shakti Abhiyan: Catch the Rain 2024' campaign is "Nari Shakti se Jal Shakti." This theme emphasizes the empowerment of women (Nari Shakti) in water conservation and management (Jal Shakti). By highlighting the role of women in sustainable water practices, the campaign aims to foster community participation and ensure effective water resource management. Therefore, the correct answer is C: Nari Shakti se Jal Shakti.

108. (A): Mahtari Vandana Yojana was launched by the Chhattisgarh state government. This scheme aims to provide financial assistance and support to mothers for better healthcare and maternal welfare.

109. (D): The 'Gulf of Tonkin Incident' is historically related to the Vietnam War. This event escalated U.S. involvement in Vietnam during the early 1960s.

110. (A): 'Inflection 2.5' refers to a Large Language Model developed by Inflection AI. It is designed to understand and generate human-like text based on the input it receives.

111. (D): The Yaounde Declaration is focused on malaria eradication, outlining strategies and commitments to eliminate the disease. This initiative aims to combat the spread of malaria through coordinated efforts and resource allocation.

112. (A): According to the recently released Council on Energy, Environment and Water (CEEW) report, the states Haryana, Karnataka, and Punjab have been placed at the top in water management. These states have implemented effective water conservation strategies and efficient usage practices, leading to exemplary water management outcomes. Therefore, the correct answer is A.

113. (D): President Droupadi Murmu was conferred the Honorary Degree of Doctor of Civil Law by the University of Mauritius. This honor recognizes her significant contributions and leadership. Therefore, the correct answer is D.

114. (C): Researchers recently discovered a new scorpion species with 8 eyes and 8 legs in Thailand. This discovery highlights the rich biodiversity of the region and adds to the understanding of scorpion species variation.

115. (A): India's first Future LABS center was inaugurated at C-DAC Thiruvananthapuram. This center focuses on advanced research and development in emerging technologies, promoting innovation and technological progress. Therefore, the correct answer is A.

116. (A): The Blue Line serves as the maritime boundary between Lebanon and Israel. It was established to resolve territorial disputes and maintain peace between the two countries. Therefore, the correct answer is A.

117. (C): The first Oil Palm Processing Mill under the Mission Palm initiative was inaugurated in Arunachal Pradesh. This project aims to boost the production and processing of oil palm, contributing to the state's agricultural and industrial growth. Therefore, the correct answer is C.

118. (A): India's first indoor athletics and aquatic centre was inaugurated in Bhubaneswar. This facility provides state-of-the-art infrastructure for athletes and promotes the development of sports in the region. Therefore, the correct answer is A.

119. (C): According to the latest United Nations Development Programme (UNDP) Global Human Development Index report, India ranks 134. This ranking reflects India's current status in terms of human development compared to other nations. Therefore, the correct answer is C.

120. (B): The Electric Mobility Promotion Scheme 2024 was introduced by the Ministry of Heavy Industries. This scheme aims to accelerate the adoption of electric vehicles (EVs) in India by providing incentives and developing necessary infrastructure. Therefore, the correct answer is B.

121. (A): The 12th edition of the India-Italy Military Cooperation Group meeting was recently held in New Delhi. This meeting serves to strengthen defense and strategic partnerships between India and Italy, fostering collaboration on various military and security initiatives.

122. (A): The naval forces of China, Iran, and Russia recently launched a joint exercise near the Gulf of Oman. This exercise aims to enhance maritime security cooperation and demonstrate collective naval capabilities in the strategically significant region.

123. (D): Prasar Bharti - Shared Audio Visuals for Broadcast and Dissemination (PB-SHABD) was recently launched by the Ministry of Information & Broadcasting. This initiative aims to streamline and enhance the distribution of audio-visual content across various broadcasting platforms.

124. (A): Alzheimer's disease is a progressive brain condition that deteriorates memory and cognitive functions. It significantly impacts an individual's ability to perform daily activities and affects overall brain health. Therefore, the correct answer is A.

125. (D): The theme state of the World's Largest International Crafts Fair, Surajkund Mela 2024, was Gujarat. This state showcased its rich cultural heritage and craftsmanship, highlighting traditional arts and crafts on an international platform. Therefore, the correct answer is D.

126. (D): eROSITA is an X-ray telescope. It is designed to perform an all-sky survey in X-rays, aiming to detect and catalog millions of X-ray sources, including galaxy clusters and active galactic nuclei. Therefore, the correct answer is D.

127. (B): Bluetongue disease is transmitted by insects, specifically by biting midges of the genus *Culicoides*. These insects act as vectors, spreading the disease among livestock.

128. (A): The theme of 'World Wetland Day' 2024 is "Wetland and Human Wellbeing." This theme emphasizes the crucial role wetlands play in sustaining human health, providing ecosystem services, and supporting biodiversity. Therefore, the correct answer is A.

129. (D): The Telangana state government recently launched 'Operation Smile X', a mission aimed at rescuing and rehabilitating child labourers. This initiative focuses on providing education, healthcare, and safe environments for rescued children. Therefore, the correct answer is D.

132. (B): In right angle triangle ABC

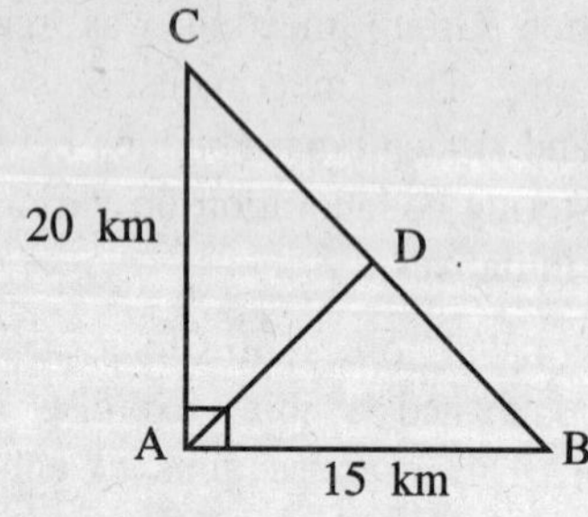

AB = 15 km, AC = 20 km

BC = hypotenuse

Let AD ⊥ BC

$\because$ Area of $\Delta ABC = \frac{1}{2} \times AB \times AC$

$\therefore$ Area of $\Delta ABC = \frac{1}{2} \times 20 \times 15 = 150 \text{ km}^2$

and Area of $\Delta ABC = \frac{1}{2} \times BC \times AD$

$\Rightarrow \quad 150 = \frac{1}{2} \times BC \times AD$

$\Rightarrow \quad BC \times AD = 300 \quad \ldots(i)$

In $\Delta ABC \Rightarrow \quad BC^2 = AB^2 + AC^2$

$\Rightarrow \quad BC^2 = 15^2 + 20^2 = 225 + 400$

$BC^2 = 625$

$\Rightarrow \quad BC = 25$

Putting the value of BC in (*i*), we get,

$AD = \frac{300}{25} = 12$

$\Rightarrow \quad AD = 12 \text{ km}$

Now, the minimum possible time, in minute, required to reach the hypotenuse from

$$A = \frac{\text{Distance}}{\text{Speed}} = \frac{12}{\frac{30}{60}} = \frac{12 \times 60}{30}$$

$= 24$ minutes.

133. (D): Given, $\log 3^x = \log 12^y = a$

$\Rightarrow \quad 3^a = x$ and $12^a = y$

$\because$ G is the geometric mean of x and y,

$\therefore \quad G^2 = xy = 3^a \cdot 12^a$

$= (3 \times 12)^a = 36^a$

$\Rightarrow \quad G^2 = 36^a = (6^2)^a$

$\Rightarrow \quad G^2 = (6^2)^a$

$\therefore \quad G = 6^a$

Now, $\log 6^G = \log 6^{6^a} = a \log 6^a = a - 1 = a$

$\Rightarrow \quad \log 6^G = a.$

134. (A): Given, $x + 1 = x^2 \Rightarrow x^2 - x - 1 = 0$

$$\therefore x = \frac{-(-1) \pm \sqrt{(-1)^2 - 4 \times 1 \times -1}}{2 \times 1} = \frac{1 \pm \sqrt{5}}{2}$$

$$\Rightarrow x^2 = \left(\frac{1+\sqrt{5}}{2}\right)^2 = \frac{1+5+2\sqrt{5}}{4}$$

$$= \frac{6+2\sqrt{5}}{4} = \frac{3+\sqrt{5}}{2}$$

$$\therefore x^4 = \left(\frac{3+\sqrt{5}}{2}\right)^2 = \frac{9+5+6\sqrt{5}}{4}$$

$$= \frac{14+6\sqrt{5}}{4} = \frac{7+3\sqrt{5}}{2}$$

Thus, $2x^4 = 2\left(\frac{7+3\sqrt{5}}{2}\right) = 7 + 3\sqrt{5}$.

137. (D): To find the number of positive integer solutions to $x - y - z = 25$ with $x \leq 40$, $y \leq 12$ and $z \leq 12$:

Rearrange the Equation:

$$x = y + z + 25$$

Apply Constraints:

$$y + z \leq 15 \text{ (since } x \leq 40)$$

Count Solutions: y and z are positive integers.

The number of solutions to $y + z \leq 15$ with $y, z \leq 12$ is 99.

Therefore, the correct answer is D: 99.

138. (C): Solve the inequality:

$(n - 5)(n - 10) - 3(n - 2) \leq 0$

Expand and Simplify:

$n^2 - 15n + 50 - 3n + 6 \leq 0$

$n^2 - 18n + 56 \leq 0$

Find Roots: $n = \dfrac{18 \pm \sqrt{324 - 224}}{2} = \dfrac{18 \pm 10}{2}$

$n = 14$

and $n = 4$

Determine Range: $4 \leq n \leq 14$

Count Integer Solutions: There are 11 integer values of n that satisfy the inequality.

Therefore, the correct answer is C: 11.

139. (A): Given: $f_1(x) = x^2 + 11x + n$

$f_2(x) = x$

Set $f_1(x) = f_2(x)$:

$x^2 + 11x + n = x$

$x^2 + 10x + n = 0$

For two distinct real roots, the discriminant must be positive:

$$D = 10^2 - 4 \cdot 1 \cdot n > 0$$

$$100 - 4n > 0$$

$$n < 25$$

The largest integer n satisfying this is 24.

Therefore, the correct answer is A: 24.

140. (B): To determine the number of ways to choose three points that form a triangle from 11 points (A, B, C, D, E, F, G, H, J, K, O):

Total Combinations:

$$\binom{11}{3} = 165$$

Subtract Collinear Triplets:

Each diameter has 3 collinear points (two endpoints and center O).

There are 5 diameters, so 5 collinear triplets.

Valid Triangles:

$$165 - 5 = 160$$

Therefore, the correct answer is B: 160.

141. (A): Let a be the first term and d be the common difference of an A.P.

Then, $t_n = n^{th} \text{ term} = a + (n - 1)d$

$\therefore$ $t_7 = a + 6d$, $t_3 = a + 2d$

and $t_{17} = a + 16d$

According to question

$(7^{th} \text{ term})^2 = (3^{rd} \text{ term})(17^{th} \text{ term})$

$\Rightarrow (a + 6d)^2 = (a + 2d)(a + 16d)$

$\Rightarrow a^2 + 36d^2 + 12ad$

$= a^2 + 16ad + 2ad + 32d^2$

$\Rightarrow 36d^2 - 32d^2 = 18ad - 12ad$

$\Rightarrow 4d^2 = 6ad$

$\Rightarrow 2d = 3a$

$\Rightarrow \dfrac{2}{3} = \dfrac{a}{d} \Rightarrow a : d = 2 : 3.$

142. (D): Distribute 7 identical erasers among 4 kids with each getting at least one and at most three erasers:

Initial Distribution: Give each kid 1 eraser. Remaining: 7 – 4 = 3 erasers.

Distribute 3 Erasers with Constraints: No kid can receive more than 2 additional erasers.

Count Solutions: Using stars and bars with restrictions, the number of valid distributions is 16.

Therefore, the correct answer is D: 16.

143. (A): In the coded addition:

	B	H	A	A	G	F
+	A	H	I	F	K	F
	A	A	I	G	C	A	F

From the Units Place: F + F = F implies F = 0.

From the Millions Place:

B + A = A with a carryover, so B = 10 – A.

From the first step: A = 1.

Substituting A: B = 10 – 1 = 9.

Therefore, the letter A represents the digit 1.

Therefore, the correct answer is A: 1.

144. (B): From the coded addition:

	B	H	A	A	G	F
+	A	H	I	F	K	F
	A	A	I	G	C	A	F

From the Millions Place:

B + A = A with a carryover of 1.

Thus, B = 10 – A.

From Question 143: A = 1.

Substituting A: B = 10 – 1 = 9.

Therefore, the letter B represents the digit 9.

145. (C): Based on the constraints and previous assignments: D cannot represent 7 to maintain unique digit assignments and avoid conflicts in the addition.

Therefore, the correct answer is C.

146. (D): From the coded addition:

	B	H	A	A	G	F
+	A	H	I	F	K	F
A	A	I	G	C	A	F

From Previous Assignments:

A = 1, B = 9, F = 0

Determining G: G cannot be 6 to avoid duplication and maintain distinct digits.

Therefore, the digit 6 cannot be represented by the letter G. Therefore, the correct answer is D: 6.

147. (D): Based on the given information:

The first performance was by Princess, assigned by Badal.

Ashman's compositions were performed consecutively.

Therefore, the second performance was composed by Dyu.

148. (C): Analyzing the statements:

Statement C claims that Queen did not perform in any item composed by Gagan.

This statement is false because, according to the given facts, Queen did perform an item composed by Gagan.

149. (D): Considering the sequence and constraints:

Ashman's compositions were performed consecutively.

Given the assignments and the sequence, the sixth performance was composed by Badal.

150. (A): Evaluating the performance pairs:

Both the first and sixth performances were composed by Badal. This makes them the pair of performances composed by the same composer.

151. (A): To determine the highest total score among the players:

Given Scores:

Tanzi: Round-2: 4, Round-4: 5

Umeza: Round-4: 1, Round-5: 2

Yonita: Round-3: 4, Round-4: 5

Zeneca: Round-4: 5, Round-5: 5

Additional Facts:

Fact 1: Tanzi, Umeza, and Yonita have the same total score.

Fact 3: The highest total score is one more than double the lowest total score.

Calculations: Let the common total score for Tanzi, Umeza, and Yonita be T.

Tanzi's Total: 4 (Round-2) + 5 (Round-4) + other rounds = T

Umeza's Total: 1 (Round-4) + 2 (Round-5) + other rounds = T

Yonita's Total: 4 (Round-3) + 5 (Round-4) + other rounds = T

After assigning appropriate scores to the missing rounds based on the constraints, the highest total score among all players is calculated to be 25.

Therefore, the correct answer is A: 25.

152. (A): To determine Zeneca's total score:

Given Scores:

Zeneca: Round-4: 5, Round-5: 5

Additional Facts:

Fact 1: Tanzi, Umeza, and Yonita have the same total score.

Fact 5: Tanzi and Zeneca had the same score in Round-1 but different scores in Round-3.

Calculations: Based on the constraints and the known scores, Zeneca's total score is calculated by summing her scores across all participated rounds: 5 (Round-4) + 5 (Round-5) + scores from other rounds, resulting in a total of 24.

Therefore, the correct answer is A: 24.

153. (D): To identify the highest scorer among the players:

Given Scores: Xyla: Round-4: 1, Round-5: 5

Additional Facts:

Fact 1: Tanzi, Umeza, and Yonita have the same total score.

Fact 3: The highest total score is one more than double the lowest total score.

Calculations: After calculating the total scores for all players based on their scores in each round and considering the given constraints, it is determined that Xyla achieved the highest total score in the tournament.

Therefore, the correct answer is D: Xyla was the highest scorer.

154. (A): To determine Tanzi's score in Round-3:

Given Scores: Tanzi: Round-2: 4, Round-4: 5

Additional Facts:

Fact 1: Tanzi, Umeza, and Yonita have the same total score.

Fact 5: Tanzi and Zeneca had the same score in Round-1 but different scores in Round-3.

Calculations: Based on the total scores and the constraints, Tanzi's score in Round-3 is calculated to balance her total score with Umeza and Yonita, resulting in a score of 1 in Round-3.

Therefore, the correct answer is A: 1.

155. (D): Key Observations:

No one is standing at intersection d (Fact 6).

X can see only U and Z (Fact 2). This suggests X is at a location where only two lines of sight are possible, likely b.

Y can see only U and W (Fact 3). Y must be positioned such that no direct line of sight exists with others except U and W.

U sees V, who is standing at the next intersection behind Z (Fact 4).

Analysis of Intersection a:

Intersection a has visibility toward b, c, and e.

Since W cannot see V or Z (Fact 5), W cannot stand at a because a would allow visibility toward intersections where V or Z might be located.

Thus, intersection a is empty.

156. (A): Key Observations:

V is located "behind Z" from U's perspective (Fact 4).

W cannot see V or Z (Fact 5), so V must be positioned such that there is no direct line of sight to W's intersection.

X can see only U and Z (Fact 2). Hence, V cannot be in a position visible to X.

Analysis of Visibility:

V can see U, as stated in Fact 4.

Since V is positioned behind Z, V can also see Z.

157. (C): Key Observations:

X can see only U and Z (Fact 2), indicating that X is at a corner of the triangle formed by three street segments.

Y can see only U and W (Fact 3), which places Y in a position adjacent to U and W's intersection.

Shortest Path:

If X is at b and Y is at e, the shortest path from X to Y is through U's intersection.

The minimum number of street segments X must cross to reach Y is 2 (b → f → e).

158. (A): To determine who a new person standing at intersection d would see:

Key Observations:

Intersection d provides visibility to c, g, and h.

Based on the placements:

U is likely at c (visible from d).

Z is positioned at g (visible from d).

W is at an intersection where it cannot see V or Z (Fact 5). Thus, W is likely at h, but d cannot see h due to the absence of a direct connection.

Conclusion: A person at intersection d would only see U (at c) and Z (at g).

Therefore, the correct answer is A: U and Z only.

159. (A): The minimum possible number of different types of prizes occurs when the distribution of items satisfies the doubling rule. Starting with 1 item of type a, the next type (b) must have at least double the items of type a, and so on. This gives:

Type a: 1 item

Type b: At least 2 items

Total: 1 + 2 = 3, which leaves 97 items to fill.

To minimize the number of types, the remaining 97 items can all belong to a single type (type c) since there is no restriction beyond doubling for the previous type. Thus, the minimum number of types is 2.

Other options are incorrect as they assume either fewer types or less strict doubling rules.

161. (A): The doubling rule requires each type to have at least double the items of the previous type:

Type a: 1 item

Type b: At least 2 items

Type c: At least 4 items

For type c to have exactly 45 items, the previous types would have to total 55 items or fewer (100 − 45 = 55). This is not possible since earlier types must follow the doubling rule. Thus, having exactly 45 items of type c violates the doubling rule.

Other options represent valid distributions based on the doubling constraint.

162. (D): Box 45 belongs to a type with:

31 items in boxes 1–44

1 item in box 45

43 items in boxes 46–100

The total number of items of this type is 31 + 1 + 43 = 75. For this to fit the doubling rule, it suggests the progression:

Type a: 1 item

Type b: 2 items

Type c: 4 items

Type d: 8 items

Type e: 16 items

Type f: 32 items

Type g: 75 items

Thus, there are 5 distinct types. Options with fewer types fail to explain the doubling progression, and higher types would require more items than available.

163. (D): To calculate the number of ways to arrange the items, consider the rules:

Cluster Rules: All items of the same type must be grouped together, with no empty shelf between items of the same type.

Empty Shelf Rules: There must be at least one empty shelf between items of different types, and at most two empty shelves can have consecutive numbers.

Placement Rules:

A and B must be placed consecutively in increasing order.

I and J must be placed consecutively in higher-numbered shelves than A and B.

D, E, and F (savouries) must be placed after all biscuits and candies.

K is fixed at shelf 16.

L must be preceded by one empty shelf, and C must be preceded by two empty shelves.

Considering the above constraints, the placement of empty shelves and clustering allows for 8 possible arrangements, accounting for different valid configurations of biscuits, candies, and savouries.

165. (D): To identify a valid set of empty shelf numbers, consider the placement rules:

Empty Shelves for C and L:

C must be preceded by two empty shelves.

L must be preceded by exactly one empty shelf.

Other Rules:

At least one empty shelf must exist between different types of items.

No more than two consecutive empty shelves are allowed.

Validation of Option D:

Shelves 1 and 2 provide the two consecutive empty shelves required for placing C.

Shelf 6 ensures a gap between the biscuits and candies.

Shelf 12 provides a gap between the candies and savouries.

This configuration satisfies all rules and constraints, making it valid.

166. (A): Based on the clustering rules:

Biscuits, candies, and savouries are placed consecutively within their groups.

The minimum spacing required between different types ensures at least four shelves are maintained between clusters.

Other options misinterpret the placement rules (e.g., some place candies before biscuits, which is invalid).

167. (D): Let the income of Bimla be 100 units.

Amala's Income:

Amala's income is 20% more than Bimla's:

$$100 \times 1.2 = 120 \text{ units.}$$

Amala's income is 20% less than Kamala's income, so Kamala's income is $120 \div 0.8 = 150$ units.

After Adjustments:

Kamala's income decreases by 4%:

$$150 \times 0.96 = 144 \text{ units.}$$

Bimla's income increases by 10%:

$$100 \times 1.1 = 110 \text{ units.}$$

Percentage by Which Kamala's Income Exceeds Bimla's:

Difference in incomes:

$$144 - 110 = 34.$$

Percentage:

$$(34/110) \times 100 = 30.91\%$$

Thus, the percentage by which Kamala's income exceeds Bimla's is 31%.

168. (D): Number of Girls and Boys:

Let the total number of students be x.

Girls: $0.6x$, Boys: $0.4x$, and $0.6x - 0.4x = 30$

Solving: $x = 150$, so there are 90 girls and 60 boys.

Students Who Passed:

68% of the total students pass: $0.68 \times 150 = 102$.

30 boys passed, so $102 - 30 = 72$ girls passed.

Girls Who Did Not Pass:

Total girls: 90, Passed: 72, Not passed:

$$90 - 72 = 18.$$

Percentage:

$$(18/90) \times 100 = 20\%$$

Thus, the percentage of girls who do not pass is 20%.

169. (A): Let the cost price of the pen be p and the book be b.

First Condition (5% Loss on Pen, 15% Gain on Book):

Profit: $-0.05p + 0.15b = 7$

Second Condition (5% Gain on Pen, 10% Gain on Book):

Profit: $0.05p + 0.10b = 13$

Solving Equations:

Adding the two equations:

$$(-0.05p + 0.15b) + (0.05p + 0.10b) = 7 + 13$$

$$0.25b = 20 \Rightarrow b = 80$$

Thus, the cost price of the book is 80 units.

170. (A): Properties of Hexagon Formed:

An equilateral triangle is divided into 6 smaller equilateral triangles when corners are cut.

The central hexagon retains 4 of the 6 smaller triangles.

Area Calculation:

Area of hexagon H = 4 × (Area of one smaller triangle).

Area of original triangle

T = 6 × (Area of one smaller triangle).

Ratio of areas:

$$H : T = 4 : 6 = 2 : 3.$$

Thus, the ratio of the area of the hexagon to the triangle is 2 : 3.

Previous Paper (Solved)

Jamia Millia Islamia (JMI)

MBA Entrance Examination-2023*

Directions (Qs. No. 1-5): *In the questions given below, there is a sentence in which one part is given in bold. The part given in bold may or may not be grammatically correct. Choose the best alternative among the four given which can replace the part in bold to make the sentence grammatically correct. If the part given in bold is already correct and does not require any replacement, choose option (D), i.e. "No replacement required" as your answer.*

1. Nobody can deny the fact that Indian economy **is very different than** American economy.
A. is so much different than
B. are very different from
C. is very different from
D. No replacement required

2. Accurate **statistics with regards** to the area occupied in different form of cultivation are difficult to obtain.
A. statistic with regards to
B. statistics with regard to
C. statistic with regard to
D. No replacement required

3. **Seldom if ever** was there any training or instructions in such tactics for either the tank crews or the infantry formations.
A. Seldom or never
B. Seldom if never
C. Seldom or ever
D. No replacement required

4. As soon as I opened the front door of my house, **than I smelled** the distinctive aroma of fresh coffee.
A. then I smelled
B. that I smelled
C. I smelled
D. No replacement required

5. The party explicitly **denies that they are not** involved in mainstream politics.
A. denied that they are not
B. denies that they were
C. denied that they are
D. No replacement required

Directions (Qs. No. 6-9): *Select the phrase/connector (it must be at the start) from the given three options which can be used to form a single sentence from the two sentences given below, implying the same meaning as expressed in the statement sentences.*

6. We see ourselves repeating our ordinary routine. We realize how much wealth surrounds our life.
(*i*) When we see ourselves ....
(*ii*) Our ordinary routine.........
(*iii*) Realizing how much wealth..............
A. Only (*i*) B. Both (*ii*) and (*iii*)
C. Only (*iii*) D. Only (*ii*)

7. There is a growing influence of the Indian Diaspora on Capitol Hill. Trump will certainly see the advantages of doing business with India.
(*i*) As there is a growing influence of...
(*ii*) The growing influence of the Indian...
(*iii*) With the growing influence of the Indian...
A. Only (*i*) is correct
B. Both (*i*) and (*ii*) are correct
C. Both (*i*) and (*iii*) are correct
D. All are correct

8. There was no democracy in British India. The rulers could take bold decisions fearlessly without bothering about repercussions.
(*i*) As there was no democracy in British India...
(*ii*) Since there was no democracy in British...
(*iii*) With the rulers taking bold decisions...
A. Only (*i*) is correct
B. Only (*ii*) is correct
C. Both (*i*) and (*ii*) are correct
D. All are correct

9. Twelve million youth enter the Indian work force every year. Eighty percent of these youth are unskilled.
(*a*) While eighty per cent .....
(*b*) Since twelve million ....
(*c*) Of the twelve million ....
A. Only (*a*) B. Only (*c*)
C. Only (*a*) and (*c*) D. None of these

1. C	**2.** B	**3.** D	**4.** C	**5.** C	**6.** A	**7.** C	**8.** C	**9.** B

* **Exam held on 20-05-2023.**

Directions (Qs. No. 10-14): *Given below are sentences each of which has been divided into five parts out of which the first part has been marked bold. Each of the questions is then followed by the four options which give the sequence of the rearranged parts. You must choose the option which gives the correct sequence of the parts. If the sentence is already arranged or the correct sequence doesn't match any of the given sequence, mark D, .i.e. "None of the above" as your answer.*

10. **The apex court had ordered that the**/of the biometric scheme and the enabling law (*a*)/deadline be extended till the five-judge constitution (*b*)/on petitions challenging the validity (*c*)/ bench delivers its judgment (*d*).
    A. (*a*)(*c*)(*d*)(*b*) B. (*b*)(*c*)(*a*)(*d*)
    C. (*b*)(*d*)(*c*)(*a*) D. None of the above

11. **Repealing the law that safeguards**/the floodgates of poaching (*a*)/and it would lead to (*b*)/marginalisation of the indigenous people (*c*)/the indigenous people would open (*d*).
    A. (*d*)(*c*)(*b*)(*a*) B. (*d*)(*a*)(*b*)(*c*)
    C. (*a*)(*c*)(*b*)(*d*) D. None of the above

12. **My thoughts are with the families**/in this unfortunate accident (*a*)/recovery of the injured (*b*)/of those who have lost their loved ones (*c*)./I pray for the speedy (*d*).
    A. (*b*)(*c*)(*a*)(*d*) B. (*d*)(*a*)(*c*)(*b*)
    C. (*a*)(*c*)(*b*)(*d*) D. (*c*)(*a*)(*d*)(*b*)

13. **Several people became leaders**/remained where they were (*a*)/and Ministers after that (*b*)/really but the people (*c*)/belonging to the community (*d*)
    A. (*a*)(*b*)(*c*)(*d*) B. (*b*)(*c*)(*d*)(*a*)
    C. (*c*)(*a*)(*b*)(*d*) D. None of the above

14. **He also directed the department**/to develop the new schools as model (*a*)/completion of construction work (*b*)/construction technology for early (*c*)/institutions and engage modern (*d*).
    A. (*a*)(*d*)(*c*)(*b*) B. (*a*)(*b*)(*c*)(*d*)
    C. (*c*)(*a*)(*d*)(*b*) D. None of the above

Directions (Qs. No. 15-20): *Read the following passage carefully and answer the questions given below. Certain words are given in bold to help you locate them while answering some of the questions.*

Have you heard that the economy is like a car? It's the most popular **analogy** in financial reporting and political discourse. The American people are repeatedly told by financial pundits and politicians that consumption is an 'engine' that 'drives' economic growth because it makes up 70% of GDP. One notable Nobel-winning economics pundit with a penchant for bizarre growth theories even recently noted that an economy can be 'based on purchases of yachts, luxury cars, and the services of personal trainers and celebrity chefs.' Conversely, other economists including Nobel-winner Joseph Stiglitz claim that our economy is stuck in 'first gear' due to inequality: too much income is concentrated among too few rich people who tend to save larger share of their income and thus have a lower 'marginal propensity to consume'.

The Keynesian message is clear: if you want to put the economic pedal to the metal, get out there and consume! Not so fast, Speed Racer. The systematic failure by Keynesian economists and pundits to distinguish between consuming and producing value is the single most damaging fallacy in popular economic thinking. If the economy were a car, consumer preferences would surely be the steering wheel, but real savings and investment would be the engine that drives it forward. Economic growth (booms) and declines (bust) have always been led by changes in business and durable goods investment, while final consumer goods spending has been relatively stable through the business cycle. Booms and busts in financial markets, heavy industry and housing have always been leading indicators of recession and recovery

As John Stuart Mill put it two centuries ago, 'the demand for commodities is not the demand for labor.' Consumer demand does not necessarily translate into increased employment. That's because 'consumers' don't employ people. Businesses do. Since new hires are a risky and costly investment with **unknown** future returns, employers must rely on their expectations about the future and weigh those decision very carefully. As economic historian Robert Higgs' pioneering work on the Great Depression suggests, increased uncertainty can depress job growth even in the face of booming consumption. As recent years have demonstrated, consumer demand that appears to be driven by temporary or unsustainable policies is unlikely to induce businesses to hire.

15. Choose the word which is **MOST SIMILAR** to the word given in passage **UNKNOWN.**
    A. Recognize B. Perceived
    C. Unpredictable D. Uncanny

16. Which of the following is the most suitable title for the passage above?
    A. Recession and Recovery
    B. Consumer: The driving force for Economy
    C. Economy: a Distant Dream?
    D. Is Consumption Necessary for Economic Growth?

10. C	11. B	12. D	13. B	14. A	15. D	16. D

17. In the statement **"consumer preferences would surely be the steering wheel, but real savings and investment would be the engine that drives it forward"**, what can we infer from the line "consumer preferences would surely be the steering wheel"?

A. Consumer likings regulate the economy individually.

B. If you want to regulate the economy, consumption is the only force.

C. The Penchant of the consumers controls the economy.

D. The consumer preferences are not at par with savings and economy in driving the economy.

18. Which of the following statements is/are correct in context with the passage?

A. Economists fail to distinguish between consuming and producing value and form a mistaken belief.

B. Economic growth and declines have always been led by changes in business and durable goods investment.

C. Only (A)

D. Both (A) and (B)

19. Which of the following is/are likely to induce businesses to hire?

A. Consumer Demand

B. Consumer Spending

C. Increased certainty in future returns

D. Both (B) and (C)

20. Choose the word which is **MOST OPPOSITE** to the word **ANALOGY** given in passage.

A. Similarity B. Narrative

C. Contrast D. Variance

Directions (Qs. No. 21-24): *In each of the questions given below a sentence is given in which a word is highlighted. Each sentence is then followed by three words. Choose the word(s) that can replace the given word in bold to make a grammatically and contextually meaningful sentence as your answer. If none of the words can replace the highlighted word then choose "None can replace" as the correct choice.*

21. There is a vending machine on the platform that **dispenses** snacks.

(*i*) Disburses (*ii*) Squander

(*iii*) Distributes

A. Only (*i*) B. Both (*i*) & (*iii*)

C. None can replace D. Only (*ii*)

22. India and Japan have devised a **mechanism** for cooperation in the steel industry at the joint secretary level.

(*i*) System (*ii*) Method

(*iii*) tools

A. Only (*i*) B. Both (*i*) & (*iii*)

C. Both (*i*) & (*ii*) D. None can replace

23. Your business premises which **qualify** for business asset taper relief have become too cramped.

(*i*) Hamper (*ii*) Measured

(*iii*) Inclined

A. None can replace B. Both (*i*) & (*iii*)

C. Both (*i*) & (*ii*) D. Only (*ii*)

24. The misuse of the Governor's office to undermine duly elected State governments is a particularly mischievous **disruption** of federalism.

(*i*) Disturbance (*ii*) Obstruction

(*iii*) Relevant

A. None can replace B. Both (*i*) & (*iii*)

C. Both (*i*) & (*ii*) D. Only (*ii*)

Directions (Qs. No. 25-27): *In each of the following sentences, parts of the sentence are left blank. Beneath each sentence, five different ways of completing the sentence are indicated. Choose the best alternative among the given options.*

25. Police ______ Notorious Gangster after relentless chase that ______ for 3 weeks.

A. Arrest, reigned B. Nabbed, lasted

C. Snatched, persist D. Contempt, endured

26. Tropical rain forests choked in fog and continuously ______ by mists and down pours are least ______ by fires.

A. Rejuvenate, impact B. Exhausted, Overwhelm

C. Drenched, affected D. Approach, Influence

27. An interview is a good chance to ______ how candidates ______ difficult situations

A. Discuss, improved B. Assess, addressed

C. Analyze, tackling D. Evaluate, approach

Directions (Qs. No. 28-30): *Improve the bold part in the following sentences, if needed.*

28. He made himself master of practically every branch of medieval learning, and **has a thoroughly knowledge of** the sources and the bibliography of his subject

A. having a thorough knowledge of

B. has had a thorough knowledge to

C. had a thorough knowledge of

D. No Correction required

17. C	**18.** D	**19.** C	**20.** D	**21.** B	**22.** C	**23.** A	**24.** C	**25.** B	**26.** C
27. D	**28.** C								

29. Gionee **has been found guilty for** intentionally inflicting malware in over 20 million phones by a Chinese court.
   A. had been found guilty for
   B. has been found guilty of
   C. has been found being guilty with
   D. No Correction required

30. Many people believe that voluntary bodies as they are today should **not entrusted with** this national responsibility.
   A. be entrust not with
   B. not being entrusted for
   C. not be entrusted with
   D. No Correction required

Directions (Qs. No. 31-34): *Read the following passage carefully and answer the questions given below. Certain words are given in bold to help you locate them while answering some of the questions.*

Renewable energy is the future, and future is finally here! Global investment in renewable energy shot up last year, far outstripping investment in fossil fuels, according to a UN report. As the price of clean energy technology plummets, it has become an increasingly attractive prospect for world governments. China was by far the world's largest investor in renewable energy in 2017, accounting for nearly half of the new infrastructure commissioned. This was mainly a result of its massive support for solar power, which globally attracted nearly a fifth more investment than in the previous year. Other countries including Australia, Sweden and Mexico more than doubled the amount of money they pumped into clean energy projects. "Yet again, this was a record year for new renewable power capacity being financed," Francoise d'Estais from UN Environment's energy and climate branch told The Independent. "We had a record 157 gigawatts commissioned last year, far outstripping the fossil fuel generating capacity, which we estimated as 70 gigawatts".

In just over a decade, concerted investment has increased the proportion of world electricity generated by wind, solar and other renewable sources from around 5 per cent to 12 per cent. *"The electricity sector remains the brightest spot for renewables with the exponential growth of solar photovoltaics and wind in recent years, and building on the significant contribution of hydropower generation."* But, electricity accounts for only a fifth of global energy consumption. The global replacement of traditional fuels with renewables led to around 1.8 gigatonnes of carbon dioxide emissions being avoided last year – the equivalent of removing the entire US transport system. According to the Wind and Solar Atlas, there are opportunities and potential for Wind and Solar plants in the East and West Nile areas that will produce around 31,150 MW from wind and 52,300 MW from solar. Egypt is also considering financing options to conduct feasibility studies for building the world largest solar power plant for both electricity generation and water desalination.

The UK has been performing well in clean energy generation, with recent figures showing wind and solar sources had overtaken nuclear as suppliers of electricity. However, despite these positive trends, 2017 saw a big drop of 65 per cent in British renewables investment.

Experts have criticised the withdrawal of UK support for onshore wind, as previous analysis has demonstrated it already has the capacity to outcompete fossil fuels as a power source. As renewable energy prices continue to fall, however, Professor Moslener said government subsidies are likely to become less and less important.

31. Which of the following facts are correct as per the given passage?
   I. The decrease in the cost of renewable energy resulted in its wide use.
   II. China massively supported solar power and became largest investor in renewable energy.
   III. Egypt is conducting feasibility studies for building largest solar power plant.
   A. Only I B. Only II
   C. Both II and III D. All I, II and III

32. What did the author mean by the line *"The electricity sector remains the brightest spot for renewables with the exponential growth of solar photovoltaics and wind in recent years, and building on the significant contribution of hydropower generation."*?
   I. The growth of renewable energy in electricity sector is not that impressive.
   II. Electric sector has performed the best for renewables.
   III. Hydropower generation has a significant contribution in the electricity sector.
   A. Only I B. Only II
   C. None D. Both II and III

33. Which of the following is/are the positive effect(s) of renewable energy?
   I. Overall increase in the global temperature.
   II. Carbon dioxide emissions were reduced to a considerable amount.
   III. Nile being converted into a biodiversity hotspot.
   A. Only I B. Only II
   C. Both II and III D. All I, II and III

29. B 30. C 31. D 32. D 33. B

34. Why government subsidies are likely to become less important?

A. As China is increasing the investment in this sector.

B. As the price of clean energy technology continues to plummet.

C. As Fossil fuels is the better alternative

D. As there are opportunities and potential for Wind and Solar plants in the East and West Nile areas

35. What least value should be replaced by * in 233*431 so the number becomes divisible by 9?

A. 3 B. 4
C. 5 D. 6

36. How many terms are there in 2, 4, 8, 16, ..., 1024 ?

A. 7 B. 8
C. 9 D. 10

37. Which of the following is a prime number?

A. 9 B. 2
C. 4 D. 8

38. Find the HCF of 54, 288, 360.

A. 18 B. 36
C. 54 D. 108

39. Reduce 368/575 to the lowest terms.

A. 30/25 B. 28/29
C. 29/28 D. 16/25

40. Two ships are sailing in the sea on the two sides of lighthouse. The angle of elevation of the top of the lighthouse is observed from the ships are 30 degree and 45 degree respectively. If the lighthouse is 100 m high, the distance between the two ships is:

A. 276 meters B. 273 meters
C. 270 meters D. 263 meters

41. From a point C on a level ground, the angle of elevation of the top of a tower is 30 degree. If the tower is 100 meter high, find the distance from point C to the foot of the tower.

A. 170 meters B. 172 meters
C. 173 meters D. 167 meters

42. A boat having a length 3 m and breadth 2 m is floating on a lake. The boat sinks by 1 cm when a man gets into it. The mass of the man is:

A. 50 kg B. 60 kg
C. 70 kg D. 80 kg

43. A cistern 6 m long and 4 m wide contains water up to a breadth of 1 m 25 cm. Find the total area of the wet surface.

A. 42 m square B. 49 m square
C. 52 m square D. 64 m square

44. Three numbers are in the ratio of 3 : 4 : 5 respectively. If the sum of the first and third numbers is more than the second number by 52, then which will be the largest number?

A. 52 B. 65
C. 67 D. 72

45. The sum of the digits of a two – digit number is 12. If the new number formed by reversing the digits is greater than the original number by 54, then what will be the original number?

A. 93 B. 28
C. 48 D. 39

46. A shopkeeper purchased 200 bulbs for ₹ 10 each. However, 5 bulbs were fused and had to be thrown away. The remaining was sold at ₹ 12 each. What will be the percentage profit?

A. 13 B. 15
C. 17 D. 22

47. The length of a rectangular field is thrice its breadth. If the cost of cultivating the field at ₹ 367.20 per square meter is ₹ 27, 540, then what is the perimeter of the rectangle?

A. 47 m B. 39 m
C. 52 m D. 40 m

48. If the fractions 8/5, 7/2, 9/5, 5/4, 4/5 are arranged in descending order of their values, which one will be fourth?

A. 9/5 B. 4/5
C. 5/4 D. 8/5

49. A and B are two taps which can fill a tank individually in 10 minutes and 20 minutes respectively. However, there is a leakage at the bottom which can empty a filled tank in 40 minutes. If the tank is empty initially, how much time will both the taps take to fill the tank (leakage is still there)?

A. 10 minutes B. 5 minutes
C. 7 minutes D. 8 minutes

50. What is 50% of 40% of ₹ 3,450?

A. ₹ 690 B. ₹ 580
C. ₹ 670 D. ₹ 570

34. B	**35.** A	**36.** D	**37.** B	**38.** A	**39.** D	**40.** B	**41.** C	**42.** B	**43.** B
44. B	**45.** D	**46.** C	**47.** D	**48.** C	**49.** D	**50.** A			

51. A started a business investing ₹ 45,000. After 3 months, B joined him with a capital of ₹ 60,000. After another 6 months, C joined them with a capital of ₹ 90,000. At the end of the year, they made a profit of ₹ 16,500. What is A's share of profit?
A. ₹ 5,500 B. ₹ 6,500
C. ₹ 6,900 D. ₹ 5,900

52. If the area of a circle is 75.44 square cm then what is the circumference of the circle?
A. 40.2 cm B. 28.9 cm
C. 29.2 cm D. 30.8 cm

53. Find the simple interest on ₹ 7000 at 50/3% for 9 months:
A. ₹ 1075 B. ₹ 975
C. ₹ 875 D. ₹ 775

54. Find the simple interest on the ₹ 2000 at 25/4% per annum for the period from 4th February, 2005 to 18th April 2005
A. ₹ 25 B. ₹ 30
C. ₹ 35 D. ₹ 40

55. In terms of percentage profit, which among following is the best transaction?
A. Cost Price 36, Profit 17
B. Cost Price 50, Profit 24
C. Cost Price 40, Profit 19
D. Cost Price 60, Profit 29

56. Sachin is younger than Rahul by 7 years. If the ratio of their age 7 : 9, find the age of Sachin:
A. 23.5 B. 24.5
C. 12.5 D. 14.5

57. The ratio between the present ages of P and Q is 6 : 7. If Q is 4 years old than P, what will be the ratio of the ages of P and Q after 4 years?
A. 7 : 8 B. 7 : 9
C. 3 : 8 D. 5 : 8

58. Ages of two persons differ by 16 years. If 6 year ago, the elder one be 3 times as old the younger one, find their present age:
A. 12, 28 B. 14, 30
C. 16, 32 D. 18, 34

59. A man walks at 5 kmph for 6 hours and at 4 km/h for 12 hours. His average speed is:
A. $4\frac{1}{3}$ km/h B. $7\frac{2}{3}$ km/h
C. $9\frac{1}{2}$ km/h D. 8 km/h

60. The ratio between the speeds of two trains is 7 : 8. If the second train runs 440 km in 4 hours, then the speed of the first train is:
A. 47.4 km/hr B. 57.19 km/hr
C. 68.13 km/hr D. 96.25 km/hr

61. Walking at the rate of 4 kmph a man covers certain distance in 2 hr 45 min. Running at a speed of 16.5 kmph the man will cover the same distance in:
A. 12 min B. 25 min
C. 40 min D. 48 min

62. 12 men can complete a work in 18 days. Six days after they stared working, 4 more men joined them. How many days will all of them together complete the remaining work?
A. 10 days B. 8 days
C. 11 days D. 9 days

63. A person borrowed 500 at the rate of 5% per annum at S.I. What amount will be pay to clear the debt after 4 years?
A. 500 B. 600
C. 450 D. 400

64. If in a frequency distribution, the mean and median are 21 and 22 respectively, then its mode is approximately:
A. 25.5 B. 24.0
C. 22.0 D. 20.5

65. The difference between 45% of a number and 18% of the same number is 145.8. What is 30% of that number?
A. 148 B. 162
C. 178 D. 184

66. A certain sum of money is borrowed by a person at 8% simple interest for 4 years. If he has to pay ₹ 384 as interest, what is the total amount he has to pay?
A. ₹ 1464 B. ₹ 1584
C. ₹ 1632 D. ₹ 1678

67. A man can row upstream at 6 km/hr and down streams at 11 km/hr. Find the rate of the current.
A. 1.5 km/hr B. 2.5 km/hr
C. 3.5 km/hr D. 4.5 km/hr

68. Perimeter of rectangle is equal to the perimeter of square whose area is 400 cm^2 and length of rectangle is 40% more than the side of a square then find the area of rectangle.
A. 248 cm^2 B. 420 cm^2
C. 356 cm^2 D. 336 cm^2

51. A	**52.** D	**53.** C	**54.** A	**55.** D	**56.** B	**57.** A	**58.** B	**59.** A	**60.** D
61. C	**62.** D	**63.** B	**64.** B	**65.** B	**66.** B	**67.** B	**68.** D		

Directions (Qs. No. 69-73): *The bar graph given below shows the foreign exchange reserves of a country (in million US $) from 1991-92 to 1998-99. Answer the questions based on graph.*

The foreign exchange reserves of a country (in million US $)

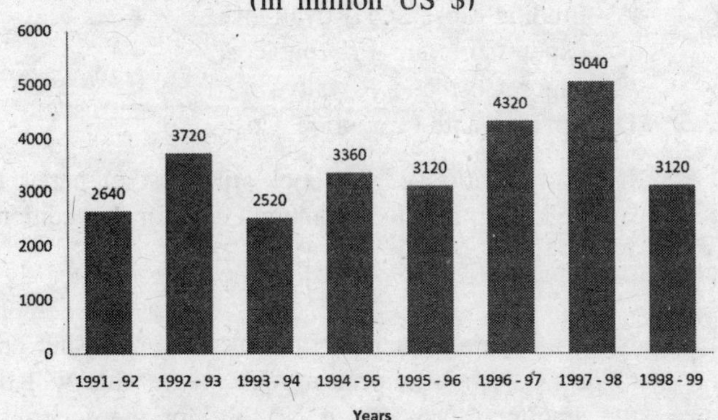

69. The foreign exchange reserves in 1997-98 was how many times that in 1994-95?

A. 1.5 B. 2
C. 3.5 D. 2.6

70. What was the percentage increase in the foreign exchange reserves in 1997-98 over 1993-94?

A. 80% B. 90%
C. 100% D. 110%

71. For which year, the percent increase of foreign exchange reserves over the previous year is the highest?

A. 1994-95 B. 1995-96
C. 1998-99 D. 1992-93

72. The foreign exchange reserves in 1996-97 were approximately what percent of the average foreign exchange reserves over the period under review?

A. 80% B. 100%
C. 125% D. 130%

73. The ratio of the number of years, in which the foreign exchange reserves are above the average reserves, to those in which the reserves are below the average is:

A. 3 : 5 B. 2 : 3
C. 4 : 7 D. 3 : 7

Directions (Qs. No. 74-78): *The following Line chart gives the ratio of the amounts of imports by a Company to the amount of exports from that company over the period from 1995 to 2001. Answer the following questions based on following Line graph:*

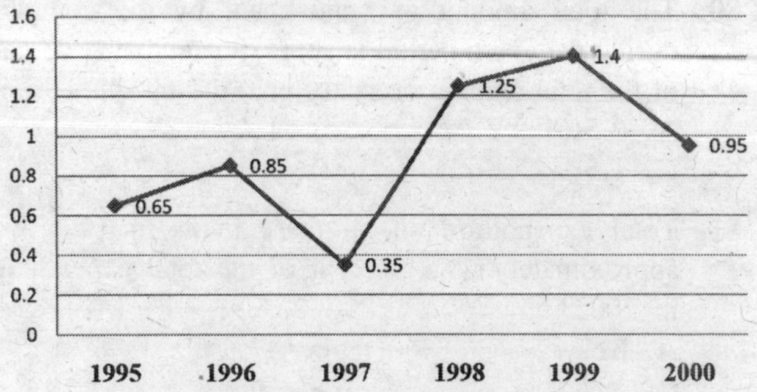

74. In how many of the given years were the exports more than imports?

A. 1 B. 2
C. 3 D. 4

75. The imports were minimum proportionate to the exports of the Company in the year:

A. 1997 B. 1995
C. 1996 D. 2000

76. If the imports of a company in 1996 was ₹ 272 crores, the exports from the company in 1996 was:

A. ₹ 120 Crores B. ₹ 220 Crores
C. ₹ 320 Crores D. ₹ 420 Crores

77. What was the percentage increase in imports from 1997 to 1998?

A. 70 B. 72
C. 74 D. Data Inadequate

78. If the imports in 1998 was ₹ 250 crores and the total exports in years 1998 and 1999 together was ₹ 500 crores, then the imports in 1999 was:

A. 320 Crore B. 420 Crore
C. 520 Crore D. 620 Crore

Directions (Qs. No. 79-83): *Study the following table chart and answer the questions based on it. Expenditures of a Company (in Lakh Rupees) per annum over the given years.*

Year	Salary	Fuel and Transport	Bonus	Interest on Loans	Taxes
1998	288	98	3.00	23.4	83
1999	342	112	2.52	32.5	108
2000	324	101	3.84	41.6	74
2001	336	133	3.68	36.4	88
2002	420	142	3.96	49.4	98

79. What is the average amount of interest per year which the company had to pay during this period?

A. ₹ 36.66 lakhs B. ₹ 36.36 lakhs
C. ₹ 36.26 lakhs D. ₹ 36.06 lakhs

69. A **70.** C **71.** D **72.** C **73.** A **74.** D **75.** A **76.** C **77.** D **78.** B
79. A

80. The total amount of bonus paid by the company during the given period is approximately what percent of the total amount of salary paid during this period?
A. 0.5% B. 1%
C. 1.5% D. 2%

81. Total expenditure on all these items in 1998 was approximately what percent of the total expenditure in 2002?
A. 61% B. 47%
C. 59% D. 69%

82. Calculate the total expenditure of the company over these items during the year 2000 from the table chart given.
A. ₹ 543.44 lakhs B. ₹ 544.44 lakhs
C. ₹ 545.44 lakhs D. ₹ 546.44 lakhs

83. The ratio between the total expenditure on Taxes for all the years and the total expenditure on Fuel and Transport for all the years respectively is approximately?
A. 4 : 13 B. 7 : 13
C. 10 : 13 D. 11 : 13

Directions (Qs. No. 84-90): *The following pie chart shows the percentage distribution of the expenditure incurred in publishing a book. Study the pie chart and answer the following questions.*

Expenditures (in percentage)

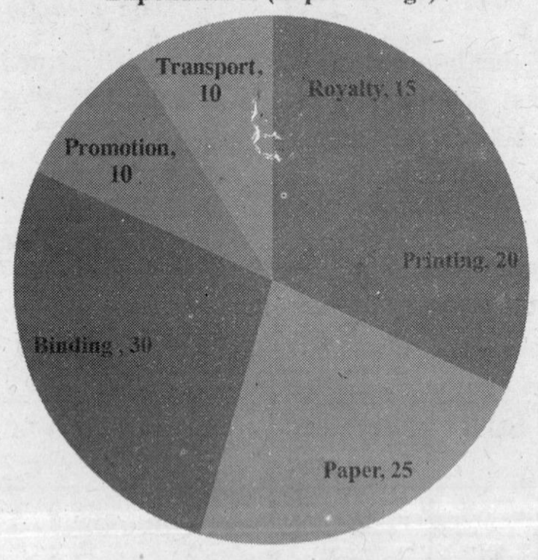

84. What is the central angle of the sector corresponding to the expenditure incurred on Royalty?
A. 54 degrees B. 48 degrees
C. 45 degrees D. 40 degrees

85. Which two expenditures together have central angle of 108°?
A. Binding Cost + Royalty Cost
B. Printing Cost + Paper Cost
C. Binding Cost + Transportation Cost
D. Printing Cost + Transportation Cost

86. If the difference between the two expenditures are represented by 18 degree in the pie-chart, then which option of following can be correct?
A. Binding Cost and Royalty Cost
B. Paper Cost and Printing cost
C. Paper Cost and Royalty
D. Royalty and Promotion Cost

87. If for an edition of the book, the cost of paper is ₹ 56250, then find the promotion cost for this edition.
A. ₹ 21500 B. ₹ 22300
C. ₹ 22500 D. ₹ 22700

88. If for the certain quantity of books, the publisher has to pay ₹ 30,600 as printing cost, then what will be the amount of royalty to be paid for these books?
A. ₹ 22650 B. ₹ 22750
C. ₹ 22850 D. ₹ 22950

89. If 5500 copies are published and the transportation cost on them amounts to ₹ 82500, then what should be the selling price of the book so that the publisher can earn a profit of 25%?
A. ₹ 180.50 B. ₹ 182.50
C. ₹ 183.50 D. ₹ 187.50

90. Royalty on the book is less than the printing cost by:
A. 20% B. 25%
C. 30% D. 35%

Directions (Qs. No. 91-95): *Bar graph below shows pens sold by a retailor on five different days. Study the data carefully and answer the following questions.*

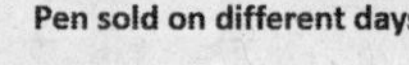

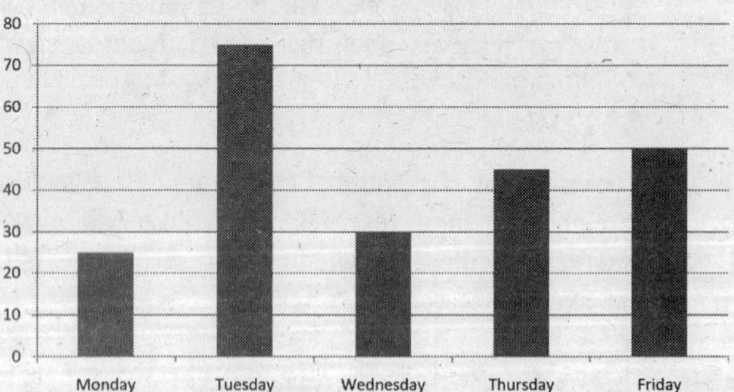

91. Find the difference between total number of pens sold on Monday and Tuesday together to total number of pens sold on Thursday and Friday together?
A. 15 B. 10
C. 5 D. 20

80. B	**81.** D	**82.** B	**83.** C	**84.** A	**85.** D	**86.** B	**87.** C	**88.** D	**89.** D
90. B	**91.** C								

92. Total number of pens sold on Saturday is 40% more than total number of pens sold on Wednesday. Find total number of pens sold on Friday and Saturday together?

A. 92 B. 110
C. 72 D. 108

93. Total number of pens sold on Tuesday are 25% more than total number of pens sold on Sunday. Find total number of pens sold on Sunday?

A. 64 B. 50
C. 94 D. 60

94. Out of total pens sold on Thursday, 20% are blue ink pen. Out of remaining 25% are red ink pen and remaining are black ink pen. Find total number of blue and black ink pen sold on Thursday?

A. 27 B. 36
C. 45 D. 39

95. Out of total pens sold on Tuesday ratio between total defective pens sold to total pens sold is 7 : 15. Find total number of non-defective pens sold on Tuesday by retailer?

A. 20 B. 25
C. 30 D. 40

Directions (Qs. No. 96-100): *Pie chart given below shows total number of workers in three different companies. Table given below shows ratio between officers and workers working in these companies. Study the data carefully and answer the following questions:*

Total workers = 900

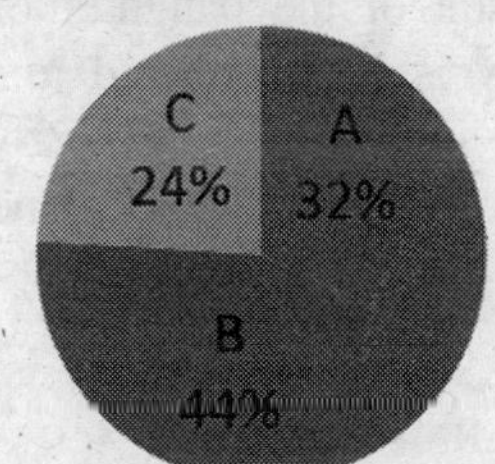

Company	Officers : Workers
A	1 : 16
B	1 : 18
C	1 : 12

Note: Total employees = Officers + Workers

96. Find the ratio between total number of workers in company A and C together to total number of officers in company A and C together.

A. 16 : 1 B. 12 : 1
C. 14 : 1 D. 18 : 1

97. Total number of employees in company 'B' is how much more than total number of employees in company 'C'.

A. 174 B. 194
C. 204 D. 184

98. Total number of officers in company 'A' is how much less than total number of officers in company 'B'.

A. 4 B. 2
C. 6 D. 8

99. Total number of officers and workers in company D is 50% and 25% more than total number of officers and workers in company 'C' respectively. Find total number of employees in company 'D'.

A. 279 B. 297
C. 342 D. 306

100. Find the difference between total number of workers in company 'A' and total number of workers in company 'B' and 'C' together.

A. 432 B. 396
C. 360 D. 324

Directions (Qs. No. 101-102): *Given bar graph shows percentage distribution of total CDs ordered by four shopkeeper (A, B, C & D) and percentage of CDs sold by these four shopkeepers out of total CDs ordered by each. Read the data carefully and answer the questions.*

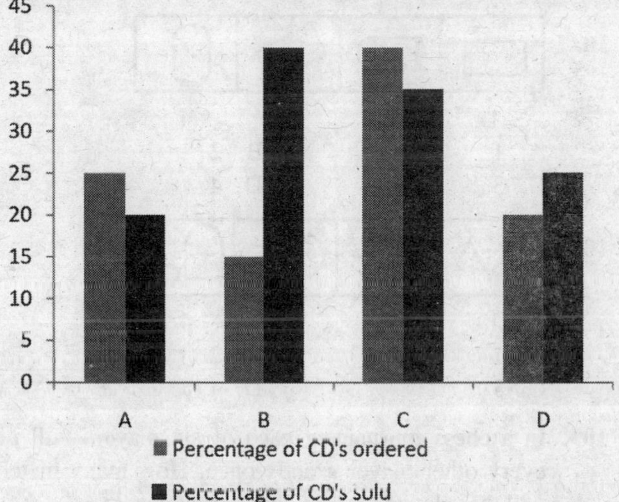

Total CD's ordered by all four shopkeepers together = 600

101. Total unsold CDs by A & D together are how much more than total sold CDs by C?

A. 126 B. 132
C. 128 D. 116

92. A **93.** D **94.** B **95.** D **96.** C **97.** D **98.** A **99.** B **100.** D **101.** A

102. If total CD's sold by shopkeeper E are 125% more than total CD's sold by B and shopkeeper E sold 27% of total ordered CD's, then find total CD's ordered by E are what percent more than total CD's ordered by C?

A. 36% B. 15%
C. 30% D. 25%

Directions (Qs. No. 103–106): *In each of the following questions a number series is given with one term missing. Choose the correct alternative that will continue the same pattern and fill in the blank spaces.*

103. 1, 4, 27, 16, ? , 36, 343

A. 125 B. 50
C. 78 D. 132

104. 20, 19, 17, ?, 10, 5

A. 15 B. 14
C. 13 D. 12

105. 7, 10, 8, 11, 9, 12, ?

A. 13 B. 12
C. 10 D. 7

106. 6, 11, 21, 36, 56, ?

A. 51 B. 71
C. 81 D. 41

Directions (Qs. No. 107 & 108): *Choose the figure which is different.*

107.

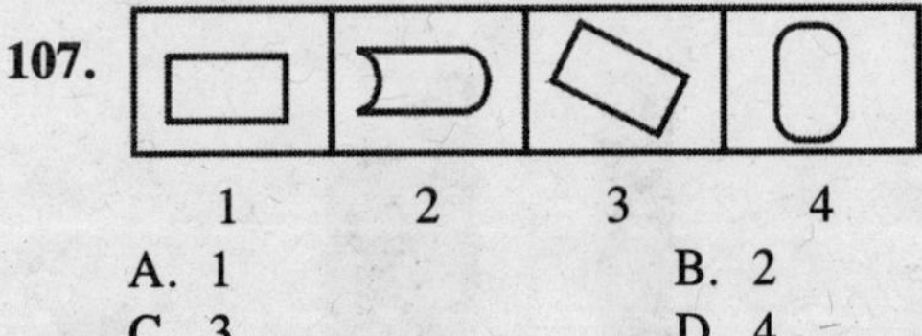

A. 1 B. 2
C. 3 D. 4

108.

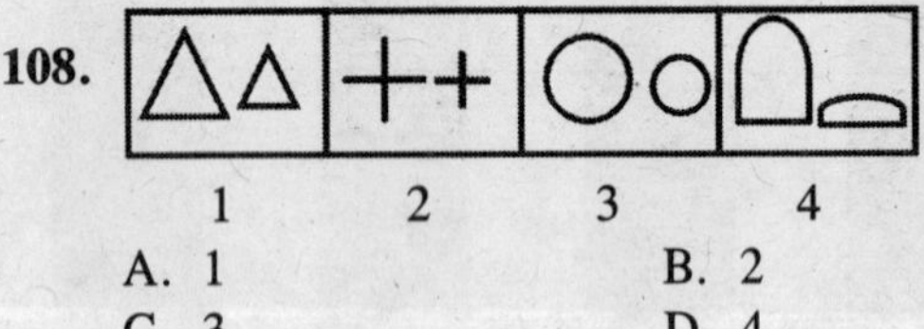

A. 1 B. 2
C. 3 D. 4

109. In a chess tournament each of six players will play every other player exactly once. How many matches will be played during the tournament?

A. 12 B. 15
C. 30 D. 36

110. A, B, C and D play a game of cards. A says to B. "if I give you 8 cards, you will have as many as C has and I shall have 3 less than what C has. Also, if I take 8 cards from C, I shall have twice as many as D has." If B and D together have 50 cards, how many cards have A got?

A. 35 B. 37
C. 38 D. 40

111. Reena is twice as old as Sunita. Three years ago, she was three times as old as Sunita. How old is Reena now.

A. 6 years B. 12 years
C. 14 years D. 16 years

112. A shepherd has 27 sheep. All but 10 died. How many he left with?

A. 10 B. 15
C. 17 D. 27

113. A group of 1200 persons consisting of captains and soldiers is travelling in a train. For every 15 soldiers there is one captain. The number of captains in the group is.

A. 70 B. 75
C. 80 D. 85

114. Aruna cut a cake into two halves and cuts one half into smaller pieces of equal size. Each of the small pieces is twenty grams in weight. If she has seven pieces of the cake in all with her, how heavy was the original cake?

A. 240 gm B. 220 gm
C. 225 gm D. 250 gm

115. Introducing a boy to her mother, Richa said that he is the son of the daughter of the father of her uncle. How is Richa related to the boy?

A. Brother-in-law B. Brother
C. Father D. Uncle

116. Choose the correct code form. If BATMAN is coded as 123416, PERMAN is coded as 987416 then TAPER is coded as:

A. 32987 B. 92897
C. 38972 D. 32978

117. Look at this series 7, 10, 8, 11, 9, 12, ... What number should come next?

A. 7 B. 12
C. 10 D. 13

118. Find the missing number in the given series:

8, 13, 10, 15, 12, ...

A. 14 B. 17
C. 18 D. 20

102. D	**103.** A	**104.** B	**105.** C	**106.** C	**107.** D	**108.** D	**109.** B	**110.** D	**111.** B
112. A	**113.** B	**114.** A	**115.** A	**116.** A	**117.** C	**118.** B			

119. Blueberries cost more than strawberries.
Blueberries cost less than raspberries.
Raspberries cost more than strawberries and blueberries.

If the first two statements are true, the third statement is:

A. True
B. False
C. Uncertain
D. Cannot be defined

120. One morning Udai and Vishal were talking to each other face to face at a crossing. If Vishal's shadow was exactly to the left of Udai, which direction was Udai facing?

A. East
B. West
C. North
D. South

121. Odometer is to mileage as compass is to:

A. Speed
B. Hiking
C. Needle
D. Direction

122. The marks obtained by 10 students in Science (out of 50) are 30, 41, 40, 41, 30, 41, 30, 28, 41, 40. The modal mark is:

A. 40
B. 30
C. 41
D. 35

123. Which word does not belong with the group?

A. Electric Crane
B. Electric Train
C. Electric Iron
D. Electric Lift

124. Y is in the East of X which is in the North of Z. If P is in the South of Z, then in which direction of Y, is P?

A. North-east
B. South-west
C. South-east
D. West

Directions (Qs. No. 125): *Read the following information carefully and answer the question.*

Dev, Kumar, Nilesh, Ankur and Pintu are standing facing to the North in a playground such as given below:
Kumar is at 40 m to the right of Ankur.
Dev is 60 m in the south of Kumar.
Nilesh is at a distance of 25 m in the west of Ankur.
Pintu is at a distance of 90 m in the North of Dev.

125. If a boy starting from Nilesh met to Ankur and then to Kumar and after this he to Dev and then to Pintu and whole the time he walked in a straight line, then how much total distance did he cover?

A. 115 m
B. 215 m
C. 251 m
D. 205 m

126. If P is 18th from the left-end and S is 10th from the right end and if there are 7 students between them, then find the number of total students in a row?

A. 35
B. 19
C. Cannot be determined
D. 16

127. In a row of persons, if A who is 10th from the left and B who is 9th from the right interchange their position, A becomes 15th from the left. How many persons are there in the row?

A. 15
B. 23
C. 22
D. 25

Directions (Qs. No. 128 & 129): *What number is wrong according to given number series pattern:*

128. 1, 3, 9, 31, 128, 651, 3913

A. 9
B. 1
C. 128
D. 31

129. 291, 147, 75, 39, 22, 12, 7.5

A. 22
B. 291
C. 147
D. 75

130. Sum of A's and B's age 6 years ago is 88. A's age 18 years ago is equal to B's age 6 years ago. Find the age of A two years hence.

A. 58 years
B. 64 years
C. 42 years
D. 52 years

Directions (Qs. No. 131-135): *Study the following information carefully and answer the questions given below:*

Seven boxes A, B, C, D, E, F, G are kept one above the other containing different number of chocolates ranging from 10 – 90. Not more than Four boxes are kept above A. Two boxes are kept between A and the box containing 41 chocolates, which is kept below Box A. D contains thrice the number of chocolates than box B. Box C contains 50 number of chocolates and is not kept at the top. The number of chocolates in box G is a cube of a number. Only one box is kept between box containing 41 chocolates and 39 chocolates. Box D has less number of chocolates than box A. One of the boxes contain 78 chocolates. Five boxes are kept between box containing 64 chocolates and Box C. Box G is immediately above box E. Box D is not kept immediately above or below box B. Three boxes are kept between box D and box F. Box D is above box F.

119. A **120.** A **121.** D **122.** C **123.** C **124.** B **125.** B **126.** C **127.** B **128.** C
129. A **130.** A

131. Which among the following box/boxes is kept exactly between Box D and Box B?
A. G, E B. B, C
C. B, A D. None of these

132. How many chocolates are kept in box E?
A. 50 B. 13
C. 41 D. None of these

133. Which among the following boxes contains the maximum and minimum number of chocolates respectively?
A. G, E B. B, D
C. F, B D. None of these

134. Which of the following combination is not true?
A. 50 – D B. 41 – E
C. 64 – A D. None of these

135. Which among the following boxes is kept immediately below box B?
A. G B. C
C. A D. F

136. In the question given below there are two conclusions followed by five statements. You have to choose the correct set of statements that logically satisfies given conclusions.
I. Some silver are not ring.
II. Some platinum are not chain.

Statements:
I. All rings are gold. Some gold is chain. Some chain is silver. No silver is platinum.
II. Some rings are gold. All gold is chain. Some chain is silver. No silver is platinum.
III. All rings are gold. All gold is chain. Some chain is silver. Some silver is platinum.
IV. Some rings are gold. Some gold is chain. No chain is silver. Some silver is platinum. No platinum is ring.
V. Some rings are gold. Some gold is chain. Some chain is silver. Some silver is platinum.
A. Only statement II B. Only statement III
C. Only statement I D. Only statement IV

137. Recently State Bank of India issued infrastructure bond. This is the first time SBI is issuing a infrastructure bond, helping it in long-term lending to the infrastructure segment at a time period of?
A. 15 years B. 10 years
C. 12 years D. 20 years

138. Yoginder K Alagh is a renowned:
A. Athlete B. Industrialist
C. Artists D. Economist

139. The Paradise of Food' is translated in four different languages wins JCB Prize for Literature in recently. Initially the author was published this book in which language?
A. Hindi B. Tamil
C. Urdu D. Sanskrit

140. Table tennis player Sharath Kamal Achanta won how many gold medals in recently concluded common-wealth games?
A. 1 B. 2
C. 3 D. 4

141. Recently in December, the 5th Scorpene class submarine of Project-75 named INS 'Vagir' has been delivered to the Indian Navy. INS Vagir belongs to which class submarine?
A. Kalvari B. Sindhugosh
C. Arihant D. Karanj

142. Which of the following Statement regarding Utkarsh 2.0 is true?
I. The Reserve Bank of India's Medium-term Strategy Framework for the period 2023-2025
II. Utkarsh 2.0' was launched by the Governor of RBI.
III. Strengthened trust of corporate
A. Only I and II B. Only I
C. Only III D. Only II and III

143. Sahyadri Farmer Producer Company (FPC) is the India's first private agriculture mandi opened recently in which district of Maharashtra?
A. Aurangabad B. Nashik
C. Pune D. Nagpur

144. Which of the following given bank has maximum share-holding in Yes Bank?
A. Bank of Baroda B. State Bank of India
C. Punjab National Bank D. Canara Bank

145. As per recent newspaper report who among the following person assume the chair of B20 India and lead the business agenda during India's G20 presidency.
A. Hon'ble Nirmala Sitharaman
B. Hon'ble Jagdeep Dhankhar
C. Hon'ble Narendra Modi
D. TCS – N Chandrasekaran

131. A	**132.** C	**133.** C	**134.** A	**135.** D	**136.** D	**137.** A	**138.** D	**139.** C	**140.** C
141. A	**142.** A	**143.** B	**144.** B	**145.** D					

146. At present how many Total credit rating agency in India?
A. 7 B. 6
C. 8 D. 10

147. The Reserve Bank of India (RBI) recently imposed a monetary penalty of ₹ 2.27 crore on RBL Bank for not complying with certain directives on ....
A. Agricultural Credit B. Loan recovery agents
C. Kisan Credit Card D. KYC norms

148. Axis Bank and Autotrac Finance Limited Ltd (AFL) announced their strategic partnership under the co-lending model through the Yubi Co. Lend platform. Autotrac Finance Limited Ltd is based in which of the following states?
A. Haryana B. Maharashtra
C. Rajasthan D. Gujarat

149. '4R' strategy' which was in news recently is related to .....
A. Startups B. Job Creation
C. Banking D. Fiscal Deficit

150. Consider the following statement regarding the Yuva Utsav. Which of the following statement is incorrect?
(*i*) Yuva Utsav on the theme of 'Panch Pran of Amrit Kaal - India @2047' was recently organized in the Siaha district of Mizoram.
(*ii*) The festival was organized by the North Eastern Council.
(*iii*) The Yuva Ustav is being celebrated marking the Azadi Ka Amrit Mahotsav in the spirit of Yuva Shakti.
A. Only (*ii*) B. Both (*i*) and (*ii*)
C. Only (*iii*) D. Both (*ii*) and (*iii*)

151. The Competition Commission of India has approved Reliance Retail Ventures' (RRVL's) acquisition of METRO Cash & Carry India for a cash consideration of ________
A. ₹ 2,450 crore B. ₹ 3,850 crore
C. ₹ 3,450 crore D. ₹ 2,850 crore

152. Consider the following statements regarding the report "Women and Men in India 2022" released by the Ministry of Statistics and Programme Implementation (MoSPI). Which of the following statement is correct?
(*i*) India's sex ratio (females per 1,000 males) is expected to improve to 952 by 2040.
(*ii*) The sex ratio at birth went up by three points to 907 in 2018-20 from 904 in 2017-19
(*iii*) India's Labour Force Participation Rate has been on the rise since 2017-2018.
A. Only (*i*) B. Both (*ii*) and (*iii*)
C. Only (*ii*) D. Both (*i*) and (*iii*)

153. Government of Maharashtra has decided to launch the second phase of the Jalyukt Shivar project. Jalyukt Shivar project targets ________
A. Slum areas
B. Drinking water supply to coastal areas
C. Mountain and hilly areas
D. Drought-prone areas

154. Who among the following has been named the 2022 recipient of the Chameli Devi Jain Award for Outstanding Women media persons?
A. Nidhi Razdan
B. Barkha Dutt
C. Sagarika Ghose
D. Dhanya Rajendran

155. According to the Federal Deposit Insurance Corp (FDIC), which of the following banks has agreed to buy a significant chunk of the Signature Bank in a $2.7 billion deal?
A. Jpmorgan Chase
B. New York Community Bank
C. Goldman Sachs
D. Bank of New York Mellon

156. Consider the following statement regarding RailTel's work order from the Centre for Development of Advanced Computing (C-DAC). Which of the following statement is incorrect:
A. RailTel Corporation of India Ltd has received the work order from the Centre for Development of Advanced Computing (C-DAC) amounting to ₹ 287.57 crores.
B. The delivery period of the project is 300 days.
C. The work order is for supply, installation, integration, testing and commissioning of IT infrastructure in green field data centre at New Delhi and Bengaluru along with training and support.
D. The C-DAC is the premier R&D organisation of the Ministry of Science and Technology.

157. Under the Stand-Up India scheme, ______ loans amounting to ₹ 39,517 crore as of February have been sanctioned since the launch in April 2016.
A. 1.65 lakh B. 2.75 lakh
C. 1.75 lakh D. None of these

146. B **147.** B **148.** A **149.** C **150.** A **151.** D **152.** B **153.** D **154.** D **155.** B
156. D **157.** C

158. Ministry of Statistics and Programme Implementation (MoSPI) released the ______ issue of "Women and Men in India 2022" (an annual statistics released by the Ministry of Statistics and Programme Implementation).

A. 22nd B. 25th
C. 24th D. None of these

159. The fertiliser cooperative major IFFCO and state-owned Coal India Ltd (CIL) will manufacture Nano DAP for a period of ______ years.

A. Two
B. Three
C. Four
D. None of these

160. Which of the following state government has decided to launch the second phase of Jalyukt Shivar project and it is a scheme that targets drought-prone areas by Undertaking water conservation measures?

A. Karnataka
B. Tamil Nadu
C. Maharashtra
D. None of these

161. The United Kingdom (UK) Treasury and the Bank of England have facilitated a private sale of the UK subsidiary of the collapsed Silicon Valley Bank to HSBC Holdings Plc's 'ring-fenced subsidiary' for ________ sterling.

A. 1 pound B. 2 pound
C. 3 pound D. None of these

162. Which of the following bank is buying troubled rival Credit Suisse for almost $3.25 billion, in an effort to avoid further market-shaking turmoil in the global banking system?

A. Union Bank of India
B. Bank of Maharastra
C. Union Bank of Switzerland
D. None of these

163. Which of the following has signed an MoU, with the Prajapati Brahma Kumari Ishwariya Vishwa Vidyalaya, Mount Abu in New Delhi for spreading the message of Nasha Mukt Bharat Abhiyaan, NMBA, among youth, women and students?

A. Department of Social Justice and Empowerment
B. Department of Social Welfare
C. Department of Social Defence
D. Department of Education

164. Which of the following statements is true about 'Yellow Journalism'?

A. Yellow Journalism refers to a reporting style that uses factual reporting and objective coverage.
B. Yellow Journalism refers to a reporting style that uses sensationalism, exaggeration, and manipulation of facts to create a sensational story.
C. Yellow Journalism refers to a type of newspaper that covers sensational stories.
D. Yellow Journalism refers to a type of investigative journalism that uncovers corrupt practices.

165. Pradhan Mantri MUDRA Yojana is aimed at:

A. bringing the small entrepreneurs into formal financial system.
B. providing loans to poor farmers for cultivating particular crops.
C. providing pensions to old and destitute persons.
D. funding the voluntary organization involved in the promotion of skill development and employment generation.

166. The 'Closed Economy' is the economy in which:

A. Only export takes place
B. Budget deficit is less
C. Only import takes place
D. There is no foreign trade

167. The Multi-billion dollar project TAPI on which work started in December, 2015 is related to:

A. Natural Gas B. Solar Energy
C. Road Construction D. Railway Line

168. 'VAT' is imposed:

A. Directly on consumer
B. On first stage of production
C. On all stages between production and sale
D. On final stage of production

169. Which bank has partnered with GIFT SEZ (special economic zone) to promote IT and financial services?

A. HDFC Bank
B. ICICI Bank
C. Axis Bank
D. State Bank of India

170. As per RBI Guidelines, what is the minimum Net – owned fund required for NBFCs to issue Credit Cards?

A. ₹ 10 Crores B. ₹ 50 Crores
C. ₹ 100 Crores D. ₹ 500 Crores

158. C **159.** B **160.** C **161.** A **162.** C **163.** A **164.** B **165.** A **166.** D **167.** A
168. C **169.** B **170.** C

EXPLANATORY ANSWERS

1. (C): "Nobody can deny the fact that Indian economy is very different than American economy."

The phrase "different than" is not grammatically correct. The correct phrase to use when comparing two things is "different from." So, the corrected sentence would be: "Nobody can deny the fact that the Indian economy is very different from the American economy."

2. (B): "Accurate statistics with regards to the area occupied in different form of cultivation are difficult to obtain." The phrase "with regards to" is incorrect. The correct phrase is "with regard to," which means concerning or in relation to something.

Additionally, the word "statistics" should be in the plural form because we are referring to more than one statistic. So, the corrected sentence would be: "Accurate statistics with regard to the area occupied in different forms of cultivation are difficult to obtain."

3. (D): No replacement required

The original sentence is grammatically correct as it is.

The sentence is structured to convey that there was rarely, if ever, any training or instructions in such tactics for either the tank crews or the infantry formations. The phrase "seldom if ever" is idiomatic and effectively communicates the intended meaning. Therefore, no replacement is necessary.

4. (C): I smelled

The corrected sentence would be:

"As soon as I opened the front door of my house, I smelled the distinctive aroma of fresh coffee."

In this context, the phrase "I smelled" effectively conveys the sequence of events after opening the front door, making the sentence grammatically correct.

5. (C): denied that they are

The corrected sentence would be:

"The party explicitly denied that they are involved in mainstream politics."

In this context, the past tense "denied" (option C) is suitable because it reflects that the denial occurred in the past. The present tense "are" is also appropriate because it refers to the ongoing status of their involvement in mainstream politics.

6. (A): Only (*i*) Forming a single sentence:

"When we see ourselves repeating our ordinary routine, we realize how much wealth surrounds our life."

This option uses the phrase "When we see ourselves" to connect the two ideas, indicating that the realization of the wealth comes about when observing the repetition of the ordinary routine.

7. (C): (*i*) "As there is a growing influence of..."

(*iii*) "With the growing influence of the Indian..."

Both options (*i*) and (*iii*) are correct because they effectively introduce the concept of causality or association between the two statements.

Option (*i*) starts with "As there is," which implies a causal relationship between the growing influence of the Indian Diaspora on Capitol Hill and Trump's perception of the advantages of doing business with India.

Correct Sentence - "As there is a growing influence of the Indian Diaspora on Capitol Hill, Trump will certainly see the advantages of doing business with India."

Option (*iii*) begins with "With the growing influence of the Indian," which also establishes a connection between the growing influence and Trump's perception of the advantages of doing business with India.

Correct Sentence - "With the growing influence of the Indian Diaspora on Capitol Hill, Trump will certainly see the advantages of doing business with India."

8. (C): (*i*) "As there was no democracy in British India..."

(*ii*) "Since there was no democracy in British..."

Option (*i*) and (*ii*) both introduce the absence of democracy in British India as a reason or condition for the subsequent statement. They effectively convey a causal relationship between the absence of democracy and the rulers' ability to make bold decisions.

9. (B): (*c*) "Of the twelve million ..."

This option specifies the group being referred to in the second statement, making it clear that it's about the twelve million youth mentioned in the first statement. It effectively connects the two statements and provides clarity about the specific group being discussed in the second statement.

15. (D): In the context of the passage, the term "UNKNOWN" implies aspects of the economy that are not well-known or understood. By choosing "uncanny," one could interpret it as suggesting that these unknown aspects of the economy have a strange or eerie quality to them. It implies a sense of mystery or unpredictability, which captures the essence of the unknown elements being discussed in the passage.

16. **(D):** Is Consumption Necessary for Economic Growth?

The passage primarily discusses the relationship between consumption and economic growth, questioning the widely held belief that consumption is the primary driver of economic growth. It examines various viewpoints on this matter, presenting arguments that challenge the notion that consumption alone fuels economic prosperity.

17. **(C):** When the statement says "consumer preferences would surely be the steering wheel," it is comparing consumer preferences to a steering wheel in a car. Just as a steering wheel directs the movement of a vehicle, consumer preferences direct or influence the movement of the economy. This analogy suggests that the choices and preferences of consumers have a significant impact on economic activity and the direction in which the economy moves. In practical terms, consumer preferences refer to the desires, tastes, and inclinations of individuals or households when making purchasing decisions. These preferences drive demand for goods and services in the market, which, in turn, affects production, investment, employment, and overall economic growth. Therefore, "The Penchant of the consumers controls the economy" is the most appropriate inference from this line. It emphasizes that consumer preferences have a considerable influence on economic activity and play a central role in shaping the behavior of markets and industries.

18. **(D):**

(*a*) "Economists fail to distinguish between consuming and producing value and form a mistaken belief." This statement accurately reflects a point made in the passage. The passage discusses how Keynesian economists and pundits often fail to distinguish between consuming and producing value, leading to a mistaken belief in the importance of consumption as the primary driver of economic growth.

(*b*) "Economic growth and declines have always been led by changes in business and durable goods investment." This statement is consistent with the information provided in the passage. The passage discusses how changes in business and durable goods investment have historically played a leading role in economic growth and declines, while final consumer goods spending has been relatively stable through the business cycle.

19. **(C):** Increased certainty in future returns refers to the confidence that businesses have in the expected profitability of their investments. When businesses feel more certain about the returns they will receive on their investments, they are more willing to undertake new projects or expand existing ones. This confidence is typically based on various factors, including market conditions, economic outlook, government policies, and industry trends.

When businesses are confident about future returns, they are more likely to make long-term investments to improve their competitiveness and profitability. These investments may include expanding operations, developing new products or services, upgrading technology and infrastructure, or entering new markets. Such investments often require additional resources, including labor, which can lead to businesses hiring new employees.

20. **(D):** While "contrast" directly focuses on highlighting differences, "variance" carries a broader meaning that encompasses not just the existence of differences but also their degree and variability. In the context of the passage, where the author criticizes relying on the "car analogy" for economic models, variance could represent the various and unpredictable factors that drive actual economic growth compared to the simplistic analogy's singular focus on consumption.

Therefore, both "contrast" and "variance" offer valid opposing ideas to "analogy" depending on the specific interpretation and emphasis. While "contrast" may be a more direct antonym, "variance" adds the nuance of variability and complexity, potentially aligning better with the author's critical argument.

21. **(B):**

(*i*) **Disburses:** Given this definition, "disburse" could also be a suitable replacement for "dispenses" in the sentence "There is a vending machine on the platform that dispenses snacks."

(*iii*) **Distributes:** This word means to give out or deliver goods or resources to multiple recipients. It is a suitable replacement for "dispenses" in the given context.

Both "disburses" and "distributes" could potentially replace "dispenses" in the sentence, although "distributes" is a more common and appropriate word choice when referring to snacks from a vending machine.

22. (C):

(*i*) **System:** A system refers to a set of interconnected or interdependent components forming a complex whole. In this context, a system for cooperation in the steel industry could involve various processes, procedures, and protocols.

(*ii*) **Method:** A method refers to a particular procedure or way of doing something. It is often a systematic approach to achieve a specific goal or objective.

Considering the meanings of the options and the context of the sentence, both "system" and "method" are suitable replacements for "mechanism."

23. (A):

(*i*) **Hamper:** This word means to hinder or obstruct the movement or progress of something. It does not accurately replace "qualify" in the context of the sentence.

(*ii*) **Measured:** This word means done with care and consideration; calculated. It does not convey the meaning of meeting the criteria or being eligible, which is the meaning of "qualify" in this context.

(*iii*) **Inclined:** This word means having a tendency or preference towards a particular action or behavior. It does not convey the meaning of meeting the criteria or being eligible, which is the meaning of "qualify" in this context.

Given the options provided, none of them accurately replace "qualify" in the context of the sentence.

24. (C):

(*i*) **Disturbance:** This word refers to a disruption of the normal functioning or order of something. It implies a state of unrest or interference that disturbs the usual flow or operation of a system. In the context of the sentence, "disturbance" accurately captures the sense of disruption caused by the misuse of the Governor's office to undermine duly elected State governments.

(*ii*) **Obstruction:** This word refers to the act of blocking or hindering progress or movement. While it may relate to impeding or interfering with something, it encompass the broader sense of "disruption" conveyed in the context of the sentence. While "obstruction" suggests a hindrance or barrier, "disruption" implies a more extensive and pervasive interference with the normal functioning of federalism.

Both "disturbance" and "obstruction" capture aspects of the disruption caused by the misuse of the Governor's office in undermining duly elected State governments. However, "disturbance" may better convey the broader sense of disruption in this context, as it implies a disturbance of the normal order or functioning.

25. (B): Nabbed, lasted

So the complete sentence would be: "Police nabbed notorious gangster after relentless chase that lasted for 3 weeks."

This option provides appropriate verbs that fit the context: "nabbed" meaning to catch or seize, and "lasted" indicating the duration of the chase.

26. (C): Drenched, affected

So the complete sentence would be: "Tropical rainforests choked in fog and continuously drenched by mists and downpours are least affected by fires."

This option provides appropriate verbs that fit the context: "drenched" describes the continuous wetting of the rainforests, and "affected" indicates the impact of fires on them.

27. (D): Evaluate, approach

So the complete sentence would be: "An interview is a good chance to evaluate how candidates approach difficult situations."

This option provides appropriate verbs that fit the context: "evaluate" means to assess or judge, and "approach" refers to the method or manner in which candidates deal with difficult situations.

28. (C): had a thorough knowledge of

So the revised sentence would be: "He made himself master of practically every branch of medieval learning and had a thorough knowledge of the sources and the bibliography of his subject."

This option maintains the correct tense and matches the past tense of "made himself master" with "had a thorough knowledge of."

29. (B): has been found guilty of

So the revised sentence would be: "Gionee has been found guilty of intentionally inflicting malware in over 20 million phones by a Chinese court."

This option provides the correct preposition "of" to indicate what Gionee has been found guilty of. The other options introduce awkward phrasing or incorrect prepositions.

30. (C): not be entrusted with

So the revised sentence would be: "Many people believe that voluntary bodies as they are today should not be entrusted with this national responsibility."

This option provides the correct verb form "not be entrusted with" to convey the idea that voluntary bodies should not be given this national responsibility. The other options introduce awkward phrasing or incorrect verb forms.

31. (D):

I. The decrease in the cost of renewable energy resulted in its wide use: This statement is supported by the passage, which mentions that the price of clean energy technology has plummeted, making it increasingly attractive for world governments.

II. China massively supported solar power and became the largest investor in renewable energy: This statement is accurate according to the passage, which highlights China's significant support for solar power and its position as the world's largest investor in renewable energy.

III. Egypt is conducting feasibility studies for building the world's largest solar power plant: This statement is also accurate based on the passage, which mentions that Egypt is considering financing options to conduct feasibility studies for building the world's largest solar power plant for both electricity generation and water desalination.

32. (D):

II. Electric sector has performed the best for renewables: This statement aligns with the author's intention. The passage emphasizes the electricity sector as the "brightest spot" for renewables due to its substantial growth and contribution from various renewable sources.

III. Hydropower generation has a significant contribution in the electricity sector: This statement is also accurate. The passage mentions the significant contribution of hydropower generation alongside solar photovoltaics and wind in the electricity sector's transition to renewable energy.

33. (B):

II. Carbon dioxide emissions were reduced to a considerable amount: This statement is accurate. The passage mentions that the global replacement of traditional fuels with renewables led to around 1.8 gigatonnes of carbon dioxide emissions being avoided last year, which is equivalent to removing the entire US transport system.

34. (B): As the price of clean energy technology continues to plummet: This statement aligns with the information provided in the passage, which mentions that the price of clean energy technology has been decreasing. As the cost of renewable energy technologies decreases, they become more economically competitive with traditional fossil fuels. Consequently, government subsidies may become less necessary to incentivize the adoption of renewable energy sources.

36. (D): 2, 4, 8, 16, ... 1024 are in G.P.

Here, $a = 2,\ cr = 2$

nth term $= ar^{n-1}$

$$1024 = 2 \times 2^{n-1} = 2 \times \frac{2^n}{2}$$

$$\Rightarrow \quad 2^n = 1024 = (2^5)^5 = 2^{10} \Rightarrow n = 10.$$

37. (B): 2 is a prime number.

38. (A): 54, 288, 360

54) 288 (5
270
18) 54 (3
54
×

18) 360 (20
36
× 0

Hence, HCF = 18.

39. (D): $\dfrac{368}{575} = \dfrac{16}{25}$

$368 \div 23 = 16$

$575 \div 23 = 25.$

40. (B):

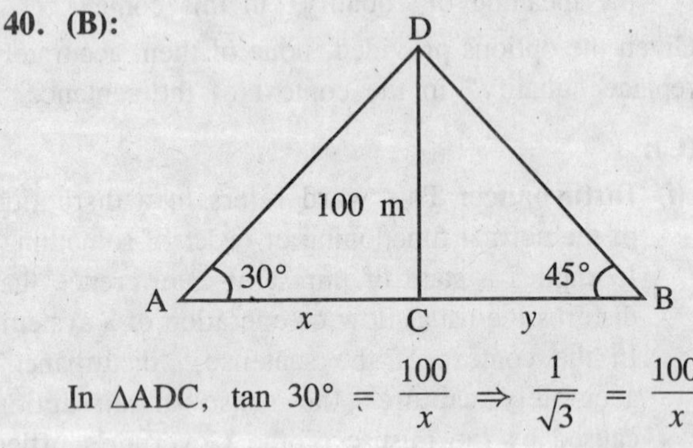

In ΔADC, $\tan 30° = \dfrac{100}{x} \Rightarrow \dfrac{1}{\sqrt{3}} = \dfrac{100}{x}$

$\Rightarrow \quad x = 100\sqrt{3}$

In ΔBCD, $\tan 45° = \dfrac{100}{y} \Rightarrow 1 = \dfrac{100}{y}$

$\Rightarrow \quad y = 100$

$\therefore \quad x + y = 100 + 100\sqrt{3}$

$= 100\left(\sqrt{3}+1\right)$

$= 100\ (1.73 + 1)$

$= 100 + 2.73 = 100\left(\dfrac{273}{100}\right)$

$= 273$ m.

41. (C):

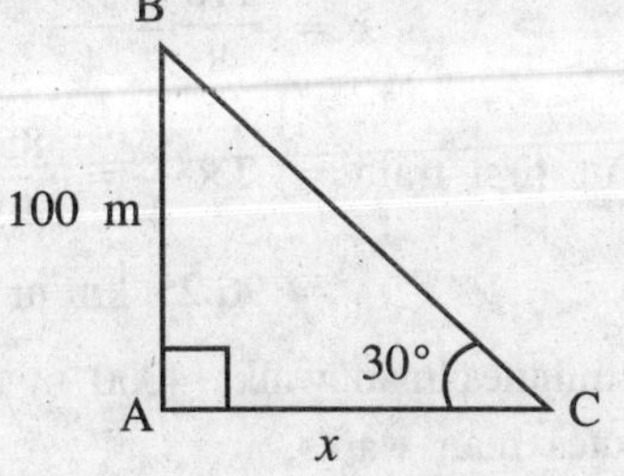

In Δ ABC, $\tan 30° = \dfrac{100}{x}$

$$\Rightarrow \quad \frac{1}{\sqrt{3}} = \frac{100}{x} \Rightarrow x = 100\sqrt{3}$$

$$\Rightarrow \quad x = 100 \times 1.73$$

$$= 100 \times \frac{173}{100} = 173 \text{ m.}$$

42. (B): The Mass of the man

$$= \frac{300 \times 200}{1000} = 60 \text{ kg.}$$

44. (B): Let numbers are $3x$, $4x$ and $5x$

According to the question,

$$3x + 5x = 4x + 52$$

$$\Rightarrow \quad 4x = 52 \Rightarrow x = 13$$

Hence, the largest number = 65.

45. (D): Let Ten's place digit number = x and unit's place digit number = y

$\therefore$ Numebr = $10x + y$

$$x + y = 12 \quad \ldots(i)$$

$$10x + y + 54 = 10y + x$$

$$\Rightarrow \quad 9x - 9y = -54$$

$$\Rightarrow \quad x - y = -6 \quad \ldots(ii)$$

From (*i*) and (*ii*), $x = 3$, $y = 9$

Hence, the original number = 39.

46. (C): C.P. = 200 × 10 = ₹ 2000

S.P. = 195 × 12 = ₹ 2340

Profit = 2340 − 2000 = ₹ 340

$$\text{Profit } \% = \frac{340}{2000} \times 100 = 17\%.$$

47. (D): Let breadth = y m

$\therefore$ length = $3y$ m

area = $3y \times y = 3y^2$

₹ 367.20 = 1 m^2

$$₹\ 27{,}540 = \frac{1}{367.20} \times 27540 \text{ m}^2 = 75 \text{ m}^2$$

$$3y^2 = 75$$

$$\Rightarrow \quad y^2 = 25 \Rightarrow y = 5$$

$\therefore$ Breadth = 5 m and length = 15 m

Perimeter of rectangle = $2(l + b) = 2(15 + 5)$

$= 2 \times 20 = 40$ m.

48. (C): $\dfrac{8}{5} = 1.6$

$$\frac{7}{2} = 3.5$$

$$\frac{9}{5} = 1.8$$

$$\frac{5}{4} = 1.25$$

$$\frac{4}{5} = 0.8$$

$\therefore \dfrac{7}{2}, \dfrac{8}{5}, \dfrac{9}{5}, \dfrac{5}{4}, \dfrac{4}{5}$ are in descending order

Hence, fourth = $\dfrac{5}{4}$

49. (D): (A + B + C)'s 1 minute work

$$= \frac{1}{10} + \frac{1}{20} - \frac{1}{40} = \frac{4 + 2 - 1}{40} = \frac{5}{40} = \frac{1}{8}$$

Hence, tank will fill in 8 minutes.

50. (A): 50% of 40% of ₹ 3450

$$= 50\% \text{ of } \frac{40}{100} \times 3450$$

$$= 50\% \text{ of } 1380$$

$$= \frac{50}{100} \times 1380 = ₹\ 690.$$

51. (A): A = 45000 × 12

B = 60000 × 9

C = 90000 × 6

A : B : C = 1 : 1 : 1

Hence, A's share of profit = $\dfrac{1}{3} \times 16500 = ₹\ 5500.$

52. (D): Area of the circle = πr^2

$$\Rightarrow \quad \frac{22}{7} \times r^2 = 75.44$$

$$\Rightarrow \quad r^2 = \frac{75.44 \times 7}{22}$$

$$\Rightarrow \quad r = \sqrt{24} = 4.9$$

$$\text{Circumference} = 2 \times \frac{22}{7} \times 4.9$$

$$= 44 \times 0.7 = 30.8 \text{ cm.}$$

53. (C): S.I. $= \frac{7000 \times 50 \times 9}{3 \times 12 \times 100} =$ ₹ 875.

54. (A): S.I. $= \frac{2000 \times 25 \times 73}{100 \times 4 \times 365} =$ ₹ 25.

55. (D): $\frac{29}{60} \times 100 = \frac{290}{6}$

$= 48.33\%$ is the best transaction.

56. (B): Let, Rahul age $= x$ years

Sachin age $= (x - 7)$ years

$$\frac{x-7}{x} = \frac{7}{9}$$

$\Rightarrow \quad 9x - 63 = 7x$

$\Rightarrow \quad 2x = 63 \Rightarrow x = 31.5$

Hence, Sachin's age $= 31.5 - 7 = 24.5$ years.

57. (A): Let P's age $= 6x$

and Q's age $= 7x$

$6x + 4 = 7x \Rightarrow x = 4$

Present age of P = 24 years

Present age of Q = 28 years

After 4 years ratio of their ages

$= \frac{28}{32} = 7 : 8.$

58. (B): Let, elder's age $= x$ years

$\therefore$ Smaller's age $= x - 16$

6 years ago, elder's age $= (x - 6)$ years

6 years ago, smaller edge $= x - 22$

$x - 6 = 3(x - 22)$

$\Rightarrow \quad x - 6 = 3x - 66$

$\Rightarrow \quad 2x = 60 \Rightarrow x = 30$

Present age of elder = 30 years

Present age of smaller = 30 − 16 = 14 years

Hence, their present age = 14, 30.

59. (A): $d_1 = 6 \times 5 = 30$ km

$d_2 = 4 \times 12 = 48$ km

Average speed $= \frac{\text{Total distance}}{\text{Total time}}$

$= \frac{78}{18} = 4\frac{6}{18} = 4\frac{1}{3}$ km/hr.

60. (D): Let speed of first train $= 7x$ km/hr

and speed of 2nd train $= 8x$ km/hr

According to the question,

$8x = \frac{440}{4} = 110$

$\Rightarrow \quad x = \frac{110}{8} = \frac{55}{4}$

$\therefore$ Speed of first train $= 7 \times \frac{55}{4} = \frac{385}{4}$

$= 96.25$ km/hr

61. (C): In 60 minutes man walks 4000 m

In 165 minutes man walks,

$\frac{4000}{60} \times 165 = 11000$ m

Now $\because$ 16500 m man runs in 60 minutes

$\therefore$ 11000 m man runs in $\frac{60}{16500} \times 11000$

$= 40$ minutes.

62. (D): 12 men can do a work in 18 days

(18 − 6) days = 12 days

12 men + 4 men = 16 men

Now, 12 men can do this work in 12 days

16 men can do this work in $\frac{12 \times 12}{16} = 9$ days.

63. (B): S.I. $= \frac{500 \times 4 \times 5}{100} =$ ₹ 100

Amount = 500 + 100 = ₹ 600

64. (B): Mode = 3 × Median − 2 × Mean

$= 3 \times 22 - 2 \times 21$

$= 66 - 42 = 24.$

65. (B): Let, number $= x$

$\left(\frac{45-18}{100}\right)x = 145.8$

$\Rightarrow \quad 27x = \frac{1458}{10} \times 100 = 14580$

$\Rightarrow \quad x = \frac{14580}{27} = 540$

Hence, $\frac{30}{100} \times 540 = 162.$

66. (B): P $= \frac{384 \times 100}{4 \times 8} = 1200$

$\therefore$ Amount = 1200 + 384 = ₹ 1584.

67. (B): Speed of the current $= \frac{(11-6)}{2} = \frac{5}{2}$

$= 2.5$ km/hr.

68. (D): Area of square = 400

$\therefore$ Side of square = 20 cm

$2(l + b) = 4 \times 20 \Rightarrow l + b = 40$

Length of rectangle = $20+\frac{40}{100}\times 20$ = 28 cm

∴ Breadth of rectangle = 40 – 28 = 12 cm

Arae of rectangle = 28 × 12 = 336 cm^2.

69. (A): From bar-graph:

The foreign exchange reserves in 1997-98 was

$\frac{5040}{3360} = \frac{3}{2}$ = 1.5 times that in 1994-95.

70. (C): Increase in 1997-98 over 1993-94

= 5040 – 2520 = 2520

∴ Percentage increase = $\frac{2520}{2520}\times 100$ = 100%.

71. (D): Percent increase over the previous year

(A) 1994-95

$\Rightarrow \frac{3360-2520}{2520}\times 100 = \frac{840}{252}\times 10 = 33.33\%$

(B) 1995-96

$\Rightarrow \frac{3120-3360}{3360}\times 100 = \frac{-2400}{336} = -7.14\%$

(C) 1998-99

$\Rightarrow \frac{3120-5040}{5040}\times 100 = \frac{-19200}{504} = -38.09\%$

(D) 1992-93

$\Rightarrow \frac{3720-2640}{2640}\times 100 = \frac{10800}{264} = 40.90\%$

Hence, (D) 1992-93 the % increase of foreign exchange reserve over the previous year is the highest.

72. (C): The average foreign exchange reserve

$= \frac{2640+3720+2520+3360+3120+4320+5040+3120}{8}$

$= \frac{27,840}{8} = 3480$

and the foreign exchange reserve in 1996-97 = 4320

Hence, Required percent = $\frac{4320}{3480}\times 100$

= 125% (Approx.).

73. (A): The average reserve

$= \frac{2640+3720+2520+3360+3120+4320+5040+3120}{8}$

$= \frac{27,840}{8} = 3480$

Now, the number of years above the average = 3 and the number of years below the average = 5

Hence, the required ratio = 3 : 5.

74. (D): From line-chart:

∵ The exports more than imports

∴ 0.65 < 1, 0.85 < 1, 0.35 < 1, 0.95 < 1

Hence, given 4 years were the exports more than imports.

75. (A): (A) 1997 ⇒ 0.35 : 1 ⇒ 7 : 20

(B) 1995 ⇒ 0.65 : 1 ⇒ 13 : 20

(C) 1996 ⇒ 0.85 : 1 ⇒ 17 : 20

(D) 2000 ⇒ 0.95 : 1 ⇒ 19 : 20

Here, the imports were minimum proportionate to the exports of the company in 1997.

76. (C): Given, the imports of a company in 1996

= ₹ 272 crores

The ratio of imports and exports in 1996

= 0.85 : 1 = 85 : 100

∴ $85x = 272 \Rightarrow x = \frac{272}{85}$

∴ $100x = 100\times\frac{272}{85} = 20\times\frac{272}{17}$

= 20 × 16 = ₹ 320 crores

Hence, the required exports from the company in 1996 was ₹ 320 crores.

78. (B): Given, the imports in 1998 = ₹ 250 crores

∴ The exports in 1998 = $\frac{250}{1.25}$ = 200 crores

Given, the total exports in years 1998 and 1999

= ₹ 500 crores

∴ The exports in 1999 = 500 – 200 = 300 crores

Hence, the imports in 1999 = 1.4 × 300

= 420.0 crores = 420 crores.

79. (A): From table-chart:

The average amount of interest per year

$= \frac{23.4+32.5+41.6+36.4+49.4}{5}$

$= \frac{183.3}{5}$ = 36.66 lakhs.

80. (B): The total amount of bonus paid by the company during the given period

= 3.00 + 2.52 + 3.84 + 3.68 + 3.96

= 17 lakhs

and the total amount of salary paid during this period

= 288 + 342 + 324 + 336 + 420 = 1710 lakhs

$\therefore$ Required per cent $= \frac{\text{Total Bonus}}{\text{Total Salary}} \times 100$

$= \frac{17}{1710} \times 100 = 1\%$ (Approx).

81. (D): Required per cent

$= \frac{\text{Total expenditure in 1998}}{\text{Total expenditure in 2002}}$

$= \frac{288 + 98 + 3.00 + 23.4 + 83}{420 + 142 + 3.96 + 49.4 + 98} \times 100$

$= \frac{495.4}{713.96} \times 100 = 69\%$ (Approx.)

82. (B): Total expenditure in 2000

= 324 + 101 + 3.84 + 41.6 + 74

= 544.44 lakhs.

83. (C): Required ratio

$= \frac{\text{Total expenditure on taxes}}{\text{Total expenditure on fuel and transport}}$

$= \frac{83 + 108 + 74 + 88 + 98}{98 + 11 + 101 + 133 + 142}$

$= \frac{451}{586} = \frac{450}{585} = \frac{10 \times 45}{13 \times 45} = \frac{10}{13} = 10 : 13.$

For Qs. No. 84-90:

From given pie-chart:

$100 = 360°$

$\Rightarrow \quad 1 = \frac{360}{100} = \frac{18°}{5}$

84. (A): Central angle of expenditure on Royalty

$= 15 = 15 \times \frac{18°}{5} = 54°.$

85. (D): (A) Binding Cost + Royalty Cost

$= 30 + 15 = 45$

$= 45 \times \frac{18°}{5} = 9 \times 18 = 162°$

(B) Printing cost + Paper cost

$= 20 + 25 = 45 = 162°$

(C) Binding cost + Transportation cost

$= 30 + 10 = 40$

$= 40 \times \frac{18°}{5} = 8 \times 18 = 144°$

(D) Printing cost + Transportation cost

$= 20 + 10 = 30$

$= 30 \times \frac{18°}{5} = 6 \times 18 = 108°.$

86. (B): (A) Binding cost – Royalty

$= 30 - 20 = 10$

$= 10 \times \frac{18°}{5} = 36°$

(B) Paper cost – Printing cost

$= 25 - 20 = 5 \times \frac{18°}{5} = 18°$

(C) Paper cost – Royalty

$= 25 - 15$

$= \frac{56250}{25} \times 10 = 36°$

(D) Royalty – Promotion cost

$= 15 - 10 = 5 \times \frac{18°}{5} = 18°$

87. (C): Given, the cost of paper = ₹ 56250

$\therefore$ The promotion cost $= \frac{56250}{25} \times 10 =$ ₹ 22500.

88. (D): Given, Printing cost = ₹ 30,600

$\therefore$ Amount of Royalty $= \frac{30600}{20} \times 15$

$= 1530 \times 15 =$ ₹ 22950.

90. (B): Royalty on the book is less than the printing cost by

$\frac{20 - 15}{20} \times 100 = \frac{5}{20} \times 100 = 25\%.$

91. (C): (Total number of pens sold on Monday and Tuesday) – (Total number of pens sold on Thursday and Friday)

= (25 + 75) – (45 + 50)

= 100 – 95 = 5.

92. (A): Total number of pens sold on Wednesday = 30

$\therefore$ Total number of pens sold on Saturday

$= 30 \times \frac{140}{100} = 42$

Hence, total number of pens sold on Friday and Saturday = 50 + 42 = 92.

93. (D): Let total number of pens sold on Sunday be x

Then total number of pens sold on Tuesday

$= x \times \frac{125}{100}$

$$\Rightarrow \quad 75 = \frac{5}{4}x$$

$$\Rightarrow \quad x = \frac{75 \times 4}{5} = 60.$$

94. (B): Total pen sold on Thursday = 45

$\therefore$ Blue ink pen = $45 \times \frac{20}{100} = 9$

Remaining = 45 – 9 = 36

$\therefore$ Red ink pen = $36 \times \frac{25}{100} = 9$

Black ink pen = 36 – 9 = 27

Hence, total number of blue and black ink pen sold on Thursday = 9 + 27 = 36.

95. (D): Total pens sold on Tuesday = 75

and (total defective pens sold) : (Total pens sold) = 7 : 15

$\therefore$ $15x = 75 \Rightarrow x = 5$

$\therefore$ Total defective pens sold = $7x = 7 \times 5 = 35$

Hence, total number of non-defective pens sold on Tuesday = 75 – 35 = 40

From Qs. No. 96-100.

From given pie-chart and table:

Total workers = 900

Workers in A = $900 \times \frac{32}{100} = 288 = 16 \times 18$

Workers in B = $900 \times \frac{44}{100} = 396 = 18 \times 22$

Workers in C = 9 × 24 = 216 = 12 × 18

Officers in A = 18

Officers in B = 22

Officers in C = 18

96. (C): Required ratio = (Total numbers of workers in A and C) : (Total number of officers in A and C)

= (288 + 216) : (18 + 18)

= 504 : 36 = 14 : 1.

97. (D): Total number of employees (B – C)

= 396 + 22 – (216 + 18)

= 418 – 234 = 184.

98. (A): Total number of officers in Company B – A

= 22 – 18 = 4.

99. (B): Total number of officers in C = 18

and total numbers of workers in C = 216

$\therefore$ Total number of officers and workers in Company D

$= 18 \times \frac{150}{100} + 216 \times \frac{125}{100}$

$= 18 \times \frac{3}{2} + 216 \times \frac{5}{4}$

= 27 + 54 × 5 = 27 + 270 = 297.

100. (D): Total number of workers in Company

= (B + C) – A = (396 + 216) – 288

= 612 – 288 = 324.

103. (A): 1, 4, 27, 16, [125], 36, 343

$\Rightarrow 1^3, \ 2^2, \ 3^3, \ 4^2, \ 5^3, \ 6^2, \ 7^3$

$\Rightarrow$ 1, 2, 3, 4, 5, 6, 7

Here, ? = the missing term = 125.

104. (B): 20 19 17 [14] 10 5

–1 –2 –3 –4 –5

Here, ? = the missing term = 14.

105. (C):

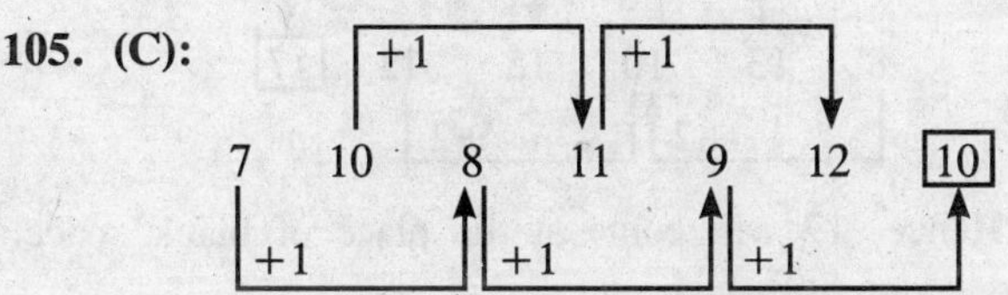

Here, ? = the missing number = 10.

106. (C):

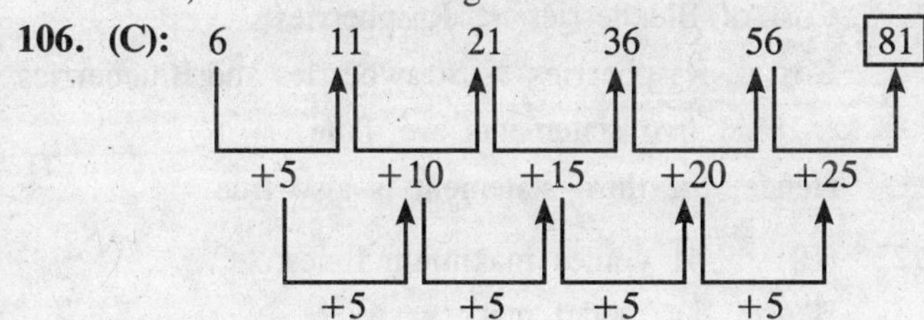

Here, ? = the missing number = 81.

109. (B): The number of matches will be played during the tournament

$$= \frac{n(n-1)}{2} = \frac{6(6-1)}{2}$$

= 3 × 5 = 15.

111. (B): Let Sunita's present age = x years

Then, Reena's present age = $2x$ years

3 years ago,

$3(x - 3) = 2x - 3$

$\Rightarrow 3x - 9 = 2x - 3$

$\Rightarrow 3x - 2x = 9 - 3$

$\Rightarrow x = 6$

$\therefore$ Reena's present age = $2x = 2 \times 6 = 12$ years.

113. (B): Total number of persons in a group = 1200 and (15 soldiers + 1 captain) = 16 persons

∴ The numbers of captains in the group

$$= \frac{1200}{16} = 75.$$

116. (A): As,

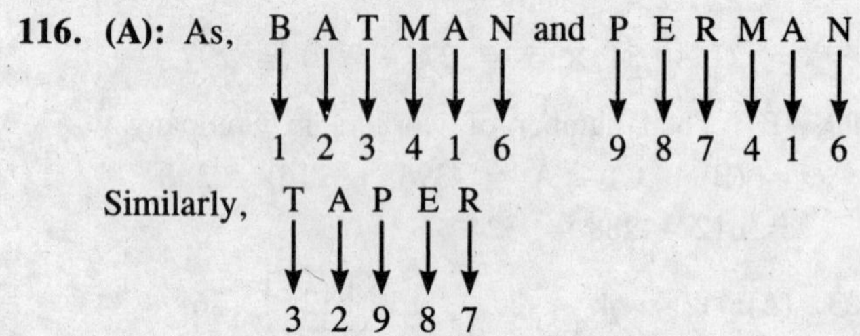

117. (C):

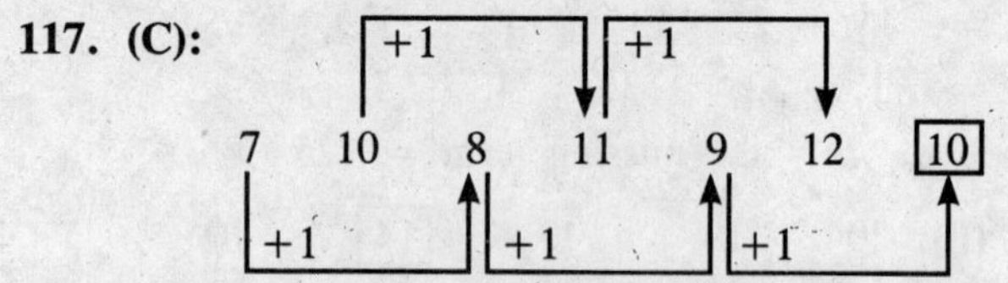

Hence, next number will come 10 in blank space.

118. (B):

+2 +2

8 13 10 15 12 17

+2 +2

Hence, 17 will come at the place of blank space.

119. (A): Cost of Blueberries > Strawberries

Cost of Blueberries < Raspberries

Cost of Raspberries > Strawberries and Blueberries

∵ First two statements are True

Hence, the third statement is also true.

122. (C): ∵ 41 comes maximum times.

Hence, the model mark = 41.

124. (B):

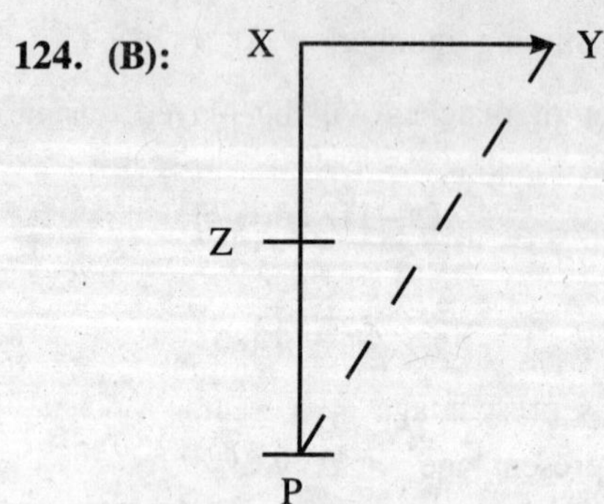

Hence, required direction is South-West.

127. (B):

10th 9th

A B

B A 15th

Number of persons = 15 + 8 = 23.

128. (C):

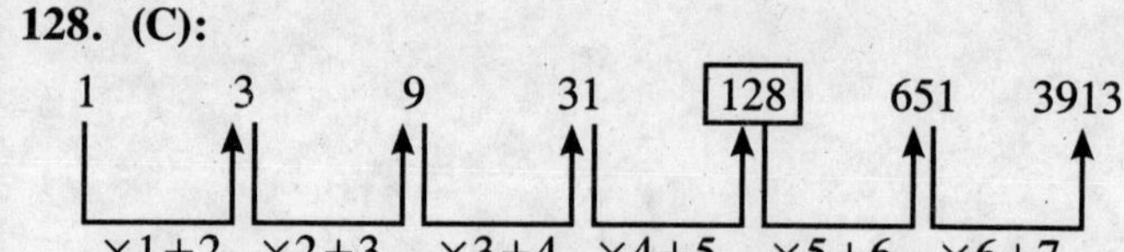

Hence, wrong number = 128.

129. (A):

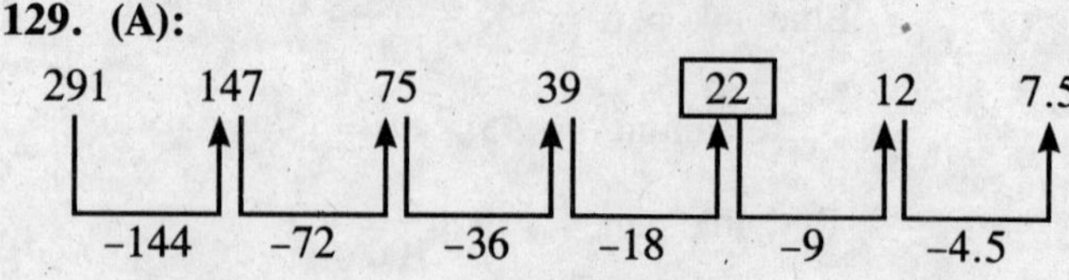

Hence, wrong number = 22.

130. (A): Let Present age of A = x years

and present age of B = y years

6 years ago A's age = $(x - 6)$ years

6 years ago B's age = $(y - 6)$ years

$$x - 6 + y - 6 = 88$$

$$\Rightarrow \quad x + y = 100 \qquad \ldots(i)$$

18 years ago,

$$\text{A's age} = x - 18$$

According to the question,

$$x - 18 = y - 6$$

$$\Rightarrow \quad x - y = 12 \qquad \ldots(ii)$$

From (*i*) and (*ii*),

$$x + y = 100$$

$$x - y = 12$$

$$2x = 112 \Rightarrow x = 56$$

$$y = 94 - 56 = 38$$

After 2 years, A's age = 56 + 2 = 58 years.

For Qs. No. 131-135.

Boxes	Number of Chocolates
A	64
D	39
G	27
E	41
B	13
F	78
C	50

131. (A): GE boxes is kept exactly between box D and box B.

132. (C): Box E = 41 Chocolates.

133. (C): Maximum number of Chocolates F = 78

Minimum number of Chocolates B = 13.

134. (A): D = 39 Chocolates.

135. (D): Box F is kept immediately below box B.

137. (A): State Bank of India (SBI) issued its first infrastructure bonds on December 2, 2022. On January 18, 2023, SBI issued a second 15-year infrastructure bond, the first time an Indian bank has issued a 15-year infrastructure bond. SBI's third infrastructure bond issuance raised ₹ 10,000 crore at a coupon rate of 7.54% on July 31, 2023.

138. (D): Yoginder K. Alagh is known as an economist. An economist is someone who studies and analyzes economic systems, policies, and trends. They often conduct research, provide insights into economic issues, and offer recommendations for economic development and policy formulation. Yoginder K. Alagh has made significant contributions to the field of economics through his research, publications, and involvement in policy-making. He may have expertise in various areas of economics such as agricultural economics, development economics, or industrial economics, depending on his specific focus and contributions.

139. (C): The Paradise of Food by Khalid Jawed was originally published in Urdu in 2014 under the title Ne'mat Khana. It was translated into English by Baran Farooqi and won the 2022 JCB Prize for Literature. The book is about an orphaned Muslim boy named Guddu Miyaan who grows up in a joint family. The JCB Prize described the book as a "bracing counter-narrative" to hyper-consumerism, and praised the translation for highlighting the original text's poetry and music.

140. (C): Sharath Kamal won three gold medals for India at the Commonwealth Games 2022. Achanta Sharath Kamal was born on July 12, 1982, in Chennai, Tamil Nadu, a city known for its table tennis prowess and multiple national champions.

141. (A): INS Vagir, the fifth Scorpene class submarine of Project 75, was delivered to the Indian Navy in December. It belongs to the Kalvari class submarine, a part of India's indigenous submarine construction program aimed at enhancing naval capabilities. These submarines are equipped with advanced stealth features and state-of-the-art technology, making them formidable assets for the Indian Navy's underwater operations. INS Vagir's delivery marks another significant milestone in India's efforts to bolster its maritime defense capabilities and strengthen its naval fleet, contributing to national security and defense readiness in the region.

142. (A): Statement I refers to the Reserve Bank of India's (RBI) Medium-term Strategy Framework for the period 2023-2025. Utkarsh 2.0 is indeed part of RBI's strategic framework aimed at achieving certain goals or objectives over the specified period. Statement II states that Utkarsh 2.0 was launched by the Governor of RBI. This indicates the official launch of the initiative by the highest authority of the RBI, emphasizing its significance and official endorsement.

143. (B): Sahyadri Farmer Producer Company (FPC), inaugurated recently, marks a significant milestone as India's first private agriculture mandi. Situated in Nashik district of Maharashtra, this initiative aims to transform agricultural trade practices by providing a platform for farmers to directly sell their produce to buyers. By bypassing traditional intermediaries, such as commission agents, farmers can potentially receive better prices for their crops, leading to increased income and empowerment. The establishment of Sahyadri FPC underscores efforts to modernize and streamline agricultural marketing systems, ultimately benefiting both farmers and consumers alike.

144. (B): State Bank of India (SBI) holds the maximum shareholding in Yes Bank, signifying a significant stake in the latter's ownership structure. This ownership arrangement highlights SBI's strategic interest and involvement in Yes Bank's operations and governance. As one of India's largest public sector banks, SBI's substantial investment in Yes Bank reflects its commitment to the stability and growth of the banking sector. The significant shareholding by SBI also underscores its role in supporting Yes Bank's restructuring efforts and facilitating its recovery from financial challenges. Overall, SBI's dominant position in Yes Bank's shareholding reinforces its influence and impact on the bank's future direction and performance.

145. (D): As reported in a recent newspaper, N Chandrasekaran, the CEO of Tata Consultancy Services (TCS), has assumed the chair of B20 India and is leading the business agenda during India's G20 presidency. This appointment highlights Chandrasekaran's influential role in shaping the business discourse and priorities within the G20 framework. With his extensive experience and leadership in the corporate sector, Chandrasekaran is well-positioned to advocate for key economic and business-related issues on behalf of India's business community. His leadership in the B20 forum underscores the importance of private sector engagement and collaboration in driving global economic growth and development agendas.

146. (B): There are six credit rating agencies registered under SEBI namely, CRISIL, ICRA, CARE, SMERA, Fitch India and Brickwork Ratings.

CRISIL (Credit Rating Information Services of India Limited): A leading agency with a strong presence in various segments, including corporate, structured finance, and infrastructure.

ICRA (Investment Information and Credit Rating Agency of India Limited): Known for its expertise in project finance, infrastructure, and public finance.

CARE (Credit Analysis & Research Limited): Emphasizes transparency and objectivity, focusing on corporate, infrastructure, and financial institutions.

India Ratings and Research Pvt. Ltd. (formerly Fitch Ratings India Pvt. Ltd.): Part of the Fitch Group, offering credit ratings across various sectors like corporates, banks, and sovereign entities.

Brickwork Ratings India Pvt Ltd.: Specializes in assigning credit ratings to small and medium enterprises (SMEs) and infrastructure projects.

SMERA Ratings Limited: Focused on evaluating the credit-worthiness of micro, small, and medium enterprises (MSMEs).

147. (B): The Reserve Bank of India (RBI) fined RBL Bank Ltd ₹ 2.27 crore in March 2023 for not complying with certain directives on loan recovery agents. The RBI's actions are based on deficiencies in regulatory compliance from 2018-19 to 2021-22. The RBI's statement says that the action is not intended to comment on the validity of any transactions or agreements between the bank and its customers.

148. (A): Autotrac Finance Limited Ltd (AFL) is based in the state of Haryana. This strategic partnership between Axis Bank and AFL under the co-lending model through the Yubi Co. Lend platform signifies a collaborative effort to offer financial products and services to customers, particularly in the domain of lending. Such partnerships leverage the strengths and resources of both entities to enhance the accessibility and efficiency of financial services, ultimately benefiting consumers and driving economic growth.

149. (C): The 4R strategy is a comprehensive strategy implemented by the Indian government to reduce the number of non-performing assets (NPAs) faced by public sector banks (PSBs). The strategy consists of the following steps: Recognition, Resolution, Recovery, Recapitalization, Reforms. The 4R strategy is a response to the twin balancesheet problem, which occurs when heavily indebted corporations cause banks to lose money and enter non-performing assets (NPAs). An NPA is a debt where the borrower has been unable to make interest and principal payments to the lender for an extended period of time.

150. (A): The Yuva Utsav, held on the theme of 'Panch Pran of Amrit Kaal - India @2047', recently took place in the Siaha district of Mizoram, marking the celebration of Azadi Ka Amrit Mahotsav in the spirit of Yuva Shakti.

151. (D): The Competition Commission of India (CCI) has approved Reliance Retail Ventures' (RRVL's) acquisition of METRO Cash & Carry India for a cash consideration of ₹ 2,850 crore. The acquisition was announced in December 2022, and the CCI approval was received in March 2023. The deal is expected to be completed by the end of 2023. METRO Cash & Carry India is a wholly-owned subsidiary of German international wholesaler METRO AG. It operates 31 wholesale distribution centers in India. Reliance Retail Ventures is a subsidiary of Reliance Industries, and is one of the largest retailers in India.

152. (B): Statement (*ii*) indicates that the sex ratio at birth increased by three points to 907 in 2018-20 from 904 in 2017-19, highlighting a positive trend towards a more balanced sex ratio among newborns in India. This suggests potential improvements in addressing gender-based discrimination and promoting gender equality at birth.

Statement (*iii*) mentions that India's Labour Force Participation Rate (LFPR) has been on the rise since 2017-2018. This indicates an increasing trend of both men and women participating in the labor force, which is essential for economic growth and development. A rising LFPR suggests improved opportunities for women in the workforce and reflects progress towards gender equality in employment.

153. (D): The Jalyukt Shivar project, initiated by the Government of Maharashtra, aims to address water scarcity and enhance water conservation measures in drought-prone areas of the state. Through this project, various interventions are implemented to augment water storage, recharge groundwater levels, and improve irrigation facilities in regions vulnerable to drought. The project employs techniques such as construction of check dams, farm ponds, contour trenches, and watershed management practices to capture and conserve rainwater effectively.

154. (D): Dhanya Rajendran has been named the 2022 recipient of the Chameli Devi Jain Award for Outstanding Women Media Persons. This prestigious award recognizes her significant contributions to the field of journalism and media.

As the co-founder and editor-in-chief of The News Minute, an independent digital media platform, Rajendran has played a pivotal role in shaping public discourse and providing insightful coverage of a wide range of socio-political issues.

155. (B): New York Community Bank has agreed to buy a significant chunk of Signature Bank in a $2.7 billion deal, as reported by the Federal Deposit Insurance Corp (FDIC). This acquisition marks a significant move in the banking sector, reflecting ongoing consolidation efforts and strategic expansion plans among financial institutions. With this deal, New York Community Bank aims to enhance its market presence and strengthen its position in the banking industry.

156. (D): RailTel Corporation of India Ltd has been awarded a work order by the Centre for Development of Advanced Computing (C-DAC) amounting to Rs 287.57 crores. The project entails the supply, installation, integration, testing, and commissioning of IT infrastructure in greenfield data centers located in New Delhi and Bengaluru, along with providing training and support services. The delivery period for the project is stipulated at 300 days, indicating a time-bound initiative to bolster IT infrastructure capabilities.

157. (C): Under the Stand-Up India scheme, loans totaling Rs 39,517 crore have been sanctioned since its launch in April 2016, as of February. This initiative aims to empower entrepreneurs from marginalized sections of society, particularly Scheduled Castes (SCs), Scheduled Tribes (STs), and Women, by facilitating access to financial assistance and promoting entrepreneurship. The scheme has provided a significant boost to economic empowerment, with approximately 1.75 lakh loans sanctioned to eligible beneficiaries.

158. (C): The Ministry of Statistics and Programme Implementation (MoSPI) released the 24th issue of "Women and Men in India 2022," an annual publication that provides comprehensive statistics on gender-related indicators and socio-economic trends in India. This report serves as a valuable resource for policymakers, researchers, and organizations working to address gender disparities and promote gender equality in various sectors. By presenting data-driven insights into areas such as education, employment, health, and empowerment, the report facilitates evidence-based decision-making and advocacy efforts aimed at advancing gender equality and women's empowerment across the country.

159. (B): The collaboration between IFFCO and Coal India Ltd (CIL) to manufacture Nano DAP (Di-Ammonium Phosphate) is set to span a period of three years. This partnership aims to leverage the expertise and resources of both organizations to produce Nano DAP, a crucial fertilizer component, ensuring its availability and contributing to the agricultural sector.

160. (C): The state government of Maharashtra has opted to initiate the second phase of the Jalyukt Shivar project, a scheme aimed at addressing water scarcity in drought-prone areas through various water conservation measures. Jalyukt Shivar, which translates to "Water-Rich Village," emphasizes the creation of water storage structures, watershed development, and efficient water management practices to recharge groundwater levels and mitigate the impact of droughts.

161. (A): The United Kingdom (UK) Treasury and the Bank of England have orchestrated a private sale of the UK subsidiary of the collapsed Silicon Valley Bank to HSBC Holdings Plc's 'ring fenced subsidiary' for a nominal sum of 1 pound sterling. This transaction, facilitated amid the fallout of the Silicon Valley Bank's collapse, symbolizes a strategic move to transfer the subsidiary's operations and assets to HSBC, a major player in the banking sector. The sale, conducted for a minimal amount, indicates a restructuring effort within the UK banking industry.

162. (C): To avert a potential financial domino effect triggered by Credit Suisse's woes, its larger and more stable Swiss counterpart, Union Bank of Switzerland (UBS), stepped in with a strategic acquisition valued at around $3.25 billion. This move not only injected much-needed financial support into Credit Suisse, but also served as a dam against wider market panic. While the deal reshaped the Swiss banking landscape by consolidating power and potentially impacting future operations for both institutions, its true significance lies in averting a broader financial crisis that could have had far-reaching consequences.

163. (A): The Department of Social Justice and Empowerment has signed a memorandum of understanding (MoU) with the Prajapati Brahma Kumari Ishwariya Vishwa Vidyalaya, Mount Abu in New Delhi. This collaboration aims to spread awareness about the Nasha Mukt Bharat Abhiyaan (NMBA) among youth, women, and students. By partnering with the Vishwa Vidyalaya, the department seeks to leverage their platforms and networks to effectively communicate the objectives and messages of the NMBA.

164. (B): Yellow journalism is a style of reporting characterized by sensationalism, exaggeration, and manipulation of facts to create attention-grabbing and often misleading stories. Originating in the late 19th century, particularly associated with certain newspapers in the United States, yellow journalism prioritizes attracting readership over accuracy and impartiality. It often involves sensational headlines, lurid illustrations, and biased or inflammatory language to evoke strong emotional reactions from readers.

165. (A): The Pradhan Mantri MUDRA Yojana (PMMY) is a government initiative aimed at bringing small entrepreneurs into the formal financial system. Through this scheme, small business owners, particularly those belonging to the Micro, Small, and Medium Enterprises (MSME) sector, are provided access to credit from formal financial institutions like banks and non-banking financial companies (NBFCs). The scheme offers financial assistance in the form of loans, categorized into three segments: Shishu, Kishor, and Tarun, based on the stage of growth and funding requirements of the business. By facilitating access to finance, PMMY aims to empower entrepreneurs, foster entrepreneurship, and boost economic growth by promoting small businesses across various sectors.

166. (D: A "Closed Economy" refers to an economic system where there is no involvement in international trade, meaning there are no imports or exports. In this type of economy, all goods and services consumed are produced domestically, and there is minimal interaction with foreign markets. This scenario often arises in countries that prioritize self-sufficiency and have strict regulations or restrictions on international trade. As a result, economic activities are largely confined within the borders of the country, and there is limited exposure to fluctuations in global markets.

167. (A): The TAPI project, which stands for Turkmenistan-Afghanistan-Pakistan-India, is a multi-billion dollar venture aimed at transporting natural gas from Turkmenistan's Galkynysh Gas Field to Afghanistan, Pakistan, and India. The project, which began construction in December 2015, involves laying down a pipeline spanning approximately 1,800 kilometers. It holds significant strategic importance for the involved countries, as it promises to meet the growing energy demands of South Asia while also fostering economic cooperation and stability in the region.

168. (C): Value Added Tax (VAT) is a consumption tax levied on the value added to goods and services at each stage of their production or distribution. Unlike a sales tax, which is imposed only at the point of sale to the end consumer, VAT is imposed on all stages of production and distribution, including manufacturing, wholesale, and retail. This means that each time value is added to a product or service, VAT is applied to that added value. Ultimately, the final consumer bears the burden of the VAT, as it is included in the price they pay for the product or service.

169. (B): In a strategic move to accelerate the development of IT and financial services within GIFT SEZ, India's first International Financial Services Centre, ICICI Bank emerged as the chosen partner. This 2018 alliance wasn't simply a handshake; it signified a joint effort to leverage ICICI's established strength in both sectors. By attracting and supporting businesses operating within GIFT SEZ, the collaboration aimed to create a flourishing hub for technological and financial innovation. More than just filling empty office spaces, the partnership envisioned nurturing an ecosystem where cutting-edge IT solutions and diverse financial services could thrive, ultimately contributing to GIFT SEZ's growth and solidifying its position as a key player in India's economic landscape.

170. (C): The Reserve Bank of India (RBI) mandates that Non-Banking Financial Companies (NBFCs) must meet certain financial criteria to issue credit cards. One such criterion is the minimum net-owned fund, which signifies the company's capital strength and ability to absorb losses. For NBFCs seeking to venture into credit card issuance, the RBI requires a substantial net-owned fund of at least ₹ 100 crores. This requirement ensures that NBFCs have a solid financial foundation to manage the risks associated with credit card operations, including credit defaults and market fluctuations. By setting this threshold, the RBI aims to safeguard the interests of credit card users and maintain the stability of the financial system.

Previous Paper (Solved)

Jamia Millia Islamia (JMI)

MBA (Full Time) Entrance Examination-2022*

Quantitative Analysis

1. The domain of the function

$f(x) = \sqrt{(2 - 2x - x^2)}$ $f(x) = (2 - 2x - x^2)$ is:

A. $-1 - \sqrt{3} \leq x \leq -1 + \sqrt{3}$ $-1 - 3 \leq x \leq -1 + 3$

B. $-2 \leq x \leq 2$ $-2 \leq x \leq 2$

C. $-2 + \sqrt{3} \leq x \leq -2 - \sqrt{3}$

D. $-\sqrt{3} \leq x \leq \sqrt{3}$ $-3 \leq x \leq 3$

2. $f(x) = \sqrt{((x + 1)(x - 3)(x - 2))}$ $f(x) = ((x + 1)(x - 3)(x - 2))$ is a real value function in the domain:

A. $(-\infty, -1] \cup [3, \infty)$ $(-\infty, -1] \cup [3, \infty)$

B. $(-\infty, -1] \cup [2, 3]$ $(-\infty, -1] \cup [2, 3]$

C. $[-1, 2) \cup [3\infty)$ $[-1, 2) \cup [3\infty)$

D. None of these

Directions (Qs. No. 3-5): *The passage given below is followed by four alternate summaries. Choose the option that best captures the essence of the passage.*

3. The four sentences (labelled 1, 2, 3, 4) given in this question, when properly sequenced, form a coherent paragraph. Each sentence is labelled with a number. Decide on the proper sequence of order of the sentences and key in this sequence of four numbers as your answer:

1. They would rather do virtuous side projects assiduously as long as these would not compel them into doing their day jobs more honorably or reduce the profit margins.
2. They would fund a million of the buzzwordy programs rather than fundamentally question the rules of their game or alter their own behavior to reduce the harm of the existing distorted, inefficient and unfair rules.
3. Like the dieter who would rather do anything to lose weight than actually eat less, the business elite would save the world through social-impact-investing and philanthro-capitalism.
4. Doing the right thing — and moving away from their win-win mentality — would involve real sacrifice; instead, it's easier to focus on their pet projects and initiatives.

A. 3421 B. 3241

C. 2134 D. 3124

4. The five sentences (labelled 1, 2, 3, 4) given in this question, when properly sequenced, form a coherent paragraph. Decide on the proper order for the sentence and key in this sequence of five numbers as your answer.

1. Scientists have for the first time managed to ed genes in a human embryo to repair a genetic mutation, fuelling hopes that such procedures may one day be available outside laboratory conditions.
2. The cardiac disease causes sudden death in otherwise healthy young athletes and affects about one in 500 people overall.
3. Correcting the mutation in the gene would not only ensure that the child is healthy but also prevents transmission of the mutation to future generations.
4. It is caused by a mutation in a particular gene and a child will suffer from the condition even if it inherits only one copy of the mutated gene.

A. 1243 B. 3214

C. 4123 D. 1234

5. As Soviet power declined, the world became to some extent multipolar, and Europe strove to define an independent identity. What a journey Europe has undertaken to reach this point. It had in every century changed its internal structure and invented new ways of thinking about the nature of international order. Now at the culmination of an era, Europe, in order to participate in it, felt obliged to set aside the political mechanisms through which it had conducted its affairs for three and a half centuries. Impelled also by the desire to cushion the emergent unification of Germany, the new European Union established a common currency in 2002 and a formal political structure in 2004. It proclaimed a Europe united, whole, and free, adjusting its differences by peaceful mechanisms.

1. Europe has consistently changed its internal structure to successfully adapt to the changing world order.
2. Europe has consistently changed in keeping with the changing world order and that has culminated in a united Europe.
3. The establishment of a formal political structure in Europe was hastened by the unification of Germany and the emergence of a multipolar world.
4. Europe has chosen to lower political and economic heterogeneity, in order to adapt itself to an emerging multi-polar world.

A. 1 B. 2

C. 3 D. 4

6. Five jumbled up sentences, related to a topic, are given below. Four of them can be put together to form a coherent paragraph. Identify the odd one out and key in the number of the sentence as your answer:

1. Talk was the most common way for enslaved men and women to subvert the rules of their bondage, to gain more agency than they were supposed to have.
2. Even in conditions of extreme violence and unfreedom, their words remained ubiquitous, ephemeral, irrepressible, and potentially transgressive.
3. Slaves came from societies in which oaths, orations, and invocations carried great potency, both between people and as a connection to the all-powerful spirit world.
4. Freedom of speech and the power to silence may have been preeminent markers of white liberty in Colonies, but at the same time, slavery depended on dialogue: slaves could never be completely muted.

A. 4 B. 1
C. 2 D. 3

7. Identify the most appropriate summary for the paragraph.

North American walnut sphinx moth caterpillars (Amorpha juglandis) look like easy meals for birds, but they have a trick up their sleeves—they produce whistles that sound like bird alarm calls, scaring potential predators away. At first, scientists suspected birds were simply startled by the loud noise. But a new study suggests a more sophisticated mechanism: the caterpillar's whistle appears to mimic a bird alarm call, sending avian predators scrambling for cover. When pecked by a bird, the caterpillars whistle by compressing their bodies like an accordion and forcing air out through specialized holes in their sides. The whistles are impressively loud - they have been measured at over 80 dB from 5 cm away from the caterpillar - considering they are made by a two-inch long insect.

A. North American walnut sphinx moth caterpillars will whistle periodically to ward off predator birds—they have a specialized vocal tract that helps them whistle.
B. North American walnut sphinx moth caterpillars can whistle very loudly; the loudness of their whistles is shocking as they are very small insects.
C. North American walnut sphinx moth caterpillars, in a case of acoustic deception, produce whistles that mimic bird alarm calls to defend themselves.
D. North American walnut sphinx moth caterpillars, in a case of deception and camouflage, produce whistles that mimic bird alarm calls to defend themselves.

8. Train service suffers when a railroad combines commuter and freight service. By dividing its attention between its freight and commuter customers, a railroad serves neither particularly well. Therefore, if a railroad is going to be a successful business, then it must concentrate exclusively on one of these two markets.

For the argument to be logically correct, it must make which one of the following assumptions?

A. Commuter and freight service have little in common with each other.
B. Unless a railroad serves its customers well, it will not be a successful business.
C. If a railroad concentrates on customer service, it will be a successful business.
D. The first priority of a railroad is to be a successful business.

Directions (Qs. No. 9): *Read the paragraph and answer the question given below:*

The term "pit bull" does not designate a breed of dog, as do the terms "German shepherd" and "poodle." It is like the terms "Seeing-Eye dog" and "police dog," which designate dogs according to what they do. If you take two German shepherds and place them side by side, you cannot tell by appearance alone which is the police dog and which is the Seeing-Eye dog.

9. Which one of the following is the main point of the passage?

A. Some breeds of dogs cannot be distinguished from other breeds of dogs by appearance alone.
B. Pit bulls can be distinguished from other kinds of dogs by appearance alone.
C. A dog is a pit bull because of what it does, not because of its breed.
D. German shepherds can function both as police dogs and as Seeing-Eye dogs.

Directions (Qs. No. 10-11): *Fill up the blanks to make the sentence appropriate.*

10. How much a man earns is as important as ______.

A. why does he earn of all
B. when does he do so
C. where does he earn
D. how does he do it

11. The notice at the petrol pump should be _____.

A. all engines must have to be switched off.
B. all engines have to be switched off.
C. all engines need to be switched off.
D. all engines must be switched off.

Directions (Qs. No. 12-14): *Choose the correct synonym of the given word.*

12. Fastidious

A. Over aspiring B. Overconfidence
C. Finicky D. Overfed

13. Alacrity

A. With suspicion B. Unwillingly
C. Eagerness D. Hesitatingly

14. Estrange

A. Miscalculate B. Alienate
C. To become puzzling D. Endanger

Directions (Qs. No. 15-18): *The given sentence below is not totally correct. Choose the correct sentence from the options given below:*

15. Only in the interest of establishing clear lines of communication among their government and ours has the President acceded to their demands in regard to the tariff dispute.

A. Only due to the interest of establishing clear lines of communication between their government and ours has the President acceded to their demands in regard to the tariff dispute.

B. Only in the interest of establishing clear lines of communication between their government and ours has the President acceded to his demands in regard to the tariff dispute.

C. Only in the interest of establishing clear lines of communication between their government and ours has the President acceded to their demands in regards with the tariff dispute.

D. Only in the interest of establishing clear lines of communication between their government and ours has the President acceded to their demands in regard to the tariff dispute.

16. The result of all these lengthy legal actions, counter-claims, and appeals, stretching over several months, were simply huge bills from the lawyers and nothing else.

A. The result of lengthy legal actions, counterclaims, and appeals, stretching over several months, were simply huge bills from the lawyers and nothing else.

B. The result of all lengthy legal actions, counterclaims, and appeals, stretching over several months, were huge bills from the lawyers and nothing else.

C. The result of all lengthy legal actions, counterclaims, and appeals, stretching over several months, were simply huge bills from the lawyers and nothing else.

D. The result of all lengthy legal actions, counterclaims, and appeals, stretching over several months, were simply huge bills from lawyers and nothing else.

17. Mother dolphins whistle to their calves frequently after birth so that the calves will learn recognizing their distinctive whistle.

A. learn to recognize their distinctive whistle.

B. will learn to recognize their distinctive whistle.

C. learn recognizing their distinctive whistle.

D. learn to recognize their mother's distinctive whistle.

18. Most people cope up with anxiety by reaching for food rather then deal with their feelings.

A. cope up with anxiety by reaching for food rather than deal with their feelings.

B. cope with anxiety by reaching for food rather than dealing with their feelings.

C. cope up with anxiety by reaching for food rather than dealing with their feelings.

D. cope with anxiety by reaching for food rather than deal with their feelings.

Directions (Qs. No. 19-45): *Read the passages and answer the questions based on it.*

Passage I

Bernard Bailyn has recently reinterpreted the early history of the United States by applying new social research findings on the experiences of European migrants. In his reinterpretation, migration becomes the organizing principle for rewriting the history of preindustrial North America. His approach rests on four separate propositions.

The first of these asserts that residents of early modern England moved regularly about their countryside; migrating to the New World was simply a "natural spillover." Although at first the colonies held little positive attraction for the English—they would rather have stayed home—by the eighteenth-century people increasingly migrated to Ameri a because they regarded it as the land of opportunity. Secon Bailyn holds that, contrary to the notion that used to flou in America history textbooks, there was never a typical N World community. For example, the economic and demograp character of early New England towns varied considerably.

Bailyn's third proposition suggests two general patterns prevailing among the many thousands of migrants: one group came as indentured servants; another came to acquire land. Surprisingly, Bailyn suggests that those who recruited indentured servants were the driving forces of transatlantic migration. These colonial entrepreneurs helped determine the social character of people who came to preindustrial North America. At first, thousands of unskilled laborers were recruited; by the 1730's, however, American employers demanded skilled artisans.

Finally, Bailyn argues that the colonies were a half-civilized hinterland of the European culture system. He is undoubtedly correct to insist that the colonies were part of an Anglo-American empire. But to divide the empire into English core and colonial periphery, as Bailyn does, devalues the achievements of colonial culture. It is true, as Bailyn claims, that high culture in the colonies never matched that in England. But what of seventeenth-century New England, where the settlers created effective laws, built a distinguished university, and published books? Bailyn might respond that New England was exceptional. However, the ideas and institutions developed by New England Puritans had powerful effects on North American culture.

Although Bailyn goes on to apply his approach to som thousands of indentured servants who migrated just prior t the revolution, he fails to link their experience with t political development of the United States. Evidence presente in his work suggests how we might make such a connectio These indentured servants were treated as slaves for the perio during which they had sold their time to American employers. It is not surprising that as soon as they served their time they passed up good wages in the cities and headed west to ensure their personal independence by acquiring land. Thus, it is in the west that a peculiarly American political culture began, among colonists who were suspicious of authority and intensely anti-aristocratic.

19. The author of the passage would be most likely to agree with which of the following statements about Bailyn's work?
   A. Bailyn's description of the colonies as part of an Anglo-American empire is misleading and incorrect.
   B. Bailyn failed to test his propositions on a specific group of migrants to colonial North America.
   C. Bailyn underestimates the effects of Puritan thought on North American Culture.
   D. Bailyn overemphasizes the experiences of migrants to the New England colonies, and neglects the southern and the western parts of the New World.

20. It can be inferred from the passage that American history textbooks used to assert that:
   A. more migrants came to America out of religious or political conviction that came in the hope of acquiring land
   B. many migrants to colonial North America failed to maintain ties with their European relations
   C. the level of literacy in New England communities was very high
   D. New England communities were much alike in terms of their economics and demographics

21. The author of the passage is primarily concerned with:
   A. suggesting that new social research on migration should lead to revisions in current interpretations of early American history
   B. providing the theoretical framework that is used by most historians in under-standing early American history
   C. refuting an argument about early American history that has been proposed by social historians
   D. discussing a reinterpretation of early American history that is based on new social research on migration

22. According to the passage, which of the following is true of English migrants to the colonies during the eighteenth century?
   A. Most of them came because they were unable to find work in England.
   B. They differed from other English people in that they were willing to travel.
   C. They were generally not as educated as the people who remained in England.
   D. They expected that the colonies would offer them increased opportunity.

23. Which of the following best summarizes the author's evaluation of Bailyn's fourth proposition?
   A. It is partially correct.
   B. It is controversial though persuasive.
   C. It is highly admirable.
   D. It is intriguing though unsubstantiated.

24. According to the passage, Bailyn and the author agree on which of the following statements about the culture of colonial New England?
   A. The cultural achievements of colonial New England have generally been unrecognized by historians.
   B. The colonists imitated the high culture of England, and did not develop a culture that was uniquely their own.
   C. The southern colonies were greatly influenced by the high culture of New England.
   D. High culture in New England never equaled the high culture of England.

25. The author of the passage states that Bailyn failed to:
   A. relate the experience of the migrants to the political values that eventually shaped the character of the United States
   B. describe carefully how migrants of different ethnic backgrounds preserved their culture in the United States
   C. take advantage of social research on the experiences of colonists who migrated to colonial North America specifically to acquire land
   D. investigate the lives of Europeans before they came to colonial North America to determine more adequately their motivations for migrating

26. Which of the following statements about migrants to colonial North America is supported by information in the passage?
   A. Migrants who came to the colonies' as indentured servants were more successful at making a livelihood than were farmers and artisans.
   B. Migrants to colonial North America were more successful at acquiring their own land during the eighteenth century than during the seventeenth century.
   C. By the 1730's, migrants already skilled in a trade were in more demand by American employers than were unskilled laborers.
   D. A significant percentage of migrants who came to the colonies to acquire land were forced to work as field hands for prosperous American farmers

Passage II

According to a recent theory, Archean-age gold-quartz vein systems were formed over two billion years ago from magnetic fluids that originated from molten granite-like bodies deep beneath the surface of the Earth. This theory is contrary to the widely held view that the systems were deposited from metamorphic fluids, that is, from fluids that formed during the dehydration of wet sedimentary rocks.

The recently developed theory has considerable practical importance. Most of the gold deposits discovered during the original gold rushes were exposed at the Earth's surface and were found because they had shed trails of alluvial gold that were easily traced by simple prospecting methods. Although these same methods still lead to an occasional discovery, most deposits not yet discovered have gone undetected because they are buried and have no surface expression.

The challenge in exploration is therefore to unravel the subsurface geology of an area and pinpoint the position of buried minerals. Methods widely used today include analysis of aerial images that yield a broad geological overview; geophysical techniques that provide data on the magnetic, electrical, and mineralogical properties of the rocks being investigated; and sensitive chemical tests that are able to detect the subtle chemical halos that often envelop mineralization. However, none of these high-technology methods are of any value if the sites to which they are applied have never mineralized, and to maximize the chances of discovery the explorer must therefore pay particular attention to selecting the ground formations most likely to be mineralized. Such ground selection relies to varying degrees on conceptual models, which take into account theoretical studies of relevant factors.

These models are constructed primarily from empirical observations of known mineral deposits and from theories of ore-forming processes. The explorer uses the models to identify those geological features that are critical to the formation of the mineralization being modeled, and then tries to select areas for exploration that exhibit as many of the critical features as possible.

27. According to the passage, methods of exploring for gold that are widely used today are based on which of the following facts?
A. Most of the Earth's remaining gold deposits are exposed at the surface.
B. Most of the Earth's remaining gold deposits are buried and have no surface expression.
C. Only one type of gold deposit warrants exploration, since the other types of gold deposits are found in regions difficult to reach.
D. Only one type of gold deposit warrants exploration, since the other types of gold deposits are unlikely to yield concentrated quantities of gold.

28. The theory mentioned in line 1 of the passage, relates to the conceptual models discussed in the passage in which of the following ways?
A. It may furnish a valid account of ore-forming processes, and, hence, can support conceptual models that have great practical significance.
B. It suggests that certain geological formations, long believed to be mineralized, are in fact mineralized, thus confirming current conceptual models.
C. It suggests that there may not be enough similarity across Archean-age gold quartz vein systems to warrant the formulation of conceptual models.
D. It corrects existing theories about the chemical halos of gold deposits, and thus provides a basis for correcting current conceptual models.

29. It can be inferred from the passage that which of the following is easiest to detect?
A. A gold-quartz vein system originating in metamorphic fluids
B. A gold deposit that is mixed with granite
C. A gold deposit that exhibits chemical halos
D. A gold deposit that has shed alluvial gold

30. Which of the following statements about discoveries of gold deposits is supported by information in the passage?
A. The number of gold discoveries made annually has increased between the time of the original gold rushes and the present.
B. It is unlikely that newly discovered gold deposits will ever yield as much as did those deposits discovered during the original gold rushes.
C. New discoveries of gold deposits are likely to be the result of exploration techniques designed to locate buried mineralization.
D. Modern explorers are divided on the question of the utility of simple prospecting methods as a source of new discoveries of gold deposits.

31. The passage implies that which of the following steps would be the first performed by explorers who wish to maximize their chances of discovering gold?
A. Surveying several sites known to have been formed more than two billion years ago
B. Limiting exploration to sites known to have been formed from metamorphic fluid
C. Using an appropriate conceptual model to select a site for further exploration
D. Using geophysical methods to analyze rocks over a broad area

32. According to the passage, the widely held view of Archean-age gold-quartz vein systems is that such systems:
A. originated in molten granite-like bodies
B. were formed from metamorphic fluids
C. were formed from alluvial deposits
D. generally, have surface expression

33. The author is primarily concerned with:
A. explaining the importance of a recent theory
B. advocating a return to an older methodology
C. enumerating differences between two widely used methods
D. describing events leading to a discovery

Passage III

In an attempt to improve the overall performance of clerical workers, many companies have introduced computerized performance monitoring and control systems that record and report a worker's computer-driven activities. However, at least one study has shown that such monitoring may not be having the desired effect. In the study, researchers asked monitored clerical workers and their supervisors how assessments of productivity affected supervisors' ratings of workers' performance. In contrast to unmonitored workers doing the same work, who without exception identified the most important element in their jobs as customer service, the monitored workers and their supervisors all responded that productivity was the critical factor in assigning ratings. This finding suggested that there should have been a strong correlation between a monitored worker's productivity and the overall rating the worker received. However, measures of the relationship between overall rating and individual elements of performance clearly supported the conclusion that supervisors gave considerable weight to criteria such as attendance, accuracy, and indications of customer satisfaction.

It is possible that productivity may be a "hygiene factor," that is, if it is too low, it will hurt the overall rating. But the evidence suggests that beyond the point at which productivity becomes "good enough," higher productivity per se is unlikely to improve a rating.

34. The primary purpose of the passage is to:
A. explain the need for the introduction of an innovative strategy
B. recommend a course of action
C. discuss a study of the use of a particular method
D. resolved a difference of opinion

35. According to the passage, a "hygiene factor" is an aspect of a worker's performance that:
A. is so basic to performance that it is assumed to be adequate for all workers
B. is not likely to affect a worker's rating unless it is judged to be inadequate
C. is given less importance than it deserves in rating a worker's performance
D. is important primarily because of the effect it has on a worker's rating

36. It can be inferred that the author of the passage discusses "unmonitored workers" primarily in order to:
A. provide an example of a case in which monitoring might be effective
B. provide evidence of an inappropriate use of CPMCS
C. illustrate the effect that CPMCS may have on workers' ratings
D. emphasize the effect that CPMCS may have on workers' perceptions of their jobs

7. According to the passage, before the final results of the study were known, which of the following seemed likely?
A. That workers who initially achieved high productivity ratings would continue to do so consistently
B. That the most productive workers would be those whose supervisors claimed to value productivity
C. That the highest performance ratings would be achieved by workers with the highest productivity
D. That supervisors who claimed to value productivity would place equal value on customer satisfaction

Passage IV

During the Victorian period, women writers were measured against a social rather than a literary ideal. Hence, it was widely thought that novels by women should be modest, religious, sensitive, guileless, and chaste, like their authors. Many Victorian women writers took exception to this belief, however, resisting the imposition of nonliterary restrictions on their work. Publishers soon discovered that the gentlest and most iddylike female novelists were tough-minded and relentless when their professional integrity was at stake. Keenly aware of their artistic responsibilities, these women writers would not make concessions to secure commercial success.

The Brontes, George Eliot, Elizabeth Barrett Browning, and their lesser-known contemporaries repudiated, in their professional lives, the courtesy that Victorian ladies might exact from Victorian gentlemen. Desiring rigorous and impartial criticism, most women writers did not wish reviewers to be kind to them if kindness meant overlooking their literary weaknesses or flattering them on their accomplishments simply because of their sex. They had expected derisive reviews; instead, they found themselves confronted with generous criticism, which they considered condescending. Elizabeth Barrett Browning labeled it "the comparative respect which means... absolute scorn."

For their part, Victorian critics were virtually obsessed with finding the place of the woman writer so as to judge her appropriately. Many bluntly admitted that they thought Jane Eyre a masterpiece if written by a man, shocking or disgusting if written by a woman. Moreover, reactionary reviewers were quick to associate an independent heroine with carefully concealed revolutionary doctrine; several considered Jane Eyre a radical feminist document, as indeed it was. To Charlotte Bronte, who had demanded dignity and independence without any revolutionary intent and who considered herself politically conservative, their criticism was an affront. Such criticism bunched all women writers together rather than treating them as individual artists.

Charlotte Bronte's experience served as a warning to other women writers about the prejudices that immediately associated them with feminists and others thought to be political radicals. Irritated, and anxious to detach themselves from a group stereotype, many expressed relatively conservative views on the emancipation of women and stressed their own domestic accomplishments. However, in identifying themselves with women who had chosen the traditional career path of marriage and motherhood, these writers encountered still another threat to their creativity. Victorian prudery rendered virtually all experience that was uniquely feminine unprintable. No nineteenth-century woman dared to describe childbirth, much less her sexual passion. Men could not write about their sexual experiences either, but they could write about sport, business, crime, and war—all activities from which women were barred. Small wonder no woman produced a novel like War and Peace. What is amazing is the sheer volume of first-rate prose and poetry that Victorian women did write.

38. The passage suggests that the literary creativity of Victorian women writers could have been enhanced if:
A. novels of the period had been characterized by greater stylistic and structural ingenuity
B. a reserved and decorous style had been a more highly valued literary ideal
C. publishers had sponsored more new women novelists
D. women had been allowed to write about a broader range of subjects

39. It can be inferred from the passage that a Victorian woman writer who did not consider herself a feminist would most probably have approved of women's:
A. entering the publishing business
B. joining the stock exchange
C. joining a tennis club
D. entering a university

40. The passage suggests that the attitude of Victorian women writers toward being grouped together by critics was most probably one of:
A. indifference B. amusement
C. ambivalence D. annoyance

41. It can be inferred from the passage that Charlotte Bronte considered the criticisms leveled at Jane Eyre by reactionary reviewers "an affront" primarily because such criticism:
A. assessed the literary merit of the novel on the basis of its author's sex
B. labeled the novel shocking and disgusting without just cause
C. denied that the novel was a literary masterpiece
D. assumed that her portrayal of an inde-pendent woman represented revolutionary ideas

42. The author of the passage quotes Elizabeth Barrett Browning in order to demonstrate that Victorian women writers:
A. felt that their works were misunderstood
B. refused to make artistic concessions
C. resented condescending criticism
D. feared derisive criticism

43. The passage suggests that Victorian criticism of works by women writers was:
A. perfunctory B. resourceful
C. timely D. indulgent

44. According to the passage, Victorian women writers "would not make concessions" to publishers primarily because they felt that such concessions would:
A. require them to limit descriptions of uniquely feminine experiences
B. make them vulnerable to stereotyping by critics
C. provide no guarantee that their works would enjoy commercial success
D. compromise their artistic integrity

45. The primary purpose of the passage is to:
A. trace the historical relationship between radical feminist politics and the Victorian novels written by women
B. show how three Victorian women writers responded to criticism of their novels
C. describe the discrepancy between Victorian society's expectations of women writers and the expectations of the women writers themselves
D. resolve the apparent contradiction between Victorian women writers' literary innovativeness and their rather conservative social views

Directions (Qs. No. 46-50): *Read the information furnished below and answer the questions given below:*

Recently, the answers of a test held nationwide were leaked to a group of unscrupulous people. The investigative agency has arrested the mastermind and nine other people A, B, C, D, E, F, G, H and I in this matter. Interrogating them, the following facts have been obtained regarding their operation. Initially the mastermind obtains the correct answer-key. All the others create their answer-key in the following manner. They obtain the answer-key from one or two people who already possess the same. These people are called his/her sources. If the person has two sources, then he/she compares the answer-keys obtained from both sources. If the key to a question from both sources is identical, it is copied, otherwise it is left blank. If the person has only one source, he/she copies the sources answers into his/her copy. Finally, each person compulsorily replaces one of the answers (not a blank one) with a wrong answer in his/her answer key. The paper contained 200 questions; so the investigative agency has ruled out the possibility of two or more of them introducing wrong answers to the same question. The investigative agency has a copy of the correct answer key and has tabulated the following data. These data represent question numbers.

Name	Wrong Answer(s)	Blank Answer(s)
A	46	
B	96	46, 90, 25
C	27, 56	17, 46, 90
D	17	-
E	46, 90	-
F	14, 46	92, 90
G	25	-
H	46, 92	-
I	27	17, 46, 90

46. Both G and H were sources to:
A. None of the nine B. B
C. I D. F

47. How many people (excluding the mastermind) needed to make answer-keys before C could make his answer-key:
A. 2 B. 3
C. 4 D. 5

48. Which one among the following must have two sources:
A. A B. C
C. B D. D

49. Card on which digit 3 is written is in which cage:
A. 2 B. 1
C. 3 D. Either 1 or 2

50. Which of the following combinations of three cards chosen for prognosis is impossible:
A. 1, 2, 3 B. 5, 8, 9
C. 7, 2, 3 D. 5, 7, 6

Directions (Qs. No. 51-52): *Read the information furnished below and answer the questions given below:*

A fortune teller has a unique way of predicting his customer's fate. He has kept three parrots in three different cages. Each cage also has three cards with a single digit non-zero number inscribed on every card. No two cards have the same number and no cages contain two cards with digits summing to ten. Further the total of the numbers on the three cards in the first cage is greater than the second by two and the third cage by four. When a customer asks for his prognosis, the fortune teller lets out the three parrots which randomly pick one card out of their respective cages. Before the prognosis is made, the fortune teller totals the digits on the three cards picked out and charges the customer the same number of rupees as the total of the cards. One day a customer paid seven rupees for his prognosis.

51. What is the maximum sum of money that someone may pay?

A. 22 B. 23
C. 24 D. 21

52. What is the lowest payment possible?

A. ₹ 5 B. ₹ 7
C. ₹ 6 D. ₹ 8

Data Analysis and Sufficiency

Directions (Qs. No. 53-56): *Read the information furnished below and answer the questions given below:*

Ampee, Bumpee, Chumpee, Dumpee and Pumpee are five ducks. Initially they had 1, 2, 3, 4, 5 eggs, not necessarily in that order. They laid 1, 2, 3, 4, 5 eggs (not necessarily in that order) and finally had 4, 5, 6, 7, 8 eggs (not necessarily in that order) in the end. Further information regarding them is given:

1. Initially Dumpee had 2 eggs and ended up with 7 eggs at the end.
2. Bumpee laid 3 eggs and did not end in 8 eggs.
3. Pumpee did not lay 1 egg or 2 eggs.
4. Ampee ended with the number of eggs Chumpee started with.

53. The duck that ended with maximum number of eggs started with how many number of egg:

A. Ampee
B. Bumpee
C. Either Ampee or Bumpee
D. Chumpee

54. What is the name of the duck that laid 1 egg?

A. Ampee B. Bumpee
C. Chumpee D. Either Ampee or Bumpee

55. How many eggs the duck that ended with 6 eggs lay?

A. Bumpee laid 3 eggs and did not end in 8 eggs.
B. Pumpee did not lay 1 egg or 2 eggs.
C. Ampee ended with the number of eggs Chumpee started with.
D. Initially Dumpee had 2 eggs and ended up with 7 eggs at the end.

56. How many eggs the duck that started with 3 eggs lay?

A. Initially Dumpee had 2 eggs and ended up with 7 eggs at the end.
B. Pumpee did not lay 1 egg or 2 eggs.
C. Ampee ended with the number of eggs Chumpee started with.
D. Bumpee laid 3 eggs and did not end in 8 eggs.

57. A sum of money is sufficient to pay Sachin's salary of 45 days and kale's salary for 60 days. For how many days can the sum pay the salary of both?

A. 25 days B. 280/11 days
C. 270/11 days D. 180/7 days

58. A and B are two alloys of iron and silver prepared by mixing metals in the ratio 4 : 5 and 7 : 5 respectively. If equal quantities of alloys are melted to form a third alloy C, the ratio of iron to silver in C is:

A. 19 : 18 B. 37 : 35
C. 31 : 25 D. 29 : 35

59. In what proportion must tea at ₹ 7.50 per kg be mixed with tea at ₹ 10.50 per kg to produce a mixture worth ₹ 8.50 per kg?

A. 1 : 2 B. 2 : 3
C. 1 : 1 D. 2 : 1

60. Two full tanks, one shaped like a cylinder and the other like a cone, contain jet fuel. The cylindrical tank holds 500 litres more than the conical tank. After 200 litres of fuel has been pumped out from each tank the cylindrical tank contains twice the amount of fuel in the conical tank. How many litres of fuel did the cylindrical tank have when it was full?

A. 1200 B. 1000
C. 1100 D. 700

61. The ratio of the age of a man and his wife is 4 : 3. After 4 years, this ratio will be 9 : 7. If at the time of the marriage, the ratio was 5 : 3, then how many years ago they were married?

A. 15 years B. 8 years
C. 10 years D. 12 years

62. Total salary of A, B & C is ₹ 350. If they spend 75%, 80% & 56% of their salaries respectively their savings are as 10 : 12 : 33. Find the salary of C?

A. 80 B. 180
C. 150 D. 120

63. The cost of diamond varies directly as the square of its weight. Once, this diamond broke into four pieces with weights in the ratio 1 : 2 : 3 : 4. When the pieces were sold, the merchant got ₹ 70,000 less. Find the original price of the diamond.

A. ₹ 1.4 lakh B. ₹ 1 lakh
C. ₹ 2.5 lakh D. None of These

64. A student gets an aggregate of 60% marks in five subject in the ratio 10 : 9 : 8 : 7 : 6. If the passing marks are 50% of the maximum marks and each subject has the same maximum marks, in how many subjects did he pass the examination?
A. 2 B. 4
C. 3 D. 5

65. Two persons A and B can do a work alone in 29 days. A takes the rest of one day after every 4 days and B takes the rest of one day after every 5 days. If A and B starts working together, then the work will be completed on:
A. 15th day B. 17th day
C. 16th day D. 18th day

66. A and B do a work in exactly 16 days, B and C do the same work in exactly 12 days while C and A do the same work in about 10 days. If A, B and C can together do the work in integral number of days, then C does the work alone in:
A. 15 days B. 18 days
C. 16 days D. none of these

67. Three labourers worked together for 30 days, in the course of work, all of them remained absent for few days. One of them was absent for 10 days more than the second labourer and the third labourer did one-third of the total work. How many days more than the third labourer was the first one absent?
A. 4 B. 6
C. 5 D. cannot be determined

68. I sell a table for ₹ 24 and thus make a percentage of profit equal to the cost price. What did the table cost me?
A. ₹ 10 B. ₹ 30
C. ₹ 40 D. ₹ 20

69. A work was completed by three persons of equal ability, first one doing *m* hours for *m* days, second one doing *n* hours for *n* days (*m* and *n* being integers) and third one doing 16 hours for 16 days. The work could have been completed in 29 days by third person alone with his respective working hours. If all of them do the work together with their respective working hours, then they can complete it in about:
A. 12 days B. 13 days
C. 14 days D. 15 days

70. A man sells two horses for ₹ 1955 each. On one he gains 15% and on the other he loses 15%. His total gain or loss is:
A. ₹ 40.00 B. ₹ 97.75
C. ₹ 90.00 D. ₹ 19.55

71. A bike costs ₹ 48000. Its value depreciates by 30% in the first year and in each subsequent year the depreciation is 20% of the value at the beginning of that year. The value of the bike after 3 years will be:
A. ₹ 26880 B. ₹ 38400
C. ₹ 39480 D. ₹ 21504

72. A jeep travels a distance of 100 km at a uniform speed. If the speed of the jeep is 5 kmph more then it takes 1 hour less to cover the same distance. The original speed of the jeep is:
A. 50 kmph B. 25 kmph
C. 30 kmph D. 20 kmph

73. Two trains 121 m and 99 m in length respectively are running in opposite directions, one at the rate of 40 kmph and the other at the rate of 32 kmph. How long will they take to be completely clear of each other from the moment they meet?
A. 110 sec B. 99 sec
C. 88 sec D. 11 sec

74. A man reaches his office 30 min late, if he walks from his home at 3 km per hour and reaches 40 min early if he walks at 4 km per hour. How far is his office from his house?
A. 7 km B. 5 km
C. 14 km D. 3 km

75. There are 3 concentric circular strips on a dart. The Probability of hitting the inner most circular lamina is 1/9, that of the central strip is 1/3 and of the outer most strip is 5/9. One gets 10 points for hitting the inner most lemma, 6 for the central strip and 2 for the outermost strip. What is the probability of getting at least 20 points in 3 attempts? Given that a target (*i.e.,* the one of the 3 strips) is never missed?
A. 1/81 B. 52/729
C. 5/81 D. 1/9

76. 5 army men are standing in a row left to right. Chetan and Chetak are charioteers. Shailendra and Surendra are the soldiers while Dinesh is a doctor. Dinesh always stands in the middle. The two soldiers and two charioteers do not stand next to each other respectively. If Shailendra is not standing immediately next to the doctor, then out of all the arrangements possible, what is the probability that a charioteer stands next to the doctor?
A. 1/4 B. 1
C. 1/3 D. 1/2

77. There are 7 boys and 8 girls in a class. A teacher has 3 items viz a pen, a pencil and an eraser, each 5 in number. He distributes the items, one to each student. What is the probability that a boy selected at random has either a pencil or an eraser?
A. 2/3 B. 2/21
C. 14/45 D. None of these

78. Glass spheres (which submerge fully in water) of radius 7 mm are dropped into a cylindrical vessel containing some water. The diameter of the vessel is 14 cm. Find how many spheres have been dropped in it if the water level rises by 3.5 cm?
A. 300 B. 375
C. 37 D. Data insufficient

79. Three identical cones with base radius r are placed on their base so that each is touching the other two. The radius of the circle drawn through their vertices is:
A. smaller than r
B. equal to r
C. depends on the height of the cones
D. larger than r

80. Two walls and the ceiling of a room meet at right angles at point P. A fly is in the air, 1 meter from one wall, 8 meters from the other wall and 9 meters from the point P. How many meters is the fly from the ceiling?
A. 14 B. 15
C. 4 D. None of these

81. The HCF of two numbers is 12 and their sum is 288. How many pairs of such numbers are possible?
A. 6 B. 4
C. 8 D. 2

82. Three company of soldiers containing 120, 192 and 144 soldiers are to be broken down into smaller groups such that each group contains soldiers from one company only and all the groups have equal number of soldiers. What is the least number of total groups formed?
A. 29 B. 49
C. 39 D. 19

83. If a book has 252 pages, how many digits have been used to number the pages?
A. 648 B. 650
C. 660 D. None of these

84. For an odd number n, find the highest number that always divides $n \times (n^2 - 1)$?
A. 12 B. 96
C. 48 D. 24

85. The cost of 3 hamburgers, 5 milk shakes, and 1 order of fries at a certain fast food restaurant is ₹ 23.50. At the same restaurant, the cost of 5 hamburgers, 9 milk shakes, and 1 order of fries is ₹ 39.50. What is the cost of 2 hamburgers, 2 milk shakes, and 2 orders of fries at this restaurant?
A. 5 B. 10
C. 7.5 D. 15

86. If x and y are positive integers and $x^2 - y^2 = 101$, find the value of $x^2 + y^2$.
A. 5050 B. 5101
C. 5150 D. None of these

87. On writing first 252 positive integers in a straight line, how many times digit 4 appears?
A. 50 B. 52
C. 55 D. 54

88. India and Australia player one-day international cricket series until anyone team win 4 matches. No match ended in a draw. In how many ways can the series be won?
A. 35 B. 105
C. 70 D. 140

89. The sum of all the possible numbers of 4 digits formed by digits 3, 5, 5, and 6 using each digit once is:
A. 64427 B. 65297
C. 43521 D. 63327

90. In CAT 2007 there were 75 questions. Each correct answer was rewarded by 4 marks and each wrong answer was penalized by 1 mark. In how many different combinations of correct and wrong answer is a score of 50 possible?
A. None of these B. 15
C. 16 D. 14

Directions (Qs. No. 91-96): *Read the paragraph and answer the questions given below.*

A small software firm has four offices, numbered 1, 2, 3 and 4. Each of its offices has exactly one computer and exactly one printer. Each of these eight machines was bought in either 1987, 1988, or 1989. The eight machines were bought in a manner consistent with the following conditions:

I. The computer in each office was bought either in an earlier year than or in the same year as the printer in that office.
II. The computer in office 2 and the printer in office 1 were bought in the same year.
III. The computer in office 3 and the printer in office 4 were bought in the same year.
IV. The computer in office 2 and the computer in office 3 were bought in different years.
V. The computer in office 1 and the printer in office 3 were bought in 1988.

91. Suppose that the computer in office 2 and the computer in office 3 had been bought in the same year as each other. If all of the other conditions remained the same, then which one of the following machines could have been bought in 1989?
A. the printer in office 1
B. the computer in office 2
C. the computer in office 4
D. the printer in office 2

92. If the computer in office 3 was bought in 1988, then which one of the following statements could be true?
A. The computer in office 4 was bought in 1987.
B. The printer in office 1 was bought in 1988.
C. The computer in office 2 was bought in 1987.
D. The printer in office 2 was bought in 1988.

93. If the computer in office 4 was bought in 1988, then which one of the following statements must be true?
A. The printer in office 1 was bought in 1988.
B. The computer in office 2 was bought in 1988.
C. The printer in office 1 was bought in 1989.
D. The computer in office 3 was bought in 1987.

94. If as few of the eight machines as possible were bought in 1987, then what is the exact number of machines that were bought in 1987?
A. 3 B. 1
C. 2 D. 0

95. Which one of the following statements could be true?
A. The printer in office 4 was bought in 1988.
B. The printer in office 1 was bought in 1987.
C. The computer in office 2 was bought in 1987.
D. The computer in office 3 was bought in 1989.

96. If the computer in office 3 was bought in an earlier year than the printer in office 3 was, then which one of the following statements could be true?
A. The computer in office 2 was bought in 1987.
B. The computer in office 4 was bought in 1988.
C. The computer in office 2 was bought in 1988.
D. The printer in office 4 was bought in 1988.

Directions (Qs. No. 97-103): *Read the paragraph and answer the questions given below.*

Exactly six trade representatives negotiate a treaty: K, L, M, N, O, P. There are exactly six chairs evenly spaced around a circular table. The chairs are numbered 1 through 6, with successively numbered chairs next to each other and chair number 1 next to chair number 6. Each chair is occupied by exactly one of the representatives. The following conditions apply:

I. P sits immediately next to N.
II. L sits immediately next to M, N, or both.
III. K does not sit immediately next to M.
IV. If O sits immediately next to P, O does not sit immediately next to M.

97. If K sits immediately next to O, then L CANNOT sit directly between:
A. K and N B. M and N
C. N and O D. M and P

98. If L sits immediately next to N, which one of the following statements must be false?
A. K sits immediately next to O.
B. L sits immediately next to M.
C. N sits directly between L and P.
D. O sits immediately next to P.

99. If L sits immediately next to M, then which one of the following is a complete and accurate list of representatives any one of whom could also sit immediately next to L?
A. K, N B. N, P
C. K, N, O, P D. K, O, P

100. If N sits immediately next to M, then K can sit directly between:
A. L and P B. N and O
C. N and P D. P and O

101. If K sits directly between L and P, then M must sit directly between:
A. L and N B. N and O
C. N and P D. L and O

102. If L sits immediately next to P, which one of the following is a pair of representatives who must sit immediately next to each other?
A. L and N B. L and O
C. K and O D. M and N

103. Which one of the following seating arrangements of the six representatives in chairs 1 through 6 would NOT violate the stated conditions?
A. K, L, M, P, N, O B. K, P, N, M, O, L
C. K, L, M, O, P, N D. K, O, P, N, L, M

Directions (Qs. No. 104-107): *Read the paragraph and answer the questions given below.*

Four couples—Ram & Sita, Laila & Majnu, Krishna & Radha and Heer & Ranjha—are sitting around a circular table on 8 chairs equidistant from each other, all of them facing the centre of the table. Each of the four men and each of the four women wear a T-shirt of one of the four colors *i.e.,* Red, Blue, Green and Yellow, such that no two men wear the same colored T-shirt and no two women wear the same colored T-shirt. The following information is also known.

1. No two men sit adjacent to each other.
2. Ram is sitting opposite Ranjha.
3. No husband is sitting adjacent to his wife.
4. Ram, Majnu, Krishna and Ranjha are males. The rest are females.
5. In a couple, the husband and wife don't wear the same-colored T-shirt.
6. Ram does not wear a green colored T-shirt.
7. No person is wearing the same-colored T-shirt as the person sitting either adjacent or opposite to him/her.
8. Sita is not sitting adjacent to Krishna.
9. Heer and Ranjha wear blue and red colored T-shirts respectively.

104. How many individuals are sitting between Krishna and Majnu?
A. 1 B. 3
C. 2 D. 4

105. If the person sitting to the immediate right of Krishna is wearing a blue colored T-shirt, then that person is:
A. Heer B. Laila
C. Either Heer or Laila D. Either Laila or Radha

106. Who are wearing the Yellow-colored T-shirts?
A. Heer & Majnu B. Ram & Laila
C. Ranjha & Radha D. Sita & Krishna

107. Which 2 people are sitting adjacent to the male wearing the Blue T-shirt?
A. Heer & Laila B. Sita & Radha
C. Laila & Sita D. Radha & Heer

Directions (Qs. No. 108-110): *Read the paragraph and answer the questions given below.*

Ten students Alex, Bryan, Charlie, Deepak, Elwin, Frank, George, Harish, Ian and Joseph are the only participants in an inter-college competition. They are all from three different colleges viz., Harvard, Stanford and Oxford. The number of participants from no two colleges is the same.

The following additional information is known:

I. Exactly two of Bryan, Elwin and George are from Harvard.

II. Frank and Alex are from different colleges and neither of them is from a college from where the maximum participants are.

III. Charlie and Ian arc from the same college.

IV. Derek, Harish and Joseph are from three different colleges.

V. Harish is from Stanford and Derek is from the same college as Alex.

108. If Joseph and Bryan are from different colleges, which of the below statements is definitely true?

A. Bryan and Alex are from Oxford.
B. Bryan is from the same college as Harish.
C. None of the above
D. Elwin and Ian are from the same college.

109. Which of these students cannot be from the college from where the least number of participants are?

A. Joseph B. Frank
C. Derek D. Alex

110. Which two of these are definitely from two different colleges?

A. Elwin and Frank B. Ian and Derek
C. Bryan and Alex D. George and Harish

Directions (Qs. No. 111-114): *Read the paragraph and answer the questions given below.*

Four friends—A, B, C and D - play a game which involves money. They all start with different amounts, and at the end of 4 rounds, they end up with ₹ 1024 each. The results of each round are as given below:

Amount with each person				
ROUND	A	B	C	D
4	1024	1024	1024	1024
3	2304	1024	512	256
2	2304	512	128	1152
1	1152	128	1664	1152
Initially	288	1568	1664	576

In each round, the amount with the person who is ranked I becomes 4 times its value, the amount with the person who is ranked II becomes twice its value, the amount with the person who is ranked III remains the same, and the person who is ranked IV loses the amount that were gained by ranks I and II (such that the sum total of the amounts with the four of them remains constant in each round).

111. Who had the least amount at the end of round 3?

A. D B. A
C. B D. C.

112. What is the maximum amount that anyone had in any of the four rounds?

A. ₹ 1152 B. ₹ 2304
C. ₹ 1728 D. ₹ 2048

113. Who had the least amount before the game started?

A. B B. C
C. A D. D

114. At the end of which round did C have the least amount among all four?

A. Round 1 B. Round 2
C. Round 3 D. Round 4

Directions (Qs. No. 115-118): *Read the paragraph and answer the questions given below.*

Sixty-four players seeded from seed 1 to seed 64 participated in a knock-out tennis tournament. Seed 1 is the highest seed and seed 64 is the lowest seed. The tournament would be played in six rounds *i.e.,* first round, second round, third round, quarterfinals, semifinals and final. In the first round, the player with the highest seed (*i.e.,* 1) would play with the player with the lowest seed (*i.e.,* 64) which is designated Match Number 1.

Similarly, the player with the second highest seed (*i.e.,* 2) would play with the player with the second lowest seed (*i.e.,* 63), which is designated Match Number 2 and so on. In the second round, the winner of the Match Number 1 of the first round would play with the winner of the Match Number 32 of the first round and this match is designated Match Number 1 of the second round.

Similarly, the winner of the Match Number 2 of the first round would play with the winner of the Match Number 31 of the first round and this match is designated Match Number 2 of the second round and so on. In the similar pattern the subsequent rounds will be played.

115. If there are only five upsets (a lower seeded player beating a higher seeded player) in the tournament, then who could be the lowest seeded player winning the tournament?

A. 32 B. 16
C. 17 D. 63

116. If one of the matches was between the players seeded 23 and 46, then one of the matches in the tournament can be between players seeded:

A. 6 and 18 B. 5 and 51
C. 17 and 15 D. 9 and 13

117. Who could be the lowest seeded player facing the player seeded 12 in the finals?

A. 57 B. 59
C. 63 D. 62

118. If the player seeded 43 won the tournament, then which of the following players cannot be the runner-up?

A. Player seeded 44 B. Player seeded 45
C. Player seeded 36 D. Player seeded 46

Reasoning and General Intelligence

Directions (Qs. No. 119-122): *Read the paragraph and answer the questions given below.*

1600 satellites were sent up by a country for several purposes. The purposes are classified as broadcasting (B), communication (C), surveillance (S), and others (O). A satellite can serve multiple purposes; however, a satellite serving either B, or C, or S does not serve O.

The following facts are known about the satellites:

1. The numbers of satellites serving B, C, and S (though may be not exclusively) are in the ratio 2 : 1 : 1.
2. The number of satellites serving all three of B, C, and S is 100.
3. The number of satellites exclusively serving C is the same as the number of satellites exclusively serving S. This number is 30% of the number of satellites exclusively serving B.
4. The number of satellites serving O is the same as the number of satellites serving both C and S but not B.

119. If the number of satellites serving at least two among B, C, and S is 1200, which of the following MUST be FALSE?

A. The number of satellites serving B is more than 1000
B. All 1600 satellites serve B or C or S
C. The number of satellites serving B exclusively is exactly 250
D. The number of satellites serving C cannot be uniquely determined

120. If at least 100 of the 1600 satellites were serving O, what can be said about the number of satellites serving S?

A. Exactly 475
B. At most 475
C. At least 475
D. No conclusion is possible based on the given information

121. What is the minimum possible number of satellites serving B exclusively?

A. 100 B. 200
C. 250 D. 500

122. What best can be said about the number of satellites serving C?

A. Must be between 450 and 725
B. Cannot be more than 800
C. Must be between 400 and 800
D. Must be at least 100

Directions (Qs. No. 123-126): *Read the information furnished below and answer the questions given below:*

Alpi is a 2-year kid who likes to play with her 5 different toys A, B, C, D, and E. She has exactly one toy of each kind. She played for seven consecutive days starting from Monday, and each day she played with at least one toy. The duration (in minutes) for which she played with each of the toys is given below:

Toy	A	B	C	D	E
Duration	1	2	3	4	5

The bar graph shows the total duration (in minutes) for which she played with the toys for seven days. All the seven days are disguised as D1, D2, D3, D4, D5, D6 and D7 (i.e., not necessarily in the order from Monday to Sunday).

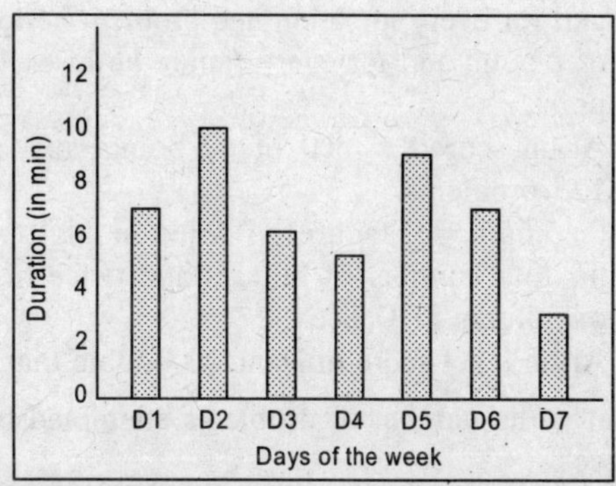

The following facts are also known:

- She plays with exactly one toy at a time and does not play with the same toy in any two consecutive days. Further, she does not play with the same toy more than once in any day.
- She played for the same duration for exactly two consecutive days.
- The duration for which she played on Saturday was half of the duration for which she played on Sunday.
- On Monday she played for 3 minutes more than she did on Wednesday, and the day on which she played for the least duration was not Tuesday.
- The day she played for 6 minutes comes before the day she played for 10 minutes in the week.

123. What could be the maximum number of days she played with exactly one toy?

A. 4 B. 5
C. 2 D. 3

124. For how many minutes did she play on Monday?

A. 8 B. 6
C. 7 D. 5

125. With which toy did she play for the maximum number of times in the week?

A. B B. C
C. Either B or C D. None of these

126. On how many days she played with more than 2 toys?

A. 2 B. 3
C. 4 D. 5

Directions (Qs. No. 127-129): *Read the information furnished below and answer the questions given below:*

The table below gives some information about the points scored by Arjun in ANC (All Hestia Championship), in each of five different mind games—Dice, Dance, Dupe, Digit and Dynasty.

Game	Total Problems	Problems Attempted	Successful Attempts	Failures	Net Score
Dice	35	29			
Dance	30				
Dupe	35	17		6	
Digit	40				11
Dynasty	45		30		

It is also known that:

1. for every successful attempt Arjun get one point and for every un attempted problem he loses 1/6th of a point and for every failure he loses 1/3rd of a point.
2. Arjun scored a total of 67 points and attempted 125 problems.
3. the number of failures of Arjun in Digit is 1/6th of his total number of failures and twice his number of failures in Dance.
4. Arjun's net score in Dance is double that in Dupe.

127. What is the number of problems attempted by him in Dance?
A. 18 B. 19
C. 20 D. 21

128. The maximum number of failures of Arjun in any game was:
A. 14 B. 13
C. 15 D. 12

129. What is the total number of failures of Arjun in the competition?
A. 36 B. 35
C. 34 D. 33

Directions (Qs. No. 130-135): *Read the information furnished below and answer the questions given below:*

In a class of 145 students, 70 like Physics, 80 like Chemistry and 90 like Mathematics. Also, 20 like Chemistry only, 30 like both Chemistry and Mathematics but not Physics and 15 like Physics and Mathematics but not Chemistry. It is also known that each of the 145 students likes at least one of the three subjects.

In another class, all the students like Biology only. This class is merged with the previous class to make a new class and as a result now the combined strength of the new class becomes 180. It is also found that in the new class, some of the students from the previous class who like Chemistry or Mathematics but not Physics started liking Biology. As a result, the ratio of number of students who now like Chemistry, Mathematics and Biology to number of students who now like Mathematics and Biology to number of students who like Chemistry and biology becomes 1 : 3 : 4.

130. In the new class, if the number of students who like exactly three subjects is 24 then, how many students like exactly only subject.
A. 84 B. 83
C. 85 D. 82

131. In the new class, if the number of students who like Physics and Chemistry only is equal to the number of students who like Mathematics and Biology only then, how many students like exactly three subjects?
A. 25 B. 26
C. 23 D. 24

132. In the new class, what could be the maximum number of students who like exactly two subjects?
A. 78 B. 79
C. 77 D. 76

133. In the new class, what could be the maximum number of students who like Biology?
A. 72 B. 70
C. 71 D. 73

134. Which of the following two groups of people had identical sources?
I. A, D and G II. E and H
A. Both I and II B. Only II
C. Neither I nor II D. Only I

135. Which of the following statements is true?
A. C introduced the wrong answer to question 27
B. E introduced the wrong answer to question 46
C. H introduced the wrong answer to question 46
D. F introduced the wrong answer to question 14

Current Affairs and Economic & Business Environment

136. Devaluation of a currency means:
A. Permitting the currency to seek its worth in the international market
B. Fixing the value of the currency in conjunction with the movement in the value of a basket of pre-determined currencies
C. Fixing the value of currency in multi-lateral consultation with the IMF, the World Bank and major trading partners
D. Reduction in the value of a currency vis-a-vis major internationally traded currencies

137. Which among the following is the largest export market for India, for its marine products?
A. USA B. China
C. EU D. Japan

138. Which Company launched M15 Petrol, with 15 per cent blend of methanol with petrol?
A. GAIL Ltd
B. Bharat Petroleum
C. Oil and Natural Gas Corporation
D. Indian Oil Corporation

139. The Madras High Court has invoked the "parens patriae jurisdiction" to declare which entity as a 'living being'?
A. Tamil Language B. Food Grains
C. Agricultural Lands D. Mother Nature

140. Which institution releases the 'Report on Currency and Finance (RCF)'?
A. Ministry of Finance
B. National Payment Corporation of India
C. Reserve Bank of India
D. NITI Aayog

141. Which Union Ministry is associated with the pilot phase of the Open Network for Digital Commerce (ONDC)?
A. Ministry of Commerce and Industry
B. Ministry of MSME
C. Ministry of Home Affairs
D. Ministry of Electronics and IT

142. 'Jivhala' is a special loan scheme launched by which state government?
A. Andhra Pradesh B. Odisha
C. West Bengal D. Maharashtra

146. India's first green-field grain-based ethanol plant has been inaugurated in which state/UT?
A. Gujarat B. Odisha
C. Bihar D. Telangana

144. India signed a pact on 'Green Hydrogen Task Force' and agreed to work on AI-startups with which country?
A. UK B. USA
C. Germany D. France

145. Which start-up recently became the 100th unicorn of India?
A. Open B. Fractal
C. Games 24 × 7 D. Livspace

146. After the May 2022 Meeting of the Monetary Policy Committee, what is the revised Repo Rate?
A. 3.75 % B. 4.25 %
C. 4.40 % D. 4.50 %

147. Cynthia Rosenzweig, who was seen in the news, is the recipient of which prestigious award?
A. Booker Prize B. World Food Prize
C. Pulitzer Prize D. Abel Award

148. Which Indian state/UT recently passed a 'Startup Policy', to support 15,000 start-ups by 2030?
A. Assam B. Rajasthan
C. Punjab D. New Delhi

149. Who is the head of the Delimitation Commission, which redrew the electoral map of Jammu and Kashmir?
A. Justice Sadasivam
B. Justice Ranjan Gogoi
C. Justice Ranjana Prakash Desai
D. Sushil Chandra

150. What is the new Total Fertility Rate (TFR) in India as per the National Family Health Survey (NFHS-5)?
A. 2.4 B. 2.0
C. 2.2 D. 1.9

151. Which state has announced incentives for farmers opting for Direct Seeding of Rice (DSR)?
A. Rajasthan B. Uttar Pradesh
C. Telangana D. Punjab

152. Which Union Ministry implements the 'PM MITRA' Scheme?
A. Ministry of Home Affairs
B. Ministry of Defence
C. Ministry of External Affairs
D. Ministry of Textiles

153. What is the mascot of the Fourth Khelo India Youth Games 2022?
A. Appu B. Veer
C. Dhakad D. Ghambhir

154. Which country established a 'Digital Markets Unit (DMU)' to curb authority of big tech companies over news publishers?
A. USA B. UK
C. France D. Australia

155. Which company has designed India's first Regional Rapid Transit System (RRTS)?
A. DRDO B. HAL
C. Alstom D. Siemens

156. Which institution releases the Periodic Labour force survey (PLFS) results in India?
A. Ministry of Labour and Employment
B. NITI Aayog
C. World Bank—India
D. National Statistics Office

157. Carlos Alcaraz, who won the Madrid Open title recently, is from which country?
A. France B. Spain
C. Switzerland D. Russia

158. Which budget among the following is known as the black budget in Indian budget history?
A. Budget of 1990-91 B. Budget of 1965-66
C. Budget of 1973-74 D. Budget of 1962-63

159. 'John Lee', who was in the news recently, is the newly elected leader of which country?
A. Taiwan B. Hong Kong
C. South Korea D. Malaysia

160. Which country has reported a rare viral infection 'Monkeypox'?
A. Japan B. Australia
C. India D. United Kingdom

161. By selling a 3.5 per cent stake in LIC, what is the total amount to be raised by the Government?
A. ₹ 64000 Crore B. ₹ 45000 Crore
C. ₹ 36000 Crore D. ₹ 21000 Crore

162. Which country has proposed a "European Political Community" for countries hopeful of joining the European Union?
A. UK B. Italy
C. Germany D. France

163. Which is the first Indian company to cross USD 100 billion annual revenue?
A. Adani Industries B. Tata Industries
C. Future Enterprises D. Reliance Industries

164. In which one of the following budgets the services tax was introduced?
A. Budget 1987-1988
B. Budget 2007-2008
C. Budget 1994-1995
D. Budget 1997-1998

165. Which country launched "Affordable Connectivity Program" to provide subsidies on internet service to lower-income households?
A. China B. USA
C. Australia D. UK

166. 'National Behaviour Change Communication Framework for Garbage Free Cities' has been launched under which scheme?
A. Swachh Bharat Mission-Gramin 2.0
B. AMRUT 2.0
C. Swachh Bharat Mission-Urban 2.0
D. HRIDAY 2.0

167. Which is the venue of the 'Semicon India Conference-2022'?
A. Mumbai B. New Delhi
C. Bengaluru D. Chennai

168. Which institution launched the 'Mandate document' for National Curriculum Framework (NCF)?
A. University Grants Commission
B. Union Education Ministry
C. AICTE
D. National Testing Agency

169. Which Indian Bank launched the 'Open-for-all' Digital ecosystem for MSMEs?
A. State Bank of India B. HDFC Bank
C. ICICI Bank D. Canara Bank

170. Which Indian state is the first to set up a Gene Bank Project?
A. Kerala B. Maharashtra
C. Telangana D. West Bengal

ANSWERS

1	**2**	**3**	**4**	**5**	**6**	**7**	**8**	**9**	**10**
A	C	B	A	C	D	C	B	C	D
11	**12**	**13**	**14**	**15**	**16**	**17**	**18**	**19**	**20**
D	C	C	B	B	B	D	D	C	D
21	**22**	**23**	**24**	**25**	**26**	**27**	**28**	**29**	**30**
D	D	B	D	A	C	B	A	D	C
31	**32**	**33**	**34**	**35**	**36**	**37**	**38**	**39**	**40**
C	B	A	C	B	D	C	D	D	D
41	**42**	**43**	**44**	**45**	**46**	**47**	**48**	**49**	**50**
D	C	D	D	C	A	C	C	*	*
51	**52**	**53**	**54**	**55**	**56**	**57**	**58**	**59**	**60**
C	C	C	C	D	D	D	B	D	A
61	**62**	**63**	**64**	**65**	**66**	**67**	**68**	**69**	**70**
D	C	B	B	B	C	C	D	C	C
71	**72**	**73**	**74**	**75**	**76**	**77**	**78**	**79**	**80**
D	D	D	C	B	B	C	B	D	C
81	**82**	**83**	**84**	**85**	**86**	**87**	**88**	**89**	**90**
B	D	A	D	D	B	C	C	D	A
91	**92**	**93**	**94**	**95**	**96**	**97**	**98**	**99**	**100**
D	A	C	D	A	C	C	D	C	D
101	**102**	**103**	**104**	**105**	**106**	**107**	**108**	**109**	**110**
D	C	A	B	A	B	B	D	A	B
111	**112**	**113**	**114**	**115**	**116**	**117**	**118**	**119**	**120**
A	B	C	B	A	D	C	D	D	B
121	**122**	**123**	**124**	**125**	**126**	**127**	**128**	**129**	**130**
C	A	C	B	C	A	A	D	A	C
131	**132**	**133**	**134**	**135**	**136**	**137**	**138**	**139**	**140**
A	B	C	*	*	D	C	D	D	C
141	**142**	**143**	**144**	**145**	**146**	**147**	**148**	**149**	**150**
A	D	C	C	A	C	B	D	C	B
151	**152**	**153**	**154**	**155**	**156**	**157**	**158**	**159**	**160**
D	D	C	B	C	D	B	C	B	D
161	**162**	**163**	**164**	**165**	**166**	**167**	**168**	**169**	**170**
D	D	D	C	B	C	C	B	C	B

Previous Paper (Solved)

Jamia Millia Islamia (JMI)

MBA (FULL TIME)

Entrance Examination-2021*

Directions (Q.No. 1-10): *Read the following passage carefully and choose the best answer for each question.*

In 1787, the twenty-eighth year of the reign of King George III, the British Government sent a fleet to colonize Australia. Never had a colony been founded so far from its parent state, or in such ignorance of the land it occupied. There has been no reconnaissance. In 1770 Captain James Cook had made landfall on the unexplored east coast of this utterly enigmatic continent, stopped for a short while at a place named Botany Bay and gone north again. Since then, no ship had called for not a word, not an observation, for 17 years, each one of which was exactly like the thousands that had preceded it, locked in its historical immensity of blue heat, blush, sandstone and the measured booming of glassy pacific rollers.

Now, this coast was to witness a new colonial experiment, never tried before, not repeated since. An unexplored continent would become a jail. The space around it, the very air and sea, the whole transparent labyrinth of the South Pacific, would become a wall 14,000 miles thick.

The late 18th century abounded in schemes of social goodness thrown off by its burgeoning sense of revolution. But here, the process was to be reversed: not utopia, but Dystopia; not Rousseau's natural man moving in moral grace amid free social contract, but man coerced, deracinated, in chains. Other parts of the Pacific, especially Tahiti, might seem to conform Rousseau. But the intellectual patrons of Australia, in its first colonial years, were Hobbes and Sade.

In their most sanguine moments, the authorities hoped that it would eventually swallow a whole class—the criminal class, whose existence was one of the prime sociological beliefs of late Georgian and early Victorian England. Australia was settled to defend English property not from the frog-eating invader across the Channel but from the marauder within. English lawmakers wished not only to get rid of the Criminal class but if possible to forget about it. Australia was a Cloaca, invisible, its contents filthy and unnamable.

To most Englishmen this place seemed not just a mutant society but another planet—an exiled world, summed up in its popular name, Botany Bay. It was remote and anomalous to its white creators. It was strange but close, as the unconscious to the conscious mind. There was as yet no such thing as Australian history or culture. For its first forty years, everything that happened in the thief-colony was English. In the whole period of convict transportation, the Crown shipped more than 160,000 men, women and children (due to defects in the records, the true number will never be precisely known) in bondage to Australia. This was the largest forced exile of citizens at the behest of a European government in pre-modern history. Nothing in earlier penology compares with it. In Australia, England drew the sketch for our own century's vaster and more terrible fresco of repression, the Gulag. No other country had such a birth, and its pangs may be said to have begun on the afternoon of January 26, 1788, when a fleet of eleven vessels carrying 1,030 people, including 548 male and 188 female convicts, under the command of captain Arthur Phillip in his flagship Sirius, entered Port Jackson or, as it would presently be called, Sydney Harbor.

1. When the author refers to "the marauder within", he is referring to:
A. the working class B. the lower class
C. the criminal class D. the Loch Ness monster

2. According to the passage, the intellectual mentors of Australia could be:
A. Hobbes and Cook
B. Hobbes and Sade
C. Phillip and Jackson
D. Sade and Phillip

3. Which of the following does not describe what the English regarded Australia to be?
A. a mutant society
B. an exiled world
C. an enigmatic continent
D. a new frontier

4. Elsewhere, according to the author, the late eighteenth century saw a plethora of:
A. moral grace
B. social welfare programs
C. free social contracts
D. social repression

* Held on 21/08/2021

5. The word sanguine means:
A. wise
B. pessimistic
C. the rise of the "criminal class" and its impact on the life of Georgian England
D. confident

6. The primary theme of the passage is:
A. the colonization of Australia
B. the first forty years of Australian history
C. the rise of the "criminal class" and its impact on the life of Georgian England
D. the establishment of Australia as a penal colony

7. One of the hallmarks of the late Georgian and early Victorian England was the belief in:
A. repression of the "criminal class"
B. convict transportation
C. colonization as a solution to social problems
D. the existence of a "criminal class" of people

8. What is penology?
A. The study of transportation of criminals
B. The study of punishment in its relation to crime
C. The study of pens
D. The study of ink flow of pens

9. According to the passage, which of the following statements is not true?
A. During the seventeen years after Captain James Cook made landfall at Botany Bay, the British made several observation trips to Australia
B. Australia was settled by the British to protect their property from some of their own kin.
C. The author implies that while Rousseau was vindicated in the functioning of the society of Tahiti, the process in Australia presented a contrary picture.
D. All are true

10. Sydney Harbor was earlier known as:
A. Port Jackson B. Botany Bay
C. Storm Bay D. Norfolk Bay

Directions (Q.No. 11-13): *In each of the following questions a part of a paragraph or sentence has been* **bold**. *From the choice given, you are required to choose the one which would best replace the underlined part.*

11. **Contemplating whether to exist** with an insatiable romantic temperature, he was the author and largely the subject of a number of memorable novels.
A. Contemplating whether to exist
B. Combining realistic details
C. Miscegenating a brilliant mind
D. Aware that he had been born

12. How many times have I asked myself: when is the world going to start to make sense? **There is a monster out there**, and it is rushing towards me over the uneven ground of consciousness.
A. There is a monster out there
B. It is as if the world is on my shoulders
C. The answer is out there somewhere
D. There is a sea of sensibility in me

13. The donation was **such that as I was expected** him to donate.
A. so that as I expected
B. such that I expected of
C. such as that I expected
D. No correction required

Question No. 14. In original paper question was missing

Directions (Q.No. 15-19): *Read the following passage carefully and choose the best answer for each question.*

At the heart of the enormous boom in wine consumption that has taken place in the English-speaking world over the last two decades or so is a fascinating, happy paradox. In the days when wine was exclusively the preserve of a narrow cultural elite, bought either at auctions or from gentleman wine merchants in wing collars and bow-ties, to be stored in rambling cellars and decanted to order by one's butler, the ordinary drinker didn't get a look-in. Wine was considered a highly technical subject, in which anybody without the necessary ability could only fall flat on his or her face in embarrassment. It wasn't just that you needed a refined aesthetic sensibility for the stuff if it was not to be hopelessly wasted on you. It required an intimate knowledge of what came from where, and what it was supposed to taste like. Those were times, however, when wine appreciation essentially meant a familiarity with the great French classics, with perhaps a smattering of other wines—like sherry and port.

That was what the wine trade dealt in. These days, wine is bought daily in supermarkets and high-street chains to be consumed that evening, hardly anybody has a cellar to store it in and most don't even possess a decanter. Above all, the wines of literally dozens of countries are available in our market. When a supermarket offers its customers a couple of fruity little numbers from Brazil, we scarcely raise an eyebrow. It seems, in other words, that the commercial jungle that wine has now become has not in the slightest deterred people from plunging adventurously into the thickets in order to taste and see. Consumers are no longer intimidated by the thought of needing to know their Pouilly-Fume from their Pouilly-Fuisse, just at the very moment when there is more to know than ever before. The reason for this new mood of confidence is not hard to find. It is on every wine label from Australia, New Zealand, South Africa and the United States: the name of the grape from which the wine is made. At one time that might have sounded like a fairly technical approach in itself. Why should native English-speakers know what Cabernet Sauvignon or Chardonnay were? The answer lies in the popularity that wines made from those grape varieties now enjoy. Consumers effectively recognize them as brand names, and have acquired a basic lexicon of wine that can serve them even when confronted with those Brazilian upstarts.

In the wine heartlands of France, they are scared to death of that trend—not because they think their wine isn't as good as the best from California or South Australia (what French winemaker will ever admit that?) but because they don't traditionally call their wines Cabernet Sauvignon or Chardonnay. They call them Chateau Ducru—Beaucaillou or Corton—Charlemagne, and they aren't about the change. Some areas, in the middle of southern France, have now produced a generation of growers using the varietal names on their labels and are tempting consumers back to French wine. It will be an uphill struggle, but there is probably no other way if France is to avoid simply becoming a specialty source of old-fashioned wines for old-fashioned connoisseurs. Wine consumption was also given a significant boost in the early 1990s by the work of Dr. Serge Renaud, who has spent many years investigating the reasons for the uncannily low incidence of coronary heart disease in the south of France. One of his major findings is that the fat-derived cholesterol that builds up in the arteries and can eventually lead to heart trouble, can be dispersed by the tannins in wine. Tannin is derived from the skins of grapes, and is therefore present in higher levels in red wines, because they have to be infused with their skins to attain the red colour. That news caused a huge upsurge in red wine consumption in the United States. It has not been accorded the prominence it deserves in the UK, largely because the medical profession still sees all alcohol as a menace to health, and is constantly calling for it to be made prohibitively expensive. Certainly, the manufacturers of anticoagulant drugs might have something to lose if we all got the message that we would do just as well by our hearts by taking half a bottle of red wine every day.

15. The tone that the author uses while asking "what French winemaker will ever admit that ?" is best describe as

A. caustic B. satirical
C. critical D. hypocritical

16. What according to the author should the French do to avoid becoming a producer of merely old-fashioned wines?

A. Follow the labelling strategy of the English-speaking countries
B. Give their wines English names
C. Introduce fruity wines as Brazil has done
D. Produce the wines that have become popular in the English-speaking world

17. The development which has created fear among winemakers in the wine heartland of France is the:

A. tendency not to name wines after the grape varieties that are used in the wines.
B. 'education' that consumers have derived from wine labels from English speaking countries.
C. new generation of local winegrowers who use labels that show names of grape varieties.
D. ability of consumers to understand a wine's qualities when confronted with "Brazilian upstarts":

18. Which one of the following, if true, would provide most support for Dr. Renaud's findings about the effect of tannins?

A. A survey showed that film celebrities based in France have a low incidence of coronary heart disease.
B. Measurements carried out in southern France showed red wine drinkers had significantly higher levels of coronary heart incidence than white wine drinkers did.
C. Data showed a positive association between sales of red wine and incidence of coronary heart disease.
D. Long-term surveys in southern France showed that the incidence of coronary heart disease was significantly lower in red wine drinkers than in those who did not drink red wine.

19. Which one of the following CANNOT be reasonably attributed to the labelling strategy followed by wine producers in English speaking countries?

A. Consumers buy wines on the basis of their familiarity with a grape variety's name.
B. Even ordinary customers now have more access to technical knowledge about wine.
C. Consumers are able to appreciate better quality wines.
D. Some non-English speaking countries like Brazil indicate grape variety names on their labels.

Directions (Q.No. 20 and 21): *In the following question, a sentence is divided into four parts, Labelled (I), (II), (III) and (IV). From among the labelled parts select the one that has an error.*

20. Threats of extortion have made (I)/ the city's good and rich (II)/ panicky and he is struggling to (III)/ ensure the safety of their loved ones. (IV)

A. I B. II
C. III D. IV

21. You and I was (I)/ supposed to finish (II)/ this work before (III)/ leaving office today. (IV)

A. I B. II
C. III D. IV

Directions (Q.No. 22 and 23): *In the following questions, a sentence has been divided into three parts, labelled (A), (B) and (C). From among the labelled parts, select the one that has an error. If there is no error in the statement, mark option (D), i.e. 'No error' as your answer.*

22. After the Colonel was done with his routine inspection, (A)/ the privates stood at ease, (B)/ though the sun scorched their faces (C)./ No error (D).

23. Having thus shorn seventeen sheep of their wool, (A)/ O'Reilley gathered the wool in a heap (B)/ and tossed it onto the rafters (C)./ No error (D).

Directions (Q.No. 24-26): *Choose the word which is most nearly the same in meaning to the **bold** word.*

24. **Gratify**
   A. Satisfy B. Disappoint
   C. Restrain D. Supply

25. **Eulogy**
   A. Curse B. Occupy
   C. Praise D. Doubt

26. Mollify
   A. Alienate B. Conciliate
   C. Coddle D. Manhandle

27. Choose the word which is most nearly the opposite in meaning to the **bold** word given below.

   Clamour
   A. Settling B. Murmur
   C. Peccant D. Quiet

28. "The battle ended in victory for the royal imperial troops," says the laconic report of success.
   A. verbose B. aphoristic
   C. succinct D. lengthy

Directions (Q.No. 29-33): *Choose the alternative which best expresses the meaning of the idiom from the options given.*

29. I can eat a horse
   A. I can do anything to reach my goal
   B. I can defeat the strong
   C. I am a foodie
   D. I am foodie

30. Rain or Shine
   A. Whatever the circumstances
   B. Live in poverty
   C. Behave moodily
   D. Relax oneself

31. Going Dutch
   A. Behave like a Dutchman
   B. Drink Jots of wine
   C. Dress elegantly
   D. Pay for your share

32. Play it by ear
   A. Follow the instructions thoroughly
   B. Say something that is emotional and sweet
   C. Play music by remembering the sound rather than reading notes
   D. Behave whimsically

33. Cut to the chase
   A. Stop following someone
   B. Quit the game
   C. Get to the point
   D. Reveal the truth

Directions (Q.No. 34 and 35): *Choose the most appropriate option for filling in the blanks. The sequence of words in the correct option should match the sequence of the sentences in which they should be used.*

34. (*i*) There is so much love .... the two of them.
   (*ii*) I have not seen Aditi .... Friday.
   (*iii*) I started my exam preparation .... January.
   (*iv*) The three sisters did not look for new friend as they were quite happy playing .... themselves.
   (*v*) I have not seen Mohan .... six months.
   A. between, from, since, among, for
   B. among, from, for, between, since
   C. among, since, for, between, from
   D. between, since, from, among, for

35. (*i*) He succeeded .... perseverance and sheer hard work.
   (*ii*) .... the power vested in me, I hereby declare these premises sealed.
   (*iii*) .... his illness he could not finish his work in time.
   (*iv*) .... need, please contact me at the emergency number indicated.
   A. by virtue of, by dint of, in case of, in consequence of
   B. by dint of, by virtue of, in consequence of, in case of
   C. by virtue of, in consequence of, by dint of, in case of
   D. by dint of, in consequence of, by virtue of, in case of

Directions (Q.No. 36 and 37): *The following questions are independent of each other.*

36. Pick the word with the correct spelling.
   A. Acqueisence B. Acquiescence
   C. Acaueiscence D. Acquescience.

37. Pick the odd word out
   A. Propitiate B. Appreciate
   C. Appease D. Conciliate

Directions (Q.No. 38-42): *The poem given below is followed by five questions. Choose the best answer to each question.*

As you set out for Ithaka
hope the journey is a long one,
full of adventure, full of discovery.
Laistrygonians, Cyclops,
angry Poseidon—don't be afraid of them:
you'll never find things like that on your way
as long as you keep your thoughts raised high,
as long as a rare excitement
stirs your spirit and your body.
Laistrygonians, Cyclops,
wild Poseidon—you won't encounter them
unless you bring them along inside your soul,
unless your soul sets them up in front of you.
Hope your road is a long one.
May there be many summer mornings when,
with what pleasure, what joy,
you enter harbors you're seeing for the first time;
may you stop at Phoenician trading stations

to buy fine things,
mother of pearl and coral, amber and ebony,
sensual perfume of every kind—
as many sensual perfumes as you can;
and may you visit many Egyptian cities
to learn and go on learning from their scholars.
Keep Ithaka always in your mind.
Arriving there is what you are destined for.
But do not hurry the journey at all.
Better if it lasts for years,
so you are old by the time you reach the island,
wealthy with all you have gained on the way,
not expecting Ithaka to make you rich.
Ithaka gave you the marvelous journey.
Without her you would not have set out.
She has nothing left to give you now.
And if you find her poor,
Ithaka won't have fooled you.
Wise as you will have become,
so full of experience,
you will have understood by then what these Ithakas mean.

38. Which of the following best reflects the central theme of this poem?
A. If you don't have high expectations, you will not be disappointed.
B. Don't rush to your goal; the journey is what enriches you.
C. The longer the journey the greater the experiences you gather.
D. You cannot reach Ithaka without visiting Egyptian ports.

39. The poet recommends a long journey. Which of the following is the most comprehensive reason for it?
A. You can gain knowledge as well as sensual experience.
B. You can visit new cities and harbours.
C. You can experience the full range of sensuality.
D. You can buy a variety of fine things.

40. In the poem, Ithaka is a symbol of
A. the divine mother B. your inner self
C. the path to wisdom D. life's distant goal.

41. What does the poet mean by 'Laistrygonians' and 'Cyclops'?
A. Creatures which, along with Poseidon, one finds during a journey.
B. Mythological characters that one should not be afraid of.
C. Intra-personal obstacles that hinder one's journey.
D. Problems that one has to face to derive the most from one's journey.

42. Which of the following best reflects the tone of the poem?
A. Prescribing B. Exhorting
C. Pleading D. Consoling

Directions (Q.No. 43-47): *In each of the following question, a word is used in four different ways. Choose the option in which the usage of the word is INCORRECT or INAPPROPRIATE.*

43. Bundle
A. The newborn baby was a bundle of joy for the family.
B. Mobile operators are offering a bundle of additional benefits.
C. He made a bundle in the share market.
D. It was sheer luck that brought a bundle of boy-scouts to where I was lying wounded

44. Distinct
A. He is distinct about what is right and what is wrong
B. Mars became distinct on the horizon in the month of August.
C. The distinct strains of Ravi's violin could be heard above the general din.
D. Ghoshbabu's is a distinct case of water rising above its own level.

45. Implication
A. Everyone appreciated the headmaster's implication in raising flood relief in the village
B. This letter will lead to the implication of several industrialists in the market scam.
C. Several members of the audience missed the implication of the minister's promise.
D. Death, by implication, is the only solution the poem offers the reader.

46. Host
A. If you host the party, who will foot the bill?
B. Kerala's forests are host to a range of snakes
C. Ranchi will play the host to the next national film festival.
D. A virus has infected the host computer.

47. Sort
A. What sort of cheese do you use in pizza?
B. Farmers of all sort attended the rally.
C. They serve tea of a sort on these trains.
D. Let's sort these boys into four groups.

Directions (Q.No. 48-50): *Data is proved followed by two statements I and II both resulting in a value, say I and II. Evaluate these values for each of the following questions separately.*

48. Nineteen year from now Jackson will be 3 times as old as Joseph is now. Joseph is three years younger than Jackson.
I. Johnson's age now
II. Joseph's age now
A. I > II B. I < II
C. I = II D. Nothing can be said

49. Last week Martin received $10 in commission for selling 100 copies of a magazine. Last week Miguiel sold 100 copies of this magazine. He received his salary of $ 5 per week plus a commission of 2 cents for each of the first 25 copies sold, 3 cents for each of next 25 copies sold and 4 cents for each copy thereafter. ($1 = 100 cents)

I. Martin's commission in the last week

II. Miguiel's total income for last week

A. I > II B. I < II

C. I = II D. Nothing can be said

Question No. 50. In original paper some part of question was missing.

I. The probability of encountering 54 Sundays in a leap year

II. The probability of encountering 53 Sundays in a non-leap year

A. I > II B. I < II

C. I = II D. Nothing can be said

Directions (Q.No. 51-53): *Read the information below and answer the question that follow.*

Alphonso, on his death bed, keeps half his property for his wife and divide the rest equally among his three sons Ben, Carl and Dave. Some years later Ben dies leaving half is property to his widow and half to his brothers Carl and Dave together, sharing equally. When Carl makes his will, he keeps half his property for his widow and the rest he bequeaths to his younger brother Dave. When Dave dies some years later, he keeps half his property for his widow and the remaining for his mother. The mother now has ₹ 1,575,000.

51. What was the worth of the total property?

A. ₹ 30 lakh B. ₹ 8 lakh

C. ₹ 18 lakh D. ₹ 24 lakh

52. What was the Carl's original share?

A. ₹ 4 lakh B. ₹ 12 lakh

C. ₹ 6 lakh D. ₹ 5 lakh

53. What was the ratio of the property owned by the windows of the three sons, in the end?

A. 7 : 9 : 13 B. 8 : 10 : 15

C. 5 : 7 : 9 D. 9 : 12 : 13

Directions (Q.No. 54-56): *The following operations are defined for real numbers a # b = a + b if a and b are positive else a # b = 1. a ∇ b = (ab)*$^{a+b}$ *if ab is positive else a ∇ b = 1*

54. $\frac{2\#1}{1\nabla 2}=$

A. $\frac{1}{8}$ B. 1

C. $\frac{3}{8}$ D. 3

55. $\{((1\#1)\#2) - (10^{1.3} \nabla \log_{10} 0.1)\}/(1 \nabla 2) =$

A. $\frac{3}{8}$ B. $4 \log_{10} 0.1/8$

C. $(4 + 10^{1.3})/8$ D. None of these

56. $\left(\frac{X\#-Y}{-X\nabla Y}\right)=\frac{3}{8}$, then which of the following must be true?

A. X = 2, Y = 1 B. X > O, Y < O

C. X, Y both positive D. X, Y both negative

Directions (Q.No. 57 and 58): *Answer the following questions based on the following information.*

In a locality, there are five small cities: A, B, C, D and E. The distances of these cities from each other are as follows. AB = 2 km; AC = 2 km; AD > 2 km; AE > 3 km; BC = 2 km; BO = 4 km; BE = 3 km; CD = 2 km; CE = 3 km; DE > 3 km.

57. If a ration shop is to be set up within 3 km of each city, how many ration shops will be required?

A. 1 B. 2

C. 3 D. 4

58. If a ration shop is to be set up within 3 km of each city, how many ration shop will be required?

A. 2 B. 3

C. 4 D. 5

59. Out of two–thirds of the total number of basket ball matches, a team has won 17 matches and lost 3 of them. What is the maximum number of matches that the team can lose and still win more than three-fourths of the total number of matches if it is true that no match can end in a tie?

A. 4 B. 6

C. 5 D. 3

Directions (Q.No. 60-62): *Each of these questions is followed by two statements, I and II.*

Choose 1. if the question can be answered with the help of statement I alone.

Choose 2. if the question can be answered with the help of statement II alone.

Choose 3. if both statement I and statement II are needed to answer the question.

Choose 4. if the question cannot be answered even with the help of both the statements.

60. If x, y and z are real numbers, is $z - x$ even or odd?

I. xyz is odd.

II. $xy + yz + zx$ is even.

A. 1 B. 2

C. 3 D. 4

61. What is the first term of an arithmetic progression of positive integers?

I. Sum of the squares of the first and the second term is 116.

II. The fifth term is divisible by 7.

A. 1 B. 2

C. 3 D. 4

62. What is the number x?

I. The LCM of x and 18 is 36.

II. The HCF of x and 18 is 2.

A. 1 B. 2

C. 3 D. 4

63. What is the total number of ways to reach A to B in the network given?

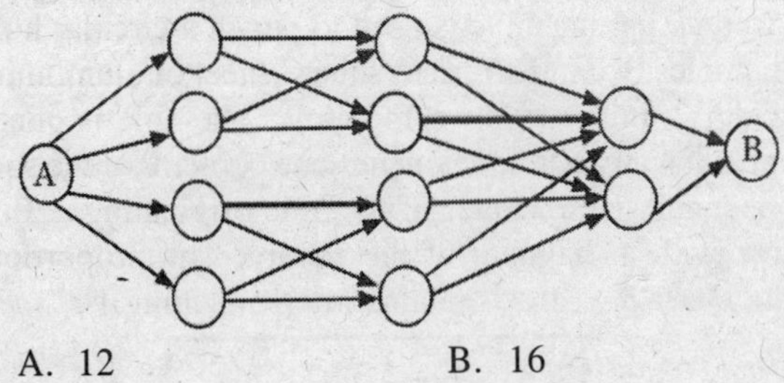

A. 12 B. 16

C. 20 D. 22

64. In a race of 200 m run, A beats S by 20 m and N by 40 m. If S and N are running a race of 100 m with exactly same speed as before, then by how many meters will S beat N?

A. 11.11 m B. 10 m

C. 12 m D. 25 m

65. If $R = \frac{30^{65} - 29^{65}}{30^{65} + 29^{65}}$ then

A. $0 < R \le 0.1$ B. $0 < R \le 0.5$

C. $0.5 < R \le 1.0$ D. $R > 1.0$

66. Rajiv reaches city B from city A in 4 hours driving at speed of 35 kmph for the first two hour and at 45 kmph for the next two hours. Aditi follows the same route, but drives at three different speeds: 30, 40 and 50 kmph, covering an equal distance in each speed segment. The two cars are similar with petrol consumption characteristics (km per litre) shown in the figure below.

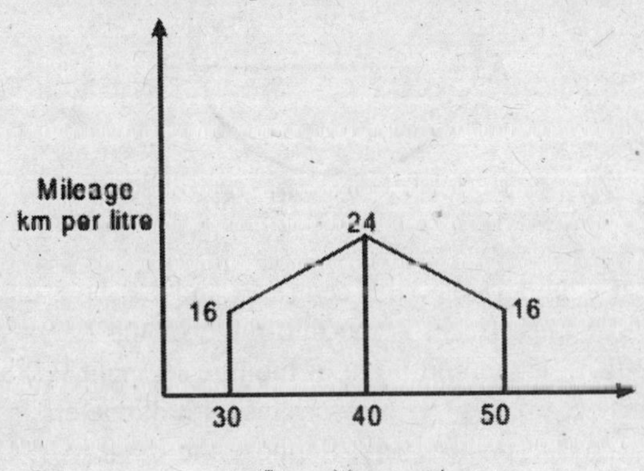

The quantity of petrol consumed by Aditi for the journey in liters is:

A. 8.3 B. 8.6

C. 8.9 D. 9.2

67. The adjoining figure shows a set of concentric squares. If the diagonal of the innermost square is 2 units, and if the distance between the corresponding corners of any two successive squares is 1 unit, find the difference between the values of the areas of the eight and the seventh squares, counting from the innermost square in square units.

A. $10\sqrt{2}$ sq units B. $35\sqrt{2}$ sq units

C. 30 sq units D. None of these

68. Two fair six-faced dice A and B be thrown simultaneously. If EI is the events that die A shows up four, E2 is the event that die B shows up two and E3 is the event that the sum of numbers on both dice is odd, then which of the following statements is NOT true?

A. E1, E2 and E3 are independent

B. E1 and E2 are independent

C. E2 and E3 are independent

D. E1 and E3 are independent

69. For which value of k does the following pair of equations yield a unique solution for x such that the solution is positive?

$$x^2 - y^2 = 0, (x - k)^2 + y^2 = 1$$

A. 2 B. 0

C. $\sqrt{2}$ D. $-\sqrt{2}$

70. A man is walking towards a vertical pillar in a straight path, at a uniform speed. At a certain point A on the path, he observes that the angle of elevation of the top of the pillar is 30°. After walking for 10 min from A in the same direction, at a point B, he observes that the angle of elevation of the top of the pillar is 60°. Then, the time taken (in minutes) by him, from B to reach the pillar, is

A. 5 B. 6

C. $\sqrt{2}$ D. $-\sqrt{2}$

71. If a E R and the equation $-3(x - [x])^2 + 2(x - [x]) + a^2 = 0$; where $[x]$ denotes the greatest integer x has no integral solution, then all possible values of a lie in the interval:

A. $(-1, 0) \cup (0, 1)$ B. $(1, 2)$

C. $(-2, -1)$ D. $(-\infty, -2) \cup (2, \infty)$

72. If the 2nd, 5th and 9th terms of a non-constant A.P. are in G.P... Then the common ratio of this G.P. is:

A. $\frac{7}{4}$ B. $\frac{8}{5}$

C. $\frac{4}{3}$ D. 1

73. If all the words (with or without meaning) having five letters, formed using the letters of the word SMALL and arranged as in a dictionary; then the position of the word SMALL is:

A. 58th B. 59th
C. 46th D. 42nd

74. A bird is sitting on the top of vertical pole 20 m high and its elevation from a point O on the ground is 45°. It flies off horizontally straight away from the point O. After one second, the elevation of the bird from O is reduced to 30°. Then the speed (in m/s) of the bird is:

A. $40(\sqrt{2}-1)$ B. $40(\sqrt{3}-\sqrt{2})$
C. $20\sqrt{2}$ D. $20(\sqrt{3}-1)$

75. A right circular cone of height h is cut by a plane parallel to the base and at a distance $h/3$ from the base, then the volumes of the resulting cone and the frustum are in the ratio:

A. 1 : 3 B. 8 : 19
C. 1 : 4 D. 1 : 7

76. Based on the figure below, what is the value of x, if $y = 10$?

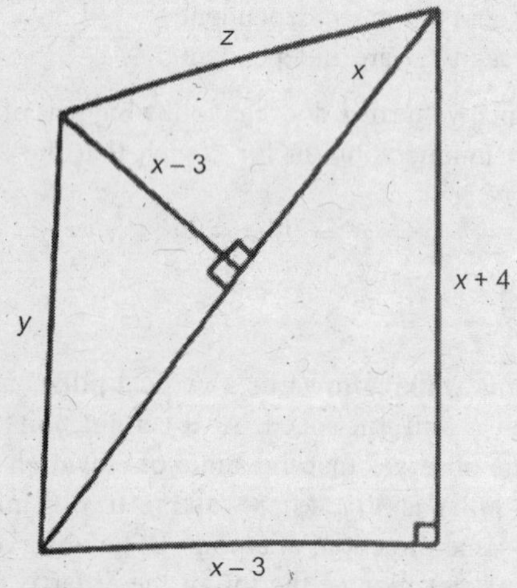

A. 0 B. 11
C. 12 D. None of these

77. Consider two different cloth-cutting processes. In the first one, n circular cloth pieces are cut from a square cloth piece of side 'a' in the following steps: the original square of side 'a' is divided into n smaller squares, not necessarily of the same size; then a circle of maximum possible area is cut from each of the smaller squares. In the second process, only one circle of maximum possible area is cut from the square of side 'a' and the process ends there. The cloth pieces remaining after cutting the circles are scrapped in both the processes. The ratio of the total area of scrap cloth generated in the former to that in the later is:

A. 1 : 1 B. $\sqrt{2}-1$
C. $\frac{n(4-\pi)}{4n-\pi}$ D. $\frac{4n-\pi}{n(4-\pi)}$

78. P, Q, S and R points on the circumference of a circle of radius r, such that PQR is an equilateral triangle and PS is a diameter of the circle. What is the Perimeter of the quadrilateral PQSR?

A. $2r(1+\sqrt{3})$ B. $2r(2+\sqrt{3})$
C. $r(1+\sqrt{5})$ D. $2r+\sqrt{3}$

79. A punching machine is used to punch a circular hole of diameter two units form a square sheet of aluminium of width 2 units as shown in below. The hole is punched such that circular hole touches one corner P of the square sheet and the diameter of the hole originating at P is in line with a diagonal of the square. The proportion of the sheet area that remains after punching is:

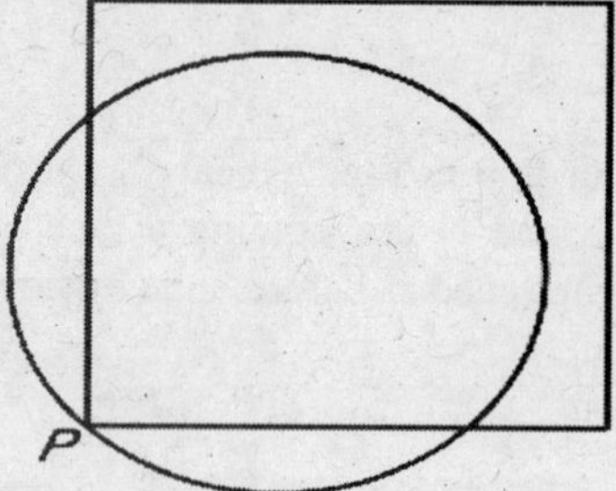

A. $\frac{6-\pi}{8}$ B. $\frac{\pi+2}{8}$
C. $\frac{4-\pi}{4}$ D. $\frac{\pi-2}{4}$

80. In the given figure, AB is diameter of the circle and points C and D are on the circumference such that $\angle CAD = 30°$ and $\angle CBA = 70°$. What is the measure of $\angle ACD$?

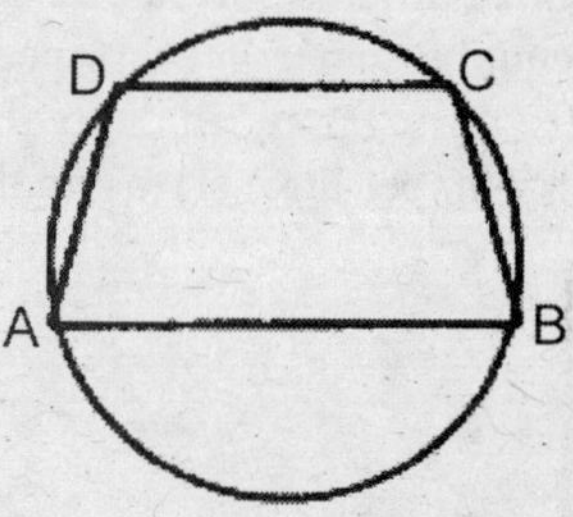

A. 40° B. 50°
C. 30° D. 90°

81. Let C be a circle with centre P_0 and AB be a diameter of C. Suppose P_1 is the mid-point of the line segment P_0B, P_2 is the mid-point of the line segment P_1B and so on. Let $C_1, C_2, C_3, \ldots$ be circles with diameters P_0P_1, P_1P_2, $P_2P_3 \ldots$ respectively. Suppose the circles C_1, C_2, C_3, are all shaded. The ratio of the area of the unshaded portion of C to that of the original circle C is:

A. 8 : 9 B. 9 : 10
C. 10 : 11 D. 11 : 12

82. The variance of first 50 even natural numbers is:

A. $\frac{833}{7}$ B. 833
C. 467 D. $\frac{467}{5}$

83. How many numbers can be made with digits 0, 7, 8 which are greater than 0 and less than a million?

A. 496 B. 486
C. 1084 D. 728

84. The figure below shows two concentric circles with centre O. PQRS is a square inscribed in the outer circle. It also circumscribes the inner circle, touching it at points B, C, D and A. What is the ratio of the perimeter of the outer circle to that of polygon ABCD?

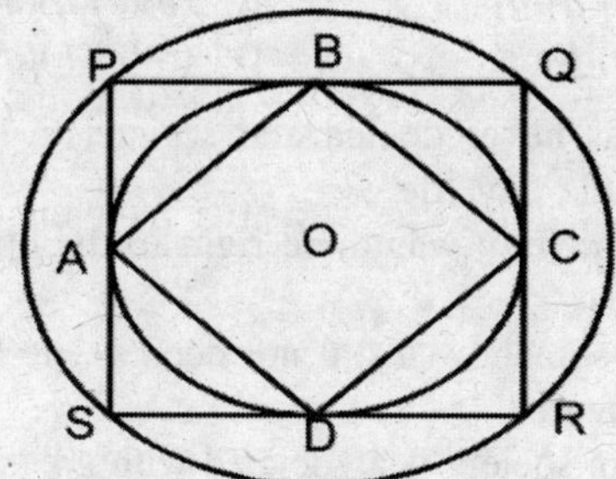

A. $\frac{\pi}{4}$ B. $\frac{3\pi}{2}$
C. $\frac{\pi}{2}$ D. π

85. If a company has a revenue function $R = 100q - q^2$, and cost function $C = q^3 - \frac{57}{2}q^2$, what is the maximum profit?

A. 4000 B. 1000
C. 13000 D. None of these

86. Complete the series 2, 6, 12, 20, 30, 42, ...?

A. 50 B. 52
C. 54 D. 56

87. In a kilometer race, if X gives Y 30 m start, X wins by 20 seconds but if X gives Y 30 seconds start, Y wins by 20 m, find the speed of Y.

A. 5.25 B. 4.75
C. 4.15 D. 4.00

88. There are 190 chairs they are to be arranged in rectangular manner. Initially, when the chairs are arranged 5 more chairs are needed. When number of rows is increased by 2, 35 more chairs are needed then how many rows were there initially?

A. 17 B. 13
C. 15 D. 18

89. Two equal sums of money were invested. One at 4% and the other at 4.5%. At the end of 7 years, the simple interest received from the latter exceeded that received from the former by ₹ 31.50. Each sum was:

A. ₹ 9000 B. ₹ 1500
C. ₹ 1750 D. None of these

90. Consider the five points comprising of the vertices of a square and intersection points of its diagonals. How many triangles can be formed using these points?

A. 3 B. 8
C. 10 D. 12

91. If a square sheet is converted into a cylinder by rolling it along its side, what is the ratio of the base radius to the side of the square?

A. $\frac{1}{2\pi}$ B. $\frac{1}{\pi}$
C. $\frac{2}{\pi}$ D. $\frac{1}{4\pi}$

92. In Nuts and Bolts factory, one machine produces only nuts at the rate of 100 nut per minute and needs to be cleaned for 5 minutes after production of every 1000 nuts. Another machine produces only bolts at the rate of 75 bolts per minute and needs to cleaned for 10 minutes after production of every 1500 bolts. If both the machines start production at the same time, what is the minimum duration required for producing 9000 pairs of nuts and bolts?

A. 130 minutes B. 135 minutes
C. 170 minutes D. 180 minutes

93. A father and his son are waiting at a bus stop in the evening. There is a lamp post behind them. The lamp post, the father and his son stand on the same straight line. The father observes that the shadows of his head and his son's head are incident at the same point on the ground. If the heights of the lamp post, the father and his son are 6 metres, 1.8 metres and 0.9 metres respectively, and the father is standing 2.1 metres away from the post, then how far (in metres) is the son standing from his father?

A. 0.9 B. 0.75
C. 0.6 D. 0.45

94. The remainder, when $(15^{23} + 23^{23})$ is divided by 19, is:

A. 4 B. 15
C. 0 D. 18

95. In some code, letters, *a*, *b*, *c*, *d* and *e* represent numbers 2, 4, 5, 6 and 10. However, we don't know which letter represents which number. Consider the following relationships:

I. $a + c = e$
II. $b - d = d$
III. $e + a = b$

A. $b = 4, d = 2$ B. $a = 4, e = 6$
C. $b = 6, e = 2$ D. $a = 4, c = 6$

96. Let *n* be the number of different 5-digit numbers, divisible by 4 with the digits 1, 2, 3, 4, 5 and 6, no digit being repeated in the numbers. What is the value of *n*?

A. 144 B. 168
C. 192 D. None of these

97. Let *x*; *y* be two positive numbers such that $x + y = 1$.

Then, the minimum value of $\left(x+\frac{1}{x}\right)^2 + \left(y+\frac{1}{y}\right)^2$ is:

A. 12
B. 20
C. 12.5
D. 13.3

98. Let $y = \cfrac{1}{2+\cfrac{1}{3+\cfrac{1}{2+\cfrac{1}{3+\ldots}}}}$ what is the value of y?

A. $\frac{\sqrt{13}+3}{2}$
B. $\frac{\sqrt{13}-3}{2}$
C. $\frac{\sqrt{15}+3}{2}$
D. $\frac{\sqrt{15}-3}{2}$

99. A jogging park has two identical circular tracks touching each other and a rectangular track enclosing the two circles. The edges of the rectangles are tangential to the circles. Two friends, A and B, start jogging simultaneously form the point where one of the circular tracks touches the smaller side of the rectangular track. A jogs along the rectangular track, while B jogs along the two circular tracks in a figure of eight. Approximately, how much faster than A does B have to run, so that they take the same time to return to their starting point?

A. 3.88%
B. 4.22%
C. 4.44%
D. 4.72%

Directions (Q.No. 100-104): *A number of sentences are given below which, when properly sequenced, from a coherent paragraph, each sentence is labelled with a letter. Choose the most logical order of sentences from among the four given chances to construct a coherent paragraph.*

100. (*a*) This is probably one of the reasons why the number of women and men remain roughly equal in most societies.
(*b*) Fortunately, or unfortunately, individual couples cannot really be concerned about this overall 'error'.
(*c*) Population growth then can be considered the error of this central process.
(*d*) Purely at the human level, it appears that most couples like to have at least one living daughter and one living son when they are in the middle ages.

A. (*c*)(*b*)(*d*)(*a*)
B. (*d*)(*a*)(*c*)(*b*)
C. (*d*)(*c*)(*b*)(*a*)
D. (*c*)(*d*)(*a*)(*b*)

101. (*a*) Against this background, the current target of 12.8 percent does not seem that high a figure.
(*b*) A better vantage point to evaluate the 12.8 percent target for export growth is our performance in the 'golden years' between 1986-87 and 1990-91, during which time exports in dollar terms increased by 17.1 percent.
(*c*) In fact, the rate of growth would have to increase still further if we are to achieve the eighth plan target of export growth in value terms of 13.6 percent per annum.
(*d*) Even in 1990-91, the year of the Gulf War, exports went up by 9 percent.

A. (*b*)(*d*)(*a*)(*c*)
B. (*b*)(*c*)(*a*)(*d*)
C. (*d*)(*a*)(*b*)(*c*)
D. (*a*)(*c*)(*b*)(*d*)

102. (*a*) Their growing costs and a growing economy must be reckoned with realistically.
(*b*) Central programmes persist and in some cases grow.
(*c*) As demand expands, programmes expand.
(*d*) It is extremely difficult to curtail them.

A. (*c*)(*d*)(*a*)(*b*)
B. (*b*)(*c*)(*d*)(*a*)
C. (*d*)(*a*)(*b*)(*c*)
D. (*a*)(*c*)(*b*)(*d*)

103. (*a*) It was never denied and seemed to be integrated into the city life.
(*b*) The poverty was there right in the open in all the streets.
(*c*) But, somehow it did not depress me as much as I had feared.
(*d*) Indian society is associated with great poverty, and indeed I saw a lot of poverty in Mumbai.

A. (*a*)(*d*)(*b*)(*c*)
B. (*b*)(*c*)(*d*)(*a*)
C. (*b*)(*c*)(*a*)(*d*)
D. (*d*)(*c*)(*b*)(*a*)

104. (*a*) This has been going on now for nearly 200 years.
(*b*) They haven't even been noticed much by central, state, or local governments, no matter how insolent or blasphemous or treasonous those writers may be.
(*c*) But writers of novels, plays, short stories or poems have never been hurt or hampered much
(*d*) Journalists and teachers are often bullied or fired in my country for saving this or that.

A. (*d*)(*c*)(*b*)(*a*)
B. (*b*)(*c*)(*d*)(*a*)
C. (*a*)(*b*)(*c*)(*d*)
D. (*d*)(*c*)(*a*)(*b*)

Directions (Q.No. 105-107): *Read the information below and answer the questions that follow –*

The seven basic symbols in a certain numeral system and their respective values are as follows: I = 1, V = 5, X = 10, L = 50, C = 100, D = 500, and M = 1000. In general, the symbols in the numeral system are read from left to right, starting with the symbol representing the largest value; the same symbol cannot occur continuously more than three times; the value of the numeral is the sum of the values of the symbols. For example, XXVII = 10 + 10 + 5 + 1 + 1 = 27. An exception to the left-to-right reading occurs when a symbol is followed immediately by a symbol of greater value; then, the smaller value is subtracted from the larger. For example, XLVI = (50 – 10) + 5 + 1 = 46.

105. The value of the numeral MDCCLXXXVII is:

A. 1687
B. 1787
C. 1887
D. 1987

106. The value of the numeral MCMXCIX is:

A. 1999
B. 1899
C. 1989
D. 1889

107. Which of the following can represent the numeral for 1995?

(*a*) MCMLXXV (*b*) MCMXCV
(*c*) MVD (*d*) MVM
A. only (*a*) and (*b*) B. only (*c*) and (*d*)
C. only (*b*) and (*d*) D. only (*d*)

Directions (Q.No. 108-115): *In each of the following questions a pair of capitalized words is followed by four pair of words. You are required to mark as the answer the pair of words which have a relationship between them most similar to the relationship between the capitalized pair.*

108. LIQUID : GASEOUSNESS
A. Serum : Fume B. Humid : Arid
C. Thaw : Distil D. Smoke : Cloud

109. FISSION : FUSION
A. Implosion : Explosion
B. Separation : Combination
C. Intrusion : Extrusion
D. Enemy : Friend

110. DOUBT : FAITH
A. Atheist : Religion B. Sceotic : Pious
C. Iconoclast : Idol D. Apostate : State

111. BRICK . BUILDING
A Word : Dictionary B. Alphabet : Letter
C. Platoon : Soldier D. Idiom : Language

112. DULCET : RAUCOUS
A. Sweet : Song
B. Crazy : Insane
C. Palliative : Exacerbating
D. Theory : Practical

113. ACTION : REACTION
A. Introvert : Extrovert
B. Assail : Defend
C. Diseased : Treatment
D. Death : Rebirth

114. MALAPROPISM : WORDS
A. Anachronism : Time
B. Ellipsis : Sentence
C. Jinjanthropism : Apes
D. Catechism : Religion

115. ANTERIOR : POSTERIOR
A. In : Out B. Too : Bottom
C. Head : Fail D. Front : Real

Directions (Q.No. 116-119): *In each of the questions given below, four different ways of writing a sentence are indicated. Choose the best way of writing the sentence.*

116. I. The main problem with the notion of price discrimination is that it is not always a bad thing, but that it is the monopolist who has the power to decide who is charged what price.
II. The main problem with the notion of price discrimination is not that it is always a bad thing; it is the monopolist who has the power to decide who is charged what price.
III. The main problem with the notion of price discrimination is not that it is always a bad thing, but that it is the monopolist who has the power to decide who is charged what price.
IV. The main problem with the notion of price discrimination is not it is always a bad thing, but that it is the monopolist who has the power to decide who is charged what price.
A. I B. II
C. III D. IV

117. I. A symbiotic relationship develops among the contractors, bureaucracy and the politicians, and by a large number of devices, costs are artificially escalated and black money is generated by underhand deals.
II. A symbiotic relationship develops among contractors, bureaucracy and politicians, and are artificially escalated with a large number of devices and black money is generated through underhand deals.
III. A symbiotic relationship develops among contractors, bureaucracy and the politicians, and by a large number of devices costs are artificially escalated and black money is generated on underhand deals.
IV. A symbiotic relationship develops among the contractors, bureaucracy and politicians, and by large number of devices costs are artificially escalated and black money is generated by underhand deals.
A. I B. II
C. III D. IV

118. I. The distinctive feature of tariffs and export subsidies is that they create difference of prices at which goods are traded on the world market and their price within a local market.
II. The distinctive feature of tariffs and export subsidies is that they create a difference of prices at which goods are traded with the world market and their prices in the local market.
III. The distinctive feature of tariffs and export subsidies is that they create a difference between prices at which goods are traded on the world market and their prices within a local market.
IV. The distinctive feature of tariffs and export subsidies that they create a difference across prices at which goods are traded with the world market and their prices within a local market.
A. I B. II
C. III D. IV

119. I. Any action of government to reduce the systemic risk inherent in financial markets will also reduce the risks that private operators perceive and thereby encourage excessive hedging.

II. Any action by government to reduce the systemic risk inherent in financial markets will also reduce the risks that private operators perceive and thereby encourage excessive gambling.

III. Any action by government to reduce the systemic risk inherent due to financial markets will also reduce that risks that private operators perceive and thereby encourages excessive hedging.

IV. Any action of government to reduce the systemic risk inherent to financial markets will also reduce the risks that private operators perceive and thereby encourage excessive gambling.

A. I B. II
C. III D. IV

Directions (Q.No. 120-125): *Analyse the information below and answer the questions that follow.*

A company manufacturing and selling vacuum cleaners started operations with cash in hand of ₹ 5 million at the beginning of 2014-15. The table below gives the production, sales price and costs of the company over the next five years.

Year	2014-15	2015-16	2016-17	2017-18	2018-19
Production (units)	14000	18000	20000	17000	15000
Sales (units)	12000	17000	16000	19000	19000
Price (₹ per unit)	10000	11000	11000	11000	12000
Fixed cost (million ₹)	18	30	30	40	40
Total Variable cost (million ₹)	84	122	141	161	172

120. The end of which year was the quantity of cumulative unsold stock the largest?
A. 2014-15 B. 2015-16
C. 2016-17 D. None of the above

121. The percentage increase in cumulative cash in hand over the preceding year was the highest in:
A. 2014-15 B. 2015-16
C. 2016-17 D. 2017-18

122. The increase in the difference between income and costs in a year over the preceding year was the largest in:
A. 2015-16 B. 2016-17
C. 2017-18 D. 2018-19

123. Assuming all cash transaction, the cumulative cash in hand with the company (in million ₹)
A. 16 B. 20
C. 82 D. 87

124. If the company was able to sell all the units that it produced during a year in the same year, the cash in hand (in million ₹) at the end of 2018-19 would be:
A. 87 B. 92
C. 102 D. 117

125. Assuming that all variable costs incurred in a year are attributable to the units produced in that year, the highest variable cost per unit was incurred in the year:
A. 2014-15 B. 2015-16
C. 2016-17 D. None of the above

Directions (Q.No. 126-131): *Read the table below and answer the questions that follow.*

Data on edible oil production and consumption for the year 2019-20 across six Countries are tabulated below:

Country	Annual edible oil production (billion liters)	Approx. population (million)	Annual edible oil consumption per capita (liters)	Projected Annual edible oil production growth rate %	Projected Annual population growth rate %	Projected Annual edible oil consumption growth rate per capita %
I	12	1000	12	10	2	5
J	7	500	13	5	5	6
K	5	300	11	5	4	7
L	10	1200	10	10	1	1
M	9	700	14	5	4	6

126. Assuming none of the above five countries export edible oil, which country would need to import the maximum quantity of edible oil in 2020-21?
A. I B. J
C. K D. None of these

127. Assuming that a country imports edible oil only to meet the gap between production and consumption, if any, which country is in a position to export the maximum quantity of edible oil in 2019-20?
A. I B. J
C. K D. None of these

128. Assuming none of the above five countries exported or imported edible oil, which country that had an export capacity in 2019-20 would need to import next year.
A. I B. J
C. K D. None of these

129. The net import requirement of edible oil (in million litres) for all the five countries put together in the year 2020-21 is closest to:
A. 450 B. 550
C. 650 D. 750

130. Which country would have the highest annual consumption of edible oil in liters per capita in the year 2021-22?
A. I B. K
C. L D. M

131. What is the approximate average per capita consumption of edible oil (in liters) for all the five countries put together in the year 2021-22?
A. 11.52 B. 12.33
C. 13.27 D. 14.31

Directions (Q.No. 132-136): *Answer the questions that follow after the graph.*

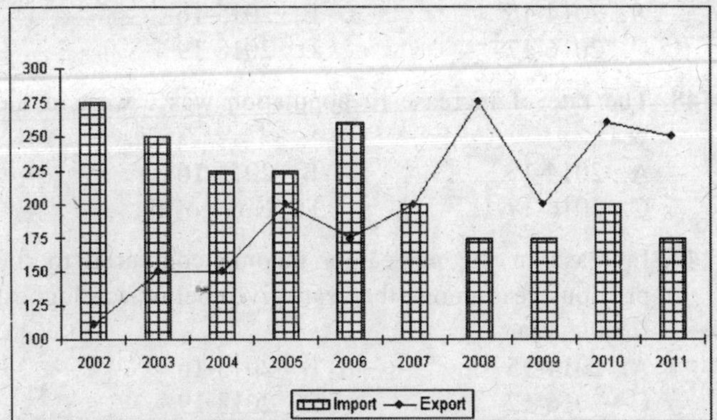

132. Approximately by what percentage are the total Exports greater/smaller than the total imports for the given period?

A. Greater by 9 per cent
B. Smaller by 10 per cent
C. Smaller by 9 per cent
D. Greater by 10 per cent

133. If the absolute difference between imports and exports are ranked in ascending order, which year gets 4th rank?

A. 2010 B. 2009
C. 2008 D. None of these

134. In which year was the fifth largest annual percentage increase in exports recorded?

A. 2007 B. 2009
C. 2008 D. None of these

135. Which year saw the second largest annual percentage increase in imports?

A. 2010 B. 2005
C. 2006 D. None of these

136. What is the approximate percentage point difference in the maximum annual percentage increase in export and the minimum annual percentage decrease in Imports?

A. 28 B. 48
C. 64 D. 12

Directions (Q.No. 137 & 138): *Study the following pie-charts regarding to sales of 5 models of cars for the years 2019 and 2020, and answer the question that follow.*

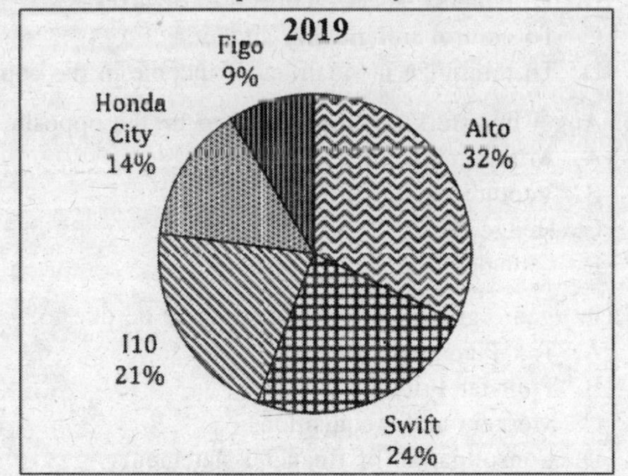

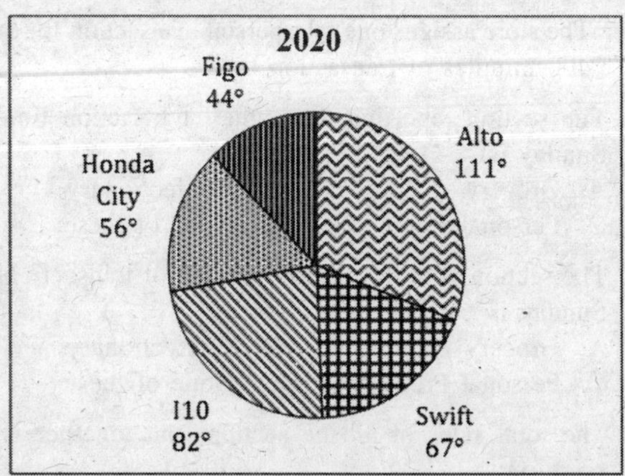

137. If the 2019 sales for all car models is 80,000 and these have grown by 25% in 2020, then what is the approximate increase in the number of Figo cars sold in 2020 over 2019?

A. 4860 B. 12200
C. 4500 D. None of these

138. If the 2019 sales for all car models is 80,000 and these have grown by 25% in 2020, then how many models have grown more than the average growth rate for all the models taken together?

A. 2 B. 3
C. 4 D. None of these

Directions (Q.No. 139-144): *Using the tables and graphs below, answer the question that follow.*

A departmental store reported the following sales data (in million ₹) for a particular week.

Day	Section					
	Grocery	Confectionary	Personal Products	Men's Apparel	Ladies' Apparel	Appliances
Monday	0.18	0.12	0.61	0.42	0.72	0.86
Tuesday	0.16	0.14	0.72	0.38	0.56	0.68
Wednesday	0.22	0.21	0.86	0.46	0.68	0.76
Thursday	0.28	0.16	0.68	0.54	0.58	0.82
Friday	0.29	0.32	0.00	0.01	0.42	0.54
Saturday	0.33	0.42	1.10	0.92	0.88	0.96
Sunday	0.38	0.58	1.22	1.42	1.46	1.42

The Average Value of a Transaction (AVT) in ₹ and the Time Taken per Transaction (TpT) in seconds, is given in the figure below:

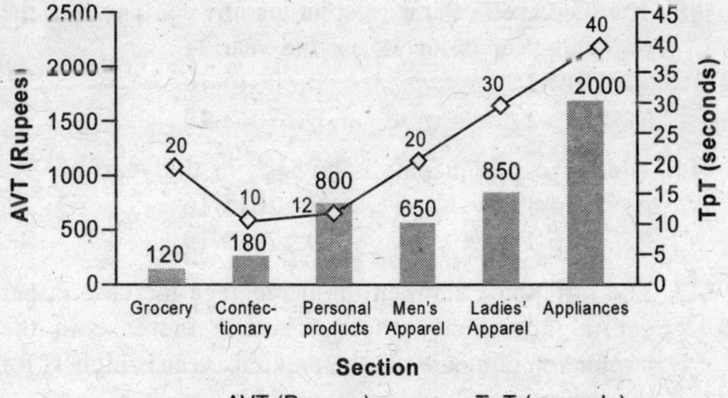

Note: The store assigns one salesperson in a section for every 400 minutes of transaction time.

139. The section reporting the highest transaction time on Sunday is:
A. Grocery B. Confectionary
C. Personal Products D. None of these

140. The section with the highest number of transactions on Sunday is:
A. Grocery B. Confectionary
C. Personal Products D. None of these

141. The total sales of all the sections put together is the same on:
A. Monday and Tuesday
B. Tuesday and Wednesday
C. Wednesday and Thursday
D. Thursday and Friday

142. The ratio of sales on the week-end (Saturday and Sunday) to total sales is nearly:
A. 1 : 2.34 B. 1 : 3.43
C. 1 : 4.48 D. 1 : 5.51

143. The section requiring the maximum number of sales persons on Saturday is:
A. Grocery B. Confectionary
C. Personal Products D. None of these

144. The ratio of salespersons required in the Appliances section on Monday to the salespersons required in the same section on Sunday is approximately:
A. 1 : 0.50 B. 1 : 1.45
C. 1 : 1.65 D. 1 : 1.95

Directions (Q.No. 145-149): *The following table gives the national income and the population of a country for the years 2013-14 to 2018-19. For each of the question following the table choose the best alternative.*

Year	National Income (in ₹ Crore)	Population (in crore)
2013-14	229,225	74.0
2014-15	261,174	75.0
2015-16	291,556	77.0
2016-17	329,934	78.5
2017-18	388,539	80.0
2018-19	433,500	81.5

145. The increase in the per capita income compared to the previous year is lowest for the year:
A. 2014-15 B. 2015-16
C. 2016-17 D. 2018-19

146. The per capita income is highest for the year:
A. 2014-15 B. 2015-16
C. 2016-17 D. 2018-19

147. The difference between the percentage increase in per capita income and the percentage increase in the population compared to the previous year is highest for the year:
A. 2014-15 B. 2015-16
C. 2016-17 D. 2018-19

148. The rate of increase in population was lowest in the year:
A. 2014-15 B. 2015-16
C. 2016-17 D. None of these

149. Increase in the per-capita income compared to the previous year among the years given below was highest for the year:
A. 2014-15 B. 2015-16
C. 2016-17 D. 2018-19

150. The practice of funding a project or venture by raising small amounts of money from a large number of people, typically via the Internet is termed as:
A. Consortium Financing
B. Bidding
C. Crowd funding
D. Sourcing

151. Cloud computing means:
A. Carbon transfers on commodity exchanges
B. Computing under disaster conditions
C. Use of computing resources which are available in a remote location and accessible over a network
D. None of these

152. A computer virus is a ....
A. operating system B. hash function
C. program D. packet

153. Which is the best way to secure an electronic document?
A. Sharing with colleagues
B. Keeping multiple copies
C. Protecting with password
D. None of these

154. With reference to Income Tax Act, 1961, advance tax payment is optional for companies. This is:
A. True B. Sometimes true
C. False D. Cannot Say

155. Repo rate is the rate used by central banks:
A. To improve the risk profile of the banks
B. To enhance speedy collection of taxes
C. To control inflationary situations
D. To minimize inequalities of income in the country

156. Angel investors are considered to be the opposite of:
A. Arbitrageurs
B. Venture capitalists
C. Hedge funds
D. Global investors

157. Inorganic growth of enterprises may be due to:
A. Tax Planning
B. Transfer Pricing
C. Mergers and Acquisitions
D. Consolidation of financial statements

158. Special purpose vehicle is:
A. Nationwide financial inclusion programme launched by RBI
B. Remedial measure in the credit provisioning problem
C. Cross border financing mechanism
D. None of these

159. As per the deposit insurance scheme, each depositor in a bank is insured up to a maximum of .... for both principal and interest amount held by him/her in the same right and same capacity as on the date of liquidation or the cancellation of bank's license or the date on which the banks get amalgamated or merged with another bank.
A. ₹ 1 lakh B. ₹ 2 lakh
C. ₹ 5 lakh D. ₹ 9 lakh

160. In India, the inflation is measured by:
A. Wholesale Price Index
B. Consumer Services Index
C. Incremental Inflation Index
D. Producer Price Index

161. The current base year for GDP measurement is:
A. 2009-10
B. 2011-12
C. 2012-13
D. 2016-17

162. The proposed bad bank in India refers to:
A. National Capital Management Company Ltd. (NCMCL)
B. National Bank Revival Corporation Ltd. (NBRCL)
C. National Asset Reconstruction Company Ltd. (NARCL)
D. National Asset Management Company Ltd. (NAMCL)

163. Method to safeguard against losses due to currency fluctuations is popularly known as:
A. Risk
B. Premium
C. Hedging
D. Rounr' Tripping D Bond Indexation

164. Which of the following is not correct about Regional Comprehensive Economic Partnership (RCEP)?
A. It is a Free Trade Agreement of 16 countries of Asia Pacific Region including India.
B. Member states account for a population of 3.4 billion people with a total Gross Domestic Product (GDP) of $49.5 trillion (at PPP).
C. RCEP potentially includes more than 3 billion people or 45% of the world's population
D. Combined GDP of negotiating member states is about $21.3 trillion, accounting for about 40 per cent of world trade

165. Which of the following is not correct for Government of India's initiative "Make in India"?
A. It is launched by Prime Minister of India in 2014.
B. It aims to attract Foreign Investment for faster industrial development of India
C. It aims to substitute the imports of India
D. It focuses on the twenty-five sectors of the economy for faster economic growth, export promotion and employment generation

166. The Economics Survey 2019 has proposed a change in the Beti Bachao Beti Padhao (BBBP) scheme. The campaign, to be labelled .... will be used to represent the change towards gender equality.
A. Bahaar
B. Betiya
C. Badlav
D. Bandhan

167. Recently, which of the following scheme has launched by Union Ministry of Skill Development and Entrepreneurship?
A. Pradhan Mantri Jeevan Jyoti Bima Yojana
B. Pradhan Mantri Yuva Yojana
C. MUDRA Bank Yojana
D. Pradhan Mantri Surakshit Matritva Abhiyan

168. The Reserve Bank of India has joined the Central Banks and Supervisors 'Network for Greening the Financial System (NGFS)' as a member. Where is the Secretariat of NGFS located?
A. Paris
B. Geneva
C. Rome
D. London

169. The 'Prime Global Cities Index Q 1 2021' report is published by which entity?
A. KPMG Global
B. Knight Frank
C. REITs
D. Cushman and Wakefield

170. Financial Inclusion is:
A. Representation of all segment of the economy in the financial system
B. Delivery of financial services at affordable costs to sections of disadvantaged and low-income segments.
C. Funding by the government to the low-income segments
D. All of above

ANSWERS

1	2	3	4	5	6	7	8	9	10
C	B	D	B	D	D	D	B	A	A
11	**12**	**13**	**14**	**15**	**16**	**17**	**18**	**19**	**20**
B	A	B	*	A	B	D	C	C	A
21	**22**	**23**	**24**	**25**	**26**	**27**	**28**	**29**	**30**
D	D	A	C	B	C	D	A	C	A
31	**32**	**33**	**34**	**35**	**36**	**37**	**38**	**39**	**40**
D	C	B	D	B	B	B	B	A	D
41	**42**	**43**	**44**	**45**	**46**	**47**	**48**	**49**	**50**
C	B	D	A	A	C	B	D	A	B[#]
51	**52**	**53**	**54**	**55**	**56**	**57**	**58**	**59**	**60**
D	D	B	C	A	B	A	A	A	A
61	**62**	**63**	**64**	**65**	**66**	**67**	**68**	**69**	**70**
A	C	B	A	D	C	C	A	C	A
71	**72**	**73**	**74**	**75**	**76**	**77**	**78**	**79**	**80**
A	C	A	D	B	B	A	A	A	A
81	**82**	**83**	**84**	**85**	**86**	**87**	**88**	**89**	**90**
D	B	D	C	D	D	B	B	D	B
91	**92**	**93**	**94**	**95**	**96**	**97**	**98**	**99**	**100**
A	C	D	C	B	C	C	D	D	B
101	**102**	**103**	**104**	**105**	**106**	**107**	**108**	**109**	**110**
A	B	D	A	B	A	C	A	B	A
111	**112**	**113**	**114**	**115**	**116**	**117**	**118**	**119**	**120**
A	B	B	A	D	C	B	C	B	C
121	**122**	**123**	**124**	**125**	**126**	**127**	**128**	**129**	**130**
B	A	C	A	D	D	C	D	B	D
131	**132**	**133**	**134**	**135**	**136**	**137**	**138**	**139**	**140**
B	C	A	A	A	A	D	B	D	B
141	**142**	**143**	**144**	**145**	**146**	**147**	**148**	**149**	**150**
D	A	D	C	B	D	A	D	D	C
151	**152**	**153**	**154**	**155**	**156**	**157**	**158**	**159**	**160**
C	C	C	C	C	B	C	D	C	A
161	**162**	**163**	**164**	**165**	**166**	**167**	**168**	**169**	**170**
B	C	C	A	C	C	B	A	B	A

* Q.No. 14 is missing [#]Error in question

EXPLANATORY ANSWERS

67. Given, the diagonal of the innermost square = 2 units.

$\therefore$ The diagonal of the seventh square

$$= 2 + 2 + 2 + 2 + 2 + 2 + 2$$
$$= 14 \text{ units}$$

$$\Rightarrow \quad \text{Side}\sqrt{2} = 14$$

$$\Rightarrow \quad \text{Side} = \frac{14}{\sqrt{2}} = 7\sqrt{2} \text{ units}$$

$\Rightarrow$ Area of the seventh square

$$= \left(7\sqrt{2}\right)^2 = 98 \text{ sq. unit}$$

and the diagonal of the eighth square

$$= 2 + 2 + 2 + 2 + 2 + 2 + 2 + 2$$
$$= 16 \text{ units}$$

$$\Rightarrow \quad \text{Side}\sqrt{2} = 16$$

$$\Rightarrow \quad \text{Side} = 8\sqrt{2} \text{ units}$$

$\Rightarrow$ Area of the eighth square

$$= \left(8\sqrt{2}\right)^2 \text{ sq. units}$$
$$= 128 \text{ sq. units}$$

Hence, the difference between the areas of the eighth and seventh squares

$$= 128 - 98 = 30 \text{ sq. units}$$

74.

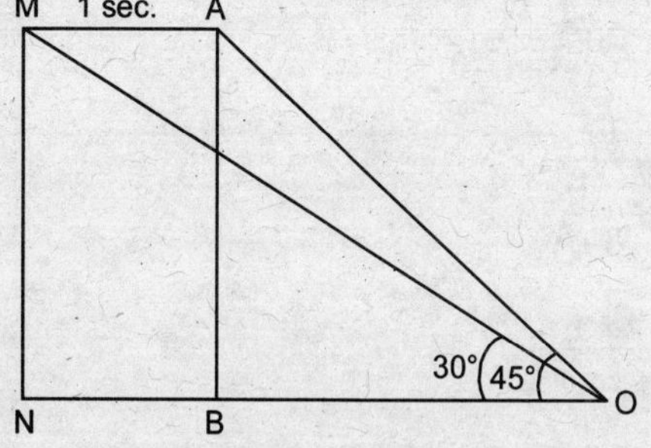

Let AB be a vertical pole.

Given, AB = 20 m

and ∠AOB = 45°

∵ AB = MN and AM = BN

After 1 second, angle of elevation

$$\angle MON = 30°$$

In ΔABO,

$$\tan 45° = \frac{AB}{BO}$$

$$\Rightarrow \quad 1 = \frac{20}{BO}$$

$$\Rightarrow \quad BO = 20 \text{ m}$$

and In ΔMNO,

$$\tan 30° = \frac{MN}{NO}$$

$$\Rightarrow \quad \frac{1}{\sqrt{3}} = \frac{20}{NO}$$

$$\Rightarrow \quad NO = 20\sqrt{3} \text{ m}$$

$$\because \quad BN = NO - BO$$

$$= 20\sqrt{3} - 20$$

$$\therefore \quad BN = 20\left(\sqrt{3}-1\right) \text{ m}$$

$$\Rightarrow \quad AM = 20\left(\sqrt{3}-1\right) \text{ m}$$

Hence, the speed of the bird

$$= \frac{\text{Distance (AM)}}{1 \text{ second}} = \frac{20\left(\sqrt{3}-1\right)\text{m}}{1 \text{ second}} = 20\left(\sqrt{3}-1\right) \text{ m/sec.}$$

80.

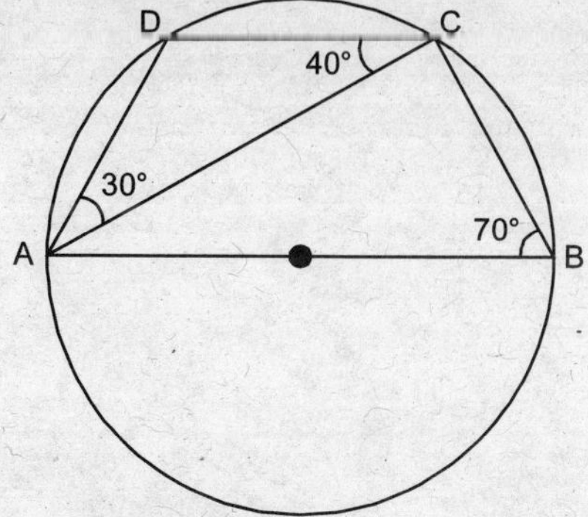

Since, ABCD is a cyclic quadrilateral

$$\therefore \quad \angle ADC + \angle ABC = 180°$$

$$\Rightarrow \quad \angle ADC + 70° = 180°$$

$$\Rightarrow \quad \angle ADC = 110°$$

In ΔACD

$$\angle DAC + \angle CDA + \angle ACD = 180°$$

$$\Rightarrow 30° + 110° + \angle ACD = 180°$$

$$\Rightarrow \angle ACD = 180° - 140°$$

$$\Rightarrow \angle ACD = 40°$$

82. Here, $a = 2$, $d = 2$, $t_{50} = 100$, $n = 50$

We know that

$$\text{Standard deviation} = d\sqrt{\frac{n^2-1}{12}}$$

$$= 2\sqrt{\frac{(50)^2-1}{12}}$$

$$= 2\sqrt{\frac{2500-1}{12}}$$

$$= 2\sqrt{\frac{2499}{12}}$$

$$= 2\sqrt{\frac{833}{4}}$$

$$= \frac{2\sqrt{833}}{2}$$

$$= \sqrt{833}$$

$$\Rightarrow \quad \text{S.D.} = \sqrt{\text{Variance}}$$

$$\therefore \quad \text{Variance} = (\text{S.D.})^2$$

$$= \left(\sqrt{833}\right)^2$$

$$= 833$$

86. 2, 6, 12, 20, 30, 42, [56]

Differences: +4, +6, +8, +10, +12, +14

Second differences: +2, +2, +2, +2, +2

Hence, the next term in the series = 56.

89. Let the sums of money = ₹ x

Then, $\quad \text{simple interest}_1 = \frac{prt}{100}$

$$= \frac{x \times 4 \times 7}{100}$$

$$= ₹\frac{28}{100}x$$

and simple interest$_2$ $= \dfrac{prt}{100}$

$$= \frac{x \times 4.5 \times 7}{100}$$

$$= \frac{x \times \frac{9}{2} \times 7}{100}$$

$$= ₹\frac{63}{200}x$$

According to question,

$$\frac{63}{200}x - \frac{28}{100}x = 31.50$$

$\Rightarrow$ $63x - 56x = 31.50 \times 200$

$\Rightarrow$ $7x = 6300$

$\Rightarrow$ $x = ₹\,900$

Hence, each sum was ₹ 900.

91. Let the length of the side of the square sheet = x units

Given, converted into a cylinder

$\therefore$ Circumference of the base of a cylinder = x

$\Rightarrow$ $2\pi r = x$

$\Rightarrow$ $r = \dfrac{x}{2\pi}$

Hence, required ratio $= \dfrac{x}{2\pi} : x$

$$= \frac{1}{2\pi} : 1 = 1 : 2\pi = \frac{1}{2\pi}$$

94. $15^{23} + 23^{23}$

$= (19 - 4)^{23} + (19 + 4)^{23}$

$= {}^{23}C_0 \,.\, 19^{23} - {}^{23}C_1 \,.\, 19^{22} \,.\, 4 + {}^{23}C_2 \,.\, 19^{21} \,.\, 4^2 + ... + (-1)^{23} \,.\, {}^{23}C_{23} \,.\, 4^{23} + {}^{23}C_0 \,.\, 19^{23} + {}^{23}C_1 \,.\, 19^{22} \,.\, 4 + {}^{23}C_2 \,.\, 19^{21} \,.\, 4^2 + ... + {}^{23}C_{23} \,.\, 4^{23}$

$= 2[{}^{23}C_0 \,.\, 19^{23} + {}^{23}C_2 \,.\, 19^{21} \,.\, 4^2 + ... + {}^{23}C_{22} \,.\, 19 \,.\, 4^{22}]$

$= 2 \times 19[{}^{23}C_0 \,.\, 19^{22} + {}^{23}C_2 \,.\, 19^{20} \,.\, 4^2 + ... + {}^{23}C_{22} \,.\, 4^{22}]$

Hence, when $(15^{23} + 23^{23})$ is divided by 19 then, the remainder is 0.

98. $y = \dfrac{1}{2 + \dfrac{1}{3 + \dfrac{1}{2 + \dfrac{1}{3 + ...}}}}$

$\Rightarrow y = \dfrac{1}{2 + \dfrac{1}{3 + y}}$

$\Rightarrow y = \dfrac{3 + y}{6 + 2y + 1}$

$\Rightarrow y = \dfrac{3 + y}{2y + 7}$

$\Rightarrow 2y^2 + 7y = 3 + y$

$\Rightarrow 2y^2 + 6y - 3 = 0$

Here, $a = 2$, $b = 6$, $c = -3$

$\therefore$ $D = b^2 - 4ac$

$= 36 + 4 \times 2 \times 3$

$= 36 + 24$

$= 60$

$\therefore$ $y = \dfrac{-b \pm \sqrt{D}}{2a}$

$= \dfrac{-6 \pm \sqrt{60}}{2 \times 2}$

$= \dfrac{-6 \pm \sqrt{4 \times 15}}{4}$

$= \dfrac{-6 \pm 2\sqrt{15}}{4}$

$= \dfrac{-3 \pm \sqrt{15}}{2}$

$= \dfrac{-3 - \sqrt{15}}{2}$ or $\dfrac{\sqrt{15} - 3}{2}$.

Previous Paper (Solved)

Jamia Millia Islamia (JMI)

MBA (EXECUTIVE)

Entrance Examination-2021*

1. What day is the fourteenth of a given month?
I. The last day of the month is a Wednesday.
II. The third Saturday of the month was seventeenth.
A. If the data in statement I alone are sufficient to answer the question
B. If the data in statement II alone are sufficient to answer the question
C. If the data either in I or II alone are sufficient to answer the question
D. If the data even in both the statements together are not sufficient to answer the question

2. Among four friends A, B, C and D, who is the heaviest?
I. B is heavier than A, but lighter than D.
II. C is lighter than B.
A. If the data in statement I alone are sufficient to answer the question
B. If the data in statement II alone are sufficient to answer the question
C. If the data even in both the statements together are not sufficient to answer the question
D. If the data in both the statements together are needed

3. It is 8.00 p.m., when can Hemant get next bus for Ramnagar from Dhanpur?
I. Buses for Ramnagar leave after every 30 minutes, till 10 p.m.
II. Fifteen minutes ago, one bus has left for Ramnagar.
A. If the data in statement I alone are sufficient to answer the question
B. If the data in statement II alone are sufficient to answer the question
C. If the data even in both the statements together are not sufficient to answer the question
D. If the data in both the statements together are needed

4. In a certain code '13' means 'stop smoking' and '59' means 'injurious habit'. What is the meaning of '9' and '5' respectively in that code?
I. '157' means 'stop bad habit'.
II. '839' means 'smoking is injurious'.
A. If the data in statement I alone are sufficient to answer the question
B. If the data in statement II alone are sufficient to answer the question
C. If the data either in I or II alone are sufficient to answer the question
D. If the data even in both the statements together are not sufficient to answer the question

5. When is Manohar's birthday this year?
I. It is between January 13 and 15, January 13 being Wednesday.
II. It is not on Friday.
A. If the data in statement I alone are sufficient to answer the question
B. If the data in statement II alone are sufficient to answer the question
C. If the data either in I or II alone are sufficient to answer the question
D. If the data even in both the statements together are not sufficient to answer the question

6. On which day the flat was purchased by Rohan in 1996?
I. Certainly before 18th December, 1996 but definitely not before 15th December, 1996.
II. Certainly after 16th December, 1996 but not later than 19th December, 1996.
A. If the data in statement I alone are sufficient to answer the question
B. If the data in statement II alone are sufficient to answer the question
C. If the data either in I or II alone are sufficient to answer the question
D. If the data in both the statements together are needed

7. Buses are always punctual in city X. How long, at the most, will Mr. Roy have to wait for the bus?
I. Mr. Roy has come to the bus stand at 9 A.M.
II. There is a bus at 10 A.M. and possibly another bus even earlier.
A. If the data in statement I alone are sufficient to answer the question
B. If the data in statement II alone are sufficient to answer the question
C. If the data even in both the statements together are not sufficient to answer the question
D. If the data in both the statements together are needed

* Held on 24/08/2021

8. Gourav ranks eighteenth in a class. What is his rank from the last?

I. There are 47 students in the class.

II. Jatin who ranks 10th in the same class, ranks 38th from the last.

A. If the data in statement I alone are sufficient to answer the question

B. If the data in statement II alone are sufficient to answer the question

C. If the data either in I or II alone are sufficient to answer the question

D. If the data even in both the statements together are not sufficient to answer the question

9. Rohit, Kajol, Tanmay and Suman are four friends. Who is the oldest among them?

I. The total age of Kajol and Tanmay together is more than that of Suman.

II. The total age of Rohit and Kajol together is less than that of Suman.

A. If the data in statement I alone are sufficient to answer the question

B. If the data in statement II alone are sufficient to answer the question

C. If the data either in I or II alone are sufficient to answer the question

D. If the data even in both the statements together are not sufficient to answer the question

10. In a certain code language, '297' means 'tie clip button'. Which number means 'button'?

I. In that language '926' means 'clip your tie'.

II. In that language '175' means 'hole and button'.

A. If the data in statement I alone are sufficient to answer the question

B. If the data in statement II alone are sufficient to answer the question

C. If the data either in I or II alone are sufficient to answer the question

D. If the data even in both the statements together are not sufficient to answer the question

11. What is Gagan's age?

I. Gagan, Vimal and Kunal are all of the same age.

II. Total age of Vimal, Kunal and Anil is 32 and Anil is as old as Vimal and Kunal together.

A. If the data in statement I alone are sufficient to answer the question

B. If the data in statement II alone are sufficient to answer the question

C. If the data either in I or II alone are sufficient to answer the question

D. If the data in both the statements together are needed

12. How is Rakesh related to Keshav?

I. Tapan's wife Nisha is paternal aunt of Keshav.

II. Rakesh is the brother of a friend of Nisha.

A. If the data in statement I alone are sufficient to answer the question

B. If the data in statement II alone are sufficient to answer the question

C. If the data either in I or II alone are sufficient to answer the question

D. If the data even in both the statements together are not sufficient to answer the question

13. Vipin's and Javed's salaries are in the proportion of 4 : 3 respectively. What is Vipin's salary?

I. Javed's salary is 75% that of Vipin's salary.

II. Javed's salary is ₹ 4500.

A. If the data in statement I alone are sufficient to answer the question

B. If the data in statement II alone are sufficient to answer the question

C. If the data either in I or II alone are sufficient to answer the question

D. If the data even in both the statements together are not sufficient to answer the question

14. A, B, C, D and E are sitting in a row. B is between A and E. Who among them is in the middle?

I. A is left of B and right of D.

II. C is at the right end.

A. If the data in statement I alone are sufficient to answer the question

B. If the data in statement II alone are sufficient to answer the question

C. If the data either in I or II alone are sufficient to answer the question

D. If the data in both the statements together are needed

15. How many gift boxes were sold on Monday?

I. It was 10% more than the boxes sold on the earlier day *i.e.*, Sunday.

II. Every third visitor to the shop purchased the box and 1500 visitors were there on Sunday.

A. If the data in statement I alone are sufficient to answer the question

B. If the data in statement II alone are sufficient to answer the question

C. If the data either in I or II alone are sufficient to answer the question

D. If the data in both the statements together are needed

16. In a certain language, 'pit nae mit' means 'red pant shirt'. Which word means 'pant' in that language?

I. 'mit tim nae sir' means 'he wore red pant'.

II. 'nee jic pit' means 'shirt is dirty'.

A. If the data even in both the statements together are not sufficient to answer the question

B. If the data in statement I alone are sufficient to answer the question

C. If the data in statement II alone are sufficient to answer the question

D. If the data either in I or II alone are sufficient to answer the question

17. How many visitors saw the exhibition yesterday?

I. Each entry pass holder can take up to three persons with him/her.

II. In all, 243 passes were sold yesterday.

A. If the data in statement I alone are sufficient to answer the question

B. If the data in statement II alone are sufficient to answer the question

C. If the data either in I or II alone are sufficient to answer the question

D. If the data even in both the statements together are not sufficient to answer the question

18. In what proportion would Raj, Karan and Altaf distribute profit among them?

I. Raj gets two-fifth of the profit.

II. Karan and Altaf have made 75% of the total investment.

A. If the data in statement I alone are sufficient to answer the question

B. If the data in statement II alone are sufficient to answer the question

C. If the data even in both the statements together are not sufficient to answer the question

D. If the data either in I or II alone are sufficient to answer the question

19. What is the price range of ordinary wall clocks?

I. The price range of ordinary wrist watches of company X is ₹ 400 to ₹ 600.

II. The price range of ordinary wall clocks of company X is 50% that of their ordinary watches.

A. If the data in statement I alone are sufficient to answer the question

B. If the data in both the statements together are needed

C. If the data either in I or II alone are sufficient to answer the question

D. If the data even in both the statements together are not sufficient to answer the question

20. Refer to the Statements and choose the most appropriate answer:

I. The Reserve Bank of India has recently put restrictions on few small banks in the country.

II. The small banks in the private and co-operative sector in India are not in a position to withstand the competitions of the bigger in the public sector.

A. Statement I is the cause and statement II is its effect

B. Statement II is the cause and statement I is its effect

C. Both the statements I and II are independent causes

D. Both the statements I and II are effects of independent causes

21. One New York publisher has estimated that 50,000 to 60,000 people in the United States want an anthology that includes the complete works of William Shakespeare. And what accounts for this renewed interest in Shakespeare? As scholars point out, his psychological insights into both male and female characters are amazing even today. This paragraph best supports the statement that:

A. Shakespeare's characters are more interesting than fictional characters today.

B. People even today are interested in Shakespeare's work because of the characters.

C. Academic scholars are putting together an anthology of Shakespeare's work.

D. New Yorkers have a renewed interested in the work of Shakespeare.

22. One of the warmest winters on record has put consumers in the mood to spend money. Spending is likely to be the strongest in thirteen years. During the month of February, sales of existing single-family homes hit an annual record rate of 4.75 million. This paragraph best supports the statement that:

A. consumer spending will be higher thirteen years from now than it is today.

B. warm winter weather is likely to affect the rate of home sales.

C. during the winter months, the prices of single-family homes are the lowest.

D. there were about 4 million homes for sale during the month of February.

23. Today's high school students spend too much time thinking about trivial and distracting matters such as fashion. Additionally, they often dress inappropriately on school grounds. Rather than spending time writing another detailed dress policy, we should make school uniforms mandatory. If students were required to wear uniforms, it would increase a sense of community and harmony in our schools and it would instill a sense of discipline in our students. Another positive effect would be that teachers and administrators would no longer have to act as clothing police, freeing them up to focus on more important issues. This paragraph best supports the statement that:

A. students who wear school uniforms get into better colleges.

B. teachers and administrators spend at least 25% of their time enforcing the dress code.

C. students are not interested in being part of a community.

D. school uniforms should be compulsory for high school students

24. Statement: "Wanted a two-bedroom flat in the court area. For immediate possession."—An advertisement.

Assumptions:

I. Flats are available in court area.

II. Some people will respond to the advertisement.

III. It is a practice to give such an advertisement.

A. All are implicit

B. Only II is implicit

C. None is implicit

D. Only I and II are implicit

25. Statement: This book is so prepared that even a layman can study science in the absence of a teacher.

Assumptions:

I. A layman wishes to study science without a teacher.
II. A teacher may not always be available to teach science.
III. A layman generally finds it difficult to learn science on its own.

A. Only I and II are implicit
B. Only II and III are implicit
C. Only I and III are implicit
D. All are implicit

26. Statement: "We do not want you to see our product on newspaper, visit our shop to get a full view."—An advertisement.

Assumptions:

I. People generally decide to purchase any product after seeing the name in the advertisement.
II. Uncommon appeal may attract the customers.
III. People may come to see the product.

A. None is implicit
B. Only I and II are implicit
C. Only II and III are implicit
D. All are implicit

27. Statement: The company has decided to increase the price of all its products to tackle the precarious financial position.

Assumptions:

I. The company may be able to wipe out the entire losses incurred earlier by this decision.
II. The buyers may continue to buy its products even after the increase.
III. The company has adequate resources to continue production for few more months.

A. Only I and III are implicit
B. Only II is implicit
C. Only II and III are implicit
D. None is implicit

28. How is 'now' written in a code language?

I. 'now and then' is written as 'ka da ta' in that code language.
II. 'then you come' is written as 'da ma pa' in that code language.

A. If the data in statement I alone are sufficient
B. If the data in statement II alone are sufficient
C. If the data either in statements I or II alone are sufficient
D. If the data in both the statements I and II together are not sufficient

29. How is Suniti related to the man in the photograph?

I. Man in the photograph is the only son of Suniti's grandfather.
II. The man in the photograph has no brothers or sisters and his father is Suniti's grandfather.

A. If the data in statement I alone are sufficient
B. If the data in statement II alone are sufficient
C. If the data either in statements I or II alone are sufficient
D. If the data in both the statements I and II together are not sufficient

30. Fact 1: Jessica has four children. Fact 2: Two of the children have blue eyes and two of the children have brown eyes. Fact 3: Half of the children are girls. If the first three statements are facts, which of the following statements must also be a fact?

I. At least one girl has blue eyes.
II. Two of the children are boys.
III. The boys have brown eyes.

A. II only
B. I and III only
C. II and III only
D. None of the statements is a known fact

31. Fact 1: All hats have brims. Fact 2: There are black hats and blue hats. Fact 3: Baseball caps are hats. If the first three statements are facts, which of the following statements must also be a fact?

I. All caps have brims.
II. Some baseball caps are blue.
III. Baseball caps have no brims.

A. I only
B. II only
C. I, II and III
D. None of the statements is a known fact

32. BRISTLE : BRUSH

A. Arm : Leg
B. Stage : Curtain
C. Recline : Chair
D. Key : Piano

33. Look at this series: 2, 1, (1/2), (1/4), ... What number should come next?

A. (1/3)
B. (1/8)
C. (2/8)
D. (1/6)

34. Look at this series: 36, 34, 30, 28, 24, ... What number should come next?

A. 20
B. 22
C. 23
D. 26

35. Look at this series: F2, ..., D8, C16, B32, ... What number should fill the blank?

A. A16
B. G4
C. E4
D. E3

36. Look at this series: V, VIII, XI, XIV, ..., XX, ... What number should fill the blank?

A. IX
B. XXIII
C. XV
D. XVII

37. Look at this series: J14, L16, ..., P20, R22, ... What number should fill the blank?

A. S24
B. N18
C. M18
D. T24

38. Yard is to inch as quart is to:
A. Gallon B. Ounce
C. Milk D. Liquid

39. Candid is to indirect as honest is to:
A. Frank B. Wicked
C. Truthful D. Untruthful

40. B2CD, ..., BCD4, B5CD, BC6D
A. B2C2D B. BC3D
C. B2C3D D. BCD7

41. DEF, DEF2, DE2F2, ..., D2E2F3
A. DEF3 B. D3EF3
C. D2E3F D. D2E2F2

42. Statement: All bags are cakes. All lamps are cakes.

Conclusions:
I. Some lamps are bags.
II. No lamp is bag.
A. Only conclusion I follows
B. Only conclusion II follows
C. Either I or II follows
D. Neither I nor II follows

43. Statement: Some kings are queens. All queens are beautiful.

Conclusions:
I. All kings are beautiful.
II. All queens are kings.
A. Only conclusion I follows
B. Only conclusion II follows
C. Either I or II follows
D. Neither I nor II follows

44. Statement: All young scientists are open-minded. No open-minded men are superstitious.

Conclusions:
I. No scientist is superstitious.
II. No young people are superstitious.
A. Only conclusion I follows
B. Only conclusion II follows
C. Either I or II follows
D. Neither I nor II follows

45. Violating an Apartment Lease occurs when a tenant does something prohibited by the legally binding document that he or she has signed with a landlord. Which situation below is the best example of Violating an Apartment Lease?
A. Tim has decided to move to another city, so he calls his landlord to tell him that he is not interested in renewing his lease when it expires next month.
B. Valerie recently lost her job and, for the last three months, has neglected to pay her landlord the monthly rent they agreed upon in writing when she moved into her apartment eight months ago.
C. Mark writes a letter to his landlord that lists numerous complaints about the apartment he has agreed to rent for two years.
D. Leslie thinks that her landlord is neglecting the building in which she rents an apartment. She calls her attorney to ask for advice.

46. People speculate when they consider a situation and assume something to be true based on inconclusive evidence. Which situation below is the best example of Speculation?
A. Francine decides that it would be appropriate to wear jeans to her new office on Friday after reading about "Casual Fridays" in her employee handbook.
B. Mary spends thirty minutes sitting in traffic and wishes that she took the train instead of driving.
C. After consulting several guidebook and her travel agent, Jennifer feels confident that the hotel she has chosen is first-rate.
D. When Emily opens the door in tears, Theo guesses that she's had a death in her family.

47. Reentry occurs when a person leaves his or her social system for a period of time and then returns. Which situation below best describes Reentry?
A. When he is offered a better paying position, Jacob leaves the restaurant he manages to manage a new restaurant on the other side of town.
B. Catherine is spending her junior year of college studying abroad in France.
C. Malcolm is readjusting to civilian life after two years of overseas military service.
D. After several miserable months, Sharon decides that the can no longer share an apartment with her roommate Hilary.

48. Embellishing the Truth occurs when a person adds fictitious details or exaggerates facts or true stories. Which situation below is the best example of Embellishing the Truth?
A. Isabel goes to the theatre, and the next day, she tells her coworkers she thought the play was excellent.
B. The realtor describes the house, which is eleven blocks away from the ocean, as prime waterfront property.
C. During the job interview, Fred, who has been teaching elementary school for ten years, describes himself as a very experienced teacher.
D. The basketball coach says it is likely that only the most talented players will get a college scholarship.

49. The film director wants an actress for the lead role of Lucy who perfectly fits the description that appears in the original screenplay. He is not willing to consider actresses who do not resemble the character as she is described in the screenplay, no matter how talented they are. The screenplay describes Lucy as an average-sized, forty something redhead, with deep brown eyes, very fair skin, and a brilliant smile. The casting agent has four actresses in mind.

Actress #1 is a stunning red-haired beauty who is 5′9″ and in her mid-twenties. Her eyes are brown and she has an olive complexion.

Actress #2 has red hair, big brown eyes, and a fair complexion. She is in her mid-forties and is 5′5″.

Actress #3 is 5′4″ and of medium build. She has red hair, brown eyes, and is in her early forties.

Actress #4 is a blue-eyed redhead in her early thirties. She's of very slight build and stands at 5′.

A. 1, 2 B. 2, 3
C. 1, 4 D. 2, 4

50. The school principal has received complaints from parents about bullying in the school yard during recess. He wants to investigate and end this situation as soon as possible, so he has asked the recess aides to watch closely. Which situation should the recess aides report to the principal?

A. A girl is sitting glumly on a bench reading a book and not interacting with her peers.
B. Four girls are surrounding another girl and seem to have possession of her backpack.
C. Two boys are playing a one-on-one game of basketball and are arguing over the last basket scored.
D. Three boys are huddled over a handheld video game, which isn't supposed to be on school grounds.

51. Zachary has invited his three buddies over to watch the basketball game on his wide-screen television. They are all hungry, but no one wants to leave to get food. Just as they are arguing about who should make the food run, a commercial comes on for a local pizze-ria that delivers. The phone number flashes on the screen briefly and they all try to remember it. By the time Zachary grabs a pen and paper, each of them recollects a different number.

#1. All of them men agree that the first three numbers are 995.
#2. Three of them agree that the fourth number is 9.
#3. Three agree that the fifth number is 2.
#4. Three agree that the sixth number is 6; three others agree that the seventh number is also 6. Which of the numbers is most likely the telephone number of the pizzeria?

A. 995-9266 B. 995-9336
C. 995-9268 D. 995-8266

52. Statement: Should India encourage exports, when most things are insufficient for internal use itself?

Arguments:

I. Yes. We have to earn foreign exchange to pay for our imports.
II. No. Even selective encouragement would lead to shortages.

A. Only argument I is strong
B. Only argument II is strong
C. Either I or II is strong
D. Neither I nor II is strong

53. Statement: Should all the drugs patented and manufactured in Western countries be first tried out on sample basis before giving licence for sale to general public in India?

Arguments:

I. Yes. Many such drugs require different doses and duration for Indian population and hence it is necessary.
II. No. This is just not feasible and hence cannot be implemented.

A. Only argument I is strong
B. Only argument II is strong
C. Either I or II is strong
D. Neither I nor II is strong

54. Statement: Should there be a ceiling on the salary of top executives of multinationals in our country?

Arguments:

I. Yes. Otherwise it would lead to unhealthy competition and our own industry would not be able to withstand that.
II. No. With the accent on liberalization of economy, any such move would be counter-productive. Once the economy picks up, this disparity will be reduced.

A. Only argument I is strong
B. Only argument II is strong
C. Both I and II is strong
D. Neither I nor II is strong

55. The Pacific yew is an evergreen tree that grows in the Pacific Northwest. The Pacific yew has a fleshy, poisonous fruit. Recently, taxol, a substance found in the bark of the Pacific yew, was discovered to be a promising new anticancer drug. Find the statement that must be true according to the given information.

A. Taxol is poisonous when taken by healthy people.
B. Taxol has cured people from various diseases.
C. People should not eat the fruit of the Pacific yew.
D. The Pacific yew was considered worthless until taxol was discovered.

56. Tim's commute never bothered him because there were always seats available on the train and he was able to spend his 40 minutes comfortably reading the newspaper or catching up on paperwork. Ever since the train schedule changed, the train has been extremely crowded, and by the time the doors open at his station, there isn't a seat to be found. Find the statement that must be true according to the given information.

A. Tim would be better off taking the bus to work.
B. Tim's commute is less comfortable since the train schedule changed.

C. Many commuters will complain about the new train schedule.

D. Tim will likely look for a new job closer to home.

57. Ten new television shows appeared during the month of September. Five of the shows were sitcoms, three were hour-long dramas, and two were news-magazine shows. By January, only seven of these new shows were still on the air. Five of the shows that remained were sitcoms. Find the statement that must be true according to the given information.

A. Only one of the news-magazine shows remained on the air.

B. Only one of the hour-long dramas remained on the air.

C. At least one of the shows that was cancelled was an hour-long drama.

D. Television viewers prefer sitcoms over hour-long dramas.

58. Statement: A large number of people in ward X of the city are diagnosed to be suffering from a fatal malaria type.

Courses of Action:

I. The city municipal authority should take immediate steps to carry out extensive fumigation in ward X.

II. The people in the area should be advised to take steps to avoid mosquito bites.

A. Only I follows B. Only II follows

C. Either I or II follows D. Both I and II follow

59. Statement: Since its launching in 1981, Vayudoot has so far accumulated losses amounting to ₹ 153 crore.

Courses of Action:

I. Vayudoot should be directed to reduce wasteful expenditure and to increase passenger fare.

II. An amount of about ₹ 300 crore should be provided to Vayudoot to make the airliner economically viable.

A. Only I follows

B. Only II follows

C. Either I or II follows

D. Both I and II follow

60. Statement: Exporters in the capital are alleging that commercial banks are violating a Reserve Bank of India directive to operate a post shipment export credit denominated in foreign currency at international rates from January this year.

Courses of Action:

I. The officers concerned in the commercial banks are to be suspended.

II. The RBI should be asked to stop giving such directives to commercial banks.

A. Only I follows

B. Only II follows

C. Neither I nor II follows

D. Both I and II follow

61. Statement: No women teacher can play. Some women teachers are athletes.

Courses of Action:

I. Male athletes can play.

II. Some athletes can play.

A. Only conclusion I follows

B. Either I or II follows

C. Neither I nor II follows

D. Both I and II follow

62. Fact 1: All chickens are birds.

Fact 2: Some chickens are hens.

Fact 3: Female birds lay eggs.

If the first three statements are facts, which of the following statements must also be a fact?

I. All birds lay eggs.

II. Hens are birds.

III. Some chickens are not hens.

A. II only

B. II and III only

C. I, II and III

D. None of the statements is a known fact.

63. Fact 1: Pictures can tell a story.

Fact 2: All storybooks have pictures.

Fact 3: Some storybooks have words.

If the first three statements are facts, which of the following statements must also be a fact?

I. Pictures can tell a story better than words can.

II. The stories in storybooks are very simple.

III. Some storybooks have both words and pictures.

A. I only

B. II only

C. III only

D. None of the statements is a known fact.

64. At the baseball game, Henry was sitting in seat 253. Marla was sitting to the right of Henry in seat 254. In the seat to the left of Henry was George. Inez was sitting to the left of George. Which seat is Inez sitting in?

A. 251 B. 254

C. 255 D. 256

65. "Bundle up," said Aunt Margaret. "I don't want you getting sick and coming down with ammonia."

A. malapropism B. solecism

C. oxymoron D. harangue

66. Jack pleaded, "Can I go on the rollercoaster one more time, Mom? Please? I really, really want to. Pretty please? I'll do extra chores this week. Please?" This little boy is:

A. gainsaying his mother
B. importuning his mother
C. disparaging his mother
D. censuring his mother

67. "You are hopeless! I cannot believe your files are in such disorder," the irritable supervisor shouted. This remark is:
A. effusive B. sententious
C. bombastic D. opprobrious

68. "Come on, Mom! You're not being fair! Why can't I stay out until midnight just like my friends? I'm old enough," stated Marissa emphatically. This teenager is:
A. remonstrating her mother
B. importuning her mother
C. gainsaying her mother
D. being sententious

69. "Oh, wow! I just can't believe it! I'm so excited! This is the best thing ever! I am very, very happy," the new homeowner declared. This remark is:
A. bombastic B. eloquent
C. effusive D. sardonic

70. The cranky old coach yelled, "You call that a pitch? I've seen rookies with better aim." This remark is:
A. derisive B. sententious
C. voluble D. effusive

Directions (Q.No. 71-75): *For the following questions, choose the person who would most likely have the characteristic or attitude noted in italics.*

71. *blithe*
A. a soldier in combat
B. a young child in a playground
C. the mother of a very sick child
D. a surgeon during an operation

72. *petulant*
A. someone who throws a tantrum because his or her soup was not warm enough
B. someone who is going on an important job interview
C. someone who needs to earn a little extra money
D. someone who doesn't like being with other people

73. *puerile*
A. an infant
B. a ten-year-old who has never been given responsibility
C. a thirty-four-year-old with too much responsibility
D. an elderly woman

74. *irascible*
A. someone who just found out he has a rare disease
B. someone who just inherited a farm with 200 acres
C. someone who has just bumped into an old acquaintance, whom she would rather not have seen, from high school
D. someone waiting for his airplane to take off, only to be told four hours later that his flight has been canceled and his luggage has been lost

75. *saturnine*
A. someone who just won the lottery
B. someone who has just fallen in love
C. someone who has just had a loved one end a relationship
D. someone who is sleeping

Directions (Q.No. 76-85): *Choose the answer that is the best response for each question below.*

76. Which of the following traits is most desirable in a roommate?
A. bumptious B. personable
C. pretentious D. puerile

77. Which of the following traits is least desirable in a roommate?
A. diffident B. gregarious
C. sanguine D. surly

78. Which kind of person would most likely make the best waiter?
A. someone who is blithe
B. someone who is overweening
C. someone who is perfidious
D. someone who is punctilious

79. Which kind of person would most likely make the best spy?
A. someone who is capricious
B. someone who is craven
C. someone who is perfidious
D. someone who is sagacious

80. Which kind of person would most likely make the best judge?
A. someone who is diffident
B. someone who is sagacious
C. someone who is sanguine
D. someone who is saturnine

81. Which kind of person would most likely make the best security guard?
A. someone who is bumptious
B. someone who is circumspect
C. someone who is gregarious
D. someone who is perfidious

82. Which kind of person would most likely be the best companion when you are feeling sad?
A. someone who is bumptious
B. someone who is irascible
C. someone who is puerile
D. someone who is sanguine

83. Which character trait would you least like to see in a soldier?
A. craven B. overweening
C. pretentious D. surly

84. Which character trait would you least like to see in a judge?
A. capricious B. circumspect
C. personable D. punctilious

85. Which character trait would you least like to see in a supervisor?
A. blithe B. bumptious
C. overweening D. petulant

Directions (Q.No. 86-90): *Read the following passage carefully and answer the questions given below. Certain words/phrases are printed in bold to help you to locate them while answering some of the questions.*

One may look at life, events, society, history, in another way. A way which might, at a stretch, be described as the Gandhian way, though it may be from times before Mahatma Gandhi came on the scene. The Gandhian reaction to all grim poverty, squalor and degradation of the human being would approximate to effort at self change and self-improvement, to a regime of living regulated by discipline from within. To change society, the individual must first change himself. In this way of looking at life and society, words too begin to mean differently. Revolution, for instance, is a term frequently used, but not always in the sense it has been in the lexicon of the militant. So also with words like peace and struggle. Even society may mean differently, being some kind of organic entity for the militant, and more or less a sum of individuals for the Gandhian. There is yet another way, which might, for want of a better description, be called the mystic. The mystic perspective measures these concerns that transcend political ambition and the dynamism of the reformer, whether he be militant or Gandhian. The mystic measures the terror of not knowing the remorseless march of time; he seeks to know what was before birth, what comes after death? The continuous presence of death, of the consciousness of death, sets his priorities and values: militants and Gandhians, kings and prophets, must leave all that they have built; all that they have unbuilt and depart when messengers of the buffalo-riding Varna come out of the shadows. Water will to water, dust to dust. Think of impermanence. Everything passes.

86. The Gandhian reaction of poverty is:
A. a regulated distribution of wealth
B. self-abnegation
C. self-discipline
D. a total war on poverty

87. According to Gandhianism, the individual who wants to change society
A. may change society without changing himself
B. must change himself
C. must re-form society
D. should destroy the existing society

88. Who, according to the passage, finds new meaning for words like revolutions, peace and struggle?
A. A Gandhian who disciplines himself from within
B. A mystic
C. A militant
D. A Gandhian who believes in non-violent revolution

89. The expression 'water will to water, dust to dust' means
A. man will become dust and water after death
B. man will one day die and become dust
C. man will become water after death
D. water and dust can mix well

90. What does society mean to a Gandhian?
A. a disciplined social community
B. a regime of living regulated by discipline from within
C. an organic entity
D. a sum of individuals

Directions (Q.No. 91-95): *Read the following passage carefully and answer the questions given below. Certain words/phrases are printed in bold to help you to locate them while answering some of the questions.*

India is a country of villages. Rural population still dominates the urban population as far as the number is considered. This is despite the fact that there is rampant migration of rural families to urban centres. Generally, the gains of being a unit of the urban population are less than the disadvantages and risks that are in-built in the urban life. Crime, riots, etc are some of the examples of such risks of urban life. The forces that generate conditions conducive to crime and riots are stronger in urban communities than in rural areas. Urban living is more anonymous living. It often releases the individual from community restraints more common in tradition-oriented societies. But more freedom from constraints and controls also provides greater freedom to deviate. And living in the more impersonalized, formally controlled urban society means that regulatory orders of conduct are often directed by distant bureaucrats. The police are strangers executing these prescriptions on an anonymous set of subjects. Minor offences in small town or village are often handled without resort to official police action. As disputable as such action may seem to be, it results in fewer recorded violations of the law compared to those in the big cities. Although perhaps causing some decision difficulties for the police in small town, formal and objective law enforcement is not always acceptable to the villagers. Urban area with mass population, greater wealth, more commercial establishments and more products of our technology also provide more frequent opportunities for theft. Victims are impersonalized, property is insured, consumer goods in more abundance are vividly displayed and are more portable. The crime rate increases despite formal moral education given in schools.

91. Which of the following would be the best title for the above passage?
A. Lure of Village Life
B. Rural-Urban Rift
C. Hazards of Urban Life
D. Crime and Punishment

92. The passage mainly emphasizes the
A. need for formal moral education to be given in schools
B. reasons for growing crime rate in urban centres as compared to that in rural areas
C. increasing crime rate in rural areas
D. None of these

93. The author thinks that risks and disadvantages are
A. outweigh the gains of rural life
B. surpassed by the gains of urban life
C. almost negligible in rural life
D. more than the gains in urban life

94. Which of the following is a characteristic of an urban setting?
A. Less forceful social control
B. Minimal opportunities of crime due to better law enforcement
C. Deviation from freedom
D. Fewer recorded violations of the law Minimal = very small in size or amount; as small as possible

95. Which of the following statements is TRUE in the context of the passage?
A. Small communities have more minor crimes than in urban centres.
B. Urban crimes cannot be prevented.
C. Lack of personal contacts increases crimes in urban areas
D. The display of consumer goods is the main cause of crime.

Directions (Q.No. 96-98): *Select the best synonym for each vocabulary word. Pick the correct answer.*

96. harbinger
A. forerunner B. harbor
C. convert D. None of these

97. elan
A. spirited B. speed
C. effective D. None of these

98. non sequitur
A. secret B. clarity
C. illogic D. None of these

Directions (Q.No. 99-101): *Select the best antonym for each vocabulary word. Pick the correct answer.*

99. surrogate
A. copy B. survivor
C. original D. None of these

100. melange
A. mix B. desert
C. sameness D. None of these

101. ado
A. trouble B. calm
C. language D. None of these

Directions (Q.No. 102-109): *Read the following sentences carefully. Decide which word best describes what is being said and circle the letter of the correct answer. Please fill in the blanks with the most suitable option.*

When you ....(102).... at an airport, you should go straight to the checkin desk where your ticket and luggage ....(103).... . You ....(104).... your hand luggage with you but your suitcases ....(105).... to the plane on a conveyor belt. You can now go to the departure lounge.

If you are on an international flight, your passport ....(106)...., and then you and your bags ....(107).... by security cameras; sometimes you ....(108).... a body search and your luggage ....(109).... by a security officer.

102. A. start B. started
C. arrive D. are arrived

103. A. are checked B. control
C. check D. is changed

104. A. kept B. keeping
C. wait D. keep

105. A. take B. took
C. are taken D. taking

106. A. check B. checked
C. is checking D. is checked

107. A. are x-rayed B. x-rayed
C. control D. check

108. A. give B. are given
C. gave D. giving

109. A. is searched B. searching
C. searched D. search

110. This bank has launched digital platform 'Merchant Stack' to provide banking services to retail merchants:
A. SBI B. HDFC
C. ICICI D. PNB

111. Who among the following publishes the Economic Survey of India?
A. National Development Council
B. Ministry of Finance
C. Institute Finance
D. Indian Statistical Institute

112. Green Golden Revolution is related to:
A. Oil Seed B. Horticulture and Honey
C. Jute D. Rice and Pulses

113. The idea of *Cultural Poverty* was given by:
A. Oscar Lewis B. Gunnar Myrdal
C. Aashish Bose D. Amartya Sen

114. Who among the following has given the concept of Human Development?
A. Amartya Sen
B. Mahbub-ul-Haq
C. Sukhamoy Chakravarty
D. G.S. Chaddha

115. The Travel and Tourism Competitive Index (TTCI) is released by:
A. World Bank
B. International Monetary Fund
C. World Economic Forum
D. United Nations Development Programme

116. Which one of the following countries is not a founding member of the New Development Bank?
A. Brazil B. Canada
C. Russia D. India

117. As on October 16, 2020 total membership of International Monetary Fund is:
A. 189 countries B. 190 countries
C. 191 countries D. 192 countries

118. In which of the following the term 'cap' and 'trade' used?
A. Share Broking
B. Mutual Fund Investments
C. Emission Trading
D. Commodity Futures

119. Food aggregator company Swiggy has partnered with which bank to launch its own digital wallet?
A. HDFC Bank B. State Bank of India
C. ICICI Bank D. Axis Bank

120. 'Samarth' is an initiative of which E-Commerce company, to help artisans enter digital marketplace?
A. Amazon B. Flipkart
C. Snapdeal D. Shopclues

121. Which organisation launched the 'National Strategy for Financial Education'?
A. RBI B. NPCI
C. SEBI D. SBI

122. Which Indian PSU regained Market Capitalization of ₹ 50,000 crore and entered 100 most valued Indian firms?
A. SAIL B. BHEL
C. NTPC D. BEML

123. Which company has partnered with a not for profit organisation, SEED to launch a community COVID-19 vaccination drive and set up COVID care centres?
A. Samsung B. Amazon
C. PepsiCo D. Apple Inc

124. Who is the winner of the 2021 UNESCO/Guillermo Cano World Press Freedom Prize?
A. Maria Ressa
B. Cheche Lazaro
C. Rodrigo Duterte
D. Mike Enriquez

125. Mahesh Balasubramanian has been appointed as the new MD of which of life insurance company?
A. Kotak Mahindra Life Insurance Company
B. ICICI Prudential Life Insurance Company
C. Aditya Birla Sun Life Insurance Company
D. HDFC Standard Life Insurance Company

126. Which Indian logistics company has launched the 'Oxygen on Wheels' project for transportation of oxygen directly from producing plants to hospitals and homes?
A. Aegis Logistics
B. Container Corporation of India Ltd
C. Adani Logistics
D. Mahindra Logistics

127. SHWAS and AROG are the two new loan products launched by which institution amid the fight against COVID-19?
A. World Bank B. SBI
C. ADB D. SIDBI

128. Which company has acquihired delivery startup Daily Joy?
A. Lenskart B. Amazon
C. Flipkart D. Google

129. Which bank has emerged as the top arranger of corporate bond deals in 2020-21 (FY21)?
A. Kotak Mahindra Bank
B. Axis Bank
C. ICICI Bank
D. HDFC Bank

130. Indian Oil signed MoU for hydrogen generation technology with which institute?
A. IISc B. IIT Kanpur
C. DTU D. None of these

131. Airtel Payments Bank partnered with this insurance company to offer "Smart Plan Shop Package Policy".
A. Bajaj Allianz General Insurance
B. Bharti AXA General Insurance
C. TATA AIG Insurance Company
D. HDFC ERGO General Insurance Company

132. Which of the following become World's first Large Scale Chemical Production Plant to completely run on Renewable Energy?
A. Sipchem
B. Asahi Kasel Corporation
C. Evonik Industries
D. SABIC

133. Which Indian company is set to acquire Mumbai based private sector general insurer Raheja QBE General Insurance Company Limited in a deal worth around $76 million?
A. Myntra B. Paytm
C. Flipkart D. PhonePe

134. Which company has decided to acquire about 25% stake in India's second largest telecom company Bharti Airtel's data centre business-Nxtra Data Ltd-for $235 million?
A. General Electric B. Wal-Mart
C. Carlyle Group D. General Motors

135. Which company will close its physical store locations permanently?
A. IBM B. Microsoft
C. Apple D. Google

136. Which Indian company became the first Indian company to reach a market capitalisation of ₹ 11 trillion?
A. Infosys
B. Reliance Industries Ltd
C. Indian Oil Corporation
D. Tata Power

137. BSNL has partnered with .... to let users connect to nearby Wi-Fi hotspots.
A. Google Pay B. PayPal
C. PhonePe D. Paytm

138. Name the financial institution which has launched 'green' bond fund for central banks to promote green finance.
A. Bank for International Settlements
B. World Bank
C. International Monetary Fund
D. Asian Development Bank

139. Samsung shifted its display manufacturing unit from China to India's which state?
A. Maharashtra B. Madhya Pradesh
C. Karnataka D. Uttar Pradesh

140. Who wrote the book "The Paradoxical Prime Minister"?
A. Khushwant Singh
B. Shashi Tharoor
C. Arundhati Roy
D. Vikram Seth

141. Twelve years ago, Budh was twice as old as Badri. If the ratio of their present ages is 4 : 3 respectively, find the difference between their present ages.
A. 5 years B. 6 years
C. 7 years D. 8 years

142. The sum of the ages of father and his son is 44 years. If 6 years after the father will be 3 times as old as his son, what are their present ages?
A. 36, 8 B. 38, 6
C. 35, 9 D. 37, 7

143. If $a : b$ is 3 : 4 and $b : c$ is 2 : 5. Find $a : b : c$.
A. 3 : 2 : 5
B. 3 : 6 : 5
C. 3 : 4 : 10
D. 2 : 3 : 4

144. The ratio of the total amount distributed in all the males and females as salary is 6 : 5. The ratio of the salary of each male and female is 2 : 3. Find the ratio of the no. of males and females.
A. 5 : 9 B. 5 : 7
C. 7 : 5 D. 9 : 5

145. In a kilometer race, A beats B by 40 metres or by 5 seconds. What is the time taken by A over the course?
A. 1 minute 57 seconds B. 2 minutes
C. 1.5 minutes D. None of these

146. A and B take part in a 100 m race. A rims at 5 km per hour. A gives B a start of 8 m and still beats him by 8 seconds. The speed of B is:
A. 5.15 km/hr B. 4.14 km/hr
C. 4.25 km/hr D. 4.41 km/hr

147. The day on 5th April of a year will be the same day on 5th of which month of the same year?
A. 5th July B. 5th August
C. 5th June D. 5th October

148. On February 5, 1998, it was Thursday. The day of the week on February 5, 1997, was:
A. Wednesday B. Monday
C. Friday D. Sunday

149. Which of the following years in not a leap year?
A. 800 B. 700
C. 1600 D. 2000

150. In a bag, there are 8 red, 7 yellow and 6 green balls. If one ball is picked up at random, what is the probability that it is neither red nor green?
A. $\frac{1}{4}$ B. $\frac{1}{2}$
C. $\frac{1}{5}$ D. $\frac{1}{3}$

151. A man tossed two dice. What is the probability that the total score is a prime number?
A. $\frac{5}{12}$ B. $\frac{5}{14}$
C. $\frac{5}{20}$ D. $\frac{5}{24}$

152. A card is drawn from a pack of 52 cards. What is the probability of getting a king of heart or a queen of club?

A. $\frac{1}{22}$ B. $\frac{1}{24}$
C. $\frac{1}{26}$ D. $\frac{1}{28}$

153. A 60 liter mixture of milk and water contains 10% water. How much water must be added to make water 20% in the mixture?
A. 8 liters B. 7.5 liters
C. 7 liters D. 6.5 liters

154. An alloy contains 14 parts of tin and 100 parts of copper. What is the percentage of tin in the alloy?
A. 12.3% B. 13%
C. 11.5% D. 11%

155. A can do a piece of work in 6 days working 8 hours a day. B can do the same work in 4 days working 6 hours a day. If they work together 8 hours a day, in how many days they will do this work?
A. 3 days B. 3.5 days
C. 2 days D. 2.5 days

156. A man swims 12 km downstream and 10 km upstream. If he takes 2 hours each time, what is the speed of the stream?
A. 1 km/hr B. 0.5 km/hr
C. 1.5 km/hr D. 0.7 km/hr

157. A man can row, 5 km/hr in still water and the velocity of the stream is 1.5 km/hr. He takes an hour when he travels upstream to a place and returns back to the starting point. How far is the place from the starting point?
A. 2.5 km B. 2.275 km
C. 3 km D. 4.5 km

158. A merchant has 1000 kg of sugar part of which he sells at 8% profit and the rest at 18% profit. He gains 14% on the whole. The Quantity sold at 18% profit is:
A. 400 kgs B. 560 kgs
C. 600 kgs D. 640 kgs

159. How many kilograms of sugar costing ₹ 9 per kg must be mixed with 27 kg of sugar costing ₹ 7 per kg so that there may be a gain of 10% by selling the mixture at ₹ 9.24 per kg?
A. 36 kgs B. 42 kgs
C. 54 kgs D. 63 kgs

160. A can contains a mixture of two liquids A and B in the ratio 7 : 5. When 9 litres of mixture are drawn off and the can is filled with B, the ratio of A and B becomes 7 : 9. How many litres of liquid A was contained by the can initially?
A. 10 B. 20
C. 21 D. 25

161. A milkman sells the milk at the cost price but he mixes the water in it and thus he gains 9.09%. The quantity of water in the mixture of 1 liter is:
A. 83.33 ml B. 90.90 ml
C. 99.09 ml D. Can't be determined

162. 39 persons can repair a road in 12 days, working 5 hours a day. In how many days will 30 persons, working 6 hours a day, complete the work?
A. 10 B. 13
C. 14 D. 15

163. If 7 spiders make 7 webs in 7 days, then 1 spider will make 1 web in how many days?
A. 1 B. 3
C. 7 D. 14

164. 2 men and 7 boys can do a piece of work in 14 days; 3 men and 8 boys can do the same in 11 days. Then, 8 men and 6 boys can do three times the amount of this work in:
A. 18 days B. 21 days
C. 24 days D. 30 days

165. If a person having ₹ 2000 and he want to distribute this to his five children in the manner that each son having ₹ 30 more than the younger one, what will be the share of youngest child?
A. ₹ 175 B. ₹ 325
C. ₹ 340 D. ₹ 260

166. By selling 45 lemons for ₹ 40, a man loses 20%. How many should he sell for ₹ 24 to gain 20% in the transaction?
A. 16 B. 18
C. 20 D. 22

167. The percentage profit earned by selling an article for ₹ 1920 is equal to the percentage loss incurred by selling the same article for ₹ 1280. At what price should the article be sold to make 25% profit?
A. ₹ 2000 B. ₹ 2200
C. ₹ 2400 D. Data Inadequate

168. A and B are partners in a business. A contributes 1 14 of the capital for 15 months and B received 2/3 of the profit. For how long B's money was used?
A. 3 months B. 6 months
C. 10 months D. 12 months

169. Michel can swim in still water at the rate of 6 km per hour. After swimming in a stream, she realized that she takes twice the time to go upstream as she takes to go downstream. What is speed of the current?
A. 2.25 km/hr B. 2 km/hr
C. 4 km/hr D. 1.5 km/hr

170. ₹ 1200 divided among P, Q and R, P gets half of the total amount received by Q and R. Q gets one-third of the total amount received by P and R. Find the amount received by R?
A. ₹ 1100 B. ₹ 500
C. ₹ 1200 D. ₹ 700

ANSWERS

1	2	3	4	5	6	7	8	9	10
B	D	D	C	A	D	D	C	D	C
11	**12**	**13**	**14**	**15**	**16**	**17**	**18**	**19**	**20**
D	D	B	D	D	A	D	C	B	B
21	**22**	**23**	**24**	**25**	**26**	**27**	**28**	**29**	**30**
B	B	D	B	B	C	A	D	C	A
31	**32**	**33**	**34**	**35**	**36**	**37**	**38**	**39**	**40**
D	D	B	B	C	D	B	B	D	B
41	**42**	**43**	**44**	**45**	**46**	**47**	**48**	**49**	**50**
D	C	D	D	B	D	C	B	B	B
51	**52**	**53**	**54**	**55**	**56**	**57**	**58**	**59**	**60**
A	A	A	C	C	B	C	D	A	D
61	**62**	**63**	**64**	**65**	**66**	**67**	**68**	**69**	**70**
C	B	C	A	A	B	D	A	C	A
71	**72**	**73**	**74**	**75**	**76**	**77**	**78**	**79**	**80**
B	A	B	D	C	B	D	D	C	B
81	**82**	**83**	**84**	**85**	**86**	**87**	**88**	**89**	**90**
B	D	A	A	C	C	B	B	D	D
91	**92**	**93**	**94**	**95**	**96**	**97**	**98**	**99**	**100**
C	B	D	A	C	A	A	C	C	C
101	**102**	**103**	**104**	**105**	**106**	**107**	**108**	**109**	**110**
B	C	A	D	C	D	A	B	A	C
111	**112**	**113**	**114**	**115**	**116**	**117**	**118**	**119**	**120**
B	B	A	B	C	B	B	C	C	D
121	**122**	**123**	**124**	**125**	**126**	**127**	**128**	**129**	**130**
A	A	C	A	A	D	D	A	D	A
131	**132**	**133**	**134**	**135**	**136**	**137**	**138**	**139**	**140**
B	D	B	C	B	B	D	A	D	B
141	**142**	**143**	**144**	**145**	**146**	**147**	**148**	**149**	**150**
B	A	C	D	B	B	A	A	B	D
151	**152**	**153**	**154**	**155**	**156**	**157**	**158**	**159**	**160**
A	C	B	A	C	B	B	C	D	C
161	**162**	**163**	**164**	**165**	**166**	**167**	**168**	**169**	**170**
A	B	C	B	C	B	A	C	B	B

EXPLANATORY ANSWERS

1. Statement II reveals that 17th was a Saturday and therefore, 14th was Wednesday.

So, only statement II is needed to answer the given question.

Hence option (B) is correct.

2. From I. we have A < B < D

From II. we have C < B

Combining (I) and (II), we can conclude that D is the heaviest.

So, both the statements are needed.

3. It is 8 p.m.

II. One bus has left, 15 minutes ago

∴ Time = 8 p.m. – 15 minutes = 7.45 p.m.

I. Next bus has left for Ramnagar

∴ Time = 7.45 + 30 minutes

= 8.15 p.m.

Hence, both the statements together are needed.

4. From Statement I, we get that

'1' stands for "stop" because that is the common term in "stop smoking" and "stop bad habit"

and that '5' means "habit" because that is common to "injurious habit" and "stop bad habit".

So in code '59', '9' means injurious.

Similarly from Statement II, we get

'1' means smoking and '9' is injurious.

So in code '13', '3' is stop and in code '59', '5' is habit.

So the data either in I or II is sufficient to answer the question.

5. Manohar's birthday = 14 January = Thursday

Hence, I alone are sufficient to answer the question.

6. I. Before 18th December, not before 15 December.

II. After 16th December, not later 19th December.

$\therefore$ On 17th December the flat was purchased by Rohan in 1996.

Hence, both the Statements together are needed.

8. I. Gourav's rank from the last

= 47 – 18 + 1 = 48 – 18 = 30th

II. Total number of students

= 10 + 38 – 1 = 10 + 37 = 47.

Hence, I or II alone are sufficient to answer the question.

33. 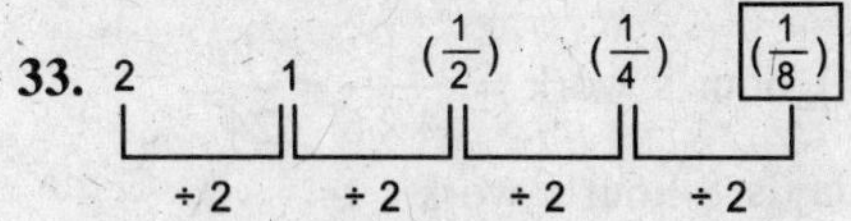

Hence, the next term is $\frac{1}{8}$.

34. 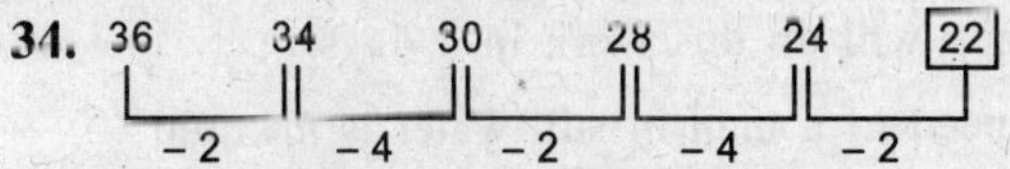

Hence, the next term is 22.

35. F 2 E 4 D 8 C 16 B 32 (× 2, × 2, × 2, × 2; – 1, – 1, – 1, – 1)

Hence, the missing term in the series = E4.

36. 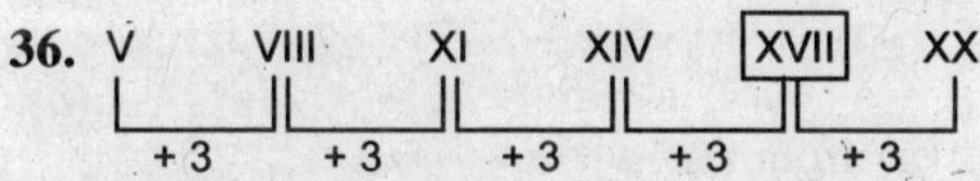

Hence, the missing number = XVII.

37. J 14 L 16 N 18 P 20 R 22 (+ 2, + 2, + 2, + 2; + 2, + 2, + 2, + 2)

Hence, the missing number = N18.

40. B2CD BC3D BCD4 D5CD BC6D (+1, +1, +1, +1)

The missing term = BC3D.

141. Let 12 years ago Badri's age = x years then, Budh's age = $2x$ years

$\therefore$ Badri's present age = $(x + 12)$ years.

and Budh's present age = $(2x + 12)$ years.

Given, Ratio of their present ages is 4 : 3

$\therefore$ $(2x + 12) : (x + 12) = 4 : 3$

$\Rightarrow 3(2x + 12) = 4(x + 12)$

$\Rightarrow 6x + 36 = 4x + 48$

$\Rightarrow 2x = 12$

$\Rightarrow x = 6$

Hence, the difference between their present ages

$= (2x + 12) - (x + 12)$

$= x$ years

= 6 years.

142. Let the present age of son and father are x years and y years

Then, $x + y = 44$ ...(*i*)

given, 6 years after

$3(x + 6) = y + 6$

$\Rightarrow 3x + 18 = y + 6$

$\Rightarrow y - 3x = 12$ ...(*ii*)

Subtracting (*ii*) from (*i*),

$4x = 32$

$\Rightarrow x = 8$

$\therefore y = 36$ [from (*i*)]

Hence, their present ages are 8 years and 36 years.

143. Given $a : b = 3 : 4$

and $b : c = 2 : 5$

$\Rightarrow b : c = 4 : 10$

Hence, $a : b : c = 3 : 4 : 10$.

144. Let the total amount = ₹ x

Then, the salary of all the males = $x \times \frac{6}{11} = ₹\frac{6x}{11}$

and the salary of all the females = $x \times \frac{5}{11} = ₹\frac{5x}{11}$

Let the number of males and females are p and q

Then, $\frac{2p}{3q} = \frac{\frac{6x}{11}}{\frac{5x}{11}}$

$\Rightarrow \frac{2p}{3q} = \frac{6}{5}$

$\Rightarrow \frac{p}{q} = \frac{6}{5} \times \frac{3}{2} = \frac{9}{5}$

Hence, the required ratio of the number of males and females is 9 : 5.

145. Given, A beats B by 40 m or by 5 seconds and total distance = 1 km = 1000 m

The time taken by B over the course

$= \frac{5}{40} \times 1000$ sec = 125 sec

Hence, the time taken by A over the course

= 125 – 5 = 120 seconds = 2 minutes.

146. Given, speed of A = 5 kmph = $\frac{5 \times 5}{18} = \frac{25}{18}$ m/sec.

Let the speed of B = x m/sec.

Then, $\frac{100 - 8}{x} - \frac{100}{\frac{25}{18}} = 8$ sec.

$$\Rightarrow \frac{92}{x} - 72 = 8$$

$$\Rightarrow \frac{92}{x} = 80$$

$$\Rightarrow x = \frac{92}{80} \text{ m/sec.} = \frac{92}{80} \times \frac{18}{5} \text{ km/h}$$

$$= \frac{23}{20} \times \frac{18}{5} = \frac{414}{100} = 4.14 \text{ km/h}$$

Hence, the speed of B = 4.14 km/hr.

148. The year 1997 is an ordinary year

So, it has 1 odd day

∴ The day on 5th February 1998 will be 1 day beyond the day on 5th February 1997. But 5th February 1998 was Thursday

∴ 5th February 1997 will be Wednesday.

150. Total number of balls = 8 + 7 + 6 = 21

Let E = event that the ball drawn is neither red nor green

= event that the ball drawn is blue

∴ $n(E) = 7$

$$\therefore p(E) = \frac{7}{21} = \frac{1}{3}.$$

151. A man tossed two dice

∴ $n(s) = 6 \times 6 = 36$

Let E = event that the total score is a prime number.

Then, E = {(1, 1), (1, 2), (1, 4), (1, 6), (2, 1), (2, 3), (2, 5), (3, 2), (3, 4), (4, 1), (4, 3), (5, 2), (5, 6), (6, 1), (6, 5)}

∴ $n(E) = 15$

$$\therefore p(E) = \frac{n(E)}{n(s)} = \frac{15}{36} = \frac{5}{12}.$$

152. Here, $n(s) = 52$

Let E = event of getting a king of heart or a queen of club.

Then, $n(E) = 2$

$$\therefore p(E) = \frac{n(E)}{n(s)} = \frac{2}{52} = \frac{1}{26}.$$

153. Given, mixture of milk and water = 60 litre

$$\text{Quantity of water} = \frac{60 \times 10}{100} = 6 \text{ litre}$$

∴ Quantity of milk = 60 – 6 = 54 litre

$$\because \frac{6+x}{54} = \frac{60 \times \frac{20}{100}}{60 \times \frac{80}{100}}$$

$$\Rightarrow \frac{6+x}{54} = \frac{12}{48}$$

$$\Rightarrow \frac{6+x}{54} = \frac{1}{4}$$

$$\Rightarrow 24 + 4x = 54$$

$$\Rightarrow 4x = 54 - 24$$

$$\Rightarrow 4x = 30$$

$$\Rightarrow x = \frac{30}{4} = \frac{15}{2} = 7.5$$

Hence, 7.5 litre water must be added in the mixture.

154. Here, total parts of alloy = 14 + 100 = 114

∴ The required percentage of tin in the alloy

$$= \frac{14}{114} \times 100 = \frac{1400}{114} = 12.2807 = 12.3\%.$$

155. A's 1 day's 1 hour's work $= \frac{1}{6 \times 8} = \frac{1}{48}$

and B's 1 day's 1 hour's work $= \frac{1}{4 \times 6} = \frac{1}{24}$

∴ (A + B)'s 1 day's 8 hour's work

$$= 8\left(\frac{1}{48} + \frac{1}{24}\right) = 8\left(\frac{1+2}{48}\right) = 8 \times \frac{1}{16} = \frac{1}{2}$$

Hence, they will do this work in 2 days.

156. Let the speed of a man in still water is u km/hr and the speed of the stream is v km/hr

Then, speed downstream $= \frac{12}{2}$ km/hr

$$\therefore u + v = 6 \quad ...(i)$$

and speed upstream $= \frac{10}{2}$

$$u - v = 5 \quad ...(ii)$$

Subtracting (*ii*) from (*i*)

$$2v = 1$$

$$\Rightarrow v = \frac{1}{2}$$

$$\Rightarrow v = 0.5 \text{ km/hr}$$

Hence, the speed of the stream = 0.5 km/hr.

157. Let the speed of a man in still water is u km/hr and the speed of the stream is v km/hr

and let the distance is the place from the starting point = d km

$$\text{Then, } \frac{d}{u-v} + \frac{d}{u+v} = 1 \text{ hr}$$

$$\Rightarrow \frac{d}{5 - \frac{3}{2}} + \frac{d}{5 + \frac{3}{2}} = 1$$

$$\Rightarrow \frac{2d}{7} + \frac{2d}{13} = 1$$

$$\Rightarrow 2d\left[\frac{13+7}{91}\right] = 1$$

$\Rightarrow \quad d = \frac{91}{40} = 2.275$ km

Hence, the place from the starting point is 2.275 km far.

158. Let the cost price of 1 kg sugar is ₹ 1

Let he sells x kg at 8% profit and rest $(1000 - x)$ kg at 18% profit

Then, $x \times \frac{108}{100} + (1000 - x) \times \frac{118}{100} = 1000 \times \frac{114}{100}$

$\Rightarrow 108x + 118\,(1000 - x) = 114000$

$\Rightarrow 108x + 118000 - 118x = 114000$

$\Rightarrow 108x - 118x = 114000 - 118000$

$\Rightarrow -10x = -4000$

$\Rightarrow x = 400$ kg

$\Rightarrow 1000 - x = 1000 - 400 = 600$ kg

Hence, he sells 600 kg at 18% profit.

159. S.P. of 1 kg mixture = ₹ 9.24, gain 10%

$\therefore$ C.P. of 1 kg mixture = ₹ $9.24 \times \frac{100}{110}$

$= \frac{924}{110} =$ ₹ 8.4

By the rule of alligation

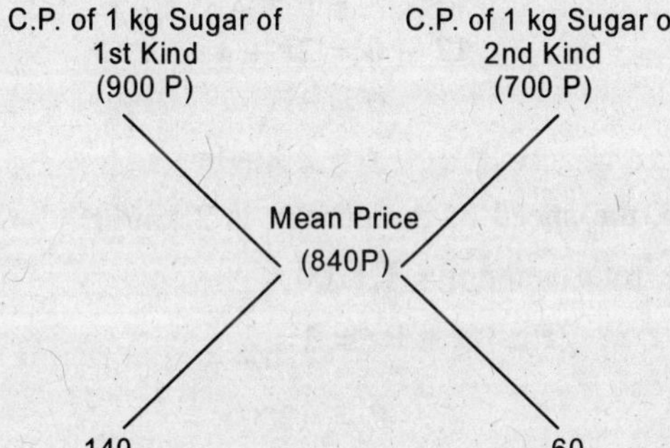

Sugar of 1st kind : sugar of 2nd kind = 140 : 60 = 7 : 3

Let x kg of sugar of 1st kind be mixed with 27 kg of sugar of 2nd kind

Then, $7 : 3 = x : 27$

$\Rightarrow \quad 3x = 7 \times 27$

$\Rightarrow \quad x = 7 \times 9 = 63$ kg.

160. Suppose the can initially contains $7x$ and $5x$ litres of mixtures A and B respectively.

Quantity of A in mixture left

$= \left(7x - \frac{7}{12} \times 9\right)$ litres $= \left(7x - \frac{21}{4}\right)$ litres

Quantity of B in mixture left

$= \left(5x - \frac{5}{12} \times 9\right)$ litres $= \left(5x - \frac{15}{4}\right)$ litres

$\therefore \quad \frac{7x - \frac{21}{4}}{5x - \frac{15}{4}} = \frac{7}{9}$

$\Rightarrow \quad \frac{28x - 21}{20x + 21} = \frac{7}{9}$

$\Rightarrow 252x - 189 = 140x + 147$

$\Rightarrow \quad 112x = 336$

$\Rightarrow \quad x = 3$

Hence, the can initially contained $7x = 21$ litre of A.

161. Let the quantity of water in the mixture of 1 litre is x ml

Then, gain % $= \frac{\text{water}}{\text{1 litre mixture} - \text{water}} \times 100\%$

$\Rightarrow \quad 9.09 = \frac{x}{1000 - x} \times 100$

$\Rightarrow \; 9090 - 9.09x = 100x$

$\Rightarrow \quad 9090 = 109.09x$

$\Rightarrow \quad x = \frac{9090}{109.09} = \frac{909000}{10909}$

$= 83.3256 = 83.33$ ml

Hence the quantity of water in the mixture of 1 litre is 83.33 ml.

162. Here, $M_1 = 39$ persons, $D_1 = 12$ days, $h_1 = 5$ hours, $W_1 = 1$ and $M_2 = 30$ persons, $h_2 = 6$ hours, $D_2 = ?$, $W_2 = 1$

$\because \quad \frac{M_1D_1h_1}{W_1} = \frac{M_2D_2h_2}{W_2}$

$\therefore \quad \frac{39 \times 12 \times 5}{1} = \frac{30 \times D_2 \times 6}{1}$

$\Rightarrow \quad D_2 = \frac{39 \times 12 \times 5}{30 \times 6}$

$= 39 \times 2 \times \frac{1}{6}$

$= 39 \times \frac{1}{3} = 13$ days

Hence, the required days = 13.

163. Here, $M_1 = 7$, $d_1 = 7$, $w_1 = 7$

$M_2 = 1$, $w_2 = 1$, $d_2 = ?$

$\because \quad \frac{M_1d_1}{w_1} = \frac{M_2d_2}{w_2}$

$\therefore \quad \frac{7 \times 7}{7} = \frac{1 \times d_2}{1}$

$\Rightarrow \quad d_2 = 7$

Hence, the required days = 7.

164. Let 1 man's 1 day's work = x

and 1 boy's 1 day's work = y

Then, $2x + 7y = \frac{1}{14}$

$\Rightarrow$ $6x + 21y = \frac{3}{14}$ ...(*i*)

and $3x + 8y = \frac{1}{11}$

$\Rightarrow$ $6x + 16y = \frac{2}{11}$ ...(*ii*)

Subtracting (*ii*) from (*i*), we get

$$5y = \frac{3}{14} - \frac{2}{11}$$

$\Rightarrow$ $5y = \frac{33-28}{154}$

$\Rightarrow$ $5y = \frac{5}{154}$

$\Rightarrow$ $y = \frac{1}{154}$

Putting the value of y in (*i*),

$\therefore$ $6x + 21 \times \frac{1}{154} = \frac{3}{14}$

$\Rightarrow$ $6x + \frac{3}{22} = \frac{3}{14}$

$\Rightarrow$ $6x = \frac{3}{14} - \frac{3}{22} = \frac{33-21}{154}$

$\Rightarrow$ $6x = \frac{12}{154} = \frac{6}{77}$

$\Rightarrow$ $x = \frac{1}{77}$

$\therefore$ (8 men + 6 boys)'s 1 day's work $= 8 \times \frac{1}{77} + 6 \times \frac{1}{154}$

$$= \frac{8}{77} + \frac{3}{77} = \frac{11}{77} = \frac{1}{7}$$

Hence, 8 men and 6 boys can do piece of work in 7 days

Hence, 8 men and 6 boys can do three times the amount of the work in $3 \times 7 = 21$ days.

165. Let the share of youngest child = ₹ x

Then, $x + x + 30 + x + 60 + x + 90 + x + 120 =$ ₹ 2000

$\Rightarrow$ $5x + 300 = 2000$

$\Rightarrow$ $5x = 2000 - 300$

$\Rightarrow$ $5x = 1700$

$\Rightarrow$ $x = 340$

Hence, the share of youngst child will be ₹ 340.

166. Here, S.P. of 45 lemons = ₹ 40, loss = 20%

$\therefore$ C.P. of 45 lemons = ₹ $40 \times \frac{100}{80}$ = ₹ 50

$\Rightarrow$ S.P. of 45 lemons at 20% gain

= ₹ $50 \times \frac{120}{100}$ = ₹ $50 \times \frac{6}{5}$ = ₹ 60

Hence, he should sell lemons for ₹ 24

$$= \frac{45}{60} \times 24 = \frac{3}{4} \times 24 = 18.$$

167. Let the C.P. of an article = ₹ x

Then, $1920 - x = x - 1280$

$\Rightarrow$ $x + x = 1920 + 1280$

$\Rightarrow$ $2x = 3200$

$\Rightarrow$ $x =$ ₹ 1600

Hence, S.P. of an article at 25% profit

$= 1600 \times \frac{125}{100} = 1600 \times \frac{5}{4} =$ ₹ 2000.

169. Let the speed of the current = x km/hr

Then, speed upstream = $(6 - x)$ km/hr

and speed downstream = $(6 + x)$ km/hr

According to the question,

$2(6 - x) = 6 + x$

$\Rightarrow$ $12 - 2x = 6 + x$

$\Rightarrow$ $12 - 6 = 2x + x$

$\Rightarrow$ $6 = 3x$

$\Rightarrow$ $x = 2$ km/hr

Hence, the speed of the current is 2 km/hr.

170. Given, total amount = ₹ 1200

P : (Q + R) = 1 : 2

$\therefore$ P $= 1200 \times \frac{1}{3}$

= ₹ 400

and Q + R = 1200 – 400

= ₹ 800

and Q : (P + R) = 1 : 3

$\therefore$ Q $= 1200 \times \frac{1}{4}$

= ₹ 300

and P + R = 1200 – 300

= ₹ 900

Hence, the amount received by R

= (P + R) – P

= 900 – 400

= ₹ 500.

ENGLISH LANGUAGE

1. Comprehension

Directions (Qs. 1-200) : *Read the following passages carefully and answer the questions given below it. Certain words/phrases are printed in* **bold** *to help you locate them while answering some of the questions.*

PASSAGE–1

It all started twenty-five years ago. I was teaching Economics at a university in Bangladesh. The country was in the middle of a famine. I felt terrible. Here I was, teaching the **elegant** theories of Economics in the classroom with all the **enthusiasm** of a brand-new Ph.D. from the United States. But I would walk out of the classroom and see skeletons all around me, people waiting to die.

I felt that whatever I had learned, whatever I was teaching, was all make-believe stories, with no meaning for people's lives. So I started trying to find out how people lived in the village next door to the university campus. I wanted to find out whether there was anything I could do as a human being to delay or stop the death, even for one single person. I **abandoned** the bird's-eye view that lets you see everything from above, from the sky. I assumed a worm's-eye view, trying to find whatever comes right in front of you-smell it, touch it, see if you can do something about it.

One particular incident took me in a new direction. I met a woman who was making bamboo stools. After a long discussion, I found out that she made only two U.S. pennies each day. I couldn't believe anybody could work so hard and make such beautiful bamboo stools yet make such a tiny amount of profit. She explained to me that because she didn't have the money to buy the bamboo to make the stools, she had to borrow from the trader-and the trader imposed the condition that she had to sell the product to him alone, at a price that he decided.

And that explains the two pennies—she was virtually in bonded labour to this person. And how much did the bamboo cost? She said, "Oh, about twenty cents. For a very good one twenty-five cents." I thought, "People suffer for twenty cents and there is nothing anyone can do about it?" I debated whether I should give her twenty cents, but then I came up with another idea—let me make a list of people who needed that kind of money. I took a student of mine and we went around the village for several days and came up with a list of forty-two such people. When I added up the total amount they needed, I got the biggest shock of my life : It added up to twenty-seven dollars! I felt ashamed of myself for being part of a society which could not provide even twenty-seven dollars to forty-two hard-working, skilled human beings.

To escape that shame, I took the money out of my pocket and gave it to my student. I said, "You take this money and give it to those forty-two people that we met and tell them this is a loan, but they can pay me back whenever they are able to. In the meantime, they can get a good price. After receiving the money, they were very excited.

1. Which of the following can be inferred about the author?
   A. He studied in Bangladesh
   B. He also belonged to a poor family
   C. His Ph.D. was on poverty in Bangladesh
   D. His Ph.D. was in Economics
   E. He started teaching in Bangladesh 25 years after getting his Ph.D. from the United States

2. The author of the passage seems to have–
   A. inspired several people through his lecture to make a living
   B. transformed himself into an action-oriented person to eradicate poverty
   C. continued his teachings excellently and with a lot of enthusiasm
   D. helped his students in their endeavour to eradicate poverty
   E. contributed money for the needy

3. Which of the following is **most opposite** of the word **'Elegant'** as used in the passage?

A. Irrelevant
B. Diluted
C. Crude
D. Ill proportioned
E. Ignoble

4. The contents of the passage prove that poverty can be alleviated if ....
1. there is a strong will to do so.
2. some funds and/or other resources are available.
3. there is a vision to identify and remedy the problems

A. Only 1 and 2
B. Only 2 and 3
C. Only 1 and 3
D. All the three
E. None of these

5. The woman described in the passage could not earn reasonably good money because ....
A. the quality of the goods she made was short of excellence
B. the sale of her products was very scanty
C. the raw material required to make finished products was in short supply
D. there were very few buyers for her goods due to the devastating famine
E. None of these

6. The trader's act to compel the woman to sell the stools only to him can be termed as..........
A. an act of kindness towards the needy woman
B. an ethical business strategy to maximize profit
C. sheer exploitation of the hopeless and needy people
D. contributing some help to the famine-stricken victims
E. None of these

7. What made the author feel ashamed of himself?
A. He lacked in thorough knowledge of Economics and therefore wanted to study more
B. He was ignorant of the fact that even a small help was also going to be significant
C. He was a party to the exploitation of the poor by the trader
D. He was not in a position to take the culprit trader to task
E. He was providing a small amount as a loan and not as donation

8. The survey conducted by the author revealed that............
A. the amount needed to help the village poor to make a living was not very big'
B. it was an unmanageable task for the author to help the needy people of the village
C. there were forty-two traders who were engaged in the act of exploitation of the poor
D. the number of the needy people in the village was very large
E. none of these

Directions (9–10): *Choose the word/group of words which is most nearly the **same** in meaning as the word given in **bold** as given in passage.*

9. Abandoned
A. Gave up
B. Escaped from
C. Accepted
D. Took away
E. Enabled

10. Enthusiasm
A. Excellence
B. Happiness
C. Force
D. Effervescence
E. Zeal

PASSAGE–2

One of the most critical demographic events in the world today is population ageing i.e. the process by which the share of older individuals in the total population starts becoming larger. The ageing phenomenon, which has been initially experienced by developed countries, is now steadily approaching the developing world. Projections show that over the next five decades, world median age will continue to increase, resulting in enhanced old age dependency ratios in all parts of the world. Thus, population ageing would be a major global public policy **concern** in the twenty-first century posing unprecedented challenges for fiscal, monetary and overall macro-economic management.

There is a general **consensus** that ageing population reduces output growth, limits economic welfare and lowers employment. One direct effect of population ageing is labour shortages that are caused by declining birth rates and increasing life **spans.** This translates itself into a higher old-age dependency ratio (i.e. proportion of population aged 65 and older to population aged 15 to 64). Consequently, with ageing, the economy's capacity to **sustain** the elderly population would decline. An important consequence of this development is reflected in increasing fiscal pressures through higher government spending on social security, health care and other welfare programmes for the elderly accompanied by lower tax buoyancy consequent to falling proportions of the productive labour force. Given the hard budget constraint for many developing countries, this could mean lower government spending for programmes that primarily benefit the young. With public pension schemes coming under increasing pressure to raise contribution levels or cut the size of social safety benefits, the issue of fiscal sustainability is one of the principal challenges facing policymakers worldwide, particularly in the context of intergenerational equity.

The experience of US, Western Europe and other Organization for Economic Cooperation and Development

(OECD) countries suggests that substantial demographic changes have occurred in the past few decades. Improvements in life standards, health care and nutrition have increased life expectancy. As a result, the old-age dependency ratio in OECD countries is projected to reach nearly 50 per cent by 2050. This is going to pose a huge fiscal burden in terms of social security, health care, pension and other related expenditures. In this regard, an OECD exercise reveals a rise in old age pension spending, on an average, by about 3-4 percentage points of GDP over the period till 2050. Expenditure relating to health and long term medical care is estimated to increase by more than 3 percentage points of GDP over the same period. Overall, total age-related expenditures relative to GDP could rise on average by about 7 percentage points over the period 2000-2050. In turn, this would imply an average decline of 6-7 percentage points in the primary balance to GDP ratio.

11. Which of the following is definitely **true** of population ageing?
A. It was almost simultaneously experienced by all the countries of the globe
B. The underdeveloped countries cannot experience the phenomenon
C. Developing and developed countries experienced the phenomenon respectively in succession
D. The challenges posed by population ageing had been witnessed in the past also
E. None of these

12. On which of the following points related to population ageing, there is no dispute among thinkers?
A. The direct effect of population ageing is abundance of labourers
B. Economic welfare will be enhanced due to availability of experienced people
C. Employment will be lowered significantly due to population ageing
D. Old age dependency ratio will be lowered significantly
E. None of these

13. The term "population ageing" refers to—
A. the proportion of senior citizens in a developed country
B. the percentage of older people in a developing nation
C. increase in the overall population of a developed country
D. enhancement in the proportion of older people in the population
E. none of these

14. Which of the following factors is responsible for increase in longevity?
(1) Substantial raise in living status
(2) Adequate and timely health care
(3) Nourishing and healthy diet
A. 1 and 2 only B. 2 and 3 only
C. 1 and 3 only D. All the three
E. None of these

15. Which of the following is most likely to happen by middle of the 21st century?
(1) In countries like US and Western Europe, the old-age dependency ratio is likely to touch 50%
(2) Six to seven points increase in primary balance to GDP ratio in OECD countries
(3) Raise to the extent of three to four percentage points of GDP in age old pension spending.
A. 1 and 2 only B. 1 and 3 only
C. 2 and 3 only D. All the three
E. None of these

16. What is most likely to happen if the dependency ratio is higher?
A. It would lower the economist's capacity to sustain the elderly population
B. Govt. spending on social security would significantly decline
C. Productive labour force will increase significantly
D. Due to increased longevity expenditure on health care will reduce
E. None of these

Directions (17–18): *Choose the word which is most nearly the* ***same*** *in meaning as the word given in* ***bold*** *as given in the passage.*

17. Consensus
A. agreement B. consent
C. harmony D. compromise
E. interaction

18. Span
A. width B. gap
C. duration D. distance
E. extent

Directions (19–20): *Choose the word which is most* ***opposite*** *in meaning of the word given in* ***bold*** *as given in the passage.*

19. Concern
A. reassurance B. comfort
C. anxiety D. indifference
E. neglect

20. Sustain
A. prolong B. uphold
C. protract D. diminish
E. quit

PASSAGE–3

Management is a set of processes that can keep a complicated system of people and technology running smoothly. The most important aspects of management include planning, budgeting, organizing, staffing, controlling, and problem solving. Leadership is a set of processes that creates organizations in the first place or adapts them to significantly changing circumstances. Leadership defines what the future should look like, aligns people with that vision, and inspires them to make it happen despite the obstacles. This distinction is absolutely crucial for our purposes here. Successful transformation is 70 to 90 per cent leadership and only 10 to 30 per cent management. Yet for historical reasons, many organizations today don't have much leadership. And almost everyone thinks about the problem here as one of managing change.

For most of this century, as we created thousands and thousands of large organizations for the first time in human history, we didn't have enough good managers to keep all those bureaucracies functioning. So many companies and universities developed management programs, and hundreds and thousands of people were encouraged to learn management on the job. And they did. But, people were taught little about leadership. To some degree, management was emphasized because it's easier to teach than leadership. But even more so, management was the main item on the twentieth-century agenda because that's what was needed. For every entrepreneur or business builder who was a leader, we needed hundreds of managers to run their ever-growing enterprises.

Unfortunately for us today, this emphasis on management has often been institutionalized in corporate cultures that discourage employees from learning how to lead. Ironically, past success is usually the key ingredient in producing this outcome. The syndrome, as I have observed it on many occasions, goes like this: Success creates some degree of market dominance, which in turn produces much growth. After a while keeping the ever-larger organization under control becomes the primary challenge. So attention turns inward, and managerial competencies are **nurtured.** With a strong emphasis on management but not leadership, bureaucracy and an inward focus take over. But with continued success, the result mostly of market dominance, the problem often goes unaddressed and an unhealthy arrogance begins to evolve. All of these characteristics then make any transformation effort much more difficult.

Arrogant managers can over-evaluate their current performance and competitive position, listen poorly, and learn slowly. Inwardly focused employees can have difficulty seeing the very forces that present threats and opportunities. Bureaucratic cultures can **smother** those who want to respond to shifting conditions. And the lack of leadership leaves no force inside these organizations to break out of the morass.

21. Which of the following is **not** the characteristic of bureaucratic culture?

A. Manager's listen poorly and learn slowly.
B. Managerial competencies are nurtured.
C. Employee clearly see the forces that present threats and opportunities.
D. Prevalence of unhealthy arrogance.
E. Managers tend to stifle initiative and innovation.

22. Which of the following statements is **not true** in the context of the passage?

A. Bureaucratic culture smother those who want to respond to changing conditions.
B. Leadership produces change and has the potential to establish direction.
C. Pressure on managers come mostly from within.
D. Leadership centres on carrying out important functions such as planning and problem solving.
E. Managers believe that they are the best and that their idiosyncratic traditions are superior.

23. Why did companies and universities develop programmes to prepare managers in such a large number?

A. Companies and Universities wanted to generate funds through these programmes.
B. The large number of organizations were created and they needed managers in good number.
C. Organizations did not want to spend their scarce resources in training managers.
D. Organizations wanted to create communication network through trained managers.
E. None of these

24. Management education was emphasized in the management programs because --------

A. establishing direction was the main focus of organizations.
B. motivating employees was thought to be done by managers.
C. strategies for producing change was the main focus of organizations.
D. organizations wanted to create powerful guiding coalition.
E. management was the main item of agenda in organizations.

25. How, the author, has defined management?

A. It is the process of adapting organizations to changing circumstances.
B. It is the system of aligning people with the direction it has taken.
C. It refers to creating a vision to help direct the change effort.
D. Creating better performance through customer orientation.
E. None of these

26. Which of the following is **similar** in meaning of the word **'smother'** as used in the passage?

A. suppress B. encourage
C. instigate D. criticize
E. attack

27. Why, according to the author, a distinction between management and leadership is crucial?
A. Leaders are reactive whereas managers are proactive.
B. Organizations are facing problems of not getting good managers.
C. Organizations are pursuing the strategy of status-quo
D. In today's context organizations need leaders much more than managers in transforming them.
E. None of these

28. What, according to the author, is leadership?
A. Process which keeps system of people and technology running smoothly.
B. Planning the future and budgeting resources of the organization.
C. Inspiring people to realize the vision.
D. Carrying out the crucial functions of management.
E. None of these.

29. Why were people taught little about leadership in management programmes?
A. Teachers were busy in understanding the phenomenon of leadership.
B. Enough study material was not available to facilitate teaching of leadership.
C. Focus of these programmes was on developing managers.
D. Leadership was considered only a political phenomenon.
E. None of these

30. What is the historical reason for many organizations not having leadership?
A. A view that leaders are born, they are not made.
B. Leaders lack managerial skills and organizations need managers.
C. Leaders are weak in carrying out traditional functions of management.
D. Leaders allow too much complacency in organizations.
E. None of these

31. Which of the following characteristics help organizations in their transformation efforts?
A. Emphasis on leadership but not management
B. A strong and dogmatic culture
C. Bureaucratic and inward looking approach
D. Failing to acknowledge the value of customers and shareholders
E. None of these

32. Which of the following statements is/are **definitely true** in the context of the passage?
1. Bureaucracy fosters strong and arrogant culture.
2. Leadership competencies are nurtured in large size organizations.
3. Successful transformation in organizations is 70 to 90 per cent leadership.
A. Only 1 and 2 B. Only 1 and 3
C. Only 2 and 3 D. Only 2
E. Only 3

33. In the passage, management is equated with—
A. organization
B. leadership
C. organizational vision
D. bureaucracy
E. managerial training

34. Which of the following is **similar** in meaning of the word **'nurtured'** as used in the passage?
A. created B. developed
C. thwarted D. surfaced
E. halted

35. Why does the attention of large organizations turn inward?
A. Their managers become arrogant.
B. They have to keep themselves under control.
C. Their success creates market dominance.
D. They want to project their predictability
E. None of these

PASSAGE–4

The University Grants Commission's directive requiring college and university lecturers to spend a minimum of 22 hours a week in direct teaching is the product of budgetary cutbacks rather than pedagogic wisdom. It may seem odd, at first blush, that teachers should protest about teaching a mere 22 hours. However, if one considers the amount of time academics require to prepare lectures of good quality as well as the time they need to spend doing research — it is clear that most conscientious teachers work more than 40 hours a week. In university systems around the world, lecturers rarely spend more than 12 to 15 hours in direct teaching activities a week. The average college lecturer in India does not have any office space. If computers are available, Internet connectively is unlikely. Libraries are poorly stocked. Now the UGC says universities must implement a complete **freeze** on all permanent recruitment, abolish all posts which have been vacant for more than a year, and cut staff strength by 10 per cent. And it is in order to ensure that these cutbacks do not affect the quantum of teaching that existing lecturers are being asked to work longer. Obviously, the quality of teaching — and academic work in general — will decline. While it is true that some college teachers do not take their classes regularly, the UGC and the institutions concerned must find a proper way to hold them accountable. An absentee teacher will continue to play truant even if the number of hours he is required to teach goes up.

All of us are well aware of the unsound state that the Indian higher education system is in today. Thanks to years of **sustained** financial neglect, most Indian universities and colleges do no research worth the name. Even as the number of students entering colleges has increased dramatically, public investment in higher education has actually declined in relative terms. Between 1995 and 2007, when public expenditure on higher education as a percentage of outlays on all levels of education grew by more than 60 per cent in Malaysia and 20 per cent in Thailand, India showed a decline of more than 10 per cent. Throughout the world, the number of teachers in higher education per million population grew by more than 10 per cent in the same period; in India, it fell by one per cent. Instead of transferring the burden of government apathy on to the backs of the teachers, the UGC should insist that the needs of the country's university system are adequately catered for.

36. Why does the UGC want to increase the direct teaching hours of university teachers?
- A. UGC feels that the duration of contact between teacher and the taught should be more
- B. UGC wants teachers to spend more time in their departments
- C. UGC wants teachers to devote some time to improve university administration
- D. UGC does not have money to appoint additional teachers
- E. None of these

37. Which of the following is the reason for the sorry state of affairs of the Indian Universities as mentioned in the passage?
- A. The poor quality of teachers
- B. Involvement of teachers in extracurricular activities
- C. Politics within and outside the departments
- D. Heavy burden of teaching hours on the teachers
- E. Not getting enough financial assistance

38. Which of the following statement(s) is/are TRUE in the context of the passage?
1. Most colleges do not carry out research worth the name.
2. UGC wants lecturers to spend minimum 22 hours a week in direct teaching.
3. Indian higher education system is in unsound state.

- A. Only (1) and (3)
- B. All (1), (2) and (3)
- C. Only (3)
- D. Only (2)
- E. Only (2) and (3)

39. Besides direct teaching, University teachers spend considerable time in/on.....
- A. administrative activities such as admissions
- B. supervising examinations and correction of answer papers
- C. carrying out research in the area of their interest
- D. maintaining research equipment and libraries
- E. developing liaison with the user organizations

40. Which of the following statements is **not true** in the context of the passage?
- A. UGC wants teachers to spend minimum 40 hours in a week in teaching
- B. Some college teachers do not engage their classes regularly
- C. The average collect teacher in India does not have any office space
- D. UGC wants universities to abolish all posts which have been vacant for more than a year
- E. All of these are true

41. Between 1995 and 2007, the number of teachers in higher education per million population, in India........
- A. increased by 60%
- B. increased by 20%
- C. decreased by 22%
- D. decreased by 10%
- E. decreased by 1%

42. Which of the following statements is **not true** in the context of the passage?
- A. Indian universities are financially neglected.
- B. All over the world, the university lecturers hardly spend more than 12 to 15 hours a week in direct teaching
- C. Indian universities are asked to reduce staff strength by 10%
- D. Public investment in higher education has increased in India
- E. Malaysia spends more money on education than Thailand

43. Choose the word which is **similar** in meaning as the word **'freeze'** as used in the passage.
- A. Cold
- B. Halt
- C. Decay
- D. Control
- E. Power

44. What is the UGC directive to the universities?
- A. Improve the quality of teaching
- B. Spend time on research activities
- C. Do not appoint any permanent teacher
- D. Provide computer and internet facilities
- E. Do not spend money on counselling services to the students

45. Choose the word which is **similar** in meaning as the word **'sustained'** as used in the passage.
A. Continuous B. Frequent
C. Careless D. Deliberate
E. Sporadic

PASSAGE–5

Comfort is now one of the causes of its own spread. It has now become a physical habit, a fashion, an ideal to be pursued for its own sake. The more comfort is brought into the world, the more it is likely to be valued. To those who have known comfort, discomfort is a real torture. The fashion which now **decrees** the worship of comfort is quite as imperious as any other fashion. Moreover, enormous material interests are bound up with the supply of the means of comfort. The manufacturers of furniture, of heating apparatus, of plumbing fixtures cannot afford to let the love of comfort die. In modern advertisements they have found a means for compelling it to live and grow. A man of means today, who builds a house is in general concerned primarily with the comfort of his future residence. He will spend a great deal of money on bathrooms, heating apparatus, padded furnishings, and having spent, he will regard his house as perfect. His counterpart in an earlier age would have been primarily concerned with the impressiveness and magnificence of his dwelling—with beauty, in a word, rather than comfort. The money our contemporary would spend on baths and central heatings would have been spent on marble staircases, frescoes, pictures and statues. I am inclined to think that our present passion for comfort is a little exaggerated. Though I personally enjoy comfort, I have lived most happily in houses **devoid of** everything that Anglo-Saxons deem **indispensable**. Orientals and even South Europeans who know not comfort and live very much as our ancestors did centuries ago, seem to go on very well without our elaborate apparatus and padded luxuries. However, comfort for me has a justification; it facilitates mental life. Discomfort handicaps thought; it is difficult to use the mind when the body is cold and aching.

46. Choose the word that is **similar** in meaning of the word **'devoid of'** as used in the passage.
A. available B. lacking
C. empty D. false
E. deficient

47. How people manage to keep the love of comfort alive?
A. By pumping in more comfort goods in the market
B. By sacrificing high profits on comfort goods
C. By targeting youth in the sales campaign
D. By appealing to the emotionality of people
E. None of these

48. What is the author's prediction about comfort?
A. The value of comfort will increase
B. People will value more spirituality thus reducing the value of comfort
C. People will desire simple life style
D. The advertisements will play down the comfort aspect of goods
E. None of these

49. What was the characteristic of affluent man of an **earlier age**?
A. He used to put higher premium on comfort
B. He was relying much on advertisements
C. He believed more in simple and cheaper things
D. He was more qualitative in his emphasis rather than being quantative
E. His emphasis was on beauty

50. What change according to the author has taken place in the attitude to comfort?
A. It is taken for granted in the modern way of living
B. It has become now an ideal to be pursued for its own sake
C. It is now believed that discomfort handicaps thought
D. It is thought that comfort helps body and mind to function effectively
E. None of these

51. Choose the word which is **similar** in meaning of the word **'decree'** as used in the passage.
A. order B. spread
C. projected D. attract
E. exhibit

52. Why does the author value comfort?
A. It helps to project one's image
B. It helps to project your values
C. It facilitates mental life
D. It encourages a blend of materialistic and spiritual thinking
E. None of these

53. Why would manufacturers of various devices not permit comfort to die?
A. They want to manufacture more and more comfort goods
B. Manufacturers' are mainly interested in creating new things
C. Manufacturers' emphasis is on producing beautiful things
D. Their prosperity is closely linked with the people's desire for comfort
E. None of these

54. Choose the word which is **most opposite** in meaning of the word **'Indispensable'** as used in the passage.
A. unattractive B. avoidable

C. favourable D. inelegant
E. comfortable

55. Which of the following statements is **not true** in the context of the passage?
A. Discomfort is not liked by those who live in comfort
B. The affluent man of an earlier age was interested more in beauty than in comfort
C. Discomfort handicaps thought
D. Orientals and South Europeans love comfort immensely
E. Author of the passage enjoys comfort

PASSAGE–6

Using infant mortality as a key indicator of the status of children, we now begin to have the broad features of a hypothesis as to the causes of higher or lower mortality rates. One aspect is the **complex** of factors involving the **access** of mothers to trained personnel and other facilities for child delivery, the nutritional status of pregnant and nursing mothers and the quality of health-care and nourishment which babies receive. The other aspect, indicated by rural-urban differentials, is the possible importance of human settlement patterns in relation to the availability of health-care and related facilities such as potable water, excreta disposal systems, etc. Thus, in a special sense, it is much cheaper to make health and other basic services available to a community when it is densely settled rather than widely dispersed.

It is possible to argue, however, that both these sets of factors are closely related to a third one, namely income levels. Poorer mothers and babies have less access to health-care facilities and nourishment than those who are better-off, urban communities are on an average much better-off than rural communities. That economic conditions play a crucial role in determining the status of both mother and child is beyond dispute. But the question really is whether this is the only decisive factor or whether factors such as the availability of medical facilities, health-care programmes and nutritional programmes have an independent role. If so, then the settlement patterns which affect service delivery to the mother and child target groups become a relevant consideration. These are clearly issues of some importance for policy and programme planning.

56. Which of the following can be inferred from the passage?
A. Infant mortality rate is higher in rural areas as compared to that of urban areas
B. Income level alone can predict the infant mortality rate
C. There, now, is more population in urban areas as compared to rural areas
D. Delivery of services to the mother and child does not depend on the settlement pattern
E. The rural areas have now become densely-populated

57. Which of the following is the issue of importance for policy?
A. Relationship of mortality and income levels
B. Growing rural-urban differentials
C. Infant-mortality rate and mortality rate inter-dependence
D. Dependence of education level of the mother and infant mortality rate
E. Independence of factors other than income on infant mortality

58. Which, according to the passage, is the other main indicator of the status of children, besides infant mortality?
A. Educational level B. Nourishment level
C. Weight at birth D. Not mentioned
E. None of these

59. What is the advantage of providing services in the urban areas, as compared to that of rural areas?
A. The services are cheaply available
B. Per-capita expenditure for setting up services is much less
C. There is more awareness about availability of services
D. The investment can be received in short duration
E. It is much easier to set up services

60. Which of the following is the **same** in meaning as the word **'access'** as used in the passage?
A. Passage B. Outburst
C. Surplus D. Demand
E. Reach

61. Which of the following is not to factor for mortality rate?
A. Settlement pattern B. Type of child delivery
C. Nutritional status D. Potable water
E. Income level

62. Which of the following is the **same** in meaning as the word **'complex'** as used in the passage?
A. Building B. Nature
C. Composite D. List
E. Types

PASSAGE–7

To open up a field of study, draw attention to its vital elements, the lecture is invaluable. To listen to a lecture can be thrilling experience from which the student may gain ideas obtainable in no other way. But possibly to a greater degree than other forms of instruction, lecturing presumes a high order of intellectual competence on the part of learners. The purposes of the lecture are to summarize, to clarify, to stimulate and to humanize the materials of the course. It should synthesize, evaluate, criticise and compare ideas and facts with which students have come in contact through out-of-class assignments.

The effectiveness of lectures could be enhanced by introducing the lecture with a brief review of the work preceding. It should also be indicated how the day's lecture fits into the course pattern. A lecture should seldom be presented in one unbroken discourse. Unless exceptionally interesting, a long lecture **strains** the capacity for concentrated listening, causing intermittent wandering of attention and loss of continuity in thought. The lecture should therefore be organized in a few block or units. As a rule, the exposition should be concluded before the end of the class period so as to allow some time for general discussion.

For students to obtain maximum benefit from a lecture, individual participation in study both precede and follow it. On their own initiative, most students would not engage in preparatory study, hence formal assignments may be necessary. The lecture should be concluded on the assumption that the assignment has been fulfilled. It pays to explore the aids available for teaching a course particularly through lectures, since verbal exposition alone, however **lucid**, has its shortcomings.

63. Which of the following is the best suited title for the passage?
A. Methods of Teaching
B. Effective Learning
C. Contrast Programmes
D. Lecture-Method
E. Teaching Without Tears

64. Which of the following is the **same** in meaning as the word '**strains**' as used in the passage?
A. Spoils
B. Damages
C. Drains energy from
D. Requires greater effort
E. Puts premium on

65. An uninterrupted discourse type method results into.........
A. loss of attention
B. a thrilling experience
C. stimulation of interest
D. humanising the course material
E. None of these

66. Which of the following is **not true** in the context of the passage?
A. Students on their own take up assignments
B. Lecture method humanises the course content
C. There are many methods of teaching
D. Improvements can be made in the traditional lecture method of instruction
E. Various aids can be used with lecture method

67. Compared to other methods, lecturing requires ....
A. more competent trainer
B. bigger number of students
C. higher level of learner
D. a new field of study
E. better presentation of ideas

68. The passage seems to be written chiefly for.........
A. students B. educators
C. parents D. researchers
E. administrators

69. The effectiveness of lectures can be enhanced by which of the following?
1. Breaking it into units
2. Showing its integration in the course
3. In the end giving some time for discussion
A. 1 and 2 only B. 3 only
C. 1 and 3 only D. 2 and 3 only
E. All 1, 2 and 3

70. Which of the following is the same in meaning as the word '**lucid**' as used in the passage?
A. long B. interesting
C. clear D. ideal
E. thrilling

PASSAGE–8

A new analysis has determined that the threat of global warning can still be greatly **diminished** if nations cut emissions of heat-trapping greenhouse gases by 70% this century. The analysis was done by scientists at the National Center for Atmospheric Research (NCAR). While global temperatures would rise, the most dangerous potential aspects of climate change including **massive** losses of Arctic sea ice and permafrost and **significant** sea-level rise, could be partially avoided.

"This research indicates that we can no longer avoid significant warming during this century," said NCAR scientist Warren Washington, the study paper's lead author. "But, if the world were to implement this level of emission cuts, we could stabilize the threat of climate change", he added.

Average global temperatures have warmed by close to degree Celsius since the pre-industrial era. Much of the warming is due to human-produced emissions of greenhouse gases, **predominantly** carbon dioxide. This heat-trapping gas has increased from a pre-industrial level of about 284 parts per million (ppm) in the atmosphere to more than, 380 ppm today. With research showing that additional warming of about 1 degree C may be the threshold for dangerous climate change, the European Union has called for **dramatic** cuts in emissions of carbon dioxide and other greenhouse gases.

To examine the impact of such Cuts on the world's climate, Washington and his colleagues ran a series of global studies with the NCAR-based Community Climate System Model (CCSM). They assumed that carbon dioxide levels could be held to 450 ppm at the end of this century. In contrast, emissions are now on track to reach about 750 ppm by 2100, if unchecked. The team's results showed that if carbon dioxide were held to 450 ppm; global temperatures would increase by 0.6 degrees Celsius above current readings by the end of the century. In contrast, the study showed that temperatures would rise by almost four times that amount, to 2.2 degrees Celsius above current readings, if emissions were allowed to continue on their present course. Holding carbon dioxide levels to 450 ppm would have other impacts, according to the climate modeling study.

Sea-level rise due to thermal expansion as water temperatures warmed would be 14 centimeters (about 5.5 inches) instead of 22 centimeters (8.7 inches). Also, Arctic ice In the summertime would **shrink** by about a quarter in volume and stabilize by 2100; as **opposed** to shrinking, at least three-quarters and continuing to melt, and Arctic warming would be reduced by almost half.

71. Why has the European Union called for dramatic cuts in carbon dioxide and greenhouse gas emissions?
A. As global warming is not an issue of concern
B. As the temperatures may rise almost by an additional one degree and this may lead to severe climate change.
C. As the NCAR has forced the European. Union to announce the cuts.
D. As all the nations have decided to cut emissions of carbon dioxide
E. None of these

72. What would **not** be one of the impacts of cutting greenhouse gas emissions?
A. Temperatures will stop soaring
B. Ice in the Arctic sea would melt at a slower pace
C. The rise in sea level would be lesser
D. All of the above would be the impact
E. None of these

73. What would be the impact of unchecked greenhouse gas and carbon dioxide emissions?
A. The temperature would rise from the current temperature by 2.2 degrees Celsius
B. The sea-level would rise by about 5.5 inches
C. The arctic ice would stabilize by 2100
D. The arctic ice would reduce by one-fourth
E. None of these

74. What can be the most appropriate title of the above passage?
A. A study of the rise in water level
B. A study of rise in temperatures
C. A study of the effects of greenhouse gas emissions
D. A study of the Arctic region
E. A study of change in seasons

75. Which of the following statements is true in context of the passage?
A. At present the carbon dioxide emission is about 284 ppm.
B. The carbon dioxide emissions will be about 450 ppm at the end of this century if unchecked.
C. The carbon dioxide emission was about 380 ppm during the pre-industrial era.
D. The carbon dioxide emissions will be about 750 ppm at the end of this century if unchecked.
E. None of these

76. What does the scientist Warren Washington mean when he says "we could stabilize the threat of climate change"?
A. Climate change can be stopped completely.
B. Climate change can be regularized.
C. Climate change and its affects can be studied extensively.
D. the ill-effects of the change in climate can be minimized.
E. None of these

77. Why did Washington and his colleagues conduct a series of studies?
A. Bcause they realized that the temperature increase was almost about 1 degree
B. So that they could stabilize the climate change.
C. So that they could help the European Union in cutting the carbon dioxide emissions
D. Because they found out that the greenhouse gas emissions could be cut by 70%
E. None of these

78. What would be the impact of holding the carbon dioxide level at 450 ppm at the end of this century?
1. Global temperatures would increase by 0.6 degrees Celcius.
2. Arctic warming would be reduced by half.
3. Thermal, expansion will stop completely.
A. Only 1
B. Only 1 and 2
C. Only 2 and, 3
D. All the three 1, 2 and 3
E. None of these

PASSAGE–9

John Maynard Keynes, the trendiest dead economist of this **apocalyptic** moment, was the godfather of government stimulus. Keynes had the radical idea that throwing money at recessions through aggressive deficit spending would **resuscitate** flatlined economies–and he wasn't too particular about where the money was thrown. In the depths of the Depression, he suggested that the Treasury could "fill old bottles with banknotes, bury them at suitable depths in disused coal mines" then sit back and watch a money-mining boom create jobs and prosperity. "It would, indeed, be more sensible to build houses and the like," he wrote, but "the above would be better than nothing."

As President-elect Barack Obama prepares to throw money at the current downturn–a stimulus package starting at about $800 billion, plus the second $350 billion chunk of the financial bailout–we all really do seem to be Keynesians now. Just about every expert agrees that pumping $1 trillion into a **moribund** economy will rev up the ethereal goods-and-services engine that Keynes called "aggregate demand" and stimulate at least some short-term activity, even if it is all wasted on money pits. But Keynes was also right that there would be more sensible ways to spend it. There would also be less sensible ways to spend it. A trillion dollars' worth of bad ideas–sprawl-inducing highways and bridges to nowhere, ethanol plants and pipelines that accelerate global warming, tax breaks for overleveraged McMansion builders and burdensome new long-term federal entitlements–would be worse than mere waste. It would be smarter to buy every American an iPod, a set of Ginsu knives and 600 Subway foot-longs.

It would be smarter still to throw all that money at things we need to do anyway, which is the goal of Obama's upcoming American Recovery and Reinvestment Plan. It will include a mix of tax cuts, aid to **beleaguered** state and local governments, and spending to address needs ranging from food stamps to computerized health records to bridge repairs to broadband networks to energy-efficiency retrofits, all designed to save or create 3 million to 4 million jobs by the end of 2010. Obama has said speed is his top priority because the faster Washington injects cash into the financial bloodstream, the better it stands to help avert a multiyear slump with double digit unemployment and deflation. But he also wants to use the stimulus to advance his long-term priorities: reducing energy use and carbon emissions, cutting middle-class taxes, upgrading neglected infrastructure, reining in health-care costs and eventually reducing the budget deficits that exploded under George W. Bush. Obama's goal is to exploit this crisis in the best sense of the word, to start pursuing his vision of a greener, fairer, more competitive, more sustainable economy.

Unfortunately, while 21st century Washington has demonstrated an impressive ability to spend money quickly, it has yet to prove that it can spend money wisely. And the chum of a 1 with 12 zeros is already creating a feeding **frenzy** for the ages. Lobbyists for shoe companies, zoos, catfish farmers, mall owners, airlines, public broadcasters, car dealers and everyone else who can afford their retainers are lining up for a piece of the stimulus. States that embarked on **raucous** spending and tax-cutting sprees when they were flush, are begging for bailouts now that they're broke. And politicians are dusting off their unfunded mobster museums, waterslides and other pet projects for rebranding as shovel-ready infrastructure investments. As Obama's aides scramble to assemble something effective and transformative as well as politically achievable, they acknowledge the tension between his desires for speed and reform.

79. John M. Keynes was advocate of which of the following suggestions?

A. Spending money recklessly during recessions is suicidal
B. Exorbitant spending during recessions is likely to boost economy
C. Aggressive deficit spending is likely to be fatal for economic meltdown.
D. Government stimulus to economy may not help because of red-tapism
E. None of these

80. Which of the following is **true** about Keynes' philosophy?

A. Actual spending money during meltdown is more important than where and on what it is spent.
B. Government should be selective in approach for spending money during recession
C. Filling old bottles with banknotes and burying them is an atrocious proposal
D. Creating jobs and prosperity during recessions is almost an impracticable proposal
E. None of these

81. The author of the passage calls Barack Obama and his team as 'Keynesians' because ....

A. Barack Obama has been reluctant to follow Keynes' philosophy
B. His team is advising Barack to refrain from Keynes' philosophy
C. Barack Obama and his team have decided to fill old bottles with banknotes
D. Building houses has been under the active consideration of Barack Obama and his team
E. None of these

82. What, according to Keynes, is the **'aggregate demand'**?

A. Goods and Services Sector
B. Stimulation of a short-term activity
C. Attempting to rev up the sluggish economy
D. Pumping one trillion dollars into economy
E. None of these

83. Highways, bridges, ethanol plants, etc. are considered by the author as ....

A. reasonably appropriate propositions to spend money on
B. measures that affect the environment adversely
C. imprudent proposals to waste money on
D. tax saving schemes bestowed on builders
E. None of these

84. Obama's upcoming American Recovery and Reinvestment Plan focuses on which of the following?
1. Recovery of all debts from the debtors in a phased manner.
2. Pumping money very liberally in projects that are mandatory.
3. Investing money recklessly in any project regardless of its utility.

A. 1 only B. 2 only
C. 3 only D. 2 and 3 only
E. All of these

85. According to the author of the passage, food stamps, bridge repairs, etc. are the projects that ....
A. do not warrant urgent spending as they have a lower utility value
B. need the least investment and priority as compared to building houses for the needy
C. may not have any favourable impact on attempts to counter recession
D. have lower value in terms of returns but require major investments
E. None of these

86. Obama desires to accelerate the process of pumping money with utmost rapidity as he believes that it would ....
1. help create reasonably high employment opportunities.
2. avoid deflation.
3. inject cash into the already troubled economy.

A. 1 and 2 only B. 2 and 3 only
C. 1 and 3 only D. All of these
E. None of these

87. Which of the following is/are corrective measure(s) as part of the long-term priorities of Obama that was an outcome of his predecessor's regime?
1. Countering recession through immediate rescue operations.
2. Reining the budget deficit.
3. Creating a more sustainable economy.

A. 1 & 2 only B. 2 & 3 only
C. 1 & 3 only D. 2 only
E. None of these

Directions (88–90): *Choose the word which is most* ***opposite*** *in meaning of the word printed in* ***bold*** *as used in the passage.*

88. Moribund
A. declining B. waning
C. thriving D. pessimistic
E. glorifying

89. Beleaguered
A. carefree B. harassed
C. stressful D. uneventful
E. evaporating

90. Raucous
A. strident B. harsh
C. rough D. unprecedented
E. soft

Directions (91–93): *Choose the word which is most nearly the* ***same*** *in meaning as the word given in* ***bold*** *as used in the passage.*

91. Apocalyptic
A. unwelcome B. disastrous
C. risk-free D. joyous
E. ceremonious

92. Resuscitate
A. melt down B. devastate
C. mislead D. save
E. deactivate

93. Frenzy
A. passion B. expression
C. succession D. habit
E. manifestation

PASSAGE–10

It is said that there is a **dismal** fall of standards everywhere. The leaders who are not equal to the task misguide their followers. The remedy of the malady that affects our political economic and social practices lies in the human individual. What is needed is a change in his nature. For that we should read great classics. Literature brings about that change for the better. It improves the quality of human beings. Great books give great thoughts, broaden our outlook and awaken our souls. They also provide a moral base as the lack of discipline and ideals is **inimical** to civilized value.

There are various kinds of books. Some arouse or instruct while others **elevate** our nature. The first kind of books destroy our ego and give us joy. Now joy is different from pleasure. The books which give joy contain emotions and thoughts recollected in tranquility. Only a seer can produce such books. They deserve not only to read but also to be digested. Through them we establish contact with the mastermind of the past. They hand on to us our tradition. But maintaining a tradition does not mean peaking or doing as our forefathers did following a tradition blindly will **render** it dead and useless. We must make **adaptations** and bring modifications. However, the individual contribution is largely determined by the pressure brought to bear up on him by the new problems of the new age.

There are three clearly marked features of the age in which we live. They are the scientific and technological revolution, the liberation of dependent countries in Asia and Africa and the growing unity of the world: We should read books which trace the history of the above mentioned three moments. The intellectual wealth of all mankind is at our disposal, we should break the barriers of language. Books build bridge between cultures, that is they bring them together. They promote understanding and love and remove suspicion, fear and hatred.

Great books come to our help when our values are at the discount many of us are mere shadows of human beings. We are the victims of contradictory impulses, we are a bundle of fear suspicion, greed, jealousy as well as kindliness and goodwill. For creating a normal harmonious human society, the former instincts should be curbed and the latter kindled, we must guard against corrupting the minds of our people with **trivialities.** A general spiritual awakening is essential.

94. What are the three chief features of our age according to the passage?
- A. It is the age of scientific and technological revolution.
- B. Many countries in Asia and Africa have no freedom from dependence.
- C. A sense of unity is growing among the different countries of the world.
- D. All of these
- E. None of these

95. According to the passage, how can we keep our tradition alive?
- A. We can do so only by following our forefathers blindly.
- B. It can be maintained only by making old traditions dead and useless.
- C. It can be achieved through a deep faith in old traditions.
- D. We can keep them alive by making critical and creative changes in them according to the demands of the age.
- E. None of these

96. What is the main argument of the passage?
- A. We should think in terms of the welfare of humanity as a whole.
- B. One should read good books and do the works relevant to one's own welfare.
- C. We should use scientific and technological know-how in terms of our welfare.
- D. All of these
- E. None of these

97. What distinction does the author make between joy and pleasure?
- A. Pleasure is a spiritual state whereas joy is physical and intellectual.
- B. Joy is a spiritual state where as pleasure is physical and intellectual.
- C. Pleasure is a sign of maturity and lasts longer than joy.
- D. Pleasure sustains even in pain, but joy is thing only felt in pleasant situation.
- E. None of these

98. How can the nature of the individual be changed according to the passage?
- A. If he reads great books, his outlook will be broad, his psychological health will improve and he will have moral contentment and spiritual joy.
- B. If he reads great books only, his psychological health will improve.
- C. If he reads great books, he will have only moral contentment and spiritual joy.
- D. Not given in the passage.
- E. None of these

99. What are the qualities of great classics according to the passage?
- (a) They are impersonal and the source of joy.
- (b) They contain emotions and thoughts recollected in tranquility.
- (c) They are written by prophets and are best interpreters of our past.
- A. Only (a) and (b)
- B. Only (b) and (c)
- C. Only (a) and (c)
- D. Only (a)
- E. All (a), (b) and (c)

100. What does the author consider essential for creating a normal harmonious human society?
- (a) We should control our emotions of fear, greed, suspicion and jealousy.
- (b) We should encourage kindliness.
- (c) We should not engage our mind in petty and mean things.
- (d) There should be a general spiritual awakening among us.
- A. Only (a) and (b)
- B. Only (a), (b) and (c)
- C. Only (b) and (d)
- D. Only (b), (c) and (d)
- E. All (a), (b), (c) and (d)

101. Which of the following statements (a), (b) and/or (c) is/are **not true** in the context of the passage?
- (a) Only those books which entertain us can elevate our nature.
- (b) Men suffer from conflicting attitudes.
- (c) All the evils of the world arise from the fact that men are unable to sit still in a place.

A. Only (b) and (c)
B. Only (a) and (b)
C. Only (a) and (c)
D. Only (b)
E. All (a), (b) and (c)

102. Which of the following statements (a), (b) and/or (c) is/are **true** in the context of the passage?
(a) Books bridge cultures and promote understanding and goodwill.
(b) The author denies silent meditation and approves only books to get spiritual joy.
(c) Most of men are not men but mere shadows of men.
A. Only (a)
B. Only (a) and (b)
C. Only (a) and (c)
D. Only (b) and (c)
E. All (a), (b) and (c)

Directions (103–105): *Choose the word or the group of words which is most nearly the* ***same*** *in meaning of the word given in* ***bold*** *at the question place as used in the passage.*

103. Dismal
A. depressing B. disabled
C. bitter D. level-heated
E. reckless

104. Adaptation
A. support B. substance
C. adjustment D. deviation
E. travail

105. Render
A. conclude B. make
C. expect D. breakout
E. confine

Directions (106–108): *Choose the word or the group of words which is most nearly* ***opposite*** *in meaning to the word given in* ***bold*** *at the question place as used in the passage.*

106. Elevate
A. argue B. convince
C. indulge D. release
E. lessen

107. Trivialities
A. essentials B. emoluments
C. promises D. details
E. interferences

108. Inimical
A. destitute B. conspicuous
C. oppressed D. compatible
E. extravagant

PASSAGE–11

China is preparing astronauts for long-term missions so that they can "carry out manned explorations of deep space in the future," an official said. A five-year programme to ready Chinese astronauts for long-term missions in space has been approved and will begin later this year, Director of the Astronaut Center of China, Chen Shanguang said. Chen told the China Daily that the programme aims to establish astronauts' operational and decision-making abilities in space, along with any psychological and physical changes they undergo living in cramped compartments in weightless conditions. The longest period Chinese astronauts remained in space so far was 115.5 hours, or nearly five days, during the mission of Shenzhou VI in 2005. "China will build a space station in 10 years and will probably carry out manned explorations of deep space in the future," Chen was quoted as saying. He said that the challenge is to find out how to enable astronauts to remain healthy and work efficiently over long periods in space and added–the findings will play a significant role in preparing the selection criteria to recruit future astronauts. "Space missions are becoming more difficult, making greater demands on astronauts. We want to find scientific answers to questions like what type of people can work as astronauts on long missions and what capabilities they should have," he said. The research will also be used to decide what a suitable workload is for astronauts on long missions.

109. What are the main concerns of a manned mission to space as quoted by Chen?
A. How to enable astronauts to remain healthy?
B. What kind of workload can astronauts bear?
C. How long can spaceships remain in space?
D. Both A and B but not C
E. A, B and C

110. Which of the following statements is **not** correct as per the passage?
A. Astronaut Center of China is planning to build a space station for star wars against America and India.
B. Longest time that the Chinese astronauts have stayed in the space so far was nearly 5 days.
C. Chen Shanguang is the Director of Astronaut Center of China.
D. China is striving to increase the capabilities of their astronauts to be successful on their space missions.
E. All are cottect

111. The passage could be a part of a —
A. newspaper report.
B. historical report.
C. school textbook.
D. research thesis on space.
E. a chinese fiction

112. According to the passage, why are the space missions becoming more difficult?
A. The working conditions have deteriorated.
B. The demands on astronauts have increased.
C. There is less time to take decisions.
D. The demands of astronauts have increased.
E. The space is being crowded by space missions

PASSAGE–12

Many people love the cute koala bear. This animal has been made into stuffed toys all over the world. But it is rare to see this creature alive and moving, because it's gradually becoming extinct. The koala, like the kangaroo, is actually a marsupial. It contains a small pouch for its young, like the kangaroo. For this reason, the koala is not related to true bears. In appearance, it is a combination of a monkey and a kangaroo. Koalas are native to Australia, and they are now chiefly found in New South Wales and Queensland. They are highly protected animals, because their number has greatly diminished in the last ten years. The koala has been hunted since the middle of this century for fur and food, which has moved it from its normal habitats. Today, anyone found harming a koala is severely punished by the law. Koalas get their endearing appearance from a covering of gray fur and little tufts of white hair on the sides of their faces. Their eyes are small and black, set in their head. They have large ears and curved noses, but no tail. They use their arms and paws to climb through the trees. Koalas have interesting living habits. They are nocturnal, which means that they move around chiefly at night. Koalas do not stay on the ground. They move from tree-to-tree, carefully lowering and raising themselves by their paws. Koalas eat only the leaves of the eucalyptus, which is another reason that they are now becoming extinct. The eucalyptus tree is disappearing, thus the koalas are fighting a battle against extinction on their own. Koalas have a surprisingly long life span, which can range from 9 to 20 years, in rare cases. The koala's worst enemy, besides hunters, is fire. When a tree is inflamed, often they cannot run fast enough to save themselves. Baby koalas are in danger around certain kinds of lizards and eagles, although they are protected today by natural habitats set up for them. It is interesting to note that many koalas die from being hit by cars, and some are even attacked by dogs!

113. What has led the koala bear to move away from its normal habitat?
A. To escape from being hunted for fur and food.
B. To avoid the danger from lizards.
C. It needs a different environment now.
D. The normal habitat does not provide sufficient food.
E. None of these

114. Which of the following are causes of danger to koala bears?
A. Fire, lizards
B. Accidents with vehicles, dogs
C. Both A and B
D. Their nocturnal habits
E. None of these

115. Which of the following statements is false about Koala bears?
A. Koala bears eat eucalyptus leaves.
B. Koala bears have large ears and curved noses.
C. Koala bears have small black eyes.
D. Koala bears have long tails.
E. None of these

116. Which of the following statements is true about koa bears?
A. They can safely live among animals and bir like dogs and eagles.
B. Koalas have a long life span.
C. Koala bears are commonly found all over the world.
D. Koalas do not use their paws as much as the arms.
E. None of these

PASSAGE–13

For achieving inclusive growth there is a critical nee d to rethink the role of the State. The early debate among economists about the size of the Government can be misleading. The need of the hour is to have an enabling Government. India is too large and complex a nation for the State to be able to deliver all that is needed. Asking the Government to produce all the essential goods, create all the necessary jobs, and keep a curb on the prices of all goods is to lead to a large cumbersome bureaucracy and widespread corruption.

The aim must be to stay with the objective of inclusive growth that was laid down by the founding fathers of the nation and also to take a more modern view of what the State can realistically deliver.

This is what leads to the idea of an enabling State, that is, a Government that does not try to directly deliver to the citizens everything that they need. Instead, it (1) creates an enabling ethos for the market so that individual enterprise can flourish and citizens can, for the most part, provide for the needs of one another, and (2) steps in to help those who do not manage to do well for themselves, for there will always be individuals, no matter what the system, who need support and help. Hence we need a Government that, when it comes to the market, sets effective, incentive-compatible rules and remains on the sidelines with minimal interference, and, at the same time, plays an important role in directly helping the poor by ensuring that they get basic eucation and helath services and receive adequate nutrition and food.

117. According to the passage:

1. The objective of inclusive growth was laid down by the founding fathers of the nation.
2. Need of the hour is to have an enabling Government.
3. The Government should engage in maximum interference in market processes.
4. There is a need to change the size of the Government.

Which of the statements given above are correct?

A. 1 and 2 only
B. 2 and 3 only
C. 1 and 4 only
D. 1, 2, 3 and 4
E. None of these

118. According to the passage, the strategy of inclusive growth can be effected by focusing on:

A. Meeting all the needs of every citizen in the country.
B. Increasing the regulations over the manufacturing sector.
C. Controlling the distribution of manufactured goods.
D. Delivery of the basic services to the deprived sections of the society.
E. All of these

119. What constitutes an enabling Government?

1. A large bureaucracy.
2. Implementation of welfare programmes through representatives.
3. Creating an ethos that helps individual enterprise.
4. Providing resources to those who are underprivileged.
5. Offering direct help to the poor regarding basic services.

Select the correct answer from the codes given below:

A. 1, 2 and 3 only
B. 4 and 5 only
C. 3, 4 and 5 only
D. 1, 2, 3, 4 and 5
E. None of these

120. Why is the State unable to deliver "all that is needed"?

1. It does not have sufficient bureaucracy.
2. It does not promote inclusive growth.

Select the correct answer from the codes given below:

A. 1 only　　B. 2 only
C. Both 1 and 2　　D. Neither 1 nor 2
E. Either 1 or 2

121. What is the essential message being conveyed by the author of the passage?

A. The objectives of inclusive growth laid down by the founding fathers of the nation should be remembered.
B. The Government needs to make available more schools and health services.
C. The Government needs to establish markets and industries to meet the needs of the poor strata of the society.
D. There is a need to rethink the role of the State in achieving inclusive growth.
E. None of these

PASSAGE–14

The concept of 'creative society' refers to a phase of development of a society in which a large number of potential contradictions become articulate and active. This is most evident when oppressed social groups get politically mobilised and demand their rights. The upsurge of the peasants and tribals, the movements for regional autonomy and self-determination, the environmental movements, and the women's movements in the developing countries are signs of emergence of creative society in contemporary times. The forms of social movements and their intensity may vary from country to country and place to place within a country. But the very presence of movements for social transformation in various spheres of a society indicates the emergence of a creative society in a country.

122. What does the author imply by "creative society"?

1. A society where diverse art forms and literary writings seek incentive.
2. A society where social inequalities are accepted as the norm.
3. A society where a large number of contradictions are recognised.
4. A society where the exploited and the oppressed groups grow conscious of their human rights and upliftment.

Select the correct answer using the codes given below:

A. 1, 2 and 3　　B. 4 only
C. 3 and 4　　D. 2 and 4
E. None of these

123. What according to the passage are the manifestations of social movements?

1. Aggressiveness and being incendiary.
2. Instigation by external forces.
3. Quest for social equality and individual freedom.
4. Urge for granting privileges and self-respect to disparaged sections of the society.

Select the correct answer using the codes given below:

A. 1 and 3 only　　B. 2 and 4 only
C. 3 and 4 only　　D. 1, 2, 3 and 4
E. None of these

124. With reference to the passage, consider the following statements:

1. To be a creative society, it is essential to have a variety of social movements.
2. To be a creative society, it is imperative to have potential contradictions and conflicts.

Which of the statements given above is/are correct?

A. 1 only B. 2 only
C. Both 1 and 2 D. Neither 1 nor 2
E. Either 1 or 2

PASSAGE–15

Today, with a Nobel Prize to its credit. Grameen is one of the largest microfinance organisations in the world. It started out lending small sums to poor entrepreneurs in Bangladesh to help them grow from a subsistence living to a livelihood. The great discovery its founders made was that even with few assets, these entrepreneurs repaid on time. Grameen and microfinance have since become financial staples of the developing world. Grameen's approach, unlike other microfinancers uses the group-lending model. Costs are kept down by having borrowers vet one another, tying together their financial fates and eliminating expensive loan officers entirely. The ultimate promise of Grameen is to use business lending as a way for people to lift themselves out of poverty.

Recently Grameen has taken on a different challenge–by setting up operations in the United States Money may be tight in the waning recession, but it is still a nation of 1,00,000 bank branches. Globally, the working microfinance equation consists of borrowing funds cheaply and keeping loan defaults and overhead expenses sufficiently low. Microlenders, including Grameen, do this by charging **colossal** interest rates–as high as 60% or 70%–which is necessary to compensate for the risk and attract bank funding. But loans at rates, much above the standard 15% would most likely be attacked as usurious in America.

So, the question is whether there is a role for a Third World lender in the world's largest economy? Grameen America, believes that in a few years it will be successful and turn a profit, thanks to 9 million United States households untouched by main-stream banks and 21 million using the likes of payday loans and pawn shops for financing. But enticing the unbanked won't be easy. After all, profit has long **eluded** United States microfinanciers and if it is not lucrative; it is not microlending–but charity. When Grameen first went to the United States, in the late 1980s, it tripped up. Under Grameen's tutelage, Banks started micro loans to entrepreneurs with a shocking 30% loss. But Grameen America says that this time results will be different because Grameen employees themselves will be making the loans, not training an American bank to do it. More often than not, the borrowers. Grameen finds in the United states already have jobs (as factory workers for example) or side businesses–selling toys, cleaning houses etc. The loans from Grameen, by and large, provide a steadier source of funding, but they don't create businesses out of nothing. But money isn't everything. More importantly for many entrepreneurs, group members are tremendous sources of support to one another. So even if studies are yet to determine if Grameen is a clear-cut pathway out of poverty, it still achieves something useful.

125. What has adversely affected the success of microfinance institutions in the United States?

A. The focus of these institutions is on making a profit a any cost instead of being charitable to the needy.
B. American banks engaged in microlending were the most severely hit during the recession.
C. Widespread perception among bankers that these institutions are better suited to developing countries
D. Their failure to attract those outside the formal banking system as customers
E. Americans are too proud to accept aid from third world countries.

126. Why has Grameen made a second attempt to launch in the United States?

A. The Willingness of U.S. banks to provide the necessary staff and funds to facilitate the spread of microfinance.
B. The rates of interest on loans in the U. S. are exorbitant making it easier to recover capital.
C. The realisation that a large percentage of the American population not reached by mainstream banks can be tapped.
D. Recognition of the fact that disbursing credit developing countries during the recession is too risky.
E. None of these

127. Which of the following can be inferred from the passage?

A. Microfinance has been successful only in Asian countries
B. Microfinance makes individual borrowers dependent rather than independent
C. America has the largest number of banks in the world
D. There is scope for microfinance institutions to profitable in developed countries
E. There are no informal sources of credit in developed countries

128. According to the author, what has enhanced the likelihood of success for Grameen America at present?

A. Its success in Bangladesh and other developing countries

B. Absence of other microfinance Institutions for competition
C. The fact that America is currently in the midst recession.
D. It provides loans at nominal rates of interest i.e. below 15 percent
E. None of these

129. Which of the following can be said about Grameen?
1. Its success in developing countries will ensure success in developed countries
2. It ensures that the poor in developing countries enjoy a subsistence standard of living.
3. It has demonstrated that the poor are far more likely to repay loans than the affluent.

A. None B. Only 1
C. Only 1 and 3 D. Only 2
E. Only 3

130. What is the central theme of the passage?
A. The contention that Grameen is doomed to fall in developed countries.
B. A comprehensive evaluation of the current status of the American economy.
C. A discussion about the prospects of Grameen and micro finance in the U.S.
D. The role of banks in facilitating rnicrolending efforts in developed nations.
E. Microfinance efforts arc useful in developing countries but are futile in developed ones.

131. Why was Grameen America's initial U. S. initiative a flop?
1. Lack of proper training to Grameen America personnel.
2. Grameen's refusal to adapt their system to meet the needs of the American poor.
3. It ended up giving loans at half their customary rates of interest.

A. None B. Only 1
C. Only 1 and 3 D. Only 2
E. Only 3

132. Which of the following is a benefit of the Grameen system of microfinance?
A. If a single member is unable to repay a loan other group members will repay it.
B. Dispensing with the expense of technology networks to monitor advances
C. It utilises the vast bank network already existing in a country
D. Group members can sanction loans and verify if borrowers have sufficient collateral.
E. Backing that borrowers receive from other group members

133. Which of the following is most similar in meaning to the word **'eluded'** as used in the passage?
A. Avoided B. Duped
C. Abandoned D. Intangible
E. Betrayed

134. Which of the following is most opposite in meaning to the word **'colossal'**, as used in the passage?
A. Short B. Lavish
C. Minority D. Frugal
E. Insignificant

PASSAGE–16

The great recession hasn't been great for free trade. As unemployment has been throughout the world, governments have become more focused on protecting their own Industries than on promoting intenational commerce. The U. S. though typically an enthusiastic supporter of open markets in duded "buy American" clauses in its stimulus package and propped up its railing auto industry with handouts.

But according to the Asian Development Bank (ADB), in the part of the world that was hit hardest by the trade crash-Asia, the number of Free Trade Agreements (FTAs) signed by Asian countries has grown from Just three in 2000 to 56 by the end of August 2009. Nineteen of those FTAs are among 16 Asian economies a trend that could help the region become a powerful trading bloc.

The drive to lower trade barriers has taken on **fresh** urgency amid, the recession. As Asian manufacturing networks become more intertwined–and as Asian consumers become wealthier–regional commerce is becoming **critical** to future economic expansion. Intraregional trade last year made up 57% of total Asian trade, up from 37% in 1980. In the past Asia produced for America and Europe, now Asia is producing for Asia.

Of course, Asia is still dependent on sales to the West. But FTAs could reduce the region's exposure to the United States by giving Asian companies preferential treatment in selling to Asian companies and consumers. These benefits could come with down-sides, however. According to experts. FTAs create a "non-level playing field with advantages for Asian countries". If the most dynamically growing part of the global economy gives the U.S. restricted access it will impact global balance. Companies in countries like the United States left out of the trade pacts could face disadvantages when trying to tap fast-growing Asian markets, This, in turn, could have a negative impact on efforts 10 rebalance excessive debt in the U.S. and excessive savings in Asia. Still, the benefits of greater regional integration could prove powerful enough to overcome the roadblocks. In Asia, the only thing everyone agrees upon is business. If it does, the world economy may never be the same.

135. What do the Asian Development Bank statistics indicate?
- A. Asian economies are financially more sound than those of the developed world
- B. The financial crisis impacted the West far more than it did Asia
- C. Asian countries have aligned themselves on lines similar to the European Union
- D. Western, countries are sceptical about trading with developing countries
- E. Asian countries have been actively opening their markets to one another.

136. What has given rise, to the large number of trade agreements between Asian countries?
- A. The need to insulate Asian economies from over-exposure to the American economy
- B. Angry reaction among Asian countries owing to America's protectionist policy
- C. The aim of empowering the poorer Asian economies and bring them on par with Western economies.
- D. The desire to achieve conditions conducive to global consensus on trade regulations and tariffs.
- E. Widespread panic in Europe and Asia as Asian economies are yet to recover from the recession.

137. Which of the following is **not true** in the context the passage?
1. Political and economic rivalries between A, countries are non-existent today.
2. Asian countries hold America responsible for recession and have imposed economic sanctions against the U.S.
3. America has adopted a protectionist strategy after the recession.

- A. Only 1 B. Only 2 and 3
- C. Only 1 and 2 D. Only 3
- E. None of these

138. Which of the following describes expert predictions' trade pacts between Asian countries?
- A. These will be beneficial and are likely to give rise to a common Asian currency
- B. Tariffs will be lowered and bureaucratic regulation will become transparent
- C. Widening of differences between participant and non-participant countries will hamper global stabillty
- D. Regional conflicts will increase as competition and inequities between Asian nations will intensify.
- E. They are likely to be short-lived as it will be difficult to get participating nations to arrive at a consensus.

139. Which of the following has/have not been (an) impact of the recession?
1. Various trade agreements signed between developed and Asian countries have not been honoured.
2. The U. S. government has restructured the automobile industry.
3. Regional conflicts in Asia have substantially reduced.

- A. Only 3 B. Only 1
- C. Only 1 and 2 D. All 1, 2 and 3
- E. None of these

140. According to the author what danger does creating an Asian trading bloc pose?
- A. Political instability in Asia will rise as some countries are wealthier than others
- B. American consumers have ceased their demand for Asian goods
- C. Unemployment in Asian countries will rise as many plants will be forced to close down.
- D. It will alter the balance of power in the World with small Asian countries becoming most dominant.
- E. None of these

141. What is the author trying to convey through the phrase "In the past Asia produced for America and Europe, now Asia is producing for Asia"?
- A. The number of wealthy consumers in Asia outnumber those in America and Europe together
- B. Asian countries do not support free trade and continue to trade among themselves despite the recession
- C. Goods manufactured in Asian countries often fail to meet the standards set by developed countries.
- D. Asian countries no longer export to Western markets alone and now clear to Asian markets as well.
- E. Interregional and barriers between Europe and Asia have weakened considerably.

142. Which of the following is most opposite in meaning to the word **'critical'** as used in the passage?
- A. Unimportant B. Complimentary
- C. Approval D. Sale
- E. Steady

143. Which of the following is most similar in meaning to the word **'fresh'** as used in the passage?
- A. Additional B. Renewed
- C. Original D. Healthy.
- E. Modem

144. Which of the following can be said about the American economy in the context of the passage?
1. Most American companies have opted to withdraw from Asia.
2. America's stand on free trade has altered because of the recession.

3. The American economy is far too dependent on Asia for trade

A. Only 1 B. Only 2
C. Only 3 D. All 1, 2 and 3
E. None of these

PASSAGE–17

There are various sectors in India that are to be assessed for their strengths, weaknesses, opportunities and threats. The total population is over 1 billion, which will increase to 1.46 billion by 2035 to cross China. The huge population will result in higher unemployment and deterioration of quality, Literacy in India is yet another factor to be discussed. According to the 1991 Census, 64.8% of the population was illiterate. The major downtrend of education is due to child labour, which has spread all over India, and this should be totally eradicated by way of **surveillance** and a good educational system implemented properly by the Government.

Pollution is one more threat to the environment and for the country's **prospects**. This has been experienced more in urban areas, mainly in metropolitan cities. The water pollution by the sewage seepage into the ground water and improper maintenance will lead to various diseases, which in turn will affect the next generation. In most of the cities there is no proper sewage disposal. The Government has to take effective steps to control population, which, in turn, will minimize the pollution.

Poverty questions the entire strength of India's political view and minimises the energetic way of approach. The shortfall of rains, enormous floods, unexpected famine, drought, earthquake and the recent tsunami hit the country in a negative way. The proactive approach through effective research and analytical study helps us to determine the effects in advance. Proper allocation of funds is a **prerequisite**. In developed countries like the US and Japan, precautionary methods are adopted to overcome this, but it has to be improved a lot in our systems.

Increased population is one of the major reasons for poverty and the Government is unable to allocate funds for basic needs to the society. India has nearly 400 million people living below the poverty-line and 90% of active population is in informal economy. The children are forced to work due to their poverty and **differential** caste system. They work in match industry for daily wages, as servants, mechanics, stone-breakers, agricultural workers, etc. To prevent child labour existing laws which favour the Anti Child Labour Act should be implemented by the Government **vigorously**.

More population results in cheap cost by virtue of the demand-supply concept. Most of the foreign countries try to utilise this factor by outsourcing their business in India with a very low capital. According to the US, India is a "knowledge pool" with cheap labour. The major advantage is pure communication and technical skill, which is adaptable to any environment. The cutting-edge skill in IT of our professionals helps the outsourcing companies to **commensurate** with the needs of the consumers in a short span. The major competitors for India are China and Philippines and by the way of an effective communication and expert technical ability, Indians are ahead of the race. The major metropolitan states are targeting the outsourcing field **vigorously** by giving various amenities to the outsourcing companies like tax concession, allotting land, etc, to start their businesses in their cities without any hurdles. Thereby most of the MNCs prefer India as their destinations and capitalise the resources to maximise their assets. Infrastructure is another key factor for an outsourcing company to start a business in a particular city. It includes road, rail, ports, power and water. The increased input in infrastructure in India is very **limited** where China's record is excellent.

India, in earlier days, gave more importance to the development of Industry and less importance to other departments. But the scenario has quite changed nowadays by allocating a special budget of funds for security. This is because of the frightening increase in terrorism all around the world, especially emerging after the 9/11 terror attack in the US. In the last ten years, budget towards the development of military forces is higher when compared to others. It shows that the threat from our neighbouring countries is escalating. India has to concentrate more on this security factor to wipe out the problem in the way of cross-border terrorism.

Making India a developed country in 2020 is not an easy task. India has to keep in check a variety of factors in order to progress rapidly. To quote China as all example is that they demolished an old building to construct a very big port to meet future demands, but India is still waiting for things to happen. The profits gained by India through various sectors are to be spent for the development and welfare of the country. India's vision for a brighter path will come true not only by mere words or speech, but extra effort is needed at all levels to overcome the pitfalls.

145. Which of the following is/are the facility (ies) available to MNCs investing in India?

1. Easy availability of land
2. Better infrastructure than China
3. Tax concessions

A. Only 3 B. All 1, 2 and 3
C. Only 1 and 2 D. Only 1 and 3
E. None of these

146. Which of the following ,according to the author, is a result of poverty in India?

A. Lack of a robust security system
B. Child labour and the resulting dearth of educated youth

C. Floods, famines and other calamities
D. Rapid increase in population
E. None of these

147. How, according to the author, can the effects of floods, famines, droughts etc be minimised?
A. By limiting pollution, thereby reducing the chances of such event taking place
B. By educating the children about the ill-effects of such calamities who in turn will help during the time of need
C. By following the US system of providing relief to its citizens
D. By allotting proper funds for research which can predict the outcome of such calamities and thus design relief measures
E. None of these

148. Why, according to the author, is India one of the favourite destinations for investment by outsourcing companies?
1. Shorter response time for clients
2. Better technical skills.
3. Availability of cheap labour.

A. Only 3 B. All 1, 2 and 3
C. Only 2 and 3 D. Only 1 and 2
E. Only 1

149. Which of the following is/are true in the context of the passage?
1. India leads the way in the amount invested in the development of infrastructure.
2. Political system in India is not influenced by poverty.
3. Indian population would increase by approximately 50 per cent in the next twenty five years.

A. Only 1 and 2 B. Only 2
C. Only 3 D. Only 2 and 3
E. All 1, 2 and 3

150. Which of the following, according to the author, is/ are result(s) of increased population in India?
1. Pollution
2. Poverty
3. Unemployment

A. Only 1 B. Only 1 and 2
C. Only 2 D. Only 1 and 3
E. All 1, 2 and 3

151. Why, according to the author, has the Indian Government allotted more funds to strengthen the military forces?
A. To improve security in order to counter increasing terrorism.
B. As the security in India over the past ten years was grossly inadequate
C. As the US too has strengthened its military forces after the 9/11 attack
D. As the Industry is developed enough and is not in need of any more funds
E. None of these

152. What is the author's main objective in writing this passage?
A. To exhort the Government to garner support from its neighbouring countries
B. To suggest to the Government to follow China's example blindly, thereby bringing about rapid development
C. To highlight the plight of the poor
D. To discuss the problem of child labour and suggest suitable remedies
E. To bring forth the problems associated with India's development and to suggest measures to counter them

Directions (153–156): *Choose the word/group of words which is most* ***similar*** *in meaning to the word/group of words printed in* ***bold*** *as used in the passage.*

153. Surveillance
A. spying B. cameras
C. security D. observation
E. alertness

154. Prerequisite
A. result B. association
C. necessity D. factor
E. mystery

155. Prospects
A. assimilation B. demand
C. future D. brochure
E. diagnosis

156. Commensurate
A. match B. extracting
C. contemplating D. request
E. employing

Directions (157–159): *Choose the word/group of words which is most* ***opposite*** *in meaning to the word/group of words printed in* ***bold*** *as used in the passage.*

157. Limited
A. abundant B. complete
C. flowing D. inadequate
E. encompassing

158. Differential
A. solitude B. homogeneous
C. synonymous D. unique
E. different

159. Vigorously
A. simply B. regularly
C. roughly D. softly
E. leniently

PASSAGE–18

In the past, the richest states often grew the fastest and the poor ones the slowest. But India's record GDP growth of 8.49% per year in the five-year period 2004-09 is a case of improved productivity and growth in customarily poor states trickling up and aggregating into rapid growth at the national level. Nobody should call this a success of trickle-down economics. Trickle-down assumes that fast growth can be had simply by changing a few policies that benefit the rich, after which some benefits trickle down to the poor.

In fact, miracle growth is globally rare, precisely because it is so difficult for countries to improve the productivity of a substantial proportion of the population. Only when productivity improvement is widespread is there enough productivity improvement from all regions and people to **add** up to fast growth. In other words, fast growth does not trickle down; it trickles up. Once a country grows fast, government revenues will boom, and can be used to accelerate spending in social sectors and welfare.

Miracle growth and record revenues enabled the Central government to finance social welfare schemes, farm loan waivers and enormous oil subsidies. This can be called the trickling down of part of the revenue bonanza into welfare and workfare. But neither welfare nor workfare could have caused the **sharp** acceleration of economic growth. The growth bonanza itself was sparked by state-level political and policy changes that accelerated local growth, which then trickled up to the national level.

160. Which of the following is TRUE in the context of the Passage?

A. India's growth was more inclusive in nature during 2004-2009 than it had been in the past.
B. Developed countries use the same model of development as India.
C. Widespread growth is best achieved through Central Government-monitored schemes.
D. At present India's traditionally poor states are more prosperous than her socially developed ones.
E. There should be no government expenditure in social sectors if the current high growth rate is not maintained.

161. Why have countries found it difficult to achieve high growth?

1. Ensuring an increase in the output among a large number of citizens is difficult.
2. Corruption of politicians at the grassroots level results in the benefits of growth not reaching the poor.
3. The government's failure to allocate sufficient income to inclusive social welfare schemes

A. Only 1 B. Only 1 & 2
C. Only 2 & 3 D. All 1, 2 & 3
E. None of these.

162. To which of the following factors does the author attribute India's high growth rate during 2004-09?

A. Tremendous growth of the vast majority of richer states
B. Change in national-level policies to benefit only large well-off states
C. Gains of richer states have been used to fund social welfare schemes in the larger states.
D. Improved productivity of traditionally low-performing states.
E. None of these

163. Which of the following best describes the author's view of trickle-down theory?

A. It ensures accountability of the government even at the grassroots level.
B. It has been effective in helping poor states catch up with richer ones.
C. It promotes inclusive growth over quick growth.
D. It targets social welfare at the cost of economic growth.
E. It has largely failed to drive sustained growth.

164. What is the author's objective in writing this passage?

A. Advocating greater autonomy for the richest states in India
B. Urging the government to invest in social development to facilitate economic growth
C. Criticising traditional economic principles on which the Indian economy is based
D. Encouraging larger states to disburse more wealth at the grassroots level
E. None of these

165. Which of the following is similar in meaning to the word 'ADD' as used in the context of the passage?

A. Aggravate B. Result
C. Include D. Compute
E. Intensify

166. Which of the following is opposite in meaning of the word 'SHARP' as used in the context of the passage?

A. Blunt B. Expected
C. Late D. Gradual
E. Indistinct

PASSAGE–19

Born out of the forces of globalisation, India's IT sector is undertaking some globalisation of its own. In search of new sources of rapid growth, the country's outsourcing giants are aggressively expanding beyond their usual stomping grounds into the developing world; setting up programming centres, **chasing** new clients and hiring local talent. Through geographic diversification, Indian companies hope to regain some momentum after the recession. This shift is being driven by a global economy in which the US is no longer the **undisputed** engine of growth. India's IT powers rose to prominence largely on the decisions made by American executives, who were quick to capitalize on the cost savings to be gained by outsourcing non-core operations, such as systems programming and call centres, to specialists overseas.

Revenues in India's IT sector surged from $4 billion in 1998 to $59 billion last fiscal, But with the recession NASSCOM forecasts that the growth rate of India's exports of IT and other business services to the US and Europe will drop to at most 7% in the current fiscal year, down from 16% last year and 29% in 2007-08.

Factors other than the crisis are driving India's IT firms into the emerging world. Although the US still accounts for 60% of the export revenue of India's IT sector, emerging markets are growing faster. Tapping these more dynamic economies won't be easy, however. The goal of Indian IT firms for the past 30 years has been to woo clients outside India and transfer as much of the actual work as possible back home, where lower wages for highly skilled programmers allowed them to offer significant cost savings. With costs in other emerging economies equally low, Indian firms can't compete on price alone.

To adapt, Indian companies which are relatively unknown in these emerging nations are establishing major local operations around the world, in the process hiring thousands of locals. Cultural conflicts arise at times while training new recruits. In addition, IT firms also have to work extra hard to woo business from emerging-market companies still unaccustomed to the concept of outsourcing. If successful, the future of India's outsourcing sector could prove as bright as its past.

167. What is the author trying to convey through the phrase "India's IT sector is undertaking some globalization of its own"?

A. India has usurped America's position as the leader in IT.
B. The Indian IT sector is competing with other emerging nations for American business.
C. The Indian IT sector is considering outsourcing to developing economies.
D. Indian IT companies are no longer able to offer comprehensive cost-effective solutions to the US.
E. Indian IT firms are engaging in expanding their presence internationally.

168. Which of the following factors made the services offered by the Indian IT attractive to the US?

1. Indian IT companies had expertise in rare core operations.
2. US lacked the necessary infrastructure and personnel to handle mass call centre operations.
3. Inability of other equally cost-efficient developing countries to comply with their strict policies.

A. None B. Only 1
C. Only 1 & 2 D. Only 2
E. Only 2 & 3

169. What has caused Indian IT firms to change the way they conduct business in developing countries?

A. The volume of work being awarded cannot be handled by Indian firms.
B. The demands of these markets are different from those of India's traditional customers.
C. Wages demanded by local workers are far higher than what they pay their Indian employees.
D. Stringent laws which are not conducive to outsourcing
E. The locals are well-versed in the latest technology and have no need for training.

170. What do the NASSCOM statistics about Indian IT exports indicate?

A. Drop in demand for IT services by Europe and the US
B. Indian IT firms charge exorbitantly for their services.
C. India has lost out to other emerging IT hubs.
D. The Indian IT sector should undergo restructuring.
E. None of these

171. According to the passage, which of the following is NOT a difficulty that Indian IT firms will face in emerging markets?

A. Mindset resistant to outsourcing
B. Local IT services are equally cost-effective
C. The US is their preferred outsourcing destination.
D. Conflicts arising during the training of local talent
E. Unfamiliarity of these markets with India's capability in IT

172. Which of the following is **not** true in the context of the Passage?

1. The recession severely impacted the US but not India.
2. India is trying to depend less on the US as a source of growth.
3. The future success of Indian IT firms depends on emerging markets.

A. Only 2 & 3 B. Only 1
C. Only 3 D. All 1, 2 & 3
E. None of these

173. Which of the following words is most similar in meaning to the word **'chasing'** as used in the passage?

A. running B. harassing
C. pestering D. pursuing
E. poaching

174. Which of the following words is most opposite in meaning to the word **'undisputed'** as used in the passage?

A. challenging B. doubtful
C. deprived D. emphasized
E. comprehend

PASSAGE–20

Goldman Sachs predicted that crude oil price would hit $200 and just as it appeared that alternative renewable energy had a chance of becoming an economically viable option, the international price of oil fell by over 70%. After hitting the all-time high of $147 a barrel, a month ago, crude oil fell to less than $40 a barrel. What explains this sharp decline in the international price of oil? There has not been any major new discovery of a hitherto unknown source of oil or gas. The short answer is that the demand does not have to fall by a very sizeable quantity for the price of crude to respond as it did. In the short run, the price elasticity of demand for crude oil is very low. **Conversely**, in the short run, even a relatively big change in the price of oil does not immediately lower consumption. It takes months, or years, of high oil price to **inculcate** habits of energy conservation. World crude oil price had remained at over $60 a barrel for most of 2005-2007 without making any major **dent** in demand.

The long answer is more complex. The economic slowdown in the US, Europe and Asia along with dollar depreciation and commodity speculation have all had some role in the downward descent in the international price of oil. In recent years, the supply of oil has been rising but not enough to catch up with the rising demand, resulting in an almost vertical escalation in its price. The number of crude oil futures and options contracts have also increased manifold which has led to significant speculation in the oil market.In comparison, the role of the Organization of Petroleum Exporting Countries (OPEC) in fixing crude price has considerably weakened. OPEC is often accused of operating as a cartel restricting output thus keeping prices artificially high. It did succeed in setting the price of crude during the 1970s and the first half of the 80s. But, with increased futures trading and contracts, the control of crude pricing has moved from OPEC to banks and markets that deal with futures trading and contracts.

It is true that most oil exporting regions of the world have remained politically unstable **fuelling** speculation over the price of crude. But there is little evidence that the geopolitical uncertainties in west Asia have improved to **weaken** the price of oil. Threatened by the downward slide of oil price, OPEC has, in fact, announced its decision to curtail output.

However most oil importers will heave a sigh of relief as they find their oil import bills decline except for those who bought options to import oil at prices higher than market prices. Exporting nations, on the other hand, will see their economic prosperity slip. Relatively low price of crude is also bad news for investments in alternative renewable energy that cannot compete with cheaper and non-renewable sources of energy.

175. Why are oil importing countries relieved?
A. Price of crude reached $ 147 not $ 200 as was predicted
B. Discovery of oil reserves within their own territories
C. Demand for crude has fallen sharply
D. There is no need for them to invest huge amounts of money in alternative sources of energy
E. None of these

176. Which of the following factors is responsible for rise in speculation in crude oil markets?
1. OPEC has not been able to restrict the oil output and control prices
2. The supply of oil has been rising to match demand
3. Existence of large number of oil futures and oil contracts

A. Only 1 B. Both 1 & 2
C. Only 3 D. All 1, 2 & 3
E. None of these

177. What does the phrase "the price elasticity of demand for crude oil is very low" imply?
A. When the price rises the demand for crude oil falls immediately
B. A small change in demand will result in a sharp change in the price of crude
C. Within a short span of time the price of crude oil has fluctuated sharply
D. Speculation in oil does not have much of an impact on its price
E. None of these

178. Which of the following is/are **true** in the context of the passage?
1. The decline in oil prices has benefited all countries
2. Renewable energy sources are costlier than non-renewable ones
3. Lack of availability of alternative renewable energy resulted in rise in demand for crude

A. Only 2 B. Both 1 & 2
C. Both 2 & 3 D. Only 3
E. None of these

179. What has been the impact of the drop in oil prices?
A. Exploration for natural gas resources has risen
B. The dollar has fallen sharply
C. OPEC has decided to restrict its production of oil
D. Economic depression in oil importing countries
E. Drastic fall in demand for crude oil

180. What led to alternative energy sources being considered economically feasible?

A. The price of oil rose by 70 per cent while renewable energy sources are cheap
B. Exorbitant crude oil prices made alternative energy sources an attractive option
C. Expert predictions that the price of oil would alternately escalate and plunge sharply
D. Evidence that no new sources of oil and gas are available
E. None of these

181. What does the author want to convey by citing the statistic of 2005-2007?
A. The prices of crude were rising gradually so people were not alarmed
B. The dollar was a strong currency during that period
C. Many people turned to alternative renewable energy sources because of high oil prices
D. If the price of oil is high for a short time it does not necessarily result in a drop in consumption
E. People did not control their demand for fuel then which created the current economic slowdown

182. Which of the following factors is not responsible for the current drop in oil prices?
A. Economic crisis in America, European and Asian nations
B. Speculation in oil markets
C. Weakening of the dollar
D. Political stability in oil exporting countries
E. All the above are not responsible for the current drop in oil prices

183. Which of the following is **not true** in the context of the passage?
1. OPEC was established in 1970 to protect the interests of oil importing countries
2. When demand for oil exceeds supply there is a sharp rise in price
3. Today futures trading markets set the oil prices to a large extent

A. Only 1　　B. Only 3
C. Both 1 & 3　　D. Only 2
E. None of these

184. Which of the following is the function of OPEC?
A. Controlling speculation in oil
B. Ensuring profits are equally distributed to all its members
C. Monitoring inflation in oil prices and taking necessary steps to lower it
D. Guaranteeing political instability in oil exporting countries does not impact output
E. Determining prices of crude oil

Directions (185–187): *Choose the word which is most **similar** in meaning to the word printed in **bold** as used in the passage.*

185. Inculcate
A. Modify　　B. Construct
C. Initiate　　D. Fix
E. Instill

186. Fuelling
A. Incentive　　B. Supplying
C. Stimulating　　D. Irritating
E. Restoring

187. Dent
A. Reduction　　B. Break
C. Tear　　D. Breach
E. Split

Directions (188–189): *Choose the word which is most **opposite** in meaning to the word printed in **bold** as used in the passage.*

188. Conversely
A. Compatibly　　B. Similarly
C. Likely　　D. Aligning
E. Resembling

189. Weaken
A. Powerful　　B. Nourish
C. Intense　　D. Boost
E. Energise

PASSAGE–21

We should recognise the indebtedness of the country to its farm families who toil to safeguard national food security. Loan waiver is the price we have to pay for the neglect of rural India over the past several decades. There has been a gradual decline in investment in key sectors related to agriculture such as infrastructure, marketing, post harvest technology etc. The four crore farmers whose debt is to be **relieved** will be eligible for institutional credit for their cultivation expenses during Kharif 2008. The challenge is to prevent them from getting into the debt trap again. For this purpose the Central and various State governments should set up an Indebted Farmers' Support Consortium, comprising scientists, panchayat raj officials and others relevant to assisting farmers to improve the profitability and productivity of their farms in an environmentally sustainable manner. The smaller the farm, the greater is the need for marketable surplus to reduce indebtedness.

The Indebted Farmers' Support Consortium should aim to get all the four crore farmers all the benefits of the government schemes such as the Rashtriya Krishi Vikas Yojana, Irrigation Benefit Programme and others. If this is done, every farm family released from the debt trap should be able to produce at least an additional half tonne per hectare of foodgrains. This should help increase food production by about 20 million tonnes by 2008-10. At a time when global and national food stocks are dwindling and prices are rising, this will be a timely gain for our national food security. We need to ensure that the outcome of the debt waiver is enhanced farmers' income and production. The prevailing **gap** between potential and actual yields in the crops of rainfed areas such as pulses and oilseeds is over 200 per cent even with the necessary technologies on the shelf. We are now importing without duty large quantities of pulses and oilseeds. If helped, farmers can produce these at a lower cost.

Opportunities for **assured** and remunerative marketing are essential if loan waiver is not to become a recurring event leading to the destruction of the credit system. This is why the Minimum Support Price is necessary for all, not just for a few crops which is the case at present. This is the single most effective step to make loan waivers history. There is another urgent step which needs to be taken. The loan waiver does not cover those who borrow from moneylenders. It will not be possible for the government to scrutinise the veracity of such private deals but steps can be taken such as giving them Smart Cards which will entitle them to essential inputs like seeds and fertilizers. The gram sabha can be entrusted with the task of identifying these farmers so that there is transparency in the process and elimination of the chances for falsification and corruption. Fear of occasional misuse should not come in the way of enabling millions of poor farmers who have borrowed from informal sources if we are to achieve the goal of four per cent growth in agriculture.

190. What is the likely impact of ensuring farmers' benefit from government schemes?
1. They can use the credit from these schemes to repay moneylenders.
2. The government can control the price rise.
3. Increased agricultural production.

A. Both 1 and 2 B. All 1, 2 and 3
C. Only 3 D. Both 2 and 3
E. None of these

191. Why does the author feel that rural India has been overlooked in the past?
1. Institutional credit was only made available for Kharif crops.
2. Drop in investment in central areas related to agriculture.
3. Records of those eligible for loan waivers have not been maintained over time.

A. Only 2 B. Both 1 and 2
C. Only 3 D. All 1, 2 and 3
E. None of these

192. How can small farmers avoid debt?
A. They need to acquire additional land holdings
B. They need to take advantage of both government schemes as well as credit from moneylenders
C. They have to ensure a sufficient amount of their farm produce is sold
D. The Government should provide periodic loan waivers
E. None of these

193. What is the objective of the Indebted Farmers' Support Consortium ?
A. It is a support group for the families of indebted farmers
B. It has to devise new government schemes for farmers
C. It has to track farmers eligible for government schemes
D. It has to evaluate government schemes and weed out the inefficient ones
E. None of these

194. What does the author mean by the phrase "indebtedness of the country to its farm families" ?
A. If farmers are in debt it impacts the entire country
B. Citizens should be grateful to farmers and their families for the hardships borne by them to cultivate crops
C. India's food production has fallen causing it to be in debt since it has to import food
D. The number of farmers' descendants taking up agriculture has fallen.
E. None of these

195. What is the author's opinion of recurring loan waivers?
A. They are beneficial to farmers
B. They are detrimental to the system of lending.
C. They will reduce the need for a Minimum Support Price for agricultural products
D. Farmers will no longer be in debt to moneylenders
E. None of these

196. Which of the following is **true** in the context of the passage?
A. The Minimum Support Price for agricultural products is yet to be implemented
B. Loan waiver is a permanent solution to indebtedness of farmers
C. Current agricultural growth is below four per cent
D. India's food production has increased in 2008
E. Moneylenders benefit from loan waivers

197. Why does the loan waiver not cover credit taken from moneylenders?
1. It is difficult to verify these contracts between farmers and moneylenders.
2. It will increase the deficit in the budget.
3. There is a risk that the funds may be misappropriated.

A. Both 1 and 3 B. All 1, 2 and 3
C. Only 2 D. Both 1 and 2
E. None of these

Directions (198–200); *Choose the word which is most* ***similar*** *in meaning to the word printed in* ***bold*** *as used in the passage.*

198. Assured

A. insured B. definite
C. doubted D. confident
E. reliance

199. Relieved

A. exempted B. backed
C. supported D. calmed
E. substituted

200. Gap

A. hole B. break
C. pause D. difference
E. interruption

ANSWERS

1	**2**	**3**	**4**	**5**	**6**	**7**	**8**	**9**	**10**
D	B	E	C	E	C	B	A	A	E
11	**12**	**13**	**14**	**15**	**16**	**17**	**18**	**19**	**20**
E	C	D	D	B	A	A	C	D	D
21	**22**	**23**	**24**	**25**	**26**	**27**	**28**	**29**	**30**
C	D	B	E	E	A	D	C	C	E
31	**32**	**33**	**34**	**35**	**36**	**37**	**38**	**39**	**40**
A	B	D	B	C	D	E	B	C	A
41	**42**	**43**	**44**	**45**	**46**	**47**	**48**	**49**	**50**
E	D	B	C	A	B	A	A	E	B
51	**52**	**53**	**54**	**55**	**56**	**57**	**58**	**59**	**60**
E	C	D	B	D	A	B	B	B	E
61	**62**	**63**	**64**	**65**	**66**	**67**	**68**	**69**	**70**
B	B	D	C	A	A	E	A	E	C
71	**72**	**73**	**74**	**75**	**76**	**77**	**78**	**79**	**80**
B	E	A	C	D	D	E	B	B	A
81	**82**	**83**	**84**	**85**	**86**	**87**	**88**	**89**	**90**
E	A	C	B	A	D	B	C	A	E
91	**92**	**93**	**94**	**95**	**96**	**97**	**98**	**99**	**100**
B	D	A	D	D	A	B	A	E	E
101	**102**	**103**	**104**	**105**	**106**	**107**	**108**	**109**	**110**
C	C	A	C	B	E	A	D	D	A
111	**112**	**113**	**114**	**115**	**116**	**117**	**118**	**119**	**120**
A	B	A	C	D	B	A	D	C	D
121	**122**	**123**	**124**	**125**	**126**	**127**	**128**	**129**	**130**
D	C	C	C	A	C	D	E	E	C
131	**132**	**133**	**134**	**135**	**136**	**137**	**138**	**139**	**140**
A	E	A	D	E	D	C	C	D	D
141	**142**	**143**	**144**	**145**	**146**	**147**	**148**	**149**	**150**
D	A	E	B	D	E	D	C	C	E
151	**152**	**153**	**154**	**155**	**156**	**157**	**158**	**159**	**160**
A	E	E	C	C	A	A	B	D	A
161	**162**	**163**	**164**	**165**	**166**	**167**	**168**	**169**	**170**
A	D	E	C	B	D	E	A	B	A
171	**172**	**173**	**174**	**175**	**176**	**177**	**178**	**179**	**180**
C	B	D	B	E	C	E	D	C	B
181	**182**	**183**	**184**	**185**	**186**	**187**	**188**	**189**	**190**
D	E	D	E	D	C	A	B	D	B
191	**192**	**193**	**194**	**195**	**196**	**197**	**198**	**199**	**200**
A	E	A	B	B	C	A	B	A	D

□□□

2. Closet Test

Directions (Qs. 1–210): *In the following passages, there are blanks, each of which has been numbered. These numbers are printed below the passage and against each, five words are suggested, one of which fits the blank appropriately. Find out the appropriate word in each case.*

PASSAGE–1

Seed quality is an **...(1)...** aspect of crop production. For ages, farmers have traditionally been selecting and **...(2)...** good quality seed, since it was in their interest to do so. They knew and understood the importance of quality seed in production.

However, with the advent of green revolution technology, based **...(3)...** on the high-yielding dwarf varieties of wheat and rice, mainstream thinking changed. Agricultural scientists, for reasons that remain **...(4)...** began to doubt, the ability of farmers to maintain seed quality **...(5)...** . Aided by the World Bank, the Ministry of Agriculture launched a National Seeds Project in 1967. Under the project spread into three phases, seed processing plants werre **...(6)...** up in nine states. Six states were covered under phase three. All that the huge processing plants were **...(7)...** to do was to provide 'certified' seeds of food crops, mainly self- pollinating crops, to farmers. In mid-1980s, the International Rice Research Institute (IRRI) in the Philippines concluded a study which **...(8)...** that there was hardly any difference in the crop yields from transplanted rice and from the crop sown by broad casted seeds. One would wonder why, in the first instance, were the farmers, asked to **...(9)...** over to transplanting paddy? The answer is simple–probably, to help the mechanical industries grow. Since rice, is the staple food in Asia, tractor sales could only grow if there was a way to move the machine in the rice fields. No wonder, the sales of tractors, puddlers, reapers and other associated **...(10)...** soared in the rice growing areas.

1. A. irrational B. main C. brilliant D. important E. empathetic

2. A. maintaining B. trusting C. selling D. processing E. creating

3. A. necessarily B. exceptionally C. primarily D. regularly E. truly

4. A. unexplained B. doubt C. some D. true E. sad

5. A. himself B. sometimes C. proper D. improve E. themselves

6. A. established B. created C. set D. wound E. thought

7. A. tried B. mattered C. meaning D. supposed E. expect

8. A. renounced B. showed C. passed D. negated E. directed

9. A. shift B. make C. turn D. mull E. switch

10. A. sell B. equipments C. people D. techniques E. creatures

PASSAGE–2

The world's climate has always changed and species have evolved accordingly to survive it. The surprising fact about the **...(11)...** between evolution and global warming **...(12)...** that it is not linear. **...(13)...** temperatures alone are not **...(14)...** of evolution. Evolution is also the **...(15)...** of seasonal changes. As the environment **...(16)...** those species which don't adapt **...(17)...** to exist. But the sheer **...(18)...** of manmade climate change today is **...(19)...**. 'Bad things are happening' and by one ...(20)... global warming could threaten up to one-third of the world's species if left unchecked. In fact; a lot of the species which will be able to survive are the ones we consider pests like insects and weeds.

11. A. difference B. similarity C. argument D. relationship E. alliance

12. A. being B. seems C. mainly D. besides E. is

13. A. However B. Mounted C. Rising D. Elevating E. Inclining

14. A. means B. triggers C. responses D. threats E. stimulus

15. A. result B. precursor C. resistance D. cause E. provocation

16. A. conserves B. stifles C. predicts D. changes E. emerges

17. A. continue B. halt C. cease D. terminate E. discontinue

18. A. luck B. value C. collapse D. pace E. attention

19. A. threatened B. pursued C. unprecedented D. record E. debated

20. A. forecast B. chance C. pattern D. occasion E. imagination

PASSAGE–3

The large number of natural disasters within a few days in late September has led to two assumptions. First, we are experiencing more natural calamities today ...(21)... ever before, and second, the distribution of disasters ...(22)... unequal. A UN report studied natural disasters ...(23)... 1975 and 2007 found that not only is the ...(24)... of catastrophes increasing because of climate change and environmental ...(25)... but also that the brunt of tragedies is borne ...(26)... poor countries least equipped to deal with such ...(27)... It is true that some countries are disaster-prone but some ...(28)... Japan for example have managed to overcome their geographical disadvantages.

...(29)... to UN estimates, equivalent populations in the Philippines and Japan ...(30)... the same number of cyclones each year but 17 times more people perish in the Philippines than in Japan. In some ways natural disasters give developed economies an excuse for technological improvement while in poorer ones it feeds a vicious cycle– since they are constantly struggling to recover from natural calamities they cannot afford the disaster prevention measures needed.

21. A. as B. than C. not D. of E. since

22. A. being B. are C. often D. is E. seem

23. A. after B. prior C. between D. separating E. affecting

24. A. response B. dances C. occurring D. damage E. frequency

25. A. degradation B. protection C. detriment D. audit E. summit

26. A. of B. by C. with D. for E. on

27. A. calm B. misbelieve C. misfortunes D. faith E. mistake

28. A. inspite B. even C. since D. how E. like

29. A. Thanks B. Comparing C. Similar D. According E. Linked

30. A. endure B. incite C. enjoys D. trigger E. encounters

PASSAGE–4

On October 2, 1983 the Grameen Bank Project ...(31)... the Grameen Bank. We invited the Finance Minister to be the Chief Guest at our ...(32)... ceremony. But when the Ministry came to ...(33)... that the ceremony would take place in a remote district, they said it would not be an ...(34)... place to launch a Bank and that the ceremony should be ...(35)... in Dhaka so that all the top Government Officials could ...(36)... We stood firm and ...(37)... to them that we did not work in urban areas so it made no ...(38)... to have the ceremony in a city ...(39)... we had no borrowers. We had the ceremony in a big open field with the Finance Minister present as Chief Guest. For all of us who had worked so hard to ...(40)... this it was a dream come true.

31. A. reorganised B. merged C. named D. converted E. became

32. A. opening B. closing C. dedicated D. inaugurate E. induction

33. A. reveal B. know C. aware D. inform E. acquaint

34. A. excellent B. available C. inauspicious D. appropriate E. obvious

35. A. invited B. assembled C. done D. shifted E. held

36. A. present B. accompany C. attend D. involve E. entertain

37. A. apologised B. told C. explained D. denied E. refused

38. A. difference B. sense C. difficulty D. meaning E. point

39. A. where B. while C. that D. however E. which

40. A. obey B. achieve C. discover D. built E. perform

41. A. gives B. researches C. introduced D. originates E. enlightened

42. A. improved B. entrusted C. fought D. cured E. dealt

43. A. thousands B. alike C. imitated D. similar E. naming

44. A. course B. less C. approximate D. period E. just

45. A. referred B. known C. perceived D. regarded E. called

46. A. denotes B. describes C. for D. explains E. means

47. A. business B. membership C. scope D. effort E. purpose

48. A. provided B. buying C. equipped D. supplied E. empowering

49. A. coming B. next C. past D. few E. previous

50. A. overlook B. curb C. protect D. enrich E. neglect

PASSAGE–5

Decades ago, China ...(41)... the concept of 'barefoot doctors'. They were community healthcare workers who successfully ...(42)... the health of China's villages. Following this example, many African, Asian and Latin American countries have started ...(43)... programmes. The largest of such community health efforts is India's National Rural Health Mission. In ...(44)... over three years, the programme has mobilized over fifty thousand new community health workers, each ...(45)... as 'Asha'. This is short for 'Accredited Social Health Activist' and translated into Hindi is the word ...(46)... hope.

Today technology companies and foundations are also joining the ...(47)... to support community health workers. Mobile phone companies are ...(48)... these workers with phones and support systems to obtain up to date medical information, call ambulances etc. In the ...(49)... years, community health workers can thus help ...(50)... the spread of many devastating but curable diseases.

PASSAGE–6

Jamshedji Tata is ...(51)... to be the path-finder of modern industrial builders. He is known as the grand-father of the Indian industry for his acumen and enthusiasm. Nobody else could have ...(52)... of the new industries started by Jamshedji at that time when industrial ...(53)... and revolution was yet to come to India.

Jamshedji's father Nasarvanji Tata used to trade in jute with China and Britain. He started ...(54)... from India. Jamshedji started a cloth mill in Nagpur more than hundred years ago. At that time almost all the ...(55)... used to come from Lancashire in England. What Jameshdji ...(56)... was praiseworthy.

Jamshedji ...(57)... very well that an industrial revolution can only be brought in the country by setting up iron and steel industry ...(58)... he did not live to see the industry he had in mind, he had done all ...(59)... work. In fact, he laid the ground work for it. He had planned the entire steel city now known as Jamshedpur, complete with streets, roads, schools, parks, play grounds, temples, mosques, churches, etc. His **...(60)...** was fulfilled by his sons, Sir Dorabji Tata and Sir Rattan Tata, when they started the Tata Iron & Steel Factory in 1907 just after three years of his death.

51. A. rewarded B. agreed C. empowered D. determined E. considered

52. A. absolved B. thought C. ventured D. set E. planned

53. A. imports B. acts C. machinery D. awakening E. factories

54. A. export B. industries C. import D. trade E. dispatch

55. A. goods B. imports C. cloth D. machines E. industries

56. A. did B. dreamt C. agreed D. told E. meant

57. A. felt B. advocated C. planned D. thought E. knew

58. A. Because B. Although C. Surprisingly D. Luckily E. Even

59. A. insignificant B. complete C. trivial D. preliminary E. external

60. A. need B. task C. dream D. industry E. sentiment

PASSAGE–7

Rabbits are among the most **...(61)...** of all animals. The rabbit of a colony, once had a **...(62)...** to discuss this **...(63)...** of theirs. They came to the **...(64)...** that as their timidity would never leave them, they were condemned to a miserable existence and it would be better to drown themselves and end their **...(65)...** once and for all. Accordingly, they began to move towards a large lake.

When the frogs in the lake saw a large number of rabbits **...(66)...** they were filled with **...(67)...** and made for the deepest part of the lake. Seeing this, the **...(68)...** of the rabbits stopped and said to his fellow-creatures: "It is true we are timid, but here are animals more timid than us. There is still some **...(69)...** for us. Let us all go back to our homes," and the **...(70)...** of rabbits headed back to their colony.

61. A. skilled B. calm C. expensive D. generous E. timid

62. A. meeting B. lecture C. assembly D. festival E. contest

63. A. tradition B. gene C. trait D. virtue E. sentiment

64. A. decision B. finate C. point D. solution E. conclusion

65. A. torture B. misery C. bad luck D. life E. species

66. A. attending B. retreating C. approaching D. swimming E. sulking

67. A. sympathy B. tear C. empathy D. gratitude E. glee

68. A. group B. army C. leader D. captain E. fellow

69. A. ray B. refuge C. doubt D. solution E. hope

70. A. multiple B. manifold C. leader D. herd E. calmest

PASSAGE–8

Once, in a forest there was a little tree covered with pointed leaves. "Ah"! It said to itself one day, "my neighbours are happy. They have leaves that are pleasing to see. Mine are like needles, I wish I could have **...(71)...** of gold!" Soon it was night and the little tree dozed, the next morning it was transformed! "What joy," it cried, "I'm covered with gold! No other tree in the forest has a similar grab." But towards evening a man came by, he threw a fearful look around him, and seeing that nobody was **...(72)...** him, took off the golden leaves, put them in a sack and **...(73)...**

"Oh," said the little tree, "I miss those lovely golden leaves which **...(74)...** in the sunlight, but leaves of glass could be just as brilliant. I would like to have leaves of glass." That evening the little tree slept, and the next morning it was **...(75)...** again. From its branches hung leaves of glass. "Ah", it said, "this is a pretty attire, my neighbours have nothing like it." But that very day, some black clouds gathered in the sky, the wind blew strongly and a storm came in. All the glass leaves from the little tree fell and broke.

"Alas," sighed the tree. This foliage that I was ambitious for is very elegant, but very ...(76)... It would be better to have a ...(77)... of good green leaves, some nice fragrant ones." The little tree slept that night, and the next morning it was dressed as it vied. But the scent of its fresh leaves attracted the ...(78)... who came to nibble them, and standing up on their hind paws, they nibbled all the way to the top of the little tree and left it entirely ...(79)... When it went to sleep that night, it longed for its original leaves, and the next morning ...(80)... to see them reappear on its branches. They had neither the splendour of gold, nor the luminous transparency of glass, nor the attraction of aromatic plants; but they were solid, nobody came to take them off and the tree had them throughout the season.

71. A. designs B. leaves C. branches D. fruits E. roots

72. A. beside B. with C. inspecting D. watching E. looking

73. A. exclaimed B. continued C. wished D. counted E. fled

74. A. dried B. sheltered C. glistened D. reflected E. warmed

75. A. new B. created C. transformed D. awake E. alive

76. A. costly B. fragile C. attractive D. good E. flimsy

77. A. bunch B. forest C. collection D. substitute E. description

78. A. neighbours B. bees C. hunters D. trees E. goats

79. A. lonely B. sad C. bare D. depressed E. hungry

80. A. excited B. proclaimed C. rejoiced D. eager E. searched

PASSAGE–9

As the country embarks on planning ...(81)... the 12th Plan (2012-17) period, a key question mark ...(82)... hangs over the process is on the energy requirements.

Growh is energy hungry, and the aspirations of growing at 9-10% will ...(83)... huge demands on the energy resources of the country. In this energy jigsaw, renewable energy will ...(84)... like never before in the 12th Plan and ...(85)....

By the rule of the thumb, India will ...(86)... about 100 gigawatts (Gw)-100,000 megawatts-of capacity addition in the next five years. Encouraging trends on energy efficiency and sustained ...(87)... by some parts of the government—the Bureau of Energy Efficiency in particular needs to be complimented for this—have led to substantially lesser energy intensity of economic growth. However, even the tempered demand numbers are ...(88)... to be below 80 Gw. As against this need the coal supply from domestic sources is unlikely to support more than 25 Gw equivalent capacity. Imported coal can add some more, but at a much ...(89)... cost. Gas-based electricity generation is unlikely to contribute anything substantial in view of the unprecedented gas supply challenges. Nuclear will be ...(90)... in the foreseeable future. Between imported coal, gas, large hydro and nuclear, no more than 15-20 Gw equivalent can be ...(91)... to be added in the five-year time block.

...(92)... ...(93)... this, capacity addition in the renewable energy based power generation has touched about 3 Gw a year. In the coming five years, the overall capacity addition in the electricity grid ...(94)... renewable energy is likely to range between 20 Gw and 25 Gw. Additionally, over and above the grid-based capacity, off-grid electricity applications are reaching remote places and ...(95)... lives where grid-based electricity supply has miserably failed.

81. A. against B. for C. onwards D. at E. on

82. A. that B. inside C. always D. who E. where

83. A. forward B. subject C. place D. demand E. replace

84. A. pass B. publish C. feature D. find E. light

85. A. likewise B. publicity C. next D. after E. earlier

86. A. waste B. require C. highlight D. generate E. consumed

87. A. structures B. efforts C. projections D. practices E. developmental

88. A. sure B. unsure C. unexpected D. unlikely E. likely

89. A. nominal B. excelled C. higher D. lower E. expected

90. A. failure B. success C. dangerous D. maximum E. marginal

91. A. certain B. linked C. remarked D. expected E. sure

92. A. When B. But C. However D. If E. As

93. A. for B. with C. is D. ever E. against

94. A. through B. project C. versus D. against E. capacity

95. A. lightening B. making C. touching D. saving E. generating

PASSAGE–10

The Right of Children to Free and Compulsory Education (RTE) Act, 2009, which came **...(96)...** effect in April this year, is meant to transform the education sector and take India closer to the goal of universal schooling. But with admissions to the new academic session just **...(97)...** the corner, it is fast becoming clear that **...(98)...** well-intentioned ideas into **...(99)...** will take some doing. For a start, the guidelines for admissions under the RTE prohibit schools from conducting any sort of student profiling. The stress on a random yet justifiable admission process means that schools will have to resort to something as quirky as a lottery system. However, leaving admission to a good school to pure **...(100)...** will only incentivise manipulations, defeating the very essence of RTE.

The main problem facing the education sector is that of a resource crunch. The provisions for ensuring universal access to education are all very well, **...(101)...** we have the infrastructure in place first. Brick and mortar schools need to precede open admission and not the **...(102)...** way around. In that sense, legislators' assessment of ground realities is **...(103)...** target when they endorse the closure of tens of thousands of low-cost private schools for not meeting the minimum standards of land plot, building specifications and playground area as laid out in the RTE Act. Instead of bearing down **...(104)...** on private schools for failing to conform to abstract bureaucratic criteria, efforts to bring about universal education should focus on upgrading and expanding the existing government school infrastructure to accommodate all. Only then can we ensure the much-needed supply-demand **...(105)...** in the education sector.

96. A. with B. for C. on D. into E. in

97. A. around B. near C. into D. about E. reaching

98. A. forming B. translating C. having D. taking E. framing

99. A. affect B. ideas C. practice D. concept E. procedure

100. A. benefit B. merit C. chance D. basis E. method

101. A. unless B. until C. executed D. provided E. exercised

102. A. other B. any C. two D. differ E. after

103. A. on B. of C. often D. taken E. off

104. A. soft B. more C. less D. only E. hard

105. A. need B. equilibrium C. expectation D. attempt E. aspects

PASSAGE–11

The U.S. is in the **...(106)...** of a cleanup of toxic financial waste that will **...(107)...** taxpayers hundreds of billions of dollars, at the very least. The primary manufacturers of these hazardous products **...(108)...** multimillion-dollar paychecks for their efforts. So why shouldn't they **...(109)...** to pay for their mop-up? This is, after all, what the U.S. Congress **...(110)...** in 1980 for **...(111)...** of actual toxic waste. Under the Superfund law **...(112)...** that year, polluters **...(113)...** for the messes they make. Environmental lawyer E. Michael Thomas sees no **...(114)...** lawmakers couldn't demand the same of financial polluters and **...(115)...** them to ante up some of the bank bailout money.

106. A. range B. depth C. midst D. essence E. debate

107. A. benefit B. cost
C. earn D. facilitate
E. save

108. A. donated B. demanded
C. dwindled D. spent
E. pocketed

109. A. hesitate B. come
C. defy D. have
E. admit

110. A. decreed B. refrained
C. commented D. admonished
E. visualized

111. A. consumers B. advocates
C. exponents D. producers
E. users

112. A. revoked B. forced
C. squashed D. abandoned
E. enacted

113. A. regain B. claim
C. pay D. demand
E. consider

114. A. practice B. reason
C. compensation D. issue
E. wonder

115. A. force B. plead
C. appeal D. dupe
E. follow

PASSAGE–12

A day light can be seen ...(116)... very small holes, so little things will ...(117)... a person's character. Indeed consists in little acts well and ...(118) performed; daily life being the ...(119)... from which build it up and rough ...(120)... the habits which form it. One of the more marked test of character is the manner in which we ...(121)... ourselves towards others, a graceful behaviour, towards superiors, inferiors, and ...(122)... is constant source of pleasure. It pleases others because it indicates ...(123)... for their personality, but it gives tenfold more ...(124)... to our selves. Every man may, to large extent be a self educator in good ...(125)... as in every else, he can be civil and kind if he thinks he has not a penny in his purse.

116. A. through B. out of
C. in D. by
E. With

117. A. darken B. characterise
C. adorn D. illustrate
E. vilify

118. A. equally B. honourably
C. roughly D. officially
E. impartially

119. A. house B. livelihood
C. quarry D. relation
E. relative

120. A. spouse B. give up
C. new D. watch
E. choose

121. A. conduct B. manage
C. nature D. present
E. dispose

122. A. equals B. juniors
C. seniors D. superiors
E. priors

123. A. happiness B. honour
C. regard D. respect
E. influence

124. A. force B. requirement
C. pleasure D. dedication
E. loudness

125. A. status B. behaviour
C. character D. career
E. condition

PASSAGE–13

With the U.S. military tied down on two fronts and the rest of the world growing ...(126)... to American power, the challenges for Rice are as ...(127)... as they have been for any Secretary of State in the past three decades. After six years of tussling with others on Bush's national-security team, Rice has seen off her rivals and ...(128)... as the principal spokes-person for Bush's foreign ...(129).... Her reward has been to ...(130)... responsibility for selling a failed policy in Iraq and ...(131)... a legacy for Bush at a time when ...(132)... in the world are in the mood to help her. "Bush is severely ...(133)... and has very little ...(134)... or support at home or abroad," says Leslie Gelb, former president of the Council on Foreign Relations. "That is ...(135)... true for his Secretary of State. So they are ...(136)... flailing around."

That's a grim assessment, since the ...(137)... to international order are ...(138)... today than at any 'other' time since the end of the cold war. The most immediate source of ...(139)... emanates from Iraq, where the country's civil war risks ...(140)... a region-wide conflict.

126. A. resistant B. subservient
C. immune D. cordial
E. indifference

127. A. obvious B. trivial
C. superfluous D. daunting
E. rewarding

128. A. renamed B. emerged
C. appointed D. entrusted
E. visited

129. A. aid B. recognition
C. policy D. acceptability
E. minister

130. A. shirk B. avoid
C. transfer D. visualize
E. inherit

131. A. focusing B. framing
C. escaping D. salvage
E. demolishing

132. A. people B. few
C. diplomats D. autocrats
E. most

133. A. intensified B. master-minded
C. weakened D. projected
E. supported

134. A. credibility B. difficulty
C. majority D. power
E. enthusiasm

135. A. not B. uniformly
C. remotely D. partially
E. also

136. A. effectively B. inadvertently
C. basically D. aimlessly
E. not

137. A. admirations B. threats
C. pleasantries D. demands
E. accolades

138. A. louder B. fewer
C. magnificent D. most
E. bigger

139. A. instability B. fuel
C. energy D. peace
E. atrocity

140. A. defusing B. demolishing
C. terminating D. igniting
E. extinguishing

PASSAGE–14

The ...**(141)**... of Bengal tigers left in the world has ...**(142)**... from 100,000 to 4,000 over the last century. The main threats are ...**(143)**... of habitat, poaching and the trade in tiger parts for Eastern medicines. Most Bengal tigers live in protected areas of India. Anti-poaching task-force have been ...**(144)**... up and there is also a trade ...**(145)**... on tiger products in many countries, as a measure to save this rare species.

141. A. from B. kind
C. glory D. number
E. species

142. A. limited B. shrunk
C. abolished D. eliminated
E. ascended

143. A. prevention B. encroaching
C. condition D. shift
E. loss

144. A. set B. brought
C. swept D. deployed
E. grown

145. A. agreement B. contract
C. ban D. link
E. policy

PASSAGE–15

Human Resources Development Department has ...**(146)**... heads of all Central Office Departments to ...**(147)**... to the notice of the employees ...**(148)**... to their departments ...**(149)**... the availability of professional counsellor engaged by our organization on contract basis to ...**(150)**... counselling services to employees of Mumbai. HRDD has also sought the ...**(151)**... of all the employees to ...**(152)**... the fears and unfounded notions, if any, about counselling so that employees were ...**(153)**... to come forward and avail of it. Counselling facility for employees was ...**(154)**... in Mumbai in September 21 with the help of a professional counsellor. The counsellor is ...**(155)**... on Mondays in the Main Building Mumbai.

146. A. reported B. indicated
C. referred D. advised
E. invited

147. A. tell B. ask
C. show D. give
E. bring

148. A. affected B. absolved
C. attached D. affixed
E. surrounded

149. A. regarding B. about
C. upon D. aforesaid
E. consequent

150. A. decide B. determine
C. provide D. takcover
E. spread

151. A. availability B. presence
C. support D. permission
E. objection

152. A. dissolve B. disperse
C. dispel D. displace
E. differ

153. A. asked B. directed
C. diverted D. encouraged
E. offered

154. A. obstructed B. observed
C. started D. laid
E. resulted

155. A. ready B. available
C. accessible D. attainable
E. approachable

PASSAGE–16

From the time I started writing this book I have come to see it as personal ...(156)... to an outstanding fellow Indian, whose ...(157)... and compassion have often moved me. Insight, not objectivity, is the key to understanding of a life as multi-layered as that of Swami Vivekananda and in the ...(158)... of writing this book, I have often felt ...(159)... by the realization that a historian may not always be a good biographer. I have also been ...(160)... by the several inconsistencies and ...(161)... of Vivekananda's life, and only by bringing these out more sharply, I felt, could one consciously ...(162)... from the hagiography that ...(163)... biographical work on him. It is impossible to reach an understanding of a personality as complex as Vivekananda's without studying his ambiguities and shifting ...(164)... on various issues. In trying to integrate these in a ...(165)... assessment of Vivekananda, I have largely gone by what the Swami has himself suggested – judge a man ultimately by his strengths, not his weaknesses.

156. A. justice B. devotion
C. contribution D. attribution
E. tribute

157. A. deliberation B. projection
C. vivacity D. acknowledgement
E. appreciation

158. A. course B. manifestation
C. objective D. implementation
E. serenity

159. A. represented B. relieved
C. compensated D. burdened
E. occupied

160. A. absorbed B. perplexed
C. carried D. ventured
E. loaded

161. A. duplications B. paradoxes
C. assumptions D. levels
E. pluralities

162. A. desist B. estranged
C. distinguish D. depart
E. abstain

163. A. evolves B. focuses
C. permeates D. empowers
E. emphasizes

164. A. positions B. engagements
C. possibilities D. provocations
E. flexibilities

165. A. modern B. conducive
C. commensurate D. diabolic
E. holistic

PASSAGE–17

Actually, everyday we all engage in this business of 'reading' people. We do it ...(166).... We want to figure others out. So we ...(167)... make guesses about what others think, value, want and feel and we do so based on our ....(168).... beliefs and understanding about human nature. We do so because if we can figure out ....(169).... and intentions of others the possibility of them ....(170).... or hurting us, ...(171).... and this well help us to ....(172).... a lot of unnecessary pain and trouble. We also make second-guesses about what they will do in future, how they will ....(173).... if we make this or that response. We do all this second guessing based upon our ....(174).... of what we believe about the person's inner nature ....(175).... his or her roles and manners. We mind-read their ....(176).... motives.

Also everyday we misguess and misread. Why? Because of the complexity, ...(177).... and multi-dimensional functioning of people. After all how well do you 'read' your own thoughts, aims, values, motives, beliefs, etc.? How well do you know your own structuring process— your own thinking and ....(178).... styles.

166. A. vehemently B. practically
C. actually D. incessantly
E. virtually

167. A. ably B. constantly
C. partly D. largely
E. positively

168. A. futuristic B. proactive
C. reactive D. decorative
E. assumptive

169. A. manifestations B. expressions
C. motives D. hopes
E. prospects

170. A. tricking B. blaming
C. furthering D. alarming
E. criticising

171. A. lessens B. happens
C. questions D. deepens
E. laments

172. A. approach B. direct
C. avoid D. implement
E. prepare

173. A. solve B. apply
C. plan D. approach
E. respond

174. A. projection B. exhibition
C. situation D. prediction
E. attribution

175. A. organising B. underneath
C. appreciating D. proposing
E. outside

176. A. cunning B. visible
C. deeper D. obvious
E. proposed

177. A. abnormality B. angularity
C. focus D. layeredness
E. contribution

178. A. proposing B. developing
C. upbringing D. lamenting
E. emoting

PASSAGE–18

Man has always cosidered himself to be the ruler of his planet. This **...(179)...** and the attendant superiority feeling has made him look down **...(180)...** other creatures who co-exist with human on this earth. The so-called 'civilized' human race has **...(181)...** and ill-treated small and large animal species and birds in an attempt to prove his **...(182)...** . It is common knowledge that **...(183)...** number of animals have been **...(184)...** for centuries under the **...(185)...** of conducting scientific experiments or for sports. Till recently, in the **...(186)...** of scientific experiments monkeys and frogs have been **...(187)...** to dissection and **...(188)...** in the laboratory.

179. A. pleasure B. fact
C. achievement D. force
E. arrogance

180. A. in B. upon
C. with D. for
E. into

181. A. criticised B. devalued
C. protected D. abused
E. enlarged

182. A. supremacy B. wisdom
C. cleverness D. instinct
E. possession

183. A. tall B. plenty
C. countless D. diverse
E. numerous

184. A. tourtured B. exposed
C. treated D. vanished
E. extinct

185. A. projection B. criticism
C. pretext D. game
E. study

186. A. matter B. set
C. scheme D. virtue
E. name

187. A. confined B. subjected
C. condemned D. allied
E. performed

188. A. cruelty B. deformation
C. study D. vivisection
E. proliferation

PASSAGE–19

Organisation ...**(189)**... is a very broad subject that appears frequently in recent management studies. Organisations have many ...**(190)**... to improve whatever it is that they do. They can reflect on their operations, study their products, ...**(191)**... to cutsomers, and encourage ...**(192)**... parts of the organisation to share knowledge as well as the results of their ...**(193)**... efforts. All firms have these opportunities, although few companies take full ...**(194)**... of them Good firms everywhere ...**(195)**... their processes and ...**(196)**... in order to learn from past successes as well as ...**(197)**... . They measures and benchmark what they do. They try to get different parts of the organisation to ...**(198)**... with one another.

189. A. learning B. system
C. building D. structure
E. conflict

190. A. systems B. incentives
C. opportunities D. methods
E. reasons

191. A. call B. refer
C. please D. pay
E. listen

192. A. significant B. different
C. all D. some
E. many

193. A. approved B. separate
C. all D. individualistic
E. hard

194. A. benefit B. credit
C. recourse D. advantage
E. stock

195. A. critique B. protect
C. design D. criticize
E. innovate

196. A. projects B. finances
C. people D. products
E. ideas

197. A. breaks B. limitations
C. gaps D. set-ups
E. failures

198. A. expand B. develop
C. cooperate D. grow
E. mingle

PASSAGE–20

With the U.S. military tied down on two fronts and the rest of the world growing **...(199)...** to American power, the challenges for Rice are as **...(200)...** as they have been for any Secretary of State in the past three decades. After six years of tussling with others on Bush's national-security team, Rice has seen off her rivals and **...(201)...** as the principal spokes- person for Bush's foreign **...(202)....** Her reward has been to **...(203)...** responsibility for selling a failed policy in Iraq and **...(204)...** a legacy for Bush at a time when **...(205)...** in the world are in the mood to help her. "Bush is severely **...(206)...** and has very little **...(207)...** or support at home or abroad," says Leslie Gelb, former president of the Council on Foreign Relations. "That is

...(208)... true for his Secretary of State. So they are ...(209)... flailing around."

That's a grim assessment, since the ...(210)... to international order are bigger today than at any 'other' time since the end of the cold war. The most immediate source of atrocity emanates from Iraq, where the country's civil war risks igniting a region-wide conflict.

199. A. resistant B. subservient C. immune D. cordial E. indifference

200. A. obvious B. trivial C. superfluous D. daunting E. rewarding

201. A. renamed B. emerged C. appointed D. entrusted E. visited

202. A. aid B. recognition C. policy D. acceptability E. minister

203. A. shirk B. avoid C. transfer D. visualize E. inherit

204. A. focusing B. framing C. escaping D. salvage E. demolishing

205. A. people B. few C. diplomats D. autocrats E. most

206. A. intensified B. master-minded C. weakened D. projected E. supported

207. A. credibility B. difficulty C. majority D. power E. enthusiasm

208. A. not B. uniformly C. remotely D. partially E. also

209. A. effectively B. inadvertently C. basically D. aimlessly E. not

210. A. admirations B. threats C. pleasantries D. demands E. accolades

ANSWERS

1	2	3	4	5	6	7	8	9	10
D	B	C	A	B	C	D	B	E	B
11	**12**	**13**	**14**	**15**	**16**	**17**	**18**	**19**	**20**
D	E	C	B	A	D	C	D	C	E
21	**22**	**23**	**24**	**25**	**26**	**27**	**28**	**29**	**30**
B	D	C	E	A	B	C	E	D	A
31	**32**	**33**	**34**	**35**	**36**	**37**	**38**	**39**	**40**
E	A	B	D	E	C	C	B	A	B
41	**42**	**43**	**44**	**45**	**46**	**47**	**48**	**49**	**50**
C	A	D	E	C	C	D	E	A	B
51	**52**	**53**	**54**	**55**	**56**	**57**	**58**	**59**	**60**
E	B	B	A	C	A	E	B	D	C
61	**62**	**63**	**64**	**65**	**66**	**67**	**68**	**69**	**70**
E	A	D	E	B	C	B	C	E	D
71	**72**	**73**	**74**	**75**	**76**	**77**	**78**	**79**	**80**
B	D	E	E	C	B	C	B	C	C
81	**82**	**83**	**84**	**85**	**86**	**87**	**88**	**89**	**90**
B	C	C	C	D	B	B	D	C	E
91	**92**	**93**	**94**	**95**	**96**	**97**	**98**	**99**	**100**
D	E	E	A	C	D	A	B	C	C
101	**102**	**103**	**104**	**105**	**106**	**107**	**108**	**109**	**110**
D	A	E	E	B	C	B	E	D	A
111	**112**	**113**	**114**	**115**	**116**	**117**	**118**	**119**	**120**
D	E	C	B	A	A	D	B	C	C
121	**122**	**123**	**124**	**125**	**126**	**127**	**128**	**129**	**130**
A	A	D	C	B	A	D	E	C	E
131	**132**	**133**	**134**	**135**	**136**	**137**	**138**	**139**	**140**
D	A	C	E	E	D	D	E	E	D

141	142	143	144	145	146	147	148	149	150
D	B	E	A	C	D	E	C	A	C
151	152	153	154	155	156	157	158	159	160
B	C	D	C	B	E	C	A	B	A
161	162	163	164	165	166	167	168	169	170
B	D	C	A	E	D	B	E	C	A
171	172	173	174	175	176	177	178	179	180
A	C	E	A	E	C	B	E	E	B
181	182	183	184	185	186	187	188	189	190
B	A	C	A	C	E	B	D	B	C
191	192	193	194	195	196	197	198	199	200
E	B	D	D	E	A	E	D	A	D
201	202	203	204	205	206	207	208	209	210
B	C	E	D	A	C	E	E	D	D

❑❑❑

3. Ordering of Sentences

Directions (Qs. 1–100): *Each of these question sets has a group of sentences marked with numbers, rearrange them in proper sequence to form a meaningful paragraph; then answer the questions given below each set.*

SET-1

1. With all the bid information being available and tracked online, corruption has considerably reduced.
2. Today, most, ie over ninety-five per cent, households, in the city enjoy broadband connection.
3. All city contracts are now bid for online.
4. Over twenty years ago the city government, Central Government and the private sector made a concerted effort to shift the economy to include IT.
5. As our cities do expand and become more complex, such a system will make governance more manageable.
6. This level of connectedness has changed not only the city's economy but also how it is governed and how business is conducted.

1. Which of the following should be the **FIRST** sentence after rearrangement?
A. 1 B. 2
C. 3 D. 4
E. 5

2. Which of the following should be the **SECOND** sentence after rearrangement?
A. 1 B. 2
C. 3 D. 4
E. 6

3. Which of the following should be the **THIRD** sentence after rearrangement?
A. 1 B. 3
C. 4 D. 5
E. 6

4. Which of the following should be the **FIFTH** sentence after rearrangement?
A. 1 B. 2
C. 3 D. 4
E. 5

5. Which of the following should be the **LAST (SIXTH)** sentence after rearrangement?
A. 2 B. 3
C. 4 D. 5
E. 6

SET-2

1. If tomorrow's children meet these two crucial criteria, they are likely to have the opportunity both to pursue work to fulfil their dreams and make an impact on the world around.
2. In the 21st century, however, this no longer holds true as the expectations of organisations have changed.
3. The concept of job in the 20th century was often equated with toil.
4. In order to meet these changed expectations, employees need commitment and access to continuous learning.
5. Jobs were acquired, learned and performed until retirement and did not have to be rewarding.
6. They demand more creativity and expertise and want employees to be responsible for both outputs and outcomes.

6. Which of the following should be the **FIRST** sentence after rearrangement?
A. 1 B. 2
C. 3 D. 4
E. 5

7. Which of the following should be the **SECOND** sentence after rearrangement?
A. 1 B. 2
C. 3 D. 4
E. 5

8. Which of the following should be the **THIRD** sentence after rearrangement?
A. 2 B. 3
C. 4 D. 5
E. 6

SET-3

1. For instance, if we measure the room temperature continuously and plot its graph with time on X-axis and temperature on the Y-axis, we get a continuous waveform, which is an analog signal. Analog is always continuous.
2. The absence or presence of something can be used to plot a digital signal.
3. An analog signal is a continuously varying signal, similar to a sinusoidal waveform.
4. Any signal can be classified into one of the two types : analog and digital.
5. In contrast, a digital signal takes the form of pulses, where we have something or nothing.

9. Which of the following should be the **FIRST** sentence after rearrangement?
A. 1 B. 2
C. 3 D. 4
E. 5

10. Which of the following should be the **FIFTH** sentence after rearrangement?
A. 1 B. 2
C. 3 D. 4
E. 5

11. Which of the following should be the **FOURTH** sentence after rearrangement?
A. 1 B. 2
C. 3 D. 4
E. 5

12. Which of the following should be the **THIRD** sentence after rearrangement?
A. 1 B. 2
C. 3 D. 4
E. 5

13. Which of the following should be the **SECOND** sentence after rearrangement?
A. 1 B. 2
C. 3 D. 4
E. 5

SET-4

1. Expansion of retail banking especially has a lot of scope, since retail assets are just 22 per cent of the total banking assets.
2. Where they do not find it viable to open branches they may open satellite offices in these areas.
3. There is tremendous scope for the expansion of banking in India.
4. Banks can also diversify beyond cities to semi-urban and rural areas.
5. In these ways a transition from class banking to mass banking can take place.
6. They can also collaborate with local stakeholders in order to extend microcredit services to those living there.

14. Which of the following should be the **THIRD** sentence after rearrangement ?
A. 2 B. 3
C. 4 D. 5
E. 6

15. Which of the following should be the **first** sentence after rearrangement ?
A. 1 B. 2
C. 3 D. 4
E. 5

16. Which of the following should be the **FIFTH** sentence after rearrangement ?
A. 2 B. 3
C. 4 D. 5
E. 6

17. Which of the following should be the **SIXTH (LAST)** sentence after rearrangement ?
A. 1 B. 2
C. 3 D. 4
E. 5

18. Which of the following should be the **SECOND** sentence after rearrangement ?
A. 1 B. 2
C. 3 D. 4
E. 5

SET-5

1. To elaborate briefly on these characteristics and dimensions that the author is talking about—NRMs are general tests intended to be used to classify students by percentile for measuring either aptitude or proficiency for admissions into or placement within a program.
2. Contrastingly, the CRM, such as a locally produced achievement test, measures absolute performance that is compared only with the learning objective, hence a perfect score is theoretically obtainable by all students who have a mastery of the pre-specified material, or conversely, all students may fail the test.
3. In most of these books the authors classify a measurement strategy as either norm-referenced (NRM) or criterion-referenced (CRM).

4. Another author points out how the type of interpretation that an NRM offers is the relative performance of the students compared with that of all the others resulting in, ideally, a bell curve distribution.
5. Numerous books on constructing and using language tests have been written by various authors.
6. CRMs, on the other hand, are more specific, achievement or diagnostic tests intended to be used for motivating students by measuring to what per cent they have achieved mastery of the taught or learned material.
7. One of the authors clearly delineates the differences of these two types by focusing on the categories of "test characteristics" and "logistical dimensions."

19. Which of the following should be the **FIRST** sentence after rearrangement?
A. 7 B. 2
C. 3 D. 4
E. 5

20. Which of the following should be the **FIFTH** sentence after rearrangement?
A. 1 B. 2
C. 3 D. 6
E. 5

21. Which of the following should be the **SEVENTH (LAST)** sentence after rearrangement?
A. 1 B. 2
C. 3 D. 4
E. 5

22. Which of the following should be the **THIRD** sentence after rearrangement?
A. 1 B. 2
C. 7 D. 4
E. 5

23. Which of the following should be the **SECOND** sentence after rearrangement?
A. 1 B. 2
C. 3 D. 4
E. 6

SET-6

1. He walked up to his teacher and asked "Why does one die, Master?"
2. "The time has come for your vase to die."
3. "Its natural", said the teacher. "Everything has a beginning and an end."
4. A young student happened to break a precious vase belonging to his teacher.
5. When he heard his teacher's footsteps, he quickly hid the broken vase behind him.
6. The student then, held out the pieces of the broken vase saying.

24. Which of the following should be **FIFTH** sentence after the rearrangement?
A. 1 B. 6
C. 3 D. 2
E. 5

25. Which of the following should be the **SIXTH (LAST)** sentence after the rearrangement?
A. 2 B. 6
C. 3 D. 5
E. 4

26. Which of the following should be the **FIRST** sentence after rearrangement?
A. 3 B. 4
C. 6 D. 1
E. 5

27. Which of the following should be the **SECOND** sentence after rearrangement?
A. 2 B. 3
C. 5 D. 1
E. 6

28. Which of the following should be the **FOURTH** sentence after rearrangement?
A. 1 B. 5
C. 2 D. 6
E. 3

SET-7

1. "It is possible" said the courtier pensively.
2. "But I don't understand how he can be the noblest."
3. The Emperor asked one of his courtier's if it was possible for a man to be the 'lowest' and the 'noblest' at the same time.
4. "He has been given the honour of an audience with the Emperor. That makes him the noblest among all beggars." said the courtier.
5. The courtier returned with a beggar. "He is the lowest among your Subject" he said to the Emperor.
6. The Emperor then requested that such is person be brought to him.

29. Which of the following should be **FIRST** sentence after the rearrangement?
A. 3 B. 4
C. 6 D. 1
E. 5

30. Which of the following should be the **SECOND** sentence after the rearrangement?
A. 2 B. 3

C. 5 D. 1
E. 6

31. Which of the following should be the **FOURTH** sentence after rearrangement?
A. 1 B. 5
C. 2 D. 6
E. 4

32. Which of the following should be the **FIFTH** sentence after rearrangement?
A. 1 B. 4
C. 3 D. 2
E. 5

33. Which of the following should be the **SIXTH (LAST)** sentence after rearrangement?
A. 6 B. 2
C. 1 D. 5
E. 4

SET-8

1. He felt that his honest ways were responsible for the poverty and starvation of his family.
2. Sixteen miles away from Mysore, there is a dense forest.
3. He told them how his honesty was useless and asked if he should try an alternative.
4. They told him that they would prefer starving to dishonesty.
5. Once there lived a poor but honest woodcutter in the forest.
6. So he wanted to discuss his feeling with his wife and children.

34. Which of the following should be **SECOND** sentence after the rearrangement?
A. 1 B. 2
C. 3 D. 4
E. 5

35. Which of the following should be the **FIFTH** sentence after the rearrangement?
A. 1 B. 2
C. 3 D. 4
E. 5

36. Which of the following should be the **FIRST** sentence after rearrangement?
A. 1 B. 2
C. 3 D. 4
E. 5

37. Which of the following should be the **SIXTH (LAST)** sentence after rearrangement?
A. 1 B. 2
C. 3 D. 4
E. 5

38. Which of the following should be the **THIRD** sentence after rearrangement?
A. 1 B. 2
C. 3 D. 4
E. 5

SET-9

1. "What a waste of my tax money", I thought, walking past the people having free Californian Chardonnay.
2. "Speak to her", he said, "She's into books".
3. The friend who had brought me there noticed my noticing her.
4. In late 2003, I was still paying taxes in America, so it horrified me that the US Consulate was hosting a "Gallo drinking appreciation event".
5. Behind them, a pianist was playing old film tunes, and a slim short woman was dancing around him.

39. Which of the following would be the FOURTH sentence?
A. 1 B. 2
C. 3 D. 4
E. 5

40. Which of the following would be the FIRST sentence?
A. 1 B. 2
C. 3 D. 4
E. 5

41. Which of the following would be the FIFTH (LAST) sentence?
A. 1 B. 2
C. 3 D. 4
E. 5

42. Which of the following would be the SECOND sentence?
A. 1 B. 2
C. 3 D. 4
E. 5

43. Which of the following would be the THIRD sentence?
A. 1 B. 2
C. 3 D. 4
E. 5

SET-10

1. In all varieties of humour, especially the subtle ones it is therefore what the reader thinks which gives extra meaning to these verses.
2. But such a verse may also be enjoyed at the surface level.
3. Nonsense verse is one of the most sophisticated forms of literature.

4. This fulfils the author's main intention in such a verse which is to give pleasure.
5. However, the reader who understands the broad implications of the content and allusion finds greater pleasure.
6. The reason being it requires the reader to supply a meaning beyond the surface meaning.

44. Which of the following is the **FIFTH** sentence?
A. 4 B. 5
C. 2 D. 3
E. 1

45. Which of the following is the **SIXTH (LAST)** sentence?
A. 6 B. 5
C. 4 D. 1
E. 3

46. Which of the following is the **FIRST** sentence?
A. 5 B. 1
C. 6 D. 4
E. 3

47. Which of the following is the **SECOND** sentence?
A. 1 B. 5
C. 6 D. 2
E. 4

48. Which of the following is the **THIRD** sentence?
A. 1 B. 2
C. 6 D. 3
E. 4

SET-11

1. Suddenly the dog saw a wolf entering the house.
2. He became alert and finally killed the wolf.
3. The dog was sleeping beside the child guarding him against any danger.
4. One day he and his wife went to the market leaving behind their child who was sleeping.
5. He used to leave the dog as a guard whenever he went out.
6. There was a hunter who has a faithful dog.

49. Which of the following will be the FIFTH sentence after rearrangement?
A. 6 B. 5
C. 2 D. 1
E. 3

50. Which of the following will be the SECOND sentence after rearrangement?
A. 1 B. 2
C. 3 D. 4
E. 5

51. Which of the following will be the THIRD sentence after rearrangement?
A. 1 B. 2
C. 4 D. 3
E. 5

52. Which of the following will be the SIXTH sentence after rearrangement?
A. 1 B. 2
C. 3 D. 4
E. 5

53. Which of the following will be the FIRST sentence after rearrangement?
A. 6 B. 5
C. 4 D. 3
E. 2

SET-12

1. There are a number of items in the atomic energy programme which are being made indigenously.
2. Given the overall energy situation in India, the use of nuclear power in some measure is inescapable even while thermal and hydro power continue to be the dominant elements.
3. However, commercial aspects of exploiting nuclear capabilities, especially for power-generation programmes, have been recently given high priority.
4. Atomic energy programmes have been subject to serve restrictions for very obvious reasons as the Department of Atomic Energy is becoming self-reliant in areas in which only a few countries have such capability.
5. Even to meet these nuclear power requirements, India critically requires a commercial-level power-generation capability, with its commensurate safety and nuclear waste management arrangements.
6. Thus, in the Indian context energy security is also crucial, perhaps much more than it is for the U.S.A., because India imports a good part of its crude oil requirements, paying for it with precious foreign exchange.

54. Which of the following will be the **FIFTH** sentence after rearrangement?
A. 1 B. 2
C. 3 D. 4
E. 5

55. Which of the following will be the **THIRD** sentence after rearrangement?
A. 1 B. 2
C. 3 D. 4
E. 5

56. Which of the following will be the **SECOND** sentence after rearrangement?
A. 1 B. 2

C. 3 D. 4
E. 5

57. Which of the following will be the **FIRST** sentence after rearrangement?
A. 1 B. 2
C. 3 D. 4
E. 5

58. Which of the following will be the **FOURTH** sentence after rearrangement?
A. 1 B. 2
C. 3 D. 4
E. 5

SET-13

1. It governs all other power, physical, mental etc.
2. The mobility of the purpose helps your thoughts to break all the boundaries.
3. The power of mind is enormous.
4. Therefore, to achieve it, one should try to kindle the mind power.
5. When thoughts transcend limitations, the goal is reachable.
6. The pre-requisite is that your mind should be inspired by some good purpose.

59. Which of the following should be the **SECOND** sentence after rearrangement?
A. 1 B. 2
C. 3 D. 4
E. 5

60. Which of the following should be the **FIRST** sentence after rearrangement?
A. 1 B. 2
C. 3 D. 4
E. 5

61. Which of the following should be the **SIXTH (LAST)** sentence after rearrangement?
A. 1 B. 2
C. 3 D. 4
E. 5

62. Which of the following should be the **FOURTH** sentence after rearrangement?
A. 1 B. 2
C. 3 D. 4
E. 5

63. Which of the following should be the **FIFTH** sentence after rearrangement?
A. 1 B. 2
C. 3 D. 4
E. 5

SET-14

1. Lastly, my thanks to Ramesh, for wanting to do this last thesis together.
2. And, as always, my appreciation to David, who often believes in me more than I do myself.
3. I would like to acknowledge the enormous help given to me in creating this book.
4. For their patience, I wish to thank Joseph and John and multitude of my friends.
5. Also special thanks to Thomas, my editor, for handling this project with the right touch.
6. Have you ever had a friend like Ramesh?

64. Which of the following will be the **SECOND** sentence after rearrangement?
A. 1 B. 3
C. 2 D. 4
E. 5

65. Which of the following will be the **THIRD** sentence after rearrangement?
A. 1 B. 4
C. 3 D. 2
E. 5

66. Which of the following will be the **FOURTH** sentence after arrangement?
A. 1 B. 2
C. 3 D. 4
E. 6

67. Which of the following will be the **SIXTH (LAST)** sentence after rearrangement?
A. 6 B. 2
C. 3 D. 4
E. 1

68. Which of the following will be the **FIRST** sentence after rearrangement?
A. 1 B. 2
C. 6 D. 4
E. 5

SET-15

1. Then, fulfill that dream, with the help we offer
2. Are you willing to set goals that will move you towards making that dream a reality?
3. But, for those who are willing to dream big,
4. This book seeks to challenge people who are willing to dream.
5. I want to ask you two questions,
6. I offer this, not for the already-achieved or those who think of themselves as hopeless.
7. Are you willing to dream of doing great things?

69. Which of the following will be the **FOURTH** sentence?
A. 4 B. 1
C. 3 D. 7
E. 2

70. Which of the following will be the **FIRST** sentence?
A. 2 B. 7

C. 5 D. 4
E. 3

71. Which of the following will be the **THIRD** sentence?
A. 3 B. 5
C. 7 D. 4
E. 2

72. Which of the following will be the **LAST** sentence?
A. 4 B. 3
C. 2 D. 1
E. 7

73. Which of the following will be the **SIXTH** sentence?
A. 3 B. 4
C. 5 D. 6
E. 7

SET-16

1. What teachers reapeatedly commented on was that she was "very creative" and had "an unusual way of thinking", etc.
2. A study done by the Institute focuses on Roma, an individual with creative abilities.
3. But nowhere were Roma's these abilities recognised on her report cards, because there was no check-off box for artwork and creativity.
4. Some of her artwork was selected to represent her school at art exhibition at state level.
5. As a child, she had been a good student—above average in most areas but not an exceptional early reader and writer.

74. Which of the following should be the **THIRD** statement after rearrangement?
A. 1 B. 2
C. 3 D. 4
E. 5

75. Which of the following should be the **FOURTH** statement after rearrangement?
A. 1 B. 2
C. 3 D. 4
E. 5

76. Which of the following should be the **SECOND** statement after rearrangement?
A. 1 B. 2
C. 3 D. 4
E. 5

77. Which of the following should be the **FIRST** statement after rearrangement?
A. 1 B. 2
C. 3 D. 4
E. 5

78. Which of the following should be **FIFTH (LAST)** statement after rearrangement?
A. 1 B. 2
C. 3 D. 4
E. 5

SET-17

79. 1. Many so-called indicators for stocks and indexes take on complex hues, such as taking on moving averages of moving averages and so on.
2. A moving-average-based indicator will always be a little late, and you should naturally be suspicious of any 'formula' that can predict the next move, based purely on moving averages of price.
3. The moving average is simply a "smoothing" function — it gets rid of periodic volatility to tell you the recent trend.
4. At best, they can tell you a trend, and if the hypothesis is that the trend will sustain, and that bears out historically in enough instances, you might have a hope with it.
5. But smoothing has its disadvantages; it reacts slowly to sudden changes, so it will only tell you that the trend has changed after the trend has changed, sometimes too late to actually take action.

A. 1 2 3 4 5 B. 4 2 3 1 5
C. 1 3 5 2 4 D. 2 5 3 1 4
E. 3 2 1 5 4

80. 1. From Sweden to the UK to Greece to even the US in the early part of the century, housing prices have fallen.
2. But wasn't that just correlation?
3. Housing bubbles have been known to go bust in the past, and in different countries.
4. "The real estate market has never gone down in any meaningful way" —this statement was often quoted by real estate agents and brokers in the US, and it might have even been statistically valid, with over 50 years of data supporting it.
5. While the argument is moot today (US House Prices are still falling, after more than three years of a downward trend) it remains alive in pockets of the world.

A. 3 4 1 2 5 B. 3 4 2 1 5
C. 4 2 3 1 5 D. 2 5 4 1 3
E. 1 2 3 4 5

81. 1. For pure vegetarians India is a heaven.
2. India can boast for its innumerable varieties of tasty and nutritious vegetarian dishes.
3. These are also prepared using different methods of cooking like baking, boiling, frying etc.
4. Vegetables are an integral part of out food and we consume them in a number of ways.
5. Indians like their vegetable curries real hot 'n' spicy and so add a number of spices to make them really exotic.

A. 2 3 1 4 5 B. 1 5 3 4 2
C. 3 5 2 4 1 D. 4 1 2 5 3
E. 5 1 2 3 4

82. 1. Over the last few decades green tea has undergone many scientific and medical studies to determine the extent of its long health benefits.
2. In China there is a proverb – "Better to be deprived of food for three days, than tea of one" – and they were using the tea as a cure for headache, depression and many other ailments.
3. But it's true that Chinese people were well aware about green tea from ancient time.
4. We came to know about this green tea very late.
5. If I had said that tea is a healthy drink some years before the introduction of green tea, I might have been ridiculed.

A. 5 4 3 2 1 B. 3 4 2 1 5
C. 5 2 4 1 3 D. 4 5 3 1 2
E. 1 2 3 4 5

SET-18

83. 1. In simpler terms, it is the Indian version of the Razzies.
2. The 3rd Golden Kela Awards will be hosted by Cyrus Broacha this year.
3. It was created in order to ridicule the bad performances and as a revenge for wasting our precious time and money on such idiotic films.
4. The Golden Kela Awards is held each year where awards are given for the year's worst in Bollywood.
5. It was created by Random magazine, India's longest running humor magazine in the year 2009.

A. 4 1 5 3 2 B. 2 1 3 4 5
C. 1 3 5 4 2 D. 3 5 1 4 2
E. 5 1 2 3 4

84. 1. Despite the strong performance of the economy in 2010–11, the outlook for 2011–12 is clouded by stubborn and persistently high inflation, and rising external risks.
2. The three key macroeconomic concerns before the Union Budget 2011-12 were high inflation, high current account deficit (CAD), and fiscal consolidation.
3. Additionally, there was an expectation that the government would restart the reform process.
4. While the Budget sets a lower nominal gross domestic product (GDP) growth target of 14%, we believe that the real GDP growth target of 9% factored in the Budget is on the optimistic side.
5. The Budget has made an attempt to address all these issues, albeit through small steps.

A. 2 3 5 1 4 B. 3 2 1 5 4
C. 4 1 3 5 2 D. 1 4 3 5 2
E. 5 1 2 3 4

85. 1. These were mainly bulwarks against winter, the hoarded dregs of more plentiful seasons.
2. The first were the earliest mince pies, which saw cooked, shredded meat, dried fruits, alcohol w[illegible] its preservative qualities and perhaps a few spi[illegible] or herbs, all encased in large pies.
3. Subsequently, people baked this into a kind of pie, adding bread-cumbers for bulk, eggs to bind it, and upping the dried fruits and called it 'plum pudding'.
4. The pudding seems to have had two principal forerunners.
5. The second main pudding was a pottage or soup called frumenty, a fast dish involving cracked wheat, currants and almonds which was ladled out at the start of a meal.

A. 5 3 4 1 2 B. 2 1 5 3 4
C. 4 1 3 5 2 D. 4 2 1 5 3
E. 5 1 2 3 4

86. 1. In a bid to placate the associate members, the ICC has decided to increase the number of participating teams to 16 in the Twenty20 World Cup, as the game's governing body feels these countries will have a greater chance of competin[illegible] on an equal footing in cricket's shortest form[illegible].
2. It is convenient just now to forget that in the last edition of the tournament, considerable criticism was heaped on the governing body for the inordinate length of the tournament, thanks in large part to the presence of the associates.
3. To be fair to the ICC, criticism of the move to restrict the number of teams in the next edition of the Cup is a case of damned if you do, damned if you don't.
4. The ICC's decision to restrict the number of teams in the 2015 World Cup has evoked mixed responses, with opinion divided among players of the full member teams.
5. Not surprisingly, the associate members aren't too thrilled about the idea of being kept out of cricket's showpiece event.

A. 5 3 4 1 2 B. 2 1 5 3 4
C. 4 1 3 5 2 D. 4 5 1 3 2
E. 1 2 3 4 5

SET-19

87. 1. The upsurge of public activism against the setting up of Special Economic Zones, which eventually forced the State government to announce the scrapping of all 15 such projects, is an impressive case in point.
2. Early last year, a similar agitation coerced the government into calling for a revision of the Goa Regional Plan 2011, a controversial document that opened up large swathes of land, including green belts and coastal stretches, for construction.

3. The broad-based agitation against SEZs has demonstrated the power of popular protest in the State.
4. Those opposed to the projects had questioned the propriety of the government acquiring large tracts of land and then selling them to promoters at low prices.
5. A coastal State with an area of 3,700 squre kilometers and a population of about 1.4 million, Goa has been extremely sensitive to the impact of unrestrained economic development.

A. 2 3 4 5 1 B. 3 4 5 1 2
C. 5 1 2 3 4 D. 4 1 2 3 5
E. 1 2 3 4 5

88. 1. The post-election crisis in Kenya remains unresolved.
2. The damage being done to the country's economy is severe: tourism, horticulture, and other industries that depend on trade beyond the Kenyan border are reeling.
3. Many countries responded, providing essential humanitarian assistance and logistical support. For this, I and many other Kenyans are very grateful.
4. Thousands of livelihoods, along with investments throughout the region, are threatened and collapsing.
5. As the situation in Kenya escalated with murders, rapes, burning of property, looting, and the displacement of thousands of people throughout the country—the international community was urged to help.

A. 1 5 4 2 3 B. 1 2 3 5 4
C. 1 3 4 5 2 D. 1 2 4 5 3
E. 1 4 5 3 2

89. 1. The US market will continue to be the dominant one in the foreseeable future. The rupee could become even stronger.
2. A greater recourse to hedging as well as striving for multi-currency revenue streams automatically suggests itself.
3. Already one company, TCS, by resorting to these methods extensively has turned in an above average performance during the first quarter.
4. Most IT companies have been grappling with more mundane problems such as a high level of attrition amidst rising wage costs and inability to secure the right type and number of American visas.
5. The BPO industry and many medium-sized software exporters are reportedly operating on thin margins.

A. 2 3 1 4 5 B. 1 2 3 4 5
C. 4 3 2 1 5 D. 5 4 1 2 3
E. 3 1 2 4 5

90. 1. Last March, I was invited to present a paper on the topic of whether the mistakes of the 20th century would be repeated in the 21st century as well.
2. The economic crisis hadn't become grave then.
3. But today the world is in the midst of the biggest economic crisis since 1929.
4. The key difference between then and now is that the old power structures have finally disappeared.
5. Now even the US is pleading for financial help from China.

A. 2 3 1 4 5 B. 1 2 3 4 5
C. 3 4 5 1 2 D. 4 5 1 2 3
E. 5 1 2 3 4

SET-20

91. 1. Downshifting doesn't necessarily mean changing your job, but taking steps to stop your work taking over your life and it can involve flexible working.
2. This trend from the US, where it is practised by ten per cent of the working population, has arrived in India.
3. If you feel bored, frustrated and trapped in your job, you are a likely candidate for not just a job change but a downshift.
4. All of these things can lead to a better quality of life.
5. A better word for downshifting would be 'reequilibrating,' suggests Judy Jones, co-author of 'Getting a Life, the Down Shifter's Guide to a Happier, Simpler Living'.

A. 5 1 3 2 4 B. 1 5 4 2 3
C. 3 2 5 1 4 D. 1 5 2 3 4
E. 1 2 3 4 5

92. 1. To avoid either of these outcomes, they will need to accumulate enough savings during their years in the workforce to support themselves with dignity for nearly twenty years after they are too old to work.
2. Most of India's 144 million informal sector workers who earn ₹ 3,000/- or less per month will become destitute as soon as they stop working.
3. But their fragile labour market attachments and modest intermittent incomes, coupled with the absence of a low cost secure long term savings mechanism has effectively put retirement planning out of reach of India's working poor.
4. Income security in old age is rapidly emerging as one of the most important causes of poverty in India.
5. Or will be forced to work till they die.

A. 1 2 4 5 3 B. 2 1 4 3 5
C. 4 2 5 1 3 D. 4 2 1 5 3
E. 2 1 3 4 5

93. 1. What was once marginal has now become central —the only possible strategy now is alliance, agreement, coalition and accommodation.
2. The shift to bottom-up political power has meant that India's reform agenda has become far more tentative, as policies can be derailed or slowed down by political parties with even small national clout.
3. Untrammeled acceptance of ineffective policies and bad ideas is no longer possible.
4. And, on the flip side coalition politics has worked its magic, and India's potential bureaucrat-visionaries now have too many feet in the aisle ready to trip them over.
5. Since then, however, India's democracy has changed and deepened.

A. 5 3 4 2 1 B. 1 3 2 5 4
C. 2 5 1 3 4 D. 4 5 3 1 2
E. 3 2 4 5 1

94. 1. The growth and activity of these NGOs is a sign of the changing nature of India's democracy.
2. These organizations are emphasizing an approach towards political democracy that is rooted in the idea of 'civil society' rather than in the divisions that now dominate India's politics.
3. This ever-widening group of middle-class Indians is using NGOs to come face-to-face with India's poorer and working classes, and to plant the idea of secular rights and liberties across these communities.
4. And while it is still early days here, this trend carries a great deal of promise, especially when we consider that the growth of such NGOs has been enabled by a middle class with an active interest in political reforms.
5. This bottom-up civil consciousness, non-political and non-partisan as it is, is a sign of a new kind of democracy in India

A. 2 4 5 1 3 B. 1 5 2 4 3
C. 3 4 1 2 5 D. 5 2 1 4 3
E. 1 2 3 4 5

95. 1. The people in the city were living in an environment where the front end of private goods had largely fallen into place, while the support infrastructure at the back end—transport, water, power—was in shambles, full of ominous creaks and missing pieces.
2. The consuming class noticed that they could buy a house, but they didn't have sewage or water connections, or garbage disposal systems.
3. In the cities, the rise of the middle class (who for the first time in India were educated as well as increasingly wealthy, engaged consumers) helped sharpen the focus on India's hopelessly dilapidated urban infrastructure.
4. But it is only since the late 1990s that the popular demand for better infrastructure became more strident.
5. If they bought a car, they had to drive it on terrible roads, and if they choose to walk, they found they could easily fall into an open storm drain or a random hole in the sidewalk that had been gouged open to lay pipes and then forgotten.

A. 4 3 2 5 1 B. 2 1 4 3 5
C. 5 4 2 1 3 D. 2 4 5 3 1
E. 3 4 2 5 1

SET-21

96. 1. After all, a story told on the large screen inevitably differs from that told on the small screen.
2. This critical difference has an impact on viewership in terms of age, income and occupation.
3. In this, the age of multimedia, we have to train ourselves to understand that as a rule, the medium is the message.
4. It also has an impact on the expectations brought by the public to bear on large and small screen performances, and on the performers.
5. Never has the myth of 'one size fits all', been shown up so effectively, therefore, as in the field of Media Studies.

A. 1 2 4 3 5 B. 3 1 2 5 4
C. 3 1 2 4 5 D. 3 4 1 2 5
E. 5 1 2 3 4

97. 1. Indeed, the reading-public of today seems to be more tolerant of this crossover than their predecessors might have been.
2. Both writers and readers seem to enjoy criss-crossing the line between documentation and fiction.
3. Beginning with Midnight's Children, there has been a steady breakdown of the disciplinary wall between literature and history.
4. Editorial cartoons, once barely recognised as a source of humour for the masses, are now studied as important sources of historical documentation and literary value.
5. This has led to a revision in the view of what constitutes historical and literary debate, and of what constitutes the sources of this debate.

A. 4 5 3 1 2 B. 3 2 1 5 4
C. 3 1 2 5 4 D. 1 2 3 5 4
E. 4 5 3 2 1

98. 1. Sub-Saharan Africa is often cited as a territory in which starvation could be significantly reduced, were GM foods brought into worldwide circulation.
2. Farmers cite the steady impoverishment of the soil, and the deterioration in the quality of seeds, as excellent reasons for protesting GM foods.
3. As with many cutting-edge discoveries, however, its long-term consequences can be difficult to handle.
4. Genetically modified, or GM foods, are marketed enthusiastically by some sections of the developed world that claim they can cure the ills of the developing world.
5. A lack of transparency concerning ethical testing is another reason given by the developing world for receiving GM foods with caution rather than with celebration.

A. 4 1 3 2 5 B. 2 5 4 1 3
C. 3 1 4 5 2 D. 4 5 2 1 3
E. 1 2 3 4 5

99. 1. For example, cars in the developing world are often seen as status symbols to be acquired, while in the developed world they are seen as liabilities to be discarded.
2. The size of the carbon footprint of nations in the developing world has again come in for serious international discussion.
3. The failed mission of Copenhagen is the immediate cause of the resumption of this debate.
4. While the main triggers of the debate are economic, social and cultural factors also have a major role to play.
5. As with so many other issues, clearly, here too 'one man's meat is another man's poison.'

A. 4 5 3 1 2 B. 3 5 4 1 2
C. 2 3 4 1 5 D. 2 1 3 5 4
E. 2 3 4 5 1

100. 1. A person is neither the product of just her environment nor just her genetic make up.
2. Let me give an example.
3. A child is born with a talent for music, which then gets nurtured through continuous training in a conducive atmosphere.
4. The transactional model of child development helps to resolve the split between nature and nurture.
5. Rather it is the complex interaction between the two that is key.

A. 1 4 2 3 5 B. 4 1 5 2 3
C. 2 3 4 1 5 D. 1 4 5 2 3
E. 3 4 5 2 1

ANSWERS

1	2	3	4	5	6	7	8	9	10
D	B	E	A	D	C	E	A	D	B
11	**12**	**13**	**14**	**15**	**16**	**17**	**18**	**19**	**20**
B	A	C	C	C	E	E	A	E	D
21	**22**	**23**	**24**	**25**	**26**	**27**	**28**	**29**	**30**
B	C	C	B	A	B	C	E	A	E
31	**32**	**33**	**34**	**35**	**36**	**37**	**38**	**39**	**40**
C	A	E	E	C	B	D	A	C	D
41	**42**	**43**	**44**	**45**	**46**	**47**	**48**	**49**	**50**
B	A	E	A	B	E	A	C	D	E
51	**52**	**53**	**54**	**55**	**56**	**57**	**58**	**59**	**60**
C	B	A	C	B	D	A	E	A	C
61	**62**	**63**	**64**	**65**	**66**	**67**	**68**	**69**	**70**
D	B	E	B	D	D	E	C	B	C
71	**72**	**73**	**74**	**75**	**76**	**77**	**78**	**79**	**80**
E	B	D	E	B	D	B	C	C	C
81	**82**	**83**	**84**	**85**	**86**	**87**	**88**	**89**	**90**
D	A	A	A	D	D	C	D	A	B
91	**92**	**93**	**94**	**95**	**96**	**97**	**98**	**99**	**100**
C	C	A	B	A	D	C	A	D	A

□□□

4. Errors in Sentences

Directions (Qs. 1–107): *Read each sentence to find out whether there is any grammatical mistake/error in it. The error if any, will be in one part of the sentence. Mark the number of the part with error as your answer. If there is 'No error' mark E. (Ignore the error of punctuation if any)*

1. We are yet starting (A)/ offering this facility to (B)/ our customers as we are (C)/ awaiting approval from the Board. (D)/ No error (E)
2. The Chairmen of all large (A)/ public sector banks met with (B)/ senior RBI officials to give its (C)/ suggestions about implementing the new policy. (D)/ No error (E)
3. They have not fully considered (A)/ the impact that relaxing (B)/ these guidelines is likely (C)/ to have with the economy, (D)/ No error (E)
4. Had this notification (A)/ been amended earlier; (B)/ we could have stopped (C)/ the transfer of funds. (D)/ No error (E)
5. There are many insurance (A)/ disputes nowadays because of (B)/ most people do not fully (C)/ understood the terms and conditions of their policies. (D)/ No error (E).
6. While most major economies set aside (A)/about 3 per cent of their GD P(B)/in research and development, India(C)/spends less than 1 per cent on this.(D)/ No error(E)
7. Owing to the poor quality of(A)/the equipment producing by Chinese firms(B)/many foreign companies have placed(C)/orders with Indian firms(D)/ No error(E)
8. We expect a hike(A)/ in the cash reserve ratio(B)/ which is the portion of deposits(C)/that banks keep with RBI.(D)/No error(E)
9. Unless these differences(A)/ will be resolved soon(B)/ there will be an adverse(C)/effect on foreign investment (D)/ No error(E)
10. We are confident that the steps(A)/ we have taken to attract talented people(B)/ and build a solid organisation(C)/ will ensure we remain profitably.(D)/ No error(E)
11. At a time which most firms(A)/were finding it difficult (B)/ to raise money, we succeeded(C)/ in raising the necessary funds(D)/ No error(E)
12. Everyone is keen in knowing(A)/ the forecast for the monsoon(B)/ this year as it has been the(C)/ major cause of inflation in Asia.(D)/No error(E)
13. Building biogas plants will help to reduce(A)/ greenhouse gas emissions by reducing(B)/the consuming of conventional fuels(C)/ such as firewood and kerosene.(D)/No error(E)
14. Since some banks may take longer(A)/ to achieve these targets, RBI(B)/has considered to revise these guidelines(C)/on a case to case basis.(D)/No error(E)
15. After joining the Hong Kong based(A)/ bank in 1990, he has(B)/ head various departments(C)/ including corporate and investment banking.(D)/No error(E)
16. Some genuine issues exist(A)/with the newly adopted(B)/system and needs to(C)/be examined seriously.(D)/ No error(E)
17. Whether or not to confront(A)/them about their role(B)/ in the matter is a decision(C)/which is yet to take.(D)/ No error(E)
18. The government is still in the(A)/ process of finalized new policy(B)/ guidelines for the allocation of land(C)/to private sector organisations.(D)/ No error(E)
19. According to government estimates(A)/at least four millions tonnes of sugar(B)/will have to be imported (C)/ this year because of a poor monsoon.(D)/ No error(E)
20. In our experience people usually(A)/ value things that they have to(B)/payoff more than those that(C)/ they receive free of cost.(D)/ No error(E)
21. At present China is the(A)/ world's leader manufacture(B)/of environment-friendly products(C)/ such as electric cars and bicycles.(D)/ No error(E)

22. Over eighty per cent from us(A)/ feel that if we had taken(B)/Some corrective measures earlier(C)/ the crisis could have been averted.(D)/ No error(E)
23. The manager of that city branch(A)/ cannot handle it with the help of(B)/ only two personnel as(C)/ business has increased substantially.(D)/ No error(E)
24. With the literacy rates in this(A)/ region as low as ten per cent(B)/ we need to encourage(C)/ local people to build schools.(D)/No error(E)
25. While-providing such facilities(A)/ online makes it covenient(B)/ and easily accessible for customers,(C)/ we face several challenges.(D)/ No error(E)
26. He has taken care to (A)/compliance with the norms (B)/so he expects the proposal (C)/to be approved without delay. (D) No error (E)
27. Under the terms of the new deal (A)/the channel can broadcast (B)/the next cricket tournament to be (C)/ played among India and Australia. (D) No error (E)
28. Our equipment gets damage (A)/very often in summer (B)/because there are (C)/frequent power cuts. (D) No error (E)
29. We have received many (A)/of the letters from customers (B)/asking us to extend (C)/the deadline to repay their loans. (D) No error (E)
30. Since I had lived there (A)/for many years the villagers (B)/were very comfortable talked (C)/to me about their problems. (D) No error (E)
31. We have been under (A)/a lot of pressure to (B)/open fifty new stores (C)/by the ending of the year. (D) No error (E)
32. The government has (A)/launched many creative schemes (B)/to make banking services (C)/available to everyone. (D) No error (E)
33. The company is in debt (A)/and has been unable (B)/ to pay their employees' salaries (C)/for the past six months. (D) No error (E)
34. This is turned out to be (A)/one of our most successful projects (B)/and we have made quite (C)/a large profit from it. (D) No error (E)
35. A non banking financial company is a (A)/financial institution similarly to a bank (B)/but it cannot issue (C)/cheque books to customers. (D) No error (E)
36. We should all try (A)/to help the police (B)/in their efforts (C)/to combating crime. (D) No error (E)
37. My name is Rahul (A)/and I am coming (B)/from a beautiful state (C)/in India (D) No error (E)
38. We were help (A)/to carry (B)/the piano upstairs (C)/ by one of our neighbours. (D) No error (E)
39. If you want to (A)/keep good health (B)/you must eats (C)/a lot of vegetables. (D) No error (E)
40. Some people who (A)/live in the Netherlands (B)/ cycle to work (C)/and back daily (D) No error (E)
41. In recent months, (A)/a large number of equipments (B)/has been steal (C)/from construction sites (D) No error (E)
42. I paid a lot of money (A)/for the camera (B)/and I expects it (C)/to work. (D) No error (E)
43. I forget (A)/to pack a set of (B)/clean clothes (C)/for the picnic. (D) No error (E)
44. It is important (A)/to be looking (B)/both ways before (C)/crossing the road. (D) No error (E)
45. The Indian Government's (A)/primary goal (B)/is to reduction (C)/of poverty (D) No error (E)
46. It was clear from the way (A)/they were behaving (B)/ that they had been (C)/lost their senses. (D) No error (E)
47. A small piece (A)/of bread is (B)/better than (C)/ having nothing to eat. (D) No error (E)
48. When he had been (A)/walked along the road (B)/a wild and ferocious dog (C)/hit him hard and knocked him down. (D) No error (E)
49. That boy possess (A)/three beautiful pens (B)/but he would not (C)/show them to any one. (D) No error (E)
50. I am grateful to you (A)/and all your friends (B)/for showing sympathy (C)/and kindness with me. (D) No error (E)
51. Though I had been (A)/his friend for quite a long time, (B)/I refused to help him (C)/because his ill nature. (D) No error (E)
52. Families are (A)/fortunate enough to own (B)/a house in the city (C)/are very few. (D) No error (E)
53. Ramesh has been both (A)/a dishonesty person (B)/ and a gambler (C)/since his childhood. (D) No error (E)
54. Everyone of us know (A)/that he is not capable (B)/ remaining under water (C)/for such a long time. (D) No error (E)
55. He is the man (A)/who I know (B)/has helped my son (C)/in the final examination (D) No error (E)
56. The number of employees (A)/reporting sick (B)/has reduced significantly (C)/because of the incentive. (D) No error (E)
57. Your television set (A)/is superior to (B)/our television set (C)/by all respects. (D) No error (E)
58. I have been (A)/living in Hyderabad (B)/at my uncle (C)/since my birth. (D) No error (E)
59. The leader was so shrewd (A)/that he could not deceive (B)/by the words of (C)/the sycophant courtiers. (D) No error (E)

60. The boy who was guilt for (A)/having broken the window glass (B)/came out (C)/with the truth. (D) No error (E)

61. The President has denied/(A) that the economy is in recession/(B) or was go into one/(C) despite a spate of downcast reports/(D). No error (E).

62. The angry being/(A) left out of the bonanza/(B) is palpable among/(C) employees of the organization/ (D). No error (E).

63. His comments came after/(A) the research group said that its/(B) consumer confidence index were/(C) slumped to Its lowest level/ (D). No Error (E)

64. If an goes well,/(A) the examination scheduled for next month/(B) is all set to be completely free/(C) from annoying power cuts and disruptios/(D). No Error (E).

65. There are just too few trains/(A) for the ever-grow/(B) number of passengers/(C) in the city /(D). No Error(E).

66. The buzz at the party was/(A) that a famous/(B) filmstar and politician, would/(C) probable drop by for a while/(D). No Error (E).

67. The Opposition disrupted proceedings/(A) in both Houses of Parliament/(B) for the second consecutive day/(C) above the plight of farmers in the country/ (D). No Error (E).

68. In response to the growing crisis,/(A) the agency is urgently asking for/(B) more contributions, to make up for/(C) its sharp decline in purchasing power/(D). No Error (E).

69. The tennis player through/(A) the opening set before her opponent,/(B) rallied to take the final two sets/ (C) for the biggest victory of her young career/(D). No Error (E).

70. Aggression in some teenage boys/(A) may be linkage to overly/(B) large glands in their brains,/(C) a new study has found/(D). No Error (E).

71. (A) Know he was dying/(B) Morrie visited with Mitch/ (C)his study every Tuesday/(D) just as they used to back in college/(E) No error.

72. (A) One Sunday when his sons/(B) Rob and Jon was home/(C) they all gathered/(D) in the living room/ (E) No error.

73. (A) He grow up the way/(B) many youngest children grow up,/(C) pampered, adored/(D) and inwardly tortured/(E) No error.

74. (A) Proper care was taken/(B) for the maintenance of accounting records/(C) as per accordance with/(D) the provisions of applicable laws/(E) No error.

75. (A) He pulled his lips together/(B) close his eyes/(C) and I watched the first teardrop/(D) fall down the side of his cheek/(E) No error.

76. (A) The Audit Committee of the Board/(B) has been constituted/(C) by the Board of Directors/(D) as per instructions of the Reserve Bank of India/(E) No error.

77. (A) Nobody knew/(B) where I spend my day/(C) and nobody really/(D) seemed to care/(E) No error.

78. (A) My father has/(B) always had a curious habit/(C) which I could never understand,/(D) of consulting astrologers/(E) No error.

79. (A) I stopped at Aurangabad,/(B) from which I make excursions/(C) to the Ajanta Caves/(D) and the temple at Ellora/(E) No error.

80. (A) We are planning/(B) to set up a Training coilege/ (C) to train our marketing team/(D) for effective marketing of our products/(E) No error.

81. We build the roof (A)/ with a steep slope (B)/ so that the rain water could (C)/ slide off easily. (D)/ No error (E)

82. My brother had (A)/ just come from abroad. (B)/ He seems to have (C)/ enjoyed his trip very much. (D)/ No error (E)

83. If I had realized (A)/ what a bad teacher you are (B)/ I would not have come (C)/ to you for any guidance. (D)/ No error (E)

84. He put his hand (A)/ into his pocket and was (B)/ astonished when he found (C)/ that his wallet is not there. (D)/ No error (E)

85. I am sorry to disappoint you (A)/ but I cannot let you (B)/ have any more money (C)/ till the end of this month. (D)/ No error (E)

86. The judge asked the man (A)/ if the bag he had lost (B)/ contain five thousand rupees. (C)/ The man replied that it did. (D)/ No error. (E)

87. I thrust you will (A)/show forbearance to me (B)/ a few minutes more (C)/ so that I can finish this work (D)/ No error. (E)

88. The ground outside the village, (A)/ abounding with frogs and snakes, (B)/ the enemies of mankind, (C)/ is soft and marshy. (D)/ No error. (E)

89. We are all short sighted (A)/ and very often see but one side of the matter. (B)/ Our views are not extended (C)/ to all that has a connection with it. (D)/ No error. (E)

90. Just laws are no restraint with (A)/ the freedom of the good, (B)/ for the good man desires nothing (C)/ which a just law interfere with. (D)/ No error. (E)

91. Had he done (A)/ his home work well (B)/ he would not have (C)/ suffered this embarrassment. (D)/ No error. (E)

92. He was angry with me (A)/ because he thought my (B)/ remark was (C)/ aimed before him. (D)/ No error. (E)

93. My daughter never (A)/ would write to me (B)/ so I never know (C)/ what she is doing (D)/. No error (E).

94. Whenever we have a puncture (A)/ she just sits in the car (B)/ and reads a book (C)/ while I changed the wheel (D)/. No error (E).

95. He walked to the market (A)/ with both his servants (B)/ on either side of his (C)/ to help him buy things (D)/. No error (E).

96. Ganesh, who has been (A)/ driving all day (B)/ was extremely tired (C)/ and wanted to stop. (D)/. No error (E).

97. Everyone was reading quietly (A)/ when suddenly the door (B)/ burst open and a (C)/ complete stranger rushed in. (D)/. No error (E).

98. A disabled child (A)/ has defined as (B)/ one who is unable to (C)/ ensure necessities by himself. (D)/ No error (E)

99. Many decision problems (A)/ involve a number of (B)/ objectives, and often (C)/ these objectives conflicts. (D)/ No error (E)

100. Various employees, whom (A)/ we met, echoed (B)/ the sentiments expressed (C)/ by the CEO of the company. (D)/ No error (E)

101. It is difficult to assume that (A)/ a increase in the number of health institutions (B)/ would automatically enhance (C)/ utilisation of health services (D)/ No error (E)

102. The challenge for us (A)/ is to engage with a potential (B)/ customer early so we can (C)/ sell him the entire range.(D)/ No error (E)

103. Having said that (A)/ let me further clarify (B)/ that this model may (C)/ not always work. (D)/ No error (E)

104. This situation probably (A)/ contributing to a (B)/ greater lack of protection (C)/ for children in the households. (D)/ No error (E)

105. The management of the organisation (A)/ must be willing to pass up (B)/ short-term gains for (C)/ long-term strategic benefit. (D)/ No error (E)

106. The amount at the minimum (A)/ payment is determined (B)/ by management and varies (C)/ from firm to firm. (D)/ No error (E)

107. Went are the days when (A)/ the leader barked instructions (B)/ and his minions scurried (C)/ to carry them out. (D)/ No error (E)

Directions (Qs. 108–132): *In each question below a sentence with four words printed in* **bold** *type is given. These are numbered as (A), (B), (C) and (D). One of these four boldly printed words, may be either wrongly spelt or inappropriate in the context of the sentence. Find out the word which is wrongly spelt or inappropriate, if any. The number of that word is your answer. If all the boldly printed words are correctly spelt and also appropriate in the context of the sentence, mark (E) i.e. 'All Correct' as your answer.*

108. This firm which is **based** (A)/ in France is **prepaired** (B)/ to **finance** small Indian **businesses** (C)/ which produce environment friendly **products**. (D)/ All correct (E).

109. Despite **intense** (A)/ **pressure** (B)/ from his superiors he refused to **discloze** (C)/ the **findings** of the report. (D)/ All correct (E).

110. Corporates have benefited **tremendously** (A)/from the government's **timely** (B)/ decision to **waive** (C)/ various **tax.** (D)/ All correct (E).

111. Since you are **unable** (A)/ to repay the loan you have no **alternate** (B)/ but to **seek** (C)/ an **extension**. (D)/ All correct (E).

112. A **major** (A)/ **disadvantage** (B)/ of this deal is that we shall have to **bear** (C)/ the **cost** of **training**/(D). All correct (E).

113. The **principal** (A)/ was asked to **indicate** (B)/ the names of **students** (C)/ who were standing for **election**. (D)/ All correct (E).

114. For years, the only **evidence** (A)/ Morrie had of his **mother** (B)/ was the **telegram** (C)/ **declaring** her death. (D)/ All correct (E).

115. He studied at **night**, (A)/ by the lamp at the kitchen table and in the **morning** (B)/ he would go to **synagogue** (C)/ to say the memorial **lecture** for the dead. (D)/ All correct (E).

116. She was short **immigrant** (A)/ with **plane** (B)/ features, curly brown **hair** (C)/ and the **energy** of two women. (D)/ All correct (E).

117. The **Fresh** (A)/ air **might** (B)/ be good for the **childrens,** (C)/ the relatives **thought**. (D)/ All correct (E).

118. Enforcement of laws, clean and **efficient** (A)/ administration was what British rulers **dispensed** (B)/ in India through the Government **machinery** (C)/ known as **bureaucreacy** (D)/ All correct (E)

119. **Copyright** (A)/ will **subsist** (B)/ in any work published within the lifetime of the author **until** (C)/ 50 years **following** (D)/ his deatlh. All correct (E)

120. Computer **surveying** (A)/ is **surfacing** (B)/ at trade shows, where participants **completing** (C)/ surveys while **making** (D)/ a visit to a company's booth. All correct (E)

121. The **pricing** (A)/ of intellectual property is more **complicated** (B)/ than most pricing because today it is **relatingly** (C)/ **inexpensive** (D)/ to make copies of most intellectual property. All correct (E)

122. **Experience** (A)/ of **extensive** (B)/ travel in parts of the **globe** (C)/ further **explored** (D)/ her vision. All correct (E)

123. The **document** (A)/ he gave me was long and **complicated** (B)/ and I **struggled** (C)/ to **understand** (D)/ it. All correct (E)

124. We shall have to **await** (A)/ and see if these **measures** (B)/ are **sufficient** (C)/ to **address** (D)/ the problem. All correct (E)

125. They are **negotiating** (A)/ to try and **reach** (B)/ an agreement which **will beneficial** (C)/ everyone **concerned**. (D)/ All correct (E)

126. The company has **decided** (A)/ to **allott** (B)/ a **substantial** (C)/ **portion** (D)/ of its profits to research and development. All correct (E)

127. It **remains** (A)/ to be seen **whether** (B)/ these **reforms** (C)/ will be **acceptable** (D)/ by the Board. All correct (E)

128. The Economic **imperatives** (A)/ for **acquiring** (B)/ technological strengths do not **warrant** (C)/ **repeatition** (D)/ here. All correct (E)

129. The combination of a base of imported technology and **Capabilities** (A)/ built up **indigenous** (B)/ led **initially** (C)/ to product and process **involvement** (D)/. All correct (E)

130. If a country does not learn to **master** (A)/ these new realities of life, our **aspirations** (B)/ to ensure the **prosperity** (C)/ of our people may come to **not** (D)/. All correct (E)

131. Since vegetable and fruit **consumption** (A)/ will increase in future, an **appropriate** (B)/ choice considering **agro-climate** (C)/ input needs and economic **returns** (D)/ should be arrived at for every region. All correct (E)

132. An **environmental** (A)/ **concern** (B)/ that is likely to have **implications** (C)/ for Indian agriculture is the **emission** (D)/ of gases like methane and carbon dioxide. All correct (E)

Directions (Qs. 133–150): *A sentence has been broken into four parts. Choose the part that has an error. If there is no error, the answer is E. (Ignore the error of Punctuation, if any)*

133. A. The sound was taken up by another dog, and then another and another,
B. till, borne on the wind which now sighed softly through the Pass,
C. a wild howling began, which seemed to come from all over the country,
D. as far as the imagination could grasp them through the gloom of the night.
E. No Error

134. A. At last there came a time when the driver went
B. further afield than he had yet gone,
C. and during its absence, the horses began to tremble
D. worse than ever and to snort and scream with fright.
E. No Error

135. A. The house was silent when we got back,
B. save for some poor creature who was
C. screaming away in one of the distant wards,
D. and a low, moaning sound from Vinod's room.
E. No Error

136. A. a temple was erected to him
B. at the foot of the Capitoline Hill,
C. at which were deposited the
D. public treasury and the laws of the state.
E. No Error

137. A. I soon lost sight and recollection of ghostly fears
B. in the beauty of the scene as we drove along,
C. although had I known the language, or rather languages, which my fellow passenger were speaking,
D. I might not have been able to throw them off so easily.
E. No Error

138. A. The Romans, according to their custom of identifying their deities
B. with those of the Greek gods whose attributes
C. were similar to their own, declared Cronus to be identical
D. from their old agricultural divinity Saturn.
E. No Error

139. A. As she said this she looked down at her hands,
B. and was surprising to see that
C. she had put on one of the Rabbit's little white
D. kid gloves while she was talking.
E. No Error

140. A. The power of displaying the grandeur of his patroness
B. to his wondering visitors, and of letting it see her civility towards himself and his wife,
C. was exactly what he had wished for; and that an opportunity of doing it should be given so soon,
D. was such an instance of Lady Catherine's condescension, as he knew not how to admire enough.
E. No Error

141. A. While they were dressing,
B. he came two or three times to their different doors,
C. to recommend their being quick,
D. as the manager was very much objecting to be kept waiting for his dinner.
E. No Error

142. A. The hardy colonist and the trained European who fought at his side,
B. frequently expended months in struggling against the rapid of the streams,
C. or in effecting the rugged passes of the mountains,
D. in quest of an opportunity to exhibit their courage in a more martial conflict.
E. No Error

143. A. She smiled, as if in pity at her own momentary forgetfulness,
B. discovering by the act a row of teeth that would have shamed the purest ivory,
C. when, replacing the veil, she bowed her face, and rode in silence,
D. like one whose thoughts were abstract from the scene around her.
E. No Error

144. A. It is impossible to say what unlooked-for remark,
B. this short and silent communication, between two such singular men,
C. might have elict from the white man,
D. had not his active curiosity been again drawn to other objects.
E. No Error

145. A. Artificial intelligence
B. is devoid of
C. intelligence although it is
D. devoid of artifice
E. No Error

146. A. If all cells are conceived primarily as a receptacles
B. of the same genetic formula – not only all
C. the individuals, but all the cells of
D. the same individuals – what are they but the cancerous extension of this base formula?
E. No Error

147. A. In the past, behind the immediate popularity
B. of the phonograph is the entire electric
C. implosion that gave such new stress and
D. importance to actual speech rhythms in music, poetry, and dance alike
E. No Error

148. A. These developments, of course, produced
B. a renewed waves of criticism of
C. advertising, and, in particular,
D. ridicule of its confident absurdities
E. No Error

149. A. Science really begins when general principles
B. have to be put to the test of fact,
C. and when practical problems and theoretical relations
D. of relevant factors is used to manipulate reality in human action
E. No Error

150. A. Men differ in their capacities
B. for excellence, yet democracy
C. insists that everyone
D. have an equal right to judge.
E. No Error

ANSWERS

1	2	3	4	5	6	7	8	9	10
A	C	D	E	B	C	B	E	B	D
11	**12**	**13**	**14**	**15**	**16**	**17**	**18**	**19**	**20**
A	A	C	C	C	C	D	B	B	C
21	**22**	**23**	**24**	**25**	**26**	**27**	**28**	**29**	**30**
B	A	C	E	E	B	D	A	B	C
31	**32**	**33**	**34**	**35**	**36**	**37**	**38**	**39**	**40**
D	E	C	A	B	D	B	A	C	D
41	**42**	**43**	**44**	**45**	**46**	**47**	**48**	**49**	**50**
C	C	A	B	C	C	E	A	C	D
51	**52**	**53**	**54**	**55**	**56**	**57**	**58**	**59**	**60**
D	E	B	A	B	E	D	C	B	A
61	**62**	**63**	**64**	**65**	**66**	**67**	**68**	**69**	**70**
C	A	C	E	B	C	D	A	B	B
71	**72**	**73**	**74**	**75**	**76**	**77**	**78**	**79**	**80**
A	B	B	C	B	E	B	B	B	E
81	**82**	**83**	**84**	**85**	**86**	**87**	**88**	**89**	**90**
A	A	B	D	C	C	C	E	D	D

91	92	93	94	95	96	97	98	99	100
D	D	B	D	C	A	B	D	D	A
101	102	103	104	105	106	107	108	109	110
B	C	C	B	B	C	A	B	C	D
111	112	113	114	115	116	117	118	119	120
B	E	A	E	D	B	C	D	B	C
121	122	123	124	125	126	127	128	129	130
C	D	E	A	C	B	D	C	D	D
131	132	133	134	135	136	137	138	139	140
E	C	D	C	C	C	C	D	B	B
141	142	143	144	145	146	147	148	149	150
D	B	D	C	C	A	B	B	D	D

□□□

5. Sentence Correction

Directions (Qs. 1–40): *Which of the phrases A, B, C and D given below each sentence should replace the phrase printed in* **bold** *in the sentence to make it grammatically correct? If the sentence is Correct as it is given and no correction is required, mark E as the answer.*

1. Although scared of heights, she **gather all her courage** and stood atop the 24-storey building to participate in the activities.
   A. gathered all her courage
   B. gathered all courageous
   C. gather all courageous
   D. is gathered all courage
   E. No correction required

2. Naturally, with everything **gone so well** for them, it was time for celebration.
   A. go so well
   B. going so well
   C. gone as well
   D. going as well
   E. No correction required

3. The ban was imposed by the state's commercial taxes department last Friday after protests by a certain community, which **had threat to burn** cinema halls screening the controversial movie.
   A. had threats of burning
   B. had throated to burn
   C. had threatened to bum
   D. had threatened to burning
   E. No correction required

4. Rakesh, an avid football player who captained his team in school and college, **will inaugurate** the match tomorrow in Pune.
   A. will be inaugurate
   B. is inauguration
   C. will inaugurating
   D. is inaugurate
   E. No correction required

5. At a musical night organised for them, the artistic side of the doctors **came as forward**, as they, sang beautifully and made the evening truly memorable.
   A. come forward
   B. come to the fore
   C. came to the forth
   D. came to the fore
   E. No correction required

6. Radha's three children, Shantana, Manu and Meera are talented, but **the latter excels** the other two.
   A. the last excels
   B. latter excel
   C. the latter excelling
   D. the last excelling
   E. No correction required

7. **Being a successful businessman demands** hard work, honesty, persuasive skills and sound market knowledge.
   A. To be a successful businessman who demands
   B. Being a successfully demanding businessman
   C. To be a successful businessman demanding
   D. For being a successful demanding businessman
   E. No correction required

8. The officer appreciated his subordinate's **many attempt to bravely confront** the miscreants.
   A. many attempting brave confronts
   B. many brave attempts to confront
   C. repeated attempts to brave confront
   D. many attempts of brave confront
   E. No correction required

9. **Was it they who were** accused of stealing the neighbour's car?
   A. Were it they who were
   B. Was it they who had
   C. Were they who
   D. Were it they who
   E. No correction required

10. We must treat any statement as a rumour **until they are confirmed** with proof.

A. till they are confirmed
B. until they are confirming
C. until it is confirmed
D. until it is confirming
E. No correction required

11. He is the only one of the **members who have paid** all the dues.
A. member who has paid
B. members who have been paying
C. member who has been paid
D. members who has paid
E. No correction required

12. The doctor has advised him **to lay in bed** at least for two weeks.
A. that he lay in bed
B. that he lays in bed
C. to lie in bed
D. to be laid in bed
E. No correction required

13. Neither any of the members of the society nor the Chairman **were present for** the annual meeting.
A. were present at
B. was present for
C. have been present
D. has been present for
E. No correction required

14. We admire **him attempting to climb** the summit in such a bad weather.
A. his attempting to climb
B. his attempt of climb
C. him for attempt of climb
D. his for attempt to climbing
E. No correction required

15. Students are not abandoning helmets, but **some avoiding use** of helmets while riding motorbikes.
A. some avoid the used
B. some avoid of the use
C. some are avoiding of use
D. some are avoiding use
E. No correction required

16. He is a healthy man, he always **uses to go** for a morning walk.
A. goes
B. has gone
C. is going
D. using to go
E. No correction required

17. I was very tired when I met you because I **was moving** in my lawn for two hours.
A. had moved
B. had been moved
C. had been moving
D. was being moved
E. No correction required

18. We left the place only after we **were promised that** we would be brought to that place again.
A. promised that
B. had promised that
C. were promised to
D. was promised that
E. No correction required

19. Yesterday I could not resist my temptation and out of curiosity. I **peep into the room.**
A. peep at the room
B. peeped at the room
C. have peeped into the room
D. peeped into the room
E. No correction required

20. I met the boy who was my friend's brother **and whom name was** Shyam.
A. and whom name is
B. and who name was
C. and whose name was
D. and whose name is
E. No correction required

21. Indian manufacturing industries after a long period of protection **is now at loggerheads** with the forces of globalisation.
A. is now at loggerhead
B. are now in loggerheads
C. are now at loggerheads
D. are now in loggerhead
E. No correction required

22. A decision to this effect **has approved** by the appointment committee of the cabinet.
A. have approved
B. has been approved
C. have been approved
D. has been approving
E. No correction required

23. The statement of the other accused recorded by the agency **has no evidenciary value.**
A. has no evidence
B. have no evidences
C. has been of no evidence
D. have been of no evidence
E. No correction required

24. An earthquake of mild intensity **has been felt yesterday** at the wee hours in the capital.
A. was being felt yesterday
B. was felt yesterday
C. has felt that day
D. had felt yesterday
E. No correction required

25. The constraints of the infrastructure rob the country **for sufficient** conditions of high growth.
A. to sufficient
B. for efficient
C. of sufficient
D. of efficient
E. No correction required

26. A nation that **had been once tried to** kill him was the first to embrace him.
A. had once been trying to
B. had once tried to
C. once had been tried to
D. had to once try and
E. No correction required

27. Had he known more about the policies of the company, he might not have accepted the offer.
A. He had known more
B. Did he know more
C. Since not more was known
D. If he would know more
E. No correction required

28. His life is an example of **how the human will can** flourish even in harsh conditions.
A. what the human will can
B. how the human can and will
C. when the human will can
D. where the human will can
E. No correction required

29. The social worker passionately stroked the annoyed passenger in order **that be pacified.**
A. to pacify him
B. that to pacify
C. to be pacified for
D. that to be pacified with
E. No correction required

30. They were no longer able to provide the **help their children need.**
A. helped their children need
B. help their children needed
C. help that their children need
D. help that their children would need
E. No correction required

31. You may be well organized in your thoughts but **what would you propose** may not be necessarily acceptable on all occasions.
A. what you would propose
B. that you would propose
C. what you propose
D. what you would have proposed
E. No correction required

32. The striking difference between the two contestants **compatible with each other** for the match was related to their age.
A. compatible with one another
B. compatible against one another
C. competing with the other
D. competing with each other
E. No correction required

33. Market research and market communication **is so far being confined to** a handful of consumer goods like soaps, cosmetics, etc.
A. is thus far being confined to
B. have so far been confined to
C. are so far being confined to
D. have so far been confined with
E. No correction required

34. If we rely on others for technology upgradation, **potential serious damage may** be caused.
A. potentially serious damage may
B. serious potentially damage may
C. seriously potential damage may
D. seriously potential damage might
E. No correction required

35. The load-shedding, however justifiable it may be, **has been aggravating** the problems.
A. has been aggravated
B. have aggravated
C. have been aggravating
D. would have been aggravated
E. No correction required

36. Good moral character **is the must be** in every walk of life.
A. is to be the most
B. is become the must
C. is a must
D. is a must be
E. No correction required

37. Our deepest fear is that we **have powerful** beyond measure.
A. were powerful at
B. are powerful about
C. have been powerful beyond
D. are powerful beyond
E. No correction required

38. He is too adamant to **be effectively** in his work
A. to become effectively
B. to be effective
C. to have been effectively
D. for being effectively
E. No correction required

39. Because the competition is **going to become fierce**, we may have some real struggles on the horizon.

A. is becoming fiercely
B. is going to be fiercely
C. has become fiercely
D. was going to become fierce
E. No correction required

40. They lost the match because they **neglected by** the coach's valuable advice.
A. ignored
B. were ignored by
C. were neglected by
D. No correction required

41. He **hesitated to listen to** what his brother was saying.
A. listened to hesitate
B. hesitated listen to
C. hesitates to listening
D. is hesitated to listen to
E. No correction required

42. Hardly **does the sun rise** when the stars disappeared.
A. have the sun rose B. had the sun risen
C. did the sun rose D. the sun rose
E. No correction required

43. The police has **so far succeeded in recovering** only a part of the stolen property.
A. thus far succeeded for recovery
B. so far succeed in the recovery of
C. as far as succeeded in recovery of
D. so far succeed to recover
E. No correction required

44. **What happens to** all those travellers on the ship was not known?
A. What happened of
B. That is what happens to
C. What is that happens to
D. What happened to
E. No correction required

45. Because of his ill health, the doctor has advised him **not to refrain** from smoking.
A. to not refrain from
B. to resort to
C. to refrain from
D. to be refrained from
E. No correction required

46. The courts **are actively to safeguard** the interests and the rights of the poor.
A. are actively to safeguarding
B. have been actively safeguarding
C. have to active in safeguarding
D. are actively in safeguarding
E. No correction required

47. He is a singer of repute, but his **yesterday's performance was** quite disappointing.
A. performances for yesterday were
B. yesterday performance was
C. yesterday performances were
D. performances about yesterday were
E. No correction required

48. **Despite of their** differences on matters of principles, they all agree on the demand of hike in salary?
A. Despite their
B. Despite of the
C. Despite for their
D. Despite off their
E. No correction required

49. The orator **had been left** the auditorium before the audience stood up.
A. had been leaving B. was left
C. left D. would leave
E. No correction required

50. This is one of the most important **inventions of this century**.
A. invention of this century
B. invention of these centuries
C. inventions of centuries
D. inventions of the centuries
E. No correction required

ANSWERS

1	2	3	4	5	6	7	8	9	10
A	B	C	E	D	A	E	B	E	C
11	**12**	**13**	**14**	**15**	**16**	**17**	**18**	**19**	**20**
D	C	B	A	D	A	C	E	D	C
21	**22**	**23**	**24**	**25**	**26**	**27**	**28**	**29**	**30**
C	B	E	B	C	B	D	D	A	B
31	**32**	**33**	**34**	**35**	**36**	**37**	**38**	**39**	**40**
A	D	B	E	E	C	D	B	E	A
41	**42**	**43**	**44**	**45**	**46**	**47**	**48**	**49**	**50**
E	B	E	D	C	B	E	A	C	E

❑❑❑

6. Synonyms

Directions (Qs. 1–82) : *Each of these following items consists of a word in capital letters, followed by five words or groups of words. Select the word or group of words that is **most similar** in meaning to the word in capital letters.*

1. PESSIMISTIC
A. Indifferent B. Ascetic
C. Unsettle D. Not hopeful
E. Sad

2. ANALOGOUS
A. Unsuitable B. Uncritical
C. Similar D. Disproportionate
E. Unfit

3. EXAGGERATE
A. Bluff B. Overstate
C. Explain D. Underestimate
E. Boast

4. EVIDENT
A. Prominent B. Seen
C. Observed D. Quite clear
E. Proved

5. PENALIZE
A. Persecute B. Punish
C. Torture D. Ruin
E. Fleece

6. REMEDIAL
A. Punitive B. Stringent
C. Corrective D. Strict
E. Educative

7. TRIVIAL
A. Unimportant B. Transparent
C. Important D. Unexpected
E. Small

8. INCREDIBLE
A. Hard to believe B. Considerable
C. Inconsistent D. Unsatisfactory
E. Indebted

9. ABSURD :
A. Senseless B. Clean
C. Abrupt D. Candid
E. Stupid

10. PHILANTHROPY :
A. Generosity B. Perversity
C. Perjury D. Flaunting
E. Prosperity

11. INSCRUTABLE :
A. Strange B. Mysterious
C. Marvellous D. Sublime
E. Hidden

12. EXACTLY ALIKE :
A. United B. Identical
C. Comparable D. Regular
E. Example

13. MUTUAL :
A. Reciprocal B. Agreed
C. Common D. Conjugal
E. Shared

14. IMBECILE :
A. Astute B. Cunning
C. Stupid D. Ludicrous
E. Clever

15. WEIRD :
A. Beastly B. Unpleasant
C. Frightening D. Unnatural
E. Ugly

16. AVARICIOUS :
A. Greedy B. Jealous
C. Angry D. Wicke
E. Kind

17. RAPACITY
A. Anger B. Cruelty
C. Pride D. Greed
E. Kindness

18. BEWITCHING
A. Enchanting B. Magical
C. Affected D. Ensnaring
E. Befooling

19. DISDAIN
A. Disown B. Condemn
C. Hate D. Criticise
E. Discard

20. DAZED
A. Shocked B. Dreamy
C. Happy D. Tired
E. Sad

21. COUNTERFEIT
A. Imitated B. Duplicate
C. Fake D. Foreign
E. Counted

22. SCARCELY
A. Hardly B. Always
C. Sometimes D. Frequently
E. Barely

23. GAIETY
A. Dexterity B. Wonder
C. Colourfulness D. Jollity
E. Gayness

24. HOSPITABLE
A. Convivial B. Liberal
C. Congenial D. Welcoming
E. Unhealthy

25. PERPLEX
A. Distract B. Intrigue
C. Perspective D. Baffle
E. Confusion

26. EXACTION
A. Accuracy
B. Left-over-portion
C. Act of demanding strictly
D. Ignorance
E. Imitation

27. STRAFE
A. To punish
B. To strengthen
C. To run away
D. To work very hard
E. To tie

28. CONTEMPORANEOUS
A. Irritating
B. Artificial
C. A very complicated problem
D. Happening at the same time
E. Insulting

29. HIATUS
A. Uphill task B. Distant place
C. Fading memory D. Gap
E. Very High

30. EXACERBATE
A. To make something more severe
B. To cause artificial shortage
C. To assume false importance
D. To flatter
E. To Overestimate

31. DELECTATION
A. Enjoyment B. Envy
C. Inspiration D. Astuteness
E. Rejection

32. FACTITIOUS
A. Humorous B. Truthful
C. Artificial D. Causing fatigue
E. Factual

33. MODICUM
A. Basic
B. Pertaining to earlier times
C. Small quantity
D. Annoying weather
E. Medium income

34. PROTAGONIST
A. Talented child
B. Reserved person
C. Leading character
D. Fearless
E. Dissident

35. PASSE
A. Lukewarm
B. Old-fashioned
C. Energy
D. Fraud
E. Successful

36. VITUPERATION
A. Questionable B. Resistance
C. Absurdity D. Bitter criticism
E. Wild Operation

37. VAUNT
A. Boast B. Desire
C. Ineptitude D. Joke
E. Locker

38. NIMBLE
A. Clamorous B. Scrap
C. Nippy D. Urbane
E. Strong

39. MOROSE
A. Humble B. Morsel
C. Sullen D. Repugnant
E. Stupid

40. BAMBOOZLE
A. Musical B. Mystify
C. Thrash D. Relinquish
E. Drink excessively

41. CANARD
A. Story B. Humid
C. Prison D. Rumour
E. Music

42. INNUENDO
A. Enquiry B. Indirect reference
C. Innovation D. Inorganic
E. Indecisive

43. ENSCONCE
A. To surround
B. To promote
C. To honour
D. To settle comfortably
E. To dishonour

44. INGRATIATE
A. To regret
B. To provoke
C. To place oneself in a favourable position
D. To feel delighted
E. To compensate

45. AUGURY
A. Dispute B. Altar
C. Place of refuge D. Omen
E. Prophecy

46. TRANSGRESS
A. To take loan
B. To go beyond the limit
C. To discuss at length
D. To show a clean pair of heels
E. To grasp

47. FERRET OUT
A. To search B. To trap
C. To hide D. To flee
E. To fly

48. USURP
A. To be lazy
B. To climb
C. To seize power or position illegally
D. To yield
E. To waste

49. MERCURIAL
A. Mechanical B. Heavy
C. Clownish D. Quick-changing
E. Liquid

50. ALLEVIATE
A. To release B. To lessen
C. To deprive D. To deceive
E. To rise

51. TEPID
A. Irreversible B. Causing fatigue
C. Fast moving D. Lukewarm
E. Coward

52. TENUOUS
A. Contentious B. Dark
C. Slender D. Malfunctioning
E. Hot

53. PROBITY
A. Integrity B. Impudence
C. Profane D. Preface
E. Investigation

54. MUSTY
A. Certainty B. Stale
C. Modern D. Mysterious
E. Essential

55. PLAUDIT
A. Applause B. Knowledgeable
C. Lazy D. Communicative
E. Enjoyable

56. TEMERITY
A. Innocence B. Tendency
C. Audacity D. Tenderness
E. Behaviour

57. RUMINATE
A. To run fast B. To reprimand
C. To think deeply D. To spend lavishly
E. To captivate

58. DEPRECATE
A. To repeat B. To belittle
C. To steal D. To search
E. To deny

59. CRAVEN
A. Greedy B. Cowardly
C. Flattering D. Restless
E. Rally

60. FORTY WINKS
A. A person beyond 40 years of age
B. A studious person
C. Ordeals of life
D. A short nap
E. A group of forty

61. VICARIOUS
A. Ambitious
B. Not experienced personally
C. Nostalgic
D. Vindictive
E. Curious

62. TO JETTISON
A. To go on trekking
B. To sail
C. To abandon
D. To fire a gun
E. To fly fast

63. TO BROWBEAT
A. To bully
B. To chase
C. To give a hint
D. To revive old friendship
E. To thrash

64. TO ASSUAGE
A. To assume B. To forget
C. To resolve D. To mitigate
E. To use

65. DEBONAIR
A. Bed-ridden B. Candid
C. Elegant D. Thrifty
E. Obscence

66. DESPOT
A. Pragmatic person
B. Cruel ruler
C. Knowledgeable historian
D. Leading industrialist
E. Dejected

67. MUSTY
A. Tiring B. Deserted
C. Swanky D. Obsolete
E. Strong

68. PERNICKETY
A. Highly talented B. Futuristic
C. Fussy D. Extravagant
E. Penury

69. ROSETTE
A. Badge B. Wild jungle
C. Exhibition D. Palatial building
E. Dish

70. ORNATE
A. Dimension B. Ancient
C. Richly decorated D. Vigour
E. Profuse

71. DIAPHANOUS
A. Cylindrical B. Almost transparent
C. Complicated D. Steep climb
E. Two dimensional

72. COMEUPPANCE
A. Retribution B. Lenience
C. Leisure
D. Competitive nature E. Richness

73. UNSCATHED
A Unstinting B. Unsociable
C. Unspeakable D. Unharmed
E. Untouched

74. EPAULETTE
A. Ammunition B. Shoulder ornament
C. Equipment D. Cockpit
E. Appealing Authority

75. EXPIATION
A. Expansion B. Atonement
C. Explanation D. Addition
E. To Exhale air

76. PROCRASTINATE
A. Intimidate B. Humiliate
C. Predict D. Postpone
E. Segragate

77. ABDOMINABLE
A. Original B. Detestable
C. Preferable D. Complimentary
E. Eatable

78. RESCIND
A. Cancel B. Enjoy
C. Praise D. Receive
E. Rejoin

79. COLLATERAL
A. Pathetic B. Tiresome
C. Guarantee D. Magnanimous
E. Partnership

80. KNAVE
A. Novice B. Dishonest
C. Futuristic D. Traditional
E. Slave

81. FINESSE
A. Skill B. Softness
C. Charm D. Gist
E. Benty

82. ARDOUR
A. Enthusiasm B. Candidness
C. Discipline D. Fairness
E. Power

Directions (83–100): *In each of these questions, you find a sentence, a part of which is **bold**. For the **bold** part, five words/phrases are suggested. Choose the word/phrase **nearest** in meaning to the **bold** part.*

83. His descriptions are **vivid**.
A. Detailed B. Categorical
C. Clear D. Ambiguous
E. Different

84. Friends have always **deplored** my unsociable nature.
A. Deprived B. Implored
C. Denied D. Regretted
E. Explored

85. Despite his enormous wealth, the businessman was very **frugal** in his habits.
A. Reckless B. Law abiding
C. Unpredictable D. Economical
E. Careless

86. He was **engrossed** in writing a story.
A. Absolved B. Absorbed
C. Interested D. Engaged
E. Drowned

87. People fear him because of his **vindictive** nature.
A. Violent B. Cruel
C. Revengeful D. Irritable
E. Killing

88. He always has a very **pragmatic** approach to life.
A. Practical B. Proficient
C. Potent D. Patronizing
E. Advanced

89. He was not at all **abashed** by her open admiration.
A. Delighted B. Piqued

C. Embarrassed D. Livid
E. Moved

90. Rahul was amazed at how **affable** his new employer was
A. Demanding B. Polite
C. Repulsive D. Quality-conscious
E. Friendly

91. Since our plans are **amorphous** we shall send you the detailed programme at a later date.
A. Impractical B. Prohibitive
C. Inimical D. Formless
E. Confidential

92. Preeti's **arduous** efforts had sapped her energy.
A. Over-ambitious B. Strenuous
C. Sterile D. Apocryphal
E. Futile

93. The manager's **articulate** presentation of the advertising campaign impressed his employers.
A. Well-prepared B. Effective
C. Superficial D. Banal
E. Colourful

94. I do not wish to be **beholden** to anyone in this office
A. Dependent B. Opposed
C. Obligated D. Sycophant
E. Assistant

95. We must prevent the **proliferation** of nuclear weapons.
A. Use B. Increase
C. Expansion D. Extension
E. Birth

96. The debate has **instigated** a full official enquiry into the incidence.
A. Initiated B. Incited
C. Forced D. Caused
E. Attracted

97. The workers were full of **applause** for the new policy of the management.
A. Approval B. Adulation
C. Praise D. Eulogy
E. Curiosity

98. Her **ostensible** calm masked a deepseated fear.
A. Illusory B. Apparent
C. Dubious D. Visible
E. Obvious

99. Sonu is an **inveterate** liar.
A. Effective B. Habitual
C. Frequent D. Familiar
E. Occasional

100. The underworld still makes solid profit out of **illicit** liquor.
A. indigenous B. illegitimate
C. illegal D. country
E. optional

ANSWERS

1	2	3	4	5	6	7	8	9	10
D	C	B	D	B	C	A	A	A	A
11	12	13	14	15	16	17	18	19	20
B	B	A	C	C	A	D	A	C	A
21	22	23	24	25	26	27	28	29	30
C	A	C	D	D	A	A	D	D	A
31	32	33	34	35	36	37	38	39	40
A	C	C	C	B	D	A	C	C	B
41	42	43	44	45	46	47	48	49	50
D	B	D	C	D	B	A	C	D	B
51	52	53	54	55	56	57	58	59	60
D	C	A	B	A	C	C	B	B	D
61	62	63	64	65	66	67	68	69	70
B	C	A	D	C	B	D	C	A	C
71	72	73	74	75	76	77	78	79	80
B	A	D	B	B	D	B	A	D	B
81	82	83	84	85	86	87	88	89	90
A	A	C	D	D	B	C	A	C	B
91	92	93	94	95	96	97	98	99	100
D	B	A	C	B	B	C	B	B	C

□□□

7. Antonyms

Directions (Qs. 1–29) : *Each of the following items consists of a sentence followed by five words. Select the* ***antonym*** *of the word (occuring in the sentence in* ***capital*** *letters) as per the context.*

1. What the critic said about this new book was **absurd**.
A. Interesting B. Impartial
C. Sensible D. Ridiculous
E. Clear

2. The issue raised in the forum can be **ignored**.
A. Removed B. Considered
C. Set aside D. Debated
E. Moved

3. After swallowing it the frog has become **lethargic**.
A. Aggressive B. Dull
C. Active D. Hungry
E. Sleepy

4. For the first time I saw him speaking **rudely** to her.
A. Softly B. Gently
C. Politely D. Slowly
E. Happily

5. Dust storms and polluted rivers have made it **hazardous** to breathe the air and drink the water.
A. Convenient B. Risky
C. Wrong D. Safe
E. Difficult

6. Only hard work can **enrich** our country.
A. Impoverish B. Improve
C. Increase D. Involve
E. Shine

7. He is man of **extravagant** habits.
A. Sensible B. Careful
C. Economical D. Balanced
E. Generous

8. They employ only **diligent** workers.
A. Unskilled B. Lazy
C. Careless D. Idle
E. Sincere

9. His success in the preliminary examination made him **complacent**.
A. Discontented B. Self-satisfied
C. Curious D. Militant
E. Adamant

10. In this competition, he has become the **victor**.
A. Beaten B. Frustrated
C. Disappointed D. Vanquished
E. Failure

11. His behaviour at social gatherings is **laudable**.
A. Condemnable B. Impolite
C. Unpleasant D. Repulsive
E. Appreciable

12. The characters in this story are not all **fictitious**.
A. Common B. Factual
C. Real D. Genuine
E. Truthful

13. The **reluctance** of the officer was obvious.
A. Eagerness B. Hesitation
C. Enjoyment D. Unwillingness
E. Lethargy

14. He is a **generous** man.
A. Stingy B. Uncharitable
C. Selfish D. Ignoble
E. Kind

15. He showed a marked **antipathy** to foreigners.
A. profundity B. fondness
C. objection D. willingness
E. aversion

16. The authorities took the corrective action with **celerity**.
A. reluctance B. delay
C. promptness D. lack of judgement
E. swiftness

17. It seems **churlish** to refuse such a generous offer.
A. wise B. sensible
C. polite D. immature
E. rude

18. A **conscientious** editor, he checked every definition for its accuracy.
A. novice B. careless

C. unscientific D. biased
E. proud

19. Sharma's **craven** refusal to join the protest was criticised by his comrades.
A. strategic B. bold
C. diplomatic D. well-thought
E. cowardly

20. The dictator **quelled** the uprising.
A. fostered B. defended
C. supported D. fomented
E. suppressed

21. People are unwilling to **follow** the rules.
A. waive B. neglect
C. dispose D. disregard
E. lead

22. That was an **impudent** remark.
A. gentle B. mild
C. modest D. unassuming
E. impertinent

23. His sudden appearance on the scene was **fortuitous.**
A. circumstantial B. unfortunate
C. sudden D. calculated
E. lucky

24. The batsman gave a **sterling** performance.
A. a risky B. a vital
C. an ordinary D. a match-saving
E. dashing

25. While facing that situation he turned out to be **dauntless.**
A. tactful B. stoical
C. bashful D. cowardly
E. fearless

26. We went to the first floor through the **rickety** wooden stairs.
A. stable B. old
C. narrow D. uncomfortable
E. slippery

27. They made a **profigate** use of scarce resources.
A. proper B. extravagant
C. effective D. thrifty
E. prudent

28. The consultant analysed the proposal carefully before he decided to **jettison** it.
A. abandon B. strengthen
C. accept D. modify
E. forward

29. The politician was **flummoxed** by the question put to him.
A. comfortable B. annoyed
C. delighted D. disconcerted
E. Insulted

Directions (30–100): *Each of the following items consists of a word or group of words in capital letters, followed by four words. Select the word that is **furthest** in meaning to the word or group of words in capital letters.*

30. RELUCTANT
A. Optimistic B. Unwilling
C. Enthusiastic D. Excited
E. Active

31. SCARCITY
A. Plenty B. Prosperity
C. Facility D. Simplicity
E. Paucity

32. THICK SKINNED
A. Thankless B. Sensitive
C. Pliant D. Resolute
E. Careful

33. BLEAK
A. Bright B. Confusing
C. Uncertain D. Great
E. Dark

34. STERN
A. Violent B. Generous
C. Mild D. Forgiving
E. Strong

35. SUPERFICIAL
A. Profound B. Difficult
C. Secretive D. Mystical
E. Unofficial

36. ELEGANCE
A. Balance B. Indelicacy
C. Clumsiness D. Savagery
E. Beauty

37. COARSE
A. Pleasing B. Rude
C. Polished D. Soft
E. Sour

38. EXPLOIT :
A. Utilize B. Alert
C. Support D. Neglect
E. Absorb

39. DETRIMENTAL :
A. Demolition B. Aversion
C. Beneficial D. Bad
E. Healthy

40. SHARP :
A. Bleak B. Blunt
C. Bright D. Blond
E. Dull

41. CONDEMN :
A. Censure B. Approve
C. Recommend D. Praise
E. Use

42. RELUCTANT :
A. Avoiding B. Anxious

C. Refuse D. Eager
E. Active

43. INTRICATE :
A. Complicated B. Simple
C. Colourful D. Good
E. Clear

44. PENURY :
A. Pompous B. Luxury
C. Poverty D. Punitive
E. Treasury

45. EXPOSTULATE :
A. Protest B. Agree
C. Follow D. Argue
E. Counter

46. INHIBIT
A. Pamper B. Breed
C. Accept D. Promote
E. Live

47. PENURY
A. Education B. Laziness
C. Wealth D. Ignorance
E. Poverty

48. VITAL
A. Trivial B. Peripheral
C. Optional D. Superficial
E. Important

49. KINDLED
A. Extinguished B. Reduced
C. Weakened D. Ignited
E. Fired

50. REPULSIVE
A. Attractive B. Colourful
C. Unattractive D. Striking
E. Acceptive

51. OBSCURE
A. Suitable B. Apt
C. Thalamus D. Clear
E. Incurable

52. CIRCUMSPECT
A. Careless B. Pusillanimous
C. Reticent D. Hostile
E. Visible

53. OBLIGATORY
A. Doubtful B. Voluntary
C. Sincerely D. Faithfully
E. Compulsory

54. EPHEMERAL
A. Temporal B. Stable
C. Permanent D. Earthly
E. Superficial

55. SOLICITOUS
A. Mild B. Showing no concern for
C. Grateful D. Cheerful
E. Thankful

56. UNDER DURESS
A. Dry B. Volition
C. Affluence D. Lack of commitment
E. Fertile

57. LACONIC
A. Sullen B. Handsome
C. Verbose D. Sharp memory
E. Terse

58. SLOTHFUL
A. Credulous
B. Highly skilled
C. Without resources
D. Sprightly
E. Weak

59. SINGULAR
A. nearby B. Ordinary
C. Wide D. Modern
E. Unique

60. RECLUSE
A. Criminal B. Wise
C. Gregarious D. Timid
E. Solitary

61. BE NO SLOUCH
A. Inefficient B. Honest
C. Saintly D. Well-known
E. Unkind

62. OPPROBRIUM
A. Very easy B. Suspenseful
C. Modern D. Praise
E. Criticism

63. IMBROGLIO
A. Pleasant situation B. Critical
C. Ambiguity D. Amnesty
E. Turmoil

64. EVANESCENT
A. Scanty B. Lasting
C. Anguish D. Scattered
E. Fading

65. IMPERTINENT
A. Polite B. Perturbing
C. Curious D. Steady
E. Hasty

66. ABHORRENT
A. Terse B. Attractive
C. Mature D. Usual
E. Disgusting

67. ABSTRUSE
A. Crazy B. Calm
C. Obvious D. Boundless
E. Nervous

68. PROFANE
A. Sacred B. Artless
C. Rigid D. Aspersion
E. Secular

69. GARRULOUS
A. Tiresome B. Harsh
C. Light D. Quiet
E. Talkative

70. CANTANKEROUS
A. Convivial B. Pliable
C. Pessimistic D. Bold
E. Argumentative

71. SAGACIOUS
A. Timid
B. Lacking sense of enterprise
C. Financially poor
D. Showing poor judgement
E. Judgemental

72. PROTRACT
A. Not to display
B. To indulge in extravagance
C. Not to be careful about future
D. To cut short
E. Prolong

73. DEBILITATE
A. To argue B. To strengthen
C. To guess D. To conspire
E. To weaken

74. PERTINACIOUS
A. Irretrievable B. Insipid
C. Irresolute D. Reproof
E. Stubborn

75. IMPECUNIOUSNESS
A. Smoothness B. Carefree nature
C. Affluence D. Stability
E. Strength

76. INIMICAL
A. Supportive B. Inquisitive
C. Lack lustre D. Coarse
E. Hostile

77. SCINTILLA
A. Unscientific B. Huge quantity
C. Mealy-mouthed D. Unpromising
E. Iota

78. KNAVE
A. Honest B. Ignorant
C. Timid D. Belligerent
E. Jack

79. APOCRYPHAL
A. Confusing B. Modern
C. True D. Unsophisticated
E. Doubtful

80. PINNACLE
A. Discipline B. Lowest point
C. Delightful D. Comfort
E. Zenith

81. RICKETY
A. Stable B. Humid
C. Rollicking D. Pleasing
E. Weak

82. SWINGEING
A. Tactful
B. Extremely hot weather
C. Little in amount
D. Hindrance
E. Severe

83. DISPARAGE
A. To cause ambiguity
B. To add to confusion
C. To spread rumours
D. To adulate
E. To understate

84. STOICAL
A. Urbane B. Flinching
C. Worldly D. Hostile
E. Calm

85. LACONIC
A. Voluble B. Jealous
C. Exhausted D. Timid
E. Terse

86. GIMCRACK
A. Notorious B. Outstanding
C. Humour D. Incorrigible
E. Showy

87. REPUDIATE
A. Explain B. Criticise
C. Accept D. Weaken
E. Disown

88. PREPOSSESSING
A. Incredible B. Arousing envy
C. Unattractive D. Recent
E. Possessing

89. ADULATION
A. Confusion B. Inertia
C. Consolidation D. Condemnation
E. Admiration

90. BLITHESOME
A. Graceful B. Sullen
C. Adventurous D. Mammoth
E. Joyous

91. SENILE
A. Suspicious B. Mentally alert
C. Corrupt D. Affluent
E. Agile

92. PREDILECTION
A. Analogy B. Anticlimax
C. Antipathy D. Argument
E. Preference

93. ON THE BLINK
A. Apologetically B. Blindly
C. Legally D. In working order
E. Defective

94. CONSANGUINE
A. Of different kind
B. Invisible
C. Urbane
D. Untenanted
E. Related

95. REDOUBTABLE
A. Truthful
B. Crafty
C. Widely travelled
D. Ordinary
E. Sure

96. INORDINATE
A. Distant B. Facile
C. Moderate D. Attractive
E. Excessive

97. CONSUMMATE
A. Sluggish B. Imperfect
C. Melancholy D. Dull
E. Complete

98. REPROOF
A. Brawl B. Omission
C. Ambiguity D. Approval
E. Rebuke

99. FELICITOUS
A. Jealous B. Inapt
C. Demanding D. Inaccessible
E. Appropriate

100. CHARLATAN
A. Knowledgeable doctor
B. Trickster
C. Comedian
D. Senior government official
E. Novice

ANSWERS

1	2	3	4	5	6	7	8	9	10
C	B	C	C	D	A	C	C	A	D
11	**12**	**13**	**14**	**15**	**16**	**17**	**18**	**19**	**20**
A	C	A	A	B	B	C	D	B	D
21	**22**	**23**	**24**	**25**	**26**	**27**	**28**	**29**	**30**
D	A	D	C	D	A	D	C	A	C
31	**32**	**33**	**34**	**35**	**36**	**37**	**38**	**39**	**40**
A	B	A	C	A	C	C	D	C	B
41	**42**	**43**	**44**	**45**	**46**	**47**	**48**	**49**	**50**
D	D	B	B	B	D	C	A	A	A
51	**52**	**53**	**54**	**55**	**56**	**57**	**58**	**59**	**60**
D	A	B	C	B	D	C	D	B	C
61	**62**	**63**	**64**	**65**	**66**	**67**	**68**	**69**	**70**
A	D	A	B	A	B	C	A	D	A
71	**72**	**73**	**74**	**75**	**76**	**77**	**78**	**79**	**80**
D	D	B	C	C	A	B	A	C	B
81	**82**	**83**	**84**	**85**	**86**	**87**	**88**	**89**	**90**
A	C	D	B	A	B	C	C	D	B
91	**92**	**93**	**94**	**95**	**96**	**97**	**98**	**99**	**100**
B	C	D	A	D	C	B	D	B	A

□□□

8. Fill in the Blanks

Directions (Qs. 1-40) : *Pick out the most effective word(s) from the given words to fill in the blanks to make the sentence meaningfully complete.*

1. You must ensure the correctness of the information before ....
A. drawing B. enabling
C. learning D. jumping
E. examining

2. The rocket .... the target and did not cause any casualty.
A. sensed B. reached
C. missed D. exploded
E. aimed

3. It is desirable to take .... in any business if you want to make profit.
A. advice B. risk
C. loan D. recourse
E. perseverance

4. They wasted all the money on purchase of some .... items.
A. excellent B. important
C. significant D. quality
E. trivial

5. When he found the wallet his face glowed but soon it faded as the wallet was ....
A. empty B. vacant
C. recovered D. stolen
E. expensive

6. He has served the country by .... many significant positions.
A. appointing B. creating
C. developing D. holding
E. encouraging

7. The frequent errors are a result of the student's ....
A. talent B. smartness
C. carelessness D. perception
E. destructiveness

8. The robbers eventually .... in breaking into the house.
A. succeeded B. decided
C. caught D. trained
E. managed

9. I finally .... her to stay another day.
A. advised B. persuaded
C. suggested D. called
E. tortured

10. Most of the people who .... the book exhibition were teachers.
A. witnessed B. presented
C. conducted D. held
E. attended

11. One requires great .... to teach and handle little children who are restless.
A. patience B. attitude
C. determination D. knowledge
E. aptitude

12. The researchers will .... some of the causes of increasing poverty in the state.
A. fund B. investigate
C. promote D. circulate
E. collaborate

13. I usually perform .... when nobody is watching me.
A. alone B. good
C. better D. hard
E. nervously

14. It was .... to everyone that the minister had been drinking.
A. observed B. known
C. discovered D. realised
E. unfortunate

15. I would rather stay indoors .... the rain stops.
A. so B. waiting
C. until D. usually
E. then

16. The process should be completed as far as possible within a week, ... which the matter should be brought to notice of the officer concerned.
A. following B. failing
C. realizing D. referring
E. regarding

17. The officers are ..... to regular transfers.
A. free B. open
C. subject D. available
E. dictated

18. All letters received from Government should ..... be acknowledged.
A. suddenly B. obviously
C. immediately D. occasionally
E. adequately

19. Mumbai office ..... a meeting of senior officials to discuss the high incidence of frauds.
A. attended B. convened
C. reported D. registered
E. asked

20. The note should be ..... to all the concerned departments for their consideration.
A. regulated B. requested
C. carried D. forwarded
E. represented

21. Your present statement does not .... what you said last week.
A. accord to B. accord in
C. accord with D. accord for
E. accord

22. I had a vague .... that the lady originally belonged to Scotland.
A. notion B. expression
C. imagination D. theory
E. dream

23. The prisoner showed no .... for his crimes.
A. hatred B. obstinacy
C. remorse D. anger
E. sorry

24. It is inconceivable that in many schools children are subjected to physical .... in the name of discipline.
A. violation B. exercise
C. violence D. security
E. training

25. We have not yet fully realised the .... consequences of the war.
A. happy B. pleasing
C. grim D. exciting
E. heroic

26. Happiness consists in being .... what we have.
A. contented to B. contented with
C. contented for D. contented in
E. contented

27. His rude behaviour is a .... his organization.
A. disgrace for B. disgrace on
C. disgrace upon D. disgrace to
E. disgrace in

28. No child is .... understanding. One has to wait and provide proper guidance.
A. dull to B. dull in
C. dull of D. dull for
E. dull into

29. I am fully .... the problems facing the industry.
A. alive with B. alive to
C. alive for D. alive on
E. alive in

30. The Romans were .... science.
A. bad in B. bad to
C. bad for D. bad at
E. bad about

31. Although I was .... of his plans, I encouraged him, because there was no one else who was willing to help.
A. sceptical B. remorseful
C. fearful D. excited
E. victim

32. You have no business to .... pain on a weak and poor person.
A. inflict B. put
C. direct D. force
E. cause

33. Her uncle died in a car accident. He was quite rich. She suddenly .... all her uncle's money.
A. succeeded B. caught
C. gave D. inherited
E. captured

34. There was a major accident. The plane crashed. The pilot .... did not see the tower.
A. likely B. probably
C. scarcely D. hurriedly
E. surely

35. The car we were travelling in .... a mile from home.
A. broke off B. broke down
C. broke into D. broke up
E. broke away

36. What are you .... in the kitchen cupboard?
A. looking in B. looking on
C. looking to D. looking for
E. looking at

37. I did not see the point of .... waiting for them, so I went home.
A. hanging around B. hang on
C. hang together D. hanging up
E. hanging down

38. He lost confidence and .... of the deal at the last minute.
A. backed out B. backed on
C. backed down D. backed onto
E. backed away

39. To the dismay of all the students, the class monitor was ..... berated by the Principal at a school assembly.
A. critically B. ignominiously
C. prudently D. fortuitously
E. thoroughly

40. All attempts to revive the fishing industry were ..... failure.
A. foredoomed to B. heading at
C. predicted for D. estimated to
E. going for

41. There are ..... parked outside than yesterday.
A. fewer cars
B. few cars
C. less cars
D. a small number of cars
E. a little cars

42. The minister had to ..... some awkward questions from reporters.
A. fend B. fend at
C. fend out D. fend off
E. fend in

43. The ..... of evidence was on the side of the plaintiff since all but one of the witnesses testified that his story was correct.
A. propensity B. force
C. preponderance D. brunt
E. cause

44. Attention to detail is ..... of a fine craftsman.
A. hallmark B. stamp
C. seal of authority D. authenticity
E. tool

45. Behaving in a .... and serious way, even in a .... situation, makes people respect you.
A. Calm, difficult
B. steady, angry
C. flamboyant, tricky
D. cool astounding
E. silly, sound

46. Along with a sharp rise in ...., a recession would eventually result in more men, women, and children living in ....
A. crime, apathy
B. fatalities, poor
C. deaths, slums
D. unemployment, poverty
E. migrations, streets

47. The government has .... to provide financial aid to the ones .... by severe floods in the city.
A. desired, troubled
B. promised, havoc
C. failed, affected
D. wanted, struck
E. decided, ill

48. An airplane with .... passengers on board made an unscheduled .... as the airport to which it was heading was covered with thick fog.
A. imitable, slip
B. faulty, stop
C. variety, halt
D. tons, wait
E. numerous, landing

49. Deemed universities .... huge fees, but have not been successful in providing .... education to our students.
A. collect, maintaining
B. pay, better
C. ask, good
D. charge, quality
E. demand, quantitative

50. If the banks desire to .... profit, they should get rid of .... measures.
A. lose, concentrate
B. increase, populist
C. earn, unhealthy
D. maximise, traditional
E. make, unsteady

51. He was immature in his young age when he became completely .... by German and writing of Shakespeare.
A. collapsed, army
B. engrossed, people
C. captivated, literature
D. seized, soldiers
E. broken, rules

52. The man who does not .... that the good of every living creature is him .... is a fool.
A. see, good
B. know, had
C. understand, ugly
D. see, worse
E. understand, better

53. Being a kind hearted master, he never .... too .... work on his servants.
A. does, much B. entrusts, easy
C. performs, little D. imposes, much
E. assigns, little

54. On account of the .... of grass on the arid plains the cattle became ....

A. dearth, emaciated
B. dearth, flippant
C. abundance, arrangement
D. sacrifice, agitated
E. crisis, jubilant

55. The teacher must ...... the unique style of a learner in order to .... it to the desired knowledge.
A. advocate ... direct
B. perpetuate .... develop
C. appreciate ... focus
D. absorb .... maintain
E. discover .... harness

56. Not all countries benefit .... from liberalisation. The benefits tend to ..... first to the advantaged and to those with the right education to be able to benefit from the opportunities presented.
A. equally ... generate
B. richly ... downgrade
C. suitably ... ascribe
D. uniformally ... percolate
E. judiciously ... facilitate

57. He has .... sense of words. Therefore, the sentences he constructs are always .... with rich meaning.
A. profound ... pregnant
B. distinguished ... loaded
C. terrific ... tempted
D. meaningful ... full
E. outstanding ... consistent

58. He was an .... musician, had been awarded the George medal during the second world war and .... with the title of Rai Bahadur.
A. outstanding ... popularised
B. underestimated ... declared
C. accomplished ... honoured
D. impressive ... assigned
E. obdurate ... proclaimed

59. Whether it be shallow or not, commitment is the ...., the bedrock of any .... loving relationship.
A. expression ... perfunctory
B. foundation ... genuinely
C. manifestation ... deep
D. key ... alarmingly
E. basis ... absorbing

60. Many people take their spirituality very seriously and ..... about those who don't, worrying about them and ...... them to believe.
A. think ... criticising
B. pride ... appraising
C. rationalise ... enabling
D. wonder ... prodding
E. ponder ... venturing

61. Unless new reserves are found soon, the world's supply of coal is being ...... in such a way that with demand continuing to grow at present rates, reserves will be ...... by the year 2050.
A. consumed ... completed
B. depleted ... exhausted
C. reduced ... argument
D. burnt ... destroyed
E. utilized ... perished

62. If you are ...., you tend to respond to stressful situations, in a calm, secure, steady and .... way.
A. resilient ... rational
B. obdurate ... manageable
C. propitious ... stable
D. delectable ... flexible
E. supportive ... positive

63. Management can be defined as the process of .... organisational goals by working with and through human and non-human resources to .... improve value added to the world.
A. getting ... deliberately
B. managing ... purposefully
C. targeting ... critically
D. realising ... dialectically
E. reaching ... continuously

64. If you are an introvert, you ...... to prefer working alone and, if possible, will .... towards projects where you can work by yourself or with as few people as possible.
A. like ... depart
B. advocate ... move
C. tend ... gravitate
D. express ... attract
E. feel ... follow

65. The society provides the individual security of life, ... of thought and sustenance for action. Every individual who .... from the society is indebted to the society.
A. serenity .... gains
B. prosperity .... benefits
C. objectivity .... profits
D. seriousness .... derives
E. semblance......... evolves

66. A hobby is an activity of interest .... for pleasure. It helps to break the monotony and tedium of our .... routine.
A. developed .... interesting
B. pursued .... humdrum
C. cultivated .... developed
D. regularized .... cultivated
E. arranged .... pursued

67. The .... growth of Indian agriculture in the last three decades has earned .... from other countries.
A. pervasive .... reputation

B. significant .... deliverance
C. superior .... regard
D. dynamic ....accolades
E. distinctive .... encouragement

68. College-going students should .... the spirit of service from the great men of ....
A. inculcate .... power
B. develop .... possession
C. invent .... wisdom
D. analyze .... wisdom
E. imbibe .... yore

69. The planning of trees on the .... of town and villages helps the .... of a counrty.
A. surface .... output
B. periphery .... output
C. joints .... production
D. vicinity .... cultivation
E. outskirts ....afforestation

70. The human infant is a life-long bundle of energy with a .... array of potentialities, and many ....
A. marvellous .... vulnerabilities
B. peculiar .... opportunities
C. critical .... competencies
D. vocational .... strengths
E. perfect .... pecularities

71. His presentation was so lengthy and .... that it was difficult for us to find out the real .... in it.
A. boring .... planning
B. tedious .... skill
C. verbose .... content
D. laborious .... coverage
E. simple .... meaning

72. There is no .... the fact that a man of knowledge .... great power.
A. justifying .... acknowledges
B. clarifying .... exhibits
C. advocating .... projects
D. denying .... wields
E. proclaiming .... develops

73. The .... of opinion which emerged at a recently concluded seminar was that the problem of dowry cannot be .... unless the law against it is made more stringent.
A. divergence .... managed
B. sympathy .... projected
C. consesus .... tackled
D. similarity .... curbed
E. convergennce .... appreciated

74. Leisure must be spent carefully and .... only, otherwise the devil will take the .... you.
A. positively .... care
B. constructively .... better
C. proactively .... thought
D. objectively .... energy
E. purposefully .... measure

75. As business pull down .... barriers and .... boundaries, integration and standardisation of work systems will become even more important.
A. competition, break
B. strong, mix
C. physical, merge
D. international, explode
E. tax, suggest

76. The co-operative model has .... well in the dairy business in India, ... it perhaps the most organised among all food business in the country.
A. evolved, projecting
B. worked, making
C. proved, marking
D. traded, rendering
E. signified, grading

77. The .... of all good companies .... faster to employee needs and, in some cases, actually know most people by name.
A. employees, work
B. officers, listen
C. employers, react
D. leaders, respond
E. mentors, consider

78. The year also saw the boom and doom of many dotcoms .... the relentless advance of the internet ....
A. although, continued
B. whereas, boomed
C. despite, slowdown
D. provided, industry
E. putting, halt

79. Our executive made a bold but, in his mind .... figure that he hoped would .... to the customer's vanity and wallet.
A. realistic, appeal
B. lower, convince
C. great, suit
D. soft, match
E. higher, favour

80. The entry of players such as Hindustan Unilever and Dabur into Glaxo's _________ turf, health drinks, has __________ in more competition.
A. home, ushered
B. strong, ushered
C. home, increased
D. own, reigned
E. ground, entered

ANSWERS

1	2	3	4	5	6	7	8	9	10
A	C	B	E	A	D	C	A	B	E
11	12	13	14	15	16	17	18	19	20
A	B	C	A	C	B	C	C	B	D
21	22	23	24	25	26	27	28	29	30
C	A	C	C	C	B	D	B	B	D
31	32	33	34	35	36	37	38	39	40
B	C	C	B	C	C	D	A	B	A
41	42	43	44	45	46	47	48	49	50
A	D	D	A	A	D	C	E	C	B
51	52	53	54	55	56	57	58	59	60
C	A	D	A	A	D	A	C	B	D
61	62	63	64	65	66	67	68	69	70
B	A	E	C	A	B	D	E	E	A
71	72	73	74	75	76	77	78	79	80
C	D	C	B	C	B	B	A	D	A

□□□

9. Ordering of Words in a Sentence

Directions (Qs. 1–75): *In the following items, some parts of the sentence have been jumbled up. You are required to rearrange these parts which are labelled P, Q, R and S to produce the correct sentence. Choose the option with proper sequence.*

1. We are doing
P : to the people
Q : to give relief
R : all we can
S : but more funds are needed
The correct sequence should be
A. P Q R S B. R Q P S
C. Q P R S D. S P Q R
E. P R Q S

2. The man
P : when he was
Q : in the office last evening
R : could not finish
S : all his work
The correct sequence should be
A. P Q R S B. Q R S P
C. R Q P S D. R S P Q
E. P R Q S

3. The people decided
P : they were going
Q : how much
R : to spend
S : on the construction of the school building
The correct sequence should be
A. Q P R S B. P Q R S
C. P R Q S D. S Q P R
E. Q R P S

4. The man said that
P : those workers
Q : would be given a raise
R : who did not go on
S : strike last month
The correct sequence should be
A. P Q R S B. P R S Q
C. Q P R S D. R S P Q
E. P R Q S

5. I think
P : the members
Q : are basically in agreement
R : of the group
S : on the following points.
The correct sequence should be
A. R Q P S B. S Q R P
C. P R Q S D. P Q S R
E. Q R P S

6. While it was true that
P : I had
Q : to invest in industry
R : some lands and houses
S : I did not have ready cash
The correct sequence should be
A. P Q R S B. P R S Q
C. S Q P R D. Q P R S
E. Q P S R

7. P : But your help
Q : to finish this work
R : it would not have been possible
S : in time
The correct sequence should be
A. P R Q S B. S P Q R
C. R P Q S D. P Q R S
E. Q P R S

8. The boy
P : in the competition
Q : who was wearing spectacles
R : won many prizes
S : held in our college
The correct sequence should be
A. P Q R S B. R P S Q
C. Q R P S D. Q P S R
E. S P Q R

9. About 200 years ago,
P : in the south of India
Q : an old king
R : ruled over a kingdom
S : called Rajavarman.
The correct sequence should be
A. Q S R P B. P Q R S
C. Q P S R D. Q S P R
E. Q P R S

10. P : his land
Q : a wooden plough
R : the Indian peasant still uses
S : to cultivate.
The correct sequence should be
A. R Q P S B. Q P S R
C. S R Q P D. R Q S P
E. Q P R S

11. He was a man,
P : even if he had to starve
Q : who would not beg
R : borrow or steal
S : from anyone.
The correct sequence should be
A. P Q R S B. P R Q S
C. Q R S P D. Q P R S
E. P S R Q

12. P : in the progress of
Q : universities play a crucial role
R : our civilization
S : in the present age.
The correct sequence should be
A. S Q P R B. Q R S P
C. Q R P S D. S Q R P
E. P Q R S

13. P : far out into the sea
Q : for the next two weeks there were further explosions
R : which hurled
S : ashes and debris.
The correct sequence should be
A. Q R P S B. R S P Q
C. Q R S P D. S R P Q
E. P Q R S

14. William Shakespeare,
P : in his lifetime
Q : the great English dramatist
R : wrote thirty-five plays
S : and several poems.
The correct sequence should be
A. P Q R S B. R S P Q
C. Q S R P D. Q R S P
E. P R Q S

15. Whenever I am,
P : with an old friend of mine
Q : in New Delhi
R : to have dinner
S : I always try.
The correct sequence should be
A. S Q P R B. Q S R P
C. R P S Q D. P R Q S
E. P Q R S

16. P : I don't know
Q : must have thought
R : what people sitting next to me
S : but I came away.
The correct sequence should be
A. R S Q P B. R Q S P
C. P Q R S D. P R Q S
E. P S R Q

17. P : in estimating the size of the earth
Q : but they were hampered by the lack of instruments of precision
R : ancient astronomers
S : used methods which were theoretically valid
Which one of the following is the correct sequence?
A. R P Q S B. P R Q S
C. R S Q P D. R P S Q
E. P Q R S

18. P : It is a pity that
Q : by offering a handsome dowry
R : a number of parents think that
S : they will be able to ensure the happiness of their daughters
Which one of the following is the correct sequence?
A. S Q R P B. P R S Q
C. P S R Q D. P R Q S
E. P Q R S

19. The common man
P : in nurturing
Q : a more active role
R : communal harmony
S : should play
Which one of the following is the correct sequence?
A. P R S Q B. S Q P R
C. S Q R P D. P R Q S
E. P Q R S

20. The doctor
P : able to find out
Q : what has caused
R : the food poisoning
S : has not been
Which one of the following is the correct sequence?
A. S P R Q B. P R Q S
C. P R S Q D. S P Q R
E. P Q R S

21. P : was suspended
Q : the officer being corrupt
R : before his dismissal
S : from service

Which one of the following is the correct sequence?
A. Q P S R B. Q P R S
C. R S Q P D. R S PQ
E. P Q R S

22. With an unsteady hand
P : on my desk
Q : from his pocket
R : he took an envelope
S : and threw it

Which one of the following is the correct sequence?
A. Q R P S B. Q R S P
C. R Q P S D. R Q S P
E. P Q R S

23. P : she gave her old coat
Q : to a beggar
R : the one with the brown fur on it
S : shivering with cold

Which one of the following is the correct sequence?
A. S Q R P B. S P R Q
C. P R Q S D. P S Q R
E. P Q R S

24. It is a privilege
P : to pay tax
Q : of every citizen
R : as well as the duty
S : as well as the duty who is well-placed

Which one of the following is the correct sequence?
A. R P S Q B. S P R Q
C. R Q S P D. S Q R P
E. P Q R S

25. It is not good
P : of the wicked persons
Q : to overthrow
R : to accept the help
S : the righteous persons

Which one of the following is the correct sequence?
A. R S Q P B. Q S R P
C. R P Q S D. Q P R S
E. P Q R S

26. Life is judged
P : and not by
Q : of work done
R : the longevity of years
S : by the quality

Which one of the following is the correct sequence?
A. Q S P R B. S Q R P
C. Q S R P D. S Q P R
E. P Q R S

27. P : When he learns that
Q : you have passed the examination
R : in the first division
S : your father will be delighted

Which one of the following is the correct sequence?
A. Q P S R B. S P Q R
C. Q R S P D. S R Q P
E. P Q R S

28. P : The journalist
Q : saw
R : countless number of the dead
S : driving across the field of battle

Which one of the following is the correct sequence?
A. P Q S R B. P Q R S
C. P S Q R D. S R Q P
E. R P Q S

29. P : Jane planned
Q : some stamps
R : to buy
S : this afternoon

Which one of the following is the correct sequence?
A. P R Q S B. P S Q R
C. Q R P S D. Q S P R
E. R P Q S

30. Her mother
P : when she was
Q : hardly four years old
R : began to teach Neha
S : English

Which one of the following is the correct sequence?
A. R S Q P B. S R P Q
C. R S P Q D. S R Q P
E. R P Q S

31. P : Bill had
Q : a friend
R : an appointment
S : to meet

Which one of the following is the correct sequence?
A. P S R Q B. P R S Q
C. Q S R P D. Q R S P
E. R P Q S

32. For fear
P : that may or may not affect them perhaps at first
Q : of upsetting young people
R : only healthy people over 80 should be sequenced
S : about their genetic propensities

Which one of the following is the correct sequence?
A. S Q P R B. Q S R P
C. S Q R P D. Q S P R
E. P Q R S

33. While traditional

P : under made-up Americans aliases pretending familiarity with a culture and climate

Q : India sleeps a dynamic young cohort of highly skilled articulate professionals

R : they've never actually experienced earning salaries that were undreamt of by their elders

S : work through the night in the call centres functioning on US time

Which one of the following is the correct sequence?

A. P R Q S   B. Q S P R
C. P S Q R   D. Q R P S
E. P Q R S

34. IITs are

P : of great self-confidence and competitive advantage for India today

Q : in science and technology which has become a source

R : as they epitomize his creation of an infrastructure for excellence

S : perhaps Jawaharlal Nehru's most consequential legacy

Which one of the following is the correct sequence?

A. Q P S R   B. S R Q P
C. Q R S P   D. S P Q R
E. P Q R S

35. As India

P : from nearly 250 years of the British rule in India

Q : first major struggle for independence from the British rule

R : celebrates the Diamond Jubilee of its independence

S : it also observes simultaneously the 150th Anniversary of the Great Indian Mutiny

Which one of the following is the correct sequence?

A. R S P Q   B. Q P S R
C. R P S Q   D. Q S P R
E. P Q R S

36. There have been

P : a day after high intensity violence left at least 50 persons

Q : sporadic clashes between

R : dead in the northern city of Tripoli

S : the Lebanese army and militants

Which one of the following is the correct sequence?

A. Q S R P   B. S Q R P
C. Q S P R   D. S Q P R
E. P Q R S

37. Although

P : of non-owner managers came to be widely appreciated

Q : political freedom from the British masters

R : came to us in 1947 it was not until

S : well into the following decade that the role

Which one of the following is the correct sequence?

A. S P Q R   B. Q R S P
C. S R Q P   D. Q P S R
E. P Q R S

38. Conditions

P : for marketing in the U.S. and Canada

Q : Mexico as a manufacturing base

R : that Indian companies aspiring to tap

S : would have to fulfil include the complex rules of origin

Which one of the following is the correct sequence?

A. R Q P S   B. S P Q R
C. R P Q S   D. S Q P R
E. P Q R S

39. Aside

P : of the same three-storey building in the military academy

Q : from eating in the same dining hall

R : half to the north of the entrance half to the south

S : the 206 troops live side by side on the ground floor

Which one of the following is the correct sequence?

A. R P S Q   B. Q S P R
C. R S P Q   D. Q P S R
E. P Q R S

40. Russia's test firing

P : to US steps that have sparked an arms race

Q : of an intercontinental ballistic missile on

R : and undermined world security

S : Tuesday was in response

Which one of the following is the correct sequence?

A. S Q P R   B. Q S R P
B. S Q R P   D. Q S P R
E. P Q R S

41. Marks, cities, civilization —

P : on the verge of globalization; poised to

Q : the slow ascent to where he is today, poised

R : it is in this order that primitive man made

S : achieve universal prosperity and abundance

Which one of the following is the correct sequence?

A. R Q P S   B. P S R Q
B. R S P Q   D. P Q R S
E. S R P Q

42. I bow my head

P : for their sense of the beautiful in

Q : nature and for their foresight in investing beautiful

R : manifestations of nature with a religious significance

S : in reverence to our ancestors

Which one of the following is the correct sequence?
A. Q R S P B. S P Q R
B. Q P S R D. S R Q P
E. P Q R S

43. With all the crime and sleaze
P : I am not sure how many parents will be able to
Q : how many will have the courage to satisfy the child's uncomfortable queries
R : that dominates the front page of the newspapers today
S : read out the headlines to their children and if they do so
Which one of the following is the correct sequence?
A. R P S Q B. S Q R P
C. R Q S P D. P R S Q
E. P Q R S

44. The way
P : processes that govern their actions
Q : nutrients become integral parts
R : depends on the physiological and biochemical
S : of the body and contribute to its functions
Which one of the following is the correct sequence?
A. Q R S P B. P S R Q
C. Q S R P D. S P R Q
E. P Q R S

45. Thus,
P : international surveys would hence forth record
Q : if dirt-poor people in the developing world
R : their wealth of happiness alongside their material poverty
S : display a general sense of well-being
Which one of the following is the correct sequence?
A. S Q R P B. Q S P R
C. S Q P R D. Q S R P
E. P Q R S

46. It's
P : someone who's grieving but
Q : natural to feel uncomfortable
R : that prevent you from being there
S : or awkward when you have to help
Which one of the following is the correct sequence?
A. Q P S R B. R S P Q
C. Q S P R D. R P S Q
E. P Q R S

47. Developing countries
P : along the equator, which
Q : could become leaders in energy production
R : are expected to face the brunt of global warming
S : with a solar energy breakthrough
Which one of the following is the correct sequence?
A. Q S P R B. P R Q S
C. Q R P S D. P S Q R
E. S R P Q

48. A diversified
P : use as a heating or power generation fuel by converting gas into
Q : adding a new dimension to the traditional use of gas
R : of natural gas is emerging
S : amongst other products, high quality diesel transportation fuel virtually free of sulphur
Which one of the following is the correct sequence?
A. R P Q S B. S Q P R
C. R Q P S D. S P Q R
E. P Q R S

49. As things stand
P : but a majority still does not have access to English
Q : linguistic edge they are equipped with
R : after globally because of the
S : Indian professionals are much sought
Which one of the following is the correct sequence?
A. R S P Q B. S R Q P
C. R S Q P D. S R P Q
E. P Q R S

50. While advocates
P : of its provisions with the
Q : there is some misguided concern about a possible clash of some
R : of social reform have generally hailed the new legislation
S : religious and customary practices in vogue in the country
Which one of the following is the correct sequence?
A. R Q P S B. Q R S P
C. R Q S P D. Q R P S
E. P Q R S

51. Public Interest Litigations
P : as they are subjected to massive misuse
Q : but today they contribute to the backlog
R : were instituted as a means to help ordinary people side-step judicial delays to secure justice
S : also called postcard petitions
Which one of the following is the correct sequence?
A. R S Q P B. S R P Q
C. R S P Q D. S R Q P
E. P Q R S

52. Among
P : the soldier's mindset from fighting
Q : the doctrine's other directives is the need to reorient
R : namely terrorists hiding among civilians
S : the enemy to fighting his own people
Which one of the following is the correct sequence?
A. P Q R S B. Q P S R

C. P Q S R D. Q P R S
E. S R P Q

53. Indeed
P : on how to nurture young talent at the grassroots level
Q : as the powerhouse of women's hockey
R : is an instructive lesson for Indian hockey bosses
S : the non-descript town's emergence
Which one of the following is the correct sequence?
A. Q S R P B. S Q P R
C. S Q R P D. Q S P R
E. P Q R S

54. With pressure
P : to submit a report on the retreat of glaciers in Uttarakhand and also its impact
Q : mounting from every corner
R : a committee comprising scientists, geologists and technical experts
S : the state government has finally constituted
Which one of the following is the correct sequence?
A. Q S P R B. S Q R P
C. Q S R P D. S Q P R
E. P Q R S

55. This could
P : while out on sea-right from an engine break down to a human problem
Q : they shoulder great responsibility and have to take care of any eventuality
R : because while seafarers do look forward to some fun on the decks
S : not be further from the truth
Which one of the following is the correct sequence?
A. P R Q S B. S Q R P
C. P Q R S D. S R Q P
E. R S P Q

56. The producer must
P : give enough information so that the consumer
Q : will understand how the product differs from the competition
R : about the product but to buy it, the producer must
S : inform the consumer of his product and if he wants the consumer to not only know.
Which one of the following is the correct sequence?
A. P R S Q B. S Q P R
C. P Q S R D. S R P Q
E. R S P Q

57. The bigoted
P : reality that additional hands also mean additional mouths to feed, cloths and house
Q : in order to augment their incomes, plead for more children, ignoring the resultant
R : not only to the national interests but also to those families which
S : belief—the more, the marrier—has done immense harm
Which one of the following is the correct sequence?
A. S Q R P B. P R Q S
C. S R Q P D. P Q R S
E. R S P Q

58. Critics
P : cover up the essentially inequalitarian
Q : and unjust nature of a Third World State
R : has been basically a sugar-coated concept that tries to
S : also point out that development administration.
Which one of the following is the correct sequence?
A. P Q S R B. S R P Q
C. P R S Q D. S Q P R
E. Q P R S

59. For
P : are determined by nature and which by nurture
Q : about two decades now
R : aspects of cognition and behaviour in the human brain
S : scientists have been trying to figure out which.
Which one of the following is the correct sequence?
A. S Q R P B. Q S P R
C. S Q P R D. Q S R P
E. P Q R S

60. A school of psychology argues that
P : is one of the manifestations of impulse control disorder, a condition in which
Q : an act harmful to oneself or others
R : motorcycling—like gambling or sky-diving—
S : an individual cannot resist the impulse or temptation to perform.
Which one of the following is the correct sequence?
A. R P S Q B. Q S P R
C. R S P Q D. Q P S R
E. P Q R S

61. With six of its neighbours
P : there is a renewed warning for India
Q : and safeguard its own strategic interests
R : ranking high on a global roster of failed states
S : to reassess its policy towards them
Which one of the following is the correct sequence?
A. P R S Q B. R P Q S
C. P R Q S D. R P S Q
E. P Q R S

62. Faced with the
P : traditional culture in the pre-independence India
Q : challenge of the intrusion of colonial culture and ideology

R : developed during the nineteenth century
S : an attempt to reinvigorate traditional institutions and to realise the potential of.

Which one of the following is the correct sequence?

A. P R Q S B. Q S P R
C. P S Q R D. Q R P S
E. S R P Q

63. Looking back,
P : two wars I had been through
Q : life in the Army had all along been truly joyous
R : and the innumerable postings and below par accommodation at many stations
S : despite the vicissitudes and hardships of the.

Which one of the following is the correct sequence?

A. S R P Q B. Q P R S
C. S P R Q D. Q R P S
E. P Q R S

64. Polluted
P : on aqua life while
Q : Kerala rivers threatens the indigenous varieties
R : rivers are wreaking havoc
S : the introduction of exotic fish in the

Which one of the following is the correct sequence?

A. R P S Q B. Q S P R
C. R S P Q D. Q P S R
E. P Q R S

65. Typically,
P : despite the overwhelming evidence of the negative role
Q : or for the destruction of natural habitats,
R : played by commercial logging and mining interest
S : it is local communities who are blamed for deforestation

Which one of the following is the correct sequence?

A. P R S Q B. S Q P R
C. P Q S R D. S R P Q
E. R Q P S

66. If the idyllic
P : and rehabilitation work being carried out across several nations,
Q : only a cursory mention in the massive restoration
R : island of Car Nicobar has found
S : part of the reason could be inaccessibility of these islands

Which one of the following is the correct sequence?

A. R Q P S B. S P Q R
C. R P Q S D. S Q P R
E. P Q R S

67. The real founder
P : and Humayun's son Akbar, the greatest ruler
Q : of the Mughal Empire was Babur's grandson
R : Ashoka a millennium and half earlier
S : to sit on an Indian throne after

Which one of the following is the correct sequence?

A. S P Q R B. Q R S P
C. S R Q P D. Q P S R
E. P Q R S

68. In the neighbourhood
P : of the equator there is little need of clothes of fire,
Q : stretched out on the bare ground beneath the shade of a tree
R : and no danger to health, to pass the livelong day
S : and it is possible with perfect comfort

Which one of the following is the correct sequence?

A. P R S Q B. Q S R P
C. P S R Q D. Q R S P
E. P Q R S

69. Hospitality
P : to commendation on this account
Q : is a virtue for which the natives of the east
R : and the people of Egypt are well entitled
S : in general are highly and deservedly admired;

Which one of the following is the correct sequence?

A. Q S R P B. P R S Q
C. Q R S P D. P S R Q
E. P Q R S

70. It is possible
P : between Finland and Sweden, which was an international accord
Q : to find a solution to the Kashmir issue
R : settling a territorial dispute on the basis of *status quo*
S : on the lines of the agreement on the Aland Islands

Which one of the following is the correct sequence?

A. Q R P S B. P S Q R
C. Q S P R D. P R Q S
E. S R P Q

71. Once an
P : Shanghai has metamorphosed into
Q : in China's economic development strategy
R : a major international city which is a key element
S : obscure fishing town,

Which one of the following is the correct sequence?

A. R P S Q B. S Q R P
C. R Q S P D. S P R Q
E. Q P R S

72. When factors
P : to the growth of biotechnology come together,
Q : it heralds the arrival of a new venture
R : and a government that is dedicated

S : like rich biodiversity, a conducive climate, a network of established research institutes, educated and skilled manpower.

Which one of the following is the correct sequence?

A. Q P R S B. S R P Q
C. Q R P S D. S P R Q
E. P Q R S

73. Brazil's Guaranis

P : from being Internet savvy
Q : are an ancient tribe who live in the country's remote jungles,
R : excluded them
S : but that has not.

The proper sequence should be:

A. P S R Q B. Q R S P
C. P R S Q D. Q S R P
E. P Q R S

74. A game host

P : that could be used at the airport duty-free shops
Q : and the winner walked away with
R : shot out ten witty questions
S : vouchers worth 200 Singapore dollars.

The proper sequence should be:

A. P S Q R B. R Q S P
C. P Q S R D. R S Q P
E. P Q R S

75. And while

P : without adequate international support
Q : the US military has been forced into remaining in Iraq
R : the overthrow of Saddam Hussein may have been quick,
S : longer than anticipated.

The proper sequence should be:

A. R S Q P B. P Q S R
C. R Q S P D. P S Q R
E. P Q R S

ANSWERS

1	2	3	4	5	6	7	8	9	10
B	D	A	B	C	C	A	C	A	D
11	**12**	**13**	**14**	**15**	**16**	**17**	**18**	**19**	**20**
C	A	C	D	B	D	C	B	B	D
21	**22**	**23**	**24**	**25**	**26**	**27**	**28**	**29**	**30**
B	D	C	C	B	D	B	C	A	B
31	**32**	**33**	**34**	**35**	**36**	**37**	**38**	**39**	**40**
B	D	B	B	C	C	C	A	B	D
41	**42**	**43**	**44**	**45**	**46**	**47**	**48**	**49**	**50**
A	B	A	C	B	C	B	A	B	A
51	**52**	**53**	**54**	**55**	**56**	**57**	**58**	**59**	**60**
D	B	C	C	D	D	C	B	D	A
61	**62**	**63**	**64**	**65**	**66**	**67**	**68**	**69**	**70**
D	B	C	A	B	A	D	C	A	C
71	**72**	**73**	**74**	**75**					
D	B	D	B	C					

□□□

Quantitative, Data Interpretation & Data Sufficiency

1

Simplification

BODMAS-RULE

This rule is very important for the arithmetical simplification. When vinculum, bracket, of, division, multiplication, addition, subtraction all or two or more than two operations are present in any question, then we can find out the result (answer) with the help of BODMAS - Rule. Details of BODMAS-Rule is given below :

Order	Abbreviated Letter Used in rule	Meaning	Notation
1.	V	Vinculum or Bar	——
2.	B	Brackets	[ ], { }, ( )
3.	O	Of	of
4.	D	Division	÷
5.	M	Multiplication	×
6.	A	Addition	+
7.	S	Subtraction	–

Note :

(*i*) Order of the letter which is used in BODMAS Rule is always fixed.

(*ii*) Absence of any operation or more than one operations does not changes the order of BODMAS.

(*iii*) 'of' means multiplication.

BRACKETS

When all brackets are present in a question, in that condition **ViCiCuSq-Rule** is applied. This ViCiCuSq-Rule stands for brackets and represents the order of calculation of brackets. Details are given below :

Order	Abbreviated Letter Used in rule	Meaning	Notation
1.	Vi	Vinculum	——
2.	Ci	Circular Bracket	( )
3.	Cu	Curly Bracket	{ }
4.	Sq	Square Bracket	[ ]

Note : This order of brackets (ViCiCuSq) is also fixed and not variable.

SOLVED EXAMPLES

Example 1: $\frac{3}{5}$ of $\frac{5}{7}$ of 357 = ?

A. 51 B. 153

C. 255 D. 159

Solution: $357\times\frac{5}{7}\times\frac{3}{5}=153$

Example 2: 125% of 860 + 75% of 480 = ?

A. 1415 B. 1385

C. 1435 D. 1365

Solution: $\frac{860\times125}{100}+\frac{480\times75}{100}$

= 1075 + 360

= 1435

Example 3: 1121.21 + 121.021 + 21.0021 = ?

A. 1263.2331

B. 1263.2121

C. 1163.2121

D. 1163.2331

Solution: 1121.21 + 121.021 + 21.0021

= 1263.2331

Example 4: $\left(\sqrt{5}-\sqrt{6}\right)^2+\left(\sqrt{3}+\sqrt{10}\right)^2=(?)^3-40$

A. 8 B. 4

C. 3 D. 6

Solution: Let ? = x

$\therefore \left(\sqrt{5}-\sqrt{6}\right)^2+\left(\sqrt{3}+\sqrt{10}\right)^2=(x)^3-40$

$\Rightarrow 5+6-2\sqrt{30}+3+10+2\sqrt{30}=x^3-40$

$\Rightarrow 24=x^3-40$

$\Rightarrow x^3=40+24$

$=64=4^3$

$\Rightarrow x=4$

MULTIPLE CHOICE QUESTIONS

1. 68% of $\sqrt{2916} \times 25 = ? + 189$

A. 728 B. 718
C. 729 D. 739

2. $\sqrt{5^2 \times 41 \times 5 - 17^2 - 75} = ?$

A. 69 B. 61
C. 71 D. 79

3. 8.88 × 88.8 × 88 = ?

A. 68301.142 B. 79391.642
C. 65365.824 D. None of these

4. $\dfrac{9 \div 2 \times 27 \div 9}{18 \div 7.5 \times 5 \div 4} = ?$

A. 4.5 B. 5.7
C. 2.5 D. 6.8

5. $\sqrt{\sqrt{2500} + \sqrt{961}} = (?)^2$

A. 81 B. 3
C. 6561 D. 9

6. $64^{12} \div 4^{15} = 64^?$

A. 9 B. 3
C. 12 D. 7

7. $\sqrt{97344} = ?$

A. 302 B. 322
C. 292 D. None of these

8. 14% of 255 + ?% of 405 = 124.8

A. 22 B. 24
C. 18 D. 15

9. 19.25 × 16.4 × ? = 3472.7

A. 15 B. 17
C. 12 D. None of these

10. 83.04 – 66.46 – 11.71 = ?

A. 5.63 B. 2.92
C. 3.87 D. None of these

11. $\sqrt{529} + 46 \times 7.4 + (8)^3 - 251 = ?$

A. 265.1 B. 246.1
C. 256.4 D. None of these

12. $(16 \times 4)^3 \div (4)^5 \times (2 \times 8)^2 = (4)^?$

A. 5 B. 6
C. 3 D. 8

13. 534.58 – 386.89 + 221.45 – 195.42 = ?

A. 162.65 B. 109.65
C. 173.72 D. None of these

14. $\sqrt{5625} \times \dfrac{3}{5} + (85)^2 = ?$

A. 7270 B. 7280
C. 7260 D. 7250

15. $(7)^3 \times (3)^3 \div (6)^2 = ?$

A. 12348 B. 85.75
C. 1543.5 D. 257.25

16. $\dfrac{17^{6.87}}{17^{4.23}} = 17^{(?)}$

A. 1.62 B. 2.64
C. 11.1 D. 29.06

17. $\sqrt{2401} \times \sqrt{3249} = ?$

A. 2793 B. 2842
C. 2679 D. 2891

18. (5967 – 2437 – 1910) ÷ ? = 27

A. 60 B. 50
C. 65 D. 45

19. $\sqrt[3]{12167} \times \sqrt{?} = 621$

A. 841 B. 27
C. 625 D. None of these

20. 4.5% of 800 ÷ 0.5% of 640 = ?

A. 11.75 B. 12
C. 112.05 D. 11.25

21. 383 ÷ 25 × 2.5 + 12 = ?

A. 50.30 B. 222.14
C. 68.30 D. 124.24

22. 5083 + 25% of ? + 289 = 6385.5

A. 4044 B. 4054
C. 4154 D. 4104

23. $0.2 \times 10^{-2} = ?$

A. 2 B. 0.02
C. 0.002 D. 0.0002

24. 15 – 10 + 5 × 2 ÷ 5 = ?

A. 70 B. 4
C. 5 D. None of these

25. 37% of 150 – 0.05% of 1000 = ?

A. 50 B. 55
C. 55.5 D. 55.55

26. $(15)^{98} \times (15)^{-95} = ?$

A. 3375 B. 225
C. 45 D. 75

27. $\sqrt[3]{?} = (36 \times 24) \div 9$

A. 884736 B. 804036
C. 854734 D. 814736

28. (43% of 2750) – (38% of 2990) = ?

A. 49.3 B. 44.7
C. 43.6 D. 46.3

29. $40 \times 2 \div 10 + 5 - 4 = ?$

A. 5 B. 8
C. 11 D. 9

30. $28 \times 104 \div (18 + 6) + 3 = ?$

A. $124\frac{1}{3}$ B. $104\frac{1}{3}$
C. $125\frac{1}{3}$ D. 128

31. $0.99 \times 14 \div 11 \div 0.7 = ?$

A. 2.9 B. 1.6
C. 1.8 D. 2.8

32. $8\frac{1}{3}+5\frac{1}{4}\times 13\frac{1}{5} \div 6\frac{3}{5} = ?$

A. $19\frac{1}{3}$ B. $18\frac{1}{2}$
C. $21\frac{1}{3}$ D. None of these

33. $\frac{14}{3}$ of $\frac{5}{8}$ of $72 = ?$

A. 209 B. 217
C. 210 D. 199

34. $10 \times 10 \times 10 \div (20 \div 10 \times 10 - 10) + 6 = ?$

A. 108 B. 111
C. 106 D. 114

35. $\dfrac{\frac{1}{3}\times 20 \div 4}{\frac{1}{4}\times 25 \div 5} = ?$

A. $\frac{7}{3}$ B. $\frac{4}{3}$
C. $\frac{5}{3}$ D. $\frac{10}{3}$

36. $\dfrac{2.70\times 2.70+4.30\times 4.30+8.60\times 2.70}{2.70+4.30} - ?$

A. 6.8 B. 7.0
C. 7.6 D. 8.5

37. $1150 \div 50 \div 23 + 15 = ?$

A. 16 B. 20
C. 22 D. 18

38. $\dfrac{(0.08)^3+(0.011)^3}{(0.08)^2-0.08\times 0.011+(0.011)^2} = ?$

A. 0.087 B. 0.091
C. 0.077 D. 0.067

39. $22 \div \left[(28-13)\div\{(32-8)\div\left(5+\frac{1}{3}\right)\}\right] = ?$

A. 7.9 B. 6.8
C. 6.6 D. 5.7

40. $\dfrac{\left(20^2-10^2\right)\div 5\times 3+10}{\frac{1}{3}\text{ of } 27+10\div 2+1} = ?$

A. $10\frac{2}{3}$ B. $14\frac{1}{3}$
C. 15 D. $12\frac{2}{3}$

41. $11^2 - 6^2 \div 6 \times \frac{5}{2} = 2$ of $10 = ?$

A. 126 B. 108
C. 110 D. 125

42. $\frac{25}{3}-\frac{4}{7}$ of $\frac{7}{5}+\frac{11}{3}\div\frac{2}{3}-4 = ?$

A. $8\frac{1}{15}$ B. $9\frac{1}{30}$
C. $7\frac{1}{30}$ D. $9\frac{1}{5}$

43. $35 \times 0.07 - 21 \times 0.03 = ?$

A. 2.75 B. 1.72
C. 1.82 D. 2.13

44. $60 \times [35 - \{25 - (18 - \overline{9-3}) \div 11\}] = ?$

A. $566\frac{5}{7}$ B. $665\frac{5}{11}$
C. $665\frac{8}{11}$ D. $765\frac{5}{11}$

45. $\dfrac{140-44\times 9\div 3}{\frac{1}{2}\text{ of } 18\div 9+2} = ?$

A. $2\frac{2}{3}$ B. $3\frac{1}{3}$
C. $4\frac{2}{3}$ D. $6\frac{4}{5}$

46. $4\frac{1}{3}\times 5\frac{1}{3}\div 6\frac{1}{3}\div\frac{1}{3}+5\frac{1}{3}-2\frac{1}{3} = ?$

A. $14\frac{14}{19}$ B. $13\frac{19}{21}$
C. $13\frac{18}{19}$ D. $17\frac{8}{11}$

47. $1+\dfrac{1}{1+\dfrac{1}{1+\frac{1}{3}}} = ?$

A. $1\frac{4}{7}$ B. $2\frac{4}{7}$
C. $3\frac{4}{7}$ D. $4\frac{4}{7}$

48. $3 - [9 + \{14 - (6 - \overline{3-21})\}] = ?$

A. 0 B. 4
C. 18 D. 6

49. (8 ÷ 88) × 8888088 = ?
A. 8008008 B. 808088
C. 808080 D. 808008

50. 1260 ÷ 15 ÷ 7 = ?
A. 588 B. 122
C. 58 D. 12

51. 2 – [2 – {2 – 2(2 + 2)}] = ?
A. 6 B. – 6
C. 4 D. – 4

52. 100 × 10 – 100 + 2000 ÷ 100 = ?
A. 979 B. 920
C. 780 D. 29

53. 3640 ÷ 14 × 16 + 340 = ?
A. 3500 B. 4500
C. 3525 D. 4480

54. 25 – 5 [2 + 3 {2 – 2 (5 – 3) + 5} –10] ÷ 4 = ?
A. 5 B. 25
C. 23.25 D. 23.75

55. $(-5)\ (4)\ (2)\left(-\frac{1}{2}\right)\left(\frac{3}{4}\right) = ?$
A. 15 B. –15
C. 30 D. –30

ANSWERS

1	2	3	4	5	6	7	8	9	10
C	A	D	A	B	D	D	A	D	D
11	**12**	**13**	**14**	**15**	**16**	**17**	**18**	**19**	**20**
D	D	D	A	D	B	A	A	D	D
21	**22**	**23**	**24**	**25**	**26**	**27**	**28**	**29**	**30**
A	B	C	D	B	A	A	D	D	A
31	**32**	**33**	**34**	**35**	**36**	**37**	**38**	**39**	**40**
C	D	C	C	B	B	A	B	C	D
41	**42**	**43**	**44**	**45**	**46**	**47**	**48**	**49**	**50**
A	B	C	B	A	C	A	B	D	D
51	**52**	**53**	**54**	**55**					
B	B	B	D	A					

SOME SELECTED EXPLANATORY ANSWERS

1. $\sqrt{2916} \times 68\% \times 25 = ? + 189$

$\Rightarrow 54 \times \frac{68}{100} \times 25 = ? + 189$

$\Rightarrow 918 = ? + 189$

$\Rightarrow ? = 918 - 189 = 729$

2. $? = \sqrt{25 \times 41 \times 5 - 17^2 - 75}$

$= \sqrt{5125 - 289 - 75} = \sqrt{4761} = 69$

3. 8.88 × 88.8 × 88 = 69391.872

4. $\frac{9 \div 2 \times 27 \div 9}{18 \div 7.5 \times 5 \div 4} = \frac{\frac{9}{2} \times \frac{27}{9}}{\frac{18}{7.5} \times \frac{5}{4}} = \frac{\frac{27}{2}}{3} = 4.5$

5. $\sqrt{\sqrt{2500 + 961}}$

$= \sqrt{\sqrt{50 + 31}} = \sqrt{9} = \sqrt{(3)^2} = 3.$

6. Let $(64)^x = 64^{12} \div 4^{15}$

$\Rightarrow 4^{3x} = 4^{36-15} = 4^{21}$

$\therefore 3x = 21 \quad \therefore x = 7$

7. $\sqrt{97344} = 312$

8. $\because$ 14% of 255 + ?% of 405 = 124.8

$\Rightarrow 35.7 + 405 \times ? = 124.8$

$\Rightarrow \frac{405 \times ?}{100} = 124.8 - 35.7 = 89.1$

$\therefore ? = \frac{98.1 \times 100}{405} = \frac{891 \times 10}{405}$

$= \frac{891 \times 2}{81} = \frac{1782}{81} = 22.$

9. $\because$ 19.25 × 16.4 × ? = 3472.7

$\therefore ? = \frac{3472.7}{19.25 \times 16.4} = 11$

10. 83.04 – 66.46 – 11.71 = 4.87

11. $\sqrt{529} \div 46 \times 7.4 + (8)^3 - 251$

$= \frac{23}{46} \times 7.4 + 512 - 251$

$= 3.7 + 512 - 251 = 264.7$

12. $(4)^? = (16 \times 4)^3 \div (4)^5 \times (2 \times 8)^2$

$(4)^? = \frac{(4)^9}{(4)^5} \times (4)^4 = (4)^{9+4-5}$

$\therefore \quad ? = 8.$

13. $534.58 - 386.89 + 221.45 - 195.42 = 172.72$

14. $\sqrt{5625} \times \frac{3}{5} + (85)^2 = 75 \times \frac{3}{5} + 7225 = 7270$

15. $343 \times 27 \div 36 = 257.25$

16. $17^{(?)} = \frac{17^{6.87}}{17^{4.23}} = 17^{6.87-4.23} = 17^{2.64}$

$\therefore \ ? = 2.64.$

17. $\sqrt{2401} \times \sqrt{3249} = 49 \times 57 = 2793.$

18. $(5967 - 2437 - 1910) \div ? = 27$

$\therefore \quad \frac{1620}{?} = 27$

$\therefore \quad ? = \frac{1620}{27} = 60$

19. $\because \sqrt[3]{12167} \times \sqrt{?} = 621$

$\Rightarrow \quad 23 \times \sqrt{?} = 621$

$\Rightarrow \quad \sqrt{?} = \frac{621}{23} = 27$

$\therefore \quad ? = (27)^2 = 729$

20. $\frac{4.5}{100}$ of $800 \div \frac{0.5}{100}$ of 640

$= 36 \div 3.2 = 11.25$

21. $383 \div 25 \times 2.5 + 12$

$= \frac{383}{25} \times 2.5 + 12 = 50.30.$

22. $\because 5083 + \frac{25}{100}$ of $? + 289 = 6385.5$

$\Rightarrow \ 0.25 \times ? = 6385.5 - 5083 - 289$

$\therefore \quad ? = \frac{1013.5}{0.25} = 4054.$

23. $0.2 \times 10^{-2} = 0.2 \times \frac{1}{100} = 0.002$

24. $15 - 10 + 5 \times 2 \div 5$

$= 15 - 10 + \frac{5 \times 2}{5} = 15 - 10 + 2 = 7$

25. 37% of $150 - 0.05\%$ of 1000

$= \frac{37}{100}$ of $150 - \frac{0.05}{100}$ of 1000

$= \frac{111}{2} - 0.5 = 55.5 - 0.5 = 55.$

26. $(15)^{98} \times (15)^{-95} = (15)^3 = 3375$

27. $(36 \times 24) \div 9 = \sqrt[3]{?}$

$\Rightarrow \ 4 \times 24 = \sqrt[3]{?}$

$\therefore \ ? = 96^3 = 884736$

28. $(43\%$ of $2750) - (38\%$ of $2990)$

$= 0.43 \times 2750 - 0.38 \times 2990 = 46.3$

29. $\because \ 40 \times 2 \div 10 + 5 - 4 = 40 \times \frac{2}{10} + 5 - 4$

$= 8 + 5 - 4 = 9$

30. $\because \ 28 \times 104 \div (18 + 6) + 3$

$= 28 \times 104 \div 24 + 3$

$= 28 \times \frac{104}{24} + 3 = 28 \times \frac{13}{3} + 3$

$= \frac{364}{3} + 3 = \frac{373}{3} = 124\frac{1}{3}$

31. $\because \ 0.99 \times 14 \div 11 \div 0.7$

$= 0.99 \times \frac{14}{11} \div 0.7 = \frac{0.99 \times 14}{11 \times 0.7} = 1.8$

32. $\because \ 8\frac{1}{3} + 5\frac{1}{4} \times 13\frac{1}{5} \div 6\frac{3}{5}$

$= \frac{25}{3} + \frac{21}{4} \times \frac{66}{5} \div \frac{33}{5} = \frac{25}{3} + \frac{21}{4} \times \frac{66}{5} \times \frac{5}{33}$

$= \frac{25}{3} + \frac{21}{2} = \frac{50+63}{6} = \frac{113}{6} = 18\frac{5}{6}$

33. $\because \ \frac{14}{3}$ of $\frac{5}{8}$ of $72 = \frac{14 \times 5 \times 72}{3 \times 8} = 210$

34. $10 \times 10 \times 10 \div (20 \div 10 \times 10 - 10) + 6$

$= 10 \times 10 \times 10 \div \left(\frac{20}{10} \times 10 - 10\right) + 6$

$= 10 \times 10 \times 10 \div (20 - 10) + 6$

$= 10 \times 10 \times 10 \div 10 + 6 = 10 \times 10 \times \frac{10}{10} + 6$

$= 10 \times 10 \times 1 + 6 = 100 + 6 = 106$

35. $\because \ \frac{\frac{1}{3} \times 20 \div 4}{\frac{1}{4} \times 25 \div 5} = \frac{\frac{1}{3} \times 5}{\frac{1}{4} \times 5} = \frac{\frac{5}{3}}{\frac{5}{4}} = \frac{4}{3}$

36. $\frac{2.70 \times 2.70 + 4.30 \times 4.30 + 8.60 \times 2.70}{2.70 + 4.30}$

$= \frac{(2.70)^2 + (4.30)^2 + 2 \times 4.30 \times 2.70}{2.70 + 4.30} = \frac{(2.70 + 4.30)^2}{2.70 + 4.30}$

$[\because a^2 + b^2 + 2ab = (a + b)^2]$

$= 2.70 + 4.30 = 7.00$

37. $1150 \div 50 \div 23 + 15 = \frac{1150}{50} \div 23 + 15$

$= 23 \div 23 + 15 = \frac{23}{23} + 15 = 1 + 15 = 16.$

38. $\frac{(0.08)^3 + (0.011)^3}{(0.08)^2 - 0.08 \times 0.011 + (0.011)^2}$

$\frac{(0.08 + 0.011)\left[(0.08)^2 - 0.08 \times 0.011 + (0.011)^2\right]}{(0.08)^2 - 0.08 \times 0.011 + (0.011)^2}$ $[\because a^3 + b^3 = (a + b)(a^2 - ab + b^2)]$

$= 0.08 + 0.011 = 0.091.$

39. $22 \div \left[(28-13)\div\left\{(32-8)\div\left(5+\frac{1}{3}\right)\right\}\right]$

$= 22\div\left[15\div\left\{24\div\frac{16}{3}\right\}\right]$

$= 22\div\left[15\div\frac{24}{\frac{16}{3}}\right] = 22\div\left[15\div\frac{9}{2}\right]$

$= 22\div\frac{15}{\frac{9}{2}} = 22\div\frac{10}{3} = \frac{22\times3}{10} = 6.6$

40. $\frac{\left(20^2-10^2\right)\div5\times3+10}{\frac{1}{3}\text{ of }27+10\div2+1}$

$= \frac{(400-100)\div5\times3+10}{9+10\div2+1} = \frac{300\div5\times3+10}{9+5+1}$

$= \frac{60\times3+10}{15} = \frac{190}{15} = \frac{38}{3} = 12\frac{2}{3}$

41. $1^2 - 6^2 \div 6 \times \frac{5}{2} + 2$ of 10

$= 11^2 - 6^2 \div 6 \times \frac{5}{2} + 20$

$= 11^2 - 6\times\frac{5}{2} + 20 = 11^2 - 15 + 20$

$= 121 + 5 = 126.$

42. $\frac{25}{3} - \frac{4}{7}\text{of}\frac{7}{5} + \frac{11}{3}\div\frac{2}{3} - 4$

$= \frac{25}{3} - \frac{4}{5} + \frac{11}{3}\div\frac{2}{3} - 4 = \frac{25}{3} - \frac{4}{5} + \frac{11}{2} - 4$

$= \frac{83}{6} - \frac{24}{5} = \frac{415-144}{30} = \frac{271}{30} = 9\frac{1}{30}$

43. $35 \times 0.07 - 21 \times 0.03 = 2.45 - 0.63 = 1.82$

44. $60 \times [35 - \{25 - (18 - \overline{9-3}) \div 11\}]$
$= 60 \times [35 - \{25 - (18-6) \div 11\}$
$= 60 \times [35 - \{25 - 12 \div 11\}]$

$= 60\times\left[35-\left\{25-\frac{12}{11}\right\}\right] = 60\times\left[35-\frac{263}{11}\right]$

$= 60\times\frac{122}{11} = 665\frac{5}{11}$

45. $\frac{140-44\times9\div3}{\frac{1}{2}\text{ of }18\div9+2} = \frac{140-44\times3}{9\div9+2}$

$= \frac{140-132}{1+2} = \frac{8}{3} = 2\frac{2}{3}$

46. $4\frac{1}{3}\times5\frac{1}{3}\div6\frac{1}{3}\div\frac{1}{3}+5\frac{1}{3}-2\frac{1}{3}$

$= \frac{13}{3}\times\frac{16}{3}\div\frac{19}{3}\div\frac{1}{3}+\frac{16}{3}-\frac{7}{3}$

$= \frac{13}{3}\times\frac{16}{19}\div\frac{1}{3}+\frac{16}{3}-\frac{7}{3}$

$= \frac{13}{3}\times\frac{48}{19}+\frac{16}{3}-\frac{7}{3} = \frac{208}{19}+\frac{16}{3}-\frac{7}{3}$

$= 10\frac{18}{19}+3 = 13\frac{18}{19}$

47. This type of questions is solved starting from the bottom.

$1+\frac{1}{1+\frac{1}{1+\frac{1}{3}}} = 1+\frac{1}{1+\frac{1}{\frac{4}{3}}}$

$= 1+\frac{1}{1+\frac{3}{4}} = 1+\frac{1}{\frac{7}{4}} = 1+\frac{4}{7} = \frac{11}{7} = 1\frac{4}{7}$

48. $3 - [9 + \{14 - (6 - \overline{3-21})\}]$
$= 3 - [9 + \{14 - (6 + 18\}]$
$= 3 - [9 + \{14 - 24\}] = 3 - [9 - 10]$
$= 3 + 1 = 4.$

49. $(8 \div 88) \times 888808 = \frac{8}{88}\times8888088 = 808008$

50. $1260 \div 15 \div 7 = 1260 \times \frac{1}{15}\times\frac{1}{7} = 12$

51. $2 - [2 - \{2 - 2(2 + 2)\}]$
$= 2 - [2 - \{2 - 8\}] = 2 - [2 + 6]$
$= 2 - 8 = -6$

52. $100 \times 10 - 100 + 2000 \div 100$
$= 100 \times 10 - 100 + 20$
$= 1000 - 100 + 20 = 920$

53. $3640 \div 14 \times 6 + 340$

$= 3640 \times \frac{1}{14} \times 16 + 340 = 4160 + 340 = 4500$

54. $25 - 5\ [2 + 3\ \{2 - 2\ (5 - 3) + 5\} - 10] \div 4$
$= 25 - 5\ [2 + 3\ \{2 - 4 + 5\} - 10] \div 4$
$= 25 - 5\ [2 + 9 - 10] \div 4$

$= 25 - 5\times1\times\frac{1}{4} = 25 - \frac{5}{4} = \frac{95}{4} = 23.75$

55. $(-5)\ (4)\ (2)\left(-\frac{1}{2}\right)\left(\frac{3}{4}\right)$

$= -5\times4\times2\times-\frac{1}{2}\times\frac{3}{4} = 15$

❋❋❋❋❋

2

L.C.M. & H.C.F.

LCM

Multiple : A number is said to be multiple of other when it is exactly divisible by the other.

Common multiple : A common multiple of two or more numbers is a number which is exactly divisible by each of them. For example, for 2 and 3, common multiples are 6, 12, 18, 24 and so on.

Explanation:

Consider the two numbers 2 and 3

Multiple of 2 are 2, 4, 6, 8, 10, 12, ...

Multiple of 3 are 3, 6, 9, 12, 15, ...

∴ Common multiples are 6, 12, 18, ...

Least Common Multiple (L.C.M.) : L.C.M. of two or more given numbers is the least number which is exactly divisible by each of them. For example,

6 is a common multiple of 2 and 3

12 is also common multiple of 2 and 3

18 is also common multiple of 2 and 3

But 6 is the least common multiple (L.C.M.) of 2 and 3.

Methods to find out L.C.M.

L.C.M. of two or more given numbers is determined by following two methods:

1. By prime factorization method
2. By division method

1. By prime factorization method : Resolve the given numbers into their prime factors and then find the product of the highest power of all the factors that occur in the given numbers. This product will be the L.C.M.

Example 1 : Find the L.C.M. of 40, 50, 60 and 80.

Sol :

$$40 = 2 \times 2 \times 2 \times 5 = 2^3 \times 5$$
$$50 = 2 \times 5 \times 5 = 2 \times 5^2$$
$$60 = 2 \times 2 \times 3 \times 5 = 2^2 \times 3 \times 5$$
$$80 = 2 \times 2 \times 2 \times 2 \times 5 = 2^4 \times 5$$

Here, the prime factors that occur in the given numbers are 2, 3 and 5 and their highest powers are respectively 2^4, 5^2 and 3.

Hence, the required L.C.M. $= 2^4 \times 3 \times 5^2 = 1200$.

2. By division method : This is the quicker method to find the prime factors and hence L.C.M.

For determining L.C.M. of the numbers 40, 50, 60 and 80, following process of division is adopted:

2	40, 50, 60, 80
2	20, 25, 30, 40
2	10, 25, 15, 20
5	5, 25, 15, 10
	1, 5, 3, 2

Now required L.C.M. $= 2 \times 2 \times 2 \times 5 \times 5 \times 3 \times 2 = 1200$

L.C.M. of decimal : First of all, we find out the L.C.M. of numbers without decimal and then, we see the number in which decimal is given in the minimum digit from right to left. We put the decimal in our result which is equal to that number of digits.

Example : Find the L.C.M. of 0.6, 9.6 and 0.36.

Sol : The given numbers are equivalent to 0.60, 9.60 and 0.36.

Now, we find out the L.C.M. of 60, 960 and 36, which is equal to 2880.

Hence, the required L.C.M. = 2880.

L.C.M. of fraction : The L.C.M. of two or more fractions is the least fraction or integer which is exactly divisible by each of them.

If $\frac{a}{b}, \frac{c}{d}, \frac{e}{f}$ be the proper fractions, then their L.C.M. is given by

$$\frac{\text{L.C.M. of numerators } a, c, e}{\text{H.C.F. of denominators } b, d, f}$$

An example : Find the L.C.M. of $\frac{1}{2}, \frac{3}{5}, \frac{4}{7}$ and $\frac{5}{12}$

Sol : $$\text{L.C.M.} = \frac{\text{L.C.M. of } 1, 3, 4, 5}{\text{H.C.F. of } 2, 5, 7, 12} = \frac{60}{1} = 60$$

HCF

Factor : One number is said to be a factor of other when it divides the other exactly. Hence, 5 and 7 are factors of 35.

Common factor : A common factor of two or more numbers is a number that divides each of them exactly. Hence, 5 is a common factor of 15, 25, 35 and 55.

Highest Common Factor (H.C.F.) : H.C.F. of two or more numbers is the largest number by which each given number is divisible without leaving any remainder.

An example : It is required to find the H.C.F. of 6 and 8.

Factors of 6 are 1, 2, 3, 6 and

Factors of 8 are 1, 2, 4, 8.

The common factors are 1, 2, but highest of these is 2. Hence, 2 is the H.C.F.

Note : *The terms Highest Common Divisor (H.C.D.) and Greatest Common Measure (G.C.M.) are often used in the sense of Highest Common Factor (H.C.F.)*

We can find H.C.F. by two methods:

1. By prime factorization method :

An example : Find the H.C.F. of 144, 336 and 2016.

Sol : $144 = 2 \times 2 \times 2 \times 2 \times 3 \times 3 = 2^4 \times 3^2$

$336 = 2 \times 2 \times 2 \times 2 \times 3 \times 7 = 2^4 \times 3 \times 7$

$2016 = 2 \times 2 \times 2 \times 2 \times 2 \times 7 \times 3 \times 3 = 2^5 \times 7 \times 3^2$

$\therefore$ H.C.F. of given numbers $= 2^4 \times 3 = 48$.

2. By division method : Divide the greater number by the smaller number, divide the divisor by the remainder, divide the remainder by the next remainder, and so on until no remainder is left. The last divisor is the required H.C.F.

An example : Find the H.C.F. of 48, 168 and 324.

Sol :

```
48 ) 168 ( 3
     144
     ----
      24 ) 48 ( 2
           48
           --
           ××
```

Thus, the H.C.F. of 48 and 168 is 24.

Now, we find out the H.C.F. of 24 and 324

```
24 ) 324 (13
     24
     ---
      84
      72
      ---
      12 ) 24 (2
           24
           --
           ××
```

$\therefore$ Required H.C.F. = 12.

H.C.F. of Decimals : First of all find the H.C.F. of the given numbers ignoring decimals and then put decimal at maximum digits from right to left.

An example : Find the H.C.F. of 0.0012, 1.6 and 2.8.

Sol : First we find the H.C.F. of 12, 16 and 28, which comes to 4.

So, H.C.F. of 0.0012, 1.6 and 2.8 will be 0.0004.

H.C.F. of Fractions : If $\frac{a}{b}, \frac{c}{d}, \frac{e}{f}, \ldots$ be the proper fraction, their H.C.F. is equal to $\frac{\text{H.C.F. of numerators}}{\text{L.C.M. of denominators}}$

An example : Find the H.C.F. of $\frac{54}{9}, 3\frac{9}{17}$ and $\frac{36}{51}$

Sol : Here, $\frac{54}{9} = \frac{6}{1}$; $3\frac{9}{17} = \frac{60}{17}$ and $\frac{36}{51} = \frac{12}{17}$

Hence, the fractions are $\frac{6}{1}, \frac{60}{17}$ and $\frac{12}{17}$

$\therefore$ H.C.F. $= \frac{\text{H.C.F. of } 6, 60, 12}{\text{L.C.M. of } 1, 17, 17} = \frac{6}{17}$.

Relationship Between Two Numbers and Their L.C.M. and H.C.F.

Product of the H.C.F. and the L.C.M. of two numbers is equal to the product of the given numbers.

i.e., 1st number × 2nd number = H.C.F. × L.C.M.

MULTIPLE CHOICE QUESTIONS

1. The largest three-digit number, when divided by 6, 9 and 12 leaves 1 as remainder in each case, will be

A. 887 B. 987
C. 973 D. 730

2. Two numbers are in the ratio of 8 : 15. If their H.C.F. is 4, the numbers are

A. 32 and 60 B. 16 and 30
C. 80 and 150 D. 64 and 120

3. The largest number that will divide 226 and 272 leaving 1 and 2 as remainders respectively, is

A. 36 B. 45
C. 55 D. 59

4. Which of the following is the greatest common divisor of 1170 and 102?

A. 8 B. 4
C. 6 D. 3

5. A number, when 3 is added to it, becomes divisible by 36, 45 and 50. The smallest such number is

A. 987 B. 798
C. 986 D. 897

6. The least perfect square number which is completely divisible by 10, 20, 30 and 40 is

A. 4800 B. 3600
C. 4400 D. 2500

7. The product of two numbers is 2160 and their H.C.F. is 12. How many such pairs of numbers can be possibly formed?

A. 3 B. 1
C. 2 D. None

8. The greatest number that will divide 366, 513 and 324 leaving the same remainder in each case is
A. 21 B. 18
C. 27 D. 42

9. The sum of two numbers is 216 and their H.C.F. is 27. These numbers are
A. 60 and 90 B. 81 and 135
C. 64 and 128 D. 30 and 84

10. The L.C.M. of two numbers is 45 times their H.C.F. If the sum of the L.C.M. and the H.C.F. of these two numbers is 1150 and one of the numbers is 125, then the other number is
A. 256 B. 225
C. 250 D. 255

11. The H.C.F. and the L.C.M. of two numbers are 50 and 250 respectively. On dividing one of these numbers by 2, 50 is obtained as quotient. The numbers are
A. 100, 125 B. 80, 100
C. 125, 100 D. 200, 250

12. The largest three-digit number, which when successively divided by 6, 9 and 12, leaves 3 as remainder in each case, is
A. 575 B. 795
C. 975 D. 525

13. The greatest number that will divide 33, 64 and 80 leaving 3, 4 and 5 as remainders respectively, is
A. 10 B. 20
C. 15 D. 22

14. The H.C.F. of three numbers is 12. If the three numbers are in the ratio of 1 : 2 : 3, then the numbers are
A. 14, 28, 42 B. 12, 24, 36
C. 15, 30, 45 D. 24, 48, 72

15. The greatest four-digit number completely divisible by 2, 3, 4 and 5 is
A. 9960 B. 9690
C. 8990 D. 9980

16. Three bells ring respectively at an interval of 15 seconds, 20 seconds and 24 seconds. If they ring continuously for 12 minutes then how many times, during this period, will they ring together?
A. 2 times B. 6 times
C. 5 times D. 3 times

17. The smallest number, on being successively divided by 5, 6, 8, 9 and 12 leaves 1 as remainder in each case and is completely divisible by 13, will be
A. 4603 B. 6305
C. 4503 D. 3601

18. If in the process of finding H.C.F. of two numbers by continued division method, 49 is the last divisor and quotients obtained (from the beginning) are 17, 3 and 2 respectively, then the numbers are
A. 432 and 4929 B. 343 and 5829
C. 388 and 5880 D. 472 and 5930

19. A, B and C start running together in a particular direction from a particular point on a 12 kms long circular path. If the speeds of A, B and C are 3 kms/h, 7 kms/h and 13 kms/h respectively, then after how many hours will they meet together again?
A. 8 B. 6
C. 12 D. 10

20. Which of the following has most numbers of divisors?
A. 182 B. 176
C. 101 D. 99

ANSWERS

1	2	3	4	5	6	7	8	9	10
C	A	B	C	D	D	C	A	B	B
11	**12**	**13**	**14**	**15**	**16**	**17**	**18**	**19**	**20**
A	C	C	B	A	B	D	B	C	B

SOME SELECTED EXPLANATORY ANSWERS

1. L.C.M. of 6, 9 and 12

3	6, 9, 12
2	2, 3, 4
	1, 3, 2

$\therefore$ LCM = 3 × 2 × 3 × 2 = 36.

$\because$ Largest 3-digit number = 999

36) 999 (27
72
279
252
× 27

$\therefore$ Largest 3-digit number which is exactly divisible by 6, 9 and 12

= 999 – 27 = 972

$\therefore$ The required number = 972 + 1 = 973

2. Let the numbers be $8x$ and $15x$

$8x = 2 \times 2 \times 2 \times x$

$15x = 3 \times 5 \times x$

$\therefore$ LCM of $8x$ and $15x = 2 \times 2 \times 2 \times x \times 3 \times 5$

$= 120x$

Now, 1st number × 2nd number = HCF × LCM

$\Rightarrow \quad 8x \times 15x = 4 \times 120x$

$\Rightarrow \quad 120x^2 = 4 \times 120x$

$\Rightarrow \quad x = 4$

$\therefore$ Numbers are $8 \times 4 = 32$ and $15 \times 4 = 60$

3. $226 - 1 = 225$ and $272 - 2 = 270$

Now, HCF of 225 and 270

```
225 ) 270 ( 1
      225
      ---
       45 ) 225 ( 5
            225
            ---
             ×
```

$\therefore$ The required number is 45.

4. $1170 = 2 \times 5 \times 3 \times 3 \times 13$

$102 = 2 \times 3 \times 17$

$\therefore$ Greatest common divisor $= 2 \times 3 = 6$

5. It is clear from the given conditions of the problem that the smallest number will be 3 less than the LCM of 36, 45 and 50.

$\therefore$ LCM of 36, 45 and 50

3	36, 45, 50
2	12, 15, 50
3	6, 15, 25
5	2, 5, 25
	2, 1, 5

$\therefore$ LCM $= 3 \times 2 \times 3 \times 5 \times 2 \times 5 = 900$

$\therefore$ Required number $= 900 - 3 = 897$.

6. LCM of 10, 20, 30 and 40

2	10, 20, 30, 40
5	5, 10, 15, 20
2	1, 2, 3, 4
	1, 1, 3, 2

$\therefore$ LCM $= 2 \times 2 \times 5 \times 3 \times 2$

But the number is a perfect square number

$\therefore$ Required number $= 2 \times 2 \times 5 \times 5 \times 3 \times 3 \times 2 \times 2 = 3600$.

7. Product of two numbers = their HCF × their LCM

$2160 = 12 \times \text{LCM}$

$\therefore \quad \text{LCM} = \frac{2160}{12} = 180$

Therefore such pairs of numbers in which product of numbers is 2160 and HCF is 12 will be only 2.

i.e., 12×180 and 36×60.

8. Difference between 366 and 513

$= 513 - 366 = 147$

and difference between 513 and 324

$= 513 - 324 = 189$

$\therefore$ HCF of 147 and 189

```
147 ) 189 ( 1
      147
      ---
      × 42 ) 147 ( 3
             126
             ---
             × 21 ) 42 ( 2
                    42
                    --
                     ×
```

$\therefore$ The required largest number is 21.

9. Let the numbers be x and y.

$\therefore x + y = 216 = 27 \times 8$

Since HCF of these two numbers is 27, hence, common factor of these two numbers is 27.

Therefore these numbers will be of the form of 27×1, 27×2, 27×3, ... etc.

According to the condition of the problem sum of these numbers is 216.

$\therefore$ The numbers will be $27 \times 3 = 81$

and $\quad 27 \times 5 = 135$

10. LCM of the two numbers $= 45 \times \text{HCF}$

and $\quad \text{LCM} + \text{HCF} = 1150$

$\Rightarrow \quad 45 \times \text{HCF} + \text{HCF} = 1150$

$\Rightarrow \quad \text{HCF}(45 + 1) = 1150$

$\Rightarrow \quad \text{HCF} = \frac{1150}{46} = 25$

$\therefore \quad \text{LCM} = 45 \times 25 = 1125$

$\because$ 1st number × 2nd number = LCM × HCF

$\therefore$ 125 × 2nd number $= 1125 \times 25$

$\therefore \quad \text{2nd number} = \frac{1125 \times 25}{125} = 225.$

11. According to the condition of the problem, 50 is obtained on dividing one of the numbers by 2

$\therefore$ One of the numbers $= 50 \times 2 = 100$

Now, 1st number × 2nd number = LCM × HCF

$\therefore \quad 100 \times \text{2nd number} = 250 \times 50$

$\therefore \quad \text{2nd number} = \frac{250 \times 50}{100} = 125$

Hence, numbers are 100 and 125.

12. LCM of 6, 9 and 12 = 36 and largest 3-digit number = 999

$\therefore$ HCF of 36 and 999

```
36 ) 999 ( 27
     72
     ---
     279
     252
     ---
      27
```

$\therefore$ Largest three-digit number completely divisible by 6, 9 and 12

$= 999 - 27 = 972$

Since 3 is left as remainder in each case,

$\therefore$ Required largest number of 3-digit

$= 972 + 3 = 975$.

13. $33 - 3 = 30$, $64 - 4 = 60$ and $80 - 5 = 75$

Now, HCF of 30, 60 and 75:

$30 = 2 \times \underline{3 \times 5}$

$60 = 2 \times 2 \times \underline{3 \times 5}$

$75 = \underline{3 \times 5} \times 5$

$\because \quad$ Common factor $= 3 \times 5 = 15$

$\therefore$ Required largest number = 15.

14. Let the numbers be x, $2x$ and $3x$ respectively. Here, HCF of the three numbers is 12, therefore 12 is the largest common factor of these three numbers. Thus, it is clear that $x = 12$

$\therefore$ These numbers are 12, 24 and 36 respectively.

15. LCM of 2, 3, 4 and 5 = 60

Largest 4-digit number = 9999

Now, 60) 9999 (166
60
399
360
× 399
360
39

$\therefore$ Largest 4-digit number completely divisible by 2, 3, 4 and 5

$= 9999 - 39 = 9960$

$\therefore$ Required number = 9960

16. LCM of 15, 20 and 24

5	15, 20, 24
4	3, 4, 24
3	3, 1, 6
	1, 1, 2

LCM = 5 × 4 × 3 × 2 = 120

$\because$ 12 minutes = 12 × 60 = 720 seconds

$\therefore$ Number of times the bells will ring together during 12 minutes

$$= \frac{720}{120} = 6 \text{ times.}$$

17. LCM of 5, 6, 8, 9 and 12 = 360. Hence, the smallest number which when divided by 5, 6, 8, 9 and 12 leaves 1 as remainder in each case will be 360 + 1 = 361. But 361 is not completely divisible by 13. Hence, on considering 360 × 2 + 1, 360 × 3 + 1,... , 360 × n + 1, we conclude that 360 × 10 + 1 = 3601 is the required number.

18. This question is based on finding HCF by continued division method. Now according to the condition of the problem,

Last divisor = 49

and Last quotient = 2

$\therefore$ dividend = 49 × 2 = 98

Now, divisor = 98 and quotient = 3

and remainder = 49

$\therefore$ dividend = 98 × 3 + 49 = 343

Now, divisor = 343

quotient = 17

and remainder = 98

$\therefore$ Dividend = 343 × 17 + 98 = 5829

Therefore, these numbers are 343 and 5829.

19. A, B and C will take 4 hours, $\frac{12}{7}$ hours and $\frac{12}{13}$ hours respectively in completing one round on the circular path.

$\therefore$ LCM of $\frac{4}{1}, \frac{12}{7}$ and $\frac{12}{13}$

$$= \frac{\text{LCM of 4,12 and 12}}{\text{HCF of 1,7 and 13}}$$

$\because$ LCM of 4, 12 and 12= 12 and HCF of 1, 7 and 13 = 1

$\therefore$ Required LCM = $\frac{12}{1} = 12$

Hence, they will meet together again after 12 hrs.

20.

Numbers	***Their divisors***
182 →	1, 2, 7, 13, 14, 26, 91 and 182
176 →	1, 2, 4, 8, 16, 22, 44, 88 and 176
101 →	1 and 101
99 →	1, 3, 9, 11, 33 and 99

Therefore, 176 has the most number of divisors.

*****

3

Ratio & Proportion

Some Important Facts:

1. If a and b are two quantities, then
   (*a*) Duplicate ratio of $a : b = a^2 : b^2$
   (*b*) Sub-duplicate ratio of $a : b = \sqrt{a} : \sqrt{b}$
   (*c*) Triplicate ratio of $a : b = a^3 : b^3$
   (*d*) Sub-triplicate ratio $a : b = \sqrt[3]{a} : \sqrt[3]{b}$
   (*e*) Inverse or reciprocal ratio of $a : b = \frac{1}{a} : \frac{1}{b}$
2. If $a : b = c : d$, then
   (*a*) Third proportional (c) to 'a' and 'b' $= \frac{b^2}{a}$
   (*b*) Fourth proportional (d) $= \frac{bc}{a}$
   (*c*) Mean proportional between a and $b = \sqrt{ab}$
   (*d*) If $\frac{a}{b} = \frac{c}{d}$ then $\frac{a+b}{a-b} = \frac{c+d}{c-d}$
   (Componendo and dividendo)
3. (*a*) Comparision of ratios $(a : b) > (c : d) \Leftrightarrow \frac{a}{b} > \frac{c}{d}$
   (*b*) Compounded ratio of $(a : b)$, $(c : d)$, $(e : f) = \frac{ace}{bdf}$
4. If A : B = $x : y$ and B : C = $p : q$, then
   (*a*) $A : C = \frac{x \times p}{y \times q}$
   (*b*) $A : B : C = px : py : qy$
5. In what *ratio* the two kinds of tea must be mixed together one at ₹ x per kg and another at ₹ y per kg, so that the mixture may cost ₹ z per kg?
   $$\text{Ratio} = \frac{z-y}{x-z}$$
6. A grey hound persues a hare as takes J_1 leaps for every J_2 leaps of the hare. If K_1 leaps of the hound are equal to K_2 leaps of the hare, then the Ratio of speeds of the hound and hare is
   $$\frac{J_2 \times K_1}{J_1 \times K_2}$$
7. The incomes of two persons are in the ratio of $a : b$ and their expenditure are in the ratio of $x : y$. If the saving of each person is ₹ s, then income of each is ₹ $\frac{as(y-x)}{ay-bx}$ and ₹ $\frac{bs(y-x)}{ay-bx}$ respectively.
8. In a mixture of z litre, the ratio of milk and water is $x : y$. If another p litres of water is added to the mixture, the ratio of milk and water in the resulting mixture $= \frac{xz}{yz + p(x+y)}$
9. There are four members a, b, c and d, then formula for
   (*a*) What should be added to each of these numbers so that the remaining numbers may be proportional $= \frac{ad-bc}{(b+c)-(a+d)}$.
   (*b*) What should be subtracted from each of these numbers so that the remaining numbers may be proportional $= \frac{ad-bc}{(a+d)-(b+c)}$.
10. In a mixture the ratio of milk and water is $a : b$. If in this mixture another K litre of water is added, then the ratio of milk and water in the resulting mixture becomes $a : m$. Then the quantity of milk in the original mixture $= \frac{ak}{m-b}$ and quantity of water $= \frac{bk}{m-b}$.

SOLVED EXAMPLES

Example 1: The ratio between the three angles of a quadrilateral is 6 : 7 : 8 respectively. The value of the fourth angle of the quadrilateral is 108°. What is the difference between the largest and the smallest angles of the quadrilateral?

Solution: $6x + 7x + 8x = 360° - 108°$

$\Rightarrow \quad 21x = 252°$

$\Rightarrow \quad x = 12°$

$\therefore$ Required difference $= 108° - 6 \times 12°$

$= 108° - 72° = 36°$.

Example 2: Three-fifth of a number is equal to 70% of another number. What is the ratio between the first number and the second number respectively?

Solution: Let the numbers are x and y respectively.

$\therefore \quad x \times \frac{3}{5} = y \times \frac{70}{100}$

$\Rightarrow \quad x \times \frac{3}{5} = y \times \frac{7}{10}$

$\Rightarrow \quad \frac{x}{y} = \frac{7}{10} \times \frac{5}{3} = 7 : 6.$

Example 3: The respective ratio between the speeds of a car, a train and a bus is 5 : 9 : 4. The average speed of the car, the bus and the train is 72 km/hr together. What is the average speed of the car and the train together?

Solution: Let the speed of car, train and bus be $5x$, $9x$ and $4x$ km/hr respectively.

$\because \quad 5x + 9x + 4x = 72 \times 3$

$\therefore \quad x = 12$

$\therefore$ Average speed of car and train

$= \frac{5x + 9x}{2} = \frac{14 \times 12}{2} = 84$ km/hr

Example 4: The ratio between the present ages of Meena and Priya is 3 : 4 respectively. Ten years ago the ratio between their ages was 4 : 7 respectively. What will be Meena's age after 5 years?

Solution: Let the present age of Meena be $3x$ years

$\therefore$ The present age of Priya = $4x$ years

$\frac{3x - 10}{4x - 10} = \frac{4}{7}$

$21x - 70 = 16x - 40$

$x = \frac{70 - 40}{5} = 6$

$\therefore$ Meena's age after 5 years = $3 \times 6 + 5$

$= 23$ years.

MULTIPLE CHOICE QUESTIONS

1. An amount of rupees 4500 is to be distributed among Shrinath, Ramnath and Raghunath in the ratio of 3 : 7 : 5 respectively. If ₹ 500 is added to each of the share, the new ratio will become ......?

A. 7 : 10 : 13 B. 9 : 16 : 13
C. 2 : 4 : 3 D. 4 : 5 : 2

2. The total number of students studying in a school is 10396. The ratio of the total number of girls to the total number of boys studying in the school is 52 : 61 respectively. What is the total number of girls studying in the school?

A. 4874 B. 4784
C. 5216 D. 5612

3. In a box the numbers of one rupee, half rupee and quarter rupee are in the ratio 3 : 4 : 5 and the total value of the coins is ₹ 100. Find the number of each kind of coins respectively—

A. 48, 64, 80 B. 48, 60, 70
C. 55, 78, 90 D. 44, 68, 80

4. The ratio of the ages of two persons is 4 : 7 and the age of one of them is more than the other by 30 years. What is the sum of their ages in years?

A. 100 B. 110
C. 120 D. 130

5. The ratio of the amounts of A and B is 4 : 3 and the sum of their amount is ₹ 700. What amount in rupees should A give B to make the ratio 1 : 1?

A. 100 B. 200
C. 150 D. 50

6. The ratio of the volumes of water and glycerine in 240 c.c. glycerine mixed with water is 1 : 3. What additional volume of water should be mixed with it so that the ratio of the volumes of water and glycerine becomes 2 : 3?

A. 70 c.c. B. 80 c.c.
C. 60 c.c. D. 50 c.c.

7. If 15% of A is the same as 20% of B, then A : B is :

A. 9 : 11 B. 4 : 3
C. 3 : 4 D. 6 : 7

8. The fourth proportional to 1, 3 and the third proportional to 1 and 3 is :

A. 9 B. 81
C. 3 D. 27

9. The ratio of third proportional to 12 and 30 and the mean proportional to 9 and 25 is :

A. 5 : 1 B. 2 : 1
C. 9 : 14 D. 7 : 15

10. If $a + b : b + c : c + a = 6 : 7 : 8$ and $a + b + c = 14$ then the value of c is :

A. 14 B. 7
C. 8 D. 6

11. ₹ 120 are divided among P, Q, R such that P's share is ₹ 20 more than Q's and ₹ 20 less than R's share. What is Q's share?

A. ₹ 20 B. ₹ 15
C. ₹ 25 D. ₹ 10

12. If four numbers are in the ratio 5 : 7 : 11 : 13 be such that the sum of their cubes is 3996, find the average of four numbers.

A. 13 B. 11
C. 12 D. 9

13. If 2A = 3B = 4C then A : B : C is :
A. 2 : 3 : 4 B. 4 : 3 : 2
C. 6 : 4 : 3 D. 3 : 4 : 6

14. If $\frac{1}{5}:\frac{1}{x}=\frac{1}{x}:\frac{1}{1.25}$, then the value of x is :
A. 1.25 B. 1.5
C. 2.5 D. 2.25

15. A fraction bears the same ratio to $\frac{1}{27}$ as $\frac{3}{7}$ does to $\frac{5}{9}$. The fraction is :
A. $\frac{7}{45}$ B. $\frac{1}{35}$
C. $\frac{45}{7}$ D. $\frac{5}{21}$

16. The fourth proportional to 0.2, 0.12 and 0.3 is:
A. 0.13 B. 0.15
C. 0.18 D. 0.8

17. A bag contains 25 paise, 10 paise and 5 paise coins in the ratio 1 : 2 : 3. If their total value is ₹ 30, the number of 5 paise coins is :
A. 50 B. 100
C. 150 D. 200

18. In a class, the number of boys is more than the number of girls by 12% of the total strength. The ratio of boys to girls is :
A. 11 : 14 B. 14 : 11
C. 25 : 28 D. 28 : 25

19. A right cylinder and a right circular cone have the same radius and the same volume. The ratio of the height of the cylinder to that of the cone is :
A. 3 : 5 B. 2 : 5
C. 3 : 1 D. 1 : 3

20. The speeds of three cars are in the ratio 3 : 4 : 5. The ratio between times taken by them to travel the same distance is :
A. 3 : 4 : 5 B. 5 : 4 : 3
C. 12 : 15 : 20 D. 20 : 15 : 12

21. A and B are two alloys of gold and copper prepared by mixing metals in proportions 7 : 2 and 7 : 11 respectively. If equal quantities of the alloys are melted to form a third alloy C, the proportion of gold and copper in C will be :
A. 5 : 9 B. 5 : 7
C. 7 : 5 D. 9 : 5

22. If $a : b = c : d$, then $\frac{ma+nc}{mb+nd}$ is equal to :
A. $m : n$ B. $na : mb$
C. $a : b$ D. $md : nc$

23. Vijay got thrice as many marks in Maths as in English. The proportion of his marks in Maths and History is 4 : 3. If his total marks in Maths, English and History are 250, what are his marks in English?
A. 120 B. 90
C. 40 D. 80

24. A mixture contains milk and water in the ratio 5 : 1. On adding 5 litres of water, the ratio of milk and water becomes 5 : 2. The quantity of milk in the mixture is:
A. 16 litres B. 25 litres
C. 32.5 litres D. 22.75 litres

25. Two equal glasses are respectively $\frac{1}{3}$ and $\frac{1}{4}$ full of milk. They are then filled up with water and the contents mixed in a tumbler. The ratio of milk and water in the tumbler is:
A. 7 : 5 B. 7 : 17
C. 3 : 7 D. 11 : 23

26. The ratio between two numbers is 3 : 4 and their L.C.M. is 180. The first number is :
A. 15 B. 20
C. 45 D. 60

27. A man has some hens and cows. If the number of heads be 48 and number of feet equals 140, the number of hens will be :
A. 22 B. 23
C. 24 D. 26

28. The ratio between the ages of Kamal and Savita is 6 : 5 and the sum of their ages is 44 years. The ratio of their ages after 8 years will be :
A. 5 : 6 B. 7 : 8
C. 8 : 7 D. 14 : 13

29. One year ago the ratio between Laxmi's and Gopi's salary was 3 : 4. The ratios of their individual salaries between last year's and this year's salaries are 4 : 5 and 2 : 3 respectively. At present the total of their salary is ₹ 4160. The salary of Laxmi now, is :
A. ₹ 1040 B. ₹ 1600
C. ₹ 2560 D. ₹ 3120

30. If 15% of x = 20% of y, then $x : y$ is :
A. 3 : 4 B. 4 : 3
C. 17 : 16 D. 16 : 17

31. If $\frac{x}{5}=\frac{y}{8}$, then $(x + 5) : (y + 8)$ is equal to :
A. 3 : 5 B. 13 : 8
C. 8 : 5 D. 5 : 8

32. The salaries of A, B, C are in the ratio 2 : 3 : 5. If the increments of 15%, 10% and 20% are allowed respectively in their salaries, then what will be the new ratio of their salaries?
A. 3 : 3 : 10 B. 10 : 11 : 20
C. 23 : 33 : 60 D. Cannot be determined

33. A sum of ₹ 1300 is divided amongst P, Q, R and S such that $\frac{\text{P's share}}{\text{Q's share}} = \frac{\text{Q's share}}{\text{R's share}} = \frac{\text{R's share}}{\text{S's share}} = \frac{2}{3}$.

Then, P's share is :

A. ₹ 140 B. ₹ 160
C. ₹ 240 D. ₹ 320

34. The ratio of the number of boys and girls in a college is 7 : 8. If the percentage increase in the number of boys and girls be 20% and 10% respectively, what will be the new ratio?

A. 8 : 9 B. 17 : 18
C. 21 : 22 D. Cannot be determined

35. The third proportional to 0.36 and 0.48 is :

A. 0.64 B. 0.1728
C. 0.42 D. 0.94

36. An alloy is to contain copper and zinc in the ratio 9 : 4. The zinc required to be melted with 24 kg of copper is :

A. $10\frac{2}{3}$ kg B. $10\frac{1}{3}$ kg
C. $9\frac{2}{3}$ kg D. 9 kg

37. 15 litres of mixture contains 20% alcohol and the rest water. If 3 litres of water be mixed with it, the percentage of alcohol in the new mixture would be :

A. 15% B. $16\frac{2}{3}$%
C. 17% D. $18\frac{1}{2}$%

38. The sides of a triangle are in the ratio $\frac{1}{2}:\frac{1}{3}:\frac{1}{4}$ and its perimeter is 104 cm. The length of the longest side is :

A. 52 cm B. 48 cm
C. 32 cm D. 26 cm

39. x varies inversely as square of y. Given that $y = 2$ for $x = 1$. The value of x for $y = 6$ will be equal to :

A. 3 B. 9
C. $\frac{1}{3}$ D. $\frac{1}{9}$

40. Which of the following ratios is greatest?

A. 7 : 15 B. 15 : 23
C. 17 : 25 D. 21 : 29

ANSWERS

1	2	3	4	5	6	7	8	9	10
E	B	A	B	D	C	B	D	A	D
11	**12**	**13**	**14**	**15**	**16**	**17**	**18**	**19**	**20**
A	D	C	C	B	C	C	B	D	D
21	**22**	**23**	**24**	**25**	**26**	**27**	**28**	**29**	**30**
C	C	C	B	B	C	D	C	B	B
31	**32**	**33**	**34**	**35**	**36**	**37**	**38**	**39**	**40**
D	C	B	C	A	A	B	B	D	D

SOME SELECTED EXPLANATORY ANSWERS

2. From question,

The total number of students in the school = 10396 and ratio of number of girls : boys = 52 : 61

∴ The total number of girls in that school

$= \frac{10396 \times 52}{(52+61)} = \frac{10396 \times 52}{113}$

= 92 × 52 = 4784.

3. $3x + 4x \times \frac{1}{2} + 5x \times \frac{1}{4} = 100$

$12x + 8x + 5x = 400$

$x = 16$

Number of 1 rupee = 48

Number of 1/2 rupee = 64

Number of quarter rupee = 5 × 16 = 80

4. ∵ $7x - 4x = 30$,

$x = 10$

∴ Sum of their ages = (4 + 7) × 10

= 11 × 10

= 110 years

5. ∵ $4x + 3x = 700$

⇒ $x = 100$

400 300

Ⓐ Ⓑ

∵ $\frac{400 - x}{300 + x} = \frac{1}{1}$

⇒ $400 - x = 300 + x$

∴ $x = 50$

6. Quantity of water in 240 cc glycerine and water

$= \frac{1}{4} \times 240 \text{ cc} = 60 \text{ cc}$

Quantity of glycerine = (240 – 60) cc

= 180 cc

$\because \quad \frac{60+x}{180} = \frac{2}{3}$

$\Rightarrow \quad x = 60$ cc.

8. First we find the third proportional to 1 and 3.

Let the third proportional to 1 and 3 is

$\Rightarrow \quad 1 : 3 :: 3 : x$

$\Rightarrow \quad x = 3 \times 3$

$\Rightarrow \quad x = 9$

The fourth proportional to 1, 3 and the third proportional to 1 and 3

= The fourth proportional to 1, 3 and 9. Let the fourth proportional to 1, 3 and 9 is y, then $1 : 3 :: 9 : y$

$\Rightarrow \quad 1 \times y = 3 \times 9$

$\Rightarrow \quad y = 27$

$\therefore$ Required answer is 27.

9. Let the third proportional to 12 and 30 be y, then $12 : 30 :: 30 : y$

$\Rightarrow \quad 12y = 30 \times 30$

$y = \frac{30 \times 30}{12} = 75$

Mean proportional to 9 and 25

$= \sqrt{9 \times 25} = 3 \times 5 = 15$

$\therefore$ The required ratio is 75 : 15 = 5 : 1

10. Given

$$\left.\begin{array}{l} a+b=6x \\ b+c=7x \text{ and } c+a=8x \end{array}\right\} \quad ...(1)$$

and $\quad a + b + c = 14 \quad ...(2)$

adding equations in (1) we get

$2(a + b + c) = 21x$

using (2) we get

$2 \times 14 = 21x$

$\Rightarrow \quad x = \frac{2 \times 14}{21}$

$= \frac{2 \times 2}{3} = \frac{4}{3}$

$a + b = 6x = 6 \times \frac{4}{3} = 8.$

Using $a + b + c = 14$ and $a + b = 8$

We get $c = 6$.

11. Given P's share = Q's share + ₹ 20

P's share = R's share – ₹ 20

let Q's share be y.

then P's share = $y + 20$

$y + 20$ = R's share – ₹ 20

$\Rightarrow$ R's share = $y + 40$

P's share + Q's share + R's share = 120

$y + 20 + y + y + 40 = 120$

$3y + 60 = 120$

$3y = 120 - 60 = 60$

$y = 20$

$\therefore$ Q's share = y = ₹ 20.

12. Let the four numbers be $5x$, $7x$, $11x$ and $13x$.

Given $(5x)^3 + (7x)^3 + (11x)^3 + (13x)^3 = 3996$.

$125x^3 + 343x^3 + 1331x^3 + 2197x^3 = 3996$

$\Rightarrow \quad 3996x^3 = 3996$

$\Rightarrow \quad x^3 = 1 \quad \Rightarrow \quad x = 1$

$\therefore$ The four numbers are 5, 7, 11 and 13. Average of these four numbers

$= \frac{5+7+11+13}{4} = \frac{36}{4} = 9.$

13. Let 2A = 3B = 4C = x.

Then, $A = \frac{x}{2}$, $B = \frac{x}{3}$ and $C = \frac{x}{4}$.

$\therefore A : B : C = \frac{x}{2} : \frac{x}{3} : \frac{x}{4} = 6 : 4 : 3.$

Hence, A : B : C = 6 : 4 : 3.

14. $\frac{1}{x} \times \frac{1}{x} = \frac{1}{5} \times \frac{1}{1.25}$

or, $\frac{1}{x^2} = \frac{4}{25}$

or, $x^2 = \frac{25}{4}$

$\therefore \quad x = \frac{5}{2} = 2.5.$

15. $x : \frac{1}{27} = \frac{3}{7} : \frac{5}{9} \Rightarrow \frac{5}{9}x = \frac{1}{27} \times \frac{3}{7}.$

$\therefore \frac{5}{9}x = \frac{1}{63}$ or $x = \left(\frac{1}{63} \times \frac{9}{5}\right) = \frac{1}{35}.$

16. Let $0.2 : 0.12 :: 0.3 : x$.

Then, $0.2x = 0.12 \times 0.3$ or

$x = \frac{0.12 \times 0.3}{0.2} = 0.18.$

17. Ratio of their values $= \frac{1}{4} : \frac{2}{10} : \frac{3}{20}$

= 5 : 4 : 3.

$\therefore$ Value of 5-paise coins = ₹ $\left(30 \times \frac{3}{12}\right)$

= ₹ 7.50.

$\therefore$ Number of 5-paise coins = $\frac{750}{5}$ = 150.

19. Let the heights of the cylinder and cone be h and H respectively. Then, $\pi r^2 h = \frac{1}{3}\pi r^2$ H or $\frac{h}{\text{H}} = \frac{1}{3}$.

So, their heights are in the ratio 1 : 3.

20. Ratio of time taken = $\frac{1}{3} : \frac{1}{4} : \frac{1}{5}$ = 20 : 15 : 12.

21. Gold in C = $\left(\frac{7}{9} + \frac{7}{18}\right) = \frac{21}{18} = \frac{7}{6}$.

Copper in C = $\left(\frac{2}{9} + \frac{11}{18}\right) = \frac{15}{18} = \frac{5}{6}$.

$\therefore$ Gold : Copper = $\frac{7}{6} : \frac{5}{6}$ = 7 : 5.

22. Let $\frac{a}{b} = \frac{c}{d} = k$. Then, $a = bk$ and $c = dk$.

$\therefore \quad \frac{ma + nc}{mb + nd} = \frac{mbk + ndk}{mb + nd} = k\left(\frac{mb + nd}{mb + nd}\right)$

$= k = \frac{a}{b}$.

23. M = 3E and $\frac{\text{M}}{\text{H}} = \frac{4}{3}$.

$\therefore$ H = $\frac{3}{4}$M = $\frac{3}{4} \times 3$E = $\frac{9}{4}$E.

Now, M + E + H = 250

$\Rightarrow$ 3E + E + $\frac{9}{4}$E = 250

$\therefore$ 25E = 1000 or E = 40.

24. Let quantity of milk and water be $5x$ and x litres.

Then, $\frac{5x}{x+5} = \frac{5}{2}$ or, $10x = 5x + 25$

or, $x = 5$.

$\therefore$ Quantity of milk = $5x$ = 25 litres.

26. Let the numbers be $3x$ and $4x$.

Then, their L.C.M. = $12x$.

$\therefore$ $12x = 180$ or $x = 15$.

Hence, the first number = 45.

27. Let the number of hens = x and number of cows = y.

Then, $x + y = 48$ and $2x + 4y = 140$.

Solving these equations, we get, $2y = 44$

or $y = 22$.

So, $x = (48 - 22) = 26$.

$\therefore$ Number of hens = 26.

28. Let their ages be $6x$ and $5x$ years.

$\therefore$ $6x + 5x = 44$ or, $x = 4$.

So, their present ages are 24 years and 20 years.

Ratio of their ages after 8 years = 32 : 28

= 8 : 7.

29. Let the salaries of Laxmi and Gopi one year before be x_1, y_1 respectively and now x_2, y_2 respectively. Then,

$\frac{x_1}{y_1} = \frac{3}{4}, \frac{x_1}{x_2} = \frac{4}{5}, \frac{y_1}{y_2} = \frac{2}{3}$ and $x_2 + y_2 = 4160$.

Solving these equations, we get $x_2 = 1600$.

30. 15% of x = 20% of y

$\Rightarrow \quad \frac{15x}{100} = \frac{20y}{100}$

$\Rightarrow \quad \frac{x}{y} = \left(\frac{20}{100} \times \frac{100}{15}\right) = \frac{4}{3}$

$\Rightarrow \quad x : y = 4 : 3$.

31. Let $\frac{x}{5} = \frac{y}{8} = k$. Then, $x = 5k$ and $y = 8k$.

$\therefore \quad \frac{x+5}{y+8} = \frac{5k+5}{8k+8} = \frac{5(k+1)}{8(k+1)} = \frac{5}{8}$

$\Rightarrow$ $(x + 5) : (y + 8) = 5 : 8$.

32. Let A = $2k$, B = $3k$ and C = $5k$

A's new salary = $\frac{115}{100}$ of $2k$

$= \left(\frac{115}{100} \times 2k\right) = \frac{23}{10}k$

B's new salary = $\frac{110}{100}$ of $3k$

$= \left(\frac{110}{100} \times 3k\right) = \frac{33}{10}k$

C's new salary = $\frac{120}{100}$ of $5k$

$= \left(\frac{120}{100} \times 5k\right) = 6k$.

$\therefore$ New ratio = $\frac{23k}{10} : \frac{33k}{10} : 6k$ = 23 : 33 : 60.

34. Originally, let the number of boys and girls in the college be $7x$ and $8x$ respectively. Their increased number is (120% of $7x$) and (110% of $8x$)

i.e., $\left(\frac{120}{100} \times 7x\right)$ and $\left(\frac{110}{100} \times 8x\right)$

i.e. $\frac{42x}{5}$ and $\frac{44x}{5}$.

$\therefore$ Required ratio = $\frac{42x}{5} : \frac{44x}{5}$ = 21 : 22.

35. Let the third proportional to 0.36 and 0.48 be *x*.

Then, 0.36 : 0.48 :: 0.48 : *x*

$\Rightarrow \quad x = \left(\frac{0.48 \times 0.48}{0.36}\right) = 0.64.$

36. Let the required quantity of copper be *x* kg.

Then, 9 : 4 :: 24 : *x* $\Rightarrow$ $9x = 4 \times 24$

$\Rightarrow \quad x = \frac{4 \times 24}{9} = 10\frac{2}{3}.$

Hence, the required quantity of copper is $10\frac{2}{3}$ kg.

37. Alcohol in 15 litres of mixture = 20% of 15 litres =

$\left(\frac{20}{100} \times 15\right)$ litres = 3 litres.

Water in it = (15 – 3) litres = 12 litres.

New quantity of mixture = (15 + 3) litres = 18 litres.

Quantity of alcohol in it = 3 litres.

Percentage of alcohol in new mixture

$= \left(\frac{3}{18} \times 100\right)\% = 16\frac{2}{3}\%.$

38. Ratio of sides = $\frac{1}{2} : \frac{1}{3} : \frac{1}{4}$ = 6 : 4 : 3.

Largest side = $\left(104 \times \frac{6}{13}\right)$ cm = 48 cm.

39. Given $x = \frac{k}{y^2}$, where *k* is a constant.

Now, $y = 2$ and $x = 1$ gives $k = 4$.

$\therefore \quad x = \frac{4}{y^2} \quad \Rightarrow \quad x = \frac{4}{6^2}$,

when $y = 6 \quad \Rightarrow \quad x = \frac{4}{36} = \frac{1}{9}$.

40. $\frac{7}{15} = 0.466$, $\frac{15}{23} = 0.652$,

$\frac{17}{25} = 0.68$ and $\frac{21}{29} = 0.724$.

Clearly, 0.724 is greatest and hence, 21 : 29 is greatest.

4

Age and Average

IMPORTANT FACTS

1. The present age of the father is x times the age of his son. T years hence, the father's age become y times the age of his son. Then the present ages of the father and his son are:

   Present age of the son $= \frac{(y-1)T}{x-y}$ years and age of the father $= \frac{(y-1)T \times x}{x-y}$ years.

2. T years ago, the father's age was x times that of his son and at present the father's age is y times the age of his son. Then their present ages are:

   Son's age $= \frac{T(x-1)}{x-y}$ years;

   Father's age $= \frac{T(x-1)}{x-y} \times y$ years.

3. Average Speed $= \frac{\text{Total travelled distance}}{\text{Total taken time}}$

4. If equal distances are travelled at the rate X and Y, then Average Speed $= \frac{2XY}{X+y}$

5. When a person leaves a group and another person joins the group in the place of person left, then
   I. In the case of increasing of average age, Age of the newcomer = Age of person left + no. of persons in the group X increase in average age.
   II. In the case of decreasing of average age, Age of the newcomer = Age of person left – no. of persons in the group X decrease in average age.

6. When a person joins a group without replacing any previous person from that group, then
   I. In the case of increasing of average age, Age of the newcomer = Previous of the age + no. of all persons (including newcomer) × increaser in average age.
   II. In the case of decreasing of average age, Age of the newcomer = Previous average age – no. of all persons (including new comer) × decrease in average age.

7. When a person leaves the group but nobody joins this group, then
   I. In the case of increasing of average age, Age of man left = Previous Average of the age – no. of present persons × decrease in the average age.
   II. In the case of decreasing of average age, Age of man left = Previous Average age + no. of present persons × increase in average age.

8. Average related to Natural Numbers

   I. Average of consecutive natural numbers till n $= \frac{(n+1)}{2}$

   II. Average of squares of numbers till n $= \frac{(n+1)(2n+1)}{6}$

   III. Average of cubes of consecutive natural numbers till $n = \frac{n(n+1)^2}{4}$

9. Average related to Even Numbers

   I. Average of n = consecutive even numbers $= n + 1$

   II. Average of consecutive even number till n $= (n/2 + 1)$

   III. Average of squares of n consecutive even numbers $= \frac{2(n+1)(2n+1)}{3}$

   IV. Average of squares of consecutive even numbers till $n = \frac{(n+1)(2n+1)}{3}$

10. Average related to Odd Numbers

   I. Average of n consecutive odd numbers $= n$

   II. Average of consecutive odd numbers till n $= \frac{n(n+1)}{3}$

   III. Average of squares of consecutive odd numbers till $n = \frac{n(n+1)}{3}$

SOLVED EXAMPLES

Example 1: Ankur's present age is 12 years more than Raman's age 5 years ago. Presently Raman is 24 years older than Raju's present age who is 12 years younger than Amit. If Amit's present age is 42 years, what is Ankur's age 3 years ago?

Solution: Amit's present age = 42 years

Raju's present age = 42 – 12 = 30 years

Raman's present age = 30 + 24 = 54 years

Ankur's present age = 54 – 5 + 12

= 61 years

∴ Ankur's age 3 years ago = 58 years

Example 2: Present ages of Leela and Shivani are in the ratio of 4 : 5 respectively. Three years hence this ratio becomes 5 : 6. What is the difference between their present ages?

Solution: Let Leela's and Shivani's present ages be $4x$ and $5x$ years respectively.

After 3 years,

$$\frac{4x+3}{5x+3} = \frac{5}{6}$$

$\Rightarrow$ $25x + 15 = 24x + 18$

$\Rightarrow$ $25x - 24x = 18 - 15 = 3$

∴ $x = 3$ = Required difference

Example 3: Radha's present age is three years less than twice her age 12 years ago. Also the respective ratio between Raj's present age and Radha's present age is 4 : 9. What will be Raj's age after 5 years?

Solution: Let the present age of Radha be x years. As per question,

$\because$ $x = (x - 12) \times 2 - 3$

$\Rightarrow$ $x = 2x - 27$

$\therefore$ $x = 27$

$\because$ Present age of Raj

$$= \frac{4}{9} \times 27 = 12 \text{ years}$$

∴ Raj's age after 5 years = 12 + 5 = 17 years

Example 4: If $12a + 12b = 45$, what is the average of a and b?

Solution: $\because$ $12a + 12b = 45$

$\Rightarrow$ $12(a + b) = 45$

$$\therefore \quad \frac{a+b}{2} = \frac{45}{12 \times 2} = 1.875.$$

Example 5: The sum of five numbers is 555. The average of first two numbers is 75 and the third number is 115. What is the average of last two numbers?

Solution: Average of last two numbers

$$= \frac{555 - 2 \times 75 - 115}{2}$$

$$= \frac{555 - 150 - 115}{2} = \frac{290}{2} = 145.$$

Example 6: The average marks of nine students in a group is 63. Three of them scored 78, 69 and 48 marks. What are the average marks of remaining six students?

Solution: The average marks of remaining 6 students

$$= \frac{9 \times 63 - (78 + 69 + 48)}{6}$$

$$= \frac{567 - 195}{6} = 62.$$

MULTIPLE CHOICE QUESTIONS

1. The sum of 8 consecutive odd numbers is 656. Also average of four consecutive even number is 87. What is the sum of the smallest odd number and second largest even number?
   A. 165 B. 175
   C. 163 D. Cannot be determined

2. The ages of Meena, Tina and Seema are in the ratio of 6 : 4 : 7 respectively. If the sum of their ages is 34 years, what is Seema's age?
   A. 12 years B. 10 years
   C. 18 years D. None of these

3. The average of 4 positive integers is 52.5. The highest integer is 76 and the lowest integer is 34. The difference between the remaining two integers is 4. Which of the following integers is higher of the remaining two integers?
   A. 52 B. 54
   C. 48 D. Cannot be determined

4. The present age of Deepa is 3 times the present age of his son. Five years hence the ratio of their ages will be 34 : 13 respectively. What is the present age of Deepa?
   A. 63 years B. 68 years
   C. 58 years D. 60 years

5. The average of 5 consecutive even numbers A, B, C, D and E is 66. What is the product of B and E?
   A. 4352 B. 4340
   C. 4620 D. None of these

6. The present age of father is 34 years more than that of his son. Twelve years ago father's age was 18 times the age of his son. What is the present age of the son in years?
   A. 16 B. 14
   C. 12 D. 18

7. A father is older than his first son by 30 years, the first son is older than the second son by 10 years.

If the sum of their ages by 95 years, find the age of father—
A. 65 years B. 55 years
C. 45 years D. 50 years

8. In 10 years, Alok will be twice as old as Babul was 10 years ago. If Alok is now 9 years older than Babul, the present age of Babul is :
A. 19 years B. 29 years
C. 39 years D. 49 years

9. The difference between the ages of two persons is 10 years. 15 years ago, the elder one was twice as old as the younger one. The present age of the elder person is :
A. 25 years B. 35 years
C. 45 years D. 55 years

10. Ratio of Anshu's age to Jolly's age is equal to 4 : 3. Anshu will be 26 years old after 6 years. How old is Jolly now?
A. 12 years B. 15 years
C. $19\frac{1}{2}$ years D. 21 years

11. The ratio between the ages of Asha and Bhushan at present is 2 : 3. Five years hence the ratio of their ages will be 3 : 4. What is the present age of Asha?
A. 10 years B. 15 years
C. 25 years D. data inadequate

12. Three years ago the average age of A and B was 18 years. With C joining them, the average becomes 22 years. How old is C now?
A. 24 years B. 27 years
C. 28 years D. 30 years

13. Ten years ago A was half of B in age. If the ratio of their present ages is 3 : 4, what will be the total of their present ages?
A. 8 years B. 20 years
C. 35 years D. 45 years

14. Out of three numbers, the first is twice the second and is half of the third. If the average of the three numbers is 56, the three numbers in order are :
A. 48, 96, 24 B. 48, 24, 96
C. 96, 24, 48 D. 96, 48, 24

15. The average of 50 numbers is 38. If two numbers, namely 45 and 55 are discarded, the average of the remaining numbers is :
A. 36.5 B. 37.0
C. 37.5 D. 37.52

16. The average temperature of the first three days is 27° C and that of the next three is 29° C. If the average of the whole week is 28.5° C, the temperature of the last day of the week is:
A. 10.5° C B. 21° C
C. 31.5° C D. 42° C

17. The average of an adult class is 40 years. 12 new students with an average age of 32 years join the class, thereby decreasing the average by 4 years. The original strength of the class was :
A. 10 B. 11
C. 12 D. 15

18. The average weight of 8 persons is increased by 2.5 kg when one of them whose weight is 56 kg is replaced by a new man. The weight of the new man is :
A. 66 kg B. 75 kg
C. 76 kg D. 86 kg

19. In a TV factory, an average of 60 TVs are produced per day for the first 25 days of the month. A few workers fell ill for the next five days, reducing the daily average for the month to 58 sets per day. The average production per day for the last 5 days is :
A. 45 B. 48
C. 52 D. 58

20. The average expenditure of a man for the first five months is ₹ 120 and for the next seven months it is ₹ 130. If he saves ₹ 290 in that years, his monthly average income is :
A. ₹ 140 B. ₹ 150
C. ₹ 160 D. ₹ 170

21. The average age of 24 students in a class is 10. If the teacher's age is included, the average increases by one. The age of the teacher is :
A. 25 years B. 30 years
C. 35 years D. 40 years

22. A batsman has a certain average runs for 11 innings. In the 12th inning he made a score of 90 runs and thereby decreased his average by 5. His average after 12th inning is :
A. 127 B. 145
C. 150 D. 217

23. The average weight of three men A, B and C is 84 kg. Another man D joins the group and the average now becomes 80 kg. If another man E, whose weight is 3 kg more than that of D, replaces A, then the average weight of B, C, D and E becomes 79 kg. The weight of A is :
A. 70 kg B. 72 kg
C. 75 kg D. 80 kg

24. A man whose bowling average is 12.4 takes 5 wickets for 26 runs and thereby decreases his average by 0.4. The number of wickets, taken by him, before his last match, is :
A. 85 B. 78
C. 72 D. 64

25. The present ages of three persons are in proportions 4 : 7 : 9. Eight years ago, the sum of their ages was 56. Find their present ages (in years).
A. 8, 20, 28 B. 16, 28, 36
C. 20, 35, 45 D. Cannot be determined

26. A is two years older than B who is twice as old as C. If the total of the ages of A, B and C be 27, then how old is B?
A. 7 B. 8
C. 9 D. 10

27. A person's present age is two-fifth of the age of his mother. After 8 years, he will be one-half of the age of his mother. How old is the mother at present?
A. 32 years B. 36 years
C. 40 years D. 48 years

28. Quasab is as much younger than Rahim as he is older than Tanveer. If the sum of the ages of Rahim and Tanveer is 50 years, what is definitely the difference between Rahim's and Quasab's age?
A. 1 year B. 2 years
C. 25 years D. Can not be determined

29. A father said to his son, ''I was as old as you are at present at the time of your birth.'' If the father's age is 38 years now, the son's age five years back was :
A. 14 years B. 19 years
C. 33 years D. 38 years

30. Asha's father was 38 years of age when she was born while her mother was 36 years old when her brother four years younger to her was born. What is the difference between the ages of her parents?
A. 2 years B. 4 years
C. 6 years D. 8 years

31. A student was asked to find the arithmetic mean of the numbers 3, 11, 7, 9, 15, 13, 8, 19, 17, 21, 14 and x. He found the mean to be 12. What should be the number in place of x?
A. 3 B. 7
C. 17 D. 31

32. If a, b, c, d, e are five consecutive odd numbers, their average is :
A. $5(a + 4)$
B. $\frac{abcde}{5}$
C. $5(a + b + c + d + e)$
D. None of these

33. Of the four numbers, the first is twice the second, the second is one-third of the third and the third is 5 times the fourth. The average of the numbers is 24.75. The largest of these numbers is :
A. 9 B. 25
C. 30 D. 45

34. Of the three numbers, the average of the first and the second is greater than the average of the second and the third by 15. What is the difference between the first and the third of the three numbers?
A. 15 B. 45
C. 60 D. None of these

35. The average temperature of the town in the first four days of a month was 58 degrees. The average for the second, third, fourth and fifth days was 60 degrees. If the temperatures of the first and fifth days were in the ratio 7 : 8, then what is the temperature on the fifth day?
A. 64 degrees B. 62 degrees
C. 56 degrees D. 46 degrees

36. The captain of a cricket team of 11 members is 26 years old and the wicket keeper is 3 years older. If the ages of these two are excluded, the average age of the remaining players is one years less than the average age of the whole team. What is the average age of the team?
A. 23 years B. 24 years
C. 25 years D. 32 years

37. A cricketer has a certain average for 10 innings. In the eleventh inning, he scored 108 runs, thereby increasing his average by 6 runs. His new average is :
A. 48 runs B. 52 runs
C. 55 runs D. 60 runs

38. The average weight of 3 men A, B and C is 84 kg. Another man D joins the group and the average now becomes 80 kg. If another man E, whose weight is 3 kg more than that of D, replaces A, then the average weight B, C, D and E becomes 79 kg. The weight of A is :
A. 70 kg B. 72 kg
C. 75 kg D. 80 kg

39. The average age of husband, wife and their child 3 years ago was 27 years and that of wife and the child 5 years ago was 20 years. The present age of the husband is :
A. 35 years B. 40 years
C. 50 years D. 36 years

40. In an examination, a pupil's average marks were 63 per paper. If he had obtained 20 more marks for his Geography paper and 2 more marks for his History paper, his average per paper would have been 65. How many papers were there in the examination?
A. 8 B. 9
C. 10 D. 11

ANSWERS

1	2	3	4	5	6	7	8	9	10
C	D	A	A	D	B	B	C	B	B
11	**12**	**13**	**14**	**15**	**16**	**17**	**18**	**19**	**20**
A	A	C	B	C	C	C	C	B	B
21	**22**	**23**	**24**	**25**	**26**	**27**	**28**	**29**	**30**
C	B	C	A	B	D	C	D	A	C
31	**32**	**33**	**34**	**35**	**36**	**37**	**38**	**39**	**40**
B	D	D	D	A	A	A	C	B	D

SOME SELECTED EXPLANATORY ANSWERS

1. Let the smallest odd and smallest even numbers are x and y respectively. Then,

$\because\ x + (x + 2) + (x + 4) + (x + 6) + (x + 8) + (x + 10) + (x + 12) + (x + 14) = 656$

$\Rightarrow \quad 8x + 56 = 656$

$\therefore \quad x = \dfrac{656-56}{8} = 75$

$\because\ y + (y + 2) + (y + 4) + (y + 6) = 4 \times 87$

$\Rightarrow \quad 4y + 12 = 348$

$y = \dfrac{348-12}{4} = 84$

$\therefore$ Reqd. sum of the smallest odd number and second largest even number

$= x + (y + 4) = 75 + (84 + 4) = 163$

2. Seema's age $= \dfrac{7 \times 34}{(6+4+7)} = 14$ years.

3. Let the 4 positive integers, kept in descending order be a, b, c and d respectively. Then from question,

$\because \quad a + b + c + d = 4 \times 52.5 = 210$

$\Rightarrow 76 + (b + c) + 34 = 210$

$\Rightarrow \quad (b + c) = 100 \quad ...(i)$

Again from question,

$b - c = 4 \quad ...(ii)$

Solving (i) and (ii), we get

$b = 52$

and $\quad c = 48$

Hence, higher integer $= b = 52$

4. Let the present age of Deepa's son $= x$ years.

Then from question,

Deepa's present age $= 3x$ years

$\because \quad \dfrac{3x+5}{x+5} = \dfrac{34}{13}$

$\Rightarrow \quad 39x + 65 = 34x + 170$

$\Rightarrow \quad 5x = 105$

$\therefore \quad x = 21$

Deepa's present age $= 3x = 3 \times 21 = 63$ years

5. From question,

$A + B + C + D + E = 66 \times 5 = 330$

Let the 1st even number A be n, then

$\because\ n + (n + 2) + (n + 4) + (n + 6) + (n + 8) = 330$

$\Rightarrow \quad 5n + 20 = 330$

$\Rightarrow \quad 5n = 310$

$\therefore \quad n = 62$

Thus the required product

$= B \times E = (n + 2) \times (n + 8)$

$= 64 \times 70 = 4480$

7. Age of 1st son $= x$

Father's age $= x + 30$

Age of 2nd son $= x - 10$

$\because\ x + (x + 30) + (x - 10) = 95$

$\Rightarrow \quad 3x + 20 = 95$

$\Rightarrow \quad 3x = 75$

$\therefore \quad x = 25$

$\therefore$ Father's age $= (25 + 30)$ years $= 55$ years

8. Let the present ages of Babul and Alok be x years and $(x + 9)$ years respectively.

Then, $(x + 9 + 10) = 2(x - 10)$ or $x = 39$.

9. Let the present age of the elder person be x years.

Then, the present age of the other person

$= (x - 10)$ years

$(x - 15) = 2(x - 10 - 15)$ or $x = 35$

$\therefore$ The present age of the elder person is 35 years.

10. Let Anshu's age $= 4x$ and Jolly's age $= 3x$ years.

$\therefore\ 4x + 6 = 26 \quad \Rightarrow \quad x = 5$

$\therefore$ Jolly's age $= 3x = 15$ years.

11. Let the ages of Asha and Bhushan be $2x$ and $3x$ years.

$\dfrac{2x+5}{3x+5} = \dfrac{3}{4}$

$\Rightarrow \quad 4(2x + 5) = 3(3x + 5)$

$\Rightarrow \quad x = 5.$

$\therefore$ Asha's present age = $2x$ = 10 years.

12. Sum of ages of A and B, 3 years ago
= (18 × 2)
= 36 years.
Sum of ages of A, B and C = (22 × 3)
= 66 years.
Sum of ages of A and B = (36 + 6) years
= 42 years.
$\therefore$ C's age = (66 – 42) years = 24 years.

14. Let second number = x. Then, first one = $2x$ and third number = $4x$.

$$\therefore \quad \frac{x+2x+4x}{3} = 56 \Rightarrow 7x = 168 \text{ or } x = 24.$$

So, the numbers are 48, 24, 96.

15. Total of 50 numbers = (50 × 38) = 1900.
Total of 48 numbers = [1900 – (45 + 55)]
= 1800.

$$\therefore \text{ Required average} = \frac{1800}{48} = \frac{225}{6} = 37.5.$$

16. $3 \times 27 + 3 \times 29 + x = 7 \times 28.5$
$\therefore \quad x = 31.5$

17. Let original strength = x. Then,
$40x + 12 \times 32 = (x + 12) \times 36$
or $40x + 384 = 36x + 432$ or $4x = 48$
or $x = 12.$

18. Total increase = (8 × 2.5) kg = 20 kg.
Weight of new man = (56 + 20) kg = 76 kg.

19. Production during these 5 days
= (30 × 58 – 25 × 60) = 240.

$$\therefore \text{ Average for 5 days} = \frac{240}{5} = 48.$$

20. Total income = ₹ 120 × 5 + 130 × 7 + 290)
= ₹ 1800.

Average monthly income = ₹ $\left(\frac{1800}{12}\right)$
= ₹ 150.

21. Age of the teacher = (25 × 11 – 24 × 10) years
= 35 years.

22. $11x + 90 = (x - 5) \times 12$ or $x = 150$.
$\therefore$ Average after 12th inning = (150 – 5)
= 145.

23. A + B + C = 3 × 84 = 252, A + B + C + D
= (4 × 80) = 320.
$\therefore$ D = (320 – 252) = 68 and so E
= (68 + 3) = 71.
Now, B + C + D + E = (4 × 79) = 316
So, A = (320 – 245) = 75 kg.

24. Let the number of wickets taken before the last match = x.

$$\text{Then, } \frac{12.4x+26}{x+5} = 12 \Rightarrow x = 85.$$

25. Let their present ages be $4x$, $7x$ and $9x$ years respectively.
Then, $(4x - 8) + (7x - 8) + (9x - 8) = 56$
$\Rightarrow 20x = 80 \quad \Rightarrow \quad x = 4.$
$\therefore$ Their present ages are 16 years, 28 years and 36 years respectively.

26. Let C's age be x years.
Then, B's age = $2x$ years.
A's age = $(2x + 2)$ years.
$\therefore (2x + 2) + 2x + x = 27$
$\Rightarrow 5x = 25 \Rightarrow x = 5.$
Hence, B's age = $2x$ = 10 years.

27. Let the mother's present age be x years. Then, the person's present age = $\left(\frac{2}{5}x\right)$ years.

$$\therefore \left(\frac{2}{5}x+8\right) = \frac{1}{2}(x+8)$$

$\Rightarrow 2(2x + 40) = 5(x + 8) \Rightarrow \quad x = 40.$

28. Rahim – Quasab = Rahim – Tanveer
$\Rightarrow$ Quasab = Tanveer
Also, Rahim + Tanveer = 50
$\Rightarrow$ Rahim + Quasab = 50.
So, (Rahim – Quasab) cannot be determined.

29. Let the son's present age be x years.
Then, $(38 - x) = x$
$\Rightarrow \quad 2x = 38$
$\Rightarrow \quad x = 19.$
$\therefore$ Son's age 5 years back = (19 – 5) years
= 14 years.

30. Mother's age when Asha's brother was born
= 36 years.
Father's age when Asha's brother was born
= (38 + 4) years = 42 years.
$\therefore$ Required difference = (42 – 36) years
= 6 years.

31. Clearly, we have

$$\left(\frac{3+11+7+9+15+13+8+19+17+21+14+x}{12}\right) = 12$$

or, $\quad 137 + x = 144$
or, $\quad x = 144 - 137 = 7.$

32. Clearly, $b = a + 2$, $c = a + 4$, $d = a + 6$ and $e = a + 8$.
$\therefore$ Average

$$= \frac{a+(a+2)+(a+4)+(a+6)+(a+8)}{5}$$

$= \left(\frac{5a+20}{5}\right) = (a + 4).$

34. Let the numbers be x, y and z.

Then, $\left(\frac{x+y}{2}\right)-\left(\frac{y+z}{2}\right) = 15$

or, $(x + y) - (y + z) = 30$

or, $x - z = 30.$

35. Sum of temperatures on 1st, 2nd, 3rd and 4th days

$= (58 \times 4) = 232$ degrees ...(*i*)

Sum of temperatures on 2nd, 3rd, 4th and 5th days

$= (60 \times 4) = 240$ degrees ...(*ii*)

Subtracting (*i*) from (*ii*), we get :

Temperature on 5th day – Temperature on 1st day

= 8 degrees.

Let the temperatures on 1st and 5th days be $7x$ and $8x$ degrees respectively.

Then, $8x - 7x = 8$ or $x = 8$.

$\therefore$ Temperature on the 5th day $= 8x = 64$ degrees.

36. Let the average age of the whole team be x years.

$\therefore\ 11x - (26 + 29) = 9\ (x - 1)$

$\Rightarrow\ 11x - 9x = 46 \Rightarrow\ 2x = 46$

$\Rightarrow\ x = 23.$

So, average age of the team is 23 years.

37. Let average for 10 innings be x. Then,

$$\frac{10x+108}{11} = x + 6$$

$\Rightarrow\ 11x + 66 = 10x + 108$

$\Rightarrow\ x = 42.$

$\therefore$ New average $= (x + 6) = 48$ runs.

39. Sum of the present ages of husband, wife and child = $(27 \times 3 + 3 \times 3)$ years = 90 years.

Sum of the present ages of wife and child

$= (20 \times 2 + 5 \times 2)$ years = 50 years.

$\therefore$ Husband's present age = $(90 - 50)$ years

= 40 years.

40. Let the number of papers be x.

Then, $63x + 20 + 2 = 65x$

or, $2x = 22$

or, $x = 11.$

*****

5

Percentage

IMPORTANT FACTS

To solve quickly the problems related to percentage, remember following rules:

Rule 1:

(*a*) Of the given two numbers if the first is $x\%$ more than the second, then the second will be $\left(\frac{100 \times x}{100+x}\right)\%$ less than the first.

(*b*) Of the given two numbers if the first is $x\%$ less than the second, then the second will be $\left(\frac{100 \times x}{100-x}\right)\%$ more than the first.

(*c*) If two numbers are respectively $x\%$ and $y\%$ more than a third number, then the first number will be $\left(\frac{100+x}{100+y} \times 100\right)\%$ of the second.

(*d*) If two numbers are respectively $x\%$ and $y\%$ less than a third number, then the first number will be $\left(\frac{100-x}{100-y} \times 100\right)\%$ of the second.

Rule 2 :

(*a*) If a number or quantity is increased by $x\%$ then in order to restore its original value it must be decreased by $\left[\frac{100 \times x}{100+x}\right]\%$.

(*b*) If a number or quantity is decreased by $x\%$ then in order to restore its original value it must be increased by $\left[\frac{100 \times x}{100-x}\right]\%$.

Rule 3 :

(*a*) If a number is successively increased by $x\%$ and $y\%$ then a single equivalent increase in that number will be $\left(x+y+\frac{xy}{100}\right)\%$

(*b*) If two successive discounts of $x\%$ and $y\%$ are allowed on a particular amount, then a single discount that is equivalent to the two successive discounts will be

$$\left(x+y-\frac{xy}{100}\right)\%$$

(*c*) If a number is successively increased by $x\%$, $y\%$ and $z\%$, then a single equivalent increase in that number will be

$$\left[(x+y+z)+\left(\frac{xy+yz+zx}{100}\right)+\frac{(xyz)}{10000}\right]\%$$

(*d*) If three successive discounts of $x\%$, $y\%$ and $z\%$ are allowed on an amount, then a single discount that is equivalent to the three successive discounts will be

$$\left[x+y+z-\frac{(xy+yz+zx)}{100}+\frac{xyz}{10000}\right]\%$$

Rule 4 :

(*a*) If a number is increased by $x\%$ and thereafter reduced by $x\%$, then the number will be reduced by $\left(\frac{x^2}{100}\right)$ per cent.

(*b*) If a number is reduced by $x\%$ and thereafter increased by $x\%$ then the number will be reduced by $\left(\frac{x^2}{100}\right)$ per cent.

(*c*) If due to an increase of $x\%$ in the selling price of certain commodity the sell/consumption of the commodity decreases by $y\%$, then gross receipts on account of sale of that commodity will be increased or decreased by $\left(x-y-\frac{xy}{100}\right)\%$, where $x > y$ and will be decreased by $\left(y-x+\frac{xy}{100}\right)\%$, where $y > x$.

SOLVED EXAMPLES

Example 1: If the numerator of a fraction is increased by 200% and the denominator is increased by 400%. The resultant fraction is $1\frac{1}{20}$. What was the original fraction?

Solution: Let original fraction = $\frac{x}{y}$; then

$$\frac{x+2x}{y+4y} = \frac{21}{20}$$

$$\frac{3x}{5y} = \frac{21}{20}$$

$$\frac{x}{y} = \frac{21\times5}{20\times3} = \frac{7}{4} = 1\frac{3}{4}.$$

Example 2: In a class of 65 students and 4 teachers, each student got sweets that are 20% of the total number of students and each teacher got sweets that are 40% of the total number of students. How many sweets were there?

Solution: The share of each student $= \frac{20}{100}\times65$
= 13 sweets

The share of each teacher $= \frac{40}{100}\times65$
= 26 sweets

Total number of sweets = 65 × 13 + 4 × 26
= 845 + 104 = 949.

Example 3: Bovina spent ₹ 44,668/- on her air tickets, ₹ 56,732/- on buying gifts for the family members and the remaining 22% of the total amount had as cash with her. What was the total amount?

Solution: Let total amount = ₹ x ; then

$$\frac{78}{100}\times x = 44668 + 56732$$

$$\Rightarrow x = \frac{101400\times100}{78} = ₹\ 1{,}30{,}000.$$

Example 4: Rubina decided to donate 16% of her monthly salary to an NGO. On the day of donation she changed her mind and donated ₹ 6,567/- which was 75% of what she had decided earlier. How much is Rubina's monthly salary?

Solution: Let her monthly salary be ₹ x ; then

$$\frac{16}{100}\times\frac{75}{100}\times x = 6567$$

$$\Rightarrow \frac{3}{25}x = 6567$$

$$\Rightarrow x = \frac{6567\times25}{3} = ₹\ 54725$$

Thus, her monthly salary = ₹ 54725.

MULTIPLE CHOICE QUESTIONS

1. Mr. Rajesh spent 20% of his monthly income on grocery and household expenses. Out of the remaining he spent 25% on children's education 20% on transport and 15% on entertainment. He is left with an amount of ₹ 14,400 after incurring above expenses. What was his monthly income?
   A. ₹ 45,000 B. ₹ 24,000
   C. ₹ 36,000 D. ₹ 32,000

2. Number of students in a school in June every year increases by 10% from the previous year. If the school had 2,400 students in 2009, how many students did it have in June 2011?
   A. 2,840 B. 2,880
   C. 2,904 D. 2,920

3. On a test consisting of 150 questions, Reema answered 40% of the first 75 questions correctly. What per cent of the other 75 questions does she need to answer correctly for her grade on the entire exam to be 60%?
   A. 80 B. 70
   C. 40 D. 50

4. If the numerator of a fraction is increased by 200% and the denominator is increased by 300%. The resultant fraction is $\frac{9}{17}$. What was the original fraction?
   A. $\frac{11}{17}$ B. $\frac{9}{11}$
   C. $\frac{13}{17}$ D. None of these

5. One-sixth of a number is 53. What will 57% of that number be?
   A. 181.26 B. 136.74
   C. 197.16 D. 149.46

6. Mrs. Sudha Jain invests 14% of her monthly salary, *i.e.* ₹ 7,014 in Insurance Policies. Later she invests 21% of her monthly salary on Family Mediclaim Policies; also she invests another 6.5% of her salary on Mutual Funds. What is the total annual amount invested by Mrs. Sudha Jain?
   A. ₹ 25,050 B. ₹ 50,100
   C. ₹ 2,42,550 D. ₹ 2,49,498

7. A sum of ₹ 817 is divided among A, B and C such that 'A' receives 25% more than 'B' and 'B' receives 25% less than 'C'. What is the 'A's share in the amount?

A. ₹ 228 B. ₹ 247
C. ₹ 285 D. ₹ 304

8. Ms. Sujan invests 7% *i.e.* ₹ 2170 of her monthly salary in mutual funds. Later she invests 18% of her monthly salary in recurring deposits also, she invests 6% of her salary on NSC's. What is the total annual amount invested by Ms. Sujan?
A. ₹ 1,25,320 B. ₹ 1,13,520
C. ₹ 1,35,120 D. ₹ 1,15,320

9. What is the 30% of 40% of $\frac{2}{5}$th of 2500?
A. 500 B. 400
C. 360 D. 120

10. A sum of ₹ 731 is divided among A, B and C, such that 'A' receives 25% more than 'B' and 'B' receives 25% less than 'C'. What is C's share in the amount?
A. ₹ 172 B. ₹ 200
C. ₹ 262 D. None of these

11. Thirty five per cent of 740 is 34 more than a number. What is two-fifth of the number?
A. 45 B. 90
C. 180 D. 120

12. Ramu scored 456 marks in an exam and Shama got 54 per cent marks in the same exam which is 24 marks less than Ramu. If the minimum passing marks in the exam is 34 per cent, then how much more marks did Ramu score than the minimum passing marks?
A. 184 B. 196
C. 190 D. 180

13. Shreyas bought an article and sold for 125% of its cost price. What was the cost price of the article, if Shreyas sold it for ₹ 30,750?
A. ₹ 24,600 B. ₹ 25,640
C. ₹ 24,250 D. ₹ 23,200

14. When 20% of a number is added to another number the number increases by 50%. What is the respective ratio between the first and the second number?
A. 3 : 2 B. 2 : 3
C. 5 : 2 D. Cannot be determined

15. If a number is added to seven-ninth of thirty five per cent of 900, the value so obtained is 325. What is the number?
A. 60 B. 120
C. 90 D. None of these

16. The difference between 60% of a number and 20% of the same number is 316. What is 35% of that number?
A. 270.5 B. 285.5
C. 276.5 D. 275

17. In an examination it is required to get 36% of the aggregate marks to pass. A student gets 174 marks and is declared failed by 96 marks. What is the maximum aggregate marks a student can get?
A. 750 B. 650
C. 600 D. Cannot be determined

18. There is a rebate of 15%, if electric bills are paid in time. A man got a rebate of ₹ 54 by paying the bill in time. What was his electric bill in rupees?
A. 300 B. 350
C. 360 D. 380

19. A number is increased by 20% then again by 20%. By what per cent the original number is changed?
A. 40% B. 50%
C. 44% D. 36%

20. In an examination 62% of the examinees got plucked in Mathematics, 52% passed in English and 22% failed in both the subjects. If 108 is the number of examinees who passed in both the subjects then find out the total number of candidates—
A. 1200 B. 900
C. 800 D. 1000

21. Ramesh gets 10% more than Mohan. How much per cent will Mohan get less than Ramesh?
A. 10% B. 9%
C. $9\frac{1}{11}\%$ D. 11%

22. By what quantity the use of coal is to be reduced to keep one's family budget same when the price of coal is increased by 25%?
A. 25% B. 20%
C. 30% D. 15%

23. The percentage equivalent to the fraction 3/4 is :
A. 75% B. 25%
C. 60% D. 80%

24. If each side of a square be increased by 10%, what is the percentage increase of the area?
A. 21% B. 10%
C. 20% D. 100%

25. Suppose 35% of the males are married. Find the percentage of unmarried females in the total population, if $\frac{5}{7}$ part of the population in a village are males.
A. 21% B. 25%
C. $3\frac{4}{7}\%$ D. 28%

26. In an examination, 80% of the students failed in English, 85% in Maths and 75% in both English and Maths. If 40 students passed in both the subjects, the total number of students is
A. 200 B. 400
C. 600 D. 800

27. If the ratio of Rohan's expenditure on food and clothes be 3 : 2 and the prices register an increase of 20% on food and 25% on clothes of expenditure. By how much should his salary be increased in order that he may maintain the same level of consumption as before, his present salary being ₹ 1750?

A. ₹ 2135 B. ₹ 1200
C. ₹ 387 D. ₹ 385

28. A hockey team lost 20% of the total number of matches it played during a year If it won 70% of the matches played by the team and 40 matches were drawn. What was the total number of matches played by the team during the year.

A. 400 B. 200
C. 500 D. 300

29. A rise of 25% in the price of groundnuts compels a person to buy 1.5 kg of groundnuts less for ₹ 240, original price of groundnuts per kg. is :

A. ₹ 40 B. ₹ 100
C. ₹ 32 D. ₹ 140

30. In an election between two candidates A and B, A got 55% of the total valid votes. 20% of the votes were declared invalid. If the total votes were 7500, the number of valid votes pulled in favour of the candidate B is :

A. 2700 B. 3300
C. 7500 D. 1500

31. The population of a city is 35000. On an increas of 6% in the number of men and an increase of 4% in the number of women, the population would become 36700. The number of men and women separately in thousand is:

A. 15, 16 B. 16, 17
C. 17, 18 D. 18, 17

32. After 30 kg of water were evaporated from a solution of salt and water which had 15% of salt, the remaining solution had 20% salt. The weight of the original solution is :

A. 30 kg B. 60 kg
C. 120 kg D. 600 kg

33. X's salary is half that of Y. If X got a 50% rise in his salary and Y got a 25% rise in his salary, then find the percentage increase in combined salaries of both.

A. 25% B. $16\frac{2}{3}\%$
C. 30% D. $33\frac{1}{3}\%$

34. In a particular school in a rural area, 80% of students with age below 14 years in the arca are enrolled; of them, 75% come regularly to the school. If 270 students are regular, how many students are there in the area who are below 14 years?

A. 270 B. 370
C. 450 D. 550

35. A's weight is 25% that of B's and 40% that of C's. What percentage of C's weight is B's weight?

A. 80% B. 60%
C. 160% D. 90%

ANSWERS

1	2	3	4	5	6	7	8	9	10
A	C	A	D	A	D	C	D	D	D
11	**12**	**13**	**14**	**15**	**16**	**17**	**18**	**19**	**20**
B	A	A	C	D	C	A	C	C	B
21	**22**	**23**	**24**	**25**	**26**	**27**	**28**	**29**	**30**
C	B	A	A	C	B	D	A	C	A
31	**32**	**33**	**34**	**35**					
D	C	D	C	C					

SOME SELECTED EXPLANATORY ANSWERS

1. Let Rajesh's monthly income be ₹ 100.

∴ Expenditure on grocery and household expenses = ₹ 20.

Expenditure on education etc.

$= \frac{80 \times 60}{100} = ₹\ 48$

Saving = 100 – 20 – 48 = ₹ 32

Now,

when saving ₹ 32 then income = ₹ 100

when saving ₹ 14400 then income

$= \frac{100}{32} \times 14400 = ₹\ 45000$

2. Required number of students

$= 2400\left(1+\frac{10}{100}\right)^2$ $\left[P = P_0\left(1+\frac{R}{100}\right)^T\right]$

$= 2400 \times \frac{11}{10} \times \frac{11}{10} = 2904.$

3. Required % $= \dfrac{150\times\frac{60}{100}-75\times\frac{40}{100}}{75}\times 100\%$

$= \dfrac{90-30}{75}\times 100\% = 80\%$

4. Let the fraction be $\dfrac{x}{y}$

$\therefore \quad \dfrac{x+2x}{y+3y} = \dfrac{9}{17}$

$\Rightarrow \quad \dfrac{3x}{4y} = \dfrac{9}{17}$

$\therefore \quad \dfrac{x}{y} = \dfrac{9}{17}\times\dfrac{4}{3} = \dfrac{12}{17}$

5. Let the number be x

$\because \quad \dfrac{x}{6} = 53$

$\Rightarrow \quad x = 53 \times 6$

$\therefore \quad x\times\dfrac{57}{100} = \dfrac{53\times 6\times 57}{100} = 181.26$

6. Let the monthly salary be ₹ x

$\because \quad x\times\dfrac{14}{100} = 7014$

$\Rightarrow \quad x = \dfrac{7014\times 100}{14} =$ ₹ 50100

$\therefore$ Total amount of annual investment

$= \dfrac{(14+21+6.5)}{100}\times 50100\times 12 =$ ₹ 249498

8. Monthly salary of Ms. Sujan $= \dfrac{2170\times 100}{7}$

= ₹ 31,000.

$\therefore$ Total money invested by her in a year

$= 31000\times\dfrac{(7+18+6)}{100}\times 12$

= ₹ 9610 × 12

= ₹ 115320

9. $2500\times\dfrac{30}{100}\times\dfrac{40}{100}\times\dfrac{2}{5} = 120.$

10. Let the share of C be ₹ x

$\therefore$ Share of B $= \dfrac{75x}{100} =$ ₹ $0.75x$

and share of A $= 0.75x\times\dfrac{125}{100} =$ ₹ $0.9375x$

$\because 0.9375x + 0.75x + x = 731$

$\therefore \quad x = \dfrac{731}{2.6875} =$ ₹ 272

11. Number $= 740\times\dfrac{35}{100} - 34 = 225$

$\therefore \dfrac{2}{5}$ of the number $= 225\times\dfrac{2}{5} = 90.$

12. Let the maximum marks of the eximination be x. Then, from question—

$\because \quad 54\%$ of $x = 456 - 24 = 432$

$x = \dfrac{432\times 100}{54} = 800$

$\Rightarrow$ Minimum passing marks $= \dfrac{34}{100}\times 800$

$= 272$

$\therefore$ Required difference = 456 − 272 = 184.

13. C.P. of the article $= \dfrac{30750\times 100}{125} =$ ₹ 24600.

14. Let the two numbers be x and y respectively. Then,

$\because \quad \dfrac{20x}{100}+y = y+\dfrac{50y}{100}$

$\Rightarrow \quad \dfrac{x}{5}+y = y+\dfrac{y}{2}$

$\Rightarrow \quad \dfrac{x}{5} = \dfrac{y}{2}$

$\Rightarrow \quad \dfrac{x}{y} = \dfrac{5}{2}$

$\therefore \quad x : y = 5 : 2$

15. Let the number be x.

$\because \quad 900\times\dfrac{35}{100}\times\dfrac{7}{9}+x = 325$

$\therefore \quad x = 325 - 245 = 80$

16. Let the number be 'n', then from question,

$\because \quad (60\% - 20\%)$ of $n = 316$

$\Rightarrow \quad 40\%$ of $n = 316$

$\Rightarrow \quad 35\%$ of $n = \dfrac{316}{40}\times 35$

$= 276.5$

17. Let the maximum marks of the exam. paper = n. Then from question,

$n\times\dfrac{36}{100} = 174 + 96$

$\Rightarrow \quad n = \dfrac{270\times 100}{36}$

$\therefore \quad n = 750$

18. 15% = ₹ 54

$100\% = ₹\ \frac{54}{15} \times 100$

= ₹ 360

19. Let the first number be 100.

After 20% increase, the number becomes = 120

After again 20% increase, the number becomes

$= 120 \times \frac{120}{100} = 144$

∴ Original number is changed by (144 – 100)% = 44%

20. Failed in Mathematics = 62%

Failed in English = (100 – 52)% = 48%

Failed in both = 22%

Failed only in Maths = (62 – 22)% = 40%

Failed only in English = (48 – 22)% = 26%

∴ Total failed = (40 + 26 + 22)%

= 88%

∴ Passed in both = (100 – 88)% = 12%

12% = 108

$100\% = \frac{108}{12} \times 100 = 900$

21. Ramesh gets = 110,

Mohan = 100

Required percentage = $\frac{10}{110} \times 100 = 9\frac{1}{11}\%$.

22. Required percentage = $\frac{25}{(100+25)} \times 100$

$= \frac{25}{125} \times 100 = 20\%$.

23. Required percentage = $\frac{3}{4} \times 100\% = 75\%$.

24. Percentage increase in area

$= \frac{(110)^2 - (100)^2}{(100)^2} \times 100\%$

$= \frac{210 \times 10}{100 \times 100} \times 100\% = 21\%$.

26. Let the total number of students be x. Number of student failed in one or both is given by

$n(A \cup B) = n(A) + n(B) - n(A \cap B)$

= 80% of x + 85% of x – 75% of x

$= \frac{90x}{100} = \frac{9x}{10}$

passed in both = $\left(x - \frac{9x}{10}\right) = \frac{x}{10}$

From question, $\frac{x}{10} = 40$

$\Rightarrow x = 400$

27. Let expenditure on food and clothes be ₹ $3x$ and ₹ $2x$.

From question, $3x + 2x = 1750$

$x = 350$

Food = 3 × 350 = 1050

Clothes = 2 × 350 = 700

New expenditure = 120% of 1050 + 125% of 700

$= \left(\frac{120}{100} \times 1050\right) + \left(\frac{125}{100} \times 700\right)$

= ₹ 2135

∴ Required increase = 2135 – 1750 = ₹ 385.

28. Let the total number of matches played be x.

From question, 20% of x + 70% of x + 40 = x

$\Rightarrow \frac{20x}{100} + \frac{70x}{100} + 40 = x$

$\Rightarrow x = 400.$

30. Total votes = 7500

Invalid votes = 20% of 7500 = $\frac{20}{100} \times 7500$

= 1500

∴ Valid votes = 7500 – 1500 = 6000

Valid votes polled in favour of the candidate A

= 55% of 6000 = $\frac{55}{100} \times 6000 = 3300$

∴ Valid votes polled in favour of the candidate B = 6000 – 3300 = 2700.

31. Increase in the population = 36760 – 35000

= 1760

Let the number of men in the population be x

∴ Increase in the men population = 6% of x

$= \frac{6x}{100}$

Population of women = 35000 – x

Increase in the women population

= 4% of (35000 – x) = $\frac{4}{100}(35000 - x)$

Now From question,

$\frac{6x}{100} + \frac{4}{100}(35000 - x) = 1760$

$\Rightarrow 6x + 4(35000 - x) = 176000$

$\Rightarrow 2x = 176000 - (35000 \times 4)$

$\Rightarrow 2x = 176000 - 140000$

$\Rightarrow 2x = 36000;\ x = \frac{36000}{2} = 18000$

∴ Numbere of men in the population of city = 18000 and Number of women in the population of city = 35000 – 18000 = 17000.

32. Let the weight of the original solution be x kg.

The weight of salt at 15% = $\frac{15}{100} \times x$

$= \frac{15x}{100}$ kg.

Weight of the remaining solution when 30 kg of water from the solution is evaporated

= $(x - 30)$ kg.

∴ Percentage of salt in the remaining solution

$$= \frac{15x/100}{x-30} \times 100\% = \left(\frac{15x}{x-30}\right)\%$$

It is given that the remaining solution had 20% salt (Given)

$$\therefore \quad \frac{15x}{x-30} = 20$$

$$\Rightarrow \quad 15x = 20(x - 30)$$

$$\Rightarrow \quad 20x - 15x = 600$$

$$\therefore \quad 5x = 600;$$

$$x = 600 \div 5 = 120$$

Hence, the weight of the original solution is 120 kg.

33. Suppose the initial salary of Y = ₹ 100

Then, initial salary of X = $\frac{1}{2}$ × ₹ 100 = ₹ 50

Increase in Y's salary = 25% of ₹ 100 = ₹ 25

Increase in X's salary = 50% of ₹ 50

$= ₹\left(50 \times \frac{50}{100}\right) = ₹ 25$

∴ Total increase = ₹ (25 + 25) = ₹ 50

∴ Percentage increase in combined salaries of both

$$= \frac{50}{(100+50)} \times 100$$

$$= \frac{50}{150} \times 100 = 33\frac{1}{3}\%.$$

34. Let total number of students with age below 14 years in the area be 100

Number of students enrolled = 80% of 100 = 80

Number of students who come regularly = 75% of 80

$$= 80 \times \frac{75}{100} = 60$$

If number of regualr students is 60, total number = 100

If number of regular students is 270, total number

$$= \frac{100}{60} \times 270 = 450.$$

❀❀❀❀❀

6

Profit & Loss

GENERAL FORMULAE

1. $\text{Gain }\% = \left(\frac{\text{Gain}}{\text{C.P}} \times 100\right)$

2. $\text{Loss }\% = \left(\frac{\text{Loss}}{\text{C.P}} \times 100\right)$

3. $\text{S.P} = \left(\frac{100 + \text{Gain }\%}{100}\right) \times \text{C.P}$

4. $\text{S.P} = \left(\frac{100 - \text{Loss }\%}{100}\right) \times \text{C.P}$

5. $\text{C.P} = \left(\frac{100}{100 + \text{Gain }\%}\right) \times \text{S.P}$

6. $\text{C.P} = \left(\frac{100}{100 - \text{Loss }\%}\right) \times \text{S.P}$

Formulae For Short Cut Solution

Type 1 :

Conditional Tricks

If cost price of X goods = Selling price of Y goods then,

I. $\text{Gain }\% = \frac{X - Y}{Y} \times 100$ (In case of $X > Y$)

II. $\text{Loss }\% = \frac{Y - X}{Y} \times 100$ (in case of $X < Y$)

Type 2 :

I. If X_1 and X_2 both are the rate of gain or both are the rate of loss, then, $\text{C.P.} = \left(\frac{100}{X_1 - X_2}\right) \times$ amount of difference between S.Ps.

II. If in X_1 and X_2 one is the rate of gain and another is the rate of loss, then $\text{C.P.} = \left(\frac{100}{X_1 + X_2}\right) \times$ amount of difference between S.Ps

Type 3 :

Miscellaneous Tricks

I. When a man buys two things on equal price and in those things one is sold on the profit of X % and another is sold on the loss of X %, then there is no loss or gain percent.

II. When a man sells two things at the same price each and in this process his loss on first thing is X % and gain on second thing is X % then in such type of questions, there is always a loss.

$$\text{Loss }\% = X\ \%\text{ of } X = \frac{X^2}{100} = \left(\frac{X}{10}\right)^2$$

III. Dishonest dealer and less weight

$$\text{Gain} = \frac{\text{Error}}{\text{True value} - \text{Error}} \times 100$$

Where, error = 100 gm – used weight of goods

IV. If A sells a thing to B at a gain of R_1 %, B sells it to C at a gain of R_2 % and C sells it to D at a gain of R_3 %

Then, cost price of D = Cost Price of $A\,(1 + R_1/100)\,(1 + R_2/100)\,(1 + R_3/100)$

V. If A sells a thing, to B at a loss of R %, B sells it to C at a loss of R % and C sells it to D at a loss of R % then, Cost price of D = Cost price of $A\,(1 - R_1/100)\,(1 - R_2/100)\,(1 - R_3/100)$

SOLVED EXAMPLES

Example 1: Suman purchased an item of ₹ 72,000 and sold it at a loss of 27 percent. With that amount she purchased another item and sold it at a gain of 30 percent. What is her overall profit/loss?

Solution: First S.P. = $\frac{72000 \times 73}{100}$ = ₹ 52560

Second S.P. = $\frac{52560 \times 130}{100}$ = ₹ 68328

Loss = 72000 – 68328 = ₹ 3672.

Example 2: Mr. Babulal purchased 100 pieces of an article at the rate of ₹ 480 per piece. He then listed the price so as to gain a profit of 25%. While selling the articles he offered a discount of 5%. What is the percentage of profit earned in the deal?

Solution: Profit per cent = $\left(x+y+\frac{xy}{100}\right)\%$

Here, $x = 25\%$, $y = -5\%$

$= \left(25-5-\frac{25\times5}{100}\right)\% = 18.75\%.$

Example 3: The profit earned after selling an article for ₹ 625 is the same as loss incurred after selling the article for ₹ 435. What is the cost price of the article?

Solution: C.P. of the article = $\frac{625+435}{2}$ = ₹ 530.

Example 4: A man sold an item for ₹ 6,750 at a loss of 25%. What will be the selling price of same item if he sells it at a profit of 15%?

Solution: C.P. of the item = $\frac{6750\times100}{75}$ = ₹ 9000

∴ Required S.P. of the item = $\frac{9000\times115}{100}$ = ₹ 10350.

Example 5: A man sold a wristwatch for ₹ 2,400 at a loss of twenty-five per cent. At what rate should he have sold the wristwatch to earn a profit of twenty five per cent?

Solution: C.P. of the wristwatch = $\frac{100\times2400}{100-25}$ = ₹ 3200

∴ Required S.P. of the wristwatch

= $\frac{125\times3200}{100}$ = ₹ 4000.

MULTIPLE CHOICE QUESTIONS

1. What profit / loss per cent did Raveena earn if she purchased an item of ₹ 5,600 and sold it at three-fourth of its cost price?
   A. Loss of 20 per cent B. Gain of 25 per cent
   C. Neither gain nor loss D. Loss of 15 per cent

2. By what per cent must the cost price be raised in fixing the sale price in order that there may be a profit of 20% after allowing a commission of 10%?
   A. 30% B. $33\frac{1}{3}\%$
   C. 25% D. 40%

3. A sold a watch to B at a loss of 10%. B sold it to C at a gain of 10%. If A had sold at the same price which C paid for it, what would have been his gain or loss per cent?
   A. 1% loss B. 10% gain
   C. 12% gain D. 11% loss

4. A shopkeeper purchased two cycles at ₹ 1600 and sold the first at 10% profit and second one at 20% profit. If he could sell the first cycle at a profit of 20% and the second one at a profit of 10% then he could get ₹ 5 more. What will be the cost price of each in rupees?
   A. 925, 675 B. 1000, 600
   C. 825, 775 D. 900, 700

5. A person makes a profit of 25%, by selling an article for ₹ 35.50. By how much should he increase his selling price so as to make a profit of 40%?
   A. ₹ 4.60 B. ₹ 4.26
   C. ₹ 4 D. ₹ 3.90

6. A man bought a pen and sold it at a loss of 20%. If he had bought it for 30% less and sold it for ₹ 60 more, he would have made a profit of 50%. Find the C.P. of the article.
   A. ₹ 200 B. ₹ 140
   C. ₹ 240 D. ₹ 210

7. The cost price of 15 article is equal to S.P. of 10 articles. The gain percent is:
   A. 50% B. 25%
   C. $16\frac{2}{3}\%$ D. 100%

8. Raghav bought a radio with 20% discount on the labelled price. Had he bought it with 25% discount, he would have saved ₹ 500. At what price did he buy the radio?
   A. ₹ 1000 B. ₹ 500
   C. ₹ 5000 D. ₹ 10000

9. A man buys mangoes at ₹ 5 a dozen and an equal number at ₹ 4 a dozen. He sells them at ₹ 5.50 a dozen and makes a profit of ₹ 50. How many mangoes does he buy?
   A. 30 dozens B. 40 dozens
   C. 50 dozens D. 60 dozens

10. How many for a rupee must a shopkeeper sell to gain 25%, if he bought toys at 10 for a rupee?
    A. 10 B. 9
    C. 8 D. 6

11. Suppose the ratio of two investment be 3 : 2. What is the gain or loss on the two investments taken together if a man loses 20% on an investment but gains 25% on another investment.
    A. 2.5% B. 0.2%
    C. 2% D. 3%

12. A shopkeeper gives 12% additional discount after giving an initial discount of 20% on the labelled price of a T.V. If the sale price of the T.V. is ₹ 704. What is the labelled price of the T.V?
A. ₹ 844.80 B. ₹ 929.28
C. ₹ 1000 D. ₹ 900

13. By selling 12 oranges for a rupee, a man loses 10%. How many oranges for a rupee be sold to gain 20%?
A. 5 B. 4
C. 9 D. 12

14. A dishonest shopkeeper professes to sell pulses at his cost price but uses a false weight of 950 gm for each kilogram. His gain per cent is :
A. $5\frac{5}{19}\%$ B. 19%
C. $4\frac{5}{19}\%$ D. 95%

15. Sushil bought two boxes for ₹ 1300. He sold one box at a profit of 20% and the other box at a loss of 12%. If the selling price of both boxes is the same. Then the cost price of each box is :
A. ₹ 850, ₹ 650 B. ₹ 750, ₹ 750
C. ₹ 550, ₹ 750 D. ₹ 750, ₹ 650

16. A producer sells his articles to a wholesaler at 10% profit. The wholesaler sells it to a retailer at 20%. The retailer sells it to a customer at ₹ 41.25 making 25% profit. Then the cost of production is :
A. ₹ 52 B. ₹ 132
C. ₹ 110 D. ₹ 25

17. A bought two oxen for ₹ 1080. He sold one at a loss of 5% and the other at a gain of 7%. He neither gained nor lost in this transaction. C.P. of each is:
A. ₹ 630, ₹ 450 B. ₹ 680, ₹ 400
C. ₹ 600, ₹ 480 D. ₹ 540, ₹ 540

18. A businessman makes a profit of 20% in the first year. In the subsequent year, he had a loss of 25% on the capital which he had at the beginning of the second year. His overall gain or loss per cent in the capital is:
A. 120% B. 90%
C. 100% D. 10%

19. A co-operative society manufactures note books. It makes a profit of ₹ 9.00 when it sells 100 copies to a local shop. The local shop, in turn, makes a profit of ₹ 2 on selling 50 copies at 69 paisa per copy. How much did it cost the society to manufacture 100 note books?
A. ₹ 65 B. ₹ 55
C. ₹ 56 D. ₹ 32.50

20. A man marks his goods at a price that would give him 40% profit. He sells three-fourths of his goods at the marked price. For the remaining, he has to lower the marked price by 40%. His per cent profit on the entire transaction is:
A. 21% B. 84%
C. 52% D. 26%

21. By reducing the selling price of an article by ₹ 80 a gain of 5% turns into a loss of 5%. Then the original selling price of the article is:
A. ₹ 1050 B. ₹ 525
C. ₹ 510 D. ₹ 515

22. A man bought a horse and a carriage for ₹ 3000. He sold the horse at a gain of 20% and carriage at a loss of 10%, thereby gaining 2% on the whole. Then the cost of the horse is:
A. ₹ 3060 B. ₹ 1200
C. ₹ 2100 D. ₹ 3000

23. If 20% more would be gained by selling a price of cloth for ₹ 45.50 than by selling it for ₹ 39. What per cent would be gained by selling if for ₹ 42.25?
A. 32% B. 42%
C. 30% D. 35%

24. There would be 10% loss if rice is sold at ₹ 5.40 per kg. At what price per kg should it be sold to earn a profit of 20%?
A. ₹ 6 B. ₹ 6.48
C. ₹ 7.02 D. ₹ 7.20

25. A fruitseller buys lemons at 2 for a rupee and sells them at five for three rupees. His gain per cent is:
A. 10% B. 15%
C. 20% D. 25%

26. By selling 100 bananas, a fruitseller gains the selling price of 20 bananas. His gain per cent is :
A. 10% B. 15%
C. 20% D. 25%

27. A shopkeeper mixes two varieties of tea, one costing ₹ 35 per kg and another at ₹ 45 per kg in the ratio 3 : 2. If he sells the mixed variety at ₹ 41.60 per kg, his gain or loss per cent is :
A. $6\frac{2}{3}\%$ gain B. $6\frac{2}{3}\%$ loss
C. 4% gain D. 4% loss

28. A dishonest dealer professes to sell his goods at cost price. But he uses a false weight and thus gains $6\frac{18}{47}\%$. For a kg, he uses a weight of :
A. 953 gms B. 940 gms
C. 960 gms D. 947 gms

29. By selling toffees at 20 for a rupee, a man loses 4%. To gain in 20%, for one rupee he must sell
A. 16 toffees B. 20 toffees
C. 25 toffees D. 24 toffees

30. A man sold two houses for ₹ 7.81 lakhs each. On one he gained 5% and on the other he lost 5%. What per cent is the effect of the sale on the whole?

A. 0.25% loss B. 0.25% gain
C. 25% loss D. 25% gain

31. By selling 45 oranges for ₹ 40, a man loses 20%. How many should he sell for ₹ 24 so as to gain 20% in the transaction?

A. 16 B. 18
C. 20 D. 22

32 A man gains 10% by selling an article for a certain price. If he sells it at double the price, the profit made is :

A. 20% B. 60%
C. 100% D. 120%

33. A man sells two horses for ₹ 4000 each, neither losing nor gaining in the deal. If he sold one horse at a gain of 25%, the other horse is sold at a loss of:

A. $16\frac{2}{3}\%$ B. $18\frac{2}{9}\%$
C. 25% D. 20%

34. Due to an increase of 30% in the price of eggs, 3 eggs less are available for ₹ 7.80. The present rate of eggs per dozen is :

A. ₹ 8.64 B. ₹ 8.88
C. ₹ 9.36 D. ₹ 9.25

35. The per cent profit when an article is sold for ₹ 78 is twice as when it is sold for ₹ 69. The C.P. of the article is :

A. ₹ 49 B. ₹ 51
C. ₹ 57 D. ₹ 60

36. 6% more is gained by selling a radio for ₹ 475 than by selling for ₹ 451. The C.P. of the radio is :

A. ₹ 400 B. ₹ 434
C. ₹ 446.50 D. ₹ 500

37. A tradesman by means of a false balance defrauds to the extent of 8% in buying goods and also defrauds to 8% in selling. His gain per cent is :

A. 15.48% B. 16%
C. 16.64% D. 20%

38. While selling a watch, a shopkeeper gives a discount of 5%. If he gives a discount of 7%, he earns ₹ 15 less as profit. The marked price of the watch is :

A. ₹ 697.50
B. ₹ 712.50
C. ₹ 787.50
D. ₹ 750.00

39. The marked price is 10% higher than the cost price. A discount of 10% is given on the marked price. In this kind of sale, the seller

A. bears no loss, no gain
B. gain 1%
C. loss 1%
D. gain 10%

40. The difference between a discount of 40% on ₹ 500 and two successive discounts of 36% and 4% on the same amount is :

A. 0 B. ₹ 2
C. ₹ 1.93 D. ₹ 7.20

ANSWERS

1	2	3	4	5	6	7	8	9	10
A	B	A	C	B	C	A	D	C	C
11	**12**	**13**	**14**	**15**	**16**	**17**	**18**	**19**	**20**
C	C	C	A	C	D	A	D	C	D
21	**22**	**23**	**24**	**25**	**26**	**27**	**28**	**29**	**30**
B	B	C	D	C	D	A	B	A	B
3	**32**	**33**	**34**	**35**	**36**	**37**	**38**	**39**	**40**
B	D	A	C	D	A	C	D	C	D

SOME SELECTED EXPLANATORY ANSWERS

1. S.P. of the item = $5600 \times \frac{3}{4}$ = ₹ 4200

$\therefore$ Loss % = $\frac{5600 - 4200}{5600} \times 100 = 25$

2. Let x% must the cost price be raised

$\therefore$ S.P. = $(100 + x)$

$\because \quad (100 + x)\frac{90}{100} = 120$

$\Rightarrow \quad 3x = 100$

$\therefore \quad x = 33\frac{1}{3}\%.$

3. Let A's C.P. = ₹ 100

A's S.P. = $100 \times \frac{90}{100}$;

B's S.P. = $100 \times \frac{90}{100} \times \frac{110}{100}$

C paid = B's S.P. = $100\times\frac{90}{100}\times\frac{110}{100}$

$= 99$

If A had sold at ₹ 99

Then, his loss = (100 – 99)% = 1%.

4. Let the C.P. of 1st cycle = ₹ x

and C.P. of 2nd cycle = ₹ $(1600 - x)$

Total S.P. in 1st case

$$= x\times\frac{110}{100}+(1600-x)\times\frac{120}{100}$$

$$= \frac{12\times1600-x}{10}$$

Total S.P. in 2nd case

$$= x\times\frac{120}{100}+(1600-x)\times\frac{110}{100}$$

$$= \frac{11\times1600+x}{10}$$

$$\because \frac{11\times1600+x}{10}-\frac{12\times1600-x}{10} = 5$$

$$\therefore x = \frac{1650}{2} = 825$$

C.P. of 1st cycle = 825

C.P. of 2nd cycle = 1600 – 825 = 775.

5. Let new S.P. be ₹ x

Then (100 + Gain%) : (1st S.P.)

= (100 + Gain%) : (2nd S.P.)

125 : 35.50 = 140 : x

$$\Rightarrow x = \frac{35.50\times140}{125} = ₹\ 39.76$$

∴ Increased in S.P. = ₹ (39.76 – 35.50)

= ₹ 4.26.

6. Let original C.P. be ₹ x

$$\text{S.P.} = 80\% \text{ of } x = \frac{80x}{100} = \frac{4x}{5}$$

$$\text{New C.P.} = 70\% \text{ of } x = \frac{70x}{100} = \frac{7x}{10}$$

$$\text{New S.P.} = 150\% \text{ of } \frac{7x}{10} = \frac{21x}{20}$$

$$\therefore \frac{21x}{20}-\frac{4x}{5} = 60$$

$$\Rightarrow \frac{x}{4} = 60$$

$x = 240$

7. Let C.P. of each article be ₹ 1

Then C.P. of 10 article = ₹ 10

S.P. of 10 article = ₹ 15

$$\text{Gain \%} = \left(\frac{15-10}{10}\times100\right)\% = \left(\frac{5}{10}\times100\right)\%$$

= 50%.

8. Let the labelled price be x

$$\therefore \text{S.P.} = 80\% \text{ of } x = \frac{4x}{5}$$

$$\text{New S.P.} = 75\% \text{ of } x = \frac{3x}{4}$$

$$\therefore \frac{4x}{5}-\frac{3x}{4} = 500$$

$\Rightarrow x =$ ₹ 10000.

9. C.P of 2 dozens of mangoes = ₹ (5 + 4)

= ₹ 9

S.P. of 2 dozens of mangoes = ₹ 11

2 dozens of mangoes are bought at a profit of ₹ 2.

If profit is ₹ 50, mangoes bought = $\frac{2}{2}\times50$

= 50 dozens.

10. C.P of 10 toys = ₹ 1

Gain = 25%

$$\text{S.P of 10 toys} = \frac{125}{100}\times1 = ₹\ \frac{5}{4}$$

Thus S.P of 10 toys is ₹ $\frac{5}{4}$

∴ For ₹ 1, Number of toys = $10\times\frac{4}{5} = 8$

So he must sell 8 toys for a rupee.

11. Let the investments are $3x$ and $2x$

Then total investment = $5x$

Receipt = (80% of $3x$ + 125% of $2x$)

= $(2.4x + 2.5x) = 4.9x$

$$\therefore \text{loss} = \left(\frac{0.1x}{5x}\times100\right)\% = 2\%$$

12. Let the labelled price of the T.V be ₹ x

$$\text{Initial S.P} = 80\% \text{ of } x = \frac{80x}{100}$$

$$\text{New S.P} = 88\% \text{ of } \frac{80x}{100}$$

$$= \frac{88}{100}\times\frac{80x}{100} = \frac{704x}{1000}$$

From question,

$$\frac{704x}{1000} = 704$$

$704x = 704 \times 1000$

$\Rightarrow \quad x = 1000$

$\therefore$ The labelled price of the T.V = ₹ 1000.

14. Let C.P. of 1 gm pulses be ₹ 1

$\therefore$ C.P. of 950 gm pulses = ₹ 950

S.P. of 950 gm = C.P. of 1 kg

= C.P. of 1000 gm = ₹ 1000

$\therefore$ Gain = ₹ (1000 – 950) = ₹ 50

$$\therefore \quad \text{Gain \%} = \frac{50}{950} \times 100 = 5\frac{5}{19}\%.$$

17. From question,

$\therefore$ Loss on one = Gain on other

$\therefore$ 5% of the C.P. of one = 7% of the C.P. of the other

$$\Rightarrow \frac{\text{C.P. of 1st}}{\text{C.P. of 2nd}} = \frac{7\%}{5\%} = \frac{7}{5}$$

or, C.P. of 1st : C.P. of 2nd = 7 : 5

Divide ₹ 1080 in the ratio of 7 : 5

$$\therefore \text{C.P. of the 1st} = \frac{7}{12} \times 1080 = ₹\ 630.$$

$$\text{and C.P. of the 2nd} = ₹\ \frac{5}{12} \times 1080 = ₹\ 450.$$

18. Let his capital at the beginning of first year be ₹ 100

Profit during first year = 20% of ₹ 100 = ₹ 20

$\therefore$ Capital at the beginning of the second year

= ₹ (100 + 20) = ₹ 120

Loss during second year = 25% of ₹ 120

$$= ₹\left(120 \times \frac{25}{100}\right) = ₹\ 30$$

$\therefore$ Capital at the end of second year

= ₹ (120 – 30) = ₹ 90

$\therefore$ Loss = ₹ (100 – 90) = ₹ 10

$$\text{Overall Loss \% on his capital} = \left(\frac{10}{100} \times 100\right)\%$$

= 10%.

19. The local shop sells 50 copies @ 69 paisa per copy

= ₹ (50 × 0.69) = ₹ 34.50

His profit = ₹ 2

$\therefore$ The local shop purchases 50 copies for

= S.P. – Profit = ₹ (34.50 – 2) = ₹ 32.50

$\therefore$ The local shop purchases 100 copies for

$$= ₹\left(\frac{32.50}{50} \times 100\right) = ₹\ 65$$

$\therefore$ Co-operative society sells 100 copies for ₹ 65

Profit = ₹ 9

$\therefore$ Co-operative society manufactures 100 copies for

= ₹ (65 – 9) = ₹ 56.

23. Let C.P. of cloth be ₹ x. Then $x \times \frac{20}{100}$

= ₹ (45.50 – 39) = ₹ 6.50

$$\Rightarrow \quad x = \frac{6.50 \times 100}{20} = ₹\ 32.50$$

Gain = ₹ (42.25 – 32.50) = ₹ 9.75

$$\therefore \text{Gain\%} = \frac{9.75}{32.50} \times 100 = 30\%.$$

24. 90 : 5.40 :: 120 : x

$$\therefore x = \frac{5.40 \times 120}{90} = 7.20.$$

So, the rice must be sold at ₹ 7.20 per kg.

25. Suppose he buys 10 lemons.

$$\text{C.P.} = ₹\left(\frac{10}{2}\right) = ₹\ 5,\ \text{S.P.} = ₹\left(\frac{3}{5} \times 10\right) = ₹\ 6.$$

$$\text{Gain\%} = \left(\frac{1}{5} \times 100\right)\% = 20\%.$$

26. Gain = (S.P. of 100 bananas) – (C.P. of 100 bananas)

(S.P. of 20) = (S.P. of 100) – (C.P. of 100)

₹ S.P. of 80 = C.P. of 100.

Let C.P. of each = ₹ 1.

C.P. of 80 = ₹ 80

S.P. of 80 = ₹ 100.

$$\therefore \text{Gain \%} = \left(\frac{20}{80} \times 100\right)\% = 25\%$$

27. Suppose he purchases 3 kg and 2 kg of tea of first and second kind respectively.

C.P. = ₹ (3 × 35 + 2 × 45) = ₹ 195.

S.P. = ₹ (5 × 41.60) = ₹ 208.

$$\text{Gain \%} = \left(\frac{13}{195} \times 100\right)\% = 6\frac{2}{3}\%.$$

28. Let the error be x gms. Then,

$$\frac{x}{1000 - x} \times 100 = \frac{300}{47} \text{ or } \frac{x}{1000 - x} = \frac{3}{47}$$

$\therefore$ $47x = 3000 - 3x$ or $x = 60$.

So, he uses a weight = (1000 – 60) gm = 940 gm for a kg.

29. Suppose he sells 20 toffees.

Then, S.P. = ₹ 1 and Loss = 4%.

$$\therefore \text{C.P.} = \left(\frac{100}{96} \times 1\right) = ₹\frac{25}{24}$$

Gain = 20%

$\therefore$ S.P. = $₹\left(\frac{120}{100}\times\frac{25}{24}\right) = ₹\frac{5}{4}$.

For ₹ $\frac{5}{4}$, toffees sold = $\left(20\times\frac{4}{5}\right)$ = 16.

So, he must sell 16 toffees for a rupee.

30. Loss % = $\left(\frac{5}{10}\right)^2 = \frac{1}{4}\% = 0.25\%$.

31. S.P. of 1 orange = $₹\left(\frac{40}{45}\right) = ₹\frac{8}{9}$.

80% of C.P. = $\frac{8}{9}$ or C.P. = $\left(\frac{8}{9}\times\frac{100}{80}\right) = ₹\frac{10}{9}$.

S.P. = $\left(120\% \text{ of } ₹\frac{10}{9}\right) = ₹\frac{4}{3}$.

For $₹\frac{4}{3}$, he sells 1 orange

For ₹ 24, he would sell $\left(\frac{3}{4}\times 24\right)$ = 18 oranges.

32. Let C.P. = ₹ x.

First S.P. = 110% of x = $₹\left(\frac{11}{10}x\right)$

Second S.P. = $\frac{22}{10}x$

New gain = $\left(\frac{22}{10}x - x\right) = \frac{12x}{10}$.

New gain % = $\left(\frac{12x}{10\times x}\times 100\right)\%$ = 120%.

33. C.P. of two horses = ₹ 8000.

S.P. of one horse = ₹ 4000, gain = 25%.

$\therefore$ C.P. of this horse = $₹\left(\frac{100}{125}\times 4000\right)$

= ₹ 3200.

C.P. of another horse = ₹ (8000 – 3200)

= ₹ 4800.

S.P. of this horse = ₹ 4000.

$\therefore$ Loss% = $\left(\frac{800}{4800}\times 100\right)\% = 16\frac{2}{3}\%$.

35. Let the C.P. be ₹ x.

Then, $\frac{2(69-x)}{100} = \frac{78-x}{100}$

or, $138 - 2x = 78 - x$

or, $x = 60$

$\therefore$ C.P. = ₹ 60.

36. Difference between two selling prices = ₹ 24

$\therefore$ 6% of C.P. = ₹ 24

Hence, C.P. = $₹\left(\frac{24\times 100}{6}\right)$ = ₹400.

37. **Rule.** In such questions we adopt the rule :

Gain % = $\frac{(100 + \text{common gain\%})^2}{100} - 100$

$= \left\{\frac{(108)^2}{100} - 100\right\}\%$ = 16.64%.

38. Let the marked price be ₹ x.

Then, (7% of x) – 15 = 5% of x

or, $\frac{7x}{100} - \frac{5x}{100}$ = 15 or x = 750.

39. Let C.P. = ₹ 100.

Marked Price = ₹ 110.

S.P. = 90% of ₹ 110 = ₹ 99.

$\therefore$ Loss = 1%.

40. Price after 40% discount = 60% of ₹ 500

= ₹ 300.

Price after 36% discount = 64% of ₹ 500

= ₹ 320.

Price after next 4% discount = 96% of ₹ 320

= ₹ 307.20.

Difference in two prices = ₹ 307.20 – ₹ 300.00

= ₹ 7.20.

❋❋❋❋❋

Mixture & Alligation

Alligation deals with calculation of values or properties of a mixture. Alligation is the rule that enables us—

(1) to find the proportion in which the two or more ingredients at the given prices must be mixed to yield a mixture at the given price. This is termed as "Alligation Alternate".

(2) to calculate the average or mean value of a mixture when the prices of two or more ingredients which are to be mixed together and proportion in which they are to be mixed are given. This is termed as "Alligation Medial".

1. Rule of Alligation:

$$\frac{\text{A of Cheap mixture}}{\text{A of Dearer mixture}} = \frac{\text{CP of Dearer} - \text{Mean Price}}{\text{Mean Price} - \text{CP of Cheaper}}$$

Here cost price of unit quantity of the mixture is called the *Mean Price.*

The above rule may be represented schematically as under:

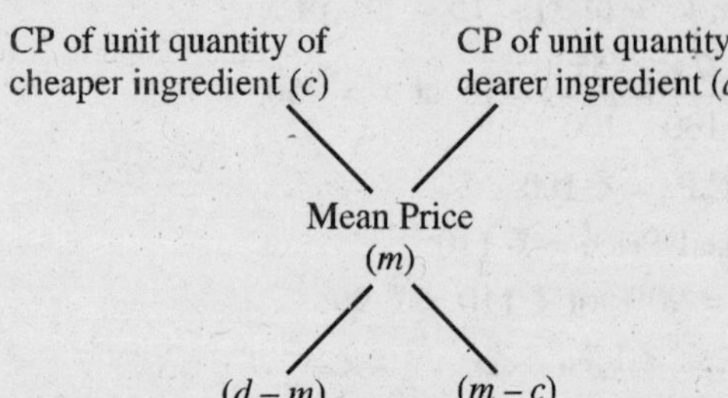

(Cheaper quantity) : (Dearer quantity)
$= (d - m) : (m - c)$

This relationship is very helpful in solving problems on mixture involving percentage values, rates, prices, speeds etc.

2. m gm of sugar solution has x % sugar in it. To increase the sugar content in the solution to y %,

quantity of sugar need to be added $= \dfrac{m(y-x)}{100-y}$

3. A vessel contains x litres of liquid A. y litres are withdrawn and replaced by liquid B. Next y litres of the mixture is withdrawn and again replaced by liquid B.

This operation is repeated n times.

$$\frac{\text{Quantity of liquid A left after } n\text{th operation}}{\text{Whole quantity of liquid A initially present}}$$

$$= \left(\frac{x-y}{x}\right)^n \text{ or } \left(1-\frac{y}{x}\right)^n$$

SOLVED EXAMPLES

Example 1: Find the quantities of two types of wheat, one @ ₹ 6 per kg and the other @ ₹ 4 per kg. to get 20 kgs. of wheat mixture worth ₹ 4.5 per kg.

Solution:

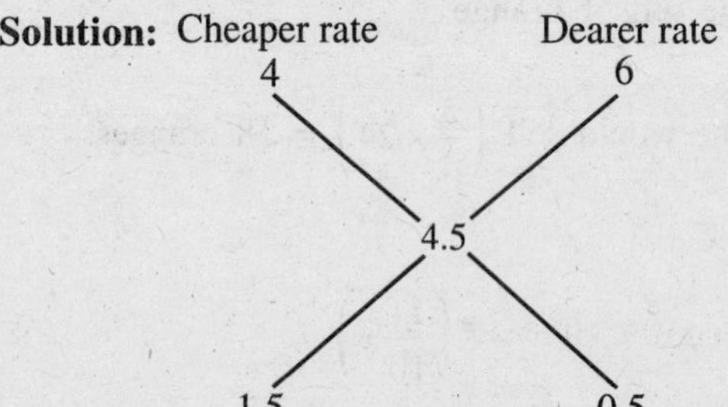

$$\frac{\text{Quantity of cheaper wheat}}{\text{Quantity of dearer wheat}} = \frac{1.5}{0.5} = \frac{3}{1}$$

Quantity of cheaper wheat

$= \dfrac{3}{3+1} \times 20 = 15$ kgs

Quantity of dearer wheat

$= \dfrac{1}{3+1} \times 20 = 5$ kgs.

Example 2: In what proportion water be mixed with pure milk in order to make a profit of 20% by selling it at cost price?

Solution: Let cost price of pure milk be Re. 1 per litre.

The SP of mixture = ₹ 1 per litre

Profit = 20%

So, CP of 1 litre of mixture

$= ₹ \left(1 \times \dfrac{100}{120}\right) = ₹ \dfrac{5}{6}$

We assume that CP of 1 litre of water is zero. Using the rule of alligation on 1 litre,

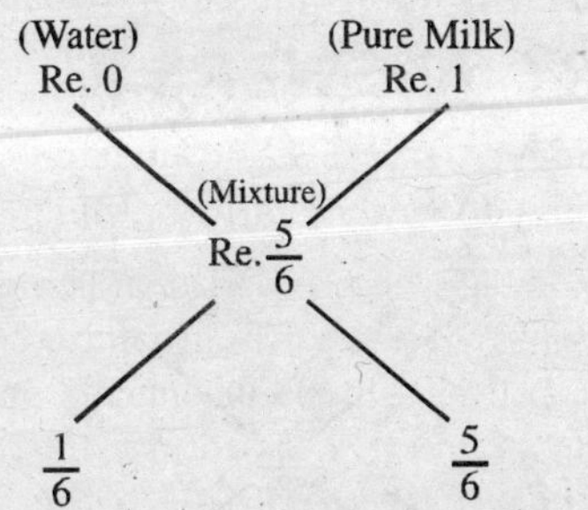

$$\frac{\text{Quantity of water}}{\text{Quantity of pure milk}} = \frac{\frac{1}{6}}{\frac{5}{6}} = \frac{1}{5}$$

or, Ratio of water to pure milk in the mixture = 1 : 5.

MULTIPLE CHOICE QUESTIONS

1. In what proportion must tea at ₹ 62 per kg be mixed with tea at ₹ 72 per kg in order to obtain the mixture worth ₹ 65 per kg?

A. 4 : 6 B. 7 : 3
C. 2 : 3 D. 4 : 7

2. Find the quantity of rice @ ₹ 10 per kg. which should be mixed with 25 kgs of rice @ ₹ 8 per kg, so that on selling the mixture @ ₹ 15 per kg there is 80% profit.

A. 6 kgs B. 7 kgs
C. 3 kgs D. 5 kgs

3. A shopkeeper buys 26 kgs of milk @ ₹ 16 per kg. He also buys from another source an inferior quality of milk @ ₹ 10 per kg. How much quantity of the latter should he buy to mix it with the former so that he can sell the mixture @ ₹ 14 per kg without making any loss?

A. 13 kgs B. 12 kgs
C. 14 kgs D. 16 kgs

4. Two vessels A and B contain milk and water in the ratio 7 : 5 and 17 : 7 respectively. In what ratio mixtures from two vessels should be mixed to get a new mixture containing milk and water in the ratio 5 : 3?

A. 1 : 2 B. 2 : 1
C. 2 : 3 D. 3 : 2

5. Two vessels A and B contain mixture of milk and water in the ratio 4 : 1 and 9 : 11 respectively. They are mixed in the ratio of 3 : 2. Find the ratio of milk : water in the resulting mixture.

A. 34 : 16 B. 33 : 17
C. 16 : 34 D. 17 : 33

6. A person has two solutions of sugar with 30% and 50% concentration respectively. In what proportion should he mix two solutions to get 45% concentration in the resulting mixture?

A. 1 : 3 B. 3 : 1
C. 2 : 3 D. 3 : 2

7. 6 litres of milk and water mixture has 75% milk in it. How much milk should be added to the mixture to make it 90% pure?

A. 8 litres B. 9 litres
C. 10 litres D. 12 litres

8. In what ratio must water be added to spirit to gain 25% by selling it at cost price?

A. 1 : 4 B. 4 : 1
C. 3 : 4 D. 4 : 3

9. A shopkeeper has 50 kgs of rice. He sells a part of it at 20% profit and the rest at 40% profit. If he gains 25% on the whole, find the quantity of each part.

A. 12.5 kgs and 37.5 kgs
B. 37.5 kgs and 12.5 kgs
C. 23.5 kgs and 21.5 kgs
D. 21.5 kgs and 23.5 kgs

10. A shopkeeper has 100 kgs of tea. He sells a part of it at 20% profit and the rest at 5% loss. If his overall profit is 10%, find the quantity for each part.

A. 20 kgs B. 25 kgs
C. 30 kgs D. 40 kgs

ANSWERS

1	2	3	4	5	6	7	8	9	10
B	D	A	B	B	A	B	A	A	D

SOME SELECTED EXPLANATORY ANSWERS

1. 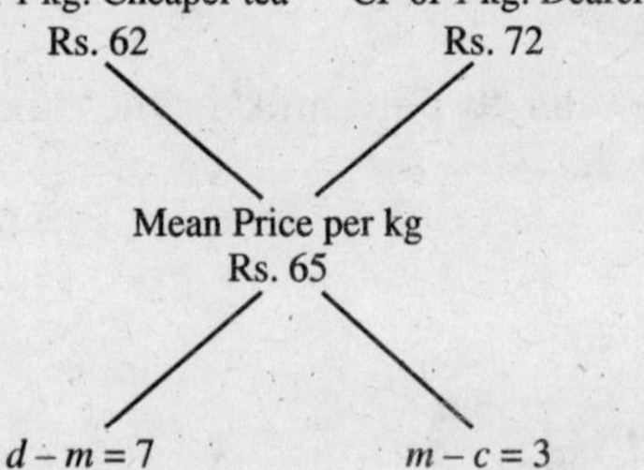

Using Alligation rule,

$$\frac{\text{Quantity of cheaper tea}}{\text{Quantity of dearer tea}} = \frac{d-m}{m-c} = \frac{7}{3}$$

Therefore, they must be mixed in the ratio of 7 : 3.

2. Cost price of the mixture $= 15 \times \frac{100}{180}$

$= ₹\ \frac{25}{3}$ per kg

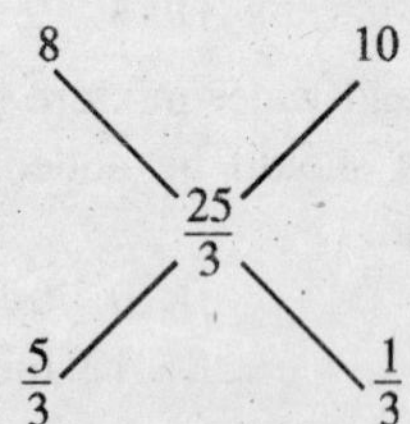

$$\frac{\text{Quantity of rice @ ₹ 8 per kg}}{\text{Quantity of rice @ ₹ 10 per kg}} = \frac{5/3}{1/3} = \frac{5}{1}$$

Quantity of rice @ ₹ 10 per kg $= 25 \times \frac{1}{5}$

= 5 kgs.

3. 16 10

14

4 2

or 2 : 1

$$\frac{\text{Quantity of milk @ ₹ 10 per kg}}{\text{Quantity of milk @ ₹ 16 per kg}} = \frac{1}{2}$$

So, quantity of milk @ ₹ 10 per kg. $= \frac{26}{2}$

= 13 kgs.

4. First of all we write the fraction of milk present in three mixtures.

In A : $\frac{7}{12}$ In B : $\frac{17}{24}$

In combination of A and B : $\frac{5}{8}$

We now apply alligation rule on these fractions.

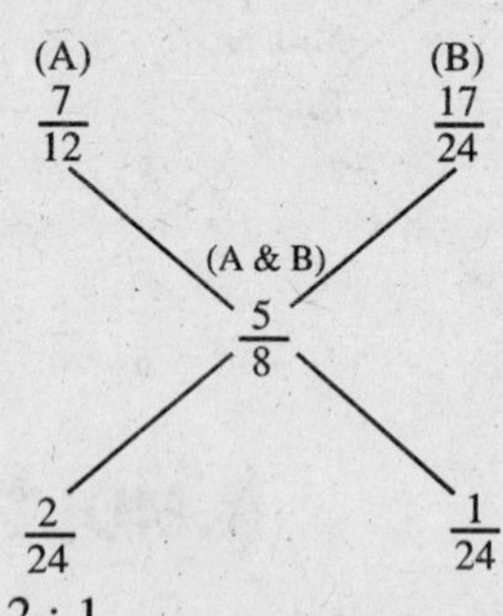

or, 2 : 1

So, Ratio of A : B = 2 : 1.

5. Fraction is *Milk* *Water*

A : $\frac{4}{5}$ $\frac{1}{5}$

B : $\frac{9}{20}$ $\frac{11}{20}$

(3A + 2B) = A and B : $\left(\frac{12}{5}+\frac{9}{10}\right)$ $\left(\frac{3}{5}+\frac{11}{10}\right)$

$\frac{33}{10}$ $\frac{17}{10}$

So, Ratio of milk : water in the resulting mixture = 33 : 17.

6. 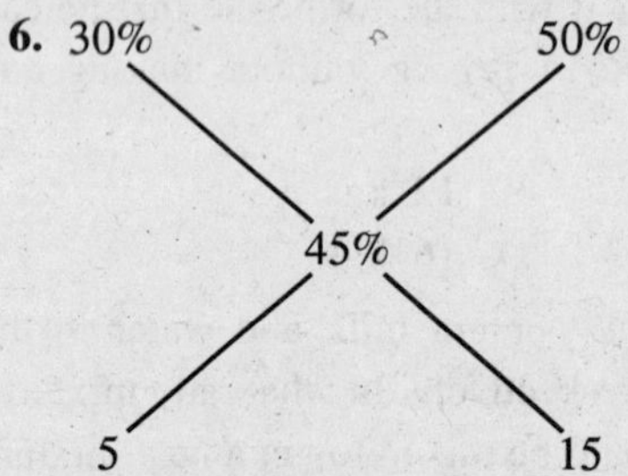

He should mix 30% and 50% in the ratio 5 : 15 or 1 : 3.

$$\frac{\text{30\% Solution}}{\text{50\% Solution}} = \frac{1}{3}$$

or 1 : 3

7. The given solution has 75% milk.

Milk to be added has 100% milk.

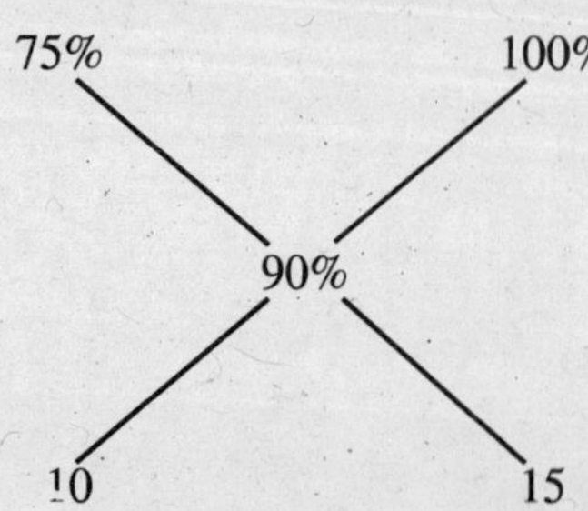

Milk should be added to the given mixture in the ratio 15 : 10 or 3 : 2.

$\therefore$ Quantity of milk to be added = $\frac{3}{2} \times 6$

= 9 litres.

8. Let cost price of spirit be Re. 1 per litre.

Then SP of mixture = Re. 1 per litre

Gain = 25%

So, CP of mixture $= 1 \times \frac{100}{125} = \text{Re. } \frac{4}{5}$

We assume that CP of water is zero.

Using alligation rule on cost price,

Water should be mixed to spirit in the ratio $\frac{1}{5} : \frac{4}{5}$ or 1 : 4.

9.

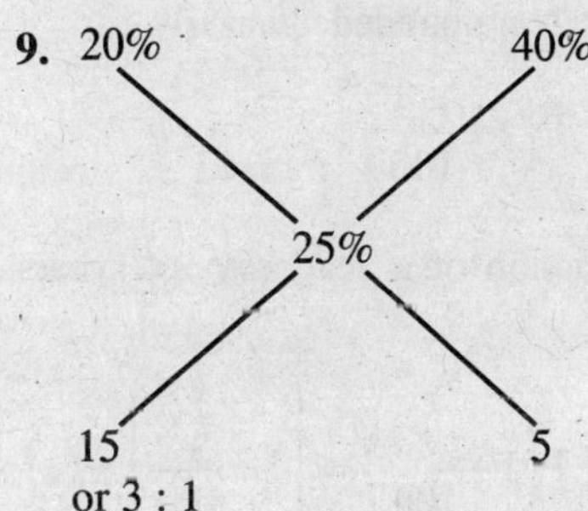

or 3 : 1

Quantity sold at 20% profit = $\frac{3}{3+1} \times 50$

= 37.5 kgs.

Quantity sold at 40% profit = (50 – 37.5)

= 12.5 kgs.

10.

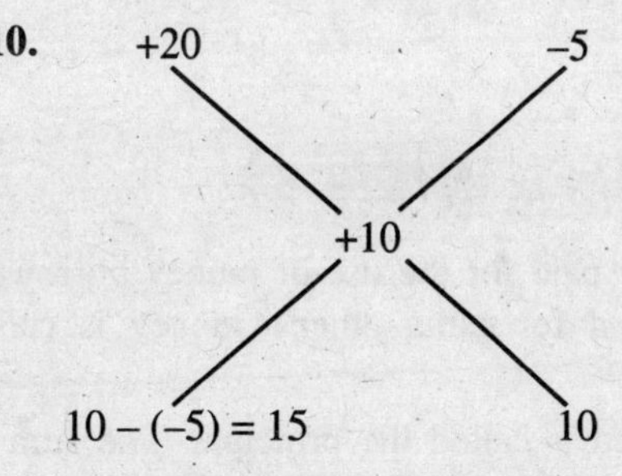

or 3 : 2

Quantity sold at 20% profit = $\frac{3}{3+2} \times 100$

= 60 kgs.

Quantity sold at 5% loss = (100 – 60)

= 40 kgs.

❋ ❋ ❋ ❋ ❋

8 Simple & Compound Interests

SIMPLE INTEREST

Interest is the money paid for the use of money borrowed, *i.e.*, extra money paid for using other's money is called *interest.*

The sum borrowed is called the principal. The sum of interest and principal is called the *Amount.*

If the interest on a certain sum borrowed for a certain period is reckoned uniformly, then it is called simple interest, denoted by S.I.

Thus, if A = Amount, P = Principal,
I = Interest, T = Time (in year),
R = Rate per cent per annum, then

(*a*) $I = \frac{P \times R \times T}{100}$ (*b*) $P = \frac{100 \times I}{R \times T}$

(*c*) $T = \frac{100 \times I}{P \times R}$ (*d*) $R = \frac{100 \times I}{P \times T}$

(*e*) $P = \frac{100\,A}{100 + RT}$ (*f*) $A = P + I.$

COMPOUND INTEREST

In business transaction if interest as it becomes due is not paid to the lender but is added on to the principal, the money is said to be lent at *compound interest* and the total sum owed after a given time is called the amount at compound interest for that time.

After a certain period, the difference between the amount and the original principal is called the compound Interest (C.I.).

Some Important Formulae :

Let Principal = P
Time = n years
Rate = r% p.a.

then, the amount,

(*a*) when interest is compounded annually:

$$\text{then, Amount} = P\left(1 + \frac{r}{100}\right)^n$$

(*b*) when interest is compounded half yearly:

$$\text{then, Amount} = P\left(1 + \frac{r/2}{100}\right)^{2n}$$

(*c*) when interest is compounded quarterly :

$$\text{then, Amount} = P\left(1 + \frac{r/4}{100}\right)^{4n}$$

(*d*) when time is fraction of a year, say $4\frac{1}{3}$ years,

$$\text{then, Amount} = P\left(1 + \frac{r}{100}\right)^4 \times \left(1 + \frac{\frac{1}{3}r}{100}\right)$$

(*e*) when rates are r_1%, r_2% and r_3% for Ist, IInd and IIIrd year respectively;

$$\text{then, Amount} = P\left(1 + \frac{r_1}{100}\right)\left(1 + \frac{r_2}{100}\right)\left(1 + \frac{r_3}{100}\right)$$

SOLVED EXAMPLES

Example 1: A man gets a simple interest of ₹ 1,000 on a certain principal at the rate of 5% p.a. in 4 years. What compound interest will the man get on twice the principal in two years at the same rate?

Solution: $\because$ Principal $= \frac{1000 \times 100}{4 \times 5} =$ ₹ 5000

$$\therefore \text{Required C.I.} = 1000\left[\left(1 + \frac{5}{100}\right)^2 - 1\right]$$

$$= 1000\left[\frac{441 - 400}{400}\right]$$

$$= 1000 \times \frac{41}{400}$$

= ₹ 102.5.

Example 2: The simple interest accrued on an amount of ₹ 25,000 at the end of four years is ₹ 8,000. What would be the compound interest accrued on the same amount at the same rate in the same period?

Solution: Rate $= \frac{8000 \times 100}{25000 \times 4}\% = 8\%$

$\therefore$ C.I. $= 25000\left[\left(1+\frac{8}{100}\right)^4 - 1\right]$

$= 25000\left(\frac{27^4 - 25^4}{25^4}\right)$

$= 25000\left[\frac{531441 - 390625}{390625}\right]$

= ₹ 9012.224

Example 3: The difference between the amount of compound interest and simple interest accrued on an amount of ₹ 26,000 at the end of 3 years is ₹ 2994.134. What is the rate of interest p.c.p.a.?

Solution: $\because$ $2994.134 = \frac{26000r^2}{(100)^2}\left(\frac{r}{100}+3\right)$

$= \frac{26r^2}{10}\left(\frac{r+300}{100}\right)$

$\Rightarrow$ $2994134 = 26r^3 + 7800r^2$

$\Rightarrow$ $115159 = r^3 + 300r^2$

$\therefore$ $r = 19$

Example 4: What would be the compound interest accrued on an amount of ₹ 45,400/- at the end of two years at the rate of 15% p.a.?

Solution: C.I. $= 45400\left[\left(1+\frac{15}{100}\right)^2 - 1\right]$

$= 45400\left[\frac{23}{20}\times\frac{23}{20} - 1\right]$

$= 45400 \times \frac{129}{400}$

$= \frac{29283}{2}$ = ₹ 14641.5

MULTIPLE CHOICE QUESTIONS

1. Anshul borrowed some money at the rate of 4% p.a. for the first three years, at the rate of 8% p.a. for the next two years and at the rate of 9% p.a. for the period beyond 5 years. If he pays a total simple interest of ₹ 19,550 at the end of 7 years, how much money did he borrow?
   A. ₹ 39,500 B. ₹ 42,500
   C. ₹ 41,900 D. ₹ 43,000

2. The simple interest accrued on an amount at the end of five years @ 12.5% p.a. ₹ 1,575. What is the amount?
   A. ₹ 2,050 B. ₹ 2,550
   C. ₹ 2,250 D. ₹ 2,520

3. Siyaram invested equal sum of money in two schemes. Under scheme X, the compound interest rate was 10% p.a. and under scheme Y, the compound interest rate was 12% p.a. The interest after two years on the sum invested in Scheme X was ₹ 63. How much is the interest earned under Scheme Y after two years?
   A. ₹ 79.0272 B. ₹ 70.56
   C. ₹ 76.32 D. Cannot be determined

4. What would be the compound interest accrued on an amount of ₹ 15,000 at the rate of 15% at the end of three years?
   A. ₹ 7813.125 B. ₹ 7762.50
   C. ₹ 7762.125 D. ₹ 11235.09375

5. If the difference between the simple interest and compound interest earned on an amount @ 15% p.a. at the end of 3 years is ₹ 595.35, what is the amount?
   A. ₹ 8,400 B. ₹ 9,200
   C. ₹ 6,800 D. Cannot be determined

6. What will be the simple interest earned on an amount of ₹ 988 @ 18% p.a., at the end of 5 years?
   A. ₹ 711.36 B. ₹ 898.2
   C. ₹ 799.25 D. None of these

7. The simple interest accrued on a sum of certain principal is ₹ 1,200 in four years at the rate of 8% p.a. What would be the simple interest accrued on thrice of that principal at the rate of 6% p.a. in 3 years?
   A. ₹ 2,025 B. ₹ 3,025
   C. ₹ 2,250 D. ₹ 2,150

8. What amount of compound interest can be obtained on an amount of ₹ 18,000 at the rate of 10% p.a. at the end of three years?
   A. ₹ 5,628 B. ₹ 5,400
   C. ₹ 5,940 D. None of these

9. Shrivastava invests ₹ 14500 for 6 years at the certain rate of simple interest. After 6 years his invested sum becomes ₹ 21460. Find out the rate of interest per annum—
   A. 4% p.a. B. 10% p.a.
   C. 6% p.a. D. 8% p.a.

10. A sum of ₹ 12,500 amounts to ₹ 15,500 in 4 years at the rate of simple interest. What is the rate of interest?
    A. 3% B. 4%
    C. 5% D. 6%

11. A sum fetched a total simple interest of ₹ 4016. 25 at the rate of 9% p.a. in 5 years. What is the sum?
    A. ₹ 4462.50 B. ₹ 8032.50
    C. ₹ 8900 D. ₹ 8925

12. ₹ 800 becomes ₹ 956 in 3 years at a certain rate of simple interest. If the rate of interest is increased by 4%, what amount will ₹ 800 become in 3 years?
A. ₹ 1020.80 B. ₹ 1025
C. ₹ 1052 D. Data inadequate

13. A certain amount earns simple interest of ₹ 1750 after 7 years. Had the interest been 2% more, how much more interest would it have earned?
A. ₹ 35 B. ₹ 245
C. ₹ 350 D. Cannot be determined

14. Neelam borrowed some money at the rate of 6% p.a. for the first three years, 9% p.a. for the next five years and 13% p.a. for the period beyond eight years. If the total interest paid by him at the end of eleven years is ₹ 8160, how much money did he borrow?
A. ₹ 8000 B. ₹ 10,000
C. ₹ 12000 D. Data inadequate

15. The simple interest on a sum of money will be ₹ 600 after 10 years. If the principal is trebled after 5 years, what will be the total interest at the end of the tenth year?
A. ₹ 600 B. ₹ 900
C. ₹ 1200 D. ₹ 1500

16. Simple interest on a certain sum at a certain annual rate of interest is $\frac{1}{9}$ of the sum. If the numbers representing rate percent and time in years be equal, then the rate of interest is :
A. $3\frac{1}{3}\%$ B. 5%
C. $6\frac{2}{3}\%$ D. 10%

17. A borrowed some money from B at 12% p.a. S.I. for 3 years. He then added some more money to the borrowed sum and lent it to C for the same period at 14% p.a. rate of interest. If A gains ₹ 93.90 in the whole transaction, how much money did he add from his side?
A. ₹ 35 B. ₹ 55
C. ₹ 80 D. ₹ 105

18. A sum of ₹ 725 is lent in the beginning of a year at a certain rate of interest. After 8 months, a sum of ₹ 362.50 more is lent but at the rate twice the former. At the end of the year, ₹ 33.50 is earned as interest from both the loans. What was the original rate of interest?
A. 3.6% B. 4.5%
C. 5% D. None of these

19. The difference between the simple interest received from two different sources on ₹ 1500 for 3 years is ₹ 13.50. The difference between their rates of interest is:
A. 0.1% B. 0.2%
C. 0.3% D. 0.4%

20. Priya invested an amount of ₹ 12,000 at the rate of 10% p.a. simple interest and another amount at the rate of 20% p.a. simple interest. The total interest earned at the end of one year on the total amount invested became 14% p.a. Find the total amount invested.
A. ₹ 20,000 B. ₹ 22,000
C. ₹ 24,000 D. ₹ 25,000

21. If the rate increases by 2%, the simple interest received on a sum of money increases by ₹ 108. If the time period is increased by 2 years, the simple interest on the same sum increases by ₹ 180. The sum is:
A. ₹ 1800 B. ₹ 3600
C. ₹ 5400 D. Data inadequate

22. A sum of ₹ 2600 is lent out in two parts in such a way that the interest on one part at 10% for 5 years is equal to that on another at 9% for 6 years. The sum lent out at 10% is:
A. ₹ 1150 B. ₹ 1250
C. ₹ 1350 D. ₹ 1450

23. A sum of 1550 was lent partly at 5% and partly at 8% p.a. simple interest. The total interest received after 3 years was ₹ 300. The ratio of the money lent at 5% to that lent at 8% is :
A. 5 : 8 B. 8 : 5
C. 16 : 15 D. 31 : 6

24. Deepak invested certain amount in three different schemes A, B and C with the rate of interest 10% p.a., 12% p.a. and 15% p.a. respectively. If the total interest accrued in one years was ₹ 3200 and the amount invested in Scheme C was 150% of the amount invested in Scheme A and 240% of the amount invested in Scheme B, what was the amount invested in Scheme B?
A. ₹ 5000 B. ₹ 6500
C. ₹ 8000 D. Cannot be determined

25. Shyam invested ₹ 15,000 @ 10% per annum for one year. If the interest is compounded half-yearly, then the amount received by Shyam at the end of the year will be :
A. ₹ 16,500 B. ₹ 16,525.50
C. ₹ 16,537.50 D. ₹ 18,150

26. The difference between simple interest and compound interest on ₹ 1200 for one year at 10% per annum reckoned half-yearly is :
A. ₹ 2.50 B. ₹ 3
C. ₹ 3.75 D. ₹ 4

27. There is 60% increase in an amount in 6 years at simple interest. What will be the compound interest of ₹ 12,000 after 3 years at the same rate?
A. ₹ 2160 B. ₹ 3120
C. ₹ 3972 D. ₹ 6240

28. The difference between compound interest and simple interest on an amount of ₹ 15,000 for 2 years is ₹ 96. What is the rate of interest per annum?
A. 8 B. 10
C. 12 D. Cannot be determined

29. The difference between the simple interest on a certain sum at the rate of 10% per annum for 2 years and compound interest which is compounded every 6 months is ₹ 124.05. What is the principal sum?
A. ₹ 6000 B. ₹ 8000
C. ₹ 10,000 D. ₹ 12,000

30. Mr Dubey invested money in two schemes A and B offering compound interest @ 8% p.a. and 9% p.a. respectively. If the total amount of interest accrued through two schemes together in two years was ₹ 4818.30 and the total amount invested was ₹ 27,000, what was the amount invested in Scheme A?
A. ₹ 12,000 B. ₹ 13,500
C. ₹ 15,000 D. Cannot be determined

31. A sum of money becomes ₹ 13,380 after 3 years and ₹ 20,070 after 6 years on compound interest. The sum is:
A. ₹ 8800 B. ₹ 8890
C. ₹ 8920 D. ₹ 9040

32. A sum of ₹ 12,000 deposited at compound interest becomes double after 5 years. After 20 years, it will become:
A. ₹ 96,000 B. ₹ 1,20,000
C. ₹ 1,24,000 D. ₹ 1,92,000

33. The least number of complete years in which a sum of money put out at 20% compound interest will be more than doubled is:
A. 3 B. 4
C. 5 D. 6

34. What annual payment will discharge a debt of ₹ 1025 due in 2 years at the rate of 5% compound interest?
A. ₹ 550 B. ₹ 551.25
C. ₹ 560 D. ₹ 560.75

35. A sum of money is borrowed and paid back in two annual instalments of ₹ 882 each allowing 5% compound interest. The sum borrowed was:
A. ₹ 1620 B. ₹ 1640
C. ₹ 1680 D. ₹ 1700

ANSWERS

1	2	3	4	5	6	7	8	9	10
B	D	C	A	A	D	A	D	D	D
11	**12**	**13**	**14**	**15**	**16**	**17**	**18**	**19**	**20**
D	C	D	A	C	A	D	D	C	A
21	**22**	**23**	**24**	**25**	**26**	**27**	**28**	**29**	**30**
D	C	C	A	C	B	C	A	B	A
31	**32**	**33**	**34**	**35**					
C	D	B	B	B					

SOME SELECTED EXPLANATORY ANSWERS

2. Required amount $= ₹\dfrac{1575\times100}{12.5\times5} = ₹\ 2520.$

3. Suppose Sriram invested ₹ P in each scheme.

$$\because \quad 63 = P\left[\left(1+\frac{10}{100}\right)^2-1\right]$$

$$\Rightarrow \quad 63 = P\left(\frac{121}{100}-1\right) - \frac{21P}{100}$$

$$\therefore \quad P = \frac{63\times100}{21} = ₹\ 300$$

Compound interest of 2 years under scheme Y

$$= 300\left[\left(1+\frac{12}{100}\right)^2-1\right]$$

$$= \frac{300\times159}{625} = ₹\ 76.32.$$

5. $\because$ Required Difference $= \dfrac{P\times r^2}{(100)^2}\left(\dfrac{r}{100}+3\right)$

$$\Rightarrow \quad 595.35 = \frac{P\times15\times15}{100\times100}\left(\frac{15}{100}+3\right)$$

$$= \frac{225P}{10000}\times\frac{315}{100}$$

$$\therefore \quad P = \frac{595.35\times1000000}{225\times315} = ₹\ 8400$$

6. S.I. $= \dfrac{988\times18\times5}{100} = ₹\ 889.20$

7. Principal $= \dfrac{1200\times100}{4\times8} = ₹\ 3750$

$$\therefore \quad \text{S.I.} = \frac{3750\times3\times3\times6}{100} = ₹\ 2025$$

9. From question,

$$(21460 - 14500) = \frac{14500 \times r \times 6}{100}$$

$$\Rightarrow \quad \frac{6960}{145 \times 6} = r$$

$$\therefore \quad r = 8$$

Hence the rate of interest per annum = 8%.

10. S.I. = ₹ (15500 – 12500) = ₹ 3000.

$$\text{Rate} = \left(\frac{100 \times 3000}{12500 \times 4}\right)\% = 6\%.$$

11. $\text{Principal} = ₹\left(\frac{100 \times 4016.25}{9 \times 5}\right)$

$$= ₹\left(\frac{401625}{45}\right) = ₹\ 8925.$$

12. S.I. = ₹ (956 – 800) = ₹ 156.

$$\text{Rate} = \left(\frac{100 \times 156}{800 \times 3}\right)\% = 6\frac{1}{2}\%.$$

$$\text{New rate} = \left(6\frac{1}{2} + 4\right)\% = 10\frac{1}{2}\%.$$

$$\text{New S.I.} = ₹\left(800 \times \frac{21}{2} \times \frac{3}{100}\right) = ₹\ 252.$$

∴ New amount = ₹ (800 + 252) = ₹ 1052.

13. We need to know the S.I., principal and time to find the rate. Since the principal is not given, so data is inadequate.

14. Let the sum be ₹ x. Then,

$$\left(\frac{x \times 6 \times 3}{100}\right) + \left(\frac{x \times 9 \times 5}{100}\right) + \left(\frac{x \times 13 \times 3}{100}\right) = 8160$$

$$\Rightarrow \quad 18x + 45x + 39x = (8160 \times 100)$$

$$\Rightarrow \quad 102x = 816000 \quad \Rightarrow \quad x = 8000.$$

15. Let the sum be ₹ x. Now, S.I. = ₹ 600, T = 10 years.

$$\text{Rate} = \left(\frac{100 \times 600}{x \times 10}\right)\% = \left(\frac{6000}{x}\right)\%.$$

$$\text{S.I. for first 5 years} = ₹\left(\frac{x \times 5 \times 6000}{x \times 100}\right) = ₹\ 300.$$

$$\text{S.I. for last 5 years} = ₹\left(3x \times 5 \times \frac{6000}{x \times 100}\right) = ₹\ 900.$$

$$\therefore \quad \text{Total interest} = ₹\ 1200.$$

16. Let sum = x. Then, S.I. = $\frac{x}{9}$.

Let rate = R% and time = R years.

$$\therefore \quad \left(\frac{x \times R \times R}{100}\right) = \frac{x}{9} \Rightarrow R^2 = \frac{100}{9}$$

$$\Rightarrow \quad R = \frac{10}{3} = 3\frac{1}{3}.$$

Hence, rate = $3\frac{1}{3}\%$.

17. Let the money added be ₹ x Then,

$$\frac{(830 + x) \times 14 \times 3}{100} - \frac{830 \times 12 \times 3}{100} = 93.90$$

$$\Rightarrow \quad 830 \times 42 + 42x - 830 \times 36 = 9390$$

$$\Rightarrow \quad 42x + 830 \times (42 - 36) = 9390$$

$$\Rightarrow \quad 42x = 9390 - 4980 \Rightarrow x = \frac{4410}{42} = 105.$$

∴ Money added = ₹ 105.

18. Let the original rate be R%. Then, new rate = (2R)%.

$$\therefore \quad \left(\frac{725 \times R \times 1}{100}\right) + \left(\frac{36250 \times 2R \times 1}{100 \times 3}\right) = 33.50$$

$$\Rightarrow \quad (2175 + 725)\ R = 33.50 \times 100 \times 3 = 10050$$

$$\Rightarrow R = \frac{10050}{2900} = 3.46.$$

∴ Original rate = 3.46%.

19. $\left(\frac{1500 \times R_1 \times 3}{100}\right) - \left(\frac{1500 \times R_2 \times 3}{100}\right) = 13.50$

$$\Rightarrow \quad 4500\ (R_1 - R_2) = 1350$$

$$\Rightarrow \quad R_1 - R_2 = \frac{1350}{4500} = 0.3\%.$$

20. Let the second amount be ₹ x. Then,

$$\left(\frac{12000 \times 10 \times 1}{100}\right) + \left(\frac{x \times 20 \times 1}{100}\right) = \left[\frac{(12000 + x) \times 14 \times 1}{100}\right]$$

$$\Rightarrow \quad 120000 + 20x = 168000 + 14x$$

$$\Rightarrow \quad 6x = 48000 \Rightarrow x = 8000.$$

∴ Total investment = ₹ (12000 + 8000) = ₹ 20000.

21. Let the sum be ₹ x, rate be R% p.a. and time be T years.

$$\text{Then,} \quad \left[\frac{x \times (R + 2) \times T}{100}\right] - \left(\frac{x \times R \times T}{100}\right) = 108$$

$$\Rightarrow \quad 2xT = 10800 \qquad ...(i)$$

$$\text{And,} \quad \left[\frac{x \times R \times (T + 2)}{100}\right] - \left(\frac{x \times R \times T}{100}\right) = 180$$

$$\Rightarrow \quad 2xR = 18000 \qquad ...(ii)$$

Clearly, from (*i*) and (*ii*), we cannot find the value of x. So, the data is inadequate.

22. Let the sum lent at 10% be ₹ x and that lent at 9% be ₹ $(2600 - x)$. Then,

$$\left(\frac{x \times 10 \times 5}{100}\right) = \frac{(2600 - x) \times 9 \times 6}{100}$$

$\Rightarrow$ $50x = (2600 \times 54) - 54x$

$\Rightarrow$ $x = \left(\frac{2600 \times 54}{104}\right) = 1350.$

$\therefore$ Sum lent at 10% = ₹ 1350.

23. Let the sum lent at 5% be ₹ x and that lent at 8% be ₹ $(1550 - x)$. Then,

$$\left(\frac{x \times 5 \times 3}{100}\right) + \left[\frac{(1550 - x) \times 8 \times 3}{100}\right] = 300$$

$\Rightarrow$ $15x - 24x + (1550 \times 24) = 30000$

$\Rightarrow$ $9x = 7200$ $\Rightarrow$ $x = 800.$

$\therefore$ Required ratio = 800 : 750 = 16 : 15.

24. Let x, y and z be the amounts invested in schemes A, B and C respectively. Then,

$$\left(\frac{x \times 10 \times 1}{100}\right) + \left(\frac{y \times 12 \times 1}{100}\right) + \left(\frac{z \times 15 \times 1}{100}\right) = 3200$$

$\Rightarrow$ $10x + 12y + 15z = 320000$ ...(*i*)

Now, $z = 240\%$ of $y = \frac{12}{5}y$ ...(*ii*)

And, $z = 150\%$ of $x = \frac{3}{2}x$

$\Rightarrow$ $x = \frac{2}{3}z = \left(\frac{2}{3} \times \frac{12}{5}\right)y = \frac{8}{5}y$ ...(*iii*)

From (*i*), (*ii*) and (*iii*), we have :

$16y + 12y + 36y = 320000 \Rightarrow 64y = 320000$

$\Rightarrow$ $y = 5000.$

$\therefore$ Sum invested in Scheme B = ₹ 5000.

25. P = ₹ 15000; R = 10% p.a. = 5% per half-year; T = 1 year = 2 half-years.

$\therefore$ Amount = ₹ $\left[15000 \times \left(1 + \frac{5}{100}\right)^2\right]$

= ₹ $\left(15000 \times \frac{21}{20} \times \frac{21}{20}\right)$

= ₹ 16537.50.

26. S.I. = ₹ $\left(\frac{1200 \times 10 \times 1}{100}\right)$ = ₹ 120.

C.I. = ₹ $\left[1200 \times \left(1 + \frac{5}{100}\right)^2 - 1200\right]$ = ₹ 123.

$\therefore$ Difference = ₹ (123 − 120) = ₹ 3.

27. Let P = ₹ 100. Then, S.I. = ₹ 60 and T = 6 years.

$\therefore$ $R = \frac{100 \times 60}{100 \times 6} = 10\%$ p.a.

Now, P = ₹ 12000, T = 3 years and R = 10% p.a.

$\therefore$ C.I. = ₹ $\left[12000 \times \left\{\left(1 + \frac{10}{100}\right)^3 - 1\right\}\right]$

= ₹ $\left(12000 \times \frac{331}{1000}\right)$ = ₹ 3972.

28. $\left[15000 \times \left(1 + \frac{R}{100}\right)^2 - 15000\right] - \left(\frac{15000 \times R \times 2}{100}\right) = 96$

$\Rightarrow$ $15000\left[\left(1 + \frac{R}{100}\right)^2 - 1 - \frac{2R}{100}\right] = 96$

$\Rightarrow$ $15000\left[\frac{(100 - R)^2 - 10000 - 200R}{10000}\right] = 96$

$\Rightarrow$ $R^2 = \frac{96 \times 2}{3} = 64 \Rightarrow R = 8.$

$\therefore$ Rate = 8%.

30. Let the investment in scheme A be ₹ x.

Then, investment in scheme B = ₹ $(27000 - x)$

$\therefore$ $\left[x \times \left\{\left(1 + \frac{8}{100}\right)^2 - 1\right\} + (27000 - x)\left\{\left(1 + \frac{9}{100}\right)^2 - 1\right\}\right]$

$= 4818.30.$

$\Rightarrow$ $\left(x \times \frac{104}{625}\right) + \frac{1881(27000 - x)}{10000} = \frac{481830}{100}$

$\Rightarrow$ $1664x + 1881\ (27000 - x) = 48183000$

$\Rightarrow$ $(1881x - 1664x) = (50787000 - 48183000)$

$\Rightarrow$ $217x = 2604000$

$\Rightarrow$ $x = \frac{2604000}{217} = 12000.$

32. $12000 \times \left(1 + \frac{R}{100}\right)^5 = 24000$

$\Rightarrow$ $\left(1 + \frac{R}{100}\right)^5 = 2$

$\therefore$ $\left[\left(1 + \frac{R}{100}\right)^5\right]^4 = 2^4 = 16$

$\Rightarrow$ $\left(1 + \frac{R}{100}\right)^{20} = 16$

$\Rightarrow$ $P\left(1 + \frac{R}{100}\right)^{20} = 16P$

$\Rightarrow$ $12000\left(1 + \frac{R}{100}\right)^{20} = 16 \times 12000 = 192000.$

33. $P\left(1+\frac{R}{100}\right)^n > 2P$ or $\left(\frac{6}{5}\right)^n > 2$

Now, $\left(\frac{6}{5}\times\frac{6}{5}\times\frac{6}{5}\times\frac{6}{5}\right) > 2$. So, $n = 4$ years.

34. Let each instalment be ₹ x. Then,

$$\frac{x}{\left(1+\frac{5}{100}\right)}+\frac{x}{\left(1+\frac{5}{100}\right)^2} = 1025$$

$$\Rightarrow \quad \frac{20x}{21}+\frac{400x}{441} = 1025$$

$$\Rightarrow \quad 820x = 1025 \times 441$$

$$\Rightarrow \quad x = \left(\frac{1025\times 441}{820}\right) = 551.25.$$

So, value of each instalment = ₹ 551.25

35. Principal = (P.W. of ₹ 882 due 1 year hence) + (P.W. of ₹ 882 due 2 years hence)

$$= \left[\frac{882}{\left(1+\frac{5}{100}\right)}+\frac{882}{\left(1+\frac{5}{100}\right)^2}\right]$$

$$= \left(\frac{882\times 20}{21}+\frac{882\times 400}{441}\right) = ₹\ 1640.$$

❋❋❋❋❋

9

Time & Work

IMPORTANT FACTS

1. If A can do a piece of work in n days, then work done by A in 1 day $= \frac{1}{n}$.
2. If work done by A in 1 day $= \frac{1}{n}$; then A can finish the whole work in n days.
3. If A is twice as good a workman as B then; Ratio of work done by A and B = 2 : 1
   Ratio of times taken by A and B to finish a work = 1 : 2.
4. If a pipe can fill a tank in x hours, then the part filled in 1 hour $= \frac{1}{x}$.
5. If a pipe can empty a tank in y hour, then the part of the tank emptied in 1 hour $= \frac{1}{y}$.
6. If two pipes can fill a tank in x and y hours respectively and both the pipes are opened simultaneously then, the part filled in 1 hour $= \frac{1}{x} + \frac{1}{y}$.
7. (*a*) A tap fills a cistern in x hours and the other can empty the cistern in y hours. If both the taps are opened simultaneously, then the net part of the tank filled in 1 hour $= \frac{1}{x} - \frac{1}{y}$; when $y > x$.

   (*b*) A tap can fill a tank in x hours and other can empty in y hours. If both the taps are opened simultaneously, then the net part of tank emptied in 1 hour $= \frac{1}{y} - \frac{1}{x}$; when $x > y$.

SOLVED EXAMPLES

Example 1: A and B together can complete a piece of work in 4 days. If A alone can complete the same piece of work in 5 days, in how many days will B alone complete it?

Solution: (A + B)'s 1 day's work $= \frac{1}{4}$

A's 1 day's work $= \frac{1}{5}$

$\therefore$ B's 1 day work $= \frac{1}{4} - \frac{1}{5} = \frac{5-4}{20} = \frac{1}{20}$

$\therefore$ B alone will complete the work in 20 days.

Example 2: Four examiners can examine a certain number of answer papers in 10 days by working for 5 hours a day. For how many hours in a day would 2 examiners have to work in order to examine twice the number of answer papers in 20 days?

Solution:

No. of exam	Hrs. per day	No. of papers	Days
4 ↓	5 ↓	1 ↓	10 ↓
2	x	2	20

$$\left.\begin{array}{l} 2 : 4 \\ 1 : 2 \\ 20 : 10 \end{array}\right\} :: 5 : x$$

$$\therefore \quad x = \frac{4 \times 2 \times 10 \times 5}{2 \times 20} = 10 \text{ hrs./day}$$

Example 3: 6 women and 6 men together can complete a piece of work in 6 days. In how many days can 15 men alone complete the piece of work if 9 women alone can complete the work in 10 days?

Solution: $\because$ Work of 1 woman for 1 day

$$= \frac{1}{9 \times 10} = \frac{1}{90}$$

$\Rightarrow$ Work of 6 women for 6 days

$$= \frac{1}{90} \times 6 \times 6 = \frac{2}{5}$$

$\Rightarrow$ Work of 6 men for 6 days

$$= 1 - \frac{2}{5} = \frac{3}{5}$$

$\Rightarrow$ Work of 1 man for 1 day

$$= \frac{3}{5 \times 6 \times 6} = \frac{1}{60}$$

∴ Work of 15 men for 1 day

$$= \frac{1}{60} \times 15 = \frac{1}{4}.$$

Hence, 15 men will complete the work in 4 days.

Example 4: Six boys or four men can complete a piece of work in 24 days. In how many days will 3 boys and 10 men together complete the same piece of work?

Solution: 4 men = 6 boys

∴ 10 men = $\frac{6}{4} \times 10$

= 15 boys

∴ 10 men + 3 boys = 15 + 3

= 18 boys

∴ Required number of days = $\frac{6 \times 24}{18} = 8.$

MULTIPLE CHOICE QUESTIONS

1. 24 men can complete a piece of work in 16 days. The same work can be completed by 8 women in 72 days, whereas 24 children take 32 days to complete it. If 10 men, 15 women and 24 children work together, in how many days can the work be completed?

A. 18 B. 8
C. 22 D. 12

2. 18 Men alone can complete a piece of work in 24 days. 54 Women alone can complete the same piece of work in 12 days and 16 children alone can complete the same piece of work in 54 days. In how many days can 3 men, 9 women and 6 children together complete the piece of work?

A. 18 B. 36
C. 27 D. Cannot be determined

3. If 80 persons can finish a work within 16 days by working 6 hours a day then how many hours per day should 64 persons work to complete that very job within 15 days?

A. 7 hrs B. 8 hrs
C. 6 hrs D. 5 hrs

4. A and B can do a piece of work in 12 days. B and C in 15 days and C and A in 20 days. In how many days A, B and C together can do the work?

A. 8 days B. 12 days
C. 10 days D. 14 days

5. 5 labourers can make 5 mats in 5 hours. How many mats will 10 labourers make in 10 hours?

A. 10 B. 20
C. 30 D. 35

6. A can do $\frac{1}{2}$ of a work in 9 days while B can do $\frac{1}{3}$ of the same work in 6 days. How long would it take for A and B together to complete the work?

A. 18 B. 6
C. 12 D. 9

7. A can do a piece of work in 40 days. He works on it for 5 days and then B completes it in 21 days. How long will A and B together take to complete the work?

A. 20 days B. 15 days
C. 30 days D. 10 days

8. A, B and C can complete a work separately in 24, 36 and 48 days respectively. They started together but C left after 4 days of start and A left 3 days before the completion of work. In how many days will the work be completed?

A. 15 days B. 18 days
C. 10 days D. 12 days

9. A and B can do a piece of work in 12 days. B and C together can do it in 15 days. If A is twice as good a work man as C, find in what time B alone can do it?

A. 12 days B. 15 days
C. 20 days D. 24 days

10. If 4 men or 6 boys can finish a piece of work in 20 days, in how many days can 6 men and 11 boys finish it?

A. 20 days B. 12 days
C. 8 days D. 6 days

11. 5 men and 2 boys together in 1 hour do 4 times work as 1 man and 1 boy do in an hour. Determine the ratio of the specified times of works of a man and a boy.

A. 4 : 1 B. 1 : 4
C. 3 : 4 D. 2 : 1

12. 75 boys finish a work in 24 days. How many men will complete twice the work in 20 days while 2 men do in a day same work as 3 boys do in a day?

A. 50 B. 24
C. 60 D. 120

13. If 3 men and 4 boys together earn ₹ 264 in 8 days and 2 men and 3 boys together earn ₹ 184 in the same time, then in how many days will 6 men and 7 boys together earn ₹ 315?

A. 5 days B. 6 days
C. 9 days D. 10 days

14. Pipes A and B can fill a tank in 36 and 48 hours respectively. Both pipes are opened together to fill the tank. After some time pipe B is closed and the tank is full in 24 hours. For how much time was the pipe B opend?

A. 20 hrs. B. 16 hrs.
C. 48 hrs. D. 36 hrs.

15. A tank is normally filled in 9 hours. But because of a leak in its bottom it takes 3 hours more to fill. How much time will it take the leak to empty the full tank?
A. 12 hrs. B. 24 hrs.
C. 36 hrs. D. 48 hrs.

16. Three pipes A, B and C are connected to a tank. A and B can fill it in 20 and 30 minutes respectively, while C can empty it in 15 minutes. If A, B and C are kept open successively for 1 minute each, how soon will the tank be filled?
A. 176 min B. 167 min
C. 180 min D. 170 min

17. Two pipes A and B can separately fill a cistern in $7\frac{1}{2}$ minutes and 5 minutes respectively and a waste pipe C can carry off 14 litres per minute. If all the pipes are opened when the cistern is full, it is emptied in 1 hour. How many litres does it hold?
A. 40 litres B. 20 litres
C. 36 litres D. 30 litres

18. Two workers A and B are engaged to do a work. A working alone takes 8 hours more to complete the job than if both worked together. If B worked alone, he would need $4\frac{1}{2}$ hours more to complete the job than they both working together. What time would they take to do the work together?
A. 4 hours B. 5 hours
C. 6 hours D. 7 hours

19. Savita can do a piece of work in 20 days. Tripti is 25% more efficient than Savita. The number of days taken by Tripti to do the same piece of work is :
A. 15 B. 16
C. 18 D. 25

20. A machine P can print one lakh books in 8 hours, machine Q can print the same number of books in 10 hours while machine R can print them in 12 hours. All the machines are started at 9 a.m. while machine P is closed at 11 a.m. and the remaining two machines complete the work. Approximately at what time will the work be finished?
A. 11:30 a.m. B. 12 noon
C. 12:30 p.m. D. 1 p.m.

21. A and B can do a piece of work in 45 days and 40 days respectively. They began to do the work together but A leaves after some days and then B completed the remaining work in 23 days. The number of days after which A left the work was :
A. 6 B. 8
C. 9 D. 12

22. A, B and C are employed to do a piece of work for ₹ 529. A and B together are supposed to do $\frac{19}{23}$ of the work and B and C together $\frac{8}{23}$ of the work. What amount should A be paid?
A. ₹ 315 B. ₹ 345
C. ₹ 355 D. ₹ 375

23. A sum of money is sufficient to pay A's wages for 21 days and B's wages for 28 days. The same money is sufficient to pay the wages of both for :
A. 12 days B. $12\frac{1}{4}$ days
C. 14 days D. $24\frac{1}{2}$ days

24. 12 men complete a work in 9 days. After they have worked for 6 days, 6 more men join them. How many days will they take to complete the remaining work?
A. 2 days B. 3 days
C. 4 days D. 5 days

25. 10 men and 15 women together can complete a work in 6 days. It takes 100 days for one man alone to complete the same work. How many days will be required for one woman alone to complete the same work?
A. 90 B. 125
C. 145 D. none of these

26. 12 men can complete a piece of work in 4 days. While 15 women can compete the same work in 4 days. 6 men start working on the job and after working for 2 days, all of them stopped working. How many women should be put on the job to complete the remaining work, if it is to be completed in 3 days?
A. 15 B. 18
C. 22 D. Data inadequate

27. 10 women can complete a work in 7 days and 10 children take 14 days to complete the work How many days will 5 women and 10 children take to complete the work?
A. 3 B. 5
C. 7 D. Cannot be determined

28. Twenty-four men can complete a work in sixteen days. Thirty two women can complete the same work in twenty-four days. Sixteen men and sixteen women started working and worked for twelve days. How many more men are to be added to complete the remaining work in 2 days?
A. 16 B. 24
C. 36 D. 48

29. A pump can fill a tank with water in 2 hours. Because of a leak, it took $2\frac{1}{3}$ hours to fill the tank. The leak can drain all the water of the tank in:

A. $4\frac{1}{3}$ hrs B. 7 hrs
C. 8 hrs D. 14 hrs

30. Two pipes A and B together can fill a cistern in 4 hours. Had they been opened separately, then B would have taken 6 hours more than A to fill the cistern. How much time will be taken by A to fill the cistern separately?
A. 1 hr B. 2 hrs
C. 6 hrs D. 8 hrs

31. A tank is filled in 5 hours by three pipes A, B and C. The pipe C is twice as fast as B and B is twice as fast as A. How much time will pipe A alone take to fill the tank?
A. 20 hrs
B. 25 hrs
C. 35 hrs
D. Cannot be determined

32. Bucket P has thrice the capacity as bucket Q. It takes 60 turns for bucket P to fill the empty drum. How many turns it will take for both the buckets P and Q, having each turn together to fill the empty drum?
A. 30 B. 40
C. 45 D. 90

33. A large tanker can be filled by two pipes A and B in 60 and 40 minutes respectively. How many minutes will it take to fill the tanker from empty state if B is used for half the time and A and B fill it together for the other half?
A. 15 min B. 20 min
C. 27.5 min D. 30 min

34. A leak in the bottom of a tank can empty the full tank in 8 hours. An inlet pipe fills water at the rate of 6 litres a minute. When the tank is full, the inlet is opened and due to the leak, the tank is empty in 12 hours. How many litres does the cistern hold?
A. 7580 B. 7960
C. 8290 D. 8640

35. Two pipes can fill a tank in 20 and 24 minutes respectively and a waste pipe can empty 3 gallons per minute. All the three pipes working together can fill the tank in 15 minutes. The capacity of the tank is :
A. 60 gallons B. 100 gallons
C. 120 gallons D. 180 gallons

ANSWERS

1	2	3	4	5	6	7	8	9	10
D	B	B	C	B	D	B	A	C	D
11	**12**	**13**	**14**	**15**	**16**	**17**	**18**	**19**	**20**
D	D	A	B	C	B	A	C	B	D
21	**22**	**23**	**24**	**25**	**26**	**27**	**28**	**29**	**30**
C	B	A	A	D	A	C	B	D	C
31	**32**	**33**	**34**	**35**					
C	C	D	D	C					

SOME SELECTED EXPLANATORY ANSWERS

1. In 16 days the work is completed by 24 men.

$\therefore$ In 1 day the work is completed by

$= 24 \times 16 = 384$ men.

Similarly in 1 day the work is completed by

$= 72 \times 8 = 576$ women

and in 1 day the work is completed by

$= 24 \times 32 = 768$ children

$\because$ 384 men = 768 children

$\therefore$ 10 men $= \dfrac{768 \times 10}{384} = 20$ children

and 576 women = 768 children

$\therefore$ 15 women $= \dfrac{768 \times 15}{576} = 20$ children

$\therefore$ (20 + 20 + 24) = 64 children

$\because$ 24 children complete the work in 32 days.

$\therefore$ 64 children complete the work in $= \dfrac{32 \times 24}{64}$

$= 12$ days.

2. Work done by 3 man + 9 women + 6 children in 1 day

$$= \frac{3 \times 1}{24 \times 18} + \frac{9 \times 1}{12 \times 54} + \frac{6 \times 1}{54 \times 16}$$

$$= \frac{1}{144} + \frac{1}{72} + \frac{1}{144} = \frac{1}{36}$$

$\because \dfrac{1}{36}$ work is done in 1 day.

$\therefore$ 1 work is done in $= \dfrac{1 \times 36}{1} = 36$ days.

3. 80 persons can do the job in 16 days by working = 6 hrs daily

1 person can do the job in 16 days by working $= 6 \times 80$ hrs daily

1 person can do the job in 1 day by working $= 6 \times 80 \times 16$ hrs daily

64 persons can do the job in 15 days by working

$$= \frac{6\times80\times16}{64\times15} \text{ hrs} = 8 \text{ hr.}$$

5. 5 labourers in 5 hrs. can make = 5 mats

1 labourer in 5 hrs. can make $= \frac{5}{5}$ mats

1 labourer in 1 hrs. can make $= \frac{5}{5\times5}$ mats

10 labourers in 10 hrs. can make

$$= \frac{5\times10\times10}{5\times5} = 20 \text{ mats.}$$

6. A's 9 day's work $= \frac{1}{2}$

$\therefore$ A's 1 day's work $= \frac{1}{2\times9} = \frac{1}{18}$

B's 6 day's work $= \frac{1}{3}$

$\therefore$ B's 1 day's work $= \frac{1}{3\times6} = \frac{1}{18}$

$\therefore$ (A + B)'s 1 day's work $= \frac{1}{18}+\frac{1}{18}$

$$= \frac{2}{18} = \frac{1}{9}$$

$\therefore$ A and B both together will complete the work in 9 days.

8. Let the work be completed in x days. Therefore, A worked for $x - 3$ days, B for x days and C for 4 days.

A's 1 day's work $= \frac{1}{24}$

B's 1 day's work $= \frac{1}{36}$

and, C's 1 day's work $= \frac{1}{48}$

$$\therefore (x-3)\times\frac{1}{24}+x\times\frac{1}{36}+4\times\frac{1}{48} = 1$$

$$\Rightarrow \frac{x-3}{24}+\frac{x}{36}+\frac{1}{12} = 1$$

$$\Rightarrow \frac{3x-9+2x+6}{72} = 1$$

$$\Rightarrow 5x - 3 = 72$$

$$\Rightarrow 5x = 75$$

$$\Rightarrow x = \frac{75}{5} = 15$$

Hence, the work was completed in 15 days.

11. Work of (5 men + 2 boys) = 4 (work of 1 man + 1 boy)

= Work of 4 men + 4 boys

$\Rightarrow$ Work of (5 men – 4 men) = Work of (4 boys – 2 boys)

$\Rightarrow$ Work of 1 man = Work of 2 boys

$\therefore$ Required ratio = 2 : 1

12. Work of 3 boys = Work of 2 men

$\therefore$ Work of 1 boy = Work of $\frac{2}{3}$ man

$\therefore$ Work of 75 boys = Work of $\frac{2}{3}\times75$

= 50 men

$\because$ 1 work is completed in 24 days by 50 men

$\therefore$ 1 work is completed in 1 day by 50×24 men

$\therefore$ 2 works are completed in 20 days by

$$\frac{50\times24\times2}{20} = 120 \text{ men.}$$

13. Let men be denoted by m and boys by b.

$3m + 4b$ earn in 8 days = ₹ 264

$\therefore$ $3m + 4b$ earn in 1 day $= \frac{264}{8}$ = ₹ 33 ...(*i*)

And, $2m + 3b$ earn in 8 days= ₹ 184

$\therefore$ $2m + 3b$ earn in 1 day $= \frac{184}{8}$ = ₹ 23 ...(*ii*)

By (*ii*) × 3 – (*i*) × 2, we have

$6m + 9b - 6m - 8b = 69 - 66$

$\Rightarrow$ $1b$ = ₹ 3

$\therefore$ $3m + 4b = 33$

$3m = 33 - 4 \times 3 - 21$

$1m = 7$

$\therefore$ Wages for 1 day of 6 men and 7 boys

$= 6 \times 7 + 7 \times 3$

= 42 + 21 = ₹ 63

$\therefore$ ₹ 63 are wages for 1 day

$\therefore$ ₹ 315 are wages for $= \frac{315}{63} = 5$ days.

15. Without the leak, in 1 hour $\frac{1}{9}$ of the tank is filled.

$\therefore$ In extra 3 hrs, the pipe fills $\frac{3}{9}=\frac{1}{3}$ of the tank more.

In (9 + 3) = 12 hours, the leak empties this extra $\frac{1}{3}$ of the tank.

$\therefore$ The leak will empty the full tank in $12\times\frac{3}{1} = 36$ hrs.

16. $\left(\frac{1}{20}+\frac{1}{30}-\frac{1}{15}\right) = \frac{1}{60}$ of the tank is filled in first 3 minutes

$$\frac{1}{20}+\frac{1}{30} = \frac{5}{60}$$

$$1-\frac{5}{60} = \frac{55}{60}$$

This $\frac{55}{60}$ part of the tank will be filled in $3 \times 55 = 165$ minutes.

The last $\frac{5}{60}$ part will be filled in 2 minutes, successively by A and B.

Total time = 165 + 2 = 167 minutes.

17. Cistern filled by (A + B) in 1 minute

$$= \left(\frac{2}{15}+\frac{1}{5}\right) = \frac{1}{3}$$

Net emptying work done by (A + B + C) in 1 minute $= \frac{1}{60}$

Work done by C in 1 minute $= \left(\frac{1}{60}+\frac{1}{3}\right)=\frac{7}{20}$

$\therefore$ C alone can empty the cistern in $\left(\frac{20}{7}\right)$ minutes

Water thrown out by C in 1 minute = 14 litres

Water thrown out by C in $\left(\frac{20}{7}\right)$ minutes =

$$\left(14\times\frac{20}{7}\right) = 40 \text{ litres}$$

$\therefore$ Capacity of the cistern = 40 litres.

18. Let A and B together take x hours to complete the work. Then,

A alone takes $(x + 8)$ hrs and B alone takes $\left(x+\frac{9}{2}\right)$ hrs to complete the work. Then,

$$\frac{1}{(x+8)}+\frac{1}{\left(x+\frac{9}{2}\right)} = \frac{1}{x}$$

$$\Rightarrow \quad \frac{1}{(x+8)}+\frac{2}{(2x+9)} = \frac{1}{x}$$

$$\Rightarrow \quad x(4x + 25) = (x + 8)(2x + 9)$$

$$\Rightarrow \quad 2x^2 = 72$$

$$\Rightarrow \quad x^2 = 36$$

$$\Rightarrow \quad x = 6.$$

19. Ratio of times taken by Savita and Tripti

= 125 : 100

= 5 : 4.

Suppose Tripti takes x days to do the work.

$5 : 4 :: 20 : x \Rightarrow x = \left(\frac{4\times20}{5}\right)$

$\Rightarrow x = 16$ days.

Hence, Tripti takes 16 days to complete the work.

21. (A + B)'s 1 day's work $= \left(\frac{1}{45}+\frac{1}{40}\right) = \frac{17}{360}$.

Work done by B in 23 days $= \left(\frac{1}{40}\times23\right)$

$= \frac{23}{40}$.

Remaining work $= \left(1-\frac{23}{40}\right) = \frac{17}{40}$.

Now, $\frac{17}{360}$ work was done by (A + B) in 1 day.

$\frac{17}{40}$ work was done by (A + B) in $\left(1\times\frac{360}{17}\times\frac{17}{40}\right)$ = 9 days.

$\therefore$ A left after 9 days.

22. Work done by A $= \left(1-\frac{8}{23}\right) = \frac{15}{23}$.

$\therefore$ A : (B + C) $= \frac{15}{23}:\frac{8}{23} = 15 : 8$.

So, A's share = ₹$\left(\frac{15}{23}\times529\right)$ = ₹ 345.

23. Let total money be ₹ x.

A's 1 day's wages = ₹$\frac{x}{21}$, B's 1 day's wages = ₹$\frac{x}{28}$.

$\therefore$ (A + B)'s 1 day's wages = ₹$\left(\frac{x}{21}+\frac{x}{28}\right)$ = ₹$\frac{x}{12}$.

$\therefore$ Money is sufficient to pay the wages of both for 12 days.

24. 1 man's 1 day's work $= \frac{1}{108}$.

12 men's 6 day's work $= \left(\frac{1}{9}\times6\right) = \frac{2}{3}$.

Remaining work $= \left(1-\frac{2}{3}\right) = \frac{1}{3}$.

18 men's 1 day's work $= \left(\frac{1}{108}\times18\right) = \frac{1}{6}$.

$\frac{1}{6}$ work is done by them in 1 day.

$\therefore$ $\frac{1}{3}$ work is done by them in $\left(6\times\frac{1}{3}\right)$ = 2 days.

25. 1 man's 1 day's work = $\frac{1}{100}$. (10 men + 15 women)'s 1 day's work = $\frac{1}{6}$.

15 women's 1 day's work = $\left(\frac{1}{6}-\frac{10}{100}\right)=\frac{1}{15}$.

1 woman's 1 day's work = $\frac{1}{225}$.

$\therefore$ 1 woman alone can complete the work in 225 days.

26. 1 man's 1 day's work = $\frac{1}{48}$; 1 woman's 1 day's work = $\frac{1}{60}$.

6 men's 2 day's work = $\left(\frac{6}{48}\times 2\right)=\frac{1}{4}$.

Remaining work = $\left(1-\frac{1}{4}\right)=\frac{3}{4}$.

Now, $\frac{1}{60}$ work is done in 1 day by 1 woman.

So, $\frac{3}{4}$ work will be done in 3 days by $\left(60\times\frac{3}{4}\times\frac{1}{3}\right)$ = 15 women.

27. 1 woman's 1 day's work = $\frac{1}{70}$; 1 child's 1 day's work = $\frac{1}{140}$.

(5 women + 10 children)'s 1 day's work

$$=\left(\frac{5}{70}+\frac{10}{140}\right)=\frac{1}{7}.$$

$\therefore$ 5 women and 10 children will complete the work in 7 days.

29. Tank emptied by the leak in 1 hour = $\left(\frac{1}{2}-\frac{3}{7}\right)=\frac{1}{14}$.

$\therefore$ Leak will empty the tank in 14 hrs.

30. Let the cistern be filled by pipe A alone in x hours.

Then, pipe B will fill it in $(x + 6)$ hours.

$$\therefore \quad \frac{1}{x}+\frac{1}{(x+6)}=\frac{1}{4}$$

$$\Rightarrow \quad \frac{x+6+x}{x(x+6)}=\frac{1}{4}$$

$$\Rightarrow \quad x^2-2x-24=0$$

$$\Rightarrow \quad (x-6)(x+4)=0$$

$$\Rightarrow \quad x=6.$$

32. Let capacity of P be x litres. Then, capacity of Q = $\frac{x}{3}$ litres.

Capacity of the drum = $60x$ litres.

Required number of turns = $\frac{60x}{\left(x+\frac{x}{3}\right)}$ = 45.

33. Part filled by (A + B) in 1 minute

$$=\left(\frac{1}{60}+\frac{1}{40}\right)=\frac{1}{24}.$$

Suppose the tank is filled in x minutes.

Then $\quad \frac{x}{2}\left(\frac{1}{24}+\frac{1}{40}\right)=1$

$$\Rightarrow \quad \frac{x}{2}\times\frac{1}{15}=1$$

$$\Rightarrow \quad x=30 \text{ min.}$$

35. Work done by the waste pipe in 1 minute

$$=\frac{1}{15}-\left(\frac{1}{20}+\frac{1}{24}\right)=\left(\frac{1}{15}-\frac{11}{120}\right)=-\frac{1}{40}.$$

[–ve sign means emptying]

$\therefore$ Volume of $\frac{1}{40}$ part = 3 gallons.

Volume of whole = (3 × 40) gallons
= 120 gallons.

❋❋❋❋❋

10

Time & Distance

IMPORTANT FORMULAE

1. Speed = Distance ÷ Time
2. Distance = Time × Speed
3. Time = Distance ÷ Speed
4. x km/hr = $\left(x \times \frac{5}{18}\right)$ m/sec
5. x m/sec = $\left(x \times \frac{18}{5}\right)$ km/hr.
6. If the speed of a body is changed in the ratio $m : n$, then the ratio of the time taken changes in the ratio $n : m$.
7. When a man covers a certain distance with a speed of x km/h and another equal distance at the rate of y km/h, then for the whole journey, the average speed is given by

   Average speed = $\frac{2xy}{x+y}$ km/h.
8. The time taken by a train in passing a signal post or a telegraph pole or a man standing near a railway line $= \frac{\text{Length of the train}}{\text{Speed of the train}}$
9. The time taken by a train of length x passing a railway bridge or a platform or a tunnel or a train of length y at rest $= \frac{x+y}{\text{Speed}}$
10. (*a*) Time taken by faster train of length x and speed u to pass the slower train of length y and speed v in the same direction $= \frac{x+y}{u-v}$

    (*b*) Time taken by the trains in passing each other while moving in opposite direction $= \frac{x+y}{u+v}$
11. (*a*) Time taken by the train of length x and speed u to cross a man moving with speed v in same direction $= \frac{x}{u-v}$

    (*b*) Time taken by the train to cross a man moving in the opposite direction $= \frac{x}{u+v}$
12. If two trains start at the same time from two points A and B towards each other and after crossing, they take a and b hours in reaching B and A respectively. Then,

    A's speed : B's speed = $\left(\sqrt{b}:\sqrt{a}\right)$

SOLVED EXAMPLES

Example 1: Distance between two railway stations A and B is 1536 kms. A train covers a journey between A to B at the uniform speed of 60 km/hr and returns from B to A at the uniform speed of 40 km/hr. What is the average speed of the train during the whole journey?

Solution: Average speed of train $= \frac{2 \times 40 \times 60}{40+60}$

$= \frac{2 \times 40 \times 60}{100} = 48$ km/hr.

Example 2: A car covers the first 39 km of its journey in 45 minutes and covers the remaining 25 km in 35 minutes. What is the average speed of the car?

Solution: Total time $= \frac{45}{60} + \frac{35}{60} = \frac{4}{3}$ hrs.

and total distance = 39 + 25 = 64 km

∴ Average speed $= \frac{64 \times 3}{4} = 48$ km/hr.

Example 3: A train covered a distance of 1235 km in 19 hours. Also, the average speed of a car is four-fifth the average speed of the train. How much distance will the car cover in 22 hours?

Solution: Speed of the train $= \frac{1235}{19} = 65$ km/hr

∴ Speed of the car $= 65 \times \frac{4}{5} = 52$ km/hr

∴ Reqd. distance = 52 × 22 = 1144 km.

Example 4: A 320 metre long train moving with an average speed of 120 km/hr crosses a platform in 24 seconds. A man crosses the same platform in 4 minutes. What is the speed of man in metre/second?

Solution: Let the length of the platform be x metre. Then,

∵ Speed of the train = 120 km/hr $= 120 \times \frac{5}{18}$

$= \frac{100}{3}$ m/sec.

From question,

$\because \quad 320m + x = \frac{100}{3} \times 24$

$\therefore \quad x = 800 - 320$
$= 480$ metre.

$\therefore$ Reqd. speed of man $= \frac{480 \text{ m}}{4 \times 60 \text{ sec}} = 2$ m/sec.

Example 5: A 260 metre long train crosses a platform thrice its length in 80 seconds. What is the speed of the train in km/hour?

Solution: Speed of the train

$= \frac{(260+780)}{80} \times \frac{18}{5}$ km/hr.

$= 46.8$ km/hr.

MULTIPLE CHOICE QUESTIONS

1. A boat while travelling upstream covers a distance of 18 km at the speed of 3 km/hr, whereas while travelling downstream it covers the same distance at a speed of 9 km/hr. What is the speed of the boat in still waters?

A. 3 km/hr B. 5 km/hr
C. 7 km/hr D. None of these

2. The speed of a car is 1.5 times the speed of a bus. If the car travels at the speed of 60 km/hr what will be the difference in the time taken by the bus and the time taken by the car to cover 720 km?

A. 5 hours B. 6 hours
C. 4 hours D. 8 hours

3. A car covers a distance of 540 km in 9 hours. Speed of a train is double the speed of the car. Two-third the speed of the train is equal to the speed of a bike. How much distance will the bike cover in 5 hours?

A. 450 km B. 360 km
C. 400 km D. 500 km

4. A train travels at a speed of 30 km per hour for 12 minutes and then for the next 8 minutes at a speed of 45 km per hour. What is the average speed for the journey?

A. 40 km/hr B. 36 km/hr
C. 43 km/hr D. 46 km/hr

5. The ratio of the speeds of two trains is 7 : 8. If the second train runs 400 km in 5 hrs., find the speed of the first train.

A. 60 km/hr B. 55 km/hr
C. 70 km/hr D. 75 km/hr

6. A train travels from Dehradun to Delhi at a speed of 40 km/hr and returns at 60 km/hr. Find the average speed for the entire journey

A. 50 km/hr B. 45 km/hr
C. 48 km/hr D. 52 km/hr

7. A car runs at 60 km per hr. A man runs at one-third the speed of the car and reaches office from his house in 15 minutes. How far is his office from his house?

A. 20 km B. 10 km
C. 5 km D. 4 km

8. Two men A and B start walking simultaneously from P to Q, a distance of 21 kms, at the speeds of 3 km and 4 km an hour respectively. B reaches Q, returns immediately and meets A at R. Then the distance from P to R is:

A. 6 km B. 12 km
C. 18 km D. 24 km

9. A monkey climbing up a greased pole ascends 12 metres and slips down 5 metres in alternate minutes. If the pole is 63 metres high, how long will it take him to reach the top?

A. $12\frac{7}{16}$ B. $7\frac{12}{16}$
C. $16\frac{7}{12}$ D. $10\frac{7}{12}$

10. A carriage driving in a fog passed a man who was walking at the speed of 6 km/hr. in the same direction. He could see the carriage for 4 minutes and it was visible to him up to a distance of 200 metres. The speed of the carriage is:

A. 9 km/hr B. 4 km/hr
C. 6 km/hr D. 8 km/hr

11. A train met with an accident 3 hours after starting, which detains it for one hour, after which it proceeds at 75% of its original speed. It arrives at the destination 4 hours late. Had the accident taken place 150 km further along the railway line, the train would have arrived only $3\frac{1}{2}$ hours late. Find the length of the trip:

A. 1200 km B. 1000 km
C. 2100 km D. 1050 km

12. Two places A and B are 162 kms apart. A train leaves A for B and at the same time another train leaves B for A. The two trains meet at the end of 6 hours. If the train travelling from A to B travels 8 km per hr. faster than the other. Then the speed of the faster train is:

A. $9\frac{1}{2}$ km/h B. 27 km/hr
C. $17\frac{1}{2}$ km/hr D. 19 km/hr

13. A train takes 18 seconds to pass completely through a station 162 metres long and 15 seconds to pass completely through another station 120 metres long. The length of the train is:

A. 60 m B. 75 m
C. 90 m D. 100 m

14. A man covered a distance of 3990 km partly by air, partly by sea and remaining by land. The time spent in air, on sea and on land is in the ratio 1 : 16 : 2 and the ratio of average speeds is 20 : 1 : 3 respectively. If total average speed is 42 km per hr, Then the distance covered by sea is :

A. 1502 kms B. 2520 kms
C. 1520 kms D. 1500 kms

15. A man is walking at a speed of 10 km/hr. After every kilometre, he takes rest for 5 minutes. How much time will he take to cover a distance of 5 km?

A. 1 hr B. 50 min
C. 20 min D. 30 min

16. Walking $\frac{5}{6}$ of his usual speed, a man reaches the station 10 min late. His usual time to reach the station is :

A. 30 min B. 40 min
C. 50 min D. 60 min

17. A is four times as fast as B and B is six times as fast as C. A certain distance is covered by B in 28 minutes. Then the time taken by C to cover the same distance is :

A. 2 : 48 hrs B. 2 : 40 hrs
C. 2 : 28 hrs D. 3 hrs

18. It takes eight hours for a 600 km journey, if 120 km is done by train and the rest by car. It takes 20 minutes more, if 200 km is done by train and the rest by car. The ratio of the speed of the train to the speed of the car is :

A. 2 : 3 B. 6 : 9
C. 3 : 4 D. 4 : 3

19. A bus takes two hours less for a journey of 300 km if its speed is increased by 5 kmph from its normal speed. The normal speed is

A. 30 kmph B. 25 kmph
C. 35 kmph D. 50 kmph

20. A boy goes to school with a speed of 3 km/hr and returns to the village with a speed of 2 km/hr. If he takes 5 hours in all, the distance between the village and the school is :

A. 6 km B. 7 km
C. 8 km D. 9 km

21. Rahim covers a certain distance in 14 hrs 40 min. He covers one half of the distance by train at 60 km/hr and the rest half by road at 50 km/hr. The distance travelled by him is :

A. 960 km B. 720 km
C. 1000 km D. 800 km

22. Two men start together to walk to a certain destination, one at 3.75 km an hour and another at 3 km an hour. The former arrives half an hour before the latter. The distance is:

A. 9.5 km B. 8 km
C. 7.5 km D. 6 km

23. A thief steals a car at 1.30 p.m. and drives it at 40 km an hour. The theft is discovered at 2 p.m. and the owner sets off in another car at 50 km an hour. He will overtake the thief at:

A. 3.30 p.m. B. 4 p.m.
C. 4.30 p.m. D. 6 p.m.

24. A man travels 35 km partly at 4 km/hr and at 5 km/hr. If he covers former distance at 5 km/hr and later distance at 4 km/hr, he could cover 2 km more in the same time. The time taken to cover the whole distance at original rate is :

A. 9 hours B. 7 hours
C. $4\frac{1}{2}$ hours D. 8 hours

25. A certain distance is covered at a certain speed. If half of this distance is covered in double the time, the ratio of the two speeds is :

A. 4 : 1 B. 1 : 4
C. 2 : 1 D. 1 : 2

26. A person sees a train passing over 1 km. long bridge. The length of the train is half that of bridge. If the train clears the bridge in 2 minutes, the speed of the train is :

A. 50 km/hr B. 45 km/hr
C. 60 km/hr D. 30 km/hr

27. Two trains are running on parallel lines in the same direction at a speed of 50 km and 30 km per hour respectively. The faster train crosses a man in slower train in 18 seconds. The length of the faster train is :

A. 170 metres B. 100 metres
C. 98 metres D. 85 metres

28. A train speeds past a pole in 15 seconds and speeds past a platform 100 metres long in 25 seconds. Its length in metres is :

A. 200 B. 150
C. 50 D. Data inadequate

29. A train overtakes two persons who are walking in the same direction in which the train is goning, at the rate of 2 kmph and 4 kmph and passes them completely in 9 and 10 seconds respectively. The length of the train is :

A. 72 metres B. 54 metres
C. 50 metres D. 45 metres

30. A boat travels upstream from B to A and downstream from A to B in 3 hours. If the speed of the boat in still water is 9 km/hr and the speed of the current is 3 km/hr, the distance between A and B is :
A. 4 km B. 6 km
C. 8 km D. 12 km

31. Speed of a boat in standing water is 6 km/hr and the speed of the stream is 1.5 km/hr. A man rows to a place at a distance of 22.5 km and comes back to the starting point. The total time taken by him, is :
A. 6 hrs 30 min. B. 8 hrs 24 min.
C. 8 hrs D. 4 hrs 12 min.

32. A man can row $9\frac{1}{3}$ km/hr in still water and he finds that it takes him thrice as much time to row up than as to row down the same distance in river. The speed of the current is :
A. $3\frac{1}{3}$ km/hr B. $3\frac{1}{9}$ km/hr
C. $1\frac{1}{4}$ km/hr D. $4\frac{2}{3}$ km/hr

33. Sound is said to travel in air at about 1100 feet per second. A man hears the axe striking the tree, $\frac{11}{5}$ seconds after he sees it strike the tree. How far is the man from the wood chopper?
A. 2197 ft B. 2420 ft
C. 2500 ft D. 2629 ft

34. Asha left for city A from city B at 5.20 a.m. She travelled at the speed of 80 km/hr for 2 hours 15 minutes. After that the speed was reduced to 60 km/hr. If the distance between two cities is 350 kms, at what time did Asha reach city A?
A. 9.20 a.m. B. 9.25 a.m.
C. 9.35 a.m. D. None of these

35. A motorist covers a distance of 39 km in 45 minutes by moving at a speed of x kmph for the first 15 minutes, then moving at double the speed for the next 20 minutes and then again moving at his original speed for the rest of the journey. Then, x is equal to :
A. 31.2 B. 36
C. 40 D. 52

36. A train when moves at an average speed of 40 kmph, reaches its destination on time. When its average speed becomes 35 kmph, then it reaches its destination 15 minutes late. Find the length of journey.
A. 30 km B. 40 km
C. 70 km D. 80 km

37. With a uniform speed a car covers the distance in 8 hours. Had the speed been increased by 4 km/hr, the same distance could have been covered in $7\frac{1}{2}$ hours. What is the distance covered?
A. 420 km
B. 480 km
C. 640 km
D. Cannot be determined

38. A 270 metres long train running at the speed of 120 kmph crosses another train running in opposite direction at the speed of 80 kmph in 9 seconds. What is the length of the other train?
A. 230 m B. 240 m
C. 260 m D. 320 m

39. Two trains running in opposite directions cross a man standing on the platform in 27 seconds and 17 seconds respecively and they cross each other in 23 seconds. The ratio of their speeds is :
A. 1 : 3 B. 3 : 2
C. 3 : 4 D. 2 : 3

40. A boat covers a certain distance downstream in 1 hour, while it comes back in $1\frac{1}{2}$ hours. If the speed of the stream be 3 kmph, what is the speed of the boat in still water?
A. 12 kmph B. 13 kmph
C. 14 kmph D. 15 kmph

ANSWERS

1	2	3	4	5	6	7	8	9	10
D	B	C	B	C	C	C	C	C	A
11	**12**	**13**	**14**	**15**	**16**	**17**	**18**	**19**	**20**
A	C	C	C	B	C	A	C	B	A
21	**22**	**23**	**24**	**25**	**26**	**27**	**28**	**29**	**30**
D	C	B	D	A	B	B	B	C	D
31	**32**	**33**	**34**	**35**	**36**	**37**	**38**	**39**	**40**
C	D	B	D	B	C	B	A	B	D

SOME SELECTED EXPLANATORY ANSWERS

1. Speed of boat in still water = $\frac{9+3}{2}$ = 6 km/hr.

2. Speed of bus = $60\times\frac{1}{1.5}$ = 40 km/hr.

Hence, required difference = $\frac{720}{40}-\frac{720}{60}$
= 18 – 12 = 6 hrs.

3. Speed of the car = $\frac{540}{9}$ = 60 km/hr.

∴ Speed of train = 60 × 2 = 120 km/hr.

and speed of bike = $120\times\frac{2}{3}$ = 80 km/hr.

∴ Reqd. distance = 80 × 5 = 400 km.

4. In 12 minutes, the train with 30 km per hour speed goes

$= 30\times\frac{5}{18}\times60\times12$ m

$= \frac{5\times5\times20\times12}{1000}$ km = 6 km

In 8 minutes, the train with 45 km per hr. speed goes

$= 45\times\frac{5}{18}\times60\times\frac{8}{1000}$ km = 6 km

Average speed = $\frac{12 \text{ km}}{20 \text{ min}} = \frac{12}{20}\times60$ km/hr
= 36 km/hr.

5. $x:\frac{400}{5} = 7 : 8$

$\Rightarrow x\times\frac{5}{400} = \frac{7}{8}$ ∴ x = 70 km/hr.

6. Reqd. average speed = $\frac{2\times40\times60}{(40+60)}$

$= \frac{2\times2400}{100}$ = 48 km/hr.

8. Let A and B meet after time t hours.

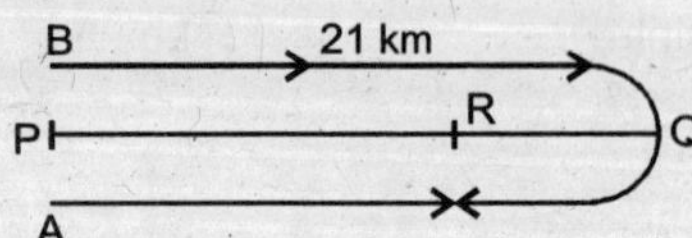

Distance covered by A in t hours = 3 t km.
Distance covered by B in t hours = 4 t km.
Total distance covered by A and B = $(3t + 4t)$ km
= 7 t km.

From the diagram we can see that the total distance covered by A and B is equal to twice the distance between P and Q.

∴ $7t = 2 \times 21$

$t = \frac{2\times21}{7}$ = 6 hours

Distance (PR) = 6 × 3 = 18 kms.

9. From question,
In 2 minutes the net ascending of the monkey is 12 – 5 = 7 metres. So, to cover 63 metres to above process is repeated $\frac{63}{7}$ = 9 times. Since on 9th time, it will climb to the top.

Hence, Time taken to cover 56 metres = $\frac{56\times2}{7}$
= 16 minutes

Remaining distance = 63 – 56 = 7 metres

Time taken to ascend 7 metres = $\frac{7}{12}$ minutes

∴ Total time taken = $16+\frac{7}{12} = 16\frac{7}{12}$ minutes.

10. The distance covered by man in 4 minutes

$= \frac{6\times1000\times4}{60}$ = 400 metres

The distance coverd by carriage in 4 minutes
= 200 + 400 = 600 metres

∴ Sepeed of carriage = $\frac{600}{4}\times\frac{60}{1000}$ km/hr.
= 9 km/hr.

12. Both trains meet after 6 hours.

∴ The relative speed of two trains = $\frac{162}{6}$ = 27 km/hr.

The speed of the slower train starting from B = $\frac{27-8}{2}$

$= \frac{19}{2} = 9\frac{1}{2}$ km/hr.

∴ The speed of the faster train = $9\frac{1}{2}+8 = 17\frac{1}{2}$ km/hr.

13. Let the length of the train = x metres
Then, in 18 sec. the train travels $(x + 162)$ metres ...(*i*)
and in 15 sec. the train travels $(x + 120)$ metres
∴ In (18 – 15) = 3 sec. the train travels $(x + 162) - (x + 120)$ = 42 m

∴ In 1 sec the train travels = $\frac{42}{3}$ = 14 metes ...(*ii*)

∴ In 18 sec. the train travels = 14 × 18
= 252 metres ...(*iii*)

From equations (*i*) and (*iii*)
∴ $x + 162 = 252$
⇒ $x = 252 - 162 = 90$
∴ Length of the train = 90 metres.

14. Total distance travelled = 3990 km

Ratio of time spent = 1 : 16 : 2

$\therefore$ Ratio of time × speeds = 20 × 1 : 16 × 1 : 2 × 3

= 20 : 16 : 6

Sum of the ratios = 20 + 16 + 6

= 42

$\therefore$ Distance covered by sea = $\frac{3990}{42} \times 16$

= 1520 kms.

15. Total time = walking time + rest time

Walking time = $\frac{5}{10}$ hour = $\frac{1}{2}$ hour = 30 min

Rest time = 4 × 5 min = 20 min

$\therefore$ Required time taken = 30 min + 20 min

= 50 min.

17. Let the speed of C be x kmph

$\therefore$ B's speed = $6x$ kmph

and A's speed = 4 × $6x$ kmph = $24x$ kmph

The distance covered by B in 28 minutes

$= 6x \times \frac{28}{60}$ km

$= \frac{28x}{10}$ km $= \frac{14x}{5}$ km

The time taken by C to cover the same distance

$= \frac{\frac{14x}{5}\text{km}}{x\text{ kmph}} = \frac{14}{5}$ hrs

$= 2\frac{4}{5}$ hours = 2 hrs 48 minutes

19. Let s be the normal speed and t be the normal time taken by the bus

$\therefore$ $s \times t = 300$ ...(1)

new speed = $s + 5$

new time = $t - 2$

$\therefore$ $(s + 5)(t - 2) = 300$

$(s + 5)\left(\frac{300}{s} - 2\right) = 300$ (from (1))

$(s + 5)(300 - 2s) = 300s$

$300s - 2s^2 + 1500 - 10s = 300s$

$\Rightarrow$ $2s^2 + 10s - 1500 = 0$

$\Rightarrow$ $2s^2 + 60s - 50s - 1500 = 0$

$\Rightarrow$ $2s(s + 30) - 50(s + 30) = 0$

$\Rightarrow$ $(s + 30)(2s - 50) = 0$

$\therefore$ $s = 25$

$\therefore$ The normal speed of the bus is 25 kmph.

20. Let the required distance be x km. Then,

$\frac{x}{3} + \frac{x}{2} = 5$

$\Rightarrow$ $2x + 3x = 30$

$\Rightarrow$ $x = 6.$

21. Let the total distance be x km. Then,

$\frac{x}{2} \times \frac{1}{60} + \frac{x}{2} \times \frac{1}{50} = \frac{44}{3}$

or $\frac{x}{120} + \frac{x}{100} = \frac{44}{3}$

or $5x + 6x = 8800$

or $x = 800.$

$\therefore$ Required distance = 800 km.

22. Let the distance be x km. Then,

$\frac{x}{3} - \frac{x}{3.75} = \frac{1}{2}$

or $\frac{3.75x - 3x}{3 \times 3.75} = \frac{1}{2}$

or $1.5x = 3 \times 3.75$

or $x = \frac{3 \times 3.75}{1.5} = 7.5$ km

23. Distance covered by thief in (1/2) hour = 20 km.

Now, 20 km is compensated by the owner at a relative speed of 10 km/hr in 2 hours.

So, he overtakes the thief at 4 p.m.

24. Suppose the man covers first distance in x hrs and second distance in y hrs. Then,

$4x + 5y = 35$

and $5x + 4y = 37.$

Solving these equations, we get $x = 5$ and $y = 3$.

$\therefore$ Total time taken = (5 + 3) hrs = 8 hrs.

25. Let x km be covered in y hrs. Then,

1st speed = $\left(\frac{x}{y}\right)$ km/hr.

2nd speed = $\left(\frac{x}{2} \div 2y\right)$ km/hr = $\left(\frac{x}{4y}\right)$ km/hr.

$\therefore$ Ratio of speed = $\frac{x}{y} : \frac{x}{4y} = 1 : \frac{1}{4} = 4 : 1.$

26. Distance covered in $\frac{2}{60}$ hr = $\left(1 + \frac{1}{2}\right)$ km

$= \frac{3}{2}$ km.

Distance covered in 1 hr = $\left(\frac{3}{2} \times \frac{60}{2}\right)$ km = 45 km.

Hence, speed of the train = 45 km/hr.

27. Relative speed = (50 – 30) km/hr = 20 km/hr.

$= \left(20 \times \frac{5}{18}\right)$ m/sec = $\left(\frac{50}{9}\right)$ m/sec.

Let the length of faster train be x

Then, $x \times \frac{9}{50} = 18 \Rightarrow x = \frac{18 \times 50}{9} = 100$ m.

28. Let the length of the train be x metres and its speed be y metres/sec.

Then, $\frac{x}{y} = 15 \Rightarrow y = \frac{x}{15}$.

Now, $\frac{x+100}{25} = \frac{x}{15} \Rightarrow x = 150$ m.

30. Speed in downstream = (9 + 3) km/hr = 12 km/hr.

Speed in upstream = (9 – 3) km/hr = 6 km/hr.

Let the distance AB = x km.

Then, $\frac{x}{6} + \frac{x}{12} = 3 \Rightarrow 2x + x = 36$

$\Rightarrow x = 12$.

$\therefore$ Distance AB = 12 km.

31. Speed in upstream = (6 – 1.5) km/hr = 4.5 km/hr.

Speed in downstream = (6 + 1.5) km/hr = 7.5 km/hr.

Total time taken = $\left(\frac{22.5}{4.5} + \frac{22.5}{7.5}\right)$ hrs. = 8 hrs.

32. Let speed in upstream = x km/hr

Then, speed in downstream = $3x$ km/hr

$\therefore$ Speed in still water = $\frac{1}{2}(x + 3x)$ km/hr = $2x$ km/hr

Speed of the current = $\frac{1}{2}(3x - x)$ km/hr = x km/hr

$\therefore 2x = \frac{28}{3}$ or $x = \frac{14}{3} = 4\frac{2}{3}$ km/hr.

33. Distance = $\left(1100 \times \frac{11}{5}\right)$ feet = 2420 feet.

34. Distance covered in 2 hrs 15 min

i.e., $2\frac{1}{4}$ hrs = $\left(80 \times \frac{9}{4}\right)$ km = 180 km.

Time taken to cover remaining distance

$= \left(\frac{350 - 180}{60}\right)$ hrs $= \frac{17}{6}$ hrs

$= 2\frac{5}{6}$ hrs = 2 hrs 50 min.

Total time taken = (2 hrs 15 min + 2 hrs 50 min) = 5 hrs 5 min.

So, Asha reached city A at 10.25 a.m.

35. $x \times \frac{15}{60} + 2x \times \frac{20}{60} + x \times \frac{10}{60} = 39$

$\Rightarrow \frac{x}{4} + \frac{2x}{3} + \frac{x}{6} = 39$

$\Rightarrow 3x + 8x + 2x = 468$

$\Rightarrow x = 36$.

36. Difference between timings = 15 min = $\frac{1}{4}$ hr.

Let the length of journey be x km.

Then, $\frac{x}{35} - \frac{x}{40} = \frac{1}{4}$

$\Rightarrow 8x - 7x = 70$

$\Rightarrow x = 70$ km.

37. Let the distance be x km. Then,

$\frac{x}{7\frac{1}{2}} - \frac{x}{8} = 4 \Rightarrow \frac{2x}{15} - \frac{x}{8} = 4$

$\Rightarrow x = 480$ km.

38. Relative speed = (120 + 80) km/hr

$= \left(200 \times \frac{5}{18}\right)$ m/sec $= \left(\frac{500}{9}\right)$ m/sec.

Let the length of the other train be x metres.

Then, $\frac{x + 270}{9} = \frac{500}{9}$

$\Rightarrow x + 270 = 500$

$\Rightarrow x = 230$.

40. Let the speed of the boat in still water be x kmph. Then,

Speed in downstream = $(x + 3)$ kmph,

Speed in upstream = $(x - 3)$ kmph.

$\therefore (x + 3) \times 1 = (x - 3) \times \frac{3}{2}$

$\Rightarrow 2x + 6 = 3x - 9$

$\Rightarrow x = 15$ kmph.

11

Mensuration

Triangle

1. Perimeter = sum of three sides
2. Area = $\frac{1}{2} \times \text{base} \times \text{height}$, or

   Area = $\sqrt{s(s-a)(s-b)(s-c)}$

   where *a, b, c,* are the lengths of the sides of triangle and $s = \frac{a+b+c}{2}$

Right Angled Triangle : It is one whose one of the angles is right angle, *i.e.,* 90°.

1. $(\text{Hypotenuse})^2 = (\text{Perpendicular})^2 + (\text{Base})^2$
2. Area = $\frac{1}{2} \times \text{Base} \times \text{Perpendicular}$

Equilateral Triangle : All three sides are equal in length and all three angles are equal to 60°.

1. Area = $\frac{\sqrt{3}}{4} \times (\text{Side})^2$
2. Area = $\frac{(\text{Height})^2}{\sqrt{3}}$
3. Height = $\frac{\sqrt{3}}{2} \times \text{side}$
4. Perimeter = 3 × side

Isosceles Triangle : Two sides are equal in lengths.

1. Area = $\frac{b}{4}\sqrt{4a^2 - b^2}$

   where a = lengths of equal sides

   b = length of unequal side
2. In an isosceles right triangle,

   (*a*) Hypotenuse = $\sqrt{2} \times$ congruent side (a)

   (*b*) Area = $\frac{1}{2} \times a^2$

   (*c*) Perimeter = $\sqrt{2} \times a\left(\sqrt{2}+1\right)$

Rectangle :

1. Area = length(l) × breadth(b)
2. Perimeter = $2(l + b)$
3. Diagonal = $\sqrt{l^2 + b^2}$

Square :

1. Area = $(\text{Side})^2$
2. Perimeter = 4 × side
3. Diagonal = $\text{side} \times \sqrt{2}$

Parallelogram: Area = Base × Height.

Trapezium : Area = $\frac{1}{2} \times \text{Height} \times$ (Sum of parallel sides).

Here, height is the distance between the two parallel sides.

Rhombus :

1. Area = $\frac{1}{2} \times$ Product of diagonals
2. Side = $\sqrt{\left(\frac{d_1}{2}\right)^2 + \left(\frac{d_2}{2}\right)^2}$, where d_1 and d_2 are diagonals
3. Perimeter = 4 × side

Quadrilateral : Area $= \frac{1}{2} \times$ One diagonal × (Sum of perpendicular to it from the opposite vertices)

$$= \frac{1}{2} \times d \times (a+b)$$

Circle :

1. Diameter = 2 × Radius
2. Area = $\pi r^2 = \frac{\pi}{4} d^2$; where d = diameter = $\sqrt{\frac{4A}{\pi}}$
3. Circumference = $2\pi r = \pi d$
4. Radius = $\frac{\text{Circumference}}{2\pi} = \frac{\sqrt{\text{Area}}}{\pi}$
5. Length of an Arc = $\frac{\theta}{360°} \times 2\pi r$
6. Area of sector = $\frac{\theta}{360°} \times \pi r^2 = \frac{1}{2} \times \text{Arc} \times r$

Polygon :

1. Interior angle + Exterior angle = 180°
2. Each interior angle = $\left(\frac{2n-4}{n}\right) \times 90°$

   where n = number of sides

3. Sum of Exterior angles = 360°
4. Perimeter = Number of sides × Length of side.
5. For an equilateral triangle of side 'a'

(a) radius of inscribed circle $= \frac{a}{2\sqrt{3}}$

and side of the triangle $= 2\sqrt{3}r$,

(b) radius of circumcircle $= \frac{a}{\sqrt{3}}$

6. Area of regular polygon $= \frac{1}{2}$(No. of sides) (Radius of the inscribed circle)

7. Area of regular hexagon $= \frac{3\sqrt{3}}{2}(\text{side})^2$

$= 2.598\ (\text{side})^2$

8. Area of a regular octagon

$= 2(\sqrt{2}+1)(\text{side})^2 = 4.828\ (\text{side})^2$

9. Area of quadrilateral, A

$= \sqrt{s(s-a)(s-b)(s-c)(s-d)}$

where, $s = \frac{a+b+c+d}{2}$

VOLUME AND SURFACE AREA OF SOLIDS

Cuboid : A cuboid has six faces, each one a ractangle. It has 12 edges. For example, a rectangular brick.

Let Length = l, Breadth = b and Height = h, then,

1. Volume = (Length × Breadth × Height)
2. Whole Surface Area = $2(lb + bh + lh)$
3. Diagonal $= \sqrt{l^2+b^2+h^2}$
4. Area of 4 walls of a room = $2 \times h\ (l + b)$

Cube : In a cube, Length = Breadth = Height

1. Volume = $(l)^3$
2. Length $= \sqrt[3]{\text{Volume}}$
3. Whole Surface Area = $6\ l^2$
4. Diagonal $= l\times\sqrt{3}$
5. Lateral Surface Area = $4\ l^2$

Cylinder :

1. Volume = $\pi r^2 h$
2. Curved Surface Area = $2\pi rh$
3. Total Surface Area = $2\pi r(r + h)$

where r = radius, h = height

Spherical Cell :

1. Volume $= \frac{4}{3}\pi(R^3 - r^3)$
2. Total Surface Area= $4\pi(R^2 - r^2)$

where R = Outer radius
r = Inner radius

Sphere :

1. Volume $= \frac{4}{3}\pi r^3$
2. Surface Area = $4\pi r^2$

Semi-sphere :

1. Volume $= \frac{2}{3}\pi r^3$
2. Curved surface area = $2\pi r^2$
3. Total surface area = $3\pi r^2$

Cone :

1. Slant height $(l) = \sqrt{r^2+h^2}$
2. Volume $= \frac{1}{3}\pi r^2 h$
3. Curved surface area = πrl
4. Total surface area = $\pi r\ (l + r)$
5. If the depth of the frustum of a cone be k and the radii of its ends are r_1 and r_2, then

(i) Slant height of the frustum of a cone

$= \sqrt{k^2+(r_1-r_2)^2}$

(ii) Curved surface of the frustum

$= \pi(r_1 + r_2)\ l.$

(iii) Volume $= \frac{\pi k}{3}\left(r_1^2+r_1r_2+r_2^2\right)$

SOLVED EXAMPLES

Example 1: What is the longest rod that can be placed in a room which is 7 m long, 9 m broad and $\sqrt{39}$ m high?

Solution: Required length of rod

$= \sqrt{7^2+9^2+(\sqrt{39})^2} = \sqrt{49+81+39}$

$= \sqrt{169} = 13$ m.

Example 2: The total area of a circle and a square is equal to 5450 sq. cm. The diameter of the circle is 70 cms. What is the sum of the circumference of the circle and the perimeter of the square?

Solution: Let side of the square = x cm

Also $\pi \times 35 \times 35 + x^2 = 5450$

$\Rightarrow \frac{22}{7}\times 35\times 35+x^2 = 5450$

$\Rightarrow x^2 = 5450 - 3850 = 1600$

$\therefore x = 40$ cm

$\therefore$ Required sum $= \pi \times d + 4x$

$= \left(\frac{22}{7}\times 70+4\times 40\right) = 380$ cm.

Example 3: Perimeter of a circle is equal to the prmimeter of a square whose area is 484 cm^2. What is the radius of the circle?

Solution: Side of a square $= \sqrt{\text{Area}} = \sqrt{484} = 22$ cm.

Perimeter of square = 4 × side = 4 × 22 = 88 cm.

$\therefore \quad 2\pi r = 88$

$\Rightarrow \quad 2 \times \frac{22}{7} \times r = 88$

$\Rightarrow \quad r = \frac{88 \times 7}{2 \times 22} = 14$ cm.

Example 4: The perimeter of a square is equal to twice the perimeter of a rectangle of length 8 cm and breadth 7 cm. What is the circumference of a semicircle whose diameter is equal to the side of the square? (Rounded off to the two decimal place)

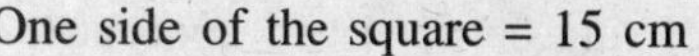

Solution: $\because$ Perimeter of the square

= 2 × Perimeter of rectangle

= 2(8 + 7) × 2 = 60 cm

One side of the square = 15 cm

Radius of the semicircle (R) = $\frac{15}{2}$ cm

$\therefore$ Perimeter of the semicircle = $\pi R + 2R$

$= \frac{22}{7} \times \frac{15}{2} + 15 = 23.57 + 15$

= 38.57 cm

MULTIPLE CHOICE QUESTIONS

1. What is the area of a circle whose radius is equal to the side of a square whose perimeter is 112 metres?

A. 176 sq m B. 2504 sq m
C. 284 sq m D. None of these

2. The sum of the circumference of a circle and the perimeter of a rectangle is 132 cm. The area of the rectangle is 112 sq cm and breadth of the rectangle is 8 cms. What is the area of the circle?

A. 616 sq cm B. 540 sq cm
C. 396 sq cm D. Cannot be determined

3. The total area of a circle and a rectangle is equal to 1166 sq cm. The diameter of the circle is 28 cm. What is the sum of the circumference of the circle and the perimeter of the rectangle if the length of the rectangle is 25 cm?

A. 186 cm B. 182 cm
C. 184 cm D. Cannot be determined

4. What would be the cost of laying a carpet on a floor which has its length and breadth in the respective ratio of 32 : 21 and where its perimeter is 212 feet, if the cost per square foot of laying the carpet is ₹ 2.5?

A. ₹ 6,720 B. ₹ 5,420
C. ₹ 7,390 D. Cannot be determined

5. A triangle's perimeter is 25 cms. Which of the following may be true or is a possibility?

(*a*) The sides are 7 cms., 7 cms. and 11 cms.
(*b*) It is an equilateral triangle.
(*c*) The value of sides can be in integer only

A. Only (*a*) B. Only (*a*) and (*b*)
C. Only (*c*) D. Only (*b*) and (*c*)

6. What will be the cost of building a fence around a circular field with area equal to 18,634 sq. metres; if the cost of building the fence per metre is ₹ 365?

A. ₹ 1,76,660 B. ₹ 68,01,410
C. ₹ 2,43,250 D. ₹ 56,60,220

7. The area of a square is 196 sq cms whose side is half the radius of a circle. The circumference of the circle is equal to breadth of a rectangle. If perimeter of the rectangle is 712 cm. What is the length of the rectangle?

A. 196 cm B. 186 cm
C. 180 cm D. 190 cm

8. The circumference of a circular plot is 484 metres. Find out the area of that circular plot—

A. 15246 m^2 B. 18634 m^2
C. 20328 m^2 D. 13552 m^2

9. A room measures 22 dm by 16 dm. I wish to buy a carpet for the floor leaving an uncarpeted margin 2 dm wide along each of the shorter sides of the room and a margin 0.5 dm wide along each of the longer sides of the room. If the price of the carpet is ₹ 500 per sq. metre, what is the cost of the whole carpet required?

A. ₹ 500 B. ₹ 2700
C. ₹ 2000 D. ₹ 1350

10. A paper is in the form of a rectangle ABCD where AB = 22 cm and BC = 14 cm. A semi-circular portion with segment BC as a diameter is cut off. Find the area of remaining paper.

A. 231 cm^2 B. 213 cm^2
C. 321 cm^2 D. 200 cm^2

11. How many plants can be put in a circular flower bed whose circumference is 880 dm allowing 35 dm^2 for each plant?

A. 880 B. 1760
C. 1000 D. 1500

12. An athletic track 14 m wide consists of two straight sections 120 m long joining semi-circular ends whose inner radius is 35 m. Calculate the area of the track :

A. 5670 m^2 B. 7065 m^2
C. 5607 m^2 D. 7056 m^2

13. A square park has each side of 100 m. At each corner of the park, there is a flower bed in the form of a quadrant of radius 14 m. Then the area of the remaining part of the park is :

A. 9384 m^2 B. 9834 m^2
C. 9000 m^2 D. 8900 m^2

14. The length of minute hand of a clock is 14 cm. Then the area swept by the minute hand in one minute is:
A. 10 m^2 B. 12.26 m^2
C. 20.26 m^2 D. 10.26 m^2

15. Find the area of ring between two concentric circles whose circumference are 77 cm and 55 cm.
A. 770 cm^2 B. 321 cm^2
C. 231 cm^2 D. 230 cm^2

16. A rectangle water reservoir is 10.8 metres long and 3.75 metres wide at base. Water flows into it at the rate of 18 m per sec. through the pipe having the cross section 7.5 cm × 4.5 cm. Then the height to which the water will rise in the reservoir in 30 minutes is :
A. 7.2 m B. 2.7 m
C. 3.7 m D. 7.3 m

17. A rectangular sheet of 44 cm × 18 cm is rolled along its length and a cylinder is formed. Then the volume of cylinder is :
A. 7227 cm^3 B. 7272 cm^3
C. 2727 cm^3 D. 2772 cm^3

18. How many metres of cloth 5 metre wide will be required to make a conical tent, the radius of whose base is 7 metre and height is 24 metre?
A. 100 m B. 110 m
C. 550 m D. 55 m

19. The surface area of a sphere whose volume is 4851 cubic metres is :
A. 1386 m^2 B. 1380 m^2
C. 1286 m^2 D. 3186 m^2

20. A hollow sphere of external and internal diameter 4 cm and 2 cm respectively, is melted into a cone of base diameter 8 cm. Then the height of the cone is :
A. 12 cm B. 14 cm
C. 20 cm D. 24 cm

21. The diamensions of a metallic rod are 19 cm × 4 cm × 2 cm and each side of a metallic cube is 4 cm. Both are melted and recast into a new cube. Find the length of edge of cube so formed.
A. 4 cm B. 5 cm
C. 6 cm D. 7 cm

22. An agricultural field is in the form of a rectangle of length 35 metres and width 15.4 metres. A pit 5.5 metres long, 4 metres wide and 2.5 metres deep is dug in the corner of the field and the earth taken out of the pit is spread uniformly over the remaining area of the field. The extent to which the level of the field has been raised is :
A. 16.6 cm B. 10.6 cm
C. 16.1 cm D. 6.10 cm

23. The side of a square exceeds the side of the another square by 4 cm and the sum of areas of two squares is 400 sq. cm. Find the dimensions of the square.
A. 8 cm, 12 cm B. 10 cm, 14 cm
C. 12 cm, 16 cm D. 14 cm, 18 cm

24. The cost of levelling a rectangular field at the rate of 85 paise per square metre is ₹ 624.75. Then the perimeter of the field if its sides are in the ratio of 5 : 3 is :
A. 35 m B. 21 m
C. 112 m D. 49 m

25. The diagonal of a rectangular field is 15 m and its area is 108 sq. m. What will be the total expenditure in fencing the field at the rate of ₹ 5 per metre?
A. ₹ 441 B. ₹ 420
C. ₹ 210 D. ₹ 120

26. The minute hand of a clock is 10 cm long. The area of the face of the clock described by the minute hand between 9 AM and 9.35 AM is :
A. 140 cm^2 B. 183.3 cm^2
C. 180 cm^2 D. 175.3 cm^2

27. The length of a rectangular plot is 60% more than its breadth. If the difference between the length and the breadth of that rectangle is 24 cm, what is the area of that rectangle?
A. 2400 sq. cm B. 2480 sq. cm
C. 2560 sq. cm D. Data inadequate

28. The area of a rectangle is 460 square metres. If the length is 15% more than the breadth, what is the breadth of the rectangular field?
A. 15 metres B. 26 metres
C. 34.5 metres D. None of these

29. The ratio between the length and the breadth of a rectangular field is 3 : 2. If only the length is increased by 5 metres, the new area of the field will be 2600 sq. metres. What is the breadth of the rectangular field?
A. 40 metres B. 60 metres
C. 65 metres D. Cannot be determined

30. If the length and breadth of a rectangular plot be increased by 50% and 20% respectively, then how many times will its area be increased?
A. $1\frac{1}{3}$ B. 2
C. $3\frac{2}{5}$ D. None of these

31. The length of a rectangle is decreased by r%, and the breadth is increased by $(r + 5)$%. Find r, if the area of the rectangle is unaltered.
A. 5 B. 8
C. 10 D. 20

32. The length and breadth of the floor of the room are 20 feet and 10 feet respectively. Square tiles of 2 feet length of different colours are to be laid on the floor. Black tiles are laid in the first row on all sides. If white tiles are laid in the one-third of the remaining and blue tiles in the rest, how many blue tiles will be there?

A. 16 B. 24
C. 32 D. 48

33. A park square in shape has a 3 metre wide road inside it running along its sides. The area occupied by the road is 1764 square metres. What is the perimeter along the outer edge of the road?

A. 576 metres B. 600 metres
C. 640 metres D. Data inadequate

34. What will be the length of the diagonal of that square plot whose area is equal to the area of a rectangular plot of length 45 metres and breadth 40 metres?

A. 42.5 metres B. 60 metres
C. 75 metres D. Data inadequate

35. The length of one pair of opposite sides of a square is increased by 5 cm on each side; the ratio of the length and the breadth of the newly formed rectangle becomes 3 : 2. What is the area of the original square?

A. 25 sq. cm B. 81 sq. cm
C. 100 sq. cm D. 225 sq. cm

36. What will be the ratio between the area of a rectangle and the area of a triangle with one of the sides of the rectangle as base and a vertex on the opposite side of the rectangle?

A. 1 : 2
B. 2 : 1
C. 3 : 1
D. Data inadequate

37. A cow is tethered in the middle of a field with a 14 feet long rope. If the cow grazes 100 sq. ft. per day, then approximately what time will be taken by the cow to graze the whole field?

A. 2 days B. 6 days
C. 18 days D. 24 days

38. A circular ground whose diameter is 35 metres, has a 1.4 m broad garden around it. What is the area of the garden in square metres?

A. 160.16 B. 176.16
C. 196.16 D. None of these

39. The cost of the paint is ₹ 36.50 per kg. If 1 kg of paint covers 16 square feet, how much will it cost to paint outside of a cube having 8 feet each side?

A. ₹ 692 B. ₹ 768
C. ₹ 876 D. ₹ 972

40. The capacity of a cylindrical tank is 246.4 litres. If the height is 4 metres, what is the diameter of the base?

A. 1.4 m B. 2.8 m
C. 14 m D. 28 m

ANSWERS

1	2	3	4	5	6	7	8	9	10
D	A	B	A	A	A	C	B	D	A
11	12	13	14	15	16	17	18	19	20
B	D	A	D	C	B	D	B	A	B
21	22	23	24	25	26	27	28	29	30
C	B	C	C	C	B	C	D	A	D
31	32	33	34	35	36	37	38	39	40
D	A	B	B	C	B	B	D	C	D

SOME SELECTED EXPLANATORY ANSWERS

1. ∵ Radius of the circle $= \frac{112}{4} = 28$ m

∴ Area of the circle $= \frac{22}{7} \times 28 \times 28 = 2464$ m^2.

2. Length of the rectangle $= \frac{112}{8} = 14$ cm.

∴ Perimeter of the rectangle = 2(14 + 8)
= 44 cm.

∴ Circumference of the circle = 132 – 44
= 88 cm.

∴ $r = \frac{88 \times 7}{2 \times 22} = 14$ cm

∴ Area of the circle

$= \frac{22}{7} \times 14 \times 14 = 616$ sq cm.

3. From question—

∵ Diameter of the circle = 28 cm.

⇒ Area of the circle $= \frac{22}{7} \times (14)^2 = 616$ cm^2

∴ Area of the rectangle = 1166 – 616
= 550 cm^2

⇒ Breadth of the rectangle $= \frac{550}{25} = 22$ cm.

$\therefore$ Required sum = $2\times\frac{22}{7}\times(14)+2(25+22)$

= 88 + 94 = 182 cm.

4. Length of the floor = $\frac{212\times32}{2\times(32+21)}$ = 64 ft.

and breadth the floor = $\frac{64\times21}{32}$ = 42 ft.

$\therefore$ Area of the floor = 64 × 42 = 2688 sq. ft.

$\therefore$ Reqd. cost = ₹ 2688 × 2.5 = ₹ 6720.

5. Only statement A may be true or possibility.

6. Area of the circular field = 18634 m^2

$\because$ $\pi r^2 = 18634$

$\Rightarrow$ $r^2 = 18634\times\frac{7}{22} = 5929$

$\Rightarrow$ $r = 77$ m

$\because$ Length of the fence = $2\times\frac{22}{7}\times77$

= 484 m

$\therefore$ Total cost = 484 × 365

= ₹ 176660.

7. One side of the square = $\sqrt{196}$ = 14 cm

$\therefore$ Radius of the circle = 28 cm

$\therefore$ Circumference of the circle = $2\times\frac{22}{7}\times28$

= 176 cm

$\therefore$ Breadth of the rectangle = 176 cm

$\therefore$ Length of the rectangle = $\frac{712}{2}-176$

= 356 – 176

= 180 cm.

8. Let r be the radius of the circular plot then from problem,

$\because$ The circumference of the circular plot = 484 m

$\Rightarrow$ $2\pi r = 484$

$r = 484\times\frac{7}{22}\times\frac{1}{2}$ = 77 metres

$\therefore$ Area of the circular plot = $\pi r^2 = \frac{22}{7}\times(77)^2$

= 18634 m^2.

10. Area of the whole paper ABCD = 22 × 14

= 308 cm^2

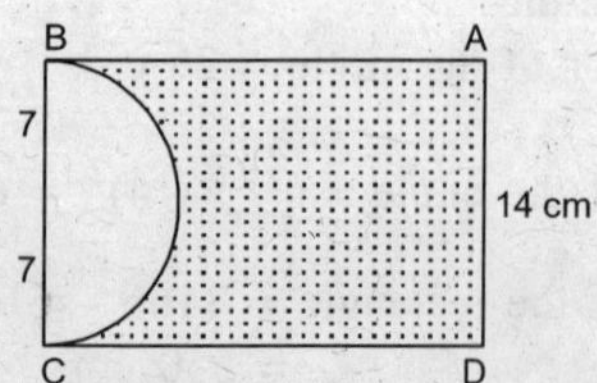

Radius of the semi-circle = $\frac{1}{2}\times14$ cm = 7 cm

$\therefore$ Area of the semi-circle = $\frac{1}{2}\pi r^2$

$= \frac{1}{2}\times\frac{22}{7}\times7\times7$

= 77 cm^2

$\therefore$ Area of the remaining part of the paper

= 308 cm^2 – 77 cm^2 = 231 cm^2.

11. Circumference of flower bed = 880 dm

$\Rightarrow$ $2\pi r = 880$ dm

$\Rightarrow$ $r = \frac{880}{2\pi}$ dm = $\frac{880\times7}{2\times22}$ = 140 dm

Area of flower bed = $\pi r^2 = \frac{22}{7}\times(140)^2$ dm^2

$\therefore$ Required number of plants

$= \frac{\frac{22}{7}\times140\times140}{35}$ dm^2

$= \frac{22}{7}\times\frac{140\times140}{35}$ = 1760.

13. Area of each quadrant = $\frac{\theta}{360}\times\pi r^2$

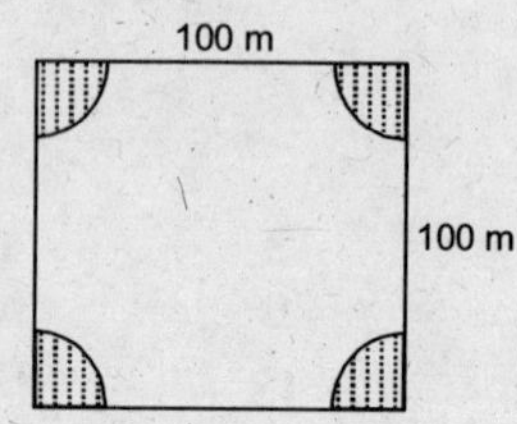

$= \frac{90}{360}\times\frac{22}{7}\times14\times14$ m^2 = 154 m^2

$\therefore$ Area of 4 quadrants = 154 × 4 m^2 = 616 m^2

Area of park = $(100)^2$ = 10,000 m^2

Hence area of the remaining part of the park

= 10,000 – 616 = 9,384 m^2.

14. Length of minute hand of clock = r = 14 cm

Central angle covered in 1 minute = $\frac{360}{60} = 6°$

$\therefore$ Area swept in one minute = Area of sector with central angle 6°

$= \frac{\theta}{360}\times\pi r^2 = \frac{6}{360}\times\frac{22}{7}\times14\times14$

$= \frac{154}{15}$ = 10.26 cm^2.

15. Let R be the radius of outer circle and r the radius of inner circle.

Circumference of outer circle = 77 cm

$\therefore\ 2\pi R = 77$

$\Rightarrow R = \dfrac{77}{2\pi} = \dfrac{77\times7}{2\times22} = \dfrac{49}{4}$ cm

Circumference of inner circle = 55 cm

$\therefore\ 2\pi r = 55 \Rightarrow r = \dfrac{55}{2\pi} = \dfrac{55\times7}{2\times22} = \dfrac{35}{4}$ cm

$\therefore$ Area of ring = $\pi(R^2 - r^2)$

$= \dfrac{22}{7}\times\left(\dfrac{49}{4}+\dfrac{35}{4}\right)\left(\dfrac{49}{4}-\dfrac{35}{4}\right) = 231\ \text{cm}^2$

16. Volume of water that flows in one second

$= (18 \times 0.075 \times 0.045)\ \text{m}^3$

Volume of water that flows in 30 minutes

$= 18 \times 0.075 \times 0.045 \times 30 \times 60$

$= 109.35\ \text{m}^3$.

Area of the base of the reservoir = $10.8 \times 3.75\ \text{m}^2$

$\therefore$ Height of water = $\dfrac{109.35}{10.8\times3.75} = 2.7$ metres.

17. Let r cm be the radius of the base and h cm be the height. Then, $h = 18$ cm.

Now, circumference of the base = Length of the Sheet

$\Rightarrow$ Circumference = 44 cm

$\Rightarrow\ 2\pi r = 44$

$\Rightarrow\ 2\times\dfrac{22}{7}\times r = 44$

$\Rightarrow\ r = 7$ cm

Volume of the cylinder = $\pi r^2 h\ \text{cm}^3$

$= \dfrac{22}{7}\times(7)^2\times18\ \text{cm}^3$

$= 2772\ \text{cm}^3$

18. Slant height, $l = \sqrt{r^2+h^2}$

$= \sqrt{7^2+24^2} = 25$ metres

Curved Surface area of cone = πrl

$= \dfrac{22}{7}\times7\times25 = 550\ \text{m}^2$

$\therefore$ Area of the cloth required = $550\ \text{m}^2$

$\therefore$ Length of the cloth = $\dfrac{550}{5} = 110$ metres.

21. Volume of the metallic rod = $19 \times 4 \times 2$

$= 152$ cu.cm.

Volume of the cube = $4^3 = 64$ cu. cm.

Total volume of both after melting them

$= 152 + 64 = 216$ cu.cm.

$\therefore$ Volume of new cube = 216 cu. cm.

$\Rightarrow$ Side = 6 cm.

23. Let S_1 and S_2 be the two squares. Let the side of the square S_1 be x cm. Then the side of the square $S_2 = (x + 4)$ cm.

$\therefore$ Area of square $S_1 = x^2$

and, Area of square $S_2 = (x + 4)^2$

$\therefore$ According to the question,

$x^2 + (x + 4)^2 = 400$

Solving the equation, weget

$x = -16$ and 12

But x cannot be negative

$\therefore$ Side of the square S_1 = 12 cm

and that of square $S_2 = x + 4 = 12 + 4$

$= 16$ cm.

26. Angle described by minute hand in 60 minutes = 360°

Angle described by minute hand in 35 minutes

$= \dfrac{360}{60}\times35 = 210°$

$\therefore$ The required area swept by the minute hand = Area of sector $r = 10$ cm

and, $\theta = 210°$

$= \dfrac{22}{7}\times10\times10\times\dfrac{210}{360}$

$= 183.3\ \text{cm}^2$.

27. Let breadth = x cm. Then, length = $\left(\dfrac{160}{100}x\right)$ cm

$= \dfrac{8}{5}x$ cm.

So, $\dfrac{8}{5}x - x = 24 \Rightarrow \dfrac{3}{5}x = 24$

$\Rightarrow\ x = \left(\dfrac{24\times5}{3}\right) = 40.$

$\therefore$ Length = 64 cm, Breadth = 40 cm.

Area = $(64 \times 40)\ \text{cm}^2 = 2560\ \text{cm}^2$.

28. Let breadth = x metres. Then, length

$= \left(\dfrac{115x}{100}\right)$ metres.

$\therefore\ x\times\dfrac{115x}{100} = 460$

$\Rightarrow\ x^2 = \left(\dfrac{460\times100}{115}\right) = 400$

$\Rightarrow\ x = 20.$

29. Let length = $(3x)$ metres and breadth $= (2x)$ metres.

Then, $(3x + 5) \times 2x = 2600$

$\Rightarrow\ 6x^2 + 10x - 2600 = 0$

$\Rightarrow\ 3x^2 + 5x - 1300 = 0$

$\Rightarrow\ (3x + 65)(x - 20) = 0$

$\Rightarrow\ x = 20.$

$\therefore$ Breadth = $2x$ = 40 m.

31. Let original length = x and original breadth = y.

Then, original area = xy.

$$\text{New area} = \left[\frac{(100-r)}{100}\times x\right]\left[\frac{(105+r)}{100}\times y\right]$$

$$= \left[\left(\frac{10500-5r-r^2}{10000}\right)xy\right]$$

$$\therefore \left(\frac{10500-5r-r^2}{10000}\right)xy = xy$$

$\Rightarrow r^2 + 5r - 500 = 0$

$\Rightarrow (r + 25)(r - 20) = 0 \quad \Rightarrow \quad r = 20.$

32. Area left after laying black tiles

= [(20 – 4) × (10 – 4)] sq. ft = 96 sq. ft.

Area under white tiles = $\left(\frac{1}{3}\times 96\right)$ sq. ft

= 32 sq. ft

Area under blue tiles = (96 – 32) sq. ft

= 64 sq. ft

Number of blue tiles = $\frac{64}{(2\times 2)} = 16.$

33. Let the length of the outer edge be x metres. Then, length of the inner edge = $(x - 6)$ m.

$\therefore \quad x^2 - (x - 6)^2 = 1764$

$\Rightarrow x^2 - (x^2 - 12x + 36) = 1764$

$\Rightarrow \quad 12x = 1800$

$\therefore \quad x = 150.$

$\therefore$ Required perimeter = $(4x)$ m

= (4 × 150) m

= 600 m.

34. Area = (45 × 40) m^2

$\Rightarrow \frac{1}{2} \times (\text{diagonal})^2 = 1800$

$\Rightarrow$ diagonal = 60 m.

35. Let original length of each side = x cm.

Then, its area = (x^2) cm^2.

Length of rectangle formed = $(x + 5)$ cm and its breadth = x cm.

$\therefore \quad \frac{x+5}{x} = \frac{3}{2} \quad \Rightarrow 2x + 10 = 3x \Rightarrow x = 10.$

$\therefore$ Original length of each side = 10 cm and its area = 100 cm^2.

36. Area of rectangle = lb sq. units.

Area of the triangle = $\frac{1}{2} lb$ sq. units.

$\therefore$ Required ratio = $lb : \frac{1}{2} lb = 2 : 1.$

37. Area of the field grazed = $\left(\frac{22}{7}\times 14\times 14\right)$ sq. ft

= 616 sq. ft.

Number of days taken to graze the field = $\frac{616}{100}$ days

= 6 days (approx.).

38. Radius of the ground = 17.5 m.

Radius of inner circle = (17.5 – 1.4) m = 16.1 m.

Area of the garden = $\pi \times [(17.5)^2 - 16.1)^2]$ m^2

$$= \left[\frac{22}{7}\times(17.5+16.1)(17.5-16.1)\right] m^2$$

$$= \left(\frac{22}{7}\times 33.6\times 1.4\right) m^2 = 147.84 \ m^2.$$

39. Surface area of the cube = (6×8^2) sq. ft

= 384 sq. ft.

Quantity of paint required = $\left(\frac{384}{16}\right)$ kg = 24 kg.

$\therefore$ Cost of painting = ₹ (36.50 × 24) = ₹ 876.

12 Permutation & Combination

IMPORTANT RESULTS

(*i*) Number of permutations of n distinct things taken r at a time, $0 \le r \le n$
$= n(n-1)(n-2) \ldots (n-r+1)$
$= n!/(n-r)! = {}^nP_r$.
This is equivalent to filling r places by r objects taking from n distinct objects.

(*ii*) The number of permutations of n distinct objects taken all at a time $= n!$

(*iii*) The number of combinations of n objects taken r at a time, $0 \le r \le n$. $= {}^nC_r$

$$= \frac{n!}{(n-r)!.r!}.$$

(*iv*) The number of permutations of n dissimilar things taken r at a time when each thing can be repeated any number of times $= n^r$.

(*v*) The number of combinations of n distinct objects taken r at a time when any object may be repeated any number of times
= coefficient of x^r in $(1 + x + x^2 + \ldots + x^r)^n$
= coefficient of x^r in $(1-x)^n = {}^{n+r-1}C_r$.

(*vi*) Number of combinations of n distinct things taken r at a time when p particular things always occur $= {}^{(n-p)}C_{(r-p)}$.

(*vii*) The number of permutations of n distinct things taken r at a time when p particular things always occur $= {}^{(n-p)}C_{(r-p)}.r!$.

(*viii*) Number of combinations of n distinct things taken r at a time when p particular things never occur $= {}^{(n-p)}C_r$.

(*ix*) Number of permutations (arrangements) of n distinct things taken r at a time when p particular things never occur $= {}^{(n-p)}C_r.r!$.

(*x*) Number of permutations of n things, taken all at a time when p_1 are alike of one kind, p_2 are alike of second kind, ..., p_r of them are alike of the r-th kind $p_1 + p_2 + \ldots + p_r \le n$, and remaining things are all different $= n!/\{p_1!p_2! \ldots p_r!\}$.

(*xi*) If $3n$ things are to be divided into three equal groups, then the number of ways $= \dfrac{(3n)!}{n!.n!.n!.3!}$.

(*xii*) If $3n$ things are to be divided equally between 3 persons (*i.e.*, division of $3n$ things into 3 equal groups with permutation of groups) then the number of ways $= \dfrac{(3n)!}{(n!)^3}$.

(*xiii*) Greatest value of ${}^nC_r$
${}^nC_r$ is greatest when $r = n/2$ if n is even
$r = (n-1)/2$ or $(n+1)/2$ if n is odd.

(*xiv*) ${}^nC_r = {}^nC_{n-r}$.

(*xv*) ${}^nC_r + {}^nC_{r+1} = {}^{n+1}C_{r+1}$.

(*xvi*) ${}^nC_r = {}^nC_s \Rightarrow r = s$ or $r + s = n$.

(*xvii*) The number of circular permutations of n different things taken all at a time $= (n-1)!$

(*xviii*) The number of arrangements of n persons on a round table $= (n-1)!$.

(*xix*) The number of arrangements of n flowers to make a garland $= \dfrac{1}{2}(n-1)!$.

SOLVED EXAMPLES

Example 1: In how many different ways can the letters of the word 'PRIDE' be arranged ?

Solution: Required number of arrangements

$$= {}^5P_5 = 5! = 120$$

Example 2: In how many different ways can the letters of the word 'PRAISE' be arranged ?

Solution: Required number of ways

$$= {}^6P_6 = 6! = 720$$

Example 3: On a shelf there are 4 books on Economics, 3 books on Management and 4 books on Statistics. In how many different ways can the books be arranged so that the books on Economics are kept together ?

Solution: Required number of different ways

$$= {}^8P_8 \times {}^4P_4 = \underline{|8} \times \underline{|4}$$

$$= 40320 \times 24 = 967680$$

Example 4: In how many different ways can the letters of the word 'PRETTY' be arranged?

Solution: Required ways $= \frac{\underline{|6}}{\underline{|2}} = 360$

Example 5: In how many different ways can the letters of the word 'PEANUT' be arranged ?

Solution: Required ways $= {}^6P_6 = \underline{|6}$

$$= 6 \times 5 \times 4 \times 3 \times 2 \times 1 = 720.$$

MULTIPLE CHOICE QUESTIONS

1. How many seven digit numbers can be made from the number 3428651, using each digit only once ?

A. 49 B. 180
C. 5040 D. 2520

2. How many words can be formed from the letters of the word 'DIRECTOR' so that the vowels are always together?

A. 2106 B. 1206
C. 360 D. 2160

3. In how many ways a committee of 5 members can be selected from 6 men and 5 ladies, consisting of 3 men and 2 ladies?

A. 120 B. 220
C. 200 D. 320

4. In how many ways can the letters of the word 'APPLE' be arranged?

A. 720 B. 120
C. 60 D. 180

5. How many words can be formed by using all the letters of the word. 'ALLAHABAD'?

A. 3780 B. 1890
C. 7560 D. 2520

6. How many words can be formed from the letters of the word 'SIGNATURE' so that the vowels always come together?

A. 720 B. 1440
C. 2880 D. 17280

7. In how many different ways can the letters of the word 'BANKING' be arranged so that the vowels always come together?

A. 120 B. 240
C. 360 D. 720

8. In how many ways can a group of 5 men and 2 women be made out of a total of 7 men and 3 women?

A. 63 B. 90
C. 126 D. 45

9. In a group of 6 boys and 4 girls, four children are to be selected. In how many different ways can they be selected such that at least one boy should be there?

A. 159 B. 194
C. 205 D. 209

10. A box contains 2 white balls, 3 black balls and 4 red balls. In how many ways can 3 balls be drawn from the box, if at least one black ball is to be included in the draw?

A. 32 B. 48
C. 64 D. 96

11. In how many ways can a team of 3 boys and 3 girls be selected from 5 boys and 4 girls?

A. 14 B. 40
C. 18 D. 140

12. The number of ways of selecting 9 balls from 6 red, 5 white and 5 blue if each selection consists of 3 balls of each colour is :

A. 1200 B. 20000
C. 2200 D. 2000

13. In how many ways can we select 4 red balls and 3 blue balls from 8 red balls and 9 blue balls?

A. 8550 B. 5850
C. 5880 D. 8580

14. Find the number of diagonals of a decagon

A. 45 B. 35
C. 55 D. 25

15. In how many ways can a student choose a programme of 5 courses if 9 courses are available and 2 specific courses are compulsary for every student?

A. 53 B. 14
C. 35 D. 28

16. Seven different lecturers are to deliver lectures in seven periods of a class on a particular day. A, B and C are three of the lecturers. The number of ways in which a routine for the day can be made such that A delivers his lecuture before B, and B before C, is

A. 420 B. 120
C. 210 D. 840

17. The number of words that can be made by rearranging the letters of the word APURBA so that vowels and consonants alternate is

A. 18 B. 35
C. 36 D. 24

18. The number of ways in which the letters of the word ARTICLE can be rearranged so that the even places are always occupied by consonants is

A. 576 B. ${}^4C_3 \times (4!)$

C. 2(4!) D. 288

19. The number of ways in which a couple can sit around a table with 6 guests if the couple take consecutive seats is

A. 1440 B. 720

C. 5040 D. 2880

20. The number of ways in which 20 different pearls of two colours can be set alternately on a necklace, there being 10 pearls of each colour, is

A. $9! \times 10!$ B. $5(9!)^2$

C. $(9!)^2$ D. $(18!)^2$

21. There are 4 mangoes, 3 apples, 2 oranges and 1 each of 3 other varieties of fruits. The number of ways of selecting at least one fruit of each kind is

A. 10! B. 9!

C. 4! D. 5!

22. The number of ways in which 6 different balls can be put in two boxes of different sizes so that no box remains empty is

A. 62 B. 64

C. 36 D. 60

23. The number of arrangements of the letters of the word BHARAT taking 3 at a time is

A. 72 B. 120

C. 14 D. 48

24. Find the number of different permutations of the letters of the word BANANA.

A. 16 B. 60

C. 61 D. 36

25. A box contains two white balls, three black balls and four red balls. In how many ways can three balls be drawn from the box if at least one black ball is to be included in the draw?

A. 16 B. 32

C. 64 D. 128

26. All the letters of the word EAMCET are arranged in possible ways. The number of such arrangement in which not two vowels are adjacent to each other is:

A. 360 B. 144

C. 72 D. 54

27. The number of arrangements which can be made by using all the letters of the word LAUGH, if the vowels are adjacent, is:

A. 10 B. 24

C. 48 D. 120

28. There are 10 lamps in a hall. Each one of them can be switched on independently. The number of ways in which the hall can be illuminated is:

A. 10^2 B. 1023

C. 210 D. 10!

29. Everybody in a room shakes hands with everybody else. The total number of hand shakes is 66. The total number of persons in the room is:

A. 11 B. 12

C. 8 D. 14

30. 20 persons are invited for a party. The number of ways in which they and the host can be seated at a circular table, if two particular persons be seated on either side of the host, is equal to:

A. 18! . 2!

B. 18! . 3!

C. 19! . 2!

D. 19! . 3!

31. The number of ways in which 5 prizes be distributed among 4 boys, while each boy is capable of having any number of prizes is:

A. 6^4 B. 4^5

C. $4! \cdot 2^4$ D. 6 . (4!)

32. In an examination there are three multiple choice questions and each question has 4 choices. Number of ways in which a student can fail to get all answers correct, is:

A. 11 B. 12

C. 27 D. 63

33. 7 men and 7 women are to sit round a table so that there is a man on either side of a woman. The number of seating arrangement is:

A. $(7!)^2$ B. $(6!)^2$

C. $6! \times 7!$ D. 7!

34. Three men have 4 coats, 5 waist coats and 6 caps. In how many ways can they wear them?

A. 178200

B. 172000

C. 172800

D. 1720800

35. To fill 12 vacancies there are 25 candidates of which 5 are from scheduled castes. If 3 of the vacancies are reserved for scheduled caste candidates while the rest are open to all, find the number of ways in which the selection can be made.

A. 4974200

B. 4947200

C. 4972400

D. 4927400

ANSWERS

1	2	3	4	5	6	7	8	9	10
C	D	C	C	C	D	D	A	D	C
11	12	13	14	15	16	17	18	19	20
B	D	C	B	C	D	C	A	A	B
21	22	23	24	25	26	27	28	29	30
C	A	A	B	C	C	C	B	B	A
31	32	33	34	35					
B	D	C	C	A					

SOME SELECTED EXPLANATORY ANSWERS

1. Required number of ways = $^7P_7 = \lfloor 7 = 5040$

2. In the given word, we treat the vowels IEO as one letter.

Thus, we have DRCTR (IEO).

This group has 6 letters of which R occurs 2 times and others are different.

Number of ways arranging these letters $= \frac{6!}{2!} = 360.$

Now 3 vowels can be arranged among themselves in 3! = 6 ways.

∴ Required number of ways = (360 × 6) = 2160.

3. (3 men out of 6) and (2 ladies out of 5) are to be chosen.

∴ Required number of ways

$= (^6C_3 \times {}^5C_2)$

$= \left(\frac{6\times5\times4}{3\times2\times1} \times \frac{5\times4}{2\times1}\right) = 200.$

4. The word 'APPLE' contains 5 letters, 1A, 2P, 1L and 1E.

∴ Required number of ways

$= \frac{5!}{(1!)(2!)(1!)(1!)} = 60.$

5. The word 'ALLAHABAD' contains 9 letters, namely 4A, 2L, 1H, 1B and 1D.

∴ Required number of words

$= \frac{9!}{(4!)(2!)(1!)(1!)(1!)} = 7560.$

6. The word 'SIGNATURE' contains 9 different letters. When the vowels IAUE are taken together, they can be supposed to form an entity, treated as one letter. Then, the letters to be arranged are SGNTR (IAUE). These 6 letters can be arranged in $^6P_6 = 6! = 720$ ways. The vowels in the group (IAUE) can be arranged amongst themselves in $^4P_4 = 4! = 24$ ways.

∴ Required number of words = (720 × 24)
= 17280.

7. In the word 'BANKING', we treat the two vowels AI as one letter. Thus, we have BNKNG (AI).

This has 6 letters of which N occurs 2 times and the rest are different.

Number of ways of arranging these letters

$= \frac{6!}{(2!)(1!)(1!)(1!)(1!)} = 360.$

Now, 2 vowels AI can be arranged in 2! = 2 ways.

∴ Required number of ways = (360 × 2) = 720.

8. Required number of ways

$= (^7C_5 \times {}^3C_2)$

$= (^7C_2 \times {}^3C_1) = \left(\frac{7\times6}{2\times1}\times3\right) = 63.$

9. We may have (1 boy and 3 girls) or (2 boys and 2 girls) or (3 boys and 1 girl) or (4 boys).

∴ Required number of ways

$= (^6C_1 \times {}^4C_3) + (^6C_2 \times {}^4C_2) + (^6C_3 \times {}^4C_1) + (^6C_4)$

$= (^6C_1 \times {}^4C_1) + (^6C_2 \times {}^4C_2) + (^6C_3 \times {}^4C_1) + (^6C_2)$

$= (6\times4)+\left(\frac{6\times5}{2\times1}\times\frac{4\times3}{2\times1}\right)+\left(\frac{6\times5\times4}{3\times2\times1}\times4\right)+\left(\frac{6\times5}{2\times1}\right)$

= (24 + 90 + 80 + 15) = 209.

10. We may have (1 black and 2 non-black) or (2 black and 1 non-black) or (3 black)

∴ Required number of ways

$= (^3C_1 \times {}^6C_2) + (^3C_2 \times {}^6C_1) + (^3C_3)$

$= \left(3\times\frac{6\times5}{2\times1}\right)+\left(\frac{3\times2}{2\times1}\times6\right)+1 = (45 + 18 + 1) = 64.$

13. 4 red balls from 8 red balls can be selected in $^8C_4$ ways 3 blue balls from 9 balls can be selected in $^9C_3$ ways

∴ Total number of selection = $^8C_4 \times {}^9C_3$

$= \frac{8\times7\times6\times5}{1\times2\times3\times4}\times\frac{9\times8\times7}{1\times2\times3}$

$= 70 \times 84 = 5880.$

14. A decagon has 10 vertices

Join any two vertices in $^{10}C_2$ lines 10 lines will be sides.

$\therefore$ Number of diagonals $= {}^{10}C_2 - 10$

$= \frac{10\times9}{1\times2} - 10$

$= 45 - 10 = 35$

16. As the order of A, B and C is not to change they are to be treated identical in arrangement. So, the required

Number of ways $= \frac{7!}{3!}$.

$= \frac{7\times6\times5\times4\times3\times2\times1}{3\times2\times1} = 840.$

18. The number of ways to fill the three even places by 4 consonants $= {}^4P_3$.

After filling the even places, remaining places can be filled in $^4P_4$ ways.

So, the required number of words

$= {}^4P_3 \times {}^4P_4$

$= 4! \times 4! = 24 \times 24 = 576.$

19. A couple and 6 guests can be arranged in $(7-1)!$ ways. But the two people forming the couple can be arranged among themselves in 2! ways.

$\therefore$ The required number of ways $= 6! \times 2!$

$= 720 \times 2 = 1440.$

20. Ten pearls of one colour can be arranged in $1/2\ (10-1)!$ ways. The number of arrangements of 10 pearls of the other colour in 10 places between the pearls of the first colour = 10!.

$\therefore$ The required number of ways $= \frac{1}{2}\times9!\times10!$

$= 5 \times 9! \times 9! = 5(9!)^2.$

22. Each ball can be put in 2 ways (either in one box or the other).

$\therefore$ 6 balls can be put in $2 \times 2 \times ...$ to six times, i.e., 2^6 ways. But in two of the ways one box is empty. So, the required number of ways $= 2^6 - 2. = 62.$

23.

Possibilities	*Selections*	*Arrangements*
One pair, one different	$^1C_1 \times {}^4C_1$	$^1C_1\times{}^4C_1\times\frac{3!}{2!} = 12$
Three different	$^5C_3$	$^5C_3 \times 3! = 60$

$\therefore$ The required number of ways = 72

24. BANANA

3A's, 2N's, B, i.e., 6 letters, 3 alike of one type and 2 of another type. Number of words taken all at a time is $\frac{6!}{3!2!} = \frac{6\times5\times4}{2} = 60.$

25. The required number of ways

$= {}^3C_1 \times {}^6C_2 + {}^3C_2 \times {}^6C_1 + {}^3C_3 = 64.$

26. First we place 3 consonant in 3! ways and then at four places (2 between them and 2 on sides) 3 vowels in which one vowels is repeated can be placed in $^4P_3/2!$ ways.

Hence, required number $= 3!\ {}^4P_3/2! = 72.$

27. Considering two vowels together as a letter, there are 4 letters in all which can be arranged in 4! ways while 2 vowels can also be arranged in 2! ways.

$\therefore$ Total number of arrangements $= 4!\ .\ 2! = 48.$

28. Each bulb has two choices, either switched on or off.

$\therefore$ Required number $= 2^{10} - 1 = 1023$

(Since in one way, when all switches are off, the hall will not be illuminated.)

29. Let there be n persons in a room.

$\therefore$ Total no. of shakehands $= {}^nC_2 = 66$

$\Rightarrow \quad \frac{1}{2}n(n-1) = 66$

$\Rightarrow \quad n^2 - n - 132 = 0$

$\Rightarrow \quad (n+11)(n-12) = 0$

$\Rightarrow \quad n = 12 \qquad (\because n \neq -11)$

30. Host can sit on any seat. Two particular guests can sit on either sides of host in 2! = 2 ways and remaining 18 guests in (18)! ways.

Hence, total ways = 2.(18)!.

31. Since every prize can be given by any of the four boys, so number of ways $= 4 \times 4 \times 4 \times 4 \times 4 = 4^5$.

32. Each question can be answered in 4 ways and all questions can be answered correctly in only one way, so the required number of ways $= 4^3 - 1 = 63.$

33. First the seven women sit round the table in 6! ways and then seven men will sit in the spaces between every pair of two women in 7! ways.

$\therefore$ Required seating arrangements $= 6! \times 7!$.

34. $^4P_3 \times {}^5P_3 \times {}^6P_3 = 172800.$

35. $5C_3 \times {}^{22}C_9 = 4974200.$

13

Probability

1. **Random Experiment:** If the result of an experiment is not certain and is any one of the several possible outcomes, the experiment is called a trial or a random experiment.
2. **Sample Space:** The set of all possible outcome of an experiment is called the sample space provided no two or more of these outcomes can occur simultaneously and exactly one of these outcomes must occur whenever the experiment is conducted.
3. **Events:** The outcomes of an experiment, *i.e.*, sample points of the sample space are usually known as simple events and any subset of the sample space 'S' is called an event.

   Thus throwing of a dice is an experiment, S = {1, 2, 3, 4, 5, 6} is the sample space, {1}, ... {6} are simple events and {1, 2}, etc., are events. The empty set ϕ is also an event as $\phi \subset S$ and it is called an impossible event. The sample space S is also a subset of S and so it is also an event. S represents the sure event, *i.e.*, certainty.
4. **Equally Likely Events:** A set of events is said to be equally likely if taking into consideration all the relevant factors there is no reason to expect one of them in preference to others.

   For example, when a fair coin is tossed, the occurrence of a tail or a head are equally likely.
5. **Exhaustive Events:** A set of events is said to be exhaustive if the performance of the experiment always results in the occurrence of atleast one of them.

   For example, if we throw a dice, then the events A_1 = {1, 2}, A_2 = {2, 3, 3} are not exhaustive as we can get 5 as outcome of the experiment which is not the member of any of the events A_1 and A_2. If we consider the events E_1 = {1, 2, 3} and E_2 = {2, 4, 5, 6}, then the set E_1, E_2, is exhaustive.
6. **Mutually Exclusive Events:** A set of events is said to be mutually exclusive if they have no point in common, *i.e.*, happening of one of them eliminates the happening of any of the remaining events. Thus E_1, E_2, E_3, ... are mutually exclusive iff $E_i \cap E_j = \phi$ for $i \neq$ E_1 and E_2 are mutually exclusive.
7. **Complement of An Events:** The complement of an event A, denoted by $\overline{A}$, A' or A^c, is the set of all sample points of the space other than the sample points in A.

   e.g., In the experiment of throwing a fair dice, S = {1, 2, 3, 4, 5, 6}. If A = {1, 3, 5, 6}, then $\overline{A}$ = {2, 4}

   Note that $A \cap \overline{A} = S$.
8. **Classical Definition of Probability:** If there are n exhaustive mutually exclusive and equally likely outcomes of an experiment and m of them are favourable to an event A, the probability of the happening of A is defined as the ratio m/n.

   Thus, denoting the probability of the happening of an event A by p, we have $p = m/n$.

   Clearly p is a positive number not greater than unity, so that $0 \leq p \leq 1$.

   Since the number of cases in which the event A will not happen is $n - m$, the probability q that the event will not happen is given by $q = \frac{(n-m)}{n} = 1 - \frac{m}{n}$ $= 1 - p. \therefore p + q = 1$

   If probability of happening of an event A is 1, then A is certain event and if probability of happening of an event A is 0, then A is impossible event.
9. **Odds in Favour and Odds against an Event:** As a result of an experiment if a of the outcomes are favourable to an event E and b of the outcomes are against it, then we say that odds are a to b in favour of E or odds are b to a against E.

   Thus, odds in favour of an event E

   $$= \frac{\text{number of favourable cases}}{\text{number of unfavourable cases}}.$$

   Similarly, odds against an event E

   $$= \frac{\text{number of unfavourable cases}}{\text{number of favourable cases}}.$$

   If odds in favour of an event are $a : b$ then the probability of the occurrence of that event is $\frac{a}{a+b}$

and the probability of the non-occurrence of that event is $\frac{b}{(a+b)}$.

Addition Theorem:

(*a*) If 'A' and 'B' are any two events in a sample space S, then $P(A \cup B) = P(A) + P(B) - P(A \cap B)$.

(*b*) If 'A' and 'B' are mutually exclusive then $P(A \cap B) = 0$ so that $P(A \cup B) = P(A) + P(B)$.

(*c*) If A is any event in S, then $P(A') = 1 - P(A)$.

Total Probability Theorem:

The probability that one of several mutually exclusive events $A_1, A_2, ..., A_n$ will happen, is the sum of the probabilities of the separate events. In symbol,

$$P(A_1 + A_2 + ... + A_n) = P(A_1) + P(A_2) + ... + P(A_n).$$

Conditional Probability:

The probability of B under the assumption that A has occurred is called the conditional probability of B under the condition that the event A has taken place and is denoted by P(B/A). P(B/A) is read as "probability at the event B given A^{B}."

Conditional Probability Theorem:

If A and B are any two events in the sample space S, the conditional probability of B relative to A is given by

$$P(B/A) = \frac{P(B \cap A)}{P(A)} = \frac{n(B \cap A)}{n(A)}, A \neq \phi.$$

Some Important Remarks about Coins, Dice and Playing Cards:

(*a*) **Coins:** A coin has a head side and a tail side. If an experiment consist of more than a coin, coins are considered to be distinct if not otherwise stated.

(*b*) **Dice:** A die (cubical) has six faces marked 1, 2, 3, 4, 5, 6. We may have tetrahedral (having four faces 1, 2, 3, 4) or pentagonal (having five faces 1, 2, 3, 4, 5) dic. As in the case of dice, if we have more than one die, all dice are considered to be distinct if not otherwise stated.

(*c*) **Playing Cards:** A pack of playing cards usually contain 52 cards.

There are 4 suits (spade, heart, diamond and club) each having 13 cards. There are two colours — red (heart and diamond) and black (spade and club) each having 26 cards.

In thirteen cards of each suit, there are 3 face cards namely king, queen and jack, so there are in all 12 face cards (4 kings, 4 queens and 4 jacks).

Also there are 16 honours cards, 4 of each suit namely ace, king, queen and jack.

SOLVED EXAMPLES

Example 1: A bag contains 7 Red balls, 4 Green balls and 5 Yellow balls. What is the probability that 3 balls drawn at random are either Green or Yellow?

Solution: Total ways $= {}^{16}C_3 = \frac{\lfloor 16}{\lfloor 13 \lfloor 3} = 560$

Favourable ways $= {}^{4}C_3 \times {}^{5}C_3 = \frac{\lfloor 4}{\lfloor 3 \lfloor 1} \times \frac{\lfloor 5}{\lfloor 3 \lfloor 2}$

$= 4 \times 10 = 40.$

$\therefore$ Reqd. Probability $= \frac{40}{560} = \frac{1}{14}.$

Example 2: A basket contains three Red and four Green balls. If four balls are drawn at random from the basket, what is the probability that two are Red and two are Green?

Solution: Reqd. Probability $= \frac{{}^{3}C_2 \times {}^{4}C_2}{{}^{7}C_4} = \frac{3 \times 6}{35}$

$= \frac{18}{35}.$

Example 3: A box contains 8 Red, 16 Blue, 4 Yellow and 12 Black bolls. Two balls are picked up randomly. What is the chance that both are Red?

Solution: Total results $= {}^{40}C_2 = \frac{40 \times 39}{2} = 780$

and favourable results $= {}^{8}C_2 = \frac{\lfloor 8}{\lfloor 2 \lfloor 6} = \frac{8 \times 7}{2}$

$= 28.$

$\therefore$ Required probability $= \frac{28}{780} = \frac{7}{195}.$

Example 4: A bag contains 8 Red, 16 Blue, 12 Black and 4 Yellow marbles. One marbles is picked up randomly. What is the probability that it is not Blue?

Solution: Total results $= {}^{40}C_1 = 40$

Favourable results when it is Blue $= {}^{16}C_1 = 16.$

$\therefore$ Favourable results when it is not Blue

$= 40 - 16 = 24$

$\therefore$ Reqd. probability $= \frac{24}{40} = 0.6.$

MULTIPLE CHOICE QUESTIONS

Directions (Qs. 1 to 3) : *Study the information carefully to answer the questions that follow.*

A bucket contains 8 Red, 3 Blue and 5 Green marbles.

1. If 4 marbles are drawn at random, what is the probability that 2 are Red and 2 are Blue?

A. $\frac{11}{16}$ B. $\frac{3}{16}$

C. $\frac{11}{72}$ D. $\frac{3}{65}$

2. If 2 marbles are drawn at random, what is the probability that both are Green?

A. $\frac{1}{12}$ B. $\frac{5}{16}$

C. $\frac{2}{7}$ D. None of these

3. If 3 marbles are drawn at random, what is the probability that none is Red?

A. $\frac{3}{8}$ B. $\frac{1}{16}$

C. $\frac{1}{10}$ D. None of these

Directions (Qs. 4 to 5) : *Study the information and answer the questions that follow.*

A basket contains 3 Red balls, 5 Blue balls and 2 Green balls.

4. If three balls are drawn at random, what is the probability that none is Blue?

A. $\frac{1}{6}$ B. $\frac{1}{12}$

C. $\frac{1}{5}$ D. $\frac{3}{10}$

5. If four balls are drawn at random, what is the probability that at least one is Green?

A. $\frac{2}{3}$ B. $\frac{1}{2}$

C. $\frac{1}{3}$ D. $\frac{2}{5}$

6. If two balls are drawn at random, what is the probability that both are Red?

A. $\frac{1}{5}$ B. $\frac{3}{10}$

C. $\frac{3}{5}$ D. $\frac{1}{15}$

7. A dice is thrown once. Find the probability of getting a number greater than 3.

A. $\frac{2}{3}$ B. $\frac{1}{3}$

C. $\frac{1}{2}$ D. $\frac{3}{2}$

8. A bag contains 5 Red balls, 8 White balls, 4 Green balls and 7 Black balls. If one ball is drawn at random, find the probability that it is Black.

A. $\frac{7}{24}$ B. $\frac{5}{24}$

C. $\frac{5}{6}$ D. $\frac{1}{4}$

9. Find the probability that a number selected from the numbers 1 to 25 is not a prime number when each of the given number is equally to be selected.

A. $\frac{9}{25}$ B. $\frac{16}{25}$

C. $\frac{21}{25}$ D. $\frac{14}{25}$

10. A bag contains 3 Red balls and 5 Black balls. A ball is drawn at random from the bag. What is the probability that the ball drawn is not Red?

A. $\frac{3}{8}$ B. $\frac{5}{8}$

C. $\frac{1}{8}$ D. $\frac{7}{8}$

11. A die is thrown once. Find the probability of getting an odd number.

A. $\frac{1}{2}$ B. $\frac{3}{2}$

C. $\frac{2}{3}$ D. $\frac{1}{3}$

12. A letter is chosen at random from the word REED the probability of choosing an E is –

A. $\frac{3}{4}$ B. $\frac{1}{2}$

C. $\frac{1}{4}$ D. $\frac{2}{3}$

13. A card is drawn at random from a well-shuffled deck of playing cards. Find the probability that the card drawn is a card of spade or an ace.

A. $\frac{11}{13}$ B. $\frac{1}{26}$

C. $\frac{4}{13}$ D. $\frac{9}{13}$

14. If a letter is chosen at random from the word TRIANGLE.
What is the probability that it a vowel?

A. $\frac{3}{8}$ B. $\frac{5}{8}$

C. $\frac{1}{4}$ D. $\frac{3}{4}$

15. What is the chance that a leap year, selected at random, will contain 53 Sundays?

A. $\frac{52}{365}$ B. $\frac{52}{366}$

C. $\frac{2}{7}$ D. $\frac{5}{7}$

16. In a book of 300 pages, if a page is opened at random; find the probability that the sum of the digits in its number is 10.

A. $\frac{8}{15}$ B. $\frac{9}{15}$

C. $\frac{7}{75}$ D. $\frac{14}{15}$

17. A die is thrown once. Find the probability of getting an even number.

A. $\frac{1}{3}$ B. $\frac{1}{2}$

C. $\frac{1}{4}$ D. $\frac{1}{6}$

18. Two friends were born in the year 2000. What is the probability that they have the same birthday?

A. $\frac{1}{500}$ B. $\frac{1}{730}$

C. $\frac{1}{365}$ D. $\frac{1}{366}$

19. A number is chosen at random from among the first 30 natural numbers. The probability of the number chosen being prime is :

A. $\frac{1}{3}$ B. $\frac{3}{10}$

C. $\frac{1}{30}$ D. $\frac{11}{30}$

20. The probability that a number selected at random from the set of numbers {1, 2, 3, 4, ..., 100} is a cube is:

A. $\frac{1}{25}$ B. $\frac{2}{25}$

C. $\frac{3}{25}$ D. $\frac{4}{25}$

21. A single letter is selected at random from the word 'COLLEGE'. Find the probability of getting a vowel.

A. $\frac{3}{7}$ B. $\frac{4}{7}$

C. $\frac{5}{7}$ D. $\frac{2}{7}$

22. A box contains 5 Red balls, 4 Green balls and 7 White balls. A ball is drawn at random from the box. Find the probability that the ball drawn is neither Red nor White.

A. $\frac{2}{7}$ B. $\frac{3}{4}$

C. $\frac{1}{4}$ D. $\frac{1}{2}$

23. In a cricket match, a batsman hits boundary 8 times out of 40 balls he plays. Find the probability that he didn't hit boundary.

A. 0.8 B. 0.6

C. 0.5 D. 0.4

24. Two coins are tossed simultaneously. The probability of getting atmost one head is :

A. $\frac{1}{4}$ B. $\frac{3}{4}$

C. $\frac{1}{2}$ D. $\frac{1}{4}$

25. A bag contains 50 coins and each coin is marked from 51 to 100. One coin is picked at random. The probability that the number on the coin is not a prime number is :

A. $\frac{1}{5}$ B. $\frac{3}{5}$

C. $\frac{2}{5}$ D. $\frac{4}{5}$

26. In a football match, a player makes 4 goals from 10 penalty kicks. The probability of converting a penalty kick into a goal by the player, is :

A. $\frac{1}{4}$ B. $\frac{1}{6}$

C. $\frac{1}{3}$ D. $\frac{2}{5}$

27. Three unbiased coins are tossed. What is the probability of getting at least 2 heads?

A. $\frac{1}{4}$ B. $\frac{1}{2}$

C. $\frac{1}{3}$ D. $\frac{1}{8}$

28. In a simultaneous throw of two dice, what is the probability of getting a total of 7?

A. $\frac{1}{6}$ B. $\frac{1}{4}$

C. $\frac{2}{3}$ D. $\frac{3}{4}$

29. What is the probability of getting a sum 9 from two throws of a dice?

A. $\frac{1}{6}$ B. $\frac{1}{8}$

C. $\frac{1}{9}$ D. $\frac{1}{12}$

30. Tickets numbered 1 to 20 are mixed up and then a ticket is drawn at random. What is the probability that the ticket drawn bears a number which is a multiple of 3?

A. $\frac{3}{10}$ B. $\frac{3}{20}$

C. $\frac{2}{5}$ D. $\frac{1}{2}$

31. A card is drawn from a pack of 52 cards. The probability of getting a queen of club or a king of heart is :

A. $\frac{1}{13}$ B. $\frac{2}{13}$

C. $\frac{1}{26}$ D. $\frac{1}{52}$

32. Two cards are drawn together from a pack of 52 cards. The probability that one is a spade and one is a heart, is :

A. $\frac{3}{20}$ B. $\frac{29}{34}$

C. $\frac{47}{100}$ D. $\frac{13}{102}$

33. A bag contains 6 white and 4 red balls. Three balls are drawn at random. What is the probability that one ball is red and the other two are white?

A. $\frac{1}{2}$ B. $\frac{1}{12}$

C. $\frac{3}{10}$ D. $\frac{7}{12}$

34. A box contains 20 electric bulbs, out of which 4 are defective. Two bulbs are chosen at random from this box. The probability that at least one of these is defective, is :

A. $\frac{4}{19}$ B. $\frac{7}{19}$

C. $\frac{12}{19}$ D. $\frac{21}{95}$

35. Two dice are tossed. The probability that the total score is a prime number is :

A. $\frac{1}{6}$ B. $\frac{5}{12}$

C. $\frac{1}{2}$ D. $\frac{7}{9}$

ANSWERS

1	2	3	4	5	6	7	8	9	10
D	A	A	B	A	D	C	A	B	B
11	**12**	**13**	**14**	**15**	**16**	**17**	**18**	**19**	**20**
A	B	C	A	C	C	B	D	A	A
21	**22**	**23**	**24**	**25**	**26**	**27**	**28**	**29**	**30**
A	C	A	B	D	D	B	A	C	A
31	**32**	**33**	**34**	**35**					
C	D	A	B	B					

SOME SELECTED EXPLANATORY ANSWERS

1. Total number of ways = ${}^{16}C_4 = \frac{\lfloor 16}{\lfloor 12 \lfloor 4}$

$= 1820$

And favourable number of ways = ${}^{8}C_2 \times {}^{3}C_2$

$= \frac{\lfloor 8}{\lfloor 6 \lfloor 2} \times \frac{\lfloor 3}{\lfloor 1 \lfloor 2} = 84$

$\therefore$ Reqd. probability $= \frac{84}{1820} = \frac{3}{65}$.

2. Total number of ways = ${}^{16}C_2 = \frac{\lfloor 16}{\lfloor 14 \lfloor 2} = 120$

And favourable number of ways = ${}^{5}C_2$

$= \frac{\lfloor 5}{\lfloor 3 \lfloor 2} = 10$

$\therefore$ Reqd. probability $= \frac{10}{120} = \frac{1}{12}$.

3. Total number of ways $= {}^{16}C_3 = \frac{\lfloor 16}{\lfloor 13 \lfloor 3} = 560$

Total number of ways when all the marbles are Red

$= {}^{8}C_3 = \frac{\lfloor 8}{\lfloor 5 \lfloor 3} = 56$

$\therefore$ Probability when all the three are Red

$= \frac{56}{560} = \frac{1}{10}$

$\therefore$ And probability when none is Red $= 1 - \frac{1}{10}$

$= \frac{9}{10}.$

4. Probability that none is blue

$= \frac{{}^5C_3}{{}^{10}C_3} = \frac{10}{120} = \frac{1}{12}$

5. Probability that none is green

$= \frac{{}^8C_4}{{}^{10}C_4} = \frac{70}{210} = \frac{1}{3}$

$\therefore$ Probability that at least one is green

$= 1 - \frac{1}{3} = \frac{2}{3}$

6. Probability that both are red

$= \frac{{}^3C_2}{{}^{10}C_2} = \frac{3}{45} = \frac{1}{15}$

7. Sample space S = {1, 2, 3, 4, 5, 6} ; n(S) = 6
Let A = "getting a number grater than 3" then
A = {4, 5, 6} ; n(A) = 3

$P(A) = \frac{n(A)}{n(S)} = \frac{3}{6} = \frac{1}{2}.$

9. We are given numbers from 1 to 25.
n(S) = 25.
Prime numbers from 1 to 25 are 2, 3, 5, 7, 11, 13, 17, 19, 23.
These are 9 prime numbers.
Let E denote the event 'Number drawn is not prime'.

$\therefore \quad n(E) = 25 - 9 = 16$

$p(E) = \frac{n(E)}{n(S)} = \frac{16}{25}.$

10. Total number of balls in the bag = 3 + 5 = 8
Let E denote the event 'ball drawn is red'.

$\therefore \quad n(E) = 3$ and $n(S) = 8$.

(*i*) $p(E) = \frac{n(E)}{n(S)} = \frac{3}{8}$

(*ii*) $p(\text{not red}) = p(\bar{E})$

$= 1 - p(E) = 1 - \frac{3}{8} = \frac{5}{8}.$

11. Sample S = {1, 2, 3, 4, 5, 6} ; n(S) = 6
Let F denote the event 'getting an odd number'.
F = {1, 3, 5} ; n(F) = 3

$\therefore \quad P(F) = \frac{n(F)}{n(S)} = \frac{3}{6} = \frac{1}{2}.$

12. The sample space is $\{R, E_1, E_2, D\}$
There are 2 ways to choose the letter E from the four letters

$\therefore \quad P(E) = \frac{2}{4} = \frac{1}{2}.$

13. There are 52 cards in a deck of 52 playing cards. There are 13 spades and 4 aces in 52 playing cards. Out of 13 spades there is one ace.
$\therefore$ Favourable no ways for the card drawn to be spade or an ace = 13 spades + 3 aces = 16.

$\therefore$ P(a card of spade or an ace) $= \frac{16}{52} = \frac{4}{13}.$

14. Since there are 3 vowels out of a total of 8 letters, the probability of choosing a vowel is 3/8.

15. A Leap year has 366 days. In a leap year, here are 52 complete weeks (52 Sundays) and 2 days over these two days can be as follows.
Sunday and Monday, Monday and Tuesday, Tuesday and Wednesday, Wednesday and Thursday, Thursday and Friday, Friday and Saturday, Saturday and Sunday. Out of these 7 possibilities, only two (Saturday and Sunday; Sunday and Monday) are favourable for having 53 Sundays)

Required chance $= \frac{2}{7}.$

17. A die is thrown once. Its sample space is
S = {1, 2, 3, 4, 5, 6}, n(S) = 6
Let E : an even number, then E = {2, 4, 6} Number of favourable cases = n(E) = 3

$P(E) = \frac{n(E)}{n(S)} = \frac{3}{6} = \frac{1}{2}.$

18. Year 2000 is a leap year. There are 366 days in the year 2000. Total number of cases in which two friends can be born on the same day are 366.
Out of 366 days, number of favourable ways in which two friends have the same birthday = 1

$\therefore$ Required probability $= \frac{1}{366}.$

19. The prime numbers from first 30 natural numbers are 2, 3, 5, 7, 11, 13, 17, 19, 23, 29.
We find that there are 10 prime numbers from 1 to 30.
$\therefore$ Probability that the number chosen being prime is

$= \frac{10}{30} = \frac{1}{3}.$

20. From the natural numbers 1 to 100 the four number 1, 8, 27 and 64 are cubes

$\therefore$ Required Probability $= \frac{4}{100} = \frac{1}{25}$.

23. Let A denote the event that the batsman did not hit a boundary.
We have, Total number of trials = 40
Number of trials in which the event A happened
$= 40 - 8 = 32$

$\therefore \quad P(A) = \frac{32}{40} = \frac{4}{5} = 0.8.$

27. Here S = {HH, HT, TH, TT}.
Let E = Event of getting at least one head = {HT, TH, HH}.

$\therefore \quad P(E) = \frac{n(E)}{n(S)} = \frac{4}{8} = \frac{1}{2}.$

28. We know that in a simultaneous throw of two dice, $n(S) = 6 \times 6 = 36$.
Let E = Event of getting a total of 7 = {(1, 6), (2, 5), (3, 4), (4, 3), (5, 2), (6, 1)}.

$\therefore \quad P(E) = \frac{n(E)}{n(S)} = \frac{6}{36} = \frac{1}{6}.$

29. In two throws of a die, $n(S) = (6 \times 6) = 36$.
Let E = Event of getting a sum 9 = {(3, 6), (4, 5), (5, 4), (6, 3)}.

$\therefore \quad P(E) = \frac{n(E)}{n(S)} = \frac{4}{36} = \frac{1}{9}.$

30. Here, S = {1, 2, 3, 4, ..., 19, 20}.
Let E = Event of getting a multiple of 3 = {3, 6, 9, 12, 15, 18}.

$\therefore \quad P(E) = \frac{n(E)}{n(S)} = \frac{6}{20} = \frac{3}{10}.$

31. Here $n(S) = 52$.
Let E = Event of getting a queen of club or a king of heart.
Then, $n(E) = 2$.

$\therefore \quad P(E) = \frac{n(E)}{n(S)} = \frac{2}{52} = \frac{1}{26}.$

32. Let S be the sample space. Then,

$$n(S) = {}^{52}C_2 = \frac{(52 \times 51)}{(2 \times 1)} = 1326.$$

Let E = Event of getting 1 spade and 1 heart.
$\therefore$ $n(E)$ = Number of ways of choosing 1 spade out of 13 and 1 heart out of 13
$= ({}^{13}C_1 \times {}^{13}C_1) = (13 \times 13) = 169.$

$\therefore \quad P(E) = \frac{n(E)}{n(S)} = \frac{169}{1326} = \frac{13}{102}.$

33. Let S be the sample space. Then,
$n(S)$ = Number of ways of drawing 3 balls out of 10

$$= {}^{10}C_3 = \frac{(10 \times 9 \times 8)}{(3 \times 2 \times 1)} = 120.$$

Let E = Event of drawing 1 red and 2 white balls
$\therefore$ $n(E)$ = Number of ways of drawing 1 red ball out of 4 and 2 white balls out of 6

$$= ({}^4C_1 \times {}^6C_2) = \left(4 \times \frac{6 \times 5}{2 \times 1}\right) = 60.$$

$\therefore \quad P(E) = \frac{n(E)}{n(S)} = \frac{60}{120} = \frac{1}{2}.$

34. P (None is defective)

$$= \frac{{}^{16}C_2}{{}^{20}C_2} = \left(\frac{16 \times 15}{2 \times 1} \times \frac{2 \times 1}{20 \times 19}\right) = \frac{12}{19}.$$

P (at least one is defective) $= \left(1 - \frac{12}{19}\right) = \frac{7}{19}.$

35. Clearly, $n(S) = (6 \times 6) = 36$.
Let E = Event that the sum is a prime number.
Then, E = {(1, 1), (1, 2), (1, 4), (1, 6), (2, 1), (2, 3), (2, 5), (3, 2), (3, 4), (4, 1), (4, 3), (5, 2), (5, 6), (6, 1), (6, 5)

$\therefore \quad n(E) = 15$

$\therefore \quad P(E) = \frac{n(E)}{n(S)} = \frac{15}{36} = \frac{5}{12}.$

Data Interpretation

TABLES

Tables are often used in reports, magazines and newspaper to present as set of numerical data. It is one of the easiest and most accurate ways of presenting data. One of the main purposes of tables is to make complicated information easier to understand. Hence, the advantage of presenting data in a table is that one can see the information at a glance. We present below an example of tabular presentation of annual expenditure of 5 families for last 4 years.

Annual Expenditure of 5 families (in ₹ Thousands)

Years → Families ↓	2005	2006	2007	2008
A	35	50	55	60
B	40	60	65	75
C	45	50	70	80
D	30	40	45	50
E	50	55	60	70

Essentials of a Tables:

(i) **Title:** Heading of the table
(ii) **Stub:** The section of the table containing row headings in called Stub.
(iii) **Column Captions :** The heading of each column is designated as column caption.
(iv) **Body**
(v) **Footnotes**
(vi) **Source**

Example 1. Directions: *Study the folloiwng table and answer the questions given below:*

Categories of students according to their enrolment in various courses in a vocational college.

Courses	*Categories (Faculty)*			
	Arts		*Science*	
	Boys	*Girls*	*Boys*	*Girls*
1. Business Management	45	25	65	25
2. Typewriting	186	23	32	20
3. Stenography	120	25	58	12
4. Typewriting and Stenography	100	12	5	3

1. If 60% boys and 70% girls pass in their respective courses, then total pass percentage is:
A. 58% B. 66% C. 54% D. 62%

2. The total number of students who have opted the course of Business Management and the course of Stenography exceeds the number of students studying in typewriting course by:
A. 44% B. 66% C. 33% D. 55%

3. In which of the following courses, percentage of girls is the highest?
A. Stenography B. Business Management
C. Typewriting D. Typewriting and Stenography

4. In the art faculty number of students who have opted the course of stenography is how much per cent of the total student in the faculty?

A. 27% B. 10% C. 18% D. 15%

5. Total number of boys studying in the college exceeds the total number of girls in the college by:

A. 321% B. 280% C. 308% D. 250%

Solution 1. ∵ Total boys = 45 + 186 + 120 + 100 + 65 + 32 + 58 + 5 = 611

∴ Number of boys who pass in their respective courses = 60% of 611 = $611 \times \frac{60}{100} = 366.60$

Total number of girls = 25 + 23 + 25 + 12 + 25 + 20 + 12 + 3 = 145

Number of girls who pass in their respective courses = 70% of 145 = $\frac{145 \times 70}{100} = 101.50$

∴ Combined pass per cent = $\frac{(366.6 + 101.5) \times 100}{611 + 145} = \frac{46810}{756} = 61.92 \simeq 62\%$

Solution 2. ∵ Number of students in Business Management course = 160
Number of students in typewriting course = 261
Number of students in stenography corse = 215

∴ Required per cent = $\left(\frac{160 + 215 - 261}{261}\right) \times 100 \approx 44\%$

Solution 3. Percentage of girls in Business Management course = $\frac{(25 + 25) \times 100}{160} = 31.25$

Percentage of girls in typewriting course = $\frac{(23 + 20) \times 100}{261} = 16.47$

Percentage of girls in stenography course = $\frac{(25 + 12) \times 100}{215} = 12.56$

And percentage of girls in typewriting and stenography course = $\frac{(12 + 3) \times 100}{120} = 12.50$

Hence, it is clear from the above that percentage of girls in Business Management course is the highest.

Solution 4. Required percentage = $\frac{(25 + 120) \times 100}{536} \times 100 \simeq 27$

Solution 5. Total number of boys = 45 + 65 + 186 + 32 + 120 + 58 + 100 + 5 = 611
Total number of girls = 25 + 23 + 25 + 12 + 25 + 20 + 12 + 3 = 145

∴ Required percentage = $\left(\frac{611 - 145}{145}\right) \times 100 \simeq 321\%$

Example 2. Directions: *Figures of biscuit exports from a country during various years are given in the following table. Study the table carefully and answer the questions that follows:*

VOLUME OF EXPORT OF BISCUITS FROM A COUNTRY

Year	*Quantity (in lakh tins)*	*Price (in crores ₹)*
2004	100	150
2005	75	150
2006	150	330
2007	160	400
2008	200	500

1. During which year per tin export price remained at lowest level?
A. 2007 B. 2006 C. 2005 D. 2004

2. During which years price per tin remained at the same level?
A. 2006 and 2008 B. 2006 and 2007 C. 2007 and 2008 D. 2006 and 2004

3. The export price of biscuit increased from 2004 to 2008 by how much per cent?
A. 100 B. $116\frac{2}{3}$ C. $233\frac{1}{3}$ D. 350

4. The difference between the number of biscuit tins exported in 2008 and that in 2007 is:
A. 40 B. 40,000 C. 4,00,000 D. 40,00,000

Solution 1. Export price per tin in 2004 = $\frac{₹\ 150 \text{ crores}}{₹\ 100 \text{ lakhs}} = ₹\ 150$

Export price per tin in 2005 = $\frac{₹\ 150 \text{ crores}}{₹\ 75 \text{ lakhs}} = ₹\ 200$

Export price per tin in 2006 = $\frac{₹\ 330 \text{ crores}}{₹\ 150 \text{ lakhs}} = ₹\ 220$

Export price per tin in 2007 = $\frac{₹\ 400 \text{ crores}}{₹\ 160 \text{ lakhs}} = ₹\ 250$

Export price per tin in 2008 = $\frac{₹\ 500 \text{ crores}}{₹\ 200 \text{ lakhs}} = ₹\ 250$

Hence, it is clear that per tin export price was at lowest level in 2004.

Solution 2. From the explanation given in the answer of Q.No. 1, it is clear that per tin export price was same in 2007 and 2008.

Solution 3. From the level of 2004 percentage increase in export price in 2008 = $\left(\frac{500-150}{150}\right)\times 100 = 233\frac{1}{3}\%$

Solution 4. Required difference = 200 – 160 = 40 lakh tins = 40,00,000 tins.

Example. 3. Directions: *Study the following table carefully and answer the questions given below:*

Number of Employees Working in Various departments of a Factory

Year	*Production Deptt.*	*Sale Deptt.*	*Procurement Deptt.*	*Administration & Accounts Deptt.*	*Research & Development Deptt.*
2003	150	25	50	45	75
2004	225	40	45	62	70
2005	450	65	30	90	73
2006	470	73	32	105	70
2007	500	80	35	132	74
2008	505	75	36	130	75

1. During which of the following years number of employees working in production deptt. of the factory was less than 50% of the total employees of the factory?
A. 2003 B. 2005 C. 2006 D. 2007

2. During which year the number of employees working in each department was more than those in the previous year and nearly equal to next year?
A. 2007 B. 2006 C. 2005 D. 2004

3. In which department of the factory number of employees remained nearly same during the years from 2003 to 2008?
A. Production B. Sale
C. Research and Development D. Administration and Accounts
E. Procurement

4. In which department of the factory number of employees are maximum from 2003 to 2008?
A. Production
B. Sale
C. Research and Development
D. Administration and Accounts
E. Sale and Procurement

5. During which year number of employees in the factory became nearly double the total number of employees working in the factory during 2003.
A. 2008
B. 2007
C. 2006
D. 2005

Solution 1. Number of total employees in 2003 = 150 + 25 + 50 + 45 + 75 = 345

∴ Percentage number of employees working in producton deptt. = $\frac{150 \times 100}{345}$ = 43.48%

Number of total employees in 2004 = 225 + 40 + 45 + 62 + 70 = 442

∴ Percentage number of employees working in production deptt. = $\frac{225 \times 100}{442}$ = 50.9%

Number of total employees in 2005 = 450 + 65 + 30 + 90 + 73 = 708

∴ Percentage number of employees working in proudction deptt. = $\frac{450 \times 100}{708}$ = 63.56%

Total number of employees in 2006 = 470 + 73 + 32 + 105 + 70 = 750

∴ Percentage number of employees working in production deptt. = $\frac{470 \times 100}{750}$ = 62.67%

Total number of employees in 2007 = 500 + 80 + 35 + 132 + 74 = 821

∴ Percentage number of employees working in production deptt. = $\frac{500 \times 100}{821}$ = 60.9%

Total number of employees in 2007 = 505 + 75 + 36 + 130 + 75 = 821

∴ Percentage number of employees working in production in deptt. = $\frac{505 \times 100}{821}$ = 61.51%

Hence, it is clear that percentage number of employees working in production deptt. was less than 50% in 2003.

Solution 2. It is clear from the table that it was the year 2007 when the number of employees working in each department was more than that in the previous year and nearly equal to next year.

Solution 3. According to the table in the research and development department number of employees remained nearly same during the year from 2003 to 2008.

Solution 4. Production.

Solution 5. Total number of employes in 2003 = 345
Total number of employees in 2005 = 708
Hence, it was the year 2005 when total number of employees in the factory became nearly double the total number of emplyees working in the factory during 2003.

Example. 4. *Study the table carefully to answer the questions that follow.*

Number of students studying in six different classes of six different schools.

Class → School ↓	V	VI	VII	VIII	IX	X
P	152	160	145	156	147	144
Q	148	166	150	155	157	143
R	161	152	140	145	143	165
S	159	142	149	140	142	168
T	147	144	158	163	154	150
U	150	160	162	160	161	140

1. What is the respective ratio of students studying in class IX of schools Q and R together to those studying in class VI of schools S and T together?
A. 143 : 150 B. 150 : 143 C. 127 : 181 D. 181 : 127

2. Number of students studying in class X from school P forms approximately what per cent of the total number of students studying in class X from all schools together?
A. 9 B. 12 C. 16 D. 24

3. Total number of students studying in school T from all classes together forms what per cent of total number of students studying in school S from all classes together?
A. 100.26 B. 101.78 C. 102.64 D. 103.52

4. The number of students studying in class VII from school U forms what per cent of the total number of students from all the classes together from that school?
A. 15.93 B. 16.14 C. 17.36 D. 18.28

5. Which class has the maximum number of students from all schools together?
A. V B. VI C. VII D. X

Solution 1. Number of students of class IX of schools Q and R = 157 + 143 = 300
Number of students of class VI of schools S and T = 142 + 144 = 286
Hence, required ratio = 300 : 286 = 150 : 143

Solution 2. Total number of students of class X from all schools = 144 + 143 + 165 + 168 + 150 + 140 = 910

$$\text{Required percentage} = \frac{144}{910} \times 100 = 15.82 \simeq 16\%$$

Solution 3. Total number of students of school T from all classes = 147 + 144 + 158 + 163 + 154 + 150 = 916
Total number of students of school S from all classes = 159 + 142 + 149 + 140 + 142 + 168 = 900

$$\text{Required percentage} = \frac{916}{900} \times 100 = 101.78\%$$

Solution 4. Total number of students of school U from all the classes = 150 + 160 + 162 + 160 + 161 + 140 = 933

$$\text{Required percentage} = \frac{162}{933} \times 100 = 17.36\%$$

Solution 5. Total number of students of class V from all the schools = 152 + 148 + 161 + 159 + 147 + 150 = 917
Total number of students of class VI from all the schools = 160 + 166 + 152 + 142 + 144 + 160 = 924
Total number of students of class VII from all the schools = 145 + 150 + 140 + 149 + 158 + 162 = 904
Total number of students of class VIII from all the schools = 156 + 155 + 145 + 140 + 163 + 160 = 919
Total number of students of class IX from all the schools = 147 + 157 + 143 + 142 + 154 + 161 = 904
Total number of students of class X from all the schools = 144 + 143 + 165 + 168 + 150 + 140 = 910
Hence, the class VI has maximum number of students.

BAR GRAPHS

Given quantity of a bar graph can be compared by the height or length. A bar graph can have either vertical or horizontal bars. You can compare different quantities or the same quantity at the different times. The bars may be placed adjacent to each other or may be separated from each other by spaces depending upon the problem.

For Example: **Registration of New Vehicles in Delhi (in thousands)**

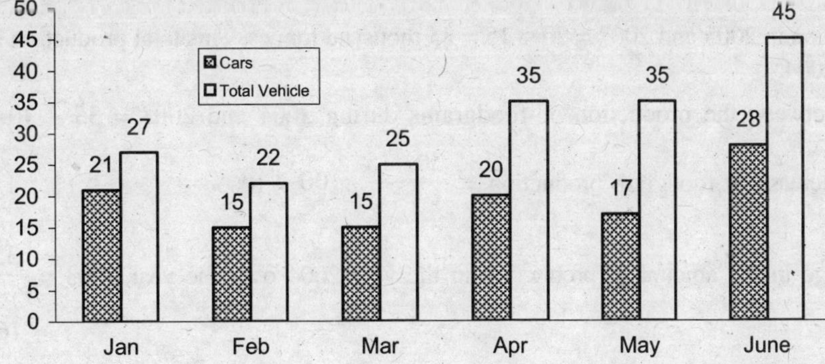

CUMULATIVE GRAPH

These are usually bar or line graphs where the height of the bar or line is divided up proportionally among various quantities presented in the graph. The representation of quantities may be done in terms of either percentage of the total or in absolute figures. These are also called sub-divided graphs. Thus, cumulative graph may be conveniently used for making comparisons.

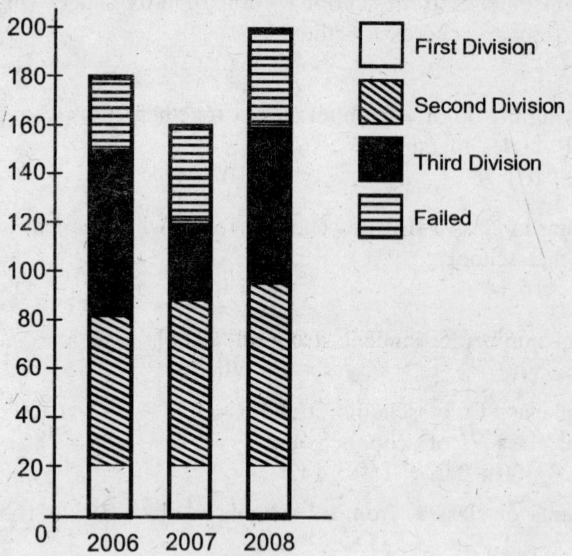

Example 1: Directions: *The following bar graph shows the production of food grains in India during certain year. Study the graph carefully and answer the questions given below:*

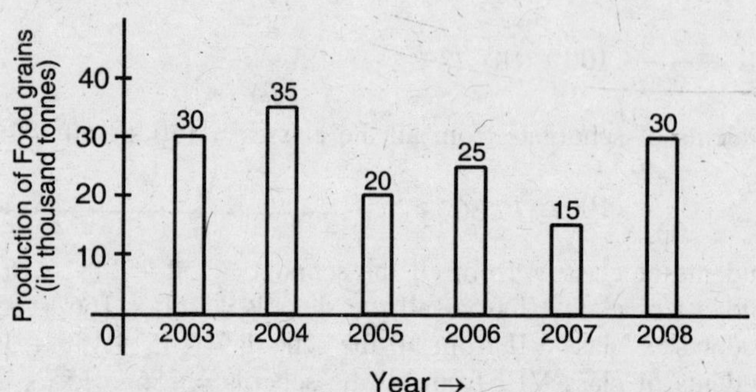

1. Total food grain production in 2005 and 2007 is equal to the production during which of the following years?
A. 2003 B. 2004 C. 2006 D. 2008

2. The difference between the foodgrain productions of 2004 and 2008 is:
A. 500 tonnes B. 1000 tonnes C. 5000 tonnes D. 10000 tonnes

3. Percentage increase in the production of foodgrains in the year 2008 over the year 2007 is:
A. 15% B. 30% C. 50% D. 100%

4. Rate of change in quantity of production in which of the following two consecutive years is at the minimum level?
A. 2003 and 2004 B. 2005 and 2006 C. 2007 and 2008 D. 2006 and 2007

Solution 1. Total production in 2005 and 2007 = 20 + 15 = 35 thousand tonnes. This total production is equal to the production in the year 2004.

Solution 2. Difference between the production of foodgrains during 2004 and 2008 = 35 – 30 = 5 thousand tonnes.

Solution 3. Percentage increase in foodgrain production = $\frac{30-15}{15} \times 100 = 100\%$

Solution 4. Rate of change in the amount of production in the year 2004 over the year 2003 = $\frac{35-30}{30} \times 100$

$= 16.67\%$

Rate of change in the amount of production in the year 2006 over the year 2005 = $\frac{(25-20)}{20} \times 100 = 25\%$

Rate of change in the amount of production in the year 2008 over the year 2007 = $\frac{(30-15)}{15} \times 100 = 100\%$

Rate of change in the amount of production in the year 2007 over the year 2006 = $\frac{(25-15)}{15} \times 100 = 66.67\%$

Hence, it is clear that the rate of change in the amount of production during the consecutive years 2007 and 2008 is at the highest level.

Example 2: Directions: *The bar graph as shown below gives information about the sale and profit details of a departmental store during the years from 2001–2008. Study the graph carefully and answer the questions asked here under.*

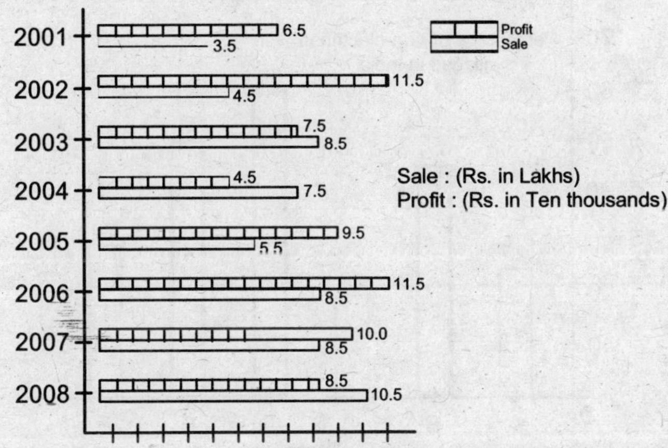

1. Mean of annual increase in sale from 2003 to 2008 (rupees in lakhs) is:
   A. 0.1 B. 0.2 C. 0.3 D. 0.4
2. Annual mean profit of the store (rupees in ten thousands) is approximately:
   A. 8.5 B. 8.6 C. 8.7 D. 9.0
3. During which of the following years percentage of profit earned by the store on the total sale was at the highest level?
   A. 2001 B. 2002 C. 2003 D. 2005
4. Assuming the profit earned during the year 2001 as base (100), the profit made by the store during the year 2008 was:
   A. 76 B. 105 C. 121 D. 131
5. During which year between 2001 to 2006 profit made by the store as compared to the previous year was more than 100%?
   A. 2008 B. 2007 C. 2005 D. 2003

Solution 1. Mean of annual increase in sale from 2003 to 2008 = $\frac{10.5-8.5}{5} = .4$

Solution 2. Annual mean profit of the store (rupees in ten thousands)

$$= \frac{(6.5+11.5+7.5+4.5+9.5+11.5+10.0+8.5)}{8} = \frac{69.5}{8} = 8.7 \text{ (approx.)}$$

Solution 3. Percentage of profit on the total sale in 2001 = $\frac{6.5 \times 10000 \times 100}{3.5 \times 100000} = 18.57$

Percentage of profit on the total sale in 2002 = $\frac{11.5 \times 10000 \times 100}{4.5 \times 100000} = 25.56$

Percentage of profit on the total sale in 2003 = $\frac{7.5 \times 10000 \times 100}{8.5 \times 100000} = 8.82$

And percentage of profit on the total sale in 2005 = $\frac{9.5 \times 10000 \times 100}{5.5 \times 100000} = 17.27$

$\therefore$ Percentage of profit on the total sale in 2002 was the highest level.

Solution 4. Required profit = $\frac{100 \times 8.5}{6.5} = 131$

Solution 5. Profit per cent during the year 2005 as compared to the previous year = $\frac{(9.5 - 4.5) \times 100}{4.5} = 111.11\%$

Hence, profit in the year 2005 was more than 100% as compared to the previous year.

Example 3: Directions: *Study the graph given below and answer the questions asked there under.*

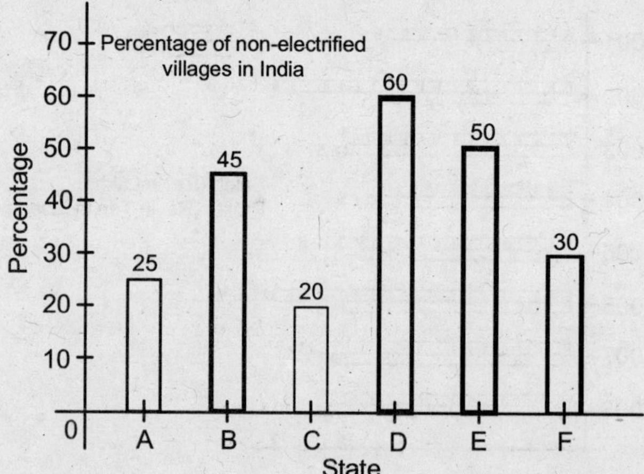

1. According to the table given below which state of India has the highest percentage of electrified villages?
   A. A B. B C. C D. D E. E
2. If central govt. decides to extend financial assistance for prompt electrification and begins with the state having the least electrified villages, then in the order of preference which of the following states will be fourth?
   A. C B. B C. A D. E E. F
3. How many states have at least 60% or more electrified villages?
   A. Five B. Three C. Four D. Two E. One
4. In which of the following states percentage of electrified villages is double the percentage of electrified villages in state (D)?
   A. C B. F C. A D. B E. E
5. What is the percentage of electrified villages in the state (A)?
   A. 65% B. 25% C. 35% D. 75% E. None of these

Solution 1. In the state (C) percentage of non-electrified villages is the least. It means the percentage of electrified villages for the state (C) is the highest.

Solution 2. The order of preference of the least electrified villages is given as: D, E, B, F, A, C.

Solution 3. In A, C and F states, percentage of non-electrified villages are 25, 20 and 30 per cent respectively. Hence, percentages of electrified villages for these three states are 75, 80 and 70 per cent respectively.

Solution 4. Percentage of electrified villages in state D = 100 – 60 = 40
Percentage of electrified villages in state C = 100 – 20 = 80
Hence, the percentage of electrified villages in the state C is double the percentage of electrified villages in state D.

Solution 5. Percentage of electrified villages in the state A = 100 – 25 = 75%

Example 4: Directions: *The following bar chart shows the amount accrued from additional taxation by the government during certain successive years. Study the chart carefully and answer the questions that follow:*

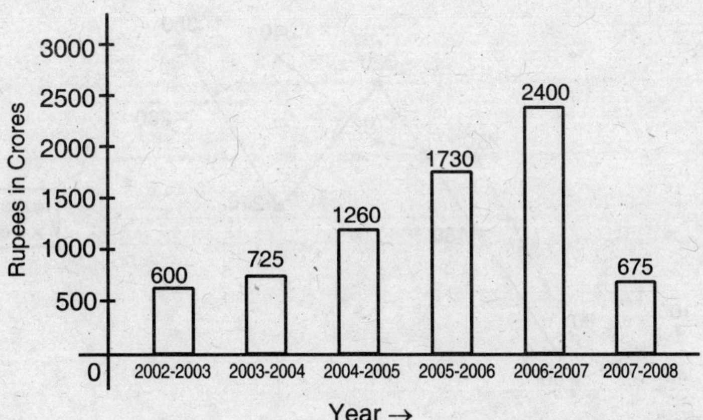

1. In between which of the following two successive financial years increase in taxation was at the highest level?
   A. 2002-2003 and 2003-04 B. 2005-06 and 2006-07
   C. 2006-07 and 2007-08 D. 2004-05 and 2005-06
2. Total increase in taxation was how much per cent between the years 2004-05 and 2005-06?
   A. 37.3% B. 35.4% C. 38.5% D. 36.6%
3. Percentage decrease in taxation in between the years 2006-07 and 2007-08 was:
   A. 71.8% B. 68.8% C. 72.6% D. 75%
4. Between the years 2005-06 and 2006-07 the taxation was increased by:
   A. ₹ 670 crores B. ₹ 650 crores C. ₹ 700 crores D. ₹ 715 crores
5. What is the average amount of taxation during all these years?
   A. ₹ 1233.7 crores B. ₹ 1433.5 crores C. ₹ 1231.7 crores D. ₹ 1400 crores

Solution 1. Between the financial years 2005-06 and 2006-07, maximum increase of ₹ 670 crores had been registered in taxation.

Solution 2. Percentage of total increase $= \dfrac{(1730-1260)}{1260} \times 100 = \dfrac{470 \times 100}{1260} = 37.3\%$

Solution 3. Percentage of total decrease in taxation between the years 2006-07 and 2007-08

$$= \frac{(2400-675)}{2400} \times 100 = \frac{1725 \times 100}{2400} = 71.8\%$$

Solution 4. Increase in taxation in between the financial years 2005-06 and 2006-07

= ₹ (2400 – 1730) = ₹ 670 crores

Solution 5. Average of the total taxation during the years $= \dfrac{600+725+1260+1730+2400+625}{6}$

$$= \frac{7390}{6} = ₹\ 1231.7 \text{ crores}$$

LINE GRAPHS

Line graphs are used to show how a quantity changes continuously. If the line goes up, the quantity is increasing; if the line goes down, the quantity is decreasing; if the line is horizontal, the quantity is not changing.

For Example:

Demand and Production of rubber (in thousand tons) in various years

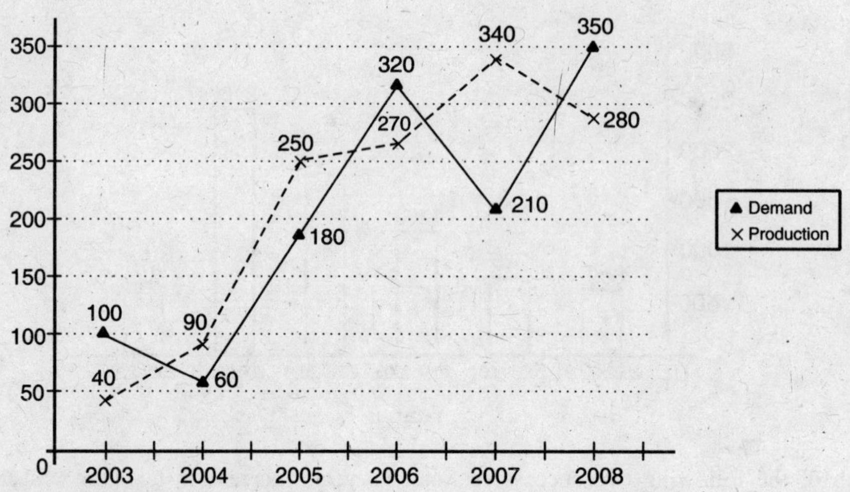

Example 1: Directions: *Study carefully the graph given below and answer the questions that follow:*

1. Price of a machine during 2005 was:

A. ₹ $5\frac{1}{3}$ thousand B. ₹ 50 thousand C. ₹ 5103 D. ₹ 3 thousand

2. The percentage decrease in the production in 2007 over the previous year 2006 was:

A. 5% B. 20% C. 25% D. 30%

3. The difference in revenue collection from the sale of machines during 2007 and 2008 was:

A. ₹ 10 lakhs B. ₹ 1 crore C. ₹ 4 crores D. ₹ 6 crores

4. Had the company sold its machines in 2008 at 25% inhanced price of 2007, what would have been the total selling price of machines produced during the year?

A. ₹ 35 crores B. ₹ 20 crores C. ₹ 12.5 crores D. ₹ 15.5 crores

5. Difference between the price of a machine in the year 2006 and that in the eyar 2007 was:

A. ₹ 1500 B. ₹ 2500 C. ₹ 1800 D. ₹ 3200

Solution 1. No. of machines produced during the year 2005 = 15000

And price of the machines = ₹ 8,0000000

∴ Price of 1 machine in 2005 = ₹ $\frac{80000000}{15000}$ =₹ $5\frac{1}{3}$ thousand

Solution 2. Percentage decrease in production of machines during 2007 over the previous year 2006

$$= \frac{(25-20)\times 100}{25} = 20\%$$

Solution 3. Difference in revenue collected from sale of machines during 2007 and 2008

= 16 – 10 = ₹ 6 crores.

Solution 4. On enhancing price by 25% in 2008, total price of the machines produced during the years 2008

$$= \frac{10\times 125}{100} = ₹\ 12.5 \text{ crores}$$

Solution 5. Price of 1 machine in 2006 = $\frac{80000000}{25000}$ = ₹ 3200

Price of 1 machine in 2007 = $\frac{100000000}{20000}$ = ₹ 5000

∴ Required difference = ₹ (5000 – 3200) = ₹ 1800

Example 2: Directions: *Study the graph carefully to answer the questions that follow:*

Percentage Increase in profit of two companies over the years

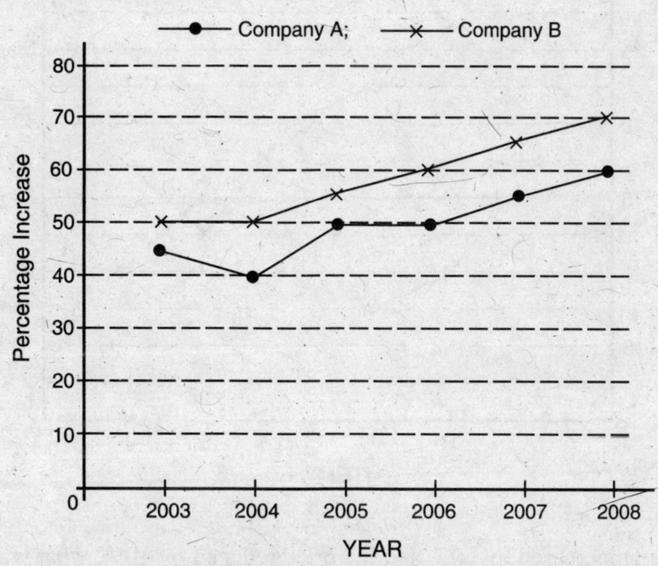

1. What is the per cent increase in profit of company A in the year 2007 from the previous year?
   A. 5　　B. 10　　C. 45　　D. 60
2. What is the per cent increase in profit of company A in the year 2008 from the previous year?
   A. 7.64　　B. 9.09　　C. 8.12　　D. 10.11
3. What is the per cent increase in profit of company A in the year 2005 from the previous year?
   A. 10　　B. 15　　C. 20　　D. 25
4. If the profit of company B in the year 2003 was ₹ 6,79,995, what would its profit have been in the year 2002?
   A. ₹ 4,24,530　　B. ₹ 4,53,330　　C. ₹ 5,01,500　　D. ₹ 5,53,330
5. Based on the graph, which of the following statements is True?
   A. Company B has made the highest profit in the year 2008
   B. Company A has made the lowest profit in the year 2004
   C. Company B has made more amount of the profit than company A over the years
   D. There is no increase in the profit of company B in the year 2005 from the previous year

Solution 1. Required percentage = $\frac{55-50}{50} \times 100 = 10\%$

Solution 2. Required percentage = $\frac{60-55}{55} \times 100 = 9.09\%$

Solution 3. Required percentage = $\frac{50-40}{40} \times 100 = 25\%$

Solution 4. Required profit = $\frac{100}{150} \times 6,79,995 =$ ₹ 4,53,330

Solution 5. It is clear from the graph that company B has made the highest profit in the year 2008, i.e., 70%

Example 3: Directions: *Study the following graph carefully to answer these questions:*

Quantity of Various items sold and price per kg

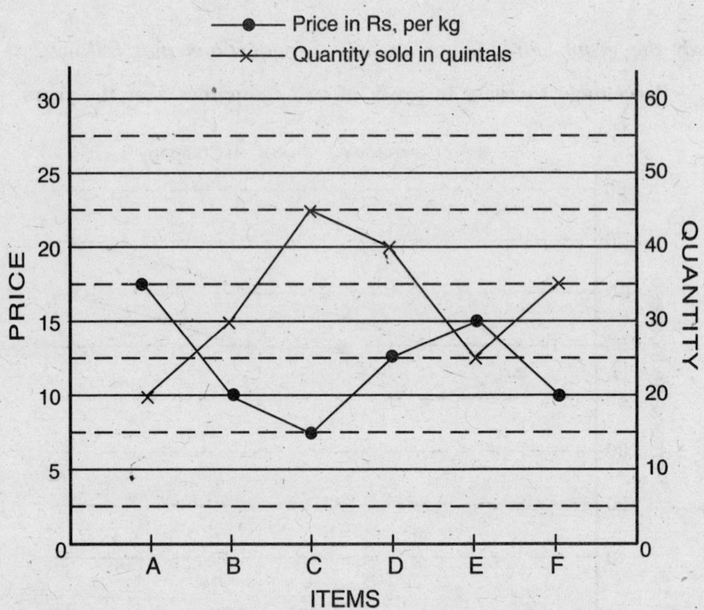

1. If the quantity sold of item D increased by 50% and the price reduced by 10%, what was the total value of the quantity sold for Item D?
   A. ₹ 675 B. ₹ 6750 C. ₹ 67500 D. ₹ 67550
2. What is the ratio between the total values of quantity sold for items E and F respectively?
   A. 3 : 2 B. 5 : 7 C. 7 : 5 D. 15 : 14
3. If the price as well as the quantity sold is increased by 20% for item A, what is the total value of quantity sold for item A?
   A. ₹ 42000 B. ₹ 48500 C. ₹ 49000 D. ₹ 50400
4. What is the average price per kg. of items A, B and C?
   A. ₹ 7.50 B. ₹ 9 C. ₹ 9.50 D. ₹ 11.67
5. Total value of quantity sold for item C is what per cent of the total value of the quantity sold for item E?
   A. 85 B. 87.5 C. 90 D. 111

Solution 1. New quantity of item D = $\frac{150}{100} \times 40 = 60$ quintal

New price per kg of item D = $\frac{90}{100} \times 12.50 =$ ₹ 11.25

Since, total value = ₹ (60 × 100 × 11.25) = ₹ 67500

Solution 2. Required ratio = (25 × 100 × 15) : (35 × 100 × 10) = 15 : 14

Solution 3. New price of item A per kg = $\frac{120}{100} \times 17.50 =$ ₹ 21

New quantity of item A = $\frac{120}{100} \times 20 = 24$ quintal

Since, total value = ₹ (24 × 100 × 21) = ₹ 50400

Solution 4. Average price per kg of items A, B and C = $\frac{17.50+10+7.50}{3}$ = ₹ 11.67

Solution 5. Required percentage = $\frac{45\times100\times750}{25\times100\times15}\times100$ = 90%

Example 4: Directions: *Study the following graph carefully and answer the questions that follow:*

Percentage profit earned by two companies over the given years

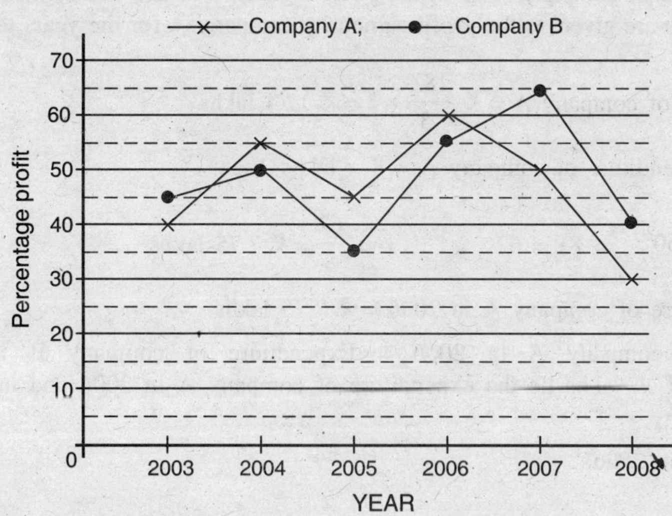

1. If the income of company A in 2005 was equal to its expenditue in 2007, what was the ratio between company's expenditure in the years 2005 and 2007 respectively?

A. 19 : 20 B. 20 : 19 C. 20 : 29 D. 29 : 20

2. If the total expenditure of the two companies in 2008 was ₹ 18 lakhs and expenditure of companies A and B in that year in the ratio of 4 : 5 respectively, then what was the income of company B in that year (in lakh ₹)?

A. 8 B. 10 C. 10.4 D. 14

3. If the total income of company A in all the years together was equal to the total expenditure of company B in all the years together, which was ₹ 265 lakhs, then what was the total percentage profit earned by Company A for all the years together?

A. 37 B. 45 C. 52 D. Cannot be determined

4. If the income of company B in 2006 was ₹ 18.6 lakhs and ratio of incomes of company A and B in 2006 was 2 : 3, what was the expenditure of company A in 2006 (in lakhs)?

A. 7.75 B. 9.75 C. 12 D. 12.4

5. If the income of company A in 2006 was equal to the total expenditure of company B in 2007, then what was the ratio of expenditure of company A in 2006 to the income of company B in 2007?

A. 10 : 13 B. 13 : 10 C. 25 : 66 D. 66 : 25

Solution 1. Let income of company A in 2005 = Expenditure of Company A in 2007 = ₹ x and also expenditure of company A in 2005 = ₹ x_1; then

For company A in 2005,

$$\frac{x-x_1}{x_1}\times100 = 45 \qquad \Rightarrow 29x_1 = 20x \qquad \therefore\ x_1 = \frac{20x}{29}$$

Since, required ratio = $\frac{20x}{29} : x$ = 20 : 29

Solution 2. In 2008, expenditure of company B = $\frac{5}{4+5} \times 18$ lakhs = ₹ 10 lakhs.

Let, income of company B in 2008 = ₹ x lakhs; then

$$\frac{x-10}{10} \times 100 = 40 \quad \Rightarrow x - 10 = 4 \quad \therefore x = ₹\ 14 \text{ lakhs}$$

Hence, income of company B in 2008 = ₹ 14 lakhs

Solution 3. Here, total income of company A in all the years together = ₹ 265 lakhs, while individual profit percentages for different years are given so the profit earned by company A for the years together can not be determined.

Solution 4. In 2006, income of company A = ₹ $\frac{18.6}{3} \times 2$ = ₹ 12.4 lakhs

Let in 2006, expenditure of company A = ₹ x lakhs, then

$$\frac{12.4-x}{x} \times 100 = 60 \quad \Rightarrow 8x = 62 \quad \therefore x = \frac{62}{8} = ₹\ 7.75 \text{ lakhs}$$

Hence, expenditure of company A in 2006 = ₹ 7.75 lakhs

Solution 5. Let income of company A in 2006 = Expenditure of company B in 2007 = ₹ x lakhs also ₹ x_1 lakhs, and ₹ x_2 lakhs be the expenditure of company A in 2006 and income of company B in 2007 respectively; then

For company A in 2006,

$$\frac{x-x_1}{x_1} \times 100 = 60 \quad \Rightarrow 8x_1 = 5x \quad \therefore x_1 = ₹\ \frac{5x}{8} \text{ lakhs}$$

For company B in 2007,

$$\frac{x_2-x}{x} \times 100 = 65 \quad \Rightarrow 20x_2 = 33x \quad \therefore x_2 = ₹\ \frac{33x}{20} \text{ lakhs}$$

Since, required ratio = $\frac{5x}{8} : \frac{33x}{20} = \frac{5x}{8} \times 40 : \frac{33x}{20} \times 40 = 25 : 66$

PIE CHARTS

These are used to show the share of various sectors in the total. They usually show the percentage share of each sector in the whole (taken as 100%). In such representation the total quantity in question is distributed over a total angle of 360°. The area of each sector is proportional to the relative frequency of the class represented by the sector.

$$\text{Sector angle} = \frac{\text{Class frequency}}{\text{Total frequency}} \times 360°$$

For Example: ***Distribution of Expenditure of a family***

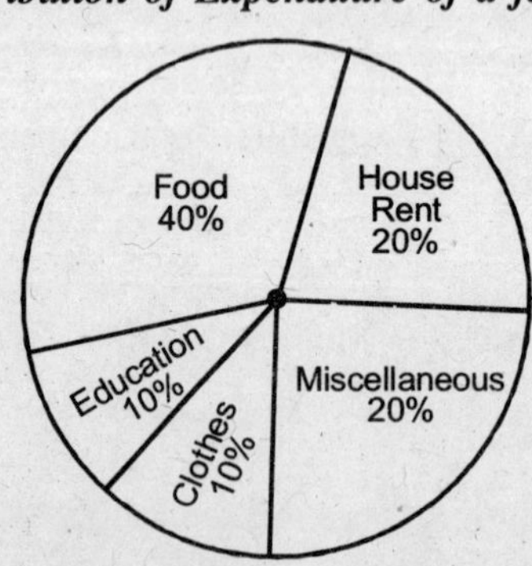

Example 1: Directions: *The pie-chart given below shows the household expenditure of a family on different items. Study the chart carefully and answer the questions that follows:*

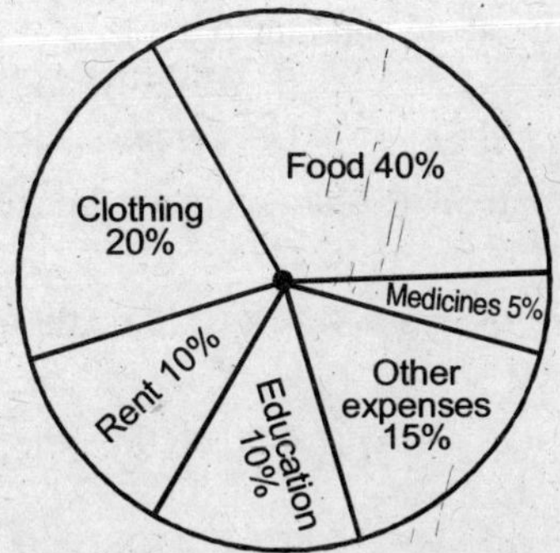

1. If the family's expenditure on education is ₹ 375 then the same amount is being expent by this family on which of the following items?
   A. Medicines B. Other expenses C. Rent D. Clothing
2. If the family expends ₹ 750 per month on food, what is the annual expenditure of this family on education?
   A. ₹ 2150 B. ₹ 1022.50 C. ₹ 2250 D. ₹ 1400
3. If total expenditure of this family is ₹ 4500, find the expenditure of the family on clothing?
   A. ₹ 800 B. ₹ 900 C. ₹ 840 D. ₹ 950
4. What is the angle subtended on the centre by the segment representing other expenses?
   A. 64° B. 54° C. 36° D. 15°
5. What is the ratio of total expenses on rent and clothing to the total expenses on medicines and other expenses of this family?
   A. 2 : 3 B. 3 : 4 C. 3 : 5 D. 3 : 2

Solution 1. Both segments representing education and rent respectively are each 10%. Hence, family's expenditure on these two items will be equal, *i.e.*, ₹ 375 will be expent on rent.

Solution 2. Here, 40% = ₹ 750

$\Rightarrow 10\% = \frac{750}{40} \times 10 = ₹\ 187.50$

$\therefore$ Annual expenditure of the family on education = 187.50 × 12 = ₹ 2250

Solution 3. Expenditure on clothing $= \frac{20}{100} \times 4500 = ₹\ 900$

Solution 4. Central angle for 15% $= \frac{15}{100} \times 360° = 54°$

Solution 5. Expenditure on rent and clothing = 10% + 20% = 30%

Expenditure on medicine and other expenses = 5% + 15% = 20%

$\therefore$ Ratio of the two = 30% : 20% = 3 : 2

Example 2: Directions: *The pie chart, drawn here, shows the spending of a country on various sports during a particular year. Study the graph carefully and answer the questions that follow:*

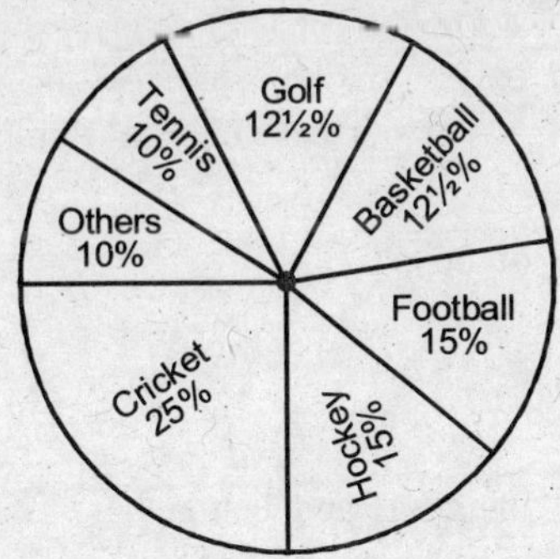

1. Graph shows that the most popular game of the country is:
   A. Football B. Hockey C. Cricket D. Tennis
2. Out of the following the country spent the same amount on:
   A. Hockey and Cricket B. Hockey and Football
   C. Hockey and Golf D. Tennis and Golf
3. The ratio of the total amount spent on football to that spent on hockey is:
   A. 2 : 1 B. 1 : 1 C. 1 : 2 D. 3 : 2
4. If the total amount spent on sports during the year was ₹ 1,20,00,000, how much was spent on basketball?
   A. ₹ 16,00,000 B. ₹ 18,00,000 C. ₹ 3,00,000 D. ₹ 15,00,000
5. If the total amount spent on sports during the year was ₹ 30,00,000, the amount spent on cricket and hockey together was:
   A. ₹ 18,00,000 B. ₹ 12,00,000 C. ₹ 15,00,000 D. ₹ 20,00,000

Solution 1. According to the graph, expenditure on cricket is the maximum. Therefore cricket is the most popular game.

Solution 2. According to the graph, equal amount has been spent on Hockey and Football.

Solution 3. Expenditure on the game of Football = 15% of total amount spent
Expenditure on the game of Hockey = 15% of total amount spent.
Therefore, the ratio of the expenditure on the two games = 1 : 1

Solution 4. 100% = ₹ 1,20,00,000
∴ Expenditure on the game of Basketball = 12½% of 1,20,00,000

$$= \frac{25 \times 1{,}20{,}00{,}000}{100} = ₹\ 15{,}00{,}000$$

Solution 5. 100% = ₹ 30,00,000
∴ Expenditure on the games of Cricket and Hockey = 25% + 15% = 40%
∴ Total expenditure on the games of Cricket and Hockey = 20% of 30,00,000

$$= \frac{40 \times 30{,}00{,}000}{100} = ₹\ 12{,}00{,}000.$$

Example 3: Directions: *Study the pie-charts carefully to answer the questions that follow.*

Percentage of Students in Six different Colleges
Total number of Students = 3500

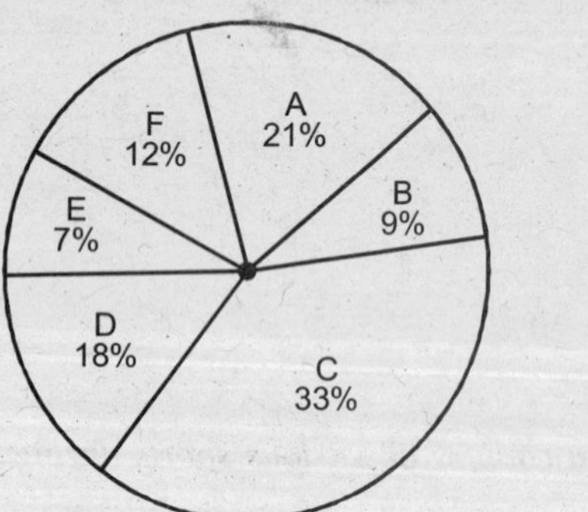

Percentage of Girls in each of the Colleges
Total number of Girls = 1800

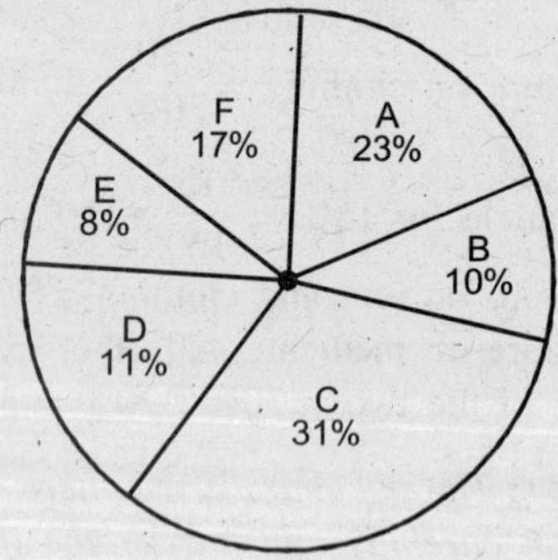

1. What is the number of girls in college D?
   A. 176 B. 188 C. 192 D. 198
2. The number of boys from College A form what per cent of total number of students from that college?
   A. 22.83 B. 38.41 C. 43.67 D. 56.29
3. Which college has the maximum number of boys?
   A. A B. B C. C D. D
4. Which college has lowest number of girls?
   A. B B. D C. E D. F
5. What is the total number of boys from Colleges E and F together?
   A. 215 B. 251 C. 283 D. 310

Solution 1. Number of girls in College D = $\frac{11}{100}\times 1800 = 198$

Solution 2. Number of students from College A = $\frac{21}{100}\times 3500 = 735$

Number of girls from College A = $\frac{23}{100}\times 1800 = 414$

Since, number of boys from college A = 725 – 414 = 321

Required percentage = $\frac{321}{735}\times 100 = \frac{2140}{49} = 43.67\%$

Solution 3. Number of boys in college A = $\frac{21}{100}\times 3500 - \frac{23}{100}\times 1800 = 735 - 414 = 321$

Number of boys in college B = $\frac{9}{100}\times 3500 - \frac{10}{100}\times 1800 = 315 - 180 = 135$

Number of boys in college C = $\frac{33}{100}\times 3500 - \frac{31}{100}\times 1800 = 1155 - 558 = 597$

Number of boys in college D = $\frac{18}{100}\times 3500 - \frac{11}{100}\times 1800 = 630 - 198 - 432$

Hence, number of boys in college C has maximum.

Solution 4. It is clear from the pie-chart that percentage of girls in college E is minimum, hence, college E has lowest number of girls.

Solution 5. Number of boys from college E = $\frac{7}{100}\times 3500 - \frac{8}{100}\times 1800 = 245 - 144 = 101$

Number of boys from college F = $\frac{12}{100}\times 3500 - \frac{17}{100}\times 1800 = 420 - 306 = 114$

Hence, their total = 101 + 114 = 215

Example 4: Directions: *Study the following pie-diagrams carefully to answer these questions.*

Number of students studying in different faculties in the years 2008 and 2009 from State X

Year-2008
Total students = 35000

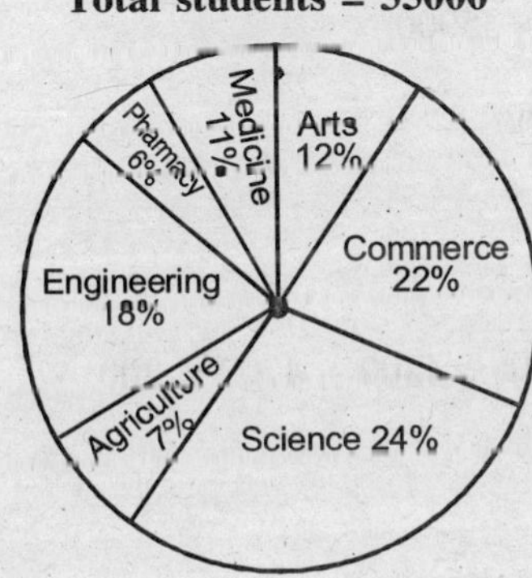

Year-2009
Total students = 40000

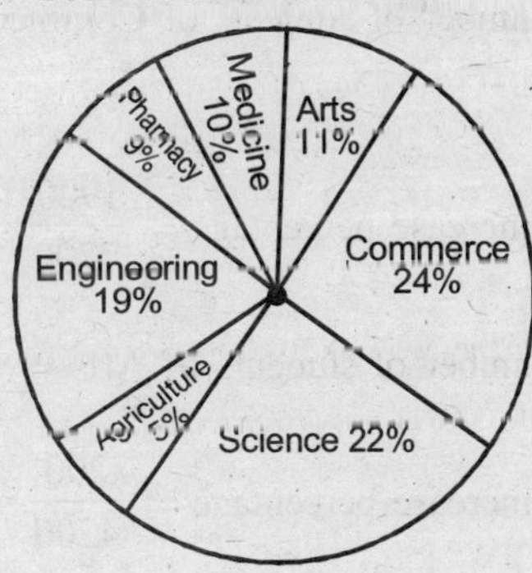

1. In which faculty there was decrease in the number of students from 2008 to 2009?
A. Arts B. Agriculture C. Pharmacy D. None of these

2. What was the approximate percentage increase in the number of students of Engineering from year 2008 to 2009?
A. 15 B. 17 C. 20 D. 25

3. In which of the following faculties the percentage increase in the number of students was minimum from 2008 to 2009?
A. Science B. Commerce C. Arts D. Medicine

4. What is the ratio between the number of students studying Pharmacy in the years 2008 and 2009 respectively?
A. 4 : 3 B. 5 : 7 C. 7 : 12 D. 8 : 13

5. In the year 2008, the number of students studying Arts and Commerce together is what per cent of the number of students studying these subjects together in 2009?
A. 76 B. 79 C. 82 D. 85

Solution 1. In 2008, number of students in Arts = $\frac{12}{100} \times 35000 = 4200$

In 2009, number of students in Arts = $\frac{11}{100} \times 40000 = 4400$

In 2008, number of students in Agriculture = $\frac{7}{100} \times 35000 = 2450$

In 2009, number of students in Agriculture = $\frac{5}{100} \times 40000 = 2000$

In 2008, number of students in Pharmacy = $\frac{6}{100} \times 35000 = 2100$

In 2009, number of students in Pharmacy = $\frac{9}{100} \times 40000 = 3600$

Hence, in Agriculture there was decrease in the number of students from 2008 to 2009.

Solution 2. In 2008, the number of students in Engineering = $\frac{18}{100} \times 35000 = 6300$

In 2009, the number of students in Engineering = $\frac{19}{100} \times 40000 = 7600$

Required percentage = $\frac{7600 - 6300}{6300} \times 100 = \frac{1300}{63} = 20.6 \approx 20\%$

Solution 3. Increase in number of students of Science = $\frac{22}{100} \times 40000 - \frac{24}{100} \times 35000$

$= 8800 - 8400 = 400$

Hence, Increase percentage = $\frac{400}{8400} \times 100 = 4\frac{16}{21}\%$

Increase in number of students of Commerce = $\frac{24}{100} \times 40000 - \frac{22}{100} \times 35000$

$= 9600 - 7700 = 1900$

Hence, their increase percentage = $\frac{1900}{7700} \times 100 = 24\frac{52}{77}\%$

Increase in number of students of Arts = $\frac{11}{100} \times 40000 - \frac{12}{100} \times 35000 = 4400 - 4200 = 200$

Hence, their increase percentage = $\frac{200}{4200} \times 100 = 4\frac{16}{21}\%$

Increase in number of students of Medicine = $\frac{10}{100} \times 40000 - \frac{11}{100} \times 35000 = 4000 - 3850 = 150$

Hence, their increase percentage = $\frac{150}{3850} \times 100 = 3\frac{69}{77}\%$

So, in Medicine the percentage increase in the number of students was minimum from 2008 to 2009.

Solution 4. In 2008, the number of students studying Pharmacy = $\frac{6}{100} \times 35000 = 2100$

In 2009, the number of students studying Pharmacy = $\frac{9}{100} \times 40000 = 3600$

Hence, their ratio = 2100 : 3600 = 7 : 12

Solution 5. In 2008, the number of students studying Arts and Commerce together = $\frac{(12+22)}{100} \times 35000 = 34 \times 350 = 11900$

In 2009, the number of students studying Arts and Commerce together = $\frac{(11+24)}{100} \times 40000 = 35 \times 400 = 14000$

Hence, required percentage = $\frac{11900}{14000} \times 100 = 85\%$

Example 5: *Study the following Graph carefully and answer the questions given below:*

Percentage of students in various courses (A, B, C, D, E, F) and Percentage of girls out of these.
Total students = 1200 (800 girls + 400 boys)

Percentage in Various Courses

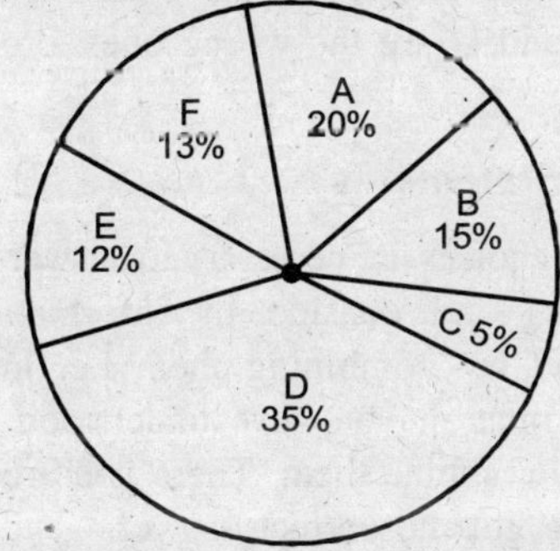

(Total girls = 800)
Percentage of Girls in Various courses

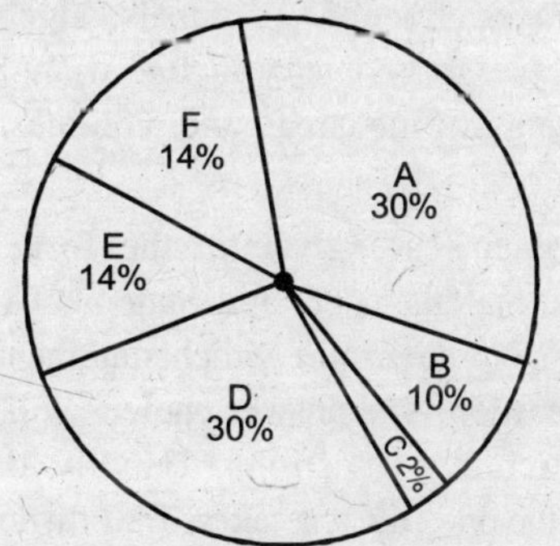

1. For which course is the number of boys the minimum?
(a) A (b) C (c) E (d) F

2. For course D what is the respective ratio of boys and girls?
(a) 3 : 4 (b) 3 : 5 (c) 4 : 5 (d) 5 : 6

Solution 1. Number of boys in course 'A' = $\frac{20}{100} \times 1200 - \frac{30}{100} \times 800 = 240 - 240 = 0$

Number of boys in course 'C' = $\frac{5}{100} \times 1200 - \frac{2}{100} \times 800 = 60 - 16 = 44$

Number of boys in course 'E' = $\frac{12}{100} \times 1200 - \frac{14}{100} \times 800 = 144 - 112 = 32$

Number of boys in course 'F' = $\frac{13}{100} \times 1200 - \frac{14}{100} \times 800 = 156 - 112 = 44$

Hence, in course 'A' number of boys is minimum *i.e.*, zero.

Solution 2. For course D,

Number of boys = $\frac{35}{100} \times 1200 - \frac{30}{100} \times 800 = 420 - 240 = 180$

Number of girls = $\frac{30}{100} \times 800 = 240$

Since, required ratio = 180 : 240 = 3 : 4

Data Sufficiency

Data sufficiency questions primary concern is to test how well you can reason quantitatively. This differs widely from quantitative section which tests your ability of manipulating numbers whereas **data sufficiency** tests your reasoning ability.

Concepts necessary to solve Data Sufficiency Questions

The data sufficiency questions covers maths and algebra concepts that are taught in High schools and colleges. In addition to basic arithmetic, you can expect questions testing your knowledge of averages, fractions, decimals, algebra, factoring, and basic principles of geometry such as triangles, circles, and how to determine the areas and volumes of simple geometric shapes.

Data sufficiency problems are given in the form of numbered statements like Statement (1) and Statement (2). The task of the test taker is to determine which statement is required to answer the question. The answer choices will be the same for data sufficiency questions. Usually data sufficiency problems are the ones the test takers find difficult to answer.

Rather than relying on your own assumptions, find out the information contained in the statement. Separate assumptions from the meaning hidden in the statement. By doing this it becomes easier to identify the correct answer.

Elimination of Answer Choices

There is one more tactic to separate the wrong answer choices from the right ones. It is nothing but simple memorization of answer choices. Practice memorizing the answer choices while preparing with practice questions.This will in turn helps a test taker to memorize the answers in the test section. Then rephrase them and arrange them. This should be done to eliminate the wrong answer choices.

Avoid Lengthy Calculations

This is the best tactic to avoid ending up with wrong answers. Calculating by depending only upon the formulae is not sufficient. This will result in long calculation. The trick for short calculations is to calculate the problem according to the information given in the statement.

Diagrams

Some of the data sufficiency problems contain figures or diagrams along with the statement. These diagrams contain information relevant to the answers. Identify the information in those diagrams and try fitting them with answer choice. This will help you in short calculations and in saving time.

Drawing Grids

To separate the assumptions, draw a grid on a scratch paper and write the alphabetical order of the choices. Now start eliminating the wrong choices in the grid. For example if the choices B, C and D are the wrong ones, cross them in the grid.

Combining the Statements

In some cases both choices are necessary to answer a question. In situations of this kind, consider the information in both the statements and try combining them i.e. information. Rephrase the information you have understood from both the statements and combine them. There you are! You will find that you have got the correct answer.

Evaluating Statements on their Own

There is a technique which is applicable for quantitative section, "Do not rely on what your mind conceives". Some statements seem to have the same idea. But the statements are designed in such a way so as to trick you. Evaluating statements is a common area where test takers tend to make errors.

Evaluating each statement on its own is the only way to avoid such errors. For example, assume that statement A is X and it may be either an odd number or even number. And also assume that statement B is Y, which might be an odd, even or prime number.

More over for real numbers used in data sufficiency, this method will end up in short and systematic calculation. As a result you will find the answer choice which is relevant to answer.

When an individual follows these strategies for data sufficiency, he/she will find it easier to answer the questions within the given time. Above all nothing can beat constant practice to be more efficient in data sufficiency section.

MULTIPLE CHOICE QUESTIONS

Directions (Qs. 1 to 7): *Each question is followed by two statements, I and II. Indicate your responses based on the following directives:*

Mark (A) if the question can be answered using I alone but not using II alone.

Mark (B) if the question can be answered using II alone but not using I alone.

Mark (C) if the question can be answered using either statement alone.

Mark (D) if the question can be answered using I and II together but not using I or II alone.

1. A man's annual salary for three consecutive years is in the ratio 4 : 5 : 6. What is the total savings of the man at the end of third year?

I. In the first two years, the man saved 30% of his salary which is ₹ 30,000 less than the third year's savings.

II. The ratio of income and expenditure of the man for the three years is 30 : 11.

2. The numerator and denominator of a fraction are positive integers. Is the numerator less than the denominator?

I. If both the numerator and the denominator are increased by 1, the fraction becomes 3/4

II. If both the numerator and the denominator are decreased by 1, the fraction becomes 5/7

3. In an exam, each correct answer gets 1 mark, a wrong answer –1/3 mark and no mark for the unanswered questions. How many marks did Kiran score in that exam, if the mark he scored is divisible by 3?

I. Out of a total of 50 questions in the paper, Kiran attempted 39.

II. 18 questions attempted by Kiran were wrong.

4. Raja and his wife have a son. The sum of the present ages of Raja and his son is 70 years. Find the present age of Raja's wife.

I. When Raja's wife would attain Raja's age, the sum of their ages would be 140 years

II. When Raja's son would attain Raja's wife's age the sum of the ages of Raja and his son would be 160 years.

5. What is the value of the positive integer x?

I. $3x + 4y + 5z = 12$; y and z are positive integers.

II. $3x + 4y + 5z = 0$; y and z are integers.

6. Amit says, "After x years, my age will be 2 times the age of Bimal". Bimal says, "After $2x$ years my age will be same as the current age of Amit". What is the value of x?

I. The age difference between Amit and Bimal is 5 years.

II. After $2x$ years Amit is five times as old as Bimal is now.

7. A maid is appointed for 30 days with the condition that for every day that she worked, she would get ₹ 50 and for every day she did not work, ₹ 10 would be deducted from her earnings. At the end of 30 days can she take home more than ₹ 500?

I. She worked for at least 16 days.

II. She worked for at most 20 days.

Directions (Qs. 8 to 14): *Each question is followed by two statements, I and II Indicate your responses based on the following directives:*

Mark (A) if the question can be answered using one of the statements alone, but cannot be answered using the other statement alone.

Mark (B) if the question can be answered using either statement alone.

Mark (C) if the question can be answered using I and II together but not using I or II alone

Mark (D) if the question cannot be answered even using I and II together.

8. A number was increased by x% and then further increased by y%. Was it effectively increased by more than 50%?

I. $x + y = 50$.

II. $x = 20$ and $y = 30$.

9. What was the cost price of an article which was sold for ₹ 144?

I. The percentage profit made was numerically equal to the cost price in rupees.

II. Profit made on the article was 45% of selling price.

10. Praveen and Rakesh started a business with investments in the ratio 2 : 3. The profit made by them at the end of a year was ₹ 60000. Find Praveen's share of profit

I. Praveen received ₹ 12000 less thatn Rakesh as his share.

II. Praveen and Rakesh stayed in the business till the end of the year.

11. A sum of ₹ P was lent for 2 years at R% p.a. at simple interest. Find R.

I. If ₹ (P + 1000) was lent for 2 years at R% p.a. at simple interest, the interest fetched would be ₹ 200 more than the interest received.

II. If ₹ P was lent for 2 years at (R + 10)% p.a. at simple interest, the interest fetched would be ₹ 200 more than the interest received.

12. A person bought an article and sold it at a loss of 10%. What is the cost price of the article?

I. If he had bought it for 20% less and sold it for ₹ 55 more, he would have made a profit of 40%.

II. If he had bought it for 20% more and sold it for ₹ 135 more, he would have made a profit of 20%.

13. Find the profit made by Somu on selling his watch.

I. If the cost price of Somu was 20% less, his profit would have been ₹ 60 more.

II. If the selling price of Somu was 20% more, his profit would have been ₹ 80 more.

14. A sum of ₹ P was lent at R% p.a. simple interest for 2 years. Find the simple interest.

I. The difference in the simple interest and the compound interest, compound interest being compounded annually on ₹ P at R% p.a. for 2 years is ₹ 10.

II. The interest earned on ₹ P in the first year in ₹ 10.

Directions (Qs. 15 to 17): *Each question is followed by two statements, I and II. Answer each question using the following instructions:*

Mark (A) if the question can be answered using statement I alone but not by using statement II alone.

Mark (B) if the question can be answered using statement II alone but not by using statement I alone.

Mark (C) if the question can be answered by using both the statements together but not by either of the statements alone.

Mark (D) if the question cannot be answered by using either of the statements alone.

Mark (E) if the question cannot be answered on the basis of the two statements.

15. When a number is divided by 18, the quotient and the remainder are 3 and x respectively. What is the value of x?

I. When the number is divided by 15, the remainder is 1.

II. When the number is divided by 8, the remainder is 2.

16. S represents the sum of the cubes of three consecutive integrers. Is S divisible by 18?

I. The middle number among the integers is divisible by 3

II. the middle number among the integers is divisible by 2.

17. A, B and C are natural numbers. Is (A + 2B + 8C) divisible by 4?

I. B and C are even numbers.

II. A is an odd number.

Directions (Qs. 18 to 19): *Each question is followed by two statements, I and II. Indicate your responses based on the following directives:*

Mark (A) if the question can be answered using I alone but not using II alone.

Mark (B) if the question can be answered using II alone but not using I alone.

Mark (C) if the question can be answered using I and II together but not using I or II alone.

Mark (D) if the question can not be answered using I and II together.

18. Is $x > y$?

I. $\log_2 x = \log_4 y$

II. $\log x - \log 4 = \log y - \log 16$

19. A is a positive integer. Is A divisible by 3?

I. $10^A - 1$ is divisible by 37.

II. $10^A + 1$ is divisible by 11.

Directions (Qs. 20 to 24): *Each question is followed by two statements, I and II. Answer each question using the following instructions:*

Mark (A) if the question can be answered by using statement I alone but not by using statement II alone.

Mark (B) if the question can be answered using statement II alone but not by using statement I alone.

Mark (C) if the question can be answered by using both the statements together but not by either of the statements alone.

Mark (D) if the question can be answered by using either of the statements alone.

Mark (E) if the question cannot be answered on the basis of the two statements.

20. Are the roots of the equation $x^2 + ax + k^2 = 0$ real where a and k are real?

I. k is a root of the equation.

II. The square of the sum of the roots is greater than the product of the roots.

21. The series S is in geometric progression. Find the common ratio.

I. The sum of the first three terms of S is 26 and all terms of S are integers.

II. If the first term is multiplied by 4 and the second term is doubled, then the first three terms of S are in arithmetic progression.

22. The ratio of the sums of the first 13 terms of two APs with positive common differences is equal to the ratio of the sums of the first 23 terms. What is the ratio of the third terms of the two APs?

I. The 4th terms of the two APs are 1 and 2 respectively.

II. The 6th term of the second AP is 0.

23. Find the sum of the first twenty five terms of an arithmetic progression.

I. Four times the twelfth term of the arithmetic progression is equal to thrice the sixteenth term of the progression.

II. Thirteenth term of the progression is 4.

24. How many terms of a A.P., whose first term is 10, must be taken to make a sum of 24?
I. Common difference d is –2.
II. 4th term is 4.

Directions (Qs. 25 to 27): *Each question is followed by two statements, I and II. Indicate your responses based on the following directives:*

Mark (A) if the question can be answered using I alone but not using II alone.

Mark (B) if the question can be answered using II alone but not using I alone.

Mark (C) if the question can be answered using I and II together but not using I or II alone.

Mark (D) if the question cannot be answered even using I and II together.

25. Is the value of x non-negative?
I. $|3x - 2| = 10$.
II. $|x - 5| = 5$.

26. A and B are real numbers. Is $A = B$?
I. $A^2 = B^3$
II. $A^3 = B^2$

27. Is X > Y?
I. $(X + Y) > X$.
II. $(X - Y) > 2Y$.

Directions (Qs. 28 to 36): *Each question is followed by two statements, I and II. Answer each question using the following instructions:*

Mark (A) if the question can be answered by using statement I alone but not by using statement II alone.

Mark (B) if the question can be answered by using statement II alone but not by using statement I alone.

Mark (C) if the question can be answered by using both the statements together but not by either of the statements alone.

Mark (D) if the question can be answered by using either of the statements alone.

Mark (E) if the question cannot be answered on the basis of the two statements.

28. The average ages of the boys and the girls in a group are 20 years and 18 years respectively. Is the average age of the group more than 19 years?
I. There are at least as many boys as there are girls in the group.
II. There are at most as many boys as there are girls in the group.

29. Find the average of N natural numbers.
I. If 3/4th of the numbers are increased by 1 and the remaining are decreased by 3, the average of the numbers would be 2.5
II. If half of the N numbers are doubled and the remaining are tripled, the average of the numbers would be 6.75.

30. A vessel had X litres of milk. Y litres was withdrawn from it and then replaced with an equal amount of water. Find the present ratio of milk and water in it.
I. X = 10 Y
II. X – Y = 90

31. A boy has a total of 45 one-rupee and fifty paise coins. Find the total value of the coins with the boy.
I. The average value per coin is $75\frac{5}{9}$ paise.
II. The value of the rupee coins is more than that of the fifty paise coins by 1350 paise.

32. A dishonest milkman professes to sell his milk at cost price but he mixes it with water. Find the percentage of water in the mixture.
I. By adding water the milkman gains 25%.
II. Milk in the new mixture is 80%.

33. The average weight of boys in a class is 28 kg and that of girls is 21 kg. Find the average weight of the class.
I. The ratio of boys to girls is 5 : 2.
II. Number of boys in the class is 30.

34. The ratio of milk to water in a mixute is 5 : 1. What quantity of water should be added to make it 5 : 3?
I. The amount of water to be added is 1/3rd of that the original mixute.
II. The ratio of half the amount of milk to water in the original mixture is 5 : 2.

35. The number of students in section A is 20 and that of section B is 25. If 5 students from section A go to section B does the average weight of class B increase or decrease?
I. The weight of the heaviest student in section A is 50 kg and the weight of the lightest student in section B is 35 kg.
II. The weight of the lightest student in section A is 45 kg and the weight of the heaviest student in section B is 40 kg.

36. Which is the smallest of the three numbers, whose average is 14?
I. One of the numbers is equal to the average of the three numbers.
II. The largest and the smallest of the numbers are equally spaced from the middle number.

Directions (Qs. 37 to 43): *Each question is followed by two statements, I and II. Indicate your responses based on the following directives:*

Mark (A) if the question can be answered using I alone but not using II alone.

Mark (B) if the question can be answered using II alone but not using I alone.

Mark (C) if the question can be answered using either statement alone.

Mark (D) if the question can be answered using I and II together but not using I or II alone.

37. Satish, Rakesh and Prakash completed a job for a total of ₹ 1000. Find the share of Satish in this amount.
I. The ratio of the times for which Satish, Rakesh and Prakash worked is 3 : 2 : 1.
II. The ratio of the parts of the job completed by Satish, Rakesh and Prakash is 3 : 2 : 1.

38. P, Q and R can complete a job in 20 days, x days and y days respectively. All the three worked together for 6 days and then P left. Q and R completed the remaining part of the job. Who completed the maximum part of the job?
I. $4x = 3y$
II. $x = 30$

39. B can do a piece of work in 12 days. In how many days can A alone do the work?
I. A and B together completed the work and distributed the total earnings in the ratio of 3 : 2.
II. Two days work of A is equal to three days work of B.

40. A and C take 20 days to do a piece of work. B and C take 15 days to do the same work. How many days does C alone take to complete the work?
I. A and B together take 12 days to complete the work.
II. A, B and C together take 10 days to complete the work.

41. A can work twice as fast as B. C can work thrice as fast as B. How many days does A alone take to complete a piece of work?
I. B and C take 15 days to complete the work.
II. A and C take 12 days to complete the work.

42. Two taps P and Q together take 3 minutes 36 seconds to fill an empty tank. How many minutes does a drain pipe R take to empty the tank when it is full?
I. P and R can fill the tank in 9 minutes.
II. Q alone takes 9 minutes to fill the tank.

43. A certain number of people can complete a work in 18 days. How many more men are required to complete the work 3 days early?
I. 270 men can complete the work in a day.
II. If the number of people is half the original number, they complete half the work in 18 days.

Directions (Qs. 44 to 62): *Each question is followed by two statements, I and II. Indicate your responses based on the following directives:*

Mark (A) if the question can be answered using one of the statements alone, but cannot be answered using the other statement alone.

Mark (B) if the question can be answered using either statement alone.

Mark (C) if the question can be answered using I and II together but not using I or II alone.

Mark (D) if the question cannot be answered even using I and II together.

44. Praveen travelled from A to B at a certain speed and returned at a lesser speed. Was his forward travel time more than 4 hours?
I. The sum of his forward and return travel times was 8 hours.
II. His forward travel time was 1 hour less than his return travel time.

45. Rajesh started from his house for his office at a kmph and reached his office b minutes early. If he started from his house at b kmph, he would have reached his office 'a' minutes late. Find the usual time he would take to reach his office.
I. $a + b = 10$
II. $\frac{ab}{a-b} = 12$

46. If Satish travelled from his home to school at a speed a % higher than his usual speed, he would reach school x minutes early. If he instead travelled at b% lower than his usual speed, he would reach school y minutes late. Is $x > y$?
I. $a = 10$
II. $b = 10$

47. Car A started from P towards Q at x kmph at 8:00 a.m. Car B started from P towards Q at y kmph at 10:00 a.m. At what time B overtook A?
I. $x : y = 2 : 3$
II. PQ = 360 km

48. Car X started from A towards B. Car Y started simultaneously from B towards A. X and Y take a hours and b hours respectively to reach their destinations from their meeting point. Find the time they would take to meet.
I. $a = \frac{2500}{b}$
II. AB = 5000 km.

49. A train crosses a bridge in 1minute at a speed of 20 kmph. What is the length of the bridge?
I. The length of the trian is 200 m.
II. A man can cross the same bridge in 5 minutes.

50. Is the radius of a cylinder C equal to its height?
I. When the radius and the height of C are interchanged, its volume remains unchanged.
II. When the radius and the height of C are interchanged, its total surface area remains unchanged.

51. S is a square and R is a rectangle but not a square. Is the side of S less than the length of R?
I. The areas of S and R are equal.
II. The reciprocal of the side of S is equal to the average of the reciprocals of the length and the breadth of R.

52. R is a rectangle. C_1 and C_2 are cylinders. Is the radius of the base of C_2 more than that of C_1?
I. C_1 was formed by folding R along its length.
II. C_2 was formed by folding R along its breadth.

53. A sphere of radius 128 cm is melted and "n" small spheres are formed. Find 'n'.
I. Radius of the each small sphere is 4 cm.
II. Radius of the large sphere is 32 times the radius of each small sphere.

54. What is the ratio of the areas of the squares ABCD and PQRS?
I. The ratio of the perimeters of ABCD and PQRS is 3 : 2.
II. The ratio of the lengths of the diagonals of ABCD and PQRS is 3 : 2.

55. Find the angle of elevation of the top of the tower at a point on the ground when the height of the flag staff standing on the tower is 7 metres.
I. Height of the tower is 30 meters.
II. The shadow of the tower is $\sqrt{3}$ times of the height of the tower.

56. A bag, has a total of 12 white and black balls. Threre are more white balls than black balls in it. Find the number of black balls in it.
I. The probability of drawing a white ball is at most 2/3
II. The probability of drawing a black ball is at most 1/3

57. Ashok purchased some apples, mangoes and oranges, each of which cost him ₹ 9, ₹ 8 and ₹ 3 respectively. Find the number of apples purchased.
I. He spent a total of ₹ 67 in purchasing them.
II. The number of apples purchased is a multiple of the number of mangoes purchased but not equal in number.

58. At a party, every person shook hands with every other person exactly once. Find the number of persons who attended the party.
I. The number of handshakes at the party is 300.
II. If instead of attending the party, each person sent a greeting card to every other person then the number of cards required is 90.

59. What is the area of the triangle AOB?
I. AOB is a right angled isosceles triangle right angled at O the origin.
II. The midpoint of AB is (3, 4)

60. Find the distance between the towers.
I. The heights of the towers are 80 metres and 62.5 metres respectively.
II. The line joining the tops of the towers makes an angle 45° with the horizontal line.

61. If A and B are two independent events, then find P(A ∩ B).
I. P (A) = P(B) = 0.4
II. P(A ∪ B) = 0.64

62. Is $a = b$?
I. ${}^nP_a = {}^nP_b$
II. ${}^nC_a = {}^nC_b$

Directions (Qs. 63 to 73): *Each question is followed by two statements, I and II. Answer each question using the following instructions:*

Mark (A) if the question can be answered by using statement I alone but not by using statement II alone.

Mark (B) if the question can be answered using statement II alone but not by using statement I alone.

Mark (C) if the question can be answered by using both the statements together but not by either of the statements alone.

Mark (D) if the question can be answered by using either of the statements alone.

Mark (E) if the question cannot be answered on the basis of the two statements.

63. Each face of a cube is painted with exactly one of the colours—Red, Blue and Green. It is then cut into 125 smaller and identical cubes. How many of the smaller cubes have all the three colours on them?
I. No two adjacent faces of the large cube were painted with the same colour.
II. Two faces of the large cube were painted in red, two faces in blue and the remaining two faces in green colour.

64. A team of three members is to be formed from a group of two managers A and B, two assistants C and D, and two accountants E and F. Who is definitely selected?
I. A is selected only if D is selected. C and F are not selected together.
II. Only one among B and E is selected.

65. All apples are not bananas. All babanas are oranges. All oranges are tasty. Is A tasty?
I. A is an apple.
II. A is not a apple.

66. All human beings are monkeys. All monkeys are vegetarian. No vegetarian is a flesh eater. Is Ravi a flesh eater?
I. Ravi is a human being.
II. Ravi is not a human being.

67. All cats are tigers. All rats are dogs. No tiger is a dog. Is X a rat?
I. X is a tiger.
II. X is a cat.

68. In a group of people, each one watches at least one of the two games—Football and Cricket. Find the ratio of the number of people who watch Football to the number of people who watch Cricket.

I. 50% of the people who watch Football also watch Cricket.

II. 40% of the people who watch Cricket also watch Football.

69. In a colony, 50 persons read "*The Hindu*". Thirty among those who read "*The Hindu*" also read "*The Telegraph*". How many persons read '*The Telegraph*' but not "*The Hindu*"?

I. 20 persons read neither "*The Hindu*" nor "*The Telegraph*".

II. 60 persons do not read "*The Hindu*".

70. In a class 50% of the students passed in English. What percentage of students failed in both English and Maths?

I. 50% of the students passed in Maths.

II. 25% of the students passed in English and Maths.

71. In a class of 100 students, if 40 students failed in Maths, 40 students filed in Science and 30 students failed in Geography, how many students were passed only in Science?

I. 20 students were failed in all the three subjefts and 30 students were failed in none of the three subjects.

II. 15 students were failed only in Science.

72. If Kishore wakes up in the morning, he goes to the office. Only if Kishore does not go to the office, then he meets his boss. Only if Kishore meets his boss, he watches a movie in the evening. Did Kishore watch a movie on Monday evening?

I. Kishore went to the office on Monday.

II. Kishoere did not go to the office on Monday.

73. Each one of Rohan, Sanjay and Sunil plays a game among Cricket, Football and Hockey. Does Sanjay play Cricket?

I. Rohan either plays Cricket or Football. If Sanjay plays Cricket then Rohan plays Hockey.

II. Sunil plays either Football or Hockey, Sanjay plays either Cricket or Football and Rohan neither plays Cricket nor Football.

Directions (Qs. 74 to 81): *Each question is followed by two statements, I and II. Answer each question using the following instructions.*

Mark (A) if the question can be answered using statement I alone.

Mark (B) if the question can be answered using statement II alone.

Mark (C) if the question can be answered using both the statements together.

Mark (D) if the question cannot be answered using both the statements and some additional information is required to answer the question.

74. Six persons—Saroj, Sathya, Sumit, Sujal, Sambhabi and Sukla are sitting in a row facing same direction. Who is sitting at the extreme left of the row?

I. Sukla is sitting to the right of Sumit but to the immediate left of Saroj and none of Saroj, Sumit and Sukla is sitting at the extreme ends.

II. Sumit and Sujal, neither of whom is sitting at the extreme right, are sitting to the right of Sambhabi, who is two places away tc the right of Saroj.

75. Abhishek, Kishore, Pratap, Ramkumar and Vijay are sitting around a circular table not necessarily in the same order. Is Pratap sitting next to Vijay?

I. Pratap and Ramkumar sit next to each other.

II. Abhishek and Kishore do not sit in adjacent chairs.

76. Six persons—Mita, Mini, Monk, Motu, Mithu and Mala are standing in a queue, may not be in the same order. Is Motu the third person from the front end of the queue?

I. Motu is standing behind Mini and is standing ahead of Mala.

II. Mithu is three places ahead of Mita.

77. Five friends Anand, Bharat, Cindra, Dravid and Estlla sit in a row facing a particular direction, not necessarily in the same order. Who is sitting exactly at the middle of the row?

I. If Bharat and Dravid interchange their positions, then Dravid is to the immediate right of Estlla.

II. If Anand interchanges his position with Cindra, then Estlla is the only person sitting adjacent to him.

78. Six persons—Ashmit, Bikash, Charan, Dinesh, Ekta and Firoj are sitting around a circular table. Who is sitting opposite Ashmit?

I. Neither Charan nor Dinesh is adjacent to or opposite Bikash.

II. Charan is not sitting adjacent to Ekta and Firoj is not sitting adjacent to Dinesh.

79. Seven books—physics, chemistry, sociology, maths, biology, history and geography are kept in a stack, may not be in the same order. Is the history book kept at the middle?

I. The physics book is kept at the bottom, but not immediately below the history book.

II. The number of books above the chemistry book is the same as the number of books below the biology book. Exactly three books are there between the history book and the geography book.

80. In a queue of 36 persons, what is the position of Manoj from the front end?

I. Manoj is equidistant from Dinesh and Komal and Komal is the 13th person from the front end of the queue.

II. Suresh is the 15th person from the rear end of the queue and there are 15 persons in between Suresh and Manoj.

81. Ravi wanted to go from his house to his office. He started from his house and travelled 15 km. He then took a right turn and travelled 12 km before taking a left turn and travelling further 6 km to reach junction B. How far and in which direction is his office from his home?

I. After reaching junction B, he travelled 8 km to reach his office

II. On reaching junction B, he took a right turn to travel towards east another 8 km to reach his office.

Directions (Qs. 82 to 96): *Each question is followed by two statements, I and II. Indicate your response based on the following directives:*

Mark (A) if the question can be answered using one of the statements alone, but cannot be answered using the other statement alone.

Mark (B) if the question can be answered using either statement alone.

Mark (C) if the question can be answered using I and II together but not using I or II alone.

Mark (D) if the question cannot be answered even using I and II together.

82. If each alphabet has a specific code and the word APPEAL is coded as 122344 and the word PILLAR is coded as 112456, then find the code for the word CATERPILLAR.

I. The word REPEAT is coded as 233467.

II. The word PLACATE is coded as 1223479.

83. Is X the cousin of Y?

I. X is the son of the father of Y.

II. Y is the daughter of the mother of X.

84. Six persons P,Q, R, S, T and U attended a party. Among them there are two couples. Is Q the husband of S?

I. P's father's mother's only child's spouse is Q.

II. R is the father of Q and they belong to different gender

85. Is P the youngest person among P, Q, R, S and T?

I. At most one person is yonger than P.

II. Exactly three persons are elder than P.

86. Avinash, Adarsh and Shashank are the top rankers in three different subjects Maths, Physics and Chemistry not necessarily in the same order. Among these no two students got the same rank in any two subjects. Who cannot be the top aanker in Chemistry?

I. Avinash got better rank than Shashank in two subjects.

II. Shashank is the 2nd ranker is Maths.

87. Is A the mother of B?

I. B is the son of A?

II. A is the sister-in-law of C whose husband is D.

88. In a code language if "man is great" is coded as "# ¥@" then what is the code for "cow is god"?

I. In the code language, "man are superman" is coded as "¥αδ" and "pinky is god" is coded as "w#λ".

II. In the code language, "cow is great" is coded as "β#@" and "man is god" is coded as "#λ¥".

89. A is the father-in-law of D whose only son is E.Is E the father of G?

I. D is the grand father of G.

II. G is the grand son of C whose husband is D.

90. If "God is Great" is coded as "Do Re Mi" and as "Humans are Good" is coded as "So La Si", then find the Code for "God".

I. "God is Good" is coded as "Re Si Do".

II. "Good are Great" is coded as "Mi Si So".

91. Five persons—P, Q, R, S, and T belong to five different cities—Mumbai, Chennai, Hyderabad, Bangalore and Delhi. Which city does Q belong to?

I. Either P or Q belongs to Bangalore. Either R or S belongs to Chennai.

II. T belongs to either Delhi or Mumbai. R belongs to either Hyderabad or Delhi.

92. A, B, C, D and E are five consecutive years of which only one is a leap year. Find which one among them is the leap year.

I. The total number of days, in A, B, C together is more than the number of days in C, D, E.

II. The total number of days in A, B, C together is equal to the number of days in C, D, E.

93. Is X a leap year?

I. In the year X, July has the same calendar as that of January.

II. In the year X October is not having the same calendar as that of January.

94. Which day is 1 March this year?

I. 1 January this year was a Sunday.

II. There was only one day of the week that occurred 53 times last year.

95. Three boxes are labelled as X, Y and Z. One box contains only red balls, another box contains only green balls while the third box contains both red and green balls. Which box contains balls of only green colour?

I. A ball is picked up from the box labelled Z and it is found to be green in colour

II. Two balls are picked each from the boxes labelled X and Y, it is found that they are in red colour.

96. A, B, C and D are four members of a family. Among them, there is a Doctor, a Lawyer, a Professor and an Engineer. Is B the Professor?

I. Among them there is a couple who have two children. The Doctor is not the husband of Professor.

II. A, the Engineer is the brother of Lawyer C. B and C belong to the same gender while A and B belong to different genders.

ANSWERS

1	2	3	4	5	6	7	8	9	10
D	C	D	D	A	A	A	B	B	B
11	**12**	**13**	**14**	**15**	**16**	**17**	**18**	**19**	**20**
A	B	C	A	A	B	B	B	D	A
21	**22**	**23**	**24**	**25**	**26**	**27**	**28**	**29**	**30**
B	C	B	E	B	C	C	B	A	A
31	**32**	**33**	**34**	**35**	**36**	**37**	**38**	**39**	**40**
D	D	A	E	B	E	B	A	C	C
41	**42**	**43**	**44**	**45**	**46**	**47**	**48**	**49**	**50**
C	D	A	A	A	C	A	A	A	B
51	**52**	**53**	**54**	**55**	**56**	**57**	**58**	**59**	**60**
B	C	B	B	D	D	C	B	C	C
61	**62**	**63**	**64**	**65**	**66**	**67**	**68**	**69**	**70**
A	C	A	C	E	A	D	C	C	C
71	**72**	**73**	**74**	**75**	**76**	**77**	**78**	**79**	**80**
A	A	D	B	C	D	C	C	B	B
81	**82**	**83**	**84**	**85**	**86**	**87**	**88**	**89**	**90**
B	C	B	B	D	C	C	A	D	D
91	**92**	**93**	**94**	**95**	**96**				
D	A	B	D	A	C				

SOME SELECTED EXPLANATORY ANSWERS

1. Neither of the statements is independently sufficient, as we do not know the savings of the third year.

Using both the statements, we have 30% of $(4k + 5k) + 30{,}000$ = Savings of the third year.

As the ratio of income and expenditure = 30 : 11, the ratio of income and savings becomes 30 : 19.

Combining the two statements, total income of 3 years $= 4k + 5k + 6k = 15k$

Total savings of 3 years = 30% of $4k$ + 30% of $5k$ + (30% of $4k$ + 30% of $5k$ + 30,000) = $5.4k + 30{,}000$

Ratio of 3 year's income to year's savings = $(15k) : (5.4k + 30{,}000) = 30:19$.

This equation can be solved for k; and savings can be calculated.

2. Let the fraction be $\frac{n}{d}$

Using statement I,

$$\frac{n+1}{d+1} = \frac{3}{4}$$

$$4n + 4 = 3d + 3$$

$$4n = 3d - 1$$

$$\therefore \quad n = \frac{3}{4}d - \frac{1}{4} < \frac{3}{4}d. \quad \therefore \frac{n}{d} < \frac{3}{4} < 1$$

I is sufficient.

Using statement II,

$$\frac{n-1}{d-1} = \frac{5}{7}$$

Let $n - 1 = 5k$ and $d - 1 = 7k$ where k is a positive integer.

$n = 5k + 1$ and $d = 7k + 1$

As k is a positive integer, $5k < 7k$. $\therefore n < d$.

II is sufficient.

3. From statement I alone, we cannot find the score as we do not know the number of mistakes he committed. His mark can be 3 or 15 or 27 or 39.

From statement II alone, we cannot find the number of marks he got as we do not know the number of questions he attempted. Each statement is not sufficient.

From statements I and II, we can find his marks as 39 $- 18 - \frac{18}{3} = 15$.

4. Let the present ages of Raja, his wife and his son be x years, y years and z years respectively.

$$x + z = 70 \quad ...(1)$$

Using statement I,

When Raja's wife would attain Raja's age, she would be x years old.

She would attain Raja's age $(x - y)$ years from now.

Raja's age then $= x + x - y = (2x - y)$ years.

$$x + 2x - y = 140$$

$$3x - y = 140 \quad \text{...(2)}$$

we have two equations (1) and (2) with three unknowns x, y and z.

$\therefore$ y cannot be found.

I is not sufficient.

Using statement II, when Raja's son would attain Raja's wife's age, he would be y years old.

He would attain Raja's wife's age $(y - z)$ years from now.

Raja's age then $= (x + y - z)$ years.

$$x + y - z + y = 150$$

$$x + 2y - z = 150 \quad \text{...(3)}$$

We have two equations (1) and (2) with three unknowns x, y and z.

$\therefore$ y cannot be found.

II is not sufficient.

Using both statements,

From (1) $\Rightarrow$ $z = 70 - x$

From (2) $\Rightarrow$ $x = \dfrac{140 + y}{3}$

$$\therefore \quad \left(\frac{140+y}{3}\right)+2y-\left(70-\left(\frac{140+y}{3}\right)\right)=160$$

y can be found.

Both statements taken together are sufficient to answer the question.

5. From statement I,

$3x + 4y + 5z = 12$

Since $x, y, z \in z^+$ (a set of positive integers)

The value of each of x, y, z should be 1

$(3)(1) + (4)(1) + 5(1) = 12$. So $x = 1$

Statement I alone is sufficient.

From statement II

$$3x + 4y + 5z = 0$$

y and z are integers.

x is positive so y and z are negative.

If $y = z = -1$; then $3x = 9 \Rightarrow x = 3$

If $y = z = -2$; then $3x = 18 \Rightarrow x = 6$.

So unique values of x is not possible.

So statement II alone is not sufficient.

6. Let the present age of Amit be a years.

Let the present age of Bimal be b years.

Given

$$a + x = 2(b + x) \quad \rightarrow \quad \text{(I)}$$

Also, $\quad b + 2x = a \quad \rightarrow \quad$ (II)

From (I) and (II), we have

$$b + 3x = 2b + 2x$$

$$b = x$$

$$= x + 2x = a \text{ so } a = 3x$$

From statement I

$$a - b = 5$$

thus, $3x - x = 5$

Hence x can be found.

So statement I alone is sufficient.

From statement II,

$a + 2x = 5b$

As $a = 3x$ and $b = x$,

we get, $5x = 5x$

From this, x can't be found out, so

Statement II alone is not sufficient.

7. Let the number of days the maid was present be x.

$\therefore$ The number of days she was absent be $(30 - x)$

$$50x - (30 - x)10 > 500$$

$$5x - (30 - x) > 50$$

$$5x - 30 + x > 50$$

$$6x > 80$$

$$x > 13.\overline{3}$$

Statement I

Number of days the maid was present is greater than $13.\overline{3}$,

$\therefore$ She will get more than ₹ 500

Statement I is sufficient.

Statement II

She was present at most for 20 days.

Statement II is not sufficient to answer the question.

8. Let the number be N initially

Its value after the x% increase $= \text{N} + \dfrac{x}{100}\text{N}$

$$= \text{N}\left(1+\frac{x}{100}\right)$$

Its value after y% increase

$$= \text{N}\left(1+\frac{x}{100}\right)+\frac{y}{100}\left[\text{N}\left[\left(1+\frac{x}{100}\right)\right]\right]$$

$$= \text{N}\left(1+\frac{x}{100}\right)\left(1+\frac{y}{100}\right)=\text{N}\left(1+\frac{x+y}{100}+\frac{xy}{100^2}\right)$$

Precentage increase in the number

$$= \frac{\text{N}\left(1+\dfrac{x+y}{100}+\dfrac{xy}{100^2}\right)-\text{N}}{\text{N}}(100)\%$$

$$= \frac{x+y}{100} + \frac{xy}{100^2}(100)\% = \left(x+y+\frac{xy}{100}\right)\%$$

Using statement I, $x + y + \frac{xy}{100} > x + y = 50$

I is sufficient.

Using statement II, x and y are known.

∴ effective percentage increase in the number can be found.

II is sufficient.

Either of the statements is sufficient.

9. Given SP = ₹ 144, if c is the cost price.

From statement I, $c(1 + c/100) = 144$

$$100c + c^2 = 14{,}400$$

$c^2 + 100c - 14{,}400 = 0$ or $c = 80$ or -180.

As c cannot be negative c is 80.

From statement II,

$$\frac{SP - CP}{SP} \times 100 = 45$$

$$\frac{144 - CP}{144} \times 100 = 45$$

So, CP can be calculated.

Either of the statements is sufficient.

10. Let the share of Praveen be ₹ p.

Share of Rakesh = ₹ $(60000 - p)$.

Using statement I, $p = 60000 - p - 12000$

$$p = 24000$$

I is sufficient.

Using statement II, ratio of profits = ratio of investments.

$$\therefore \quad p = \frac{2}{2+3}(60000) = 24000$$

II is sufficient. Either of the statements is sufficient.

11. Using statement I, extra interest $= (1000)\left(\frac{R}{100}\right)(2)$

$$= 200$$

$$R = 10$$

I is sufficient.

Using statement II, extra interest $= (P)\left(\frac{10}{100}\right)(2)$

$$= 200$$

$$P = 2000$$

II is not sufficient.

12. Given, SP = 0.9 (CP)

From statement I, 0.8 (CP) + 55 = (1.4)(0.9)(CP). Hence, CP can be found by solving it with the given equation.

From statement II, 1.2 CP + 135 = 1.2(1.2) (CP). Hence, CP can be found by solving it together with the given equation. Hence, each statement by itself is sufficient.

13. Let the cost price of Somu and his selling price be ₹ x and y respectively.

Using statement I, extra profit = decrease in the cost

price $= \frac{20}{100}x$ = ₹ 60

$$x = ₹\ 300$$

y is unknown.

∴ profit cannot be found. I is not sufficient.

Using statement II, extra profit = increase in the selling

price $= \frac{20}{100}y = 80$

$$y = 400$$

x is unknown. ∴ profit cannot be found.

II is not sufficient.

Using both statements, x and y are both known.

∴ profit can be found.

Both statements taken together are required to answer the question.

14. Using statement I, different between CI and SI for

2 years $= P\left(\frac{R}{100}\right)^2 = 10$

P and R are both unknown. I is not sufficient.

Using statement II, $\left(\frac{PR}{100}\right) = 10$

Simple interest $= P\left(\frac{R}{100}\right)2 = 20$

Since the interest for one year is known, interest for two years can be found.

∴ Statement II is sufficient.

15. When the number is divided by 18 the quotient is 3, so the number is greater than or equal to 54 and less than 71.

From statement I, the value of the number is only 61 as from the number 54 to the number less than 74 there is only one number (61) which leaves remainder 1 when divided by 15.

So when 61 is divided by 18 the remainder is 7. hence $x = 7$.

Statement I alone is sufficient.

From Statement II, the possible values of the number are 58 and 66.

When 58 is divided by 18 the remainder is 4.

When 66 is divided by 18 the remainder is 12. Hence, x can be 4 or 12. As x is not unique, statement II alone is not sufficient.

16. Using Statement I,

If the numbers are 2, 3 and 4S = 99.

In his case, S is not divisible by 18.

If the numbers are –1, 0, 1, S = 0.

In this case, S is divisible by 18.

I is not sufficient.

Using Statement II,

If the numbers are –1, 0 and 1, S = 0.

If the numbers are 1, 2 and 3, S = 36.

If the numbers are 3, 4 and 5, S = 216.

It can be seen that in all the cases considered, S is divisible by 18.

∴ S must always be divisible by 18.

II is sufficient.

17. From statement I, B and C are even numbers.

So 2B + 8C is divisible by 4, but we do not know whether A is divisible by 4 or not.

So statement I alone is not sufficient.

From statement II

A is an odd numbers so (A) + (2B + 8C)

= (odd) + (even) = odd

(A + 2B + 8C) is an odd number

Odd number are not divisible by even numbers.

So A + 2B + 8C is not divisible by 4.

Statement II alone is sufficient.

18. Using statement I, $\log_2 x = \dfrac{\log_2 y}{\log_2 2^2} = \dfrac{\log_2 y}{2} = \log_2 y^{\frac{1}{2}}$

$\therefore\ x = y^{\frac{1}{2}}$

If $y = \dfrac{1}{4}$ then $x = \dfrac{1}{2}$. In this case, $x > y$. If $y = 4$, $x = 2$. In this case, $x < y$.

Statement I is not sufficient.

Using statement II $\log x - \log 4 = \log y - \log 16$

$$\log\left(\frac{x}{4}\right) = \log\left(\frac{y}{16}\right)$$

$$\frac{x}{4} = \frac{y}{16}$$

$$y = 4x. \quad \therefore \quad y > x$$

Using statement II we can answer the question.

19. From statement I, if A = 1, $10^A - 1 = 0$.

If A = 3, $10^A - 1 = 999$.

In both cases $10^A - 1$ is divisible by 37.

Only in the second case, A is divisible by 3.

I is not sufficient.

From statement II, if A = 1, $10^A + 1 = 11$

If A = 3, $10^A + 1 = 1001$

In both cases, $10^A + 1$ is divisible by 11.

Only in the second case, is divisible by 3.

II is not sufficient.

Even both statements taken together are not sufficient to answer the question.

20. Using statement I, if one root is real, the other is also real, as all the coefficients are real.

Using statement II, $a^2 > k^2$

Let $a^2 = ck^2$ where $c > 1$

The discrimination $= \sqrt{a^2 - 4k^2} = \sqrt{(c-4)k^2}$

If $c \geq 4$ roots are real otherwise they are complex.

We can answer the question from statement I but not from statement II.

21. Let the first terms be a and the common ratio be r.

Using statement I, $a + ar + ar^2 = 26$

$\Rightarrow\ a(1 + r + r^2) = 26$

As all the terms are integers, a and r are integers.

Hence a can be 1 or 2 or 13 or 26

When $a = 1$, $1 + r + r^2 = 26$,

$r^2 + r - 25 = 0$

$$r = \frac{-1 \pm \sqrt{(-1)^2 - 4(1)(25)}}{2} = \frac{-1 \pm \sqrt{101}}{2}$$

Similarly, we can find the value of r for other values of a.

Only when a = 2 or 26, we get the corresponding integer value of r.

From statement II, if the first three terms of S are a, ar and ar^2, then we have $4a + ar^2 = 2(2ar)$

$\Rightarrow \quad r^2 + 4 = 4r$

$\Rightarrow \quad r^2 - 4r + 4 = 0$

$\Rightarrow \quad (r - 2)^2 = 0$

$\Rightarrow \quad r = 2$

∴ Statement II alone is sufficient.

22. Let the two APs be a, $a + 2d$. .... and b, $b + e$, $b + 2e$, ...

We have $\dfrac{a+6d}{b+6e} = \dfrac{a+11d}{a+11e} = \dfrac{d}{e}$

$\left(\text{If } \frac{N_1}{D_1} = \frac{N_2}{D_2},\right.$ both expression are equal to $\left.\frac{N_2 - N_1}{D_2 - D_1}\right)$

Therefore $\frac{a+6d}{b+6e} = \frac{d}{e} = \frac{-6d}{-6e} = \frac{a}{b}$

The ratio of any two corresponding terms is the same.

From I, it follows that the ratio of any two corresponding terms is 1/2 provided, both the terms are not 0.

From II, it follows that the third terms are not 0 (as $d > 0$ and $e > 0$ and $a + 5d = b + 5e = 0$)

Therefore, even statement II is needed to make sure that the third terms are not both 0. We need both the statements.

23. From statement I, if a is the first term and d is the common ratio, then we have $4(a + 11d) = 3(a + 15d)$. But with this, we cannot find any value.

From statement II, we know the thirteenth term. Sum of the first twenty-five terms

$= 25/2[a + (a + 24d)]$

$= 25/2[2(a + 12d)] = 25/2[2 \times t_{13}]$

As we know t_{13}, we can find the sum from statement I alone.

24. $a = 10$, $s = 24$

$24 = n/2[2a + (n - 1)d]$ ..... (1)

From statement I, $d = -2$

On solving $n = 3$ or 8, so not sufficient.

From statement II, $10 + 3d = 4 \Rightarrow d = -2$

Substituting $d = -2$ in (1) $n = 3$ or 8, so not sufficient.

25. Statement I

$|3x - 2| = 10$

$3x - 2 = 10$

$3x = 12$	$-3x + 2 = 10$
$x = 4$	$-8 = 3x$

$x = \frac{-8}{3}$

Statement I is not sufficient.

Statement II; $|x - 5| = 5$.

$x - 5 = 5$ or $-x + 5 = 5$

$x = 10$ or $x = 0$

Statement II is sufficient.

26. Statement I,

A = 8, B = 4, In this case, A > B. Say A = 0, B = 0. In this case, A = B.

I is not sufficient.

Statement II,

Say A = 4, B = 8. In this case, A < B.

Say A = 0, B = 0. In this case, A = B. II is not sufficient.

Using both statements,

$A^2 = B^3$ and $A^3 = B^2$

$\therefore A = B^{\frac{3}{2}}$ and $A^3 = \left(B^{\frac{3}{2}}\right)^3 = B^2$

$B^2\left(B^{\frac{5}{2}} - 1\right) = 0$

$B^2 = 0$ or $B^{\frac{5}{2}} = 1$

$B = 0$ or $B^5 = 1^2 = 1$

$B = 0$ or 1.

If $B = 0, A = 0$

If $B = 1, A = 1$

In either case, A = B.

Both statements taken together are required to answer the question.

27. From statement I alone, as $(X + Y) > X \Rightarrow Y > 0$.

So, we cannot conclude whether X > Y or X < Y. Hence I alone is not sufficient. From statement II alone, as $(X - Y) > 2Y \Rightarrow X > 3Y$

For X = –3, Y = –2

X > 3Y but X < Y

For X = –1, Y = –2

X > 3Y and X > Y

Hence II alone is not sufficient.

From statements I and II together, we have Y > 0 and X > 3Y.

For Y > 0, 3Y > Y and X > 3Y (given) hence X > Y.

So, I and II together are sufficient to answer the question.

28. The average age of the group will be more than 19 years if there are more boys than girls.

Using statement I, if there are more boys than girls, average age will be more than 19 years. If there are equal number of boys and girls it will be 19 years. I is not sufficient.

Using statement II, if there are equal number of boys and girls the average age will be 19 years. If there are more girls than boys, the average age will be less than 19 years. In any case, the average will never be more than 19 years. II is sufficient.

29. Using statement I, new sum = 3/4(N) (+1) + 1/4(N) (–3) initial sum

$\therefore$ old average (–1) new average = 2.5. I is sufficient.

Using statement II, let the averages of the half which

is doubled and that which is tripled be a and b respectively. Initial sum = $\frac{N}{2}a+\frac{N}{2}b$.

Old average = $\frac{a+b}{2}$.

New sum = $\frac{N}{2}(2a)+\frac{N}{2}(3b)$ = 6.75 N

i.e., $a + b = 6.75 - b/2$.

b is unknown. ∴ $\frac{a+b}{2}$ can not be found.

II is not sufficient.

30. After Y litres was withdrawn, the vessel would have (X – Y) litres of milk.

∴ the vessel would finally have X – Y litres of milk and Y litres of water

∴ required ratio = $\frac{X-Y}{Y}=\frac{X}{Y}-1$

Using statement I,

$\frac{X}{Y}$ = 10. I is sufficient.

Using statement II, neither both X and Y known nor is $\frac{X}{Y}$ known.

∴ the question cannot be answered with the information in statement II. Ii is not sufficient.

31. Using statement I, total value of the coins = $75\frac{5}{9}(45)$ paise.

I is sufficient.

Let the number of one rupee coins and fifty paise coins be a and b respectively.

$a + b = 45$ and $100a - 50b = 1350$

solving these, $a = 24$ and $b = 21$.

The question cannot be answered. II is sufficient.

32. From statement I, we can know that the milkman added 20% water. From statement II, we can know that the milkman added 20% water.

33. Statement I, average weight = 5/7(28) + 2/7(21)

= 26kg.

Statement II is not sufficient as the number of girls are unknown.

34. From statement I, we do not get an idea of either the total volume of the initial mixture or of the volume of either of the components. Hence, statement I alone is not sufficient.

From statement II also, we do not get any information regarding the volumes of the total mixture or of the components and hence, statement II alone is not sufficient. Even when we take both the statements together, we have the same problem.

35. From statement I, if the total weight of 5 students who are transferred from section A to section B is more than 35(5) = 175 kg, then the average weight of the class B will increase. Otherwise, we can't say anything as we don't know the average weight of the section A. So first statement alone is not sufficient.

From statement II, if the total weight of the five students who are transferred from section A to section B is more than 40(5) = 200 kg, the average weight of class B will increase. The total weight of the five students is definitely more than 45(5) = 225 kg. Therefore, the average weight of section B will increase. We can answer the question from II alone.

36. Statement I says that one number is 14 and does not give any information about the remaining numbers. Statement II tells us that the numbers are of the form $14 - d$, 14, $14 + d$, but do not give any information to determine d uniquely. Even if we take both the statements together, we cannot determined uniquely and hence data is still insufficient.

37. As we do not have any information about the efficiencies. I alone is not sufficient.

Ratio of wages = Ratio of parts of the job done. We obtain the ratio of the parts of the job done only from statement II. II is sufficient.

38. Part of the job completed by P = $\frac{6}{20}=\frac{3}{10}$

Remaining part = $\frac{7}{10}$

This will be completed by Q and R. Parts of the job completed by Q and R will be in the ratio $\frac{1}{x}:\frac{1}{y}=y:x$

Using statement I, $\frac{y}{x}=\frac{4}{3}$

Parts of the remining part done by Q and R can be found. I is sufficient.

Using statement II, y is unknown.

∴ Parts of the remaining part done by Q and R cannot be found. II is not sufficient.

39. From statement I,

The earnings are distributed in the ratio of work done, as one days work ratio of A and B is 3 : 2, so the time taken by A and B is in the ratio 2 : 3.

Hence we can find the time taken by A to complete the work.

Statement I alone is sufficient.

From statement II,

A's 2 day's work = $3\times\frac{1}{12}$ = 1/4

A's 1 day's work = 1/8

So time taken by A to complete the work is 8 days

So statement II alone is sufficient. Hence either statement alone is sufficient.

40. Question statement gives, A + C do 1/20 ...(1) of the work in 1 day B + C do 1/15 ...(2) of the work in 1 day.

Statement I gives A + B do 1/12 in 1 day ...(3) we can get C from the three equations and hence, statement I alone is sufficient.

Statement II gives A + B + C do 1/10 in 1 day ...(4). By solving (1), (2) and (4), we can get C and hence, statement II alone is also sufficient.

41. Already in the question statement, relationship between efficiencies of A, B and C is given.

From statements I, B and C 1 day's work = 1/15

As B and C can be expressed in terms of A, time taken by A can be found.

∴ Statement I alone is sufficient.

From statement II, A and C 1 day's work 1/12

As C can be expressed in terms of A, time taken by A can be found.

∴ Statement II alone is sufficient.

42. Given P + Q = 1/216.

Statement I gives P + R = 1/540. It is clear that statement I alone is not sufficient as it gives another equation, but not the values of P and R. Statement II gives Q = 1/540. This statement also gives one more equation and hence is not sufficient by itself to find R. When both the statements are taken together, we get three equations and by solving we get P, Q and R and hence can answer the question.

43. Statement I gives that the work requires 270 man days and hence the number of men required to complete in 15 days is 18. Hence, statement I alone is sufficient. Statement II does not mention anything about the total quantity of work and hence is insufficient.

44. Let the forward and return travel times of Praveen be f hours and r hours respectively.

Using statement I, $f + r = 8$ ...(1)

Forward speed > Return speed

$\therefore f < r$

$\therefore f < 4$ as $f + r = 8$

I is sufficient.

Using statement II, $f = r - 1$

r is unknown

∴ the question cannot be answered. II is not sufficient.

45. Let the usual time be t hours.

Distance = $a\left(t-\frac{b}{60}\right)$km $= b\left(t+\frac{a}{60}\right)$km

$\Rightarrow t = \frac{ab}{30(a-b)}$

Using statement I,

$\frac{ab}{a-b}$ is not know.

t cannot be found

I is not sufficient.

Using statement II,

$\frac{ab}{a-b}$ is known.

t can be found

II is sufficient.

46. Let the usual time of travel of Satish be t minutes. If his speed was a % higher, it would be $\frac{100+a}{100}$ times his usual speed. His time would then be $\left(\frac{100}{100+a}\right)t$ minutes. If his speed was b% lower, it would be $\frac{100-b}{100}$ times his usual speed. His time would then be $\left(\frac{100}{100-b}\right)-t$ minutes.

If $b = a$, $x = t - \frac{100t}{100+a}$ and $y = \frac{100t}{100-a} - t$

$x - y = 2t - \left(\frac{(100t)(200)}{100^2 - a^2}\right)$

$\therefore y > x$ whenever $a = b$

Both statements taken together are required to answer the question.

47. Distance travelled by A by 10 : 00 a.m. = $2x$ km.

Time of overtaking = $\frac{2x}{y-x}$ hours after 10:00 a.m.

$$\frac{2x}{y-x} = \frac{2}{\frac{y}{x}-1}$$

If $\frac{y}{x}$ is known, or both y and x known, the required time can be found. Using statement I,

$$\frac{y}{x} = \frac{3}{2}$$

I is sufficient.

Using statement II,

neither $\frac{y}{x}$ nor both y and x are known. II is not sufficient.

48. Let the meeting point be M.

Let the time taken to meet be t hours.

X would take t hours to travel AM for which Y would take b hours. Y would take t hours to travel BM for which X would take a hours.

Let the speeds of X and Y be x kmph and y kmph respectively.

$$AM = xt = yb \quad ...(1)$$

$$BM = yt = xa \quad ...(2)$$

Multiplying (1) and (2),

$$(xt)(yt) = (yb)(xa)$$

$$t > 0. \quad \therefore t = \sqrt{ab}$$

If ab or both a and b are known, then t can be found.

Using statement I, ab – 2500

I is sufficient.

Using statement II, neither ab nor both a and b are known.

II is not sufficient.

49. Time taken to cross the bridge

$$= \frac{\text{length of the bridge + length of the train}}{\text{speed of the train}}$$

Since we know, the time taken by the train to cross the bridge, the train's speed and the length of the train, so we can uniquely determine the length of the bridge. Statement I alone is sufficient.

Statement II alone is not sufficient as we do not have any information about the trains speed.

50. Let the radius and the height of C be r and h respectively.

Using statement I, $\pi r^2 h = \pi h^2 r$.

$$\pi rh\,(r - h) = 0$$

$$rh > 0$$

$$\therefore \quad r - h = 0 \quad i.e., \quad r = h$$

I is sufficient.

Using statement II, $2\pi\, r(r + h) = 2\pi h(h + r)$

$$2\pi(r^2 - h^2) = 0 \; i.e., \; 2\pi(r + h)(r - h) = 0$$

$$2\pi(r + h) \neq 0$$

$$\therefore \quad r - h = 0 \quad i.e., \; r = h$$

II is sufficient.

Either of the statements is sufficient.

51. R is not a square.

$\therefore$ Its lenght is not equal to its breadth. Let the side of S be a. Let the lenght and the breadth of R be ℓ and b respectively

$$\ell \neq b.$$

$$\therefore \quad \ell > b$$

Using I, $a^2 = \ell b < \ell^2$

$$\therefore \quad a < \ell$$

I is sufficient.

Using statement II, $\frac{1}{a} = \frac{\frac{1}{\ell}+\frac{1}{b}}{2} > \frac{\frac{2}{\ell}}{2} = \frac{1}{\ell}$

$$\therefore \quad a < \ell$$

II is sufficient.

$\therefore$ Either of the statements is sufficient.

52. Let the length and the breadth of R be ℓ and b respectively.

As the information about C_1 and C_2 are given in different statements, the question cannot be answered by using either of the statements. Using both statements, the length of R would form the circumference of C_1 and its breadth would form the height of C_1.

$$\therefore \quad \text{Radius of } C_1 = \frac{\text{lenght of R}}{2\pi}$$

Similarly, radius of $C_2 = \frac{\text{breadth of R}}{2\pi}$

$\therefore$ Radius of $C_2 \leq$ radius of C_1.

$\therefore$ Radius of C_2 can never exceed the radius of C_1.

Both statements taken together are required to answer the question.

53. Volume of the sphere = $\frac{4}{3}\pi r^3$

Where r is radius of the sphere.

from statement I,

$$n = \frac{\frac{4}{3}\pi(128)^3}{\frac{4}{3}\pi(4)^3}$$

So statement I alone is sufficient.

From statement II, $\frac{R}{r} = 32$

$$n = \frac{\frac{4}{3}\pi R^3}{\frac{4}{3}\pi r^3} = \left(\frac{R}{r}\right)^3 = (32)^3$$

So statement II alone is also sufficient.

54. From statement I, the ratio of the sides will also be 3 : 2 or the ratio of the areas will be 3 : 2 i.e., 9 : 4. From statement II, the area of the square = (diagonal)/2 we have the ratio of two areas of squares will be $\frac{3^2}{2}:\frac{2^2}{2}$ = 9 : 4. Hence each statement alone is sufficient.

55. Statement I

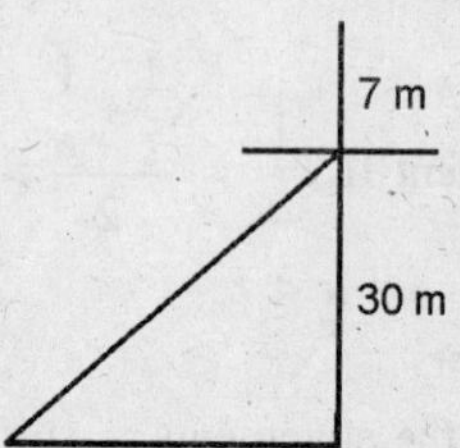

Data is not sufficient to compare the sides and get the angle of the right angled triangle.

∴ Statement I alone is not sufficient.

Statement II

Shadow of the tower is $\sqrt{3}$ times of the tower. But, the point at which the angle is measured is not known.

∴ Statement II alone is not sufficient.

Both the statements even combined the question cannot be answered.

56. There are more white balls than black balls in a total of 12 balls.

∴ There are more than 6 white balls and less than 6 black balls. Let us say there are w white balls and b black balls.

Using statement I, $\frac{w}{12} \leq \frac{2}{3}$

$w \leq 8$

∴ $w = 7$ or 8

∴ $b = 5$ or 4

Statement I alone is not sufficient

Using statement II, $\frac{b}{12} \geq \frac{1}{3}$

∴ $b \geq 4$

∴ $b = 4$ or 5

Statement II alone is not sufficient

Using both the statements we get,

$b = 4$ or 5, *i.e.,* when both the statements combined together also we cannot answer the question.

57. Given the cost of each of apple, mango and orange respectively is ₹ 9, ₹ 8 and ₹ 3

From statement I Ashok spent an amount of ₹ 67. The following table gives the possible number of fruits of each variety

Apples	*Mangoes*	*Oranges*	*Total cost*
1	2	14	67
2	2	11	67
3	2	8	67
4	2	5	67

We cannot uniquely determine the number of apples purchased.

∴ Statement I alone is not sufficient.

From statement II, we do not know the total amount spent. We cannot find the number of apples.

But combining the statements I and II only the 4th row of table i.e., 4 apples, 2 mangoes and 5 oranges satisfies the given conditions.

∴ Number of apples purchased = 4.

58. From statement I, the number of hand shakes = 300 *i.e.,* ${}^nC_2 = 300$

$\Rightarrow \frac{n(n-1)}{2} = 300$ or $n(n-1) = 600 = 25\ (24)$

$\Rightarrow n = 25$

∴ Statement I is sufficient.

From statement II: The number of cards required = 90

$\Rightarrow {}^nP_2 = 90 \Rightarrow n(n-1) = 10\ (9) \Rightarrow n = 10$

∴ Statement II is also sufficient.

We can answer the question, either of the statement.

59. From statement I, we get the location of one vertex. This is not enough to find the area of the triangle

∴ Statement I alone is not sufficient.

From statement II: We know only the mid-point of AB. We cannot find the area of the triangle.

But combining the two statements, the triangle is right angled and isosceles. The length of the median to the hypotenuse is 5. Each leg in $5\sqrt{2}$ and the are is 25.

We can get the area by combining the two statements.

60. Since angle of elevation is not given in statement I.

∴ I alone is not sufficient.

Since heights of the towers are not given

Statement II alone is also not sufficient.

When I and II are combined

We get AB = 80 m; CD = 62.5 m and ∠EDB = 45°.

In Δ DEB tan 45 = BE/DE

DE = BE = AB – AE = 80 – 62.5 = 17.5

∴ The distance between two towers is 17.5 m.

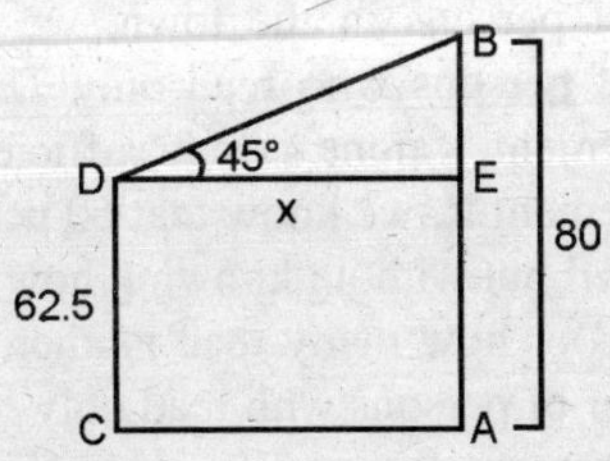

Combining both the statements, we can answer the question.

61. Since A and B are independent

$P(A \cap B) = P(A)\, P(B)$ _____(2)

Using statement I, $P(P \cap B) = (0.4)^2 = 0.16$.

I is sufficient to answer the question.

Using statement II, $P(A \cup B) = P(A) + P \cup B - P(A \cap B)$

$0.64 + P(A).\ P(B) = P(A) + P(B)$

We have only one equation with two unknowns P(A) and P(B)

So P(A) and P(B) cannot be found.

II alone is not sufficient to answer the question.

62. Statement I

$\therefore\ {}^nP_a = {}^nP_b \Rightarrow a \neq b\ (\because\ {}^6P_5 = {}^6P_6)$

$a = b + 1 = n.$

Statement I is not sufficient.

Using statement II. ${}^nC_a = {}^nC_b \Rightarrow a \neq b$

$\because\ {}^5C_3 = {}^5C_2$ or $a = n - b.$

$\therefore$ Combining both the statements, we get $a = b$.

63. From statement I, we can find the number of cubes which will have all three colours on them.

Since no two adjacent faces are painted with the same colour, opposite faces are painted with the same colour. Cubes which are at the corners of the original cube will have three colours on them. There will be eight such cubes.

Statement I alone is sufficient.

From statement II, we cannot find the number of cubes which will have all the 3 colurs on them.

If adjacent cubes are painted in the same colour, then 2 cubes will have all three colours on them.

Whereas if opposite faces are painted in the same colour, then 8 cubes will have three colour on them.

Thus statement B alone is not sufficient.

64. From I either ADC,ADF, ADE, ADB, BCD, DCE, DBF, DEF, BCE can be selected. So, I alone is not sufficient.

From II as we do not have any information about the remaining people we cannot determine who is definitely selected.

So, II alone is not sufficient.

Combining I and II, among four people B, C, E and F only two can be selected, as we need three people D must be selected. (A need not be selected every time as his selection depends on D).

65. The statements gives are as follows.

	Subject	Predicate
(*i*) particular negative	Apples	Bananas
(*ii*) universal affirmative	Bananas	Oranges
(*iii*) universal affirmative	Oranges	Tasty

From statement I,

A is an apple ⇒ A may or may not be a banana. (from (*i*))

Hence, I alone is not sufficient.

From statement II,

A is not an apple ⇒ A may or may not be a banana.

Hence, II alone is not sufficient.

Even by using both the statements we cannot answer the question.

66. The statements given are as follows.

	Subject	Predicate
(*i*) Universal affirmative	Humans	Monkeys
(*ii*) Universal affirmative	Monkey	Vegetarian
(*iii*) Universal negative	Vegetarian	East flesh

From statement I,

Ravi is human ⇒ Ravi is monkey (from (*i*))

⇒ Ravi is vegetarian (from (*ii*)) ⇒ Ravi is not a flesh eater (from (*iii*)).

Hence, statement I alone is sufficient.

From statement II, Ravi is not a human. So we cannot say if Ravi would be a flesh eater or not.

67. The statements can be classified as follows.

	Subject	Predicate
(*i*) Universal affirmative	Cats	Tiger
(*ii*) Particular affirmative	Cats	Dogs
(*iii*) Universal affirmative	Rats	Dogs
(*iv*) Universal negative	Tiger	Dogs

From statement I, X is a tiger ⇒ X is not dog (from (*iv*)) ⇒ X is not rat (from (*iii*)).

Hence, I alone is sufficient.

From statement II,

X is cat ⇒ X is tiger (from (*i*)) ⇒ X is not dog (from (*iv*))

⇒ X is not rat (from (*iii*)).

Hence, II alone is sufficient.

Thus each statement alone is sufficient.

68. From statement I, the ratio of the number of persons who love watching both the games to those who love watching football = 1/2

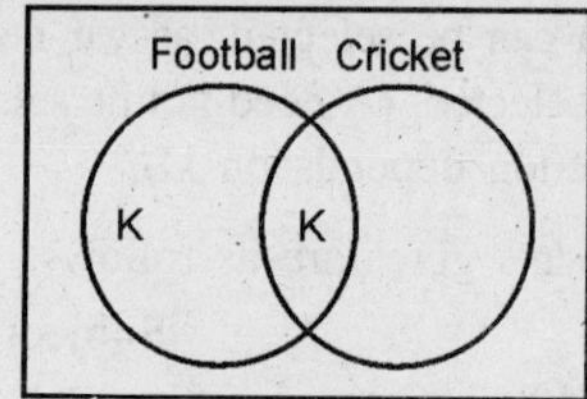

Le the number of persons who love watching Football be 2K.

$\therefore$ The number of persons who watch both is K.

But we do not know as to how many love to watch Cricket.

So statement I alone is not sufficient.

From statement II, the ratio of the no. of persons who love watching both the games to those who love watching Cricket = 2/5.

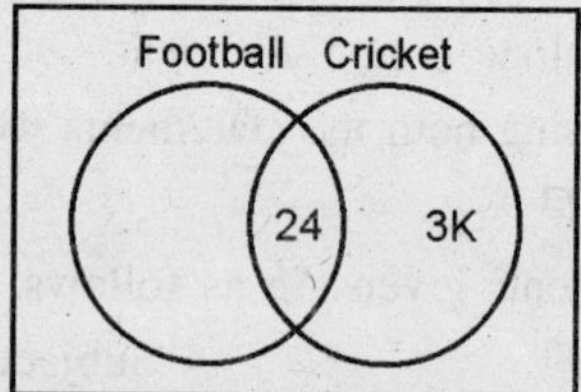

Let the number of persons who love watching cricket

be $5K_1$ $\frac{40}{100}(5K_1) = 2K_1$

But we do not know the number of persons who love watching Football.

So statement II alone is not sufficient.

Using both the statements together those who love watching both the games $K = 2K_1$

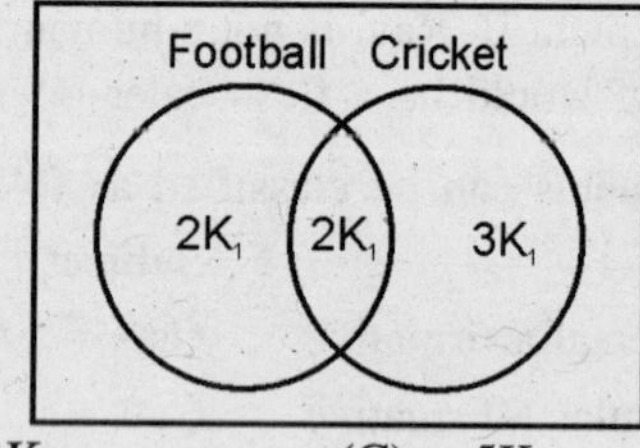

$n(F) = 4K_1$ $\quad n(C) = 5K_1$

The required ratio = $\frac{n(F)}{n(C)} = \frac{4}{5}$

We can answer the question using both the statements together.

69.

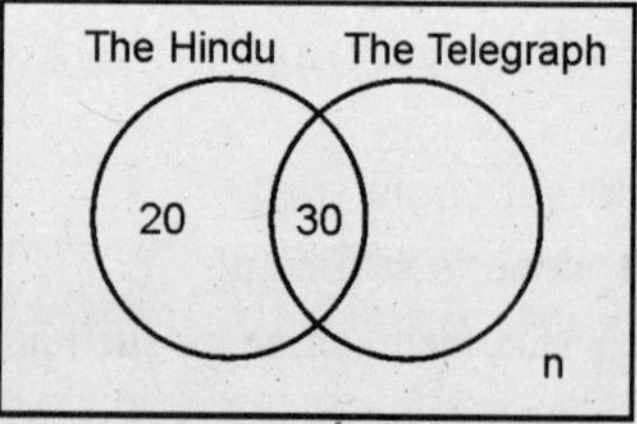

From statement I, we know that $n = 20$, but without knowing how many read '*The Telegraph*' or the total number of persons in the town, we cannot find the number of persons who read only *The Telegraph*.

Thus statement I alone is not sufficient.

From statement II, we know that 60 people do not read '*The Hindu*' but without knowing how many read '*The Telegraph*' or how many read neither, we cannot find the number of persons who read only '*The Telegraph*'.

Hence statement II alone is not sufficient.

Using both the statements together, we can find the number of persons reading only '*The Telegraph*'.

The number of persons not reading '*The Hindu*' = 60

The number of person who read '*The Telegraph*' only = 60 – 20 = 40.

70. From statement I alone we do not know the percentage of students who passed in only Maths or in only English or both the subjects. Hence statement I alone is not sufficient.

From statement II alone, we do not know the percentage of students who pass only in Maths or Maths.

Statement B alone is not sufficient.

Combining both the statements, those who passed only in English = 50% – 25% = 25%

Those who passed only in Maths = 50% – 25%

Those who have passed either in English or Maths = 25% + 25% + 25% = 75%

Those who failed in both English and Maths = 100% – 75% = 25%.

71. The given information can be represented in the following venn-diagram, where the venn-diagram represents the number of students who passed in Maths, Science and Geography.

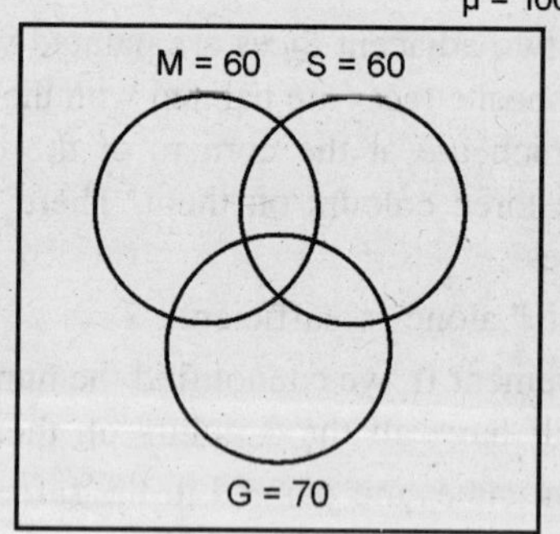

Now from I alone, the venn-diagram is as follows:

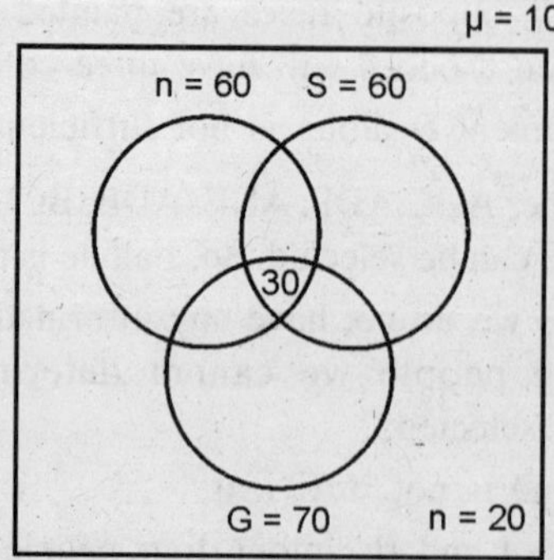

From the given information we can find out thc following:

Exactly three = 30, none = 20.

Exactly 1 + Exactly 2 + Exactly 3 = 80 ...(1)

Also, exactly 1 + 2 × exactly 2 + 3 × exactly 3 = 190 ...(2)

By subtracting (1) from (2), we get

Exactly 2 + 2 × exactly 3 = 190 – 80

Exactly 2 = 110 – 2 × 30 = 50

From (1),

Exactly 1 = 0.

The number of students who were passed only in science is 0.

I alone is sufficient.

From II alone, there is no information regarding exactly 3.

Hence, II alone is not sufficient.

72. Let the statements be denoted by p, q, r and s respectively, where

p = Kishore wakes up in the morning.

q = he goes to office.

r = he meets his boss.

s = he watches a movie in the evening.

The problem statements and their implications are as follows.

If p, then q; $p \Rightarrow q$ and $\sim q \Rightarrow \sim p$

Only if $\sim p$, then r; $r \Rightarrow \sim q$ and $\sim q \Rightarrow \sim r$.

Only if r, then s; $s \Rightarrow r$ and $\sim r \Rightarrow \sim s$

From statement (I) q is true.

$\sim q \Rightarrow \sim r$, *i.e.*, he does not meet his boss on Monday.

$\Rightarrow$ He does not watch a movie in the evening.

Thus statement I alone is sufficient.

From statement II, q is false.

$\sim q \Rightarrow \sim p$, from this we cannot conclude anything.

Hence statement II alone is not sufficient.

73. From I alone, Rohan does not play Hockey.

Hence Sanjay does not play Cricket.

So I alone is sufficient.

From II alone, Rohan plays Hockey,

Sanjay plays Cricket and Sunil plays Football

So, II alone is sufficient.

74. From I alone, any one among Sathya, Sujal and Sambhabi can sit at the extreme left. Hence statement I alone is not sufficient.

From II alone, as Sumit and Sujal are not sitting at the extreme right, they can sit at second and third position from the right end in any order.

Sambhabi must sit at the fourth place from the right end as she is two places away to the right of Saroj.

75. From statement I, we cannot conclude if Pratap is sitting next to Vijay for we only know that Pratap and Ramkumar are sitting next to each other.

So statement I alone is not sufficient.

From statement II, we only know that Abishek and Kishore fo not sit next to each other. From this we cannot conclude if Pratap is sitting next to Vijay or not. So statement II alone is not sufficient.

Using both the statements together. We can conclude the Pratap is not sitting next to Vijay.

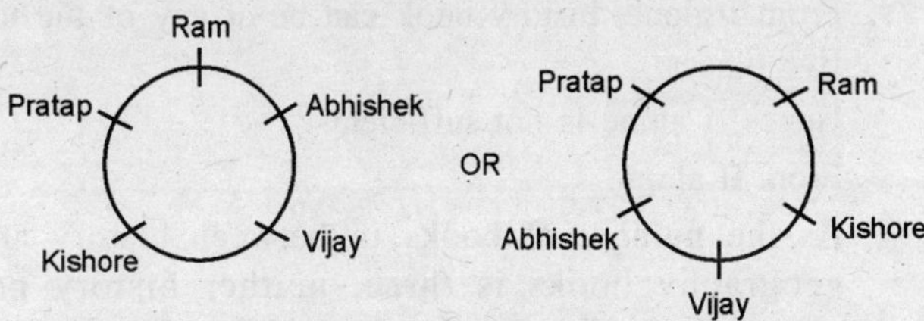

The above two possiblilities show that Vijay must be sitting between Kishore and Abishek, so he cannot be next to Pratap.

76. From I alone, we cannot get the definite position of any of the persons.

Hence I alone is not sufficient.

In II alone, only partial information is given.

∴ Hence, II alone is also not sufficient.

Combining I and II also, we cannot get that who is standing at the third position from the front end of the queue.

77. From statement I, we know that B and E are adjacent to each other and B is to the immediate right of E, but as we do not know the positions of the other people, we cannot determine who is sitting in the middle of the row.

So, statement I alone is nor sufficient.

From statement II as E is the only person sitting adjacent to C, C is at either of the ends of the row.

C E A/B/D A/B/D A/B/D

A/B/D A/B/D A/B/D E C

So, statement II alone is not sufficient.

From I and II, we get,

C E B D A or

C E B A D

Hence, we can find that Bharat is sitting at the middle of the row.

78. From I alone,

We get the positions of Bikash, Charan and Dinesh as follows:

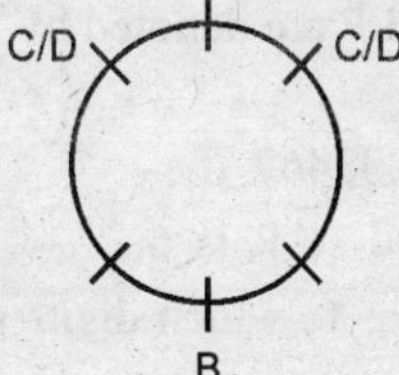

From II alone,

As Charan and Ekta are not adjacent to each other. Ekta can sit any of the other three places. Therefore, we cannot determine the position of Ashmit.

Combining I and II, we get Charan and Ekta are sitting opposite each other. Similarly, Firoj is sitting opposite Dinesh.

∴ Bikash must sit opposite Ashmit.

∴ Both the statements together are sufficient.

79. From I alone, history book can be at any of the top five places.

Hence, I alone is not sufficient.

From II alone,

As the number of books in between history and geography books is three, neither history nor geography book can be at the middle of the stack.

II alone is sufficient.

80. From I alone, there is no information regarding the number of people between Manoj and Komal.

Hence, I alone is not sufficient.

From II alone, as Suresh is the 15th person from the rear end, Manoj cannot be behind Suresh as there are 15 persons in between them.

Manoj mus be ahead of Suresh.

There are (15 + 15) = 30 people behind Manoj in the queue.

Position of Manoj is (36 – 30) = 6th from the front end.

∴ II alone is sufficient.

81. From the given information, we do not know in which direction he started his journey. With the information given in the question and that given in statement I, we can find the distance but not the direction.

Hence, I alone is not sufficient.

Statement II, we know the direction in which he is finally travelling. Hence, we can find the initial direction in which he started the journey.

Hence, using II alone we can find both distance dnd direction.

82. From statement I, we can find the code for the letters L, E, R and T.

APPEAL 122344

PILLAR 112456

So L is 1. A and P are denoted by 2 and 4 or by 4 and 2. Thus E is 3.

REPEAT 233467

T must be 7 and so R is 6.

But cannot say as to which digits represents C, A and P respectively.

Thus statement I alone is not sufficient.

From statement II,

APPEAL 122344

PILLAR 112456

PLACATE 1223479

We cannot say the digits representing C, T, I and R.

We acan say that A is represented by 2 and P by 4.

So statement II alone is not sufficient.

Now, by using both the statements together, we can conclude the alphabets and the corresponding digits will be as follows.

C A T E R P I L

9 2 7 3 6 4 5 1

So the code for the word CATERPILLAR is 11223456679

Thus we can answer the question by using both the statements together.

83. From statement I,

Z_1 is the father of Y and X. X is the brother of Y since X is the son. Hence we can say that X is not the cousin of Y.

First statement alone is sufficient.

From statement II, Y is the daughter of the mother of X. Therefore Y is the sister of X.

Hence we can say that X is not the cousin of Y.

Second statement alone is also sufficient.

Thus, either of the statements is also sufficient.

84. From statement I, P's father's mother's only child is none other than P's father. As his spouse is Q, Q is the mother of P. As Q is the female she cannot be the husband.

So, statement I alone is sufficient.

From statement II, R is the father of Q and they belong to different gender which implies that Q is a female. So Q cannot be the husband.

So statement II alone is sufficient.

85. From statement I,

P may or may not be the youngest.

From statement II,

since exactly three persons are elder to P, the fourth person may be of equal age as of P or may be younger than P. Hence second statement alone is not sufficient.

Using both the statements also we have the possibility that the fourth person may be younger than P, as at the most one person is younger than P or of same age as P. Hence P may or may not be the youngest.

86. From statement I alone as we do not have any information regarding the remaining two students, we cannot determine who is not the top ranker in chemistry. From statement II, alone also we cannot determine who is not the topper in Chemistry.

Combining the statements I and II, we know that Shashank got 2nd rank in Maths. As Avinash got a better rank than Shashank in two subjects, one of them should be Maths. [As Shashank got 2nd rank in Maths, he has to get 1st rank in either Physics or Chemistry.] So, to get better rank than Shashank, Avinash has to get the first rank in Maths. So, he cannot get the first rank in Chemistry.

87. From statement I, we cannot say if A is the mother of B, or A can be the father of B. So statement I alone is not sufficient.

From statement II, we cannot say whether A is the mother of B or not as nothing is mentioned about B.

So statement II alone is not sufficient.

Using both the statements together we can say that A is the mother of B for in statement I, it is given that B is A's son. Where as in statement. II, it is given that A is a female. So by using both we can conclude that A is B's mother.

88. From I alone, we can find the code for "man" as ¥ and 'is' as #.

I alone is not sufficient.

From II alone, we can find out the code for "is" as '#'.

'great' as @.

'cow' as 'β'.

'god' as 'λ'.

∴ II alone is sufficient.

89. From statement I, we cannot say if E is the father of G. D being the grandfather of G, does not make E as the father of G, or it is possible that D had a daughter whose child is G.

So statement I, alone is not sufficient.

From statement II, we cannot say regarding E being G's father or not as we do not know if D had any other child other than E.

So statement II, alone is not sufficient.

Even by using both the statements together, we cannot conclude whether E is the father of G or not.

Thus both the statements together are not sufficient to answer.

90. From statement I, we can find the code for the words Great and Good.

"God is Great" coded as "Do Re Mi"

"God is Good" codes as "Re Si Do"

We see that "God" and "is" is common among the two statements given. So the code for "God is" is "Do Re" in any order.

Code	Word
Si	Good
Mi	Great

But we cannot say what is the code for the word "God".

So statement I alone is not sufficiet.

From statement II, we can find the code for the words:

Words	Code
Humans	La
Great	Mi

But we cannot find the code for the word God.

Now, by using both the statements together we can conclude that the code for the word "God is" is "Do Re"

Words	Code
Great	Mi
Good	Si
Are	So
Humans	La

But individually, we cannot say what will be the code for the word God. So even by using both the statements together we cannot answer regarding the code for the word God.

91. From I alone,

Bangalore – P or Q

Chennai – R or S

Q may belong to any city other than Chennai.

∴ I alone is not sufficient.

From II alone,

T – Delhi/Mumbai

R – Hyderabad/Delhi

Q can be from any city.

∴ II alone is also not sufficient.

Combining I and II we get

S is from Chennai.

Q can be from any city other than Chennai.

∴ Neither of the statements is sufficient.

92. Let us consider the years such that only one among them is a leap year.

A	2001	2002	2003
B	2002	2003	2004
C	2003	2004	2005
D	2004	2005	2006
E	2005	2006	2007

But we take years where the centre year is not a leap year, we get any one of the five years as leap year.

A	1896	1895	1894	1893	1900
B	1897	1896	1895	1894	1901
C	1898	1897	1896	1895	1902
D	1899	1898	1897	1896	1903
E	1900	1899	1898	1897	1904

From statement I, we cannot say which are among them is the leap year.

Since A + B + C > C + D + E

A + B > D + E

It is possible that one of A or B is the leap year, but we cannot say which one.

Statement I alone is not sufficient.

From statement II, we can conclude that year C is the leap year.

Since (A + B + C) = (C + D + E)

A + B = D + E

Since there is only one leap year among the given 5 years, it has to be year C. So statement II alone is sufficient.

93. In a leap year, calendar of January matches with that of July. So, the year X is a leap year.

I alone is sufficient.

In any non-leap year, the calendar of January matches with that of October. As October is not matching with January the year X is a leap year. So, II alone is sufficient.

94. Statement I does not specify whether the year is a leap year or not. Statement II also is not sufficient as this suggests that last year was not a leap year.

Using both the statements also the question cannot be answered as we do not know whether the given year is leap or not.

95. Using statement I alone the box labelled Z may contain only green or both green and red.

Using statement II alone, we can conclude that Z has only green colour.

Hence only statement II alone is sufficient.

96. From I, as there is no information regarding A, B C and D we cannot determine whether B is the professor or not. So, I alone is not sufficient.

From II, we do not have the relation between B and D to A and C. So II alone is not sufficient.

Combining I and II, we get A and C are the children of B and D. As A is a male B is a female and D is a male. Hence, B is the Doctor and D is the professor as doctor is not the husband, doctor is female.

❋❋❋❋❋

REASONING

1. Critical Analysis

Directions (Q. 1–10): *Study the following information carefully answer the questions given below.*

1. In Los Angeles, a political candidate who buys saturation radio advertising will get maximum name recognition.

The statement above logically conveys which of the following?

A. Radio advertising is the most important factor in political campaigns in Los Angeles.

B. Maximum name recognition in Los Angeles will help a candidate to win a higher percentage of votes cast in the city.

C. Saturation radio advertising reaches every demographically distinct sector of the voting population of Los Angeles.

D. For maximum name recognition a candidate need not spend on media channels other than radio advertising.

E. A candidate's record of achievement in the Los Angeles area will do little to affect his or her name recognition there.

2. The rate of violent crime in this state is up by 30 per cent from last year. The fault lies entirely in our court system: Recently our judges' sentences have been so lenient that criminals can now do almost anything without fear of a long term prison

The argument above would be weakened if it were true that

A. 85 per cent of the other states in the nation have lower crime rates than does this state.

B. white collar crime in this state has also increased by over 25 per cent in the last year.

C. 35 per cent of the police in this state have been laid off in the last year due to budget cuts.

D. polls show that 65 per cent of the population in this state oppose capital punishment.

E. the state has hired 25 new judges in the last year to compensate for deaths and retirements.

3. The increase in the number of newspaper articles exposed as fabrications serves to bolster the contention that publishers are more interested in boosting circulation than in printing the truth. Even minor publications have staffs to check such obvious fraud.

The argument above assumes that

A. newspaper stories, exposed as fabrications, are a recent phenomenon.

B. everything a newspaper prints must be factually verifiable.

C. fact checking is more comprehensive for minor publications than for major ones.

D. only recently about newspapers admitted to publishing intentionally fraudulent stories.

E. the publishers of newspapers are the people who decide what to print in their newspapers.

4. Time and again it has been shown that students, who attend colleges with low faculty/student ratios, get the most well-rounded education. As a result, when my children are ready to attend college, I'll be sure they attend a school with a very small student population.

Which of the following, if true, identifies the greatest flaw in the reasoning above?

A. A low faculty/student ratio is the effect of a well-rounded education, not its source.

B. Intelligence should be considered as the result of childhood environment, not if advanced education.

C. A very small student population does not by itself, ensure a low faculty/student ratio.

D. Parental desires and preferences rarely determines a child's choice of a college or university.

E. Students must take advantage of the low faculty/student ratio by intentionally choosing small classes.

5. All German philosophers, except Marx, are idealists.

From which of the following can the statement above be most properly inferred?

A. Except for Marx, if someone is an idealist philosopher, then he or she is German.

B. Marx is the only non-German philosopher who is an idealist.

C. If a German is an idealist, then he or she is a philosopher, as long as he or she is not Marx.

D. Marx is not an idealist German philosopher.

E. Aside from the philosopher Marx, if someone is a German, then he or she is an idealist.

6. Bill earns more commission than does Sandra. But since Andrew earns more commission than does Lisa, it follows that Bill earns more commission than does Lisa.

Any of the following, if introduced into the argument as an additional premise, makes the argument above logically correct EXCEPT:

A. Andrew earns more commission than Bill
B. Sandra earns more commission than Lisa
C. Sandra earns more commission than Andrew
D. Sandra and Andrew earn the same amount of commission
E. Bill and Andrew earn the same amount of commission

7. During the SARS days, about 23,500 doctors who had treated SARS sufferers died and about 23,670 doctors who had not been engaged in treatment for SARS sufferers died. On the basis of these figures, it can be concluded that it was not much more dangerous to participate in SARS treatment during the SARS day than it was not to participate in SARS treatment.
Which of the following would reveal most clearly the absurdity of the conclusion drawn above?

A. Counting deaths among doctors who had participated in SARS treatment in addition to deaths among doctors who had not participated in SARS treatment.
B. Expressing the difference between the numbers of deaths among doctors who had treated SARS sufferers and doctors who had not treated SARS suffers as a percentage of the total number of deaths
C. Separating deaths caused by accidents during the treatment to SARS suffers from deaths caused by infect of SARS suffers.
D. Comparing death rates per thousand members of each group rather than comparing total numbers of deaths.
E. Comparing deaths caused by accidents in the United States to deaths caused by infection in treating SARS suffers.

8. In 2003, an airline in United State lost more than half, on average, of the foreign passengers they had previously served each year. Researchers have alleged that this extreme drop resulted from a rise in price of tickets for international lines from $60 to $90 per 1,000 miles.

Which of the following, if feasible, offers the best prospects for alleviating the problem of the drop in passengers as the researchers assessed it?

A. Cooperating with other airlines to provide more international lines.
B. Allowing foreign passengers to pay the same as the previous international line.
C. Reemphasizing the goals and mission of the airline as serving both domestic passengers and foreign passengers.
D. Increasing the financial resources of the airline by raising the ticket price for domestic passengers.
E. Offering superior VIP service for foreign passengers.

9. Our work proves to be very successful. In the past three years, each of our five clients has experienced the fastest growth of sales in their history. Therefore, if your company wants to increase sales, do not hesitate to call Sigma & Max, since we are the solution.

Which of the following, if true, most seriously jeopardizes the validity of the argument by the speaker above?

A. Most of the consultants at Sigma & Max hold MBA degrees.
B. Even without the help of Sigma & Max, the five clients of Sigma & Max will achieve the same growth rate in sale.
C. Sigma & Max is one of the five leading management consulting companies.
D. Sigma & Max uses an updated accounting approach to help companies to cut cost.
E. All of the five clients of Sigma & Max are doing business in financial industry.

10. A life insurance company allows people to prepay their endowment insurance at current rates. The policyholder then pays the premium every year. People should participate in the program as a means of decreasing the cost for their living after retirement.
Which of the following, if true, is the most appropriate reason for people NOT to participate in the program?

A. People are unsure about which insurance company they will choose after retirement.
B. The amount of money accumulated by putting the prepayment funds in an interest-bearing account today will be greater than the total cost of insurance when they retire.
C. The annual cost of premium is expected to increase at a faster rate than the annual increase in the cost of living.
D. Some of the insurance companies are contemplating large increases in premium next year.
E. The prepayment plan would not cover the cost of hospitalization.

Directions (Q. 11–12): *Answer the questions based on the following information.*
If highways were restricted to cars and only those truck with capacity of less than 8 tons, most the truck traffic would be forced to run outside highway. Such a reduction in the amount of truck traffic would reduce the risk of collision in highway.

11. The conclusion drawn in the first sentence depends on which of the following assumptions?

A. The roads outside highway would be as convenient as highway for most drivers of truck.

B. Most roads outside highways are not ready to handle truck traffic.
C. Most trucks that are currently running in highway have a capacity of more than 8 tons.
D. Cars are at greater risk of becoming involved in collisions than are trucks.
E. A reduction in the risk of collision would eventually lead to increases in car traffic.

12. Which of the following, if true, would most strengthen the conclusion drawn in the second sentence?
A. Cars with a capacity of more than 8 tons are already excluded outside highways.
B. Highways are experiencing overcrowded traffic primarily because of sharp increases in car traffic.
C. Many drivers of trucks would rather buy truck with a capacity of less than 8 tons than be excluded from highways.
D. The number of collisions that occur near highways has decreased in recent years.
E. Trucks that have a capacity of more than 8 tons cause a disproportionately large number of collisions in highways.

13. The price of purchasing a car in Country Q is 120 percent less than the price of purchasing a car in Country Y. Even after transportation fees and tariff charges are added, it is still cheaper for a buyer to import car from Country Q to Country Y than to buy car in Country Y.

The statements above, if true, best support which of the following assertions?
A. Gasoline prices in Country Q are 120 percent below those in Country Y.
B. Importing cars from Country Q to Country Y will eliminate 120 per cent of the sales of cars in Country Y.
C. The tariff on a car imported from Country Q to Country Y is less than 120 per cent of the price of a car in Country Y.
D. The fee for transporting a car from Country Q to Country Y is more than 120 per cent of the price of a car in Country Q.
E. It takes 120 per cent less time to transport a car in Country Q than it does in Country Y.

14. In 1992, 5 percent of every dollar paid in tax went to support the unemployed citizens. In 1998, 8 per cent of every dollar paid in tax went to such funds, although that unemployment rate has decreased in 1998 than in 1992.

Each of the following, if true, could explain the simultaneous increase in per cent of every dollar paid in tax to support the unemployed citizens and decrease in the number of unemployment rate EXCEPT:
A. On average, each unemployed citizen received more money in 1998 than 1992.
B. On average, people paid less tax in 1998 than in 1992.
C. The individuals had paid more tax than did enterprises during this period.
D. Income before tax has significantly decreased since 1992.
E. The number of tax evaders rose sharply between 1992 and 1998.

15. Something must be done to stop spam. In early days, people seldom received unsolicited email advertisement; but now that numerous bulk email software and email address finders are developed to collect email address all around the world. Advertisers use email addresses to market their products and even sell such email lists to other advertisers. **As a result, almost everyone ever get junk email, and sometime several and even tens of annoying emails a day.** So, relevant anti-spam regulations should be framed to stop unsolicited advertising.
The two portions in **boldface** play which of the following roles?
A. Background that the argument depends on and conclusion that can be drawn from the argument.
B. Part of evidence that the argument includes, and inference that can be drawn from this passage.
C. Pre-evidence that the argument depends on and part of evidence that supports the conclusion.
D. Background that argument depends on and part of evidence that supports the conclusion.
E. Pre-evidence that argument includes and a method that helps to supports that conclusion.

16. Stock analyst: "We believe Company A's stock will appreciate at 35% a year for the next 5 to 7 years. Company A just became the leader in its industry and we expect its sales to grow at 8% a year."
Commentator: "But how can the stock's price be expected to grow more quickly than the company's underlying sales?"
Which of the following facts would best support the stock analyst?
A. The company's expenses will be declining over the next 5 to 10 years.
B. The company just won a patent on a new product.
C. Company A's stock is currently overvalued by a significant amount.
D. The 5 to 7 year time frame is too long for anyone to accurately forecast.
E. Company A's industry peer group is expected to experience stock appreciation rates of 30% over the same time horizon.

17. Acme brand aspirin claims to be the best headache relief available in the market today. To prove this claim, Acme called 10 people and asked them their thoughts on headache relief products. All 10 of them stated that they unequivocally use Acme brand aspirin on a regular basis and that they believe it to be the best headache relief available in the market today.

Which of the following would most weaken this argument?

A. Acme brand aspirin is highly addictive.
B. The 10 people called were married to the company's top 10 executives, and they were coached on what to say.
C. Most people choose to suffer silently through their headaches and take no medicines whatsoever.
D. This survey was conducted by an independent company.
E. The 10 people were selected at random.

18. My neighbour's dogs bark and howl every time their owner lets them outside. My CPA told me that dogs tend to bark and howl when they see birds resting in the top branches of their favourite trees. I personally believe they bark and howl because they enjoy disrupting my meditations.

Which of the following can be inferred from the preceding passage?

A. The dogs must be abused by their owners.
B. The dogs' owners do not care how they are viewed by their neighbours.
C. There are many pedestrians who walk by this neighbour's house, and the dogs are starving for attention.
D. The dogs enjoy being outside.
E. The dogs will bark and howl at 3 a.m. if they are outside at that time.

19. Most citizens are very conscientious about observing a law when they can see the reason behind it. For instance, there has been very little need to actively enforce the recently-implemented law that increased the penalty for motorists caught leaving a gas station without paying for gas they had pumped into their vehicles. This is because citizens are very conscientious of the high cost of gasoline and they know that stealing gas will only further increase the price of gasoline for everyone.

Which of the following statements would the author of this passage be most likely to believe?

A. The increased penalty alone is a significant motivation for most citizens to obey the law.
B. There are still too many inconsiderate citizens in the local community.
C. High gasoline prices can be brought down if everyone does his or her part and pays for the gasoline they use at the pumps.
D. Society should make an effort to teach citizens the reasons for its laws. People would be more likely to speed on a stretch of deserted highway than to not pay for gasoline.

20. Nearly one in three subscribers to Financial Forecaster is a millionaire, and over half are in top management. Shouldn't you subscribe to Financial Forecaster now? A reader who is neither a millionaire nor in top management would be most likely to act in accordance with the advertisement's suggestion if he or she drew which of the following questionable conclusions invited by the advertisement?

A. Among finance-related periodicals. Financial Forecaster provides the most detailed financial information.
B. Top managers cannot do their jobs properly without reading Financial Forecaster.
C. The advertisement is placed where those, who will be likely to read it, are millionaires.
D. The subscribers mentioned were helped to become millionaires or join top management by reading Financial Forecaster.
E. Only those who will in fact become millionaires, or at least top managers, will read the advertisement.

ANSWERS

1	2	3	4	5	6	7	8	9	10
D	C	E	C	E	A	D	B	B	B
11	**12**	**13**	**14**	**15**	**16**	**17**	**18**	**19**	**20**
C	E	C	C	B	A	B	D	D	D

☆☆☆☆☆☆

2. Distinguishing Arguments

TYPE-I

Directions (Q. 1–30) : *In making decisions about important questions, it is desirable to be able to distinguish between 'strong' arguments and 'weak' arguments. 'Strong' arguments must be both important and directly related to the question. 'Weak' arguments may not be directly related to the question and may be of minor importance or may be related to the trivial aspects of the question.*

Each question below is followed by two arguments numbered I and II. You have to decide which of the arguments is a 'strong' argument and which is a 'weak' argument.

Give answer:

- (A) If only argument I is strong
- (B) If only argument II is strong
- (C) If either I or II is strong
- (D) If neither I nor II is strong and
- (E) If both I and II are strong.

1. **Statement:** Should all the drugs patented and manufactured in Western countries be first tried out on sample basis before giving licence for sale to general public in India?
   Arguments:
   I. Yes. Many such drugs require different doses and duration for Indian population and hence it is necessary.
   II. No. This is just not feasible and hence cannot be implemented.

2. **Statement:** Should India give away Kashmir to Pakistan?
   Arguments:
   I. No. Kashmir is a beautiful state. It earns a lot of foreign exchange for India.
   II. Yes. This would help settle conflicts.

3. **Statement:** Should Indian scientists working abroad be called back to India?
   Arguments:
   I. Yes. They must serve the motherland first and forget about discoveries, honours, facilities and all.
   II. No. We have enough talent; let them stay where they want.

4. **Statement:** Should cottage industries be encouraged in rural areas?
   Arguments:
   I. Yes. Rural people are creative.
   II. Yes. This would help to solve the problem of unemployment to some extent.

5. **Statement:** Should there be an upper age limit of 65 years for contesting Parliamentary/Legislative Assembly elections?
   Arguments:
   I. Yes. Generally, people above the age of 65 lose their dynamism and will power.
   II. No. The life span is so increased that people remain physically and mentally active even up to the age of 80.

6. **Statement:** Should articles of only deserving authors be allowed to be published?
   Arguments:
   I. Yes. It will save a lot of paper which is in short supply.
   II. No. It is not possible to draw a line between the deserving and the undeserving.

7. **Statement:** Should the prestigious people who have committed crime unknowingly, be met with special treatment?
   Arguments:
   I. Yes. The prestigious people do not commit crime intentionally.
   II. No. It is our policy that everybody is equal before the law.

8. **Statement:** Can pollution be controlled?
   Arguments:
   I. Yes. If everyone realizes the hazards it may create and cooperates to get rid of it, pollution may be controlled.
   II. No. The crowded highways, factories and industries and an ever-growing population eager to acquire more and more land for constructing houses are beyond control.

9. **Statement:** Should the railways in India be privatized in a phased manner like other public sector enterprises?
Arguments:
I. Yes. This is the only way to bring in competitiveness and provide better services to the public.
II. No. This will pose a threat to the national security of our country as multinationals will enter into the fray.

10. **Statement:** Should all the unauthorized structures in the city be demolished?
Arguments:
I. No. Where will the people residing in such houses live?
II. Yes. This will give a clear message to general public and they will refrain from constructing unauthorized buildings.

11. **Statement:** Is buying things on instalments profitable to the customer?
Arguments:
I. Yes. He has to pay less.
II. No, paying instalments upsets the family budget.

12. **Statement:** Should adult education programme be given priority over compulsory education programme?
Arguments:
I. No. It will also help in success of compulsory education programme.
II. Yes. It will help to eliminate the adult illiteracy.

13. **Statement:** Should Government close down loss-making public sector enterprises?
Arguments:
I. No. All employees will lose their jobs, security and earning, what would they do?
II. Yes. In a competitive world the rule is 'survival of the fittest'.

14. **Statement:** Should there be a cap on maximum number of contestants for parliamentary elections in any constituency?
Arguments:
I. Yes. This will make the parliamentary elections more meaningful as the voters can make a considered judgement for casting their vote.
II. No. In a democracy any person fulfilling the eligibility criteria can contest parliamentary elections and there should be no restrictions.

15. **Statement:** Should so much money be spent on advertisements?
Arguments:
I. Yes. It is an essential concomitant in a capitalist economy.
II. No. It leads to wastage of resources.

16. **Statement:** Should 'computer knowledge' be made a compulsory subject for all the students at secondary school level?
Arguments:
I. No, our need is 'bread' for everyone, we cannot follow western models.
II. Yes. We cannot compete in the international market without equipping our children with computers.

17. **Statement:** Should there be uniforms for students in the colleges in India as in the schools?
Arguments:
I. Yes, this will improve the ambience of the colleges as all the students will be decently dressed.
II. No. The college students should not be regimented and they should be left to choose their clothes for coming to the college.

18. **Statement:** Should India engage into a dialogue with neighbouring countries to stop cross border tension?
Arguments:
I. Yes. This is the only way to reduce the cross border terrorism and stop loss of innocent lives.
II. No. Neighbouring countries cannot be relied upon in such matters, they may still engage in subversive activities.

19. **Statement:** Should there be a world government?
Arguments:
I. Yes. It will help in eliminating tensions among the nations.
II. No. Then, only the developed countries will dominate in the government.

20. **Statement:** Should India become a permanent member of UN's Security Council?
Arguments:
I. Yes. India has emerged as a country which loves peace and amity.
II. No. Let us first solve problems of our own people like poverty, malnutrition.

21. **Statement:** Should fashionable dresses be banned?
Arguments:
I. Yes. Fashions keep changing and hence consumption of cloth increases.
II. No. Fashionable clothes are a person's self expression and therefore his/her fundamental right.

22. **Statement:** Should there be a ceiling on the salary of top executives of multinationals in our country?
Arguments:
I. Yes. Otherwise it would lead to unhealthy competition and our own industry would not be able to withstand that.
II. No. With the accent on liberalization of economy, any such move would be counter-productive. Once the economy picks up, this disparity will be reduced.

23. Statement: Should children be legally made responsible to take care of their parents during their old age?
Arguments:
I. Yes. Such matter can only be solved by legal means.
II. Yes. Only this will bring some relief to poor parents.

24. Statement: Should judiciary be independent of the executive?
Arguments:
I. Yes. This would help to curb the unlawful activities of the executive.
II. No. The executive would not be able to take bold measures.

25. Statement: Are nuclear families better than joint families?
Arguments:
I. No. Joint families ensure security and also reduce the burden of work.
II. Yes. Nuclear families ensure greater freedom.

26. Statement: Should government stop spending huge amounts of money on international sports?
Arguments:
I. Yes. This money can be utilized for upliftment of the poor.
II. No. Sports persons will be frustrated and will not get international exposure.

27. Statement: Should there be compulsory medical examination of both the man and the woman before they marry each other?
Arguments:
I. No. This is an intrusion to the privacy of an individual and hence cannot be tolerated.
II. Yes. This will substantially reduce the risk of giving birth to children with serious ailments.

28. Statement: Should the sex determination test during pregnancy be completely banned?
Arguments:
I. Yes. This leads to indiscriminate female foeticide and eventually will lead to social imbalance.
II. No. People have a right to know about their unborn child.

29. Statement: Should persons convicted of criminal offences in the past be allowed to contest elections in India?
Arguments:
I. No. Such persons cannot serve the cause of the people and country.
II. Yes. It is democracy - let people decide whom to vote.

30. Statement: Should officers accepting bribe be punished?
Arguments:
I. No. Certain circumstances may have compelled them to take bribe.
II. Yes. They should do the job they are entrusted with, honestly.

TYPE-II

Directions (Q. 31–40): *Each question below is followed by three or four arguments numbered I, II, III and IV. You have to decide which of the argument(s) is/are 'strong' argument(s) and which is/are 'weak' argument(s).*
Give answer:
(A) If only argument II is strong
(B) If only argument III is strong
(C) If only arguments II and III are strong.
(D) If all arguments are strong
(E) None of these

31. Statement: Should people with educational qualification higher than the optimum requirements be debarred from seeking jobs?
Arguments:
I. No. It will further aggravate the problem of educated unemployment.
II. Yes. It creates complexes among employees and affects the work adversely.
III. No. This goes against the basic rights of the individuals.
IV. Yes. This will increase productivity.

32. Statement: Should all the school teachers be debarred from giving private tuitions?
Arguments:
I. No. The needy students will be deprived of the expertise of these teachers.
II. Yes. This is an injustice to the unemployed educated people who can earn their living by giving tuitions.
III. Yes. Only then the quality of teaching in schools will improve.
IV. Yes. Now salary of these teachers is reasonable.

33. Statement: Should education be made compulsory for all children up to the age of 14?
Arguments:
I. Yes. This will help to eradicate the system of forced employment of these children.
II. Yes. This is an effective way to make the entire population educated.
III. No. We do not have adequate infrastructure to educate the entire population.
IV. Yes. This would increase the standard of living.

34. Statement: Is caste-based reservation policy in professional colleges justified?

Arguments:

I. Yes. The step is a must to bring the underprivileged at par with the privileged ones.

II. No. It obstructs the establishment of a classless society.

III. Yes. This will help the backward castes and classes of people to come out of the oppression of upper caste people.

35. Statement: Should all the management institutes in the country be brought under government control?

Arguments:

I. No. The government does not have adequate resources to run such institutes effectively.

II. No. Each institute should be given freedom to function on its own.

III. Yes. This will enable to have standardized education for all the students.

IV. Yes. Only then the quality of education would be improved.

36. Statement: Should the number of holidays of government employees be reduced?

Arguments:

I. Yes. Our government employees are having the maximum number of holidays among the countries of the world.

II. Yes. It is a sign of British legacy, why should we carry it further?

III. Yes. It will speed up work and all the pending jobs can be completed well in time.

IV. No. Employees must be given ample spare time to spend with their families.

37. Statement: Should all those, who are convicted for heinous crimes like murder or rape, beyond all reasonable doubts be given capital punishment or death penalty?

Arguments:

I. No. The death penalty should be given only in very rare and exceptional cases.

II. Yes. This is the only way to punish such people who take others' lives or indulge in inhuman activities.

III. Yes. Such severe punishments only will make people refrain from such heinous acts and the society will be safer.

IV. No. Those who are repentant for the crime they committed should be given a chance to improve and lead a normal life.

38. Statement: Should the government ban all forms of protests including strikes and processions?

Arguments:

I. Yes. This is the only way to teach discipline to the employees.

II. No. Government cannot deprive its citizens of their basic rights.

III. Yes. This is the only way to ensure maximum productivity without disruption of work.

39. Statement: Should mercy death be legalized, *i.e.*, all those who are suffering from terminal diseases be allowed to end their lives if they so desire?

Arguments:

I. No. Nobody should be allowed to end his/her life at his/her will as this goes against the basic tenets of humanity.

II. Yes. Patients undergoing terrible suffering and having absolutely no chance of recovery should be liberated from suffering through mercy death.

III. No. Even mercy death is a sort of killing and killing can never be legalized.

40. Statement: Should women be given equal opportunity in the matter of employment in every field?

Arguments:

I. Yes. They are equally capable.

II. No. They have to shoulder household responsibilities.

III. Yes. They should also go to the outside world.

ANSWERS

1	2	3	4	5	6	7	8	9	10
A	A	D	B	D	B	B	C	D	B
11	**12**	**13**	**14**	**15**	**16**	**17**	**18**	**19**	**20**
D	B	A	E	A	B	B	A	B	A
21	**22**	**23**	**24**	**25**	**26**	**27**	**28**	**29**	**30**
B	B	D	A	E	B	B	A	A	B
31	**32**	**33**	**34**	**35**	**36**	**37**	**38**	**39**	**40**
B	E	A	A	E	B	B	C	D	C

EXPLANATORY ANSWERS

1. Clearly, health of the citizens is an issue of major concern for the Government. So, a product like drugs, must be first studied and tested in the Indian context before giving licence for its sale. So, only argument I holds strong.

2. Clearly, India cannot part with a state which is a major foreign exchange earner to it. So, argument I holds strong. Further, giving away a piece of land unconditionally and unreasonably is no solution to settle disputes. So, argument II is vague.

3. Clearly, every person must be free to work wherever he wants and no compulsion should be made to confine one to one's own country. So, argument I is vague. However, talented scientists can be of great benefit to the nation and some alternatives as special incentives or better prospects may be made available to them to retain them within their motherland. So, argument II also does not hold.

4. Clearly, cottage industries need to be promoted to create more job opportunities for rural people in the villages themselves. The reason that rural people are creative is vague. So, only argument II holds.

5. The age of a person is no criterion for judging his mental capabilities and administrative qualities. So, none of the arguments holds strong.

6. Clearly, I does not provide a strong reason in support of the statement. Also, it is not possible to analyze the really deserving and not deserving. So, argument II holds strong.

7. The Constitution of India has laid down the doctrine of 'equality before the law'. So, argument II holds strong. Also, we cannot judge the intentions of a person behind committing a crime. So, argument I is vague.

8. The control of pollution, on one hand, seems to be impossible because of the ever-growing needs and the disconcern of the people but, on the other hand, the control is possible by a joint effort. So, either of the arguments will hold strong.

9. Privatization would no doubt lead to better services. But saying that this is the 'only way' is wrong. So, argument I does not hold. Argument II also seems to be vague.

10. The demolition of unauthorized buildings would teach a lesson to the unscrupulous builders and also serve as a warning for the citizens not to indulge in such activities in the future. This is essential, as unauthorized constructions impose undue burden on the city's infrastructure. So, only argument II holds strong.

11. In buying things on instalments, a customer has to pay more as the interest is also included. So, argument I does not hold. Moreover, one who buys an item on instalments maintains his future budget accordingly as he is well acquainted with when and how much he has to pay, beforehand. So, argument II is also not valid.

12. Clearly, argument I gives a reason in support of the statement and so it does not hold strong against it. The adult education programme needs to be given priority because it shall eliminate adult illiteracy and thus help in further spread of education. So, only argument II is strong enough.

13. Closing down public-sector enterprises will definitely throw the engaged persons out of employment. So, argument I holds. Also, closing down is no solution for a loss-making enterprise. Rather, its causes of failure should be studied, analyzed and the essential reforms implemented. Even if this does not work out, the enterprise may be privatized. So, argument II is vague.

14. Clearly, if there were less candidates, the voters would find it easy to make a choice. So, argument I holds. Also, every person satisfying the conditions laid down by the constitution must be given an opportunity and should not be denied the same just to cut down the number of candidates. So, argument II also holds strong.

15. Clearly, the advertisements are the means to introduce people with the product and its advantages. So, argument I holds strong. But argument II is vague because advertisements are an investment for better gain and not a wastage.

16. Nowadays, computers have entered all walks of life and children need to be prepared for the same. So, argument II is strong. Argument I holds no relevance.

17. Clearly, after being in strict discipline and following a formal dress code in the schools for so many years, the students must be granted some liberty in college life, as they have to take on the responsibilities of life, next. Besides, schools adopt uniforms to take care of the security of the child—an aspect which doesn't matter much in the colleges. So, argument II holds strong. Also, the environment of the college depends on the students' dedication and etiquettes and not on their uniforms. So, argument I is vague.

18. Clearly, peaceful settlement through mutual agreement is the best option, whatever be the issue. So, argument I holds strong. Moreover, the problem indicated in argument II can be curbed by constant check and vigilance. So, argument II seems to be vague.

19. Clearly, a world government cannot eliminate tensions among nations because it will also have the ruling group and the opposition group. Further, the more powerful and diplomatic shall rule the world according to their interests. So, only argument II holds.

20. A peace-loving nation like India can well join an international forum which seeks to bring different nations on friendly terms with each other. So, argument I holds strong. Argument II highlights a different aspect. The internal problems of a nation should not debar it from strengthening international ties. So, argument II is vague.

21. Clearly, imposing ban on fashionable dresses will be a restriction on the personal choice and hence the right to freedom of an individual. So, only argument II is strong.

22. In the absence of such a ceiling, the companies would be involved in a mutual competition of salaries, in a bid to attract the most competent professionals. So, argument I holds. Also, the prospects of increase in salary would encourage the officials to perform better in the interest of the company they serve, which would otherwise not be so if a ceiling is imposed. So, argument II also holds strong.

23. Taking care of the parents is a moral duty of the children and cannot be thrust upon them legally, nor such a compulsion can ensure good care of the old people. So, none of the arguments holds strong.

24. Clearly, independent judiciary is necessary for impartial judgement so that the executive does not take wrong measures. So, only argument I holds.

25. Clearly, with so many people around in a joint family, there is more security. Also, work is shared. So, argument I holds. In nuclear families, there are lesser number of people and so lesser responsibilities and more freedom. Thus, II also holds.

26. Clearly, spending money on sports cannot be avoided merely because it can be spent on socio-economic problems. So, argument I does not hold. Also, if the expenses on sports are curtailed, the sports persons would face lack of facilities and training and our country will lag behind in the international sports competitions. So, argument II holds.

27. Clearly, such a step would help to prevent the growth of diseases like AIDS. So, only argument II is strong.

28. Parents indulging in sex determination of their unborn child generally do so as they want only a boy child and do away with a girl child. So, argument I holds. Also, people have a right to know only about the health, development and general well-being of the child before its birth, and not the sex. So, argument II does not hold strong.

29. Clearly, persons with criminal background cannot stand to serve as the representatives of the common people. So, they should not be allowed to contest elections. Thus, only argument I holds, while II does not.

30. Clearly, officers are paid duly for the jobs they do. So, they must do it honestly. Thus, argument II alone holds.

31. The issue discussed in the statement is nowhere related to increase in unemployment, as the number of vacancies filled in, will remain the same. Also, in a working place, it is the performance of the individual that matters and that makes him more or less wanted, and not his educational qualifications. So, neither argument I nor II holds strong. Besides, the needs of a job are laid down in the desired qualifications for the job. So, recruitment of more qualified people cannot augment productivity. Thus, argument IV also does not hold strong. However, it is the right of an individual to get the post for which he fulfils the eligibility criteria, whatever be his extra merits. Hence, argument III holds strong.

32. Only argument III is strong. The lure of earning private tuitions reduces the efforts and devotion of the teachers towards the students in schools. So, if tuitions are banned, students can benefit from their teachers' knowledge in the school itself. So, argument III holds strong while I does not. However, a person cannot be barred from earning more just because he already has a good salary. So, argument IV is vague. Further, the unemployed people thriving on tuitions can survive with the school teachers holding tuitions too, if they are capable enough to guide the students well. So, argument II also does not hold strong.

33. Clearly, today's children are to make up future citizens of the country and so it is absolutely essential to make them learned, more responsible, more innovative and self-dependent by imparting them education. So, argument II holds strong while I and IV do not. Besides, the goal of literacy cannot be denied for want of infrastructure. So, argument III also does not hold.

34. Clearly, capability is an essential criteria for a profession and reservation cannot ensure capable workers. So, neither I nor III holds strong. However, making one caste more privileged than the other through reservations would hinder the objectives of a classless society. So, argument II holds strong.

35. Clearly, the government can pool up resources to run such institutes, if that can benefit the citizens. So, argument I does not hold strong. Argument II does not provide any convincing reason. Also, it is not obligatory that government control over the institutes would ensure better education than that at present. So, both argument III and IV also do not hold.

36. Reducing the number of holidays just because no other country gives so many holidays or it is a feature of a certain system which we have renounced, does not seem convincing. So, neither argument I nor II holds strong. However, this step would surely help to reduce the backlog of pending cases and dispense with the new cases much more quickly than before. So, argument III holds strong. Even if the holidays are reduced, only the avoidable or seemingly unnecessary ones shall be cut short and the national holidays shall still remain to enjoy. So, argument IV also does not hold.

37. Clearly, a person committing a heinous crime like murder or rape should be so punished as to set an example for others not to attempt such acts in future. So, argument III holds strong. Argument I is vague while the use of the word 'only' in argument II makes it weak. Also, it cannot be assured whether a criminal is really repentant of his acts or not, he may also exhibit so just to get rid of punishment. So, argument IV also does not hold.

38. Clearly, strike is not a means of indiscipline but only a practice in which the workers exercise their fundamental right to voice their protest against the atrocities of the management. So, argument I is vague while II holds. Also, the option of resorting to strikes often aggravates petty issues and disrupts work for long periods, thus affecting productivity. So, argument III also holds strong.

39. Clearly, mercy death will serve as a liberation to those to whom living is more difficult and painful. But then, it is an inhuman act and does not appeal. So, both arguments II and III hold strong. Besides, it becomes our moral duty to encourage such people to live their lives to the fullest and support them through the crisis and not demoralize them by allowing them to die if they wish to. Hence, argument I also holds strong.

40. In present times, women are being imparted education at par with the men and are capable of competing with them in all professions and fields. So, argument II holds. Also, women cannot be confined to the household and kept away from the challenges of the outside world against their will. They too have the right to be self-dependent. Besides, present-day women are well looking to outside jobs together with the household jobs. So, argument III holds while I does not.

☆☆☆☆☆☆

3. Statement and Assumptions

Directions (Q. 1–35): *In each question below a statement is given followed by two assumptions numbered I and II. You have to consider the statement and the following assumptions and decide which of the assumptions is implicit in the statement.*

Give answer

- (A) If only assumption I is implicit
- (B) If only assumption II is implicit
- (C) If either I or II is implicit
- (D) If neither I nor II is implicit
- (E) If both I and II are implicit.

1. **Statement:** Be humble even after being victorious.
   Assumptions:
   I. Many people are humble after being victorious.
   II. Generally people are not humble.

2. **Statement:** The government has decided to pay compensation to the tune of ₹ 1 lakh to the family members of those who are killed in railway accidents.
   Assumptions:
   I. The government has enough funds to meet the expenses due to compensation.
   II. There may be reduction in incidents of railway accidents in near future.

3. **Statement:** Films have become indispensable for the entertainment of people.
   Assumptions:
   I. Films are the only media of entertainment.
   II. People enjoy films.

4. **Statement:** Of all the newspapers published in Mumbai, readership of the 'Times' is the largest in the Metropolis.
   Assumptions:
   I. 'Times' is not popular in mofussil areas.
   II. 'Times' has the popular feature of cartoons on burning social and political issues.

5. **Statement:** Apart from the entertainment value of television, its educational value cannot be ignored.
   Assumptions:
   I. People take television to be a means of entertainment only.
   II. The educational value of television is not realised properly.

6. **Statement:** The State government has decided to appoint four thousand primary school teachers during the next financial year.
   Assumptions:
   I. There are enough schools in the state to accommodate four thousand additional primary school teachers.
   II. The eligible candidates may not be interested to apply, as the government may not finally appoint such a large number of primary school teachers.

7. **Statement:** A warning in a train compartment—"To stop train, pull chain. Penalty for improper use ₹ 500."
   Assumptions:
   I. Some people misuse the alarm chain.
   II. On certain occasions, people may want to stop a running train.

8. **Statement:** If it is easy to become an engineer, I don't want to be an engineer.
   Assumptions:
   I. An individual aspires to be a professional.
   II. One desires to achieve a thing which is hard earned.

9. **Statement:** The concession in rail fares for a journey to hill stations has been cancelled because it is not needed for people who can spend their holidays there.
   Assumptions:
   I. Railways should give concession only to needy persons.
   II. Railways should not encourage people to spend their holidays at hill stations.

10. **Statement:** "The bridge was built at the cost of ₹ 128 crores and even civil bus service is not utilizing it, what a pity to see it grossly underutilized." A citizen's view on a new flyover linking east and west sides of a suburb.

Assumptions:

I. The building of such bridges does not serve any public objective.

II. There has to be some accountability and utility of money spent on public projects.

11. Statement: Beware of dogs, our dogs do not bark, but they are trained to distinguish between genuine guests and intruders.

Assumptions:

I. Barking dogs bite rarely.

II. Our dogs could be dangerous for intruders.

12. Statement: Because of the large number of potholes in road X, reaching airport in time has become difficult.

Assumptions:

I. Reaching airport in time may not always be necessary.

II. There is no other convenient road to the airport.

13. Statement: Safety and health practices in many Indian companies are well below the international standards.

Assumptions:

I. International standards of health and safety are ideal and unrealistic.

II. Indian organizations do not consider safety and health management as their prime social responsibility.

14. Statement: Greater public participation results in good civic governance. Statement of Municipal Commissioner of City A.

Assumptions:

I. The municipal office is not competent to effect good civic administration.

II. Good civic governance is a matter of collective will and effort of the people and administration.

15. Statement: The regulatory authority has set up a review committee to find out the reasons for unstable stock prices.

Assumptions:

I. The investors may regain confidence in stock market by this decision.

II. The review committee has the expertise to find out the causes for volatility in the stock market.

16. Statement: 'Please note that the company will provide accommodation to only outside candidates if selected.' A condition in an advertisement.

Assumptions:

I. The local candidates would be having some other arrangement for their stay.

II. The company plans to select only local candidates.

17. Statement: Cases of food poisoning due to consumption of liquor are increasing in rural areas.

Assumptions:

I. Percentage of people consuming liquor is more in rural areas.

II. There are many unauthorized spurious liquor shops in the rural areas.

18. Statement: Shalini made an application to the bank for a loan of ₹ 1,80,000 by mortgaging her house to the bank and promised to repay it within five years.

Assumptions:

I. The bank has a practice of granting loans for ₹ 1,00,000 and above.

II. The bank accepts house as collateral security against such loans.

19. Statement: "Computer education should start at schools itself."

Assumptions:

I. Learning computers is easy.

II. Computer education fetches jobs easily.

20. Statement: "As there is a great demand, every person seeking tickets of the programme, will be given only five tickets."

Assumptions:

I. The organizers are not keen on selling the tickets.

II. No one is interested in getting more than five tickets.

21. Statement: Please consult us before making any decision on investment.

Assumptions:

I. You may take a wrong decision if you don't consult us.

II. It is important to take a right decision.

22. Statement: The Parent Teacher Association (PTA) of a school has informed the Principal that they will not send their children to the school unless the school-authority reduces the fees with immediate effect.

Assumptions:

I. Majority of the parents may agree with the PTA and may not send their wards with the school.

II. The school authority may accede to the demand of the PTA and reduce the fees.

23. Statement: The company has the right to reject any application form without furnishing any reason while sorting the list of candidates for interview—A condition mentioned in the employment notice.

Assumptions:

I. It is desirable to call only eligible candidates for interview.

II. The company believes in following impartial practice in all its functions.

24. Statement: Kartik left for Delhi on Tuesday by train to attend a function to be held on Friday at his uncle's house in Delhi.

Assumptions:

I. Kartik may reach Delhi on Wednesday.

II. Kartik may reach Delhi before Friday.

25. Statement: "Avon Cycles — Fast, easy to ride, impressive, reliable, crafted and up-to-date automation." An advertisement.

Assumptions:

I. There is no other cycle with any of these features.

II. People do not bother about the cost.

26. Statement: The entire north India, including Delhi and the neighbouring states remained 'powerless' the whole day of 19th December as the northern grid supplying electricity to the seven states collapsed yet again.

Assumptions:

1. The northern grid had collapsed earlier.
2. The grid system of providing electricity to a group of states is an ineffective type of power supply system.

27. Statement: It is through participative management policy alone that indiscipline in our industries can be contained and a quality of life can be ensured to the worker.

Assumptions:

I. Quality of life in our industries is better.

II. Indiscipline results in poor quality of life.

28. Statement: Municipal Corporation has decided to ban the entry of vehicles from sub-urban areas to the main city through main routes during peak hours to avoid traffic congestion.

Assumptions:

I. The people of sub-urban areas should not bring their vehicles during peak hours.

II. There is no traffic congestion by the vehicles of people residing in the main city.

29. Statement: World Health Organisation has decided to double its assistance to various health programmes in India as per-capita expenditure on health in India is very low compared to many other countries.

Assumptions:

I. The enhanced assistance may substantially increase the per-capita expenditure on health in India and bring it on a par with other countries.

II. The Government funding is less than adequate to provide medical facilities in India.

30. Statement: The General Administration Department has issued a circular to all the employees informing them that henceforth the employees can avail their lunch break at any of the half-hour slots between 1.00 p.m. and 2.30 p.m.

Assumptions:

I. The employees may welcome the decision and avail lunch break at different time slots.

II. There may not be any break in the work of the organization as the employees will have their lunch break at different time slots.

31. Statement: Government aided schools should have uniformity in charging various fees.

Assumptions:

I. The Government's subsidy comes from the money collected through taxes from people.

II. The Government while giving subsidy may have stipulated certain uniform conditions regarding fees.

32. Statement: In spite of less than normal rainfall in the catchment areas during the first two months of monsoon of the lakes supplying water to the city, the authority has not yet affected any cut in the water supply to the city.

Assumptions:

I. The rainfall during the remaining period of the monsoon may be adequate for normal water supply.

II. The present water level of the lakes supplying water to the city may be adequate for normal supply.

33. Statement: The head of the organization congratulated the entire staff in his speech for their sincere effort to bring down the deficit and urged them to give their best for attaining a more profitable position in future.

Assumptions:

I. The employees may get motivated and will maintain and if possible, enhance their present level of work.

II. The employees may now relax and slow down in their day to day work as there is no immediate threat of huge deficit.

34. Statement: The host in one of the popular T.V. programmes announced that the channel will contact the viewers between 9.00 a.m. to 6.00 p.m. on weekdays and the lucky ones will be given fabulous prizes.

Assumptions:

I. The people may remain indoors to receive the phone call.

II. More people may start watching the programme.

35. Statement: There is big boom in drug business and a number of jhuggi-jhopari dwellers in Delhi can be seen pedalling with small pouches of smack and brown sugar.

Assumptions:

I. Drug addiction is increasing in the country, specially in the capital.

II. Most of the jhuggi-jhopari dwellers would do anything for the money.

ANSWERS

1	2	3	4	5	6	7	8	9	10
B	A	B	D	E	A	E	B	A	B
11	12	13	14	15	16	17	18	19	20
B	B	B	B	E	A	B	E	A	D
21	22	23	24	25	26	27	28	29	30
E	E	A	B	D	A	B	D	E	B
31	32	33	34	35					
B	E	A	E	D					

EXPLANATORY ANSWERS

1. Clearly, nothing is mentioned about the nature of the people. So, assumption I is not implicit. Also, the statement gives an advice of being humble even after being victorious. This means that generally people are not humble. So, assumption II is implicit.

2. Clearly, the amount of compensation must have been decided keeping in mind the monetary position of the Government. So, assumption I is implicit. However, nothing can be said about the frequency of railway accidents in future. So, assumption II is not implicit.

3. 'Films are indispensable' does not mean that they are the only means of entertainment. So, assumption I is not implicit. Clearly, assumption II follows from the statement. So, it is implicit.

4. Neither the volume of readership of the 'Times' in areas other than the Metropolis nor the reason for its huge acclamation is evident from the statement. So, neither assumption I nor II is implicit.

5. The statement makes the first assumption clear though educational value is not to be ignored. So, assumption I is implicit. Educational value must not be ignored also shows that the educational value is not realised properly. So, assumption II is also implicit.

6. Such decisions as given in the statement are taken only after taking the existing vacancies into consideration. So, assumption I implicit while II isn't.

7. Clearly, the penalty is imposed to prevent people from misusing the alarm chain. This means that some people misuse it. So, assumption I is implicit. The alarm chain is provided to stop the running train in times of urgency. So, assumption II is also implicit.

8. Clearly, nothing is mentioned about the professional nature of the job. So, assumption I is not implicit. The statement hints that one rejects a thing that is easy to achieve. So, assumption II is implicit.

9. The statement mentions that concessions should not be given to people who can afford to spend holidays in hill stations. This means it should be given only to needy persons. So, assumption I is implicit. But, II does not follow the statement and is not implicit.

10. Clearly, the statement expresses grave concern over a newly-built flyover not being utilized by public. This implies that such projects need to be taken up only after working out their utility and that the huge expenditure incurred on building such structures is worthwhile only if they prove useful for the public. Thus, only assumption II is implicit.

11. The statement clearly warns the visitors to beware of dogs as they are trained to welcome the guests and intruders differently. So, assumption II is implicit. assumption I is vague and hence, it is not implicit.

12. The statement presents the issue of 'not reaching airport in time' as a problem. This means that reaching airport in time is necessary. So, assumption I is not implicit. Besides, it is mentioned that reaching airport in time has become difficult due to large number of potholes in road X. This implies that road X is the only possible way. So, assumption II is implicit.

13. The statement talks about the safety and health practices in Indian companies being far below international standards. It is clearly a criticism of Indian organizations not paying considerable attention to these aspects. So, assumption II is implicit The international standards demand perfection and are, in no way, non-achievable. So, assumption I is not implicit.

14. The statement stresses on the fact that though civic governance is the task of the municipal body, but all the tasks done come out to be more fruitful if the general public lends a helping hand in the same. So, only assumption II is implicit.

15. Clearly, assumption I mentions the aim for which the step talked about in the statement, has been undertaken while assumption II mentions the essential requirement for it. So, both assumption I and II are implicit.

16. The statement mentions that the company intends to provide accommodation only to outside candidates. This means that local candidates would have to arrange accommodation on their own and that the company may select local as well as outside candidates. Thus, only assumption I is implicit.

17. The statement talks of number of cases of food poisoning due to consumption of liquor and not of the number of cases consuming liquor. So, assumption I is not implicit. Besides, the statement indicates that people in rural areas are getting spurious or low-grade liquor and no check is being kept on shops selling liquor there. So, assumption II is implicit.

18. The fact that Shalini has applied for a loan of ₹ 1,80,000 implies that the bank can grant a loan above ₹ 1,00,000. So, assumption I is implicit. assumption II also follows directly from the statement and so is implicit.

19. Clearly, computer education can be started at the school level only if it is easy. So, assumption I is implicit. In the statement, nothing is mentioned about the link between jobs and computer education. So, assumption II is not implicit.

20. Clearly, the organisers are adopting this policy not to reduce the sale but to cope up with great demand so that everyone can get the ticket. So, assumption I is not implicit. Also, due to great demand, the maximum number of tickets one person can get has been reduced to five. So, assumption II is also not implicit.

21. Clearly, the statement was spoken for fear that the other person may take a wrong decision. So, assumption I is implicit. Again, the statement confirms that it is important to take the right decision. So, assumption II is also implicit.

22. The PTA is an association which would surely reflect the parents' interests and act to get them fulfilled. So, both assumption I and II are implicit.

23. Since the statement talks of the company short-listing the candidates to be called for interview, so assumption I is implicit. However, nothing can be deduced about whether the company would make a partial or fair selection of candidates. So, assumption II is not implicit.

24. Clearly, it cannot be deduced as to which day Kartik would reach Delhi. But Kartik has left for Delhi to attend a function to be held on Friday. So, he must have planned his journey to reach Delhi before Friday. Thus, only assumption II is implicit.

25. The advertisement is for Avon cycles and nothing about the cost or the features of other brands of cycles, are mentioned. So, neither assumption I nor II is implicit.

26. The statement mentions that the northern grid collapsed 'yet again'. This means that it had collapsed earlier also. So, assumption I is implicit. Also, the statement talks of a particular fault in the system but does not condemn the grid system. So, assumption II is not implicit.

27. The statement mentions that participative management policy 'will' provide quality life to the workers. So, assumption I is not implicit. Clearly, the statement mentions that participative management will contain the indiscipline and ensure quality life to workers. So, assumption II is implicit.

28. It is mentioned that entry only through main routes has been banned. So, assumption I is not implicit. Besides, the entry has been banned to reduce the volume of traffic on roads and ease congestion. It could only be done at the entrances to the city and not within the city itself. So, congestion by the city vehicles is unavoidable. Hence, assumption II is also not implicit.

29. The fact that WHO has extended its assistance to India implies that government funding here is not adequate. So, assumption II is implicit. Besides, WHO has decided to provide assistance to health programmes in India keeping in mind the considerably low per-capita expenditure on health. So, assumption I is also implicit.

30. The employees' reaction to the new decision cannot be deduced from the statement. So, assumption I is not implicit. However, assumption II denotes the most probable consequence of the new decision. So, assumption II is implicit.

31. Nothing about the source of Government's subsidy can be deduced from the statement. So, assumption I is not implicit. However, assumption II follows from the statement and so it is implicit.

32. The statement clearly indicates that at present the water level of the lakes is adequate. There is nothing of a shortage to induce a cut in water supply and still there is time to wait and watch the performance of rains during the remaining monsoon period. So, both assumption I and II are implicit.

33. The appreciation received from the head of the organization would surely motivate the employees to keep up their spirits and strive hard for the progress of the organization. So, only assumption I is implicit.

34. Clearly, the organisers of the programme have adopted the viewer interaction scheme and announced prizes for some lucky viewers so that more people are enticed into staying at home and viewing the programme. So, both assumption I and II are implicit.

35. The statement talks of boom in drug business and cites examples from the capital city. This makes I implicit. Further, it is given that most jhuggi-jhopari dwellers are seen to indulge in transactions of drug pouches. This implies that they give in to their lust for money quite easily and do not hesitate to get involved in illegal activities or the same. So, assumption II is implicit.

☆☆☆☆☆☆

4. Courses of Action

Directions (Q. 1–25): *In each question below a statement is given followed by two courses of action numbered I and II. You have to assume everything in the statement to be true and on the basis of the information given in the statement, decide which of the suggested courses of action logically follow(s) for pursuing.*

Give answer

- (A) If only I follows
- (B) If only II follows
- (C) If either I or II follows
- (D) If neither I nor II follows
- (E) If both I and II follow.

1. **Statement:** Since its launching in 1881, Vayudoot has so far accumulated losses amounting to ₹ 153 crore.

   Courses of Action:

   I. Vayudoot should be directed to reduce wasteful expenditure and to increase passenger fare.

   II. An amount of about ₹ 300 crore should be provided to Vayudoot to make the airline economically viable.

2. **Statement:** Exporters in the capital are alleging that commercial banks are violating a Reserve Bank of India directive to operate a post shipment export credit denominated in foreign currency at international rates from January this year.

   Courses of Action:

   I. The officers concerned to the commercial banks are to be suspended.

   II. The RBI should be asked to stop giving such directives to commercial banks.

3. **Statement:** A large number of people die every year due to drinking polluted water during the summer.

   Courses of Action:

   I. The government should make adequate arrangements to provide safe drinking water to all its citizens.

   II. The people should be educated about the dangers of drinking polluted water.

4. **Statement:** If the retired professors of the same institute are also invited to deliberate on restructuring the organisation, their contribution may be beneficial to the institute.

   Courses of Action:

   I. Management may seek opinion of the employees before calling retired professors.

   II. Management should involve experienced people for the systematic restructuring of the organisation.

5. **Statement:** There is an unprecedented increase in migration of villagers to urban areas as repeated crop failures have put them into precarious financial situation.

   Courses of Action:

   I. The villagers should be provided with alternate source of income in their villages which will make them stay put.

   II. The migrated villagers should be provided with jobs in the urban areas to help them survive.

6. **Statement:** Most of those who study in premier engineering colleges in India migrate to developed nations for better prospects in their professional pursuits.

   Courses of Action:

   I. All the students joining these colleges should be asked to sign a bond at the time of admission to the effect that they will remain in India at least for ten years after they complete education.

   II. All those students who desire to settle in the developed nations should be asked to pay entire cost of their education which the government subsidises.

7. **Statement:** Doordarshan is concerned about the quality of its programmes particularly in view of stiff competition it is facing from STAR and other satellite TV channels and is contemplating various measures to attract talents for its programmes.

Courses of Action:

I. In an effort to attract talents the Doordarshan has decided to revise its fee structure for the artists.

II. The fee structure should not be revised until other electronic media also revise it.

8. Statement: The Chairman stressed the need for making education system more flexible and regretted that the curriculum has not been revised in keeping with the pace of the changes taking place.

Courses of Action:

I. Curriculum should be reviewed and revised periodically.

II. System of education should be made more flexible.

9. Statement: The availability of imported fruits has increased in the indigenous market and so the demand for indigenous fruits has been decreased.

Courses of Action:

I. To help the indigenous producers of fruits, the Government should impose high import duty on these fruits, even if these are not of good quality.

II. The fruit vendors should stop selling imported fruits. So that the demand for indigenous fruits would be increased.

10. Statement: On an average, about twenty people are run over by trains and die every day while crossing the railway tracks through the level crossing.

Courses of Action:

I. The railway authorities should be instructed to close all the level crossings.

II. Those who are found crossing the tracks, when the gates are closed, should be fined heavily.

11. Statement: It is necessary to adopt suitable measures to prevent repetition of bad debts by learning from the past experiences of mounting non-performing assets of banks.

Courses of Action:

I. Before granting loan to customers, their eligibility for loan should be evaluated strictly.

II. To ensure the payment of instalments of loan, the work, for which loan was granted, should be supervised minutely on regular basis.

12. Statement: There has been an unprecedented increase in the number of requests for berths in most of the long distance trains during the current holiday season.

Courses of Action:

I. The railway authority should immediately increase the capacity in each of these trains by attaching additional coaches.

II. The people seeking accommodation should be advised to make their travel plan after the holiday.

13. Statement: It is reported that though Vitamin E present in fresh fruits and vegetables is beneficial for human body, capsule Vitamin E does not have the same effect on human body.

Courses of Action:

I. The sale of capsule Vitamin E should be banned.

II. People should be encouraged to take fresh fruits and vegetables to meet the body's requirement of Vitamin E.

14. Statement: There has been less than forty per cent voter turnout in the recent assembly elections.

Courses of Action:

I. The election commission should cancel the entire election process as the votes cast are not adequate to represent people.

II. The election commission should take away the voting rights of those who did not exercise their rights.

15. Statement: The Committee has criticized the institute for its failure to implement a dozen of regular programmes despite an increase in the staff strength and not drawing up a firm action plan for studies and research.

Courses of Action:

I. The broad objectives of the institute should be re-defined to implement a practical action plan.

II. The institute should give a report on reasons for not having implemented the planned programmes.

16. Statement: India has been continuously experiencing military threats from its neighbouring countries.

Courses of Action:

I. India should engage into an all out war to stop the nagging threats.

II. India should get the neighbours into a serious dialogue to reduce the tension at its borders.

17. Statement: Financial stringency prevented the State Government from paying salaries to its employees since April this year.

Courses of Action:

I. The State Government should immediately curtail the staff strength at least by 30%.

II. The State Government should reduce wasteful expenditure and arrange to pay the salaries of its employees.

18. Statement: Courts take too long in deciding important disputes of various departments.

Courses of Action:

I. Courts should be ordered to speed up matters.

II. Special powers should be granted to officers to settle disputes concerning their department.

19. Statement: Footpaths of a busy road are crowded with vendors selling cheap items.

Courses of Action:

I. The help of police should be sought to drive them away.

II. Some space should be provided to them where they can earn their bread without blocking footpaths.

20. Statement: Many medical and engineering graduates are taking up jobs in administrative services and in banks.

Courses of Action:

I. All the professionals should be advised to refrain from taking up such jobs.

II. The government should appoint a committee to find out the reasons for these professionals taking up such jobs and to suggest remedial measures.

21. Statement: Due to substantial reduction in fares by different airline services, large number of passengers so far travelling by upper classes in trains have switched over to airline services.

Courses of Action:

I. The railways should immediately reduce the fare structure of the upper classes substantially to retain its passengers.

II. The railways should reduce the capacity of upper classes in all the trains to avoid loss.

22. Statement: There has been large number of cases of internet hacking in the recent months creating panic among the internet users.

Courses of Action:

I. The government machinery should make an all out effort to nab those who are responsible and put them behind bars.

II. The internet users should be advised to stay away from using internet till the culprits are caught.

23. Statement : Although the Indian economy is still heavily dependent on agriculture, its share in global agricultural trade is less than the share of agricultural exports to total exports.

Courses of Action :

I. Efforts should be made to increase our agricultural production.

II. The exports of non-agricultural commodities should be reduced.

24. Statement : About 30 to 40 per cent of children who are enrolled, do not attend school on any given day.

Courses of Action :

I. More schools should be started.

II. Reasons for this absenteeism should be found out.

25. Statement : Certain mining industries in Gujarat may come to a standstill because of the notification issued by the Ministry of Environment and Forest banning mining operations and industries alike within 25 kms of National Park, the bird sanctuary and reserve forest areas.

Courses of Action :

I. The Ministry should be asked to immediately withdraw the notification.

II. The Government should make efforts to shift the parks, sanctuaries and reserve forests to other non-mining areas.

ANSWERS

1	2	3	4	5	6	7	8	9	10
A	D	E	B	A	B	A	E	D	B
11	**12**	**13**	**14**	**15**	**16**	**17**	**18**	**19**	**20**
E	A	B	D	E	B	B	E	E	B
21	**22**	**23**	**24**	**25**					
A	A	D	D	D					

EXPLANATORY ANSWERS

1. Clearly, for better economic gain, losses should be reduced and income increased. So, only course I follows.

2. The statement mentions that the commercial banks violate a directive issued by the RBI. The remedy is only to make the banks implement the Act. So, none of the courses follows.

3. The situation demands creating awareness among people about the dangers of drinking polluted water so that they themselves refrain from the same, and at the same time taking steps to provide safe drinking water. So, both the courses follow.

4. Clearly, the statement stresses that the contribution of retired professors shall be beneficial. This means that these people's experience of working in the organisation is helpful. So, only course II follows.

5. Clearly, increased migration would add extra burden on city's infrastructure. So, attempts should be made to make the villagers feel comfortable in the villages itself. So, only course I follows.

6. Clearly, no student can be bound to live and work in the country against their wish. So, course I does not follow. However, it is quite right to recover the extra benefits awarded to students if they do not serve their own country. So, only course II follows.

7. Clearly, the decision to revise its fee structure for artists is taken by Doordarshan as a remedy to the challenging problem that had arisen before it. It cannot wait till other media take action. So, only course I follows.

8. Clearly, the situation demands making the education system more flexible and changing it periodically according to the needs of the time. So, both the courses follow.

9. The ideas suggested in both course I and II represent unfair means to cut competition. The correct way would be to devise methods and techniques such that the indigenous producers could produce better quality fruits and make them available in the market at prices comparable with those of the imported ones. Hence, neither course I nor II follows.

10. The accidents can clearly be prevented by barring people from crossing the tracks when the gates are closed, So, only course II follows.

11. To ensure that debts taken are repaid promptly, the customer's requirements and future prospects ought to be studied and their work constantly checked. Thus, both the courses follow.

12. People cannot be deprived of going to a certain destination merely for lack of berths. Instead it, it is the duty of the railway authority to accommodate all the bookings by all means. So, only course I follows.

13. The statement implies that capsule Vitamin E does not function so effectively as natural Vitamin E. Since no negative effect of capsule Vitamin E is mentioned, so course I does not follow. Hence, only course II follows.

14. Re-election would demand repeated expenses and following course II would reduce the voter base permanently. Instead, awareness should be created among the people to use their right to vote effectively. So, neither course I nor II follows.

15. The problem is that despite an increase in staff strength, the institute has failed in its objective of implementing its plan. So, either there should be reasons for the failure or the plans are a failure and must be revised for practical implementation. Thus, both the courses follow.

16. Clearly, war is the last resort. First, peaceful talks and negotiations should be indulged in, to settle the issues of dispute. So, only course II follows.

17. Clearly, curtailing of the staff strength will only increase the panic and discontent, and the satisfaction of the employees is a must. So, the Government should arrange for payment of wages. Thus, only course II follows.

18. Clearly, either the work in the court needs to be sped up or the system be reorganised so that more number of problems can be resolved at the lower levels itself, to provide speedy justice to the people. So, both the courses follow.

19. Crowding on footpaths is a great inconvenience for walkers. So, stern action needs to be taken to remove the vendors. But at the same time these people ought to be provided alternative means of livelihood. So, both the courses follow.

20. Following course I would be an infringement of the right to freedom of individuals. However, if the lacking of their respective fields are found out and removed, the professionals would surely give up the idea of opting for other jobs. Hence, only course II follows.

21. Airlines, being convenient and faster means of transport, people would surely prefer it to the railways if there is a marginal difference between the fares. Hence, a considerable gap between the two fares is a must for the railways. So, course I follows. Following course II would reduce the volume of passengers. Hence, course II does not follow.

22. Clearly, internet users should not suffer on account of certain individuals who indulge in internet hacking. However, such wrong-doers ought to be penalised so that there are no hassles in the use of internet. So, only course I follows.

23. India's share in global agricultural trade is less than the share of agricultural exports to total exports. Therefore, there is no necessity of increasing the agricultural production. Reducing the exports of non-agricultural commodity will not affect the share of agricultural exports. So, neither course of action follows.

24. About 30 to 40 per cent of enrolled children do not attend schools. Therefore, the decision to start more schools is pointless. The statement does not mention that a particular group of children do not attend schools. This means the percentage of absent children comprises of various children who are absent at different times. There cannot be specific reasons for this absenteeism. So, neither course of action follows.

25. The department cannot withdraw the notification because environment pollution must be checked around the sanctuary and reserve forest areas. Further, it is coherent to shift the mining industries. So, neither course of action follows.

☆☆☆☆☆

5. Cause and Effect

Directions (Q. 1–20): *In each of the questions below two statements I and II are given. These statements may be either independent causes or may be effects of independent causes or a common cause. One of these statements may be the effect of the other statements. Read both the statements and decide which of the following answer choice correctly depicts the relationship between these two statements.*

Mark Answer

(A) If statement I is the cause and statement II is its effect.
(B) If statement II is the cause and statement I is its effect.
(C) If both the statements I and II are independent causes.
(D) If both the statements I and II are effects of independent causes.
(E) If both the statements I and II are effects of some common cause.

1. Statements:

I. Rural and semi-urban areas in the country have been suffering due to load-shedding for quite some time.

II. If the Government is not able to overcome the power crisis, load-shedding will be extended even to the urban areas.

2. Statements:

I. The Government has increased rates of petrol and diesel by 10% with immediate effect.

II. Oil producing countries have decided to increase 10% of production on crude oil from the last quarter.

3. Statements:

I. The vegetable prices in the local market have increased manifold during the past few days.

II. Incessant rain have created flood like situation in most rural parts of the State.

4. Statements:

I. The performance of Indian sports persons in the recently held Olympics could not reach the level of expectations the country had on them.

II. The performance of Indian sports person in the last Asian games was far better than any previous games.

5. Statements:

I. Large numbers of people have fallen sick after consuming sweets from a particular shop in the locality.

II. Major part of the locality is flooded and has become inaccessible to outsides.

6. Statements:

I. The life today is too fast, demanding full of variety in all aspects which at times leads to stressful situation.

II. Number of suicide cases among teenagers is on increase.

7. Statements:

I. The university authority has instructed all the colleges under its jurisdiction to ban use of cell phones inside the college premises.

II. Majority of the teachers of the colleges signed a joint petition to the university, complaining about the disturbances caused by cell phone ring tones inside the classrooms.

8. Statements:

I. The Government has reduced the prices of petroleum products by five per cent a week after increasing the prices by ten per cent.

II. The rate of inflation dropped marginally during the last week.

9. Statements:

I. The committee appointed by the Government on the fee structure of the professional courses has drastically reduced the fees of various courses in comparison to those charged in the last year.

II. The parents of aspiring students seeking admission to professional courses had launched a severe agitation protesting against the high fees charged by the professional institutes and the admission process was delayed considerably.

10. Statements:

I. The Government has decided to hold a single entrance test for admission to all the medical colleges in India.

II. The State Government has debarred students from other States to apply for the seats in the medical colleges in the State.

11. Statements:

I. Large number of Primary Schools in the rural areas are run by only one teacher.

II. There has been a huge dropout from the primary schools in rural areas.

12. Statements:

I. The car manufacturing companies have recently increased the prices of mid-sized cars.

II. The Government recently increased the duty on mid-sized cars.

13. Statements:

I. The State Government has announced special tax package for the new industries to be set-up in the State.

II. Last year the State Government had hiked the taxes for all industrial activities in the State.

14. Statements:

I. Standard of living among the middle class society is constantly going up since part of few years.

II. Indian Economy is observing remarkable growth.

15. Statements:

I. The Meteorological Department has issued a statement mentioning deficient rainfall during monsoon in many parts of the country.

II. The Government has lowered the revised estimated GDP growth from the level of earlier estimates.

16. Statements:

I. The staff of Airport Authorities called off the strike they were observing in protest against privatization.

II. The staff of Airport Authorities went on strike anticipating threat to their jobs.

17. Statements:

I. A huge truck overturned in the middle of the road last night.

II. The police had cordoned off entire area in the locality this morning for half of the day.

18. Statements:

I. Importance of yoga and exercise is being realized by all sections of the society.

II. There is an increasing awareness about health in the society particularly among middle-age group of people.

19. Statements:

I. The prices of food grains and other essential commodities in the open market have risen sharply during the past three months.

II. The political party in opposition has given a call for general strike to protest against the government's economic policy.

20. Statements:

I. The employees of the biggest bank in the country have given an indefinite strike call starting from the third of the next month.

II. The employees of the Central Government have withdrawn their week long demonstrations.

ANSWERS

1	2	3	4	5	6	7	8	9	10
E	D	B	E	D	E	B	D	B	E
11	**12**	**13**	**14**	**15**	**16**	**17**	**18**	**19**	**20**
A	B	B	A	D	D	A	B	A	A

EXPLANATORY ANSWERS

1. If certain preventive measures are practiced at the rural and semi-urban areas, the problem will be solved. But if the same is not practiced even at the cities, the problem may roll into the city also, so the two effects are of some common cause.

2. Both statements I and II are the effects of independent causes.

3. The transportation gets effect due to the flood created by incessant rains in the most rural parts of State. Therefore, on account of this, it is possible to increase the vegetable prices in the local market.

4. Both the statements are effects of some common cause.

5. Both statements I and II are the effects of independent causes.

6. Both the statements are effects of some common cause.

7. Since the teachers of the colleges complained to the university about the disturbances caused by cell phone ring-tones inside the class-rooms, the university authority has instructed all the colleges under its jurisdiction to ban use of cell phones inside the college premises.

8. Both the statements I and II are effects of independent causes.

9. Since the parents of aspiring students seeking admission to professional courses had launched a severe agitation protesting against the high fees charged by the professional institutes.
So, the committee was appointed by the Government on the fee structure of professional courses has drastically reduced the fees of various courses.

10. Both the statements are effects of some common cause.

11. Since large number of primary schools in the rural areas are run by only one teacher so, there has been a huge dropout from the primary schools in rural areas.

12. Since the government has recently increased the duty on mid-sized cars, therefore, the car manufacturing companies have recently increased the prices of mid-sized cars.

13. Because of the hike in taxes last year, the State Government has announced special tax package for the new industries to be set up in the State.

14. Since the standard of living among the middle class society is constantly going up so, Indian Economy is observing remarkable growth.

15. Both the statements I and II are effects of independent causes.

16. Both the statements I and II are effects of independent causes.

17. Since a huge truck overturned in the middle of the road last night, the police had cordoned off the entire area in the locality last morning for half of the day.

18. As the awareness about health in the society is increasing particularly, among middle-aged group of peole, the importance of Yoga and exercise is being realized by all sections of the society.

19. Since the prices of food grains and other essential commodities in the open market have been raised sharply during the past three months, the political party in opposition has given a call for general strike to protest against the government's economic policy.

20. Both the statements are effects of different causes.

☆☆☆☆☆☆

6. Data Sufficiency

Directions (Q. 1–50) : *Each of the questions below consists of a question and two statements numbered I and II. You have to decide whether the data provided in the statements are sufficient to answer the question. Read both the statements and—*

Give answer

- (A) If the data in statement I alone are sufficient to answer the question, while the data in statement II alone are not sufficient to answer the question
- (B) If the data in statement II alone are sufficient to answer the question, while the data in statement I alone are not sufficient to answer the question
- (C) If the data either in statement I alone or in statement II alone are sufficient to answer the question
- (D) If the data given in both statements I and II together are not sufficient to answer the question and
- (E) If the data in both statements I and II together are necessary to answer the question.

1. Question: How many children does M have ?
Statements:
I. H is the only daughter of X who is wife of M.
II. K and J are brothers of M.

2. Question: The last Sunday of March, 2006 fell on which date?
Statements:
I. The first Sunday of that month fell on 5th.
II. The last day of that month was Friday.

3. Question: What is the code for 'sky' in the code language?
Statements:
I. In the code language, 'sky is clear' is written as 'de ra fa'.
II. In the same code language, 'make it clear' is written as 'de ga jo'.

4. Question: How many children are there between P and Q in a row of children?
Statements:
I. P is fifteenth from the left in the row.
II. Q is exactly in the middle and there are ten children towards his right.

5. Question: How is T related to K?
Statements:
I. R's sister J has married T's brother L, who is the only son of his parents.
II. K is the only daughter of L and J.

6. Question: How is J related to P?
Statements:
I. M is brother of P and T is sister of P.
II. P's mother is married to J's husband who has one son and two daughters.

7. Question: How is X related to Y?
Statements:
I. Y and Z are children of D who is wife of X.
II. R's sister X is married to Y's father.

8. Question: Who is to the immediate right of P among five persons P, Q, R, S and T facing North?
Statements:
I. R is third to the left of Q and P is second to the right of R.
II. Q is to the immediate left of T who is second to the right of P.

9. Question: On which date of the month was Anjali born in February 2004?
Statements:
I. Anjali was born on an even date of the month.
II. Anjali's birth date was a prime number.

10. Question: How is X related to Y?
Statements:
I. Y says, "I have only one brother".
II. X says, "I have only one sister".

11. Question: How is F related to P?
Statements:
I. P has two sisters M and N.
II. F's mother is sister of M's father.

12. Question: B is the brother of A. How is A related to B?
Statements:
I. A is the sister of C.
II. E is the husband of A.

13. Question: How many children are there in the row of children facing North?
Statements:
I. Vishakha who is fifth from the left end is eighth to the left of Ashish who is twelfth from the right end.
II. Rohit is fifth to the left of Nisha who is seventh from the right end and eighteenth from the left end.

14. Question: How many doctors are practising in this town?
Statements:
I. There is one doctor per seven hundred residents.
II. There are 16 wards with each ward having as many doctors as the number of wards.

15. Question: On which day of the week was birthday of Sahil?
Statements:
I. Sahil celebrated his birthday, the very next day on which Arun celebrated his birthday.
II. The sister of Sahil was born on the third day of the week and two days after Sahil was born.

16. Question: How many pages of book X did Robert read on Sunday?
Statements:
I. The book has 300 pages out of which two-thirds were read by him before Sunday.
II. Robert read the last 40 pages of the book on the morning of Monday.

17. Question: How is Tanya related to the man in the photograph?
Statements:
I. Man in the photograph is the only son of Tanya's grandfather.
II. The man in the photograph has no brothers or sisters and his father is Tanya's grandfather.

18. Question: On which day in April is Gautam's birthday?
Statements:
I. Gautam was born exactly 28 years after his mother was born.
II. His mother will be 55 years 4 months and 5 days on August 18 this year.

19. Question: What is the code for 'is' in the code language?
Statements:
I. In the code language, 'shi tu ke' means 'pen is blue'.
II. In the same code language, 'ke si re' means 'this is wonderful'.

20. Question: Among A, B, C, D and E, who is in the middle while standing in a row?
Statements:
I. C, who is third to the left of D, is to the immediate right of A and second to the left of E.
II. C is second to the left of E, who is not at any of the ends and who is third to the right of A. D is at one of the ends.

21. Question: Among A, B, C, D, E and F, who is the heaviest?
Statements:
I. A and D are heavier than B. E and F but none of them is the heaviest.
II. A is heavier than D but lighter than C.

22. Question: Among T, V, B, E and C, who is the third from the top when arranged in the descending order of their weights?
Statements:
I. B is heavier than T and C and is less heavier than V who is not the heaviest.
II. C is heavier than only T.

23. Question: Which word in the code language means 'flower'?
Statements:
I. 'de fu la pane' means 'rose flower is beautiful' and 'la quiz' means 'beautiful tree'.
II. 'de la chin' means 'red rose flower' and 'pa chin' means 'red tea'.

24. Question: How many students in a class play football?
Statements:
I. Only boys play football.
II. There are forty boys and thirty girls in the class.

25. Question: Who is C's partner in a game of cards involving four players A, B, C and D?
Statements:
I. D is sitting opposite to A.
II. B is sitting right of A and left of D.

26. Question: On a T.V. channel, four serials A, B, C and D were screened, one on each day, on four consecutive days but not necessarily in that order. On which day was the serial C screened?
Statements:
I. The first serial was screened on 23rd, Tuesday and was followed by serial D.
II. Serial A was not screened on 25th and one serial was screened between serials A and B.

27. Question: Who among P, Q, T, V and M is exactly in the middle when they are arranged in ascending order of their heights?
Statements:
I. V is taller than Q but shorter than M.
II. T is taller than Q and M but shorter than P.

28. Question: Which code word stands for 'good' in the coded sentence 'sin co bye' which means 'He is good'?
Statements:
I. In the same code language, 'co mot det' means 'They are good'.
II. In the same code language, 'sin mic bye' means 'He is honest'.

29. Question: What is the numerical code for 'water' in a certain code?
Statements:
I. The code for 'give me water' is '719'.
II. The code for 'you can bring water for me' is written as '574186'.

30. Question: How many visitors saw the exhibition yesterday?
Statements:
I. Each entry pass holder can take up to three persons with him/her.
II. In all, 243 passes were sold yesterday.

31. Question: Gaurav ranks eighteenth from the top in a class. What is his rank from the last?
Statements:
I. There are 47 students in the class.
II. Jatin who ranks 10th in the same class, ranks 38th from the last.

32. Question: What is the rank of P from the bottom in a class of 30 students?
Statements:
I. M is third from the top and there are five students between M and P.
II. The rank of K is fourth from the bottom and there are 17 students between K and P.

33. Question: In a row of five buildings—P, Q, R, S and T, which building is in the middle?
Statements:
I. Buildings S and Q are at the two extreme ends of the row.
II. Building, T is to the right of building R.

34. Question: How many speeches were delivered in the two days' programme?
Statements:
I. 18 speakers were invited to give at least one speech (maximum of two speech), out of which one-sixth of the speakers could not come.
II. One-third of the speakers gave two speeches each.

35. Question: Among five friends, who is the tallest?
Statements:
I. D is taller than A and C.
II. B is shorter than E but taller than D.

36. Question: In a certain code language 'Pe nop con' means 'we like roses.' Which word means 'roses'?
Statements :
I. 'nop to cop' means 'we are honest.'
II. 'Pe me say' means they like flowers.'

37. Question: Rajiv's rank is 17th in his class. What is his rank from the last?
Statements :
I. There are 70 students in his class.
II. Abhijeet, who ranks 20th in Rajiv's class is 51st from the last.

38. Question: How many daughters does 'L' have?
Statements :
I. R's father has three daughters.
II. T is R's sister and daughter of L.

39. Question: Who is the heaviest among Amol, Prabhu, Narayan and Navin?
Statements :
I. Amol and Prabhu are of the same weight.
II. Prabhu weighs more than Narayan, but less than Navin.

40. Question: In which year was Rahul born?
Statements :
I. Rahul at present is 25 years younger to his mother.
II. Rahul's brother, who was born in 1964, is 35 years younger to his mother.

41. Question: Who is C's partner in a game of cards involving four players A, B, C and D?
Statements :
I. D is sitting opposite to A.
II. B is sitting right of A and left of C.

42. Question: What is the height of Ashok?
Statements :
I. Pranab is 5'9" tall and is 4" taller than Ashok.
II. Vikash is 3" shorter than Pranab.

43. Question: In which year was Suhas born?
Statements :
I. Suhas's mother was 44 years old in 1989.
II. Suhas was born three years after his mother's marriage.

44. Question: By how much is Utpal heavier than Vilas?
Statements :
I. Vilas's weight is 65 kgs.
II. Amar is 10 kg heavier than Utpal.

45. Question: How is D related to A?
Statements :
I. B is the brother of A.
II. B is D's son.

46. Question: How many matches will be played between A and B in this tournament?
Statements :
I. A has already won three matches against B and with this third win he has won the tournament.
II. The fifth match will be played next week.

47. Question: When is Chandra's birthday this year?
Statements :
I. It is between February 11 and 13 (February 11 being Thursday).
II. It is not on Saturday.

48. Question: What time did the train leave today?
Statements :
I. The train normally leaves on time.
II. The scheduled departure is at 14:30.

49. Question: Among five friends who is tallest?
Statements :
I. D is taller than A and C.
II. B is shorter than E but taller than D.

50. Question: Is the number of girl students more in the B.Ed. course?
Statements :
I. The girls performance in the annual examination is better than boys.
II. The proportion of female teachers have been increasing over the last two years.

ANSWERS

1	2	3	4	5	6	7	8	9	10
D	C	D	E	E	B	C	C	E	D
11	**12**	**13**	**14**	**15**	**16**	**17**	**18**	**19**	**20**
E	C	C	B	B	E	C	E	E	C
21	**22**	**23**	**24**	**25**	**26**	**27**	**28**	**29**	**30**
A	A	D	D	C	E	E	C	D	D
31	**32**	**33**	**34**	**35**	**36**	**37**	**38**	**39**	**40**
C	C	D	E	E	E	C	E	E	E
41	**42**	**43**	**44**	**45**	**46**	**47**	**48**	**49**	**50**
C	A	D	D	E	E	A	D	E	D

EXPLANATORY ANSWERS

1. From statement I, we conclude that H is the only daughter of M. But this does not indicate that M has no son. The information given in statement II is immaterial.

2. From statement I, we conclude that 5th, 12th, 19th and 26th of March, 2006 were Sundays.
So, the last Sunday fell on 26th.
From statement II, we conclude that 31st March, 2006 was Friday. Thus, 26th March, 2006 was the last Sunday of the month.

3. The only word common to statement I and II is 'clear' and as such, only the code for 'clear' can be ascertained from the given information.

4. From statement II, Q being in the middle, there are 10 children to his right as well as to his left. So, Q is 11th from the left. From statement I, P is 15th from the left. Thus, from both statement I and II, we conclude that there are 3 children between P and Q.

5. From statement I, we know that L is T's brother and J's husband. Since L is the only son of his parents, T is L's sister.
From statement II, we know that K is L's daughter.
Thus, from statement I and II, we conclude that T is the sister of K's father i.e. T is K's aunt.

6. From statement II, we know that P's mother is married to J's husband, which means that J is P's mother.

7. From statement I, we conclude that Y is the child of D who is wife of X i.e. X is Y's father.
From statement II, X is married to Y's father. This implies that X is Y's mother.

8. From statement I, we have the order: R, ..., P, Q.
From statement II, we have the order: P, Q, T.
Clearly, each one of the above two orders indicates that Q is to the immediate right of P.

9. From statement I and II, we conclude that Anjali was born in February 2004 on a date which is an even prime number. Since the only even prime number is 2, so Anjali was born on 2nd February, 2004.

10. The statements I and II do not provide any clue regarding relation between X and Y.

11. From statement I and II, we conclude that P is M's brother and so M's father is P's father. So, F is the child of the sister of P's father i.e., F's mother is P's aunt or F is P's cousin.

12. B is A's brother means A is either brother or sister of B. Now, each one of statement I and II individually indicates that A is a female, which means that A is B's sister.

13. Since 8th to the left of 12th from the right is 20th from the right, so from statement I, we know that Vishakha is 5th from left and 20th from right i.e. there are 4 children

to the left and 19 to the right of Vishakha. So, there are (4 + 1 + 19) i.e. 24 children in the row.
From statement II, Nisha is 7th from right and 18th from left end of the row.
So, there are (6 + 1 + 17) = 24 children in the row.

14. From statement I, total number of doctors in town = (1/700 × N) , where N = total number of residents in town. But, the value of N is not known.
From statement II, total number of doctors in town
= (Number of wards in town) × (Number of doctors in each ward)
= 16 × 16 = 256.

15. Statement I does not mention the day of the week on the birthday of either Arun or Sahil.
According to statement II, Sahil's sister was born on Wednesday and Sahil was born two days before Wednesday i.e., on Monday.

16. From statement I and II, we find that Robert read (300 × 2/3) i.e., 200 pages before Sunday and the last 40 pages on Monday.
This means that he read [300 – (200 + 40)] i.e., 60 pages on Sunday.

17. From statement I, we conclude that the man is the only son of Tanya's grandfather i.e., he is Tanya's father or Tanya is the man's daughter.
From statement II, we conclude that the man's father is Tanya's grandfather. Since the man has no brothers or sisters, so he is Tanya's father or Tanya is the man's daughter.

18. Clearly, the birthday of Gautam's mother can be found out from statement II and then Gautam's birthday can be determined using the fact given in statement I.

19. In statement I and II, the common word is 'is' and the common code word is 'ke'. So, 'ke' is the code for 'is'.

20. From each one of statement I and II, we get the order : A, C, B, E, D. Clearly, B is in the middle.

21. From statement I, we conclude that since none of A and D is the heaviest and each one of B, E and F is lighter than both A and D, so C is the heaviest.

22. From statement I, we have: B > T, B > C, V > B. Thus, V is heavier than each one of B, T and C. But V is not the heaviest. So, E is the heaviest.
Thus, we have the order. E > V > B > T > C or E > V > B > C > T. Clearly, B is third from the top.

23. From the two statements given in statement I, the code for the only common word 'beautiful' can be determined.
From the two statements given in statement II, the code for the only common word 'red' can be determined.
In statement I and II, the common words are 'rose and 'flower' and the common code words are 'de' and 'la'. So, the code for 'flower' is either 'de' or 'la'.

24. It is not mentioned whether all the boys or a proportion of them play football.

25. Clearly, each of the given statements shows that B is sitting opposite to C or B is the partner of C.

26. From statement I, we know that the serials were screened on 23rd, 24th, 25th and 26th.
Clearly, D was screened second i.e., on 24th, Wednesday.
From statement II, we know that one serial was screened between A and B.
So, A and B were screened first and third, i.e., on 23rd and 25th. But, A was not screened on 25th.
So, A was screened on 23rd and B on 25th. Thus, C was screened on 26th, Friday.

27. From statement I, we have: M > V > Q.
From statement II, we have: T > Q, T > M, P > T.
Combining the above two, we have: P > T > M > V > Q i.e. Q < V < M < T < P.
Clearly, M is in the middle.

28. In the given statement and statement I, the common word is 'good' and the common code word is 'co'. So, 'co' is the code for 'good'.
In the given statement and statement II, the common words are 'He' and 'is' and the common code words are 'sin' and 'bye'. So 'sin' and 'bye' are the codes for 'He' and 'is'. Thus, in the given statement, 'co' is the code for 'good'.

29. In statement I and II, the common words are 'me' and 'water' and the common code numbers are '7' and '1'. So, the code for 'water' is either '7' or '1'.

30. From statement I and II, we find that maximum (243 × 3) i.e. 729 visitors saw the exhibition.
But the exact number cannot be determined.

31. From statement I, we conclude that in a class of 47 students, Gaurav ranks 18th from the top and hence 30th from the last.
From statement II, we conclude that there are 9 students above and 37 students below Jatin in rank. Thus, there are (9 + 1 + 37) = 47 students in the class.
So, Gaurav who ranks 18th from the top, is 30th from the last.

32. From statement I, we conclude that P is 9th from the top. Thus, in a class of 30 students, P ranks 22nd from the bottom.
From statement II, we conclude that P is 22nd from the bottom.

33. From statement I, we have the order : S, -, -, -, Q. From statement II, we have the order : R, T. Combining the above two, we get two possible orders : S, R, T, P, Q or S, P, R, T, Q. Thus, either T or R is in the middle.

34. From statement I, we find that number of speakers who attended programme =18 – (1/6) of 18 = 15.
From statement II, we find that one-third of 15 i.e., 5 speakers gave 2 speeches each, while each of the remaining 10 speakers delivered only one speech.
So, total number of speeches delivered
$= (5 \times 2 + 10 \times 1) = 20.$

35. From statement I, we have: D > A, D > C.
From statement II, we have: E > B > D.
Combining the above two, we get : E > B > D > A > C or E > B > D >C > A.
Thus, E is the tallest.

36. From the question and statement I it is known that 'nop' stands for 'we'. From question and statement II it is known that 'pe' stands for 'like'. Hence 'con' stands for 'roses'. Both the statements are required to answer the question.

37. Statement I and statement II alone are sufficient to answer the question. From statement I Rajiv's rank from the last = 70 – 17 + 1 = 54th.
From statement II we can calculate the total number of students in the class = 20 + 51 – 1 = 70.
Now, we can calculate the Rajiv's rank from the last.

38. From statement II it is clear that T is R's sister and it is given in statement I that R's father has three daughters it means that L is the father of R and T both. Hence, L has three daughters.

39. From both the statements using together it is ascertained that Navin is the heaviest.

40. From both of the given statements, we find that Rahul is (35 – 25) = 10 years elder than his brother, who is born in 1964. So, Rahul was born in 1954. Thus, both of the given statements are needed to answer the query.

41. Clearly, each one of the given statements shown that the partner of C is B.

42. From statement I only, we find that the height of Ashok is 5'5". From statement II, we can not find the height of Ashok.

43. Even from both the statements, the date of Suhas's mother's marriage is required. So, the year in which Suhas was born cannot be determined.

44. Even from both the given statements, we are not able to compare the weights of Utpal and Vilas.

45. From both the statements together, we find that D is the father of B and B is the brother of A. So, D is the father of A. So, both of the given statements are needed.

46. From statement II, we find that four matches have already been played. Since statement I shows that A has won with the third win, so the number of matches played between A and B is four. Thus, both the statements are needed.

47. From statement I, we conclude that Chandra's birthday is on 12th February, which was Friday, this year. So, only statement I is needed.

48. Clearly, even both the statements together do not reveal the exact time of departure of the train today.

49. From statement II, we find that D < B < E. And, from statement I, we find that A < D and C < D. So, (A and C) < D < B < E i.e., E is tallest.

50. None of the given statements tells the strength of girls in B.Ed. course.

❑❑❑

7. Sitting Arrangements

CIRCULAR ARRANGEMENTS

Directions (Q. 1–5) : *Study the following information to answer the given questions :*

(*i*) Eight persons E, F, G, H, I, J, K and L are seated around a square table two on each side.

(*ii*) There are three lady members and they are not seated next to each other.

(*iii*) J is between L and F.

(*iv*) G is between I and F.

(*v*) H, a lady member, is second to the left of J.

(*vi*) F, a male member, is seated opposite to E, a lady member.

(*vii*) There is a lady member between F and I.

1. How many persons are seated between K and F?
A. One
B. Two
C. Three
D. Can't be determined
E. None of these

2. Who among the following is to the immediate left of F.
A. G
B. J
C. I
D. Can't be determined
E. None of these

3. Who among the following is seated between E and H?
A. I
B. J
C. F
D. Can't be determined
E. None of these

4. Which of the following is true about J?
A. J is a male member.
B. J is a female member.
C. Sex of J cannot be determined.
D. Position of J cannot be determined.
E. None of these

5. Who among the following are the three lady members?
A. E, H and J
B. E, G and J
C. G, H and J
D. Can't be determined
E. None of these

Directions (Q. 6–7) : *Eight friends A, B, C, D, E, F, G and H are sitting in a circle facing the centre. B is sitting between G and D. H is third to the left of B and second to the right of A. C is sitting between A and G & B and E are not sitting opposite to each other.*

6. Which of the following statement is not correct?
A. D and A are sitting opposite to each other.
B. C is third to the right of D.
C. E is sitting between F and D.
D. A is sitting between C and F.
E. E and C are sitting opposite to each other.

7. Who is third to the left of D?
A. F
B. E
C. A
D. Can't be determined
E. None of these

Directions (Q. 8–10) : *Four ladies A, B, C and D and four gentlemen E, F, G and H are sitting in a circle around a table facing each other.*

(*i*) No two ladies or two gentlemen are sitting side by side.

(*ii*) C, who is sitting between G and E, is facing D.

(*iii*) F is between D and A and is facing G.

(*iv*) H is to the right of B.

8. Who are immediate neighbours of B?
A. G and H B. E and F
C. E and H D. F and H
E. None of these

9. E is facing whom?
A. F B. B
C. G D. H
E. None of these

10. Who is sitting to the left of A?
A. E B. F
C. G D. H
E. None of these

Directions (Q. 11–13) : *Six girls are sitting in a circle. Sonia is sitting opposite to Radhika. Poonam is sitting right of Radhika but left of the Deepti. Monika is sitting left of the Radhika. Kamini is sitting right of Sonia and left of Monika. Now Deepti and Kamini, Monika and Radhika mutually exchange their positions.*

11. Who will be sitting left of Deepti?
A. Sonia B. Monika
C. Radhika D. Poonam
E. Can't be determined

12. Who will be sitting left of Kamini?
A. Poonam B. Deepti
C. Radhika D. Sonia
E. None of these

13. Who will be opposite to Sonia?
A. Radhika B. Monika
C. Kamini D. Sonia
E. None of these

Directions (Q. 14–17) : *P, Q, R, S, T, U, V and W are sitting round the circle and are facing the centre:*
(*i*) P is second to the right of T who is the neighbour of R and V.
(*ii*) S is not the neighbour of P.
(*iii*) V is the neighbour of U.
(*iv*) Q is not between S and W. W is not between U and S.

14. Which two of the following are not neigbours?
A. RV B. UV
C. RP D. QW
E. TV

15. Which one is immediate right to the V?
A. P B. U
C. R D. T
E. Q

16. Which of the following is correct?
A. P is to the immediate right of Q
B. R is between U and V
C. Q is to the immediate left of W
D. U is between W and S
E. None of these

17. What is the position of S?
A. Between U and V
B. Second to the right of P
C. To the immediate right of W
D. Data inadequate
E. None of these

Directions (Q. 18–21): *Six friends are sitting in a circle and are facing the centre of the circle. Deepa is between Prakash and Pankaj. Priti is between Mukesh and Lalit. Prakash and Mukesh are opposite to the each other.*

18. Who is sitting opposite to Prakash?
A. Mukesh B. Deepa
C. Pankaj D. Lalit
E. Priti

19. Who is just right to Pankaj?
A. Deepa B. Lalit
C. Prakash D. Priti
E. Mukesh

20. Who are the neighbour of Mukesh?
A. Prakash and Deepa
B. Deepa and Priti
C. Priti and Pankaj
D. Lalit and Priti
E. Pankaj and Deepa

21. Who is sitting opposite to Priti?
A. Prakash B. Deepa
C. Pankaj D. Lalit
E. Mukesh

Directions (Q. 22–25): *Six friends P, Q, R, S, T and U are sitting around the hexagonal table each at one corner and are facing the centre of the hexagonal. P is second to the left of U. Q is neighbour of R and S. T is second to the left of S.*

22. Which one is sitting opposite to P?
A. R B. Q
C. T D. S
E. P

23. Who is the fourth person to the left of Q?
A. P B. UT
C. R D. Data inadequate
E. None of these

24. Which of the following are the neighbours of P?
A. U and P B. T and R
C. U and R D. Data inadequate
E. None of these

25. Which one is sitting opposite to T?
A. R
B. Q
C. Cannot be determined
D. S
E. None of these

Directions (Q. 26–29):

(*i*) 8 persons E, F, G, H, I, J, K and L are seated around a square table - two on each side.

(*ii*) There are 3 ladies who are not seated next to each other.

(*iii*) J is between L and F.

(*iv*) G is between I and F.

(*v*) H, a lady member is second to the left of J.

(*vi*) F, a male member is seated opposite to E, a lady member.

(*vii*) There is a lady member between F and I.

26. Who among the following is to the immediate left of F?

A. G B. I
C. J D. H
E. L

27. What is true about J and K?

A. J is male, K is female
B. J is female, K is male
C. Both are female
D. Both are male
E. None of these

28. How many persons are seated between K and F?

A. 1 B. 2
C. 3 D. 4
E. 5

29. Who among the following are three lady members?

A. E, H and J B. E, F and G
C. E, H and G D. C, H and J
E. None of these

30. Five boys are sitting in a circle. Ajay is between Ramesh and Damanik. Suleman is left to Vikas. Ramesh is left to Suleman. Who is sitting immediate right to Ajay?

A. Suleman
B. Damanik
C. Vikas
D. Ramesh
E. Suleman or Damanik

LINEAR ARRANGEMENTS

Directions (Q. 31–33): *Read the following information and answer the questions :*

(*i*) A, B, C, D, E, F, G and H are sitting in a row facing north.

(*ii*) A is fourth to the right of E.

(*iii*) H is fourth to the left of D.

(*iv*) C and F, which are not at the ends, are neighbours of B and E respectively.

(*v*) H is next to the left of A and A is the neighbours of B.

31. Who are sitting at the ends?

A. E and C
B. F and D
C. G and B
D. Can't be determined
E. None of these

32. Which of the following statements is not true?

A. H is second to the right of F.
B. E is fourth to the left of A.
C. D is fourth to the right of H.
D. A is third to the left of D.
E. None of these

33. Which of the following statements is not true?

A. G is the neighbour of H and E.
B. B is next to the right of A.
C. E is at left end.
D. D is next to the right of B.
E. None of these

34. There are six houses in a row. Mr. Lal has Mr. Bhasin and Mr. Sachdeva as neighbours. Mr. Bhatia has Mr. Gupta and Mr. Sharma as neighbours. Mr. Gupta's house is not next to Mr. Bhasin or Mr. Sachdeva and Mr. Sharma does not live next to Mr. Sachdeva. Who are Mr. Bhasin's next door neighbour?

A. Mr. Lal and Mr. Bhasin
B. Mr. Lal and Mr. Sachdeva
C. Mr. Sharma and Mr. Lal
D. Only Mr. Lal
E. None of these

Directions (Q. 35–37) : *Study the following information carefully and answer the questions given below it :*

(*i*) Eleven students A, B, C, D, E, F, G, H, I, J and K are sitting in a row of the class facing the teacher.

(*ii*) D, who is to the immediate left of F, is second to the right of C.

(*iii*) A, is second to the right of E, who is at one of the ends.

(*iv*) J is the immediate neighbours of A and B and third to the left of G.

(*v*) H is to the immediate left of D and third to the right of I.

35. If E and D, C and B, A and H & K and F interchange their positions, which of the following pairs of students is sitting at the end?

A. D and E B. E and F
C. D and K D. K and F
E. None of these

36. Which of the following statements is true in the context of the above sitting arrangements?

A. There are three students sitting between D and G.
B. G and C are neighbours sitting to immediate right of H.

C. B is sitting between J and I.
D. K is sitting between A and J.
E. None of these

37. In the above sitting arrangement, which of the following statements is superfluous?
A. (*i*) B. (*ii*)
C. (*iii*) D. (*iv*)
E. None is superfluous

Directions (Q. 38–40) : *Read the following information and answer the questions based on it.*
Ten students A, B, C, D, E, F, G, H, I and J are sitting in a row facing west.
(*i*) B and F are not sitting on either of the edges.
(*ii*) G is sitting to the left of D and H is sitting to the right of J.
(*iii*) There are four persons between E and A.
(*iv*) I is to the north of B and F is to the south of D.
(*v*) J is in between A & D and G is in between E and F.
(*vi*) There are two persons between H and C.

38. If G and A interchange their positions, then who become the immediate neighbours of E?
A. G and F B. F only
C. A only D. J and H
E. D only

39. Who among the following is definitely sitting at one of the ends?
A. C
B. H
C. E
D. Can't be determined
E. None of these

40. Who is sitting at the seventh place counting from the left?
A. H B. C
C. J D. Either H or C
E. None of these

Directions (Q. 41–43) : *Read the following information carefully and answer the questions given below it .*
Five friends A, B, C, D and E are sitting on a bench.
(*i*) C is sitting next to D.
(*ii*) E is on the left end of the bench.
(*iii*) A is sitting next to B.
(*iv*) D is not sitting with E.
(*v*) A is on the right side of B and to the right side of E.
(*vi*) C is on second position from right.
(*vii*) A and C are sitting together.

41. What is the position of D?
A. Extreme left B. Extreme right
C. Third from left D. Second from left
E. None of these

42. What is the position of B?
A. Second from right
B. Centre
C. Extreme left
D. Second from left
E. None of these

43. At what position is A sitting?
A. Between B and C
B. Between D and C
C. Between E and D
D. Between C and E
E. None of these

Directions (Q. 44–46) : *Read the following information carefully and answer the questions based on it.*
(*i*) Eight rooms A, B, C, D, E, F, G and H are located adjacent to one another in two different rows, four on each row.
(*ii*) Doors of the rooms of one row open to the doors of the rooms of another row.
(*iii*) No room of consecutive letter is either adjacent or opposite to each other.
(*iv*) A and B are the rooms located at the end of two different rows.
(*v*) C is just left of E and is located in the same row in which A is located.
(*vi*) F is just left of B.

44. Which of the following rooms is not located at either ends?
A. B B. G
C. D D. H
E. A

45. Which room is just opposite to C?
A. F B. H
C. B D. Can't be determined
E. None of these

46. Which room is diagonally opposite to D?
A. B B. H
C. G D. Can't be determined
E. None of these

Directions (Q. 47–49) : *Read the following information carefully and answer the questions given below :*
(*i*) Six flats on a floor in the rows facing north and south are allotted to P, Q, R, S, T and U.
(*ii*) Q gets a north facing flat and is not next to S.
(*iii*) S and U get diagonally opposite flats.
(*iv*) R next to U, gets a south facing flat and T gets a north facing flat.

47. To arrive at the answer to the above questions, which of the following statements can be dispensed with?
A. None B. (*ii*) only
C. (*iii*) only D. (*i*) only
E. None of these

48. If the flats of T and P are interchanged, whose flat will be next to that of U?

A. Q B. T
C. P D. R
E. None of these

49. Which of the combinations get south facing flats?
A. URP B. UPT
C. QTS D. Data inadequate
E. None of these

50. Five boys are sitting in a row. Raghu is not adjacent to Shyam or Amit. Ajay is not adjacent to Shyam. Raghu is adjacent to Mayank. If Mayank is at the middle in the row, then Ajay is adjacent to whom out of the following?
A. Amit B. Raghu
C. Mayank D. Shyam
E. Data inadequate

51. Mini is to the right of Rajni but to the left of Ananta. Saya is to the right of Mini but to the left of Jaya. Who is on the extreme left if all the girls are facing North?
A. Jaya B. Mini
C. Rajni D. Saya
E. Ananta

52. Kittu is in-between Mohan and Sohan. Raju is to the left of Sohan and Shyam is to the right of Mohan. If all of the friends are sitting facing South, then who is on their extreme right?
A. Mohan B. Sohan
C. Kittu D. Shyam
E. Data inadequate

Directions (Q. 53–55) : *Read the following statements and answer the questions given below :*

Nine family members are sitting in a theatre in one row. They are J, K, L, M, N, O, P, Q and R. L is at the right of M and at third place at the right of N. K is at one end of the row. Q is immediately next to O and P. O is at third place at the left of K. J is right next to the left of O.

53. Which of the following statement is true?
A. There is one person between L and O
B. R and P are neighbours
C. M is at one extreme end
D. N is at two seats away from J.
E. None of the above

54. The family members sitting on the right of O are :
A. RML B. JQP
C. QPK D. KPR
E. Cannot be determined

55. Who is sitting in the centre of the row?
A. L B. J
C. O D. Q
E. None of the above

Directions (Q. 56–58) : (*a*) There are five friends; (*b*) They are standing in a row facing south; (*c*) Jayesh is to the immediate right of Alok; (*d*) Pramod is between Babir and Subodh; (*e*) Subodh is between Jayesh and Pramod.

56. Who is at the extreme left end?
A. Alok B. Babir
C. Subodh D. Data inadequate
E. None of these

57. Who is in the middle?
A. Babir B. Pramod
C. Subodh D. Jayesh
E. Alok

58. To find answers to the above two questions, which of the given statements can be dispensed with?
A. None B. A only
C. B only D. C only
E. D only

59. A, P, R, X, S and Z are sitting in a row. S and Z are in the centre. A and P are at the ends. R is sitting to the left of A. Who is to the right of P?
A. A B. X
C. S D. Z
E. None of these

60. There are 8 houses in a line and in each house only one boy lives with the conditions as given below:
1. Jack is not the neighbour Siman.
2. Harry is just next to the left of Larry.
3. There is at least one to the left of Larry.
4. Paul lives in one of the two houses in the middle.
5. Mike lives in between Paul and Larry.

If at least one lives to the right of Robert and Harry is not between Taud and Larry, then which one of the following statement is not correct?
A. Robert is not at the left end.
B. Robert is between Simon and Taud.
C. Taud is between Paul and Jack.
D. There are three persons to the right of Paul.
E. None of these

61. A, B, C, D and E are sitting on a bench. A is sitting next to B, C is sitting next to D, D is not sitting with E who is on the left end of the bench. C is on the second position from the right. A is to the right of B and E. A and C are sitting together. In which position A is sitting?
A. Between B and D B. Between B and C
C. Between E and D D. Between C and E
E. None of these

Directions (Q. 62–65): *In an exhibition seven cars of different companies—Cadillac. Ambassador, Fiat, Maruti, Mercedes, Bedford and Fargo are standing facing to east in the following order:*
1. Cadillac is next to right of Fargo.
2. Fargo is fourth to the right of Fiat.
3. Maruti car is between Ambassador and Bedford.

4. Fiat which is third to the left of Ambassador, is at one end.

62. Which of the following statement is correct?
A. Maruti is next left of Ambassador
B. Bedford is next left of Fiat.
C. Bedford is at one end.
D. Fiat is next second to the right of Maruti.
E. None of these

63. Which one of the following statements is correct?
A. Fargo car is between Ambassador and Fiat.
B. Cadillac is next left to Mercedes car.
C. Fargo is next right of Cadillac.
D. Maruti is fourth right of Mercedes.
E. None of these

64. Which of the following groups of cars is to the right of Ambassador?
A. Cadillac, Fargo and Maruti
B. Mercedes, Cadillac and Fargo
C. Maruti, Bedford and Fiat
D. Bedford, Cadillac and Fargo
E. None of these

65. Which one of the following is the correct position of Mercedes?
A. Next to the left of Cadillac
B. Next to the left of Bedford
C. Between Bedford and Fargo
D. Fourth to the right of Maruti
E. None of these

ANSWERS

1	2	3	4	5	6	7	8	9	10
C	B	E	A	E	C	A	A	D	B
11	12	13	14	15	16	17	18	19	20
A	A	A	A	D	C	C	A	A	C
21	22	23	24	25	26	27	28	29	30
B	D	A	B	B	C	D	C	C	D
31	32	33	34	35	36	37	38	39	40
E	E	D	C	C	C	E	C	C	D
41	42	43	44	45	46	47	48	49	50
B	A	A	D	A	C	A	D	A	B
51	52	53	54	55	56	57	58	59	60
C	D	A	C	B	A	C	B	B	C
61	62	63	64	65					
B	A	B	B	D					

EXPLANATORY ANSWERS

For Qs. Nos. (1 to 5): On the basis of the information given in the question, the position of all the eight persons sitting around the square table is given below as per figure .

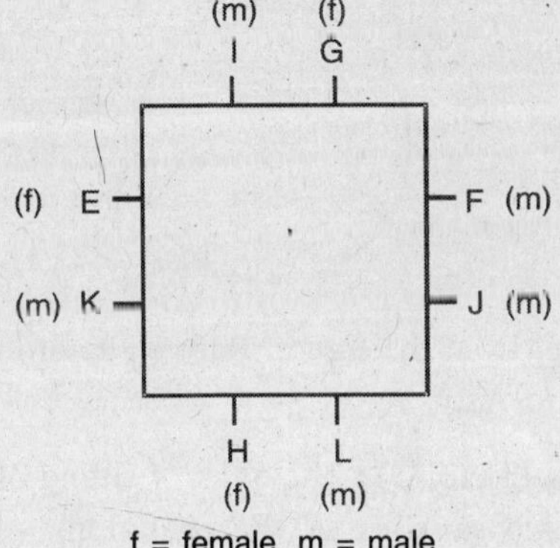

1. There are three persons seated between K and F.

2. J is sitting immediately left of F.

3. K is sitting between E and H.

4. It is clear that J is a male member.

5. It is clear from the figure that the three lady members are H, E, G. Since none of the options shows this combination, hence E is our answer.

For Qs. Nos. (6 & 7) : Figure shows the correct position of persons sitting around the circular table.

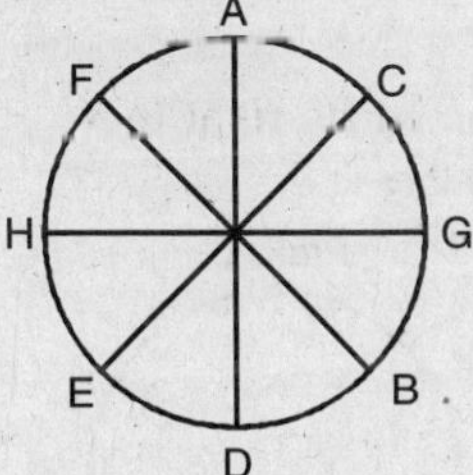

6. E is sitting between H and D. Hence, alternative (C) is not correct.

7. F is third to left of D.

For Qs. Nos. (8 to 10) : On the basis of information given in the question the sitting arrangement of the persons will be as given in the figure.

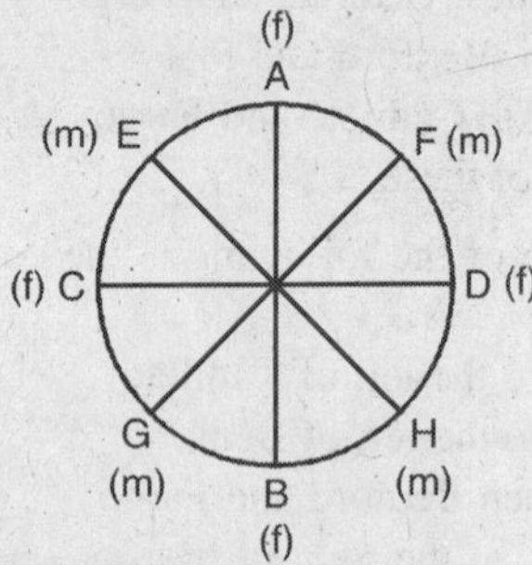

8. G and H are immediate neighbours of B.

8. E is facing H.

10. From the figure it is clear that F is sitting to the left of A.

For Qs. Nos. (11 to 13): After changing their positions as given in the questions, we have the order of sitting of persons as given in the figure.

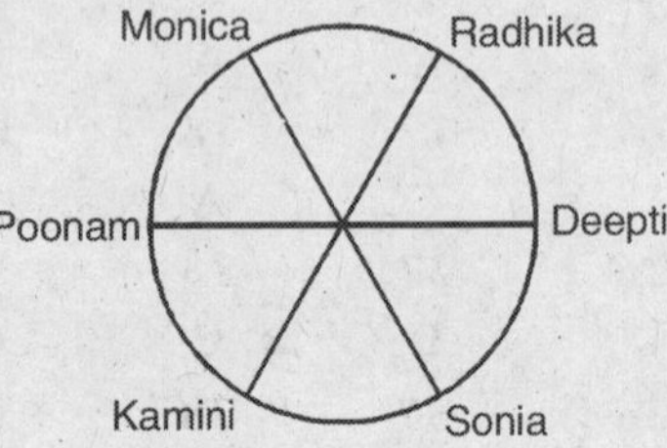

11. Sonia is sitting just left of Deepti.

12. Poonam sitting just left of Kamini.

13. Monika is sitting just opposite of Sonia.

For Qs. Nos. 14 to 17:

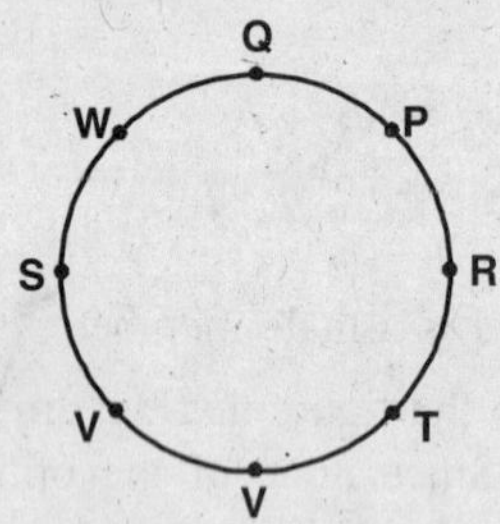

14. R and V are not neighbours.

15. T is immediate right to V.

16. Q is to the immediate left to W. Hence, C is correct option.

17. S is to the immediate right to W.

For Qs. Nos. 18 to 21:

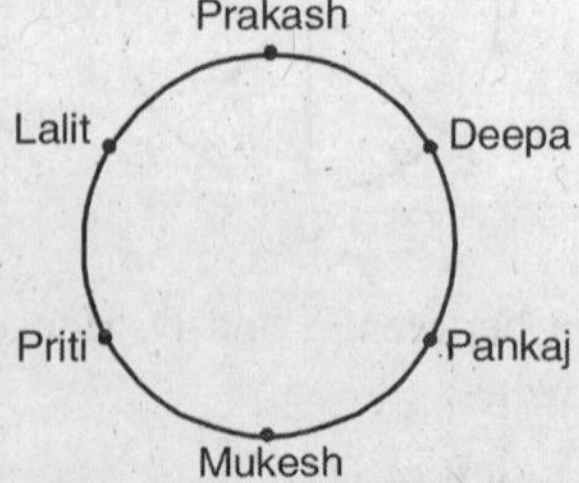

18. Mukesh is sitting opposite to Prakash.

19. Deepa is sitting just right to Pankaj.

20. Priti and Pankaj are neighbours of Mukesh.

21. Deepa is sitting opposite to Priti.

For Qs. Nos. 22 to 25:

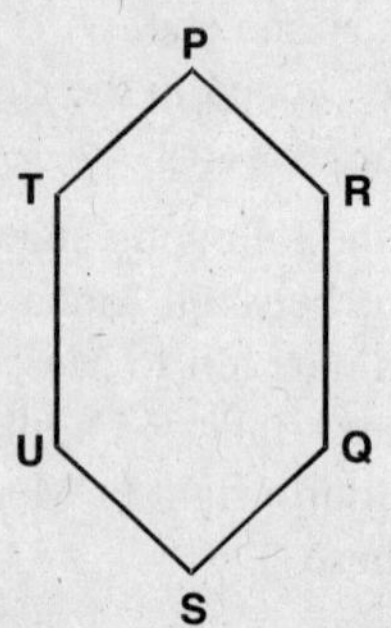

22. S is sitting opposite to P.

23. P is fourth person to the left of Q.

24. T and R are the neighbours of P.

25. Q is sitting opposite to T.

For Qs. Nos. 26 to 29:

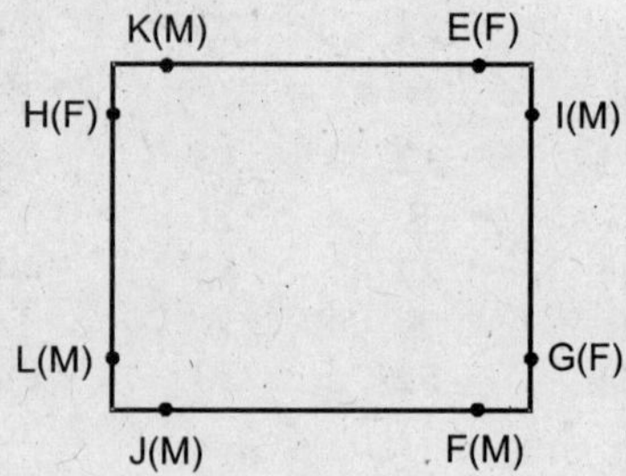

26. J is to the immediate left of F.

27. Both are male.

28. Three persons are seated between K and F (H, L and I or, E, I and G)

29. The three lady members are E, H and G.

30. The sitting arrangement of five boys are shown below:

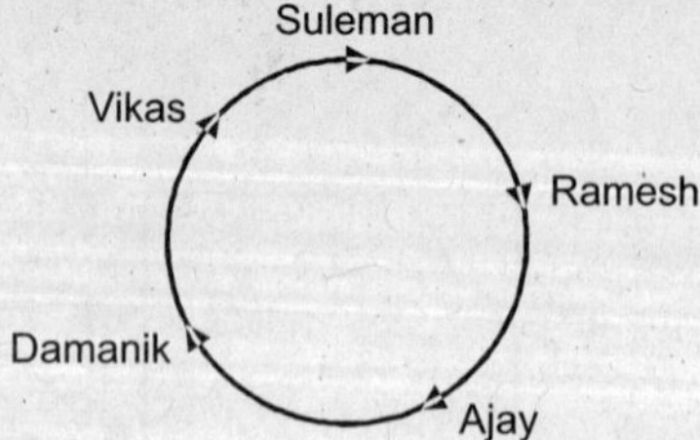

Hence, from the figure, Ramesh is sitting immediate right to Ajay.

For Qs. Nos. (31 to 33) : The order of sitting of all the eight persons which satisfies all the conditions will be as per figure.

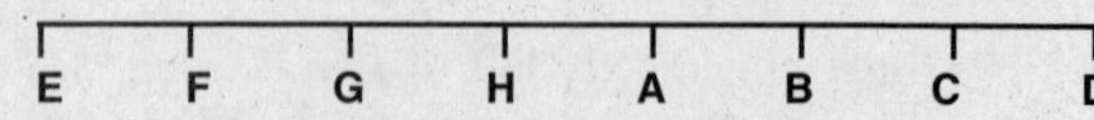

31. E and D are sitting at the extreme ends.

32. All the statements are correct.

33. Statement D is wrong because C is next to the right of B.

34. We see from the figure that Mr. Bhasin's next door neighbours are Mr. Lal and Mr. Sharma.

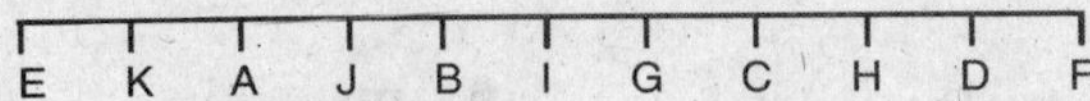

For Qs. Nos. (35 to 37) : Eleven students occupy the position in a row as shown in the figure.

E K A J B I G C H D F

35. D and K will be sitting at the two ends if the positions as given in the question are interchanged.

36. B is sitting between J and I.

37. All informations are required to know the position of all students in the row.

For Qs. Nos. (38 to 40) : Figure show the order of sitting arrangement of ten students. On the basis of the information exact position of C and H cannot be determined. However, they will occupy either first or fourth place from the right end.

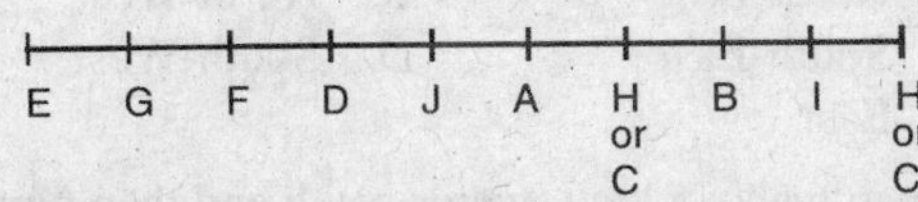

38. If positions of G and A are interchanged. A will become the immediate neighbour of E.

39. E is sitting at the left end.

40. Since the exact position of H and C is not known. However, they will occupy either seventh or tenth position from the left end.

For Qs. Nos. (41 to 43) : Figure shows the correct position of five persons sitting in a row.

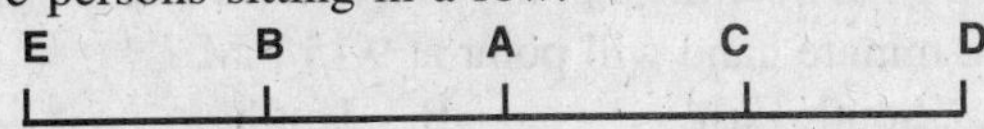

41. D is sitting at the extreme right of the bench.

42. B is second from the left.

43. A is sitting between B and C.

For Qs. Nos. (44 to 46) : Following the informations given in the questions, the location of all the eight rooms in two different rows can be shown in the figure.

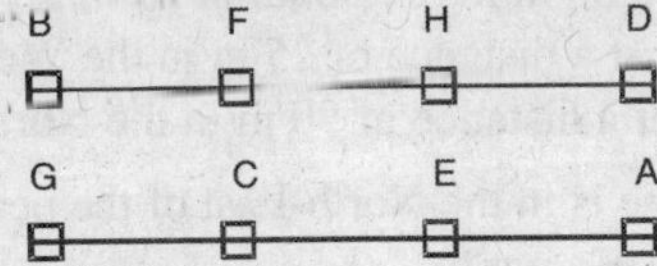

44. Room H is not located at either ends.

45. Room F is opposite to room C.

46. Room G is diagonally opposite to room D.

For Qs. Nos. (47 to 49) : On the basis of the information, the position of all the six flats can be shown as per figure.

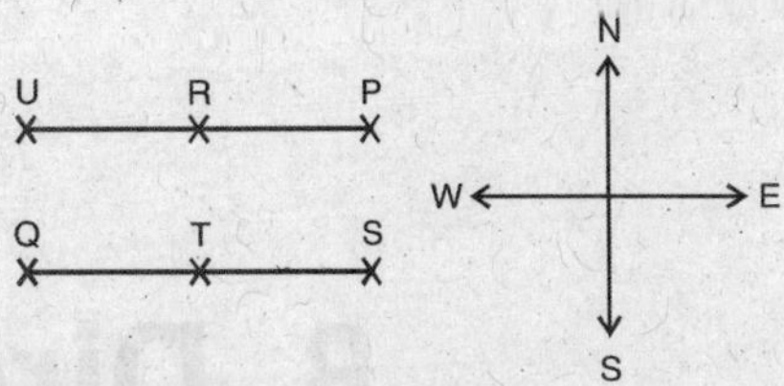

47. All the informations are required to answer the question.

48. After interchanging T and P, R's position does not get affected and R is next to U.

49. URP get the south facing flats.

50. The order of sitting is :

Amit, Shyam, Mayank, Ajay, Raghu

or

Ajay, Raghu, Mayank, Amit, Shyam

51. The order in which the girls are positioned is :

Rajni, Mini, Ananta, Saya, Jaya

or

Saya, Jaya, Ananta

or

Saya, Ananta, Jaya

52. The order of sitting while facing South is: Shyam, Mohan, Kittu, Sohan, Raju.

53-55. Order of sitting for questions 53 to 55 is : N, R, M, L, J, O, Q, P, K.

56-58. Five friends are standing in this order : Alok, Jayesh, Subodh, Pramod, Babir

59. The seating arrangement is as follows:

P X S Z R A

Therefore, right of P is X.

60.

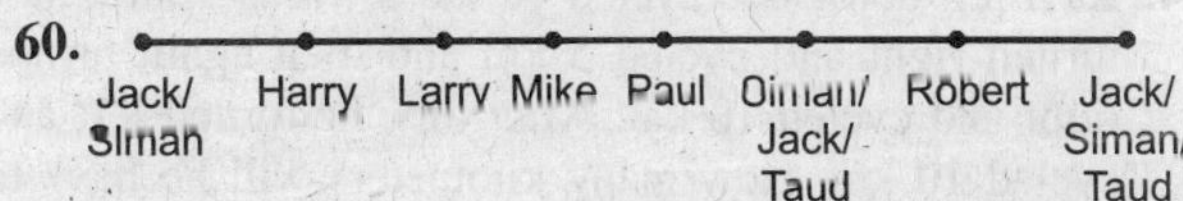

Hence, Taud can not be between Paul and Jack.

61. E B A C D

Therefore, A is sitting in between B and C

For (Qs. Nos. 62 to 65):

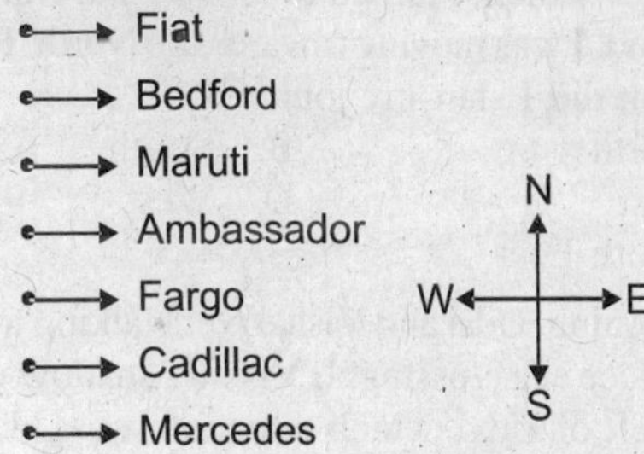

☆☆☆☆☆☆

8. Direction Sense

1. If A × B means A is to the south of B; A + B means A is to the north of B; A % B means A is to the east of B; A – B means A is to the west of B; then in P % Q + R – S, S is in which direction with respect to Q?
   A. South-West B. South-East
   C. North-East D. North-West
   E. None of these

2. One morning after sunrise Nivedita and Niharika were talking to each other face to face at Dolphin crossing. If Niharika's shadow was exactly to the right of Nivedita, which direction Niharika was facing?
   A. North B. South
   C. East D. Data is inadequate
   E. None of these

3. Reena walked from A and B in the East 10 feet. Then she turned to the right and walked 3 feet. Again she turned to the right and walked 14 feet. How far is she from A?
   A. 4 feet B. 5 feet
   C. 24 feet D. 27 feet
   E. 15 feet

4. Ravi left home and cycled 10 km towards South, then turned right and cycled 5 km and then again turned right and cycled 10 km. After this, he turned left and cycled 10 km. How many kilometers will he have to cycle to reach his home straight?
   A. 10 km B. 15 km
   C. 20 km D. 25 km
   E. 30km

5. After walking 6 km, I turned to the right and then walked 2 km. After then, I turned to the left and walked 10 km. In the end, I was moving towards the North. From which direction did I start my journey?
   A. North B. South
   C. East D. West
   E. South-East

6. One morning, Udai and Vishal were talking to each other face to face at a crossing. If Vishal's shadow was exactly to the left of Udai, which direction was Udai facing?
   A. East B. West
   C. North D. South
   E. North-East

7. Y is in the East of X which is in the North of Z. If P is in the South of Z, then in which direction of Y, is P?
   A. North B. South
   C. South-East D. All of the above
   E. South-East

8. If South-East becomes North, North-East becomes West and so on. What will West become?
   A. North-East B. North-West
   C. South-East D. South-West
   E. East

9. A man walks 5 km towards south and then turns to the right. After walking 3 km he turns to the left and walks 5 km. Now in which direction is he from the starting place?
   A. West B. South
   C. North-East D. South-West
   E. South-East

10. Rahul put his timepiece on the table in such a way that at 6 P.M. hour hand points to North. In which direction the minute hand will point at 9.15 P.M.?
    A. South-East B. South
    C. North D. West
    E. South-West

Directions (Q. 11–12): *Dev, Kumar, Nilesh, Ankur and Pintu are standing facing to the North in a playground such as given below:*

(*i*) Kumar is at 40 m to the right of Ankur.
(*ii*) Dev is are 60 m in the South of Kumar.
(*iii*) Nilesh is at a distance of 25 m in the West of Ankur.
(*iv*) Pintu is at a distance of 90 m in the North of Dev.

11. Which one is in the North-East of the person, who is to the left of Kumar?
    A. Dev B. Nilesh
    C. Ankur D. Pintu
    E. Pintu and Kumar

12. If a boy starting from Nilesh, met Ankur and then Kumar and after this he met Dev and then Pintu and all the time he walked in a straight line, then how much total distance did he cover?

A. 215 m B. 155 m
C. 245 m D. 185 m
E. 225m

Directions (Q. 13–15): *Each of the following questions is based on the following information:*

(*i*) Six flats on a floor in two rows facing North and South are allotted to P, Q, R, S, T and U.
(*ii*) Q gets a North facing flat and is not next to S.
(*iii*) S and U get diagonally opposite flats.
(*iv*) R next to U, gets a South facing flat and T gets North facing flat.

13. If the flats of P and T are interchanged then whose flat will be next to that of U?

A. P B. Q
C. R D. T
E. S

14. Which of the following combination get South facing flats?

A. QTS B. UPT
C. URP D. Data is inadequate
E. None of these

15. The flats of which of the other pair than SU, is diagonally opposite to each other?

A. QP B. QR
C. PT D. TS
E. QS

Directions (Q. 16–18): *Each of the following questions is based on the following information:*

(*i*) 8-trees → mango, guava, papaya, pomegranate, lemon, banana, raspberry, and apple are in two rows, 4 in each facing North and South.
(*ii*) Lemon is between mango and apple but just opposite to guava.
(*iii*) Banana is at one end of a line and is just next in the right of guava or either banana tree is just after guava tree.
(*iv*) Raspberry tree which is at one end of a line, is just diagonally opposite to mango tree.

16. Which of the following statements is definitely true?

A. Papaya tree is just near to apple tree.
B. Apple tree is just next to lemon tree.
C. Raspberry tree is either left to Pomegranate or after.
D. Pomegranate tree is diagonally opposite to banana tree.
E. None of these

17. Which tree is just opposite to raspberry tree?

A. Papaya
B. Pomegranate
C. Papaya or Pomegranate
D. Data is inadequate
E. Papaya or Banana

18. Which tree is just opposite to banana tree?

A. Mango B. Pomegranate
C. Papaya D. Data is inadequate
E. None of these

Directions (Q. 19–21): *Each of the following questions is based on the following information:*

(*i*) A # B means B is at 1 metre to the right of A.
(*ii*) A $ B means B is at 1 metre to the North of A.
(*iii*) A * B means B is at 1 metre to the left of A.
(*iv*) A @ B means B is at 1 metre to the south of A.
(*v*) In each question, first person from the left is facing North.

19. According to X @ B * Y, Y is in which direction with respect to X?

A. North B. South
C. North-East D. South-West
E. North-East

20. According to M # N $ T, T is in which direction with respect to M?

A. North-West B. North-East
C. South-West D. South-East
E. None of these

21. According to P # R $ A * U, in which direction is U with respect to P?

A. East B. West
C. North D. South
E. North-East

22. One morning after sunrise, Suresh was standing facing a pole. The shadow of the pole fell exactly to his right. To which direction was he facing?

A. East B. South
C. West D. Data is inadequate
E. None of these

23. A child went 90 m in the East to look for his father, then he turned right and went 20 m. After this he turned right and after going 30m, he reached to his uncle's house. His father was not there. From there, he went 100 m to his north and met his father. How far did he meet his father from the starting point?

A. 80 m B. 100 m
C. 140 m D. 260 m
E. 110m

24. Four friends A, B, C and D live in a same locality. The house of B is in the east of A's house but in the north of C's house. The house of C is in the west of D's house. D's house is in which direction of A's house?

A. South-East B. North-East
C. East D. Data is inadequate
E. None of these

25. Umesh directly went from P, to Q which is 9 feet distant. Then he turns to the right and walked 4 feet. After this he turned to the right and walked a distance which is equal from P to Q. Finally he turned to the right and walked 3 feet. How far is he now from P?

A. 6 feet B. 5 feet
C. 1 feet D. 10 feet
E. 4 feet

26. Shyam walks 5 km towards East and then turns left and walks 6 km. Again he turns right and walks 9 km. Finally he turns to his right and walks 6 km. How far is he from the starting point?

A. 26 km B. 21 km
C. 14 km D. 9 km
E. 15 km

27. Some boys are sitting in three rows all facing North such that A is in the middle row. P is just to the right of A but in the same row. Q is just behind of P while R is in the North of A. In which direction of R is Q?

A. South B. South-West
C. North-East D. South-East
E. North

28. Amit started walking positioning his back towards the sun. After some time, he turned left, then turned right and towards the left again. In which direction is he going now?

A. North or South B. East or West
C. North or West D. South or West
E. None of these

29. Village Q is to the North of the village P. The village R is in the East of village Q. The village S is to the left of the village P. In which direction is the village S with respect to village R?

A. West B. South-West
C. South D. North-West
E. South-East

30. Sundar runs 20 m towards East and turns to right and runs 10 m. Then he turns to the right and runs 9 m. Again he turns to right and runs 5 m. After this he turns to left and runs 12 m and finally he turns to right and 6 m. Now to which direction is Sundar facing?

A. East B. West
C. North D. South
E. North-West

ANSWERS

1	2	3	4	5	6	7	8	9	10
B	A	B	B	B	C	D	C	D	D
11	12	13	14	15	16	17	18	19	20
D	A	C	C	A	B	C	A	D	B
21	22	23	24	25	26	27	28	29	30
C	B	B	A	C	C	D	A	B	C

EXPLANATORY ANSWERS

1. According to P % Q + R – S

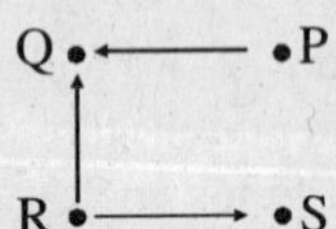

S is in the South-East of Q.

2.

Nivedita
Niharika's shadow
Niharika's
N
W
E
S

In the morning, sun rises in the East. Hence, any shadow falls in the West. Since Niharika's shadow was exactly to the right of Nivedita. Hence Niharika is facing North.

3.

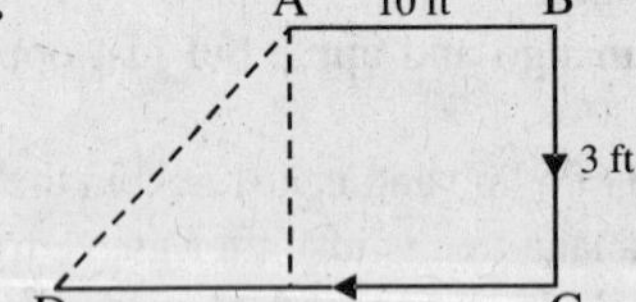

Required distance = AD

$= \sqrt{3^2 + (14-10)^2}$

$= \sqrt{9+16} = \sqrt{25} = 5$ ft

4.

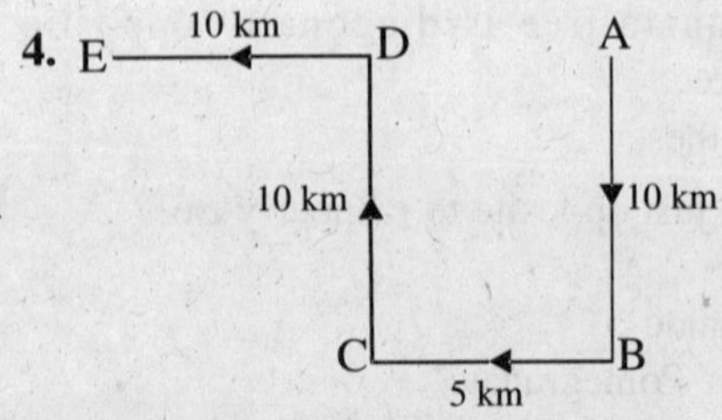

Required distance = AE

= 5 + 10 = 15 km.

5. 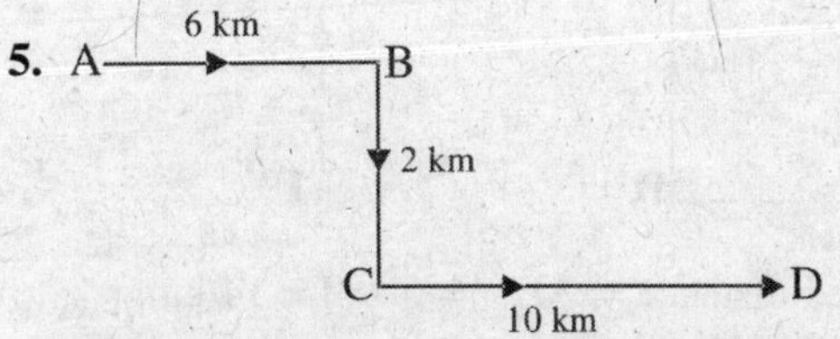

The journey was started from the South.

6. 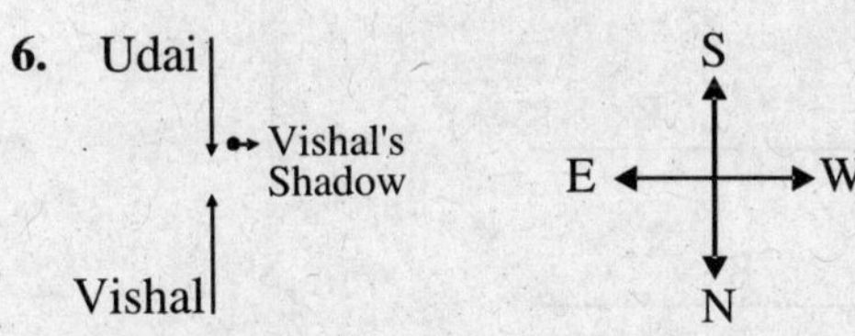

7. 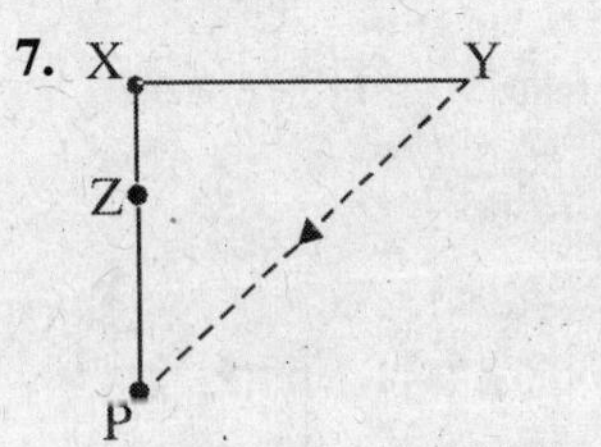

P is in South-West of Y.

8. 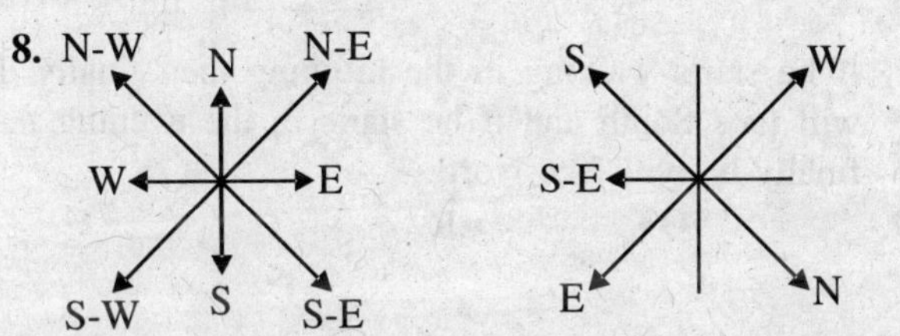

It is clear from the diagrams that new name of West will become South-East.

9. 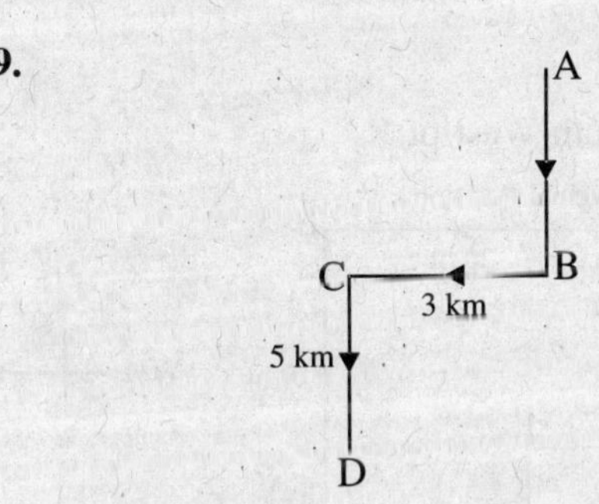

Hence, required direction is South-West.

10. 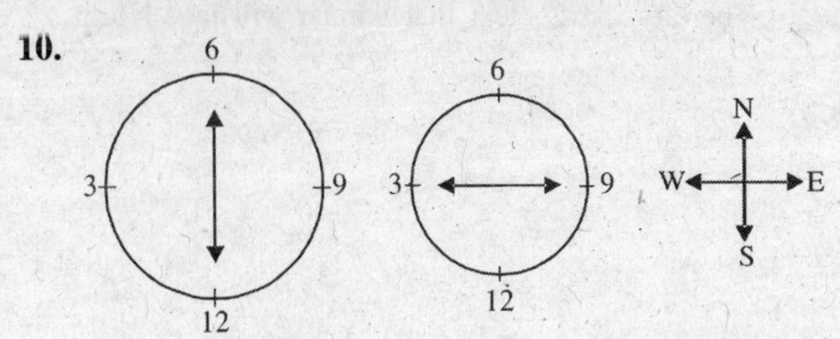

At 9.15 P.M., the minute hand will point towards West.

11. 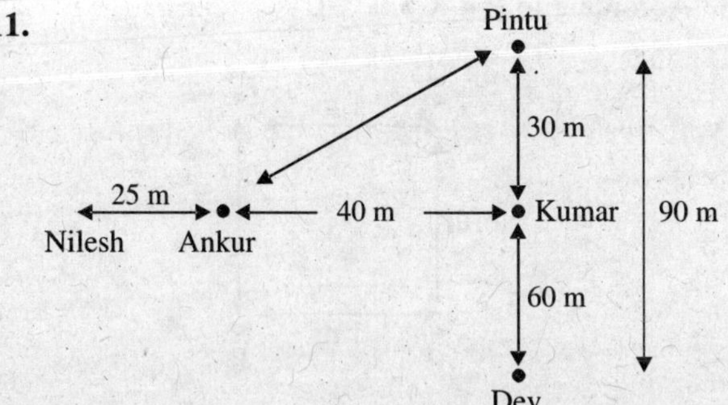

Ankur is in the left of Kumar. Hence Pintu is in North-East of Ankur.

12. Required distance = 25 m + 40 m + 60 m + 90 m

Required distance = 215 m

Answer For Q.No. 13 to 15:

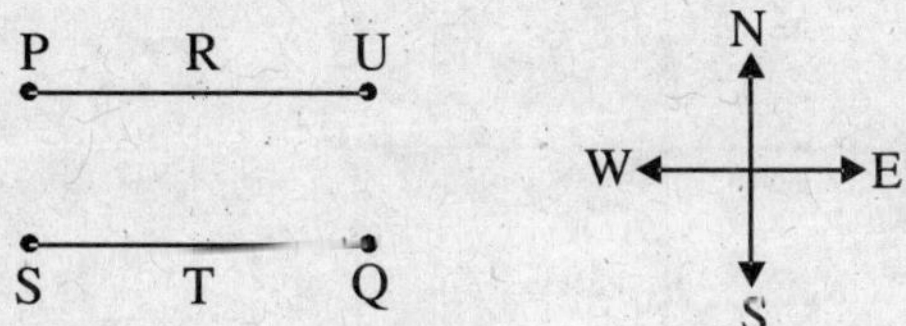

13. Flat R will be next to U.

14. URP flat combination get south facing flats.

15. OP is diagonally opposite to each-other.

Answer For Q.No. 16 to 18:

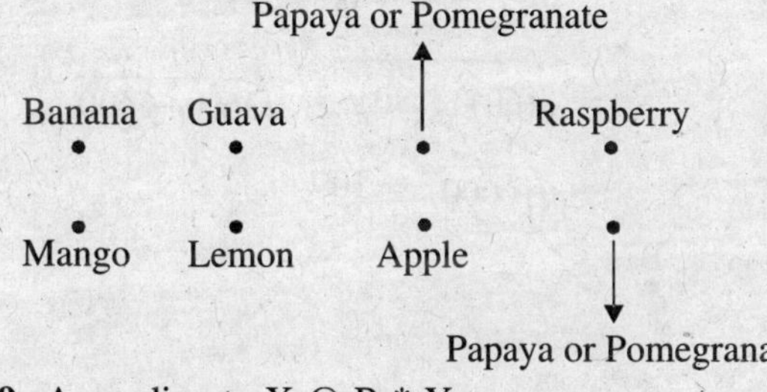

19. According to X @ B * Y

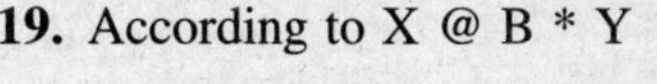

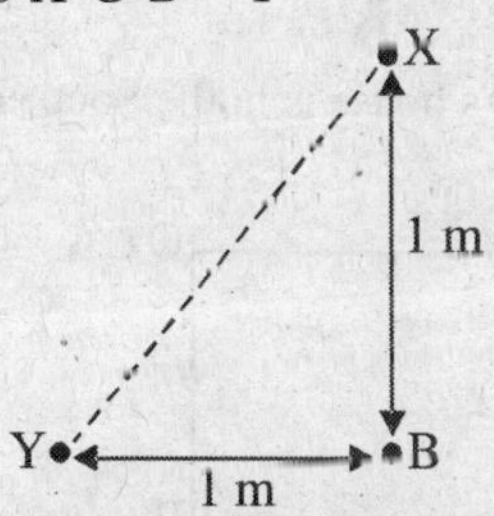

Hence Y is in South-West of X.

20. According to M # N $ T

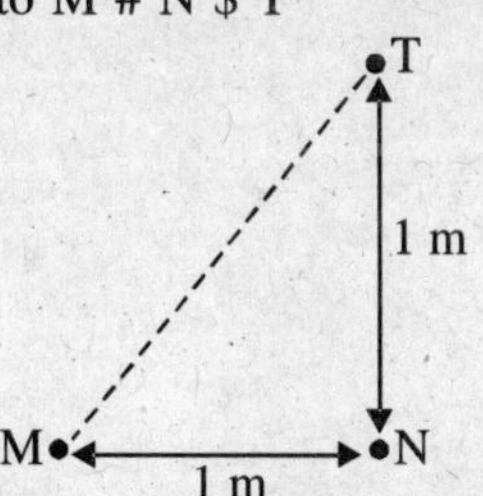

Hence, T is in the North-East of M.

21. According to P # R $ A * U

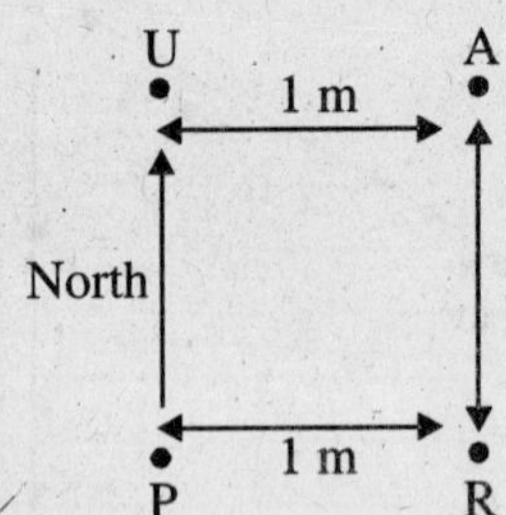

Hence, U is in North direction with respect to P.

22. Sun rises in the east in the morning. Since the shadow of Suresh falls to his right. So, he is facing South.

23.

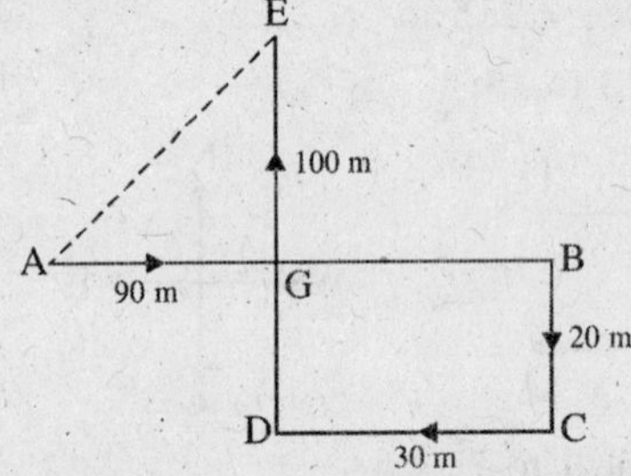

Required distance $= AE = \sqrt{AG^2 + EG^2}$

$= \sqrt{(90-30)^2 + (100-20)^2}$

$= \sqrt{(60)^2 + (80)^2} = \sqrt{3600+6400}$

$= \sqrt{10000} = 100$ m.

24. A B

C D

Therefore, D's house is in the South-East direction of A.

25.

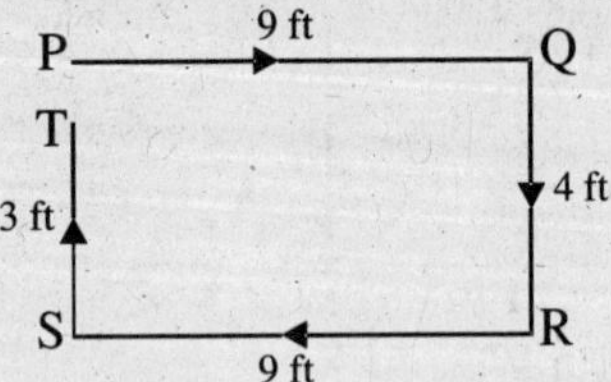

Required distance = PT = 4 – 3 = 1 ft

26.

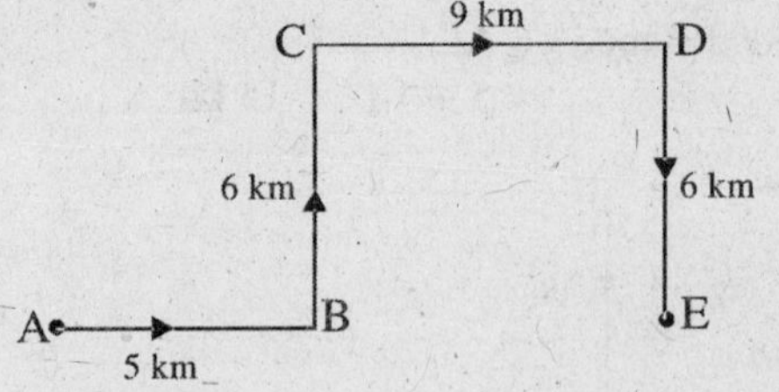

Required distance = AE = 5 + 9 = 14 km.

27.

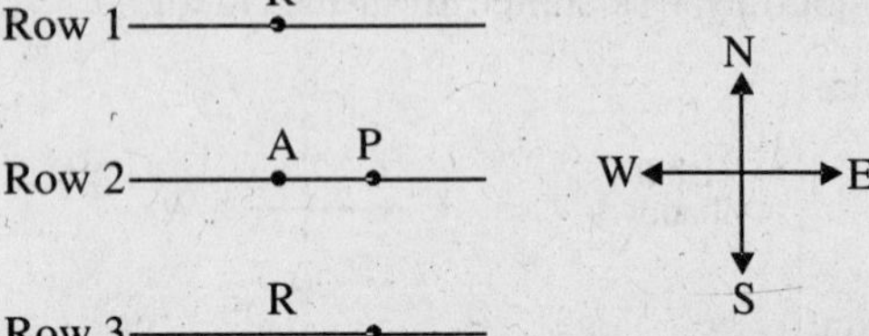

Q is in South-East of R.

28.

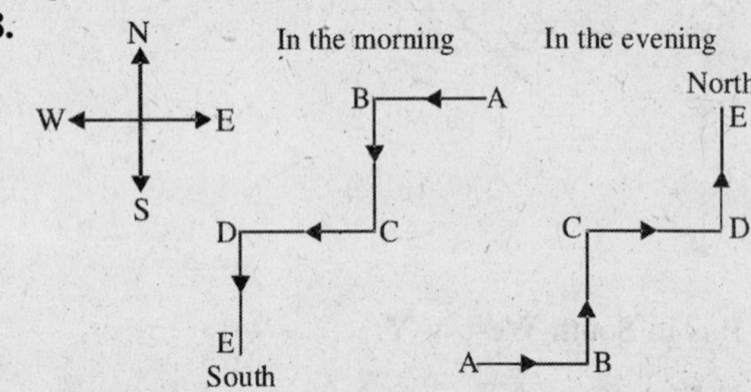

If he starts walking in the morning then finally, he will face South and if he starts in the evening then finally he will face North.

29.

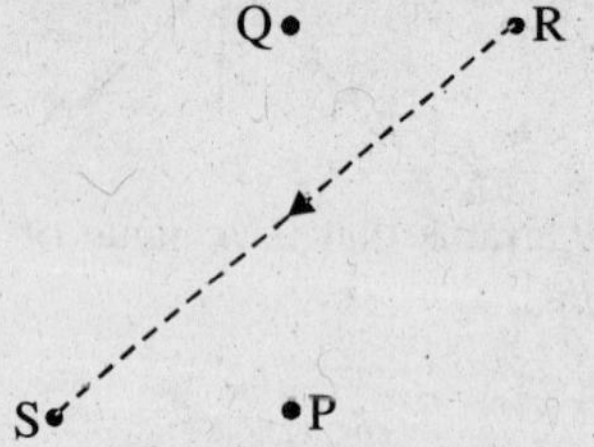

S is to the South-West of R.

30.

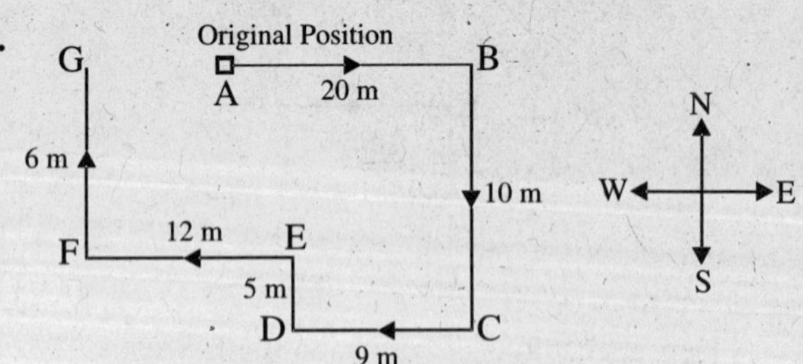

Therefore, it is clear that Sundar will face North.

☆☆☆☆☆☆

9. Input/Output

Directions (Q. 1–5) : *A word arrangement machine, when given an input line of words, first splits the line in two parts and then rearranges them following a particular rule in each step. The following is an illustration of input and the steps of rearrangements.*

Input : a bird in hand is better than two stuck in the bush.

Step I : a better bird in hand is bush than two stuck in the.

Step II : a better bird hand in is bush in than two stuck the.

Step III : a better bird hand in is bush in stuck than two the.

Step IV : a better bird hand in is bush in stuck than the two.

(Step IV is the last step for this input)

As per the rules followed in the above steps, find out in given question the appropriate step for the given input.

1. If step given below is the step I, then which of the following is definitely an input?
'all am zoo to a meet in circus'.
A. cannot be determind.
B. am all zoo to meet in a circus.
C. am zoo to all meet a in circus.
D. am zoo all to meet in circus a.
E. None of these.

2. What will be the step I of the following input?
Input : 'always look around before you leap.'
A. always look around before leap you.
B. always around look before you leap.
C. always around look before leap you.
D. always around before look you keep.
E. None of these.

3. Input : 'ill go all fate do in dart damn.'
Which step has following rearranged input line of words?
'all fate go ill damn dart do in'
A. III
B. II
C. IV
D. Cannot be determind
E. None of these

4. Which step will be the last step of the input given below?
Input : 'take it on as it where is basis.'
A. II
B. IV
C. III
D. Cannot be determind
E. None of these

5. What will be the step III of the given input?
Input : 'in every thing you always try to find some fault'.
A. always every in thing you fault find try to some.
B. always every in thing you fault find some try to.
C. always every in thing you fault find some to try.
D. always in every thing you fault try to find some.
E. none of these.

Directions (6–10) : *An electronic device, when fed with the numbers rearranges them in a particular order following certain rules. The following is a step by step process of rearrangements for the given input of numbers:*

Input : 5, 28, 12, 74, 3, 11, 31, 42.
Step I : 74, 5, 28, 12, 3, 11, 31, 42.
Step II : 74, 3, 5, 28, 12, 11, 31, 42.
Step III : 74, 3, 42, 5, 28, 12, 11, 31.
Step IV : 74, 3, 42, 5, 28, 11, 12, 31.

6. Which of the following will be the step III for the given input?
Input : 25, 08, 35, 11, 88, 67, 24, 78.
A. 88, 11, 78, 25, 24, 08, 35, 67.
B. 88, 11, 78, 25, 08, 35, 67, 24.
C. 88, 25, 08, 35, 11, 67, 24, 78.
D. 88, 11, 25, 08, 35, 67, 24, 78.
E. None of these.

7. Which of the following will be the step III for the given input?

Input : 89, 24, 44, 25, 9, 14, 5, 2.

A. 44, 5, 14, 25, 89, 9, 2, 24.
B. 44, 5, 14, 9, 24, 2, 89, 25.
C. 44, 5, 24, 9, 85, 25, 14, 2.
D. 44, 5, 89, 24, 25, 9, 14, 2.
E. None of these.

8. Which will be the IIIrd step for the given Input?

Input : 03 25 12 48 22 07

A. 48, 03, 22, 25, 12, 07.
B. 48, 03, 25, 12, 22, 07.
C. 48, 03, 22, 07, 12, 25.
D. 48, 03, 22, 07, 25, 12.
E. None of these.

9. Which of the following will be the last step for the given input?

Input : 05, 27, 50, 14, 24, 9.

A. III B. IV
C. VI D. VII
E. None of these.

10. If the step IV is as given below, which of the following will be the input?

Step IV : 48, 03, 22, 7, 12, 25.

A. 03, 25, 12, 48, 22, 07.
B. 03, 25, 48, 12, 22, 07.
C. 03, 48, 25, 12, 22, 07.
D. None of these.
E. Cannot be determined.

Directions (Q. 11–15): *Study the following information and answer the questions given below:*

An alphabetical machine, when given an input of words rearranges them following a particular rule in each step. The following is an illustration of input and steps of rearrangement.

Input : all that glitters is not gold but silver
Step I : but silver glitters is not gold all that
Step II : but silver not gold glitters is all that
Step III : silver not but gold glitters that is all
Step IV : silver not glitters that but gold is all
Step V : not glitters silver that but all gold is
Step VI : not glitters but all silver that gold is

11. If step V is "almost every week we celebrate some family function". Then what will be the step II?

A. celebrate week almost family every function some we
B. week almost celebrate family every we function some
C. celebrate week every function almost family some we
D. some we every function almost family celebrate week
E. None of these

12. Following the same sequence what will be the step VII for the input "make hay while the sun or moon shines"?

A. sun moon while make shines or hay the
B. while moon shines the sun make hay or
C. sun while moon make shines hay or the
D. while moon sun make shines the hay or
E. None of these

13. If input is "our villages are totally committed only to agriculture", then which of the following will be step IV?

A. committed are agriculture villages to our only totally
B. agriculture committed are villages to only totally our
C. agriculture committed to only are villages totally our
D. committed are to our agriculture villages only totally
E. None of these

14. If the input is "is replaced your defective get it if booklet" then what will be the step V?

A. booklet get your replaced if it defective is
B. get your booklet replaced if is it defective
C. get your booklet replaced if it is defective
D. get your if is booklet replaced it defective
E. None of these

15. If the second step is "doctor away keeps the a day an apple" then which of the following will be the step V?

A. a doctor keeps an away day apple the
B. away keeps a apple doctor the day an
C. keeps a away apple doctor an the day
D. keeps a doctor an away apple the day
E. None of these

Directions (Q. 16–20): *Study the following information carefully and answer the given questions:*

A word and number arrangement machine when given an input line of words and numbers rearranges them following a particular rule in each step. The following is an illustration of input and rearrangement.

Input : by now 25 72 sight 37 15 home
Step I : sight by now 25 72 37 15 home
Step II : sight 15 by now 25 72 37 home
Step III : sight 15 now by 25 72 37 home
Step IV : sight 15 now 25 by 72 37 home
Step V : sight 15 now 25 home by 72 37
Step VI : sight 15 now 25 home 37 by 72

And Step VI is the last step of the rearrangement.

As per the rules followed in the above steps, find out in each of the following questions the appropriate step for the given input.

16. **Input :** ask for me 49 32 64 and 24

Which of the following will be Step III?

A. me 24 for 32 ask 49 and 64
B. me 24 ask for 49 32 64 and
C. me 24 for 32 ask 49 64 and
D. me 24 for ask 49 32 64 and
E. None of these

17. Step III of an input is:
yellow 12 tire 92 84 36 goal life
How many more steps will be required to complete the rearrangement?
A. Three B. Four
C. Five D. Six
E. None of these

18. Step II of an input is:
victory 19 22 34 age bear high 24
Which of the following will be Step VII?
A. victory 19 high 22 bear 24 age 34
B. victory 19 high 22 bear 24 34 age
C. victory 19 high 22 bear 34 age 24
D. victory 19 high 22 34 age bear 24
E. There will be no Step VII

19. Input : go now and come 72 34 57 25
How many steps will be required to complete the rearrangement?
A. Four B. Five
C. Six D. Seven
E. None of these

20. Step IV of an input is : now 17 mother 23 can know 47 31
How many more steps will be required to complete the rearrangement?
A. Two B. Three
C. Four D. Five
E. None of these

Directions (Q. 21–25) : *Given an input a machine generates passcodes step by step following certain rules as illustrated below:*

Input : talk seven 37 48 given 83 likely 62
Step I : 37 talk seven 48 given 83 likely 62
Step III : 37 talk 48 seven given 83 likely 62
Step IV : 37 talk 48 seven 62 likely given 83
Step V : 37 talk 48 seven 62 likely 83 given
Step V is the last step for this input.

In the following questions same logic as illustrated above is to be used.

21. Step II for an input is "23 working 48 32 park blossom 26 garden". What will we be the fifth step?
A. 23 working 26 park 48 32 blossom garden
B. 23 working 26 park 32 48 blossom garden
C. 23 working 26 32 park 48 blossom garden
D. 23 working 26 48 park 32 blossom garden
E. None of these

22. Second step of an input "12 where 82 33 great wall 49 just". Which step will be the last step?
A. VI B. VII
C. VIII D. IV
E. None of these

23. What will be Step III for the following input?
Input : phone computer 32 link 18 75 46 dairy
A. 18 phone 46 link computer 75 32 diary
B. 18 phone 32 link 46 computer 75 diary
C. 18 phone 32 computer link 75 46 diary
D. 18 phone 32 link computer 75 46 diary
E. None of these

24. Step IV of an input "22 united 37 trading killer 45 72 jogger". What will be the input definitely?
A. United 22 37 jogger 45 trading 72 killer
B. United trading 22 37 jogger 45 72 killer
C. United 22 trading jogger 37, killer 45 72
D. Cannot be determined
E. None of these

25. What will be the third step of an input whose first step is "17 45 follow rule examination 36 85 hut"?
A. 17 rule 36 45 follow examination 85 hut
B. 17 rule 36 45 follow 85 examination hut
C. 17 rule 36 45 examination follow 85 hut
D. Cannot be determined
E. None of these

Directions (Q. 26–30): *Study the following information carefully to answer the questions given below.*

A word arrangement machine when given an input line of words, rearranges them following a particular rule in each step. The following is an illustration of input and steps of rearrangement.

Input: prime minister said he would soon raise this matter in the cabinet.

Step I : he prime minister said would soon cabinet raise this matter in the
Step II : he minister prime said would soon cabinet in raise this matter the
Step III : he minister prime said soon would cabinet in matter raise this the
Step IV : he minister prime said soon would cabinet in matter raise the this

As per the rules followed in the above steps, find out in the given questions the appropriate step for the given input.

26. Which of the following will be 3rd step of input: "experts in their field have helped us design the curriculum".
A. experts field have in their curriculum, helped us design the
B. experts field .have in their curriculum design helped the us
C. experts field in their have curriculum helped us design the
D. Cannot be determined
E. None of these

27. Input : "work hard to get first position in this renowned institution." Which of the following would be the step IV for this input?

A. first get hard work to in institution position renowned this
B. first get hard to work in institution position renowned this
C. first get hard to work in institution this renowned position
D. first work hard to get in position this renowned institution.
E. None of these

28. If step II of an input is "beat he threatened to confessed he him unless", what would be the input?

A. he threatened to beat him he confessed unless
B. he confessed unless he threatened to beat him
C. he threatened to beat him unless he confessed
D. he beat him unless he confessed threatened to
E. None of these

29. If step IV of an input is, "his opinion or right whatever concern does me of wrong," what would be the input?

I. his opinion or right whatever concern does me wrong not
B. his opinion whatever right or concern wrong does not me
C. his opinion whatever right or wrong does not concern me
D. his opinion right whatever or wrong does not concern me
E. None of these

30. If step II of an input is "closely examined this one fact if be guilty proves the man to", which of the following steps would read as "closely examined fact if this one be guilty man proves the to"?

A. Step III B. Step IV
C. Step V D. Step I
E. None of these

Directions (Q. 31–35) : *Study the following information carefully and answer the given questions:*

A word and number arrangement machine when given an input line of words and numbers rearranges them following a particular rule in each step. The following is an illustration of input and rearrangement.

Input : rose petal 29 32 86 goal 41 toll
Step I : 29 rose petal 32 86 goal 41 toll
Step II : 29 toll rose petal 32 86 goal 41
Step III : 29 toll 32 rose petal 86 goal 41
Step IV : 29 toll 32 rose 41 petal 86 goal
and Step IV is the last step of the rearrangement.

31. Input : man 79 over 63 like 43 joy 15
How many steps will be required to complete the rearrangement?

A. Six B. Seven
C. Eight D. Nine
E. None of these

32. Step II of an **Input :** 27 world go 57 48 stem 35 kite
How many more steps will be required to complete the rearrangement?

A. Five B. Four
C. Three D. Six
E. None of these

33. Input : 94 join for 81 style home 32 48
Which of the following steps will be the last?

A. VI B. V
C. VII D. IX
E. None of these

34. Step III of an Input : 18 tower 38 basket 82 76 hall new
Which of the following will be step VII?

A. 18 tower 38 hall 76 new basket 82
B. 18 tower 38 new 76 hall 82 basket
C. 18 tower 38 hall 76 new 82 basket
D. There will be no such step
E. None of these

35. Step III of an input is : 15 yes 24 80 today never go 59
Which of the following will definitely be the input?

A. 24 80 today never go 59 15 yes
B. 24 80 today yes never go 59 15
C. 24 15 yes 80 today never go 59
D. Cannot be determined
E. None of these

ANSWERS

1	2	3	4	5	6	7	8	9	10
A	C	A	C	B	B	E	D	B	E
11	**12**	**13**	**14**	**15**	**16**	**17**	**18**	**19**	**20**
A	E	B	B	C	D	B	E	B	A
21	**22**	**23**	**24**	**25**	**26**	**27**	**28**	**29**	**30**
B	A	D	D	A	B	B	C	C	B
31	**32**	**33**	**34**	**35**					
E	A	A	B	D					

EXPLANATORY ANSWERS

For Q. Nos. (1 to 5) : Rule given in the illustration suggests that first split the input into two halves and then arrange each half in alphabetical order simultaneously in each step.

1. We cannot determine the input for any given step.

2. Input : always look around before you leap.
Step I : always around look before leap you.

3. Input : ill go all fate do in dart damn.
Step I : all ill go fate damn do in dart.
Step II : all fate ill go damn dart do in.
Step III : all fate go ill damn dart do in.

4. Input : take it on as it where is basis.
Step I : as take it on basis it where is.
Step II : as it take on basis is it where.
Step III : as it on take basis is it where.

5. Input : In everything you always try to find some fault.
Step I : always in every thing you fault try to find some.
Step II : always every in thing you fault find try to some.
Step III : always every in thing you fault find some try to.

For Qs. Nos. (6 to 10) : Pattern of the arrangement of steps of given input suggests that given input is splitted into two sections—One for even numbers and other for old numbers. Then arrange these numbers in such a way that even numbers are arranged in descending order and old numbers are arranged in ascending order.

6. Input : 25, 08, 35, 11, 88, 67, 24, 78.
Step I : 88, 25, 08, 35, 11, 67, 24, 78.
Step II : 88, 11, 25, 8, 35, 67, 24 , 78.
Step III : 88, 11, 78, 25, 8, 35, 67, 24.

7. Input : 89 24 44 25 9 14 5 2
Step I : 44 89 24 25 9 14 5 2
Step II : 44 5 89 24 25 9 14 2
Step III : 44 5 24 89 25 9 14 2

Since, none of the given options contain correct order of the input as shown by step III, hence, our answer is options E.

8. Input : 03, 25, 12, 48, 22, 07.
Step I : 48, 03, 25, 12, 22, 07.
Step II : 48, 03, 22, 25, 12, 07.
Step III : 48, 03, 22, 07, 25, 12.

9. Input : 05, 27, 50, 14, 24, 9.
Step I : 50, 05, 27, 14, 24, 9.
Step II : 50, 05, 24, 27, 14, 9.
Step III : 50, 05, 24, 9, 27, 14.
Step IV : 50, 05, 24, 9, 14, 27.

Step IV is the last step for the given input as it arranges the input completely.

10. We cannot determine the input for the given step because exact placement of the numbers in input be known. As a result option (A) and (B) both reflect the probable input.

For Qs. 11 to 15: On the basis of given inputs and various steps of rearrangement we can analyse the rule in the following manner:

	1	**2**	**3**	**4**	**5**	**6**	**7**	**8**
Input :	All	that	glitters	is	not	gold	but	silver
Step I :	7	8	3	4	5	6	1	2
Step II :	7	8	5	6	3	4	1	2
Step III :	8	5	7	6	3	2	4	1
Step IV :	8	5	3	2	7	6	4	1
Step V :	5	3	8	2	7	1	6	4
Step VI :	5	3	7	1	8	2	6	4
Therefore,								
Step VII :	3	7	5	1	8	4	2	6

16. Input : ask for me 49 32 64 and 24
Step I : me ask for 49 32 64 and 24
Step II : me 24 ask for 49 32 64 and
Step III : me 24 for ask 49 32 64 and

Hence, step III is – me 24 for ask 49 32 64 and

17. Step III : yellow 12 tire 92 84 36 goal life
Step IV : yellow 12 tire 36 92 84 goal life
Step V : yellow 12 tire 36 life 92 84 goal
Step VI : yellow 12 tire 36 life 84 92 goal
Step VII : yellow 12 tire 36 life 84 goal 92

Hence, Four more steps are required.

18. Step II(given) – victory 19 22 34 age bear high 24
Step III : victory 19 high 22 34 age bear 24
Step IV : victory 19 high 22 bear 34 age 24
Step V : victory 19 high 22 bear 24 34 age
Step VI : victory 19 high 22 bear 24 age 34

The arrangement has completed in six steps only.
Hence, there will be no step VII.

19. Input : go now and come 72 34 57 25
Step I : now go and come 72 34 57 25
Step II : now 25 go and come 72 34 57
Step III : now 25 go 34 and come 72 57
Step IV : now 25 go 34 come and 72 57
Step V : now 25 go 34 come 57 and 72

Hence, five steps are required to complete the rearrangement.

20. Step IV : now 17 mother 23 can know 47 31 (Given)
Step V : now 17 mother 23 know can 47 31
Step VI: now 17 mother 23 know 31 can 47
Hence, two more steps are required to complete the rearrangement.

21. Step II : 23 working 48 32 park blossom 26 garden (Given)
Step III: 23 working 26 48 32 park blossom garden
Step IV: 23 working 26 park 48 32 blossom garden
Step V : 23 working 26 park 32 48 blossom garden
Hence, the fifth step is – 23 working 26 park 32 48 blossom garden.

22. Step II : 12 where 82 33 great wall 49 just Given,
Step III : 12 where 33 82 great wall 49 just
Step IV : 12 where 33 wall 82 great 49 just
Step V : 12 where 33 wall 49 82 great just
Step VI : 12 where 33 wall 49 just 82 great
Hence, the sixth step will be the last step.

23. Input : phone computer 32 link 18 75 46 dairy
Step I : 18 phone computer 32 link 75 46 dairy
Step II : 18 phone 32 comptuer link 75 75 46 dairy
Step III : 18 phone 32 link computer 75 46 dairy
Hence, the third step is –
18 phone 32 link computer 75 46 dairy.

24. The input can not be determined.

25. Step I : 17 45 follow rule examination 36 85 hut (Given)
Step II : 17 rule 45 follow examination 36 85 hut
Step III : 17 rule 36 45 follow examination 85 hut.
Hence, the step III is — 17 rule 36 45 follow examination 85 hut.

26. Input : experts in their field have helped us design the curriculum
Step I : experts field in their have curriculum helped us design the
Step II : experts field have in their curriculum design helped us the
Step III : experts field have in their curriculum design helped the us
Hence, the third step is—
experts field have in their curriculum design helped the us.

27. Input : work hard to get first position in this renowned institution.
Step I : first work hard to get in position this renowned institution
Step II : first get work hard to in institution position this renowned
Step III : first get hard work to in institution position renowned this
Step IV : first get hard to work in institution position renowned this.
Hence, the step IV is—first get hard to work in institution position renowned this.

28. Since, the input of the conditional part is a correct sentence, hence, input of the given step will be–"he threatened to beat him unless he confessed".

29. Since, the input of the conditional part is a correct sentence, hence, input of the given step will be– "his opinion wheather right or wrong does not concern me."

30. Step II : closely examined this one fact if be guilty (Given) proves the man to.
Step III : closely examined fact this one if be guilty man proves the to
Step IV : closely examined fact if this one be guilty man proves the to.
Obviously, the given rearrangement is of the fourth step.

31. Input : man 79 over 63 like 43 joy 15
Step I : 15 man 79 over 63 like 43 joy
Step II : 15 over man 79 63 like 43 joy
Step III : 15 over 43 man 79 63 like joy
Step IV : 15 over 43 man 63 79 like joy
Step V : 15 over 43 man 63 like 79 joy
and Step V is the last step of the rearrangement.

32. Step II : 27 world go 57 48 stem 35 kite
Step III : 27 world 35 go 57 48 stem kite
Step IV : 27 world 35 stem go 57 48 kite
Step V : 27 world 35 stem 48 go 57 kite
Step VI : 27 world 35 stem 48 kite go 57
Step VII: 27 world 35 stem 48 kite 57 go
Thus, five more steps will be required to complete the rearrangement.

33. Input : 94 join for 81 style home 32 48
Step I : 32 94 join for 81 style home 48
Step II : 32 style 94 join for 81 home 48
Step III : 32 style 48 94 join for 81 home
Step IV : 32 style 48 join 94 for 81 home
Step V : 32 style 48 join 81 94 for home
Step VI : 32 style 48 join 81 home 94 for
Thus, Step VI is the last step.

34. Step III : 18 tower 38 basket 82 76 hall new
Step IV : 18 tower 38 new basket 82 76 hall
Step V : 18 tower 38 new 76 basket 82 hall
Step VI : 18 tower 38 new 76 hall basket 82
Step VII: 18 tower 38 new 76 hall 82 basket

35. Input can not be determined.

☆☆☆☆☆☆

10. Logical Deduction

Directions (Q. 1–30): *In each quesiton below there are two statements followed by two conclusions numbered I and II. You have to take the two given statements to be true even if they seem to be at variance from commonly known facts and then decide which of the given conclusions logically follows from the two given statements, disregarding commonly known facts.*

Give Answer

(A) If only conclusion I is follows.

(B) If only conclusion II is follows.

(C) If either I or II follows.

(D) If neither I nor II follows.

(E) If both I and II follows.

1. Statements: No women teacher can play. Some women teachers are athletes.

Conclusions:

I. Male athletes can play.

II. Some athletes can play.

2. Statements: All bags are cakes. All lamps are cakes.

Conclusions:

I. Some lamps are bags.

II. No lamp is bag.

3. Statements: All mangoes are golden in colour, No golden-coloured things are cheap.

Conclusions:

I. All mangoes are cheap.

II. Golden-coloured mangoes are not cheap.

4. Statements: Some kings are queens. All queens are beautiful.

Conclusions:

I. All kings are beautiful.

II. All queens are kings.

5. Statements: All good athletes win. All good athletes eat well.

Conclusions:

I. All those who eat well are good athletes.

II. All those who win eat well.

6. Statements: All film stars are playback singers. All film directors are film stars.

Conclusions:

I. All film directors are playback singers.

II.. Some film stars are film directors.

7. Statements: All hill stations have a sun-set point. X is a hill station.

Conclusions:

I. X has a sun-set point.

II. Places other than hill stations do not have sun-set points.

8. Statements: Some dreams are nights. Some nights are days.

Conclusions:

I. All days are either nights or dreams.

II. Some days are nights.

9. Statements: All jungles are tigers. Some tigers are horses.

Conclusions:

I. Some horses are jungles.

II. No horse is jungle.

10. Statements: All poles are guns. Some boats are not poles.

Conclusions:

I. All guns are boats.

II. Some boats are not guns.

11. Statements: Many scooters are trucks. All trucks are trains.

Conclusions:

I. Some scooters are trains.

II.. No truck is a scooter.

12. Statements: Some papers are pens. Angle is a paper.

Conclusions:

I. Angle is not a pen.

II. Angle is a pen.

13. Statements: All birds are tall. Some tall are hens.

Conclusions:

I. Some birds are hens.

II. Some hens are tall.

14. Statements: Some papers are pens. Some pencils are pens.

Conclusions:

I. Some pens are pencils.

II. Some pens are papers.

15. Statements: Some men are educated. Educated persons prefer small families.

Conclusions:

I. All small families are educated.

II. Some men prefer small families.

16. Statements: All educated people read newspapers. Rahul does not read newspaper.

Conclusions:

I. Rahul is not educated.

II. Reading newspaper is not essential to be educated.

17. Statements: All pens are chalks. All chairs are chalks.

Conclusions:

I. Some pens are chairs.

II. Some chalks are pens.

18. Statements: Some ants are parrots. All the parrots are apples.

Conclusions:

I. All the apples are parrots.

II. Some ants are apples.

19. Statements: All the windows are doors. No door is a wall.

Conclusions:

I. Some windows are walls.

II. No wall is a door.

20. Statements: All lions are tigers. All tigers are goats.

Conclusions :

I. All lions are goats.

II. All goats are lions.

21. Statements: Some doctors are doors. All doors are table.

Conclusions :

I. Some doctors are tables.

II. Some tables are doctors.

22. Statements: All birds are crows. All parrots are sparrows.

Conclusions :

I. All birds are parrots.

II. All crows are sparrows.

23. Statements: All bowls are spoons. No spoon is a plate.

Conclusions :

I. No plate is a bowl.

II. No bowl is plate.

24. Statements: Some parrots are crows. No crows is green.

Conclusions :

I. No parrot is green.

II. No crow is brown.

25. Statements: All tubes are handles. All cups are handles.

Conclusions :

I. All cups are tubes.

II. Some handles are not cups.

26. Statements: All coins are crows. Some crows are pencils.

Conclusions :

I. No pencil is coin.

II. Some coins are pencils.

27. Statements: All windows are boys. All boys are doors.

Conclusions :

I. All windows are doors.

II. Some doors are boys.

28. Statements: All birds are parrots. No parrot is box.

Conclusions :

I. All parrots are birds.

II. No bird is box.

29. Statements: Some dramatists are poets. All artists are poets.

Conclusions :

I. Some dramatists are artists.

II. All poets are artists.

30. Statements: All mats are chairs. All chairs are tickets.

Conclusions :

I. All mats are tickets.

II. Some tickets are mats.

Directions (Q. 31–50) : *In each question given below two statements are followed by four conclusions numbered I, II, III and IV. You have to take the two given statements to be true even if they seem to be at variance from commonly known facts. Read the statements and conclusions and decide which of the conclusions logically follows from the two given statements, disregarding commonly known facts.*

31. Statements: All the phones are scales. All the scales are calculators.

Conclusions:

I. All the calculators are scales.

II. All the phones are calculators.

III. All the scales are phones.

IV. Some calculators are phones.

A. Only I and IV B. Only III and IV

C. Only II and IV D. Only I and II

E. Only I and III

32. Statements: No door is dog. All the dogs are cats.

Conclusions:

I. No door is cat.

II. No cat is door.

III. Some cats are dogs.

IV. All the cats are dogs.

A. Only II and IV B. Only I and III

C. Only III and IV D. Only III

E. All the four

33. Statements: Some tables are T.V. Some T.V. are radios.

Conclusions:

I. Some tables are radios.
II. Some radios are tables.
III. All the radios are T.V.
IV. All the T.V. are tables.

A. Only II and IV B. Only I and III
C. Only IV D. Only I and IV
E. None of the four

34. Statements: All men are vertebrates. Some mammals are vertebrates.

Conclusions:

I. All men are mammals.
II. All mammals are men.
III. Some vertebrates are mammals.
IV. All vertebrates are men.

A. Only IV B. Only II
C. Only III D. Only I
E. Only I and III

35. Statements: All green are blue. All blue are white.

Conclusions:

I. Some blue are green.
II. Some white are green.
III. Some green are not white.
IV. All white are blue.

A. Only I and II B. Only I and III
C. Only I and IV D. Only II and IV
E. None of the four

36. Statements: Some pens are books. Some books are pencils.

Conclusions:

I. Some pens are pencils.
II. Some pencils are pens.
III. All pencils are pens.
IV. All books are pens.

A. Only I and III B. Only II and IV
C. All the four D. None of the four
E. Only I

37. Statements: All the research scholars are psychologists. Some psychologists are scientists.

Conclusions:

I. All the research scholars are scientists.
II. Some research scholars are scientists.
III. Some scientists are psychologists.
IV. Some psychologists are research scholars.

A. Only III and IV B. None of the four
C. All the four D. Only III
E. Only II and IV

38. Statements: All the goats are tigers. All the tigers are lions.

Conclusions:

I. All the goats are lions.
II. All the lions are goats.
III. Some lions are goats.
IV. Some tigers are goats.

A. All the four B. Only I, II and III
C. Only I, III and IV D. Only II, III and IV
E. None of these

39. Statements: All members are students. No student is a girl.

Conclusions :

I. All students are members.
II. No members is a girl.
III. Some students are members.
IV. Some members are girls.

A. Only I follows
B. Only I, II and III follow
C. All follows
D. Only II and III follows
E. None follows

40. Statements : All soaps are clean. All clean are wet.

Conclusions :

I. Some clean are soaps.
II. No clean is soap.
III. Some wet are soaps.
IV. All wet are soaps.

A. Only I follows
B. Only I and II follow
C. Only either III and IV follow
D. Only I and III follow
E. None follows

41. Statements: All scientists are fools. All fools are illiterates.

Conclusions :

I. All scientists are illiterates.
II. All illiterates are scientists.
III. All illiterates are fools.
IV. Some illiterates could be scientists.

A. Only I and IV follow
B. Only II follows
C. Only II and III follow
D. Only IV follows
E. All follow.

42. Statements: All players are teachers. Some teachers are jokers.

Conclusions :

I. All players are jokers.
II. Some players are jokers.
III. Some jokers are teachers.
IV. Some teachers are players.

A. All follow
B. Only III and IV follow
C. Only II and IV follow
D. Only either IV or I and II follow
E. None follows

43. Statements: All pins are scales. All scales are caves.

Conclusions :

I. All caves are scales.
II. All scales are pins.
III. All pins are caves.
IV. Some caves are pins.

A. All follow
B. Only I, II and III follow
C. Only either III or II and IV follow
D. Only III and IV follow
E. None follows

44. Statements: Some men are goats. All goats are jackals.

Conclusions :

I. Some men are jackals.
II. Some jackals are men.
III. All jackals are goats.
IV. Some goats are men.

A. Only I and II follow
B. Only III and IV follow
C. Only IV follows
D. All follow
E. None of these

45. Statements: Some frogs are bricks. All bricks are cakes.

Conclusions :

I. Some cakes are not frogs.
II. Some cakes are frogs.
III. No cake is frog.
IV. All frogs are cakes.

A. Only I and II follow
B. All follow
C. None follows
D. Only II, III and IV follow
E. Only I, II and IV follow

46. Statements: Some pencils are papers. Some papers are boxes.

Conclusions :

I. Some pencils are boxes.
II. Some boxes are pencils.
III. Some boxes are papers.
IV. Some papers are pencils.

A. Only I and II follow
B. All follow
C. Only III and IV follow
D. None follows
E. None of these

47. Statements : Some clothes are marbles. Some marbles are bags.

Conclusions :

I. No cloth is a bag.
II. All marbles are bags.
III. Some bags are clothes.
IV. No marble is a cloth.

A. Only either I or IV follows
B. Only I or II follows
C. Only I or III follows
D. None follows
E. All follow

48. Statements: Some camels are ships. No ship is a boat.

Conclusions :

I. Some ships are camels.
II. Some boats are camels.
III. Some camels are not boats.
IV. All boats are camels.

A. Only I follows
B. Only II and III follow
C. Only I and III follow
D. Only I and II follow
E. Only either III or IV follows

49. Statements: Some green are blue. No blue is white.

Conclusions :

I. Some blue are green.
II. Some white are green.
III. Some green are not white.
IV. All white are green.

A. Only I follows
B. Only II and III follow
C. Only I and II follow
D. Only I and III follow
E. Only either II or IV follows

50. Statements: Some students are brilliant. Sushma is a student.

Conclusions :

I. Some sutdents are dull.
II. Sushma is brilliant.
III. Sushma is dull.
IV. Students are usually brilliant.

A. Only I follows
B. Only I and II follows
C. Only II follows
D. All follow
E. None follows

Directions (Q. 51–60) : *Every question below has a few statements, followed by four conclusions numbered I, II, III and IV. You have to consider every given statement as true, even if it does not conform to the well known facts. Read the conclusions and then decide which of the conclusions can be logically derived.*

51. Statements: Some keys are staplers. Some staplers are stickers. All the stickers are pens.

Conclusions:

I. Some pens are staplers.
II. Some stickers are keys.
III. No sticker is key.
IV. Some staplers are keys.

A. Only I and II
B. Only II and IV
C. Only II and III
D. Only I and IV and either II or III
E. None of these

52. Statements: All the locks are keys. All the keys are bats. Some watches are bats.

Conclusions:

I. Some bats are locks.
II. Some watches are keys.
III. All the keys are locks.
IV. Some keys are locks.

A. Only I and II
B. Only I and IV
C. Only II and III
D. Only I and III
E. None of these

53. Statements: All the papers are books. All the bags are books. Some purses are bags.

Conclusions:

I. Some papers are bags.
II. Some books are papers.
III. Some books are purses.
IV. Some papers are purses.

A. Only I and IV
B. Only II and III
C. Only I and II
D. Only I and III
E. None of these

54. Statements: All the bottles are boxes. All the boxes are bags. Some bags are trays.

Conclusions:

I. Some bottles are trays.
II. Some trays are boxes.
III. All the bottles are bags.
IV. Some trays are bags.

A. Only III and IV
B. Only I and II
C. Only II and III
D. Only I and IV
E. None of these

55. Statements: Some rats are cats. Some cats are dogs. No dog is cow.

Conclusions:

I. No cow is cat.
II. No dog is rat.
III. Some cats are rats.
IV. Some dogs are cats.

A. Only I and IV
B. Only I and II
C. Only I and III
D. Only II and III
E. Only III and IV

56. Statements: Some cups are pots. Some pots are vessels. All vessels are drums.

Conclusions:

I. Some cups are vessels.
II. Some pots are drums.
III. Some cups are drums.
IV. No pot is drum.

A. Only I, II and III follow
B. Only II follows
C. Either II or IV follows
D. Only I and III follow
E. Only I, III and either II or IV follow.

57. Statements: All teachers are doctors. All doctors are engineers. All engineers are typists.

Conclusions:

I. Some typists are teachers.
II. All doctors are typists.
III. Some engineers are teachers.
IV. All doctors are teachers.

A. Only I and II follow
B. Only I and III follow
C. Either II or IV follows
D. Either I or II and III follows
E. None of these.

58. Statements: All apples are brinjals. All brinjals are lady's fingers. Some lady's fingers are oranges.

Conclusions:

I. Some oranges are brinjals.
II. All brinjals are apples.
III. Some apples are oranges.
IV. All lady's fingers are apples.

A. None follows
B. Either I or III follows
C. All follow
D. Only I and III follow
E. None of these

59. Statements: Some novels are epics. All epics are dramas. No drama is a book.

Conclusions:

I. Some dramas are novels
II. No novel is a book.
III. Some novels are not books.
IV. No book is a drama.

A. Only I, II and IV follow
B. All follow
C. Only I, III and IV follow
D. Either I or IV follows
E. None of these

60. Statements: All chairs are tables. No table is a book. All tables are stones.

Conclusions:

I. No chair is a book.

II. No stone is a book.
III. Some stones are books.
IV. All tables are chair.
A. Only I follows
B. I and either II or III follow
C. I and III follow
D. Either II or III follows
E. None of these

ANSWERS

1	2	3	4	5	6	7	8	9	10
D	C	B	D	D	E	A	B	C	D
11	12	13	14	15	16	17	18	19	20
A	C	B	E	B	A	B	B	B	A
21	22	23	24	25	26	27	28	29	30
E	B	E	D	D	D	E	B	D	E
31	32	33	34	35	36	37	38	39	40
C	D	E	C	A	D	A	C	D	D
41	42	43	44	45	46	47	48	49	50
A	B	D	E	A	C	D	C	D	A
51	52	53	54	55	56	57	58	59	60
D	B	B	A	E	B	E	A	C	A

EXPLANATORY ANSWERS

1. Since one premise is negative, the conclusion must be negative. So, neither conclusion follows.

2. Since the middle term 'cakes' is not distributed even once in the premises, no definite conclusion follows. However, conclusion I and II involve only the extreme terms and form a complementary pair. So, conclusion either conclusion I or II follows.

3. Clearly, the conclusion must be universal negative and should not contain the middle term. So, it follows that 'No mango is cheap'. Since all mangoes are golden in colour, we may substitute 'mangoes' with 'golden-coloured mangoes'. Thus, conclusion II follows.

4. Since one premise is particular, the conclusion must be particular. So, neither conclusion I nor II follows.

5. Since the middle term 'good athletes' is distributed twice in the premises, the conclusion must be particular and should not contain the middle term. So, it follows that 'Some of those who win, eat well'.

6. Since both the premises are universal and affirmative, the conclusion must be universal affirmative and should not contain the middle term. So, conclusion I follows. Conclusion II is the converse of the second premise and so it also holds.

7. Since both the premises are universal and affirmative, the conclusion must be universal affirmative and should not contain the middle term. So, only conclusion I follows.

8. Since both the premises are particular, no definite conclusion follows. However, conclusion II is the converse of the second premise and thus it holds.

9. Since the middle term 'tigers' is not distributed even once in the premises, no definite conclusion follows. However, conclusion I and II involve only the extreme terms and form a complementary pair. So, either conclusion I or II follows.

10. Clearly, the term 'guns' is distributed in both the conclusions without being distributed in any of the premises. So, neither conclusion follows.

11. Since the first premise is particular, the conclusion must be particular and should not contain the middle term. Thus, only conclusion I follows.

12. Since the middle term 'papers' is not distributed even once in the premises, no definite conclusion follows. However, conclusion I and II involve only the extreme terms and form a complementary pair. Thus, either conclusion I or II follows.

13. Since the middle term 'tall' is not distributed even once in the premises, no definite conclusion follows. However, conclusion II is the converse of the second premise and so it holds.

14. Since both premises are particular, no definite conclusion follows. However, conclusion I is the converse of second premise, while conclusion II is the converse of the first premise. So both of them hold.

15. Since one premise is particular, the conclusion must be particular and should not contain the middle term. Thus, only conclusion II follows.

16. Since both the premises are universal and one premise is negative, the conclusion must be universal negative and should not contain the middle term. So, only conclusion I follows.

17. Since the middle term 'chalks' is not distributed even once in the premises, no definite conclusion follows. However, conclusion II is the converse of the first premise and so it holds.

18.

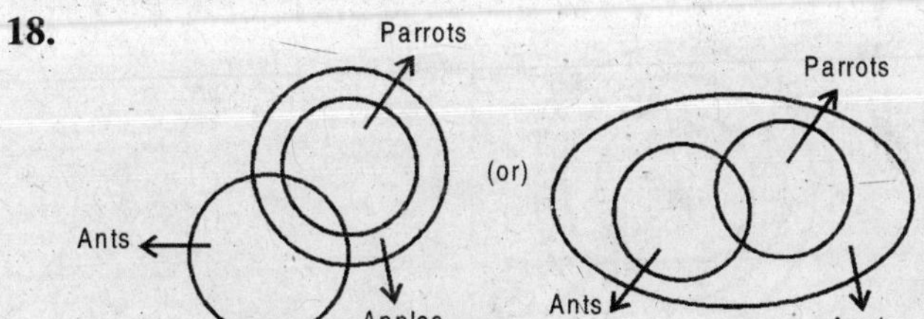

19.

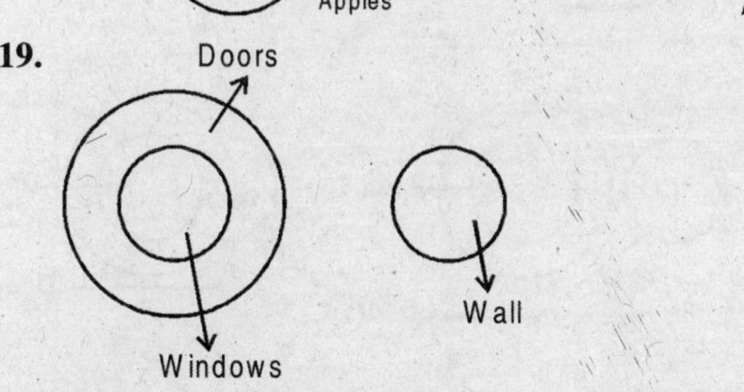

20. In the premises middle term is tiger, which is distributed in either or premises so conclusion I follows.

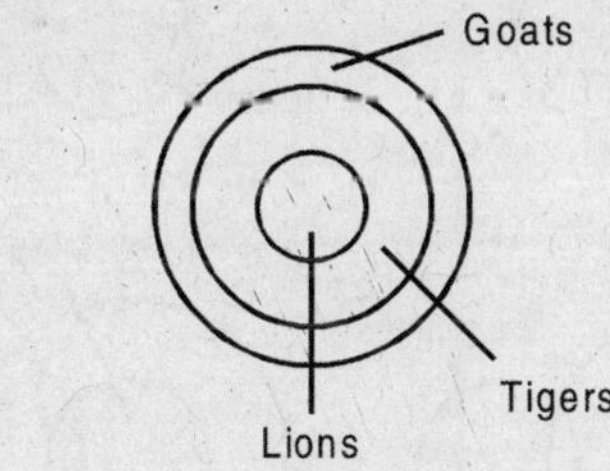

21.

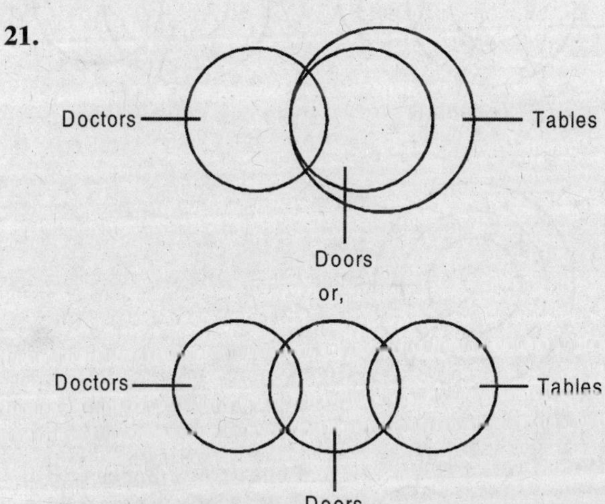

Since one premises is particular affirmative, the conclusions must be particular. Therefore, conclusion I and II follow.

22.

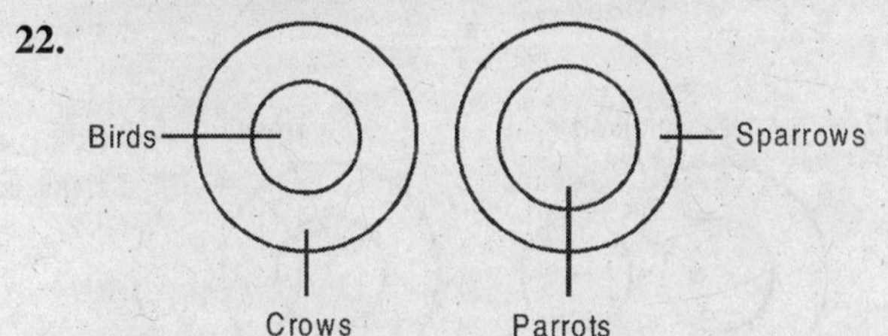

There is no middle term in the premises, therefore, no conclusion follows.

23.

Bowls
Plates
Spoons

Therefore, conclusion II follows. Conclusion I is the conversion of second conclusion.

24.

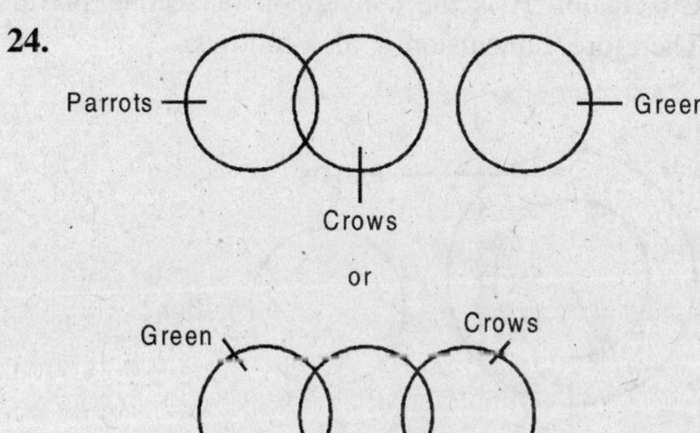

Since one premise is negative the conclusion must be particular negative. So, neither conclusion follows.

25.

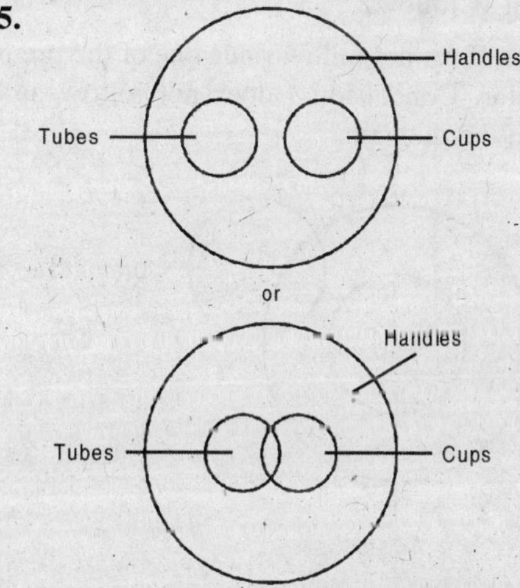

The middle term is not distributed in any of the premises. Hence, no conclusion can be drawn.

26.

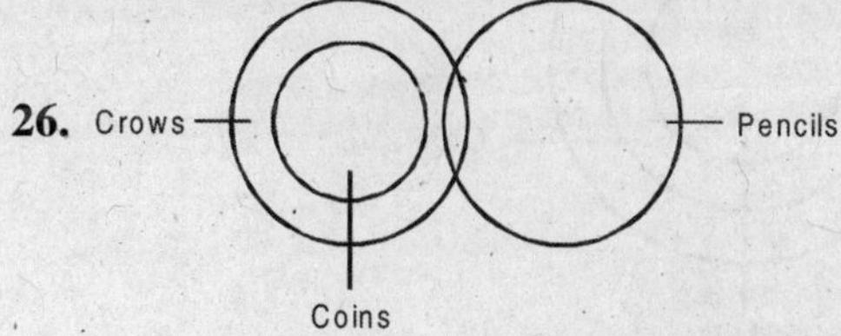

The middle term is not distributed in any of the premises. Hence, no conclusion can be drawn.

27.

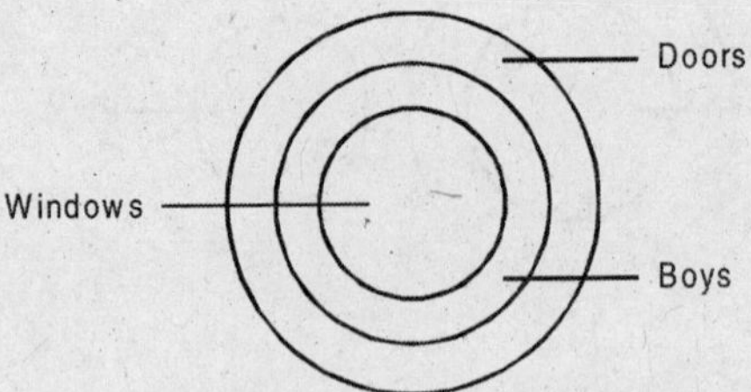

The region corresponding to windows lies entirely within that of doors. Hence, conclusion I follows. Conclusion II is the conversion of second premise. Therefore, conclusion II also follows.

28.

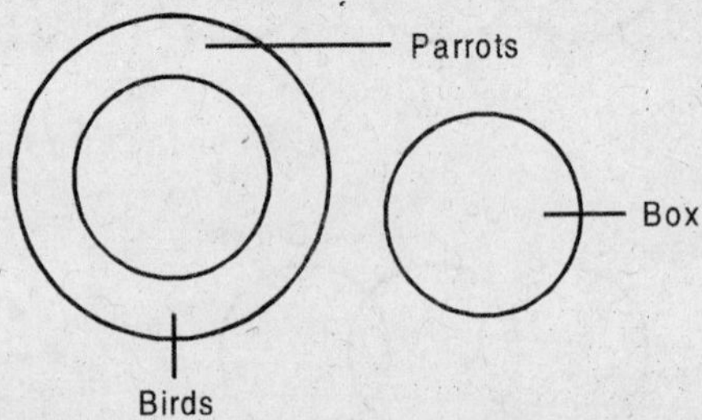

Both the premises are already aligned. We know that A + E ⇒ E and in the conclusion the subject should be the subject of the first premise and the predicate should be the predicate of the second premise. Hence, conclusion II follows.

29. Conclusion II cannot follow since one of the premises is particular. Conclusion I does not follow as it is clear from the diagram.

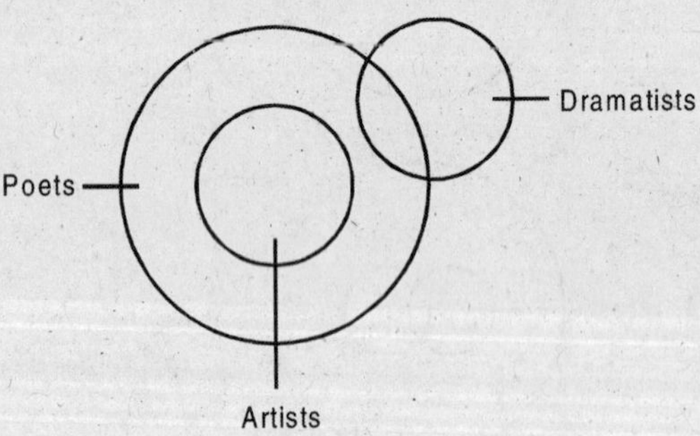

30.

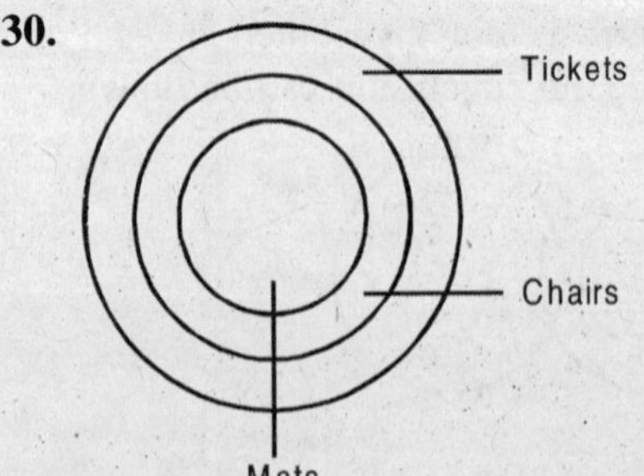

Conclusion II is the converse of conclusion I.. Therefore, it may also be true.

31.

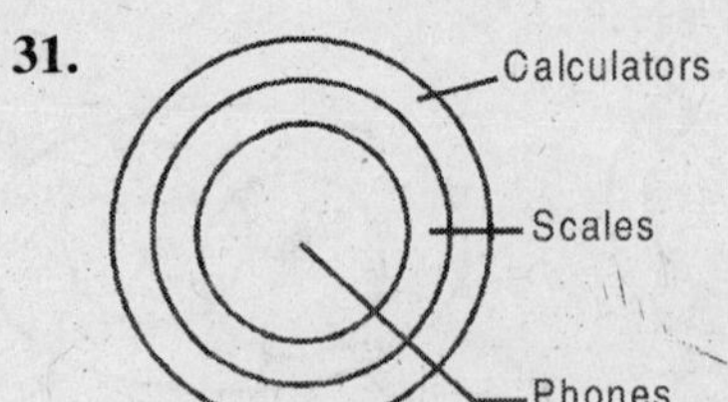

32.

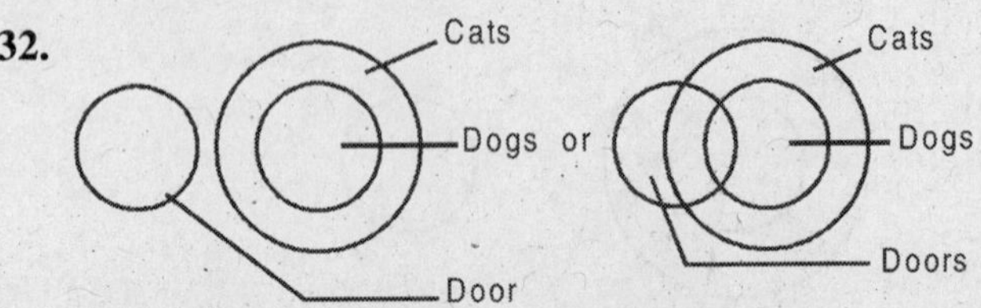

33.

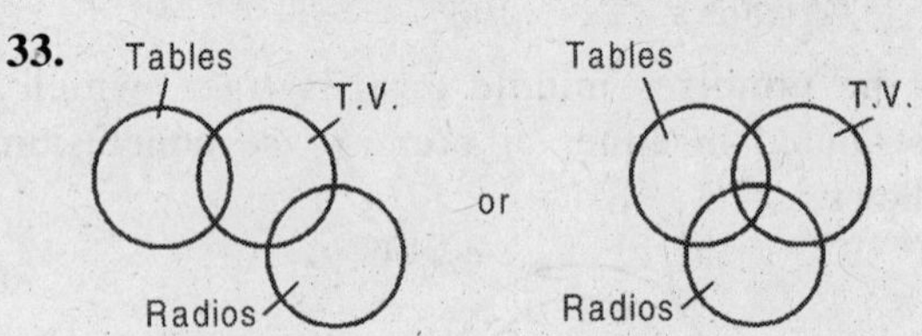

34.

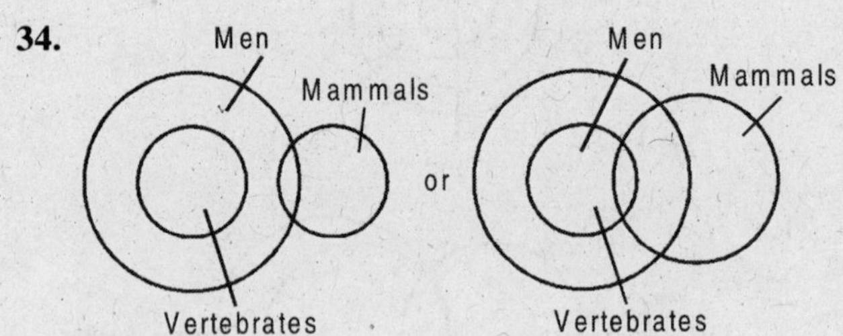

35.

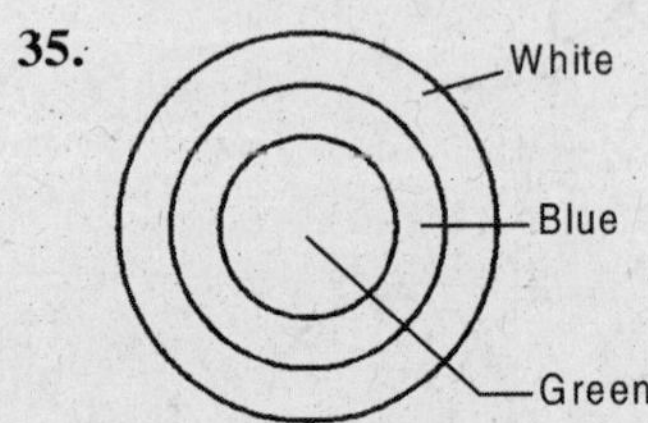

36.

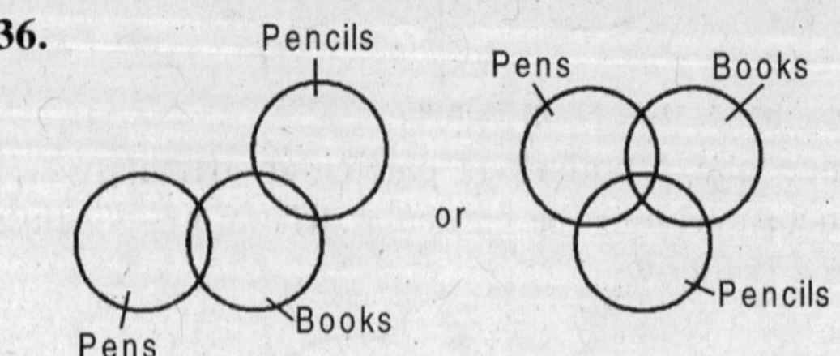

37.

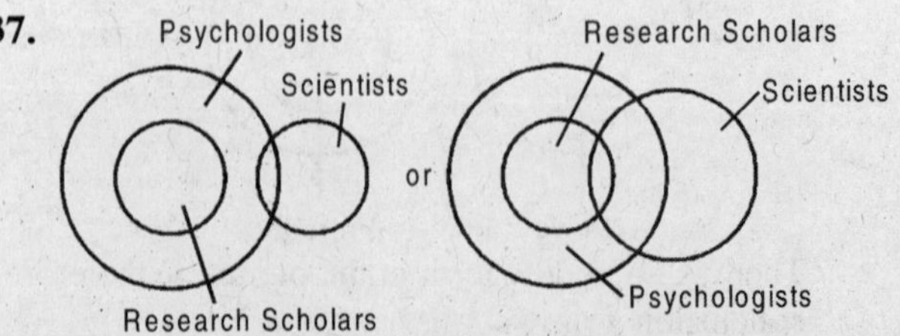

38.

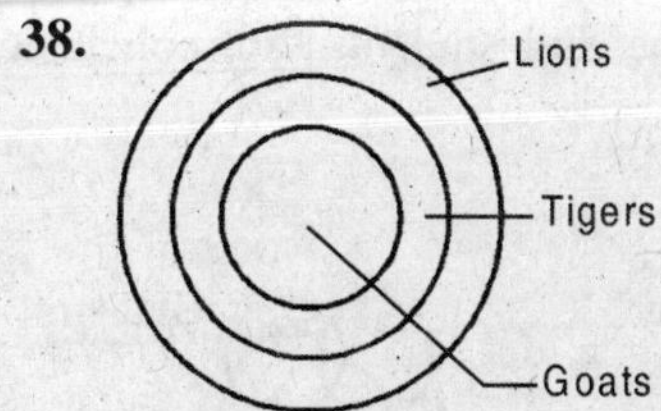

39.

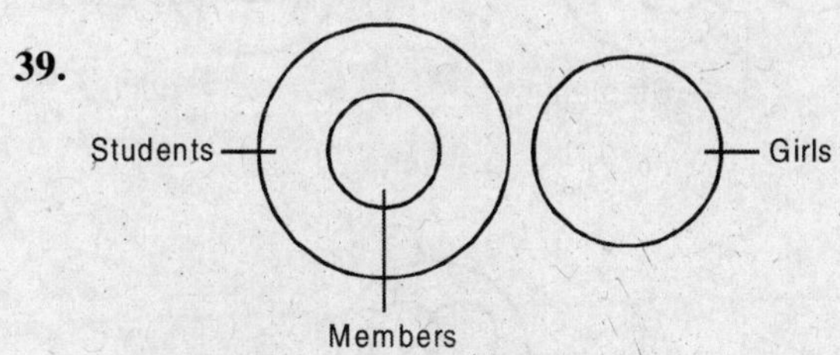

Since Members and Girls are disjoint, it follows that no members is girl. Since Members and Students have a common area, it follows that some student are members.

40.

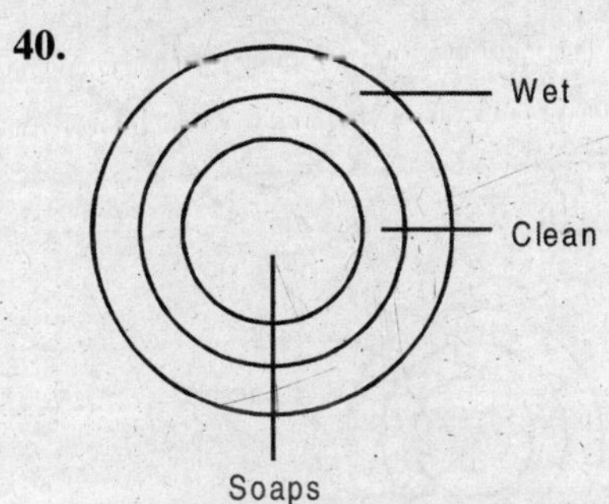

According to diagram, Clean and Soaps have a common area. So, some clean are soaps. Also wet and soaps have a common area. So, some wet are soaps.

41.

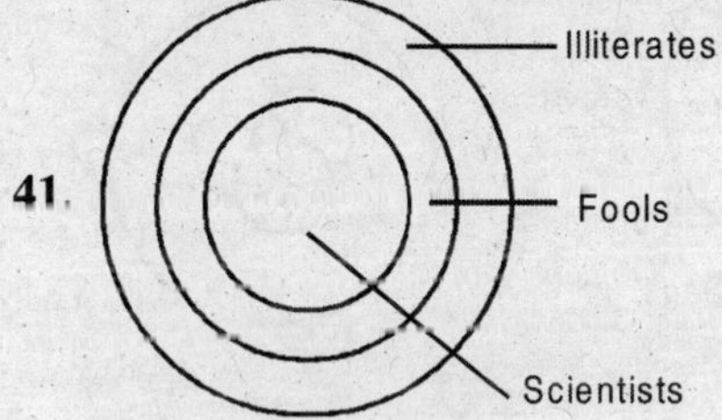

The area of scientists lies entirely in the area for illiterates so conclusion I follows. The area for conclusion I does not lie completely within scientists or fools. So conclusions II and III cannot follow. Since illiterates and scientists have a common area, conclusion IV follows.

42.

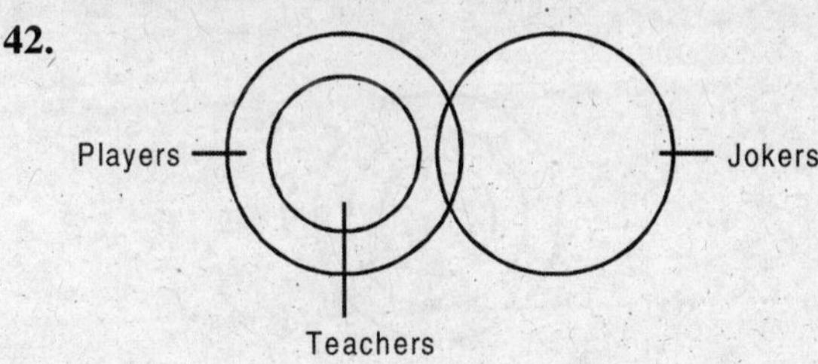

A + I ⇒ No conclusion. But conclusion III is the conversion of second premise and conclusion IV is the conversion of first premise.

43.

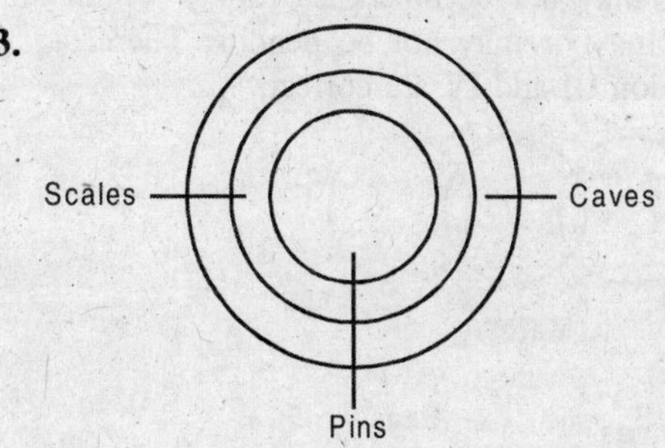

We know that A + A ⇒ A type conclusion, thus, ''All pins are caves''.

Conclusion IV is the conversion of our derived conclusion.

44.

When some men are goats then some goats are men. When all goats are jackals then some men must be jackals and vice versa. Also, some (not all) jackals must be goats. Therefore, conclusions I, II and IV are correct.

45.

When some frogs are bricks which are all cakes then some frogs must be cakes and vise versa. Also some cakes are not frogs, and all frogs cannot be cakes. Therefore, conclusion I and II are correct.

46.

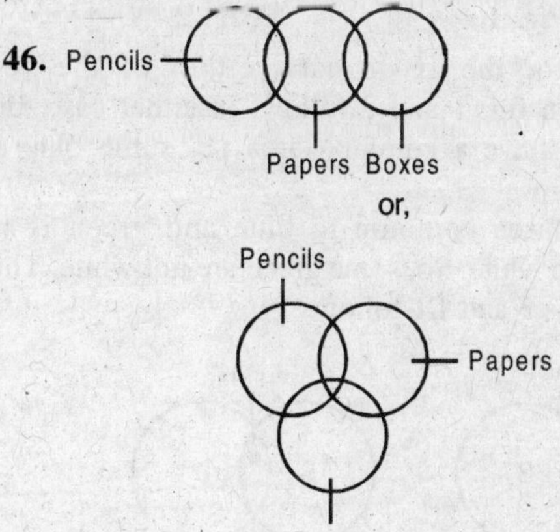

When some pencils are papers then some papers must be pencils. When some papers are boxes then some boxes must be papers. Pencils which are not papers may or may not be boxes and boxes which are not papers may or may not be pencils. Therefore, only conclusion III and IV are correct.

47.

Clothes Marbles Bags

or

Clothes Bags Marbles

Since both are premises are particular no conclusion follows.

48.

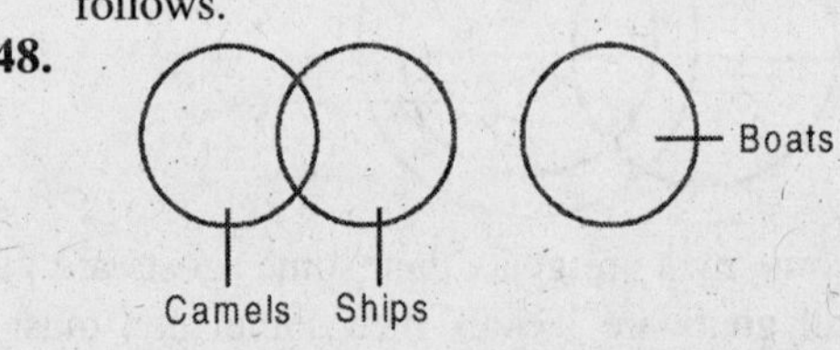

or,

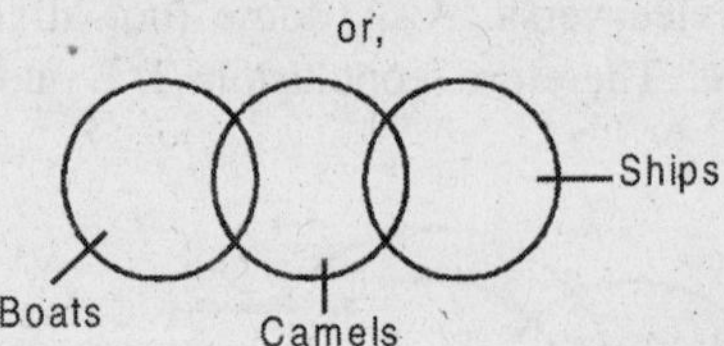

Clearly, since ships and camels have a common area in the venn diagram, it follows that some ships are camels. Also, it follows that some camels are not boats. Thus, only conclusion I and III follow.

49.

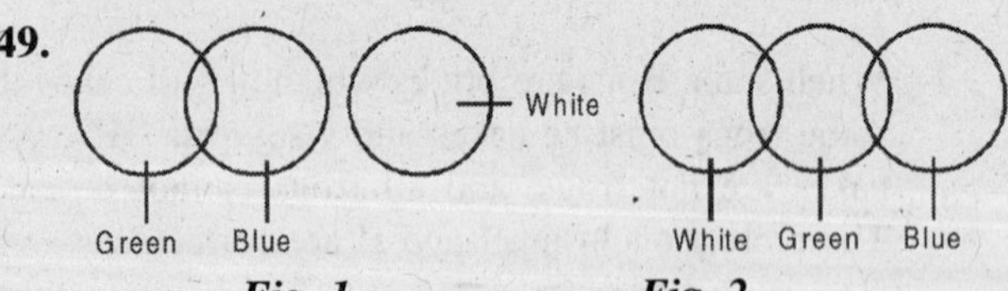

Fig. 1 *Fig. 2*

Clearly, for the given data, either of the venn diagrams in fig. 1 and 2 follow. In either case, blue and green have a common area i.e. some blue are green.

Also, the area common to blue and green is not common to white. So, some green are not white. Thus, conclusions I and III follow.

50.

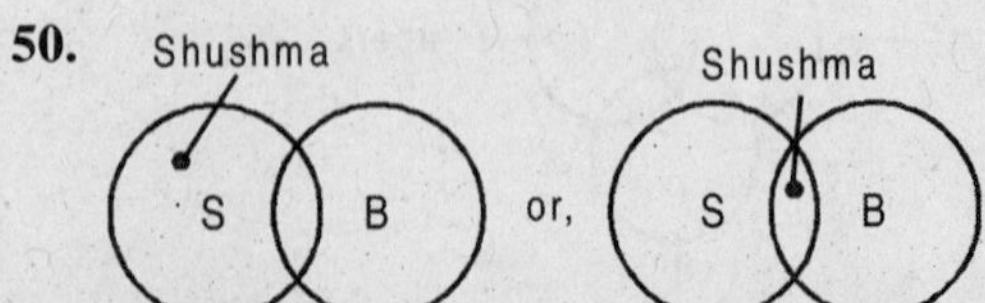

Clearly, in S the area not common to students and brilliant represents the dull students. So, conclusion I follows.

51.

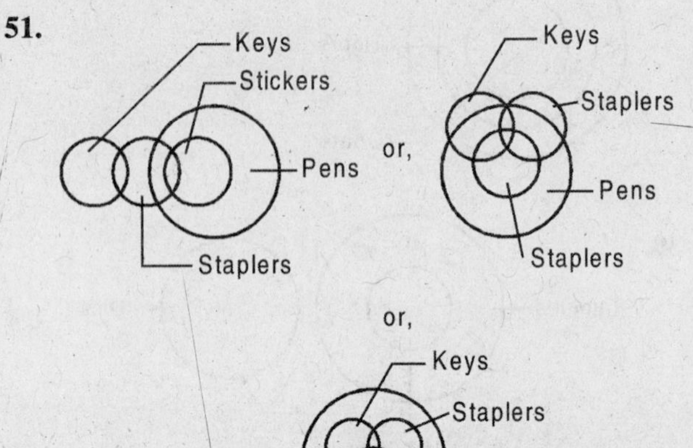

52.

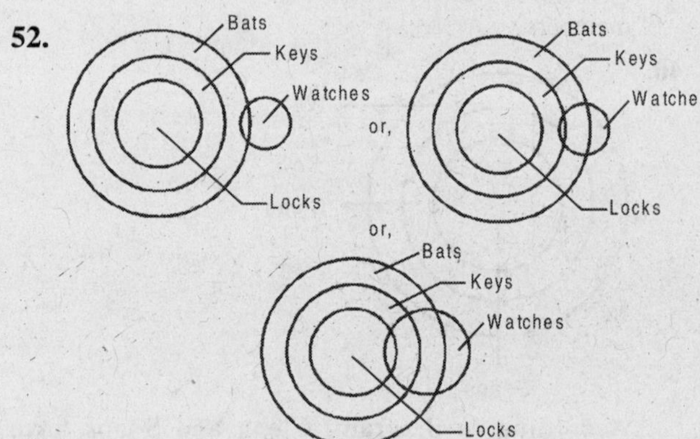

53.

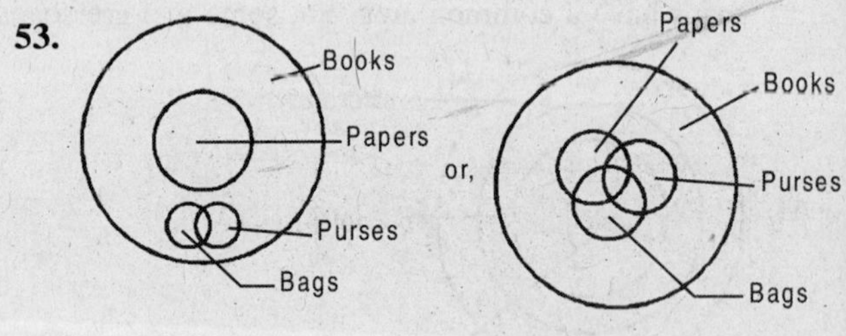

54.

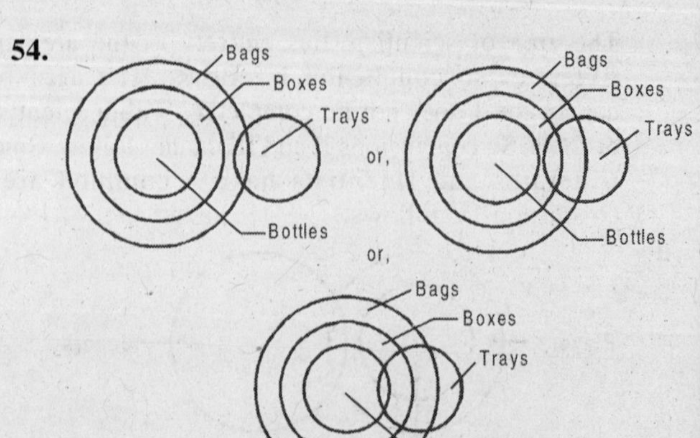

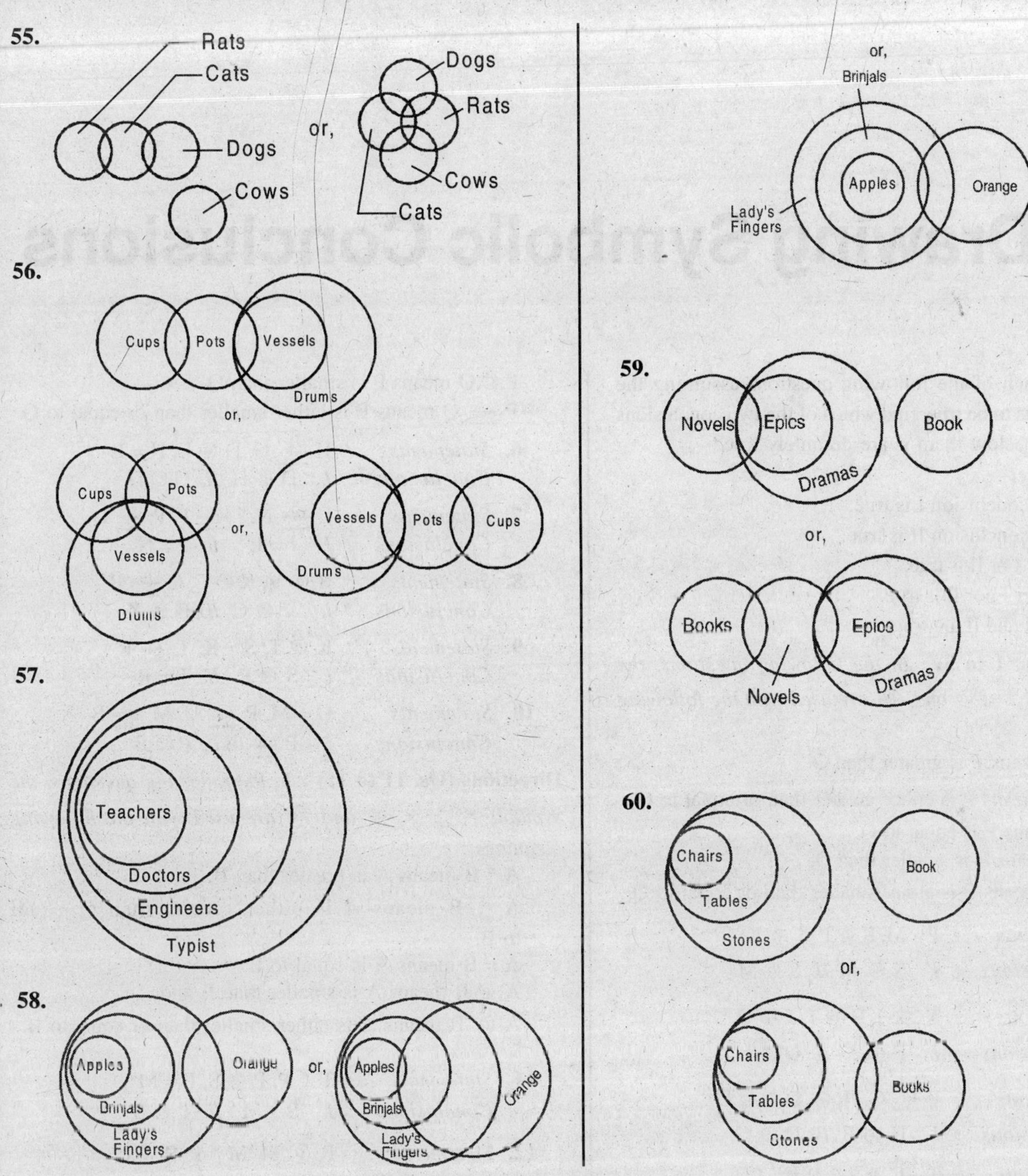
55.
Rats
Cats
Dogs
Cows
or,
Dogs
Rats
Cows
Cats
56.
Cups
Pots
Vessels
Drums
or,
Cups
Pots
Vessels
Drums
or,
Vessels
Pots
Cups
Drums
57.
Teachers
Doctors
Engineers
Typist
58.
Apples
Orange
Brinjals
Lady's Fingers
or,
Apples
Brinjals
Orange
Lady's Fingers
or,
Brinjals
Apples
Orange
Lady's Fingers
59.
Novels
Epics
Book
Dramas
or,
Books
Epics
Novels
Dramas
60.
Chairs
Tables
Stones
Book
or,
Chairs
Tables
Books
Stones

☆☆☆☆☆☆

11. Drawing Symbolic Conclusions

Now in each of the following questions assuming the given statements to be true, find which of the two conclusions I and II given below them is/are definitely true?

Give answer—

A. if only conclusion I is true.
B. if only conclusion II is true.
C. if either I or II is true.
D. if neither I nor II is true.
E. if both I and II are true.

Directions (Qs. 1 to 5) : *In the following questions, the symbols* $\oplus$, $\underline{\oplus}$, =, @ *and* $\underline{@}$ *are used with the following meanings :*

P $\oplus$ Q means P is greater than Q.

P $\underline{\oplus}$ Q means P is either greater than or equal to Q.

P = Q means P is equal to Q.

P @ Q means P is smaller than Q.

P $\underline{@}$ Q means P is either smaller than or equal to Q.

1. *Statements* : P = M, K @ P, S $\oplus$ K
Conclusions : *I.* S $\oplus$ M *II.* S @ M

2. *Statements* : T $\underline{\oplus}$ J, F $\oplus$ T, J $\oplus$ O
Conclusions : *I.* F $\oplus$ J *II.* O @ T

3. *Statements* : E $\underline{@}$ G, H $\underline{\oplus}$ D, E @ D
Conclusions : *I.* H $\oplus$ E *II.* D $\oplus$ G

4. *Statements* : T = U, R > P, P $\underline{@}$ T
Conclusions : *I.* R > U *II.* R @ U

5. *Statements* : L $\underline{\oplus}$ B, N $\underline{@}$ C, B @ N
Conclusions : *I.* L $\oplus$ N *II.* C $\oplus$ B

Directions (Qs. 6 to 10) : *In the following questions the symbol* @, $\underline{@}$, =, © *and* $\underline{©}$ *are used with the following meanings :*

P @ Q means P is greater than Q.

P $\underline{@}$ Q means P is either greater than or equal to Q.

P = Q means P is equal to Q.

P © Q means P is smaller than Q.

P $\underline{©}$ Q means P is either smaller than or equal to Q.

6. *Statements* : H $\underline{@}$ G, D @ E, H = E
Conclusions : *I.* D @ H *II.* G © D

7. *Statements* : L $\underline{@}$ N, J $\underline{©}$ P, P $\underline{@}$ L
Conclusions : *I.* J = L *II.* P = N

8. *Statements* : B @ V, K © C, C $\underline{©}$ B
Conclusions : *I.* V @ C *II.* B @ K

9. *Statements* : K @ T, S = K, T $\underline{©}$ R
Conclusions : *I.* S @ R *II.* T = R

10. *Statements* : U = M, P $\underline{@}$ U, M $\underline{@}$ B
Conclusions : *I.* P $\underline{@}$ B *II.* P © B

Directions (Qs. 11 to 15) : *In the following questions, the symbols* *, $\underline{*}$, =, @ *and* $\underline{\underline{@}}$ *are used with the following meanings :*

A * B means A is greater than B,

A $\underline{*}$ B means A is either greater than or equal to B.

A = B means A is equal to B.

A @ B means A is smaller than B and

A $\underline{\underline{@}}$ B means A is either smaller than or equal to B.

11. *Statements* : T $\underline{*}$ P, P @ S, P = M
Conclusions : *I.* S * M *II.* T @ S

12. *Statements* : R $\underline{\underline{@}}$ M, M * P, R $\underline{*}$ L
Conclusions : *I.* M = L *II.* P = L

13. *Statements* : M = T, T $\underline{\underline{@}}$ Z, S * M
Conclusions : *I.* Z $\underline{*}$ M *II.* Z @ M

14. *Statements* : L @ C, C * Z, Z $\underline{\underline{@}}$ F
Conclusions : *I.* C * F *II.* F = C

15. *Statements* : Z @ B, N $\underline{*}$ S, B @ N
Conclusions : *I.* B = Z *II.* S $\underline{\underline{@}}$ B

Directions (Qs. 16 to 20) : *In the following question the symbol @, $\underline{\underline{@}}$, =, □ and $\underline{\underline{\square}}$ used with the following meanings:*

P @ Q means P is greater than Q.

P $\underline{\underline{@}}$ Q means P is either greater than or equal to Q.

P = Q means P is equal to Q.

P □ Q means P is smaller than Q.

P $\underline{\underline{\square}}$ Q means P is either smaller than or equal to Q.

16. *Statements* : H @ W, W $\underline{\underline{\square}}$ S, M @ S
Conclusions : *I.* M = H *II.* M @ H

17. *Statements* : M @ N, N $\underline{\underline{\square}}$ T, T = P
Conclusions : *I.* P @ N *II.* P = N

18. *Statements* : M = N, N @ B, B □ P
Conclusions : *I.* P = N *II.* B □ M

19. *Statements* : P $\underline{\underline{\square}}$ Q, Q $\underline{\underline{\square}}$ R, T $\underline{\underline{\square}}$ Q
Conclusions : *I.* R @ T *II.* R @ P

20. *Statements* : G $\underline{\underline{\square}}$ S, F @ S, T □ G
Conclusions : *I.* F @ T *II.* T = S

Directions (Qs. 21 to 25) : *In the following questions, the symbols ©, *, = @, ← are used as follows :*

A © B means A is greater than B.

A * B means A is either greater than or equal to B.

A = B means A is equal to B.

A @ B means A is smaller than B.

A ← B means A is either smaller than or equal to B.

21. *Statements* : P @ Q, Q © K, K @ M
Conclusions : *I.* M = Q *II.* M © Q

22. *Statements* : P * F, M ← F, F © N
Conclusions : *I.* M = P *II.* M @ P

23. *Statements* : Q @ R, R @ M, M © D
Conclusions : *I.* D © R *II.* D © Q

24. *Statements* : M @ K, K © R, R © P
Conclusions : *I.* P @ K *II.* P @ M

25. *Statements* : T © M, M = P, P © R
Conclusions : *I.* P @ T *II.* T © R

Directions (Qs. 26 to 30) : *In the following questions the symbols, +, →, @, ⇒ and = are used with the following meanings :*

\+ means *greater than*

→ means either greater than or equal to

@ means smaller than

⇒ mean smaller than or equal to and

= means equal to.

26. *Statements* : Z @ P, T = M, M → Z
Conclusions : *I.* M + Z *II.* T + P

27. *Statements* : B ⇒ P, C + N, P = N
Conclusions : *I.* P @ C *II.* C + B

28. *Statements* : M ⇒ N, L + N, M = P
Conclusions : *I.* N = P *II.* N @ P

29. *Statements* : A ⇒ C, M ⇒ F, C + F
Conclusions : *I.* M = A *II.* C + M

30. *Statements* : K @ P, Z + K, K → M
Conclusions : *I.* Z = M *II.* Z + M

Directions (Qs. 31 to 35) : *In the following questions, the symbols #, %, @, © and δ are used with the following meanings illustrated:*

'P % Q' means 'P is not greater than Q'.

'P δ Q' means 'P is not smaller than Q'

'P # Q' means 'P is neither equal to nor smaller than Q'.

'P © Q' means 'P is neither smaller than nor greater than Q'.

'P @ Q' means 'P is equal to Q'.

In each questions, three statements showing relationships have been given, which are followed by three conclusions I, II & III. Assuming that the given statements are true, find out which conclusion(s) is/are definitely true.

31. *Statements* : M © K, K δ T, T © J
Conclusions : *I.* J # K, *II.* T # M,
III. M # J

A. None is true
B. Only I is true
C. Only II is true
D. Only III is true
E. Only II and III are true

32. *Statements* : J δ H, H @ B, B % N
Conclusions : *I.* N δ H, *II.* N @ J,
III. J δ B

A. Only I and II are true
B. Only II and III are true
C. Only I and III are true
D. All are true
E. None of these

33. *Statements* : B # T, T © K, K % M
Conclusions : *I.* K # B, *II.* M # T,
III. B # M

A. Only I is true
B. Only II is true
C. Only III is true
D. Only II and III are true
E. None of these

34. *Statements* : D % F, F δ K, K @ R
Conclusions : *I.* R % F, *II.* R % D,
III. R @ D

A. Only I is true
B. Only II is true
C. Only III is true
D. Only I and II are true
E. None of these

35. *Statements* : W © M, M % F, D # F
Conclusions : *I.* D # M, *II.* W © F, *III.* W © D

A. Only I is true
B. Only I and II are true
C. Only II and III are true
D. Only I and III are true
E. All are true

ANSWERS

1	2	3	4	5	6	7	8	9	10
D	E	A	B	B	E	D	B	D	A
11	**12**	**13**	**14**	**15**	**16**	**17**	**18**	**19**	**20**
A	D	C	D	D	D	C	B	D	B
21	**22**	**23**	**24**	**25**	**26**	**27**	**28**	**29**	**30**
D	D	D	A	E	D	E	D	B	B
31	**32**	**33**	**34**	**35**					
A	C	B	A	E					

EXPLANATORY ANSWERS

1. $P = M, K < P, S > K$
$\Rightarrow K < M, K < S$

2. $T \geq J, F > T, J > O$
$\Rightarrow F > J > O$
$\Rightarrow F > J$ & $O < J$
$\Rightarrow T \geq J > O$
$\Rightarrow T > O$

3. $E \leq G, H \geq D; E < D$
$\Rightarrow H > E$

4. $T = U, R \leq P, P \leq T$
$\Rightarrow R \leq U$

5. $L \geq B, N \leq C, B < N$
$\Rightarrow B < C \Rightarrow C > B \Rightarrow$ II

6. $H \geq G, D > E, H = E$
$\Rightarrow D > H,$
$\Rightarrow H \geq G, E \geq G$
$\Rightarrow D > G \Rightarrow G < D$

7. $L \geq N, J \leq P, P \geq L$
Hence, both conclusions are false.

8. $B > V, K < C, C \leq B$
$\therefore K < C, C \leq B \Rightarrow K < B$
$\Rightarrow B > K \Rightarrow$ Conclusion II is true.

9. $K > T, S = K, T \leq R$
from these relations both conclusions are false.

10. $U = M, P \geq U, M \geq B$
$\Rightarrow P \geq M, M \geq B \Rightarrow P \geq B$

11. $T \geq P, P < S, P = M$
$\therefore S > M$

12. $R \leq M, M > P, R \geq L$
$\therefore L \leq R \leq M$

13. $M = T, T \leq Z, S > M$
If $T = Z$, then $Z = M$
If $T < Z$, then $Z > M$

14. $L < C, C > Z, Z \leq F$
Hence, both conclusions are false.

15. $Z < B, N \geq S, B < N$
Hence, both conclusions are false.

16. $H > W, W \leq S, M > S$
$\Rightarrow H > W, S \geq W, M > S$
$\Rightarrow H > W, M > S, S \geq W$
No relationship can be established bet-ween M and H.

17. $M > N, N \leq T, T = P$
$\Rightarrow M > N, T \geq N, T = P$
$T = P \geq N$

18. $M = N, N > B, B < P$
$\Rightarrow M = N > B$
& $P > B$

19. $P \leq Q, Q \leq R, T \leq Q$
$\Rightarrow P \leq Q \leq R, T \leq Q \leq R$
I. $R > T$ may/may not be true.
II. $R > P$ may/may not be true.

20. $G \leq S, F > S, T < G$
$\Rightarrow F > S \geq G > T$
I. $F > T$ is true.
II. $T = S$ is not true.

21. P @ Q $\Rightarrow P < Q$
Q © K $\Rightarrow Q > K$
K @ M $\Rightarrow K < M$

22. $P * F \Rightarrow P \geq F$
$M \leftarrow F \Rightarrow M \leq F$
$F © N \Rightarrow F > N$
from statements (1) and (2),
$P \geq F \geq M$
$\Rightarrow P > M$ or $P = M$

23. $Q @ R \Rightarrow Q < R$
$R @ M \Rightarrow R < M$
$M © D \Rightarrow M > D$

24. $M @ K \Rightarrow M < K$
$K © R \Rightarrow K > R$
$R © P \Rightarrow R > P$
$\therefore K > M$ and $K > P$
i.e., $P < K$, *i.e.*, $P @ K$

25. $T © M \Rightarrow T > M, M = P$
$P © R \Rightarrow P > R$
$\therefore T > P > R \Rightarrow T > R \Rightarrow T © R$
Also $T > M \Rightarrow P < T \Rightarrow P @ T$

26. $Z < P, T = M, M \geq Z$
So, $M \geq Z$, or $T \geq Z$ and $P > Z$
As $M \geq Z$, it cannot be said that $M > Z$ is valid. As there is no relationship between T and P, it cannot be said whether $T > P$ or not. So, neither I nor II is true.

27. $B \leq P, C > N, P = N$
From statements (1), (2), (3)
$\Rightarrow C > N \geq B$ or $C > B$ (Conclusion II)
From statements (2) and (3) $\Rightarrow C > P$
or, $P < C$ (Conclusion I)

28. $M \leq N, L > N, M = P$
From the three statements $\Rightarrow P \leq N < L$.
Or $P \leq N$. Thus neither I nor II, *i.e.*,
$P = N$ or $P > N$ should be correct.

29. $A \leq C, M \leq F, C > F$
From statements (2) and (3)
$\Rightarrow C > F \geq M$ and $C \geq A$
Thus only (II) is correct.

30. $K < P, Z > K, K \geq M$
From statements (2) and (3) $\Rightarrow Z > K \geq M$
and $P > K$ (from statement I)
$Z > K \geq M \Rightarrow Z > M$
As $Z > M$, it cannot be equal to M.
Thus II is valid.

31. $M © K \Rightarrow M < K$
$K \delta T \Rightarrow K \geq T$
$T © J \Rightarrow T < J$
I. $J \# K \Rightarrow J > K$ (false)
II. $T \# M \Rightarrow T > M$ (false)
III. $M \# J \Rightarrow M > J$ (false)

32. $J \delta H \Rightarrow J \geq H$
$H @ B \Rightarrow H = B$
$B \% N \Rightarrow B \leq N$
$\Rightarrow J \geq H = B \leq N$
I. $N \delta H \Rightarrow N \geq H$ (true)
II. $N @ J \Rightarrow N = J$ (false)
III. $J \delta B \Rightarrow J \geq B$ (true)

33. $B \# T \Rightarrow B > T$
$T © K \Rightarrow T < K$
$K \% M \Rightarrow K < M$
$B > T < K \leq M$
I. $K \# B \Rightarrow K > B$ (false)
II. $M \# T \Rightarrow M > T$ (true)
III. $B \# M \Rightarrow B > M$ (false)

34. $D \% F \Rightarrow D \leq F$
$F \delta K \Rightarrow F \geq K$
$K @ R \Rightarrow K = R$
$\Rightarrow D \leq F \geq K = R$
I. $R \% F \Rightarrow R \leq F$ (true)
II. $R \% D \Rightarrow R \leq D$ (false)
III. $R @ D \Rightarrow R = D$ (false)

35. $W © M \Rightarrow W < M$
$M \% F \Rightarrow M \leq F$
$D \# F \Rightarrow D > F$
$\Rightarrow W < M \leq F < D$
I. $D \# M \Rightarrow D > M$ (true)
II. $W © F \Rightarrow W < F$ (true)
III. $W © D \Rightarrow W < D$ (true)

☆☆☆☆☆☆

12. Decision Making

Directions (Qs. 1 to 5) : *Read the following information carefully and answer the questions given below it.*

Following are the criteria for admitting a student in the first year engineering course in a college.

The student must—

(*i*) have passed XII standard examination in science with at least 80% marks.

(*ii*) not be more than 20 years old as on 1. 8. 1998.

(*iii*) have secured at least 90 marks in the entrance test out of a total of 150 marks.

(*iv*) be able to pay ₹ 15,000 as tuition fees for the first semester and ₹ 5,000 admission charges at the time of taking admission.

In the case of a candidate, who satisfies all other criteria except at—

(*a*) (*iv*) above but can pay at least 60% of the stipulated fees, the case may be referred to the Admission Committee.

(*b*) (*iii*) above but has secured more than 95% marks in the XIIth standard examination, the case may be referred to Chairman–Admissions.

You are given the following cases as on 1. 8. 1998. Depending upon the information provided in each case and based on the criteria mentioned above, recommend your decision. You are not to assume anything. If the information provided is not adequate to take a decision, mark 'Data inadequate' as the answer.

1. Subodh Mohaptara was 19 years old as on 20th December, 1997. He has secured 98% marks in XIIth standard examination with science and 80 marks in the entrance test. He can pay the requisite tuition fees and admission charges.

A. Admit
B. Refer to Admission Committee
C. Data inadequate
D. Do not admit
E. Refer to Chairman–Admissions

2. Reema Jaiswal was born on 20th July, 1978. She has secured 85% and 75% marks in XIIth standard with science and entrance test respectively. She can pay the requisite tuition fees and admission charges.

A. Refer to Chairman–Admission
B. Refer to Admission Committee
C. Data inadequate
D. Do not admit
E. Admit

3. Ashok Dubey was born on 27th November, 1978. He has secured 90% marks in the XIIth standard examination with science and 95 marks in the entrance test. He can pay ₹ 10,000 tuition fees and ₹ 3,500 admission charges.

A. Admit
B. Data inadequate
C. Refer to Admission Committee
D. Do not admit
E. Refer to Chairman–Admissions

4. Sudha Mirchandani has secured 95% marks in XIIth standard science stream and 70% marks in the entrance test. She can pay only 65% of the requisite tuition fees and admission charges.

A. Do not admit
B. Admit
C. Data inadequate
D. Refer to Chairman–Admissions
E. Refer to Admission Committee

5. Salil Malhotra was born on 25th September in 1979. He has secured 85% and 95% marks in the XIIth standard examination in science stream and entrance test respectively. He can pay the requisite tuition fees and admission charges.

A. Admit
B. Do not admit
C. Refer to Chairman–Admissions
D. Refer to Admission Committee
E. Data inadequate

Directions (Qs. 6 to 12) : *Read the following information to answer the given questions :*

Following are the criteria for selecting candidates for

Research Fellowship :

The candidate must—

(*i*) be a post-graduate with minimum of 65% marks.
(*ii*) not be more than 30 years as on 15. 10. 1993.
(*iii*) have at least 3 years research experience.
(*iv*) have diploma in Statistics.
(*v*) have secured at least 50% marks in the entrance test.
(*vi*) have finalised the topic for research.

However, in case a candidate who fulfills all other criteria except

(*a*) (*iii*) above, but has M. Phil degree, should be referred to Dean.
(*b*) (*iv*) above, should be referred to Chairman.
(*c*) (*i*) above, but has at least 55% marks in post–graduation and 65% in the entrance test, should be given fellowship.
(*d*) (*v*) above, but has at lest 45% marks, should be wait–listed.

Based on these criteria and information provided below, decide the course of action in each case. You are not to assume anything. If the data provided is not adequate to decide the given course of action, your answer will be "data inadequate". These cases are given to you as on 15. 10. 1993.

6. 26 years old, Mamta Deo is a post graduate with 58%. She has got four years' research experience and has finalised topic for research. She got 70% marks in diploma in Statistics and 54% marks in the entrance examination.

A. Fellowship not to be granted
B. Refer to Dean
C. Refer to Chairman
D. Grant Fellowship
E. Data inadequate

7. Shushila Nair has 65% marks in her post–graduation and is M. Phil. She has 5 years research experience. She has secured 65% in the entrance test and has finalised the research topic. Her date of birth is 11. 8. 65

A. Grant fellowship B. Wait–list
C. Refer to Dean D. Refer to Chairman
E. Data inadequate

8. Ameer Khan has got 58% in the entrance test. He has 68% in his post-graduation and 55% in M. Phil. He has got diploma in Statistics and has also finalised the topic for research.

A. Grant Fellowship B. Refer to Dean
C. Refer to Chairman D. Wait-list
E. Data inadequate

9. 28 years old Neetu Singh is M. Phil with 60% marks. She has secured 70% marks in entrance examination and has finalised the topic for research. She has also got diploma in Statistics.

A. Grant Fellowship
B. Fellowship not to be granted
C. Refer to Chairman
D. Refer to Dean
E. Data inadequate

10. Sadhana Suman has got diploma in Statistics with 60% marks and post-graduation with 56% marks. Her date of birth is 12. 12. 1968. She has got one year research experience and is still doing her M. Phil. She has secured 65% marks in entrance exam and has also finalised the research topic.

A. Grant Fellowship
B. Fellowship not to be granted
C. Refer to Dean
D. Data inadequate
E. Wait-list

11. Amar Sikka is 28 years old and has got 65% marks in post-graduation and 60% marks in M. Phil. He has got 65% marks in entrance examination and has finalised the topic for research. He also has a diploma in Statistics.

A. Grant Fellowship
B. Fellowship not to be granted
C. Refer to Dean
D. Refer to Chairman
E. Data inadequate

12. Madan Paul has got 5 years' research experience and has finalised the research topic. He has got 56% marks in post-graduation. His date of birth is 15. 2. 1966. He has also got diploma in Statistics. He got 70% marks in the entrance test.

A. Grant Fellowship
B. Fellowship not to be granted
C. Refer to Dean
D. Data inadequate
E. None of these

Directions (Qs. 13 to 19) : *Read the following information to answer the given questions :*

Following are the conditions for selecting candidates for Research Fellowship :

The candidate must—

(*i*) be a post-graduate with minimum of 60% marks.
(*ii*) not be more than 30 years as on 1. 9. 1993.
(*iii*) have at least 3 years' research experience.
(*iv*) have diploma in statistics.
(*v*) have secured at least 55% marks in the entrance test.
(*iv*) have finalised the topic for research.

However, in the case of a candidate who fulfills all other criteria except—

(*a*) (*iii*) above but has M. Phil degree, should be given fellowship.

(*b*) (*iv*) above should be referred to Dean.

(*c*) (*i*) above but has atleast 55% marks in post–graduation, should be wait-listed.

(*d*) (*v*) above but has atleast 50% marks, should be referred to Chairman.

Based on these criteria and information provided below, decide the course of action in each case. You are not to assume anything. If the data provided is not adequate to decide the given course of action, your answer will be "data inadequate". These cases are given to you as on 1. 9. 1993.

13. Vijay Gupta is 24 years old and has got 58% marks in the entrance examination. He has secured 63% marks in his post-graduation and 55% marks in M. Phil. He has got diploma in Statistics and has also finalised the topic for research.

A. Grant Fellowship B. Refer to Dean
C. Refer to Chairman D. Wait-list
E. Data inadequate

14. Ajoy Dwivedi has secured 65% marks in the post-graduation and has secured 5 years research experience. He has secured 65% marks in the entrance test and has finalised the research topic. His date of birth is 11. 8. 1965.

A. Grant Fellowship B. Wait-list
C. Refer to Dean D. Data inadequate
E. None of these

15. Madan Soren has got diploma in Statistics with 60% marks and post-graduation with 56% marks. His date of birth is 12. 12. 1968. He has got 1 year research experience and is still doing his M. Phil. He has secured 60% marks in the entrance exam and has also finalised the research topic.

A. Grant fellowship
B. Fellowship not to be granted
C. Refer to Dean
D. Data inadequate
E. Wait-list

16. 26 years old Mamta Kulkarni is M. Phil with 60% marks. She has secured 70% marks in the entrance examination and has finalised the topic for research. She has also got diploma in Statistics.

A. Grant Fellowship
B. Fellowship not to be granted
C. Refer to Chairman
D. Refer to Dean
E. Data inadequate

17. Chander Manoj has got 5 years' research experience and has finalised the research topic. He has got 56% marks in post-graduation and 60% marks in the entrance test. His date of birth is 15. 2. 1966. He has also got diploma in Statistics.

A. Grant Fellowship
B. Fellowship not to be granted
C. Refer to Dean
D. Data inadequate
E. None of these

18. Raman Hooda is 28 years old and has got 65% marks in Post-graduation and 60% marks in M. Phil. He has got 65% marks in the entrance examination and has finalised the topic for research. He also has a diploma in Statistics.

A. Grant Fellowship
B. Fellowship not to be granted
C. Refer to Dean
D. Refer to Chairman
E. Data inadequate

19. 26 years old Janaki Deo is a post-graduate with 58% marks. She has got four years research experience and has finalised the topic for research. She got 70% marks in the diploma in Statistics and 54% marks in the entrance examination.

A. Fellowship not to be granted
B. Refer to Dean
C. Refer to Chairman
D. Grant Fellowship
E. Data inadequate

Directions (Qs. 20 to 27) : *Read the following information carefully and answer the questions given below :*

Following are the criteria of promotion from Junior Officer's Cadre to Senior Officer's Cadre in an organisation:

The candidate must—

(*a*) have completed atleast 5 years in the organisation.

(*b*) have secured 65% marks in the written test for promotion.

(*c*) have secured 60% marks in the Group Discussion.

(*d*) have secured 70% marks in the interview.

(*e*) have good record of his work performance.

(*f*) have good communication skill and get along well with his colleagues.

(*g*) not be more than 40 years and less than 30 years as on 1. 9. 93.

(*h*) have good academic record with an average of at least 65% marks.

However, in the case of a candidate who—

(*i*) satisfies all other conditions except (*d*) above but has secured 75% marks in the written test and 65% marks in he Group Discussion, the case is to be referred to the General Manager (Personnel)–GM(P) for the decision.

(*j*) satisfies all other criteria except (*h*) above but has secured an average of more than 60% marks, the case is to be referred to the Managing Director (MD) of the organisation.

Now read the information provided in the case of each candidate in each of the questions given below and decide on the basis of the information provided and based on the above conditions, which of the courses of action you would suggest. These cases are given as on 5. 9. 1993. (Remember you are not to assume anything which is not provided in the question). If complete information is not provided, the answer would be Data inadequate.

20. 38 years old Rajesh has secured 65% marks in the written test for promotion, 73% marks in interview and 62% marks in Group Discussion. He has good record of his work performance, good communication skills and gets along well with his colleagues. He has good academic record with an average of 61% marks and has completed 7 years in the organisation.

A. Refer to GM(P) B. Refer to MD
C. Promote D. Do not promote
E. Data inadequate

21. 34 years old Sudha has secured 60% marks in the written test for promotion, 72% marks in inteview and 69% marks in Group discussion. She has good communication skill and gets along well with her colleagues. Her record of work performance is good and she has completed 6½ years in the organisation.

A. Refer to MD B. Do not promote
C. Refer to GM(P) D. Promote
E. Data inadequate

22. Surekha has secured 70% marks in written test for promotion, 69% marks in Group Discussion and 72% marks in the interview. She has a good academic record with an average of 67% marks. She has good record of work performance and gets along well with her colleagues. She has good communication skill and has completed 7 years in the organisation.

A. Do not promote
B. Promote
C. Refer to GM(P)
D. Refer to MD
E. Data inadequate

23. 39 years old Pawan has secured 66% marks in written promotion test and has a good academic record with an average of 62% marks. He has secured 65% marks in Group Discussion and 72% marks in interview. He has good record of his work performance, communication skill and gets along well with his colleagues. He has completed 6 years in the organisation.

A. Do not promote
B. Refer to MD
C. Refer to GM(P)
D. Promote
E. Data inadequate

24. 34 years old Sudhir has secured 76% marks in the written test for promotion, 66% marks in Group Discussion and 67% marks in interview. He has good academic record with an average of 68% marks, good communication skill and gets along well with his colleagues. His work performance is good and he has completed 6 years in the organisation.

A. Promote B. Refer to MD
C. Refer to GM(P) D. Do not promote
E. Data anadequate

25. 32 years old Manjula has good academic record with an average of 66% marks. She has secured 67% marks in Group Discussion, 75% marks in interview and 60% marks in written test for promotion. She has good communication skill and gets along well with her colleagues. She has good record of her work performance and has completed 7 years in the organisation.

A. Do not promote B. Refer to MD
C. Promote D. Refer to GM(P)
E. Data inadequate

26. 31 years old Krishna secured 65% marks in written test for promotion, 72% marks in interview and 62% marks in Group Discussion. He has good academic record with an average of 67% marks and good communication skill. He has completed 9 years in the organisation. He gets easily annoyed and irritated with his colleagues and his record of work performance since the last two years is just average.

A. Promote B. Refer to GM(P)
C. Refer to MD D. Do not promote
E. Data inadequate

27. 33 years old Neelima has secured 63% marks in Group Discussion, 71% marks in interview and 66% marks in written test for promotion. She hase good academic record with an average of 68% marks and has good communication skill. She gets along well with her colleagues and has good record of her work performance. She has completed 6 years in the organisation.

A. Refer to GM(P) B. Do not promote
C. Promote D. Refer to MD
E. Data inadequate

Directions (Qs. 28 to 35) : *Read the following information carefully and answer the questions based on the given information. Following are the criteria for admitting a student in Medical course.*

The student must—

(*a*) have passed XIIth Std. Science examination with Biology amd have secured at least 60% marks.
(*b*) be of 18 years of age as on September 1, 1994.
(*c*) have obtained 70% marks in the entrance test.
(*d*) be able to pay ₹ 20,000 at the time of admission.

In the case of a candidate, who satisfies all other criteria except at—

I. (*c*) above, but has obtained 90% marks in the XIIth Std. Science examination, should be referred to the Principle.

II. (*d*) above, but can pay ₹ 10,000 at the time of admission, can be provisionally admitted.

You are given the following cases as on September 1, 1994. Depending upon the information provided in each case and based on the criteria mentioned above, recommend your decision. You are not to assume anything. Give answer

A. if the students is to be admitted;
B. if the student is not to be admitted;
C. if the student is to be referred to the principle;
D. if the student is to be admitted provisionally, and give answer;
E. if the data are inadequate.

28. Mahesh Sagar has secured 75% marks in the entrance test and can pay admission fee of ₹ 15,000 at the time of admission. He has secured 60% marks in the XIIth Std. Science examination with Biology.

29. Sunil Agarwal has passed XIIth Std. Science examination with Biology and secured 95% marks. His date of birth is July 15, 1976. He has obtained 60% marks in the entrance test. He can pay the fee of ₹ 20,000 at the time of admission.

30. Jayaesh Ozha was 17 years old as on 11th September, 1993. He has secured 90% marks in his XIIth Std. Science examination with Biology. He has secured 75% marks in the entrance test and can pay the admission fee of ₹ 20,000.

31. Pramod Lohia was born on 5th April, 1973. He has secured 80% marks in the XIIth Std. Science examination with Biology and can pay admission fee of ₹ 20,000. He has secured 85% marks in the entrance test.

32. Usha Jethmalani has secured 68% marks in her XIIth Std. Examination in Science with Biology and has secured 75% marks in the entrance test. She was born on 20th October, 1975. She can pay the admission fee of ₹ 20,000.

33. Sudha Malhotra has secured 70% marks in the entrance test and 60% marks in her XIIth Std. Science Examinaion with Biology. She can pay the admission fee of ₹ 20,000 and was born on 7th November, 1978.

34. Rajesh Gupta has secured 90% marks in the XIIth Std. Science Examination with Biology and 60% marks in the entrance test. He was born on 3rd Obtober, 1973. He can pay the admission fee of ₹ 20,000.

35. Prasad Mehra was born on 4th July, 1976. He has secured 80% marks in the entrance test. He has secured 85% marks in the XIIth Std. Science Examination with Biology. He can pay the admission fee of ₹ 15,000.

Directions (Qs. 36 to 45) : *Study the following information to answer the questions.*

The following are the criteria for organising the Training Programme of an Institute, in different Hotels.

To organise the programme in Hotel Taj, the following criteria must be fulfilled:

(*i*) The Programme Coordinator should be of the rank of Deputy Director or Joint Director.

(*ii*) The Programme should be in one of these areas—HRD, Advertising, Computers or Statistics.

(*iii*) The duration of the Programme should not be more than seven days.

(*iv*) The fee per participant should not be less than ₹ 5,000/-

(*v*) The number of participants should be at least 50.

If all the other criteria are fulfilled except—

(*a*) the duration of the course is more than seven days—the programme is to be organised in Hotel Ritz.

(*b*) the Programme Coordinator is of the rank of Assistant Director, but the fee per participant is more than ₹ 7,000, the Programme will be organised in Taj.

(*c*) the number of participants being less than 50 but more than 30, the Programme will be organised in Hotel Sideways.

(*d*) the fee, per participant is less than ₹ 5000 but more than ₹ 3,500, the Programme should be organised in Hotel Sansy.

(*e*) the Programme is in other than the areas mentioned in (*ii*) above, but the Programme Coordinator is of Joint Director level, the Programme should be organised in Hotel Sideways.

Based on the above criteria and the information provided in each question, decide about the appropriate course of action. You are not to assume anything. If some information is not available to decide the course of action, the answer would be "data inadequate".

Give answer

A. if the Programme is to be organised in Hotel Taj;
B. if the Programme is to be organised in Hotel Sideways;
C. if the Programme is to be organised in Hotel Ritz;
D. if the Programme is to be organised in Hotel Sansy; and
E. if the data are inadequate.

36. Prof. V. D. Dixit, Assistant Director, has offered four days' programme for 60 participants in the area of HRD. The fee per participant is ₹ 8,000.

37. Dr. Ashwani Dolke, Joint Director is organising five days' programme on Research Methodology. The total number of participants are 60 and the fee per participant is ₹ 7,000.

38. Dr. (Mrs.) Saroj Rao, Deputy Director of the institute wants to organise a programme for 55 candidates with a fee of ₹ 6,000 per participant. The duration of the course is four days and it is in the area of computers.

39. A Training Programme on Advertising is to be organised for 45 participants. The fee per participant is ₹ 6,000 and the duration of the course is six days.

40. A Training Programme on Statistics is proposed by the Deputy Director with ₹ 3,30,000 fee for 50 participants. The duration will be 8 days.

41. A five days' Training Programme by Joint Director is to be organised in the field of Statistics. The total fee for the Programme is ₹ 2,10,000 for 50 participants.

42. Nikhil Mukesh, Joint Director, is an expert on Computers. He is offering five days' programme on Mathematics for 60 participants. The fee per participant is ₹ 5,300.

43. A five days' Training Programme for 55 participants is to be organised by Shri Jacob Singh, Assistant Director. The fee per participant is ₹ 8,000.

44. Dr. Narayan Shiva, Deputy Director is offering a Programme on HRD with a total fee of ₹ 1,92,500 at the rate of ₹ 5,500 per participant. The duration of the course is five days.

45. Mrs. Shiela D'souza, Deputy Director has submitted a proposal to organise four days' Programme on Computers. The fee per participant would be ₹ 4,000 for 60 participants.

ANSWERS

1	2	3	4	5	6	7	8	9	10
E	D	C	C	A	A	D	E	E	B
11	**12**	**13**	**14**	**15**	**16**	**17**	**18**	**19**	**20**
C	A	A	C	B	E	E	A	A	B
21	**22**	**23**	**24**	**25**	**26**	**27**	**28**	**29**	**30**
B	E	B	C	A	D	C	E	C	B
31	**32**	**33**	**34**	**35**	**36**	**37**	**38**	**39**	**40**
A	A	B	C	D	A	B	A	E	C
41	**42**	**43**	**44**	**45**					
D	B	E	B	D					

EXPLANATORY ANSWERS

1. Criterion (*iii*) is not satisfied but Criterion (*b*) gives the decision.

2. Both Criterion (*iii*) and Criterion (*b*) are not satisfied.

3. Criterion (*iv*) is not satisfied but Criterion (*a*) gives the decision.

4. Criterion (*ii*) is not given.

6. Both Criterion (*i*) and Criterion (*c*) are not satisfied.

7. Criterion (*iv*) is not given but Criterion (*b*) gives the decision.

8. Both Criteria (*ii*) and (*iii*) are not given and Criterion (*a*) alone cannot give the decision.

9. Both Criterion (*i*) and Criterion (*iii*) are not given and criterion (*a*) alone cannot give the decision.

10. Both Criterion (*iii*) and Criterion (*a*) are not satisfied.

11. Criterion (*iii*) is not satisfied but Criterion (*a*) gives the decision.

12. Criterion (*i*) is not satisfied but Criterion (*c*) gives the decision.

13. Criterion (*iii*) is not satisfied but Criterion (*a*) gives the decision.

14. Criterion (*iv*) is not satisfied but Criterion (*b*) gives the decision.

15. Both Criterion (*iii*) and Criterion (*a*) are not satisfied.

16. Criterion (*i*) is not given and Criterion (*c*) is not satisfied.

17. Criterion (*i*) is not satisfied but Criterion (*c*) gives the decision of "wait–list." This option is not given.

18. Criterion (*iii*) is not satisfied but Criterion (*a*) gives the decision.

19. Both Criterion (*i*) and Criterion (*iii*) are not satisfied, Criterion (*c*) and Criterion (*d*) gives different decisions.

20. Criterion (*h*) is not satisfied but Criterion (*j*) gives the decision.

21. Criterion (*b*) is not satisfied.

22. Criterion (*g*) is not given.

23. Criterion (*h*) is not satisfied but Criterion (*j*) gives the desicion.

24. Criterion (*d*) is not satisfied but Criterion (*i*) gives the decision.

25. Criterion (*b*) is not satisfied.

26. Both Criterion (*e*) and Criterion (*f*) are not satisfied.

28. Criterion (*a*) is not given.

29. Criterion (*c*) is not satisfied but Criterion (*I*) gives the decision.

30. Criterion (*b*) is not satisfied.

33. Criterion (*b*) is not satisfied.

34. Criterion (*c*) is not satisfied but Criterion (*I*) gives the decision.

35. Criterion (*d*) is not satisfied but Criterion (*II*) gives the decision.

36. Criterion (*i*) is not satisfied but Criterion (*b*) gives the decision.

37. Criterion (*ii*) is not satisfied but Criterion (*e*) gives the decision.

39. Criterion (*i*) is not given.

40. Criterion (*iii*) is not satisfied but Criterion (*a*) gives the decision.

41. Criterion (*iv*) is not satisfied but Criterion (*d*) gives the decision.

42. Criterion (*ii*) is not satisfied but Criterion (*e*) gives the decision.

43. Criterion (*ii*) is not given.

44. Criterion (*v*) is not satisfied but Criterion (*c*) gives the decision (No. of participants is 1, 92, 500 ÷ 5,500, *i.e.,* 35)

45. Category (*iv*) is not satisfied but category (*d*) gives the decision.

☆☆☆☆☆☆

13. Coding and Decoding

Directions (Qs. 1-15) : *In the following questions select the right option which indicates the correct code for the word or letter given in the question.*

1. In a certain code ABCD is written as 2468 and EFGH as 1357. How will CAGE be written in that code?

A. 6453 B. 6251
C. 6521 D. 6215
E. None of these

2. If 341782 denotes MONKEY and 0596 denotes RAGS, then 75195044 will denote.

A. KANGAROO B. PALMANTT
C. HANGAMEE D. KARNAGOO
E. None of these

3. If HARD is coded as 1357 and SOFT as 2468, what will 21448 stand for?

A. SHAFT B. SHORT
C. SHOOT D. SHART
E. None of these

4. In a certain code COUNTRY is coded as KVASXUA. How will INDIA be coded in the same manner?

A. PTIMD B. QUJNE
C. QUINE D. RVKOF
E. None of these

5. If GASP is coded as LNPQ and BROW as XABF, then SPARROW will be coded in the same manner as :

A. PQAANBF B. PQANNBF
C. PQNAABF D. PQNBBAF
E. None of these

6. If CORRESPONDENCE is coded as NUTTRAXUPQRPNR in a certain code, how will SCOPE be coded?

A. AUXNR B. ANUXR
C. RNUXA D. XUPAR
E. None of these

7. In a certain code language SECRET is written as UIIZOF. How will MYSTERY be written in the same code?

A. OCYANCN B. OCYBOCM
C. OCYAODM D. OCYBODM
E. None of these

8. In a certain code LOCATE is written as 981265 and SPARK as 47230, CASKET will be coded in the same manner as :

A. 124056 B. 210465
C. 164025 D. 124506
E. None of these

9. If HALT is coded as SZOG in a certain code, how will STOP be coded in the same manner?

A. GFLK B. HGLK
C. HGKJ D. IHML
E. None of these

10. In a certain code language DELAY is coded as ABIXV. In the same code what will BXOIV stand for?

A. EARTH B. EARNS
C. EARLY D. ELDER
E. None of these

11. In a certain code TRANSMISSION is written as RTANMSISISON. How will COMMUNICATIONS be written in the same code?

A. OCMMUNCIATIONS
B. OCMMNUICTAIONS
C. OCMMNUICTAISNO
D. OCMMNUICTAIOSN
E. None of these

12. In a certain code REGISTRY is written as VAKEWPVU. How will ENTRY be written in the same code?

A. IJXNC B. ARPVW
C. ARPVU D. IJXMC
E. None of these

13. AUSTRALIA is written in a certain code language as 973609429 and CANADA as 591989. How should CRUST be written in the same code?

A. 50763 B. 53076
C. 50376 D. 50736
E. None of these

14. DAZE is written as 41265 in a certain code. How will BOY be written in the same code?

A. 41425 B. 5120
C. 21525 D. 359
E. None of these

15. If MEDAL is coded as XPOLW, then how will CADGE be coded in the same manner?

A. NLORP B. PNQTR
C. LJMPN D. MLOQP
E. None of these

Directions (Qs. 16-26) : *In the following questions study the coded patterns and then select the right option from the given alternatives.*

16. In a certain code language, (1) 'lo ni hie pun' stands for 'he is drinking coke'; (2) 'hol ful gui pun' stands for 'she is eating food'; and (3) 'ne ful ni lo' stands for 'drinking coke and food'. Which of the following words is the code for 'he'?

A. hie B. lo
C. pun D. ni
E. None of these

17. In a certain code language,

1. Gor Paku Means 'Best Gift'
2. Mull Gor Sot Means 'Gift of Love'
3. Sot Hed Paku Means 'Best of Luck' and
4. Hed Sot Paku Means 'Love is Best'

Which of the following codes stand for the word 'Love'?

A. Paku B. Hed
C. Sot D. Mull
E. None of these

18. In a certain code language, 'pe sa de mi' means 'yes well no mean' and 'pa mi sa de' means 'sell mean well no'. What would 'yes' mean in that language?

A. de B. pe
C. mi D. sa
E. None of these

19. In a certain code 'hua pih uf pu' means 'he is very intelligent'; 'pih hua kup kit' means 'she is very fair'; 'luck uf hua' means 'Jai is intelligent'; and 'uf kit pod' means 'fair and intelligent'.
Which of the following codes stand for 'Jai'?

A. kit B. hua
C. luck D. pih
E. None of these

20. In a certain code language 'jo mi rei ma' stands for 'rest work no play'; 'rei kol puihi mesi' for 'less ground play tour'; and 'puihi ma jo mati' for 'rest group ground work'.
Which of the following codes stand for word 'no'?

A. mi B. mesi
C. rei D. jo
E. None of these

21. In a certain code language '1 2 3' means 'hot filter coffee', '3 5 6' means 'very hot day' and '5 8 9' means 'day and night'. Which digit in that language means 'very'?

A. 8 B. 6
C. 9 D. 5
E. None of these

22. In a certain code, '3 5 7' means 'get me toy', '8 4 3' means 'bring good toy' and '7 4 6' means 'bring me water'. Which of the following digits represents 'good' in that code?

A. 7 B. 6
C. 5 D. Data inadequate
E. None of these

23. In a certain code 721 means 'good college life'. 526 means 'you are good' and 257 means 'life are good', which digit stands for 'you' as the code?

A. 6 B. 5
C. 7 D. 8
E. None of these

24. In a certain code language 'dom pul ta' means 'bring hot food', 'pul tir sop' means 'food is good' and 'tak da sop' means 'good bright boy'. Which of the following does mean 'hot' in that language?

A. dom B. pul
C. ta D. Cannot be determined
E. None of these

25. In a certain code '3 7' means 'which class' and '5 8 3' means 'caste and class'. What is the code for 'caste'?

A. 3 B. 7
C. Either 5 or 3 D. Either 5 or 8
E. None of these

26. In a code language 'mu kay cit' means 'very lucky person' and 'dis hu mu' means 'fortunate and lucky'. Which is the word in that language for 'lucky?'

A. mu B. kay
C. cit D. dis
E. None of these

Directions : (Qs. 27 and 28) : *In a code language, (a) 'pit dar na' means 'you are good'; (b) 'dar tok pa' means 'good and bad'; (c) 'tim na tok' means 'they are bad'.*

27. In that language, which word stands for 'they'?

A. na B. tok
C. tim D. dar
E. None of these

28. To find the answer to the above question, which of the following statements can be dispensed with?

A. Only (*a*) B. Only (*b*)
C. (*a*) or (*b*) D. Only (*c*)
E. None of these

Directions : (Qs. 29 and 30) : *In a certain code language :*

(*a*) 'tom na rod' means 'give me sweet'.

(*b*) 'jo ta rod' means 'you and me'.

(*c*) 'pot ta noc' means 'you are good'.

(*d*) 'jo mit noc' means 'good and bad'.

29. Which of the following represents 'bad' in that language?

A. mit B. noc
C. jo D. rod
E. None of these

30. To arrive at the answer to the above question which of the following can be dispensed with?

A. All are necessary B. (*a*) or (*b*) only
C. (*a*) or (*c*) only D. (*b*) or (*c*) only
E. None of these

ANSWERS

1	2	3	4	5	6	7	8	9	10
B	A	C	B	C	B	D	A	B	C
11	**12**	**13**	**14**	**15**	**16**	**17**	**18**	**19**	**20**
D	A	D	C	A	A	C	B	C	A
21	**22**	**23**	**24**	**25**	**26**	**27**	**28**	**29**	**30**
B	E	A	D	D	A	C	E	A	E

EXPLANATORY ANSWERS

1. The letters of the given groups are coded by numbers and the word CAGE is formed by letters from the given words. So, to find the answer, select the respective numbers.

A B C D E F G H → letters
2 4 6 8 1 3 5 7 → codes
So, C A G E → letters
6 2 5 1 → answer codes

2. The numbers represent letters and to find the answer, select the respective letters.

3 4 1 7 8 2 0 5 9 6 → codes
M O N K E Y R A G S → letters
So,
7 5 1 9 5 0 4 4 → codes
K A N G A R O O → answer letters

3. The numbers represent letters and to find the answer, select the respective letters.

1 3 5 7 2 4 6 8 → codes
H A R D S O F T → letters
So, 2 1 4 4 8 → codes
S H O O T → answer letters

4. The word is coded by moving the first letter eight steps forward, and reducing the difference by one.

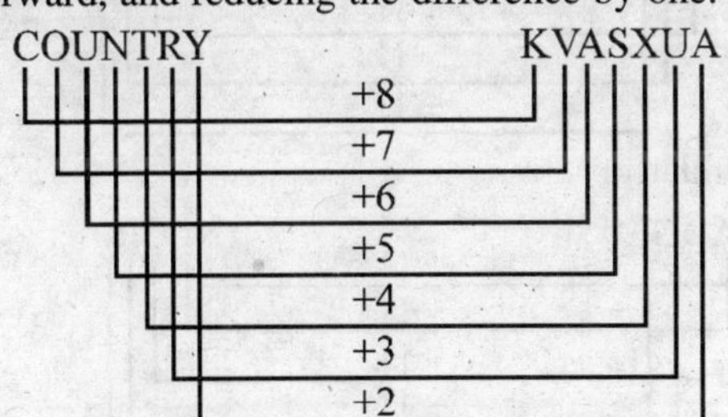

(The series restarts from A on reaching Z)

Similarly,

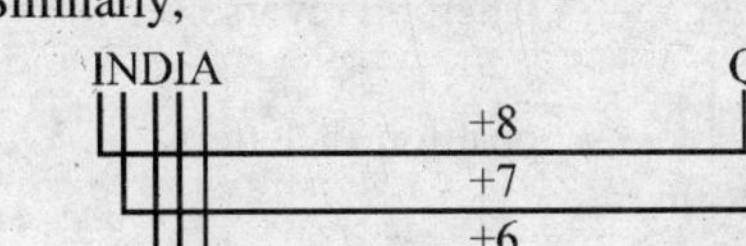

5. The letters of the words are coded by substituted letters. To find the answer code, select the respective substituted letters.

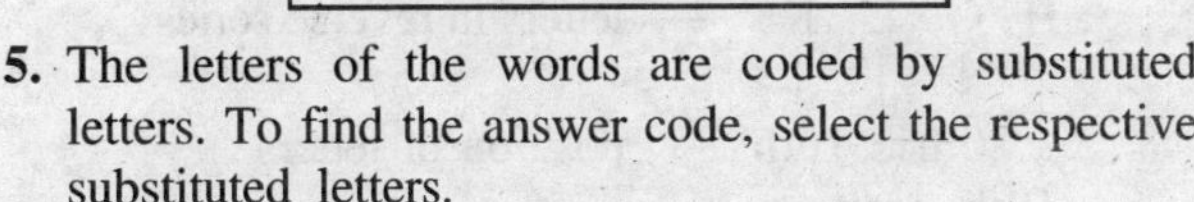

GASP BROW → letters
LNPQ XABF → substituted letter codes
So,
SPARROW → letters
PQNAABF → substituted letter answer codes

6. The letters of the word are coded by substituted letters. To find the answer code, select the respective substituted letters.

C O R R E S P O N D E N C E → letters
N U T T R A X U P Q R P N R → substituted letter codes

So,
S C O P E — letters
A N U X R — substituted letter answer codes

7. The word is coded by moving the letters forward by consecutive even numbered steps.

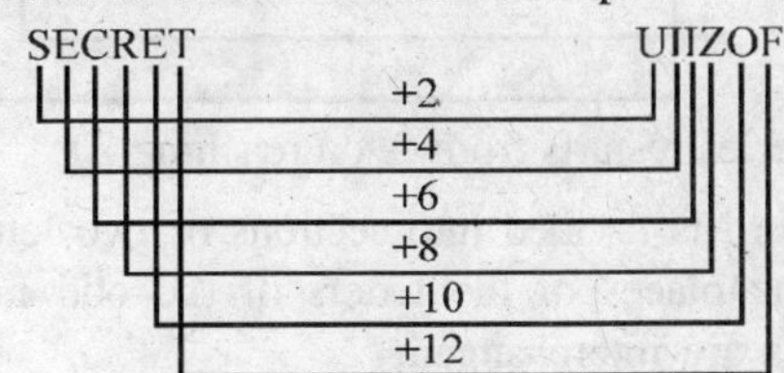

Similarly,

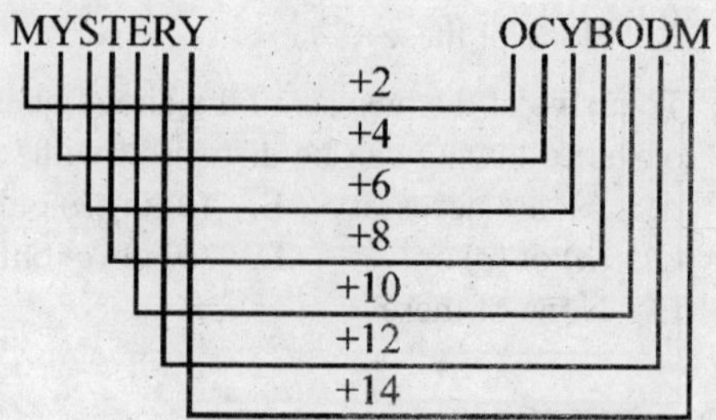

(The series restarts from A on reaching Z)

8. The letters are coded by numbers and to find the answer code, select the respective numbers.

L O C A T E S P A R K → letters
9 8 1 2 6 5 4 7 2 3 0 → codes

So,

C A S K E T → letters
1 2 4 0 5 6 → answer codes

9. The letters of the word are coded by their represented letters in reverse series.

H A L T → letters in natural series
S Z O G → letters in reverse series
8th 12th → position of letters
1st 20th

So,

S T O P → letters in natural series
H G L K → letters in reverse series
20th 16th → position of letters
19th 15th

10. The word is obtained by decoding the letters. The coded letters are moved three steps forward.

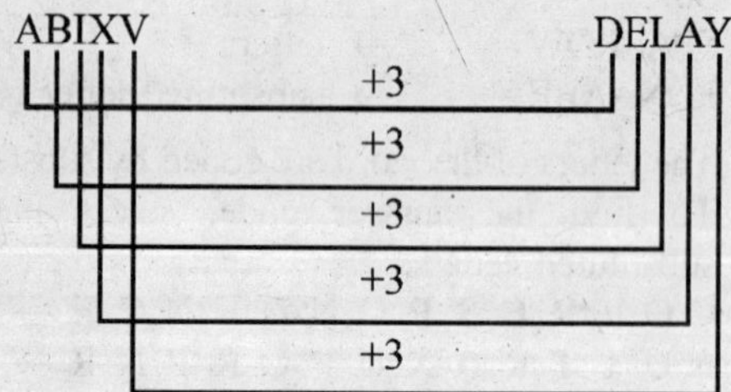

Similarly,

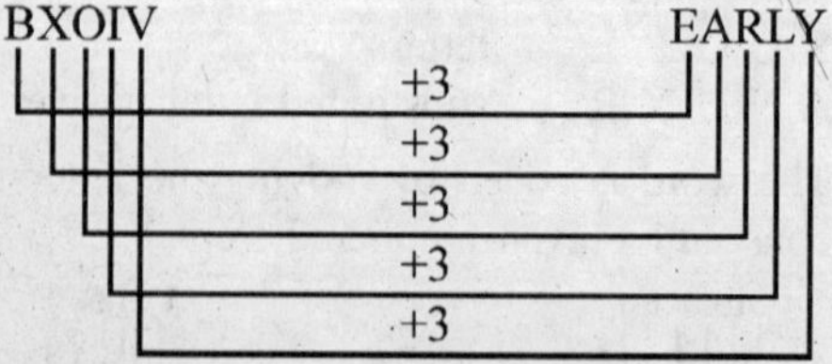

(The series restarts from A on reaching Z)

11. The word is divided into sections of two letters, and then the places of the letters of the odd numbered sections are interchanged.

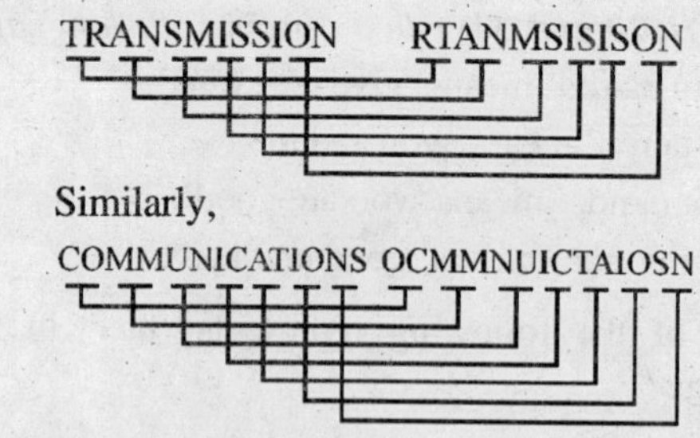

12. The letters of the word are coded by moving four steps forward and four steps backward alternately.

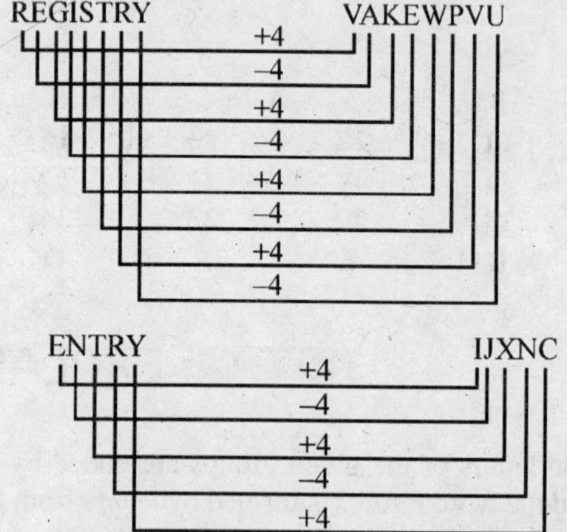

(The series restarts from A on reaching Z)

13. The letters are coded by numbers. To find the answer code, select the respective numbers.

AUSTRALIA CANADA → letters
9 7 3 6 0 9 4 2 9 5 9 1 9 8 9 → number codes

So, C R U S T → letters
5 0 7 3 6 → answer codes

14. The letters of the word are coded by the numbers representing their position in the natural series.

D A Z E → letters
4 1 26 5 → position of letters in natural series

Similarly, B O Y → letters
2 15 25 → position of letters in natural series

15. The word is coded by moving the letters eleven steps forward.

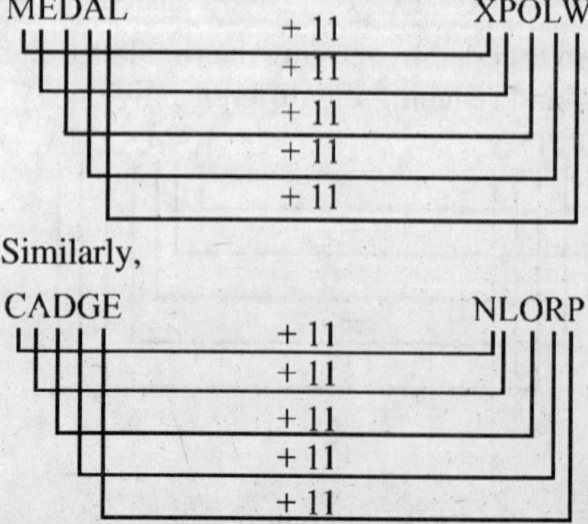

16. *Code* *Sentence*

1. *lo ni* **hie** *pun* → **he** *is drinking coke*
2. hol ful gui *pun* → she *is* eating food
3. ne ful *ni lo* → *drinking coke* and food

In the 1st and 2nd sentences, the code 'pun' for 'is' is repeated but the word 'he' is not. In the 1st and 3rd sentences, the codes 'ni' and 'lo' are repeated. So, the code 'hie' stands for 'he'.

17. *Code* *Sentence*

1. Gor Paku → Best Gift
2. Mull Gor *Sot* → Gift of *Love*
3. Sot Hed Paku → Best of Luck
4. Hed *Sot* Paku → *Love* is Best

Only in sentences 2nd and 4th, the word 'Love' is repeated and the only code repeated is 'Sot'.

18. *Code* *Sentence*

1. **pe** *sa de mi* → **yes** *well no mean*
2. pa *mi sa de* → sell *mean well no*

In both the sentences, "well no mean" is repeated and so the coded words 'sa de mi' So, only 'pe' stands for 'yes'.

19. *Code* *Sentence*

1. *hua* pih uf pu → he *is* very intelligent
2. pih *hua* kup kit → she *is* very fair
3. **luck** *uf hua* → **Jai** *is intelligent*
4. *uf* kit pod → fair and *intelligent*

The word 'Jai' is in 3rd sentence. Of the three codes, 'hua' is repeated in 1st and 2nd sentences and 'uf' is repeated in 3rd and 4th sentences. So, code 'luck' stands for 'Jai'.

20. *Code* *Sentence*

1. *jo* **mi** *rei ma* → *rest work* **no** *play*
2. *rei* kol puihi mesi → less ground *play* tour
3. puihi *ma jo* mati → *rest* group ground *work*

The word 'no' is only in 1st sentence. Of the other codes 'rei' is repeated in 2nd sentence and 'jo' and 'ma' are repeated in 3rd sentence. So, 'mi' code stands for word 'no'.

21. *Code* *Sentence*

1. 1*23* *hot* filter coffee
2. *35***6** **very** *hot day*
3. *5*89 *day* and night

The word 'very' is in 2nd sentence only. The word 'hot' is common in 1st and 2nd sentences and so is the code '3'. The word 'day' is common in 2nd and 3rd sentences and so is the code '5'. The only code remaining is '6' which stands for 'very'.

22. *Code* *Sentence*

1. *3*5*7* get me *toy*
2. **8***43* *bring* **good** *toy*
3. 7*4*6 *bring* me water

The word 'good' is in 2nd sentence only. The word 'bring' is common in 2nd and 3rd sentences and so is the code '4'. The word 'toy' is common in 1st and 2nd sentences and so is the code '3'. The only code remaining is '8' which stands for 'good'.

23. *Code* *Sentence*

1. 721 good college life
2. *52***6** **you** *are good*
3. *25*7 life *are good*

The word 'you' is in 2nd sentence only. The words 'are good' are common in 2nd and 3rd sentences and so are the codes '2' and '5'. The only code remaining is '6' which stands for 'you'.

24. *Code* *Sentence*

1. dom *pul* ta bring **hot** *food*
2. *pul* tir sop *food* is good
3. tak da sop good bright boy

From 1st and 2nd codes and sentences it is clear that code for 'food' is 'pul'. Neither the words 'bring' and 'hot' are repeated nor the codes 'dom' and 'ta'. So, the codes for the words cannot be detected.

25. *Code* *Sentence*

1. *37* which *class*
2. 58*3* caste and *class*

In both the codes and sentences code '3' stands for 'class'. So the code for 'caste' can be either '5' or '8'. The same applies for word 'and'. More information is needed.

26. *Code* *Sentence*

1. *mu* kay cit very *lucky* person
2. dis hu *mu* fortunate and *lucky*

In both the codes and sentences word 'lucky' is common and so is the code 'mu'.

27. *Code* *Sentence*

A. pit dar *na* you *are* good
B. dar *tok* pa good and *bad*
C. **tim** *na tok* **they** *are bad*

The word 'they' is in sentence B only. The word 'are' is repeated in sentence A and so is the code 'na'. The word 'bad' is repeated in sentence B and so is the code 'tok'. The only code remaining is 'tim' which stands for 'they'.

28. The answer to the above question was arrived at only after comparing all the three codes and sentences.

29. *Code* *Sentence*

A. tom na rod give me sweet
B. *jo* ta rod you *and* me
C. pot ta *noc* you are *good*
D. *jo* **mit** *noc* *good* and **bad**

The word 'bad' is in sentence 'D' only. The word 'good' is repeated in sentence 'C' and so is the code 'noc'. The word 'and' is repeated in sentence 'B' and so is the code 'jo'. The only code remaining is 'mit' which stands for 'bad'.

30. The answer to the above question was arrived at by comparing codes and sentences B, C and D. Only sentence 'A' could be dispensed with.

☆☆☆☆☆☆

14. Non-Verbal Series

Directions (Q. 1–30) : *In each of the following questions which one of the five answer figures given below should come after the problem figures if the sequence are continued?*

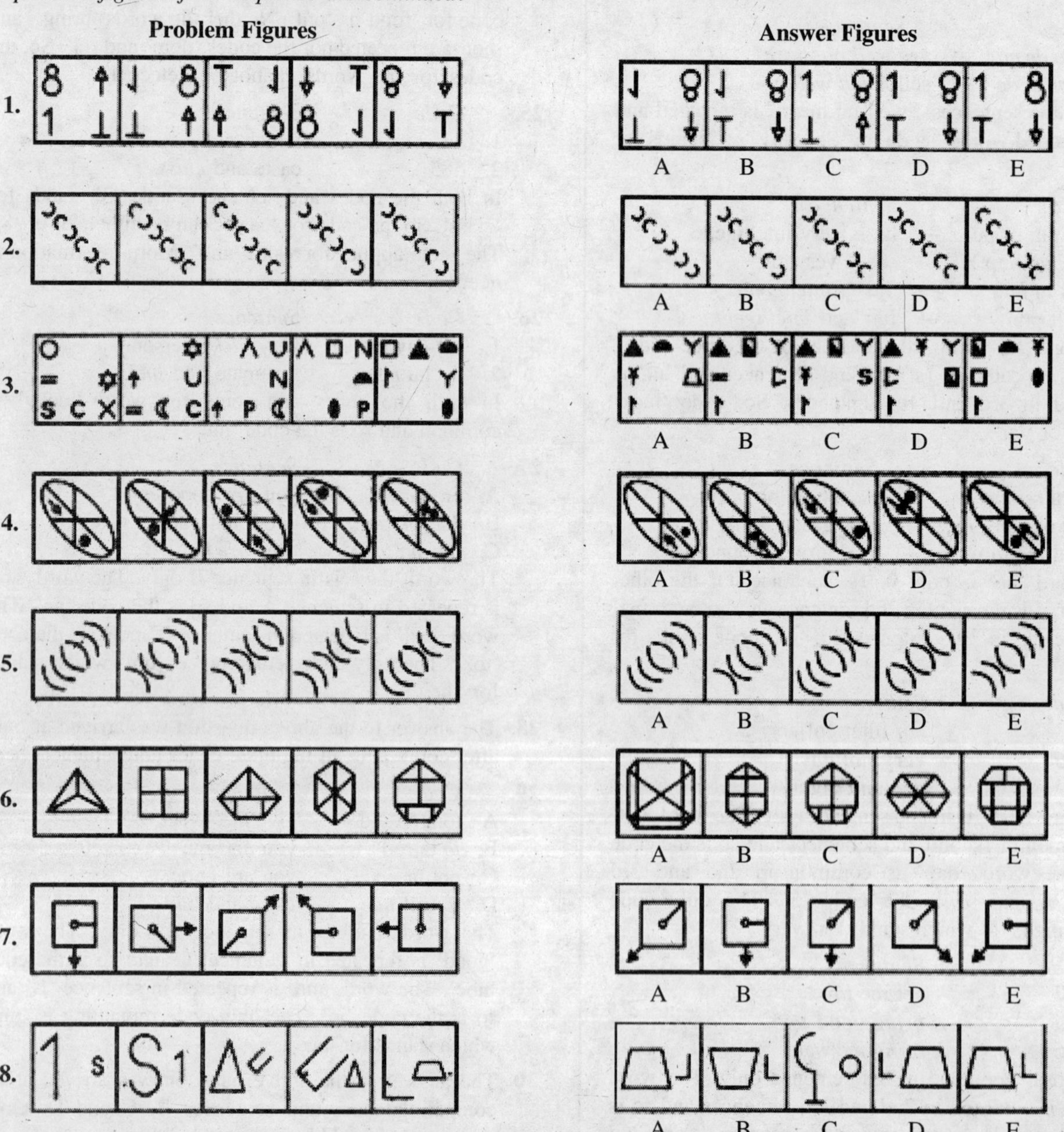

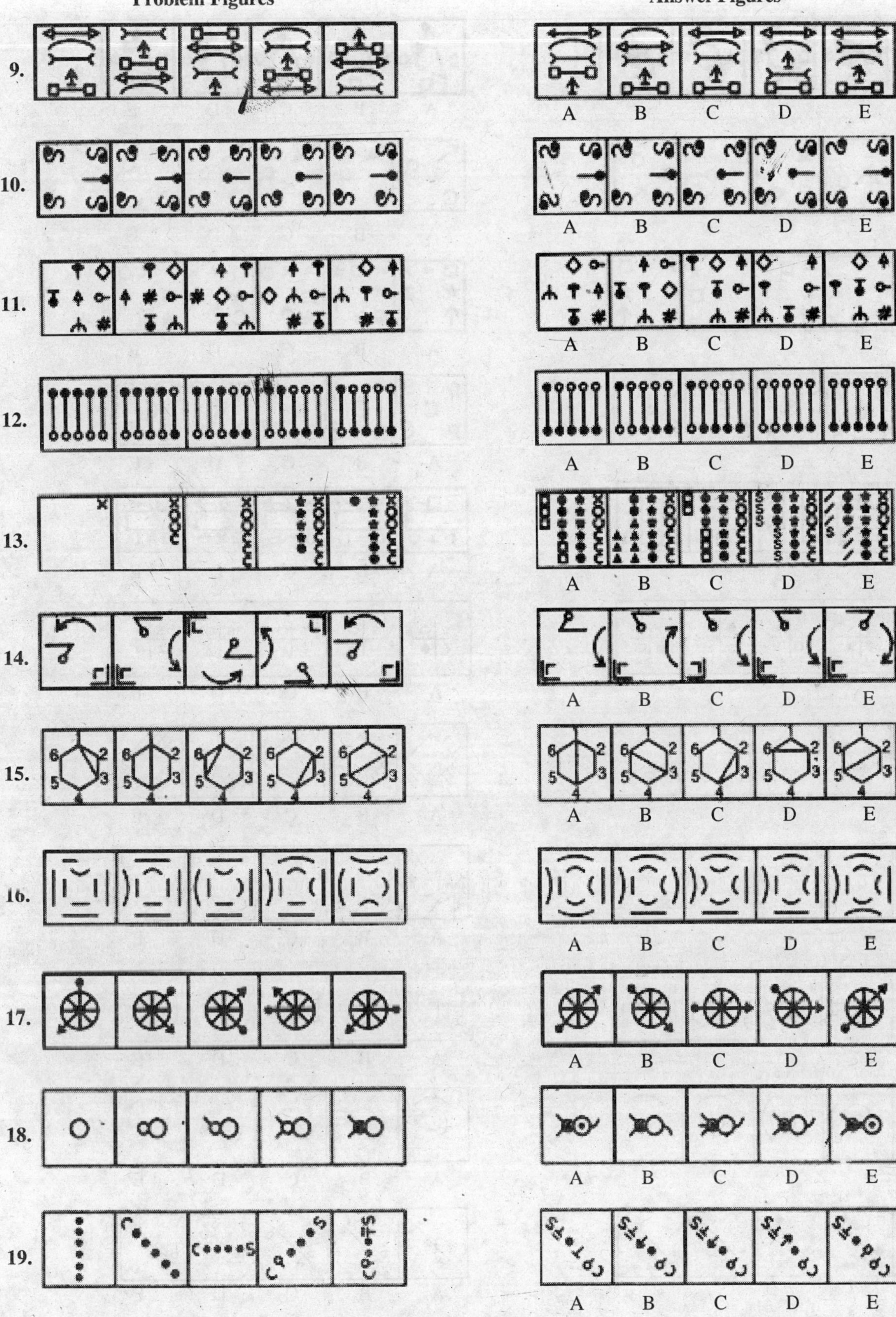
Problem Figures
Answer Figures
9.
10.
11.
12.
13.
14.
15.
16.
17.
18.
19.
A
B
C
D
E

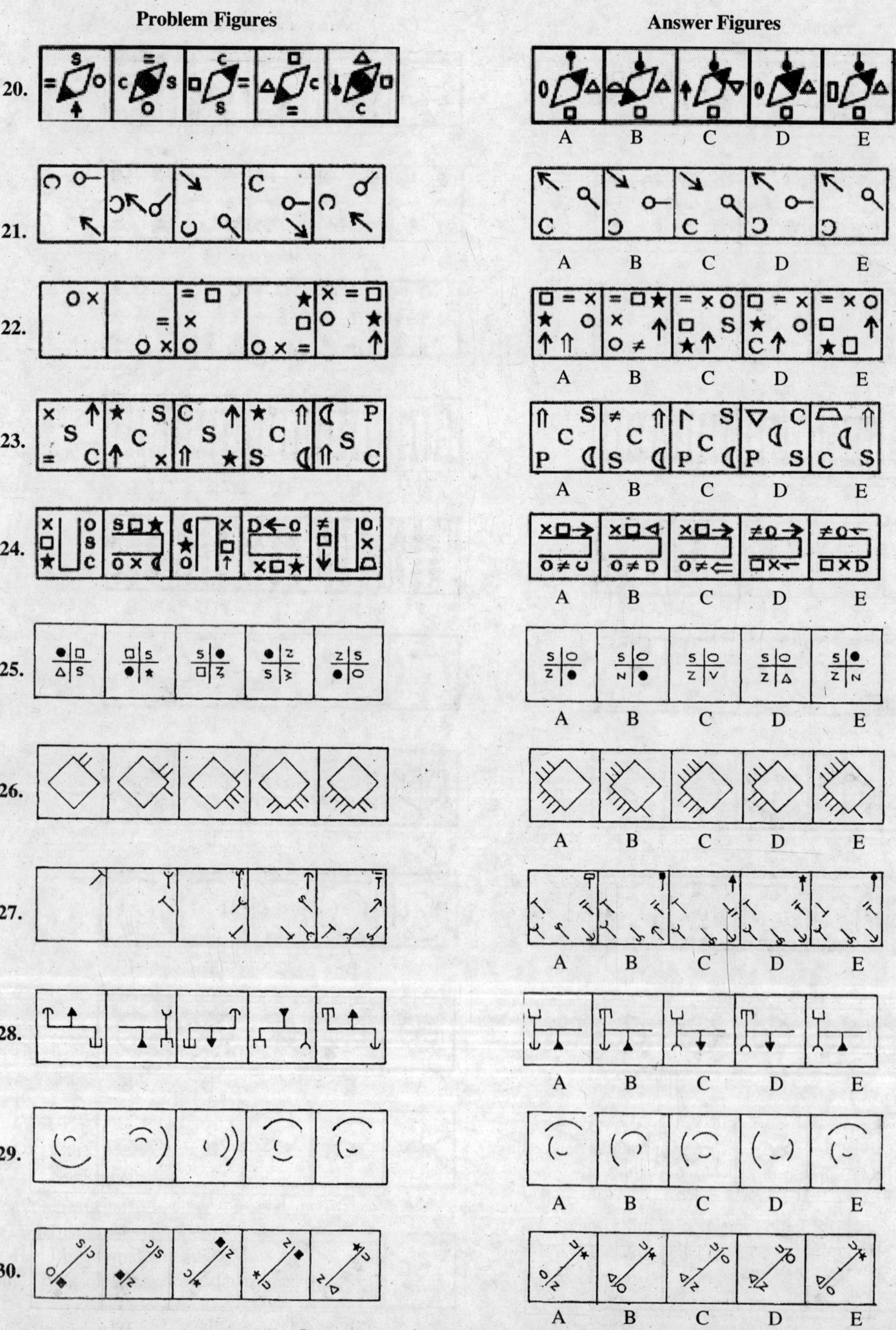
Problem Figures
Answer Figures
20.
21.
22.
23.
24.
25.
26.
27.
28.
29.
30.
A B C D E

Directions (Q. 31-50) : *In each of these questions, a series begins with an unmarked figure on the extreme left in the row of figures. One and only one of the five lettered figures in the series does not fit into the series. The two unmarked figures, one on the extreme left and the other on the extreme right fit into the series. Take as many aspects into account as possible of the figures in the series and find out the one and only of the five marked figures which does not fit into the series. The letter of that figure is the answer.*

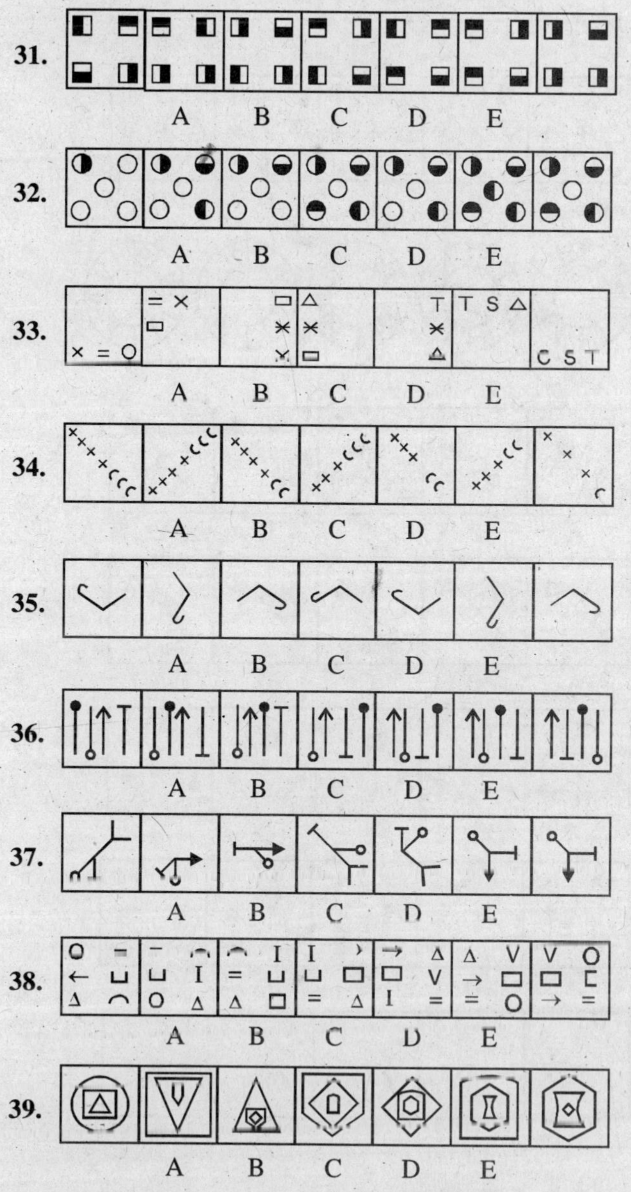

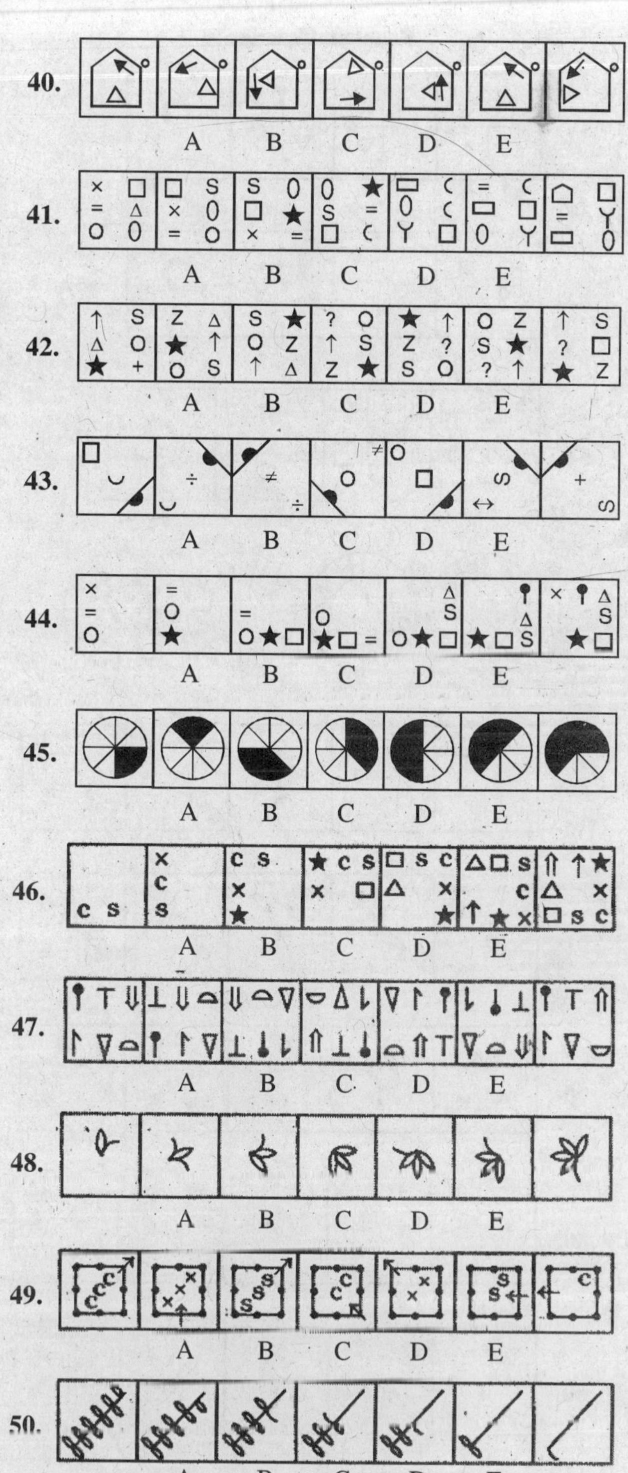

Directions (Q. 51–60) : *Each of the following questions consist of problem figures followed by answer figures. Select a figure from amongst the answer figures which will continue the same series or pattern as established by the problem figures.*

Problem Figures **Answer Figures**

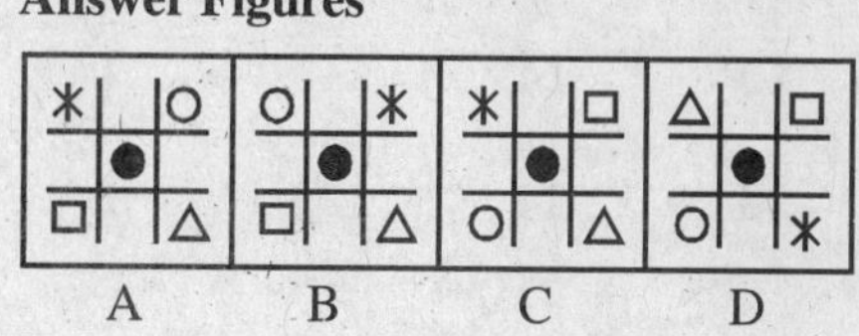

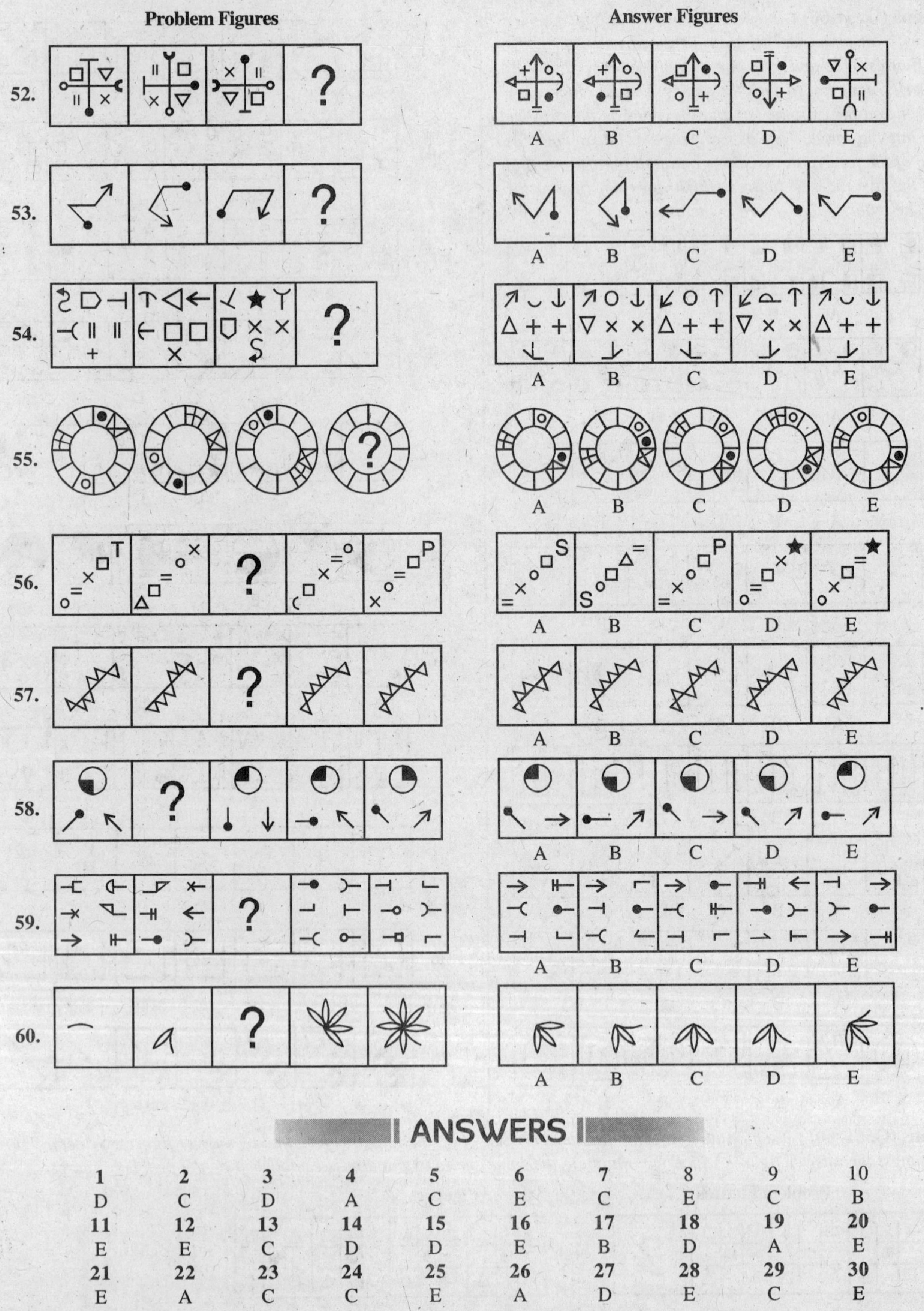

ANSWERS

1	2	3	4	5	6	7	8	9	10
D	C	D	A	C	E	C	E	C	B
11	**12**	**13**	**14**	**15**	**16**	**17**	**18**	**19**	**20**
E	E	C	D	D	E	B	D	A	E
21	**22**	**23**	**24**	**25**	**26**	**27**	**28**	**29**	**30**
E	A	C	C	E	A	D	E	C	E

31	32	33	34	35	36	37	38	39	40
A	E	A	C	C	E	E	E	A	A
41	**42**	**43**	**44**	**45**	**46**	**47**	**48**	**49**	**50**
D	E	D	C	E	C	D	E	B	D
51	**52**	**53**	**54**	**55**	**56**	**57**	**58**	**59**	**60**
A	E	A	E	A	A	C	C	A	A

EXPLANATORY ANSWERS

1. In each step, all the elements move to the adjacent corner (of the square boundary) in a CW direction and the element that reaches the upper-left corner gets vertically inverted.

2. We can label the arcs as shown . The arcs get inverted in the sequence (1 & 2), (3, 4 & 5), (6 & 1), (2, 3 & 4), (5 & 6), ...

3. All the elements move half-a-side of the square boundary in ACW direction in each step. Also, first, third and fifth elements are replaced by new elements in one step and second, fourth and sixth elements are replaced by new elements in the next step. The two steps are repeated alternately.

4. In each step, the dot moves one space CW and the arrow moves two spaces CW.

5. One arc and four arcs get inverted alternately.

6. The number of parts increases by one along with the number of sides in the figure.

7. The pin rotates 45°CW and 90°CW alternately and moves one space (each space is equal to half-a-side of the square) and two spaces CW alternately. The arrow rotates 90°ACW and 45°ACW alternately and moves two spaces and one space.

8. In one step, the two elements interchange positions and the smaller element gets enlarged while the larger element gets reduced in size. In the next step, the smaller element is replaced by a new small element and the larger element is replaced by a new large element.

9. In each step, the elements move in the order .

10. The upper-left element gets laterally inverted in first, third, fifth. .... steps; the upper-right element gets rotated through 180° is first, fourth, seventh,.... steps; the lower-left element gets laterally inverted in second, fourth, sixth, ... steps; the lower-right element gets rotated through 180° in third, sixth,... steps and the pin at the middle-right position gets laterally inverted in every second step.

11. In one step, the elements move in the sequence  and in the next step, the elements move in the sequence . The two steps are repeated alternately.

12. One of the pins gets inverted in each step. The pins get inverted sequentially from right to left.

13. The number of symbols added sequentially is 3, 2, 5, 2, 7, 2, ... These symbols are added to form a sequence of 1, 2, 3, 4, 5, 6 identical symbols.

14. The bent pin gets laterally inverted and vertically inverted alternately and moves to the adjacent side (of the square boundary) in a CW direction in each step,. The curved arrow rotates 90°ACW and moves to the adjacent side CW in each step. As for the third element — in one step the outer 'L' shaped symbol gets laterally inverted and in the next step the element gets vertically inverted. Or, similar figure reappears in every fourth step. So, after fig. (E), the fig. (B) should reappear.

15. The diagonals of the hexagon are drawn in a sequence— (1, 3), (1, 4), (1, 5), (2, 4), (2, 5), (2, 6), (3, 5), (3, 6), (4, 6).

16. In each step all the existing curves get inverted and one of the line segments gets converted into a curve.

17. The pin moves 1, 2, 3, 4, 5, ... spaces CW sequentially. The arrow moves two steps ACW each time.

18. A new feature is added at each step (in a set order).

19. One circle is replaced by a new symbol in each step and this replacement takes place on either ends alternately. The complete figure rotates 45°ACW in each step.

20. The shading moves upwards sequentially from lower-left corner to the upper-right corner of the rhombus and once it reaches the upper-right corner, it moves to the lower-left corner in the next step. Also, in each step, all the symbols move to the adjacent side (of the rhombus) in a CW direction and the symbol that reaches the LHS position gets replaced by a new symbol.

21. The curve rotates through 90° clockwise in each subsequent figure and descends stepwise but ascends in one step. Therefore, Answer Figures (A) and (C) can be ruled out. The pinhead rotates respectively through 45° anticlockwise, 90° clockwise, 45° anticlockwise and 90° clockwise in the subsequent figures and descends or ascends stepwise. Therefore, Answer

Figures (B) and (D) can be ruled out. At this stage we can mark our answer. Now consider the movement of arrow. The arrow moves upward diagonally stepwise but moves downward in one step. The arrow is reversed after every two steps.

22. In each subsequent figure, one new design is added infront of the pre-existing designs and behind the Pre-existing designs alternately pre-existing designs move two & half steps in anticlockwise direction and interchange positions. Thus, from Problem Figure (E) to Answer Figure, all the designs would move half-step in anticlockwise direction and the first and sixth designs would interchange positions and so as the second and the fifth design and the third and the fourth designs. A new design would be added in front of the pre-existing designs.

23. The movement of designs and other changes in designs can be shown as :

From Problem Figure

A to B B to C C to D

C to D D to Answer Fig.

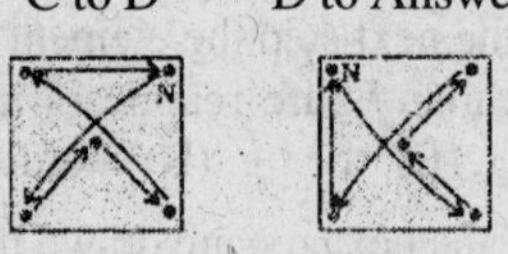

24. Whole figure rotates 90°ACW. In question figure 1 to 2 four upper elements of the figure *i.e.,* X, □, S and O move one step ACW. Lower left element moves to lower right and a new element appears at lower left place. Same changes will occur in question figure 5 to answer figure.

25. The dark circle moves two times one place and one time two places respectively in anticlockwise direction. After continuation of the sequence answer figure (E) is the required answer.

26. In each subsequent figure, one line is added to two sides of the square alternatively. After continuation of the sequence answer figure (A) is the required answer.

27. In every question figure, a new element appears. The first element rotates 90°ACW. Next element rotates 45°, 90°, 90° .... CW. Similarly, the third element from the third question figure rotates 45°, 90°, 90° ... ACW and these changes continues.

28. In each next figure, one design changes its place and also the direction of all other designs are reversed properly. After continuation of sequence answer figure (E) is the required answer.

29. Outer and inner arcs move one step alternatively in anticlockwise direction while middle arc in clockwise direction. After continuation of the sequence answer figure (C) is required answer.

30. Elements change their places across the diagonal line and then same side of diagonal line alternatively. A new element takes place instead of lower right element of the diagonal line.

31. The shade in the top left square is moved one step clockwise till figure B and then reversed, the process is repeated. The shade in the top right square is moved one step anticlockwise till figure D and then reversed. The shade in the bottom left square is moved one step clockwise in alternate figures and the shade in bottom right square is moved one step clockwise after two figures. In figure 'A' the rule is isolated by the shade in the bottom left square.

32. In alternate figures a new circle is shaded clockwise. The pattern of the shade is also moved clockwise. In figure 'E' right half of the circle in the centre should have been shaded.

33. The three elements are placed either horizontally or vertically. In option 'A' neither of the placements can be applied.

34. The placement of elements is same in alternate figures. The number and type of elements is same in two subsequent figures. In this manner, figure 'C' should have four crosses and two C shapes.

35. The element is moved one step anticlockwise and the arc at one end is turned outside and inside alternately. In figure 'C' the element should be on the right side with the arc turned outside on the top side.

36. The left most element, line segment with the dot is moved one step towards right till figure C where it reaches the extreme right position. This process is repeated from figure D where the element on the extreme left, line segment with a circle, is moved. In figure 'E' the placement of the elements does not follow the rule of the series.

37. The 'T' line is rotated 45° clockwise and the line with the circle 45° anticlockwise. The 'Y' shape and the arrow are repeated twice after two figures. In option E, the 'T' shape and the line with the circle are rotated by 90°.

38. First the elements in the four corners are moved one step anticlockwise, next the four elements from the top are moved one step anticlockwise and then the four elements from the bottom are moved one step anticlockwise. Of the remaining two elements, the one on the left is made new each time and then their places are interchanged. This process is repeated from figure D. In option 'E' open square should have been in place of circle to continue the series.

39. At each step the outermost figure is removed and a new figure is placed right in the centre of other two figures. In option 'A' the triangle is turned upside down, which violates the rule of the series.

40. The arrow is moved one step anticlockwise and the triangle one step clockwise. In figure 'A' the triangle should have been on the left side of the figure.

41. All the elements are moved anticlockwise in a set pattern and only one of the elements made new in clockwise manner. Option 'D' violates the rule.

42. The movement of elements is—top left element is moved to the middle right position, the middle right element is moved to the bottom left position, the bottom left element is moved to the middle left position, the middle left element is moved to the top right position, the top right element is moved to the bottom right position, and the bottom right element is moved to the top left position. In alternate figures, the top left element is made new. In option 'E' this element is not changed.

43. The diagonal line is moved anticlockwise and the shade moved outside and inside alternately. The element in the centre is moved to the corner opposite the diagonal and a new element is placed in the centre. In option 'D' there should have been a double arrow instead of square in the centre.

44. In figure 'A' the elements are moved clockwise, the first element is moved to the last and made new. In figure 'B' the elements are moved anticlockwise and new element is added adjacent to the new element in previous figure. This process is repeated from figure 'C' which violates the rule. 'S' shape should have been in place of equal to (=) sign.

45. The shade is moved 3 steps and 4 steps anticlockwise in alternate figures. After four steps one section clockwise is also shaded. The process is continued. In figure 'E' wrong sections are shaded.

46. According to trend of the question figures the correct series will be

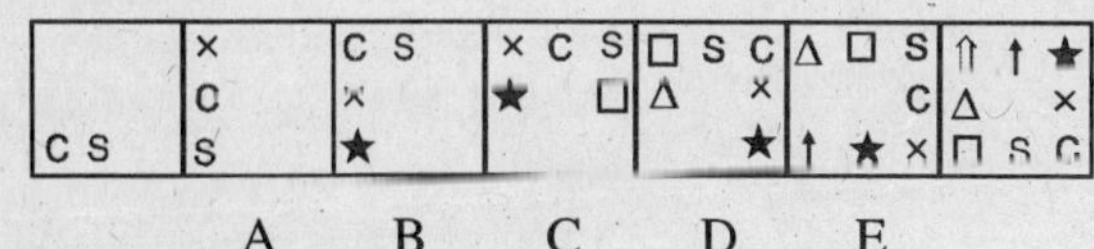

Thus, option C is correct answer.

47. In each subsequent figure each design moves half step in anticlockwise direction and respectively one, two, three, four, five, six designs are inverted. In figure (D), four designs should be inverted instead of five.

48. In each subsequent figure, the pre-existing leaflets rotate through 45° in clockwise direction and half leaflet is added behind and in front of the pre-existing leaflets alternately. The figure (E) should be as follows:

49. The inner designs are repeated after every two figures and one design is deleted. The arrow points outward and inward alternately. The arrow rotates through 45° anticlockwise alternately.

50. In the subsequent figures, two leaflets and one and half leaflets are deleted alternately.

51. The places of star, circle and square are moved one step clockwise at each step.

52. The elements in the four quadrants are moved one step clockwise and the elements at the ends of the cross are moved one step anticlockwise in this series.

53. In alternate figures, the line with the dot is turned 90° clockwise and the arrow 180° clockwise.

54. In alternate figures, the element in the top left position is horizontally inverted and moved one and half steps anticlockwise, the top middle element is turned 90° clockwise and moved one step anticlockwise, the top right element is turned 135° clockwise and moved one step anticlockwise, the element at the bottom is replaced by a new element and moved to the top middle position, and the two identical elements are replaced by two new identical elements.

55. The cross and the circle move one and two steps clockwise respectively (at each step), the plus moves 3, 4 and 5 steps clockwise, and the dot 6, 5 and 4 steps clockwise.

56. At first step, the fifth or the bottom most element is moved to the second place from top, the second element moved to the fourth place, the fourth element is moved to the third place, the third element is moved to the first or the topmost place and the element on the top, which is made new, is moved to the last or the fifth place. At second step i.e., from second problem figure to third problem figure the above process is reversed. The bottom most element is the first and the top most element is the last or fifth. Hereafter, the process is repeated from the beginning. Option 'A' is the right answer.

57. Starting from the bottom, one triangle is moved to the opposite side at each step in upward order. Option 'C' fits into the question marked space.

58. The shade inside the circle is rotated clockwise in alternate figures; the line segment with a dot is rotated

135° clockwise in alternate figures and the arrow is rotated 135° anticlockwise in alternate figures. By this process answer figure 'C' completes the series.

59. At each step the elements are moved diagonally upward and then laterally inverted, and the top two elements are made new and placed at the bottom line. By this process, option figure 'A' completes the series.

60. The number of arcs making the petals of the flower are increased by one, one and half, two, two and half respectively at each step. Also, the flower is turned 45° anticlockwise. By this process, option 'A' is the right answer.

☆☆☆☆☆☆

15. Non-Verbal Analogy

TYPE-I

Directions (Q. 1-30): *The second figure in the first unit of the Problem Figures bears a certain relationship to the first figure. Similarly, one of the figures in the Answer Figures bears the same relationship to the first figures in the second unit of the Problem Figures. Locate the figure which would fit the questions marks.*

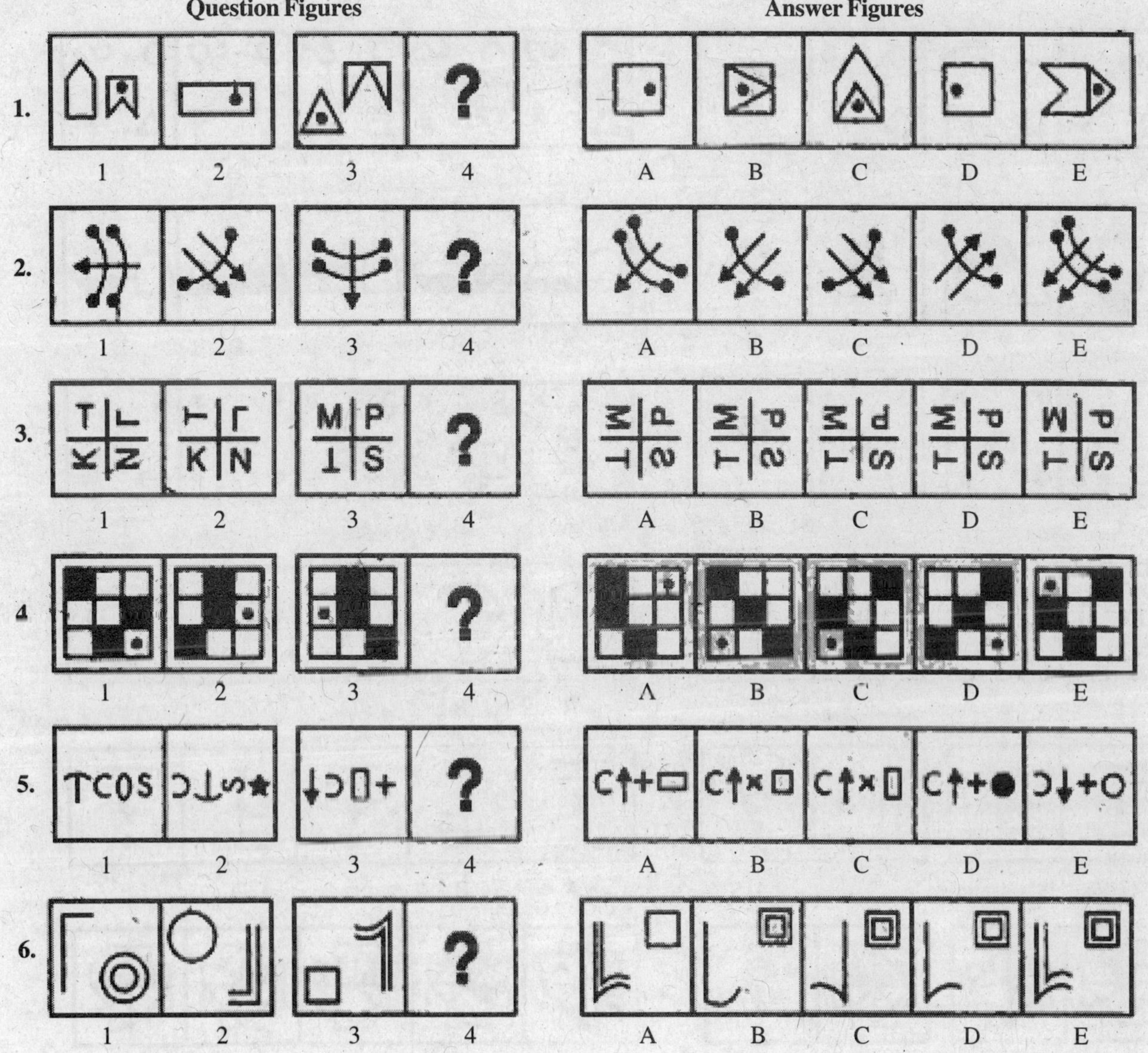

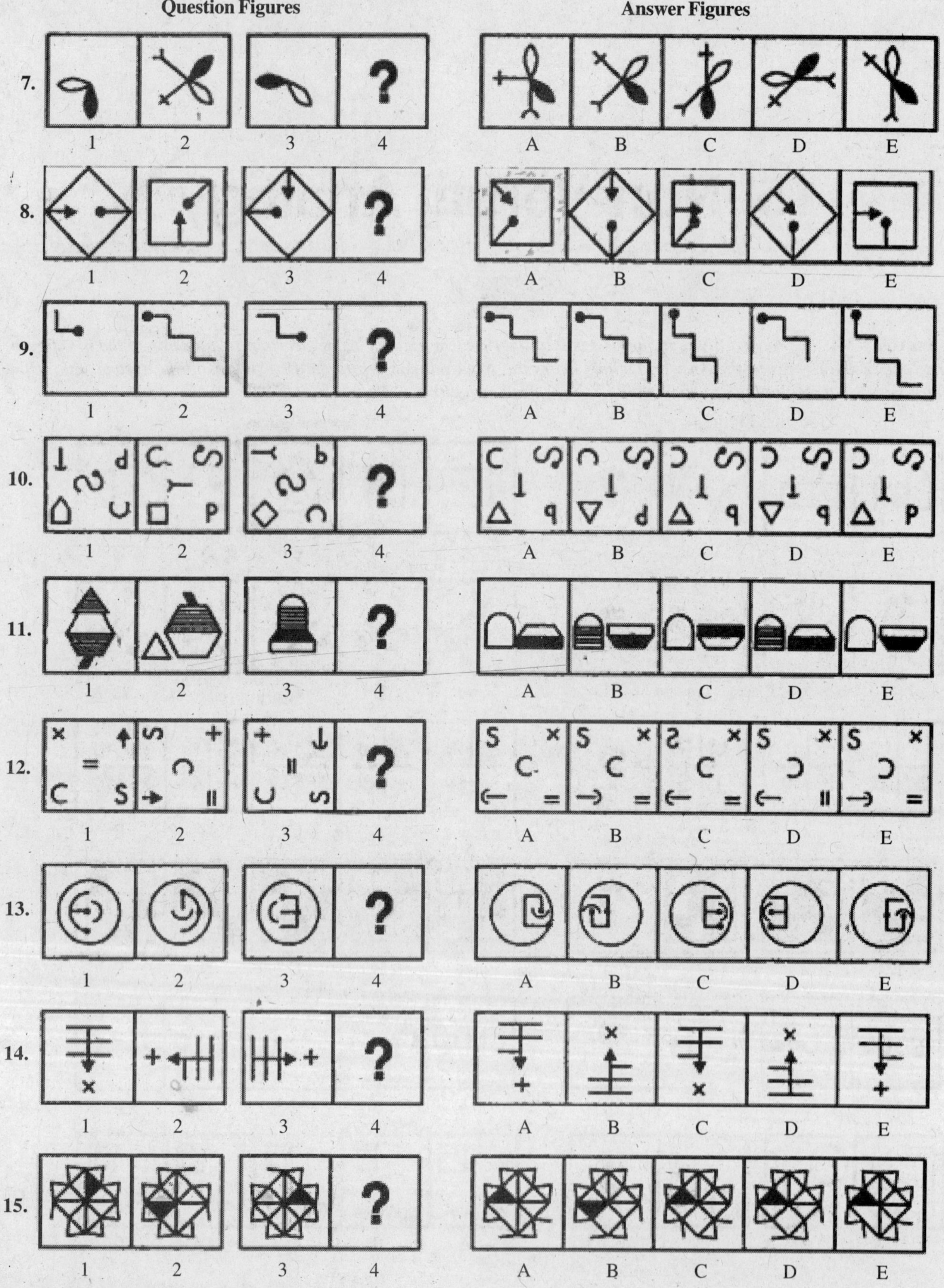
Question Figures
Answer Figures
7.
8.
9.
10.
11.
12.
13.
14.
15.
1
2
3
4
?
A
B
C
D
E

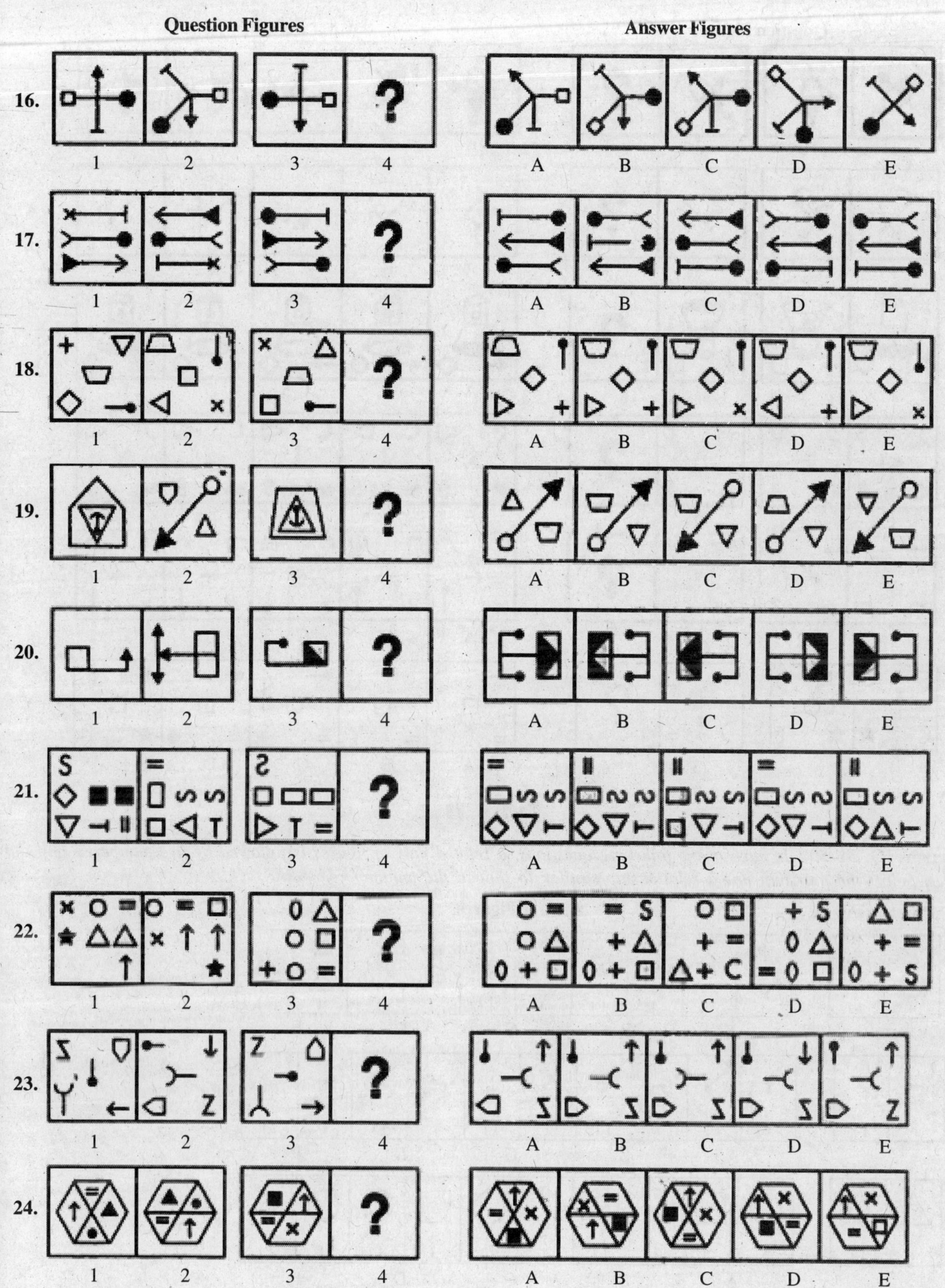

Question Figures
Answer Figures
16.
17.
18.
19.
20.
21.
22.
23.
24.
1 2 3 4
A B C D E

Question Figures **Answer Figures**

25.
1 2 3 4 A B C D E

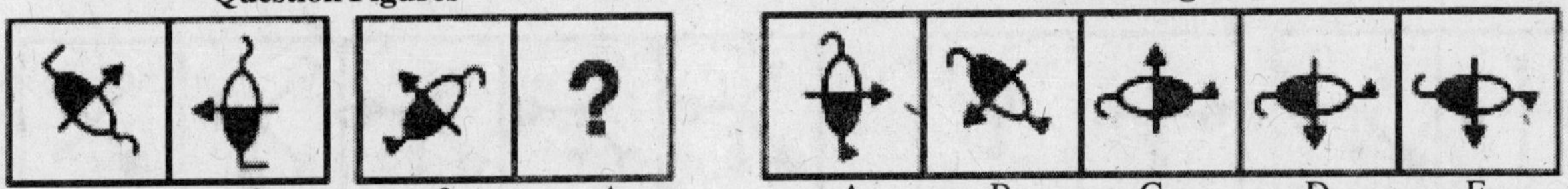

26.
1 2 3 4 A B C D E

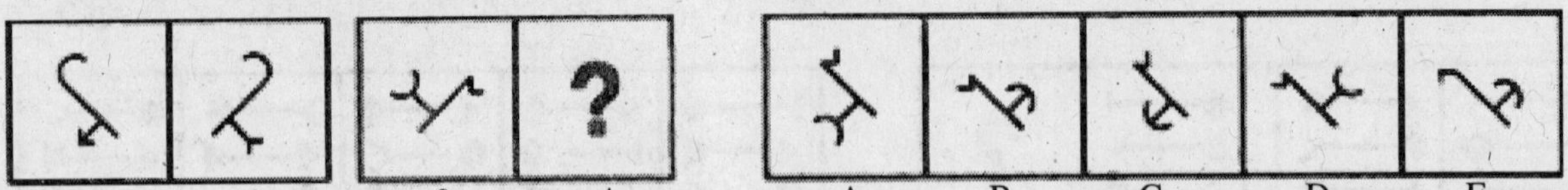

27.
1 2 3 4 A B C D E

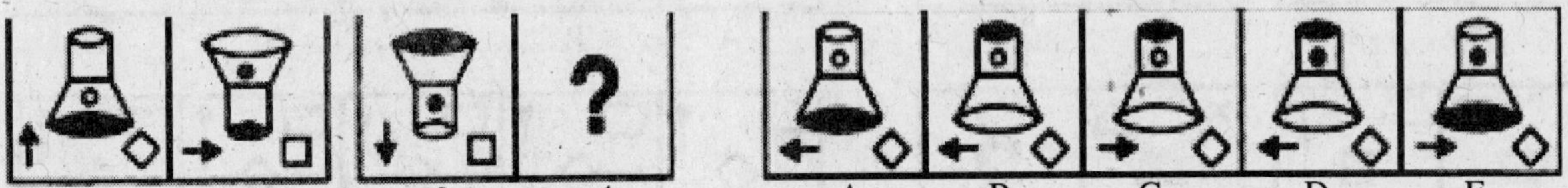

28.
1 2 3 4 A B C D E

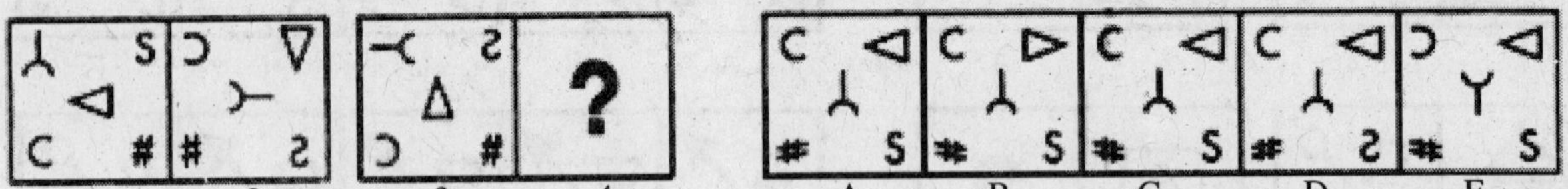

29.
1 2 3 4 A B C D E

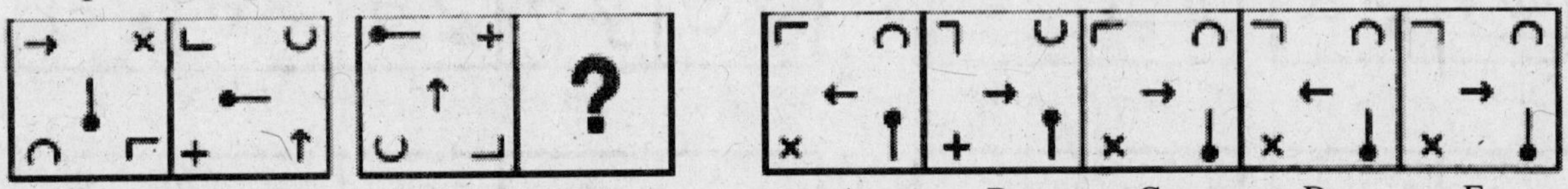

30.
1 2 3 4 A B C D E

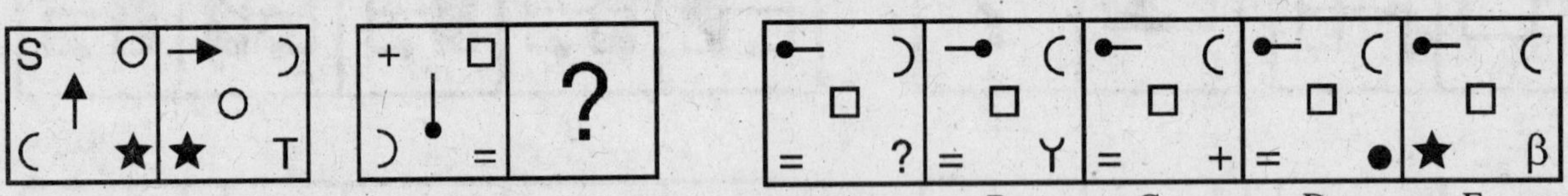

TYPE-II

Directions (Q. 31–50): *In each of the following questions, a related pair of figures is followed by five numbered pairs of figures. Select the pair that has a relationship* ***similar*** *to that in the unnumbered pair.*

Problem Figure **Answer Figures**

31.
A B C D E

32.
A B C D E

33.
A B C D E

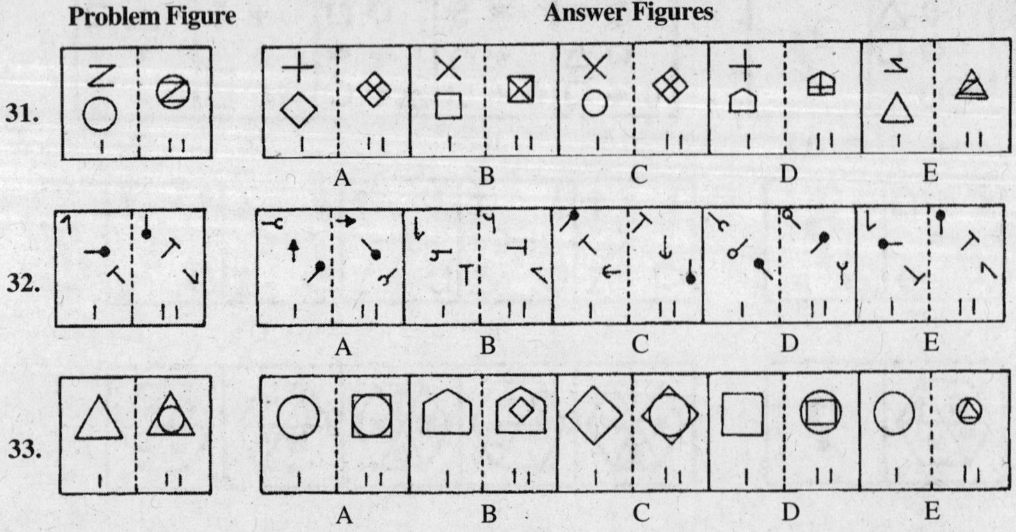

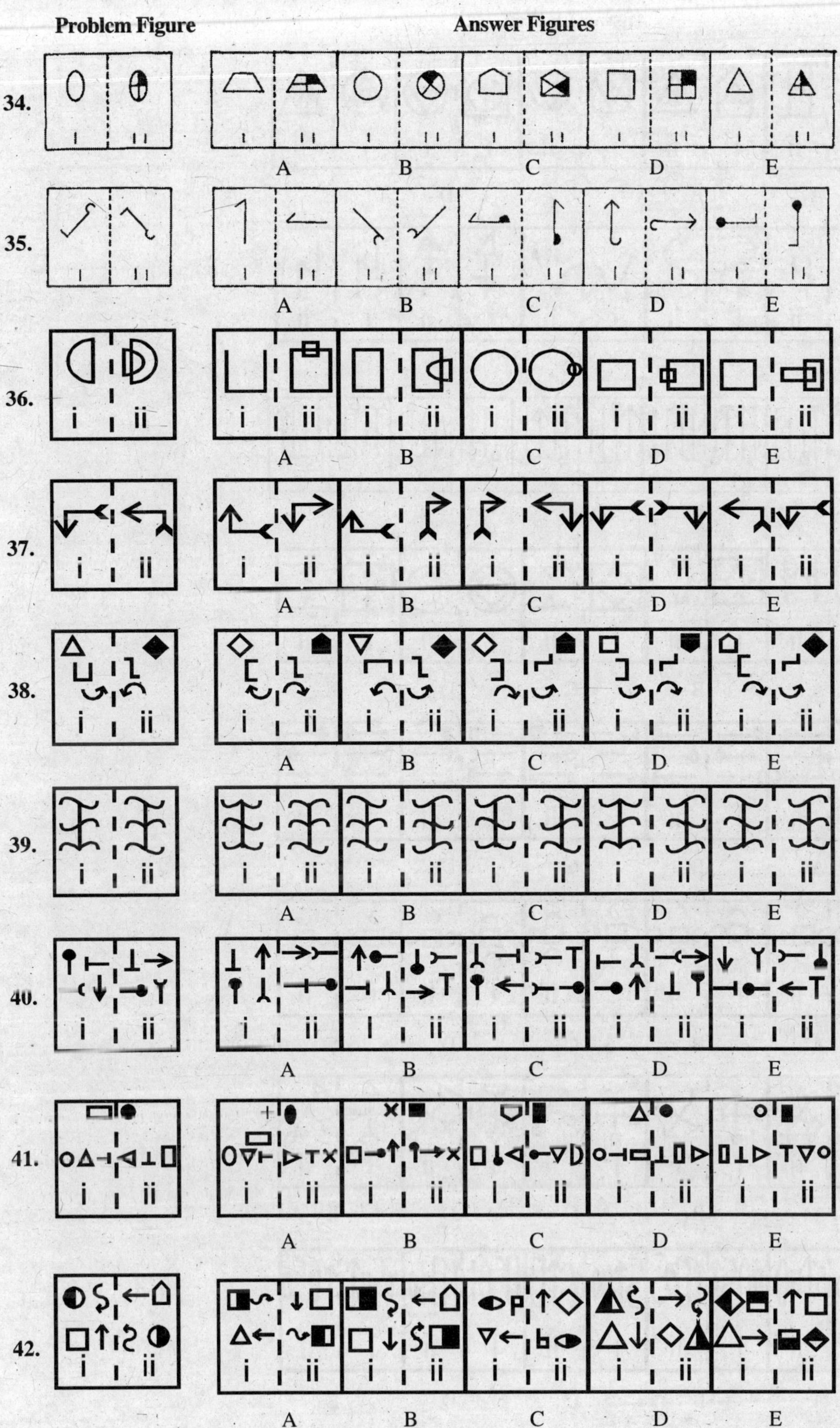
Problem Figure
Answer Figures
34.
35.
36.
37.
38.
39.
40.
41.
42.
i
ii
A
B
C
D
E

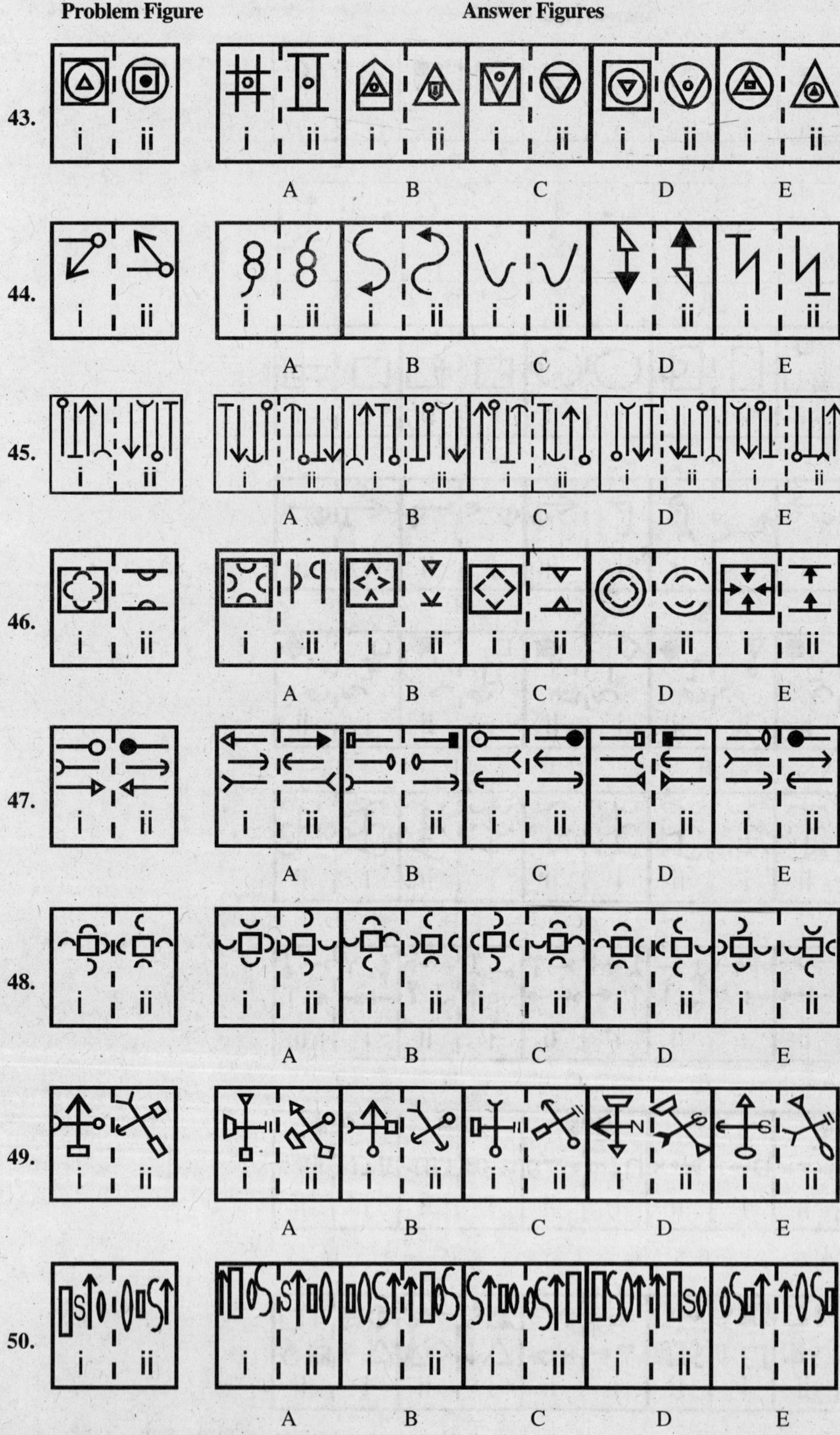
Problem Figure
Answer Figures
43.
44.
45.
46.
47.
48.
49.
50.
i
ii
A
B
C
D
E

ANSWERS

1	2	3	4	5	6	7	8	9	10
B	B	D	E	D	D	E	C	B	D
11	12	13	14	15	16	17	18	19	20
E	A	E	C	D	C	E	B	B	C
21	22	23	24	25	26	27	28	29	30
B	E	B	D	D	B	B	A	E	D
31	32	33	34	35	36	37	38	39	40
B	A	E	D	E	D	E	C	A	B
41	42	43	44	45	46	47	48	49	50
B	A	E	B	B	C	C	D	E	A

EXPLANATORY ANSWERS

1. The R.H.S. figure is fitted into the L.H.S. figure and the resulting figure is rotated 90° CW.
2. The figure rotates 45° ACW, the arrow changes to a curved line with dotted ends and the curved lines with dotted ends get converted to arrows.
3. The top left symbol rotates 90° ACW while all other symbols rotate 90° CW.
4. The black portion in top layer moves one step to the right; the black portions in the middle and the lower layers move one step to the left and the dot moves one step upwards.
5. The first and second symbols from the left interchange positions and the other two symbols also interchange positions. The symbol that reaches the first position from the left gets laterally inverted; the symbol that reaches the second position gets inverted, the third symbol rotates 90° CW and the fourth symbol gets replaced by a new one.
6. The single figure is replaced by a figure similar to the double figures and the double figures are replaced by figures similar to the single figure.
7. The figure rotates 135° ACW; a 'T' appears diagonally opposite to the black leaf and a 'Y' appears diagonally opposite to the white leaf.
8. The square rotates through 45°. The arrow moves 90° ACW and the pin moves 45° ACW.
9. The figure rotates through 180° and three lines forming a zig-zag, get attached to its lower end.
10. The symbols move in the order

The symbol that reaches the central position rotates 90° CW and its arc gets inverted; the 'P' shaped symbol rotates through 180°; the 'C' shaped symbol rotates 90° CW; the 'S' Shaped symbol gets laterally inverted and the fifth symbol gets replaced by a new one.

45°, the symbol that reaches the lower right corner rotates 90° ACW and a new symbol appears in middle-left position.

11. The upper and the lower parts of the figure get separated. Shading is removed from the upper part and the lower part is inverted. The two parts are then placed side by side.
12. The symbols move in the order

The symbol that reaches the top-left corner rotates 90° ACW; the symbol in the top-right corner rotates through 45°; the symbols in the lower-left corner and in the central positions rotates 90° CW and the symbol that reaches the lower-right corner rotates through 90°.

13. The figure gets laterally inverted. The dot on the larger arc, the pin and the small arc rotate 90° ACW. Also, the pin gets inverted.
14. The figure rotates 90° CW. One half of one of the lines on the arrow is lost. The figure in front of the arrowhead rotates through 45°.
15. The missing line segment in the first figure is replaced in second. Then moving ACW, the third line segment is removed along the two next consecutive sides of the square. Shaded portion in the first figure moves three steps ACW. Similarly, the third figure gives figure (D).
16. The lower & L.H.S. portions rotate 135° ACW; the R.H.S. and the upper portions rotate through 180°.
17. All the arrows get laterally inverted and the uppermost and the lowermost arrows interchange positions.
18. The symbols move in the order

The triangle and pin rotate 90° CW; the square and the '+' symbols rotate through 45° and the trapezium gets inverted.

19. The innermost symbol rotates 135° ACW, the arc at its one end gets replaced by a black triangle and the black circle is replaced by a white circle and this symbol gets enlarged. The middle symbol gets diminished and inverted and appears on the lower side. The outermost symbol gets diminished and inverted and appears on the upper side.

20. The figure gets laterally inverted and the inverted image of the figure formed, gets attached to it.

21. The symbols move in the order

The symbols that reach the upper position in the leftmost column, middle and lower positions in the middle column, middle position in the rightmost column rotate 90° CW. The symbol that reaches the lower position in the leftmost column rotates through 45° and a new symbol appears in the middle position in the leftmost column. The symbol in the lower position in the right most column rotates 90° ACW.

22. The symbols move in the order

and a new symbol appears in upper-right corner, to give the second figure from the first figure. The movement of symbols in the order

(obtained by rotating the initial order 90° CW) and the appearance of a new symbol in the lower right corner, gives the answer figure i.e., figure (E) from the third figure.

23. The symbols move in the order

The 'Z'-shaped symbol gets inverted; the clamp and the arrow rotate 90° ACW; the pin and the pentagon rotate 90° CW.

24. The contents of the hexagon rotate one step CW and the diagonally opposite symbols interchange positions.

25. The figure rotates 45° CW and then turns about the arrow. The arrow also gets reversed.

26. The figure gets laterally inverted and the arrowhead or the arc reverses in direction.

27. The main figure gets inverted. The end of the lamp which is white turns black and the other end turns white. The circle turns black, if initially white and it turns white, if initially black. The arrow at the bottom rotates 90° CW and the square rotates through 45°.

28. The symbol move in the order

The 'C' and 'S' shaped symbols get laterally inverted. The triangle rotates 90° ACW; the hook rotates 90° CW and the fifth symbol rotates 45° ACW.

29. The symbols move in the order

The symbol that reaches the lower-right corner gets rotated 90° ACW; the symbols that reach the upper-left and upper-right positions, get inverted; the central symbol rotates 90° CW and the symbol that reaches the lower-left corner rotates through 45°.

30. The element in the top left corner is made new and moved to the bottom right corner position, the element in the bottom right corner is moved to the bottom left corner position, the element in the bottom left corner is laterally inverted and moved to the top right corner position, the element in the top right corner is moved to the centre, and the element in the centre is turned 90° clockwise and moved to the top left corner position.

31. The uppermost design enters into innerside side of the lower design from Ist figure to the IInd figure.

32. In element I to II upper left design comes at lower right rotating 135° C.W. Middle design goes to upper left and rotates 90° CW. While lower right design goes to middle and it also rotates 90° C.W. The same changes occur in option A.

33. In element I to II and ellipse is put in the triangle. Similarly in option E a triangle is put in the ellipse.

34. From first figure to IInd figure, design is divided into four equal parts and right side of the upper portion becomes shaded.

35. From Ist figure to IInd figure, design is reversed after moving 90° anticlockwise direction.

36. The figure in the first part is laterally inverted and a similar but smaller design is placed on its left side in the second part.

37. The element in first part is moved by 90° and the places of short and long line segments are interchanged.

38. The number of sides making the top left figure is increased by one and a new figure is made, shaded and moved to the top right position. The element in the centre is turned 90° anticlockwise and the small line on the other side is turned by 180°. The element in the bottom right is turned upside down and moved to the bottom left position.

39. The direction of both arcs on the top, are on the middle right and arc on the bottom left in first part are turned to the other side in the second part.

40. From part one to part two, the element in the top left is turned 90° clockwise and the other three 90° anticlockwise, also the elements are moved one step anticlockwise.

41. From part one to part two, the top right element is turned by 90° and moved down, the lower right and middle elements are turned 90° clockwise and 90° anticlockwise respectively and moved to the left and the lower left element is shaded and moved up.

42. All the four elements exchange place diagonally and in doing so the top left element is laterally inverted, the top right element is horizontally inverted, the bottom right element is turned 90° anticlockwise and the number of lines making the element in bottom left is increased by one.

43. The innermost figure is removed and the new innermost figure also encloses the other two figures. The innermost and smallest figure is then shaded.

44. The design in the first part is horizontally inverted in the second.

45. All the elements in the first part are turned upside down and then 1st, 2nd, 3rd and 4th positioned elements become 3rd, 4th, 1st and 2nd elements in the second part.

46. The left and right sides and also the inner elements along the two sides in first part are removed in the second part. The inner elements along the other two sides are inverted.

47. The units attached to the straight lines in first part are moved to the other side. Then the topmost blank unit is shaded and the bottom unit is laterally inverted in the second part.

48. The arcs are turned 90° anticlockwise in the second part.

49. The cross is turned 45° anticlockwise in the second part. Then the direction of the elements attached to the cross is changed and the element on the top right is replaced by a new element.

50. The larger and the smaller elements in first part become smaller and larger respectively in the second. Also, the fourth element on the right becomes the first element on the left in the second part.

☆☆☆☆☆☆

16. Odd Man Out

Directions (Q. 1–25) : *In each question below five figures are given. Four are similar in a certain way and so form a group. The question is— which one of the figures* **does not** *belong to that group?*

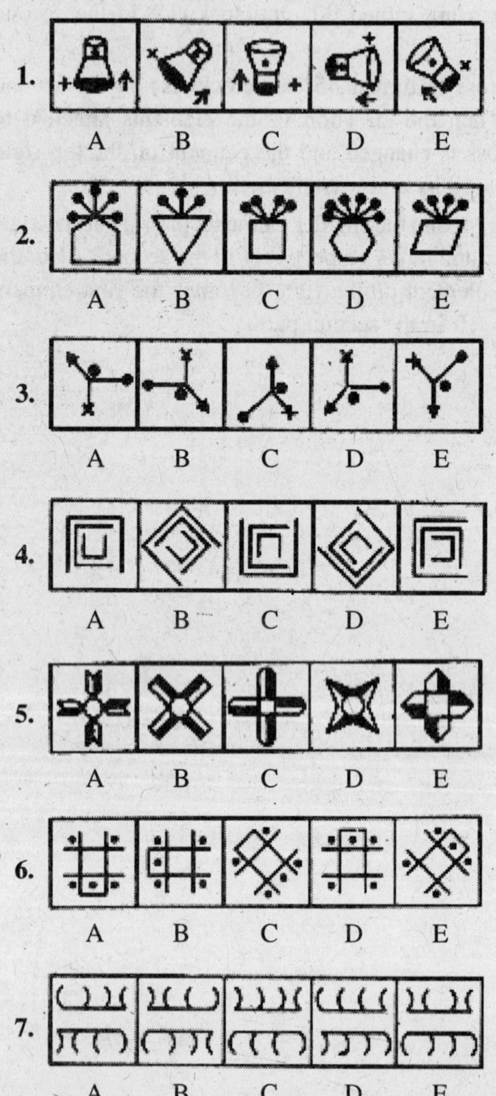

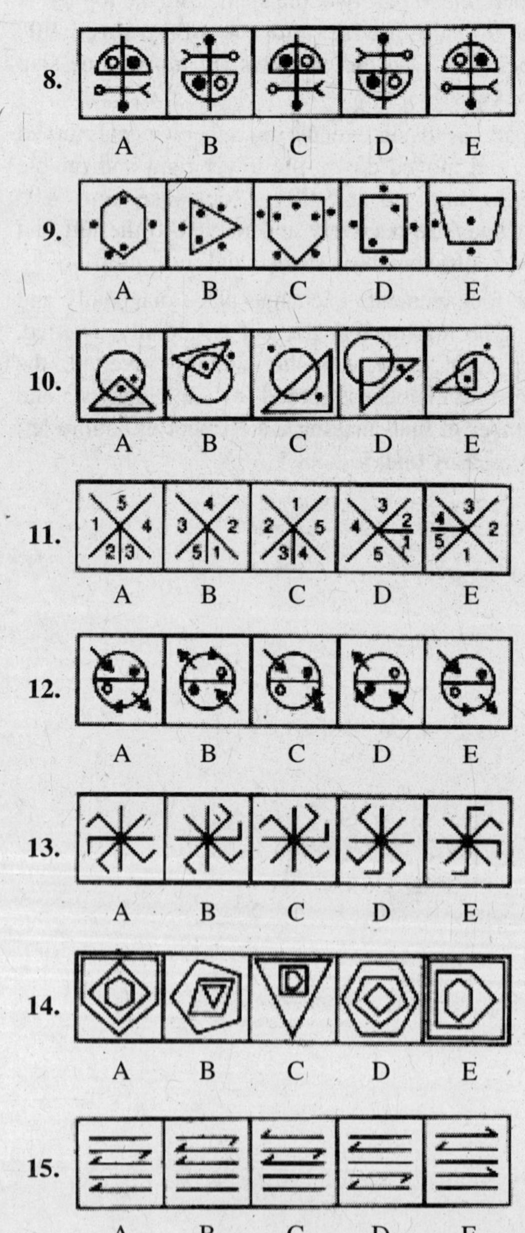

16.

A B C D E

17.

A B C D E

18.

A B C D E

19.

A B C D E

20.

A B C D E

21.

A B C D E

22.

A B C D E

23.

A B C D E

24.

A B C D E

25.

A B C D E

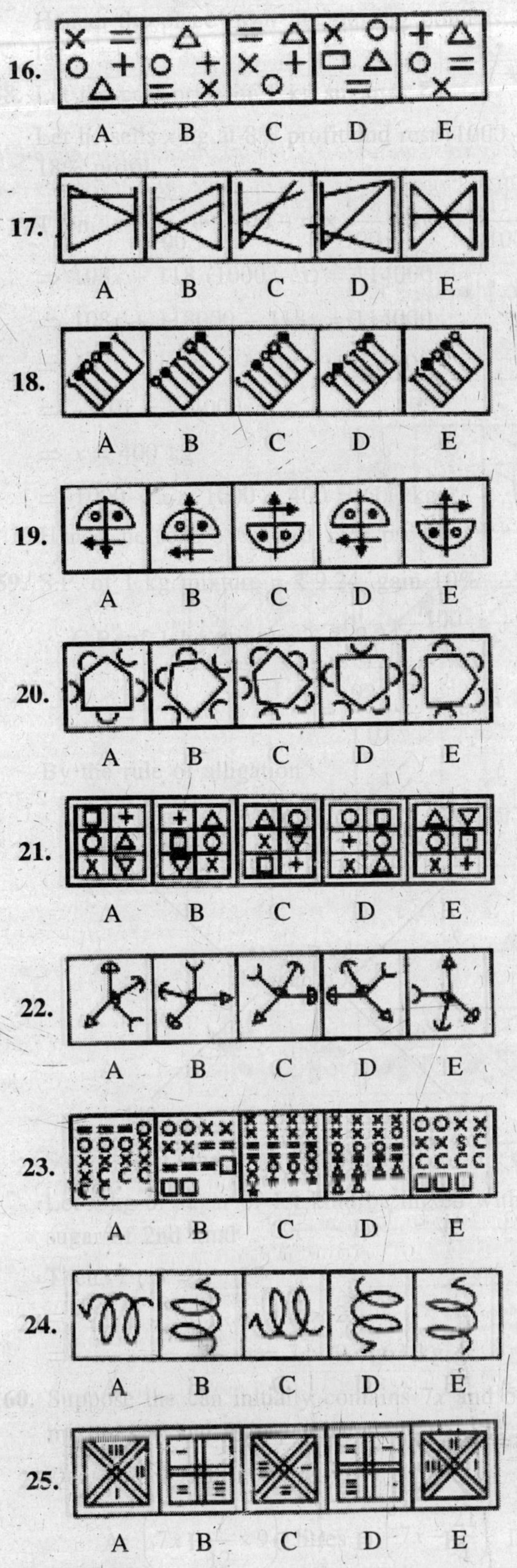

Directions (Q. 26–40) : *In each of the following questions, in four out of the five figures, element I is related to element II in the same particular way. Find out the figure in which the element I is* ***not*** *so related to element II.*

26.

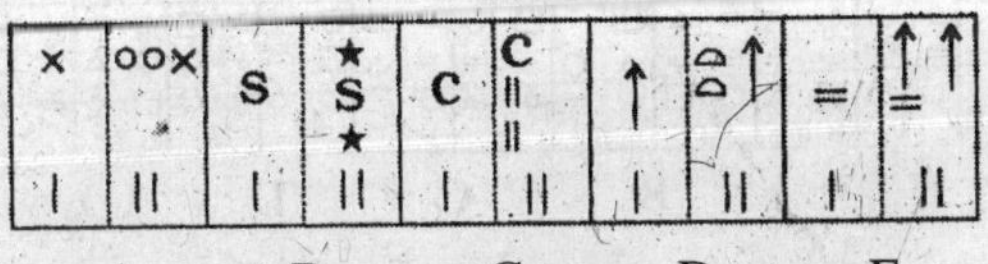

A B C D E

27.

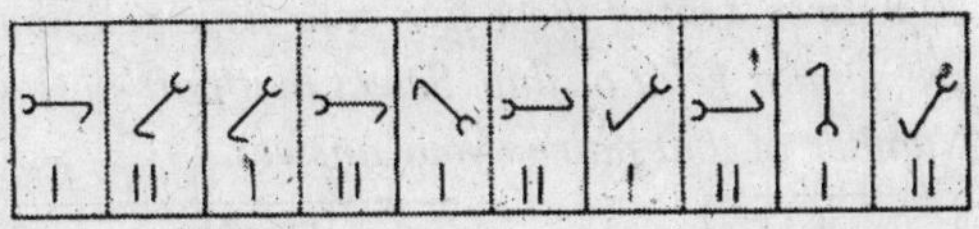

A B C D E

28.

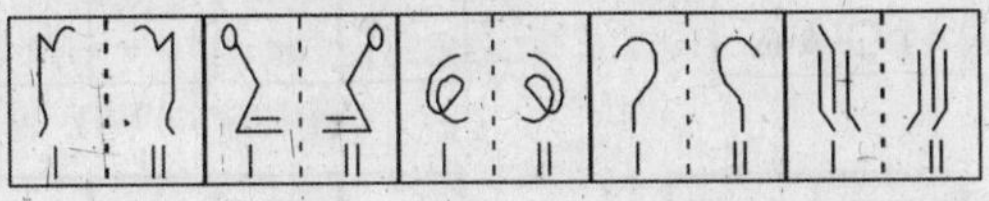

A B C D E

29.

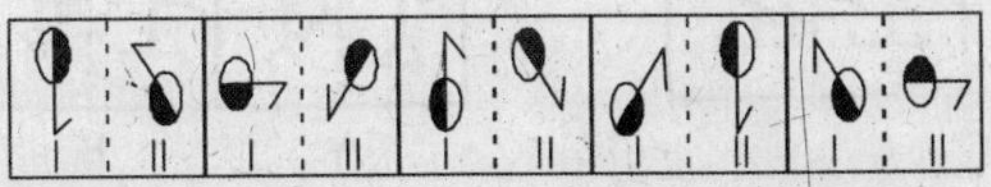

A B C D E

30.

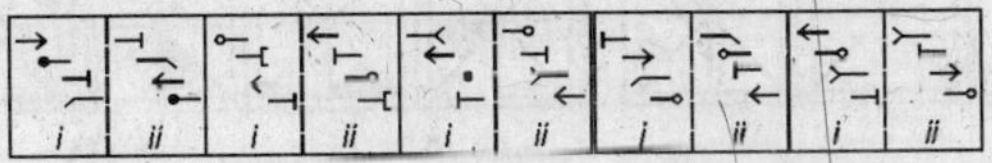

A B C D E

31.

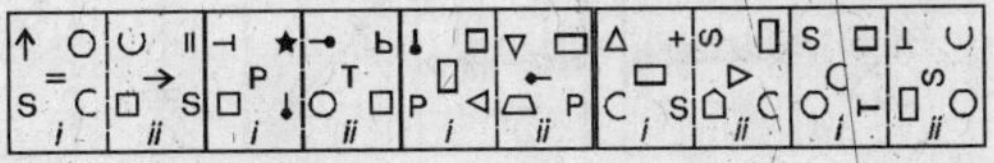

A B C D E

32.

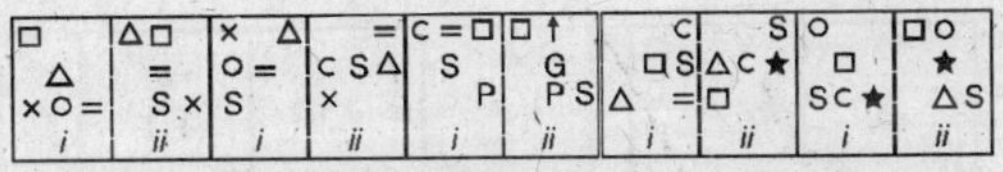

A B C D E

33.

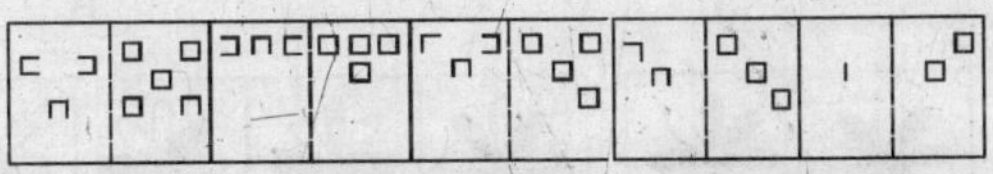

A B C D E

34.

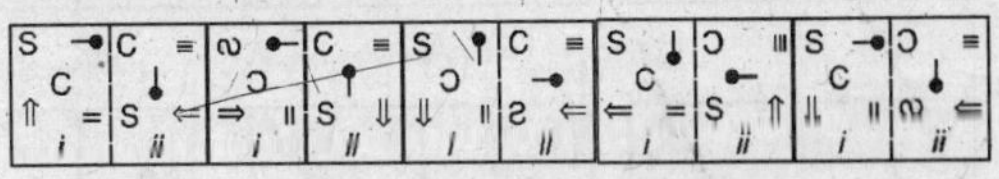

A B C D E

35.

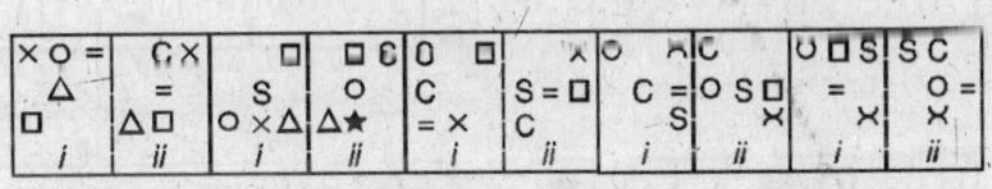

A B C D E

36.

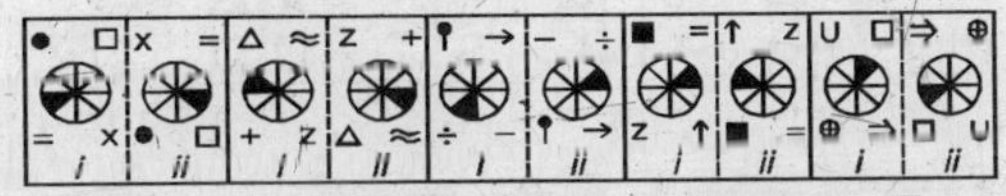

A B C D E

37.

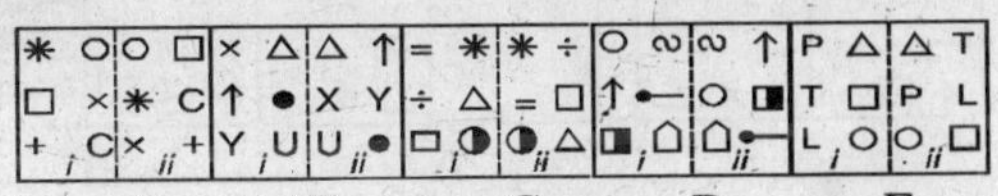

A B C D E

38.

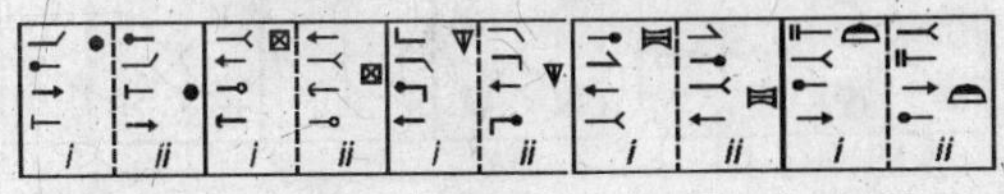

A B C D E

39. 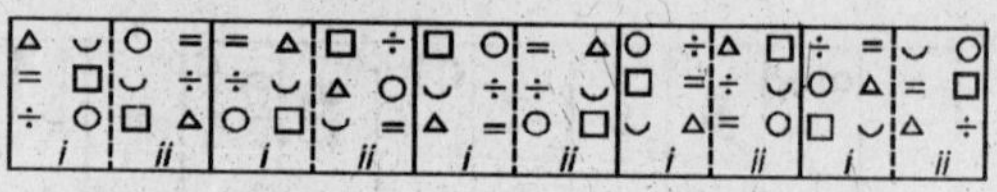 A B C D E

40. 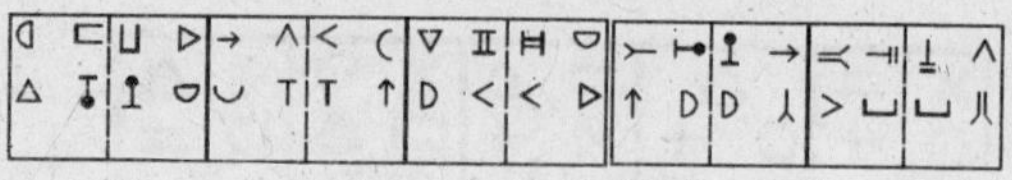 A B C D E

Directions (Q. 41–50) : *In each of the following questions, a related pair of figures (unnumbered) is followed by five numbered pairs of figures. Out of these five, four have relationship similar to that in the unnumbered pair. Only one pair of figures does not have similar relationship. Select that pair of figures which does not have a similar relationship to that in the unnumbered pair. Number of that pair is your answer.*

41. 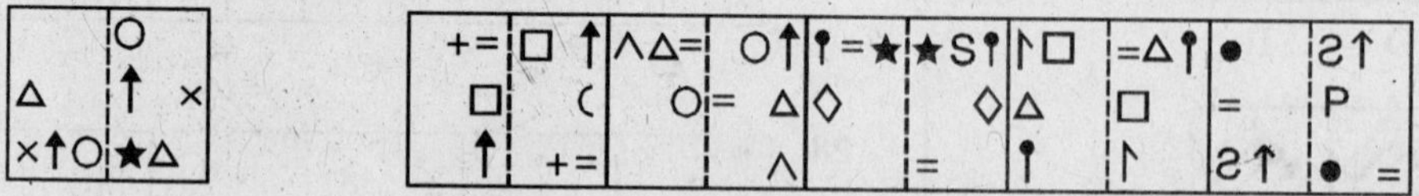 A B C D E

42. 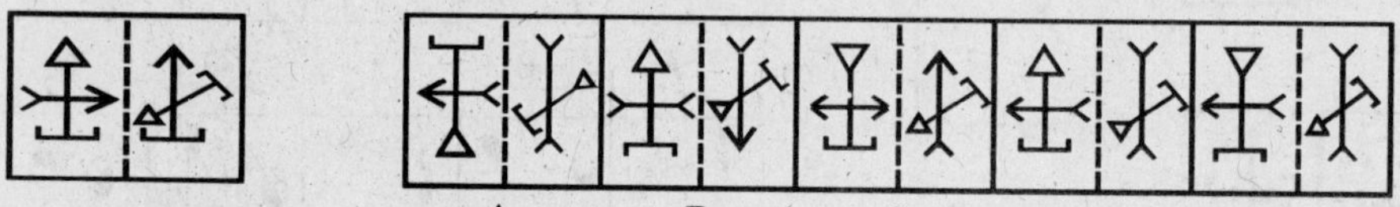 A B C D E

43. 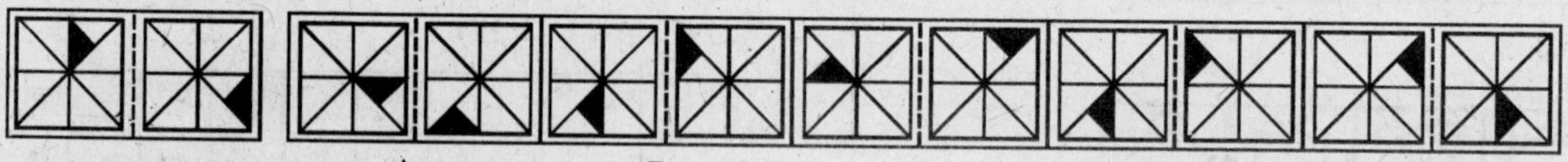 A B C D E

44. 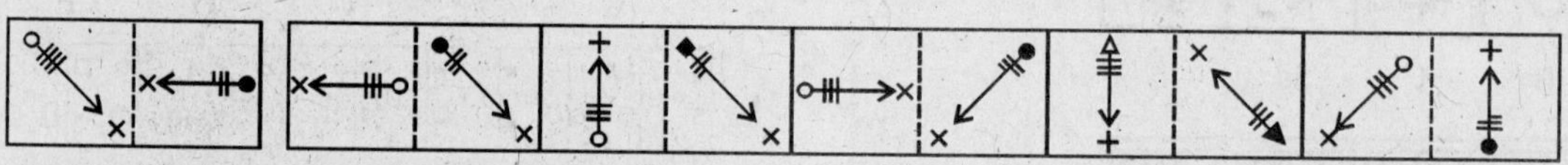 A B C D E

45. 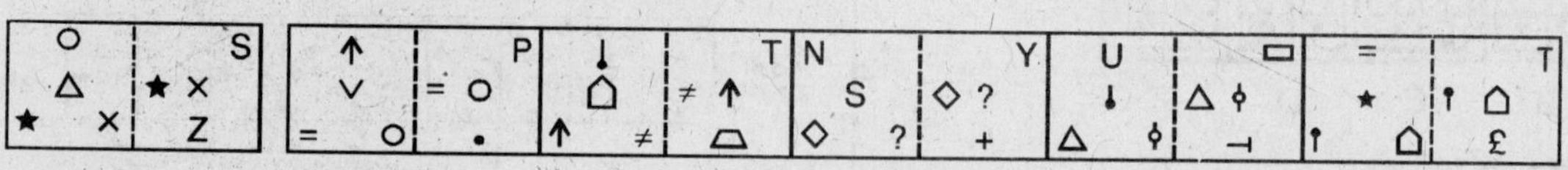 A B C D E

46.  A B C D E

47. 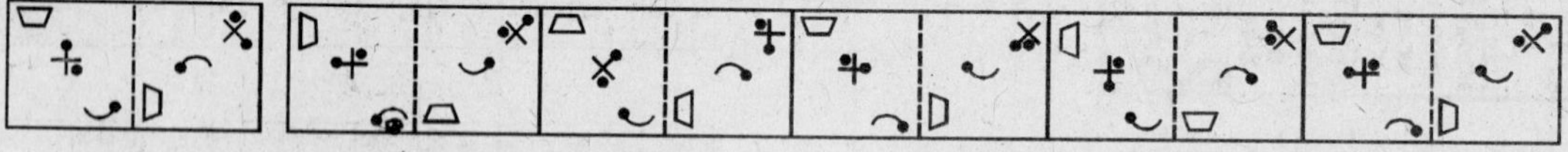 A B C D E

48. 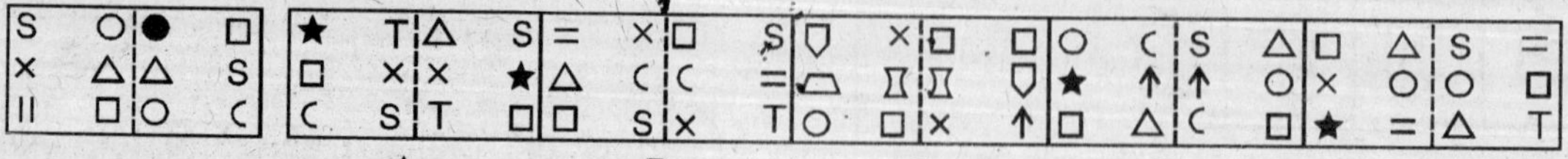 A B C D E

49. 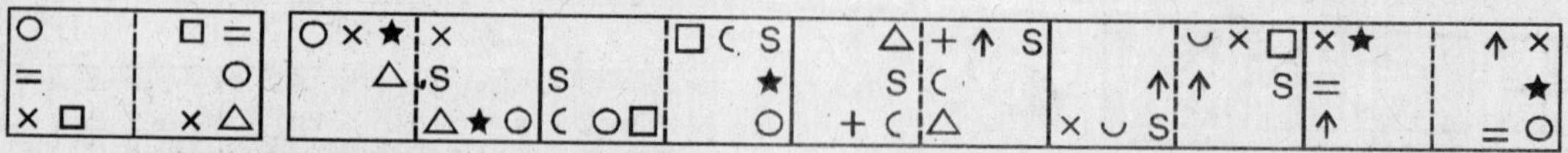 A B C D E

50. 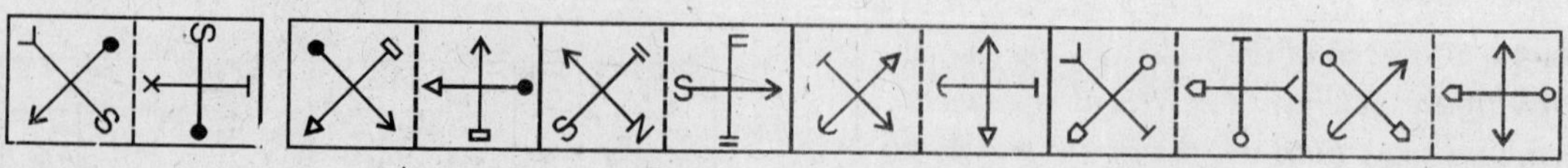 A B C D E

ANSWERS

1	2	3	4	5	6	7	8	9	10
D	A	C	A	C	C	E	C	D	A
11	**12**	**13**	**14**	**15**	**16**	**17**	**18**	**19**	**20**
B	E	B	A	E	D	C	A	B	B
21	**22**	**23**	**24**	**25**	**26**	**27**	**28**	**29**	**30**
D	C	C	C	C	E	C	A	B	D
31	**32**	**33**	**34**	**35**	**36**	**37**	**38**	**39**	**40**
B	D	A	A	C	B	A	C	C	E
41	**42**	**43**	**44**	**45**	**46**	**47**	**48**	**49**	**50**
D	E	E	A	B	C	B	A	E	E

EXPLANATORY ANSWERS

1. In all other figures, the arrow and the + sign lie towards the black end of the main figure.

2. The pins, equal in number of sides in the main figure are attached to the midpoint of a side of the main figure in case of figures (B), (C), (D) and (E). In figure (A), these pins are attached to a vertex of the main figure.

3. In all other figures, the dot appears in the angle formed between the arrow and the pin.

4. All other figures can be rotated into each other. (In each figure except figure (A), the middle element is obtained by rotating the outer element through 90° CW and the inner element is obtained by rotating the middle element through 90° CW).

5. All other figures have at least one line of symmetry.

6. All other figures can be rotated into each other.

7. In each one of the other four figures, four arcs are curved towards the left and four other arcs are curved towards the right.

8. All other figures can be rotated into each other.

9. In all other figures, the number of dots outside the main figure is one more than the number of dots inside the main figure.

10. In all other figures, one of the dots lies outside the triangle as well as the circle.

11. Only in figure (B), while moving in an ACW direction, the numbers do not form a sequence.

12. Only in figure (E), the arrowhead along the circumference of the circle indicates motion in an ACW direction.

13. Figure (A) and figure (C) can be rotated into each other and figure (D) and figure (E) can be rotated into each other.

14. In all other figures, as we move from the innermost to the outermost element, the numbers of sides of the elements either increase or decrease in a sequence.

15. In each one of the figures except figure (E), two arrows point towards left and one arrow points towards right.

16. Figure (D) has a rectangle in place of a '+' sign.

17. All other figures contain five line segments while figure (C) contains four line segments.

18. In all other figures, the black rhombus appears adjacent to white square; the black circle appears adjacent to white circle and the clamp appears adjacent to the T-shaped element.

19. In all other figures, both the arrowheads lie towards the diameter of the semicircle.

20. In each one of the figures except figure (B), three cups open towards the pentagon and two cups open outwards.

21. Only figure (D) contains two circles while all other figures have only one circle.

22. All other figures can be rotated into each other.

23. In each one of the figures except figure (C), the numbers of different types of elements are in a sequence such as there are three '=' signs, four circles, five 'C'-shaped elements and six X signs in figure (A).

24. All other figures can be rotated into each other.

25. Only in figure (C), one, two and three parallel lines appear sequentially in a CW direction In all other figures, one, two and three parallel lines appear sequentially in an ACW direction.

26. Except in figure (B), in all other figures, from element I to II two new designs are added in one side of the main design.

27. In each figure from element I to II the main design rotates through 135° clockwise or anticlockwise. Except in figure (C), in all other figures, the smaller line segment moves to other side from element I to II.

28. In all other figures the element II can be obtained by the lateral inversion of the element I. In figure (A), the lower design has not been inverted.

29. In figure (B), the small segment is on the same side as that of the half shaded circle in both the elements.
30. The first design is inverted and moved to third place, the second design is moved to the fourth place, third design to the first place and fourth design is inverted and moved to the second place. Option (D) violates this.
31. In all other options the top-left element is moved to the centre with 90° clockwise rotation. Here, it is rotated anticlockwise.
32. All the designs are shifted in a set pattern one behind the other. The fourth design in all others is changed and placed in the last. Here, the fifth and last designs are changed.
33. In all other pair of figures, all incomplete squares in the first elements are completed and an extra square is added in the second element.
34. From element I to element II, the 'S' shape is turned 90° clockwise and moved down, the double arrow shape '⇒' is turned 90° clockwise and moved to the right, the two parallel lines one turned by 90°; one parallel line is added and all three lines are moved up, the line with a dot is turned 90° clockwise and moved to the centre and the 'C' shape in the centre is turned by 180° and moved to top left position. Here, the double arrow is turned anticlockwise.
35. Starting from one unit, all units are moved in a set pattern, the places of last two units moved are interchanged and the last unit is then made new. Here, no changes are made in the last two units.
36. Irrespective of the four small items in all figures which are moved in a set pattern, the shade inside the circle in element I is moved three steps anticlockwise in element II. Here, it is moved four steps.
37. The two items on the top and middle left item in element I are moved one step anticlockwise in element II. Also, the middle right item and the two bottom items in element I are moved one step clockwise in element II. Here, both sets of items are moved anticlockwise.
38. The places of two items on the top are interchanged, the two items at the bottom are laterally inverted and their places are interchanged and the single item on the right is moved half way down. Here, the four items on the left violate the above rule.
39. From element I to element II the places of top left and bottom right item, middle left and top right items and bottom left and middle right item are interchanged respectively.
40. From element I to element II the two designs on the left side are moved diagonally and the two designs on the right are shifted to the left, top left and bottom right designs are turned 180° anticlockwise, and the top right design is turned 90° clockwise. In this option the direction of turn is the opposite.
41. From element I to element II clockwise the first unit is moved 2 steps forward, the second unit 1 step forward, the third unit 2½ steps forward and the fourth unit 3 steps forward. In option 'D' the third unit violates the rule.
42. From element I to element II, the horizontal bar is turned 135° anticlockwise and the unit at the lower end is turned by 180°. The vertical bar is turned 90° anticlockwise and the unit at the lower end is turned by 180°. In option 'E' one more unit at the top is turned by 180°.
43. In element II, the shade is moved two sections clockwise and shifted from the centre to the base. In option 'E' it is not so.
44. In element II, the arrow is turned 135° clockwise. In option 'A' it is turned anticlockwise.
45. From element I to element II, the bottom right unit and bottom left unit are moved to the centre and middle left position respectively. The other two units are removed and two new elements are placed in the top right and bottom centre position respectively. In option 'B' the placement of bottom right and left elements is not right.
46. In element II, the shades are shifted one petal clockwise. In option 'C' one of the shades is not moved.
47. From element I to element II, the unit on the top left is turned 90° anticlockwise and moved to the bottom right corner position, the unit in the centre is turned 135° anticlockwise and moved to the top right position, and the unit in the bottom right is turned by 180° and moved to the centre. In option 'B', the middle unit is turned 135° clockwise.
48. From element I to element II, a new unit is placed in the top left position, the top left unit is moved to the middle right position, the middle right unit is moved to the left position, the middle left unit is replaced by a new unit and placed in bottom right position, the bottom right unit is moved to the top right position, and the top right unit is moved diagonally to replace the bottom left unit. In option 'A', the middle left unit is not changed when moved to the bottom right position.
49. From element I to element II starting anticlockwise, the first and second units are moved 1½ steps clockwise respectively, the third unit ½ step anticlockwise, the fourth unit 2 steps clockwise, and a new unit is placed ahead of the first unit. Option 'E' violates the rules.
50. In element II, the cross is turned 135° clockwise and then the positions of left and top units on the cross are interchanged. In option 'E' it is not so.

☆☆☆☆☆☆

BUSINESS & ECONOMIC ENVIRONMENT

BUSINESS ENVIRONMENT

The term 'business environment' means the sum total of all individuals, institutions and other forces that are outside the control of a business enterprise but that may affect its performance. As one writer has put it— "Just take the universe, subtract from it the subset that represents the organisation, and the remainder is environment". Thus, the economic, social, political, technological and other forces which operate outside a business enterprise are part of its environment. So also, the individual consumers or competing enterprises as well as the governments, consumer groups, competitors, courts, media and other institutions working outside an enterprise constitute its environment. The important point is that these individuals, institutions and forces are likely to influence the performance of a business enterprise although they happen to exist outside its boundaries. For example, changes in government's economic policies, rapid technological developments, political uncertainty, changes in fashions and tastes of consumers and increased competition in the market — all influence the working of a business enterprise in important ways. Increase in taxes by government can make things expensive to buy. Technological improvements may render existing products obsolete. Political uncertainty may create fear in the minds of investors. Changes in fashions and tastes of consumers may shift demand in the market from existing products to new ones. Increased competition in the market may reduce profit margins of firms.

On the basis of the foregoing discussion, it can be said business environment, has the following features:

(*i*) **Totality of external forces:** Business environment is the sum total of all things external to business firms and, as such, is aggregative in nature.

(*ii*) **Specific and general forces:** Business environment includes both specific and general forces. Specific forces (such as investors, customers, competitors and suppliers) affect individual enterprises directly and immediately in their day-to-day working. General forces (such as social, political, legal and technological conditions) have impact on all business enterprises and thus may affect an individual firm only indirectly.

(*iii*) **Inter-relatedness:** Different elements or parts of business environment are closely interrelated. For example, increased life expectancy of people and increased awareness for health care have increased the demand for many health products and services like diet Coke, fat-free cooking oil, and health resorts. New health products and services have, in turn, changed people's life styles.

(*iv*) **Dynamic nature:** Business environment is dynamic in that it keeps on changing whether in terms of technological improvement, shifts in consumer preferences or entry of new competition in the market.

(*v*) **Uncertainty:** Business environment is largely uncertain as it is very difficult to predict future happenings, especially when environment changes are taking place too frequently as in the case of information technology or fashion industries.

(*vi*) **Complexity:** Since business environment consists of numerous interrelated and dynamic conditions or forces which arise from different sources, it becomes difficult to comprehend at once what exactly constitutes a given environment. In other words, environment is a complex phenomenon that is relatively easier to understand in parts but difficult to grasp in its totality. For example, it may be difficult to know the extent of the relative impact of the social, economic, political, technological or legal factors on change in demand of a product in the market.

(*vii*) **Relativity:** Business environment is a relative concept since it differs from country to country and even region to region. Political conditions in the USA, for instance, differ from those in China or Pakistan. Similarly, demand for sarees may be fairly high in India whereas it may be almost non-existent in France.

IMPORTANCE OF BUSINESS ENVIRONMENT

Just like human beings, business enterprises do not exist in isolation. Each business firm is not an island unto itself; it exists, survives and grows within the context of the element and forces of its environment. While an individual firm is able to do little to change or control these forces, it has no alternative to responding or adapting according to them. A good understanding of environment by business managers enables them not only to identify and evaluate, but also to react to the forces external to their firms. The importance of business environment and its understanding by managers can be appreciated if we consider the following facts:

(*i*) **It enables the firm to identify opportunities and getting the first mover advantage:** Opportunities refer to the positive external trends or changes that will help a firm to improve its performance. Environment provides numerous opportunities for business success. Early identification of opportunities helps an enterprise to be the first to exploit them instead of losing them to competitors. For example, Maruti Udyog became the leader in the small car market because it was the first to recognise the need for small cars in an environment of rising petroleum prices and a large middle class population in India.

(*ii*) **It helps the firm to identify threats and early warning signals:** Threats refer to the external environment trends and changes that will hinder a firm's performance. Besides opportunities, environment happens to be the source of many threats. Environmental awareness can help managers to identify various threats on time and serve as an early warning signal. For example, if an Indian firm finds that a foreign multinational is entering the Indian market with new substitutes, it should act as a warning signal. On the basis of this information, the Indian firms can prepare themselves to meet the threat by adopting such measures as improving the quality of the product, reducing cost of the production, engaging in aggressive advertising, and so on.

(*iii*) **It helps in tapping useful resources:** Environment is a source of various resources for running a business. To engage in any type of activity, a business enterprise assembles various resources called inputs like finance, machines, raw materials, power and water, labour, etc., from its environment including financiers, government and suppliers. They decide to provide these resources with their own expectations to get something in return from the enterprise. The business enterprise supplies the environment with its outputs such as goods and services for customers, payment of taxes to government, return on financial investment to investors and so on. Because the enterprise depends on the environment as a source of inputs or resources and as an outlet for outputs, it only makes sense that the enterprise designs policies that allow it to get the resources that it needs so that it can convert those resources into outputs that the environment desires. This can be done better by understanding what the environment has to offer.

(*iv*) **It helps in coping with rapid changes:** Today's business environment is getting increasingly dynamic where changes are taking place at a fast pace. It is not the fact of change itself that is so important as the pace of change. Turbulent market conditions, less brand loyalty, divisions and sub-divisions (fragmentation) of markets, more demanding customers, rapid changes in technology and intense global competition are just a few of the images used to describe today's business environment. All sizes and all types of enterprises are facing increasingly dynamic environment. In order to effectively cope with these significant changes, managers must understand and examine the environment and develop suitable courses of action.

(*v*) **It helps in assisting in planning and policy formulation:** Since environment is a source of both opportunities and threats for a business enterprise, its understanding and analysis can be the basis for deciding the future course of action (planning) or training guidelines for decision making (policy). For instance, entry of new players in the market, which means more competition may make an enterprise think afresh about how to deal with the situation.

(*vi*) **It helps in improving performance:** The final reason for understanding business environment relates to whether or not it really makes a difference in the performance of an enterprise. The answer is that it does appear to make a difference. Many studies reveal that the future of an enterprise is closely bound up with what is happening in the environment. And, the enterprises that continuously monitor their environment and adopt suitable business practices are the ones which not only improve their present performance but also continue to succeed in the market for a longer period.

DIMENSIONS OF BUSINESS ENVIRONMENT

Dimensions of, or the factors constituting the business environment include economic, social, technological, political and legal conditions which are considered relevant for decision-making and improving the performance of an enterprise. In contrast to the specific environment, these factors explain the general environment which mostly influences many enterprises at the same time. However, management of every enterprise can benefit from being aware of these dimensions instead of being disinterested in them. For instance, scientific research has discovered a technology that makes it possible to produce an energy efficient light bulb that lasts at least twenty times as long as a standard bulb. Senior managers in the lighting divisions at General Electric and Phillips recognised that this discovery had the potential to significantly affect their unit growth and profitability, so they have carefully followed the progress on this research and profitably used its findings. A brief discussion of the various factors constituting the general environment of business is given below:

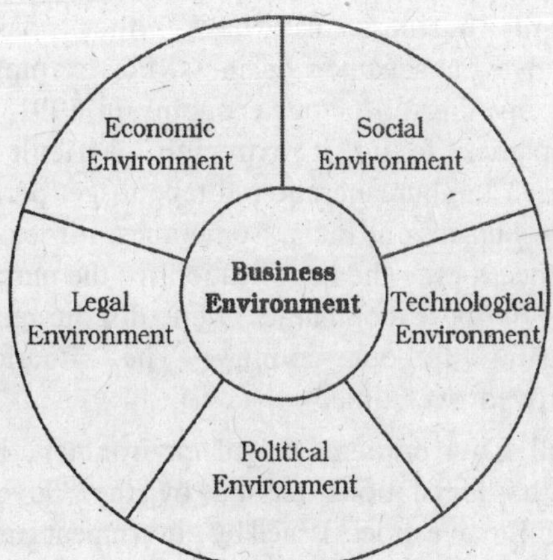

(*i*) **Economic Environment:** Interest rates, inflation rates, changes in disposable income of people, stock market indices and the value of rupee are some of the economic factors that can affect management practices in a business enterprise. Short and long term interest rates significantly affect the demand for product and services. For example, in case of construction companies and automobile manufacturers, low longer-term rates are beneficial because they result in increased spending by consumers for buying homes and cars on borrowed money. Similarly, a rise in the disposable income of people due to increase in the gross domestic product of a country creates increasing demand for products. High inflation rates generally result in constraints on business enterprises as they increase the various costs of business such as the purchase of raw materials or machinery and payment of wages and salaries to employees.

Components of Economic Environment

- Existing structure of the economy in terms of relative role of private and public sectors
- The rates of growth of GNP and per capita income at current and constant prices
- Rates of saving and investment
- Volume of imports and exports of different items
- Balance of payments and changes in foreign exchange reserves
- Agricultural and industrial production trends
- Expansion of transportation and communication facilities
- Money supply in the economy
- Public debt (internal and external)
- Planned outlay in private and public sectors

(*ii*) **Social Environment:** The social environment of business include the social forces like customs and traditions, values, social trends, society's expectations from business, etc. Traditions define social practices that have lasted for decades or even centuries. For example, the celebration of Diwali, Id, Christmas, and Guru Parv in India provides significant financial opportunities for greetings card companies, sweets or confectionery manufacturers, tailoring outlets and many other related business. Values refer to concepts that a society holds in high esteem. In India, individual freedom, social justice, equality of opportunity and national integration are examples of major values cherished by all of us. In business terms, these values translate into freedom of choice in the market, business's responsibility towards the society and non-discriminatory employment practices. Social trends present various opportunities and threats to business enterprises. For example, the health-and-fitness trend has become popular among large number of urban dwellers. This has created a demand for products like organic food, diet soft drinks, gyms, bottled (mineral) water and food supplements. This trend has, however, harmed business in other industries like dairy processing, tobacco and liquor.

Major Elements of Social Environment

- Attitudes towards product innovations, lifestyles, occupational distribution and consumer preferences
- Concern with quality of life
- Life expectancy
- Expectations from the workforce
- Shifts in the presence of women in the workforce
- Birth and death rates
- Population shifts
- Educational system and literacy rates
- Consumption habits
- Composition of family

(*iii*) **Technological Environment:** Technological environment includes forces relating to scientific improvements and innovations which provide new ways of producing goods and services and new methods and techniques of operating a business. For example, recent technological, advances in computers and electronics have modified the ways in which companies advertise their products. It is common now to see CD-ROM's, computerised information kiosks, and Internet/World Wide Web multimedia pages highlighting the virtues of products. Similarly, retailers have direct links with suppliers who replenish stocks when needed. Manufacturers have flexible manufacturing systems.

Airline companies have Internet and World Wide Web pages where customers can look for flight times, destinations and fares and book their tickets online. In addition, continuing innovations in different scientific and engineering fields such as lasers, robotics, biotechnology, food preservatives, medicine, telecommunication and synthetic fuels have provided numerous opportunities and threats for many different enterprises. Shifts in demand from vaccum tubes to transistors, from steam locomotives to dieseland electric engines, from fountain pens to ballpoint, from propeller airplanes to jets, and from typewriters to computer based word processors, have all been responsible and creating new business.

(*iv*) **Political Environment:** Political environment includes political conditions such as general stability and peace in the country and specific attitudes that elected government representatives hold towards business. The significance of political conditions in business success lies in the predictability of business activities under stable political conditions. On the other hand, there may be uncertainty of business activities due to political unrest and threats to law and order. Political stability, thus, builds up confidence among business people to invest in the long term projects for the growth of the economy. Political instability can shake that confidence. Similarly, the attitudes of government officials towards business may have either positive or negative impact upon business. For example, even after opening up of our economy in 1991, foreign companies found it extremely difficult to cut through the bureaucratic red tape to get permits for doing business in India. Sometimes, it took months to process even their application for the purpose. As a result these companies were discouraged from investing in our country. The situation has improved over time.

Major Elements of Political Environment

- The Constitution of the country
- Prevailing political system
- The degree of politicisation of business and economic issues
- Dominant ideologies and values of major political parties
- The nature and profile of political leadership and thinking of political personalities
- The level of political morality
- Political institutions like the government and allied agencies
- Political ideology and practices of the ruling party
- The extent and nature of government intervention in business
- The nature of relationship of our country with foreign countries

(*v*) **Legal Environment:** Legal environment includes various legislations passed by the Government administrative orders issued by government authorities, court judgments as well as the decisions rendered by various commissions and agencies at every level of the government—centre, state or local. It is imperative for the management of every enterprise to obey the law of the land. Therefore, an adequate knowledge of rules and regulations framed by the Government is a pre-requisite for better business performance. Non-compliance of laws can land the business enterprise into legal problems. In India, a working knowledge of Companies Act 1956; Industries (Development and Regulations) Act 1951; Foreign Exchange Management Act and the Imports and Exports (Control) Act 1947; Factories Act, 1948; Trade Union Act; 1926; Workmen's Compensation Act, 1923; Industrial Disputes Act, 1947, Consumer Protection Act, 1986, Competition Act, 2002 and host of such other legal enactments as amended from time to time by the Parliament, is important for doing business. Impact of legal environment can be illustrated with the help of government regulations to protect consumer's interests. For example, the advertisement of alcoholic beverages is prohibited. Advertisements, including packets of cigarettes carry the statutory warning 'Cigarette smoking is injurious to health'. Similarly, advertisements of baby food must necessarily inform the potential buyer that mothers milk is the best. All these regulations are required to be followed by advertisers.

ECONOMIC ENVIRONMENT IN INDIA

The economic environment in India consists of various macro-level factors related to the means of production and distribution of wealth which have an impact on business and industry. These include:

(*a*) Stage of economic development of the country.

(*b*) The economic structure in the form of mixed economy which recognises the role of both public and private sectors.

(*c*) Economic policies of the Government, including industrial, monetary and fiscal policies.

(*d*) Economic planning, including five year plans, annual budgets, and so on.

(*e*) Economic indices, like national income, distribution of income, rate and growth of GNP, per capita income, disposal personal income, rate of savings and investments, value of exports and imports, balance of payments, and so on.

(*f*) Infrastructural factors, such as, financial institutions, banks, modes of transportation communication facilities, and so on.

Business enterprises in India do realise the importance and impact of the economic environment on their working. Almost all annual company reports presented by their chairpersons devote considerable attention to the general economic environment prevailing in the country and an assessment of its impact on their companies.

The economic environment of business in India has been steadily changing mainly due to the government policies. At the time of Independence:

(*a*) The Indian economy was mainly agricultural and rural in character;

(*b*) About 70% of the working population was employed in agriculture;

(*c*) About 85% of the population was living in the villages;

(*d*) Production was carried out using irrational, low productivity technology;

(*e*) Communicable diseases were widespread, mortality rates were high. These was no good public health system.

In order to solve economic problems of our country, the government took several steps including control by the State of certain industries, central planning and reduced importance of the private sector. The main objectives of India's development plans were:

(*a*) Initiate rapid economic growth to raise the standard of living, reduce unemployment and poverty;

(*b*) Become self-reliant and set up a strong industrial base with emphasis on heavy and basic industries;

(*c*) Reduce inequalities of income and wealth;

(*d*) Adopt a socialist pattern of development — based on equality and prevent exploitation of man by man.

In accordance with the economic planning, the government gave a lead role to the public sector for infrastructure industries whereas the private sector was broadly given the responsibility of developing consumer goods industry. At the same time, the government imposed several restrictions, regulations and controls on the working of private sector enterprises. India's experience with economic planning has delivered mixed results. In 1991 the economy faced a serious foreign exchange crisis, high government deficit and a rising trend of prices despite bumper crops.

As a part of economic reforms, the Government of India announced a new industrial policy in July 1991.

The broad features of this policy were as follows:

(*a*) The Government reduced the number of industries under compulsory licensing to six.

(*b*) Many of the industries reserved for the public sector under the earlier policy, were dereserved. The role of the public sector was limited only to four industries of strategic importance.

(*c*) Disinvestment was carried out in case of many public sector industrial enterprises.

(*d*) Policy towards foreign capital was liberalised. The share of foreign equity participation was increased and in many activities 100 per cent Foreign Direct Investment (FDI) was permitted.

(*e*) Automatic permission was now granted for technology agreements with foreign companies.

(*f*) Foreign Investment Promotion Board (FIPB) was set up to promote and channelise foreign investment in India.

Appropriate measures were taken to remove obstacles in the way of growth and expansion of industrial units of large industrial houses. Small-scale sector was assured all help and accorded due recognition.

In essence, this policy has sought to liberate industry from the shackles of the licensing system (liberalisation), drastically reduce the role of the public sector (privatisation) and encourage foreign private participation in India's industrial development (globalisation).

Liberalisation: The economic reforms that were introduced were aimed at liberalising the Indian business and industry from all unnecessary controls and restrictions. They signalled the end of the licence-pemit-quota raj. Liberalisation of the Indian industry has taken place with respect to:

(*i*) abolishing licensing requirement in most of the industries except a short list,

(*ii*) freedom in deciding the scale of business activities *i.e.*, no restrictions on expansion or contraction of business activities,

(*iii*) removal of restrictions on the movement of goods and services,

(*iv*) freedom in fixing the prices of goods services,

(*v*) reduction in tax rates and lifting of unnecessary controls over the economy,

(*vi*) simplifying procedures for imports and experts, and

(*vii*) making it easier to attract foreign capital and technology to India.

Privatisation: The new set of economic reforms aimed at giving greater role to the private sector in the nation building process and a reduced role to the public sector. This was a reversal of the development strategy pursued so far by Indian planners. To achieve this, the government redefined the role of the public sector in the New Industrial

Policy of 1991, adopted the policy of planned disinvestments of the public sector and decided to refer the loss making and sick enterprises to the Board of Industrial and Financial Reconstruction. The term disinvestments used here means transfer in the public sector enterprises to the private sector. It results in dilution of stake of the Government in the public enterprise. If there is dilution of Government ownership beyond 51 per cent, it would result in transfer of ownership and management of the enterprise to the private sector.

Globalisation: Globalisation means the integration of the various economies of the world leading towards the emergence of a cohesive global economy. Till 1991, the Government of India had followed a policy of strictly regulating imports in value and volume terms. These regulations were with respect to (*a*) licensing of imports, (*b*) tariff restrictions and (*c*) quantitative restrictions. The new economic reforms aimed at trade liberalisation were directed towards import liberalisation, export promotion through rationalisation of the tariff structure and reforms with respect to foreign exchange so that the country does not remain isolated from the rest of the world. Globalisation involves an increased level of interaction and interdependence among the various nations of the global economy. Physical geographical gap or political boundaries no longer remain barriers for a business enterprise to serve a customer in a distant geographical market. This has been made possible by the rapid advancement in technology and liberal trade policies by Governments. Through the policy of 1991, the government of India moved the country to this globalisation pattern.

A Truly Globalised Economy

A truly global economy implies a boundaryless world where there is:

(*i*) Free flow of goods and services across nations;

(*ii*) Free flow of capital across nations;

(*iii*) Free flow of information and technology;

(*iv*) Free movement of people across borders;

(*v*) A common acceptable mechanism for the settlement of disputes;

(*vi*) A global governance perspective.

IMPACT OF GOVERNMENT POLICY CHANGES ON BUSINESS AND INDUSTRY

The policy of liberalisation, privatisation and globalisation of the Government has made a significant impact on the working of enterprises in business and industry. The Indian corporate sector has come face-to-face with several challenges due to government policy changes. These challenges can be explained as follows:

(*i*) **Increasing competition:** As a result of changes in the rules of industrial licensing and entry of foreign firms, competition for Indian firms has increased especially in service industries like telecommunications, airlines, banking, insurance, etc. which were earlier in the public sector.

(*ii*) **More demanding customers:** Customers today have become more demanding because they are well-informed. Increased competition in the market gives the customers wider choice in purchasing better quality of goods and services.

(*iii*) **Rapidly changing technological environment:** Increased competition forces the firms to develop new ways to survive and grow in the market. New technologies make it possible to improve machines, process, products and services. The rapidly changing technological environment creates tough challenges before smaller firms.

(*iv*) **Necessity for change:** In a regulated environment of pre-1991 era, the firms could have relatively stable policies and practices. After 1991, the market forces have become turbulent as a result of which the enterprises have to continuously modify their operations.

(*v*) **Need for developing human resource:** Indian enterprises have suffered for long with inadequately trained personnel. The new market conditions require people with higher competence and greater commitment. Hence the need for developing human resources.

(*vi*) **Market orientation:** Earlier firms used to produce first and go to the market for sale later. In other words, they had production oriented marketing operations. In a fast changing world, there is a shift to market orientation in as much as the firms have to study and analyse the market first and produce goods accordingly.

(*vii*) **Loss of budgetary support to the public sector:** The central government's budgetary support for financing the public sector outlays has declined over the years. The public sector undertakings have realised that, in order to survive and grow, they will have to be more efficient and generate their own resources for the purpose.

On the whole, the impact of Government policy changes particularly in respect of liberalisation, privatisation and globalisation has been positive as the Indian business and industry has shown great resilience in dealing with the new economic order. Indian enterprises have developed strategies and adopted business processes and procedures to meet the challenge of competition. They have become more customer-focused and adopted measures to improve customer relationship and satisfaction.

MULTIPLE CHOICE QUESTIONS

1. Which statement is false about the business environment?
A. Internal factors include the vision and mission of the organization and other internal mechanism of the organization.
B. External factors are the ones which lie beyond the control of business.
C. External environment relates with the suppliers, customers.
D. None of the above is correct.

2. Who paid under given statement?
"The nature of the global business environment guarantees that no matter how hard we work to create a stable and healthy organisation, our organisation will continue to experience dramatic changes far beyond our control.
A. W. Keats B. Margaret J Wheatley
C. Y. Zenim D. Johnson

3. Who said "Environment consists of atoms and molecules, agglomeration of things in motion, alive, of men and emotions, of physical and social law, social ideas, norms of actions, of forces and resistance".
A. Barnard B. Margaret J. Wheatly
C. Johnson D. W. Keats

4. The purposes of business that goes beyond earning profits are
A. For the supply of goods and services
B. Creating job opportunities
C. Offering better quality of life
D. All of the above

5. Identify the incorrect statement
A. The success of every business depends on adapting itself to the environment within which it functions.
B. The business environment poses threats to a firm or offers immense opportunities for potential market exploitation.
C. A change in the fashion or customers' taste may shift the demand in the market for a particular product.
D. None of the above

6. A Vision Statement describes the desired .... position of the company.
A. Current B. Past
C. Future D. None of the above

7. The features of business environment are as follows
A. Totality of External Forces
B. Dynamic Nature
C. Uncertainty
D. All of the above

8. Business environment can be understood by the following ways
A. Identification of Threats
B. Giving Direction for Growth
C. Image Building
D. All of the above

9. A .... defines the company's business, its objectives and its approach to reach those objectives.
A. Vision Statement B. Mission Statement
C. Both A and B D. Strategy

10. Which is not a mission/vision statement?
A. Help define performance standards
B. Guide employee's decision making
C. Help establish a framework for ethical behaviour
D. None of theme

11. Whose mission statement is given below?
"To bring inspiration and innovation to every athlete in the world".
A. Face book B. Nike
C. Google D. ICSI

12. Which mission statement is internal to organisation?
A. enlist external support
B. create better communication with customers and suppliers
C. serves as a public relations tool
D. Nome of them

13. Which statement is true about vision statement?
A. Your vision statement is where you want your business to reach at
B. It is your future dream for your business
C. It should keep your business reaching for new heights
D. All of the above

14. Whose mission statement is given below?
"To give people the power to share and make the world more open and connected".
A. Face book B. Nike
C. Google D. ICSI

15. Whose mission statement is given below?
"To organize the world's information and make it universally accessible and useful"
A. Face book B. Nike
C. Google D. ICSI

16. Whose mission statement is given below?
"To develop high caliber professionals facilitating good corporate governance"
A. ICSI B. Face book
C. Nike D. Google

17. Competitive Advantage involves
A. identifying the actual competitors
B. assessing competitors' objectives
C. selecting the strategies to deal with competitors
D. All of the above

18. Micro environmental factors includes
A. Employees B. Suppliers
C. Media D. All of the above

19. Which is not a part of an internal environment?
A. Machinery B. Loan
C. Marketing resources D. Money

20. Internal environment contains
A. the owner B. the shareholders
C. the non-managers D. All of the above

21. Which is not a part of an internal environment?
A. Research and development
B. Company image
C. Non competitive advantage
D. Value system

22. The human resource in any organization must have characteristics like
A. skills B. quality
C. attitude D. All of the above

23. Which financial factors don't affect internal environment of a business?
A. Financial policies B. Budget for next year
C. Financial positions D. Capital Structure

24. Which statement is false about shareholders?
A. Balance in favour of business should be more than shareholders.
B. They own shares of the company thereby end up owning the company itself.
C. Shareholder pressure to increase profits will affect organizational strategy
D. To keep shareholder's motivation, appropriate dividends are needed to be distributed.

25. Which is relevant for competitor from micro environmental factors angle?
A. Does the business have a unique selling point
B. Competitor analysis and monitoring is crucial
C. It should add value to the business
D. All of the above

26. The acronym for the macro analysis is
A. STEP B. STEEP
C. STEPP D. None of the above

27. Which area of interest does not affect business macro environment?
A. Technology
B. Ecology and Physical Environment
C. Political and Legal
D. None of the above

28. The social environment of business excludes social factors like
A. Technology B. Values, beliefs
C. Poverty, literacy D. Customs, traditions

29. The changes in culture and lifestyle may come from many sources like
A. Medical Science B. Physical Science
C. Economic D. All of the above

30. NAFTA was signed among following countries
A. US, Canada, Mexico B. India, US, Pakistan
C. US, Canada, UK D. None of the above

31. Free Market Economy is also known as
A. Capitalist economy B. Socialist economy
C. Mixed economy D. Others

32. .... is the spirit of capitalism
A. Inspiration B. Motivation
C. Innovation D. Invention

33. Give an example of non-profit organization
A. Tata B. Reliance
C. HAL D. Red Cross

34. Expand ILO
A. International Labour Organization
B. Indian Labour Organisation
C. Indian Language Organisation
D. None of these

35. .... is viewed as an organized economic activity
A. Commerce B. Industry
C. Business D. Economics

36. The most fundamental feature of capitalism is
A. Right to own property
B. Right to transfer property
C. Right to own and transfer property
D. None of these

37. The corporate entity in India is governed by
A. Companies Act, 1956
B. Partnership Act, 1932
C. Co-operative societies Act, 1904
D. Others

38. .... form of organization is suitable for small business
A. Company B. Partnership
C. Co-operative society D. Sole Proprietorship

39. The trust is governed by
A. Managing trustee B. Trust Act
C. Board D. Trust document

40. Partnership in India is governed by
A. Partnership Act, 1932
B. Companies Act, 1956
C. Co-operative Society Act, 1904
D. Others

41. The document that defines the internal affairs of the company is

A. Articles of Association
B. Memorandum of Association
C. Table A
D. None of these

42. A company which is incorporated in a country outside India under the law of that country is
A. Domestic company B. Foreign company
C. Subsidiary company D. Others

43. An entity which is formed between two or more parties to undertake economic activities together is known as
A. Joint Venture B. Merger
C. Acquisition D. None of these

44. Farming is an example of
A. Primary Sector B. Secondary Sector
C. Tertiary Sector D. None of these

45. The second sector of the economy includes
A. Agriculture
B. Tourism
C. Manufacturing and Construction
D. None of these

46. Tertiary sector is also known as
A. Service sector B. Agriculture sector
C. Business sector D. None of these

47. India's economic reforms were launched in
A. 2000 B. 1991
C. 1995 D. 1990

48. Government of India nationalized 14 banks in the year
A. 1957 B. 1950
C. 1965 D. 1969

49. The second stage of nationalization of banks were enacted in
A. 1995 B. 1980
C. 1990 D. 1975

50. The economic development of a nation depends
A. Industrial development
B. Agricultural growth
C. The development of Business
D. All the above

51. Expand BPO
A. Business Process Outsourcing
B. Business Promoting Organization
C. Business Process Organization
D. None of these

52. To liberalise means
A. Complete freedom B. Free from narrowness
C. Transform D. None of these

53. The World Trade Organization was established in
A. 1990 B. 1995
C. 1991 D. 1980

54. The process of integrating the economy with world economy known as
A. Globalization B. Privatization
C. Liberalisation D. None of these

55. TNC stands
A. Transnational Commission
B. Transnational Company
C. Transnational Committee
D. None of these

56. One of the measures of Globalization is
A. Economic growth
B. GDP
C. Devaluation of rupee
D. None of these

57. MRTP Act stands
A. Monopolistic Restrictive Trade Practice Act
B. Minimum Restrictive Trade Practice Act
C. Monopolistic Restrictive Trade Promotion Act
D. None of these

58. Expands FEMA
A. Functional Efficiency in Management Aptitude
B. Foreign Exchange Management Act
C. Foreign Exchange Management Awareness
D. None of these

59. The system by which the companies are directed and controlled is called
A. Corporate Management
B. Corporate Governance
C. Corporate Control
D. None of these

60. The main goal of business firm is
A. Minimise cost
B. Maximise profit
C. Maximise the owners value
D. None of these

61 The process of changing ideas into commercial opportunities and creating value is known as
A. Innovation B. Invention
C. Adventure D. Entrepreneurship

62. The dark side of entrepreneurship is
A. Risk B. Time
C. Investment D. None of these

63. .... is the lifeblood of every business activity
A. Finance B. Economics
C. Commerce D. Business

64. The skill that states the ability to conceive new ideas and products known as
A. Technical skills B. Conceptual skill
C. Management skill D. None of these

65. Expand IDBI
A. Industrial Development Board of India
B. Industrial Development Bank of India

C. International Development Banking Institution
D. None of these

66. The first development financial institution in India
A. IDBI B. IFCI
C. ICICI D. None of these

67. The first State Financial Corporation was established
A. Kerala in 1953 B. Karnataka in 1950
C. Gujarat in 1950 D. Punjab in 1953

68. The issue of shares by a company to its existing shareholders
A. Private placement B. Offer for sale
C. Public Issue D. Right Issue

69. OTCEI stands
A. Over The Counter Exchange Institution
B. Over The Counter Exchange of India
C. Over The Counter Exchange Institute
D. None of these

70. The members of the stock exchange are popularly known as
A. Intermediaries B. Dealers
C. Stock Brokers D. Brokers

71. Indian market is a .... competitive market
A. Perfect B. Imperfect
C. Highly D. Moderate

72. Expand the term QOL
A. Quality Oriented License
B. Quality of Life
C. Quality of Learning
D. None of these

73. Assembling of goods produced at different production centres at a common market place is
A. Dispersion B. Cartel
C. Concentration D. None of these

74. Monopoly firm charges different prices from different groups of customers called
A. Discriminating Monopoly
B. Price Discrimination
C. Differential Pricing
D. Both A and B

75. A market with two buyers
A. Duopoly B. Dupsony
C. Monopsony D. Oligopoly

76. Market with few buyers and sellers
A. Duopoly B. Dupsony
C. Monopsony D. Oligopsony

77. A Market situation with single buyer and single seller
A. Bilateral Monopoly B. Duopoly
C. Dupsony D. Monopsony

78. .... is the literal meaning of the word 'Business'
A. Manufacturing B. Production and dealing
C. State of being busy D. Exchange

79. In which year Income Tax Act was passed
A. 1961 B. 1951
C. 1964 D. 1952

80. The person who carries one man business known as
A. Partner B. Sole trader
C. Stake holder D. None of these

81. In which year Indian Co-operative Societies Act was passed
A. 1912 B. 1913
C. 1951 D. 1954

82. In which year Limited Liability Partnership Act was passed in India
A. 2006 B. 2005
C. 2008 D. 2010

83. MOU stands
A. Memorandum of Understanding
B. Ministry of Union
C. Neither A or B
D. Both A and B

84. Agriculture belongs to
A. Primary sector B. Secondary sector
C. Tertiary sector D. Quaternary sector

85. FDI stands
A. Fixed Deposit Interest
B. Foreign Direct Investment
C. Fixed Deposit Interest
D. Financial Direct Investment

86. FRBM Act stands
A. Fiscal Responsibility and Budget Management Act
B. Fiscal Resources Budget Management
C. Financial Responsibility Budget Management Act
D. None of the above

87. RBI Act was passed in
A. 1935 B. 1936
C. 1934 D. 1936

88. ROR stands
A. Rate of return B. Return to return
C. Return on return D. None of these

89. Under perfect competition firms producing .... product
A. Heterogeneous B. Homogeneous
C. Either A or B D. Neither A or B

90. Traditional concept of Marketing is ....
A. Selling
B. Buying and Selling
C. Customer satisfaction
D. None of these

91. Monopolist is a ....
A. Price maker B. Price taker
C. Price manager D. Both A and B

92. In monopoly demand curve shows .... curve
A. Upward slopping B. Horizontal
C. Vertical D. Downward slopping

93. Give an example for service monopoly
A. Service of a Doctor B. Service of a Teacher
C. Both A and B D. Neither A or B

94. Charging different prices from different groups of customers called
A. Price Discrimination
B. Pricing Under Collusion
C. Discriminating Monopoly
D. Both A and C

95. Combination of monopoly and competition is known as
A. Perfect Competition
B. Imperfect Competition
C. Monopolistic Competition
D. Monopsony

96. .... is the market situation in which few sellers or firms exist
A. Oligopoly
B. Monopoly
C. Monopolistic Competition
D. Monopsony

97. Give an example of Oligopoly
A. Automobile Industry B. Cement Industry
C. Software Industry D. All of these

98. EXIM policy stands
A. Extra Import B. Excess of Import
C. Export Import D. None of these

99. In which of the following basic categories can business environment be divided
A. Local and Regional
B. Regional and National
C. Internal and External
D. Financial and Non-Financial

100. .... is a statement which derives the role that an organization plays in a society.
A. Goals B. Mission
C. Objective D. Success

101. Economic Environment refers to all forces which have a .... impact on business.
A. political B. natural
C. economic D. social

102. .... environment is within the control of the business.
A. Internal B. External
C. Micro D. Macro

103. .... environment is beyond the control of the business.
A. Internal B. External
C. Micro D. Macro

104. Micro environment is also called as...............
A. general environment
B. operating environment
C. economic environment
D. political environment

105. Macro environment is also called as ....
A. general environment
B. operating environment
C. economic environment
D. political environment

106. Study of human population is called as .... environment.
A. political B. social
C. demographic D. economic

107. In which year the essential commodities act introduced ....
A. 1954 B. 1955
C. 1956 D. 1957

108. A systematic application of scientific knowledge to practical task is known as ....
A. technology B. culture
C. demographic D. legal

109. .... is defined as systematic assessment of the social impact of the activities of a business firm.
A. Social audit B. Social responsibility
C. Social interaction D. Social benefit

110. What are the elements of business ethics?
A. Values rights and duties
B. Attitudes pressure and environment
C. Value environment and attitude
D. Responsibilities

111. Corporate values are the .... of the corporate sector.
A. shared values B. moral beliefs
C. customer satisfaction D. goodwill

112. The economic system in which business units or factors of production are privately owned and governed is called as ....
A. capitalism B. socialism
C. democratic D. republic

113. Under .... economic system, all the economic activities of the country are controlled and regulated by the Government in the interest of the public.
A. capitalism B. socialism
C. democratic D. republic

114. The economic system in which both public and private sectors co-exist is known as .... economy.
A. capitalism B. socialism
C. democratic D. mixed

115. Fiscal policy refers to the policy of government regarding taxation, public expenditure and ....

A. public debt B. budgets
C. policies D. deposits

116. National stock exchange was set up as a joint stock company by all Indian financial institution and banks on November 27 ....

A. 1991 B. 1992
C. 1993 D. 1994

117. The benefit of OCTEI is ....

A. it offers complete transparency in dealings
B. it offers both liquidity and security
C. transactions are made fast and quick
D. it is not investor friendly

118. In India liberalization and privatization began from ....

A. 1991 B. 1971
C. 1981 D. 1947

119. Obsolesce scene means .... of products.

A. implementation B. outdated
C. assessment D. quality

120. Identification of companies technological assets that may provide .... in new businesses.

A. opportunities B. development
C. failure D. authority

121. .... occupies the central place in business.

A. People B. Raw material
C. Labour D. Finished goods

122. Businesses represent the organized efforts of enterprises to supply .... with goods and services.

A. producers B. consumers
C. intermediaries D. suppliers

123. India is good example for .... economy.

A. socialist B. mixed
C. capitalist D. communist

124. .... are a primary mechanism for motivating business activities.

A. Social relationship B. Profit
C. Customers D. Assets

125. According to whom, business environment is defined as total of all things external to firms and industries which effect their organization and operations.

A. Arthur. M. Welmer B. John Wick
C. Bayord O. Wheeler D. Mathew Smith

126. Business includes ....

A. non-economic activities
B. economic activities
C. social activities
D. production activities

127. What is the single word that can best describe todays business?

A. Technology B. Profit Making
C. Change D. People

128. Which of the following is not an economic activity?

A. A doctor practicing
B. A lawyer practicing law
C. A professional cricketer playing cricket
D. A student playing cricket

129. .... refers to the system of moral principles and rules of conduct applied to business.

A. Business culture B. Business ethics
C. Business D. Society

130. Competition is beneficial to the competing firms besides benefiting the ....

A. producers B. intermediaries
C. finances D. consumers

131. What are the main concepts concerning about business goals (or) objectives?

A. Mission objectives
B. Mission targets
C. Mission objectives target
D. Target objectives

132. .... is the primary motive for a business enterprise.

A. Profit B. Maximize customers
C. Human objective D. Maximize suppliers

133. .... is the business through which new ideas and innovations are given a sharp and are converted into useful products and services.

A. Market Leadership B. Challenge
C. Joy of Creation D. Growth

134. Among the following, what is the nature of business environment

A. Aggression
B. Relative
C. Uncertain
D. Aggression Relative and Uncertain

135. What is the significance of business environment?

A. First Mover Advantage
B. Competition
C. Information
D. Globalization

136. .... refers to all forces which have an economic impact.

A. Technological Environment
B. Political Environment
C. Economic Environment
D. Social Environment

137. The environment analysis that provides inputs for strategies decision making is ....

A. Strategic management
B. Environmental analysis
C. Business environment
D. Business analysis

138. Economic growth can be measured by ....
A. the CPI B. the CBI
C. GDP D. MPC

139. Free trade is based on the principle of ....
A. comparative advantage
B. comparative scale
C. economies of advantage
D. production possibility advantage

140. Marxism is otherwise called as ....
A. socialism B. economics
C. communism D. capitalism

141. FERA is foreign exchange regulation act for ....
A. industries B. small scale
C. labour D. owner

142. GDP is ....
A. Gross Domestic Product
B. Gross Domestic Percentage
C. Gross Domestic Personnel
D. Gross Domestic Public

143. NDP is ....
A. Net Domestic Product
B. Net Domestic Percentage
C. Net Domestic Personnel
D. Net Domestic Public

144. Business Environment is effected by .... factors.
A. Internal B. External
C. Both A and B D. None of above

145. Environmental factor which are beyond the control of individual is known as ....
A. Internal B. External
C. Both A and B D. None of above

146. Change in technology, political factors, demand of population are .... factors.
A. Internal B. External
C. Both A and B D. None of above

147. .... affects the organization and not necessary to the whole economy.
A. Micro factors B. Macro factors
C. Both A and B D. None of above

148. It is the .... which tells the purpose of existence of business.
A. Mission B. Vision
C. Both A and B D. None of above

149. To develop caliber professionals facilitating good corporate governance is .... of ICSI.
A. Mission B. Vision
C. Both A and B D. None of above

150. Which of the following would have unlimited liability?
A. Cooperative society B. Company
C. Shareholders D. Sole proprietorship

151. Which of the following are the advantages of Sole proprietorship?
A. Better control
B. Quick decision
C. Easy to form and Shut
D. All of above

152. The affairs of the business is managed by head of the family known as Karta in ....
A. Hindu undivided family
B. Partnership firm
C. Company
D. Cooperative society

153. What is the maximum strength of HUF ?
A. 20 B. 10
C. 50 D. No limit

154. Mutual agency is the important feature of ....
A. Hindu undivided Family
B. Partnership firm
C. Company
D. Cooperative society

155. Company is having perpetual succession and work under common seal. This statement is ....
A. True B. False
C. Partly true D. Partly false

156. Scale of business determines the ....
A. Size of the business
B. Capital involved in business
C. Production of such business
D. All of above

157. For the goods having artistic features .... size of enterprise is preferred.
A. Small scale B. Large scale
C. Corporation D. Very large

158. Economical advantages can be taken from ....
A. Small scale production
B. Large scale production
C. Both A and B
D. Cooperative society

159. Economics derived from large scale of business are ....
A. Internal B. External
C. Both A and B D. None of above

160. Advantages of Multi-national companies are ....
A. Funds availability
B. Provision of employments
C. Increasing competitions
D. All of above

161. Financial suitability and job opportunity is the advantages in .... scale of operation.
A. Small scale B. Large scale
C. Corporation D. Very small

162. BPO stands for ....
A. Business Process Outsourcing

B. Business Public Organization
C. Business Private Organization
D. Business People Organization

163. Providing permission to use technical know how by parent organization to another individual is known as ....
A. Franchising B. Agency
C. Marketing D. Dealership

164. Sales forecast is difficult in ....
A. Network marketing B. E commerce
C. M commerce D. Marketing

165. KPO stands for ....
A. Knowledge Process Outsourcing
B. Knowledge Public Organization
C. Key Public Offer
D. Know Potential Output

166. PDA, smart phone, computer mediated network are the need in ....
A. Network marketing B. E-commerce
C. M commerce D. Marketing

167. B2B, B2C, C2B are the types of ....
A. Network marketing B. E-commerce
C. M commerce D. Marketing

168. .... is the primary function of management.
A. Planning B. Budgeting
C. Controlling D. Organization

169. Choice of production, need of customer, gaining over competitor is .... level strategy.
A. Corporate level B. Business unit
C. Operational level D. All of above

170. SCM stands for ....
A. Supply chain management
B. Supply chain material
C. Supply choice material
D. Source concept management

171. Film production is the example of ....
A. Low technology job B. High technology job
C. Complex job D. Both B and C

172. Financial management comprises of ....
A. Financial decision B. Investment decision
C. Dividend decision D. All of above

173. Selling + customer satisfaction =
A. Network marketing B. E-commerce
C. M-commerce D. Marketing

174. Principle of equitable and good is .... part of law.
A. Natural B. Positive
C. Sociological D. Realistic

175. Hindu and Mohammedan law is ....
A. Personal law B. Principle law
C. Customary law D. Historical law

176. Company work under a ....
A. Seal B. Common seal
C. Stamp D. None of above

177. Company has .... Succession.
A. Longer B. Continue
C. Perpetual D. Limited

178. .... have homogeneous Member.
A. Hindu undivided family
B. Partnership firm
C. Company
D. Cooperatives

179. If company do not follow the principle of separate legal entity .... can be done.
A. Lifting of corporate veil
B. Principle of equity
C. Principle of natural justice
D. All of above

180. The word entrepreneurship is derived from the French word ....
A. Entreprendre B. Entreprendur
C. Entrepreneurde D. Entropre

181. "Entrepreneur is someone who actually searches for change responds to it and exploits those changes as an opportunity" this statement is given by ....
A. Peter Drucker B. H.N. Hansen
C. Koontz o'donnel D. Joseph Schumpeter

182. Which one of the following does not include in personal attribute of an entrepreneur ....
A. Dedication B. Passion
C. Flexibility D. Biasness

183. To start ones new business, entrepreneur needs to leave .... and enter into ....
A. Safe, unsafe
B. Comfort zone, twilight zone
C. Twilight zone, comfort zone
D. Unsafe zone, safe

184. Principle of innovation was given by ....
A. Steve jobs B. H.N. Hansen
C. Koontz o'donnel D. Joseph Schumpeter

185. PESTLE is part of which type of environment ....
A. Micro B. Macro
C. External D. Business

186. T in SWOT stands for ....
A. Threats B. Tasks
C. Tactics D. Technology

187. Industry analysis is given by which of the following ....
A. Porter B. H.N. Hansen
C. Koontz o'donnel D. Joseph Schumpeter

188. Which of the following is an economic factor?
A. Exchange rates B. Licensing regulations
C. Labour courts D. Employment needs

189. Sell .... and not .... is the statement given by steve jobs.
A. Company, customers B. Desire, wants
C. Product, dreams D. Dreams, product

190. Which of the following, entrepreneurship does not offer?
A. Independence and freedom
B. Recognition
C. Opportunity of being own boss
D. Less income

191. Bill gates is considered which of the type of entrepreneur
A. Visionary B. Superstar
C. Sustainer D. Idealist

192. Charm and high energy relates to which of the following
A. Visionary B. Superstar
C. Sustainer D. Idealist

193. Intrapreneur faces competition from ....
A. Entrepreneurs
B. Managers
C. Employees within the organisation
D. All the above

194. Which of the following is not the characteristics of entrepreneurship?
A. Innovation
B. Organising skills
C. Indifference approach
D. Risk taking

195. Entrepreneurship work for ....
A. Profits B. Salary
C. Remuneration D. Commission

196. Which of the following is not technique is not used in business environment scanning?
A. PESTEL analysis B. Industry analysis
C. Swot Analysis D. Government analysis

197. Ongoing scanning at an almost unconscious level is ....
A. Directed scanning B. Active scanning
C. Passive scanning D. Indirect Scanning

198. Which of the following does not include in marketing assessment process?
A. Defining the problem
B. Fastering Ideas
C. Feedback
D. Designing a plan

199. Business plans are only for start up companies, it is a ....
A. Myth B. Reality
C. Both A and B D. None of the above

200. Who claimed that entrepreneurship requires no ordinary skill?
A. Mill B. Smith
C. Ricardo D. None of the above

201. Alfred Marshall gave the necessity of entrepreneurship in ....
A. 1880 B. 1867
C. 1890 D. 2002

202. Employees relate to which of the following ....
A. Work smart
B. Work hard
C. Do not wok
D. Work all day all night

203. Overcoming the obstacles of right attitude in entrepreneurship is not matter of which of the following ....
A. Desire B. Discipline
C. Both A and B D. Fraudulent

204. Peter Drucker suggested entrepreneurship is ....
A. Science B. Art
C. Profession D. Practice

205. Entrepreneurship should always ready to accept the ....
A. Modernization B. Expansion
C. Diversification D. All of the above

206. Introduction of new products and services and adding it to product line is known as ....
A. Modernization B. Expansion
C. Diversification D. All of the above

207. Entrepreneur should have access to ....
A. Right skill B. Right environment
C. Smart capital D. All of the above

208. Which of the following is not the stage of entrepreneur firm?
A. Seed B. Start
C. Growth D. Final stage

209. Which of the following is needed to grow the entrepreneurship?
A. Media B. Society
C. Government D. All of above

210. Which of the following is a form of business organization?
A. Church B. Sole Proprietorship
C. Temple D. Mosque

211. The following factors are key drivers of globalisation:
A. Government action, exchange rates, competition and socio demographic factors
B. Market convergence, competition, exchange rates and cost advantages.
C. Cost advantages, government action, economic cycles and competition.
D. Market, cost, competition and government policies.

212. Sole proprietorship form of business organizations has the characteristic of:

A. Dual ownership B. Sharing of Profit
C. Limited liability D. One man's Capital

213. The affairs of business are managed by the head of the family, who is known as ....
A. Co-partner B. Karta
C. Owner D. Shareholder

214. Internal business environment refers not to:
A. Man (Human Resource)
B. Government Policies
C. Money (Financial Factors)
D. Marketing Resources

215. Mission and Vision Statements are commonly used to:
A. Guide management's thinking on strategic issues, especially during times of significant change
B. Help establish a framework for ethical behaviour
C. Create wider linkages with customers, suppliers and alliance partners
D. Inspire employees to work more productively by providing focus and common goals

216. What is human capital?
A. The development of robots in industry
B. The rise of Information technology
C. The skills and abilities of humans
D. Technological ideas of people

217. By Electronic Commerce, we mean:
A. Commerce of electronic goods
B. Commerce which depends on electronics
C. Commerce which is based on the use of internet
D. Commerce which is based on transactions using computers connected by telecommunication network

218. One of the main characteristic of MNCs is their large size. The other one is:
A. the localization of businesses in different countries
B. that their worldwide activities are centrally controlled by the parent company
C. delivering service or managing production in one more country
D. None of the above

219. The primary objective of public sector enterprises is to
A. serve the public
B. maximize profit
C. act as a catalyst for community development
D. provide agricultural products

220. Which one of the following is NOT an external factor?
A. New regulations B. Competition
C. Social changes D. Manufacturing

221. Which of the following is not a method of supply chain management?
A. Job Method B. Batch Method
C. Flow Method D. Cash Method

222. Selling and marketing have synonymous meaning.
A. True, both can be used interchangeably
B. False, selling is narrow concept
C. False, marketing is narrow concept
D. The concepts cannot be compared

223. Features of business environment are:
A. Uncertainty
B. Relativity
C. Static Nature
D. Specific and General Forces

224. Micro environmental factors can be described as .... close to a business that have a direct impact on its strategy.
A. Employees relationship
B. Internal factors
C. Media relation
D. Competitive environment

225. Liberalization does not includes:
A. Abolishing industrial licensing requirement in most of the industries
B. Freedom in deciding the scale of business activities
C. Restriction in fixing prices of goods and services
D. Simplifying the procedure for imports and exports

226. Statutory body is a body that is created under an Act, enacted by
A. Association of people
B. Association of ministers
C. Both A and B
D. Judiciary

227. Who said, "state ownership and operation of industrial, agricultural, financial and commercial undertakings"
A. N.N. Malaya B. I.V. Starke
C. A.H. Hansom D. O.L. Rehan

228. B2C commerce
A. includes services such as legal advice
B. means only shopping for physical goods
C. means only customers should approach customers to sell
D. means only customers should approach business to buy

229. The organization form of public sector enterprise does not include:
A. Departmental Undertaking
B. Statutory (or Public) Corporation
C. Government Company
D. Subsidiary to Public Company

230. What is the reason for MNCs Growth?
A. Reduce transport and distribution costs
B. Meet different rules and regulations

C. Avoid trade barriers
D. All the above

231. Disadvantages of E-Commerce in India are:
(*i*) Internet access is not universally available;
(*ii*) Credit card payment security is not yet guaranteed;
(*iii*) Transactions are de-personalized and human contact is missing;
(*iv*) Cyber laws are not in place.
A. (*i*) and (*ii*) B. (*ii*) and (*iii*)
C. (*i*), (*ii*), (*iii*) D. (*i*), (*ii*), (*iii*), (*iv*)

232. Marketing mix includes ....
A. Product or services
B. Financing
C. Retailers
D. Consumers

233. In which of the following, the ownership of venture is reflected by ownership of shares of stock?
A. Partnership B. Corporations
C. HUF D. Trusts

234. Franchising is
A. Purchasing all parts of the company
B. Allowing another party to use product or service under owner's name
C. Joining two or more companies
D. A company acquiring another company at its will

235. Where you want your business to be in 10 years time. This can be termed as:
A. Mission statement
B. Vision statement
C. Statement of purpose
D. Memorandum of understanding

236. Small scale industries are highly
A. Capital intensive B. Machine intensive
C. Labour intensive D. None of the above

237. The Food Corporation of India is an example of:
A. Departmental undertaking
B. Government company
C. Statutory corporation
D. None of the above

238. Which of the following is NOT included in liberalization?
A. Reduction in tax matters
B. Abolition of licensing
C. Simplification of policies
D. Imposition of tariff barriers

239. Agreement under a bilateral mistake is........... .
A. Void B. Lawful
C. Voidable D. Illegal

240. The Partnership Deed must be properly drafted and stamped according to the provision of:
A. Indian Partnership Act
B. Indian Stamp Act
C. Income Tax Act
D. The Companies Act

241. A contract that is wholly in writing, or evidenced in writing, or oral, or partly written and partly oral, is called:
A. an implied contract B. a void contract
C. a quasi-contract D. an express contract

242. If a contract required by statute to be wholly in writing is not in writing, it is:
A. voidable B. void
C. unenforceable D. valid

243. Where only one party is legally obligated to do something, the contract is classified as:
A. An executory contract
B. A unilateral contract
C. An executed contract
D. A bilateral contract

244. Contingent Contract to do or not to do anything on the happening of an uncertain future event:
A. is never enforceable
B. is enforceable since the time of making it
C. becomes enforceable in the immediate possibility of happening of that event
D. becomes enforceable only on the happening of that event

245. In relation to the PESTEL framework which of the following statements is correct:
A. It assists in the assessment of organisational strengths and weaknesses.
B. It allows a detailed analysis of the structure of an industry.
C. It can be used as a checklist to understand the different environmental influences in the macro environment.
D. Takes an historical perspective on the main political, economic, sociocultural, technological, environmental and legal factors.

246. The five forces that affect the level of competition in an industry are:
A. Threat of entrants; power of buyers; power of suppliers; threat of substitutes; competitive rivalry.
B. Threat of buyers; power of entry; power of substitutes; threat of suppliers; threat of recession.
C. Threat of recession; power of buyers; power of suppliers; threat of management failure; competitive rivalry
D. Threat of entry; power of buyers; power of suppliers; threat of substitutes; government action

247. Buyers cannot exercise high bargaining power over their suppliers if:
A. The volume they buy accounts for a large percentage of their suppliers' sales.
B. There are few buyers in the market.

C. They have many suppliers to choose from.
D. There is a high concentration of suppliers.

248. All of the following are recognized as potential sources of entrepreneurial ideas, EXCEPT:
A. Work experiences, skills, and abilities
B. Familiar and unfamiliar products and services
C. Personal interests or hobbies
D. All of the above are recognized as potential sources of entrepreneurial ideas

249. An .... is an individual who creates something for the first time, is a highly driven individual motivated by his or her own work and personal ideas.
A. Entrepreneur B. Inventor
C. Juggler D. None of the above

250. An entrepreneur's primary motivation for starting a business is:
A. To make money B. To be independent
C. To be famous D. To be powerful

251. The .... plan should contain control points to ascertain progress.
A. Business B. Marketing
C. Financial D. Operational

252. What out of the following is entrepreneurship which is totally internal in an organisation:
A. Internal Entrepreneurship
B. Internal Intrapreneurship
C. Both A and B
D. None of the above

253. .... is the one to go through minimum income risk:
A. Manager B. Entrepreneur
C. Both A and B D. None of them

254. Industry analysis should include information on:
A. Market size of competitor's product
B. Growth rate of suppliers
C. New products entry
D. Economic conditions

255. The man to coin the word 'Intrapreneur':
A. Thomas Malthus B. Gifford Bentinck
C. Gifford Pinchot D. Thomas Pogge

256. Market innovation refers to.......... .
A. Discovering new product and market
B. Setting up of a new shop
C. Acquiring a market place and bring innovation to it.
D. Procurement of capital to buy market

257. Concept of entrepreneurship was referred as .... by British economists.
A. Board Management
B. Business Administration
C. Board Administration
D. Business Management

258. What is the full form of LDC?
A. Low Division Countries
B. Less Developed Countries
C. Low Development Countries
D. Less Development Countries

259. The feature of business should be:
A. Unlawful business B. No risk
C. Distinct ownership D. No status

260. "Enterprise" means an industrial undertaking or a business concern or any other establishment, by whatever name called, engaged in the manufacture or production of goods, in any manner, pertaining to any industry specified in the .... to the Industries (Development and Regulation) Act, 1951.
A. Part 3 B. Section 34
C. First Schedule D. Preamble

261. The advantage of e-commerce is:
A. Local market B. Higher transaction cost
C. Quick delivery D. Lower margin

262. In India, which sector provides more job opportunities than any other sector?
A. Large scale
B. Medium level
C. Public sector undertakings
D. Agriculture sector

263. Large scale industries refers to those industries which require huge ...., man power and a have influx of capital assets.
A. infrastructure B. human resource
C. technology D. ownership

264. The .... entrepreneur category includes persons who enjoy putting in long hours to build a larger and more profitable business.
A. Optimizer B. Jugglers
C. Healer D. Hard worker

265. Which two work environments should be good for spawning the new enterprises?
A. Finance and marketing
B. Finance and R&D
C. Marketing and R&D
D. Marketing and IT

266. The resistance of employees in an organization against flexibility, growth, and diversification can be overcome by developing:
A. Entrepreneurship
B. Intrapreneurship
C. Managerial domain
D. Administrative domain

267. An intrapreneur needs to have a blend of:
A. Communication skills and intelligence
B. Managerial skills and entrepreneurial skills
C. Business skills and corporative skills
D. Intrapersonal skills

268. Which of the following are constraints to operational planning?
A. Time and resources B. Taxes and subsidies
C. Political instability D. None of the above

269. What is the logical order for stages of development in entrepreneurial firm?
(*i*) corporate (*ii*) start up
(*iii*) established (*iv*) seed stage
(*v*) early growth
A. (*i*) (*ii*) (*iii*) (*iv*) (*v*) B. (*v*) (*iii*) (*iv*) (*ii*) (*i*)
C. (*iv*) (*ii*) (*v*) (*iii*) (*i*) D. (*v*) (*iv*) (*iii*) (*ii*) (*i*)

270. In SWOT analysis the 'O' stands for
A. Obstacles B. Opportunities
C. Openings D. Objections

271. In the PESTEL framework for environmental analysis what does the letter S stand for?
A. Socio cultural B. Society
C. Surroundings D. Superior

272. The advantages of competition rivalry are:
A. Identifying the actual competitors
B. Assessing competitors' objectives, strategies, strengths & weaknesses, and reaction patterns
C. To root out the competitors
D. All the above

273. Assessment of competitive rivalry does NOT include an understanding of:
A. The extent to which competitors are in balance.
B. Market growth rates
C. Fixed costs, exit barriers and operational efficiency
D. The management structure of an organisation

274. Someone who works with and through other people by coordinating their work activities in order to accomplish organizational goals are ....
A. A very intelligent individual
B. A supervisor of production work
C. A manager
D. An operation supervisor

275. Managers who are responsible for making organization wide decision and establishing the plans and Goals that affect the entire organization are ....
A. First line managers B. Top managers
C. Production managers D. Research managers

276. All levels of management between the supervisory level and the top of the organization are termed ..... .
A. Middle managers B. First line managers
C. Supervisors D. Forman

277. Executive Vice president, president, managing director, chief operating officers or chairman of the board are associated with the following levels of management.
A. Team leaders B. Middle managers
C. First line managers D. Top managers

278. Agency head or plant manager is most likely associated with which of the following?
A. Team leaders B. Middle managers
C. First line managers D. Top managers

279. .... is the process of getting activities completed and effectively with and through other people.
A. Leading B. Management
C. Supervision D. Controlling

280. The distinction between a managerial position and a non managerial position is ....
A. Planning the work of others
B. Coordinating the work of others
C. Controlling the work of others
D. Organizing the work of others

281. .... distinguishes a managerial position from a non managerial one.
A. Manipulating others
B. Concern for the Law
C. Increasing efficiency
D. Coordinating and Integrating other's work

282. Effectiveness is synonymous with ....
A. Cost minimization B. Resource control
C. Good attainment D. Efficiency

283. Effectiveness refers to ....
A. The relationship between inputs and outputs
B. The addictive relationship between cost and benefit
C. The exponential nature of costs and outputs
D. None of these

284. The management process function consist of ....
A. Planning, Organizing, Staffing and Directing
B. Planning, Organizing, Leading and Directing
C. Planning, Organizing, Leading and Staffing
D. Planning, Organizing, Leading and Controlling

285. In successful organizations, ...
A. Low efficiency and high effectiveness go hand in hand
B. High efficiency and low effectiveness go hand in hand
C. High efficiency and high effectiveness go hand in hand
D. High efficiency and high equity go hand in hand

286. .... was a French industrialist who identified the basic management functions.
A. Weber B. Taylor
C. Herzberg D. Fayol

287. Writing an organizational strategic plan is an example of the .... management function.
A. Leading B. Coordinating
C. Planning D. Organizing

288. Organizing includes ....
A. Defining organizational goals
B. Hiring organizational members

C. Motivating organizational members
D. Determining who does what tasks

289. A manager resolving conflict among organizational members is performing what function?
A. Controlling B. Commanding
C. Directing D. Leading

290. The process of monitoring, comparing and correcting is called ....
A. Controlling B. Coordinating
C. Leading D. Organizing

291. Mentoring is primarily associated with the management function of ....
A. Planning B. Organizing
C. Leading D. Controlling

292. The .... role is more important for lower–level managers than it either middle or top level managers.
A. Leader B. Entrepreneur
C. Spoke person D. Disseminator

293. Manager with good .... are able to get the best out of their people.
A. Human skills B. Conceptual skills
C. Technical skills D. Visual skills

294. An organization is ....
A. The physical location where people work
B. A collection of individuals working for the same company
C. A deliberate arrangement of people to accomplish specific purpose
D. A group of individuals focused on profit-making for their shareholders

295. A difference between traditional organization and new organization is the new organization will be more ....
A. Static B. Command oriented
C. Rule oriented D. Dynamic

296. .... is a technique that manager used to improve resource allocation decision.
A. Liner programming
B. Work scheduling
C. Economic order quantity modeling
D. Regression analysis

297. Which of the early advocates of organizational behaviour was concerned about deplorable working condition?
A. Robert owan B. Huge meensterburg
C. Mary parker follett D. Chester Burnard

298. While trying to discover a problem, one manager utilizes analysis of basic work tasks that are performed in the organization, it is most likely that this manager has studied the work of ....
A. Fredrick Taylor B. Edward Deming
C. Max Weber D. Henri Fayol

299. Organizational culture is similar to an individuals ....
A. Skills B. Personality
C. Motivation D. Ability

300. An organization's specific environment ....
A. Is unique and changes with conditions
B. Is the same regardless of the organization's age
C. Is determined by the top level management
D. Is quantified to determine its objective

301. Environmental scanning creates the foundation for ....
A. Project management B. Forecasts
C. Bench marking D. Budgeting

302. Managers need forecasts that will allow them to predict future events effectively and ....
A. Accurately B. Efficiently
C. Specifically D. In a timely manner

303. Quantitative forecasting applies a set of mathematical rules to ....
A. Develop predictions of outcomes from customer's opinions
B. A series of past data to predict outcomes
C. Analyze what has happened in the past and determine when it will occur again
D. Estimate the number of products that should be produced at a given time

304. The goal of forecasting is to managers ....
A. Accurate predictions of trends and events
B. Decisions as to what customers will be demanding and when
C. Informations about the dynamics of environmental change
D. With information that will facilitate decision making

305. The accuracy of forecasts decrease as the ....
A. Quantity of data increase
B. Simplicity of the forecasts method increase
C. Period you were trying to predict increase
D. Number of customers increase

306. Forecasting techniques fall into two categories.
A. Fixed asset and human capital
B. Predictive and confirmatory
C. Quantitative and qualitative
D. Empirical and conceptual

307. What type of forecasting technique relies on the judgement and opinion of knowledgable individuals?
A. Qualitative B. Short-term
C. Confirmatory D. Predictive

308. Forecasting techniques are most accurate when the environment is ....
A. Changing inversely
B. Dynamic on the long term, so turning points can be identified

C. Not rapidly changing
D. Seasonal but not cyclical

309. On what basis are jobs grouped in order to accomplish organizational goals?
A. Departmentalization B. Centralization
C. Formalization D. Coordination

310. Organizational design is based on decisions about ....
A. Work specialization and departmentalization
B. Chain of command and span of control
C. Centralization and decentralization
D. All of these

311. Grouping activities on the basis of customer is ....
A. Functional departmentalization
B. Product departmentalization
C. Customer departmentalization
D. Geographical departmentalization

312. Today's competitive business environment has greatly increased the importance of what type of departmentation?
A. Geographic B. Customers
C. Product D. Process

313. Functional departmentation groups jobs by ....
A. Task they perform
B. Territories they serve
C. Products or services they manufacture or produce
D. Type of customer they serve

314. Assigning designers, production workers, and sales people to a common work group to develop a new product is known as a .... team.
A. Differentiated B. Product
C. Cross-functional D. Weak

315. Departmentation based on .... groups, jobs based on the territory or physical location
A. Functional B. Product
C. Geographic D. Metric

316. .... departmentation is based on the product or customer flow through the organization
A. Product B. Functional
C. Process D. Organizational structure

317. .... is the obligation or expectation to perform a duty.
A. Responsibility B. Unity of command
C. Unity of direction D. Span of control

318. .... the theory that a person should report to only one manager is called
A. Authorized line of responsibility
B. Unity of command
C. Responsibility factor
D. Chain of command

319. .... refers to the rights inherent to a position that allows a manager to tell subordinate what to do and expect them to do it.
A. Responsibility B. Unity of command
C. Chain of command D. Authority

320. The degree to which jobs are standardized and guided by rules and procedures is called ....
A. Work specialization B. Centralization
C. Decentralization D. Formalization

321. The degree to which decision making is confined at a single point in an organization is described as ....
A. Unity of command B. Chain of command
C. Span of management D. Centralization

322. In an effort make organizations more flexible and responsive to competitive pressures firms have adopted more .... decision making.
A. Centralized B. Decentralized
C. Vertically integrated D. Stable

323. A small business with low departmentalization wide spans of control, centralized authority and limited formalization can be said to posses a .... structure.
A. Simple B. Functional
C. Divisional D. Matrix

324. As the number of employees in an organization grows, structure tends to become more ....
A. Specialized B. Informal
C. Centralized D. A and B

325. When an organization assigns specialists to group according to the projects they are working on, this is called ....
A. Divisional structure B. Functional structure
C. Product structure D. Matrix structure

326. Span of management depends up on the ability of whom?
A. Employees B. Employers
C. Managers D. Subordinates

327. Who said, "Management is a multiple organ that manages a business, manages a manager and manages workers and work"?
A. Maslow B. Peter Drucker
C. Fayol D. Taylor

328. What type of control is most important for effective delegation?
A. Feed forward B. Spontaneous
C. Feedback D. None of these

329. Planning is mainly concerned with looking ahead in the future, what is it that provides the necessary raw material for correct planning?
A. TQM B. Controlling
C. Planning D. Forecasting

330. Management is the combination of Arts, Science and ....
A. Profession B. Science
C. Arts D. All the above

331. Who included Espirit De Corps as a management principle?
A. Abraham Maslow B. Henry Fayol
C. Peter Drucker D. F.W. Taylor

332. Which kind of approach did Fayol contributed to the management literature?
A. Divisional B. Scientific
C. Functional D. Professional

333. Who is called "The father of Modern Management Theory"?
A. F.W. Taylor B. Peter Drucker
C. Abraham Maslow D. Henry Fayol

334. Which need includes the basic human needs of food, clothing and shelter?
A. Physiological needs B. Psychological needs
C. Self esteem D. Self actualization

335. Many organizational problems have their root cause in what?
A. Lack of control
B. Misunderstanding
C. Lack of communication
D. None of these

336. Profession requires definite period of what?
A. Planning B. Controlling
C. Learning D. Organizing

337. Science is a body of which type of knowledge?
A. Unorganized B. Systematic
C. Structured D. Organized

338. What articulates the long-term goals of an enterprise?
A. Vision statement B. Mission
C. Objectives D. All of these

339. Who propounded the theory of X and Y?
A. Mc Cllends B. McGregor
C. Herzberg D. Fayol

340. What is essential for the management to get things done in the organization?
A. Responsibility B. Controlling
C. Delegation D. None of these

341. Name the type of the supervisor who takes care of the number being produced today?
A. Route clerk B. Time and cost clerk
C. Inspector D. Speed Boss

342. Who proposed expectancy theory of motivation?
A. Victor H Vroom B. Maslow
C. Henri Fayol D. Taylor

343. In the process of delegation, to whom is some part of the authority alotted?
A. Superiors B. Subordinates
C. Employers D. None of these

344. This is a type of motivational technique training given to the groups of managers themselves so that they may behave with and motivate their subordinates better.
A. In-basket training B. Apprenticeship
C. Sensitivity training D. Vestibule training

345. Span of control also refers to a span of what?
A. Authority B. Accountability
C. Control D. Responsibility

346. What forces managers to think about planning for results rather than merely planning activities or work?
A. Management by objectives
B. Span of management
C. Span of control
D. All of these

347. Who proposed the first theory called the hierarchy of needs theory?
A. Henri Fayol B. Abraham Maslow
C. Peter Drucker D. None of these

348. Management is a creative and .... process.
A. Systematic B. Organized
C. Continuous D. Planned

349. ...., weakness, threats, opportunities are the long form SWOT analysis.
A. Weakness B. Threat
C. Opportunity D. Strength

350. The problem solving process begins with.
A. Clarification of the situation
B. Establishment of alternatives
C. Identification of the difficulties
D. Isolation of the cause

351. Policies are sometimes defined as a ....
A. Shortcut for thinking
B. Action plan
C. Substitute for strategy
D. Substitute for management authority

352. According to Herzberg, which of the following is a maintenance factor?
A. Salary B. Work itself
C. Responsibility D. Recognition

353. Which of the following is a strength of Divisional Structure?
A. It focuses on results
B. It gains advantage due to work specialization
C. Employees have more than one boss
D. It is based solely on teams

354. Standing plan that furnish broad guidelines for channeling management thinking in specified direction are called ....

A. Single-use plan B. Programs
C. Procedures D. Policies

355. Which of the following is a factor that affects delegation of authority from the delegant's aspect?
A. Love for authority
B. Fear of exposure
C. Experiences of the superior
D. Fear of criticism

356. Fayol recognized that there was no limit to the principles of management, but he advocated 14. They included ....
A. Division of work
B. Remuneration of personnel
C. Centralization
D. All the above

357. Brech identifies four main elements of management. They are planning, control, co-ordination and ....
A. Motivation B. Centralization
C. Discipline D. Division of work

358. Which of the following might a manager be responsible for?
A. Implementing policy decisions
B. Formulating policies
C. Determining organization objectives
D. All the above

359. One of the most popular ways of defining management is that it involves getting work done.
A. Through the efforts of other people
B. As quickly as possible
C. Through the efforts of other managers
D. With as little effort as possible

360. Managers require a combination of technical competence, social and human skills and conceptual ability Conceptual ability may be defined as ....
A. The ability to view the complexities of the operations of the organization as a whole, including environmental influences
B. The ability to apply specific knowledge, methods and skills to discrete tasks
C. The ability to secure the effective use of human resources of the organization
D. All the above

361. In a detailed study of American General Managers Kotter Found that ....
A. They were all constantly setting agendas and establishing a network of co-operative relations
B. They rarely spoke to those they did not manage and often gave orders
C. They constantly set agendas but had little contact with others
D. They had no significant activities in common

362. Theory X and Theory Y represent two suppositions about human nature and behaviour at work from which styles of management are adopted. These theories were put forward by ....
A. McGregor B. Ouchi
C. Maslow D. Mayo

363. Which of the following statements is not an assumption of a manager who might adopt a Theory X style of management?
A. The intellectual potential of the average person is only partially utilized
B. The average person is lazy and has an inherent dislike of work
C. People must be threatened with punishment if the organization is to meet its objectives
D. The average person avoids responsibility

364. A Theory Y approach is more suitable where a job offers ....
A. The ability to exercise initiative
B. A high degree of intrinsic satisfaction
C. An element of problem solving
D. All of these

365. Which of the following statements about MBO is/are true?
A. Measurement of performance is in terms of the subordinates degree of accomplishment rather than the ability to follow detailed instructions on how to perform
B. Subordinates are given freedom of action to decide how to achieve objectives and targets of the organization
C. The central feature of MBO is that objectives and targets are not imposed but established and agreed through participation of subordinates with superiors
D. All of these

366. When you first turn on a computer, the COU is preset to execute instructions stored in ....
A. RAM B. Flash memory
C. ROM D. The CD-ROM

367. Which of the following is **not** a function of the control unit?
A. Read instructions B. Interpret instructions
C. Execute instructions D. Direct operations

368. What are .bas, .doc, .htm examples of in computing?
A. Extensions
B. Protocols
C. Databases
D. Other than those given as options

369. Documents converted to .... can be published to the web.
A. a doc file
B. http

C. Other than those given as options
D. HTML

370. What kind of software would you most likely use to keep track of a billing account?
A. Web authoring B. electronic publishing
C. spreadsheet D. word processing

371. A computer virus normally attaches itself to another computer program known as a ....
A. host program B. target program
C. backdoor program D. Trojan horse

372. When a file contains instructions that can be carried out by the computer. It is often called a(n) .... file.
A. Other than those given as options
B. information
C. application
D. executable

373. Data duplication wastes the space, but also promotes a more serious problem called ....
A. Isolated data
B. Data inconsistency
C. Other than those given as options
D. Program dependency

374. Which of the following is **not** a version of the Windows operating system software for the PC?
A. ME B. 98
C. XP D. 10

375. The main directory of a disk is called the .... directory.
A. network B. folder
C. root D. File

376. Which of the following is **not** an example of application software?
A. Word processing software
B. Spreadsheet software
C. Operating system software
D. Database software

377. Which of the following is **not** true about RAM?
A. RAM is the same as hard disk storage
B. RAM is a temporary storage area
C. RAM is volatile
D. RAM is a primary memory

378. The data storage hierarchy consists of ....
A. Bits, Bytes, Records, Fields, files and databases
B. Characters, fields, records, files and databases
C. Bytes, bits, fields, records, files and databases
D. Bits, bytes, fields, records, files and databases

379. = Sum (B1 B0) is an example of a ....
A. function B. cell address
C. formula D. value

380. .... are often delivered to a PC through an email attachment and are often designed to do harm.
A. Portals
B. Spam
C. Viruses
D. Other than those given as options

381. Decreasing the amount of space required to store data and programs is accomplished by ....
A. Crashing B. Disk caching
C. RAID D. file compression

382. What is the difference between a CD-ROM and CD-RW?
A. They are the same – just two different terms used by different manufacturers
B. A CD-Rom can be written to and a CD-RW cannot
C. Other than those given as options
D. A CD-RW can be written to but a CD-ROM can only be read from

383. Computer program are written in a high-level programming language, however, the human readable version of a program is called ....
A. word size B. source code
C. instruction set D. Read & Write code

384. The clock rate of a processor is measured in ....
A. megabytes or gigabytes
B. milliseconds
C. megahertz or gigahertz
D. nanoseconds

385. When cutting and pasting, the item cut is temporarily stored in the ....
A. dashboard B. ROM
C. hard drive D. clipboard

386. Copying the Excel 2007 formula = SUM (A1:A5) from cell A6 to cell B6 will result in what formula for cell B6?
A. = SUM (B6:A6) B. < SUM (A1:B6)
C. = SUM (B1:A5) D. > SUM (B1:B5)

387. RAM is used as a short memory because it—
A. has small capacity B. is very expensive
C. is programmable D. volatile

388. The Num Lock Key and Caps Lock Key are considered .... because their function changes each time you press them.
A. toggle B. dual
C. function D. cursor control

389. OLE stands for—
A. Offline Linking and Embedding
B. Online Link Emulation
C. Object Link Export
D. Object Linking and Embedding

390. Microsoft Word is an example of—
A. Application software
B. An input device
C. System software
D. A processing system

ANSWERS

1	2	3	4	5	6	7	8	9	10
D	B	B	D	D	C	D	D	B	D
11	12	13	14	15	16	17	18	19	20
B	D	D	A	C	A	D	D	B	D
21	22	23	24	25	26	27	28	29	30
C	D	B	A	D	B	D	A	D	A
31	32	33	34	35	36	37	38	39	40
A	C	D	A	C	C	A	D	D	A
41	42	43	44	45	46	47	48	49	50
A	B	A	A	C	A	B	D	B	D
51	52	53	54	55	56	57	58	59	60
A	B	B	A	B	C	A	B	B	B
61	62	63	64	65	66	67	68	69	70
D	A	A	B	A	B	D	D	B	C
71	72	73	74	75	76	77	78	79	80
A	B	C	D	A	D	A	C	A	B
81	82	83	84	85	86	87	88	89	90
A	C	A	A	B	A	C	A	B	A
91	92	93	94	95	96	97	98	99	100
A	D	C	D	B	A	D	C	C	B
101	102	103	104	105	106	107	108	109	110
C	A	B	B	A	C	B	A	A	A
111	112	113	114	115	116	117	118	119	120
B	A	B	B	B	B	D	A	B	A
121	122	123	124	125	126	127	128	129	130
B	A	B	A	A	B	C	D	B	D
131	132	133	134	135	136	137	138	139	140
C	A	C	D	A	C	B	C	A	A
141	142	143	144	145	146	147	148	149	150
A	A	A	C	B	B	A	A	A	D
151	152	153	154	155	156	157	158	159	160
D	A	D	B	A	D	A	B	C	D
161	162	163	164	165	166	167	168	169	170
B	A	A	A	A	C	B	A	B	A
171	172	173	174	175	176	177	178	179	180
D	D	D	A	A	B	C	A	A	A
181	182	183	184	185	186	187	188	189	190
A	D	B	A	B	A	A	B	D	D
191	192	193	194	195	196	197	198	199	200
A	B	C	C	A	D	D	C	A	A
201	202	203	204	205	206	207	208	209	210
C	B	D	D	D	C	D	D	D	B
211	212	213	214	215	216	217	218	219	220
D	D	B	B	D	C	C	A	A	D
221	222	223	224	225	226	227	228	229	230
D	B	A	B	C	B	C	B	D	D

231	**232**	**233**	**234**	**235**	**236**	**237**	**238**	**239**	**240**
C	A	B	B	B	C	C	D	A	B
241	**242**	**243**	**244**	**245**	**246**	**247**	**248**	**249**	**250**
B	C	B	D	C	A	D	D	B	B
251	**252**	**253**	**254**	**255**	**256**	**257**	**258**	**259**	**260**
D	D	A	D	C	A	C	B	C	C
261	**262**	**263**	**264**	**265**	**266**	**267**	**268**	**269**	**270**
C	D	A	D	B	B	B	A	C	B
271	**272**	**273**	**274**	**275**	**276**	**277**	**278**	**279**	**280**
A	D	D	C	B	A	D	B	B	B
281	**282**	**283**	**284**	**285**	**286**	**287**	**288**	**289**	**290**
D	C	A	D	C	D	C	D	D	A
291	**292**	**293**	**294**	**295**	**296**	**297**	**298**	**299**	**300**
C	A	A	C	D	A	A	A	B	A
301	**302**	**303**	**304**	**305**	**306**	**307**	**308**	**309**	**310**
B	D	B	D	C	C	A	C	A	D
311	**312**	**313**	**314**	**315**	**316**	**317**	**318**	**319**	**320**
C	B	A	C	C	C	A	B	D	D
321	**322**	**323**	**324**	**325**	**326**	**327**	**328**	**329**	**330**
D	B	A	A	D	A	B	C	D	A
331	**332**	**333**	**334**	**335**	**336**	**337**	**338**	**339**	**340**
B	C	D	A	B	C	D	A	B	C
341	**342**	**343**	**344**	**345**	**346**	**347**	**348**	**349**	**350**
D	A	B	C	D	A	B	C	D	C
351	**352**	**353**	**354**	**355**	**356**	**357**	**358**	**359**	**360**
A	A	A	D	D	D	A	A	A	A
361	**362**	**363**	**364**	**365**	**366**	**367**	**368**	**369**	**370**
A	A	A	D	D	C	D	A	D	C
371	**372**	**373**	**374**	**375**	**376**	**377**	**378**	**379**	**380**
D	D	B	A	C	C	A	D	C	C
381	**382**	**383**	**384**	**385**	**386**	**387**	**388**	**389**	**390**
D	D	B	C	D	A	D	A	D	A

OOOO

GENERAL AWARENESS

NATIONAL SYMBOLS

STATE EMBLEM

State Emblem of India is an adaptation from the Sarnath Lion Capital of Ashoka. It was adopted by the Government of India on January 26, 1950. In the adapted form, only three lions are visible, the fourth being hidden from the view. The wheel (Dharma Chakra) appears in relief in the centre of the abacus with a bull on the right and a horse on the left.

The bell-shaped lotus has been omitted. The words "Satyameva Jayate" meaning "Truth alone triumphs" are inscribed below the Emblem in Devanagari script.

NATIONAL FLAG

The National Flag of India is a horizontal tricolour of deep saffron (Kesari), white and dark green in equal proportion. In the centre of the white band there is a wheel in navy blue colour. It has 24 spokes. The ratio of the length and the breadth of the flag is 3 : 2. Its design was adopted by the Constituent Assembly of India on July 22, 1947.

NATIONAL ANTHEM

Rabindranath Tagore's song 'Jana-gana-mana' was adopted by the Constituent Assembly as the National Anthem of India on January 24, 1950.

Jana-gan-mana-adhinayaka jaya he, Bharata-bhagya-vidhata
Punjab-Sindh-Gujarat-Maratha-Dravida-Utkala-Banga
Vindhya-Himachala-Yamuna-Ganga Uchhala-jaladhi-taranga.
Tava subha name jage, Tava subha asisa mange,
Gahe tava jaya gatha,
Jana-gana-mangala-dayak, jaya he Bharata bhagya vidhata,
Jaya he, jaya he, jaya he, Jaya jaya jaya, jaya he.

NATIONAL SONG

Bankim Chandra Chatterji's 'Vande Mataram' which was a source of inspiration to the people in their struggle for freedom, has been adopted as National Song. It has an equal status with the National Anthem.

Vande Mataram
Sujalam, suphalam, malayaja-shitalam,
Shasya shyamalam, Mataram
Shubhrajyotsna,pulkita yaminim,
Phulla kusumita drumadalashobhinim,
Subhasinim sumadhura—bhashinim,
Sukhadam, Varadam, Mataram.

NATIONAL CALENDAR

It is based on the Saka era with Chaitra as its first month and a normal year of 365 days. It was adopted from March 22, 1957. Dates of the national calendar have a permanent correspondence with dates of Gregorian calendar as Chaitra I falls on March 22 in a normal year and March 21 in a leap year. In official communications, both Saka and Gregorian calendar dates are written. Months of the national calendar are Chaitra, Vaishakha, Jaishtha, Ashada, Shravan, Bhadra, Ashvina, Kartika, Margashirsha, Pausha, Magha and Phalguna.

NATIONAL ANIMAL

The magnificent tiger — Panthera tigris (Linnaeus) is the national animal of India. Tiger is found in several parts of the country and is known for its grace, strength, agility and enormous power. 'Project Tiger' was launched in 1973 to check their dwindling population in India.

NATIONAL BIRD

The Indian Peacock — Pavo Christatus (Linnaeus) is the national bird of India. It is a colourful, swan-sized bird with a fan-shaped crest of feathers on its head and a long-slander neck. The male species is more colourful with blue breast and a spectacular bronze-green train of around 200 elongated feathers.

National Flower Lotus

National Tree—Banyan

National Fruit—Mango

National Currency—Rupee '₹' (One Rupee = 100 Paise)

National Aquatic Animal—Dolphin

BOOKS AND AUTHORS

Name of Book	Author
Ain-e-Akbari	Abul Fazal
Anand Math	Bankim Chandra Chatterjee
An Unknown Indian	Nirad C. Chaudhuri
Arthshastra	Kautilya
Coolie	Mulk Raj Anand
Das Kapital	Karl Marx

Name of Book	Author
Discovery of India	Jawaharlal Nehru
Eternal India	Mrs. Indira Gandhi
Godan	Prem Chand
Gitanjali	Rabindranath Tagore
Gora	Rabindranath Tagore
Geet Govinda	Jayadeva
Harsha Charit	Bana Bhatta
Hindu View of Life	Dr. S. Radhakrishnan
India Wins Freedom	Maulana Abul Kalam Azad
Jobs of Millions	V.V. Giri
Jungle Book	Rudyard Kipling
Kamayani	Jai Shankar Prasad
Kadambari	Bana Bhatta
Life Divine	Sri Aurobindo
Last days of Netaji	G.D. Khosla
Les Miserables	Victor Hugo
Mahabharat	Veda Vyas
Macbeth	William Shakespeare
Mein Kempf	Hitler
Meghduta	Kalidas
Mother (Maa)	Maxim Gorky
Mother India	Katherine Mayo
My Experiments with Truth	Mahatma Gandhi
My Presidential Years	R. Venkataraman

Name of Book	Author
Neeti Shatak	Bhartrihari
Nehru and His Vision	Dr. K.R. Narayanan
Old Man and the Sea	Ernest Hemingway
One World	Wendell Wilkie
Panchtantra	Vishnu Sharma
Paradise Lost	John Milton
Ramayana	Valmiki (in Sanskrit)
Raghuvansham	Kalidas
Rajtarangini	Kalhan
Ram Charit Manas	Tulsi Das
Abhijnan Shakuntalam	Kalidas
Satanic Verses	Salman Rushdie
Saket	Maithili Sharan Gupta
Speed Post	Shobha De
The God of Small Things	Arundhati Roy
Treasure Island	R.L. Stevenson
Twelfth Night	William Shakespeare
Train to Pakistan	Khuswant Singh
Uttara Ram Charitra	Bhava Bhuti
Vanity Fair	W.M. Thackeray
War and Peace	Leo Tolstoy
Wealth of Nations	Adam Smith
Wake up India	Annie Besant

INVENTIONS AND DISCOVERIES

Discovery	Discoverer
Geographical Discoveries	
America	Columbus
Brazil	Cabral
North Pole	Robert Peary
Everest (Conquered)	Tabie Junko
Planetary Motion	Kepler
Hawaiian Islands	Captain Cook
South Pole	Amundsen
Solar System	Copernicus
Chemistry and Physics	
Atom Bomb	Otto Hahn
Atomic Theory	Dalton
Atomic Numbers	Moseley
Cosmic Rays	R.S. Millikan
Dynamite	Alfred Nobel
Electrons Theory	Bohr
Electricity (current)	Volta
Electric Telegraphy (Code)	S. Morse
Gravitation	Newton
Gas Light	Murdock
Oxygen	J. Priestly
Photography	L. Daguerre

Discovery	Discoverer
Printing for the blind	Louis Braille
Radium	Madame Curie
Telegraph	Samuel Morse
Television	J.L. Baird
Telephone	Graham Bell
Wireless	G. Marconi
X-rays	W.K. Roentgen
Mechanical	
Aeroplane	Wright Brothers
Bicycle	Macmillan
Computer	Charles Babbage
Dynamo	Michal Faraday
Diesel Engine	Rudolf Diesel
Engine (Railway)	Stephenson
Fountain Pen	Waterman
Gramophone	Edison
Locomotive Power of Steam	James Watt
Helicopter	Brequet
Life Boat	Henry Greathead
Microscope	Z. Jansen
Printing Press	Gutenberg
Revolver	Colt

Discovery	Discoverer
Sewing Machine	Elias Howe
Thermometer	Fahrenheit
Transistor	W. Shockley
Typewriter	Sholes
Telescope	Hans Lippershey
Tank (Military)	Swinton
Medical	
Antiseptic Surgery	Lord Joseph Lister
Bacteria	Leeuwenhock
Circulation of Blood	William Harvey

Discovery	Discoverer
Homoeopathy (Discovered)	Hahnemann
Insulin	F. Banting
Penicillin	Alexander Flemming
Malaria Parasite	Dr. Ronald Ross
Stethoscope	Laennec
Vitamins	Funk
Anti-Rabies Treatment	Pasteur
General	
Nylon	Carouthers
Science of Geometry	Euclids

WORLD'S GEOGRAPHICAL SURNAMES

• City of Sky-scrapers—New York • City of Seven Hills—Rome • City of Dreaming Spires—Oxford • City of Golden Gate—San Francisco • City of Magnificent Buildings—Washington D.C. • City of Eternal Springs—Quito (S. America) • China's Sorrow—Hwang Ho • Cockpit of Europe Belgium • Dark Continent—Africa • Emerald Isle—Ireland • Eternal City—Rome • Empire City—New York • Forbidden City—Lhasa (Tibet) • Garden City—Chicago • Gate of Tears—Strait of Bab-el-Mandeb • Gift of the Nile—Egypt • Granite City—Aberdeen (Scotland) • Hermit Kingdom—Korea • Herring Pond—Atlantic Ocean • Holy Land—Jerusalem • Island Continent—Australia • Islands of Cloves—Zanzibar • Isle of Pearls—Bahrein (Persian Gulf) • Key to the Mediterranean—Gibralter • Land of Cakes—Scotland • Land of Golden Fleece—Australia • Land of Maple Leaf—Canada • Land of Morning Calm—Korea • Land of Midnight Sun—Norway • Land of the Thousand Lakes—Finland • Land of the Thunderbolt—Bhutan • Land of White Elephant—Thailand • Land of Thousand Elephants—Laos • Land of Rising Sun Japan • Loneliest Island—Tristan De Gunha (Mid-Atlantic) • Manchester of Japan—Osaka • Pillars of Hercules—Strait of Gibraltar • Pearl of the Antilles—Cuba • Playground of Europe—Switzerland • Quaker City—Philadelphia • Queen of the Adriatic—Venice • Roof of the World—The Pamirs, Central Asia • Sugar bowl of the world—Cuba • Venice of the North—Stockholm • Windy City—Chicago • Whiteman's grave—Guinea Coast of Africa • Yellow River—Huang Ho (China) • Sickman of Europe—Turkiye

CURRENCIES OF DIFFERENT COUNTRIES

Country	Currency
Australia	Australian Dollar
Bangladesh	Taka
Belgium	Euro
Britain	Pound (Sterling)
Myanmar	Kyat
Canada	Canadian Dollar
Germany	Euro
Iran	Rial
India	Rupee
Sri Lanka	Rupee
China	Yuan
Czech Republic	Koruna
Denmark	Krone
France	Euro
Pakistan	Rupee

Country	Currency
Poland	Zloty
Spain	Euro
Indonesia	Rupiah
Iraq	Dinar
Italy	Euro
Japan	Yen
Mexico	Peso
The Netherland	Euro
European Union	Euro
Sweden	Krona
Switzerland	Swiss Franc
Turkiye	Lira
U.A.E.	Dirham
U.S.A.	Dollar
Russia	Rouble

CAPITAL OF COUNTRIES

Country	Capital	Country	Capital
Austria	Vienna	Kenya	Nairobi
Afghanisatan	Kabul	Kuwait	Kuwait
Algeria	Algiers	Laos	Vientiane
Angola	Luanda	Lebanon	Beirut
Australia	Canberra	Mexico	Mexico City
Argentina	Buenos Aires	Malaysia	Kualalumpur
Bangladesh	Dhaka	Morocco	Rabat
Belgium	Brussels	Mozambique	Maputo
Bolivia	Lapaz	New Zealand	Welington
Bulgaria	Sofia	Netherlands	Amsterdam
Bhutan	Thimpu	Panama	Panama City
Brazil	Brasilia	Portugal	Lisbon
Canada	Ottawa	Poland	Warsaw
China	Beijing	Sri Lanka	Colombo
Cyprus	Nicosia	Sweden	Stockholm
Columbia	Bagota	Switzerland	Bern
Denmark	Copenhegan	Sudan	Khartoum
Ethiopia	Addis Ababa	Sierra Leone	Freetown
Finland	Helsinki	South Africa	Capetown
France	Paris	Saudi Arabia	Riyadh
Germany	Berlin	Spain	Madrid
Greece	Athens	Thailand	Bangkok
Guatemala	Guatemala City	Turkiye	Ankara
Hungary	Budapest	Russia	Moscow
Iran	Tehran	Azerbaijan	Baku
India	New Delhi	Armenia	Yerevan
Indonesia	Jakarta	Latvia	Riga
Iraq	Baghdad	Ukrain	Kiev
Italy	Rome	U.S.A.	Washington
Ireland	Dublin	U.K.	London
Japan	Tokyo	Egypt	Cairo
Combodia	Phnom Penh	Vietnam	Hanoi
Korea (North)	Pyong Yang	Zambia	Lusaka
Korea (South)	Seoul		

INDIAN CITIES AND THEIR RIVERS

City	State	River	City	State	River
Agra	U.P.	Yamuna	Kanpur	Uttar Pradesh	Ganga
Ahmedabad	Gujarat	Sabarmati	Ludhiana	Punjab	Sutlej
Prayagraj	U.P.	Confluence of the Ganga, Yamuna, and invisible Saraswati	Lucknow	Uttar Pradesh	Gomati
			Nasik	Maharashtra	Godavari
			Patna	Bihar	Ganga
			Srinagar	J & K	Jhelum
Alwaye	Kerala	Periyar	Surat	Gujarat	Tapti
Kolkata	West Bengal	Hooghly	Tiruchirapally	Tamil Nadu	Kaveri
Cuttack	Odisha	Mahanadi	Ujjain	Madhya Pradesh	Shipra
Delhi	Delhi	Yamuna	Vijayawada	Andhra Pradesh	Krishna
Haridwar	Uttarakhand	Ganga	Varanasi	Uttar Pradesh	Ganga

WONDERS OF THE WORLD

Seven Wonders of the Ancient World: (1) the Pyramids of Egypt, built in approximately 2700 BC; (2) the Hanging Gardens at Babylon; (3) the temple of Artemis at Emphesus; (4) the statue of Zeus at Olympia; (5) the tomb of Mausolus at Halicarnassus, built in nearly 350 BC; (6) the Colossus of Rhodes, built in nearly 280 BC; (7) the Pharos Lighthouse at Alexandria.

Seven Wonders of the Medieval World: (1) the Colosseum of Rome; (2) the Great Wall of China; (3) the Porcelain Tower of Nanking; (4) the Mosque at St. Sophia (Constantinople); (5) Stonehenge; (6) the Catacombs of Rome; (7) the Leaning Tower of Pisa.

Seven New Wonders of the World: (1) Taj Mahal of Agra (India); (2) Pyramid at Chichen Itza (Mexico); (3) Machu Picchu (Peru); (4) Statue of Christ The Redeemer (Brazil); (5) Great Wall of China; (6) Roman Colosseum, Italy; (7) Ruins of Petra, Jordan.

STATES AND UNION TERRITORIES OF INDIA (CAPITALS, PRINCIPAL LANGUAGES)

States/Union Territories	*Capitals*	*Principal Languages*
■ Andhra Pradesh	Amravati	Telgu and Urdu
■ Arunachal Pradesh	Itanagar	Monpa, Adi, Nissi etc.
■ Assam	Dispur	Assamese and Bengali
■ Bihar	Patna	Hindi and Maithili
■ Chhattishgarh	Raipur	Hindi
■ Goa	Panaji	Konkani
■ Gujarat	GandhiNagar	Gujarati
■ Haryana	Chandigarh	Hindi
■ Himachal Pradesh	Shimla	Hindi and Pahari
■ Jharkhand	Ranchi	Hindi
■ Kerala	Thiruvananthpuram	Malyalam
■ Karnataka	Bengluru	Kannada
■ Madhya Pradesh	Bhopal	Hindi
■ Maharashtra	Mumbai	Marathi
■ Meghalaya	Shillong	Khashi, Jayantia and Garo
■ Manipur	Imphal	Manipuri
■ Mizoram	Aizawl	Mizo and English
■ Nagaland	Kohima	Naga, Assamese and English
■ Odisha	Bhubaneshwar	Odiya
■ Punjab	Chandigarh	Punjabi
■ Rajasthan	Jaipur	Hindi, Rajasthani
■ Sikkim	Gangtok	Sikkimese and Lepcha
■ Tamil Nadu	Chennai	Tamil
■ Tripura	Agartala	Bengali, Tripuri
■ Uttar Pradesh	Lucknow	Hindi
■ Uttarakhand	Dehradun	Hindi
■ West Bengal	Kolkata	Bengali
■ Telangana	Hyderabad	Telgu and Urdu
■ Jammu & Kashmir	Srinagar/Jammu	Kashmiri, Dongri, Urdu, Dardi and Pahari
■ Andaman and Nicobar Islands	Sri Vijaya Puram	Hindi, Nicobarese, Bengali, Malayalam, Tamil, Telugu
■ Chandigarh	Chandigarh	Hindi, Punjabi, English
■ Dadar and Nagar Haveli and Daman and Diu	Daman	Gujarati, Hindi
■ Delhi	Delhi	Hindi, Punjabi
■ Lakshadweep	Kavaratti	Malayalam
■ Puducherry	Puducherry	Tamil, Telugu, Malayalam, English and French
■ Ladakh	Leh	Ladakhi

HIGH COURTS IN INDIA

Name	Year	Territorial Jurisdiction	Seat
Allahabad	1866	Uttar Pradesh	Prayagraj (Bench at Lucknow)
Andhra Pradesh	2019	Andhra Pradesh	Amaravati
Bombay	1862	Maharashtra, Goa, Dadar & Nagar Haveli and Daman & Diu	Mumbai (Benches at Nagpur, Panaji and Aurangabad (Sambhaji Nagar)
Calcutta	1862	West Bengal and Andaman & Nicobar Islands	Kolkata (Circuit Benchs at Port Blair (Shri Vijaya Puram) and Jalpaiguri
Chhattisgarh	2000	Chhattisgarh	Bilaspur
Delhi	1966	Delhi	Delhi
Gauhati	1948	Assam, Nagaland, Mizoram and Arunachal Pradesh	Guwahati (Benches at Kohima, Aizawl and Itanagar)
Gujarat	1960	Gujarat	Ahmedabad
Himachal Pradesh	1971	Himachal Pradesh	Shimla
Jammu & Kashmir and ladakh	1928	Jammu & Kashmir, Ladakh	Srinagar and Jammu
Jharkhand	2000	Jharkhand	Ranchi
Karnataka	1884	Karnataka	Bengaluru (Circuit Benches at Dharwar and Gulbarga)
Kerala	1958	Kerala & Lakshadweep	Ernakulam
Madhya Pradesh	1956	Madhya Pradesh	Jabalpur (Benches at Gwalior and Indore)
Madras	1862	Tamil Nadu & Puducherry	Chennai (Bench at Madurai)
Orissa	1948	Odisha	Cuttack
Patna	1916	Bihar	Patna
Punjab and Haryana	1966	Punjab, Haryana and Chandigarh	Chandigarh
Rajasthan	1949	Rajasthan	Jodhpur (Bench at Jaipur)
Sikkim	1975	Sikkim	Gangtok
Uttarakhand	2000	Uttarakhand	Nainital
Tripura	2013	Tripura	Agartala
Telangana	2019	Telangana	Hyderabad
Meghalaya	2013	Meghalaya	Shillong
Manipur	2013	Manipur	Imphal

FAMOUS HILL STATION

	Hill Station		State/UT
1.	Almora, Mussoorie Nainital	:	Uttarakhand
2.	Cherrapunji (Shillong), Khasi Hills (Shillong)	:	Meghalaya
3.	Ooty, Kodaikanal Yereaud	:	Tamil Nadu
4.	Dalhousie, Kassauli	:	Himachal Pradesh
5.	Darjeeling	:	West Bengal
6.	Gulmarg, Srinagar	:	Jammu and Kashmir
7.	Mahabaleshwar	:	Maharashtra
8.	Mt. Abu	:	Rajasthan
9.	Panchmarhi	:	Madhya Pradesh
10.	Ranchi	:	Jharkhand

FAMOUS NATIONAL PARKS

1. Corbett National Park : Nainital, Uttarakhand
2. Dudhwa National Park : Lakhimpur Kheri, UP
3. Kaziranga National Park : Jorhat, Assam
4. Kanha National Park : Jabalpur, Bhedaghat
5. Gir National Park : Rajkot, Junagarh, Gujarat
6. Guindy National Park : Guindy, Chennai, Tamil Nadu
7. Nagairhole National Park : Coorg, Karnataka
8. Bandipur National Park : Mysore, Karnataka

FAMOUS NATIONAL WILDLIFE SANCTUARIES

1. Dachigam Wildlife Sanctuary : Srinagar, Jammu and Kashmir
2. Sariska : Alwar, Rajasthan
3. Hazaribagh Wildlife Sanctuary : Hazaribagh, Jharkhand
4. Tiger Project : Sawai Madhopur, Rajasthan
5. Mudhumali Wildlife Sanctuary : Mudhumalia, Nilgiri, Tamil Nadu
6. Periyar Wildlife Sanctuary : Idukki, Kottayam, Kerala

HOLY PLACES IN INDIA

1. Amarnath	Jammu and Kashmir
2. Ayodhya	Uttar Pradesh
3. Badrinath	Uttarakhand
4. Dwarka	Gujarat
5. Haridwar	Uttarakhand
6. Kancheepuram	Tamil Nadu
7. Kedarnath	Uttarakhand
8. Mathura	Uttar Pradesh
9. Puri	Odisha
10. Rameswaram	Tamil Nadu
11. Tirupati	Andhra Pradesh
12. Ujjain	Madhya Pradesh
13. Varanasi	Uttar Pradesh
14. Bodh Gaya	Bihar

SPORTS

Terms Associated With Sports :

Cricket : Ashes, Bye, Bodyline, Bowling, Break, Cover-point, Creases, Chinaman, Chucker, Drive, Duck, Follow on, Googly, Hit-Wicket, Hat-trick, Leg-before-wicket, Leg break, Leg-bye, Maiden over, No ball, Night-watchman, Runner, Run-out, Stumped, Silly-point, Slip.

Football : Handball, Corner kick, Dribble, Free Kick, Hat-trick, Off-side, Penalty Kick, Try, Throw in, Wembley.

Hockey : Bully, Carry, Corner kick, Corner, Penalty stroke, Off-side, Penalty, Roll in scoop, Sticks, Sudden death, Striking circle, Short Corner, Scoop, Tie-breaker, Under-cutting, Hat-trick.

Tennis : Backhand drive, Deuce, Fault, Half-volley, Net, Let, Volley, Smash, Service.

Billiards : Break, Cannons, Cue, Pot, Jigger, Scratch, In Bauk, In, Off.

Bridge : Dummy, Finesse, Grand-slam, Little Slam, Revoke, Ruff slam, Trump, Tricks, Vulnerable.

Volley Ball : Booster, Love, Service, Volley, Smasher.

Badminton : Smash, Drop, Let.

Chess : Check, Checkmate, Gambit, State-mate.

Golf : Bogy, Caddie, Hole, Links, Stymie, Tee, Put.

Polo : Chukker, Mallet, Bunder.

Baseball : Bunting, Diamond, Pitcher, Put-out, Strike, Home.

Boxing : Knockout, Punch, Upper-cut, Jab, Hook.

FAMOUS TROPHIES

Agha Khan Cup	Hockey
Beighton Cup	Hockey
Corbillion Cup	World Table Tennis (Women)
Davis Cup	Lawn Tennis
Duleep Trophy	Cricket
Durand Cup	Football
Ezra Cup	Polo
I.F.A. Shield	Football
Irani Cup	Cricket (India)
Jayalaxmi Cup	Table Tennis (Women)
Lady Rattan Tata Trophy	Hockey (Women)
Nehru Cup	Hockey (India)
Obaidullah Cup	Hockey
Ranji Trophy	Cricket (India)
Rangaswamy Cup	Hockey (India)
Rovers Cup	Football (India)
Santosh Trophy	Football (India)
Subroto Cup	Football
Thomas Cup	Badminton
Uber Cup	Badminton (Women)
Wellington Trophy	Rowing (India)

BIGGEST, LARGEST, TALLEST OF THE WORLD

Largest Desert	Sahara (Africa)
Tallest Statue	Statue of Unity (India)
Rainiest Place	Mowsynram near Cherrapunjee (Meghalaya, India)
Biggest Ocean	Pacific Ocean
Deepest Ocean	Pacific Ocean
Largest Mammal	Whale
Fastest Animal	Cheetah
Lightest Substance	Hydrogen gas
Longest River	Nile
Highest Waterfalls	Salto Angel Falls (Venezuela)
Tallest Animal	Giraffe
Largest Bird (Land)	Ostrich
Hardest Mineral	Diamond
Largest Delta	Sunderbans (W.B. India)
Largest Museum	American Museum of Natural History (New York)
Longest Day	June, 21
Shortest Day	December, 22
Biggest Army	People's Liberation Army, China
Largest Salt Water Lake	Caspian Sea
Highest Mountain Peak	Everest (8848 metre high)
Longest Wall	Great Wall of China
Largest Peninsula	Arabia
Largest Planet	Jupiter
Smallest Continent	Australia
Largest Lake	Caspian Sea

Deepest Lake	Baikal, 3200 ft.
Finest Harbour	Sydney Harbour
Smallest Planet	Mercury
Largest Continent	Asia
Planet nearest to the Sun	Mercury
Longest Highway Tunnel	Laerdal Tunnel (Norway)
Highest Building	Burj Khalifa, Dubai
Country Biggest	Russia (17075000 sq. km.)
Electorate, Largest	India (over 90 crores)
Longest Epic	Mahabharat
Island, Biggest in the World	Greenland
Population, Largest	China
Longest Railway Platform	Shree Siddharoodha Swamiji Railway Station Hubballi, Karnataka (India)
Swimming Course	English Channel

FIRST IN INDIA

Governor General of Independent India — Lord Mountbatten

Cosmonaut — Sq. Ldr. Rakesh Sharma

Field Marshal — S.H.F.J. Manekshaw

Indian Governor General of Indian Union — C. Rajagopalachari

Indian I.C.S. Officer — Satyendra Nath Tagore

Indian to swim across English Channel — Mihir Sen

Indian Women to swim across English Channel — Miss Arti Saha

Man to climb Mount Everest — Tenzing Norgay

Man to climb Mount Everest without Oxygen — Phu Dorjee

Man to climb Mount Everest twice — Nwang Gombu

Nobel Prize Winner — Rabindra Nath Tagore

President of Indian National Congress — W.C. Banerjee

President of Indian Republic — Dr. Rajendra Prasad

Talkie Film — Alam Ara (1931)

Test Tube Baby (Documented) — Indira

Viceroy of India — Lord Canning

Woman Minister of Indian Union — Rajkumari Amrit Kaur

Woman Governor — Mrs. Sarojini Naidu

Woman President of Indian National Congress — Dr. Annie Besant

Woman Prime Minister — Mrs. Indira Gandhi

Chief of Defence Staff (CDS) — General Bipin Rawat

Woman Speaker of a State Assembly — Mrs. Shanno Devi

Prime Minister of India — Pt. Jawaharlal Nehru

Muslim President of Indian Union — Dr. Zakir Hussain

Speaker of Lok Sabha — G.V. Mavlankar

Women to Climb Mount Everest — Bachhendri Pal

Woman Judge in Supreme Court — Mrs. Meera Sahib Fatima Biwi

Women Chief Justice of a High Court — Smt. Leela Seth

The First Indian Weightlifter to Win bronze medal in Olympics — Karnam Malleshwari (Sydney, in 2000)

World Chess Champion — Vishwanathan Anand

India's First Woman Merchant Navy Officer — Sonali Banerjee

The First Woman Air Vice-Marshal — P. Bandopadhyaya

The First Indian to be appointed as United Nations Civilian Police Advisor — Ms. Kiran Bedi

The First Women to be appointed Deputy Governor of Reserve Bank of India — K.J. Udeshi

The First Indian Lady to win a medal in World Athletic Championship — Anju Bobby George

The First Sikh Prime Minister of India — Dr. Manmohan Singh

IMPORTANT DAYS

✶ **January**

5-11	Road Safety Week
12	National Youth Day
15	Army Day
23	National Day of Patriotism
26	Republic Day
30	Martyr's Day

✶ **FEBRUARY**

1-14	Oil Conservation Fortnight
14	Valentine's Day

✶ **MARCH**

4	National Safety Day
8	International Women's Day
15	Consumers' Day
21	World Forest Day
22	World Day for Water
24	World Meteorological Day

✶ **APRIL**

7	World Health Day
7-13	Handloom Week
14-20	Fire Service Week
18	World Heritage Day
22	World Earth Day

✶ **MAY**

1	May Day
5	National Labour Day
8	World Red Cross Day

11 National Technology Day
15 International Day of the Family
17 World Telecommunication Day
24 Commonwealth Day
31 World No-Tobacco Day

✶ **JUNE**

5 World Environment Day
21 International Day of Yoga
26 International Day against Drug Abuse and Illicit Trafficking

✶ **JULY**

11 World Population Day

✶ **AUGUST**

1-7 World Breast feeding Week
10 Sanskrit Divas
15 Independence Day
20 Sadbhavana Divas

✶ **SEPTEMBER**

1-7 National Nutrition Week
5 Teachers' Day
8 International Literary Day
14 Hindi Diwas
23 World Deaf Day
27 World Tourism Day

✶ **OCTOBER**

2 ✶ Gandhi Jayanti
✶ International Day of Non Violence
✶ Anti-Leprosy Day
4 World Animal Day
6 World Habitat Day (Ist Monday)
8 Indian Air Force Day
14 World Standard Day
15 International Day of Rural Women
16 World Food Day
24 United Nations Day
27 Infantry Day
28 World Thrift Day
31 Anti-Terrorism Day

✶ **NOVEMBER**

2 All Saints Day
14 Children's Day
15-21 National Cooperative Week
19 25 Quami Ekta Week
20 Child Rights Day
26 Constitution Day

✶ **DECEMBER**

1 World AIDS Day
3 World Day for the Disabled
4 Naval Day
7 Flag Day
8 SMRC Day
10 Human Rights Day
14 National Energy Conservation Day

PARLIAMENTS OF IMPORTANT COUNTRIES

Afghanistan	—	Shora
Britain	—	Parliament House of Commons, House of Lords
Denmark	—	Folketing
The Netherlands	—	States General
India	—	Sansad
Israel	—	Knesset
Iran	—	Majlis
Ireland	—	Airetann
Iceland	—	Althing
Japan	—	Diet
Norway	—	Storting
Russia	—	Supreme Soviet
Spain	—	Cortes
Sweden	—	Riksdag
U.S.A.	—	Congress Senate
Germany	—	Bundestag

MINERAL RESOURCES OF THE WORLD

Articles	Producers	Articles	Producers
Aluminium	China	Asbestos	Russia
Boxide	Australia	Chromium	South Africa
Copper	Chile	Cobalt	Congo (Kinshasa)
Diamonds	Russia	Gold	China
Iron-ore	China	Lead	China
Platinum	South Africa	Silver	Mexico
Silicon	China	Sulfur	China
Tin	China	Titanium	China
Tungsten	China		

TEN LARGEST COUNTRIES AND THEIR AREAS

Rank by Area	Country	Area (sq. km.)
1.	Russia	17,075,400
2.	Canada	9,976,139
3.	China	9,561,000
4.	U.S.A.	9,363,123
5.	Brazil	8,511,965
6.	Australia	7,686,848
7.	India	3,287,263
8.	Argentina	2,776,889
9.	Kazakhstan	2,724,900
10.	Algeria	2,381,741

PRESIDENT OF INDIA

He is the constitutional head of the Republic but not the real executive.

Qualifications: (1) Indian citizen; (2) age not less than 35 years; (3) should have qualifications for election to Lok Sabha; (4) should not hold any office of profit; (5) should not be a Member of Parliament or State Legislature.

Election: He is elected by the elected Members of Parliament and State Legislative Assemblies in accordance with the system of proportional representation by means of single transferable vote.

Powers: He makes appointment to all the Constitutional posts. He can address either House of Parliament and send message to them. He can summon and prorogue either House of Parliament and dissolve Lok Sabha. All Bills passed by Parliament must receive his assent to become an Act. He issues Ordinance when Parliament is not in session. No money Bill can be introduced in Lok Sabha without his recommendation. He can grant pardon, reprieve or remit punishment and he can commute death sentences. He can declare national emergency, state emergency and financial emergency.

VICE-PRESIDENT OF INDIA

The Vice-President acts as the ex-officio Chairman of Rajya Sabha and acts as the President when the latter is unable to discharge his functions due to illness, absence or any other reason, or till the election of a new President when a vacancy is caused by the death, resignation or removal of the President.

The Vice-President is elected by an electoral college consisting of the members of both Houses of Parliament in accordance with the system of proportional representation by means of the single transferable vote. He must be a citizen of India, not less than 35 years of age, and should be eligible for election as a member of the Council of States.

COUNCIL OF MINISTERS

Council of Ministers is to aid and advise the President in exercise of his functions. Prime Minister and other ministers are appointed by the President.

Cabinet: Every member of the Council of Ministers is not a Cabinet Minister. Cabinet is a small body consisting of only senior members of Council of Ministers. The Cabinet functions like the executive committee of the Council of Ministers.

PRIME MINISTER OF INDIA

Art. 74(1) of our Constitution states that the Prime Minister shall be at the head of council of ministers. He has the power of selecting and advising the President to dismiss them individually. He is the chairman of the cabinet. Art. 78 provides that it shall be the duty of the Prime minister –

- To communicate to the president all the decisions of the council of ministers relating to the administration of the affairs of the union and proposals for legislation.
- To furnish such information relating to the administration of the affairs of the union and proposals for legislation as the president may call for and
- If the President so requires to submit for the consideration of the council of ministers any matter on which a decision has been taken by a minister but which has not been considered by the council.

THE SOLAR SYSTEM: SOME FACTS

Number of Planets: 8—Mercury, Venus, Earth, Mars, Jupiter, Saturn, Uranus and Neptune.

Largest most

Massive planet .... Jupiter
Brightest planet .... Venus
Brightest star .... Sirius
Fastest orbiting planet .... Mercury
Longest (Synodic) day .... Mercury
Planet with largest moon .... Jupiter
Greatest average density .... Jupiter
Tallest mountain .... Earth
Strongest magnetic fields .... Jupiter
Most circular orbit .... Venus
Shortest (synodic) day .... Jupiter
Hottest planet .... Venus
No moons .... Mercury, Venus
Planet with moon with most eccentric orbit ...... Neptune
Lowest average density .... Saturn
Greatest amount of liquid on the surface .... Earth

THE EARTH: FACTS AND DATA

Composition of the Earth: Aluminium (0.4%), Sulphur (2.7%), Silicon (13%), Oxygen (28%), Calcium (1.2%), Nickel (2.7%), Magnesium (17%), Iron (35%)

Surface area	: 510100500 sq km
Land Surface (29.1%)	: 148950800 sq km
Ocean Surface (70.9%)	: 361149700 sq km
Type of water	: 97% salt, 3% fresh
Total area of water	: 382672000 sq km
Equatorial diameter	: 12753 km
Equatorial Circumference	: 40066 km
Polar Circumference	: 39992 km
Polar diameter	: 12710 km
Equatorial radius	: 6376 km
Polar radius	: 6335 km

Mass (estimated weight)	: 594×10^{19} metric tons
Mean distance from the Sun	: 149407000 km
Earth's orbit speed (around sun)	: 107320 kmph
Period of Revolution (round the sun)	: 365 days 5 hrs 48 min. 45.51 seconds
Time of Rotation (on its axis)	: 23 hrs 56 min 4.09 seconds
Inclination of the axis (to the plane of the ecliptic)	: 23°27'

PRINCIPAL MOUNTAIN PEAKS OF THE WORLD

	Mountains	Height in Metres	Range	Date of First Ascent
1.	Mount Everest	8,848	Himalayas	May 29, 1953
2.	K-2 (Godwin Austen)	8,611	Karakoram	July 31, 1954
3.	Kanchenjunga	8,597	Himalayas	May 25, 1955
4.	Lhotse	8,511	Himalayas	May 18, 1956
5.	Makalu I	8,481	Himalayas	May 15, 1955
6.	Dhaulagiri I	8,167	Himalayas	May 13, 1960
7.	Mansalu I	8,156	Himalayas	May 9, 1956
8.	Chollyo	8,153	Himalayas	Oct. 19, 1954
9.	Nanga Parbat	8,124	Himalayas	July 3, 1953
10.	Annapurna I	8,091	Himalayas	June 3, 1950
11.	Gasherbrum I	8,068	Karakoram	July 5, 1958
12.	Broad Peak I	8,047	Karakoram	June 9, 1957
13.	Gasherbrum II	8,034	Karakoram	July 7, 1956
14.	Shisha Pangma (Gosainthan)	8,014	Himalayas	May 2, 1964
15.	Gasherbrum III	7,952	Karakoram	Aug. 11, 1975

POPULAR NICK NAMES OF SOME FAMOUS PERSONALITIES

Andhra Kesari	T. Prakasam
Anna	C.N. Anna Durai
Bang Bandhu	Sheikh Mujibur Rehman
Bapu	Mahatma Gandhi
Bard of Avon	William Shakespeare
Desh Bandhu	C.R. Das
Frontier Gandhi	Khan Abdul Gaffar Khan
Fuhrer	Adolf Hitler
Grand Old Man of India	Dadabhai Naoroji
Grand Old Man of Britain	Gladstone
Guru Dev	Rabindra Nath Tagore
Guruji	M.S. Golwalkar
Iron Man of India	Sardar Patel
Lok Nayak	Jayaprakash Narayan
Lady with the Lamp	Florence Nightingale
Lal, Bal, Pal	Lala Lajpat Rai, Bal Gangadhar Tilak, Bipin Chandra Pal
Little Corporal	Napoleon Bonaparte
Lokmanya	Bal Gangadhar Tilak
Mahamana	Pt. Madan Mohan Malaviya
Maid of Orleans	Joan of Arc
Missile Man	A.P.J. Abdul Kalam
Man of Destiny	Napoleon Bonaparte
Netaji	Subhash Chandra Bose
Nightingale of India	Sarojini Naidu
Panditji	Jawaharlal Nehru
Punjab Kesari	Lala Lajpat Rai
Shastriji	Lal Bahadur Shastri
Uncle Ho	Ho Chi Minh
Wizard of the North	Walter Scott

FAMOUS INTERNATIONAL ORGANISATIONS, HEADQUARTERS AND YEAR OF ESTABLISHMENT

International Organisations	*Headquarters*	*Year of Establishment*
United Nations Organisations (U.N.O.)	New York	1945
International Monetary Fund (I.M.F.)	Washington D.C.	1945
World Health Organisation (W.H.O.)	Geneva	1948
Food & Agricultural Organisation (FAO)	Rome	1945
International Labour Organisation (ILO)	Geneva	1919
UNESCO	Paris	1946
International Court of Justice	The Hague	1946
Universal Postal Union (UPU)	Berne	1874
International Civil Aviation Organisation (ICAO)	Montreal	1945
UNIDO	Vienna	1966
International Atomic Energy Agency (IAEA)	Vienna	1957
International Finance Corporation (IFC)	Washington	1956
United Nations Development Programme (UNDP)	New York	1965
UNICEF	New York	1946
International Maritime Organisation (IMO)	London	1948
World Meteorological Organisation (WMO)	Geneva	1950
International Telecommunication Union (ITU)	Geneva	1865
Arab League	Cairo	1945
Commonwealth of Nations	London	1949
World Trade Organisation (WTO)	Geneva	1995
International Development Association (IDA)	Washington D.C.	1960
International Bank for Reconstruction and Development (IBRD)	Washington D.C.	1945
World Intellectual Property Organisation (WIPO)	Geneva	1967
Organisation of Islamic Conference (OIC)	Jeddah (Saudi Arabia)	1969
European Union (EU)	Brussels	Changed form of EEC Established in 1958
Red Cross	Geneva	1863
Interpol	Lyons	1923
Asian Development Bank (ADB)	Manila	1966
North Atlantic Treaty Organisation (NATO)	Brussels	1949
Association of South East Asian Nations (ASEAN)	Jakarta	1967

ART AND CULTURE

☞ Classical Dances

Dance	*State*	*Famous Artists*
Bharat Natyam	Tamil Nadu	Yamini Krishnamurthy, Rukmini Devi Arundale, Swapna Sundari, Sonal Mansingh, Vaijanti Mala, Mrinalini Sarabhai, Chandralekha, Indrani, Ram Gopal, Bal Saraswati
Kathakali	Kerala	Gopinath, K.K. Nayar, Kunju-Kurup, T.K. Chandu
Kuchipudi	Andhra Pradesh/ Telangana	Sapna Sundari, Raja Reddy, Shobha Nayar, Radha Reddy, Vedantam Satyanarayan, Vimpanti Chinna Satyam.
Kathak	North India	Birju Maharaj, Gopi Krishna, Shambhu Maharaj, Sitara Devi, Vishnu Sharma, Durga Lal, Shobhana Narayan
Odissi	Odisha	Kelucharan Mahapatra, Indrani Rehman, Madhavi Mudgal, Pratima Bedi, Samyukta Panigrahi, Sonal Mansingh, Debudas
Manipuri	Manipur	Uday Shankar, Bipin Singh, Suryamukhi, Darohra Jhaveri

☞ Famous Folk Dances

State/UT	Folk Dance
Andhra Pradesh/ Telangana	Dandari, Banjara
Assam	Bihu, Keli Gopal, Sataria
Bihar	Chhau, Magahi, Durga dance
W. Bengal	Kirtan, Kalatri, Asweabadh, Brita, Kalidance
Chhattisgarh	Saila, Karama, Bhagoria
Gujarat	Garba, Rasalila, Tippani, Dandia,
Haryana	Damyal, Lahoor
Himachal Pradesh	Dussehra dance, Hikat, Notio
J&K	Dumhal, Kud
Ladakh	Spao, Jabro, Brokpa
Jharkhand	Jhau, Ghumakudia, Jadur, Sarhul, Soharai, Karama, Vaima, Loojhari, Jat-Jatin, Vidayat
Karnataka	Yakshagan, Dolu Kunitha
Kerala	Mohini Attam, Padayuni
Madhya Pradesh	Lota Nritya, Jawara
Maharashtra	Tamasha, Dahi Handi, Gof, Deepak Dindi
Manipur	Dhol Cholam
Meghalaya	Nongakarem
Nagaland	Bamboo dance
Odisha	Chhau, Maya Shabari, Dalachai
Punjab	Gidda, Bhangra, Panihari
Rajasthan	Thumar, Kathaputali, Tera Tali
Tamil Nadu	Terukalathu, Kabalatam, Kargam, Pulivesham
Tripura	Hazagiri
Uttar Pradesh	Rasalila, Nautanki, Thali, Dhurang, Jhumela, Huraka, Bol.
Uttarakhand	Kajari, Karan
Goa	Dhode Modini

MUSIC

Main Schools of Classical Music

- There are two main schools of classical music, namely, the Hindustani and the Carnatic. The Hindustani school of classical music is in vogue in north-western India, eastern India and northern parts of the South India.

Musical Instruments

- *They are:* Tabla, Mridangam, Pakhawaj, Chandai, Dholak, Veena, Sitar, Sarod, Gootuvadhyam, Sarangi, Flute, Nadaswaram, Shehnai, Shringi and Turahi.

NATIONAL AWARDS

Bharat Ratna

- Bharat Ratna is India's highest Civilian Award. It was first awarded in 1954.
- The actual award is designed in the shape of a *peepal* leaf with Bharat Ratna inscribed in Devanagri script in the Sun Figure. This is India's highest civilian award. It is given for exceptional work on art, literature, science and recognition of public service of the highest order.
- The emblem, the Sun and the rim are of platinum. The inscriptions are in burnished bronze.
- Government servants are not eligible for it.

Republic Day Awards

Padma Awards

They fall in line after the Bharat Ratna. They are also discontinued in 1977 along with the Bharat Ratna and award was started again in 1980. There are three Padma Awards:

- ***Padma Vibhushan:*** This award is given for exceptional and distinguished service in any field, including service rendered by Govt. servants.
- ***Padma Bhushan:*** This award is given for distinguished service of a high order in any field, including service rendered by Govt. servants.
- ***Padma Shri:*** This award is given for distinguished service in any field, including service rendered by Government servants.

Gallantry Awards

- ***Param Vir Chakra:*** The highest award for bravery or some daring and pre-eminent act of valour or self-sacrifice in the presence of the enemy, whether on land, at sea or in the air.
- ***Mahavir Chakra:*** It is the second highest decoration and is awarded for acts of conspicuous gallantry in the presence of the enemy, whether on land, at sea or in the air.
- ***Vir Chakra:*** It is the third in order of awards given for acts of gallantry in the presence of enemy, whether on land, at sea or in the air.
- ***Ashok Chakra:*** This medal is awarded for the most conspicuous bravery or some daring or pre-eminent act of valour or self-sacrifice on land, at sea or in the air but not in the presence of enemy.
- ***Vishishta Sewa Medal:*** It is awarded to personnel of all the three Services in class I, II and III in recognition of distinguished service of the "most exceptional" and "exceptional" and a "high" order respectively. Prefixes Parma and Ati are added before first two categories of medals respectively.
- ***Jeewan Raksha Padak:*** Awarded for meritorious acts or a series of acts of a human nature displayed in saving life from drowning, fire and rescue operations in mines etc.

INTERNATIONAL AWARDS

Nobel Prizes

- These Prizes were instituted in 1901 by a Swedish scientist, Dr. Alfred Nobel; the discoverer of Dynamite.
- Six prizes are awarded annually for (*i*) Chemistry, (*ii*) Physics, (*iii*) Medicine, (*iv*) Literature, (*v*) Peace and (*vi*) Economics —started since 1969.
- The following Indians so far have been awarded these prizes:
  (*i*) Dr. Rabindra Nath Tagore (1913) for his "Geetanjali".
  (*ii*) Dr. C.V. Raman for Physics in 1930
  (*iii*) Mother Teresa for Peace in 1979

(*iv*) Prof. Amartya Sen in 1998 for Economics
(*v*) Kailash Satyarthi in 2014 for Peace.

- In addition, few non-resident Indians have also been awarded the Nobel Prize.

Gandhi Peace Prize

- The government instituted this ₹ 1 crore prize on the lines of the Nobel Peace Prize in 1995.
- It is the highest Civilian International award by the Govt. of India.

Indira Gandhi Prize for Peace, Disarmament and Development

- The award was instituted in the memory of Mrs. Indira Gandhi to foster creative cooperation among nations of the world.

FAMOUS INTERNATIONAL AIR SERVICES

Air Service	*Name of Country*	*Air Service*	*Name of Country*
Air India	India	K.L.M. Royal Airlines	The Netherlands (Holland)
British Overseas Airways Corporation	Britain	Lufthansa Airlines	Germany
		Iraqi Airways	Iraq
Trans World Airlines	America	National Airlines	Iran
Russian Airlines	Russia	Quantas Airlines	Australia
Japan Airlines	Japan	Hong-Kong Airlines	Hong-Kong
Pakistan International Airlines	Pakistan	Egypt Airlines	Egypt
Malaysia Airlines	Malaysia	Slovak Airlines	Slovakia
Royal Nepal Airlines	Nepal	S.I.A.	Singapore
Swiss Airways	Switzerland	Garuda Airways	Indonesia
Air France	France	Bangladesh Viman Sewa	Bangladesh
Kuwait Airways	Kuwait	Air Lanka	Sri Lanka
Pan American World Airways	America	Elitalia Airlines	Italy
		Air Canada	Canada

FAMOUS RELIGIONS, FOUNDERS, HOLY BOOKS & PLACES OF WORSHIP

Religion	*Founder*	*Holy Books*	*Place of Worship*
Hinduism	Hinduism has no one Founder. (This religion is based upon the religion of original Aryan Settlers)	Ramayan, Vedas, Puranas and Geeta	Temple
Sikh	Guru Nanak Dev	Guru Grantha Sahib	Gurdwara
Christianity	Jesus Christ	Bible	Church
Islam	Prophet Mohammed	Koran (Quran)	Mosque
Parsi	Zoroaster	Zend Avesta	Fire Temple
Jainism	Adinath Rishavdev	Jain Granth	Jain Temple
Buddhism	Gautam Buddha	Tripitaka	Buddha Temple
Jew	Moosa	Torah	Synagogue

INTELLIGENCE AGENCIES OF SOME PROMINENT COUNTRIES

Country	*Intelligence Agency*	*Country*	*Intelligence Agency*
India	Research & Analysis Wing (RAW), Intelligence Bureau (I.B.), Central Bureau of Investigation (C.B.I.)	U.S.A.	Central Intelligence Agency, Federal Bureau of Investigation
Pakistan	Inter Service Intelligence (I.S.I.)	Britain	Military Intelligence (M.I.)-5 and 6, Special Branch, Ultra, Joint Intelligence Organisation

Country	Intelligence Agency	Country	Intelligence Agency
Israel	Mosad	Iran	Sabak
Egypt	Mukhabarat	Iraq	Al-Mukhabarat
Japan	Nicho	Australia	Australian Security and Intelligence Organisation
Russia	K.G.B. (Komitel Gosudars-tvennoy Bezopasnosty) (Committee for State Security)	France	S.D.E.C.E.
Canada	Security Intelligence Service	Spain	C.E.S.I.D.
S. Africa	Bureau of State Security	Cuba	D.G.I.

SOME PROMINENT RACES OF THE WORLD

Races	Country	Races	Country	Races	Country
Veddas	Sri Lanka	Bantu	Central and South Africa	Lapps	European Tundra
Somaid	West Siberia				
Masai	East Africa	Tartars	Siberia	Hausa	Nigeria
Muree	New Zealand	Baddu	Arab's Desert	Kirghiz	Steppes (Russia)
Yakoot	Russian Tundra	Semang	Malaysia	Bushman	Kalahari Desert
Papuans	New Guyana	Eskimo	Canada, Tundra Region		
Pygmy	Congo Basin			Red Indian	North America

FAMOUS STRAITS OF THE WORLD

Strait	Between	Country
Malacca Strait	Andaman Sea and South China Sea	Indonesia
Palk Strait	Mannar and Bay of Bengal	India-Sri Lanka
Magellan Strait	Pacific and South Atlantic Ocean	Chile
Dover Strait	English Channel and North Sea	England-France
Berring Strait	Berring Sea and Chukasi Sea	Alaska-Russia
Sugaroo Strait	Japan Sea and Pacific Ocean	Japan
Sunda Strait	Java and Indian Ocean	Indonesia
Gibralter Strait	Mediterranean Sea and Atlantic Ocean	Spain
Harmuj Strait	Persia and Bay of Oman	Oman Iran
Hudson Strait	Bay of Hudson and Atlantic Ocean	Canada

FAMOUS NEWSPAPERS OF THE WORLD

Newspaper	Place of Publishing	Language
Daily News	New York (America)	English
Guardian	London (Britain)	English
Pravada	Moscow (Russia)	Russian
Al-Ahram	Cairo (Egypt)	Arabic
Merdeca	Jakarta (Indonesia)	Indonesian
Times	London (Britain)	English
People's Daily	Beijing (China)	Chinese
New Statesman	Britain	English
Daily Mirror	Britain	English

Newspaper	Place of Publishing	Language
Hindu, Hindustan, Times of India, Tribune, Statesman, Indian Express, Economic Times	India	English
Hindustan, Nav Bharat Times, Dainik Bhaskar, Dainik Jagaran, Punjab Kesari	India	Hindi

IMPORTANT BOUNDARY LINES

Boundary Line	Countries	Boundary Line	Countries
Durand Line	Pakistan and Afghanistan	Seigfrid Line	Germany-France
		24th Parallel	India-Pakistan
Hindenberg Line	Germany-Poland	17th Parallel	The line which defined the boundary between North Viet-nam and South Vietnam before the two were united.
Maginot Line	France and Germany		
Mannerhein Line	Russia-Finland		
Mc Mahon Line	India-China		
Order Niesse Line	Germany-Poland	38th Parallel	North Korea and South Korea
Radcliff Line	India-Pakistan	49th Parallel	U.S.A. and Canada

SIGNALS/SIGNS AND MEANING

Signal/Sign	Meaning	Signal/Sign	Meaning
Red Triangle	Family Planning	White Flag	Treaty or Surrender
Red Cross	Medical Help	Yellow Flag	Vehicles with patients of contagious diseases
Red Light	Danger, 'Stop' for the movement of vehicles	Two Bones across with a Skull	Danger of electricity
Green Light	Go		
Olive Branch	Peace	Half mast flown Flag	National mourning
White Pigeon or Dove	Peace	Lotus and culture	Sign of civilization
Black Strip on Arm	(i) Opposition (ii) Sorrow	Wheel (Chakra)	Sign of Progress
Black Flag	Opposition	A blind folded woman with scale in hand	Sign of Justice
Red Flag	(i) Danger (ii) Revolution	Reversed flown	National calamity flag

NATIONAL EMBLEMS OF IMPORTANT COUNTRIES

Country	National Emblem	Country	National Emblem
Australia	Kangaroo	New Zealand	Kiwi, Fern Southern Cross
Ireland	Shamrock	Norway	Lion
Italy	White Lily	Nepal	Kukri
Israel	Candelabrum	Pakistan	Crescent
Iran	Rose	Poland	Eagle
Canada	White Lily	France	Lily
Great Britain	Rose	Belgium	Lion
Chile	Candor and Huemul	Bangladesh	Water Lily
Germany	Corn Flower	Mongolia	The Soyombo
Japan	Chrysanthemum	Russia	Double headed eagle
Zimbabwe	Zimbabwe Bird	Lebanon	Cedar Tree
Denmark	Beach	Sudan	Secretary Bird
Turkiye	Crescent and Star	Syria	Eagle
The Netherlands	Lion	India	Lioned Capital

CONTINENTS : SOME FACTS

Continent	Biggest Counrty	Highest Peak	Longest River
Asia	China	Mt. Everest (8848 m)	Yangtze Kiang
Africa	Algeria	Mt. Kilimanjaro (5895 m)	Nile
North America	Canada	Mt. Mckinley (6194 m)	Mississippi Missouri
South America	Brazil	Mt. Acancagua (6960 m)	Amazon
Europe	Russia	Mt. Elbrus (5642 m)	Ob
Australia	Australia	Mt. Coscuisco (2228 m)	Darling
Antarctica	—	Vinson Massif (5140 m)	—

COMPUTER

The computer is the system of that electronic device through which various informations are processed on the basis of a definite set of instructions called program and mathematical (numerical) and non-mathematical both types of informations are processed.

The first mechanical computer was composed or fabricated by Blaise Pascal in 1642 and it is called Pascalene. But in 1833, Charles Babbage first time conceived an automatic calculator or computer. Charles Babbage is called the father of modern computer. Herman made an electronic tabulating machine based on punch cards which operates automatically.

In 1937, first mechanical computer mark-I was fabricated by Howard Akeen. The most outstanding contribution in the development of modern computer goes to John Wan Newmaan who brought the 2nd revolution in the area of computer in 1951. He discovered EDVAC (Electronic Discrete Variable Automatic Computer) and utilised the stored program and the binary number system in the computer.

FUNCTIONS OF COMPUTER

1. Collection and composition (input) of datas;
2. Storage of datas.
3. Processing of datas.
4. Retrieval or output of the proccessed informations and datas.

UNITS OF COMPUTER

1. Input unit.
2. Central processing unit–CPU.
3. External Memory unit.
4. Output unit.

The CPU of the computer is called brain of the computer and sometimes CPU is also called Micro Processor of the computer. The data is entered through the input unit in the computer and through the central processing unit with the help of External Memory Unit datas are arranged and processed. Ultimately by the output unit these datas or informations are issued or released.

PARTS OF COMPUTER

- **Monitor :** The monitor of the computer is like a television in which the picture appears in the form of doted points on the screen and these are called pixcels.
- **Hard Disc and Floppy Disc :** The Hard Disc is the permanent disc in the computers while the Floppy Disc is the disc utilised when datas or informations are to be transferred from one computer to another.
- **Mouse :** The mouse of the computer is like the remote control of TV through which computer is directly regulated or controlled without utilising the key-board.
- **Printer :** The printer is a device which prints any documents or processed informations of the computer.

SOME HIGH LEVEL LANGUAGES

1. **FORTRAN :** This language was developed for solving the mathematical formulae very quickly and conveniently.
2. **COBOL :** This language was developed for the commerical purposes. For the processing of this language a group of sentences is selected called paragraph and all paragraphs composed are called a section, while all sections composed are called a division.
3. **BASIC :** In basic a definite part of the prescribed instruction is only inserted in the computer.
4. **ALGOL :** This was basically fabricated and désigned for the complex algebraic calculations.

5. **PASCAL :** It is an amplified and modified form of ALGOL.
6. **COMAL :** This computer language is used for the students of secondary level.
7. **LOGO :** This language is used for children and kids for drawing Graphic line diagrams.
8. **PROLOG :** This language is developed in 1973 in France and this language is used for Artificial Intelligence which is capable and equivalent to the logical program.
9. **FORTH :** This language was invented by Charles Mure which is frequently used in all types of the works in the computer.

COMPUTER VIRUS

The computer virus is an electronic code which is used to abolish or erradicate the inclusive informations or programs of the computer. Some important computer viruses are Micheleanjalo, Dork Avangor, kilo, filip, Macmug, Scores, Casecade, Jeruslem, Date crime, Coloumbs crime, Internet virus, Pachcom, Pach EXE, COM-EXE, Marizuana, C-brain, bloody, Chenge Mungu and Desi etc.

COMPUTER NETWORKING

There are two types of networkings which are usually occur— Local Area Networking (LAN) and Wide Area Networking (WAN). By LAN all the computers of the same buildings are connected like the computers of university premises, computers of offices etc.

By WAN all the comptuers of a large area are connected like the computers of all the offices of a city or town etc. In India a very large computer network namely INDONET has been installing through which all the main towns and cities has to be interlinked.

COMPUTER TERMINOLOGY

- **Bit :** The bit is a unit of measurement of the electronic data. One bit is either 0 or 1 but not both. On composing 8 bits, 1 byte is formed.
- **Bug :** The Bug is the error in the computer program or system and its eradication is called Debug.
- **Byte :** Total eight bits compose a byte. Thus 8 bits = 1 byte.
- **CD-ROM :** A CD like of music CD in which data can be stored substantially called CD-ROM. In a CD with comparison to floppy extremely more datas can be stored but one problem in it is that one time recorded data can not be deleted or modified.
- **Chip :** It is a thin slice on which by a special mechanism a circuit is designed which is normally made from Silicon.
- **Memory System :** The place where computer data and program are temporarily kept is called Memory system. Usually memory is implied from RAM.
- **Modem :** The device which converts digital signals into analogue signals and vice-versa is called Modem.
- **RAM :** It is Random Access Memory (a place) where datas to be processed are kept temporarily and it is unstable memory.
- **ROM :** It is Read Only Memory and it is stable or Non-valatile memory which doesn't ended after power off.
- **Scanner :** It is a device through which graphic image is transformed to digital image and the scanners are of usually two types one desktop and another hand operating.

PROGRAMING

Computers perform phenomenal feats of calculation, but they do not do so in a complicated way. They actually carry out very simple operations, such as addition and subtraction. They achieve their fantastic computing power by carrying out these operations at incredible speed.

The programme, or set of instructions for operating the computer, is therefore written as a sequence of very simple steps. (See box below) Several computer languages have been developed for different applications, including BASIC, COBOL, FORTRAN and PASCAL. Writing programmes is very skilled and time-consuming work. But for most typical computer applications ready-written programmes are available, called "packages".

☞ How A Programme Works

Without a programme to tell it what to do and how to do it, a computer is unable to function. If, for example, you wanted to know how many times the word 'the' appears in this paragraph, or in the whole book, it would not be enough merely to put the text into a computer and then ask it how many times the word appears. For the computer to accomplish the calculations it has to be told what to do in simple steps. The instructions might be:

1. Scan the text until a space followed by 'T' or 't' is found.
2. If the next letter is not 'h', go back to step 1.
3. If the letter is 'h', is the next letter 'e'?
4. If not, go back to step 1. If it is, go to step 5.
5. If 'e' is followed by a space, add 1 to the total.
6. Go back to step 1.

A full computer programme for this operation would need to be broken down into even more simple steps, but a series of such programmes could enable a computer to analyse any amount of text in great detail.

DEFENCE

The Supreme Command of the Armed Forces is vested in the hands of the President of the Country. The responsibility for national defence, however, rests with the Cabinet. All important questions having a bearing on defence are decided by the Cabinet Committee on Political Affairs, which is presided over by the Prime Minister. The Defence Minister is responsible to Parliament for all matters concerning the Defence Services. All the administrative and operational control of Armed Forces are exercised by the Ministry of Defence. The three services – Army, Navy and Air Force function through their respective service headquarters headed by the chief of Staff.

COMMISSIONED RANKS IN DEFENCE SERVICES

Army	*Navy*	*Air Force*
General	Admiral	Air Chief Marshal
Lieutenant-General	Vice-Admiral	Air Marshal
Major General	Rear-Admiral	Air Vice-Marshal
Brigadier	Commodor	Air Commodor
Colonel	Captain	Group Captain
Lieutenant-Colonel	Commander	Wing Commander
Major	Lt.Commander	Squadron Leader
Captain	Lieutenant	Flight Lieutenant
Lieutenant	Sub-Lieutenant	Flying Officer

INTERNAL SECURITY ORGANISATIONS OF INDIA

S. No.	Name of Organisation	Year of Creation	Headquarters
1.	Assam Rifles (A.R.)	1835	Shillong
2.	Central Reserve Police Force (C.R.P.F.)	1939	New Delhi
3.	National Cadet Corps (N.C.C.)	1948	New Delhi
4.	Territorial Army	1948	In different States
5.	Indo-Tibetan Border Police	1962	New Delhi
6.	Home Guard	1962	In different States
7.	Coast Guard	1978	New Delhi
8.	Border Security Force (B.S.F.)	1965	New Delhi
9.	Central Industrial Security Force (C.I.S.F.)	1969	New Delhi
10.	National Security Guard	1984	New Delhi
11.	Police	—	In different States

COMMANDER-IN-CHIEFS

1. General Sir Rob Lockhart	Aug. 15, 1947 — Dec. 31, 1947
2. General Sir Roy Bucher	Jan. 1, 1948 — Jan. 14, 1949
3. General K. M. Kariappa	Jan. 15, 1949 — Jan. 14, 1953
4. General Maharaj Rajendra Sinhji	Jan. 15, 1953 — March 31, 1955

CHIEF OF DEFENCE STAFF (CDS)

To bring in reform in higher defence management in the country, the post of Chief of Defence Staff (CDS) was created in the rank of a four-star General with salary and prerequisites equivalent to a Service Chief. The Chief of Defence Staff also heads the Department of Military Affairs (DMA), created within the Ministry of Defence and functions as its Secretary. General Bipin Rawat asumed the office as the first CDS of the country from January 1, 2020 for a three-year tenure till his death on December 8, 2021 in a helicopter crash.

ARMY INSTITUTES

1. Sainik Schools upto +2 Level	33 places in India
2. Rashtriya Indian Military College (prepare for entrance to N.D.A)	Dehradun
3. National Defence Academy (three services)	Khadakwasla, Pune
4. Indian Military Academy (Army)	Dehradun
5. Officers Training Academy (3 services) Short Courses	Chennai
6. National Defence College	New Delhi
7. The College of Combat	Mhow
8. The College of Military Engineering	Kirkee
9. Military College of Telecommunication Engineering	Mhow
10. The armoured Corps Centre and School	Ahmed Nagar
11. The School Artillery	Deolali
12. The Infantry School	Mhow and Belgaum
13. College of Material Management	Jabalpur

AIR FORCE INSTITUTIONS

Air Force Academy	Hyderabad
Helicopter Training School	Hakimpet
Flying Instructors School	Tambaram, Chennai
The College of Air Warfare	Secunderabad
Air Force Administrative College	Coimbatore
Air Force Technical College	Jalahalli

DEFENCE PRODUCTION UNITS

1. Bharat Dynamites Ltd.	Hyderabad	8. Mazagaon Dock	Mumbai
2. Praga Tools	Hyderabad	9. Goa Shipyard	Marmugao
3. Mishra Dattu Nigam	Hyderabad	10. Hindustan Shipyard Ltd.	Vishakhapatnam
4. Bharat Electronics Ltd.	Bengaluru	11. Hindustan Aeronautics Ltd.	Bengaluru, Hyderabad, Nasik, Koraput, Kanpur, Lucknow
5. Bharath Earthmovers Ltd.	Bengaluru		
6. Heavy Vehicles Ltd.	Avadi, Chennai		
7. Garden Reach Ship Builders and Engineers Ltd.	Kolkata		

☞ Indian Army Commands

Command	HQ Location	Command	HQ Location
Eastern Command	Kolkata	Western Command	Chandigarh
Northern Command	Udhampur	Southern Command	Pune
Central Command	Lucknow	Training Command	Shimla
South-Western Command	Jaipur		

☞ Indian Air Force Commands

Command	HQ Location	Command	HQ Location
Western Air Command	New Delhi	South-Western Air Command	Gandhinagar
Central Air Command	Prayagraj	Eastern Air Command	Shillong
Southern Air Command	Thiruvananthapuram	Training Command	Bengaluru

☞ Indian Navy Commands

Command	HQ Location	Command	HQ Location
Eastern Naval Command	Vishakhapatnam	Western Naval Command	Mumbai
Southern Naval Command	Kochi		

☞ Missile and Other Weapons

Name	Class	Range	Name	Class	Range
✶ Agni I	SRBM	850 km	✶ Brahmos	Supersonic Cruise Missile	290 km
✶ Agni II	MRBM	2500 km	✶ Brahmos 2	Hypersonic Cruise Missile	290 km
✶ Agni III	IRBM	3500 km-5500 km	✶ Prithvi I	SRBM	150 km
✶ Agni IV *or* Agni II Prime	IRBM	4000 km	✶ Prithvi III	SRBM	350 km
✶ Agni V	ICBM	5000 km-6000 km	✶ Sagarika	SLBM	700 km-2200 km
✶ Agni VI	ICBM	8000 km-10000 km	✶ Shaurya	TBM	700 km-2200 km
✶ Agni 3SL	ICBM	5200 km-11600 km	✶ Astra	Air to Air Missile	80 km-100 km
✶ Dhanush	SRBM	350 km			
✶ Nirbhay	Subsonic Cruise Missile	1000 km			

MULTIPLE CHOICE QUESTIONS

1. Match List-I with List-II and select the correct answer from the codes given below the lists:

List-I

(*a*) Napoleon Bonaparte
(*b*) Jean Jacques Rousseau
(*c*) Croce
(*d*) Madame Roland

List-II

1. 'A history is contemporary history'
2. 'Liberty what crimes are committed in thy name'
3. 'Man is born free but everywhere he is in chains.'
4. 'I am the Child of Revolution'

Codes :

	(*a*)	(*b*)	(*c*)	(*d*)
A.	1	2	3	4
B.	4	3	1	2
C.	3	4	2	1
D.	3	4	1	2

2. Abraham Lincon was elected the President of United States in:
A. 1862 B. 1860
C. 1875 D. 1855

3. Who was known as the 'Prince of Humanists'?
A. Francisco Petrarch B. Dante
C. Boccacio D. Erasmus

4. D-Day is the day when:
A. Germany declared war on Britain
B. US dropped the atom bomb on Hiroshima.
C. Allied Troops landed in Normandy
D. Germany surrendered to the allies

5. Whose teachings inspired the French Revolution?
A. Locke
B. Rousseau
C. Hegel
D. Plato

6. At a time when empires in Europe were crumbling before the might of Napoleon which one of the following Governor-Generals kept the British flag flying high in India?
A. Warren Hastings B. Lord Cornwallis
C. Lord Wellesley D. Lord Hastings

7. Which one of the following statements regarding Fascism in Italy is *not* true?
A. The Fascists came to power as a result of popular uprising
B. In 1926, all political parties except Mussolini's party were banned
C. The Fascists suppressed the Socialist movement
D. The Fascists were hostile to the Communists

8. The fall of Czar Nicholas-II is known as:
A. Bloody Sunday
B. Bolshevik Revolution
C. February Revolution
D. October Revolution

9. Industrial Revolution took place first in:
A. France B. Germany
C. United Kingdom D. Japan

10. The British Prime Minister at the outbreak of World War II was :
A. Churchill B. Baldwin
C. Attlee D. Chemberlain

11. The 'Great Depression' (1929) economic crisis was met by adopting the policy of
A. Stimulus B. Marshall Plan
C. New Deal D. Open Door

12. The slogan "No taxation without representation" was raised during the:
A. American War of Independence
B. Russian Revolution
C. French Revolution
D. Indian Freedom struggle

13. In the nineteenth century the people of Europe started moving from the villages to the cities due to the impact of :
A. Epidemics
B. War
C. Industrialisation
D. Population explosion in villages

14. The important cause of the Civil War in America was:
A. Abolition of slavery
B. Quest for freedom
C. Industrialisation
D. Rebellion by the native Americans

15. Industrial Revolution could not have come about without:
A. Merchant capitalism
B. The Enclosure Movement
C. The services of the proletariat class
D. An agricultural revolution

16. Consider the following statements :
The French Revolution came about mainly due to the :
1. Extreme poverty of the people
2. Impact of the works of great writers
3. Cruelty of the rulers
4. Impact of impulsive reaction

Which of the above statements are correct?
A. 1, 2 and 4 B. 2 and 3
C. 1, 3 and 4 D. 1, 2, 3 and 4

17. Asia's oldest and largest Buddhist monastery is situated in :
A. Tawang (Arunachal Pardesh)
B. Lhasa (Tibet)
C. Trincomallee (Sri Lanka)
D. Ulan Bator (Mongolia)

18. Who was the main architect of the Russian Revolution?
A. Karl Marx B. Lenin
C. Stalin D. Tolstoy

19. V.I. Lenin is associated with :
A. Russian Revolution of 1917
B. Chinese Revolution of 1949
C. German Revolution
D. French Revolution of 1789

20. Which one of the following statements is *not* correct?
A. Voltaire believed in Natural Religion
B. Rousseau wrote *Social Contract*
C. Montesquieu authored *The Spirit of Laws*
D. Necker believed in 'General Will'

21. 6th April, 1930 is well known in the history of India because this date is associated with..........
A. Dandi March by Mahatma Gandhi
B. Quit India Movement
C. Partition of Bengal
D. Partition of India

22. Which ruler enforced the system of 'Price Control' in India?
A. Mohammad Tughlak
B. Razia Begum
C. Alauddin Khilji
D. Sher Shah Suri

23. The concept of 'Din-e-Elahi' was founded by which king?
A. Dara Shikoh B. Akbar
C. Sher Shah Suri D. Shahjahan

24. Who are supposed to be the earliest inhabi-tants of India? Where did they come from?
A. Aryans from Central Asia
B. Dravidians from Mediterranean
C. Negroids from Africa
D. Bhils and the Santhals from West Asia

25. The one chief characteristic of temple architecture of the Gupta Age was :
A. Absence of dome
B. Huge size
C. Beautiful carvings
D. absence of a covered courtyard for the gathering of worshippers

26. The Rigveda consists of :
A. 1000 hymns B. 2028 hymns
C. 1028 hymns D. 1038 hymns

27. The central point in Ashoka's dharma was :
A. royalty to kings
B. peace and non-violence
C. respect to elders
D. religious tolerance

28. The social evil which was conspicuously absent during ancient India was :
A. *Sati*-System B. *Devadasi*-System
C. Polygamy D. *Purdah*-System

29. Which, among the following, can be accepted as a novelty introduced by Mughal emperors to their buildings?
A. Domes B. Minarets
C. Arches D. Attached gardens

30. The first ruler of India who defeated Muhammud of Ghur was :
A. Mularaja II of Gujarat
B. Prithviraja Chauhan of Delhi
C. Jayachand of Kannauj
D. Parmaldeva of Bundelkhand

31. What important event happened in India in 1911?
A. Bengal was partitioned
B. Non-Cooperation movement was launched
C. India's capital was shifted from Calcutta to Delhi
D. Mahatma Gandhi presided over the Congress session

32. The first phase of the Congress Party (1885-1905) was characterized by its efforts to secure:
A. limited independence
B. complete freedom
C. Indianization of services
D. constitutional reforms

33. The Muslim League demanded a separate homeland for the Indian Muslims openly for the first time at its annual session held in Lahore in the year :
A. 1931 A.D. B. 1936 A.D.
C. 1940 A.D. D. 1941 A.D.

34. Under whose governorship did the East India Company secure the Diwani Rights in Bengal, Bihar and Odisha from Emperor Shah Alam?
A. Lord Cornwallis
B. Lord William Bentinck
C. Lord Clive
D. Lord Wellesley

35. The Simon Commission was generally boycotted by the Indian political parties. What was the reason for this general non-cooperation?
A. the Commission aimed at dividing the people
B. it was an 'all white' Commission
C. it came after the Jallianwala Bagh carnage
D. it was an eye wash

36. Aligarh Muslim University was founded by :
A. Dr. Saifuddin Kitchlu
B. Mohammad Ali Jinnah
C. Sir Syed Ahmed Khan
D. Maulana Mohammad Ali

37. Ibn Batutah was an African traveller visiting India during the time of :
A. Alivardi Khan
B. Ala-ud-din Khalji
C. Iltutmish
D. Mohammad-bin-Tughlaq

38. The battle of Wandiawash was fought in :
A. 1726 B. 1760
C. 1818 D. 1857

39. The abolition of *Sati* by government regulation was at the time of :
A. Warren Hastings B. Lord Wellesley
C. Lord Bentinck D. Lord Ahmerst

40. Pick out the wrong combination :
A. Dilwara Temple : Mt. Abu
B. Pashupati Temple : Kathmandu
C. Padmanabh Temple : Bangalore
D. Minakshi Temple : Madurai

41. Match the following:
(*a*) Chanhudaro (*b*) Kalibangan
(*c*) Lothal (*d*) Surkotada
1. Alleged discovery of the skeleton of horse.
2. Bead making.
3. Traces of a dock and ship on seal.
4. Evidence of ploughing the fields.

The Correct code is :

	(*a*)	(*b*)	(*c*)	(*d*)
A.	2	4	3	1
B.	2	1	3	4
C.	1	2	3	4
D.	2	1	4	3

42. Match the Harappan settlements with the banks of rivers on which they were located :

(*a*) Harappa	1. Ravi
(*b*) Mohenjodaro	2. Indus
(*c*) Ropar	3. Sutlej
(*d*) Kalibangan	4. Ghaggar
(*e*) Lothal	5. Bhogava

Codes :

	(*a*)	(*b*)	(*c*)	(*d*)	(*e*)
A.	1	2	3	4	5
B.	1	2	3	5	4
C.	2	1	3	5	4
D.	2	1	4	3	5

43. The Goddess 'Kannagi' whose many temples were erected during the 'Sangam Age' was the goddess of:
A. Chastity B. Love
C. Prowess D. Wisdom

44. The Jain goal of life is to attain deliverance from the fetters of mudane existence, the way to which lies through three jewels. Which one of the following was not included among the 'three jewels' of Jainism?
A. Right faith B. Right action
C. Right knowledge D. Right conduct

45. The most striking feature of the Ashokan pillar is polish. Name the Ashokan pillar which is considered to be the most graceful of all Ashokan pillars.
A. Sarnath
B. Rampurva
C. Laurya-Nandangarh
D. Rummindei

46. Which are the correct statements?
1. The land grants, started in Satavahana period, paved the way for feudal developments in India.
2. Silk and spices were the Chief Indian export articles of Indo-Roman trade.
3. The Guptas issued the largest number of gold coins in ancient India.
4. The first memorial of a 'SATI' dated 510 A.D. is found at Eran in Madhya Pradesh.

A. 1 and 2 B. 1, 3, and 4
C. 1 and 4 D. 1, 2, 3 and 4

47. Who among the following patronised the 'Gandhara' (Indo-Greek style) School of Art?
A. Ashoka, the Great
B. Harsha Vardhana
C. Kanishka
D. Chandragupta Vikramaditya

48. The Sultanate of Delhi had five ruling dynasties. The dynasty having longest and shortest period were :
A. Ilbari and Khalji
B. Tughlaq and Khalji
C. Tughlaq and Sayyid
D. Ilbari and Lodis

49. Which one of the following events took place at the last during reign of Muhammad-bin-Tughlaq?
A. Introduction of token currency
B. Increase of land-revenue in Doab
C. Transfer of Capital from Delhi to Devagiri.
D. Conquest of Khurasan and Iraq

50. The most learned medieval Muslim ruler who was well versed in various branches of learning including astronomy, mathematics and medicine was :
A. Jalaluddin Khilji
B. Sikander Lodi
C. Ghiyasuddin Tughlaq
D. Muhammad-bin-Tughlaq

51. The 'Sufis' had 12 silsilas. They propounded the idea of Union with God through:
A. Love B. Rituals
C. Fasts D. Prayers

52. Match the following:
(*a*) Peshwa 1. Foreign affairs
(*b*) Panditrao 2. Audit and accounts
(*c*) Amatya 3. Providing grants to scholars
(*d*) Sumant 4. General supervision
5. Military affairs

Select the correct code :

	(*a*)	(*b*)	(*c*)	(*d*)
A.	2	3	4	5
B.	4	1	2	3
C.	4	3	2	1
D.	3	1	4	2

53. The Regulating Act of 1773 can be regarded as the first measure to :
A. assert the right of British Parliament to legislate for India
B. separate the legislature from the executive
C. separate the judiciary from the executive
D. centralise law-making

54. What was the exact constitutional status of the Indian Republic on 26th January, 1950?
A. A Democratic Republic
B. A Sovereign, Democratic Republic
C. A Sovereign, Secular, Democratic Republic
D. A Sovereign, Socialist, Secular, Democratic Republic

55. When the British obtained the grant of Diwani of Bengal, Bihar and Odisha they acquired the right to :
A. maintain law and order in these territories
B. administer civil justice and collect revenue in these territories
C. collect revenue and establish revenue administration in these territories
D. militarily defend these territories

56. Which of the following were responsible for the growth of nationalism in India during the British rule?
1. Economic exploitation of India.
2. Impact of western education.
3. Role of the Press.

Select the correct answer using the codes given below :
Codes:
A. 1, 2 and 3 B. 1 and 2
C. 2 and 3 D. 1 and 3

57. Which one of the following nationalist leaders has been described as being radical in politics but conservative on social issues?
A. G.K. Gokhale
B. B.G. Tilak
C. Lala Lajpat Rai
D. Madan Mohan Malviya

58. Provincial Autonomy in British India was envisaged by the :
A. Act of 1909 B. Act of 1919
C. Act of 1935 D. Act of 1947

59. Dyarchy means :
A. double government
B. a government in which the centre is very powerful
C. a government based on division of power between centre and provinces
D. None of the above

60. The Indian National Congress observed 'Independence Day' for the first time on 26th January in :
A. 1920 B. 1925
C. 1930 D. 1947

61. ....is situated near the banks of Sabarmati River
A. Bhavnagar B. Aurangabad
C. Ahmedabad D. Rajkot

62. Sericulture is:
A. science of the various kinds of serum
B. artificial rearing of fish
C. art of silkworm breeding
D. study of various cultures of a community

63. The most abundant constituents of earth's crust are:
A. Igneous rocks
B. Sedimentary rocks
C. Metamorphic rocks
D. Granite

64. Indian Standard Time is based on:
A. 80°E longitude B. 82½°E longitude
C. 110°E longitude D. 25°E longitude

65. Tides in the oceans are caused by :
A. Gravitational pull of the moon on the earth's surface including sea water
B. Gravitational pull of the sun on the earth's surface only and not on the sea water
C. Gravitational pull of the moon and the sun on the earth's surface including the sea water
D. None of these

66. Nagarjunasagar Project is situated on the river:
A. Tungabhadra
B. Cauvery
C. Krishna
D. Godavari

67. The difference between the Indian Standard Time and the Greenwich Mean Time is:
A. – 3½ hours B. + 3½ hours
C. – 5½ hours D. + 5½ hours

68. Which of the following dams is not on Narmada river?
A. Indira-Sagar Project
B. Maheshwar Hydel Power Project
C. Jobat Project
D. Koyna Power Project

69. Which of the following statements is **not true** about the availability of water on the earth, the crisis for which is going to increase in the years to come?
A. About 97.5 per cent of the total volume of water available on the earth is salty
B. 80 per cent of the water available to us for use comes in bursts as monsoons
C. About 2.5 per cent of the total water available on the earth is polluted water and cannot be used for human activities
D. Possibility is that some big glaciers will melt in the coming ten-fifteen years and sea level will rise by 3-4 metres all over the earth

70. Which of the following is **not** a cash crop?
A. Jute B. Paddy
C. Cashewnut D. Sugarcane

71. Through which States does Cauvery River flow?
A. Gujarat, M.P., Tamil Nadu
B. Karnataka, Kerala, Tamil Nadu
C. Karnataka, Kerala, Andhra Pradesh
D. M.P., Maharashtra, Tamil Nadu

72. Indian Standard Time is the local time of 82½°E which passes through :
A. Guntur B. Delhi
C. Allahabad D. Kolkata

73. The 17th parallel defines the boundary between:
A. North and South Korea
B. USA and Canada
C. North and South Vietnam
D. China and Russia

74. During the period of south-west monsoon, Tamil Nadu remains dry because:
A. the winds do not reach this area
B. there are no mountains in this area
C. it lies in the rain shadow area
D. the temperature is too high to let the winds cool down

75. Which of the following device measures depth of a sea?
A. Fathometer B. Anemometer
C. Altimeter D. Barometer

76. The biggest reserves of thorium are in :
A. India B. China
C. The Soviet Union D. U.S.A.

77. The Girnar Hills are situated in which of the following states?
A. Gujarat B. Karnataka
C. Madhya Pradesh D. Maharashtra

78. During December 22nd the sun is vertically over:
A. Tropic of Cancer
B. Tropic of Capricorn
C. The Equator
D. None of the above

79. Photosphere is described as the :
A. Lower layer of atmosphere
B. Visible surface of the sun from which radiation emanates
C. Wavelength of solar spectrum
D. None of the above

80. Broadly, there are three layers of the earth of the crust, the mantle and the core. The crust forms what percentage of the volume of the earth?
A. 0.5% B. 2.5%
C. 7.5% D. 12.5%

81. The grassland of Argentina is known as :
A. Pampas B. Campos
C. Savanna D. None of the above

82. Different seasons are formed because :
A. Sun is moving around the earth
B. of revolution of the earth around the Sun on its orbit
C. of rotation of the earth around its axis
D. All of the above

83. Eskers and Drumlins are features formed by:
A. underground water
B. running water
C. the action of wind
D. glacial action

84. Match List-I and List-II and select the correct answer using the codes given below the Lists :

List-I *(Rivers)*	**List-II** *(Towns)*
(*a*) Ghaghara	1. Lucknow
(*b*) Brahmaputra	2. Hoshangabad
(*c*) Narmada	3. Ahmedabad
(*d*) Sabarmati	4. Guwahati
	5. Ayodhya

	(a)	(b)	(c)	(d)
A.	4	5	1	2
B.	5	4	2	3
C.	5	4	3	1
D.	3	5	2	1

85. Which of the statements as regards the consequences of the movement of the earth is not correct?
A. Revolution of the earth is the cause of the change of seasons.
B. Rotation of the earth is the cause of days and nights.
C. Rotation of the earth causes variation in the duration of days and nights.
D. Rotation of the earth effects the movement of winds and ocean currents.

86. The world is divided into :
A. 12 time zones
B. 20 time zones
C. 24 time zones
D. 36 time zones

87. The 'Kiel' canal links the :
A. Pacific and Atlantic Oceans
B. Mediterranean Sea and Red Sea
C. Mediterranean Sea and Black Sea
D. North Sea and Baltic Sea

88. Match the following :

List-I	List-II
(a) Himadri	1. Outer Himalayas
(b) Shivalik	2. Inner Himalayas
(c) Himanchal	3. Middle Himalayas
(d) Sahyadri	4. Western Ghats

Codes:

	(a)	(b)	(c)	(d)
A.	1	2	3	4
B.	4	2	3	1
C.	2	1	3	4
D.	1	2	3	4

89. The term 'Regur' refers to:
A. Laterite soils
B. Black Cotton soils
C. Red Soils
D. Deltaic Alluvial Soils

90. Location of sugar industry in India is shifting from north to south because of:
A. cheap labour
B. expanding regional market
C. cheap and abundant supply of power
D. high yield and high sugar content in sugarcane

91. Consider the following statements :
1. Ozone is found mostly in the Stratosphere.
2. Ozone layer lies 55-75 km above the surface of the earth.
3. Ozone absorbs ultraviolet radiation from the Sun.
4. Ozone layer has no significance for life on the earth.

Which of the above statements are correct?
A. 1 and 3 B. 2 and 4
C. 2 and 3 D. 1 and 4

92. Which of the following is not a chemical coagulant used in water treatment?
A. Polyaluminium Chloride (PAC)
B. Nitrogen dioxide
C. Aluminium Sulfate (Alum)
D. Aluminium Chloride

93. Darjeeling and Dharamsala would be the right places to visit if one wanted to get a clear view respectively of :
A. Kanchanjunga and Dhauladhar ranges
B. Nandadevi and Dhauladhar ranges
C. Kanchanjunga and Nandadevi ranges
D. Nandadevi and Nanga Parvat

94. Atmosphere exists because:
A. The Gravitational force of the Earth
B. Revolution of the Earth
C. Rotation of the Earth
D. Weight of the gases of atmosphere

95. Victoria lake is located in the continent:
A. Africa
B. Asia
C. North America
D. South America

96. The famous Lagoon Lake of India is :
A. Dal Lake
B. Chilka Lake
C. Pulicat Lake
D. Mansarover

97. Where are most of the earth's active volcanoes concentrated?
A. Indian Ocean
B. Pacific Ocean
C. Aral Sea
D. Atlantic Ocean

98. Through which of the following states does the river Chambal flow?
A. U.P., M.P., Rajasthan
B. M.P., Gujarat, U.P.
C. Rajasthan, M.P., Bihar
D. Gujarat, M.P., U.P.

99. In which year was the Swachh Bharat Mission launched?
A. 2014 B. 2010
C. 2018 D. 2020

100. The area covered by forest in India is about:
A. 46% B. 33%
C. 23% D. 21.76%

101. A closed economy is the one which :
A. does not permit emigration or immigration
B. permits emigration but no immigration
C. engages in no foreign trade
D. engages in no foreign and domestic trade or transit

102. In a developed economy the major share of employment originates in the :
A. primary sector B. tertiary sector
C. secondary sector D. any of the above

103. The Economic and Social Commission for Asia and Pacific (ESCAP) is located at :
A. Bangkok B. Kuala Lumpur
C. Manila D. Singapore

104. Commercial vehicles are not produced by which of the following companies in India?
A. TELCO B. Ashok Leyland
C. DCM Daewoo D. Birla Yamaha

105. What is 'RuPay'?
A. New Currency of RBI
B. New name of Credit Cards of Banks
C. Credit Card for Farmers
D. Card Payment Network

106. The main argument advanced in favour of small scale and cottage industries in India is that:
A. cost of production is low
B. they require small capital investment
C. they advance the goal of equitable distribution of wealth
D. they generate a large volume of employment

107. The most serious economic problems of India are:
A. Poverty and unemployment
B. Stagnation, not poverty
C. Unemployment, not poverty
D. Underdevelopment, not poverty

108. Which of the following is not one of the three central problems of an economy?
A. What to produce B. How to produce
C. When to produce D. For whom to produce

109. If saving exceeds investment, the national income will:
A. fall B. rise
C. fluctuate D. remain constant

110. In which of the following industries in India are the maximum number of workers employed?
A. Sugar B. Jute
C. Textiles D. Iron and Steel

111. Terrace Cultivation is practiced mostly:
A. in urban areas
B. on slopes of mountains
C. on tops of hills
D. in undulating tracts

112. Which of the following is a Selective Credit Control method?
A. Bank Rate
B. RBI directives
C. Cash Reserve Ratio
D. Open market operations

113. Which of the following taxes is not shared by the Central Government with the States?
A. Union excise duties
B. Customs duty
C. Income tax
D. Estate duty

114. ICICI is the name of a:
A. Financial Institution
B. Chemical Industry
C. Cotton Industry
D. Chamber of Commerce and Industry

115. Structural Unemployment arises due to
A. Deflationary conditions
B. Heavy industry bias
C. Shortage of raw material
D. Inadequate productive capacity

116. What is the full form of NPA in Context of Banking system?
A. Non-Performing Assests
B. National Productivity Authority
C. National Productivity Association
D. Non-Paying Assets

117. The largest public sector bank in India is:
A. Central Bank of India
B. Punjab National Bank
C. State Bank of India
D. Indian Overseas Bank

118. Which of the following statements best explains the term contraband goods?
A. Goods produced only for exports
B. Goods produced in joint sector only
C. Goods for the trading of which licence is not required
D. Goods that are forbidden, from export, import or even possession, by law

119. Price in the market is fixed by:
A. Stock exchange rates
B. The demand and supply ruling in the market at a particular time
C. The Finance Minister
D. None of the above

120. Devaluation of currency helps to promote:
A. National Income
B. Savings
C. Imports at lower cost
D. Exports

121. Balanced economic growth can be achieved only if:
A. All the sectors of economy grow at the same rate
B. Population growth is arrested
C. All the inter dependent sectors grow in harmony
D. Basic and heavy industries are assigned highest priority

122. P.V. Sindhu is associated with which of the following sport?
A. Badminton
B. Weightlifting
C. Swimming
D. Tennis

123. 'MODVAT' stands for:
A. Ad Valorem tax on output
B. Deduction of cost of inputs from the value of output
C. Reduction in import duties
D. Imposition of tax on professions

124. Who among the following is the first to receive 'Dada Saheb Phalke' award?
A. Shivaji Ganeson
B. Devika Rani
C. Dr. Raj Kumar
D. None of the above

125. The term 'devaluation' means:
A. Reducing the value of a currency in terms of another currency
B. Increasing the value of a currency
C. Revising the value of a currency
D. None of the above

126. Per capita net availability of pulses has shown a tendency of:
A. Increase over time
B. Decrease over time
C. Constant over time
D. First increase then decrease

127. National Income is the same as:
A. Net national product at market price
B. Net domestic product at market price
C. Net national product at factor cost
D. Net domestic product at factor cost

128. Which one of the following is not an example of indirect tax?
A. Goods and Services Tax
B. Excise duty
C. Customs duty
D. Expenditure tax

129. The major aim of devaluation is to:
A. encourage imports
B. encourage exports
C. encourage both exports and imports
D. discourage both exports and imports

130. Structural unemployment arises due to:
A. deflationary conditions
B. heavy industry bias
C. shortage of raw materials
D. inadequate productive capacity

131. When was the Family Planning Programme officially started in India?
A. 1950 B. 1952
C. 1956 D. 1962

132. When was the Reserve Bank of India nationalised?
A. 1947 B. 1949
C. 1950 D. 1951

133. Which of the following is *not* a feature of the Indian economy?
A. High rate of population growth
B. Disguised unemployment
C. Lowest rate of adult literacy
D. High rate of exports

134. The 'Relative Deprivation' approach for measuring poverty has been adopted by:
A. developing countries
B. developed countries
C. under-developed countries
D. None of the above

135. One of the main factors that led to rapid expansion of Indian exports is:
A. Imposition of import duties
B. Liberalisation of the economy
C. Recession in other countries
D. Diversification of exports

136. Sustainable economic development means an increase in the rate of growth of real:
A. total and per capita product
B. total and per capita product and level of literacy rate
C. total and per capita product and life expectancy at birth
D. total and per capita product, taking into account the cost of degradation of the quality of environment in this process

137. Functional unemployment occurs when:
A. unemployed have no qualification for job
B. people frequently change their job
C. people were thrown out from job due to recession
D. None of these

138. Which among the following does **not** have a 'free trade zone'?
A. Kandla B. Mumbai
C. Visakhapatnam D. Thiruvanantpuram

139. Sun Belt of USA is important for which one of the following industries?
A. Cotton textile
B. Petrochemicals
C. Hi-tech electronics
D. Food Processing

140. Commercial banking system in India is
A. unit banking B. branch banking
C. mixed banking D. None of the above

141. Who gives recognition to political parties in India?
A. Parliament
B. President
C. Supreme Court
D. Election Commission

142. The Quorum of the Legislative Council is :
A. one-fourth of its total membership
B. one-third of its membership
C. one-tenth of its membership
D. 25

143. The Indian Constitution is:
A. federal
B. unitary
C. a happy mixture of the federal and unitary
D. federal in normal times and unitary in times of emergency

144. Universal adult franchise implies a right to vote to all:
A. adult residents of the State
B. adult male citizens of the State
C. residents of the State
D. adult citizens of the State

145. When a resolution prefering a charge against the President has been passed by a specified majority in the House, it is sent to the other House for investigation. If, as a result of such an investigation, a resolution is passed through a specified majority by the other House, declaring that the charge has been sustained, the President shall leave his office. The specified special majority must not be less than :
A. two-third of the members present and voting
B. one-third of the members present and voting
C. three-fourth of the members present and voting and two-third of the total membership
D. two-third of the total membership

146. Which one of the following judicial powers of the President of India has been *wrongly* listed?
A. he appoints the Chief Justice and other judges of the Supreme Court
B. he can remove the judges of the Supreme Court on grounds of misconduct
C. he can consult the Supreme Court on any question of law or fact which is of public importance
D. he can grant pardon, reprieves and respites to persons punished under Union Law

147. The Vice-president of India can be removed from his office before the expiry of his term if :
A. the Rajya Sabha passes a resolution by a majority of its members and the Lok Sabha agrees with the resolution
B. if the Supreme Court of India recommends his removal
C. the President so desires
D. None of the above

148. The Chief Justice of a High Court in India is appointed by the :
A. Governor of the State
B. Prime Minister of India
C. Chief Justice of the Supreme Court
D. President of India

149. Which of the following statements is constitutionally not true about the passing of the Union Budgets and Finance Bill in India?
1. Under the law, Finance Bill should be adopted by both the Houses of the Parliament within 45 days of its introduction.
2. If the Finance Bill is not adopted within specified period, the government loses its authority to levy the taxes proposed in the budgets.
3. In the absence of full budget, a vote-on-account gives the power to the government to spend.
4. Government cannot raise revenues without a proper approval of the Finance Bill

A. Only 2 B. Only 3
C. Only 4 D. Only 1, 2 and 3

150. Normally, on whose advice the President's Rule is imposed in a State?
A. Chief Minister
B. Legislative Assembly
C. Governor
D. Chief Justice of High Court

151. Which Article of the Indian Constitution deals with Amendment procedure?
A. Article 368 B. Article 358
C. Article 367 D. All of these

152. Government is the agency through which the will of:
A. the state is expressed
B. the people is expressed
C. the head of the state is expressed
D. the majority is expressed

153. In a unitary system of government :
A. The centre is all powerful
B. The centre is weaker than the states
C. The centre and states stand at par
D. The states and centre are supreme in their respective spheres

154. In Cabinet System of Government the real executive authority rests with :
A. The Council of Ministers
B. The Prime Minister
C. The Constitution
D. The Parliament

155. The Head of the State under a parliamentary government:
A. is an elected representative
B. is a hereditary person
C. is a nominated person
D. may be any one of the above

156. In the event of a ministerial proposal being defeated on the floor of the legislature, under the parliamentary system :
A. the government waits for a general no-confidence motion
B. the minister concerned is taken to task by the Prime Minister
C. the minister is forced to resign
D. the whole Council of Ministers resign

157. The "due process of law" is an essential characteristic of the judicial system of:
A. UK B. France
C. USA D. India

158. Under the Constitution it is :
A. obligatory for the President to accept the advice of the Council of Ministers but is not obliged to follow it
B. obligatory for the President to accept the advice of the Council of Ministers
C. not obligatory for the President to seek or accept the advice of the Council of Ministers
D. obligatory for the President to seek the advice of the Council of Ministers if his own party is in power

159. Which one of the following statements is correct?
A. the Presiding Officer of Rajya Sabha is elected every year
B. the Presiding Officer of Rajya Sabha is elected for a term of two years at a time
C. the Presiding Officer of Rajya Sabha is elected for a term of six years
D. the Vice-President of India is the ex-officio Presiding Officer of Rajya Sabha

160. The introduction of "no confidence" motion in the Lok Sabha requires the support of at least:
A. 50 members B. 70 members
C. 60 members D. 80 members

161. The High Court comes under :
A. State List B. Union List
C. Concurrent List D. None of the above

162. Which one of the following has been wrongly listed as a Fundamental Duty of the Indian citizens?
A. to develop scientific temper, humanism and spirit of inquiry and reform
B. to work for raising the prestige of the country in the international sphere
C. to protect and improve the natural environment
D. to strive towards excellence in all spheres of individual and collective activity

163. Which one of the following is not a Fundamental Duty as outlined in Article 51A of the Constitution?
A. to abide by the Constitution and respect its ideals
B. to defend the country and render national service when called upon to do so
C. to work for the moral upliftment of the weaker sections of society
D. to preserve the rich heritage

164. The main characteristics of the Directive Principles of State Policy given in the Indian Constitution are :
A. not enforceable by any court
B. fundamental in the governance of the country
C. 'Like instruments, instructions, political manifesto and a code of moral precepts which have to guide governors of the country'
D. no law can be passed, which is opposed to these principles

165. Of the following which are true?
A. In a State, the Legislative Council is dominant with regard to non-financial bills and the Legislative Assembly with regard to financial (money) bills
B. Vidhan Parishad can virtually block legisla-tion even if the same is passed by the Vidhan Sabha
C. In case of a tie between the two Houses, the Governor is duty-bound to call a joint session of the two Houses to have the issue settled on a majority verdict

D. If a Bill is twice approved by the Vidhan Sabha, it becomes law even if rejected by the Vidhan Parishad

166. Which one of the following types of emergency can be declared by the President?
A. Emergency due to threat of war and external aggresion
B. Emergency due to break-down of constitu-tional machinery in a State
C. Financial emergency on account of threat to the financial credit of India
D. all the three emergencies

167. The chairman of which of the following parliamentary committees is invariably from the members of ruling party?
A. Committee on public undertakings
B. Public accounts committee
C. Estimates committee
D. Committee on delegated legislation

168. Which of the following is not a formally prescribed device available to the members of parliament?
A. Question hour
B. Zero hour
C. Half-an-hour discussion
D. Short duration discussion

169. Which of the following is not a tool of executive control over public administration?
A. Power of appointment and removal
B. Line agencies
C. Appeal to public opinion
D. Civil services code

170. If the Speaker of the State Legislative Assembly decides to resign, he should submit his resignation to the:
A. Judges of the High Court
B. Deputy Speaker
C. Chief Minister
D. Finance Minister

171. The President of India can nominate to the Rajya Sabha:
A. 6 members B. 9 members
C. 15 members D. 12 members

172. India is a Federal State because of:
A. dual judiciary
B. dual citizenship prevalent here
C. share of power between the Centre and the States
D. rigid Constitution

173. Residuary Subjects are those subjects which are:
A. contained in the State list
B. contained in the Union list
C. contained in the Concurrent list
D. not covered by any of the three lists

174. Which of the following writs can be issued, by the Supreme Court, to enforce Fundamental Rights?
A. Writ of Habeas Corpus
B. Writ of Mandamus
C. Writ of Quo Warranto
D. All of these

175. When the offices of both the President and the Vice-President of India are vacant, who will discharge their functions?
A. Prime Minister
B. Home Minister
C. Chief Justice of India
D. The Speaker

176. The Supreme Court tenders advice to the President of India on a matter of law or fact:
A. on its own
B. only when such advice is sought
C. only if the matter relates to some basic issue
D. only if the issue poses a threat to the unity and integrity of the country

177. Six months shall **not** intervene between two sessions of the Indian Parliament because :
A. it is the customary practice
B. it is the British convention followed in India
C. it is an obligation under the Constitution of India
D. None of the above

178. The States of the Indian Union can be recognised or their boundaries altered by:
A. the Union Parliament by a simple majority in the ordinary process of legislation
B. two-thirds majority of both the Houses of Parliament
C. two-thirds majority of both the Houses of Parliament and the consent of the legisla-tures of concerned States
D. an executive order of the Union government with the consent of the concerned State governments

179. The Basic Feature theory of the Constitution of India was propounded by the Supreme Court in the case of:
A. Minerva Mills Vs. Union of India
B. Golaknath Vs. State of Punjab
C. Maneka Gandhi Vs. Union of India
D. Keshavananda Vs. State of Kerala

180. Which one of the following writs is issued by a court in case of illegal detention of a person?
A. Habeas corpus
B. Mandamus
C. Certiorari
D. Quo-warranto

181. Name the instrument with the help of which a sailor in a submarine can see the objects on the surface of the sea.
A. Telescope B. Periscope
C. Gycroscope D. Stereoscope

182. 'HEMOPHILLIA' is the disease of ....
A. liver B. blood
C. brain D. bones

183. Vitamin A is abundantly found in ....
A. Brinjal B. Tomato
C. Carrot D. Cabbage

184. .... is not soluble in water.
A. Vitamin A B. Vitamin B
C. Vitamin C D. None of these

185. The blood vessels with the smallest diameter are called ....
A. capillaries B. arterioles
C. venules D. lymphatics

186. Out of the following .... has the greatest elasticity.
A. steel B. rubber
C. aluminium D. annealed copper

187. Cooking gas is a mixture of which of the following two gases?
A. Carbon Dioxide and Oxygen
B. Butane and Propane
C. Carbon Monoxide and Carbon Dioxide
D. Methane and Ethylene

188. The substance most commonly used as a food preservative is:
A. sodium carbonate B. tartaric acid
C. acetic acid D. benzoic acid

189. Normally, the substances that fight against diseases in human systems are known as:
A. dioxyribonucleic acids
B. carbohydrates
C. enzymes
D. antibodies

190. The SI unit of temperature is ....
A. Kelvin B. Celsius
C. Fahrenheit D. None of the above

191. One of the common fungal diseases of man is :
A. plague B. ringworm
C. cholera D. typhoid

192. A clear sky is blue because:
A. red light is scattered more than blue
B. ultraviolet light has been absorbed
C. blue light is scattered more than red
D. blue light has been absorbed

193. Jenner introduced the method of making people immune to :
A. small pox B. rabies
C. cholera D. polio

194. The largest cell in the human body is :
A. Nerve cell B. Live cell
C. Muscle cell D. Kidney cell

195. What is the device that steps up or steps down the voltage?
A. Dynamo B. Conductor
C. Inductor D. Transformer

196. The protein deficiency disease is known as :
A. Kwashiorker B. Cirrhosis
C. Eczema D. Clycoses

197. Iron deficiency causes :
A. rickets B. anaemia
C. cirrhosis D. goitre

198. Blood group of an individual is controlled by :
A. Haemoglobin B. Shape of RBC
C. Shape of WBC D. Genes

199. In a normal man the amount of blood pumped out by the heart per minute is about :
A. 1 litre B. 3 litres
C. 4 litres D. 5 litres

200. Red/green colour blindness in man is known as :
A. Protanopia
B. Deutetanopia
C. Both A and B above
D. Marfan's syndrome

201. The blue colour of the water in the sea is due to :
A. Reflection of the blue light by the impurities in sea water
B. Reflection of the blue sky by sea water and scattering of blue light by water molecules
C. Absorption of other colours by water molecules
D. None of the above

202. The image formed on the retina of the eye is:
A. upright and real
B. larger than the object
C. small and inverted
D. enlarged and real

203. Unit of loudness of sound is:
A. bel B. decibel
C. phon D. none of these

204. Oil rises up the wick in a lamp :
A. because oil is volatile
B. due to the capillary action phenomenon
C. due to the surface tension phenomenon
D. because oil is very light

205. The 'stones' formed in human kidney consist mostly of :
A. calcium oxalate
B. sodium acetate
C. magnesium sulphate
D. calcium

206. We hear the sound later, while the light is seen earlier:
A. because light's speed is more than that of sound
B. because lights travel in a straight direction while sound in a zigzag direction
C. because sound's frequency is lower than light
D. All of the above

207. Which part of an eye is transplanted?
A. Cornea B. Retina
C. Iris D. Sciera

208. The Operation Olivia is related to the protection of which of the following?
A. Turtle B. Dolphin
C. Crocodile D. Gharial

209. The green colour of the leaf is due to :
A. Presence of Chloroplast
B. Presence of Chromium
C. Presence of Nicoplast
D. Presence of excess of oxygen

210. Voice of a child is more shrill than that of an elderly person because:
A. the pitch of the child's voice is higher than that of the person
B. the pitch is lower
C. the child is more energetic
D. None of the above

ANSWERS

1	2	3	4	5	6	7	8	9	10
B	C	D	C	B	C	A	C	C	D
11	12	13	14	15	16	17	18	19	20
C	A	C	A	A	D	A	B	A	D
21	22	23	24	25	26	27	28	29	30
A	C	B	C	D	C	B	D	D	B
31	32	33	34	35	36	37	38	39	40
C	D	C	C	B	C	D	B	C	C
41	42	43	44	45	46	47	48	49	50
A	A	A	B	C	D	C	B	B	D
51	52	53	54	55	56	57	58	59	60
A	C	A	B	B	A	B	C	A	C
61	62	63	64	65	66	67	68	69	70
C	C	B	B	C	C	D	D	D	B
71	72	73	74	75	76	77	78	79	80
D	C	C	C	A	A	A	B	B	A
81	82	83	84	85	86	87	88	89	90
A	B	D	B	C	C	D	C	B	D
91	92	93	94	95	96	97	98	99	100
A	B	A	A	A	B	B	A	A	D
101	102	103	104	105	106	107	108	109	110
C	B	A	D	D	D	A	C	D	C
111	112	113	114	115	116	117	118	119	120
B	B	B	A	D	A	C	D	B	D
121	122	123	124	125	126	127	128	129	130
C	A	A	B	A	D	C	D	B	D
131	132	133	134	135	136	137	138	139	140
B	B	D	A	B	D	B	D	D	C
141	142	143	144	145	146	147	148	149	150
D	C	D	D	D	B	A	D	C	C

151	152	153	154	155	156	157	158	159	160
A	B	A	A	A	D	C	B	D	A
161	162	163	164	165	166	167	168	169	170
B	B	C	B	D	D	C	B	B	B
171	172	173	174	175	176	177	178	179	180
D	C	D	D	C	B	C	A	D	A
181	182	183	184	185	186	187	188	189	190
B	B	C	A	A	A	B	D	D	A
191	192	193	194	195	196	197	198	199	200
B	C	A	A	D	A	B	D	D	A
201	202	203	204	205	206	207	208	209	210
B	B	B	B	A	A	A	A	A	A

2602-SP